THE HISTORY OF THE KING'S WORKS

GENERAL EDITOR: H. M. COLVIN

Volume VI

1782-1851

J. MORDAUNT CROOK
Lecturer in History,
Bedford College, London

M. H. PORT
Senior Lecturer in History,
Queen Mary College, London

LONDON: HER MAJESTY'S STATIONERY OFFICE

1973

SBN   11 670286 9*

THE HISTORY OF THE KING'S WORKS
VOLUME VI

Frontispiece

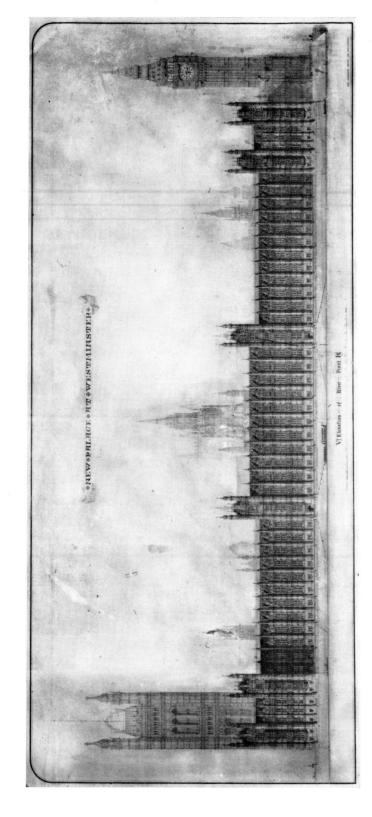

The Houses of Parliament, from the River (The Architectural Association, London)

DEDICATED
by gracious permission
to Her Majesty
QUEEN ELIZABETH II

Foreword

BY THE SECRETARY OF STATE
FOR THE ENVIRONMENT

This volume of the *History of the King's Works* continues, for the period 1782 to 1851, those published in 1963. Three further volumes covering the three centuries between 1485 and 1782 and completing the *History* are in active preparation.

As successor to those who through the ages have exercised responsibility for the construction and care of the official buildings of the Crown, I welcome this further instalment of the *History*, whose first two volumes were finished during my tenure of the Ministry of Public Building and Works. I would like to repeat the thanks I expressed then to Mr. Colvin and the distinguished scholars who have contributed to the History.

GEOFFREY RIPPON

Editor's Preface

This is the sixth and concluding volume of the *History of the King's Works* sponsored by the former Ministry of Public Building and Works, which now forms part of the Department of the Environment. The works of the medieval kings of England were dealt with in Volumes I and II published in 1963. Volumes III, IV and V will be concerned with the building activities of the Tudor, Stuart and Hanoverian governments up to the reform of the Office of Works in 1782. Although all these volumes are well advanced, none of them is yet ready for publication, and it has accordingly been decided to issue the present volume in advance of its chronological predecessors. It covers an unsettled period in the history of the Royal Works which was brought to an end only in 1851, with the establishment of a ministry under full parliamentary control in place of an office which had only recently ceased to rank as a department of the Royal Household. The history of the transition, complicated as it was by the irresponsible behaviour, first of a Surveyor General (James Wyatt) and then of a Sovereign (George IV), forms the main theme of this volume.

In form this volume follows the pattern established by those published in 1963. The first nine chapters treat of the changes in organisation, personnel and policy which determined the course of the Works between 1782 and 1851. The remainder describe the individual works carried out under the direction of the officers of the Works during the same period. Read in chronological order from one volume to another these narrative sections will (when the series is complete) provide the reader with a continuous architectural history of all the royal palaces and of many other buildings that were at one time or another the responsibility of the Office of H.M. Works. It must, however, be pointed out that the *History of the King's Works* is confined to works carried out by that office, and does not extend to works conducted by other official bodies such as the Board of Ordnance, the Commissioners of Greenwich Hospital, and the various revenue departments. To have attempted to include these within the scope of this history would have converted a task already sufficiently formidable into one whose completion might never have been accomplished at all. As it is, the reader can judge of the extent of the research involved by a perusal of the list of sources printed on pages xxv–xxvi. No one, however, who has not worked long hours in the Public Record Office can fully appreciate the sustained endeavour that lies behind the writing of this volume.

In the course of their research Dr. Crook and Mr. Port have both been greatly assisted by the curators of many archives and records, including the Public Record Office, the House of Lords Record Office, the Royal Mint, H.M. Customs and Excise, the Bedfordshire and Surrey County Record Offices, the Department of Manuscripts at the British Museum, the Department of Manuscripts at Nottingham University, the Department of Palaeography and Diplomatic at Durham University, the Victoria and Albert Museum, Sir John Soane's Museum, the R.I.B.A. Drawings Collection, the Archives Department of Westminster City Library, and the former Ministry of Public Building and Works itself. Documents in the Royal Archives at Windsor Castle are cited by gracious permission of Her Majesty the Queen, and to successive Librarians at Windsor, Sir Owen Morshead, G.C.V.O., and Mr. R. C. Mackworth-Young, C.V.O., both the authors and the Editor are much indebted for their help and for their interest in this history. Quotations from the papers of the Earl of Lincoln as First Commissioner of Works, now in the Department of Manuscripts at Nottingham University, are made by permission of the Trustees of the seventh Duke of Newcastle, deceased. Permission to make use of the Goulburn Papers in the Surrey Record Office has kindly been given by Major-General E. H. Goulburn. A passage from Earl de Grey's unpublished memoirs is printed on page 290 by kind permission of Lady Lucas and Dingwall. Professor Phoebe Stanton has kindly allowed certain quotations to be made from her Ph.D. thesis on 'Welby Pugin and the Gothic Revival'.

For access to buildings the contributors wish to acknowledge the assistance given by the Lord Chamberlain's Department and the authorities of the Houses of Parliament.

Her Majesty the Queen has graciously given permission for the reproduction of several drawings in the Royal Collections. For permission to reproduce drawings in other collections we are indebted to the Society of Antiquaries of London, the Architectural Association, the Visitors of the Ashmolean Museum, Oxford, the Librarian of the Royal Botanic Gardens, Kew, the Trustees of the British Museum, the Trustees of the London Museum, the House of Lords Record Office, the G.L.C. Record Office, the National Portrait Gallery, the R.I.B.A. Drawings Collection, the Trustees of Sir John Soane's Museum, and the Librarian of Westminster City Library.

All the plans reproduced in this volume have been prepared for publication in the Drawing Office of the Ancient Monuments Branch of what has now become the Department of the Environment. The Index has been compiled by Mr. L. M. Harrod, F.L.A.

H.M.C.

Contents

PART I

The Administration of the Office of Works 1782–1851

PART II

WORKS IN PROGRESS 1782–1851

by J. MORDAUNT CROOK and M. H. PORT[1]

[1] The exclusive authorship of the account of any individual building is indicated by appending the author's initials in brackets. Where no initials are given the text has been written jointly by the two authors.

List of Plates

List of Figures

ABBREVIATIONS USED IN REFERENCES

B.M.	British Museum.
Colvin, *Dictionary*	H. M. Colvin, *A Biographical Dictionary of English Architects 1660–1840* (1954).
Creevey Papers	*The Creevey Papers*, ed. Sir H. Maxwell, 2 vols. (1904).
D.N.B.	*Dictionary of National Biography.*
Econ. Hist. Rev.	*The Economic History Review.*
E.H.R.	*The English Historical Review.*
Farington	The Diaries of Joseph Farington, complete typescript in the Royal Library, Windsor Castle, and Print Room, British Museum.
Gent's. Mag.	*The Gentleman's Magazine.*
Greville, *Diary*	*The Greville Memoirs 1814–60*, ed. L. Strachey and R. Fulford, 8 vols. 1938.
Hist. Mon. Comm.	Historical Monuments Commission.
Hist. MSS. Comm.	Historical Manuscripts Commission.
Hope	W. H. St. John Hope, *Windsor Castle, An Architectural History*, 2 vols. 1913.
Parl. Deb.	Cobbett and Hansard, *Parliamentary Debates*, 1803 onwards.
Parl. Hist.	Cobbett, *Parliamentary History of England, 1066–1803*, 36 vols. (1806–20).
Parl. Pap.	*Parliamentary Papers* (House of Commons).
Parl. Pap. H. L.	*Parliamentary Papers* (House of Lords).
Parl. Reg.	Almon and Debrett, *Parliamentary Register 1774–1803*, 82 vols. (1775–1804).
Political Mag.	*The Political Magazine*, 21 vols. (1780–91).
P.R.O.	Public Record Office.
RA	The Royal Archives, Windsor Castle.
R.A.	The Royal Academy of Arts, or Royal Academician.
R.I.B.A.	The Royal Institute of British Architects.
V.C.H.	*The Victoria County History.*
Wellington Despatches	*Wellington Despatches, Correspondence and Memoranda*, ed. Gurwood and Wellington, 25 vols. (1845–73).
Wmk.	Watermark.
1813 Report	'Report of the Commissioners of Inquiry into the Office of Works', *Parl. Pap.* 1812–13 (258) v.
1828 Report	'Report from the Select Committee on the Office of Works', *Parl. Pap.* 1828 (446) iv.
1831 Report	'Second Report of the Select Committee on Windsor Castle and Buckingham Palace', *Parl. Pap.* 1831 (329) iv.

REFERENCES TO THE PUBLIC RECORDS

Adm.		Admiralty.
A.O.		Exchequer and Audit Department
B.T.		Board of Trade.
C.O.		Colonial Office.
Crest		Crown Estate Commissioners.
L.C.		Lord Chamberlain's Department.
L.R.R.O.		Office of Land Revenue Records and Enrolments.
MP, MR etc.		Maps and Plans.
Mepol		Metropolitan Police Offices.
P.C.		Privy Council Office.
T.		Treasury.
Works	1	Letter Books.
	2	Correspondence with the Treasury.
	3	Miscellaneous correspondence.
	4	Minutes.
	5	Accounts.
	6	Miscellaneous.
	8	Deeds.
	10	Public Buildings, Overseas.
	11	Houses of Parliament.
	12	Public Buildings, England.
	13	Contract Rolls.
	14	Ancient Monuments and Historic Buildings.
	16	Royal Parks.
	17	Art and Science Buildings.
	19	Royal Palaces.
	20	Statues and Memorials.
	21	Ceremonial.
	22	Establishment.
	29	Maps and Plans: Houses of Parliament.
	30	Maps and Plans: Public Buildings.
	31	Maps and Plans: Ancient Monuments and Historic Buildings.
	32	Maps and Plans: Royal Parks.
	33	Maps and Plans: Art and Science Buildings.
	34	Maps and Plans: Royal Palaces.
	36	Maps and Plans: Ceremonial.

PART I

The Administration of the Office of Works
1782–1851

Chapter I

THE OFFICE OF WORKS AND ECONOMICAL REFORM
1780–82

A STUDY of the Office of Works between 1782 and 1851 repays the labour of research in at least three ways. Economically, this was a period of violent changes, and in the building trade, particularly its public sector, we have an excellent barometer recording price fluctuations and varying labour conditions. Architecturally, these years saw an unprecedented volume of building activity, several revolutions in matters of style and structural technique, as well as the emergence of the architectural profession, in all of which the Office of Works played a crucial part. The face of England was transformed, and the Office of Works helped to transform the face of London. Administratively, this was a time when bureaucracy replaced amateurism and salaries replaced perquisites. The action of political ideas upon the structure of government is nicely reflected in the history of a single administrative unit, the Office of Works. As an administrative microcosm the Office of Works provides an interesting case-study in the fallibility of reformist pretensions. It was reformed by the Whigs in 1782, by the Tories in 1815, by the Whigs in 1832, and by the Whigs again in 1851: four reformations in eight decades, and still the expenditure increased. In 1782, as a result of Economical Reform, all sinecures were abolished and the Office itself was absorbed into the re-organised royal household under the jurisdiction of the Lord Chamberlain. In 1815 the department regained its administrative autonomy, lost it in 1832 through amalgamation with the Commission of Woods, Forests and Land Revenues, and finally regained it once more in 1851. The whole series of reforms gave periodic publicity to the rising cost of labour and materials, and crystallised public dissatisfaction with the expansion of the royal household in the first half of the period, and of government departments in the second.

The first reform, that of 1782, is intelligible only in its parliamentary context. Economical Reform has usually been interpreted either in political or else in financial terms.[1] But this campaign for retrenchment cannot be explained exclusively in terms either of party politics or of economic theory. The Rockingham Whigs maintained a threefold purpose: to purge an extravagant system of administration, to eliminate royal influence in Parliament, and to drive Lord North's ministry from office. 'The

---

[1] Sir D. L. Keir, 'The Economical Reform Movement', *Law Quarterly Rev.* l (1934), pp. 368–85; J. E. D. Binney, *British Public Finance and Administration, 1774–92* (1959), pp. 270–71.

whole of our grievances', Burke complained, 'are owing to the fatal and overgrown influence of the Crown, and that influence itself to our enormous prodigality. They move in a circle; they become reciprocally cause and effect.'[1]

Burke's speech on this occasion (15 December 1779) attempted to justify the campaign of the Rockingham Whigs against North's ministry on the grounds of constitutional theory. It was claimed that the executive had become too powerful. In this way an opposition campaign to break the government's monopoly of power was dressed up as a battle between the executive and the legislature. But the Rockingham Whigs were a group of opposition malcontents, not a coherent political party. If they had a consistent programme, it assumed a different form in the mouths of each of their principal spokesmen. Burke's order of priorities was quite clear: 'Firstly. The *Principle* of oeconomy by the appropriation of Civil List—which is the *great* point. Secondly. The suppression of Offices—which is a detached part rather than a member. Thirdly. The destruction of *all* subordinate Treasuries, by subjecting every expence in every department to the Treasury. Fourthly. The *appropriation* of the money saved'.[2]. Had this programme been purely financial he must surely have aimed his blows not at the Household but at the Exchequer. But if Burke emphasised the constitutional aspect, Shelburne looked to the financial side and Fox to the parliamentary. Once their temporary alliance in the wilderness had been dissolved these differences of approach were revealed as fundamental differences of opinion. Before long it became apparent that Burke's real interest lay in preserving the 'Whig' constitution unchanged, that Shelburne was primarily concerned with administrative and financial reform along the lines followed by North and Pitt, and that Fox's true inclination was towards radical parliamentary reform. Rockingham's nebulous leadership prevented disintegration until July 1782. This was long enough to ensure the success of the Economical Reform movement, but not long enough to secure its implementation. The campaign represented the collective wisdom of the Rockingham group, but the actual process of reform turned out to be largely Shelburne's work.

The Rockingham Whigs came to power in March 1782. 'At last', admitted George III, 'the fatal day is come'.[3] Abroad, the battle of Yorktown marked the triumph of the American colonists. At home, the King capitulated to the Rockingham 'clan', and the spirit of 'Oeconomical Reform,' 'virtue run mad' as Lord Hillsborough christened it, was in the ascendant.[4] The stage was set for a 'good stout blow' against those supposedly reciprocal evils, public extravagance and royal influence.[5] Clerke's Act excluded government contractors from the House of Commons.[6] Crewe's Act disfranchised revenue officers.[7] Burke's Act purged the Civil List.[8] Finally an Act

---

[1] *Parl. Hist.* xx (1778–80), p. 1297, 15 December 1779. 'My object was to give real Strength and Energy to Government, by taking from it a considerable portion of . . . Influence. . . . Fortunately in the means necessary to this great End was involved a very considerable Saving of Money, an object, in itself, very necessary and of daily increasing importance' (*Correspondence of Edmund Burke*, iv, 1963, ed. J. A. Woods, p. 208, Burke to J. W. Jepson, 28 February 1780).

[2] *Ibid.* p. 424, memorandum from Burke to Rockingham, March 1782.

[3] *Correspondence of George III*, ed. J. Fortescue, v, No. 3593, George III to Lord North, 27 March 1782.

[4] *Last Journals of Horace Walpole*, ed. Doran and Steuart ii (1910), p. 299, 13 April 1780.

[5] *Memorials and Correspondence of Charles James Fox*, ed. Lord John Russell i (1853), p. 316, 28 April 1782.

[6] 22 G. III c. 45. Sir Philip Jennings Clerke (1722–88) was M.P. for Totnes.

[7] 22 G. III c. 41. John, 1st Baron Crewe (1742–1829) was M.P. for Cheshire. Betty Kemp, 'Crewe's Act, 1782', *E.H.R.* lxviii (1953), pp. 258–63.

[8] 22 G. III c. 82; *Statutes at Large* xiv (1786), p. 262.

regulating Burke's own office of Paymaster General completed this spasm of reformatory legislation.[1]

With the encouragement of Rockingham and the county associations, Burke had formulated his proposals during November 1779.[2] His object was '*radical:* Systematick Oeconomy; a plan of *prevention;* the establishment of order and responsibility; the taking away corruption under the name of general and secret services; the permanent reduction of influence . . . not the reduction of a few places and pensions'.[3] The chequered progress of this master-plan qualifies as an index of parliamentary discontent during the declining years of North's ministry. Burke introduced his scheme three times: in February 1780, February 1781, and again in April 1782. On the first occasion, with a shaky post-electoral majority, Lord North was obliged to accept it in principle and kill it in committee.[4] At the same time he managed to dish the Whigs by pushing through his own rival scheme for administrative reform: the Commissioners for Examining Accounts.[5] On the second occasion, with a stronger majority, he felt able to deal more summarily with Burke's proposals.[6] But this proved to be almost the last time when the government was able to rely on support from uncommitted back-bench gentlemen. Losing this support, and with it his control over the Commons, North gladly relinquished office. From the opposite side of the House, he watched the passage, at the third attempt, of a modified version of Burke's scheme.

Backbench opposition to Burke arose from concern for the integrity of the royal household. 'To seize upon the civil list revenue', complained Perceval, would be to 'reduce the Sovereign to a state of humiliating dependency'.[7] Even so committed an 'oeconomist' as Thomas Gilbert hesitated to extend his criticism to the perquisites of the royal entourage. Against this the Rockingham Whigs set forth the principle of parliamentary sovereignty. If 'Parliament had no control over the civil list revenue', Lord John Cavendish maintained, 'then the people of this country . . . were all

---

[1] 22 G. III c. 81. This Act proved inadequate and was subsequently redrafted by Barré as 23 G. III c. 50.

[2] Plans were circulating among leading Whigs by 27 November (*Correspondence of Edmund Burke* iv, 1963, ed. J. A. Woods, p. 171, Rockingham to Burke, 27 November 1779). Rockingham was strongly in favour (*Memoirs of the Marquess of Rockingham and his Contemporaries,* ed. Earl of Albemarle, ii, 1852, pp. 398–9, 28 February 1780) but inclined to caution: 'The means of power, and the means of corrupt influence in the Commons must soon submit to be *shorn*. N.B. I must prefer the shears to the Hatchets' (*Correspondence of Edmund Burke* iv, 1963, ed. J. A. Woods, p. 163, Rockingham to Burke, 3 November 1779). See also N. C. Phillips, *Yorkshire and English National Politics, 1783–4* (Christchurch, New Zealand, 1961) and I. R. Christie, *Wilkes Wyvill and Reform* (1963).

[3] *Correspondence of Edmund Burke* iv (1963), ed. J. A. Woods, pp. 219–20, Burke to J. Harford, 4 April 1780.

[4] Abolition of the Board of Trade was carried on 8 March, but the turning point came on 20 March with the defeat of the clause abolishing the autonomous Treasury of the Chamber, 'the very pith and marrow of his plan . . . the very first office of the household that he had laid his fingers on' (*Parl. Hist.* xxi, 1780–81, pp. 303, 309). According to Burke, North 'paid compliments to the principle, and opposed it by detail. At first crowded Houses were seen at every stage of the business, and there was an appearance of conviction on the minds of men . . . but when they came down to precise reform, they left him and his course' (*Parl. Register* i, 1780–81, p. 487). See also *Correspondence of Edmund Burke* iv (1963), ed. J. A. Woods, pp. 214–17.

[5] *Parl. Hist.* xxi (1780–81), pp. 145, 278, 552; 20 G. III c. 54. The Commissioners' fifteen Reports, 1780–87 (*Commons Jnls.* xxxviii–xlii) formed a basis for Pitt's administrative and financial reforms, and a model for the Commission for Inquiring into Fees in Public Offices (10 Reports, 1786–88, *Parl. Pap.* 1806, vii, pp. i–x), the Select Committees on Public Finance (4 Reports, 1782–97, *Parl. Pap.* 1st Series, 1715–1801, xi–xiii) and the Commission for Inquiry into Crown Lands (17 Reports 1787–93, *Commons Jnls.* xlii–xlviii).

[6] *Parl. Hist.* xxi (1780–81), pp. 1387–98, 26 February 1781. Dunning's second motion, the indissolubility of the present Parliament, received equally short shrift (*ibid.* pp. 494-53).

[7] *Parl. Register* ii (1781), p. 12.

slaves'.[1] Such statements presupposed a convenient Opposition fallacy: that Lord North's parliamentary majority depended solely upon a battalion of placemen drawing Civil List pensions. As Wilkes put it, 'the nation suspects that the Crown has made a purchase of this House with the money of the people . . . Inward corruption is the canker, which gnaws the vitals of Parliament'.[2] In fact the parliamentary influence of the Crown was largely an intangible phenomenon. Its tangible influence, that is its disposal of offices and pensions, decreased during the first two decades of George III's reign. Dunning's famous motion was merely a clever political gambit.[3] In 1761 there were 250 placemen in the House of Commons, in 1780 fewer than 200. Between these years the number of government seats fell from 30 to 24, and continued to fall. When the Civil List registers were finally made public in 1783, they were found to contain very few pensions of a purely political nature. It was the independent gentry whose support kept North in power. However inaccurate, it was the opposition's call for retrenchment, just as much as the government's mismanagement of the American war, which persuaded them to transfer their allegiance.

The real trouble with the Civil List was its confusion of governmental and royal expenditure. But the Speaker of the House of Commons, Sir Fletcher Norton, was almost alone in envisaging separation.[4] Instead, attention was directed not to re-allocation but to retrenchment. Sensible arguments based upon the inadequacy of the Civil List to cope with expanding administrative costs were therefore ruled out of court from the start. Each application by the Crown for a larger allowance, or for the liquidation of debt, was treated as an attempt to increase parliamentary corruption. Consequently North's applications to Parliament in 1769[5] and 1777[6] supplied the Rockingham Whigs with additional ammunition. On ascending the throne George III had surrendered some of the Crown's hereditary revenues, and his parliamentary allowance had been fixed at £800,000 per annum. In 1769 this sum was claimed to be insufficient, and a debt of £513,511 was settled by Parliament. In 1777 the Civil List was raised to £900,000 and another debt of £618,340 9s. 6¼d. was discharged.[7] But still the deficits continued to pile up: by 1782 they totalled almost £300,000. It was at this stage that Burke's Act became law.

In its final form Burke's Act was far less severe than its progenitor, the Bill of 1780. Two of its original principles, Treasury omnicompetence and supply by contract,

---

[1] *Ibid.* xvii (1780), p. 241.   [2] *Parl. Hist.* xix (1777–78), p. 116, 16 April 1777.

[3] 'That the influence of the Crown has increased, is increasing and ought to be diminished'. Carried by a majority of 18, 6 April 1780 (*ibid.* xxi, pp. 340–368). For the decline of Crown influence cf. A. S. Foord, 'The Waning of the Influence of the Crown', *E.H.R.* lxii (1947), pp. 484–507; I. R. Christie, 'Economical Reform and "the Influence of the Crown", 1780', *Cambridge Historical Jnl.* xii (1956), pp. 144–54.

[4] *Parl. Hist.* xix (1777–78), pp. 213 and 227–34; xxi (1780–81), p. 262; *Correspondence of George III*, ed. J. Fortescue iii, No. 1998, George III to North, 9 May 1777. See also J. E. Tyler, 'Lord North and the Speakership in 1780', *Parl. Affairs* viii (1955), pp. 363–75; *History of Parliament, 1754–90* iii (1964), pp. 214–17.

[5] *Annual Register* 1769, pp. 62*—64*; *Parl. Hist.* xvi (1765–71), pp. 599 and 842–52; *Commons Jnls.* xxxii, pp. 255, 465–603.

[6] *Parl. Hist.* xix (1777–78), pp. 103–188 and 211–13; *Commons Jnls.* xxxvi, pp. 331–98. 'These repeated applications and debts unaccounted for', complained Shelburne's satellite, Richard Price, 'might perhaps without any impropriety be styled—The Extraordinaries of the King's civil list' (*Facts addressed to the Landholders, Stockholders, merchants, etc . . . of Great Britain and Ireland*, 1780, p. 31, n.b.). See also Price's analysis of the public debt: *The State of the Public Debt and Finances in 1783* (1783) and its *Postscript* (1784); and Burke's *Thoughts on the Causes of the Present Discontents* (1770), *Works* i (Bohn ed., 1854), pp. 343–4 and 360–63.

[7] 'Debt on the Civil List, 1775–88', B.M. Add. MS. 29470, ff. 34–5. This included a debt of £36,788 for His Majesty's Works and Gardens. For details of the grants of 1760 and 1777 cf. 1 G. III c. 1 and 17 G. III c. 21.

were abandoned. In 1780 Burke had envisaged the elimination of those administrative anachronisms the Duchies of Cornwall and Lancaster and the Counties Palatine of Chester and Durham, as well as the sale of Crown lands and a thorough cleansing of several Augean stables in the Mint, the Ordnance Office, the Pay Office and the Board of Trade and Plantations.[1] 'Some parts' of the Bill, wrote the King, are 'more revolting than others'. He objected in principle to the reform of the royal household by 'Public Regulations' instead of 'Interior Regulations'. In particular, he refused to countenance the abolition of 'such Offices as had any Peculiar Attendance on the Person of the King', or the reduction of the Privy Purse, 'which in reality is the only fund from whence I pay every act of private benevolence, every improvement in my Gardens and many articles of convenience for the Queen as well as myself'. Finally, he concluded, 'there is something very grating in furnishing the Crown, as an hospital, by open Contract'.[2] George III's opposition and Shelburne's prevarication forced Burke to accept a compromise.[3]

The scope of Burke's Civil Establishment Act, 1782,[4] was therefore limited to the implications of its title. For the sake of economy 'and for the better security of the liberty and independency of Parliament', the following offices were suppressed with all their attendant posts:[5]

The [third] Secretaryship of State for the Colonies.[6]

The Board of Trade and Plantations.[7]

The Offices of the Lords and Gentlemen of Police in Scotland.[8]

The Principal Officers of the Office of Works, Great Wardrobe and Jewel Office.

The Treasurer of the Chamber, Cofferer of the Household and Six Clerks of the Board of Green Cloth.[9]

The Paymaster of Pensions, 'and virtually the Paymasters of the late Queen's and late Princess Dowager of Wales's Servants'.

The Masters of the Harriers, Fox Hounds and Stag Hounds, 'with their several dependents'.

[1] Burke's plan was contained in his great speech of 11 February 1780 (*Parl. Hist.* xxi, 1780–81, p. 1 *et seq.*; *Works* iii, 1826, p. 229 *et seq.*) praised by Dunning as 'a monument . . . of uncommon zeal, unrivalled industry, and invincible perseverance' (*Parl. Hist.* xxi, 1780–81, p. 342). Burke's 1780 programme (original draft: *Correspondence of Edmund Burke* ed. Earl Fitzwilliam and Sir R. Bourke ii, 1884, pp. 321–4) was in practice divided into five separate bills concerning the Civil Establishment, Crown Lands, Wales, Lancaster and Cornwall. For the text of his first Civil Establishment Bill cf. *Parl. Hist.* xxi (1780–81), p. iii.

[2] *Correspondence of George III*, ed. J. Fortescue v, Nos. 3648, 3665 and 3698; Fitzmaurice, *Shelburne* ii (1912), pp. 105–7.

[3] *Parl. Hist.* xxiii (1782–83), pp. 122–7; *Correspondence of George III*, ed. J. Fortescue vi, Nos. 3792–3.

[4] *Statutes at Large* xiv (1786), p. 262; *Abstracts of Public Acts* 22 G. III sess. II c. 82. 'An Act for enabling His Majesty to discharge the Debt contracted on his Civil List revenues; and for preventing the same from being in Arrear for the future, by regulating the Mode of Payments out of the said Revenues, and by suppressing or regulating certain Offices therein mentioned, which are now paid out of the Revenues of the Civil List'.

[5] 'Expenses of the Civil List', iii (1785–96), B.M. Add. MS. 29466, ff. 15, 29.

[6] Created in 1768 and abolished in 1782, the third Secretaryship was revived in 1793 (*Parl. Hist.* xxxiii, 1797–8, pp. 963, 1141).

[7] Duties assumed by an *ad hoc* committee of the Privy Council in 1784 and formally reconstituted in 1786 (Sir H. Llewellyn Smith, *The Board of Trade*, 1928, pp. 33–43). For the old Board of Trade cf. A. H. Basye, *The Lords Commissioners of Trade and Plantations, 1748–82* (1925).

[8] Duties assumed by the Convention of Royal Burghs in Scotland.

[9] The Board of Green Cloth was responsible for the administration of the Household. Before 1782 its membership consisted of the Lord Steward, Treasurer of the Chamber, Comptroller, Cofferer and Master of the Household, three Clerks and three Clerks Comptrollers. After reform the Board became the responsibility of the Lord Steward and the Master of the Household.

C

The Office of Works, Great Wardrobe and Jewel Office were reconstituted under the direction of the Lord Chamberlain's Office, enlarged by the addition of a Superintendent of Payments, an Inspector of Wardrobe Bills, and three Assistant Clerks.[1] In all, 134 household or ministerial posts were abolished. The Pension List was reduced to £90,000 and the Secret Service Fund to £10,000. All pensions were to be paid publicly at the Exchequer. Compensation for loss of office was to be made only on grounds of ownership or hardship. From 5 April 1783, payments out of the Civil List were to follow a new method of classification, Treasury officials being paid last as a stimulus to speed and economy:

1. Pensions and allowances for the royal family (Privy Purse).
2. Judges' salaries.
3. Ambassadors' salaries.
4. Tradesmen's bills.
5. Salaries for servants of the royal household (including the Lord Chamberlain's Office and the departments of the Master of the Horse and the Lord Steward).
6. Pensions and compensations.
7. Other salaries payable out of the Civil List (including the Office of Works, Ordnance Office and Exchequer).
8. Salaries for officers of the Treasury.
9. Contingencies or Occasional Payments.[2]

The Lord Chamberlain, the Lord Steward and the Master of the Horse were made responsible for the preparation of accurate monthly estimates. In this way Civil List expenditure was to be kept within the statutory annuity of £900,000, and an annual saving of £72,368 was to be effected. This drastic diminution in what Burke described as 'the cumbrous charge of a gothic establishment' was to offset an accumulated debt of £295,877 18s. 4d. at the rate of £12,500 per quarter.[3]

Strictly speaking, Economical Reform was a parliamentary fiction. In attacking corruption the Rockingham Whigs were attacking the Crown. But several of the departments listed in Burke's Act were vulnerable targets on both financial and political grounds. Among these the Office of Works was particularly notorious. Apart from William Varey, titular Surveyor of His Majesty's Gardens and Waters at a salary of £800 per annum, its principal sinecurists, Whitshed Keene, Henry Fane and George Selwyn, all sat in the House of Commons as ministerialist supporters. When Dunning's resolution rallied a Commons majority against the government, all three were to be found, as usual, in their customary places behind Lord North.[4] Being three of North's staunchest supporters, their names were high on the Opposition's proscription list.

[1] The combined salaries of these five new posts amounted to £560 per annum: £40 less than the salary of *one* abolished office, the Resident Clerkship of the Wardrobe ('Inquiry into . . . the Office of Works', *Parl. Pap.* 1812–13, v, pp. 361, 491). For a comparison of the Lord Chamberlain's Department before and after reform cf. *Parl. Register* xvi (1779–80), p. 241: 1779 establishment; L.C. 3/20 and T. 38/221: 1792 establishment.

[2] Not being subject to statutory limitation, this item proved to be a principal cause of excessive expenditure in the following years.

[3] *Parl. Hist.* xxi (1780–81), p. 2; xxii (1781–82), p. 1411; *Annual Register* 1782, pp. 180–1. The total debt was calculated as on 5 April 1782; quarterly repayments were to begin on 10 October 1782.

[4] Division lists, *Parl. Hist.* xxi (1780–81), p. 368. Salaries enjoyed by Keene, Fane and Selwyn were the subject of a report in 1780 (Works 6/19, f. 322, 3 November 1780; 'Inquiry into . . . the Office of Works', *Parl. Pap.* 1812–13, v, p. 329).

As Surveyor General (1779–82) Keene received an Exchequer salary of £45 per annum, a Treasury allowance of 13s. 2d. per day, an extra allowance of £400 per annum, customary fees worth £80 per annum, and a house in Stable Yard, St. James's.[1] As political head of the department, it was he who had to defend the Office of Works in the Commons against the wrath of the Rockinghamites.[2] Deprived of his high estate in 1782, he was compensated by reappointment to his former post as Secretary to the Lord Chamberlain (1783).[3] Keene owed this reappointment as Lord Hertford's secretary partly to the persistence of his wife. North informed the King that Burke's Act had made her 'uneasy and importunate. The loss of both places will go very deep in their means of subsistence.'[4] Having loyally served Lord North for many years, he lived on as a Pittite until 1822.[5]

Keene's administrative functions in the Office of Works were minimal. But the burdens shouldered by Fane and Selwyn were non-existent. As nominal Keeper of the King's private roads, gates and bridges, and Conductor of the King's person on all royal progresses, Fane drew the enormous salary of £918 per annum.[6] As nominal Paymaster of the establishment, Selwyn drew a salary of £400 per annum, plus an allowance for stationery upon which he seldom wrote, plus £25 6s. 0d. per annum in lieu of lodgings for which he had no need, plus 1s. 8d. per day for his deputy and administrative factotum, Gabriel Matthias. More profitable still, he received 3d. in every £ issued by the Exchequer to the Office of Works. In this way, his total salary as Paymaster (1756–82) averaged considerably more than £1000 per annum. When the Rockingham Whigs abolished his Paymastership, Pitt compensated him with the Surveyor Generalship of Crown Lands (1784–91).[7]

The careers of Keene, Fane and Selwyn made it obvious that the old Office of Works was corrupt. It was also extravagant. In less than twenty years, 1760–79, its expenditure totalled £881,000.[8] 'For all this expence', exclaimed Burke, 'we do not see a building of the size and importance of a pidgeon house'.[9] The first two decades of George III's reign were scarcely years of royal extravagance. Not public works but running costs, salaries and allowances were responsible for this heavy expenditure:[10]

[1] For Keene's previous career and the circumstances of his appointment to the Office of Works see vol. v of this *History*.

[2] 'Mr. Whitshed Keene was on his legs three quarters of an hour' (*Parl. Register* xvii, 1780, pp. 901–3).

[3] From April to December, 1783, he was also one of the Seven Commissioners for executing the office of High Admiral of Great Britain and Ireland (*Gent's. Mag.* 1783, pt. i, p. 366).

[4] *Correspondence of George III*, ed, J. Fortescue v, No. 3622, North to George III.

[5] He died, aged 89, on 27 February 1822 at Hawthorn Hill, Berkshire (*History of Parliament, 1754–1790* iii, 1964, pp. 3–4).

[6] For details of Fane's career see vol. v of this *History*.

[7] He succeeded another placeman, Hon. J. St. John (Almon and Debrett's list of M.P.s, 1780, B.M. Add. MS. 27837, ff. 7–8). For details of Selwyn's career see vol. v of this *History*.

[8] *Parl. Hist.* xxi (1780–81), p. 551. For details of Office of Works expenditure 1761–82, cf. 'Expenses of the Civil List', ii (1751–82), B.M. Add. MS. 29465, f. 36; Works 6/20, ff. 36–8; 'Public Income and Expenditure', *Parl. Pap.* 1868–9, xxxv, 146 *et seq.*

[9] *Parl. Hist.* xxi (1780–81), pp. 35–7. Or as Wilkes put it: 'we have scarcely the appearance of a court, even in the capital. . . . No stately buildings or proud palaces, no "imperial works or worthy kings"' (*ibid.* xix, 1777–78, p. 116).

[10] Abstracted from Works 6/20, ff. 36–8, 10 April 1782; Works 5/71; Works 3/3, 14 April 1786; 'Expenses of the Civil List' ii (1751–82), B.M. Add. MS. 29465, f. 191. The figure for 'Extra Payments' in 1783 is artificially low: it no longer includes gardening charges, and merely represents the average annual cost of lighting the Houses of Parliament.

	Before Reform		After Reform
	year ending *5 January 1780*	*year ending* *5 January 1781*	*year ending* *5 January 1784*
Ordinary works (running repairs)	£15,643 8s. 9¼d.	£17,841 17s. 10¼d.	£10,063 7s. 9d.
Extraordinary works (new building)	£14,626 18s. 1½d.	£17,646 17s. 8¾d.	£6067 2s. 0¼d.
Extra payments (gardens, lamps, etc.)	£6390 11s. 5d.	£6447 2s. 2d.	£331 16s. 3d.
Salaries	£9289 0s. 9¾d.	£9261 6s. 3¼d.	£3818 3s. 4d.
Totals	£45,949 19s. 1½d.	£51,197 4s. 0¼d.	£20,280 9s. 4¼d.

Between 1770 and 1779 the average annual expenditure in the Office of Works was £46,368. After the reforms of 1782, the annual estimate was £25,000.[1] Indeed as a result of Burke's Act, the annual estimate for the whole of the new Lord Chamberlain's department, comprising the Office of Works, the Wardrobe, the Jewel Office and the day to day administration of the Household, was only £43,000. Nor was this general estimate seriously exceeded until the Napoleonic period of rising prices and royal extravagance. Keene found it difficult to deny the evidence of his own accounts.[2]

Rockingham's death on 1 July 1782 transferred responsibility for Economical Reform to Shelburne's shoulders. The Rockingham ministry's approach to the subject had hardly been systematic. Now it was Shelburne's turn: he had little more than six months to prove his own competence as a reformer.

Shelburne's instrument of reformation was Thomas Gilbert (?1719–98), the scourge of the sinecurist. Gilbert was a barrister who had made his political reputation as a Poor Law reformer. He 'had formerly made laws for the poor', remarked Walpole; 'now [he] was making poor for the laws'.[3] With regard to poor relief, the measures he had supported from 1765 onwards were directed towards the improvement of workhouse conditions and the grouping of parishes into larger administrative units.[4] With regard to sinecures he became almost obsessively involved in the investigation, taxation and elimination of placemen. In 1772 he sat on the Select Committee appointed by North to investigate the East India Company.[5] In 1778 'he could not be easy in mind without proposing' a wartime tax of 25% on all pensions and places held under the Crown.[6] 'A noble patriotism this', commented one critic,

[1] 'Expenses of the Civil List', ii (1751–82), B.M. Add. MS. 29465, f. 191. Figures for Office of Works expenditure ('Public Income and Expenditure', *Parl. Pap.* 1868–9, xxxv, pp. 181–189; 'Inquiry into . . . the Office of Works', *Parl. Pap.* 1812–13, v, p. 329) in the years immediately preceding reform are as follows:

year ending 10 October 1778: £49,100 6s. 0d.
year ending 10 October 1779: £55,925 16s. 2d.
year ending 10 October 1780: £43,179 19s. 7d.
year ending 10 October 1781: £53,599 7s. 9d.
year ending 10 October 1782: £54,495 11s. 1d.

[2] For his attempts cf. *Parl. Register* xvii (1780), pp. 601–3; *Parl. Hist.* xxi (1780–81), p. 551; *Political Mag.* i (1780), p. 473.

[3] H. Walpole, *Last Journals*, ed. Doran and A. F. Steuart ii (1910), p. 492, 6 March 1783.

[4] Newcastle Papers, cclxxxi, B.M. Add. MS. 32966, f. 110; *Parl. Hist.* xvi (1765–71), p. 6; xvii (1771–74), p. 791; xviii (1774–77), p. 541; xxii (1781–82), p. 300; xxvi (1786–88), p. 1278; Rev. [Fitz John] Brand, *Observations on . . . Mr. Gilbert's Bill [and] Dr. Price's Account of the National Debt* (1776), B.M. pressmark 104e 39.

[5] H. Walpole, *Last Journals* ed. Doran and A. F. Steuart i (1910), p. 161, 26 November 1772.

[6] 'Even Burke spoke against it' (*ibid.* ii, pp. 129–30, 9 March 1778; *Parl. Hist.* xix, 1777–78, p. 874; *Annual Register* xxi, 1778, p. 143).

'a heroic generosity, to dispose of money not your own'.[1] In 1787 he proposed a tax on dogs, increased turnpike charges on Sundays and the abolition of country ale-houses, except for *bona fide* travellers. In 1783 it was he who implemented Burke's Act. Gilbert occupied an ambivalent position throughout the campaign for Economical Reform. As M.P. for Newcastle under Lyme (1763–8) and Lichfield (1768–94) he formed part of Earl Gower's *bloc* which stood by Lord North until early in 1782. Although in favour of drastic retrenchment, he therefore opposed parliamentary reform of the royal household. Indeed between 1763 and 1782 he himself, as Comptroller of Accounts to the Treasurer of the Chamber, held a court post worth £300 per annum. In this capacity, however, he claimed to have made economies worth £900 per annum.[2] He was in fact more of a 'King's Friend' than a Rockinghamite by inclination. His sympathies lay with Shelburne rather than Burke, with Barré rather than Fox. For Gilbert, Economical Reform meant a more efficient executive, not a weaker one. As James Harris once described him, he was 'a kind of demi-courtier, demi-patriot'. Gravitating naturally from Shelburne to Pitt, he became in 1784 Chairman of the Committee of Ways and Means, holding the post until his retirement in 1794, and half its emolument until his death.[3] He is remembered, not as Shelburne's agent, but as a friend of Bridgewater and Brindley, a promoter of road and canal improvements, and the author of Gilbert's Act, 1782, which permitted the combinations of poor houses known as Gilbert Unions[4].

Shelburne took office at the beginning of July. Within three weeks a full scale investigation of the royal household was in progress. On 19 July the Treasury directed the Lord Steward, Lord Chamberlain and Master of the Horse to produce detailed estimates and accounts.[5] Four days later it was the turn of officers representing those departments suppressed by Burke's Act: the Master of the Jewel Office, Master of the Great Wardrobe, Treasurer of the Chamber and Cofferer of the Household, the Board of Green Cloth, the Office of Works, the Lords of Trade and the Secretary of State for the Plantations.[6] The Paymaster of Pensions received a similar summons forty-eight hours later.[7] On 1 October Shelburne made Gilbert responsible for the organisation of this inquest. He was also given additional powers to broaden the scope of his inquiries, so as to bring in other departments included in Burke's 1780 scheme but omitted in 1782. As the Treasury put it, he was indeed 'a very proper man for that service'.[8] Three weeks later he was also given responsibility for the preparation of official Instructions for each of the household departments which were to be reconstituted. Gilbert was assisted by a battery of departmental secretaries and independent investigators: Secker and Fanshawe for the Lord Chamberlain's Office, Parker for the department of the Master of the Horse, Samuel Garbett for the Mint, and Russell, Holdsworth and Call for the Woods and Forests

---

[1] *Letters of [James Harris] 1st Earl of Malmesbury*, ed. 3rd Earl of Malmesbury i (1870), pp. 380–1.
[2] *History of Parliament 1754–90* ii (1964), pp. 499–501; *Parl. Register* xvi (1779–80), p. 198 and xvii, p. 590. He was also 'Paymaster to widows of sea officers' (Place Papers, xlix, B.M. Add. MS. 27837 ff. 7–8; *Royal Kalendar 1779*, p. 76).
[3] *Gent's. Mag.* 1784, pt. i, p. 460; 1798, pt. ii, pp. 1090 and 1146.
[4] 22 G. III c. 83. For Gilbert's connection with Bridgewater, cf. Samuel Smiles, *Lives of the Engineers* i (1861), pp. 347–51.
[5] T. 29/52, f. 271, 19 July 1782.   [6] T. 29/52, f. 280, 23 July 1782.
[7] T. 29/52, f. 282, 25 July 1782.   [8] T. 29/52, ff. 297–8, 1 August 1782.

and Duchy of Lancaster.[1] These investigations lend substance to Shelburne's legendary status as an administrative reformer *manqué*. Richard Price, his satellite and mentor, claimed that the effect of these contemplated reforms would be a saving of £500,000 per annum.[2] With Shelburne at the Treasury, Pitt at the Exchequer and Gilbert everywhere, economy was given top priority. References to the extension of Gilbert's work were included in the King's speech at the re-opening of Parliament in December 1783.[3] But the new ministry proved too brief to permit any action on those reports which went beyond the immediate scope of Burke's Act. Even so, information received about the Jewel Office, Great Wardrobe, Board of Trade, Board of Green Cloth, Office of Works and the departments of the Lord Steward and Master of the Horse provided Gilbert with ample data for the preparation of two elaborate reports in October and November 1782.[4] These dealt with both expenditure and personnel, and incorporated annual estimates as well as compensation lists.

The principal household officers proved less than co-operative. In particular the Duke of Manchester as Lord Chamberlain resented Gilbert's interference and pressed for legal confirmation of his customary authority and patronage.[5] The Earl of Carlisle resigned as Lord Steward rather than accept dictation from Shelburne's nominee. Before Rockingham's death, the Master of the Horse, the Lord Chamberlain and the Master of the Household, Sir Francis Drake, had each prepared their own plans for the reform of their respective departments in accordance with Burke's provisions.[6] These schemes were now superseded by Gilbert's proposals.

Gilbert found that the Civil List expenditure in the year preceding reform had been £957,709 5s. 3½d. 'at the lowest computation'; after reform it was estimated at £841,014 14s. 6½d. 'or thereabouts'.[7] Theoretically this left £50,000 to be applied annually to the cancellation of Exchequer Bills, with a remainder of £8985 for 'certain contingent pensions' not included in Burke's estimate. Gilbert had to translate these estimates into concrete economies. With the help of Thomas Orde, Secretary to the Treasury, he scrutinised the pension lists and secret service funds, and found that their total expenditure amounted to £166,668 8s. 2½d.[8] The most that subtraction and re-allocation could secure was a reduction of £40,000, although Burke predicted a saving under this head of £72,000.[9] Shelburne and Gilbert were scarcely more successful in cutting down the household establishment. Gilbert's

---

[1] T. 29/52, f. 315, 8 August; f. 326, 15 August; f. 354, 25 August; f. 430, 23 October; f. 440, 26 October; ff. 453–4, 31 October; ff. 474–6, 18 November 1782; T. 29/53, ff. 210–12, 8 March and 260, 21 March 1783; T. 29/54, ff. 114–5, 3 June and 418, 7 November 1783. Shelburne also encouraged investigations of the Customs, Post Office, Navy, Police and Plantations. After Shelburne's resignation, Pitt attempted to implement several of these proposals, but succeeded only with regard to that for the Plantations (Fitzmaurice, *Shelburne* ii, 1962, pp. 226–9).

[2] R. Price, *State of the Public Debt and Finances in January, 1783* (1783), pp. 18–19.

[3] *Parl. Hist.* xxiii (1782–83), pp. 208–9 and 225. For George III's grudging acceptance of Gilbert's work cf., *Correspondence of George III* ed. J. Fortescue, vi, nos. 3947–9, 7 October 1782 and 4287, 6 April 1783.

[4] Gilbert's first report was approved by the Treasury on 9 October 1782: T. 29/52, f. 401. For a draft of Gilbert's second report cf. T. 38/507.

[5] T. 29/52, ff. 288, 26 July and 310, 6 August 1782; Manchester to George Rose 12 July 1782: P.R.O. Chatham Papers, vol. 155.

[6] Shelburne Papers, vol. 125, William L. Clements Library, Ann Arbor, Michigan, U.S.A.

[7] T. 29/53, f. 232, 14 March 1783. For similar estimates comparing details of expenditure before and after reform, cf. 'Expenses of the Civil List' ii (1751–82), B.M. Add. MS. 29465, ff. 184–193, a general account laid before the House of Lords 12 May 1786.

[8] J. Norris, *Shelburne and Reform* (1963), pp. 186–98, analyses the various lists.

[9] 'Expenses of the Civil List' ii (1751–82), B.M. Add. MS. 29465, ff. 217–21.

second report proposed a saving of £35,332 per annum under this head, 'over and above the savings computed in his former report', and besides 'many others to emerge from further investigation'.[1]

Lord Chamberlain's Department:	£2500	(fittings and furnishings)
	£1500	(stationers' bills)
	£1832	(stationery for officers of Secretaries of State)
Jewel Office	£1500	(silversmith's bills etc.)
Office of Works	£18,000	(excluding salaries)
Master of the Horse's Department:	£1500	
Lord Steward's Department:	£4000	(coal, candles, lamps, wine, beer, pastry, spicery, etc.)
	£2500	('fruit and garden stuff')
Kitchen gardens	£2000	(to be transferred from the Office of Works to the Board of Green Cloth)
Total:	£35,332	per annum

Gilbert's largest economy in household expenditure lay therefore in his reform of the Office of Works. Here he had to deal with rigid opposition from the principal officer of the department, Sir William Chambers. The old salary list, for administrative staff alone, had amounted to £3782 per annum. Gilbert's preliminary estimate, for staff at all levels, was only £2916 2s. 10d. Chambers suggested first £5302 2s. 10d., then £3882 2s. 10d., and finally agreed to £3767 14s. 2d. Allowing for ancillary charges, the new figure was eventually fixed at £3818 3s. 4d.[2]

Burke's Act had been more concerned with abolition than with reorganisation. Its vagueness allowed Gilbert not only to carry through a radical reorganisation of the royal household, but even to propose himself as director of the new system. His resounding title, Superintendent of the Household and Paymaster of the Civil List for life, was regarded as an insult by the principal household officers. In return for a £1000 salary and a £320 allowance,[3] he was to act as sole intermediary between the Treasury and the Exchequer on the one hand, and the Royal Household on the other. He was to perform the functions of co-ordinating accountant for each household department. He was to preside over every important function of the remodelled Office of Works: its monthly collection of estimates, its quarterly presentation of bills to the Lord Chamberlain, and its annual submission of accounts to the Auditors of the Imprest. Burke had attempted to professionalise the great household officers. Gilbert subordinated them to one supreme professional, himself. But this self-made apotheosis proved short-lived. Shelburne went out of office in the spring of 1783. Gilbert followed him soon afterwards, a victim of the Fox-North Coalition. Quite rightly, George III had objected to his appointment on the grounds that it broke the spirit of Clause IV of Burke's Act: 'I believe it had never occurred to Lord Shelburne that Mr. Gilbert was to be a member of the Board of Works; it would certainly be in

---

[1] T. 38/507.
[2] 'Inquiry into . . . the Office of Works', *Parl. Pap.* 1812–13, v, pp. 334, 393; Shelburne Papers, vol. 125.
[3] In 1783 he was paid an initial sum of £761 5s. 0d. 'for settling the Reforms directed by Act of Parliament' ('Debt on the Civil List, 1775–88', B.M. Add. MS. 29470, f. 109; T. 29/53, f. 232, 14 March 1783).

the teeth of the Act, for the members are declared to be bred in the profession of building, which he certainly has not been'.[1] The 'infamous coalition' was more concerned with the fact that Gilbert had trodden on too many toes. Even Shelburne had good cause to remark ruefully: 'we have had a good deal of difficulty with Mr. Gilbert'.[2]

A comparative analysis of the Office of Works before and after Burke's Act and Gilbert's investigations is best digested in tabular form. There is no change of title. Both before and after 1782 the Office of Works, by a process of contraction, is occasionally referred to as the Board of Works. Strictly speaking, the Board consisted only of the senior officers of the Office of Works, that is, those of administrative rank.[3] The table printed below (pp. 14–21), showing the principal officers of the department, illustrates the complexity of the unreformed establishment and the economy and simplicity of the new organisation.[4]

The complexity of the unreformed salary system testified to its medieval origins and haphazard development. Salaries had been drawn from several sources and paid in at least two ways: daily wages and annual allowances. All these offices carried an official house or its monetary substitute. Exchequer salaries paid to Office of Works personnel represented traditional conversions from marks into pounds. Salary deductions totalled $3\frac{1}{4}\%$, that is $2\frac{1}{2}\%$ Civil List duty, $\frac{1}{2}\%$ Paymaster's fee and $\frac{1}{4}\%$ Deputy Paymaster's fee. Tradesmen's bills were also subject to these deductions and, unlike salaries, remained so until 1815.[5] As the corporate descendant of the medieval clerkships of works, the unreformed Office of Works was a curious amalgam of the archaic and the honorific. Selwyn's lucrative backwater survived as the vestigial relic of its financial independence. Livery allowances were still received as payments from the Great Wardrobe, and officers of the Removing Wardrobe were still listed among the minor posts of the Office of Works. The establishment was divided into two categories: officers and artisans, both holding office by royal patent. Officers drew a triple income from salaries, fees and traditional perquisites. Patent Artisans—Master Joiner, Serjeant Painter, Serjeant Plumber, etc., enjoyed two sources of income. On the one hand their traditional payment had

[1] *Correspondence of George III*, ed. J. Fortescue vi, No. 4031, George III to Shelburne 17 December 1782.

[2] *Ibid.* No. 4144, Shelburne to George III, 1 March 1783.

[3] The question of nomenclature occasionally puzzled contemporaries. When in 1815 the Sheriff of Middlesex issued a warrant requiring the Commissioners of H.M.'s Board of Works to appear in the Court of King's Bench, the Office of Works solicitor replied that 'there are no such persons in existence as the Commissioners of H.M.'s Board of Works and no notice need be taken therefore of the said Warrant' (T. 29/135, f. 891, 27 June 1815).

[4] This table is a conflation of several lists which are complementary but in themselves inaccurate or incomplete: Works 1/5, ff. 29 and 45; Works 6/20, ff. 57–61; Works 5/69; Works 5/71; *Parl. Register* xvi (1779–80), pp. 225 and 322–6. For a briefer comparison cf. *Royal Kalendar* 1782, p. 85 and 1785, p. 280.

[5] After 1782 salaries were paid nett. But bills were still subject to the Civil List duty (7 G.I. sess. I c. 27, section 19) in theory until 1809 (48 G. III c. 2; 49 G. III c. 32) and in practice until 1815, while the Paymaster's fees continued to be collected by the Treasury's Receiver of Fees of Suppressed Officers (Works 1/5. ff. 51–2, f. 77, 27 March, 4 April 1783; L.C. 1/40, 28 July 1783; 'Inquiry into . . . the Office of Works', *Parl. Pap*, 1812–13, v, p. 363 and 1830, ix, p. 141). By Common law, Royal property was exempt from rates and taxes. But before 1782 officers of the King's Works were liable to Land Tax, House Tax, Window Tax, Commutation Tax, Poor Rates, etc.; after 1782 their liability was transferred to the Lord Chamberlain's Department (Works 1/5, f. 77, 17 December 1784; Works 5/72, 75, 76 and 78; Works 4/18, f. 282, 23 March 1798; Works 6/23, f. 57, 8 May 1798; L.C. 1/39, 5 December 1794; L.C. 3/35, 1798; L.C. 1/2, f. 32, 2 April 1798; L.C. 1/4, 14 December 1810; 'Inquiry into . . . the Office of Works', *Parl. Pap.* 1812–13, v, pp. 492–5).

ossified as an annual retaining fee varying from £10 to £52; and on the other, as contracting tradesmen, they drew the profits accruing from their monopoly of building commissioned by the Crown. In the case of the Master Mason and the Master Carpenter special circumstances had elevated the occupants of these posts from the ranks of the tradesmen into the ranks of the administrators. James Stuart (1713–88), Hogarth's successor as Serjeant Painter to the King, occupied a position half way between Sir Robert Taylor's status as an administrator and Richard Cobbett's status as a titled contractor. 'Athenian' Stuart had all the dignity of a sinecurist, with few of the rewards of a tradesman. The title of Master Smith had vanished in 1716. Those of Master Bricklayer and Purveyor followed in 1768 and 1777.[1] Now Gilbert's reforms abolished Sandby's post as well as Taylor's and Stuart's. Away went the last of the artisans' titular relics, and with them went their traditional stipends. The tradesmen were left in enjoyment of a rationalised monopoly.

At each of the royal houses or palaces, all work was directed by a Clerk of the Works and supervised by a Labourer in Trust. Both of these posts were accompanied by official lodgings. What the reforms of 1782 accomplished in this sphere was a regrouping of the various houses and palaces according to geography and administrative convenience. The existence of separate clerkships for Kensington Gardens and Winchester Palace had been recognised as unnecessary in 1761 and 1775.[2] St. James's, Whitehall and Westminster had long been regarded as one administrative unit, as had Richmond and Kew, Hampton Court and Bushy Park, and Windsor Castle and its neighbouring lodges. The same principle was now extended, by bringing the Tower, Newmarket, Winchester and Greenwich under one Clerk of the Works, and Buckingham House, Carlton House, the King's Mews, Kensington Palace and the King's Private Roads under another. One of those who lost by this process of amalgamation was Kenton Couse, who held the clerkship for Buckingham House in conjunction with the posts of Secretary and Clerk to the Board and Clerk Itinerant. By way of compensation he was raised to the newly-created office of Examining Clerk. His situation resembled that of Richard Ripley, who was treated with equal leniency. Ripley owed his position as Chief Clerk and Clerk Engrosser to his father's influence. Now, deprived of these emoluments, he was compensated by the award of a new post, that of Resident Clerk.

By pruning the Office of Works Burke had envisaged an annual saving of £7463.[3] This was almost double the saving he hoped to effect by the abolition of the Great Wardrobe which, as he wittily put it, served, 'not to furnish the palace with its hangings, but the Parliament with its *dependent* members'.[4] Gilbert's economies went far beyond Burke's proposals. Part of the saving lay in the abolition of communal perquisites as well as individual offices: the Riding Charges, or as we would call them, travelling expenses, averaging 5s. od. per day for senior officers, the Christmas Rewards at £15 per annum, and the Officers' Entertainments at £2 per month.[5]

---

[1] *Parl. Register* xvi (1779–80), pp. 322–6; on Floodman's death in 1781, the office of Serjeant Plumber was allowed to lapse as being 'of no further use or advantage to His Majesty's service' (Works 6/20, f. 19, 25 March 1781).
[2] *Parl. Register* xvi (1779–80), pp. 322–6. [3] *Parl. Hist.* xxii (1781–82), p. 1411.
[4] *Ibid.* xxi (1780–81), p. 351. [5] Works 5/69.

BEFORE 1782

Title	Name	Daily wage	Annual salary	Exchequer salary
Surveyor General	Whitshed Keene, M.P.	13s. 2d.	£80 0s. 0d. (fees)	£45 0s. 0d.
	riding charges	4s. 10d.		
	Surveyor's man	3s. 0d.		
	additional salary		£400 0s. 0d.	
	livery allowance		£12 15s. 0d.	
Comptroller	Sir William Chambers*	8s. 8d.		£27 7s. 6d.
	riding charges	6s. 10d.		
	Comptroller's man	3s. 0d.		
	in lieu of house at Kensington		£60 0s. 0d.	
	livery allowance		£8 9s. 4d.	
Master Mason			£200 0s. 0d.	
Deputy Surveyor	Sir Robert Taylor*		£100 0s. 0d.	
	riding charges	5s. 4d.		
Master Carpenter	Thomas Sandby*		£200 0s. 0d.	
	riding charges	5s. 4d.		
Joint Architects	James Adam*		£300 0s. 0d.	
	James Paine*		£300 0s. 0d.	
Paymaster	G. A. Selwyn, M.P.		£400 0s. 0d.	
Paymaster's Clerk	Gabriel Matthias**	1s. 8d.		
	lodging allowance		£25 6s. 0d.	
	plus 3d. in the £ on issues from the Exchequer			
Clerk Engrosser *Chief Clerk of Works*	Richard Ripley**	2s. 10d.	£66 13s. 4d.	
	riding charges	5s. 0d.		
Clerk Itinerant *Secretary* *Clerk to the Board*	Kenton Couse**	7s. 6d.	£50 0s. 0d. £100 0s. 0d.	

AFTER 1782

Deductions	Salary per annum	Title
£156 18s. 3¼d.		abolished
£50 6s. 2½d.	£500 0s. 0d. £10 0s. 0d. (stationery allowance)	Surveyor General and Comptroller**
£63 19s. 8¾d.		abolished
		abolished
£43 9s. 8¾d.		abolished
£61 10s. 0d.		abolished
£61 10s. 0d.		abolished
£81 7s. 10d.		abolished
		abolished
£26 15s. 9¾d.	£170 0s. 0d. £21 0s. 0d. (office books and papers) £20 0s. 0d. (office candles, coals and baskets)	*Resident Clerk**
£57 18s. 5¼d.	£350 0s. 0d. £5 0s. 0d. (stationery allowance)	*Examining Clerk**

BEFORE 1782

Title	Name	Daily wage	Annual Salary	Exchequer salary
Comptroller's Clerk	Thomas Fulling**	2s. 6d.		
Writing Clerk	George Horsley**		£54 16s. 5d.	
Writing Clerk	Edward Crocker**		£54 16s. 5d.	
Writing Clerk	M. E. Lloyd**		£54 16s. 5d.	
Auditors of the Imprest			£140 0s. 0d.	
Master Joiner	William Greenell	1s. 6d.		£52 12s. 6d
	livery allowance		£16 2s. 6d.	
Master Plasterer	Thomas Clark	2s. 0d.		£18 5s. 0d
Serjeant Painter	James Stuart			£10 0s. 0d
Serjeant Plumber	Daniel Floodman			£18 5s. 0d
	Plumber at Windsor and			
	Keeper of the Conduit			£18 5s. 0d
Master Carver	Samuel Norman	2s. 9d.		£27 7s. 6d
	livery allowance		£8 0s. 0d.	
Master Glazier	Richard Cobbett			£19 9s. 0d
Ranger of St. James's Park	Earl of Orford		£80 0s. 0d.	
Surveyor of King's Roads	Hon. H. Fane, M.P.		£918 0s. 0d.	
Surveyor of King's Gardens	William Varey		£800 0s. 0d.	

Clerks of the Works at:
  Richmond Palace
    and Park
  Kew House and Gardens
	}Thomas Fulling	3s. 3d.	£66 16s 2d.	

New Park Lodge, *Richmond*	John Yenn in lieu of house and coals		£100 0s. 0d. £25 0s. 0d.	

AFTER 1782

Deductions	Salary per annum	Title
£7 13s. 9¾d.		abolished
£1 7s. 5d.	£60 0s. 0d.	*Assistant Clerk***
£1 7s. 5d.	£60 0s. 0d.	*Assistant Clerk***
£1 7s. 5d.		abolished
£3 10s. 0d.		abolished
£12 1s. 8d.		abolished
		abolished
		abolished
		abolished
		abolished
£4 12s. 6d.		abolished
		abolished
£2 0s. 0d.		unaltered
190 8s. 6d.		abolished
		abolished
		Clerks of the Works at:
£9 13s. 8½d.	£250 0s. 0d.	*Richmond, Kew and New Park Lodge*
£43 13s. 10½d.	£220 0s. 0d.	*Queen's Palace, Carlton House, King's Mews, Kensington and King's Roads*

*: member of the Board of Works.
**: member of the office staff.

BEFORE 1782

Title	Name	Daily wage	Annual salary	Exchequer salary
Clerks of the Works at:				
Whitehall, St. James's and Westminster	John Woolfe riding charges plus allowance for brooms, baskets and dog meat	4s. 8d. 4s. 0d.	£133 18s. 8d.	
Hampton Court Palace Hampton Court Gardens Bushy Park	} William Rice	2s. 3d. 1s. 0d. 2s. 3d.	£105 10s. 6d. £12 0s. 0d.	
Hampton Court House Park	Thomas Rice	1s. 0d.		
Windsor Castle and Lodges	Thomas Tildesley	2s. 3d.	£150 9s. 6d.	
Greenwich	William Leach	£120 0s. 0d.		
The Tower Newmarket	} S. P. Cockerell in lieu of house and coals plus allowance for candles, brooms, baskets, dog meat and travel	2s. 3d. 2s. 3d.	£82 4s. 0d. £15 0s. 0d.	
King's Mews	Henry Holland	2s. 3d.	£82 1s. 0d.	
Kensington Palace and Gardens	John Smith		£168 7s. 0d.	
Carlton House Queen's [Buckingham] House	} Kenton Couse	2s. 3d. 2s. 3d.	£58 19s. 0d.	
Labourers in Trust at:				
Richmond and Kew	Robert Browne, Snr.	2s. 2d.	£2 18s. 2d.	
Queen's [Buckingham] House	Richard Wetherill care of water engine	2s. 2d.	£3 5s. 0d. £40 0s. 0d.	
Whitehall and St. James's	Jason Harris	2s. 2d.	£60 3s. 10d.	

AFTER 1782

Deductions	*Salary per annum*		*Title*
			Clerks of the Works at:
£8 8s. 4½d.	£200 0s. 0d.	unaltered	
£4 7s. 3½d.	£200 0s. 0d.		*Hampton Court Palace, Park and Gardens, Bushy Park, the Water Works and Longford River*
£0 18s. 1½d.			
£1 4s. 6½d.			
£0 9s. 1½d.		abolished	
£6 4s. 3½d.	£180 0s. 0d.		*Windsor Castle and the Queen's Lodges*
£16 2s. 0d.	£100 0s. 0d.		*The Tower, Newmarket, Greenwich and Winchester*
£23 17s. 4½d.		abolished	
		abolished	
£9 2s. 1d.		abolished	
£11 5s. 2d.		abolished	
£1 4s. 6½d.		abolished	
£8 2s. 6d.		abolished	
			Labourers in Trust at:
£0 19s. 9¼d.	£80 0s. 0d.		*Richmond, Kew and New Park Lodge*
£0 19s. 9¼d.	£80 0s. 0d.	unaltered	
£3 9s. 7½d.	£55 0s. 0d.		*Whitehall and Westminster*

BEFORE 1782

Title	Name	Daily wage	Annual salary	Exchequer salary
Labourers in Trust at:				
Clerk's Assistant	Thomas Bevan	2s. 2d.		
Hampton Court	} Mark Banks	2s. 2d.		
Bushy Park		1s. 0d.		
Hampton Court House Park		0s. 4d.		
Windsor Castle and Lodges	John Kempshead	2s. 2.d		
Clerk's Assistant	John Bender	2s. 2d.		
King's Mews	C. A. Craig	2s. 2d.		
Kensington Palace and Gardens	George Marshall	2s. 2d.	£26 8s. 0d.	
Greenwich	Robert Browne, Jnr.	2s. 2d.		
The Tower	Thomas Kilvington	2s. 2d.		
King's Private Roads	Samuel Warren	2s. 2d.	£24 0s. 0d.	
New Park Lodge, Richmond	Isaac Leyton	2s. 2d.		
Westminster	Samuel Saxon	2s. 2d.		
Newmarket	William Macbean	2s. 2d.		

AFTER 1782

Deductions	Salary per annum		Title
			Labourers in Trust at:
	£50 0s. 0d.		St. James's
£0 19s. 9¼d.	£55 0s. 0d.	unaltered	
£0 9s. 1½d.			
£0 3s. 0d.			
£1 5s. 9¼d.	£55 0s. 0d.	unaltered	
£0 19s. 9¼d.	£50 0s. 0d.	unaltered	
	£50 0s. 0d.	unaltered	
£0 19s. 9¼d.	£50 0s. 0d.		*The Tower*
£0 19s. 9¼d.	£50 0s. 0d.		*Newmarket*
£1 11s. 9¼d.		abolished	
£1 1s. 3¼d.		abolished	
£0 19s. 9¼d.		abolished	
£0 19s. 9¼d.		abolished	

D

Personal stationery allowances were abolished and absorbed into the new scale.[1] The old Office of Works was abolished on 11 July 1782. Its successor came into operation at the start of the following quarter, 10 October 1782.[2] During the intervening period only urgent repairs were undertaken and the office was left in the hands of Chambers, Couse, Ripley and Fulling. For this additional work they eventually received compensation.[3]

The distribution of pensions and compensations was Gilbert's responsibility. The Office of Works, the Lord Chamberlain's Department, the Jewel Office, the Office of Robes, the Board of Trade, the Board of Police in Scotland and the Departments of the Master of the Horse and Lord Steward were all subjected to careful scrutiny. All these departments had supplied salaries not only for sinecurists, but for old employees, the aged, the infirm and the incompetent. Top level sinecurists were dealt with individually, mainly through offers of alternative posts. At the lower level prospective pensioners were divided into three classes. Firstly, there were 'those who possessed small sinecure places now abandoned, made so great a dependence upon them and thought themselves so secure in the enjoyment of 'em for their lives, that they neglected all other means of acquiring livelihoods . . . and will be reduced to great distress if no provision is made for them'. Secondly, Gilbert listed those 'who have enjoyed places with larger salaries' but are now in 'much the same predicament . . ., and having placed themselves in a rank, and situation of life, and formed social connections, upon planes suitable to their apparent income will suffer many hardships, if not relieved by some provision . . . as may enable them with a becoming oeconomy to live decently, without being too much degraded by so unexpected a dismission'. Finally, there were those 'who have been dismissed from offices of real business and are fitter for employments than pensions, but are recommended for allowances or pensions till employments can be procured'.[4]

The Office of Works contained no pensioners in either the second or third categories. The unreformed department had been chiefly burdened with sinecurists and incurables. However it was involved in the compensation of at least one second-class pensioner from the Lord Chamberlain's department, namely Benjamin Vulliamy, Clockmaker to the King. Gilbert recommended that Vulliamy's salary of £150 per annum should be retained as a pension, provided that in addition to his customary care for the King's indoor clocks, he relieved the Office of Works of the duties involved in cleaning, repairing and winding up all his Majesty's turret clocks.

---

[1] For the three years, 1779–81, Cust's, the stationers in Parliament St., had charged the Office of Works an average of £215 per annum. Prices 'per rheam' for Imperial paper were as follows: Royal £7; Demy £3 10s. 0d.; Foolscap £17 17s. 0d.; Quarto Gilt £1; Blue Elephant £2 10s. 0d.; Common Blue 13s. 4d.; Blotting 15s. 0d. Wax was 7s. 0d. per lb.; Ink 11s. 3d. per quart; tape 1s. 0d. per knot; and quill pens 6s. 0d. per 100 (Works 6/20, ff. 85–6, 12 February 1783.)

[2] The first list of new senior appointments bore a royal warrant dated 24 December 1782. On 1 January 1783 Chambers brought this list to the Office of Works and formally added a list of junior appointments in his own gift. Both these lists were replaced by a full and final list bearing a royal warrant dated 1 February 1783. Salaries were to be retrospective ('Inquiry into . . . the Office of Works', *Parl. Pap.* 1812–13, v, pp. 392–3; Works 6/13; F. S. Thomas, *Notes of Materials for the History of the Public Departments*, 1846, p. 109).

[3] Couse negotiated with the Treasury for payment (R.I.B.A. MSS., Couse to Chambers 17 October 1782). On 28 February 1783 Chambers complained: 'I am fearful it has been forgot'. Payment was made three weeks later ('Debt on the Civil List, 1775–88', B.M. Add. MS. 29470, ff. 58–9; Works 6/20, ff. 75, 98–100; T. 29/53, f. 66).

[4] T. 38/507.

Pensions amounting to no less than £1188 per annum were granted to Office of Works staff. Fifteen of the recipients were pensioners in Gilbert's first category, old, infirm and unemployable.[1]

	Age	Years' service	Old salary	Pension	Died
John Bishop: fire-engine carpenter, 'very infirm'	70	20	£39 2s. 6d.	£35 0s. 0d.	18 April 1783
John Poole: joiner	70	30	£39 2s. 6d.	£35 0s. 0d.	31 December 1784
Aaron Powell: sluice attendant	50	8	£52 0s. 0d.	£30 0s. 0d.	after 1804
Ephraim Brooks: fire-engine-keeper at St. James's	50	20	£33 10s. 0d.	£20 0s. 0d.	1797
Dorothy Lacey: labourer's widow			£13 pension	£13 0s. 0d.	1792
Robert Churchill: bricklayer at St. James's	70	4	£39 2s. 6d.	£35 0s. 0d.	1786
William Macbean: Labourer in Trust at St. James's	60	19	£39 10s. 10d.	£35 0s. 0d.	1791
James Scaddon: joiner at Hampton Court	80	30	£39 2s. 6d.	£40 0s. 0d.	16 May 1789
Robert Mitchell: labourer at Hampton Court —'blind'	70	40	£26 1s. 8d.	£30 0s. 0d.	7 April 1783
Isaac Goodchild: labourer at Hampton Court —'blind'	70	29	£30 8s. 4d.	£30 0s. 0d.	1794
George Smith: labourer at Hampton Court	70	37	£26 1s. 8d.	£30 0s. 0d.	8 September 1783
Benjamin Mist: Keeper of Longford River —'maimed'	60	12	£20 0s. 0d.	£20 0s. 0d.	16 October 1793
Isaac Layton: Labourer in Trust at New Park Lodge	60	17	£39 10s. 10d.	£35 0s. 0d.	1794
Thomas Blakeley: engine keeper at St. James's —'very infirm'	83	29	£45 12s. 6d.	£40 0s. 0d.	1785
Ralph Clayton, labourer	90	36	£30 8s. 4d.	£35 0s. 0d.	1786

Another nineteen members of the department were given long-term supplementary pensions covering a wider range.[2]

[1] Figures abstracted from several lists: T. 38/221; T. 38/507; Works 5/69; Works 6/13, 14 February 1783; Works 1/5, f. 61, 14 June 1783; Works 4/16, 11 April, 20 September 1783, 7 January 1784.
[2] *Ibid.*

	Old salary	Pension	Died
John Smith: Clerk of the Works at Kensington	£168 7s. od.	£100 os. od.	
Sir William Chambers: Comptroller	see p. 14	£150 os. od.[1]	8 March 1796
George Horsley: Office Clerk	see p. 16	£20 os. od.	
Edward Crocker: Office Clerk	see p. 16	£20 os. od.	
Ann and Mary Towersey: 'keepers of the buckets, who stood in the name of [Samuel] Betty, who did the duty'	£28 os. od. each	£10 os. od. each	
Samuel Saxon: Labourer in Trust at Westminster	£39 10s. 10d.	£35 os. od.	after 1804
John Ranspach: engine attendant at the Treasury	£40 os. od.	£20 os. od.	after 1804
Thomas Rice: Clerk of the Works at Hampton Court House Park	£18 5s. od.	£30 os. od.	after 1804
George Baynes: labourer	£30 8s. 4d.	£20 os. od.	1804
Samuel Norman: Master Carver	£50 os. od.	£50 os. od.	1798
Catherine Dunn ⎱ 'widows of two old men	£18 os. od.	£18 os. od.	before 1791
Jane Beighton ⎰ long with the service'	£13 os. od.	£13 os. od.	1798
John Bedford ⎫	£27 os. od.	£20 os. od.	before 1791
Benjamin Durant ⎬ labourers: 'very old	£42 os. od.	£25 os. od.	1 July 1783
Samuel Ostridge ⎭ and infirm'	£42 os. od.	£25 os. od.	before 1791
John Spence: ⎰ Office Keeper	£41 6s. od.	£25 os. od.	after 1804
⎱ Lamplighter	£78 os. od.		
John Bankes: Office messenger		£20 os. od.	after 1804
Samuel Warren: Labourer in Trust for King's Roads	£63 10s. 10d.	£40 os. od.	after 1804
Gabriel Matthias: Assistant Paymaster	£63 os. od.	£70 os. od.	

On 17 April 1783 the Office of Works received the following directive from the Lord Chamberlain's Secretary: 'Mr. Herbert wishes Mr. Couse would direct all those who have compensations in lieu of their abolished offices to be at the Pay Office under the Piazza [in] Stable Yard on Tuesday next at 2 o'clock exactly'.[2]

The government's compensation of dispossessed office-holders was sensible, even generous. But by an odd quirk of fortune, the only real casualties in this minor avalanche of reform were four professionals: the architects Thomas Sandby, S. P. Cockerell, James Paine and James Adam, perhaps the most talented members of the old establishment, apart from Taylor and the indispensable Chambers. Ripley and Couse, Whitshed Keene, and even the incorrigible Selwyn, all received alternative posts. Matthias was given half his salary of £140 after losing his place as Selwyn's deputy, and, incidentally, another £80 per annum for losing his sinecure as Brusher of the King's Robes[3]. But the Treasury deemed that 'Artists or Tradesmen, employed merely as such', were not fit 'objects for compensation'.[4] Sandby, Paine and Adam

---

[1] This sum covered the loss of his official residences at Hampton Court and Scotland Yard, previously sublet for £233. T. 38/507; T. 29/52, f. 441, 20 October 1782; 'Inquiry into . . . the Office of Works', *Parl. Pap.* 1812–13, v, p. 338. He was luckier than two labourers in trust, Thomas Browne, Snr. and Wetherill, who retained office but without compensation for lost perquisites (T. 29/53, ff. 91–2, 14 January 1783; Works 6/20, f. 76, 10 January 1783).

[2] Works 1/5, f. 56, 17 April 1783.   [3] T. 29/53, ff. 140–1, 24 March 1783.

[4] T. 29/54, f. 394, 25 October and f. 461, 25 November 1783. One crumb of comfort remained: that 'in case of vacancies', Chambers was 'to make the first offer to such as were displaced' (Works 6/20, f. 314, 13 November 1784).

were all middle-aged men at the top of their profession. But for Cockerell, this dismissal was a major setback at the very start of his career. 'Mr. Cockerell', Chambers complained to Sheridan, 'is very able in his profession, was very diligent and regular while in His Majesty's Service and only was removed by Mr. Gilbert from thence on the reduction of the Establishment, for being Junior in Office to those who remained; his Case . . . was certainly hard'.[1] Cockerell had been a pupil of Sir Robert Taylor. In 1775 he was appointed Clerk of the Works at the Tower at only 2s. 3d. per day, one-third of the salary carried by more important clerkships.[2] Then in 1780 he was given Newmarket. In 1782 he was superseded at both places by William Leach. Perhaps as a form of indirect compensation he inherited a few years later three of Taylor's positions; the Surveyorship of the Admiralty and the Surveyorships of the Foundling and Pulteney estates.[3]

As a result of Burke's Act and Gilbert's economies, compensation for loss of office in all departments totalled £18,392 18s. 2d. in 1786. Thenceforward the total declined as the older pensioners died, and in 1804 the sum involved was estimated at £11,258 12s. od. Of this nearly one-third was payable to pensioners included in the new Lord Chamberlain's Department.[4]

Out of office, and out of sympathy with Shelburne, Burke dissociated himself from Gilbert's reforms. They were 'as mean and inhuman as his [were] public and generous. He had aimed only at the destruction of parliamentary influence, and of sinecures for parliamentary men; but they aimed their blows at poor inferior officers of twenty, thirty and forty pounds a year . . . [whereas] his oeconomy was gentle as well as systematic'.[5] Furious at the investigation of the Stationery Office and the Exchequer, Horace Walpole took up the cry. He contrasted the pensions bestowed on Shelburne's favourites, Grantham, Thurlow, Barré and Dunning, with the abolition of so many minor posts, and concluded: 'the whole scene of reformation was a mummery that at once insulted the nation, virtue and charity, and enriched only the principal reformers'.[6] One contemporary lampoon ran as follows:

> 'No catcher of vermin destroys the whole race:
> Gilbert took away twenty to gain one good place. . .
> Reformation's a trade that enriches the cunning,
> From Luther to Barré, from Calvin to Dunning'[7].

But then Shelburne had fallen foul of 'the clan', as he christened the Whig aristocracy, and in doing so he exposed the contradictions and inconsistencies which made up the Economical Reform movement. Back in office a few months later, this time in unholy alliance with Lord North, Fox was heard to announce 'that it was impossible

---

[1] Works 1/5, f. 70, 7 November 1783.　　　[2] Works 1/5, f. 69, 6 November 1783.
[3] Colvin, *Dictionary*, p. 147. On his deathbed, Taylor 'suspended the consolations of religion, literally full half an hour, till he had finished various letters in favour of Mr. Cockerell and Mr. Craig, the architects, who had been his pupils, to get them new patronage, to secure them better in what they had got. In half an hour after, he died!' (*Gent's. Mag.* 1788, pt. ii, p. 931).
[4] *Commons Jnls.* lix (1803–4), Appendix 30, p. 637.
[5] *Parl. Hist.* xxiii (1782–83), pp. 263–4, 1070.
[6] H. Walpole, *Last Journals* ed. Doran ii (1859), pp. 557–8; *Letters*, ed. Toynbee, viii, pp. 264, 396 and ix, p. 2. Burke's transfer of pensions to the Exchequer, as well as their limitation in size, only took effect after 5 April 1783 (*Parl. Hist.* xxiii, 1782–83, p. 583).
[7] Quoted by Walpole, *Last Journals*, ed. Doran and Steuart ii (1910), pp. 492–3.

for the Government of a great kingdom to go on, unless it had certain lucrative and honourable situations to bestow on its officers'.[1] However the Coalition fell before it could reverse Shelburne's measures. The consolidation of Gilbert's work became Pitt's responsibility.

In the short run, Burke's Act was a failure. It failed to halt the accumulation of deficits on the Civil List.[2] All Shelburne's theories and Gilbert's cheeseparing could not constrict the expanding cost of government. In 1784 and 1786 Pitt was forced to follow North in begging Parliament for supplementary grants.[3] Sixteen years later a further application led to the progressive reorganisation of the Civil List in 1802, 1816 and 1830.[4] But in the long run, Burke's attack on royal influence confirmed parliamentary control over the Civil List and began the slow process by which the Crown was removed from the political scene. At the same time his division of the Civil List into eight categories pointed the way to an eventual separation of royal and governmental expenditure.

As for the Office of Works, 1782 proved to be the year of its grand climacteric. In essence, its organisation had been professionalised. Instead of being, as Burke put it, with characteristic exaggeration, 'a junto of members of Parliament', it had become the 'concern of builders, and such like, and of none else'.[5] In the attenuated department which emerged from the reforms of 1782, Ripley and Couse, Horsley and Crocker, constituted the entire administrative staff of the small office in Little Scotland Yard directed by Sir William Chambers. As it happened, Horsley proved subject to recurrent bouts of insanity. So did the intemperate and unstable Thomas Tildesley, who was reappointed Clerk of the Works at Windsor. However, the periodic news of their 'calamitous situation' was sympathetically received by George III, and temporary deputies were appointed in their place.[6] But such personal troubles were to be less of a worry to Chambers than the novel administrative problems produced by reform. As his title suggests, Chambers' new position was a conflation of two earlier offices, the Surveyorship and the Comptrollership.[7] As Comptroller he had only been *de facto* head of department. Now, as Surveyor General and Comptroller, he was no longer understudy to Whitshed Keene, but *de jure* architect to the King. Unfortunately, he was also a servant with three masters: the Treasury, the Lord Chamberlain and George III.

---

[1] *Parl. Register* x (1783), p. 272. This debate on the Exchequer Regulation Bill revealed the Coalition ministers in their true colours. Burke had always proclaimed the sanctity of freehold offices as private property; he was to reiterate his position in face of Pitt's proposals (*Parl. Hist.* xxv, 1785–86, pp. 310 and 371–4).

[2] See the figures set out in *Parl. Pap.* 1868–9, xxxv, pp. 181–97.

[3] *Parl. Hist.* xxiv (1783–85), p. 1241; xxv (1785–86), p. 1348; 'Public Income and Expenditure', *Parl. Pap.* 1868–9, xxxv, p. 599. Optimistic estimates made in April 1783, were thus proved inaccurate (B.M. Add. MS. 29466 ff. 12–13, 32–43). Parliamentary grants covering Civil List debts were as follows: 1784, £60,000; 1786, £210,000; 1802, £990,053; 1804, £591,842; 1805, £10,458 (*Parl. Debates* xxx, 1815, Appendix p. lxxxvii).

[4] cf. Sir T. Erskine May, *Constitutional History of England*, ed. F. Holland i (1912), pp. 163–7; Sir D. L. Keir, *Constitutional History of Modern Britain, 1485–1951* (1960 ed.), pp. 387–9. For the constitutional implications of Burke's Act cf. E. A. Reiton, 'The Civil List in 18th century politics', *Historical Jnl.* ix (1966), pp. 318–37.

[5] *Parl. Hist.* xxi (1780–81), p. 36.

[6] Eg. Works 4/18, f. 198, 9 September 1796; T. 29/66, f. 41, 11 July 1793.

[7] Chambers himself frequently used both titles as alternatives. So widespread was this practice that in 1796 the Royal Warrant appointing James Wyatt refers to its subject as 'Surveyor *or* Comptroller' (Works 6/13, 16 March 1796).

Chapter II

THE SURVEYORSHIP OF SIR WILLIAM CHAMBERS, 1782–1796

BY 1782 Sir William Chambers had been a government architect for more than two decades. His conservative temperament and his friendship with the King made him doubly averse to change. His popularity in the department and his enormous practical experience were additional deterrents to outside reform. An architect of genius, witty, worldly and humane, a scholar as well as an industrious and method-ical administrator, Chambers was not a man to trifle with. As early as 1755, young Robert Adam, a potential rival, had conceded that Englishmen abroad considered him a 'prodigy for genius, for sense and good taste . . . his appearance is genteel and his personage good . . . He despises others as much as he admires his own talents which he shows with a slow and dignified air, conveying an air of great wisdom which is no less useful than all his other endowments'.[1] Now, at the age of 59, he found himself at the top of the architectural profession: an artist turned civil servant, bound hand and foot by politicians.

Chambers' tenure of office was memorable for one architectural masterpiece and a number of petty squabbles. As Surveyor of Somerset House, he presided over the completion of his greatest work. As Surveyor General and Comptroller he guided the Office of Works through a difficult period of readjustment. He accepted reform with reluctance, co-operating in the removal of sinecurists but resisting every move which seemed to threaten the autonomy of his department. In January 1782 he wrote to Burke:[2]

> I am sorry to find still inserted in your bill, the Clause relative to calling in Surveyors to certify to the Treasury, that works have been fairly and properly executed: it must, I apprehend, be an oversight, as by His Majesty's plan of the Office of Works, two persons are [already] appointed as standing checks upon the Surveyor's conduct . . . I must confess to you that this clause seems to me very distressing; it will subject the Surveyor, who I apprehend should be chosen from among the first of the profession, to the control of the meanest . . . ; it is calculated to keep him constantly in hot water,

---

[1] Quoted by J. Fleming, *Robert Adam* (1962), p. 160. For a summary of Chambers' governmental career cf. J. Mordaunt Crook, 'Sir William Chambers and the Office of Works, 1761–96', in John Harris, *Sir William Chambers* (1970), pp. 108–27.

[2] Fitzwilliam MSS., Sheffield City Library, Bk. 1, f. 149, 18 June 1782. The letter was written in response to a reminder from Kenton Couse (R.I.B.A. Chambers MSS. 55, 17 May 1782).

and to place him . . . in a very contemptible light. Besides which . . . [it] will be attended with considerable expense. I therefore flatter myself that you will have the goodness to give the clause in question its due consideration before it passes into an act.[1]

In the following May Chambers made a last attempt to stay the avalanche. In another letter to Burke he defended the efficiency of the old system and laid down his minimum requirements for a new establishment.[2] With regard to the new post of Surveyor General and Comptroller, he complained, 'I fear no single man would be able to go through with it. He should . . . have the help of two other able architects . . . With respect to the whole inferior arrangement of the intended new establishment, permit me to assure you from more than twenty years' experience, that the nearer it approaches to the old one the better it will be: for that had few, if any, unnecessary officers, they were moderately paid for their services, and being checked by each other and ultimately by the Board, they had no opportunity either of defrauding the Crown, or taking to themselves unwarrantable perquisites'. 'In general', he concluded, 'His Majesty's buildings were better executed, and (all things considered) cheaper than those of any other private gentleman whatever'. A head of department and two assistant architects, a chief clerk and three office clerks, eight clerks of works, sixteen or eighteen labourers in trust, as well as engine keepers, labourers and messengers, all these Chambers considered essential personnel for any new establishment: 'I think it cannot be more reduced without prejudice to the service'. But reduced it was, and the story of his next fourteen years in office is one of rising costs, expanding business and lack of staff.

Chambers attributed most of his administrative difficulties to Gilbert's over-stringent economies. When in 1783 the Treasury called, via the Lord Chamberlain, for a full survey of all official houses, he insisted that additional work required additional staff: 'the Office of Draughtsman is abolished; and the Clerks who are left . . . have been loaded with so much additional business that it will not be in their power to [prepare plans]: if they are to be done, persons must be hired for that purpose'.[3] Similarly he maintained that Gilbert's cheeseparing reductions had in several cases deprived his colleagues of their lawful perquisites. In 1787 he vainly attempted to regain for his Clerks of the Works their £80 stationery allowance lost in 1782. Gilbert had imposed an overall allowance of £21 for office stationery. The old allowance, Chambers claimed, 'was not thought more than sufficient to enable them to purchase the Paper, Measuring Books, Day Books, Account Books and other articles necessary . . . and though there are now fewer Clerks, the number of Books and Papers are not diminished, as there . . . must be distinct Books, Estimates and Accounts kept for every separate building . . . I have allowed to each Clerk out of Mr. Gilbert's £21 no more than a guinea a year . . . and the remainder was not near sufficient to supply the Office. They certainly have been considerable sufferers by so scanty an allowance, as has likewise the Resident Clerk, who has . . . supplied the deficiency in the Office

    [1] ' . . . that I do not like this Clause at all . . . that you will upon due consideration leave [it] out. . . .' (Draft MS.) The sanction in question (22 G. III c. 82 clause IX) was in fact seldom invoked.
    [2] Chambers to Burke 5 May 1782. Chambers sent a copy to George III; in 1804, when reform was again in the air, the King presented it to Wyatt (Works 4/19, 17 February 1804), who made sure that a further copy was preserved (Works 6/23, f. 237). The original is among the Fitzwilliam MSS., Sheffield City Library, Bk. I, f. 115.   [3] Works 1/5, f. 57, 2 May 1783.

at his own expense'.[1] The Treasury ignored this complaint, and no change was made until 1811, when further government economies and a petition from J. W. Hiort, then Resident Clerk, brought matters to a head.[2]

Between 1782 and 1796, Chambers served under three Lord Chamberlains: the Duke of Manchester, the Marquess of Hertford and the Marquess of Salisbury. Manchester held office (April 1782 to April 1783) as the Rockinghams' nominee. Hertford's brief tenure (April to December 1783) marked the limits of the Fox–North régime. Salisbury held office (December 1783 to May 1804) as a Pittite.

George Montagu, 4th Duke of Manchester (1737–88) amply possessed the three attributes requisite for a Foxite: dissipation, dignity and talent. Wraxall noticed that 'his figure, which was noble, his manners, affable and corresponding with his high rank, prepossessed in his favour, but his fortune bore no proportion to his dignity. Though a man of very dissipated habits and unaccustomed to diplomatic business, he did not want talents'[3]. Fox sent him to negotiate peace as Ambassador to Paris in 1783. Five years later he caught one chill while watching the trial of Warren Hastings and another while watching a cricket match at Brighton. This double affliction 'baffled the skill of his physicians', and he died 'with great serenity and resignation'.[4] By contrast, his successor, Francis Seymour-Conway, 4th Marquess of Hertford (1718–94) was notorious for his cautious and miserly disposition.[5] Indeed his pernickety presence was to prove far more of a clog on Office of Works administration than Manchester's casual acquaintance with the principles of Economical Reform. Having been Lord Lieutenant of Ireland (1765–6) and Master of the Horse (1766), Hertford held the position of Lord Chamberlain between November 1766 and April 1782, prior to his reappointment in April 1783. Commenting on his reputation for 'niggardly avarice', Walpole admitted that he was also 'the most decent, cautious, discreet and submissive of courtiers'.[6] Indeed the most that could be said of Hertford was that 'the love of money only excepted, his character was negatively good'.[7] The chief cause of his disputes with Chambers seems merely to have been his pettiness and lack of imagination. But the fact that Hertford's secretary happened to be Chambers' ex-colleague and rival Whitshed Keene, can hardly have made things easier. The third of Chambers' superiors, James Cecil, 1st Marquess of Salisbury (1748–1823), was fortunately more reliable than Manchester and less parsimonious than Hertford. In fact he was noted firstly for his wife and secondly for his generosity. Lady Salisbury was the Tory answer to Georgiana, Duchess of Devonshire. Her political blandishments had rivalled those of the Whig Queen in the famous Westminster election of

[1] Works 6/21, f. 106, 25 April 1787; T. 29/58, ff. 329 and 384; Works 4/17, 4 May 1787.

[2] The Treasury decided that 'all newspapers, court calendars, pocket books and almanacs and other allowances of that description hitherto supplied for private use should be immediately discontinued' (Works 4/20, 5 October 1810). Hiort's total allowance for stationery, heat and light was £41. 'The coals alone', he complained, 'have cost near double the whole allowance' (Works 6/25, f. 188, 21 October 1811 and f. 128, 28 February 1814). After this, excess expenditure was charged to the Lord Chamberlain's office.

[3] Sir N. Wraxall, *Memoirs* iii (1884 ed.), p. 59 and v, p. 172. He also held the office of Collector of Customs outward in the Port of London.

[4] *Gent's. Mag.* 1788, pt. ii, p. 839. 'Though his opinions were rather favourable to the side of opposition, he was never a party zealot'.

[5] 'But cautious Hertford shrinks when risks are run' (W. Combe, *The Diaboliad*, 1777).

[6] *Royal Register*, v, p. 153; H. Walpole, *Last Journals* ed. Doran i (1910), p. 258.

[7] *MSS. and Correspondence of the 1st Earl of Charlemont*, Hist. MSS. Comm. 12th Report i (1891), p. 23. Hertford supported first North's ministry, then the Fox–North Coalition, and finally became a Pittite.

1784. Indeed Salisbury seems to have owed both his appointment as Lord Chamberlain and his elevation to the Marquessate to her talent for political intrigue.[1] His staunch Protestantism and munificent hospitality made him a firm favourite with George III. On one occasion, in 1800, he spent £3000 in entertaining the Cabinet, the Royal Family and 1500 Hertfordshire Volunteers.[2] As an administrator, Salisbury proved competent and sensible, less of a nuisance than Hertford and more of an asset than Manchester.

Gilbert's plan had been that he himself should co-ordinate the different departments of the reformed royal household in his capacity as Superintendent and Paymaster. This piece of empire-building had been defeated. But his influence survived in the person of John Jones, appointed according to the Instructions of 1783 as Inspector of His Majesty's Works, Contracts and Business in the departments of the Lord Steward, Lord Chamberlain, Master of the Horse, and Office of His Majesty's Robes. In particular, Jones was to act as link between the Office of Works and the Lord Chamberlain. 'For the better encouragement of him . . . diligently and faithfully to attend the duty', he was awarded a salary of £400 per annum.[3] Understandably enough, since Burke's Act included no mention of such a post, the principal Household officers soon made sure that Jones's Inspectorship followed Gilbert's Paymastership into oblivion. In theory Jones was to exercise a general supervision over all surveys, contracts and accounts. In practice his duties were confined to the Office of Works, and before long even these duties had become nominal. His salary was charged as a pension on the Office of Works establishment and he was given the use of an official house in Scotland Yard. At his death in 1807, the appointment was allowed to lapse.[4]

Burke's Act was also circumvented with regard to the management of the royal gardens. Burke had envisaged a separate department under the direction of a Surveyor of Gardens, he 'being by Profession a Gardener, or Improver of Grounds'. This proposal was one of the few measures which made Economical Reform palatable for Farmer George.[5] But Gilbert's Instructions ensured that the royal gardens remained under the control of the various Clerks of the Works, except for the kitchen gardens which became the responsibility of the Board of Green Cloth. St. James's Park and Hyde Park also remained within the Office of Works, although still under the jurisdiction of their own Ranger, the Earl of Orford.

Orford's relationship with the Office of Works, and still more so those of his successors Lord Grenville and Lord Euston, remained tenuous in the extreme. Dignified, charming and eccentric, George Walpole, 3rd Earl of Orford (1730–91),

[1] Lady Gwendolen Cecil, *Life of Robert Cecil, Marquess of Salisbury* i (1921–32), p. 2. Joseph Farington and James Wyatt believed that Salisbury owed his position to the Marquess of Downshire (Farington, p. 1119, 6 November 1797).

[2] *Gent's. Mag.* 1823, pt. i, pp. 563–4. Salisbury ended his political career as Joint Postmaster-General, 1816–23.   [3] Works 6/13, 3 February 1783.

[4] 'Inquiry into . . . the Office of Works', *Parl. Pap.* 1812–13, v, p. 331; *Commons Jnls.* lix (1803–4), Appendix 30, p. 634, Class vii; Crest 2/918, 17 May 1783. The Duke of Portland decided that 'there did not appear to be any necessity for appointing a successor' (Works 4/20, 18 September 1807). Wyatt held the same view, although he received several applications, one at least being supported by the Duke of Kent (J. Wyatt to M. C. Wyatt, 8 Sept. 1807, Victoria and Albert Museum MSS. Box iv, 86 DD).

[5] 22 G. III c. 82, clause vii. 'A Comptroller of the Gardens, bred a Gardener, will be an useful Officer in a branch the Comptroller of Buildings cannot be supposed to understand' (*Correspondence of George III*, ed. J. Fortescue v, no. 3698, George III to Rockingham 28 April 1782).

drew the Ranger's nominal salary of £80 per annum from 1763 until the day he died. William Wyndham Grenville, 1st Baron Grenville (1759–1834), Ranger between 1791 and 1794, was still more of a conventional political appointment. The son of one Prime Minister (George Grenville) and the cousin of another (William Pitt), he eventually achieved the same distinction himself as leader of the All Talents administration in 1806–7. Cox described him as 'the proudest looking man I ever saw . . . cold and unbending even to great people'.[1] An austere scholar, a die-hard Whig and an inveterate sinecurist, he exchanged his Rangership for the Auditorship of the Exchequer, a post worth £4000 per annum. His successor, George Fitzroy, Lord Euston (1760–1844), heir to the Dukedom of Grafton, and Ranger between 1794 and 1807, was rather more conscientious. A staunch Pittite turned moderate Whig, Euston carefully discharged the duties of an office riddled with jurisdictional anomalies. His salary was paid by the Office of Works. But his duties both complemented and competed with those of the Office of Woods and Forests. The grass in the two London parks was the responsibility of the Ranger, the trees belonged to the Office of Woods and Forests, and the walls, gates and lodges to the Office of Works.[2] During his time he planted 25,000 trees. 'Everybody knows', remarked his successor Lord Sydney, 'with what judgment Lord Euston has planted Hyde Park'.[3]

Burke's Act made the Office of Works subordinate to the Lord Chamberlain. Gilbert's Instructions[4] turned subordination into dependence. Burke had vowed to demolish the 'whole ill-contrived scaffolding, which obstructs, rather than forwards our public works; to take away its Treasury; to put the whole into the hands of a real builder, who shall not be a member of Parliament; and to oblige him by a previous estimate and final payment, to appear twice at the Treasury before the public can be loaded'.[5] He had therefore stipulated that only works of less than £1000 could be executed on the Surveyor General's authority. Works estimated at more than £1000 were to be authorised by the Lord Chamberlain, the Treasury and the King's Sign Manual. Works of more than £5000 were to be executed by gross contract, subject to Treasury approval. Gilbert was still more stringent. According to his Instructions the Surveyor General's discretion was limited to 'Ordinary' works of less than £100. 'Extra' works of more than £100 were to be authorised by the Lord Chamberlain; those over £500 by both Chamberlain and Treasury; and those over £1000 by gross contract subject to Chamberlain, Treasury and Sign Manual.

---

[1] *Complete Peerage*, ed. G.E.C. etc., vi, p. 116; *Gent's. Mag.* 1834, pt. i, pp. 327–9. 'The routine of office was almost hereditary in him'.

[2] Crest 8/3, f. 310; Works 16/35/1, ff. 1–9; T. 28/38, 1790–1800 *passim*, 30 July 1823. This confusion baffled even the industrious Craig: 'Has the Office of Works [he was asked] any communication or connection in business, with the Ranger of St. James's Park, which office appears to be a part of the establishment of the Department of Works?'.

(Craig)   'I cannot say; possibly yes, as some works in St. James's Park are performed by the Office of Works, and thence communications may occasionally be made between the Ranger and the Clerk of the Works'.

('Inquiry into . . . the Office of Works', *Parl. Pap.* 1812–13, v, p. 416).

[3] T. 28/38, 20 April 1807 and 11 February 1808. John Thomas Townshend, 2nd Viscount Sydney (1764–1831), a Pittite, M.P. for Newport (1786–90) and Whitchurch (1790–1800), Ranger 1807–31 (*Gent's. Mag.* 1831, pt. i, p. 267).

[4] Works 6/368/7, 12 March 1783; 'Inquiry into . . . the Office of Works', *Parl. Pap.* 1812–13, v, pp. 389–92.   [5] *Parl. Hist.* xxi (1780–81), p. 37.

In practice, however, these regulations were far from absolute. Treasury approval was seldom sought for works of less than £1000. The strict hierarchy of organisation was sometimes ignored. Works were occasionally ordered by direct Treasury command, without reference to the Lord Chamberlain, or even by direct royal command, independently of both Treasury and Chamberlain. Contracts in gross were seldom employed in place of the usual Office of Works contract based on the principle of measure and value. And by the 1790s the Lord Chamberlain was more concerned with the honouring of estimates than with detailed examination of bills.[1]

As a sub-department of the Lord Chamberlain's Office, the reformed Office of Works retained few vestiges of financial autonomy. Requests for building operations by a government department or member of the royal family were made in the first instance to the Surveyor General. However, his authority was occasionally by-passed by applications made directly to the Lord Chamberlain or to the Treasury. Minor running repairs were executed at the discretion of the Clerk of the Works by Office of Works tradesmen, on the authority of the Surveyor General and under the supervision of the resident Labourer in Trust. For specific operations costing more than £100, the Clerk of the Works' estimate had to be delivered, via the Surveyor General, to the Lord Chamberlain, as a preliminary to execution. Treasury approval and the King's Sign Manual were required for all works of more than £1000, notably for the repairs ordered in consequence of the annual General Survey, usually held in April, when the principal officers of the department personally surveyed all the houses and palaces in their care.[2] After execution the cost of each operation was entered by the Clerk of the Works in that portion of the Quarterly Accounts pertaining to his department. In 1813 the Commissioners of Inquiry described this process as follows:

> The first Assistant Clerk sees, in the first place, that Abstracts [of work done] are correctly cast; next, he and the Examining Clerk ascertain whether the amounts of the Abstracts are correctly transcribed into the Book of Bills transmitted by the Clerks of the Works, and reference is made by the two Assistant Clerks, in the presence of the Examining Clerk, to the Book of Dimensions, when the quantities in the Tradesmen's Bills differ from those produced by the Clerks of the Works; but no other use is made of this Book, for it is presumed . . . that both [sets of] Bills are made out from the Abstracts taken from the same Book, after the Dimensions contained in it have been agreed upon by the two Measurers employed, namely, one on behalf of the Office of Works, and the other by the Tradesman. . . . The next step is to put the prices in pencil in the blank Bills, as taken from the Office Book of Prices, leaving blanks or making queries where these do not apply; in which the Examining Clerk is assisted by the Resident Clerk. The Bills in this state are produced at the Board, at which the Surveyor [General], the Examining and Resident Clerks and the Clerk of the Works, under whose direction the Work included in the Bill under consideration has been executed, should all attend; and the Bills are then read over article by

---

[1] 'Inquiry into . . . the Office of Works', *Parl. Pap.* 1812–13, v, p. 362. Special Treasury warrants were required for the settlement of bills which exceeded authorised estimates (eg. Works 4/17, 29 July 1791; Works 6/22, f. 94, 15 March 1793; Works 4/19, 19 February 1800).

[2] Eg. Works 6/23, f. 204, 26 November and f. 207, 17 December 1802; Works 4/19, 17 December 1802; L.C. 1/39, 30 March 1787; T. 29/58, f. 313, 26 April 1797. Directions given in April were followed by another survey in July 'to observe the progress, and another in October, to satisfy themselves as to the execution' ('Inquiry into . . . the Office of Works', *Parl. Pap.* 1812–13, v, p. 333). Travelling expenses thus incurred were repaid by the Lord Chamberlain (*ibid*, p. 405).

article, by the Resident Clerk, and the prices to each affixed. The several Items are then computed, according to these prices, by the two Assistant Clerks; and after the Resident Clerk has examined this computation, the amounts of the Items are added up by the Assistant Clerks, and the castings proved by the Examining and Resident Clerks. The sums total of each Bill are next entered by the Resident Clerk in an Abstract Book under the heads of the different departments or places, from which is made out the aggregate Quarterly Account transmitted to the Lord Chamberlain, together with a Pay List containing alphabetically the names of the Tradesmen, with the amounts of their respective claims, [minus] deductions . . . on account of the Civil List and Stamps; all which different Accounts are signed by the Surveyor and the Examining and Resident Clerks.[1]

The amounts were then authorised by the Lord Chamberlain, who compared them with the original estimate and then obtained the necessary Treasury warrant permitting payment of officers and tradesmen out of the Exchequer. Finally, the annual accounts were passed to the Commissioners for Auditing Public Accounts.

Gilbert's Instructions had stipulated that all Quarterly Accounts were to be submitted within fifteen days of the end of the relevant quarter.[2] But by the 1790s they were frequently several quarters in arrear, and tradesmen occasionally waited more than a year for payment. In all, three to four years might easily elapse between a demand by a Lady of the Bedchamber that her apartments might be whitewashed, and the re-appearance of that demand as an item of expenditure among the declared annual accounts.

The weakness of this complex system of check and double check lay firstly in the heavy responsibility thrust upon the Surveyor General as lynchpin of the whole system. Still more important were the difficulties involved in the production of accurate long-term estimates. There were two dangers here: the possibility of rapid price changes, and the likelihood of arbitrary demands for reconstruction and repair emanating from the royal family. As an administrator Chambers was more than adequate for the onerous burdens of office. His successor, James Wyatt, was not. Wyatt's inefficiency, the extravagance of George III's children, and excessive price-fluctuation during the Napoleonic period, strained the system to breaking point. The result was another investigation in 1810-12 and another reform in 1815.

Chambers was steeped in the customs and practices of his department. Burke's Act had stipulated that the Surveyor General must be '*bona fide* by Profession an Architect or Builder'.[3] Chambers was a professional to the core. He was also eminently humane and almost excessively loyal to his subordinates.[4] All three characteristics soon brought him into conflict with the Treasury and, more immediately, with the Treasury's nominee, the Lord Chamberlain. Trouble began almost at once. The point at issue was the method of presenting accounts; and the battle hinged upon the Lord Chamberlain's power of authorising, or refusing to authorise, quarterly payments. The whole episode is worth examining in detail, if only for the flood of

---

[1] *Ibid.* p. 360. A similar description was produced by J. W. Hiort in 1812 ('Estimates and Accounts', *Parl. Pap.* 1812, ix, p. 409).
[2] 'Inquiry into . . . the Office of Works', *Parl. Pap.* 1812-13, v, p. 357.
[3] 22 G. III c. 82, clause vi.
[4] For examples of Chambers' humanity in private practice cf. H. Martiensson, 'Chambers as a Professional Man', *Architectural Review* cxxxv (1964), pp. 277-83.

light it throws upon the personnel and organisation of the Office of Works in the months immediately following Burke's Act. These were months when 'Oeconomical' principles were being painfully translated into administrative practice, months when Chambers himself confessed to being 'entirely in the Dark as to what may be deemed right or wrong'.[1]

Burke's Act had enjoined upon the Lord Chamberlain a strict examination of Office of Works accounts. Manchester interpreted 'accounts' as monthly lists of wages, labour and materials. Chambers disagreed. 'It is indeed absurd enough', he wrote,[2] 'to remind the Treasury twelve times a year of a thing they must well be acquainted with, yet to do even a little more will be exceedingly troublesome, without answering any purpose; and to give a full account of the monthly expence incurred in the King's works, or in any other works, is absolutely Impossible, unless all the men should strike off at the end of the month and stand still 'till the measurements were taken, which would occasion much loss of time, a vast deal of trouble and a degree of confusion which even Mr. Burke would find it difficult to unravel'. Nevertheless Hertford reiterated his predecessor's demands and then added a request for detailed annual estimates. 'Such an estimate', Chambers replied,[3] 'cannot possibly be made with any degree of certainty, as it cannot be known what it may be His Majesty's pleasure to command . . . nor what further defects may be discovered in a great number of Old Buildings always tending to decay'. The most that could be offered was a general estimate based on the annual General Survey and the average expenditure of previous years.[4] As for daily wage lists, 'they are of no use whatever, as they do not tend to give the least idea of the expences incurred . . . I flatter myself the Lord Chamberlain and Lords Commissioners of His Majesty's Treasury will allow the inutility of this ceremony, for it can be nothing more, and suffer it to be discontinued'.[5]

Hertford, however, remained firm.[6] Indeed, he seized the occasion of some minor repairs at Hampton Court as an excuse to impose stringent regulations. His demand for itemised accounts, giving separate details of prices and quantities, provoked a furious and very revealing outburst from the Surveyor General:[7]

> All these requisitions are without precedent, and . . . totally impracticable in the present state of the Office of Works, of which it would increase the Business Tenfold and Consequently would be Attended with Considerable Expence in Salaries to Additional Clerks. It would moreover Create much discontent and Occasion Great Confusion by the Vast Increase of Books, Dimensions, Calculations, Abstracts, Bills, Entries, Transcripts etc., etc., and would render the Accounts so very Voluminous that the Auditors and other Officers of Inquest would find and certainly declare it impracticable, to Examine them in the Common Course of Business. . . . Your Lordship is not to Learn, I am sure, that an Estimate means nothing More than to give a General State for the Satisfaction of the Employer of the Expence Likely to be Incurr'd. If it be made too full it cannot profit the Maker, at Least not in the King's

---

[1] Works 6/20, f. 110, 24 March 1783.
[2] Works 6/20, f. 96, 15 February 1783, Chambers to Herbert.
[3] Works 6/20, f. 132, 27 June 1783, Chambers to Keene.
[4] The average expenditure for the previous seven years had been £25,633, excluding salaries (*ibid*).
[5] Works 6/20, ff. 134–5, 27 July 1783.   [6] Works 6/20, f. 138, 3 July 1783.
[7] L.C. 1/39, 26 September 1783; Works 6/20, ff. 166–179.

Service; But if it be made too Scanty it affects his Character and Subjects him in the end to Censure, perhaps to worse Treatment. There can therefore be no Reason to Suspect any Estimate after it has been Carefully made by the Respective Clerk of the Works; and as carefully examined by Mr. Couse, whose province it is to Examine them pursuant to the King's Instructions, and I confess to your Lordship that upon this present Occasion, where even the Probability of a Fraud Cannot Exist, I do not See either the Necessity, the Policy or the Justice, of Attacking the Character of Men whose Abilities Cannot be disputed, whose fidelity has been proved by More than Forty Years faithful Services, and who, serving by His Majesty's Own Immediate Appointment, should be Treated with all the deference due to so high a Patronage.

I have the honour to be, with the Greatest Respect, My Lord,
Your Lordship's most faithful and most
Obedient Humble Servant,
William Chambers

Hertford's reply was brief and to the point.[1] 'The Letter and Spirit' of Burke's Act must be obeyed, 'whether they are without precedent or not. That Act in all its provisions is Novel, and without precedent; it is however none the less binding on every Subject of this Country'. He followed this by refusing to authorise the accounts for Midsummer Quarter, 1783, thus holding up the payment of tradesmen for several months.[2] Chambers refused to relinquish his position: the accounts had been presented in the same way as they had been 'for more than a century past'; indeed 'they have even twice since the new regulations, been admitted and paid in the Lord Chamberlain's Office . . . we have . . . nothing to conceal, our books and papers will all be opened to any person duly appointed to inspect them'. If Hertford will not give way, 'immediate application must be made to the Lords of the Treasury for an Additional Detachment of Clerks . . . For all the bills [for the quarter in question] only amount to 370; being for works ordered upon 99 estimates. But if the method prescribed were pursued, there would be 1100 estimates and 1100 bills, which must each be separately measured, abstracted, calculated and made out, by the Clerk of the Works, each be read and valued by the Comptroller and his assistants in the Office, and afterwards be three times cast and as often copied over'.[3]

At this stage, Hertford was out of town and Sir Francis Drake, who had actually ordered the work at Hampton Court, was in Devonshire. Wearying of his proxy battle with the Lord Chamberlain's Secretary, Whitshed Keene, Chambers turned his attention to the Treasury and submitted an outspoken memorandum.

If a man were dishonest enough to impose upon his Lordship in a *Mock* estimate of four lines, he would I fear have more than Ingenuity enough to dress his imposition in four hundred, without danger of detection; and however important a multiplication of Bills may at first appear towards a discovery of the Truth, it can in reality only produce additional confusion, by diverting the attention of the examiner into a hundred or five hundred channels instead of ten, and by affording an opportunity of subdividing the imposition (if such there be) into as many parts as there are separate bills. . . . What I would humbly beg leave to propose . . . is that upon every occasion

[1] L.C. 1/39, 26 September 1783.   [2] L.C. 1/39, 10 October 1783.
[3] Works 6/20, ff. 179–183, 17 October 1783.

when the least doubt exists in the breasts of the Lords of the Treasury or the Lord Chamberlain, . . . a Person skilful in Builders' Accounts should be sent to the Office of Works, where he would find materials to trace an estimate of four lines, up to four hundred, and still upwards to the minutest article of which it is composed, and Bills whenever they were doubted might be examined in like manner: materials would be found in the Office to trace every article contained in each bill to the ten, twenty or sometimes two hundred original articles of which it is composed.[1]

At the same time Chambers sent Burke a private letter designed to counteract Keene's malicious influence:

The Secretary to the Lord Chamberlain has made out such an interpretation of what he calls the spirit of the regulating Act . . . as makes the Comptroller of the King's Works (what I dare say you never intended him to be) a mere footboy to the Lord Chamberlain's Office, and he . . . will, I think, very soon complete the business he has laboured at with unremitting assiduity these four years past, which is my removal from the King's Service. At present everything in the Office of Works is thrown into confusion. . . . As the correspondence [with the Treasury] is long and comes to their Lordships so weakly recommended, I have not the confidence to hope for much relief, without the interference of some powerful friend. . . . You, my dear sir, have very often honoured me with distinguishing marks of friendship and good will. I never needed your protection more than at this time. . . . And setting apart my own [interest] your humanity will I am sure be cheerfully exerted in favour of many needy and many very distressed tradesmen and servants of the Crown, who, some of them, must really starve, should the embargo in the Chamberlain's Office upon their pay be long continued.[2]

Chambers won his point. The dispute ended with a Treasury directive substantiating the Surveyor General's position.[3] Indeed Hertford received scant sympathy from the Treasury Lords. In August 1783, he received this peremptory missive:

My Lords cannot conceive it possible that any Regulation or Instruction can exist of such an absurd Tendancy as to prevent an immediate Compliance with [Burke's request for a statement of accounts]. . . . The payment of His Majesty's Civil List for the Quarter ending 5th July is exceedingly disarranged. . . . [Let] the Lord Chamberlain furnish the Accounts forthwith, or show specifically what Regulation or Instruction prevents his Lordship from knowing the Expenditure of his own office for a Quarter ended now a month since.[4]

After delaying the accounts for as long as five months, from July to November, Hertford capitulated. And with the change of government a few weeks later, he went out of office, unlamented.

---

[1] Works 6/20, ff. 194–6, 30 October 1783.

[2] Fitzwilliam MSS. Sheffield City Library, Bk. i, f. 285, 18 October 1783. The letter concludes: 'P.S. If you should upon enquiry think me deserving of protection, may I flatter myself with a recommendation to your brother's favour, whose particular situation will render it of great service'. This postscript was then endorsed by Richard Burke: 'Bon–car je n'aime pas ces éscrosqueries là'. Richard Burke (d. 1794), Edmund's youngest brother, was Secretary to the Treasury (1782–3) and Recorder of Bristol (1783–94).

[3] T. 29/54, ff. 449–50, 20 November 1783. The Treasury emphasised the necessity of a quick settlement of all outstanding demands on the Civil List, as 'Tradesmen have a just, and now a legal Priority to most others'. Cf. also Works 6/20, f. 212, 28 November 1783.

[4] T. 29/54, f. 134, 7 August 1783. Hertford produced a satisfactory reply within twenty-four hours (T. 29/54, f. 272, 8 August 1783).

But this was not before he had provoked another administrative crisis which dragged on well into 1785. This time, the point at issue was the Surveyor General's authority to order immediate repairs, independently of the Lord Chamberlain. Once more victory went to Chambers. He might be prepared to obey Hertford's order for the whitewashing of Fox's office, even if he denied its validity.[1] But he was not prepared to abrogate one jot of his statutory authority with regard to the direction of running repairs and emergency work.[2] He held this position with Hertford, and he held it again with Salisbury. Works costing more than £100 had, of course, to receive the Lord Chamberlain's assent. But Chambers determined to resist the extension of this principle to every kind of repair. The Lord Chamberlain countered by refusing to sanction such quarterly bills until they had been passed by the Treasury. This occasioned several months' delay in the payment of tradesmen. Salisbury made much of the fact that he was 'liable to be called to account for every shilling expended'.[3] Chambers in turn emphasised the practical utility of his own discretionary power, and the necessity for 'some little necessary elbow room'.[4] 'Some confidence', he added, 'some latitude, the nature of the service certainly requires. Parliament has given the Comptroller a great deal, His Majesty's [i.e. Gilbert's] Instructions have confined it to one tenth part. But even the exercise of that privilege must become superfluous if the payment of what he finds necessary to order by His Majesty's command, at the requisition of the principal officers, or from the emergency of the occasion, is to be made optional'.[5] The Lord Chamberlain must trust the judgement of the Surveyor General and his staff, and refrain from adding 'additional Clogs to a Business already too much encumbered with obstacles'.[6]

This dispute ended with a compromise: Chambers retained his discretionary control but agreed to send Salisbury weekly block estimates and *post hoc* reasons for every minor work. This note of co-operation was to characterise their relationship over the next ten years. We leave the principal contestants solving their differences by personal conference. As Chambers put it, 'a few minutes . . . to explain myself' is much more valuable than an hour of epistolary argument; administrative co-operation is more easily effected 'by a few words, than by many letters'.[7] Hertford must surely have relinquished office with a profound sense of relief. His over-scrupulous nature had been tormented by what he himself called 'the general Spirit of Oeconomy which is carried to such length at this moment'.[8] Chambers agreed that the new regulations were likely to prove troublesome: 'our present plan of proceeding is so very oeconomical'.[9] Nevertheless, he and Salisbury managed to maintain a level of co-operation and efficiency which was never reached during the Surveyorship of James Wyatt.

[1] Works 6/20, f. 17, 9 September 1783.
[2] T. 29/56, f. 319, 24 March and f. 348, 16 April 1785; Works 4/16, 17 June 1785.
[3] Works 6/21, f. 34, 4 May 1785.
[4] Works 6/21, f. 39, 17 May 1785. He instanced one occasion 'a few years ago, [when] by the imprudent removal of the Terrace at Windsor one front of the Castle began to settle; it moved with such rapidity that a few hours delay in securing it might have occasioned the fall of the building' (Works 6/21, ff. 44–5, 27 May 1785).   [5] Works 6/21, f. 32, 2 May 1785.
[6] Works 6/21, ff. 36–7, 17 May 1785.   [7] Works 6/21, ff. 44–5, 27 May 1785.
[8] Works 6/20, f. 137, 1 July 1783. Hertford complained to George III about the burdens of his office (*Correspondence of George III* ed. J. Fortescue vi, no. 4367, Hertford to George III 24 May 1783).
[9] Works 6/20, f. 291, 27 July 1784.

E

While Chambers wrangled with the Treasury Board or the Lord Chamberlain's Office, he never lost sight of the fact that administrative inefficiency frequently meant immediate hardship for government employees. When official insistence on the protocol of Treasury directives delayed the payment of bills and compensations during the hard winter of 1783–4, he reminded his superiors that while they disputed, the very livelihood of many tradesmen and pensioners was at stake. 'The keeping back of the Salaries and Compensations of this Office', he told the Treasury, 'the former of which are now three Quarters in arrear and the latter half a year in arrear, is a very great hardship upon the inferior Officers, Servants and Pensioners . . ., who having no other dependence whatever, and consequently little or no credit, are at this time absolutely in a starving condition. Their Lordships' humanity will I am confident find some speedy remedy for this evil, which is the more distressing as a great part of it falls upon very old, helpless and sick people unfit to struggle with hunger and all the other Miserys of Poverty'. Thanks to his intercession, the Treasury was moved on this occasion to pay off at least the oldest bills by distributing some £600 which still remained in the hands of Gabriel Matthias, Selwyn's deputy in the old Office of Works.[1] Chambers had begged for £900.

As Surveyor General Chambers frequently acted as a channel for the distribution of government charity. Nowhere does his transparent humanity show more clearly. The old Board of Works had regularly recommended widows and other 'real objects of charity' as worthy recipients of the Royal Maundy.[2] Chambers continued this custom, as when he recommended John Chant and Ann Gadd to the Lord Almoner, the Archbishop of York.[3] He also kept up the custom of providing a coffin and funeral expenses for deceased members of the Office staff, for example Robert Churchill, an office bricklayer, and Robert Clayton, an office labourer.[4] But he went further than either custom or duty required in petitioning the Treasury for generous allowances on behalf of disabled labourers and craftsmen. In almost every case the Treasury awarded less than Chambers recommended. For example, in 1793 he urged that a Treasury pension of £20 to £25 per annum be given to Jane Garnett. Her husband John, who had long acted as a foreman to the smith John Davis, had been killed 'in fixing an Engine to a Well to supply a Bath for the use of His Majesty at Windsor . . . Though the rope which he had brought expressly for the purpose was a very good one and had been used with much greater weights, yet by the Machinery catching the side of the well, and the timber across the same, and from the necessary circumstance of the windlass and men being at a distance from the well and the deceased, it is presumed they were incapable of observing the signal which he might give. They continued to heave, the great strain broke the rope, the man fell and was killed . . . He was a very sober, industrious, attentive, honest and ingenious man,

---

[1] Works 6/20, ff. 244–5, 26 March 1784, Chambers to Rose. In his efforts to secure prompt payment of smaller salaries, Chambers was supported by Kenton Couse (Works 3/3, 3 and 4 June 1789). See also Works 4/16, 26 March and 19 November 1784; T. 29/55 f. 161, 10 April 1784; Works 6/20, f. 243, 26 March and f. 246, 2 April 1784.

[2] Works 1/5, f. 38, 22 February 1782.

[3] Works 4/16, 28 February 1783; Works 1/5, f. 76, Christmas, 1784.

[4] Works 5/75, December, 1786; Works 5/76, December, 1787; Works 4/17, 21 December 1787. In 1814 similar arrangements were made for Francis Cobb, Constant Labourer at Hampton Court, who died aged 'about ninety' (Works 6/26, f. 164, 30 August 1814; Works 4/21, 26 August 1814, 30 August 1814). Expenses on such occasions varied between £2 and £5.

and . . . has left a widow without the least means of supporting herself, and who, from the melancholy state of her mind, the very worst consequences are to be dreaded'. The Treasury awarded a mere £12, less than half Chambers' recommendation.[1]

Another example was the case of Charles Rolfe, labourer to Palmer the plasterer. Working at George Rose's house in Scotland Yard, he 'had the misfortune to fall from the Stone Landing of the Steps going into the Yard upon the stones of the same; by which he broke his thigh and was otherwise so much bruised as to render him incapable of work . . . [with] but a distant prospect of ever being able to get his Bread'. Chambers recommended 10s. per week. The Treasury awarded 7s.[2] Rolfe's case, however, began as misfortune and ended as fraud. His allowance was paid over by Palmer's clerk, William Mears, 'every Saturday at the Pay Table'. But one day 'finding himself very infirm he brought a woman whom he called his wife, and requested the money might [in future] be paid to her, to save the fatigue of walking three or four miles, he being very lame. The request was complied with on condition she brought a weekly note from him, which she regularly did'. More than a year afterwards, Mears called to see the old man, only to discover that Rolfe had long since died, leaving scores of signed notes for presentation by his 'wife'. The woman in question, Mary Denby, was committed to Tothill Fields Bridewell, and Palmer claimed compensation for this 'very singular fraud'.[3]

But such a case was really no more than the result of grotesquely inadequate pension schemes. When Edward Gurney, a carpenter, had his leg smashed by falling timber, his family's only source of income was a temporary gratuity from a Benefit Club.[4] Like Rolfe, he was awarded 1s. per day. So was Christopher Godlington, a half blind bricklayer aged seventy-seven who had been struck by a falling tile. But Godlington's petition had been publicly supported by John Yenn, Lord Molesworth and several other residents at Kensington Palace, his place of work for over thirty years.[5] Seven shillings per week soon became the standard rate of compensation for injury, as with the case of James Davis, a painter who fell from a ladder while decorating a staircase at Windsor.[6] But Chambers persuaded the Treasury to follow the practice of the old Office of Works and award 10s. od. per week in one particularly tragic case, that of Henry Young. Young had been employed for fifteen years by the mason John Devall. On 8 October 1785, 'being at work in the Painted Chamber adjoining the House of Lords . . . he fell from the height of 33 feet on some wooden Steps which were broken by the violence of his fall . . . [he] had his Thigh broken in two places and two Bones of his right foot came out, and the wrist of his left hand was strained in so violent a Manner that the Surgeon says he will never have the use of it again so as to be fit for Labour. [He] has a wife and four

---

[1] Works 6/22, f. 132, 13 October and f. 134, 8 November 1793; T. 29/66, f. 205, 14 November 1793; Works 3/3, f. 50, 5 February 1794; Works 4/18, f. 41, 25 October 1793, and f. 56, 7 February 1794.
[2] Works 6/21, f. 156, 16 May 1789; T. 29/60, f. 373, 27 May 1789; Works 6/21, f. 158, 22 May 1789; Works 4/17, 22 May and 12 June 1789.
[3] Works 6/23, f. 50, 16 February 1798.
[4] T. 29/66, f. 48, 11 July 1793; Works 6/22, f. 86, 22 February 1793; Works 4/18, f. 8, 22 February and f. 11, 15 March 1793.
[5] T. 29/67, ff. 268–9, 4 November 1794; Works 6/22, f. 169, 24 October 1794; Works 4/18, f. 94, 24 October and f. 99, 28 November 1794.
[6] Works 6/22–3, 16 October 1795; Works 4/18, f. 146, 16 October 1795 and 19 August 1796.

children whose sole dependence for Maintenance and Support was on [his] industrious Labour . . . and at the time of the accident, his Wife being with Child, the fright so affected her as to turn her Milk to Water and Corruption and occasioned both her Breasts to break. The man', Chambers concluded, 'is . . . truly an object of compassion'.[1]

Office of Works pensions, even for established personnel, remained haphazard for many years. A part-contributory superannuation scheme for Customs officers was set up in 1802–3 and supplemented in 1807.[2] This was modified and applied to all departments in 1809–10.[3] As regards the Office of Works, the following system was proposed:

Retirement with	10 years service:		$\frac{1}{3}$ salary
,,	,,	10–20 years service, aged less than 60:	$\frac{1}{2}$ salary
,,	,,	over 20 years service aged less than 60:	$\frac{2}{3}$ salary
,,	,,	15 years service, aged more than 60:	$\frac{2}{3}$ salary

Previously the Office of Works had occasionally rewarded long service with a pension equivalent to an average salary calculated over the last three years of service.[4] In 1821, as a measure of economy, the Treasury stipulated that all future pensions for established officers were to be based upon annual contributions.[5] Before 1810 pensions for officers' dependents remained irregular. When John Woolfe, Couse's successor as Examining Clerk, died in 1793, he left his daughter Anne unprovided for. 'A series of unfortunate circumstances, and the death of her two brothers, her only relatives, reduced her to extreme indigence and misery'. From this state she was only rescued in 1811 when the Prince Regent authorised the grant of a £50 Treasury pension, to be placed in the hands of a government trustee.[6]

Although subordinate to the Lord Chamberlain, the Surveyor General's control of his own department was absolute. Higher appointments were made by the Treasury and ratified by the King in accordance with his advice. Lower posts formed part of his own personal patronage. As the Clerks of the Works 'are under my direction', Chambers informed Hertford in 1784, 'and I am made responsible for their conduct, they are, by virtue of His Majesty's general warrant, appointed by me . . . . With respect to higher offices . . . they have been, ever since his present Majesty's accession, constantly appointed by his own command to the Surveyor General'.[7] Clerks of the Works had little scope for personal initiative. Hiort defined their duties as 'to attend and receive designs and instructions from the Surveyor [General], to prepare estimates, and direct the execution of the works, and, when

---

[1] Works 1/5, f. 85, February 1786; T. 29/57, ff. 477–8, 14 July 1786; Works 4/17, 28 July 1786.

[2] T. 29/79, f. 305, 30 July 1802; T. 29/81, ff. 364–50, 10 August 1803; T. 29/92, ff. 403–5, 7 November 1807; T. 29/110, ff. 297–302, 28 March 1811.

[3] L.C. 1/3, 14 September 1809. For pension schemes before and after 50 G. III c. 177 cf. 'Report from the Select Committee on Civil Service Superannuation', *Parl. Pap.* 1856, ix, 17 *et seq.* One of those who benefitted from this statute was William Leach, ex-Clerk of the Works at Windsor, who retired with a pension of £120 per annum, two-thirds of his old salary (Works 4/20, 21 February 1812).

[4] In this way, W. Ranspach, messenger, received £212 per annum when he retired after 40 years' service (L.C. 1/40, f. 304, 9 January 1783).

[5] Works 1/10, f. 520, 10 August 1821.   [6] T. 29/111, f. 570, 25 October 1811.

[7] Works 6/20, f. 314, 13 November 1784. Clerks of the Works were appointed by a royal warrant, signed by the Treasury Commissioners: 'we reposing especial Trust and Confidence in the Ability, Care and Fidelity of . . .' etc. (Works 6/13, *passim*).

complete to measure and deliver the accounts of the same'.[1] Labourers in Trust owed both their appointments and prospects of promotion directly to Chambers. Gilbert's Instructions 'held out to them . . ., as an encouragement to a right discharge of their duties, that such of them as have given proof of their integrity and abilities to act in an advanced station [should] not be overlooked in the appointment of Clerks of the Works'.[2]

However, even in the appointment of junior officers, the King's influence might occasionally be decisive. In 1783 Chambers successfully persuaded the Treasury to retain Robert Browne Snr. and Richard Wetherell as Labourers in Trust at Richmond and the Queen's House. He maintained that they were 'well known to His Majesty' and had won his 'entire approbation', these being 'the King's usual places of residence', and added that it was wise 'to avoid the introduction of Strangers about His Majesty's Person'.[3] More explicitly, George III managed in 1789 to remove Thomas Tildesley from his Clerkship at Windsor and replace him first by Robert Browne Jnr. and then by William Leach.[4] When in 1805 Leach in turn proved incapable, he was pensioned off at the King's direction and replaced by William Matthew, a builder sufficiently humble and sufficiently energetic to act as personal assistant to James Wyatt.[5]

But Tildesley's was an exceptional case. His vile temper and intemperate habits made him the stormy petrel of the department. In 1782 Mrs. Charlotte Boyle Walsingham hired her own workmen to repaint her apartments at Windsor, since she doubted 'the abilities of the old Gentlemen usually employed'. Tildesley turned out these interlopers 'with very abusive language', and then had to be ordered to apologise for his incivility.[6] A year later Henry Emlyn, the resident carpenter, resigned because Tildesley 'had found fault with his Timber frivolously'.[7] Twelve months after that he was involved in a violent dispute with the local land-tax collector.[8] After his transference to Hampton Court, Tildesley's accounts were discovered to be in disorder and he was concerned in a furore over a quantity of stolen

[1] 'Inquiry into . . . the Office of Works', *Parl. Pap.* 1812–13, v, p. 429.

[2] *Ibid.* p. 341. Labourers in Trust were directly appointed by the Surveyor General: 'to have, hold, exercise and enjoy . . . with all Wages, Profits, Lodgings, Privileges and Advantages' (Works 6/13, *passim*).

[3] Works 6/20, f. 76, 10 January 1783.

[4] 'I find the Clerk of the Works at Hampton Court [William Rice, d. 6 May 1789] is near expiring; I have ordered Sir William Chambers to wait on Mr. Rose that Mr. Pitt may be reminded when it shall happen of what I now mention that I would have Tinsley [sic] . . . removed to that place . . . [and replaced by] Browne, the Labourer in Trust at the Mewze . . . who is an active and discreet man, [and] has had a mortification on a prior occasion' (*Later Correspondence of George III*, ed. A. Aspinall i, no. 494, George III to Pitt. 15 March 1789).

[5] 'I am extremely sorry to inform you that his Majesty has . . . directed that you should be removed from your situation' (Wyatt to Leach, Works 6/25, f. 177, 24 August 1811). The king had 'expressed a wish that . . . Leach . . . be removed to some other employment and that . . . Matthew be appointed in his stead, and that a warrant should accordingly be made out for the purpose from 5 April 1805 when the above arrangement took place' (Works 4/19, 30 May 1806). After forty years in public service, weighed down by 'infirmities . . . indigence and poverty', Leach was transferred first to the Ordnance Office, then to Hampton Court, and finally retired on pension (Works 6/25, ff. 53–4, 158, 162; T. 29/101, f. 345, 25 June 1809).

[6] Works 1/5, f. 35, 15 November 1781 and f. 40, 24 February 1782. The repair of 'grace and favour' apartments was a recurrent problem. After 1782 the Office of Works was permitted only to ensure that they were 'wind and water tight' at each General Survey. Internal decorations were to be the subject of specific requests addressed to the Surveyor General (e.g. a dispute at Kensington, Works 3/3, ff. 19–20, 29 June 1787–31 January 1794).

[7] Works 4/16, 19 December 1783.

[8] Works 1/5, f. 77, 17 December 1784.

lead.[1] Soon afterwards, his 'unfortunate wife and lame child . . ., dreading the vehemence of his Temper, [were] forced to fly from him'. Thanks to Chambers' intercession late in 1792, this 'Sick Child and worthy, very decent woman' were allowed £50 per annum, being the proceeds from three official houses illegally rented out by Tildesley.[2] Pending the sale of this property, the Treasury permitted the continuance of this extra income after 'the difference' between Tildesley and his wife had been 'made up . . . for the benefit of [their] family'.[3] Less than two years later, at the height of an administrative fracas over the use of stables at Hampton Court by the King's Cavalry, Tildesley was found to be 'indisposed even to incapacity'.[4] Indeed a doctor certified the patient as insane. Periods of mental derangement punctuated Tildesley's remaining years and only Chambers' intervention prevented his replacement in 1794 by William Tyler, R.A., an established sculptor and architect patronised by the Duke of Gloucester.[5]

Chambers' argument on this latter occasion was partly emotive and partly prudential. He was of course determined not to allow the 'utter ruin of an unfortunate man, his wife and five helpless children'. But he was equally resolute in insisting that architects of independent reputation or independent means made for inefficiency and discontent in the department.

> My real sentiments are that the Clerkships of the Office of Works will be much better served by plain Builders than by famous Architects, who deeming themselves much greater than the Comptroller will scarcely be controuled by him. Having more business of their own than they can manage they will find no leisure for that of the Crown, and having spacious town houses of their own, will scarcely quit them and their business to shift in small official habitations, and bury themselves in the Country for the inadequate reward of £150 or £200 per annum. To a common plain Builder such a reward is a powerful inducement to him; such a house becomes a commodious dwelling. Having been accustomed to subservience he obeys without difficulty, and having little or no business of his own, the greater part of his time will be spent in the management of the Crown.[6]

Under Chambers, therefore, the Office of Works was served by efficient mediocrities: John Woolfe Senior and Junior, Thomas Browne Senior and Junior, William and Thomas Rice, and worst of all, the intolerably officious Charles Alexander Craig.

[1] Works 4/17, 13 August 1792; Works 1/5, f. 108, 12 October 1792.

[2] 'Since she left her husband some months ago, [she] has never received from him more than 5 guineas tho' he agreed to pay her regularly £40 p.a., and . . . unless the poor woman can be humanely assisted . . . both she, and her child, must throw themselves upon the Parish' (Works 6/22, f. 71, Chambers to Rose 5 November 1792; Works 4/17, 9 November 1792).

[3] Works 6/22, f. 146, 13 December 1793; Works 1/5, January 1794; Works 4/18, f. 53, 24 January 1794.

[4] Works 4/18, f. 65, 11 April 1794. He was temporarily replaced on this and other occasions by Thomas Rice, who had previously assisted his uncle William Rice, Tildesley's predecessor at Hampton Court.

[5] Works 1/5, f. 131, 4 August 1794; T. 29/67, f. 171, 19 August 1794; Works 6/22, f. 167, 29 August 1794; Works 4/18, f. 198, 9 September 1796; Works 4/19, 15 May and 26 September 1800. In 1797 Wyatt urged Tildesley 'to observe the strictest Oeconomy and assiduity . . . as the only chance left you of securing to yourself the situation you now hold' (Works 6/23, f. 18, 17 February 1797). Three years later he emphasised once more the necessity for 'steady and temperate conduct' in the case of 'a Complaint like yours' (Works 6/23, f. 135, 26 September 1800).

[6] Works 6/22, ff. 163–4, 24 July 1794. In 1806 the Duke of Kent successfully insisted that part of Tildesley's duties at Hampton Court be delegated to Robert Browne Jnr. (Works 6/24, f. 51, 5 July 1806; f. 53, 7 July and f. 56, 26 July 1806). Two years later he died. In 1812 his long-suffering wife, Catherine, was awarded an annuity of £75 per annum by the Treasury (Works 4/20, 26 March 1812).

Only Kenton Couse (1721–90) and John Yenn, R.A. (1750–1821), were architects of any calibre, and they, like Chambers, were survivals from an earlier age. Robert Furze Brettingham, appointed Resident Clerk in 1794, really belongs to the age of Wyatt. Both Yenn and Couse had been bred in the Office of Works; both were tolerant and scrupulous administrators, intensely loyal to Sir William Chambers. As Clerk of the Works at St. James's, Whitehall and Westminster, Couse had been responsible for the rebuilding of 10 Downing Street,[1] before his promotion to administrative rank in 1782. Yenn's patience was to be severely taxed over many years by his responsibilities as Clerk of the Works for Kensington Palace, Buckingham House, the Royal Mews and Carlton House. Couse's obituarist praised his personal qualities, and at the same time hinted at the strength of his connections in Court and Cabinet: 'few men underwent more business . . . with greater credit and integrity. Liberal, honourable and punctual in all his engagements, he deservedly gained numberless friends, and never lost one in the practice of his profession for nearly fifty years. To the applause of others, the written testimony of a very great Personage might be added; but Delicacy forbids us to insist upon it'.[2] Chambers himself described Yenn as 'an ingenious, faithful and intelligent servant', and indeed Yenn was perhaps his closest colleague, a pupil who lived to become his successor as Treasurer of the Royal Academy.[3] But among all Chambers' assistants there was only one architect of exceptional talent, and he displayed several of the more infuriating symptoms of genius. The architect in question was the future Sir John Soane (1753–1837).

Chambers was usually on excellent terms with his subordinates. But Soane's behaviour was, almost from the beginning, truculent and conceited. He had been grateful enough at the time of his appointment in October 1790. Indeed, on that occasion, his letters to William Pitt and the Pittite banker Joseph Smith, had been fulsome in the extreme.[4] But as his private practice grew, his reputation increased and he cared less and less for his trivial commitments as Clerk of the Works at St. James's, Whitehall and Westminster. His discontent was magnified by Craig's promotion from Resident Clerk to Examiner. As the backlog of Soane's unexecuted business accumulated during 1793, so Chambers' exasperation grew greater. In December the storm broke. Soane received an official summons from the Surveyor General. 'I sent last Friday to request your attendance at this Office', wrote Chambers, 'when a Message was returned that *you were at home if I had anything to say*. My answer was that I had, and wished to speak to you here, as it was upon official Business.

[1] See vol. v of this *History*.

[2] *Gent's. Mag.* 1790, pt. ii, p. 959. See also J. Nichols, *Literary Anecdotes* iii (1812), pp. 642–3; *D.N.B.*; Colvin, *Dictionary*, pp. 155–6. On Chambers' recommendation, the Office of Works purchased Couse's collection of drawings soon after his death for 35 guineas. They included 'several plans and other designs proper to be consulted on various public occasions' (Works 4/18, f. 7, 15 February 1793; T. 29/66, f. 41, 11 July 1793).

[3] Sir William Chambers' Letter Books, B.M. Add. MS. 41135, f. 26; Colvin, *Dictionary*, pp. 741–2. A foundation member of the Architect's Club (1791), he succeeded Sir Robert Taylor as Surveyor of Greenwich Hospital in 1788. As Chambers' pupil he entered the Office of Works in 1774 as nominal Labourer in Trust at Buckingham House ('Inquiry into . . . the Office of Works', *Parl. Pap.* 1812–13, v, p. 447). In 1780 he became Clerk of the Works at Richmond. As R.A. Treasurer (1796–1820) he sided with Wyatt, fell foul of the ruling clique and was supplanted by Robert Smirke Jnr., the excuse being his 'increasing imbecility' (Farington, p. 7759, 8 April 1820). George IV 'knew the appointment was in his gift', but decided to 'waive his own partiality to gratify the wishes of the Academy' (*ibid.* p. 7785, 26 May 1820).

[4] A. T. Bolton, *Portrait of Sir John Soane* (1927), p. 48, 27 October 1790.

I remained a considerable time after at the Office, in expectation of seeing you, but you neither came nor sent any excuse, and I was of course under the necessity of giving those directions to others which should have been given to you'.[1] Several weeks later Soane had still made no move. 'Though repeatedly called upon by me', Chambers complained to Rose, 'the same inconvenience still remains unremedied, the consequences of which are great delays and uncertainties in all places belonging to his Clerkship . . . His Majesty has signified to me his displeasure upon that subject'.[2]

Soane was forced to explain his conduct. He claimed that his comments on the dilatory repair of Winchester Palace and on the inadequate construction of Somerset House and the Fleet Prison, had made him 'particularly obnoxious' to Chambers.[3] Besides which he objected to Craig's recent promotion on grounds of professional status.

> You Sir, . . . thought proper to recommend (to a situation which repuires great professional skill and practical knowledge, and therefore hitherto filled by Architects) a person who . . . has been brought up to measuring and accounts, is now a District Surveyor . . . deeply engaged in the Lime and Coal Trade, [and] consequently, not a person by whom any regular Architect would submit to be directed, however long his services may have been in the Office of Works. When you lately stated to the King the length of these Services, I presume you did not forget, that a very large part of them had been performed as Labourer in Trust at the King's Mewse. It is true the wages were only 2s. 2d. per day, but the duty, as you well know, was merely to attend at the Office four times a year to receive them, and which without doubt, was most conscientiously attended to. As you were pleased, Sir, lately to make mention of me to His Majesty, and perhaps did not recollect all the circumstances . . . , may I therefore request you to inform the King, *in my own words*, of the causes which have compelled me to adopt my present conduct.[4]

Chambers' reply was heavy with sarcasm.

> In answer to your Letter . . . I must beg to assure you that your first reason for non-attendance . . . is founded upon an entire Mistake. The Surveyor General, whose mind I ought to know, seldom or ever resents real injuries done to him, much less such trifles as are enumerated by you . . . Every free man is free to gratify his spleen, and I have only to remark, that measures taken with spiteful intent however speciously they may be justified, seldom do the Assailant much service, but . . . often recoil upon himself with doubled force. What squabbles may have been between yourself and Mr. Craig, or what animosities still exist between you, cannot concern me. I shall neither attempt his justification, which appears to me superfluous, nor a removal of your strong prejudice against him, which does not seem to me material to the business of this Office, but am sorry to hear from you that his great inferiority and my violent resentment prevent, and will prevent, your attendance at this Office.

[1] Works 6/22, f. 143, 6 December 1793.
[2] Works 6/22, f. 144, 7 December 1793 and f. 147, 3 January 1794. 'By reason of . . . [Soane's absenteeism] the public service received material injury' (Works 4/18, f. 50, 3 January 1794).
[3] See below, pp. 372, 627 and (for Somerset House) vol. v of this *History*.
[4] Works 6/22, ff. 150–1, 17 January 1794; Works 4/18, f. 52, 17 January 1794.

I have already assured you that the latter never existed, and the dangerous consequences of the former might I think be very much alleviated by an expedient for which the World is indebted to German Sagacity. In Germany when a great man connects with a Lady a few quarters inferior to him in rank, the great man preserves his own dignity, by performing on all connubial occasions with his left hand. The application is obvious, and I am very truly,

> Sir,
> Your most obedient and humble servant,
> William Chambers[1]

Soane resigned the following month.

Nor was this the only occasion when Chambers was forced to act the part of disciplinarian. Office hours were normally 10 a.m. to 1 or 2 p.m. When in 1787 George Horsley, the First Assistant Clerk, and John Bankes, the Messenger and Porter, refused to attend regularly, they were 'mulcted in their pay' for unpunctuality.[2] Horsley's recalcitrance, however, turned out to have a deeper cause than was at first suspected. In 1790 he was suspended for persistent non-attendance, and in 1793 he was certified as incurably insane.[3] 'Being totally unfit for business', Chambers informed the Treasury, 'and sometimes so wild that the Tradesmen and other persons frequenting the Office did not think themselves in safety, I found it necessary to forbid his coming, and (that the business of the Office might not be impeded) to appoint another person to do his part . . ., a Person who had done it on several former Occasions, whenever Horsley laboured under fits of Insanity. He is a very intelligent young man, very industrious and attentive to Business, very sober and tractable, his name is John William Hiort'.[4] Horsley's salary, originally £60, was increased to £80 per annum. Half this sum was for many years regularly made over to Horsley's family, and half to the industrious Hiort. Architect, accountant and inventor, Hiort (1772–1861) became the most reliable member of the department. It was upon his versatility, in a succession of different offices, that the operation of the Office of Works was to depend during the Surveyorship of the negligent Wyatt.

Chambers handled cases like those of Tildesley, Horsley and Soane with considerable tact and sympathy. His sense of humour was equal to every sort of occasion. His response to one of Gilbert's less palatable reforms was a sly letter to Thomas Orde, Secretary to the Treasury:

> The Surveyor of the Board of Works and the Officers of that Board were allowed by ancient Custom till the time of their suppression two Bucks and two Does annually; and a revival of our Places has also revived our Appetite for Vension [sic]. I beg leave to request in behalf of myself and Brethren, that the Allowance of the two

---

[1] Works 6/22, ff. 151–2, 20 January 1794.
[2] They both forfeited 'one week's allowance' (Works 4/17, 3 March 1786, 24 and 31 August 1787).
[3] Works 4/17, 16 January 1789 and 22 January 1790; Works 4/18, f. 22, 21 June 1793; T. 29/66, f. 41, 11 July 1793.
[4] Works 6/22, f. 99, 17 May 1793; Works 4/18, f. 17, 17 May and f. 28, 2 August 1793. Hiort was succeeded as Horsley's substitute first by John Spence and then by George Russell (T 29/69, f. 335, 28 July 1796; Works 6/24, f. 270, 7 June 1809). For details of Hiort's career cf. Colvin, *Dictionary*, pp. 288–9. In 1796 Chambers reported that Horsley 'will never be capable of returning to his duty' (Works 4/18, f. 185, 24 June 1796).

Bucks may still be continued to us, which will enable us to eat as well as Drink their Majesty's health on the usual days of festivity.

> I am with Great Truth and Respect,
>> Dear Sir,
>>> Your faithful and Obedient Servant,
>>>> William Chambers

P.S. Mr. Secker [of the Board of Green Cloth] informs me the Secretaries of the Treasury are also Treasurers of the Vension.[1]

Appropriately enough, Chambers received an answer which was not only favourable but suitably elegant: Orde decorated his reply 'with just enough of learning to misquote' both Virgil and Milton.

As an administrator Chambers was not impeccable. In 1780, for example, he dared to by-pass the Exchequer by drawing money for the Office of Works directly from the Excise and Stamp Offices, thus depriving the Tellers of their fees.[2] His accounts as Treasurer of the Royal Academy were frequently in arrear.[3] But the efficiency of the Office of Works during his period of office as Surveyor General and Comptroller contrasts markedly with the state of the department before 1782 and after 1796. He set his subordinates a high standard. During his fifteen years as chairman, he attended all but 65 of the 643 weekly and extraordinary meetings of the administrative Board of the Office of Works.[4] His painstaking correspondence with the private occupants of royal buildings, the secretaries of government departments, the Lord Chamberlain and the Treasury, demonstrates his immediate control over every aspect of administration and finance. 'Never any business', recalled Craig, 'was better conducted than in Sir William Chambers' time'.[5]

Chambers died on 8 March 1796. His will made ample provision for his son, his five daughters, his eight grandchildren and his wife.[6] His funeral was the occasion of a remarkable display of public respect. For nearly thirty years he had been Treasurer to the Royal Academy. Indeed, he was remembered as 'the first mover' at the time of its foundation.[7] Sir Joshua Reynolds once remarked that 'though he was President, Sir William was Vice-Roy over him'.[8] Chambers was too strong an advocate of economy and royal control to be popular with all the members.[9] Nevertheless, they gave him a solemn, 'Academical' funeral.[10]

[1] Works 1/5, f. 48. For Orde's reply see R.I.B.A. MS. 63, 9 March 1783.

[2] Hardwicke Papers, liv (1768–73), B.M. Add. MS. 35402, f. 240. 'Chambers was unquestionably extravagant and muddled his accounts' (J. Norris, *Shelburne and Reform*, 1963, p. 181).

[3] RA 17259 and 17284 (Privy Purse Accounts 1771–2).

[4] Office of Works minutes 1782–96 (Works 4/16–4/18).

[5] 'Inquiry into . . . the Office of Works', *Parl. Pap.* 1812–13, v, p. 406.

[6] 'Sir William has left Lady Chambers £800 per annum and £2500 to dispose of. He has made up the fortunes of his five daughters £6000 each. £1500 to each of his grandchildren, Mr. Chambers' children, eight in number, to accumulate till they come of age. £1100 per annum to Mr. Chambers the residuary Legatee. The will is much approved of' (Farington, p. 566, 17 March 1796).

[7] *Ibid.* p. 559, 10 March 1796. At the time there was even talk of his being President (*ibid.* p. 2854, 12 December 1804).

[8] *Ibid.* p. 2852, 10 December 1804. The Treasurer occupied a permanent post on the Council.

[9] Farington, pp. 494–6, 31 December 1795.

[10] Chambers directed 'that not more than £100 should be expended, which seemed to show that he desired no ostentation; of course nothing could be undertaken similar to the expence on account of Sir Joshua Reynolds funeral, which . . . amounted to near £1000' (*ibid.* p. 557, 10 March 1796).

On 18 March, Joseph Farington noted in his diary:

> Sir William Chambers' funeral I went to this morning as one of the Council of the Royal Academy. Mourning coaches were sent round to us and we assembled at his house in Norton St. at 10 o'clock. The three executors, Mr. Collins, Mr. Brown and Mr. Andre were there.[1] Sir Richard Kaye, Rev. Mr. Pennock, Wyatt and Yenn as visitors. Mr. West, Bacon, Lawrence, Tyler, Hoppner, Stothard, Westall, Richards and Wilton were there from the Academy. Mr. Craig, Brettingham, Groves, from the Board of Works. About 11 the procession moved to Westminster Abbey. 19 coaches in all. Mr. Chambers, Sir William's son, followed the corpse from the West door as Chief Mourner; after him Sir William Harwood, Mr. Milbanke, Major Cotton, Sir William's sons in law, and his nephew, Mr. George Chambers, followed. Then the executors, then the Academy, and lastly the Board of Works. The body was interred about 1 o'clock in the Poet's Corner. There were no Pall Bearers and the Common Funeral Service only was read. After the ceremony we separated at the West door. A considerable number of respectable tradesmen of the Board of Works attended and formed two lines to show their respect to the memory of Sir William.[2]

Chambers' death left the Office of Works without a head. With the passing, in Yenn's words, of 'that good and eminent artist',[3] the department slipped into less responsible hands. Although Soane had contemptuously resigned his junior post after his epistolary duel in 1794, he was quite prepared to intrigue for the highest office two years later. Within twenty-four hours of Chambers' death, he was calling on Joseph Smith and George Rose in the hope of influencing Pitt's choice.[4] George Dance seems also to have 'exerted himself' as the battle for the succession drew near.[5] But the Surveyor Generalship did not depend solely upon Treasury nomination: it was of course a Crown appointment, and George III had already chosen James Wyatt. It was on 7 June 1793 that, as Farington reported, 'The King voluntarily promised him the place of Surveyor General . . . in case he survived Sir William Chambers . . . The King told Wyatt that . . . he considered [him] the first Architect of the Kingdom and most proper for it. Wyatt bowed and expressed his gratitude'.[6] During the 1790s Wyatt had succeeded Chambers as George III's favourite architect. Now he succeeded also to Chambers' title. On 16 March 1796, Wyatt was appointed Surveyor General and Comptroller of the King's Works.[7]

---

[1] Yenn declined to act as executor, his reason being overwork. West and Farington suspected that he had latterly been 'upon cool terms with Sir William'. But their hope that Tyler might succeed Chambers as Treasurer was not fulfilled. Yenn became Treasurer, having neatly transferred his allegiance from Chambers to Wyatt (Farington, p. 556, 9 March 1796, p. 558 10 March and p. 566, 17 March 1796.)

[2] *Ibid.* p. 565, 18 March 1796. 'The master workmen belonging to the Board of Works . . . attended, unsolicited, to testify their regret . . . and their esteem' (*Gent's. Mag.* 1796, pt. i, p. 260).

[3] 'Inquiry into . . . the Office of Works', *Parl. Pap.* 1812–13, v, p. 447.

[4] A. T. Bolton, *Portrait of Sir John Soane* (1927), p. 50.

[5] Farington, pp. 302–3, 17 February 1795.

[6] *Ibid.* p. 131, 14 February 1794. The King 'told Wyatt that he had declared this to Mr. Pitt to prevent applications'.

[7] Works 6/13, 16 March 1796; *Later Correspondence of George III*, ed. A. Aspinall, ii, No. 1379, Pitt to George III, 9 March 1796; Farington, p. 566, 18 March 1796.

Chapter III

THE SURVEYORSHIP OF
JAMES WYATT, 1796–1813

FOR the Office of Works 1796 marked a change of location as well as a change of head. Chambers' replacement by Wyatt coincided with the department's removal from its old quarters to the house lately belonging to Mr. Bownas in Little Scotland Yard.[1] While the old Surveyor General lay dying, the new house, bought for £560 9s. od.[2], was being fitted up with an extra storey 'at a moderate expence' from designs by J. T. Groves.[3] As the Destroyer entered upon his inheritance, the old premises were symbolically demolished to make way for a new house and office for the Surveyor General of Crown Lands.[4] At the first Board meeting in the new office a petition from the employees of the department was presented and granted: that 'a painting of the late Sir William Chambers . . . be hung in the Board Room'.[5]

Wyatt's arrival inaugurated a period of extravagance and confusion. The extravagance was supplied by the royal family. The confusion was largely his own creation. Quite simply, the new Surveyor General was an incurable absentee. He had the temperament of an artist and the habits of a rake. As a designer his fluency and inventiveness stopped little short of genius. As an administrator he was little less than disastrous. He was a bad correspondent and a born procrastinator. Surveyor to Westminster Abbey, Architect to the Board of Ordnance (£280 per annum),[6] Deputy Surveyor of the Office of Woods and Forests, Surveyor at Somerset House (£200 per annum),[7] as well as Surveyor General and Comptroller of the Office of Works, James Wyatt was a pluralist who forgot to delegate. He owed his success firstly to fashion, and secondly to the favour of the Crown. His post at the Office of Woods and Forests was a Treasury appointment, and so was easily terminated when his negligence became too much even for that tolerant department.[8] But his place at the Office of Works was held under the royal sign manual, and so, given the favour of George III, was terminated only by his death. After 1800, therefore, Wyatt was usually to be found, not in his office in Whitehall, but at Windsor,

---

[1] Works 4/18, f. 144, 2 October 1795.
[2] 3rd Report of the Select Committee on Finance, 1797, *Parl. Pap.* 1st Series, 1715–1801, xii, pp. 49–53. Craig protested strongly against the move, see below, pp. 541–2.
[3] Works 4/18, f. 150, 13 November 1795. For details see below p. 542.
[4] Works 4/18, f. 135, 7 August 1795 and f. 160, 15 January 1796.
[5] The first meeting in the new office was held on 24 March, 1796 (Works 4/18, f. 170).
[6] 'Inquiry into . . . the Office of Works', *Parl. Pap.*, 1812–13, v, pp. 334–5.
[7] Below, p. 480.   [8] L.C. 1/40, f. 21, 1 March 1806.

directing the Gothic casing of the Caroline state apartments so magnificently obliterated by Wyatville's baronial reconstruction of the 1830s.

Wyatt's absenteeism began as occasional, and ended as habitual desertion. Between 1796 and 1806 he attended only 303 out of 558 meetings of the administrative Board of the Office of Works.[1] In 1807 he was absent for 'fifty successive weeks'.[2] During the three years 1808–10, he attended only 38 out of a possible 183 meetings.[3] In 1811–13, under heavy pressure from government investigators, his record improved: 87 out of 165 meetings.[4] But by then the damage had been done. Business was performed spasmodically, whenever Wyatt happened to be in town. Instructions were sent from Windsor or Fonthill, from Ashridge or Wilton, or wherever Wyatt happened to be working. On one occasion in 1807, the minutes break off while the Surveyor General is asked to return some official letters; the documents arrive seven years later.[5] When fire breaks out at St. James's Palace in 1809, Craig has to send the news by express messenger to Wilton, where Wyatt is staying with the Earl of Pembroke.[6]

Wyatt's official orders were not only epistolary but dilatory in the extreme. His unpunctuality soon became notorious. One of the many who suffered from his unreliability was Queen Victoria's father, the Duke of Kent. Kent had good reason to complain of Mr. Wyatt's 'long known want of punctuality'.[7] While his apartments at Kensington Palace crumbled away with dry rot, or in Yenn's words, with 'the acrimonious effects . . . of mildews, damps and rottenness',[8] repeated letters and personal visits over a period of several months failed to stir the culprit into writing the necessary report. The Lord Chamberlain's Secretary even abandoned departmental protocol in an attempt to break through to the Surveyor General: 'Mr. Wyatt attends so little to any Official communication, no matter by whose authority it is made, that I have tried what effect a private letter would have', demanding a mere 'three lines . . . in as strong terms as I was able'.[9]

Apart from his first and last two years of office, Wyatt was an absentee administrator, conferring responsibility without authority on the willingly officious Charles Alexander Craig. After the death of Jones in 1807,[10] Craig's flamboyant signature frequently appears as the sole authority for departmental decisions. Born in Rochester and encouraged and tutored by Sir Robert Taylor, Craig was one of those industrious mediocrities whom Chambers made it his policy to promote.[11] In contrast to Wyatt he missed no more than half a dozen Board meetings during his career.[12] On those rare occasions when he did, he always gave his reasons. Having missed the meeting held on 12 July 1811, he explained that 'he had sprained his ankle, which had caused him to keep his Bed'.[13] In private practice Craig was a surveyor rather

---

[1] Figures compiled from minutes, 1796–1806 (Works 4/18–19).
[2] 'Inquiry into . . . the Office of Works', *Parl. Pap.*, 1812–13, v, p. 344; Works 4/20. 1807 was, however, the year of Wyatt's serious illness, see below p. 54.
[3] The practice grew up of sending him the minutes by post (Works 4/20, 11 March 1811).
[4] Works 4/20–21.   [5] Works 4/20, 20 February 1807.
[6] Works 4/20, 27 January 1809.   [7] L.C. 1/4, 9 January 1811.
[8] L.C. 1/4, 30 June 1809.   [9] L.C. 1/4, 4 February 1811.
[10] Works 4/20, 4 September 1807.
[11] Some details of his career are given in Farington, p. 6896, 12 April 1816.
[12] 'Inquiry into . . . the Office of Works', *Parl. Pap.*, 1812–13, v, p. 406.
[13] Works 4/20, 19 July 1811.

than an architect: Surveyor to the Commissioners of Westminster Bridge, Surveyor, Clerk and Treasurer to the Commissioners for Paving Westminster, and a Surveyor under the Building Act of 1774 for regulating buildings and party walls.[1] The evidence which he gave in 1812 to the Commissioners of Military Inquiry sums up the irregularity of work in the department even after the reforms of 1782–3:

> What portion of your time is usually occupied in business relating to the Office of Works?
> —I really cannot tell, sometimes for a great many hours together; and at other times whole days pass without my having anything to do; at all times keeping myself much in London, to give His Majesty's service the utmost dispatch in my power. [Occasionally I have worked] from twelve to fifteen hours together, with the exception of one hour to my dinner.[2]

Craig's promotion from Resident Clerk to Examiner had infuriated Soane. In assuming the position of deputy Surveyor General, he sorely tried the patience of the Lord Chamberlain's Office,[3] the Treasury and his own subordinates in the Office of Works.

Wyatt's professional practice was enormous. The list of his executed designs extends to more than 200 items. In 1796 he told Farington that he travelled 4000 miles a year on business.[4] For this he charged half a crown per mile, plus five guineas a day while stationary, plus another five guineas a day for advice. Unlike most of his competitors he seems not to have charged the usual 5% commission on the overall cost of private building. Instead he received this percentage only on his agreed estimate.[5] This meant that although he never profited directly from soaring expenditure, he was under rather less of a moral obligation to complete his commissions within the temporal and financial limits of his estimate. But then Wyatt possessed little or no sense of professional obligation. His irresponsibility was almost pathological. It bedevilled the Department of Woods and Forests, bankrupted the Office of Works, disturbed the Royal Academy and came near to wrecking his private practice. When his interest was aroused, he was capable of bouts of intense application. According to Jeffry Wyatt, he was 'one of the best-tempered men living'. But he lacked stamina. Still worse, he lacked organisation.[6] By 1806 he was 'in straight-

---

[1] 'Inquiry into . . . the Office of Works', *Parl. Pap.*, 1812–13, v, p. 404.   [2] *Ibid.* p. 416.

[3] On at least two occasions Craig was put in his place by the Lord Chamberlain. In 1793 Chambers was ill, and sent Craig to negotiate with Salisbury, who 'refused to take the papers from Mr. Craig, alledging that he would not treat with anyone but Sir William' (Works 4/18, f. 16, 10 May 1793). Sixteen years later Craig dared to address a letter, as though he were Surveyor General, not to the Lord Chamberlain's Secretary or First Clerk, but to the Lord Chamberlain himself. Dartmouth's Secretary replied: 'I am commanded by his Lordship to express to you his surprise that Mr. Craig should have thus assumed a consequence in his Lordship's opinion very foreign to the situation he holds' (L.C. 1/40, f. 141, 22 March 1809).

[4] Farington, p. 708, 20 July 1796.

[5] Farington, p. 295, 2 February 1795; p. 1117, 2 November 1797 and p. 3472, 16 October 1806. Farington mentions 'a house [Henham Hall, Suffolk] for Lord Rous which he estimated at £12,000. It cost £20,000 but he only received the percentage on his estimate'.

[6] Jeffry Wyatt 'said his uncle is a very singular man. He will often employ himself upon trifling professional matters, which others could do, while business of importance is waiting for him. When a [new] commission . . . is proposed . . . he will eagerly attend to it till he has got all the instructions necessary for the commencement of the work, but then he becomes indifferent to it, and has lost many great commissions by such neglect. . . . At times he will, when at the house of an employer, work very hard in making designs and will frequently leave the company and bottle after dinner to go to his clerk. Such is the irregularity of his habits' (Farington, p.3472, 16 October 1806). Wyatt once worked 'incessantly' at Ashridge for three weeks. 'That, said Jeffry [Wyatt] is just what he should not have done . . . there were many other works standing still, which, if he had divided his time properly would not have been the case' (Farington, p. 6153, 2 November 1812).

ened circumstances instead of being worth £10,000, as he might have been'.[1] Seven years later, he died heavily in debt. Lord Liverpool's verdict is indisputable: though 'a man of the most considerable talents as an architect, he was certainly one of the worst Public Servants I recollect in any office, not I am persuaded from dishonesty, or want of zeal, but from carelessness and from his always choosing to engage in a great deal more business than he was capable of performing'.[2]

Royal favour made Wyatt's position at the Office of Works impregnable. It also made him a focus for intrigue and suspicion in that 'nest of vermin',[3] the Royal Academy. His influence over George III dated back to his work at Frogmore in 1793 for Queen Charlotte and Princess Elizabeth.[4] Soon afterwards the King's plans for the reconstruction of Windsor Castle were entrusted to him, but delayed for the sake of decency until the death of Sir William Chambers.[5] With Wyatt's elevation to the Surveyorship work began in earnest. Before long he was living in the apartments once occupied by Sir Christopher Wren,[6] and dining at the Equerries' table with the Lord Chamberlain.[7] From this vantage point he was able to act as the spearhead of an opposition group within the Royal Academy. For more than a decade the Academy had been dominated by an inner clique: the President, Benjamin West, his heir apparent Thomas Lawrence, Joseph Farington, the 'Dictator of the Academy', and his Abbé Siéyès, Robert Smirke, Senior. The opposition was led by Hoppner, Beechey, Tresham, Shee, Bourgeois, Soane and Yenn. Making good use of the inequalities of the Academy's constitution and the King's obsessional fear of Radicalism, the rebels managed to force West into resignation and carry Wyatt's election to the Presidency in November, 1805. But the rebels had mistaken their man. Instead of rejuvenating the Council and initiating a rotating Presidency, Wyatt slept in committee, mumbled his speeches and infuriated political patrons by his 'old habits of delay'.[8] Within a year West was back in office. Wyatt had merely

---

[1] Farington, p. 3230, 21 April 1806.

[2] Liverpool Papers, cccv, B.M. Add. MS. 38568, f. 225, Liverpool to Richmond, 7 July 1814

[3] *Conversations of James Northcote, R.A.*, ed. E. Fletcher (1901), p. 164.

[4] 'Wyatt designed the decorations at Frogmore for the entertainments given by the Queen. He was paid by the Queen therefore. But the King was so well pleased with the effect . . . that His Majesty presented Wyatt with a watch' (Farington, p. 55, 23 November 1793). 'Wyatt owed his situation with the King and the place of Surveyor General . . . to the Queen and Princess Elizabeth . . . [as] compensation for the trouble and loss of time which he had suffered in . . building Frogmore . . . for which it is believed he never received any pecuniary recompense'. Indeed Wyatt claimed 'that his expence and great loss of time in attending upon the Royal Family had been the ruin of him' (Farington, p. 1123, 9 November 1797 and p. 3527, 11 December 1806).

[5] 'The King has an intention of doing many things at Windsor, but defers it during the life of Sir William Chambers' (Farington, p. 131, 14 February 1794). For details, see Farington, p. 110, 19 January 1794 and p. 173, 8 June 1794; also p. 375 below.

[6] Wren had occupied these rooms in the days when Windsor possessed a separate works establishment. Wyatt justified his tenuous claim on the grounds that 'his attendance is more required where the King resides, in order to give His Majesty information respecting the Works carrying on in other places. It was perhaps for this reason that residences were assigned to the Surveyor General at Hampton Court and Kensington, these palaces having been formerly the residences of King William III and George I' ('Inquiry into . . . the Office of Works', *Parl Pap* 1812–13, v, p. 338).

[7] 'Wyatt considers the Queen a very warm friend of his . . . [and] is always treated with great respect at Windsor. He always dines at the Equerries Table . . . Lord Harcourt is the only nobleman who dines with the royal family, and [Wyatt] has dined at the Equerries table with Marquess Salisbury etc.' (Farington, p. 131, 14 February 1794).

[8] Farington, p. 3234, 23 April 1806. At the R.A. Birthday Dinner in 1806, sitting next to the Prince of Wales, he made 'a sad President', and 'gave the Toasts in so low a voice that he could scarcely be heard' (Farington, pp. 3260, 3 May, 3263, 5 May 1806). Characteristically, the 'Dinner Bill was enormous' (Farington, p. 3418, 14 September 1806).

succeeded in making almost as many enemies in the Royal Academy as he had in the Society of Antiquaries.[1] The comment made by Wyatt's third son is perhaps worth noticing: 'Why should not my father be President? A President has nothing to do'.[2]

Wyatt's private clients found him equally exasperating. In 1789 alterations at New College, Oxford and Salisbury Cathedral proceeded sluggishly thanks to Wyatt's intermittent attendance.[3] In 1809 Farington reported that 'after Wyatt's conduct in neglecting Lord Pembroke's alterations at Wilton . . . Lord Muncaster said Lord Pembroke had given him up, his patience having been exhausted'.[4] But the classic case was that of Fonthill Abbey. Between 1796 and his death in 1813 Wyatt was almost continuously employed on the construction of this Gothic extravaganza, commissioned by William Beckford, the millionaire nabob. Here architect and patron had much in common. Both shared the fantasies and self-indulgence of born Romantics. But Beckford's enthusiasm soon turned to fury as Wyatt's initial panache gave way to his customary lethargy. Beckford's impetuosity and Wyatt's negligence had brought about the collapse of the great tower in 1800. Undeterred, this bizarre couple pressed on with their megalomaniac enterprise although operations ground to a halt at least twice, in 1807 and 1811, when Wyatt's absence coincided with moments of crisis in Beckford's financial affairs. 'Who can ever rely on such a person?' thundered the Caliph of Fonthill. 'The atrocious neglect by the great Cloaca [Beckford's descriptive nickname for Wyatt] cannot lightly be forgiven . . . Curse the infamous Bagasse [whoremonger] . . . "Where infamous Beast, where are you? What putrid inn, what stinking tavern or pox-ridden brothel hides your hoary and gluttonous limbs?" '[5] Beckford, like the Lords of the Treasury, soon discovered that Wyatt was usually to be found snoring in his country seat or else paying court to the King: 'this twisting and turning between Hanworth and Windsor and Dixon is unbearable, but . . . I'm sure he'll be findable all right, tomorrow being the King's birthday, a ceremony which he is never in the habit of missing'.[6]

Wyatt's 'negligent apathy' was peculiarly annoying because it was interspersed with periods of intense application. As the Bishop of Durham remarked, 'you forgave Wyatt his disappointing you, when he appeared'.[7] At moments like these Beckford's

---

[1] The 'Destroyer' of Durham, Hereford, Lichfield and Salisbury Cathedrals was blackballed at the Society of Antiquaries in September, 1797. Despite this 'Popish Plott' by John Carter and Sir Henry Englefield, he was elected in December, thanks to Samuel Lysons and the Earl of Leicester (Farington, p. 1054, 6 July; p. 1076, 6 August; p. 1124, 9 November; p. 1146, 6 July; p. 1148, 4 December; pp. 1150–52, 7 December; p. 1168, 11 December 1797; p. 6439, 8 March 1814). Wyatt had less difficulty in becoming a Fellow of the Royal Society, an honour which he particularly coveted 'as Sir William Chambers was one' (Farington, p. 1055, 7 July and p. 1076, 6 August 1797).

[2] Farington, pp. 2864–5, 21 December 1804.

[3] 'The work . . . goes on very slowly for want of Mr. Wyatt' (J. Nichols, *Literary Anecdotes* iii, 1812, p. 700, Daniel Prince to Richard Gough 17 September 1789). 'Should I get sight of Mr. Wyatt, which is not easy to do, I will remonstrate against the intended alteration' (*ibid.* iv, 1812, p. 172, Horace Walpole to Richard Gough, 24 August 1789).

[4] Farington, p. 4348, 22 May 1809.

[5] B. Alexander, *Life at Fonthill, 1807–22* (1957), p. 74, 30 June 1808; p. 80, 16 September 1808 and p. 104, 5 October 1811. West recalled that 'when Wyatt has been confined in a Spunging House, Mr. Beckford has bailed him from that situation' (Farington, pp. 6394–5, 7 September 1813).

[6] Alexander, *op. cit.*, p. 67, 3 June 1808 and p. 71, 25 June 1808. Hanworth Farm, between Teddington and Staines, was Wyatt's 'small estate of about ninety acres' (Farington, p. 1808, 28 August 1797). John Dixon was Wyatt's principal draughtsman for many years. Wyatt seldom allowed him to exhibit, 'as he says the designs are borrowed from his drawings' (Farington, p. 733, 4 August 1796).

[7] Farington, p. 616, 12 May 1796.

F

'stupid, lazy, Mr. Wyatt'[1] became 'my dear, angelic, most p.p.p.p.perfect Bagasse . . . killing himself with work' in the panelled library at Fonthill known as the 'Board of Works'.[2] 'Every hour, every moment, he adds some new beauty . . . with a brio, a zeal, an energy, a faith that would move the largest mountain in the Alps'.[3]

Such flashes of inspiration became increasingly rare as the brilliant young architect of the Pantheon declined into besotted old age. Years before Peter Pindar had complained:

> '. . . . . the foolish Kingdom all runs riot,
> Calling aloud for Wyat, Wyat, Wyat'.[4]

Now it was common knowledge that 'if Wyatt can get near a large fire, and have a bottle by him he cares for nothing else'.[5] By 1800 he was suffering from kidney trouble.[6] In 1804 Lysons reported that 'Wyatt was paralytic, and had his mouth drawn aside'.[7] In September 1807 Beckford crudely noted that Wyatt was suffering from 'the most watery and pissful Tertian Fever. He is of a deathly cadaverousness and stinks only as those beneath ground do'.[8] West hinted darkly at the cause of this illness, and added that the patient's 'mind seemed to be gone'.[9] In 1811 Dance noticed that the years of dissipation had left their mark.[10] During the following year Wyatt made a rearguard attempt to diet his way back to health. 'My Bagasse shows a moderation at the table worthy of a Carthusian monk', wrote Beckford. Even so, his complexion still betrayed 'a shameful flush that is the colour of port-wine . . . Ah my God, how slow, silent and null he is!'[11] Five months later he was dead. Beckford's wry epitaph came unpleasantly close to the truth: 'alas, my poor Bagasse had already sunk from the plane of genius to the mire; and for some years now he has only dabbled in the mud'.[12]

As Surveyor General and Comptroller Wyatt served under three Lord Chamberlains: the Marquess of Salisbury, the Earl of Dartmouth and the Marquess of Hertford. Salisbury was of course a legacy from Chambers' period of office. Both his successors were representatives of traditional Court families, ex-followers of Lord North who had supported the Fox–North Coalition and then come to terms with the Pittite regime. As Lord Lewisham, George Legge, 3rd Earl of Dartmouth (1755–1810) had been M.P. for Plymouth (1778–80) and Staffordshire (1780–4) and Lord Warden of The Stannaries (1783–98). As a peer he conscientiously served first as President of the India Board (1801–2), then as Lord Steward (1802–4) and finally as

---

[1] Alexander, *op. cit.*, p. 100, 24 June 1811.

[2] *Ibid.* p. 226, 17 October 1817. It was usually called the Oak Library (J. Rutter, *Delineations of Fonthill and its Abbey*, 1823, pp. 14–15).

[3] Alexander, *op. cit.*, p. 131, 26 and 31 August 1812.

[4] Peter Pindar [Dr. J. J. Wolcot], 'The Progress of Knowledge', *Works* iii (1794), p. 241.

[5] Farington, pp. 2595–6, 29 March 1804. Wyatt 'lately left [Beckford] at the Abbey on the pretence of being obliged to go immediately to town. He stopped at Fonthill House, . . . three miles from the Abbey, there found Foxhall the Carver, and staid with him there *secretly* a day and a half enjoying himself, which Beckford a week after discovered'.

[6] 'Sir Lucas Pepys has recommended . . . Mephytic water' (Farington, p. 1758, 3 February 1800).

[7] Farington, p. 2843, 1 December 1804.   [8] Alexander, *op. cit.*, p. 43, 23 September 1807.

[9] Farington, p. 3860, 20 November 1807. 'The cause of the illness was as follows . . .' [the remainder of the page left blank].

[10] Farington, p. 5715, 3 February 1811 and p. 6070, 20 April 1812.

[11] Alexander, *op. cit.*, p. 135, 27 April 1813.   [12] *Ibid.* p. 137, 23 September 1813.

Lord Chamberlain (May 1804–10).[1] With Dartmouth's death, the Chamberlaincy remained empty until 1812. In that year the coveted vacancy was filled by the Regent's nominee, Lord Hertford, and the position of Vice-Chamberlain was bestowed on Hertford's son, Prinney's notorious companion, Lord ('Bloaters') Yarmouth.[2] Francis Ingram-Seymour-Conway, 5th Marquess of Hertford (1743–1822) had represented Lostwithiel (1766–8) and Orford (1768–94) as Lord Beauchamp and voted consistently with the Opposition Whigs between 1783 and 1793 before assuming the dignities of Master of the Horse (1804–6) and Lord Chamberlain (1812–21). Like his father, Chambers' pernickety antagonist of the 1780s, Hertford was a born courtier. Wraxall described his manner as 'noble yet ingratiating'.[3] His promotion was due largely to the fact that his celebrated wife Isabella, Lady Hertford, was the Regent's current mistress. As far as self-interest was concerned, this 'infamous rascal'[4] was apparently 'far more odious than his father'.[5]

> 'Without one virtue that can grace a name,
> Without one vice that e'er exalts to fame . . .
> If [the Devil's] pale Crown by meanness could be won
> Who'd have so fair a claim as H . . . .'s son?'[6]

Whatever their temperamental differences, Dartmouth and Hertford were together responsible for two significant changes in the organisation of the Lord Chamberlain's Office. Since the reforms of 1782–3, money issued from the Exchequer to the Lord Chamberlain's Office had been kept in the Chamberlain's bank account. Hertford was the first to maintain a separate official account at the Bank of England.[7] During Salisbury's tenure of office, the practice had also grown up of impresting Exchequer issues not to the Chamberlain's Secretary but direct to the Lord Chamberlain himself. Dartmouth protested in 1809 that this unwelcome activity as public accountant was 'not only inconvenient but in some cases incompatible with the Privileges of my Office and in others detrimental to the Public Service'.[8] Hertford repeated this complaint four years later,[9] and the system was amended in the reform of 1815.

Throughout the period 1784–1830, the Secretaryship to the Lord Chamberlain, a post reported to be worth £1389 per annum,[10] was held by one man, John Calvert (?1758–1844). Both his predecessors, Whitshed Keene and Charles Herbert, had necessarily brief tenures.[11] Through his inherited interest with the Cecils, Calvert

---

[1] *D.N.B.*

[2] Yarmouth succeeded Lord John Thynne in March 1812, but was himself succeeded by Viscount Jocelyn in July (L.C. 3/55; *Diary and Correspondence of Charles Abbot, Lord Colchester*, ed. Colchester ii, 1861, p. 355).

[3] Sir N. Wraxall, *Memoirs* iii (1804 ed.), p. 137.

[4] H. Walpole, *Last Journals*, ed. Doran ii (1910), p. 95.

[5] *MSS. and Correspondence of 1st Earl of Charlemont* i (Hist. MSS. Comm. 12th Report 1891), p. 23.

[6] W. Combe, *The Diaboliad* (1777).

[7] 'Inquiry into . . . the Office of Works', *Parl. Pap.*, 1812–13, v, p. 362.

[8] L.C. 1/40, f. 160 25 May 1809.   [9] L.C. 1/40, f. 306, 14 January 1813.

[10] *Parl. Debates* xiii (1809), Appendix p. cclxxv. The same source gives the Vice-Chamberlain's salary as £740 per annum, although the *Royal Kalendar* gives £1159 8s. 4d. with £1200 for the Lord Chamberlain.

[11] Whitshed Keene was Secretary to the Marquess of Hertford. Herbert (1743–1816; M.P. for Wilton 1775–80) was Manchester's Secretary and brother-in-law (*Gent's. Mag.* 1816, pt. ii, p. 286; *History of Parliament, 1754–90* ii, p. 610).

took office with Salisbury and retained his post unobtrusively under five Lord Chamberlains (Salisbury, Dartmouth, Hertford, Devonshire and Montrose) and seven Vice-Chamberlains: Lord Herbert (1784–94),[1] the Hon. Charles Greville (1794–1809),[2] Lord John Thynne (1809–12), Lord Yarmouth (1812), Viscount Jocelyn (1812–21),[3] the Marquess of Graham (1821–27)[4] and General Sir Samuel Hulse (1827–31).[5] As M.P. for Malmesbury (1780–4), Tamworth (1784–90), St. Albans (1790–6) and Huntingdon (1796–1831), Calvert silently supported each successive government out of gratitude for the permanence of his place.[6] Much of the clerical work in the Lord Chamberlain's Office was performed not by Calvert but by his successive First Clerks: James Ely, John Hale and T. B. Mash. They in their turn were assisted by a Superintendent of Payments, an Inspector of Bills and three Assistant Clerks.[7]

The Lord Chamberlain's Office was of course no more than the administrative heart of the Lord Chamberlain's Department. Holding the purse strings of the Office of Works was only the most onerous of its many functions. The Lord Chamberlain was responsible for the organisation of the Household above stairs, just as the Lord Steward was responsible below stairs. As accountant, censor and courtier, his duties were bewilderingly various. In the spring of 1808, for example, Dartmouth was faced with an administrative deadlock in the Office of Works.[8] At the same time he was being asked by Queen Charlotte to 'put off the drawing room until next week on account of Princess Amelia having the measles'.[9] In addition, he was having to stand up to Beilby Porteus, Bishop of London. The Bishop informed him that a certain Mr. Wilkinson was protesting at Madame Catalani's intention to appear on the stage in male attire, in defiance of the biblical injunction (*Deuteronomy* XXII, 5), 'the woman shall not wear that which pertaineth to man'. 'The land is defiled', complained the Bishop's correspondent, 'the *Feasts of Isis* [the title of the production] in a Christian country and exhibited before the nobles, the priests and the rulers of our land, and this in the solemn season of Lent'. Dartmouth's reply displayed the sort of *sang froid* which served him so well throughout several encounters with Wyatt and Craig: he merely cited the precedent of Shakespeare's transvestite heroines.[10] The establishment of the Lord Chamberlain's Department reflected the multiplicity of his responsibilities. The Poet Laureate, Henry James Pye (£100 per annum), the Principal Painter, Thomas Lawrence (£50 per annum),

---

[1] George Herbert (1759–1827, M.P. for Wilton 1788–94), later 11th Earl of Pembroke, a Pittite (*History of Parliament 1754–90* ii, pp. 610–12).

[2] Greville (1749–1809) has only one claim to fame: his liaison with Emma Hart, later Nelson's Lady Hamilton (*History of Parliament, 1754–90* i, p. 550; *Gent's. Mag.* 1809, pt. i, p. 482).

[3] Jocelyn (1788–1870; M.P. for Louth 1806–7 and 1810–20), later Earl of Roden and Lord Clanbrassil, was an ardent Tory and Orangeman.

[4] James Graham, Marquess of Graham, later Duke of Montrose (1799–1874), Tory M.P. for Cambridge (1825–32), a well known sporting figure.

[5] General (later Field Marshal) Sir Samuel Hulse (1747–1837), Treasurer and Receiver-General to the Prince of Wales; Treasurer, Vice-Chamberlain and Ranger of Windsor Home Park under George IV (*Gent's. Mag.* 1837, pt. i, p. 320).

[6] *History of Parliament, 1754–90* ii, p. 177.

[7] For details of their clerical duties cf. 'Inquiry into . . . the Office of Works', *Parl. Pap.*, 1812–13, v, pp. 361–2, 490–4.   [8] See p. 69 below.

[9] Hist. MSS. Comm. *15th Report, MSS. of the Earl of Dartmouth* iii (1896) p. 291, 7 March 1808.

[10] *Ibid.* 5 April 1808.

the Surveyor of Pictures, Benjamin West (£200 per annum), the various house-keepers for each royal palace, the ushers, pages, trumpeters and Yeomen of the Guard, the Keeper of the Swans (£30 per annum) and the King's Rat Killer, John Mitchell (£80 per annum), apothecaries, surgeons and physicians, pumpers of water and removers of ashes, all received their salaries from the hands of the Lord Chamberlain's Paymaster. At the foot of this list of courtiers, servants, pensioners and sinecurists came the names of a score or more professional men, the Officers of the King's Works.[1]

Scarcely had Wyatt achieved his new position when the political implications of his office became apparent. The Westminster election of June 1796 saw the new Surveyor General actively campaigning on behalf of the Pittite candidate, Sir Alan (later Lord) Gardner.[2] That arch-politician, Joseph Farington, 'strongly solicited him to use his influence as Surveyor General of the Board of Works, which he said he would do . . . there would be a Board Day on Saturday and many of the trades-men . . . would dine together at the Freemasons' Tavern; he would then take oppor-tunities of soliciting them and would endeavour to fix them' by polling day.[3] Most Royal Academicians were for Gardner. Farington's own efforts were so prodigious as to bring on a severe chill. He even 'went to Warwick Hill and brought a lame milkman in a coach to vote'.[4] On two occasions Wyatt himself produced coachloads of tradesmen. In the end, Gardner and Fox were elected, despite riots in favour of the Radical parson Horne Tooke. Two years later the Office of Works made a collective contribution at a time of national crisis. In 1779 'three hundred of the artificers and workmen employed by the Board of Works' had 'offered to be associated and trained upon the same footing as the Westminster and Middlesex Corps, to be employed in keeping the Peace of this City and County; their Officers to be the Master-Artificers'.[5] Now, in 1798, we find Wyatt and Craig, not forming a company, but visiting the Bank of England and paying in '£900 as the amount of the Voluntary Contributions of the Officers and Tradesmen of this Office'.[6]

As Surveyor General Wyatt always maintained his 'power of employing who I please in any of His Majesty's works'.[7] His prerogative was only advisory with regard to senior officers; but it was absolute with regard to Labourers in Trust, Constant Labourers, Gate Keepers on the King's Roads, the Office Keeper and Messenger, and all the King's tradesmen. Constant Artificers also came under Wyatt's plenary jurisdiction. But these he considered unnecessary. No more were appointed after William Lush at Carlton House.[8] This attempt to cut down the establishment is one of the very few reforms with which Wyatt can be credited. Some of his appointments left him open to the charge of nepotism. Gilbert's Instructions had expressly forbidden the employment of any contractor who was related to the Clerk of the Works or

---

[1] For comparative establishment lists of the whole Lord Chamberlain's Department cf. *Parl. Register* xvi (1779–80), p. 241; L.C. 3/20; T. 38/221; L.C. 3/49, 1812.
[2] On his mother's side Admiral Gardner (1742–1809) was related to Farington. As a member of the Board of Admiralty he represented Plymouth (1790–96) before moving to Westminster (1796–1806) (*History of Parliament, 1754–90* ii, p. 483; *Gent's. Mag.* 1809, pt. i, p. 89).
[3] Farington, p. 644, 1 June 1796.   [4] Farington, p. 659, 11 June 1796.
[5] *Correspondence of George III*, ed. Fortescue iv, No. 2768, (?) 8 September 1779, Lord North to George III.
[6] Works 4/18, f. 282, 23 March 1798.   [7] Works 6/24, f. 215, 3 September 1808.
[8] 'Inquiry into . . . the Office of Works', *Parl. Pap.* 1812–13, v, pp. 335, 344. Lush's presence was required in the absence of Wyatt's nephews, see below p. 58.

Labourer in Trust.[1] But at Carlton House the carpenter was a Wyatt and the Labourer in Trust was a Wyatt. At the Lazaretto both the carpentry and copper contracts were held by Wyatts. At Windsor the commissions for gilding and decorative painting were given to two more Wyatts. It was Sir William Chambers who had awarded the carpentry contract for Westminster and Somerset Place to James Wyatt's brother Samuel (1737–1807).[2] Naturally enough he continued to be employed after 1796, notably at Somerset House and the Lazaretto. But the supply of a patent form of tinned copper for the Lazaretto was also given to one of the Surveyor General's numerous nephews[3]. Another nephew, Jeffry Wyatt, later Sir Jeffry Wyatville (1776–1840),[4] served a double apprenticeship under Samuel and James Wyatt before achieving the status of Labourer in Trust at Carlton House in 1797. He was succeeded in 1800 by yet another of the Surveyor General's talented nephews, Lewis William Wyatt (1777–1853),[5] who had also served fourteen years' apprenticeship: as a builder under Samuel, as an architect under James. Jeffry Wyatt received the carpentry contract for Carlton House when he surrendered the position of Labourer in Trust to his cousin. Lewis Wyatt was also Assistant Architect to James Wyatt at the Ordnance.[6] In 1798 another kinsman, Edward Wyatt, was appointed 'gilder at all the Palaces etc. under the direction of this Office'.[7] But at Windsor Farington noted a still more blatant example. For the decoration of the reconstructed apartments, 'he had his son Matthew [Cotes] Wyatt [1777–1862], a young inexperienced artist, appointed, to the exclusion of artists of known ability'.[8]

The situation at Carlton House came in for severe comment from the Commissioners of Military Inquiry. Alone among the Labourers in Trust, Lewis Wyatt was discovered to be non-resident. He 'follows private practice, in the Architectural line, [and] has not given that attendance in his District, and taken that account of the Workmen employed on daywork, or of the materials used . . . which seem to be the proper duty of such an Officer'. Instead the work was left to William Lush, who also received 28s. od. per week from Jeffry Wyatt, although Lewis Wyatt could 'not recollect ever seeing him work as a Carpenter'. The Labourer in Trust left Lush 'to see that the different Workmen do their duty, to examine the materials, to direct the conversion of them agreeably to the Drawings furnished by him and also to take an account of the people employed, and to sign the weekly notes'. All these services Lewis Wyatt did not apparently consider 'to be any part of his duty'.[9] The chain of command at Carlton House was indeed complicated, beginning with James Wyatt, by-passing the Clerk of Works (Yenn), and descending via Lewis and Jeffry Wyatt to West the measuring clerk and Nixon the supernumerary Clerk of the Works, to end up with the indispensable William Lush.

During Wyatt's Surveyor Generalship the upper ranks of the Office of Works continued to show the usual disproportion of mediocrity to talent. The best of his

[1] *Ibid.* p. 333. [2] Colvin, *Dictionary*. pp. 734–6.
[3] 'Inquiry into . . . the Office of Works', *Parl. Pap.* 1812–13, v, p. 397.
[4] Colvin, *Dictionary*, pp. 736–40; *Gent's. Mag.* 1840, pt. i, pp. 545–9.
[5] Colvin, *Dictionary*, pp. 732–4; *Gent's. Mag.* 1853, pt. i, p. 670.
[6] 'Inquiry into . . . the Office of Works', *Parl. Pap.*, 1812–13, v, p. 461; 4th Report of Commissioners of Military Inquiry 1806, p. 288.
[7] Works 4/18, f. 323, 28 December 1798. [8] Farington, p. 4603, 21 July 1810.
[9] 'Inquiry into . . . the Office of Works', *Parl. Pap.* 1812–13, v, pp. 341–3.

lieutenants, Yenn, Brettingham and Hiort, all owed their appointment to Chambers. But then so did the worst, John Thomas Groves. Most of Wyatt's appointments followed the dynastic pattern established long before Chambers. The Rices and the Crockers continued to follow the Woolfes and the Brownes up the ladder of official preferment. Robert Browne Snr. (d. 1796) had served throughout Chambers' Surveyor Generalship, first as Labourer in Trust at Richmond and Kew and then as Clerk of the Works at the Tower, Newmarket, Greenwich and Winchester. His son, Robert Browne Jnr. (1756–1827) began as Labourer in Trust at Greenwich and the King's Mews and rose, via the Clerkship at Windsor, to Clerk of the Works at Richmond and Kew. Educated as an architect, with a small private practice, his future lay in administration after 1815. Meanwhile he considered his salary 'very inadequate', and took pains to supplement it by acting as Clerk of the Works at Somerset Place (£100 per annum), Examiner of Bills and Accounts to the Ranger of Windsor Great Park (£100 per annum) and Surveyor of Buildings at the Marshalsea (2% on expenditure)[1]. Edward Crocker I (d. 1779) had held the position of First Clerk long before the reforms of 1782–3. Edward Crocker II (*c.* 1757–1836) served the Office of Works in different capacities for more than forty years. He began by helping his father with clerical duties, and became Assistant Clerk in 1774. Twenty years later he became temporary Resident Clerk and Labourer in Trust at the Tower. In 1796 on account of 'his good conduct and long service', he was given the post vacated by Robert Browne Snr. as Clerk of the Works there and retained it until 1818. He also supplemented his income by assisting in the operations at Windsor and by acting as Clerk of the Works at the King's Bench and Fleet Prisons and at the House of the Master of the Rolls.[2] John Woolfe Snr. (d. 1793) passed the whole of his official career under Chambers, first as Labourer in Trust at Westminster, then as Clerk of the Works at the Mews and the Tower, Clerk of the Works at St. James's, Whitehall and Westminster and finally as Examiner. He is remembered, however, not for his official labours, but for his joint authorship with James Gandon of the two final volumes of *Vitruvius Britannicus* (1776 and 1771).[3] His son, John Woolfe Jnr. (d. 1806), spent the whole of his career as Labourer in Trust at Whitehall and Westminster, apart from a brief spell as acting Clerk of the Works in the same department, a quiet interlude between the stormy tenancies of John Soane and J. T. Groves.[4] William Rice (d. 1789) had been Clerk of the Works at Richmond and at Hampton Court under Chambers. For many years he was assisted by his nephew, Thomas Rice (d. 1810), Labourer in Trust at Richmond and Kew, who also deputised for Tildesley on several occasions before succeeding him as Clerk of the Works at Hampton Court.[5]

---

[1] *Ibid.* pp. 339, 442–3, 445; Colvin, *Dictionary*, p. 104.

[2] Works 6/22, 24 June 1796; Works 4/18, f. 185, 24 June and f. 196, 26 August 1796; 'Inquiry into . . . the Office of Works', *Parl. Pap.* 1812–13, v, pp. 341, 439; Colvin, *Dictionary*, p. 158. He had a small private practice as architect and surveyor. He lived at Upper Belgrave Place, Pimlico, letting off his official house at the Tower for £30 per annum, and a room on Tower Parade to the Officers' Mess at £4 per annum. In addition, 1 gn. per annum was due to him from the Company of Watermen plying at Tower Stairs. He received £10 expenses for each visit to Newmarket.

[3] Colvin, *Dictionary*, p. 698.

[4] Works 4/18, f. 43, 15 November 1793 and f. 59, 27 February 1794. In 1789 he assisted his father in the preparation of a report on the state of the Houses of Parliament (below, p. 497).

[5] Works 6/22, f. 164, 24 July 1794; Works 4/17, 15 May 1789, 12 March 1790; Works 4/18, f. 198, 9 September 1796 and f. 223, 17 February 1797; T. 29/93, f. 278, 4 February 1808; Works 4/18, 3 January, 15 May, 26 September 1800; Works 6/13, 12 February 1808, 10 May 1810; Works 4/20, 15 January 1808.

Only two of Wyatt's Clerks of the Works were drawn from outside this family circle, Thomas Hardwick and William Matthew. Hardwick (1752–1829)[1] had been a pupil of Sir William Chambers and remained his lifelong admirer. After several years of travel, training and professional practice, he was appointed Clerk of the Works at Hampton Court in 1810. Both Yenn and Wyatt considered him worthy of a place in the Royal Academy and described him as 'a very respectable man . . . a regular bred classical Architect'.[2] Wyatt also thought Brettingham worthy of this distinction, though he was 'not personally much relished, besides having something of a vicious [i.e. Palladian?] taste'.[3] Hardwick and Brettingham certainly fulfilled Hiort's dictum that Clerks of the Works 'ought to be men eminent in their profession as architects'.[4] By comparison with either of them William Matthew was a person of far lower calibre. He alone among Wyatt's Clerks of the Works was not a fully trained surveyor.[5] Educated as a carpenter, joiner and builder, he served twelve years at the Tower of London as Clerk of the Works to the Ordnance before being chosen by Wyatt as Leach's successor at Windsor. He had no private practice. As the Surveyor General's personal nominee he was therefore well suited to act as Wyatt's assistant in Gothicising the royal apartments. Wyatt may even have felt a little guilty about the circumstances of Matthew's appointment. He certainly went to a great deal of trouble to secure a suitable pension for Leach. 'He is an old servant of the public', Wyatt informed the Treasury, 'removed . . . not upon any ground which ought to exclude him from remuneration, but merely because the works at Windsor were of a nature to require the utmost exertions of a very active man . . . He is now so infirm as to be totally unfit for active employment, and very much distressed in his pecuniary circumstances. Indeed I feel I should not discharge my duty properly . . . if I did not strongly recommend [his] case'.[6] Leach's son was even employed as a temporary assistant to George Horsley, still absent and insane.[7] Leach Snr. was eventually pensioned off at the rate of two thirds of his old salary, and Matthew received the extra burden, and extra profit, of work at Windsor. When the accounting became too onerous, Matthew was helped by Edward Crocker Jnr.[8]

Similar emergency duties were performed for Wyatt by Hiort. In return for an extra £100 per annum Hiort accepted responsibility for the complex accounting involved in Wyatt's work at the Speaker's House and the Houses of Parliament.[9] After thirteen years as Assistant Clerk he succeeded Brettingham as Resident Clerk in 1805. In both these positions he found his salary far from excessive. In 1803 it

[1] 'Inquiry into . . . the Office of Works', *Parl. Pap.* 1812–13, v, pp. 341, 456; Colvin, *Dictionary*, pp. 264–5.

[2] Farington, p. 1442, 20 January and p. 1624, 27 August 1799. Hardwick could be strict with his subordinates. In 1815 he reported that William Miles Stone was incompetent 'to execute the duties of Labourer in Trust under the new regulations . . . from his general conduct, being frequently intoxicated, and his inability to make out and keep accounts, [he] is by no means efficient' (Works 6/27, f. 218, 21 March 1815). Whereupon Stone was told that he would be dismissed 'unless he could induce Mr. Hardwick to continue him' (Works 4/21, 3 April 1815).   [3] Farington, p. 1442, 20 January 1799.

[4] 'Inquiry into . . . the Office of Works', *Parl. Pap.* 1812–13, v, p. 430.   [5] *Ibid.* pp. 339, 341, 454–5.

[6] Works 6/25, ff. 53–4, 5 June 1809, 25 April 1810 and f. 112, 27 July 1811; Works 4/20, 19 July, 4 October 1811, 21 February 1812.

[7] Wyatt described 'young Leach' as 'a promising youth for that situation. . . . He continued to do duty for some time, but meeting with another situation more advantageous, he quitted' (Works 6/24, f. 270, 7 June 1809; Works 4/20, 11 December 1807).

[8] 'Inquiry into . . . the Office of Works', *Parl. Pap.*, 1812–13, v, pp. 341, 439.   [9] *Ibid.* pp. 335–6.

required a strong testimonial from Wyatt to obtain him an official house in Scotland Yard: his job 'is a responsible one and requires much of his attendance. He is well qualified for it, and I have always found him faithful and assiduous, and I have no hesitation in saying his residing near the office will be of infinite advantage'.[1] As Resident Clerk he had to employ a personal assistant if his duties were not to occupy him during office hours every day. Normally he attended only on Fridays, like everyone else in the department.[2] His £20 allowance for candles, coals and brooms was woefully inadequate: four fires every Friday plus one in the Board Room cost £50 per annum alone.[3] It is hardly surprising that he had to supplement his income by acting as Inspector to the Commissioners for Paving Westminster,[4] and by selling timber. 'I am a timber merchant', he admitted, 'and some of the persons employed may have purchased of me articles [to be] used in the King's Works'.[5]

At a lower level, Wyatt's Labourers in Trust were on the whole a worthy band: T. F. Hunt at St. James's, 'well qualified [and] . . . very satisfactory' in coping with work inherited from his ailing predecessor, John Lawrence;[6] William Alexander Arnold, 'strictly sober and honest and perfectly capable' in a backwater at Newmarket;[7] William Child at Windsor, living off the capital of work executed by his predecessor, Robert Goodworth;[8] Adam Lee at Whitehall and Westminster, able, conscientious and energetic;[9] Edward Jarman at the King's Mews, coming in twice a day from Marsham Street, Westminster;[10] William Miles Stone at Hampton Court, hovering on the brink of dismissal, 'frequently intoxicated' and 'unable to make out and keep accounts'.[11] During Wyatt's Surveyor Generalship Labourers in Trust became increasingly responsible for the day to day supervision of building projects. As Robert Browne Jnr. remarked, 'in my opinion the Clerks of the Works are at present Surveyors, and the Labourers in Trust Clerks of the Works'.[12]

During Wyatt's tenure of office the Office of Works was beset by a single, chronic problem: the soaring rate of expenditure. In 1786 the yearly estimate for tradesmen's bills in the Lord Chamberlain's Department of the Household had been fixed at £43,000. Between 1786 and 1793 this estimate, 'with an exception too trifling to require notice', had been sufficient. But between 1793 and 1804 rising prices and extraordinary royal demands had forced up the average annual charge to £66,000.

[1] Works 6/23, ff. 210–11, 28 February, 5 March 1803; Works 4/19, 11 March 1803. When Spence succeeded Hiort, Wyatt assured the Treasury that 'he is as fully entitled to [this] favour as Mr. Hiort was' (Works 6/24, f. 159, 7 January 1808).

[2] 'Inquiry into . . . the Office of Works', *Parl. Pap.* 1812–13, v, p. 427.

[3] *Ibid.* pp. 335, 425.   [4] *Ibid.* p. 426.

[5] *Ibid.* p. 425. This contravened Gilbert's Instructions (*ibid.* p. 333).

[6] Works 6/27, f. 222, 3 April 1815. For his numerous architectural publications see Colvin, *Dictionary*, pp. 303–4. He designed the Burns Mausoleum at Dumfries in 1816.

[7] Works 6/27, f. 227, 12 April 1815. Arnold had been an assistant clerk to Hiort ('Inquiry into . . . the Office of Works', *Parl. Pap.* 1812–13, v, p. 439).

[8] Works 6/27, f. 224, 5 April 1815.

[9] Works 6/27, f. 222, 3 April 1815. Lee had been trained, and was in practice, as a carpenter and builder. He had acted as foreman for the building of the Bridport Barracks and the Military Hospital, Portsmouth. His volume of work was increased by Groves' incapacity. He enjoyed two official apartments, at Whitehall and at Westminster, living in that at Cotton Garden and letting out the other for £20 per annum ('Inquiry into . . . the Office of Works', *Parl. Pap.* 1812–13, v, p. 465).

[10] *Ibid.* pp. 461–2. He was a joiner by profession, being appointed joiner at Buckingham House and Kensington Palace in 1783.   [11] Works 6/27, f. 218, 21 March 1815.

[12] 'Inquiry into . . . the Office of Works', *Parl. Pap.*, 1812–13, v, p. 445.

In 1804, therefore, the estimate was raised to £65,000.[1] Out of this sum, the Office of Works received the following share:[2]

Yenn (Kensington, Buckingham House, Mews, Carlton House, King's Roads)	£6800
Groves (St. James's, Whitehall, Westminster)	9700
Crocker (Tower, Newmarket, Greenwich, Winchester)	1900
Browne (Richmond, Kew)	2500
Tildesley (Hampton Court, Bushy Park)	4200
Matthew (Windsor)	6900
	————
	£32,000 per annum

It was laid down by the Treasury that this 'computation . . . was not to be exceeded on any account whatever'. The system of advance quarterly estimates prescribed by Gilbert's Instructions therefore became irrelevant.[3] The new figures had been prepared by Craig, and covered 'Ordinary' works only; 'Extra' works and General Surveys were excluded. From the start the distribution of these quotas caused endless disputes and juggling arrangements whereby excess expenditure in one sub-department in any one quarter was either not declared or else held over into the next quarter.[4]

	1804 estimate	*Year ending 5 July 1805*
Lord Chamberlain's Office Bills	8000	10,356 6s. 0d.
Privy Council Warrants	1100	1236 19s. 11d.
Messenger's Bills	1400	1352 6s. 7d.
Grooby's Bills (for lighting)	500	431 13s. 0d.
Wardrobe Bills	16,000	31,260 2s. 2d.
Office of Works Bills	32,000	72,564 12s. 5½d.
Jewel Office Bills	6000	18,795 11s. 7d.
	————	————
	£65,000	£135,997 11s. 8½d.

The Treasury's allocation of money was tempered by stringent precautions: strict economy and punctual accounting was urged upon all departments. Indeed Dartmouth's opening gesture had been to co-operate with Treasury policy to the extent of imposing a general moratorium on Office of Works activity. 'The heavy expences lately incurred in the department of the Office of Works having much excited the notice of the Lords of the Treasury, the Lord Chamberlain desires that no alteration, addition or repair may henceforth be commenced at any of His Majesty's Palaces or Houses but such as the Surveyor General may deem absolutely

[1] L.C. 1/40, f. 6, Huskisson to Calvert, 26 July 1804. The allowance for the Lord Steward's Department was similarly raised from £50,000 (1786) to £75,000 (1804). Details in 44 G. III c. 80, as stipulated by the Parliamentary Committee for the Consideration of the Civil List and approved by the House of Commons 9 July 1804.   [2] Works 4/20, 9 January 1807.
[3] 'Inquiry into . . . the Office of Works', *Parl. Pap.*, 1812–13, v, p. 551.
[4] e.g. Works 4/20, 22 July 1808, 23 December 1808.

and indispensably necessary for the preservation of the Buildings'.[1] Nevertheless, by 1806 expenditure in the Lord Chamberlain's Department, and in the Office of Works in particular, was again beginning to cause alarm. In the year ending 5 July 1805, expenditure more than doubled the 1804 allowance.[2]

As an explanation of this excessive expenditure, the Lord Chamberlain was able to point to several unusual commitments during 1805: furnishings for the Committee Rooms of both Houses of Parliament, furnishing and redecoration at Windsor and Kew, and extraordinary demands for ambassadorial plate, and for robes, insignia and decorations in connection with the Garter Installation at Windsor.[3] But the Treasury was more concerned with administrative irregularities. Copies of Treasury instructions were despatched both to the Office of Works and to James Wyatt himself, accompanied by a questionnaire as 'to what extent, and on what grounds, they have been departed from, and whether any and what obstacles . . . prevent [them] from being . . . invariably adhered to'.[4] The result was a flurry of extraordinary meetings of the Board of Works, and a fresh set of Treasury orders. Once more the Office of Works was urged to keep within the 1804 estimate of £8000 per quarter, to submit its accounts within a fortnight of the end of each quarter, and to take care that excess expenditure in any one quarter was carried over into the next.[5] The Treasury was prepared to tolerate a small margin of error: 'so long as the extra expences of the Lord Chamberlain's Department did not exceed upon the average £200 per quarter, their Lordships would be perfectly satisfied'.[6] But a margin of such precision implied a degree of control, of the Office of Works by the Lord Chamberlain, and of both by the Treasury, which could hardly be expected under the existing régime. As T. B. Mash, Dartmouth's First Clerk, informed the Treasury, 'with respect to the necessary and effectual control of the Lord Chamberlain over the Board of Works as directed by Act of Parliament, I have . . . to acquaint you . . . that his Lordship regrets much the improbability of any such being established without that complete regularity in the Department of the Office of Works which seems by no means to be expected under the superintendence of Mr. Wyatt'.[7]

Burke's Act and Gilbert's Instructions had placed a heavy burden upon the Surveyor General and Comptroller. Consequently Wyatt's absence threw the whole system into confusion. Without him there was no clearly defined chain of command, no acceptable division of responsibility. 'The most glaring deficiency in the present system', Hiort complained, 'is that it has never been properly defined, or clearly understood, who are the principal officers, what powers they are vested with, or what

---

[1] Works 4/19, 20 July 1804.
[2] Table given in L.C. 1/40, f. 21, 1 March 1806. The Treasury complained that the 1804 estimates had been exceeded by 50% in the Lord Chamberlain's Department and by 75% in the Lord Steward's Department (T. 29/87, f. 356, 24 July 1806).
[3] L.C. 1/40, ff. 23–24.   [4] Works 4/19, 6 May 1806.
[5] Works 4/19, 31 October 1806; L.C. 1/40, ff. 33–4, 25 October 1806. Similar instructions were sent to the Lord Steward, the Master of the Horse and the Master of the Robes. The Treasury added that 'a notification to the Master Tradesmen employed by this Office [of Works] be stuck up in the Outer or Waiting Room, as to the delivery of their Accounts to the Clerks of the Works in proper time, and that copies thereof should be sent to the several Clerks of the Works' (Works 4/19, 26 December 1806). All Clerks of the Works are to 'send all their bills for works done to this Office on every Quarter day, and at the same time a Probable Estimate of the ensuing Quarter, independent of the General Survey' (Works 4/19, 12 December 1806).
[6] L.C. 1/40, f. 83, 10 March 1807.   [7] L.C. 1/40, ff. 121–2, 15 January 1806.

particular department of the service they are to be individually responsible for . . . This deficiency has occasioned . . . that want of unanimity among the superior officers, and [of] that proper subordination in those of inferior status, so requisite for the well government of every establishment'.[1] Wyatt considered that in theory 'as Head Clerk', Craig had 'a general superintendance of the other Clerks'. In practice, however, he lacked the requisite authority. It was soon discovered that 'the orders of the Examining Clerk have not at all times been readily submitted to by the Clerks of the Works'.[2] At moments of crisis the 'Constitution of the Department' was invoked.[3] But of course few people could remember seeing such a document. Gilbert's Instructions had modified Burke's Act and had themselves been modified in turn by custom and necessity. As a result, much depended upon the ability and scrupulosity of individual officers, and too much upon the integrity of the head of department.

As Surveyor General and Comptroller Wyatt considered his primary allegiance due not to the Treasury, still less to the Lord Chamberlain, but first and foremost to the King and, by extension, to the Royal Family. It was royal patronage which maintained Wyatt in office despite his inefficiency; and it was arbitrary royal demands, as much as rising prices, which upset the mechanism of Office of Works administration. For example, Wyatt's responsibility for the reconstruction of Windsor Castle made him the direct recipient of George III's commands. When Wyatt's assistant and Clerk of the Works, William Matthew, presented an estimate for 1807 he therefore announced that the sum involved was 'exclusive of any works ordered by His Majesty, or which His Majesty may be pleased to command'. Such a casual *carte blanche* nullified the whole basis of Treasury control. Consequently the Treasury ordered Craig to produce further details, adding that 'it does not belong to the Surveyor General . . . but to the Lord Chamberlain and the Lords of the Treasury only, to receive His Majesty's pleasure for works to be carried on'. More explicitly, Dartmouth demanded an explanation as to 'why the Act of Parliament . . . has not been attended to'.[4] Craig quickly despatched these peremptory letters to Windsor, where Matthew showed them to Wyatt, 'who happened [as usual] to be at that place'.[5] Wyatt promised to write to Dartmouth, and then promptly forgot about it. Understandably, Craig was 'highly offended' at Matthew's apparent discourtesy. In return, Matthew's apology was profuse: 'You surely, Sir, cannot conceive . . . that I should personally offer you any offence . . . .'.[6] Nevertheless payment of Matthew's salary was delayed, along with the quarterly settlement of excess bills, until Wyatt had bestirred himself to obtain the necessary Treasury *fiat* 'without which no payment can be made'.[7]

Matthew's statement contained a grain of truth which the Treasury was slow to

---

[1] 'Inquiry into . . . the Office of Works', *Parl. Pap.*, 1812–13, v, p. 429.   [2] *Ibid.* p. 335.
[3] In 1810 'an attested copy of the late Mr. Jones's constitution' was delivered to the Audit Office (Works 4/20, 27 April 1810). In 1811 a copy was sent to 'C. W. Flint of the Irish Office for William Plunkett, Secretary to the Commissioners of Inquiry in Ireland' (*ibid.* 11 March 1811). And in 1812 'a copy of the Constitution . . . and divers other Papers and Account' were sent to the Commissioners of Military Inquiry (*ibid.* 1 May 1812). Charles Bacon admitted that he had 'never been able to get at [the Constitution] so as to read it through' ('Inquiry into . . . the Office of Works', *Parl. Pap.*, 1812–13, v, p. 435).
[4] Works 4/19, 19 December 1806.
[5] Works 4/20, 16 January 1807.   [6] Works 6/24, f. 87, 11 January 1807.
[7] Works 4/20, 23 January 1807.

accept: that long-term estimates could not stop rising prices or curtail arbitrary royal demands. The quotas fixed in 1804 were consistently exceeded. The Office of Works figures for 1807 and 1808 were £47,536 5s. 2½d. and £45,432 17s. 2¼d., plus £9003 18s. 0¼d. for the General Survey of 1808 and £10,738 3s. 6½d. for that held in 1809.[1] In 1810 the Treasury made one final attempt to stem the tide. To guard against this 'frequency of excess' it was laid down that estimates were to be regarded as contractual obligations which might be exceeded only on specific Treasury authority.[2] But such measures confused symptoms and causes. Instead of imposing a series of irrelevant estimates, the Treasury should have tried to find out why the efficiency of the Office of Works seemed to vary in inverse proportion to the expansion of its business. It was left to the Commissioners of Military Inquiry to discover the reasons. Meanwhile, Craig had an answer of his own: Office of Works personnel were overworked and underpaid.

Chambers had adopted this attitude in 1783. He reiterated his protest in 1796 when Carlton House became actually, as well as formally, the responsibility of the department. Less than a month before his death, in what must surely be regarded as a disinterested petition, he asked the Treasury not only for additional staff at Carlton House but also for extra salaries for the established office staff. In particular, he instanced the Surveyor General and Examiner as being underpaid, because they received fewer perquisites than their subordinates. Chambers proposed the following increases:[3]

To myself, the Surveyor General for the time being	:	£200 per annum
To the Examiner	:	120
To the Resident [Clerk] including coals, candles, and stationery	:	50
To an additional Clerk in the Office	:	60
To the Office Keeper	:	10
To the Messenger	:	8
To the Clerk of the Works at Carlton House	:	100
To the Labourer in Trust at Carlton House	:	60
To an Office Bricklayer there	:	42 ⎱ new
To an Office Carpenter there	:	42 ⎰ posts
total increase	:	£692 per annum

One of Wyatt's first actions as Surveyor General was to repeat this claim.[4] Both petitions were buried in Treasury files, and forgotten. According to Craig the situation had grown very much worse during the following years. Salaries had remained unchanged since 1783, but the business of the department had quadrupled.[5]

[1] L.C. 1/4, 7 October 1809, 21 February 1810.
[2] L.C. 1/40, f. 180, 26 January 1810; Works 6/25, f. 43, 26 January 1810.
[3] Works 6/22, 19 February 1796.   [4] Works 6/22, 11 May 1796.
[5] 'Inquiry into . . . the Office of Works', *Parl. Pap.*, 1812–13, v. p. 405.

In reply to an enquiry by John Lewis Mallet of the Audit Office in 1808, Craig produced the following catalogue of woe:[1]

> The late Surveyor General did solicit . . . the Treasury for an increase of salaries . . . I think mine to have been £150 or £200 per annum, but Sir he was not honoured with an answer to the best of my recollection . . . I presented a petition about seven years ago, but I have never had interest enough to get a sight of the Petition in order to take a copy of it, the original draft having been given by me to the Surveyor General. Your letter demands to know the duties of the Principal Officers. I cannot make any other reply than a general one, because their duties are so multifarious: they are Architects, Surveyors and Agents to His Majesty's Buildings, and that to an immense extent, say perhaps to more than £100,000 a year!!! The Commissioners [of Audit] have examined the Minute and Letter books, the Weekly books of one Clerk of the Works . . ., the Rough books of bills, the Abstract books, and compared some of them of the present day, with others when the Office was in commission; I think I may venture to assert, the trouble of these times is more than double, . . . and yet not any addition to our salaries, although the absolute necessary articles of subsistence are in many cases double and treble what they were then.

Craig made little of the perquisites which had always been available for Office of Works staff: official houses, gardens and lodgings, and 'a brace of birds now and then'. Rather less plausibly, he also minimised the system of additional gratuities which had grown up during the previous twenty years. These allowances were based on the traditional distinction between 'Ordinary' works and 'Extra' works. 'Ordinary' works consisted mostly of running repairs, and were therefore assumed to form part of the responsibilities incurred by acceptance of an annual salary. 'Extra' works, that is new or large commissions, were somehow felt to lie outside the normal run of duty and to require additional payment. As official and royal demands increased, 'Extra' became usual if not 'Ordinary' and haphazard gratuities turned into a permanent supplementary allowance. The rate of these gratuities varied according to the decision of the Surveyor General or Examiner. But it normally amounted to $2\frac{1}{2}\%$ on each item of 'Extra' expenditure, that is 1% for the Clerk of the Works, plus $1\frac{1}{2}\%$ for his assistants.[2] For example, between 1806 and 1812 Matthew received a total of £228 17s. 0d. for supervising 'Extra' works at Windsor.[3] Besides these allowances officers of the Works frequently received substantial Christmas presents from contracting tradesmen, such as the five guineas Holroyd the plumber gave to John Lawrence or the £10 he gave to Adam Lee.[4] In 1814 Craig supplied the Treasury with a detailed list of all gratuities for 'extra services' between 1794 and 1813.[5]

---

[1] Works 6/24, ff. 201–2, 15 July 1808. Salary claims by John Spence and George Russell, Assistant Clerks, and by Adam Lee, Labourer in Trust at St. James's, Whitehall and Westminster, were also refused by the Treasury in 1813 and 1815 (T. 29/125, f. 666, 26 October 1813; T. 29/133, f. 428, 27 January 1815).

[2] 'Inquiry into . . . the Office of Works', *Parl. Pap.*, 1812–13, v, pp. 340, 420. Wyatt claimed that *salaries* were only to be considered 'as for the common duties of office, for repairs, or ordinary accounts'. A similarly haphazard system of gratuities prevailed elsewhere in the Lord Chamberlain's Department. In 1810 its validity was questioned by the Commissioners of Audit with regard to the accounts for 1805. Their attempt to rationalise the practice produced a stern reply from Dartmouth in defence of his 'discretionary power' (L.C. 1/40, ff. 204–6, 28 August 1810). Nevertheless, gratuities in the Lord Chamberlain's Department were drastically cut in 1815 (L.C. 1/6, f. 384, 30 May and f. 393, 18 July 1815).

[3] 'Inquiry into . . . the Office of Works', *Parl. Pap.*, 1812–13, v, pp. 454–5.

[4] *Ibid.* p. 479.

[5] Works 6/26, ff. 156–7, 8 July 1814.

The total expenditure involved was £156,858 17s. 0d. The distribution of allowances on four typical occasions was as follows:

	Marriage of the Prince of Wales at St. James's 1795	Trial of Lord Melville 1806	Funeral of Lord Nelson 1806	Repair of Whitehall Chapel 1810
Total expenditure	£1543 11s. 5¾d.	£6341 6s. 0½d.	£5061 0s. 6½d.	£15,980 9s. 10½d.
Surveyor General	—	160 0s. 0d.	241 10s. 0d.	—
Examiner	—	50 0s. 0d.	50 0s. 0d.	—
Resident Clerk	5 5s. 0d.	20 0s. 0d.	6 6s. 0d.	10 10s. 0d.
First Assistant Clerk	4 4s. 0d.	10 0s. 0d.	4 4s. 0d.	6 6s. 0d.
Joint Assistant Clerk	3 3s. 0d.	8 0s. 0d.	6 6s. 0d.	5 5s. 0d.
Clerk of the Works	38 12s. 0d.	100 0s. 0d.	105 5s. 0d.	35 0s. 0d.
Labourer in Trust	—	6 0s. 0d.	10 10s. 0d.	20 0s. 0d.
Office Keeper	2 2s. 0d.	—	1 1s. 0d.	2 2s. 0d.
Messenger	1 1s. 0d.	—	3 3s. 0d.	1 1s. 0d.

On only four occasions was extra payment made to Wyatt and Craig: the Trial of Lord Melville and the Funeral of Lord Nelson, both in 1806, and the Installation of the Knights of the Bath at Westminster and the construction of the new Stationery Office, Whitehall, both in 1813. In 1810 Craig pressed for the regularisation of these gratuities. After all, they amounted to no more than 'some trifling remuneration for . . . extraordinary services'.[1] Two years later, when asked if he had any suggestions for the improvement of the department, he at first replied in the negative. But, when pressed, he conceded that 'if I dare offer an opinion, [Clerks of the Works] as well as every other officer in His Majesty's Office of Works, are not sufficiently paid for their time, trouble and experience in the business of the Office'.[2]

But in the eyes of outsiders, the officials of the Office of Works must have seemed less remarkable for their penury than for their inability to agree among themselves. Long before 1807, Craig and Wyatt were at loggerheads. But in that year their private hostility assumed public importance. The cause of the dispute was John Thomas Groves (d. 1811). Groves had been one of the first to be infected with Wyatt's lethargy. With the Surveyor General out of London and the Examiner out of favour, he was able to defy regulations with impunity. Under Chambers, leave of absence had been seldom granted. When in 1795 Brettingham wished to execute some work for the Marquess of Downshire at Hillsborough in Ireland, he took the precaution of applying for permission to both the Surveyor General and the Lord Chamberlain.[3] Brettingham's behaviour on this occasion contrasts markedly with Soane's. He informed Chambers that his inability 'to compleat and sign the Abstract of the Quarter's Books within the time prescribed . . . gives me much concern. However, that the blame may lie where it really ought, and not the smallest imputation unjustly attach itself to any other Gentleman [who is] my Brother Officer in the Board of Works, the Marquess of Downshire . . . will . . . write to his brother-in-law Lord Salisbury, to account for the Irregularity of which he is the cause . . . Hoping

[1] Works 6/25, f. 83, 7 September 1810.
[2] 'Inquiry into . . . the Office of Works', *Parl. Pap.*, 1812–13, v, p. 416.
[3] Works 4/18, f. 130, 10 July 1795.

you will have the kindness to excuse this involuntary appearance of inattention and with many wishes for the perfect restoration of your health, I am, Dear Sir William, Your sincere friend and humble servant, Robert Brettingham'.[1] But under Wyatt's permissive rule such elaborate courtesy was unnecessary. Yenn was in a position to 'notify' Craig whenever he wished to leave London,[2] and Groves was able to turn an announcement of 1806 that he was 'setting off for the Sea side' into a recuperative holiday lasting three years.[3]

In a small way, Groves was a successful pluralist: Architect to the Post Office, Architect to the Ordnance Office in Old Palace Yard, and Surveyor to the Commissioners for the Improvement of Westminster, as well as Clerk of the Works at St. James's, Whitehall and Westminster.[4] His responsibility for the Houses of Parliament gave him an extra allowance of £25 per annum.[5] He seems also to have been a man after Wyatt's own heart. In return for additional duties, Wyatt secured him extra accommodation in 1799 and an extra salary in 1801.[6] In dealing with subordinates Groves was moody and vindictive. For several years he harboured a grudge against Thomas Bevan, Labourer in Trust at St. James's. In 1799 he secured Bevan's dismissal by singling him out as an example of a very common malpractice: appropriating surplus building materials. Bevan always maintained that the lead and wood in question was his 'just perquisite', and in 1802 Wyatt showed a certain sympathy by awarding him a pension of £40 per annum.[7] This was however irregularly paid,

---

[1] Works 6/22, 3 July 1795.

[2] Works 4/19, 1 October 1802, 13 June 1806; Works 4/21, 11 June 1813, 26 August 1814. Thomas Hardwick was able to leave town 'for a few days' in 1810 and 'to go to Lincoln for about a week' in 1811 (Works 4/20, 13 July 1811). Hiort was given permission in 1796, 1798 and 1813 (Works 4/18, f. 199, 16 September 1796 and f. 301, 22 July 1798; Works 4/21, 26 June 1813) and Leach in 1795, 1796, 1797 and 1799 (Works 4/18, f. 143, 25 September 1795; f. 197, 2 September 1796; f. 253, 8 September 1797; f. 358, 6 September 1799).

[3] Works 4/20, 8 April 1808. Craig's control over the movements of Labourers in Trust was more stringent, e.g. the cases of John Lawrence, Adam Lee and William Rose (Works 4/20, 14 October 1808, 22 July 1809; Works 4/21, 23 July, 1 October, 26 November 1813, 30 September 1814). The permission given to Edward Crocker in 1813, enabling him to spend the day in Oxford, was presumably a mere formality (Works 4/21, 12 October 1813). In 1815 Lewis Wyatt was given leave to visit North Wales, following the death of his mother. 'In consequence of the distance, no time was fixed for his return, but he was desired to be absent no longer than was absolutely necessary' (Works 4/21, 1 May 1815). In 1814 George Russell was given leave to recuperate in Sicily, 'the climate . . . most likely . . . to effect a permanent recovery' (Works 4/20, 27 May 1814).

[4] *Gent's. Mag.* 1811, pt. ii, p. 494; Farington p. 236, 10 October 1794 and p. 3737, 6 June 1807; Colvin, *Dictionary*, pp. 249–50.

[5] 'Inquiry into . . . the Office of Works', *Parl. Pap.*, 1812–13, v, p. 435.

[6] The Treasury allowed Groves to alter his house in Scotland Yard, following a recommendation by Wyatt, who 'conceives Mr. Groves' conduct deserving any little attention their Lordships may be inclined to shew him', since his house is not 'at all equal, either in point of space or convenience to those of other Clerks of the Works' (T. 29/77, f. 336, 19 December 1799). After a further recommendation, the Treasury authorised a salary increase of £50 to cover his additional responsibility for the Exchequer Buildings (T. 29/77, f. 287, 9 March 1801). In 1800 we find him 'Travelling from Kingston to Weymouth and back to examine the state of the Church Edifice by his Majesty's command'; 108 miles at 1s. 8d.: £9 plus three days' time: 9 gns.=£18 9s. 0d. (Works 5/89, Whitehall, Ladyday Quarter, 1800).

[7] Works 6/24, f. 248, 17 February 1809. In 1804 the compensation list of the Lord Chamberlain's Department includes £5 per annum for Bevan backdated to January 1797 (T. 38/221). Bevan was accused of selling 'a large quantity of stores . . . clandestinely purloined' (Works 4/18, ff. 368–9, 7 December 1799; Works 4/19, 7 February 1800). In 1800 William Bedborough was committed to prison for stealing lead at Windsor (Works 6/23, f. 126, 20 June 1800). But two years later Edward Astley, Labourer at the Exchequer, was not dismissed when he admitted taking 'some old wood . . . serviceable and unserviceable', even though Groves told Wyatt that 'this is not the first time' (Works 4/19, 26 November 1802; Works 6/23, f. 205, 26 November 1802). Apparently Wyatt promised 'to forbear to acquaint Mr. Addington' following Astley's pledge 'of not offending again' (Works 4/19, 10 December 1802).

and thirteen years later, at the age of seventy-one, Bevan was still petitioning for adequate relief.[1]

On at least two occasions Groves caused friction between Wyatt and Craig, and deadlock in the Office of Works, by failing to produce adequate accounts on time. The first dispute arose during the autumn of 1807, when illness forced Groves to delegate some of his official duties. Instead of choosing an official substitute, he chose his own brother, Frederick, who was quite unconnected with the Office of Works. Frederick transmitted estimates by Groves for repairs at Westminster Hall direct to the Treasury. 'Why this person', Craig complained, 'should arrogate to himself making Statements to [the Treasury], is unknown to [me]'. The Examiner solemnly emphasised 'the propriety of keeping up the common routine of Office'; if not, 'there will be an end of all subordination'.[2]

By April, 1808, the department had reached an administrative *impasse*. The backlog of paperwork had become enormous. It was only on 12 May 1809 that several books and bills were formally signed concerning Extra works at the Fleet and King's Bench Prisons dating back to 1794.[3] Payment of bills was four quarters in arrear. Tradesmen were clamouring for settlement. Money for Ladyday Quarter 1808 had been imprested to the Lord Chamberlain, but could not be released until Craig applied his signature to the accounts; and this he refused to do on the grounds that accounts submitted by Groves contained glaring irregularities. The accounts for Michaelmas Quarter 1808 had been in the Lord Chamberlain's hands since December, and those for Christmas Quarter since January. Those for Ladyday 1809 were also threatened with delay because Craig refused to countenance the excessive expenditure of Groves' sub-department. At this stage Craig presented a memorandum to the Treasury.[4] 'With profound respect', he 'most solemnly' urged their Lordships 'to restore that subordination, which seems almost annihilated in this Office, and without which I fear the utmost disgrace will attach to it . . . I hope [you] will excuse this language; it is no more than I conceive to be my duty to My Most Gracious Sovereign, whose Commissions, Civil and Military, I bear. [If you] could but imagine but one half of the suffereings of the Petitioners [your] humanity would grant them instant relief'. He added that non-payment had resulted in 'loss of credit, bankruptcies, and I have much reason to believe, of what I *dare not write* . . . I have long courted enquiry, and I dread the consequences if relief is not soon granted'.

Seven months later nothing had been done. Craig renewed the attack. In another letter to the Treasury he held up Groves as the chief culprit responsible for the breakdown of office discipline and the abandonment of quotas fixed in 1804.[5] In Wyatt's absence Craig had assumed the administrative duties of the Surveyor General. 'Particularly [he has received] official letters and papers, returned answers,

---

[1] 'I may date the commencement of my troubles to the alteration of the chimney-breast in General Goldsworthy's drawing room [at St. James's]. . . . From that time I could never give Mr. Groves satisfaction, and for years before I was dismissed, he said he would do it'.—Signed 'Thomas Bevan and Mary, 1 Wallis Place, Pimlico' (Works 19/19/1, f. 18, 16 February 1815).

[2] Works 4/20, 30 October 1807; Works 6/24, f. 135, 29 October 1807.

[3] Works 4/20, 12 May 1809. Other bills concerning extra works at the King's Bench and Old Marshalsea Prisons in 1802–4 were passed on to Wyatt with this laconic comment: 'it is imagined [that these] were signed many years ago' (*ibid*).

[4] Works 6/24, ff. 254–5, 11 April 1809.   [5] Works 6/24, f. 256, 19 November 1809.

G

referred the contents where necessary to the Clerks of the Works, examined them on their reports thereon, and their estimates, and if he thought proper, ordered by his signature the works to be done. Also signing minutes'. But Groves 'has frequently, nay generally, acted in contradiction to this authority, and has even gone so far as, rather than submit his estimates to me, has sent them to the Surveyor General, for his order, even at a distance . . . Some have been sent to Falmouth; at other times he has not passed any estimate for many weeks together'. Bills for Ladyday Quarter 1809 in Groves' sub-department grossly exceeded both his own estimates and the 1804 quota. Worst of all, alterations estimated at £200 for Groves' official house, had cost more than £1000 and had been executed without any higher authority. Such 'frequent dereliction', Craig concluded, and 'this sort of garbling the accounts', was 'highly blameable', 'contrary to all order and regularity and disgraceful to His Majesty's Service'.

Deadlock was broken by Wyatt. Calling an impromptu Board meeting on 3 September 1808, he passed the accounts for Ladyday Quarter 1808 in Craig's absence, and then, retrospectively, justified his action to the Treasury. That afternoon Craig wrote off post haste to Dartmouth: 'I have great reason to believe that the Surveyor General has this day adopted the most unprecedented measures to make up the accounts'.[1] But on the same day Wyatt also sent off a letter in which he ascribed the inadequacy of the accounts to Groves' temporary incapacity, and blamed the excess of expenditure over estimate on Craig's mishandling of the 1804 quotas. 'If I have done wrong I shall be very sorry, but I can assure you that I have been actuated only by compassion for Mr. Groves' situation and justice to the Artificers'. The Lords of the Treasury expressed themselves 'satisfied with Mr. Wyatt's explanation', and decided that Craig's signature, 'however usual', was not vital.[2]

Craig was persuaded to sign the accounts for Christmas Quarter 1809. But having uncovered 'gross malversation' by Groves as well as 'tortuous acts', he was 'determined not to be hurried into a signature in future'. By refusing to sign the accounts for Ladyday Quarter 1810 and for several succeeding quarters, he once again produced an administrative stalemate. In a letter to George Harrison, Assistant Secretary to the Treasury, Craig complained that 'Mr. Groves scarce ever appears at the Office, and when I have written to him, he has desired me to keep my letters to myself as they served but to fill his pigeon holes and drawers unnecessarily. Is it, Sir, too much to ask if His Majesty's Service can be carried on with proper effect whilst such matters are in existence?'[3] During his illness, Groves had on occasion refused to delegate duties to his Labourer in Trust Adam Lee.[4] Now he delegated too much and too often.[5] Once more, however, Wyatt passed the accounts in Craig's absence by a series

---

[1] L.C. 1/3, 3 September 1808.
[2] T. 29/101, f. 492, 18 July 1809; Works 4/20, 2 September, 3 September, 28 October, 4 November, 25 November 1808, 28 July 1809; L.C. 1/3, 29 October 1808; L.C. 1/40, 21 July 1809.
[3] Works 6/25, f. 67, 13 July 1810.
[4] In 1807 Lee's estimate for work at the Colonial Secretary's Office appeared over Groves' signature, under his private address, Dudley Grove, Paddington (Works 6/24, f. 124, 29 September and f. 125, 2 October 1807). In 1809 Groves forbade Lee to order any more works without his superior's written authority (Works 4/20, 30 June 1809).
[5] In 1810 Craig refused to accept estimates prepared by Lee 'seeing that Mr. Groves was in town at the time of the Examiner's coming to the Office' (Works 4/20, 14 September 1810).

of extraordinary Board meetings, held either at Whitehall or at Windsor.[1] But this time the Treasury directed that the whole business be investigated by the Commissioners of Audit.[2]

Scarcely had the investigation begun when Groves, stricken with paralysis while descending the Treasury steps, died soon afterwards at his house in Great Scotland Yard.[3] His accounts proved to be just as irregular as Craig had suspected. Edward Crocker Jnr., Clerk of the Works at the Tower, Newmarket, Greenwich and Winchester, was made personally responsible for their elucidation.[4] He discovered 'that the whole appeared . . . to have been done in a hurry, and consequently very incorrect, many things being put into the [wrong] department . . . and bills made out without proper attention to fluctuations in time and price'.[5] For example, bills amounting to £60 for work at Groves' official house and £40 for work at the Foreign Secretary's, had been transferred to the account relating to work at the Office of the Auditor of the Land Revenue. Work at the Auditor's Office had itself been executed without authority. Unpaid bills amounted to more than £5000.[6]

Charles Bacon (c. 1784–1818),[7] Groves' pupil, assistant and successor, inherited the confusion of his predecessor's sub-department as well as the hostility of the Examiner. He owed his official career to Groves, and its beginning was characteristically irregular: between 1805 and 1811 he held a newly created, semi-official post as Labourer in Trust at the Speaker's House and Exchequer, for which he was secretly paid an allowance by one of the tradesmen.[8] When called upon to say how much had been spent on the residences of George III's children, he could only reply that Groves had left him insufficient evidence.[9] No doubt he agreed with Craig that the accounts 'have been so ill made out for many years past as to defy almost all scrutiny whatever'.[10] Only in January 1813 were the claims of Groves' widow with regard to her husband's work as Wyatt's assistant at the Speaker's House and the Houses of Parliament during 1806–7, finally settled by the Commissioners of Military Inquiry.[11] But the errors made by Groves were still coming home to roost three years after the culprit's death. Day labour had been listed under lump sums instead of being itemised under the usual headings of name, work and time. One item for £172 10s. od. was found to relate to refreshment expenses claimed by six master tradesmen

[1] For details cf. Works 4/20, 3 August, 3 October, 10 November 1810, 19 February, 11 March, 13 March, 18 March, 10 May, 22 May, 8 November 1811. When Wyatt held a General Survey at Newmarket on 4 April 1811, Craig absented himself 'for reasons which he intended to state' to the Treasury (Works 4/20, 5 April 1811).

[2] T. 29/106, f. 370, 20 July 1810.   [3] *Gent's. Mag.* 1811 pt. ii, p. 287.

[4] Works 4/20, 3 July 1812.   [5] Works 6/27, f. 56, 5 March 1813.

[6] For work at Whitehall Chapel, Dorset House, Treasury Chambers, Auditor of Land Revenue's Office, India Board, Board of Control, Treasury Board Room and Library, and the House of Commons Private Bill Office, cf. 'Inquiry into . . . the Office of Works', *Parl. Pap.*, 1812–13, v, pp. 440–1.

[7] Colvin, *Dictionary*, p. 51. In 1809 he won half the first premium with his design for the Westminster Improvements (Works 8/10 B/24).

[8] T. 29/111, f. 801, 28 June 1811; 'Inquiry into . . . the Office of Works', *Parl. Pap.*, 1812–13, v, pp. 340, 433.

[9] 'He cannot collect sufficient information from the Labourer in Trust at St. James's or the Assistant employed by Groves, to enable him to make any satisfactory return, as . . . he did not consider it necessary to keep those Works distinct from the general repairs' (Works 4/20, 20 December 1811).

[10] Works 6/26, f. 154, 8 July 1814. But Bacon seems also to have inherited some of his master's bad habits. In 1813 he dared to send in estimates directly to the Lord Chamberlain. This provoked Craig into reminding him of 'the irregularity of anyone's presenting estimates . . . but through the medium of this Office' (Works 4/20, 24 September 1813). In 1815 bills for works ordered by Bacon without proper authority were still perplexing the Treasury (T. 29/133, f. 222, 13 January 1815; Works 6/26, f. 179, 9 January 1815).

[11] T. 29/118, ff. 919–20, 28 August 1812; T. 29/121, f. 123, 12 January 1813.

involved in the repair of St. James's Palace after the fire. Craig's memorandum to the Treasury on this occasion ended with a splendid flourish: 'the expences under the head of Beer given to Workmen has been most scandalously abused', for 'if I am rightly informed, this was for an open house by Mr. Groves' order'.[1]

However, a few months before his death Groves had taken revenge on Craig by reopening a controversy dormant for many years. This dispute concerned the distribution and tenure of official houses. Even among the hostilities of the Office of Works it must surely rank as a classic. The trouble began in March 1783, with Gilbert's proposals for the sale of all Crown property made redundant by the abolition of sinecures.[2] Houses scheduled for disposal included several neighbouring properties in Scotland Yard: the Office of Works, the Surveyor General's two houses, the Comptroller's house and the Resident Clerk's house. The Office of Works was to move into the Master Glazier's house and the Resident Clerk into the adjoining Master Mason's.[3] For more than a year the project hung fire while elaborate surveys and rough valuations were prepared.[4] Auction arrangements and reservations produced another year's delay.[5] Meanwhile the houses in question were either left empty or else illegally occupied rent-free, like the Glazier's house.[6]

The story of one particular house is sufficiently bizarre to merit a brief digression. In December 1790, Chambers discovered that an attorney named Priddle had been living rent free in a house scheduled for auction in 1783. In a memorandum to the Treasury he noticed that Priddle had 'made it over to William Richardson, who is to be heard of at Mr. Cutt's Eating House in the Old Bailey. He lived three or four years in the house, and has since that time been in Prison, so that it has remained unoccupied since by anything but Mrs. Priddle, who died about two years ago, but is not yet buried. Mr. Priddle is himself in the King's Bench. Mr. Richardson, having been released from prison, has offered to deliver up the key . . . but I declined taking it till I had apprized you, and received such directions as would enable me to proceed with proper caution, in a business I do not understand, and with People of such uncommon descriptions'.[7] After consulting a solicitor, the Treasury advised Chambers to accept the keys: 'if on Entrance . . . the corpse of Mrs. Priddle should

[1] Works 6/26, f. 154, 8 July 1814.

[2] The Treasury ordered 'the sale of several useless Houses, the Repairs of which are now a considerable annual Burden, and which are inhabited either by Persons who held no Office or Persons whose Offices neither entitle them to, nor require any Official Residence, which is an Abuse that ought not to continue' (T. 29/53, f. 236, 14 March 1783).

[3] A full list of Gilbert's proposals is contained in Works 6/20, ff. 103–8, 17 March 1783. For the topography of Scotland Yard see p. 541 below.

[4] Chambers estimated the cost of hiring additional draughtsmen at £300 (Works 1/5, f. 57, 29 April, 2 May, 3 May, 9 May 1783; Works 4/16, 12 March, 21 March, 28 March 1783, 29 March 1784). Plans and freehold valuations were despatched to the Treasury in 'the great portfolio deposited in the Closet' (Works 6/20, f. 109, 21 March, f. 233, 24 March 1783, f. 245, 31 March 1784; T. 29/53, f. 258, 18 March and f. 272, 22 March 1783; T. 29/55, f. 60, 12 February 1784). Chambers was forced to surrender his walled fruit garden at Hampton Court, originally part of the royal garden (Works 1/5, f. 57, 27 April, 2 May 1783).

[5] Works 4/16, 4 March, 27 May 1785; T. 29/56, f. 299, 12 March 1785; Works 6/20, ff. 15–16, 11 February, 1 March, 4 March 1785, f. 43, 27 May 1785 and f. 85, 21 July 1786.

[6] Crest 2/918, 23 February 1787. Chambers complained to Richard Burke that he could hardly be held responsible for the fact that 'several of the Buildings have been tenanted ever since the suppression of the Board of Works by persons who have no right to inhabit them . . . that others are inhabited by persons who actually did pay rent till the suppression of the Board but have not . . . paid any since, and that the remainder . . . are going to ruin' (Works 6/20, f. 214, 5 December 1783, and f. 224, 6 February 1784). No repairs were to be executed without specific Treasury authority (Works 6/21, f. 172, 7 August 1790).

[7] Works 6/22, f. 4, 10 December 1790.

be found therein, the Parish Officers should be immediately sent for, to remove it for interment as they would be bound to do in the case of a dead body of a pauper accidentally found in the street . . . and if furniture of any sort should be found . . . a regular Distress [should] be made upon the same for payment of the arrears of rent'.[1] Craig, Soane, Woolfe and Richardson were therefore despatched to the house. 'On their arrival they found a padlock on the door, which Mr. Richardson tore off, and with his key opened the door. They went upstairs. Mr. Richardson forced open several room doors . . . in one . . . was a leaden coffin, which by the inscription . . . was supposed to contain . . . Mrs. Priddle . . . The Churchwardens not choosing to take charge of the coffin, on supposition of the uncertainty of its contents, and if a body, whether murdered or dying a natural death, the house was locked up . . . and sealed with the Office seal'.[2] In April 1791, while the Attorney General deliberated, Richardson was given permission to remove a box of tools. When he arrived, however, he found the place infested by squatters. 'And the house', Chambers informed the Treasury, 'is now actually occupied by several persons unknown who refuse to give their names and set all enquiries at Defiance'.[3] Not for another year did the Office of Works solve the problem of Mrs. Priddle and her property. Unfortunately the records provide no indication as to what that solution was.

It was during this period of private chicanery and official confusion that the problem of Craig's accommodation arose. The Act of 1787[4] authorising the sale of redundant houses was first ignored and then repealed by the Acts of 1792[5] and 1794.[6] Another redevelopment scheme was proposed in 1801, but nothing more was done until 1815.[7] The Office of Works had never moved into the Glazier's house, nor the Resident Clerk into the Mason's. Instead the Office of Works moved into Mr. Bownas' house, leaving the old Office of Works and the adjoining Surveyor General's house to be rebuilt for the Office of Woods and Forests. As Resident Clerk, Richard Ripley retained his old house, and supplemented his income by letting the Mason's house. In this reshuffle Kenton Couse was allowed to retain the house which he had held as Clerk of the Works and Secretary despite his promotion to the rank of Examiner. The adjoining house, which had belonged to the Comptroller, was never sold but given to the new Inspector, John Jones. And the Clerk of the Works, John Woolfe, was given the Examiner's house. When Woolfe succeeded Couse as Examiner in 1790 he remained in the same house, and the allocation thus returned to normal. Unfortunately, by this time Craig had become Resident Clerk in 1786 and installed himself in the Inspector's house, while letting the Resident Clerk's house to John Holroyd. When he became the Examiner in 1793, J. W. Hiort took over the perquisites of the Resident Clerk. But Craig retained the Inspector's house, paying no

---

[1] Works 6/22, f. 4, 30 December 1790.
[2] Works 6/22, f. 5, 7 January 1791; T. 29/62, f. 388, 18 December 1790 and f. 443, 11 February 1791.
[3] Works 6/22, f. 11, 11 April and f. 12, 27 May 1791; T. 29/63, f. 60, 5 April 1991.
[4] 27 G. III c. 22.　　　[5] 32 G. III c. 24.
[6] 34 G. III c. 75. In 1796 the Office of Woods and Forests received little co-operation from the Office of Works in their attempt to catalogue official houses (Works 4/18, f. 188, 8 July and f. 193, 12 August 1796).
[7] T. 29/133, f. 854, 24 February 1815. In that year compensation was paid to Hiort, Crocker and Temphany, the messenger, for loss of property (Works 6/26, f. 239, 6 June and f. 252, 5 July 1815; T. 29/135, f. 818, 20 June 1818; Works 4/21, 6 June 1815). Two years before, Craig had wisely warned Temphany '*viva voce*, that it appears improper to trouble the Lords of the Treasury with the subject at the present time' (Works 4/21, 5 November 1813).

rent after Jones's death in 1807, while letting the Examiner's house to Hiort. At the same time he laid claim to the house once occupied by Couse, then by Soane and now by Groves. In other words, as Examiner, Craig was living rent free in the Inspector's house, renting out the Examiner's house plus its attendant stables, and laying claim to rent from the Clerk of the Works' house on the grounds that it had once been occupied by an Examiner, Couse.[1]

Such was the situation when, in 1811, Groves exposed Craig's profitable secret. He first of all refused to pay rent to Craig and then suggested to the Treasury that the Commissioners for the Improvement of Westminster might well make use of both the Inspector's house and the Examiner's house as accommodation for a new Stationery Office.[2] Craig was asked 'to state . . . by what tenure' he held his various premises, and so the whole tangle was unravelled. His claim to the Inspector's house was easily dismissed. His claim to the Clerk of the Works' house was described by Bacon as 'one of the most absurd . . . ever offered to the consideration of a public body'.[3] Nevertheless Bacon was for long unable to take over his predecessor's house, since Craig had managed to obtain the key from Mrs. Groves. Instead he was forced to become a commuting Clerk, living out at Ealing and directing his sub-department from 'one small room' at the Exchequer and 'two little rooms' in Cotton Garden.[4] Accounts were prepared showing Craig's profits over a period of thirty years.[5] These revealed that from coach houses and stables he had been drawing a personal profit of £77 11s. od. per annum. In addition, he had accumulated £1737 15s. od. in his capacity as receiver of rents due to the Crown. This latter sum he agreed to place at the Treasury's disposal. But no mention was made of the interest which must have accrued in Craig's bank account over such a lengthy period.[6]

Craig's defence was a masterpiece of prevarication. 'The period at which he commenced to receive these Rents, he states to be so distant (probably near thirty years) that he cannot tell under what authority he has received them, but he presumes it was by order of the Treasury at the time he was appointed Resident Clerk. No account, however, of Rents received during this long period had been rendered to the Treasury; or to any other Authority . . . and . . . only once [in October 1806] . . . did the Treasury recognise that any Rents of this description were due to the Crown, by ordering that money received should be paid into the Exchequer. But what were the circumstances of this Order, or why it was not obeyed, were not recollected by Mr. Craig'.[7]

Craig's empire lasted little longer than Wyatt's. Wyatt ended his Surveyor

---

[1] Craig covered his tracks fairly well, but this seems to be the sense of evidence given by Edward Crocker and Charles Bacon ('Inquiry into . . . the Office of Works', *Parl. Pap.*, 1812–13, v, pp. 336–8, 434, 439–40). Crocker, who entered the Office of Works in 1774, was regarded as being 'very accurately informed of the state of the Department long previously to the change in the constitution of it'.

[2] T. 29/110, f. 456, 5 April and f. 262, 24 September 1811; T. 29/111, f. 552, 13 June 1811; Works 4/20, 21 June, 5 July 1811.   [3] Works 6/27, f. 23, 29 June 1812.

[4] Works 4/20, 26 June 1812; 'Inquiry into . . . the Office of Works', *Parl. Pap.*, 1812–13, v, pp. 340, 434.

[5] *Ibid.* p. 489; T. 29/118, f. 314, 21 July 1812.

[6] These sums should have been paid into the Exchequer at regular intervals by the Resident Clerk (T. 29/58, f. 246, 24 February 1787 and f. 277, 22 March 1787).

[7] 'Inquiry into . . . the Office of Works', *Parl. Pap.*, 1812–13, v, pp. 364–5. It is hardly surprising that in 1809 John Wilson Croker refused to pay Craig any more rent for the coach house and stable which he had occupied for several years. In 1812 he is listed as retaining occupation on sufferance (*ibid.* p. 489; T. 29/118, f. 314, 21 July 1812).

Generalship as he began it, with a brief burst of activity. In 1798 he had produced a directive enforcing the prompt presentation of quarterly accounts.[1] In 1800, following the dismissal of Thomas Bevan for 'embezzling of the King's Stores', he had ordered regular returns to be prepared of all stocks of building materials.[2] Neither command had the slightest permanent effect. Now, in 1811–3, with the Commissioners of Military Inquiry breathing over his shoulder, he made a final attempt to recover his reputation as an administrator. Board meetings were properly conducted. Greater care was to be taken of accounts, books and drawings.[3] Works were to be limited to those endorsed by proper authority and sanctioned by the quotas of 1804. In February 1813, Wyatt reminded Yenn and Bacon that 'if works should . . . be directed without proper authority, the Lords of the Treasury would hold the party giving such orders personally liable for the amount of such excess'. When Bacon pleaded illness, Wyatt replied that he would then 'do well to charge the Labourers in Trust with dereliction of their duties'; for the accounts must be passed, as 'it would be a great breach of humanity to attempt to compel the tradesmen to lose such large sums, occasioned by the want of regularity'.[4] He even went to the lengths of visiting Bacon in Cotton Garden in order to settle outstanding accounts.[5] In a last bid to clear up the backlog of paper work, Yenn was given a deadline for the submission of accounts, after which none would be permitted 'under any head or pretext whatever'.[6] As for Crocker, he was given a stern rebuke by the Surveyor General in May 1813. 'I really was very much surprized', wrote Wyatt, 'on coming to the Office today, with an intention to complete the passing of the Ladyday Quarter's accounts, to find that yours is not yet delivered here; there is no excuse for this neglect and I therefore now assure you that unless they are sent here [within] time enough to have them ready for passing on Friday next, they shall be totally left out, which will oblige me to state the cause for so doing'.[7]

But of course it was all too late. Four months later the Surveyor General and Comptroller was dead. And even as he penned those last, uncharacteristic commands, the Commissioners of Military Inquiry were putting the finishing touches to a report which would publicly expose all the follies and scandals of the Office of Works during the period of Wyatt's misrule.

[1] Clerks of the Works were to send in bills and books to the Examiner on the Tuesday preceding whichever Friday Board meeting constituted the quarterly passing day. Failing this, bills would be postponed to the following quarter (Works 4/18, f. 298, 6 July 1798). Quarterly accounts were to run to the Saturday succeeding each new quarter day (Works 4/18, f. 319, 7 December 1798). On the Friday after each quarter day Clerks of the Works were supposed to produce estimates for the ensuing quarter (Works 4/19, 10 August 1804).

[2] Clerks of the Works were formally to read out the relevant section of Gilbert's Instructions to their assembled Labourers in Trust and employees. Quarterly Inventories were to be prepared by Labourers in Trust and presented to the Board with each quarterly account (Works 4/19, 7 March 1800; Works 6/184/1, f. 53). In 1813 it was reported that this practice had not been maintained ('Inquiry into . . . the Office of Works', *Parl. Pap.*, 1812–13, v, pp. 356–7).

[3] Following the disappearance of a carpenter's contract, it was 'ordered that in future no Person be allowed to take Contracts out of this Office without first having obtained the Surveyor General's permission' (Works 4/20, 22 May 1811). Chambers had always taken great care of official drawings. When plans of Windsor Castle were required (1790) or when the Office of Woods and Forests were preparing a survey of Crown property in the metropolis (1793), he allowed copies but not originals to be removed from the office (Works 1/5, f. 97, 31 December 1790; Works 6/22, f. 117, 29 July 1793; Works 4/18, f. 52, 17 January 1794). Plans which had been in Groves' possession at his death were obtained only with difficulty from his widow, three years afterwards (Works 4/20, 7 August 1812; Works 4/21, 4 February 1814).

[4] Works 6/27, ff. 51–2, 16 February 1813.

[5] Works 6/27, f. 57, 12 March 1813 and f. 59, 19 March 1813.

[6] Works 6/27, f. 68, 1 May 1813. Much the same directive was sent to all the other Clerks of the Works (Works 4/20, 1 May 1813).   [7] Works 6/27, f. 73, 28 May 1813.

Chapter IV

INVESTIGATION AND REFORM, 1813–15

WYATT held office for seventeen years. Of these the first seven were hardly trouble free, but the final decade was a period of uninterrupted investigation and recrimination. In all, there were no less than four consecutive investigations: by the Treasury, by the Commissioners for Auditing Public Accounts, by the Treasury's nominees George Dance and George Saunders, and by the Commissioners of Military Inquiry. Severally and collectively, they represented a formidable indictment of the Office of Works under the stewardship of James Wyatt and a cogent argument for the reform of 1815. What began as an inquiry into the Surveyor General's personal accounts ended as a blueprint for departmental reform.

Serious inquiries started as early as 1806.[1] As the penultimate and final checks upon Office of Works expenditure it was natural that the Treasury and the Audit Office should initiate this process of investigation. Treasury inquiries normally proceeded by delegation. In this way Dance and Saunders followed Sir Robert Taylor as official inquiry agents. Investigations by the Commissioners of Audit were almost continuous after 1806, complementing and correlating those of Dance and Saunders. No pains were spared. For example, during June 1806 Craig was called to the Audit Office in Somerset House on several occasions. There he was put on oath and 'interrogated as to the mode and nature of conducting the business of this office, to all [of] which he [gave] such answers as came within the pale of his knowledge and recollection'. Extraordinary Board meetings were also held at the Office of Works, at one of which 'Mr. Sergeant Praed and John Wishaw Esq., two of the Commissioners . . . during an hour and a half examined the Minute book for the last eighteen months, one of the Clerk's weekly books, the Memorial book and the Rough books of the accounts . . . all in the presence of the Examiner, assisted by the Office Clerks'.[2] In December 1809 Craig and Russell were examined once more 'as to where certain drawings, books and papers might be, to which they could not give any answer other than they were not to be found in the Office, but by whom they might have been taken they could not tell'.[3] Such 'accidents' made investigation difficult. In February 1808 the Treasury told the Commissioners of Audit that since 'Mr.

---

[1] Works 4/19, 6 May 1806. In 1812 the Treasury sent the Commissioners of Military Inquiry the text of replies made by Wyatt and Craig to questions put to them on 15 May 1806 by the then Treasury Secretary, Vansittart (T. 29/117 f. 498, 5 June 1812).

[2] Works 4/20, 1 July, 9 July, 29 July 1808, 15 December 1809.

[3] Works 4/20, 22 December 1809.

Wyatt's accounts had been delivered to [Dance] and afterwards taken back by Mr. Wyatt's direction', they were to call upon Mr. Wyatt, and if necessary, enforce the delivery into their office of his accounts in order that they may undergo . . . examination'.[1]

The difficulties involved in elucidating Wyatt's accounts were enormous. Besides investigating his ineptitude at the Office of Works, the Audit Commissioners had to examine his work at the Office of Woods and Forests,[2] as well as his responsibility for several separate projects covered by specific parliamentary grants. It was these peripheral works which produced the greatest confusion. They were government projects in so far as Treasury grants and Office of Works tradesmen were involved. But they were private commissions in so far as Wyatt received 5% commission on expenditure and employed, or failed to employ, his own methods of accounting. The Treasury thought it necessary to inform the Audit Commissioners that these works were not paid for out of the Civil List nor were they 'executed under the superintendance of any Existing Department of Government'.[3] They were direct grant projects. Wyatt's 5% commission on such works was made up of $2\frac{1}{2}$% from the Treasury and $2\frac{1}{2}$% deducted from tradesmen's bills. Tradesmen's bills for direct grant works were not subject to the usual 3% discount in the Lord Chamberlain's Office. Wyatt claimed that his $2\frac{1}{2}$% on tradesmen's bills had been authorised by Vansittart during Addington's administration. He also claimed that his authority for the $2\frac{1}{2}$% from the Treasury lay in the verbal agreement of George Rose, acting on Pitt's instructions. It was hardly surprising that the Audit Commissioners were urged to find some way of regularising this process, or that the Commissioners of Military Inquiry condemned the whole arrangement as 'extremely loose and inaccurate'.[4] Grant succeeded grant and so the financial backlog multiplied. By 1808 the Audit Commissioners were able to inform the Treasury that between 29 June 1798 and 5 July 1807 Wyatt had received the following sums which were still unaccounted for:

Lazaretto at Chetney Hill	£95,000	0s.	0d.
Somerset House	23,771	7s.	$8\frac{1}{2}$d.
Houses of Lords and Commons and Speaker's House	57,199	2s.	$1\frac{1}{4}$d.
King's Bench, Fleet and Marshalsea	19,304	10s.	$8\frac{1}{2}$d.
Duchy of Cornwall Office	698	12s.	5d.
	£195,973	12s.	$11\frac{1}{4}$d.[5]

By 5 July 1809, the total had swollen to £217,146 5s. $8\frac{1}{2}$d.[6] Complaints from tradesmen were becoming 'numerous and urgent'. But 'repeated and peremptory commands' to Wyatt for 'some explanation on these points' proved fruitless. Thereupon the Treasury decided on 'an immediate and full investigation . . . into the present Establishment as well as the Arrangement and Conduct of the whole Business

---

[1] T. 29/93, f. 277, 4 February 1808. Dance had begun inquiries a year previously (T. 29/91, f. 387, 13 August 1807).
[2] For Wyatt's defence of his incompetence cf. Crest 8/6, f. 214, 5 January 1811.
[3] T. 29/118, f. 86, 7 July 1812.
[4] T. 29/95, f. 74, 31 May 1808; 'Inquiry into . . . the Office of Works', *Parl. Pap.*, 1812–13, v, pp. 372–4.
[5] T. 29/95, f. 74, 31 May 1808.
[6] 'Inquiry into . . . the Office of Works', *Parl. Pap.*, 1812–13, v, p. 375.

in the . . . Office of Works, and also into the . . . Execution of Public Works the Expences of which are specially rated by Parliament, and which may not come under the immediate Controul and direction of the Office of Works'. The Audit Commissioners were urged 'to proceed therein with all convenient dispatch', and to keep in mind four objectives: 'prompt and efficient execution'; 'constant and efficient controul'; 'the greatest practical economy'; and 'early settlement of accounts'.[1]

With these objects in view, Dance was made responsible for the investigation of Somerset House, and Saunders for the remainder of Wyatt's commissions.[2] Both were given considerable discretionary powers of search and interrogation. Dance (1741–1825) had supervised Office of Works accounts before, in connection with work after the Gordon Riots and at Somerset House.[3] As Professor of Architecture at the Royal Academy and a famous City architect of forty years' standing, he was in many ways the doyen of the architectural profession.[4] Saunders (*c.* 1762–1839) was a less obvious choice. A metropolitan architect with some pretensions to scholarship and engineering skill, he was principally known as Surveyor to the County of Middlesex, the Royal Society and the Trustees of the British Museum. In the last capacity he had recently completed the short-lived Townley Gallery.[5] As far as the accountancy was concerned, Saunders did most of the work. Wyatt's accounts for Chetney Hill, Windsor Castle, the King's Bench, Fleet and Marshalsea Prisons, the Office of the Secretary of State for War in Parliament Street and the Royal Military College at Sandhurst, Groves' accounts for Whitehall and Westminster, Smirke's accounts for the extension of the Mint, and the accounts of Thomas Rice as Clerk of the Works at Hampton Court and Surveyor of the Guards Buildings—Saunders examined them all between 1809 and 1815, and received £1000 per annum for his trouble.[6]

Between November 1809 and June 1812 he produced no less than thirty-two reports, to the Audit Office, to the Treasury, to the War Office and to the Commons Committee on Public Expenditure.[7] He found that, except in cases of internal dispute, as for example the dispute between Groves and Craig in 1808 and 1810, Office of Works bills payable at the Lord Chamberlain's Office seldom lingered more than a year unpaid. In fact tradesmen employed by the government normally allowed for the cost of one year's credit in fixing their prices.[8] It was the projects covered by direct parliamentary grant which accumulated the greatest deficits, and it was with

---

[1] T. 29/95, f. 74, 31 May 1808.
[2] T. 29/100, f. 67, 28 March 1809 and f. 269, 11 April 1809; Works 4/20, 30 March 1809. Saunders was appointed on 20 December 1808 and received his instructions on 29 March 1809 ('Inquiry into . . . the Office of Works', *Parl. Pap.*, 1812–13, v, p. 506).
[3] See p. 627 below and vol. v of this *History*.
[4] For his architectural career cf. Colvin, *Dictionary*, pp. 165–8. As Clerk of the City Works his income averaged £2000 (Farington, p. 1260, 24 June 1798).
[5] See below p. 404. For his career cf. Colvin, *Dictionary*, p. 527.
[6] T. 29/104, ff. 409–10, 8 May 1810; T. 29/107, f. 122, 28 August and f. 101, 4 September 1810; T. 29/111, f. 455, 7 June 1811; T. 29/112, f. 360, 30 July 1811; T. 29/118, f. 733, 11 August, f. 920, 28 August, f. 663, 7 August 1812; T. 29/120, ff. 284–5, 20 November 1812; T. 29/122, f. 781, 27 April 1813; T. 29/122, ff. 148–9, 9 March and f. 442, 2 April 1813; T. 29/123, f. 257, 21 May 1813; T. 29/131, f. 554, 4 October and f. 816, 28 October 1814; T. 29/134, f. 83, 7 March and f. 537, 28 March 1815. While examining Smirke's accounts at the Mint, Saunders was given two assistants each paid £350 per annum by the Treasury. See also '7th Report . . . on Public Expenditure', *Parl. Pap.*, 1810, ii, p. 524.
[7] They are listed in 'Inquiry into . . . the Office of Works', *Parl. Pap.*, 1812–13, v, pp. 512–3; '11th Report . . . on Public Expenditure', *Parl. Pap.*, 1810–11, iii, pp. 1101–3.   [8] *Ibid.* 1812–3, v, p. 508.

these that Saunders was primarily concerned. One of the contractors who had never been paid was the Surveyor General's own brother, Samuel Wyatt. In April 1808, his widow Ann Wyatt claimed that £30,000 remained due to her husband as a result of carpentry contracts at the Lazaretto, Somerset House, the Speaker's House and the Houses of Parliament.[1] Encouraged by Samuel Wyatt's executor, a Mr. Cobb, Saunders set about unravelling these bills. As examiner in chief he took over Wyatt's responsibility for the payment of tradesmen in such cases, thus depriving the Surveyor General of his percentage. In this way John Holroyd, master plumber, received payment from a variety of sources: from the Lord Chamberlain for regular Civil List works; from Wyatt for such Extra works as he found time to finish; from Saunders and Browne for work at the Marshalsea and Fleet; and from Wyatt, Groves and Bacon for work at the Houses of Parliament.[2] With Saunders acting as his accountant and paymaster, Wyatt's presence became redundant. When in 1812 Saunders was charged with distributing the parliamentary grant for work on the royal vault at Windsor, the Treasury therefore ordered that Wyatt's commission be 'witheld for the present'.[3]

But worse penalties were in store for Wyatt. As the investigations progressed it became very obvious that the backlog of unsettled accounts did more than leave tradesmen unsatisfied. Interest on unliquidated balances, consciously or unconsciously accumulated, supplied the Surveyor General with an increment which was notoriously unearned.[4] In April 1813 the Secretary to the Royal Military College asked the Treasury whether payment should be made to Wyatt of architect's fees totalling £1260. By way of reply the Treasury directed Saunders to publish 'the present state of Wyatt's account with the public, and whether it is probable that upon the final settlement thereof there will be any balance remaining due from him to the public'.[5] Saunders' conclusion was simply stated: 'It appears there will be a balance due from Mr. Wyatt to the public'. Payment of Wyatt's fees was therefore withheld.[6] Farington noted with satisfaction that Saunders had been made responsible for the completion of the work since the 'government had taken the superintendance of the building from [Wyatt] most probably owing to his own neglect'.[7] Doubt was thrown upon the reliability of all Wyatt's accounts when it was discovered that some tradesmen's receipts bore dates considerably later than the date of payment. One bill certified by Wyatt proved to contain an error of £2000 in the tradesman's favour. Not surprisingly, the Commissioners of Military Inquiry later came to the conclusion that 'it is impossible to consider Mr. Wyatt as having performed this part of his duty'. Since Saunders had been doing a job which should have been done by Wyatt, they recommended that his four years' salary as investigator in chief should be charged to the Surveyor General's account.[8]

However, Wyatt's crowning humiliation came at the hands of a widow living in Windsor, Mrs. Ann Cherington. On 1 May 1800 the Treasury had issued £225 to

---

[1] T. 29/94, f. 268, 20 April 1808; T. 29/95, f. 261, 29 June 1808; T. 29/100, f. 70, 28 March 1808.
[2] 'Inquiry into . . . the Office of Works', *Parl. Pap.*, 1812–13, v, p. 479.
[3] T. 29/120, ff. 284–5, 20 November 1812.
[4] 'Inquiry into . . . the Office of Works', *Parl. Pap.*, 1812–13, v, pp. 372–4, 398.
[5] T. 29/122, f. 781, 27 April 1813.   [6] T. 29/123, f. 257, 21 May 1813.
[7] Farington, p. 5715, 3 February 1811 and p. 6021, 4 February 1812.
[8] 'Inquiry into . . . the Office of Works', *Parl. Pap.*, 1812–13, v, pp. 375–6.

Wyatt for the purpose of buying two houses in Thames Street, Windsor. The property changed hands but not the money. Twelve years later the sum in question had still not been paid over. The Treasury expressed 'surprize and displeasure that . . . [Wyatt] should have suffered this business to remain so long unsettled to the serious injury of the parties interested and the great discredit of His Majesty's government'.[1] Three months later Wyatt had still made no move, but Mrs. Cherington's solicitors had succeeded in forcing immediate payment out of the Civil List of the £225, plus 5% interest. Thereupon the Treasury Lords once more assured the Surveyor General of their 'very serious displeasure at his Conduct throughout the whole of this transaction'. As he had apparently 'not thought fit to take any notice' of repeated letters, the Lord Chamberlain was directed 'to withold the payment of any salary to Mr. Wyatt as Surveyor General . . . until the said sum with interest shall be repaid'.[2]

After Wyatt's death his son and executor Benjamin Dean Wyatt pleaded that at least he might be excused repayment of interest on the £225.[3] This request was refused by the Treasury, but the offer of a blanket indemnity was accepted. In 1809 Wyatt had admitted that he owed the government £1367 8s. 4½d. In 1812, with several accounts still unexamined, he admitted responsibility for another £997 1s. 10¼d.[4] £3000 in Exchequer bills was therefore put down in 1814 as security for the balance presumed due to the public pending the sale of Wyatt's estate.[5] At last, in October 1814, it was announced that Saunders was bringing this 'special business' to a close.[6] Wyatt's debt to the public had been posthumously paid.

In 1812 Saunders had produced an interim report on the state of the Office of Works which found its way via the Audit Commissioners and the Treasury to the Commissioners of Military Inquiry.[7] It was the latter body which produced the definitive report. The Commission of Inquiry into the Conduct of Business in the Office of Works grew out of the Commission appointed in 1805 to inquire into public expenditure in military departments.[8] The original Commissioners of Military Inquiry were Major General H. Oakes,[9] Lieutenant General J. Drinkwater,[10] Samuel C. Cox, Master in Chancery, Henry Peters and Charles Bosanquet,[11] merchants, Colonel B. C. Stephenson and Giles Templeman. The Commission was prolonged in 1808,[12] and in 1811 its terms of reference were extended to include the Office of

---

[1] T. 29/120, ff. 976–7, 29 December 1812.   [2] T. 29/122, ff. 148–9, 9 March 1813.
[3] T. 29/126, f. 478, 30 November 1813. B. D. Wyatt shared his father's reputation for improvidence (Farington, p. 3472, 16 October 1806).
[4] 'Inquiry into . . . the Office of Works', *Parl. Pap.*, 1812–13, v, pp. 375, 511.
[5] T. 29/128, f. 743, 19 April 1814.   [6] T. 29/131, f. 554, 4 October 1814.
[7] T. 29/115, f. 422, 18 February 1812. The Architectural Publication Society's *Dictionary* vii (1887), p. 25 gives the date of the report as 15 October 1812.
[8] 45 G. III c. 47; *Parl. Deb.* iv (1805), pp. 492–7; v (1805), pp. 14–22, 26–7. In 1806, for purposes of comparison, they had asked the Office of Works for information about 'the mode adopted in the erection of public buildings, particularly respecting plans furnished to the artificers, the agreements as to the prices and mode of payment, the superintendance during the progress of the work, the measuring and mode of ascertaining the quantity of materials used and work done, and the final settlement of the artificers' account' (Works 4/19, 16 January 1806).
[9] Later Sir Hildebrand Oakes (1754–1822), soldier and administrator. He was the Commissioners' first chairman (*Gent's. Mag.*, 1822, pt. ii, p. 373).
[10] Later Sir John Drinkwater Bethune, F.S.A. (1762–1844), military and naval historian. He succeeded Oakes as Chairman of the Commissioners, and held the post until 1811. Between 1811 and 1835 he held office as Comptroller of Army Accounts (*Gent's. Mag.*, 1844, pt i, pp. 220, 431–3).
[11] Charles Bosanquet (1769–1850), governor of the South Sea Company and economic theorist (*Gent's. Mag.*, 1850, pt. ii, p. 325).   [12] *Parl. Deb.* xi (1808), p. 802.

Works.[1] In the Spring of 1812 the Commission was granted an extra year for the preparation of a comprehensive report.[2] For this purpose five non-military Military Commissioners were appointed: Templeman, Peters, Bosanquet, Stephenson and L. Bradshaw. They together received £7500 for their pains.[3]

The Treasury, the Audit Commissioners, Dance and Saunders, had all been concerned with cancelling debts, exposing malpractices and remedying specific evils. The Commissioners of Military Inquiry, however, were given a much wider brief. They were directed to 'inquire . . . into the Public Expenditure and Conduct of Business in the Office of Works, and also into the Mode and System pursued in the Conduct and Execution of the Public Works, the Expences of which are specially voted by Parliament, and are not included in the Estimates of any Public Department and which may not come under the Immediate Controul and Direction of the Office of Works; and whether any and what Abuses or Irregularities exist . . . and [to] report on the most effectual Means of remedying the same'.[4] In short, they were presented with a mandate to reform the department.

The Commissioners operated from their headquarters at 17 Buckingham Street, Adelphi. But much of their time was spent in examining papers elsewhere, as on the occasion in May 1812, when several of the Commissioners visited the Office of Works and examined 'divers books', accounts and lists of official houses.[5] Their interrogation of Office of Works personnel lasted several weeks. In July Craig was examined on oath four hours a day for four days on end.[6] Later that month he spent two more days answering questions from 12 to 4.15 p.m.[7] Saunders had been examined for four days and Hiort for three during the previous July.[8] Yenn went before the Commissioners on four successive days in August 1812.[9] Wyatt was interrogated for four days during June, and for another four during November.[10] Similar examinations were endured by most officials of the department.

Not surprisingly, the Commissioners' report failed to appear in time to influence the Report of the Select Committee on the Civil List, 1812. Instead the Committee members were privately supplied with Office of Works accounts by J. W. Hiort. For this delay, Templeman apologised in June 1812 to Davies Giddy, Secretary to the Select Committee:

> we have procured many books from the Office of Works, as well as many papers from that Office and from the Treasury, which we are at present employed in perusing and extracting, with a view to ascertaining in what manner the Business of the Office of Works has been conducted in detail, previously to and subsequently to the Civil List Act [1782]; we have also been employed for some days past in examining Mr. Wyatt, relative to his conduct in superintending such other Works under his arrangement, the expences of which are not included in the Civil List Expenditure, but specially voted by Parliament . . . I trust you will give us credit for pursuing the object of our present inquiries with the most anxious diligence.[11]

[1] 51 G. III c. 19.   [2] 52 G. III c. 41; T. 29/115, f. 509, 25 February 1812.
[3] T. 29/126, f. 767, 17 December 1813.   [4] 51 G. III c. 19.
[5] Works 4/20, 29 May 1812.   [6] Works 4/20, 17 July 1812.   [7] Works 4/20, 24 July 1812.
[8] 'Inquiry into . . . the Office of Works', *Parl. Pap.*, 1812–13, v, pp. 335–6, 506–9.
[9] *Ibid.* pp. 447–53.   [10] *Ibid.* pp. 395–401, 417–25.
[11] 'Report from the Select Committee upon the Civil List', *Parl. Pap.*, 1812, ii, p. 457, Appendix H. iii. [reprinted, *Parl. Pap.*, 1830, ix, p. 199].

The Select Committee were more than satisfied with this explanation, and took care to assure the House of Commons that the Commissioners of Military Inquiry were showing 'a degree of zeal and ability which has frequently attracted the notice of this House'.[1]

The results of the Commissioners' investigations were well worth waiting for. They found that on 5 January 1812, the Office of Works debt stood at £67,004 16s. 7¾d.[2] Of this sum more than half could be easily accounted for: the expenditure on Extra works for 1811 was £35,001 5s.1¾d., mostly on the Duke of Kent's apartments at Kensington. But the remainder, as much as £32,003 11s. 6d., comprised Extra works executed without regular authority and excess expenditure on Ordinary works. The list of unauthorised works of recent execution nicely illustrates the different pressures to which the Office of Works was subject.

Carlton House		£15,897	0s.	0d.	Royal Command[3]
St. James's		484	2s.	1¼d.	Emergency repairs following fire[4]
Whitehall	Office of Auditor of Land Revenue:	2315	6s.	11d.	Departmental order[5]
	Treasury Office:	1932	17s.	7d.	Departmental order[6]
	India Board Office:	2993	4s.	7¼d.	Departmental order[7]
Westminster	House of Commons Private Bill Office:	245	10s.	10½d.	Parliamentary order[8]

Until such extraordinary demands were regularised by the reforms of 1815 and 1830, the department was unlikely to balance its budget. Most difficult of all to control was the impromptu royal command. As T. B. Mash recalled in 1815, 'the orders of the King were always considered paramount to every other authority, and His Majesty's commands to any extent were instantly obeyed without any communication being made to the Treasury till the amount of the Bills in the Quarterly accounts were transmitted for the issue of the Money in discharge thereof'.[9] The result was soaring expenditure at Windsor, Carlton House and Kensington.

Excess expenditure on Ordinary works had produced a debt of £10,068 6s. 5d. These unpaid bills had accumulated on a weekly or monthly basis over several years. Yenn explained to the Commissioners that part of the trouble was due to rising prices and the bad state of several palaces. Wyatt was more candid. He admitted that these debts on ordinary works were 'the accumulation of several years, and were not known to the Office, because, being exceedings on the estimates which had been

---

[1] *Ibid.* p. 423.

[2] For details cf. 'Inquiry into . . . the Office of Works', *Parl. Pap.*, 1812–13, v, p. 409. It was later discovered that the total was in fact £69,306 15s. 9¼d., owing to the festivities at Carlton House (L.C. 1/40, f. 340, 20 October 1813).

[3] Prepared estimates were invalidated by the Regent's conflicting orders ('Inquiry into . . . the Office of Works', *Parl. Pap.*, 1812–13, v, p. 423).   [4] See below p. 366.

[5] The lack of authority for this work was perhaps Groves' most notorious error of omission. Wyatt assured the Commissioners that 'no intimation of any kind was received at this Office till after the work was completely finished' ('Inquiry into . . . the Office of Works', *Parl. Pap.*, 1812–13, v, pp. 349, 422).

[6] The works, in Board Room and Library, were by direct Treasury command.

[7] These works, ordered by the President of the India Board, were not even executed by Office of Works tradesmen. The cost was none the less charged to the Civil List because the rooms in question were situated over the Office of the Secretary of State for the Home Department.

[8] See below pp. 534–5.   [9] L.C. 1/41, f. 23, 5 May 1815.

allowed at the Office, the Clerks of the Works did not bring them forward in the quarterly accounts; and it would perhaps not now be known to the Office that there existed such outstanding debts, had there not been orders from the Treasury for collecting all outstanding demands'.[1] However he agreed with Yenn in blaming the rigidity of the 1804 quota system. Craig had of course been the author of that system. Nevertheless he tacitly admitted to the Commissioners that the whole arrangement had been a failure. He explained the accumulation of arrears in this way: weekly excesses plus the lack of authorities from the Treasury or the Lord Chamberlain 'may have occasioned a laches on the part of Clerks of the Works to submit them to me for examination [each week], knowing that such authorities were wanting'.[2]

As might have been expected, the Commissioners discovered several notorious instances of Extra works in which expenditure grossly exceeded estimate. Whitehall Chapel and Dorset House were singled out as conspicuous examples.[3] Such un-covenanted expenditure went far beyond the minor excesses which had been considered acceptable during the 1780s and 1790s.[4] The Commissioners of Audit had already discovered in 1810 that irregular and excessive expenditure between 1804 and 1810 amounted to £57,343 10s. 3d.[5] The Commissioners of Military Inquiry therefore recommended that such excesses should be immediately accounted for to the Treasury. The system should follow that employed by Saunders at the British Museum: 'indorsing on the Abstracts of the Bills, the several items of the Estimates, and the correspondent Costs, and by adding explanatory observations of the differences either of increase or diminution'.[6]

The Commissioners of Military Inquiry set out to expose the weaknesses of the Office of Works. Their general conclusions were based on a mass of particular discoveries; for example, discoveries in one administrative microcosm, the sub-department presided over by John Yenn. Yenn's position as Clerk of the Works for Kensington, Carlton House, Buckingham House and the King's Mews was one of the most difficult in the whole department. As he grew older and more deaf, he became less able to cope with his increasing responsibilities.[7] He also became discontented because the rewards of office hardly compensated for the fact that the burdens of administration seemed to be stifling his talents as an architect.[8] The King's Mews were troublesome without being too onerous. Buckingham House was not yet the subject of extravagant expense. At Carlton House expenditure was certainly extravagant, but Yenn himself had merely to suffer the humiliation of being superseded in practice by the Wyatt family. But at Kensington he suffered more than any other Clerk of the

---

[1] 'Inquiry into . . . the Office of Works' *Parl. Pap.*, 1812–13, v, p. 423.
[2] *Ibid.* p. 406.   [3] See below pp. 546, 550.
[4] E.g. excess expenditure 1784–6 (T. 29/63, f. 386, 6 August 1791), 1787–9 (Works 6/22, f. 94, 15 March 1793) and 1794–7 (Works 6/23, f. 141, 17 December 1800).   [5] L.C. 1/40, ff. 196–7, 6 July 1810.
[6] 'Inquiry into . . . the Office of Works', *Parl. Pap.*, 1812–13, v, pp. 350–51. Previously the Lord Chamberlain's Office had been more concerned with testing whether works had been properly authorised than with investigating the reasons for the excess of expenditure over estimate (*ibid.* p. 362).
[7] In December 1813 he was unable to attend a Board meeting 'in consequence of a prior Engagement and being obliged to undergo a Surgical operation on account of deafness' (Works 4/21, 10 December 1813).
[8] 'Yenn as Clerk of the Queen's House, Kensington, the Mews and Carlton House has a salary of £250 per annum besides a house at Kensington and emoluments making the whole about £500. [His Surveyorship at] Greenwich is £250 per annum' (Farington, p. 1088, 28 August 1797). 'Yenn complains that the places he holds at about £900 p.a. have so employed him, that he has had no opportunity of exerting himself as an Architect, and that his talents have been shackled. Wyatt bid him be content' (Farington, p. 1401, 22 December 1798).

Works from arbitrary demands by members of the royal family, the Dukes of Kent and Sussex, and the ill-starred Caroline, Princess of Wales. As he admitted to the Commissioners of Military Inquiry, he was often obliged to abandon the official procedure of estimate, authority and warrant, in order to accelerate work 'for fear of incurring the royal displeasure'.[1] The caprices of the Duke of Kent consistently forced Ordinary expenditure in Yenn's sub-department well above the 1804 quota. Fixed at £6800 in 1804, and confirmed in 1807, this figure bore no relation to the average annual expenditure on Ordinary works, which between 1801 and 1807 stood at £9569.[2] The cost of Extra works reached unprecedented heights. During 1808 Extra work valued at £14,104 13s. 9¾d. had been executed for the Princess of Wales alone. Unpaid bills accumulated in an alarming fashion. In March 1809 'several of the Master Tradesmen employed . . . came to the Board [meeting] and solicited the Examiner to acquaint the Lord Chamberlain with the amount of their bills . . . as some of them were in great distress for the Monies'.[3] By 5 January 1812 the Office of Works debt for Ordinary works stood at more than £10,000, of which more than half had been incurred in Yenn's sub-department. Yenn's explanation was the obvious one: 'the arrear has been progressively accumulating, and has arisen from the increased price of labour and materials, and the increased quantity of work'.[4]

But part of the trouble arose from the fact that under Wyatt's lethargic régime general surveys had been irregular, infrequent and inadequate. This meant that the accumulation of repairs was thrown upon that overloaded section labelled Ordinary works, thus forcing up expenditure beyond the 1804 quota.[5] The rigidity of this quota in turn forced deficits to be carried over from one quarter to the next. Basically, however, it was a question of royal demands. In July 1807 the Treasury requested a full account of expenditure at each of the palaces occupied by younger members of the royal family. Tildesley replied that there were no such members in residence at Hampton Court. Browne answered that the houses of the Dukes of Cumberland and Cambridge at Kew had merely been kept wind and water-tight, the cost for the years 1790–1807 being £3450 and £875 respectively. Matthew contended that a full account for Windsor Castle could not be produced, and, despite Treasury 'disapprobation' of this 'very unsatisfactory answer', no account was forthcoming. Yenn's reply was itself an explanation of rising expenditure in his sub-department:[6]

---

[1] 'Inquiry into . . . the Office of Works', *Parl. Pap.*, 1812–13, v, p. 450. Estimates for work at Kensington and Carlton House were frequently submitted only after work had been completed, although Wyatt 'had opportunities of communicating to the Treasury that such works were going on, and of intimating as nearly as he could guess what would be the cost of them' (*Ibid.* p. 349).

[2] Works 6/27, ff. 54–5, 27 February 1813.   [3] Works 4/20, 17 March 1809.

[4] 'Inquiry into . . . the Office of Works', *Parl. Pap.*, 1812–13, v, p. 346.

[5] General surveys had never reached the statutory number of three a year, but under Chambers the Spring Survey was never omitted, except at distant palaces like Winchester and Newmarket (*Ibid.* p. 347). In April 1813 John Calvert told Wyatt, 'I am directed to express to you [the Lord Chamberlain's] surprise that so long a time should have elapsed without a General Survey . . . and to call your particular attention to the state of the Housekeeper's apartments at St. James's' (L.C. 1/40, f. 320, 13 April 1813).

[6] Works 4/18, 3, 10 and 17 July 1807. Expenditure in the Lord Chamberlain's Department was also overburdened by the cost of furnishing royal residences, amounting in the case of the Dukes of Clarence and Kent to £13,421 and £19,116 respectively between April 1807 and November 1811. In 1815 furnishing expenses (apart from those for the King or Prince Regent) were transferred from the general Civil List to the allowances of individual members of the royal family (L.C. 1/6, f. 385, 6 June 1815; L.C. 1/41, f. 23, 5 May 1815). For the administrative process by which furniture was ordered, installed and paid for prior to 1815 cf. 'Estimates and Accounts', *Parl. Pap.*, 1812, ix, p. 407.

H

1798–1807	Ordinary works at Kensington for the Duke of Kent	£8797	16s.	6½d.
1802–1807	Extra works at Kensington for the Duke of Kent	18,247	6s.	8¾d.
1805–1807	Ordinary works at Kensington for the Duke of Sussex	947	2s.	1¼d.

During 1808 and 1809 Extra works for the Duke of Kent totalled as much as £16,793 7s. 5½d.,[1] and in 1811 works valued at another £10,010 1s. 0d. were authorised by the Treasury.[2]

Apart from information about expenditure, examination of Yenn's sub-department yielded several administrative irregularities. One discovery was the secret payment of officers by tradesmen. John Benson, Constant Carpenter at the Mews, was found to be in receipt of a regular allowance of 4s. a week from the paviour William Meredith; as was Edward Gurney from Watts the carpenter, who sub-contracted from Mrs. Elizabeth Arrow. Watts was also responsible for the payment of 4s. 5d. per day to John Stone, Constant Carpenter at Whitehall and St. James's. Meredith also distributed payments of £2 2s. 0d. and £1 15s. 0d. per week to William Rose and John Spence, temporarily employed as Labourers in Trust at the King's Bench and the Marshalsea. William Lush, Constant Carpenter at Carlton House, received some 28s. a week from Jeffry Wyatt, the contracting carpenter. All these surreptitious payments were disguised in the tradesmen's weekly accounts under the umbrella heading of 'day work'. Indeed the system had become so elaborate that Meredith normally received 15% or 20% commission on the sums he paid out as allowances.[3] In other words, here was a contractor profitably co-operating in a book-keeping juggle whereby salaries on the Office of Works establishment were kept artificially low through the payment of subsidiary allowances via tradesmen's accounts. But on the whole it was Groves and Bacon who were chiefly involved in such irregularities. Yenn was merely accused of excessive expenditure, and on this point he had a sound alibi in the shape of rising prices.

Drastic price changes played havoc with Office of Works expenditure. During the period of the Revolutionary and Napoleonic Wars, novel imposts and embargoes combined with sudden trade fluctuations to make the production of accurate, long-term estimates almost impossible. For example, between Yenn's estimate in 1806 for works at Kensington and his presentation of accounts three years later, English timber rose from £5 to £18 and £20 per load, foreign lengths of deal rose from £40 to £100 per hundred, and painters' materials and turpentine were increased from 70 to 800 guineas per ton by reason of the American embargo.[4] On other occasions the long delay which occurred between the execution of work at the Lazaretto and the production of bills, enabled tradesmen to charge for their work at the highest price

---

[1] 'Report from the Select Committee upon the Civil List', Appendix H, iii. *Parl. Pap.*, 1812, ii, p. 457, and 1830, ix, p. 199.
[2] L.C. 1/5, f. 330, 17 September 1813.
[3] 'Inquiry into . . . the Office of Works', *Parl. Pap.*, 1812–13, v, pp. 340–44, 433, 473–6. Stone at first denied on oath that he had received such an allowance, but later retracted his statement.
[4] L.C. 1/4, 19 July 1809.

available during a period of fluctuation. The difference this could make to the final account can be measured by the fact that prices for certain building materials in 1801 were 25% higher than in 1802.[1]

The Office of Works possessed no automatic price-fixing mechanism. Instead there operated a traditionally *ad hoc* system of petition and advice. In 1783 a new Book of Prices had been prepared covering the cost of all types of labour and materials. As a standard of reference its influence on the building trades of London was considerable. But as a barometer of market prices it was slow and cumbersome. Only a few of the contracts were revised in 1783; many tradesmen were left with prices fixed in 1774. This meant that the Treasury was constantly involved in a process of retrospective compensation for contractors. Market fluctuations were registered only after a tedious process of negotiation. In 1799, carpenters, joiners, bricklayers, plasterers and masons, twenty-one tradesmen in all, applied for compensation. The Treasury suggested that it might be 'advisable in future to make the Contracts accommodate with the Actual Price of the Materials'.[2] But this was a counsel of perfection. Prices refused to stand still until a particular work was completed. The ultimate solution would have been a sliding scale, but this was regarded as too complicated to be practicable.

Under Chambers tradesmen normally addressed their petitions to the Treasury, and these were in turn referred via the Surveyor General to the Clerks of the Works, and so back to the Treasury for endorsement. Under Wyatt this process was usually abbreviated by the Surveyor General authorising price changes after consulting with the Clerks of the Works.[3] When new prices had to be fixed they were settled at weekly Board meetings 'by comparison with other prices, by precedent or otherwise'.[4] The whole process was quite independent of the Lord Chamberlain. It had always been accepted that 'quantities and prices are under the peculiar and immediate direction of the Surveyor [General]'.[5]

Only rarely did an intermediary come between the Office of Works and its contractors. Such manoeuvres were not exactly welcomed by the department. The minutes of the Board meeting of 3 February 1809 laconically record: 'Received a paper purporting to be a List of prices settled by the Masonic Society in London'. Six weeks later a Mr. Robert Spitter arrived to present to the Board 'from the Masonic Society certain prices which they have come to a resolution to charge on different articles from Christmas 1808 in consequence of the rise of some of them by the Stone Merchants'.[6] This practice does not seem to have been repeated.

In general the free market system worked to the advantage of both government and contractor. Whenever market prices fell, the tradesmen passed on the saving to the Office of Works. In July 1794, John Holroyd was able to inform Chambers that because of 'alterations made by the Merchants in the price of pig lead, I am

[1] 'Inquiry into . . . the Office of Works', *Parl. Pap.*, 1812–13, v, p. 507.
[2] T. 29/77, ff. 311–12, 18 December 1799; Works 6/23, f. 90, 19 September, f. 95, 9 August and f. 107, 23 December 1799; Works 4/18, f. 362, 11 October and f. 372, 27 December 1799.
[3] 'Inquiry into . . . the Office of Works', *Parl. Pap.*, 1812–13, v, p. 396. 'It is to be observed that when a reference is made to all or any one Clerk of the Works, the same is usually done for his opinion only and not a rule of Guidance' (Works 4/20, 6 January 1809, 13 January 1809).
[4] 'Inquiry into . . . the Office of Works', *Parl. Pap.*, 1812–13, v, p. 553.
[5] *Ibid.* p. 361.   [6] Works 4/20, 3 February 1809, 23 March 1810.

enabled to reduce the Articles of sheet lead and water pipe 1s. od. per cwt. from Midsummer last. Should any further diminution take place you may depend upon having immediate notice'.[1] Both Chambers and Wyatt operated this reciprocal arrangement with a sense of responsibility. Craig was less co-operative. In 1809 a petition for higher prices from several master tradesmen was endorsed by the Clerks of the Works without being implemented by Craig. For this dereliction of duty the Examiner received an unusually stern reprimand from the Surveyor General, who warned him that to ignore their petition would mean 'a great defalcation of their just claims', considering 'the immoderate increase of the different prices of materials, particularly in timber, deals, oils etc.'[2] Five years later Craig was similarly rebuked by the Treasury for refusing to backdate the increased prices recently awarded to contractors. 'The increased prices', he was told, 'are fair and reasonable in themselves and only such as from the extraordinary rise of timber the parties had a fair right to claim . . . No circumstance of mere official inconvenience should prevent them from being allowed'.[3]

Office of Works prices always included an extra 3% in order to allow for deductions made on tradesmen's bills in the Lord Chamberlain's Office. In addition, besides the tradesman's percentage of profit, some allowance was also made for losses incurred by government contractors during the six or twelve months delay between execution and settlement. All in all, prices for building materials by Office of Works contractors were normally about 15% higher than prices charged by wholesale merchants.[4] Office of Works specifications always stipulated the use of 'the best workmanship and materials'. The Commissioners of Military Inquiry confirmed that 'such are in fact used', and remarked that on the whole office prices were 'as low, and in some instances lower than those usually charged'. Indeed the Commissioners had no quarrel with the pricing system as such, assuming that competitive tenders could not be introduced: 'the present . . . practice . . . is perhaps as unobjectionable as any which can be imagined, as long as it is the rule to employ none but the established tradesmen'.[5] The system of contracting monopolies was to remain unbroken until 1831.

By virtue of its synoptic structure, the building industry has always been peculiarly susceptible to market changes and price fluctuations. Naturally enough, the accounts of the Office of Works clearly reflect the economic impact of the war with France. There is an overall price rise between 1783 and 1815, with a period of maximum variation for the years 1796–7. A few examples, iron, lead, bricks, stone, glass and painters' materials, are sufficient to illustrate the general graph.

During the twenty years 1776–96 the cost of bar iron showed the following progression:[6]

[1] Works 1/5, f. 128, 10 July 1794.
[2] Works 6/24, f. 259, 12 April 1809.
[3] T. 29/128, f. 647, 14 April 1815.
[4] 'Inquiry into . . . the Office of Works', *Parl. Pap.*, 1812–13, v, pp. 397, 445.
[5] *Ibid.* p. 553. The Commissioners did however suggest that tenders should be submitted occasionally by regular tradesmen, following the practice of the Ordnance Department (cf. 13th Report of the Commission of Military Inquiry, Appendix 14). Another suggestion was that during the execution of lengthy work, such as the Lazaretto, contracts should vary according to price levels.
[6] Works 6/22, 27 May, 7 July 1796; Works 4/18, f. 181, 27 May 1796.

1776	£18 per ton	
1791–1792	£21 10s. 0d.	during this period wages rose by
1795	£24 10s. 0d.	1s. 0d. per day and coal by 8s. 0d.
1796	£25 10s. 0d.–£26 10s. 0d.	per chauldron

Between 1793 and 1808, the cost of painters' materials was subject to the following increases:[1]

	1793–1796	*1796–1800*	*1800–1808*
White lead	17%	10%	24%
Linseed oil	60.5%	15%	90%
Turpentine	137.5%		162%
Brushes	25%		132%
Colours	25%	20%	
Varnish	50%		
Wages		15%	

The rising cost of plastering between 1776 and 1797 was rather less dramatic:[2]

Laths	from 10d. to 1s. 3d. per bundle
Lime	from 8s. 0d. to 10s. 0d. per load
Hair	from 8d. to 1s. 2d. per bushel
Sand	from 5s. 6d. to 6s. 10d. per load
Size	from 1s. 6d. to 2s. 9d. per firkin
Plasterer's Wages	from 2s 8d. and 3s. 0d. to 3s. 6d. per day
Labourer's Wages	from 2s. 0d. to 2s. 4d. per day
Boy's Wages	from 10d. to 1s. 2d. per day

Stone masons were particularly subject to the pressure of rising costs during wartime. In 1792 it was reported that freight charges had risen from 10s. 0d. to 14s. 0d. per ton for Portland stone, and from 11s. 0d. to 16s. 0d. per 100 ft. for Purbeck and Yorkshire paving.[3] Contractors were therefore granted a 'War Freightage of 4d. per ft. on cube Portland, 7s. 0d. per cwt. on all paving carried Coastways, and 10s. 0d. per cwt. on Moorstone and Purbeck step'.[4] Besides this, additional duties were imposed in 1794 on all 'Portland, Purbeck, Yorkshire and Moorstone, and all stones carried coastways'. As a result, prices rose in some cases by as much as 25%:[5]

[1] Works 6/22, 22 February 1796; Works 4/18, f. 168, 26 February 1796; T. 29/69, f. 459, 15 October 1796; Works 6/23, f. 137, 17 October 1800; Works 6/24, ff. 205–6, 29 July 1808.

[2] Works 6/23, f. 30, May 1797.

[3] Works 1/5, f. 118, October 1792; Works 4/17, f. 42, 8 November 1793. 'The dearness of horses now . . . makes a great additional expence' (Works 6/23, f. 77, 7 December 1792).

[4] Works 6/22, f. 181, 19 December 1794.

[5] Works 1/5, f. 121, 20 March 1794, ff. 134–5, September 1794; T. 29/67, f. 239, 17 October 1794. The Treasury waived the imposition of this duty for the construction of Chepstow Bridge (1815), but refused to do so during the simultaneous construction of Westgate Bridge, Gloucester. The stone in the latter case was brought coastwise from Bristol and Cornwall (T. 29/133, f. 727, 17 February 1815). Higher duties forced up the cost of Dutch clinkers in 1799 from 7s. 3d. per yard to 8s. 3d. (Works 6/23, f. 77, 18 January 1799). For the effect of duties imposed in 1794 on the cost of slate cf. Works 1/5, f. 135; Works 4/18, f. 90, 26 September and f. 95, 31 October 1794; T. 29/67, f. 219, 16 October 1794.

	Before 1794	Duty and Fees	After 1794
9 in. granite per yd.	9s. 0d.	1s. 6d.	10s. 6d.
Carriageway Purbeck squares per yd.	8s. 0d.	1s. 3d.	9s. 3d.
Pebbles per yd.	5s. 0d.	10d.	5s. 10d.
Clinkers per yd.	7s. 0d.	3d.	7s. 3d.
Cube Portland per ft.	2s. 4d.	7d.	2s. 11d.
1½ in. Portland paving per ft.	1s. 7d.	1d.	1s. 8d.
Moorstone step 14 in. wide per ft.	2s. 0d.	6d.	2s. 6d.
Yorkshire paving per ft.	8d.	2d.	10d.

Less than three years later, further additions were called for. The cost of marble rose alarmingly, and the market price of labour rose 'in proportion to the dearness of Provisions and every requisite of Life'.[1]

	Before 1797	After 1797
Statuary marble per ft. cube	£1 15s. 0d.	£4 15s. 6d.
Veined marble per ft. cube	1 4s. 0d.	1 18s. 6d.
Slit firestone per ft.	1s. 0d.	1s. 1d.
Mortar per hod	5d.	6d.
Tarras per hod	3s. 6d.	5s. 0d.
Mason per day	3s. 4d.	3s. 8d.
Labourer per day	2s. 3d.	2s. 6d.
Marble polisher per day	2s. 6d.	3s. 0d.

But by 1808 these figures were outdated, and tradesmen were claiming the following prices:[2]

Cube Portland per ft.	4s. 10d.
Mason per day	5s. 6d.
Marble Polisher per day	4s. 6d.
Labourer per day	3s. 6d.

The fact that the government had a vested interest in the Portland stone quarries made no difference to the sums awarded by the Office of Works to contracting masons. The government took with one hand and paid out with the other, both actions being quite unconnected. As Wyatt explained to John Fordyce, although 'the stone quarries in the Island of Portland belong to His Majesty, and a Pier, Cranes and roads there for transporting stone from the said Quarries are maintained at the charge of the Crown . . . it has always been the practice of the present establishment of the Office of Works to contract with Masons at such prices as were considered reasonable according to the nature of the work, they finding Labour and Materials as in the common practice of business'.[3]

The rising cost of glass similarly reflects the varying state of the market. In 1794 higher duties forced John Cobbett, the chief contracting glazier, to petition for

[1] Works 6/23, f. 29, April 1797.
[2] Works 6/24, f. 218, 7 September 1808. Similar petitions for higher prices were received during 1808–9 from plasterers, carpenters, painters and bricklayers (e.g. Works 4/20, 6 and 13 January 1809).
[3] Works 4/19, 14 September 1804; Works 6/23, f. 273, 8 February 1805.

higher prices. Eleven years later he was obliged to present another petition. He gave as his reasons the increasing cost of glass from 'the manufactories, particularly in this year in consequence of the duty laid on by Parliament, and also on the several materials used in trade, such as lead, oyl, tin, etc., and on increase in journeymen's wages from 18 to 24s. od. per week, which makes it impossible for me to carry on my business on the same terms as before without sustaining a very considerable loss'. Prices therefore showed the following increases:[1]

	1793	*1794*	*1805*	*1808*
Plate glass	13s. od. per ft.	14s. 6d.	17s. od.	
Crown glass in sash	1s. 7d. per ft.	1s. 10½d.	2s. 2d. (out of town 2s. 3d.)	2s. 3d.
Crown glass in lead	1s. 2d. per ft.	1s. 5½d.	1s. 8d. (out of town 1s. 9d.)	1s. 9d.
Ground glass	2s. 6d. per ft.	3s. od.	3s. 6d.	3s. 6d.
Repairing lights	1d. per ft.	2d.	8d.	

Increases in the cost of bricks were still more drastic. In 1784 the Office of Works was paying 25s. od. per 1000 for grey stock bricks. But in that year brickmakers took advantage of the government's imposition of new duties to lay down a new set of wholesale prices. These prices in turn forced bricklayers to petition the Treasury for revised contracts. The duty imposed by Parliament had been 2s. 6d. per 1000 on bricks. The increase demanded by brickmakers was 4s. od. per 1000. Chambers considered this demand excessive, and agreed to grant contracting bricklayers an increase of only 3s. od. 'With this', he told the Treasury, 'though double what ought to be allowed but for the brickmakers' combination, the bricklayers were not satisfied. However hard it may be for the bricklayers to pay upwards of 4s. od. for what I think it reasonable to allow them 3s. od. the additional allowances to them on account of the tax should not be exceeded, and whenever the combination of the brickmakers can be broken through, and the prices of their commodities reduced to reason, these allowances should be diminished proportionably'.[2] The Office of Works therefore paid its contracting bricklayers 28s. 10d. per 1000, of which about 10d. disappeared in deductions made at the Lord Chamberlain's Office. Regional variations soon underlined the fact that contractors stood to make a regular loss. In 1786 Chambers granted an extra 2s. 6d. on bricks transported by cart from Middlesex and subject to bridge tolls at Richmond and Kew.[3] During the following year contractors handling bricks and tiles from Brentford and Ripley were also reported to be making a loss. After conducting a personal investigation 'at the kilns', Chambers agreed to further increases.[4] Falling costs around 1790, increases awarded

[1] Works 4/18, f. 101. 12 December 1794 and f. 105, 16 January 1795; Works 6/22, f. 178, 12 December 1794; Works 6/24, f. 6, 14 June 1805; Works 5/95–113, 1806–14.
[2] Works 6/21, ff. 25–6, 19 March, 2 April, 8 April 1785; Works 4/16, 31 December 1784, 7, 21 and 28 January, 8 April 1785; Works 1/5, f. 80, 15 April 1785.
[3] 'As the bricks arrive by such conveyance in much better condition than when they have been five times moved (which is the case if brought in barges) they are fitter for use and liable to less waste' (Works 6/21, f. 90, 24 July and f. 95, 18 August 1786; Works 4/17, 4 August, 18 August, 22 December 1786; T. 29/58, f. 92, 17 November 1786).
[4] Works 6/21, ff. 124–5, 12 December 1787 and f. 135, 8 February 1788.

in 1792 and 1797, and spasmodic rises during the later war years, produced the following price-table:[1]

		1784	1785	1788	1792	1797
Grey stock bricks	*per 1000*	25s. 0d.	28s 10d.	35s. 0d.	32s. 10d.	37s. 6d.
Plain tiles	*per 1000*	25s. 0d.	28s. 7d.	34s. 6d.	33s. 7d.	35s. 0d.
10 in. tiles	*per 100*	12s. 0d.	13s. 9d.	14s. 3d.	14s. 9d.	15s. 9d.
Pantiles	*per 1000*	105s. 0d.	114s. 7d.	114s. 7d.	120s. 0d.	120s. 0d.
Bricklayer	*per day*	3s. 4d. *summer*	3s. 4d.	3s. 4d.	3s. 8d.	3s. 10d.
		3s. 0d. *winter*	3s. 0d.	3s. 0d.	3s. 4d.	3s. 6d.
Bricklayer's labourer	*per day*	2s. 2d. *summer*	2s. 2d.	2s. 2d.	2s. 4d.	2s. 6d.
		2s 0d. *winter*	2s. 0d.	2s. 0d.	2s. 2d.	2s. 4d.

1799	1801	1803	1805	1808	1811	1814
39s. 0d.	44s. 3d.	48s. 0d.	53s. 0d.	55s. 0d.	61s. 0d.	61s. 0d.
39s. 0d.	53s. 0d.	53s. 0d.	53s. 0d.	55s. 6d.	65s. 0d.	57s. 6d.
22s. 2d.	26s. 0d.	26s. 0d.	26s. 0d.	29s. 0d.	—	—
120s. 0d.	130s. 6d.	130s. 6d.	130s. 6d.	130s. 6d.	143s. 3d.	135s. 0d.
3s. 8d.	4s. 4d.	4s. 10d.	5s. 0d.	5s. 2d.	5s. 6d.	5s. 6d.
3s. 6d.	3s. 10d.	4s. 4d.	4s. 8d.	4s. 8d.	3s. 8d.	3s. 8d.
2s. 4d.	2s. 8d.	2s. 10d.	3s. 0d.	3s. 2d.	3s. 8d.	3s. 8d.
2s. 2d.	2s. 6d.	2s. 8d.	2s. 10d.	2s. 10d.	3s. 4d.	3s. 4d.

The price of lead fluctuated more violently than that of any other building material. For instance, in 1785, 1789, 1790 and 1794 the principal contractors were able to announce lower prices.[2] But in almost every other year between 1783 and 1815 higher prices were requested and granted. 1787 was described as a year of 'extraordinary rise', from £1 1s. 0d. to £1 3s. 0d. per ton.[3] But the Summer of 1788 saw Chambers recommending that George Holroyd, master plumber at Somerset House and elsewhere, be paid £1 6s. 0d. per cwt. for lead instead of £1 3s. 0d. Otherwise he would be 'a considerable looser', because 'the lead merchants have now raised the price of Lead in Piggs from £19 15s. 0d. to £23 0s. 0d. per ton, owing to the diminished produce of the Scotch Mines and the vast demand from abroad . . . particularly from Russia'.[4] The price of lead supplied by contractors normally included 'labour and carriage'. In 1787 Kenton Couse explained to John Vidgeon of the Ordnance Office that 'labour' meant 'loading and unloading, hoisting and laying lead flatts, gutters etc'.[5] Between 1783 and 1790 prices fluctuated by as much as 4s. 0d. per cwt. on the cost of sheet lead and lead piping.[6] But in 1802 the

[1] Works 6/21, f. 26, 8 April, f. 28, 22 April 1785 and f. 135, 8 February 1788; T. 29/59, f. 105, 14 February and f. 115, 19 February 1788; T. 29/65, f. 72, 30 August and f. 193, 15 November 1792; Works 6/23, f. 41, 20 October 1797; Works 5/88–103, 1799–1814.

[2] Works 4/16, 1 April 1785; Works 4/17, 18 December 1789, 8 January, 23 April 1790; Works 4/18, f. 79, 11 July 1794; Works 1/5, f. 128, 10 July 1794.

[3] Works 6/21, f. 119, 27 July 1787; T. 29/58, f. 484, 15 August 1787.

[4] Works 6/21, f. 139, 2 May and f. 140, 18 June 1788; Works 4/17, 13 June 1788; T. 29/57, f. 321, 14 June 1788.   [5] Works 1/5, f. 92, 25 October 1787.   [6] Works 5/72–79.

price leapt another 15s. od.;[1] in 1805 prices were up another 25%.[2] Many of the variations on the graph, notably in 1797 and 1800–2, lasted only a matter of weeks.[3] All in all, between 1782 and 1805 sheet lead rose from 21s. od. to 51s. od. per cwt. Thereafter the price declined a little, standing at roughly 48s. od. per cwt. from 1806 to 1814.[4]

The cost of labour fluctuated less violently than the cost of building materials during the period under review. Wages remained static between 1782 and 1790: 1s. 10d. per day for 'common labourers', 2s. od. for semi-skilled men, 3s. od. for masons, painters, slaters, plumbers, joiners, carpenters, paviours and smiths, and 3s. od. or 3s. 4d. and 3s. od. or 3s. 6d. for bricklayers and plasterers according to season.[5] But in 1792 bricklayers received an extra 4d. and semi-skilled men an extra 2d.[6] In 1796 paviours went up from 3s. od. to 3s. 6d. per day; the pay of their skilled labourers rose from 2s. od. to 2s. 3d.; and the unskilled 'common labourer', casually employed, achieved parity of reward if not of status, by rising from 1s. 10s. to 2s. 3d. per day.[7] Smiths received another 6d. per day in 1803.[8] In 1806 slaters were granted as much as 5s. 6d. per day, and their semi-skilled assistants 3s. 3d.[9] In 1786 Chambers had to agree to cut down building operations in order to break a demand by carpenters and joiners for increased wages.[10] Five years later capitulation to the demands of labourers working on the Fleet Prison for 'half a crown a day and an allowance of 3½d. for Porter', was only avoided by employing the prisoners themselves.[11] In thus co-operating with the contracting tradesmen against their employees, Chambers seems to have been acting out of conviction. In 1792 he informed the Treasury that an increase in the master masons' charges was justified on the grounds that 'the Workmen in all branches almost of the Building business, are become so exorbitant in their demands that it is almost impossible to get business done'.[12] Under the stress of wartime conditions, labourers managed to improve their financial position appreciably. But it must be remembered that the figures quoted are for prices awarded to contracting tradesmen. These wages were in turn subject to the usual 3% deduction before they reached the hands of the employee.

It was generally recognised by informed critics that the increasing cost of the Civil List was largely due to rising prices. In the Parliamentary Report on the State of the Civil List, 1802, it was observed that sharp increases in expenditure in the years ending January 1796, January 1800, January 1801 and January 1802, were due to the fact that 'the Price of almost every Article of Consumption has been proportionately enhanced during the Whole of that Period, and the Necessaries of Life advanced still more rapidly for a Time, in consequence of the Scarcity in the Years 1795, 1799 and 1800'. This, it was concluded, has been 'confirmed in many Instances by Public Documents, and in all by private Experience'. In all departments 'the Continuance of War alone . . . would account for the most considerable Part of

[1] Works 4/19, 1 October 1802. [2] Works 4/19, 7 June 1805.
[3] Works 4/18, f. 218, 13 January and f. 357, 30 August 1797; Works 4/19, 14 May, 12 December 1800, 9 October, 18 December 1801, 4 June 1802. [4] Works 5/95–103, 1806–14.
[5] Works 5/72–5/79, 1782–90. [6] T. 29/65, f. 193, 15 November 1792.
[7] Works 6/22, 2 July 1796. [8] Works 4/19, 22 July 1803.
[9] Works 4/19, 1 August 1806, 28 November 1806. [10] Works 4/17, 6 July 1787.
[11] T. 29/66, f. 209, 14 November 1793. Apparently workmen 'wrought much more briskly when so refreshed' (Works 6/22, f. 77, 7 December 1792). [12] Works 6/22, f. 62, 17 August 1792.

the Excess'.[1] In January 1804, unpaid bills incurred by the Lord Chamberlain's Department as a whole amounted to £54,246 5s. 1¼d. out of a total Civil List debt of £444,816 18s. 6¼d. In that year, therefore, the old estimates were abandoned as irrelevant and the general Civil List estimate was raised from the 1786 figure of £897,400 6s. 0d. to a total of £979,043 10s. 9d.[2] But once again expenditure outstripped expectations. In seven years, 1805–11, excesses in Civil List expenditure over and above the 1804 estimate, totalled £868,707 16s. 0½d.[3] Of this, £612,013 was incurred under Class IV, that is, tradesmen's bills; out of that sum more than £400,000 represented excess expenditure incurred by the Lord Chamberlain's Department alone; and among the various sub-departments controlled by the Lord Chamberlain the Office of Works was of course the most expensive. These conclusions are best demonstrated in tabular form.[4]

			Civil List	*Lord Chamberlain's Department*	*Office of Works*
1786 estimate			£897,400 6s. 0d.	£43,000 0s. 0d.	£25,000 0s. 0d.
year ending	5 January	1787		41,393 12s. 1½d.	19,142 4s. 6½d.
		1788		36,942 5s. 8d.	19,178 14s. 5¼d.
		1789		36,460 17s. 11d.	18,951 9s. 1¼d.
		1790		46,407 15s. 6¼d.	20,009 19s. 0d.
		1791		42,767 5s. 4¾d.	22,559 7s. 2½d.
		1792		49,152 9s. 4½d.	19,828 2s. 0½d.
		1793		53,768 16s. 2¼d.	29,784 9s. 2½d.
		1794		45,545 8s. 1¼d.	29,941 6s. 5d.
		1795		61,423 13s. 4½d.	26,321 1s. 5d.
		1796		70,147 11s. 7d.	39,929 11s. 3½d.
		1797		59,866 3s. 9d.	35,893 10s. 4¼d.
		1798		59,094 14s. 0¼d.	28,181 4s. 4½d.
		1799		48,919 1s. 2d.	27,489 12s. 10½d.
		1800		66,152 4s. 7¾d.	31,887 2s. 2¼d.
		1801	1,039,289 4s. 5d.	74,449 13s. 1½d.	40,659 17s. 11½d.
		1802	997,678 3s. 0d.	78,541 6s. 0½d.	45,979 17s. 8¾d.
		1803	1,100,160 2s. 8½d.	94,192 14s. 0¾d.	43,324 6s. 5¾d.
		1804	1,148,851 2s. 1¼d.	74,973 11s. 9d.	37,693 3s. 6¼d.
1804 estimate			979,043 10s. 9d.	65,000 0s. 0d.	32,000 0s. 0d.
half year ending	5 July	1804		45,740 11s. 7½d.	23,717 19s. 11¼d.
year ending	5 July	1805	1,099,421 14s. 10¾d.	133,809 9s. 2½d.	73,033 12s. 4¼d.
		1806	1,142,680 6s. 11¾d.	136,386 15s. 5½d.	87,484 15s. 5d.
		1807	1,117,450 7s. 5d.	124,108 4s. 4½d.	77,920 11s. 11¾d.
		1808	1,068,282 8s. 6½d.	95,151 16s. 10¼d.	47,062 10s. 7¾d.
		1809	1,082,186 1s. 7¼d.	149,618 0s. 5¼d.	67,401 2s. 9¼d.
		1810	1,122,937 16s. 6½d.	118,091 4s. 7¾d.	56,755 12s. 10¼d.
		1811	1,089,053 15s. 3¾d.	101,669 15s. 8½d.	48,269 8s. 1¼d.

1 'Report from the Committee on the Civil List Accounts', *Parl. Pap.*, 1801–2, ii, p. 20.

2 *Commons Jnls.*, lix (1803–4), Appendix 30, p. 624 *et seq.* The Civil List was increased by £60,000 per annum and certain charges totalling £82,000 per annum were removed (44 G. III c. 80).

3 'Report from the Select Committee upon the Civil List', *Parl. Pap.*, 1812, ii, p. 423 and 1830, ix, p. 165.

4 This composite table has been compiled from several complementary lists: 'Report from the Committee on the Civil List Accounts', *Parl. Pap.*, 1801–2, ii, p. 13; 'Report . . . upon His Majesty's Civil List Revenue', *Parl. Pap.*, 1802–3, v, p. 335; 'Report . . . upon His Majesty's Civil List Revenue', *Parl. Pap.*, 1803–4, v, p. 219; 'Report from the Select Committee upon the Civil List', *Parl. Pap.*, 1812, ii, p. 423 and 1830, ix, p. 165; *Commons Jnls.*, 1803–4, Appendix 30, p. 624.

After 1810 Civil List expenditure ceased to fluctuate so violently. In October 1813 Charles Bacon claimed that the cost of labour and materials had risen by 25% over the seven years since 1806.[1] But between 1810 and 1813 prices seem to have remained stationary or even declined a little. In 1810 Wyatt asked the Clerks of the Works to advise him as to 'whether any and what reductions might be proper to make in the prices of the Carpenters, Joiners, Painters and Plumbers'.[2] In January 1813 'the whole of the subsisting Contracts' were ordered to be 'referred to the Clerks of the Works . . . to revise them and report whether any and what abatements can be made therefrom'.[3] The average annual expenditure of the Office of Works for the seven years ending 5 July 1811 had been £65,420. Between 5 April 1812 and 5 January 1815 expenditure showed a lower annual average of £64,500. Since this sum included £28,000 for a temporary room at Carlton House and £22,600 for permanent additions to that palace, Office of Works expenditure 1812–15 can therefore be seen as considerably less than for 1804–11.[4] Such a drastic diminution speaks volumes for the usefulness of restrictions imposed on spending during these three years, especially as the other sections of the Lord Chamberlain's Department showed a steady rise in expenditure. But in 1815 the process of reorganising the Office of Works was symbolised by its withdrawal from the Lord Chamberlain's control.[5]

The Report of the Select Committee on the Civil List, 1815, adopted a sensible attitude towards expenditure. In the first place, even allowing for the persistent accumulation of debt, Civil List expenditure between 1760 and 1815 had not equalled the income accruing from the hereditary revenues surrendered by George III at the start of his reign.[6] In the second place, the system adopted in 1760 made 'the occurrence of Debt in some degree almost unavoidable'. The application of a fixed rate of income to an expanding rate of expenditure had been little less than an attempt at squaring the circle. Many items were so variable as to defy regulation. Besides, 'the price of all articles of consumption, since the accession of his present Majesty, has so rapidly advanced, and particularly in latter times, as to render any estimate, however justly formed at the time, totally inadequate; and the continuance of peace or war must have materially affected the calculations'.[7] Civil List responsibilities, concluded the Committee, should be limited to predictable items, and their predictability should be secured by an independent system of audit allied to stringent Treasury control. 'It is to the vigilant superintendance of the Treasury that Parliament should look for . . . confining the expenditure of the Civil List'.[8] It was around this pious hope that much of the controversy concerning the Office of Works was to be centered during the period after 1815.

Meanwhile, the Commissioners of Military Inquiry had concluded their postmortem on the Office of Works under James Wyatt. Broadly speaking, they produced three sets of recommendations, concerning administration, buildings and

---

[1] Works 6/27, f. 99, 2 October 1813.   [2] Works 4/20, 2 February 1810, 12 October 1810.
[3] Works 4/20, 15 January 1813.   [4] *Parl. Deb.* 1815, xxx, Appendix pp. xcv, xcix.
[5] 54 G. III c. 157.
[6] Income from Surrendered revenues, 1760–1815: £67,494,368. Civil List plus occasional grants, 1760–1815: £61,184,960 (*Parl. Deb.* xxx, 1815, Appendix pp. lxxxvii–ix; xxxi, 1815, pp. 1000–1).
[7] *Ibid.* xxx (1815), Appendix p. cvii.   [8] *Ibid.* xxx (1815), Appendix p. cx.

finance.[1] At administrative level, they toyed with the idea of amalgamating the Office of Works and the Office of Woods, Forests and Land Revenues, before abandoning the scheme as unwieldy. Instead 'the controuling power of the Department' was to be removed from the Lord Chamberlain's Office and vested in a triumvirate: a superintendant concerned with patronage and finance, plus two professional architects. At executive level, responsibility for royal palaces and public buildings was to be redistributed between six Clerks of the Works. The King's Private Roads, now no longer private, should become public, thus saving the Civil List £600–£700 per annum. Buildings cared for by the Office of Works at the Tower of London should be transferred to the Ordnance Office or the Barrack Office. Buildings in the royal parks should be transferred to the Office of Woods, Forests and Land Revenues, along with the salary anomalously paid for so long to the Ranger of St. James's Park. The King's Bench, Marshalsea and Fleet Prisons, the Rolls House, the Houses of Parliament and Speaker's House, the Exchequer Offices, Court of Exchequer and Westminster Hall, the Horse Guards and Somerset House—all these were to be made the direct instead of indirect responsibility of the Office of Works. Financially, there was to be one radical change. Increasing charges on the Civil List were to be offset by distinguishing for the first time between royal palaces and public buildings. The King's palaces were to remain as a charge upon the Civil List. Government buildings were to be covered by parliamentary grants apportioned annually according to estimate. Office of Works operations were thus to be charged to one of three accounts: the Civil List account, the Parliamentary account, and the account of the Office of Woods and Forests.[2] Estimates were to be anchored to a system of open tenders and public contracts, 'to excite a competition of offers'. Otherwise, the day to day methods of office administration were to be retained, but with greater emphasis on the duties of Labourers in Trust: 'the chief reliance for the accuracy of bills must rest on [their] ability and integrity'.

In 1810 the Treasury had directed that all Extra works should be executed by specific contracts based on absolute estimates. In his evidence to the Commissioners Wyatt recommended that this system should be extended to Ordinary works as well.[3] But between 1810 and 1813 such contracts were seldom employed, almost the only examples being new quarters in Whitehall for the Stationery Office and the Privy Council Office.[4] According to the Commissioners, open contracts should henceforth take the form either of contracts in gross or of contracts for prices.[5] Wyatt found himself in a minority in favouring gross contracts with general contractors who in turn subcontracted with master tradesmen. Saunders considered this system 'very injudicious' except for 'small, plain or rough works' where 'the goodness of the work' is 'of much less importance than the completion of it within a fixed and short period. If no such reasons exist, making a contract in the gross may be attributed to a motive, in the Architect who promotes it, for saving his own labour; or to want of ability in

---

[1] For full details cf. 'Inquiry into . . . the Office of Works', *Parl. Pap.*, 1812–13, v, p. 365 *et seq.*
[2] As eventually adopted in 1815 (Works 4/21, 27 March 1815).
[3] 'Inquiry into . . . the Office of Works', *Parl. Pap.*, 1812–13, v, p. 551.   [4] Below, pp. 543, 550.
[5] Following evidence by James Morgan, joint architect to the Office of Woods, Forests and Land Revenues, and William Pilkington, architect to the Board of Customs and Transport Board (*ibid.* pp. 371, 377–384, 504–5). Contracts in gross were used at Dartmoor Prison and Yarmouth Naval Hospital. Contracts for prices were used at the Mint, the British Museum and Greenwich Naval Asylum.

laying out and directing the construction of the various parts'.[1] The argument between Wyatt and Saunders remained unresolved. Indeed it was repeated fifteen years later by the dialogue between Nash and Smirke. Between 1813 and 1815 competitive tenders were seldom employed. The only examples are all non-specialist works: the new boundary wall of the Marshalsea (1813), the demolition of buildings at Newmarket (1814) and the re-paving of Whitehall (1814).[2]

In several respects the recommendations of the Commissioners of Military Inquiry agreed with proposals already made by George Saunders.[3] He had however suggested an administrative committee composed of Surveyor General, Inspector and Examiner. This body was to be guided by an independent Board led by three eminent architects and concerned with policy and finance. Saunders had concluded his submission by remarking that 'the office of Surveyor of His Majesty's Works is regarded as the most eminent in the profession, and it is adviseable to take all possible means to secure respect for that appointment'. But the Commissioners of Military Inquiry disagreed. After examining Wyatt's career they judged the Surveyor Generalship to be less an object of emulation than a source of temptation. They considered that the interests of department and profession alike would best be served by its abolition.

Wyatt once remarked to Dance that he hoped for a sudden death.[4] His wish was amply fulfilled. Farington tells the story, in the words of Wyatt's close friend Dr. Thorpe. On Saturday, 4 September 1813, Wyatt

> was on his way to London with Mr. Codrington [of Dodington Park], a gentleman of fortune in Wiltshire, in Mr. Codrington's carriage with four horses. While driving at a great rate a person on horseback met the carriage in a place where another carriage or cart stood, which made the passage between the carriages so narrow that the horse and his rider were thrown down and the wheels of Mr. Codrington's carriage passed over the rump of the horse [and] the carriage was overturned. Wyatt, at the time, was reading a newspaper and had his hat off. The *top of his head* struck with great violence the *roof of the carriage*, and the concussion caused his *instant death*. A red spot appeared in his forehead, which was owing to the blood which had settled there.[5]

Wyatt died at an opportune moment. He was heading for public disgrace and private disaster. He had already been dismissed from his post as Deputy Surveyor to the Office of Woods, Forests and Land Revenues. As Surveyor General and Comptroller he could hardly have survived the reorganisation of the Office of Works. As for his private affairs, he owed Bertolini his plasterer £3000; he owed Dixon his draughtsman £900. His London house in Foley Place was mortgaged to

---

[1] *Ibid.* pp. 514–5. 'To make what is called a Close Estimate of a building, requires drawings and descriptions of all parts in detail; of the internal mechanism, dimensions and materials, as well as of all the outward forms; the necessary time not being devoted for doing this effectually in making a contract in the gross, much is estimated by guess, either involving the contractor in difficulties, or if he is artful, furnishing him with the means of easily wronging his employer'. The classic instance of such a fraud occurred during the construction of the London Custom House, see p. 427 below.

[2] T. 29/124, f. 1026, 26 August 1813; T. 29/129, f. 785, 28 June 1814.

[3] 'Inquiry into . . . the Office of Works', *Parl. Pap.*, 1812–13, v, pp. 518–20.

[4] Farington, p. 6700, 3 July 1815.

[5] Farington, p. 7389, 17 May 1818. Just before his death, Wyatt had made arrangements with Thorpe 'for them to take jointly a house at Brighton for the accommodation of their families'.

the hilt. One of his housemaids was pregnant by him and 'within three weeks of her confinement'.[1]

The news of Wyatt's death burst like a thunderclap over the professional world of the metropolis. Naturally enough, his enemies were delighted. Benjamin West confessed himself 'much struck . . . he said it would be upon his mind for forty eight hours'.[2] Among junior officials of the Office of Works the news produced an appropriate reaction: they set up a memorial to Sir William Chambers.[3] But others were pleased to see Wyatt dead merely for reasons of professional ambition. Robert Smirke rapidly marshalled his supporters: the ruling coterie of Royal Academicians and a battery of influential Tories. Soane trusted to his contacts in Whitehall, Nash to his friends at Windsor and St. James's. News of the accident in a hasty letter from his father prompted Smirke to take a chaise from Hastings to London in time to send letters by the evening post. He wrote to the Earl of Lonsdale and Earl Bathurst 'for their interest to obtain for him the situations which Wyatt held, or whatever could be obtained under such regulations as may be adopted'. Bathurst's reply was 'kind, but apprehended that Nash would be recommended by the Regent'; he added that Wyatt's Office of Works position would probably be abolished. Thomas Lawrence was very active on Smirke's behalf. He wrote to Lonsdale, then spoke to Lord Castlereagh who promised that 'if Dance should not offer he would do all he could for Smirke', and then took a chaise to Sydenham 'to know from Mr. Adams who was Private Secretary to Mr. Pitt, in whose gift the appointment of Comptroller was vested'. West remarked that 'he pitied those who had obligations upon them to leave London at this season so favourable for professional application'.[4] Meanwhile Lonsdale had written to Lords Liverpool and Mulgrave to obtain for Smirke at least Wyatt's Surveyorship of the Ordnance. Prime Minister Liverpool replied characteristically that when arrangements had been made he would then consider who was the most proper choice. Mulgrave answered that he had already bestowed the post on William Atkinson as he had known his large family for twenty years. However Smirke thought that the real reason was the fact that Atkinson, who owned a wharf in Westminster, purchased materials for cement from Mulgrave. Another architect who tried in vain for Wyatt's Ordnance post was William Porden. Perhaps, he wrote to General Turner, you could mention 'my name to the Prince Regent'.[5]

Some of Wyatt's own family acted with equal celerity. One of his sons, Matthew Cotes Wyatt, announced the accident to Soane in dramatic terms: 'How can I tell you that we have in an instant lost our father, and ah, our all, it impresses me with horror . . . the best of fathers, the kindest of friends . . . Great God, how awful, he never spoke or sighed, poor soul. That no body could defend him from the blow!

[1] Farington, p. 6396–7, 18 September 1813 and p. 7389, 17 May 1818.

[2] Farington, p. 6395, 7 September 1813. He turned down Soane's suggestion that Wyatt be given an 'Academical' funeral (Farington, p. 6396, 18 September 1813).

[3] A bust to be placed 'at the Upper End of the Board Room over the Chimney', upon 'a marble console agreeably to the . . . design of the late James Wyatt Esq'. Thomas Hardwick was chairman of the memorial committee (Works 4/21, 24 December 1813). The bust had been given by Westmacott in 1801, and the console was designed by Wyatt in 1811 (Works 4/19, 25 September 1801; Works 4/20, 19 February 1811). The bust was presented to Sir John Soane in 1832, and is now in the Soane Museum, London.

[4] Farington, p. 6396, 11 September 1813.

[5] RA 20863, 9 September 1813.

His countenance is heaven'.[1] The eldest, Benjamin Dean Wyatt, tried, via his wife Catherine, to enlist the support of Samuel Whitbread, M.P.: he wanted all three of his father's chief posts in the Office of Works, the Ordnance Office and Westminster Abbey.[2] In the event, he received only the least profitable of these, the Surveyorship to the Dean and Chapter. The youngest son, Philip, known to Beckford as 'Sweetness' because of his ingratiating manner,[3] rushed to Ragley, the Warwickshire seat of the Marquess of Hertford where the Regent was staying. There he burst into the royal bedchamber at 3 a.m. with the 'melancholy account' which 'very much affected the Regent even to shedding tears'. But when the messenger proceeded with the 'real business', namely 'to solicit the Regent to bestow upon him such of the advantages possessed by his late father as his Royal Highness might think proper', the Regent merely 'returned a civil answer in a general way'.[4] Nor was he any more generous to Wyatt's widow, Rachel. In May 1814 she confessed to Soane: 'I have now no home whatever, or bed to sleep upon', for, as Richard Holland expected, 'poor Wyatt's affairs . . . [turned] out to be very much embarrassed'. Soane and S. P. Cockerell made unsuccessful efforts to raise a subscription for her. 'There will be a large deficiency', remarked Cockerell; 'professional men whom I have spoken to are very lukewarm'.[5] Lukewarm also was Lord Liverpool, to whom Rachel Wyatt addressed repeated cries for help. Six weeks after her husband's death she presented a multiple petition requesting a pension for herself and employment for her sons: the Surveyor Generalship for Benjamin, an administrative post for Charles, a sinecure at Court for Matthew and a surveyorship at Carlton House for Philip.[6] Liverpool awarded her a pension of £130 per annum, but only after he had received two more hysterical letters giving details of her summary imprisonment for debt and her 'state of miserable and deplorable dependence'.[7] Jeffry Wyatt wrote no less than fifteen letters to different people 'soliciting their interest to get something that his uncle enjoyed'. With Wellington abroad, Benjamin Wyatt fell back on the Duke of Richmond's

---

[1] A. T. Bolton, *The Portrait of Sir John Soane* (1927), pp. 191–2.

[2] Beds. Record Office, Whitbread Papers 3388–9, 5 and 29 September 1813.

[3] Benjamin Dean Wyatt was correspondingly known as 'Bitterness' (B. Alexander, *Life at Fonthill 1807–22*, 1957, p. 131, 26 August 1812 and p. 142, 25 January 1814). Beckford described Philip Wyatt as 'more hirsute, bearded and baboon-like than the fantastic faces one can see on coconuts; very aimiable, very thin, pretty poor I don't doubt, but bursting with sublime plans' (*ibid.* p. 295, 10 March 1819).

[4] Farington p. 6397, 18 September 1813.

[5] Bolton, *op. cit.* pp. 192–3. Rachel Wyatt's appearances in contemporary MSS. are generally sad and fleeting. In December 1794 Farington noted that 'Mrs. Wyatt was so affected by the loss of her daughter five years ago that she has not since been in the dining parlour, and is only lately come into the drawing room' (Farington, p. 260, 14 December 1794).

[6] Liverpool Papers, lxvii, B.M. Add. MS. 38256, ff. 12–16, 15 October 1813. Benjamin claimed to be 'established in his profession, with a high reputation as a man of business, personally known to . . . some of the ministers', and 'of sufficient distinction . . . to hold any position of responsibility'. Matthew coveted the title of Groom of the Privy Chamber or Gentleman Usher. Charles explained that his previous dismissal from the Surveyor Generalship of Crown Lands in Upper Canada had been investigated by Lord Castlereagh and proved to be in no way damaging to his professional reputation (*ibid.* f. 107, January 1814). Philip later claimed that his father had intended to take him into partnership, he 'being the only one of his sons whom he educated properly for that profession' (Liverpool Papers, lxxvi, B.M. Add. MS. 38265, f. 193, 24 March 1817).

[7] 'My sufferings are beyond what I can describe. . . . The transition of my situation almost deprives me of my understanding. . . . Oh what a shocking reverse . . . my fate is hard indeed' (B.M. Add. MS. 38259, f. 269, 19 September 1814 and 38260, f. 289, 7 December 1814). Rachel Wyatt's pension was worth £100 per annum nett (Liverpool Papers lxxi, B.M. Add. MS. 38260, f. 290, 13 December 1814). After her death in 1817 Philip Wyatt unsuccessfully laid claim to its reversion on the grounds that he was 'left inconsolable and without a house or any present employment' (Liverpool Papers, lxxvi, B.M. Add. MS. 38265, f. 194, 24 March 1817).

influence.[1] Smirke believed Soane most likely to succeed to the inheritance, 'he being employed by Lord Liverpool and indefatigable in pursuing any object he had in view'.[2] But Soane was more than a little worried by rumours of Nash's inordinate influence at Court, his lavish hospitality at East Cowes Castle, his responsibility for work at Carlton House and Windsor. Two of Soane's correspondents stimulated his worst fears. 'Pray is it true', wrote Richard Burdon, 'that Mr. N. is the P–'s right hand man?'.[3] 'Who would cast a thought', wrote James Spiller, 'upon the marshes of Lambeth [Nash's birthplace] amidst the Circean voluptuousness of the Isle of Wight? Oh you must have observed how much is done by gratifying animal propensities, the lovers of good eating and drinking will be found to constitute a very large majority in the Pig Sty and the Palace . . .; I have heard of such gourmandising and drenching that the recital has created a vertigo; whence came the original supplies I wonder, and by what means are architectural compositions prepared under a sick headache?'.[4] Soane could never match Nash's hospitality; nevertheless he himself was not ungifted in what he called the 'art of puffing'.

Another candidate was Richard Wharton (1764–1828), joint Secretary to the Treasury, who aspired to the Surveyor Generalship as a safe non-parliamentary office with a good salary.[5] But he ultimately renounced his claims to it, probably because he found that he could not obtain a grant of it for life.[6]

In the event, no appointment was made to the vacant post. But, at the personal behest of the Prince Regent, responsibility for all the royal palaces was given to Nash, pending a Treasury decision as to 'what arrangements it may be expedient to adopt in the Office of Works in consequence of the report of the Commissioners specially appointed to inquire into the State of this Office'.[7] In this way Nash enjoyed for a few months the status of acting Surveyor General, but the day to day business of the Office devolved on C. A. Craig, who for fifteen months conducted its affairs with an efficiency and decorum that had rarely been known since the days of Sir William Chambers. Meticulous care was taken of official drawings;[8] in financial matters the prescribed routine was followed to the letter;[9] and in March 1814 a General Survey was held with due formality.[10] But it was now too late to avert the consequences of Wyatt's mismanagement. As Jeffry Wyatt later admitted, his uncle's 'neglect [had] destroyed the Office of Works as it was'.[11] What form the Office was to take in the future the government had yet to decide.

[1] Liverpool Papers, cccv, B.M. Add. MS. 38568, ff. 224–5, 7 July 1814. Liverpool replied that Richmond's advocacy came too late, besides which his protégé was 'new in the profession' and scarcely helped by his father's reputation.　　[2] Farington, p. 6397, 18 September 1813.

[3] Bolton, *op. cit.* p. 202, 18 May 1814.　　[4] *Ibid.* p. 196, 13 March 1814.

[5] Lonsdale MSS., Cumberland and Westmorland Record Office, Carlisle, Lord Lowther to Lord Lonsdale, 2 October 1813; C. Long to Lord Lonsdale, 2 December 1813. In March 1814 there was mention of appointing Wharton to the Office of Woods (*ibid.* 21 March 1814). See also *Letters of George IV*, ed. A. Aspinall (1938) i, p. 303, C. Arbuthnot to J. McMahon, 5 October 1813.

[6] His having 'formally declined' the post is announced in Lord Liverpool's letter to the Regent, 31 August 1814 (B.M. Add. MS. 38259, ff. 67–8).

[7] Works 4/21, 4 October 1813.　　[8] Works 4/21, 6 May 1814.

[9] In August 1814 Craig made a special visit to the Audit Office in Somerset House in order to attest on oath the sums he had received by way of imprest for works at the Marshalsea and King's Bench Prisons (Works 4/21, 15 and 22 April 1814). This was in conformity with the Act of 46 G. III c. 141 s. 8 requiring 'all Persons accountable for Public Monies' to attest their accounts on oath before a Baron of the Exchequer, or one of the Commissioners of Audit.

[10] Works 4/21, 11 March 1814.　　[11] *1828 Report*, p. 99.

Chapter V

THE NEW OFFICE OF WORKS: STEPHENSON AND HIS STAFF

DRAMATIC though Wyatt's death was, it did not immediately clear the way for changes on the lines recommended by the Commissioners of Military Inquiry. That could only be accomplished by legislation. The act passed in July 1814 (54 George III c. 157), 'for the better Regulation of the conduct of the Business of the Office of Works and Expedition thereof', modified in some respects the Commissioners' suggestions. Though any 'fit and proper person' might become Surveyor General, at a salary of not more than £1500 per annum, it was clear that there was no intention to appoint an architect.[1] A professional man was to hold the post of Assistant Surveyor and Cashier;[2] and not more than three other 'Architects attached to the Office of Works' were to assist the Surveyor General in 'preparing Plans, Estimates, working Drawings and Reports, and also in making surveys, inspecting workmen, and superintending the execution of contracts'. The appointment of Nash, Soane and Smirke as 'attached architects' had already been decided upon.[3] When introducing the bill, Nicholas Vansittart, Chancellor of the Exchequer, claimed that this would enable government to dispense with 'many officers who were now employed to superintend particular buildings . . . and a considerable saving would accrue to the public'; but events did not justify his optimism.[4] The 'attached architects' were not to be debarred from private practice; and the same concession was, by an amendment to the bill, extended to Clerks of the Works and Labourers in Trust, provided this did 'not interfere with the due and faithful execution of their duties'. All others serving in the Office were forbidden to engage directly or indirectly in business as architects,

---

[1] The Commissioners had stated: 'We do not see that any advantage would be gained by appointing an Architect or Surveyor by profession, to this Office'; but if such were appointed he should give up all private practice (*1813 Report*, p. 46). See also Vansittart's speech introducing the bill, 29 June (*Parl. Deb.* xxviii, 419).

[2] It is not clear why the Commissioners' proposal that the Surveyor General should be the accountant was not adopted.

[3] B.M. Add. MS. 38568, f. 224, Liverpool to Duke of Richmond, January 1814.

[4] *Parl. Deb.* xxviii, 419 ff., 29 June 1814. Subsequently the new arrangements came under fire from Brougham, who was out of Parliament in 1814. Speaking to Althorp's motion for a committee on the public offices, 7 May 1816, he remarked on the 'little revolution' in the Office of Works, which increased salaries and new posts. 'A new office was created, too, for what were called the three attached architects. What the meaning of attached architects was, he did not pretend to know; he supposed it has one meaning, that the individuals were cordially attached to their salaries. . . . There were five Clerks of the Works, with salaries amounting to £1600; 12 labourers in trust (another official term which baffled his comprehension), with a salary of £100 p.a. each. Ignorant as he was of the arcana of Office, he could not be expected to understand the nature of the service performed by those persons, which rendered them necessary; but he knew that more offices were created by the new arrangement than what had subsisted under the old' (*Parl. Deb.* xxxiv, 327–8).

I

builders or contractors. The taking by officers of any perquisite or fee (except the professional commission for private practice) was forbidden on pain of dismissal. The Treasury obtained full power to change the Office establishment and superannuate any officers; and was to formulate a code of instructions for the conduct of business and the regulation of expenditure in the Office of Works, conformably to the intent of the Regulating Act of 1782. These instructions, to be laid before Parliament, might be altered by the Treasury, subject to parliamentary consent.

The bill had an easy passage, the old system being generally condemned. The current preparations in the Parks for victory celebrations were seized on to demonstrate the need for reform.[1] The chief opposition spokesman, George Tierney, hoped the reform would 'serve as an effectual check to all those embryo palaces and villas that, as he understood, were about to start up'. Henry Bankes,[2] who always spoke on such questions, insisted on the need for the House of Commons to control building expenditure by means of previous estimates.[3]

Armed with its new powers, the Treasury on 13 September 1814 announced that it intended 'very shortly' to review the whole establishment, and warned Craig as acting head of the Office not to fill any vacancies.[4] Liverpool had already declared to the Regent that 'no consideration but that of the competency of the Individual should have any Influence in the appointment—and that it is quite essential likewise that the Individual who is selected for it should not only be capable of performing correctly the duties of the Situation but should be known to Parliament and the Public as a Person tried and approved in [some][5] other important stations'.[6] The man now recommended was the effective head of the King's Household at Windsor, Benjamin Charles Stephenson (*c.* 1766–1839).[7] Like so many of the men of business in the service of the later Hanoverians, he was a soldier by profession. But as one of the Commissioners of Military Inquiry, he was already conversant with the affairs of the Office of Works. As its administrative head, he was to prove in many respects an excellent Treasury watch-dog, displaying the 'unfailing zeal, perfect disinterestedness, and spotless integrity' referred to in a laudatory obituary.[8] Nevertheless, the appointment of this 'amiable man' as Surveyor General came as a surprise.[9]

On 3 October 1814 the Treasury directed Stephenson temporarily 'to conduct the current business of the Office of Works according to the instructions now in force and give such directions to the present officers of that establishment' as he might think

[1] *Ibid.* xxviii, 421.

[2] M.P. for Corfe Castle 1780–1826, Dorset 1826–31, d. 1834. He was for many years a vociferous critic of public works. A trustee of the British Museum and author of a *Civil and Constitutional History of Rome*, he was prejudiced and arrogant; and William Wilkins attacked his unmannerly conduct as an arbiter of taste in his *Letter to Lord Viscount Goderich* (1832). J. C. Herries declared, 16 September 1831, 'Old Bankes has never done anything but mischief in his life' (*Corr. of Charles Arbuthnot*, ed. A. Aspinall, Camden Soc. 3rd. ser. lxv., 1941, p. 144). Wraxall put his qualities in a more favourable light (*Memoirs* iv, p. 79).

[3] *Parl. Deb.* xxviii, 421. He was supported by Baring.

[4] Works 6/26, pp. 167v–8.   [5] In pencil.

[6] B.M. Add. MS. 38259, ff. 67–8, 31 August 1814.

[7] Entered Hanoverian service May 1788 as 2nd lt., 9 Lt. Drag.; 1796 transferred to English Army; 1803 Dep. Judge-Advocate, S.W. District; 1805 Capt. 46 Ft.; 1806–10, Groom of the Bechamber to the Duke of Cumberland; 1812 Comptroller of George III's household; 1814 Lt.-Col. in Hanoverian service; 1830 Major-Gen., K.C.H.; 1834 G.C.H.; *m.* 1805 Maria, da. of Sir Peter Rivers Gay, Bt.

[8] *Gent's. Mag.* 1839, ii, p. 317. Castlereagh, defending George III's establishment at Windsor, 4 February 1819, referred to 'Colonel Stephenson, to whose attention to economy, the gentlemen opposite him would do justice' (*Parl. Deb.* xxxix, 300).   [9] W. Wilkins, *Letter to Vct. Goderich* . . . (priv. printed 1832).

necessary.[1] He took up his duties on 7 October, but the new establishment as a whole did not come into effect until 6 April 1815. For some weeks Craig was allowed to conduct the ordinary office business while Stephenson mastered his new role.[2] On 11 November responsibility for the royal residences was transferred from Nash to Stephenson,[3] with the exception of the Royal Pavilion at Brighton which the Regent proposed to maintain from his Privy Purse.[4] Stephenson soon galvanised his department. Attendance, hitherto required only one day in the week,[5] was henceforth to be a daily duty. The Surveyor General himself, the Clerks of the Works were notified, would 'give daily attendance at the office (Sundays excepted)'. One member of his staff who did not accept the new régime with a good grace was Craig. When he obstructed an order to examine the accounts for the previous two quarters it was clear that he would have to go,[6] and in December 1814, after 39 years of service, he disappeared into retirement.[7] His place in the Office was taken by Robert Browne (1756–1827), with the title of Assistant Surveyor and Cashier.[8]

Stephenson then drew up interim regulations,[9] giving the Assistant Surveyor 'under the directions of the Surveyor-General . . . the superintendence and controul' over all officers and employees of the Office of Works 'in whatever may relate to the discharge of their respective public duties'. The Examiner was to continue to check the accounts and make them out for payment quarterly, assisted by the Resident Clerk, who was also to keep minute and letter books up-to-date and to file original papers. The office clerks were to continue their duties as before, and a messenger was to attend on weekdays from 11.00 a.m. to 4.00 p.m.

Permanent regulations for implementing the new Act were now essential. Soane and Smirke had taken an early interest in this question. Soane had obtained information on the procedure of the Barrack Board[10] and had asked James Spiller[11] to examine the new Regulating Act. In his memorandum of 16 September 1814,[12] Spiller noted that the Act had divided the business of the Office of Works into an 'internal' department under the Surveyor General and the Assistant Surveyor, handling the financial aspects, and an 'external' side in which the architect would be left with a free hand in the execution of works. The existing Clerks of the Works, he thought, should be subordinated to the architects, and primarily charged with measuring: ordinary clerks of works as found in private employ would also be necessary. Tradesmen might be appointed by the Board of Works, and should sign an agreement to

[1] Works 6/26, p. 172v; 4/21, p. 315.   [2] *Ibid.* p. 316.
[3] Works 6/26, pp. 172–4; Treasury minute, 11 November 1814 (Works 4/21, p. 327).
[4] Works 4/21, p. 381, 14 March 1815.
[5] Works 1/8, pp. 196–7.   [6] Works 6/27, p. 197.
[7] Works 4/21, p. 337. Craig complained to Farington 'about his having been removed from the Board of Works' after 39 years' service (Farington, p. 6896, 12 April 1816). He was, however, treated generously by the Treasury, who bestowed on him a pension of £220 ('the largest . . . which with reference to his length of service the law will allow'), plus a grant of £150 in respect of extra duties during the interregnum (Works 6/26, f. 211, 14 April 1815; Works 6/27, 17 April 1815; Works 4/21, 31 March, 15 April 1815).
[8] Works 4/21, p. 337. Browne, Clerk of the Works at Richmond and Kew since 1790, and son of another clerk of works in the Office, had applied to the Regent for appointment as one of the attached architects, and the Queen had described him to Lord Liverpool as 'very deserving of the King's good opinion and protection which he enjoyed in a high degree during many years' (B.M. Add. MS. 38252, f. 262). See above, p. 59.
[9] Works 4/21, p. 337.
[10] Soane Museum, Corr. 2, xii, F(1) 3.
[11] An unsuccessful architect who was employed by Soane to execute various commissions.
[12] Soane Museum, Corr. 2, xii, F(1) 4.

accept office rates and prices, and the valuation of the architect under whom they were employed. This would dispense with 'contracts in the gross, by competition'.[1] Smirke also sent Soane a memorandum on the most effectual manner of carrying the Act into execution.[2] On these bases was compiled a joint memorandum from Nash, Soane and Smirke.[3] Stephenson for his part had been engaged in discussions at least since 21 January 1815, when he and Browne 'had a long conversation respecting the future regulations for conducting the business of this Office' with George Harrison, Assistant Secretary of the Treasury.[4] Further conferences of officials, lawyers and ministers during February and March included one between Liverpool, Vansittart and Stephenson on 18 February.[5] Quite late in these proceedings it was decided to re-allocate various responsibilities between the Office of Works and that of Woods and Forests. A Treasury minute of 10 February proposed that the Office of Works should take over the maintenance of buildings in the parks and forests, and that the Woods and Forests should be responsible for roads and fences. The cost of the works carried out was, however, to be charged to the departments formerly responsible. The Commissioners of Woods and Forests agreed in principle, but thought the transfer should include the charges also.[6] The Treasury however declined to alter the financial arrangements. As most of the buildings concerned were privately occupied, it was perhaps thought that little expenditure would arise under the new regulations. Stephenson's final draft, in which the architects' views appear to have been taken into account, was closely followed in the code of instructions approved by the Treasury on 10 March 1815.[7]

This code provided that definition of the powers and responsibilities of officers which had been so lacking in the establishment of 1782,[8] and endeavoured to make Treasury control a reality. To this end, the Office of Works was removed from its dependence on the Lord Chamberlain and placed directly under the Treasury (art. iv), to which the Surveyor General was to apply for instructions 'in all cases of doubt or difficulty which may arise in the discharge of his official duties', and to which he was to report 'all such occurrences within his department as may appear to him necessary or proper for their information' (art. ix). Soane commented on his own copy, 'If so it may be presumed the Commissioners of Treasury will be fully occupied';[9] and Spiller, who examined the regulations for Soane, thought that the Treasury would soon be driven to rescind this article. The general survey of buildings was to form the basis of each year's activities: as the architects had suggested, only such repairs and alterations (save for accidental damage) as were then noted were to be undertaken, so that the year's expenditure would be limited to a predetermined sum. But two exceptions were allowed: works for the immediate convenience of the

---

[1] See pp. 161–2.   [2] Soane Museum, Corr. 2, xii, F(1) 5, dated 27 September 1814.
[3] T. 1/4378, f. 4109/15.
[4] For Harrison and his significance in the history of the Civil Service see J. R. Torrance, 'Sir George Harrison and the growth of bureaucracy in the early nineteenth century', *E.H.R.* lxxxiii (1968).
[5] Works 4/21, pp. 352, 367, 369, 377, 378.   [6] T. 1/4378, 17 February 1815.
[7] T. 1/4378. The principal differences were: longer time was allowed for the transmission of the various accounts; art. v: ten o'clock was substituted for eleven as the hour of opening the office; art. xiv: the attached architects were to be allowed a commission of 3% upon the cost of new works and major buildings, instead of a fixed payment; art. xlii: no near relation was to be employed by any officer on a building of which he was in charge.
[8] *1813 Report*, Hiort's and Saunders' evidence, pp. 109, 199.   [9] Soane Museum Pamphlets.

Queen or the Regent, and works approved by the Treasury. Stephenson's proposal for a discretionary allowance of £5000 for minor works was dropped (arts. xvi–xviii). Buildings in residential occupation were not to be repaired, unless to secure the structure, without express permission from the Treasury (art. xxi).

The Surveyor General was made the linch-pin, as the Inquiry Commissioners had recommended, with 'supreme controul and directing power over all persons, matters and things belonging to or connected with' the Office (art. vi), and power to suspend unsatisfactory subordinates, subject to Treasury decision (art. vii). He was frequently to inspect works in progress, and by a 'faithful and zealous discharge' of his duty, 'prevent all wasteful expenditure of public money, directing all his endeavours to establish throughout the Office of Works' the best 'system of management and economy' (art. viii). But his authority was 'subject always to such orders, directions and instructions, as he shall from time to time receive from the Commissioners of the Treasury'. In fact, as Stephenson told the Duke of Kent in 1815, his powers were 'circumscribed by the most positive rules and regulations'.[1] Henry Rowles[2] emphasized this aspect in his remarks to the 1828 Select Committee on the Office of Works:

> The Surveyor General has none of the important responsibility of his office put upon him; if any work is under consideration, he receives instructions from the Treasury, upon which he is to consult and report the opinion of those under him; if it be ordered to be executed, he is to consult others, and abide by their judgment as to the proper amount to be paid, without its being necessary that he should be himself qualified to judge or decide on so material a point; when it is to be paid for, the money is to be issued to his under officer, and that officer is to pay it away and to be accountable; thereby leaving the office of Surveyor General, from the beginning to the end, nothing but a registry of the deeds of others, a mere channel of communication.[3]

His authority, indeed, did not go beyond sanctioning an estimate of £50.[4] Even his exercise of the patronage of the Office, which the Inquiry Commissioners had proposed entrusting to him, was subject to Treasury control; and a nominee for any post in which professional knowledge might be required was to undergo a 'strict and satisfactory examination by the Assistant Surveyor and Attached Architects, in the presence of the Surveyor General', who was to report the result to the Treasury (art. xi). In practice, he seems to have been able to nominate the office clerks and to put forward suitable candidates for the professional posts.

Stephenson performed his duty with the utmost conscientiousness. In private amiable, his official *persona* appears to have been that of a martinet. His rigid and legalistic attitude may have been developed by his service in the Judge-Advocate-General's department and his experience as a Commissioner of Military Inquiry. The investigation into the Office of Works had shown the consequences of failure to observe regulations. But he appears to have lacked that touch in the handling of men which would enable him to maintain rules without friction, that ability to turn the

---

[1] Works 1/6, p. 231.
[2] Henry Holland's nephew, and sometime carpenter and joiner at the Mint (resigned 1818) (Works 1/9, pp. 161–2.) [3] *1828 Report*, p. 101. [4] Works 1/9, p. 437.

blind eye when occasion might demand it. In a private letter to Lord Liverpool in 1823 he declared: 'No part of my official Conduct has ever been influenced by any Motive, than that of endeavouring faithfully to discharge the Duties of my Situation; and I have the more zealously pursued this line of conduct, as the only means I had, of shewing my Gratitude, for the very flattering selection Your Lordship made of me, to fill the situation of Head of this Department'.[1] Liverpool acknowledged his assiduity, writing to Arbuthnot[2] that, 'as at the head of the Treasury, I would undertake things with him as the instrument which I should have great difficulty in undertaking with any person in whom I could not have the same confidence'.[3] To Peel he wrote: 'I conscientiously believe him better qualified for it [the Surveyor General-ship] than any other man in the Kingdom'.[4]

The high estimation in which Liverpool held Stephenson was shown in October 1823, when by a 'great error of judgement' the new Surveyor General incurred the King's wrath.[5] Finding a pulpit removed from the King's private chapel in Windsor Great Park to the Castle, Stephenson had reprimanded the tradesman responsible, ignorant that the original order came from the King himself. Liverpool believed that Mash of the Lord Chamberlain's Office (responsible for the internal arrangements of the palaces) had seized the opportunity to bring about Stephenson's dismissal. 'The King has', wrote George IV, 'had so many difficulties with this Colonel Stevenson, of a similar description, that it is impossible to go on, and the King there-fore desires that Lord Liverpool, will immediately place the Board of Works, on a different footing, and that Colonel Stevenson be removed'.[6] Liverpool at once promised to consider 'what new arrangement can be made for conducting the business of the Board of Works in a way most advantageous to your Majesty's service, and most agreable to your Majesty',[7] but at the same time swung into action to save 'so valuable a servant of the Government'.[8]

To Arbuthnot he wrote, 'The first point is to save Stephenson if possible; he will be a severe loss to us, and I am quite sure with the King's projects as to Windsor Castle he will be a great loss to him, as it will be difficult if not impossible to replace him with any person equally conversant in the business, and in whom the Treasury have equal confidence'.[9] Though the King had explicitly refused to accept any apology, Liverpool asked Peel (who was in London) to urge Stephenson to make one, and to seek Sir Charles Long's assistance in appeasing the royal wrath.[10] Stephenson's obsequious letter to Liverpool was clearly intended to be shown to the King.[11] In forwarding it, Liverpool begged George IV to 'overlook what has passed'. Consciously magnanimous, the King agreed, but commented: 'If bare Honesty, is to get rid of all

[1] B.M. Add. MS. 38576, f. 17, 21 October 1823.
[2] 1767–1850; joint secretary of the Treasury, 1809–23; First Commissioner of Woods and Forests, 1823–7 and January–June 1828; Chancellor of the Duchy of Lancaster, 1828–30
[3] *Correspondence of C. Arbuthnot*, ed. A. Aspinall, Camden Soc. 3rd ser. xv (1941), p. 61.
[4] *Ibid.* p. 60.   [5] *Ibid.*
[6] *Ibid.* p. 59, 17 October 1823; B.M. Add. MS. 38576, ff. 13 ff. Stephenson's rigid insistence on protocol had been illustrated in the previous July, doubtless to the annoyance of the King and the household officers, when he had refused to act upon a statement of the King's wishes respecting St. James's Palace without the formal authority of the Lord Chamberlain (B.M. Add. MS. 38295, ff. 310–313).
[7] *Letters of George IV*, ed. Aspinall, iii, p. 28.
[8] *Correspondence of C. Arbuthnot*, p. 59   [9] *Ibid.* p. 61, 21 October 1823.
[10] *Ibid.* p. 60.   [11] *Letters of George IV*, ed. Aspinall, iii, pp. 30–1.

those Rules of conduct, which form the Duties of civilized Life, there is an end of everything'. The reorganisation of the Office should be put into the hands of Arbuthnot, 'who will be likely to put it, on a good footing'.[1] In a holograph memorandum of the same date he remarked: 'The King has had so many Instances of this Gentleman's improper conduct that it will be well, that Lord Liverpool should impress upon him, humility and obedience.'[2] Assuring the King that he would 'lose no time in endeavouring in conjunction with Mr. Arbuthnot . . . to make such Arrangements as to the Conduct of the Business of the Board of Works, as may relieve Your Majesty from any further Inconvenience or Trouble',[3] Liverpool urged the reprieved Surveyor-General to observe

> the greatest caution and delicacy as to the Mode of conducting the Business of your Department, particularly with respect to those Palaces in which H.M. actually Resides.
>
> I have always felt that there was the greatest possible Distinction between those Palaces which became Royal Residences and those in which the King did not Reside—and this Distinction becomes more Important when a King happens to have a Personal Taste and Pleasure in making His own Arrangements and giving His own Orders.
>
> For whatever the Strict legal Etiquette of Office may be, no one would like to be subject to all the Inconveniences of it in the Daily occurrences of his private life.[4]

Stephenson's zeal for the public service involved him in difficulties with his subordinates, too. John William Hiort, who had entered the Office in 1793, and who since 1814 had been head of the indoor office staff as Chief Examining Clerk, was the inventor of a patent curved brick for lining flues to prevent smoking chimneys. Nash wished to use these in Buckingham Palace, but Hiort, doubtful whether he might legitimately supply them under article xli of the Treasury Instructions, applied for Treasury sanction, which was readily granted.[5] But Stephenson nevertheless urged Hiort to give up his patent. Reviewing the report of the 1828 Select Committee he remarked to the Treasury on this point: 'there appears full cause for strongly recommending that no similar exception be allowed in future'.[6] Shortly afterwards, Hiort wrote to the Surveyor General complaining of 'the accumulated annoyances', 'perpetually exercised' towards him in the past two years.[7] 'By almost imperceptible degrees' Stephenson had deprived him of all his importance; in effect he had been

---

[1] B.M. Add. MS. 38564, f. 118, 23 October 1823. Mrs. Arbuthnot wrote in her journal for 24 October 1823, 'Mr. Arbuthnot has succeeded in pacifying the King, & Col. Stevenson, having made a humble apology, is forgiven. I believe it has been done by Knighton [the king's private secretary], to whom Mr. Arbuthnot wrote remarking that the dismissal of Col. Stevenson might impede the King's improvements, &c, at Windsor' (*Jnl. of Mrs. Arbuthnot, 1820–1832*, ed. F. Bamford and the Duke of Wellington, i, p. 267). Greville refers to the King's subsequent ill-humour with the Duke of York as a consequence of this affair: 'Stephenson is a friend and servant of the Duke's, and in his ill-humour he [the King] tried to revenge himself upon the Duke as well as on Stephenson and he thwarted the Duke in his military arrangements' (*Greville Memoirs*, ed. L. Strachey and R. Fulford, 1938 i, p. 151).
[2] B.M. Add. MS. 38564, f. 120.
[3] B.M. Add. MS. 38576, f. 19, 23 October 1823. Printed (modern punctuation), *Letters of George IV*, ed. Aspinall, iii, p. 34.
[4] B.M. Add. MS. 38576, ff. 20–1, 23 October 1823.
[5] Their use was also permitted in other government works, e.g. Smirke's new General Post Office (Works 1/14, pp. 23, 52), and Poynter's St. Katharine's Hospital (Works 1/14, p. 524).
[6] Works 1/17, p. 58.   [7] *Ibid.* pp. 69–72, 19 December 1828.

suspended from performing his official functions.[1] Forty-two years' experience gave him a judgement in the details of his duty 'somewhat preferable to that of any Person of recent appointment'.

In reply Stephenson suggested Hiort should appeal to the Treasury. He denied wishing to diminish Hiort's role, but 'in the future discharge of these Duties I must require a more regular attendance, than you have for some time past bestowed upon them, as it is from the want of this proper attendance on your part I must in a great measure attribute the present accumulated arrear of unexamined Accounts in this Office'.[2] Hiort retorted that it was not his place to make a report to the Treasury. He would clear off arrears of business if the clerks were allowed to return to their duties as he had arranged them, and such additional aid as the Assistant Surveyor might think necessary was obtained. His own short absences were made up by working late. But as for the root cause of dispute, he would neither relinquish his patent nor surrender his office until he was 'absolutely unfit for Service'.[3] Stephenson declined to allow any arrangements to be made without his previous approval; Hiort was to confine his services 'to those exclusively belonging to the situation of Chief Examining Clerk'. After further irritated correspondence, Hiort on 31 December bowed to authority, recalling that his experience had materially assisted in arranging the existing system, and protesting his devotion to duty. Stephenson then prolonged these exchanges by again blaming Hiort for the arrears of unexamined accounts. Hiort, stung to self-defence, stated that no arrear existed in his individual duties but only in the 'operative branch',[4] the efficient strength of which, as he had repeatedly declared, was inadequate. The examining branch itself was operating less efficiently than if he had been allowed to 'regulate the occupation of the clerks in the various branches of the business, suited to their respective capacities, as was the case formerly'. Stephenson nevertheless maintained his opinion; and although it is hardly possible to say whose strictures were justified, the running of the office cannot have proceeded altogether smoothly after this quarrel.

Whereas the Inquiry Commissioners had proposed an effective Board of Works, consisting of the Surveyor General, with a veto, and two architects of eminence, the system adopted attached three architects to the Office of Works only in an executive and advisory capacity. The Inquiry Commissioners had expected them to perform, though on a part time basis, 'all those duties in the business put under the management of this Office, which are usually executed by Architects', for which they were to receive £500 per annum and two and a half per cent commission on new works. But the Treasury Instructions had confined them to 'affording, by their superior professional abilities, such assistance as may occasionally be required of them, *in making drawings, plans, designs, and elevations for any Public Buildings, which shall be executed under the direction of the Surveyor General of H.M.'s Works*'; to preparing estimates for such works; and to making specifications and working drawings to be

---

[1] As later emerged, Hiort particularly resented a minute of 31 July 1828: 'The Surveyor General desires in future, that all persons applying for copies of the office prices, or requiring information respecting the measurement of works or the mode of conducting any other parts of the business of this department may be referred in the first instance to himself or the Assistant Surveyor General who will direct the persons so applying being furnished with the necessary information' (Works 4/29, p. 117).

[2] Works 1/17, pp. 72–3, 20 December.

[3] *Ibid.* pp. 82–4, 26 December.   [4] Presumably the measuring of works.

laid before the Surveyor General.[1] In Spiller's opinion, this was to reduce the architects to a 'mere suit of superior clerks',[2] for the role assigned to them was indistinguishable from that of 'competent clerks in an Architect's office'. All necessary contracts were to be made by the Surveyor General. The architect was then to direct and generally to superintend the work, being responsible for its quality and for its execution in accordance with his designs; the Office of Works was to furnish whatever professional assistance might be required, measuring and checking the work, and making out, examining and paying the bills. The architects had in their joint memorandum stated it to be 'indispensable' that the Clerks of Works and Labourers in Trust should receive their directions from the architect executing a building; but this power was only granted so far as such directions did not conflict with regulations, or with instructions given by the Surveyor General or his assistant.[3]

Stephenson had proposed that in addition to their basic salaries of £500 the architects should be paid for designs for large works, 'such payments to be regulated according to the custom and usage of the profession in similar cases. But no remuneration to be made to the said Architects, for any Works, or Buildings, executed by them, upon the principle of a percentage, or commission, to be calculated upon the cost and expenses of the same'.[4] The Inquiry Commissioners' proposals were followed instead and the commission on new works was even increased to three per cent. Though this was two per cent less than the usual professional commission, the architect was relieved of some duties such as measuring and making up accounts, which normally formed part of his duties. Nash however was later to complain that this system, by taking the preparation of bills out of the hands of the architect, deprived him of control of expenditure, and that he could not, therefore, be held accountable for any exceeding of his estimates;[5] and Soane noted, 'Here, then, the Architects have no check over the making out the bills etc.'[6]

The canvassing that had taken place on James Wyatt's death was vainly renewed when the establishment of 'attached architects' was announced. In reply to one application, Lord Liverpool stated on 7 January 1814 that 'The Prince Regent is naturally desirous of employing his own architect Mr. Nash . . . and it has been settled to add Mr. Soane and Mr. Smirke as two of the architects of the more established character in the country'.[7] John Nash (1752–1835), eldest of the Attached Architects, was in many ways representative of older customs in the profession, in particular the combination of the roles of architect, builder and land developer. Having served as acting Surveyor General with control over the royal residences from 2 October 1813,[8] he clearly had a strong claim. John Soane (1753–1837), Professor of Architecture at the Royal Academy, Architect to the Bank of England, sometime Clerk of the Works for Westminster and Deputy Surveyor of the Woods and Forests, was another man with outstanding claims and powerful patronage, notably that of Lord Liverpool himself.[9] Robert Smirke (1780–1867), at thirty-three

---

[1] Art. xxii.   [2] Soane Museum memorandum.
[3] Nash at Carlton House in 1814–15 'found it impracticable to communicate my directions through the Clerk of the Works or Labourer in Trust, their other avocations allowing them very seldom to be there' (Works 6/27, p. 216).   [4] T. 1/4378.   [5] See pp. 160, 162, 171 below.
[6] Soane Museum, copy of Treasury instructions.
[7] B.M. Add. MS. 38568, f. 224, Liverpool to Duke of Richmond applying on behalf of B. Wyatt.
[8] T. 27/72, pp. 264, 500.   [9] Farington, p. 6397.

hardly more than half his colleagues' age, possessed less obvious claims. Through his father, an Academician, Smirke had become an intimate of Academy circles, gaining the particular friendship of Sir Thomas Lawrence, who went to considerable trouble to further his protégé's career.[1] Smirke built up a large country house practice which brought him an influential acquaintanceship including Lord Lonsdale,[2] the major borough patron among ministerialists, and Lord Bathurst,[3] who in 1807 as Master of the Mint had gratified Lonsdale by appointing Smirke architect to that department.[4]

The buildings under the care of the Office of Works were divided into three notional districts, each placed in the charge of one of these architects. Although in 1828 it was stated that there had been no intention of giving each a monopoly in his district,[5] such would appear to be the purport of article xxii of the Treasury Instructions:

> Any new buildings therefore, or any extraordinary additions to, or alterations or repairs of any existing buildings, wherein, from the nature or extent of them, or from their liability to affect the solidity or security of the building, particular architectural taste, or the judgment and skill of the Attached Architect may . . . be requisite or desirable, shall be referred by the Surveyor General to the Attached Architect in whose particular district it may be . . .

These districts were not strictly geographical divisions: Nash's was made up of St. James's Palace, Carlton House, the King's Mews, Kensington Palace and Gardens, St. James's Park, the Green Park, Hyde Park, and Windsor Great Park. Soane received the Queen's Palace (Buckingham House), the buildings in Whitehall and Westminster including the Houses of Parliament, Hampton Court and Bushy Park. To Smirke were allotted Windsor Castle, Greenwich Park, Somerset House, the Tower of London, the Mint, the Rolls House and Chapel, the King's Bench, Fleet and Marshalsea Prisons, and the British Museum.

The architects were to act only upon the instructions of the Surveyor General, not even being allowed to make surveys of the buildings in their districts without his authority, and were to have no control over any of the Office of Works personnel except when employed by the Surveyor General in superintending works. They were expected 'at all times to attend the Surveyor General whenever he may require their assistance in making drawings, plans and estimates, in the settlement of prices for building materials and workmanship, in making surveys; and on all occasions when their professional abilities are required, to assist the Surveyor General in the discharge of his duty'.[6] The direction of the Attached Architects was not the easiest of Stephenson's tasks. Though clearly subordinated to him by the Treasury Instructions, they were only part-time servants of the public, men of importance in their own right with direct access to sources of influence.

---

[1] Farington, p. 6395–6.
[2] Lonsdale's son and heir, Lowther, was a member of the Treasury Board which signed the Code of Instructions.
[3] (1762–1834); third Earl; Sec. of State for War and Colonies, etc.
[4] Farington, p. 3765–7. For a summary of Smirke's career see J. Mordaunt Crook, *The British Museum* (1972), chap. iii.
[5] *1828 Report*, pp. 13–14.   [6] Treasury Instructions, art. xlvii.

Nash, good-natured but unmethodical, often ran foul of Stephenson, impervious in his rectitude; and relations between them appear to have been uneasy almost from the start of the new establishment. Smirke was careful and accurate, Soane was difficult to fault and ready to defend himself waspishly if criticized, but Nash's carelessness for official forms constantly laid him open to the Surveyor General's rebuke. 'Having been informed (Stephenson wrote in June 1816) that directions were given by you for making a Doorway through the East Front of the Great Lodge in Windsor Park, I have to request you will inform me by what Authority such Directions were given, and why the same was not communicated to this Office, or to the Clerk of the Works at Windsor who is in charge of that building'.[1] Thirteen days later Nash replied that he 'conceived the Prince Regent's commands were sufficient' to justify his ordering the alterations. The Surveyor General retorted:

> I have to acknowledge the receipt of your Letter of this Day, but as it contains an Answer to only one part of mine to you of the 25th Ultimo; I must again request you will inform me, why the Commands of his Royal Highness the Prince Regent respecting the making of a new Doorway through the East Front of Cumberland Lodge were not communicated to this Office; that the work might have been done in a regular manner, and not occasion Bills being hereafter brought forward that have not a proper Authority to justify their being admitted into the Accounts of this Department—I must beg leave particularly to request your Attention to the Treasury Instructions for the Regulation and Conduct of this Office in whatever may regard his Majesty's Buildings within your District, as it is one of my principal Duties to see that they are strictly attended to, by every Person belonging to the Department.[2]

Nash then called at the office 'to explain further his reasons for directing the alteration being made without sending to Mr. Matthew'[3]—so they remain unknown to us.

They were soon at it again. A few weeks later the Surveyor General wrote to Nash:

> I was very much surprized to find that one of your Private Clerks had been at Carlton House, making Inquiries and giving Directions respecting Works belonging to that Building, an Interference with the Business of this Department, which I cannot allow. And I must therefore most positively request that you will in future confine all directions you may have to give respecting that Building or any other belonging to your District, under this Department; to the regular Official Persons who are appointed to those Buildings, as this Department has suffered many serious Inconveniences, by allowing of these Irregularities.[4]

To this Nash replied in an equally high tone:

> I beg to state that it was Mr. Repton (united with me in business) and not a 'private Clerk' who I desired in my Absence to 'enquire' for *my Information* what the Workmen were doing at Carlton House.

[1] Works 1/7, p. 126, 25 June 1816.
[3] Clerk of the Works at Windsor.
[2] Works 1/7, p. 147; 4/22, p. 41.
[4] Works 1/7, p. 181, 28 July.

Mr. Repton confined himself to 'enquiries' and gave no directions whatever—but without enquiry I do not see how I could give the directions which the latter part of your Letter seems to allow—but I will attend the Office on Tuesday for the explanation of that power which it seems I have not clearly understood.[1]

Misunderstandings continued. When Nash reported that the Prince Regent wished only necessary repairs to be done at Carlton House, 'the sum intended to be laid out in more substantial repairs, to be reserved in aid of a general reparation and arrangement of plan'[2], Stephenson replied,

> by the Act of the 56th of the King cap. 46 for the better Regulation of the Civil List, it is placed out of my power to make a reservation of Money for the Alterations and Repairs to any of the Royal Palaces beyond the year; and this I thought to have very fully explained, when I last had the pleasure of seeing you upon the subject of the Repairs, and Alterations which might be required at Carlton House.[3]

In comparison with his colleagues, Nash accordingly bulks large in the official correspondence with the Surveyor General. But if the other architects were on better terms with authority, they were not necessarily on good terms with each other. Friction between Soane and Smirke went back to the few unhappy months which the latter had spent as a pupil in Soane's office in 1796, and had been renewed in 1810 by a public criticism of Smirke's Covent Garden Theatre made by Soane in his lectures as Professor of Architecture at the Royal Academy. Soane's relations with Nash were equally uneasy. In November 1821 Nash remarked to Farington on Soane's 'temper being irritable'.[4] Four months earlier Soane had been in a fever of rage and anxiety at the news that he was to be superseded by Nash as the architect of the King's new palace at Buckingham House.[5] A bantering letter from his successful rival cannot have done much to assuage his jealousy:

> Brother Soane [Nash wrote from Cowes],
> You was in a miff when I saw you at the head of Your Masons. One of the Masonic rules, I am told, is to acquire a meek and humble spirit. I fear therefore You are not qualified for Grand Master. Now, if You will but come here and copy me for a month, You will certainly be appointed to a higher niche in Your Lodge when You next meet, and see poor Bloomfield[6] with kinder aspect than You were wont to do, and do penance for the hard thoughts You expressed of him. He is as innocent of the crime You imputed to him, as You are of *any* crime . . . . When I left You—musing upon Your wild-goose chase of Bloomfield—it occurred to me that our appointments are perfectly Constitutional, I, the King, You, the Lords, and *Your* friend Smirke, the Commons, and the blood instantly rushed to my face seeing, or fancying that You wanted to dethrone me. It then struck me that You wanted to be both King and Lords, and in fancy I heard You cry out 'Off with his head, so much for *Buckingham*'[7], and I sighed 'why should he so long for my empty chair when a few years would give him that without offense which has occasioned in him so offensive an act', for I am old, but feeling my head on my shoulders I marched off to Buckingham House . . . .[8]

[1] Works 1/7, p. 188.   [2] *Ibid.* p. 417, 29 December 1816.
[3] *Ibid.* p.419, 13 January 1817.   [4] Farington, p. 8080.
[5] See his much-altered drafts to Stephenson, Soane Mus. Corr. 2 xii, G(2) f. 6.
[6] The King's private secretary, who had informed Stephenson of Soane's supercession.
[7] In reference to the re-allocation of Buckingham House.
[8] Soane Mus. Corresp., printed by A. T. Bolton, *Portrait of Sir John Soane* (1927), p. 351.

Although each had a monopoly of major works in his own district, on other matters their common opinion might be sought, or the views of one referred to the others. Thus Nash's incidental charges for the celebrations in the Parks in 1814 were referred to Soane and Smirke;[1] the pricing of labour on the Marble Arch was referred, at Nash's request, to his colleagues;[2] the problem whether the Custom House contract was still effectual was referred to them generally;[3] and Nash's proposal to build the new Royal Mews by a contract in gross was considered by them and the Assistant Surveyor before being reluctantly assented to.[4]

Stephenson's principal subordinate was Robert Browne, who as Assistant Surveyor was intended to supply the professional knowledge necessarily lacking in a superior chosen for administrative rather than architectural ability. As a creative architect Browne was a nonentity. But his long experience of public works made him a useful subordinate. He was required to attend all meetings of the Clerks of the Works, to assist in regulating the official prices for building materials and workmanship, to inspect and give his opinion on all plans and estimates, and generally to supervise the work of the Office (art. xlvi). His salary was £1000 per annum. The indoors office staff was to consist of a Chief Examining Clerk, 'Master of the Building Profession in all its branches', who would supervise the assistant clerks and examine all measurements and accounts (art. 1). John William Hiort, who was so appointed at a salary of £500 per annum, had been Resident Clerk since 1805. He had worked privately for Vansittart and Arbuthnot.[5] Under Hiort was a Drawing and Measuring Clerk at £350 per annum. He was required to 'understand the building profession, and be capable of making fair and accurate architectural drawings'. He was also to help with the accounts (art. li). This post was given to John Spence, junior (d. 1825), son of the office-keeper, in the service as a clerk since 1796. He was assisted by two Measuring Clerks, George Russell (1790–1828) and George Davis (d. 1823), at £300 and £250 per annum respectively. They had to 'understand measuring and making up all Building Accounts'. When not making actual measurements of works, they were to be in daily attendance at the office with the other clerks, from 10 to 4 o'clock, or longer if the pressure of business required it (art. lii). Russell, who had joined the Office in 1807, was a sick man; abroad for his health from May 1814 to July 1815, his work was executed by a deputy, Timothy Bligh.[6] Again ill from January to July 1817, he had to pay 2 guineas a week for a substitute.[7] In January 1822 he was allowed to retire after the Surveyor General had reported that 'he has long appeared to me, inadequate from his infirmities to discharge the duties of his employment'.[8] Davis was engaged in February 1815 as an extra clerk, and recommended for the established post in May.[9] William Leckenby was appointed First Copying Clerk (£200 per annum), assisted by John Oliver French (£150 per annum);[10] both joined the office in April 1815[11]. Professional experience was not required of these subordinate clerks, but they had to 'understand accounts, and write a

[1] Works 6/26, pp. 233–6; Soane Mus. Corr. 2 xii, H(2).
[2] Works 4/29, p. 144.   [3] Works 4/24, p. 414; Soane Mus. Corr. 2 xii, C.
[4] Works 1/15, p. 486. See p. 303 below.   [5] Colvin, *Dictionary*, p. 288
[6] Works 5/107; Works 4/21, pp. 189, 266.   [7] Works 4/22, pp. 248, 335.
[8] Works 1/11, pp. 49–50.   [9] Works 5/107; 4/21, p. 431.
[10] Works 22/2/3.   [11] Works 5/107.

fair and expeditious hand' (art. liii). The office staff was completed by an office keeper, John Spence, senior (d. 1825), and a messenger, John Tempany (d. 1849). Temporary staff were employed from time to time at the Surveyor General's discretion.[1]

The outdoor staff, in addition to the architects, consisted of Clerks of the Works (£300 per annum), Labourers in Trust (£100 per annum), an inspector of engines (£40 per annum), turncocks at Windsor and Kensington (£50 per annum), and a plumber for the pipes and conduits at Hampton Court (£150 per annum).

The traditional title of Clerk of the Works was retained for the men in immediate charge of the various palaces and public buildings, though as Browne, Hiort and Yenn had pointed out to the Inquiry Commissioners, their duties were more extensive than that title suggested. Henry Rowles told the 1828 Select Committee that 'Government require in those offices all the information of an architect, and such professional gentlemen used formerly to hold those offices, and it was not derogatory to them to do so'.[2] The Treasury Instructions (art. xlviii) stated they were 'at present to be persons brought up as Architects or Surveyors, and sufficiently masters of their profession to be capable of conducting any building or work which may be committed to their care or inspection'. The Clerks of the Works' duties were essentially to superintend routine maintenance, inspecting the work in their departments, measuring and making up the accounts,

> to check the accounts of all day time, quantities and weight of goods and materials delivered, and of those returned as kept by their Labourers in Trust, to attend at the Office one day in each week . . . to lay before the Surveyor General . . . estimates of such works as may be ordered to be done in their several departments; to make up their accounts quarterly, and to deliver the same, within 15 days after each quarterly day, to the Chief Examining Clerk, with all measuring books, abstracts, and every other voucher or document that may be required . . . and . . . to attend the Surveyor General and his Assistant while passing the same.

As well as being responsible for bringing forward all their accounts every quarter for examination and settlement, the Clerks were to prevent alterations or repairs being carried out without proper authority and to ensure that official regulations were 'strictly, punctually and promptly obeyed in every particular'. They were allowed to carry on private practice, so long as it did not interfere with their official duties. This privilege was liable to abuse. Although the Clerks' duties were not consistently burdensome, as much could legitimately be left to their Labourers in Trust, yet delegation of functions could be carried to the point of neglect.

Five such officers were appointed, all from the old establishment. Charles Bacon (*c.* 1784–1818), in charge of the Whitehall and Westminster districts, with St. James's Palace and the King's Mews, had been trained as an architect under J. T. Groves, whom he succeeded as Clerk of the Works in 1811, after six years as Labourer in Trust at the Speaker's House. The addition in 1815 of the Mews to his department brought him an additional personal allowance of £100 per annum. Bacon told the Inquiry Commissioners that his duties did not leave him much time for private

---

[1] See below p. 126.   [2] p. 102.

practice.[1] The same point had been emphasized in his evidence by John Yenn (1750–1821), who retained his old charge as Clerk of the Works for Kensington and the Queen's Palaces, Carlton House and Hyde and St. James's Parks. Yenn was a pupil of Chambers, who had brought him into the Office of Works in 1774, and he had come to manage much of Chambers' business, later succeeding him as Treasurer of the Royal Academy. He was also Surveyor of Greenwich Hospital, and had been employed privately by George III at Windsor and at the Queen's Palace.[2] In December 1815 Farington thought Yenn was 'manifestly declining and that he could not live long';[3] six months later the Duke of Kent complained of his 'lethargy and hatred of trouble';[4] and in July 1817 Stephenson wrote that a vacancy in the clerkship at Kensington 'cannot be very distant'; but not till August 1819 did Yenn seek to retire.[5]

Another pupil of Chambers, Thomas Hardwick (1752–1829), had since 1810 superintended Hampton Court, Bushy Park and Longford River; to this was now added Browne's former charge at Richmond and Kew. Unlike his colleagues, Hardwick conducted an extensive private practice. He did not regularly occupy his official house at Hampton Court, and it is not altogether surprising to find that he was subsequently criticised for negligence.[6] Edward Crocker (*c.* 1757–1836), Clerk of Works at the Tower of London, also carried on a private practice. In 1818 he succeeded Bacon in the Westminster and Whitehall district. William Matthew, in charge of the Windsor district, alone of the Clerks had not received a formal architectural training. Apprenticed to a carpenter and builder, he then served for twelve years as clerk of the works in the Ordnance Department at the Tower and in 1806 was particularly recommended by James Wyatt to George III for the Windsor post. There he was to remain until 1832. He was 'under an express obligation to abandon all private business, and received a special promise of consideration for the future, as an inducement to accept his situation'.[7]

Clearly much depended on the efficiency of the Clerks of the Works, and Stephenson was somewhat handicapped by the personnel he had had to take over. New broom that he was, he could not sweep out the old staff entirely. To have removed men like Hardwick and Yenn from their posts would have been to arouse greater hostility in an architectural profession already critical of his own appointment as that of a non-professional man; nor was government anxious to add to its list of superannuations. But for Stephenson the situation must have been irksome. For four years he had to put up with the lethargic Yenn, whom he longed to replace by Kidd, the energetic Surveyor to the Horse Guards, 'whose professional abilities, and general steadiness, and activity of character, makes it an object of great importance to have placed in that particular district'; and he reiterated his desire to put such a 'very efficient man, in a situation where firmness and active professional abilities are very much required'.[8] The problem of men growing old in office and reluctant to retire

---

[1] He was County Surveyor for Middlesex (*1813 Report*, p. 114). See above, p. 71.
[2] *1813 Report*, p. 128. See above, p. 43.
[3] Farington, p. 6816.   [4] Works 19/16/1, f. 29.
[5] T. 1/1642, f. 13561; Works 1/9, p. 440. In December 1819 his ill-health and consequent lack of attention to his duty were blamed for some private accounts being charged with public accounts in his tradesmen's bills (Works 1/9, p. 519).
[6] Works 1/11, p. 176. See p. 120.   [7] T. 1/4378.   [8] T. 1/1642, f. 13561.

on small pensions was serious at a time when there was no age of compulsory retirement. Edward Crocker was another who, like Yenn, retained his post too long. Even in 1825 he had tended to leave matters to the Labourer in Trust, but he did not retire until the end of 1829, when he was in his seventy-second year.[1] Nevertheless, Stephenson endeavoured to make the Office as efficient as possible. He introduced an improved form for the Clerks' weekly estimates, giving a total for each major repair, instead of dividing the whole estimate under the heads of the various trades. The Clerks were to certify that estimates had been 'properly calculated and that the repairs and labour therein stated are all actually necessary and shall be done at the places and for the purposes as above specified and at and for no other'.[2] Before presenting his accounts for the Christmas quarter 1814, each Clerk was to enter a declaration upon the title page of each book of accounts that 'there are no bills or demands whatsoever due or outstanding for work done or materials supplied . . . which have not been included in my accounts'.[3]

In general, the success of this system depended on vigilance and a high attention to duty all along the line. If the Labourers in Trust neglected theirs, the tradesmen could make excessive charges for day work and even for materials. The Clerks of Works were even more important. Neglect on their part allowed the Labourers in Trust to scamp their own duties, and the tradesmen might have almost a free hand, making the estimates, carrying out the work unsupervised, and submitting exaggerated accounts hard to controvert. Their vigilant eye was required at almost every stage. The Surveyor General explained excess expenditure on a house in New Palace Yard, Westminster, by the 'neglect of the Clerk of the Works in not having sufficiently examined this building, and provided a reasonable sum to meet what are called unforeseen circumstances', which if not anticipated should at least have been reported as they occurred.[4] The day to day repairs which were in the hands of the Clerks of the Works could amount over the year to a very considerable sum, and their cooperation was essential in keeping down expenditure. So the Surveyor General wrote sharply to Yenn:

> I am under the necessity of calling your attention to the repairs now going on in the kitchen, and to the chimnies of Miss Cheveley's apartments at the Queen's Palace; as the latter are going on very slowly, and the former are executed in a very slovenly manner, neither creditable to the place, to the workmen employed,—or to the Clerk of the Works under whose superintendence that Palace is placed.[5]

In 1819, another Clerk of Works, William Matthew at Windsor, allowed extra works to be done during the repair of Bagshot Lodge for the Duke of Gloucester. This resulted in years of controversy between the Office and the tradesmen—who failed to get their money until 1826—and earned for Matthew a reprimand from the Treasury.[6] A 'want of proper attention and foresight' in Bacon, Clerk of the Works for Whitehall and Westminster, in making out his estimate (£4491), resulted in an excess of £1900 on repairs to the State Stables at Charing Cross in 1815–16: 'this

---

[1] T. 1/4378, f. 16121/29; Works 1/13, p. 223 (23 February 1825); 1/17, p. 523 (8 December 1829).
[2] Works 6/27, p. 207ᵛ, 24 January 1815.   [3] *Ibid.* p. 211.
[4] Works 1/13, p. 418, 29 July 1825.   [5] Works 1/6, p. 416, 27 February 1816.
[6] Works 1/9, p. 545; 1/11, p. 132; 1/14, p. 251.

excess was not known to me, until the accounts were made up, and delivered into this office for examination', complained Stephenson.[1] Bacon had already been in trouble; in December 1815 he was obliged to explain

> that an exceeding of £7 occurred in executing the flat round the skylight on a staircase of the Court of Common Pleas, that I myself ordered the planking of the wooden Bridge to be repaired by the 9th of November last, that no accidents might occur upon the landing of the Lord Mayor, as I happened to be prevented coming to Town on that day I unfortunately omitted to pass an estimate for the amount which was £23. The third article which relates to sweeping the streets and carting the slop and rubbish being difficult to estimate correctly, has been improperly omitted amounting to £17.[2]

This sum of £47 was however not the whole of the story. A further expenditure of £249 had been incurred by the officer in charge of the building, Adam Lee, on his own authority:

> My repeated remonstrances to Mr. Adam Lee my Labourer in Trust for the Department [of Westminster], since my appointment in 1811, has failed to impress upon him the absolute necessity of refraining from commencing works of every description without my previous knowledge and consent, except those called for by the bursting of pipes, overflowing of gutters etc between which and other repairs there is too distinct a difference to admit of mistake; and even these circumstances I have particularly desired should be immediately reported. Circumstances have occurred, that have provided for the payment of works undertaken by Mr. Lee on no responsibility but his own, and I fear he to this hour retains an opinion of the duties of his situation, so different from what they really are: that unless he is completely undeceived, I have little hopes of his avoiding the conduct in future which has produced the estimates of works I have transmitted to you.

Lee was threatened with suspension if he repeated such conduct, and seems to have mended his ways.[3] Bacon however, was a backslider, and Stephenson severely rebuked him for exceeding his estimates for the last quarter of 1817, commenting on the 'repeated occasions' he had had to notice this carelessness.[4] The explanation, no doubt, lay in Bacon's wretched health, which caused him to be frequently absent from duty;[5] although he was assisted by three Labourers in Trust in his department, his presence was necessary to the efficient functioning of the system. The Clerks' constant attention to their departments was indeed essential. Old habits died hard, and some localities presented particular difficulties. One source of frequent troubles was Somerset House with its congeries of independently-minded government departments. Crocker reported that 'Sir Byam Martin in direct opposition to the instructions I received from you when I delivered up to him the key of the apartments belonging to the late Mr. Rose as Labourer in Trust, is proceeding to repair the same, without having given me any intimation of his intentions, or its being done by the workmen employed under your directions'.[6] The numerous 'grace and favour'

---

[1] Works 1/6, pp. 439–40, 9 March 1816; 4/21, p. 207.   [2] Works 1/6, pp. 331–3, 22 December 1815.
[3] *Ibid.* pp. 333–4.   [4] Works 1/8, pp. 485–6, 5 May 1818.
[5] He died on 10 June 1818.   [6] Works 1/7, p. 357, 16 December 1816.

K

apartments at Hampton Court were another headache. Lady Albinia Cumberland, a resident since 1794, complained in August 1815 that the Clerk of the Works was making a lot of unnecessary objections to her request for the construction of a water-closet next her apartments. Stephenson replied that the work would be done as soon as proper authority had been obtained from the Lord Chamberlain; although at her expense, the work must be done by the official tradesmen, 'under the immediate directions of the Clerk of the Works, in charge of the building'.[1] Sir Thomas Brooke Pechell then applied for a similar installation, but was refused because it would have involved cutting through a main wall of the palace—which, without special instructions, was specifically forbidden by the Treasury Regulations.[2]

Each Clerk of the Works was assisted by a number of Labourers in Trust, under his immediate orders. In his evidence to the 1828 Select Committee Rowles described a Labourer in Trust as 'a practical person, a foreman of workmen, capable from his experience of making out working drawings, setting out the works for the men in the building, and to be at all times present at them, to look at the correct execution and sound work, both as to the labour and the goodness of the materials'.[3] By the Treasury Instructions the Labourers in Trust were to 'reside constantly at the place of their appointment, where a convenient habitation or apartments shall be allowed them' (art. xlix). They were not specifically instructed to give that 'constant daily attendance' that the Inquiry Commissioners had advised; but they were 'to attend the workmen, to keep an exact account of their time and materials, when working by the day, and when on measured work, to see that the materials are of the best sort and the work done in a substantial manner' (art. xlix). They were also to check the number of men at work to ensure that 'no labourers are improperly charged in the accounts of day-work'.[4] Responsible for the safe care of building materials entrusted to them, they were to keep a 'regular and accurate Debtor and Creditor Account of all old and new stores placed under their care, agreeably to an official form'. Like their superiors, they were allowed to practise privately, in which they were encouraged by the fixing of their salary at the moderate figure of £100 per annum.[5] Their official duties were 'usually considered as determined, at 6 o'clock in the Evening'.[6]

In accord with the Commissioners' suggestions, the Labourers in Trust also assumed the functions of the former 'constant carpenters' and 'constant labourers', who were pensioned off. Although provision was made in the new Office for twelve, initially only ten were appointed. Most of these were already in the service. The Clerks were called upon to report whether their existing Labourers in Trust were capable of the duties to be entrusted to them. Hardwick reported that he considered William Miles Stone, Labourer at Hampton Court, 'from his general conduct being frequently intoxicated and from his inability to make out and keep the accounts required of him by no means efficient'; he was accordingly superannuated.[7] Among

---

[1] Works 1/6, pp. 96–7, 107–9.   [2] *Ibid.* pp. 307–8, 316.   [3] *1828 Report*, p. 102.
[4] Treasury instructions, art. xlix. This practice was one of the easiest ways of overcharging, and various instances had been denounced by the Inquiry Commissioners. The practice, however, did not cease with the reform of the Office, see pp. 120, 122 below.
[5] Lewis Wyatt and T. F. Hunt at least had a private practice, see Colvin, *Dictionary*.
[6] Memorial of Adam Lee to the Speaker, 16 July 1828 (Soane Mus. corr. 2, xi, D. 28)
[7] Works 4/21, p. 389; 6/27, p. 219ᵛ.

the ten appointed may be distinguished those with, and those without architectural training. Wyatt, Kidd, Hunt, and probably Crocker fall into the first class. Lewis William Wyatt (*c.* 1778–1853) had, like his cousin Jeffry, served seven years as a builder under his uncle Samuel, and a further seven years as an architect under his uncle James. He succeeded Jeffry as Labourer in Trust at Carlton House in 1800, and for several years was assistant architect to the Ordnance. Absent from duty in 1815, he was found to be visiting Paris, and was suspended; but satisfactorily explained his conduct. In 1818 he succeeded Crocker as Clerk of the Works for the eastern department; he was allowed six months leave during 1820 to visit Italy for professional improvement. In 1829 on the death of Hardwick he was transferred to Hampton Court.[1] Robert Charles Kidd was a pupil of Robert Browne, the Assistant Surveyor, under whom he had served at Kew and Richmond as an extra Labourer in Trust from 1794. He acted there as Clerk for the first half of 1815, until the department was combined with Hampton Court. Stephenson promoted this reliable and efficient officer to the Kensington clerkship when Yenn retired in October 1819. Kidd was also Surveyor to the Horse Guards, for which he remained responsible when that department was brought under the Office in 1817. An accident in the course of his duties led to his retirement early in 1829.[2] Thomas Frederick Hunt (*c.* 1791–1831) was re-appointed Labourer in Trust at St. James's Palace in 1815, being described as 'well qualified to fulfil the duties required'.[3] He began exhibiting at the Academy the following year; and his private activities led to bankruptcy in 1820. He was an acknowledged expert on medieval and especially Tudor architecture, and two copies of his *Architectural Designs* were bought for the Office.[4] Promoted in 1829 to the clerkship at Kensington, he was excused the customary examination by the architects, being too ill to leave his bedroom; more illness led to his death in 1831.[5] Edward Crocker, junior, was the third generation of his family in the Office of Works; he probably received an architectural training under his father. He was performing the duties of Labourer in Trust at Westminster from 1812. Bacon, in recommending him for the post, praised his assiduity, commenting 'his abilities are more than adequate'. In 1826 he was responsible for repairs to the buildings at Newmarket and gave assistance in the office in examining accounts.[6] He practised privately as a measurer, and applied unsuccessfully in July 1827 to do this for his client Harrison, one of the tradesmen engaged on Buckingham Palace. He resigned on 29 October 1827, having accepted an 'incompatible post' at some distance from town.[7]

Adam Lee (*c.* 1772–1843) bridges the two groups. Trained as a carpenter, he was articled to a Clerk of the Works. As a foreman carpenter he worked on barracks at Bridport and the Military Hospital at Portsmouth before joining the Office of Works

[1] *1813 Report*, App. 19; Works 6/27, p. 212; 4/21, pp. 345, 351, 361–2, 369, 378; 1/8, p. 533; 4/24, p. 137; 4/29, p. 267. See above, p. 58.

[2] Colvin, *Dictionary*; Works 1/12, p. 202; 4/21, p. 338; 5/107; T. 1/1642/13561; Works 4/24, p. 40; 1/17, p. 22. See above, p. 115.

[3] Works 6/27, p. 222.   [4] Works 5/109, 110; 4/24, p. 186.

[5] Works 5/107; 4/24, p. 186; 4/29, p. 282; 4/30, pp. 404, 443; 5/110.

[6] Works 6/27, p. 221; 4/21, p. 393; 5/109.

[7] Works 1/15, pp. 301, 489, 514. An Edward William Crocker was employed at Buckingham Palace as measurer in 1846 and as clerk of works in 1849/50 (Works 19/7, f. 2383; 19/8, ff. 2700, 2724).

in 1801 as a clerk of works serving under Browne at the New Park Lodge in Richmond Park. In 1806 he was promoted Labourer in Trust at Whitehall and Westminster. He did occasional private business as a builder, and acquired sufficient experience to be able to prepare plans for alterations at the Privy Council Office (*c.* 1810), and to design a new front for the Office of the Auditors of Land Revenue.[1] Bacon reported in April 1815 that 'he possesses abilities that certainly qualify him to perform the duties specified'; but found him (as we have seen) a difficult subordinate, insolent, disobedient and independent.[2] In 1832, when the Office of Works was combined with the Woods and Forests, he was put in charge of the Horse Guards and Whitehall; and in 1833 he was among those who laid plans before the Select Committee on rebuilding the House of Commons.[3]

The other Labourers in Trust appear all to have been brought up to a trade. William Lush (d. 1818), appointed to the Tower in 1815, was a carpenter and joiner who became Constant Carpenter at Carlton House about 1807, and at the same time did work for Jeffry Wyatt. In 1812–13 he superintended works at the Royal Pavilion at Brighton.[4] Thomas March, Labourer in Trust at the Mint, had super-intended repairs at Sholebrook Lodge in July 1815 for General Fitzroy, Ranger of Whittlebury Forest, who described him as 'dependable'. When Lush died, March took over his department also. But he became a drunkard, and was repeatedly reprimanded for disorderly conduct. Then he removed building materials from the Tower to premises of his own at Clapham Common; when a warrant was issued for his arrest in May 1825 he absconded.[5] Another corrupted by the opportunities his position afforded was William Alexander Arnold. Described in 1815 by Crocker (under whom he was Labourer in Trust at Newmarket) as 'strictly sober and honest and perfectly capable of the situation which he now holds', he was nominated to Kensington when it was decided to sell Newmarket Palace. But the Woods and Forests sought to retain his services there until the buildings were finally disposed of in 1819, and he was ultimately made Labourer in Trust at Kew. In 1829 he was found to have connived with a tradesman in making false returns of workmen employed on the King's Works from 1824 to 1828, whereby about £280 were paid improperly. When informed that he would be reported to the Treasury, he resigned, ostensibly because of ill-health from an accident five years before; but as Stephenson refused to recommend him, he secured no pension.[6] His colleague across the river at Hampton Court, George Slade, was also accused of misconduct at this and other times, but curiously enough was retained on the revised establishment in 1832—only to be dismissed the following year. In 1822 he had to be admonished for making improper charges for labour in his accounts. But the Clerk of the Works, Hardwick, was blamed for leaving him unsupervised.[7] In 1828 William Hart, a labourer at

---

[1] *1813 Report*, App. pp. 148 ff. qq. 1–3, 15, 38, 89–90.

[2] Works 1/7, pp. 331–3 (see p. 117 above); 6/27, p. 221.

[3] *Parl. Pap.* 1833, xii, p. 568. He collected a set of drawings of the old palace of Westminster which the Office of Works wished in 1844 to purchase from his executor for £500, but the Treasury refused approval (Works 1/26, pp. 474, 479, 492).   [4] *1813 Report*, App. 21; Works 1/8, p. 266.

[5] Works 4/21, p. 474; 1/6, pp. 456, 458; 1/8, p. 509; 5/109; 1/14, p. 459.

[6] Works 6/27, p. 227; 1/6, p. 392; 1/7, pp. 65, 157, 429; 4/23, pp. 325, 339; 4/29, pp. 326, 333, 343, 398; 1/17, pp. 309–11.

[7] Works 1/11, pp. 93, 180. This caused Stephenson to enforce more stringent regulations: *ibid.*, pp. 185–7.

Hampton Court, made allegations against him and Arnold. After investigation by Hardwick and the Attached Architects, Stephenson advised Hart to initiate legal action; but apparently his witnesses were reluctant to come forward. Hart then wrote to the Duke of Wellington accusing Slade of transferring from the palace materials which were used to build five houses in Cottage Place, Hampton, as well as two at Hampton Court 'fit for the residence of any Nobleman'. Slade must have been able to rebut these allegations, as no action was taken. In August 1832, however, another workman, Fraser, accused him of having employed men paid by the public on private works. More accusations of overcharges in Slade's accounts were then made, and his explanations proving unsatisfactory he was dismissed in December 1833.[1]

The Clerks and Labourers were assisted by a number of 'constant workmen'. Although the old posts of 'constant' carpenter or labourer by warrant had been discontinued, several men had still to be employed for similar work, though in unestablished posts. A protest from the Speaker obliged Stephenson to continue at the Speaker's House 'the attendance of a constant Labourer as heretofore . . . had his Duties been properly pointed out to me [wrote Stephenson] at the time I suggested these alterations, I should not for a moment have entertained an idea of depriving your Residence of so very useful and necessary [a] person'.[2] These constant workmen might secure promotion to the status of Labourer in Trust. When Joseph Morris was so promoted in 1820, he had been for 'upwards of 20 years employed as a carpenter' at Carlton House.[3] Charles Molinix (b. *c.* 1767), who joined the Office of Works about 1793, served for some 37 years in an unspecified but established capacity before appointment as Labourer in Trust.[4] Other Labourers were appointed from 'temporary' staff. James Peacock (b. *c.* 1760) had worked in Ireland for James Wyatt, who in 1800 employed him on the lodges in Whittlebury Forest; in 1803 he superintended works at the King's Bench Prison and served until 1813 in a similar capacity at Kensington Palace, where his 'steadiness and honesty' earned the Duke of Kent's commendation. He was then without official employment for a short time. In 1815 he was temporary Labourer at Kensington and from 1816 to 1819 was acting Labourer in Trust superintending repairs in St. James's and Hyde Parks. Promoted to the established post at Richmond and Kew in 1819 as a 'very deserving man', he at length ended his career as Labourer at Kensington.[5]

Employment under one of the Attached Architects was another means of entry into official employment. Richard Whibley, appointed in 1824 as Labourer in Trust at Somerset House, had been 'long in the employ of Mr. Smirke', and had served there as foreman for the building of the new Legacy Duty Office, 1818–19.[6] William Evans (b. *c.* 1778) became Labourer at Windsor Castle in 1827, after working for Soane as clerk of works at the new Board of Trade and Council Offices;[7] and William Craib, similarly employed by Soane on the restoration of Whitehall

[1] *Ibid.*, p. 180; 1/17, pp. 9, 194–7, 211, 220; 1/20, pp. 67–8, 192–3, 245, 289.
[2] Works 6/27, pp. 226v–7.   [3] Works 1/9, p. 172.
[4] Works 1/18, p. 330; T. 1/4378. Molinix was probably 'constant labourer' at the Speaker's House.
[5] Works 6/26, pp. 161–2; T. 1/4378; Works 5/107; 1/7, p. 143; 1/9, p. 441; 1/18, p. 330.
[6] Works 1/12, p. 111; 4/23, p. 378.
[7] T. 1/4378; Works 5/109, 110; Soane Mus. Corr. 2, xii, A.

Chapel, was appointed to succeed Slade at Hampton Court.[1] The conduct of such clerks of works specifically employed to superintend new works was regarded as a matter for the architect concerned, and not for the Office of Works. Thus allegations against William Roles, when clerk of works at Buckingham Palace, were referred to Nash, and no official notice was taken of them.[2] William Evans, accused by a craftsman he had discharged for drunkenness and damaging the plaster ornaments in the new Privy Council Chamber, had to make his defence to Soane.[3]

Of the tradesmen appointed by warrant under the Office of Works there is little that need be said. They survived the changes of 1814–15, though some rationalization of their appointments and districts was undertaken.[4] They were entrusted only with minor repairs under the superintendence of the Clerks of the Works. Jobs of some size were put out to limited competition, in which no special privileges were afforded to warrant holders.[5] But even ordinary repairs could amount to considerable sums in total; and some of the regular tradesmen found opportunities of obtaining an illicit profit. In July 1829, after the enquiries in the Hampton Court district, Stephenson circularised the tradesmen, referring to his

> painful discovery . . . of several Instances, where the Public have been considerably injured by Tradesmen with the connivance of the Laborers in Trust; or of those employed in checking, and vouching day work, having made false returns of the Men employed upon the King's Works, charging the pay, and wages, of fictitious Men, as though they had been actually employed, as described in the Weekly Notes—A practice most injurious to His Majesty's service, as well as highly discreditable to the Character of a fair Tradesman.
>
> It was but too well known, that impositions of this description had existed—But the Surveyor General hoped, and trusted, that under the present Official Regulations, and from the general respectability of the Tradesmen, the Department was sufficiently protected against a continuance of such improper Practices, but in this he has unfortunately been deceived, and where he considers the Tradesmen as principally to blame, for without their immediate knowledge, and assistance, these abuses could never have existed.
>
> From the great difficulty that necessarily attends detecting impositions of this nature, it is quite impossible for the Surveyor General to ascertain either how long, or to what extent they have been carried on, but from recent discoveries he is convinced, the loss to the Public must have been considerable.[6]

---

[1] Soane Mus. Corr. 2, xii, E.   [2] Works 4/29, pp. 313 ff, 388.
[3] Soane Mus. Corr. 2, xii, A, f. 122, 21 December 1826.
[4] Works 1/9, p. 265; 4/25, p. 30; 4/26, p. 268.
[5] Soane appears to have stretched a point in dividing the new Law Courts carpentry contract between Jeffry Wyatt and Martyr, arguing that Wyatt had 'been the Office Tradesman for a great length of time' (Soane Mus. New Law Courts Corr. 'Tenders and Estimates', ff. 3, 14–16, 19).
[6] Works 1/17, pp. 397–9.

Chapter VI

THE NEW OFFICE AT WORK
1815—1828

THE vast extent of public works undertaken in the ensuing decade was to tax the new organization to the uttermost. Except at Somerset House, most of the great officers and departments of the state were housed in old, often ill-adapted accommodation; and new functions and increased state activity caused departments to outgrow their old homes. George IV, as Regent and King, added to the burdens of the Office by his determination to indulge a love of building that took little heed of financial constraints. It was largely at the cost of the Privy Purse that his private residence at Brighton was transformed into a quasi-oriental palace, but the embellishment of his 'cottage' at Windsor, though charged to the Woods and Forests, was directed by the Office of Works; and the reconstruction of Windsor Castle and the rebuilding of Buckingham Palace, as the two official residences of the sovereign, were carried on by special parliamentary grants under the scrutiny of the Office. St. James's Palace, where the King performed his state duties, was extensively repaired, and those royal palaces, such as Hampton Court and Kensington, that were no longer inhabited by the monarch, had to be kept weathertight. In 1815 the Office became responsible for the Houses of Parliament, where extensive new works were undertaken to facilitate the growing business of a legislature whose membership had itself expanded with the addition of Irish representatives in 1801. Close at hand, Westminster Hall required a major restoration, and the increasing activity of the judicature called for the erection of new courts of justice. In Whitehall, the Banqueting House was soon to require thoroughgoing repair, as were numerous government offices; and for the Board of Trade and the Privy Council new premises were erected. Additional offices were built at Somerset House, the rebuilding of the British Museum was started, the Mint had to be reinstated after a disastrous fire, and a new General Post Office was erected and the Custom House repaired by the Office of Works on behalf of the departments concerned. The Church Building Commission constantly referred plans of new churches to the Office. The introduction of gas lighting for the public departments had to be supervised. The ceremonials of state had to be conducted, the burials of princes, the coronation of the King. The total expenditure of the Office up to the death of George IV in 1830, a period of some fifteen years, was nearly two and a half million pounds (exclusive of the rebuilding of Buckingham House and Windsor Castle.)

Despite the extension of its responsibilities the Office of Works was one of those services that had to bear the brunt of the axe of economy, wielded by ministers with an eye on the House of Commons. Of the principal classes of public expenditure, interest on the national debt was an unavoidable charge; naval and military expenditure was pared after the war and thereafter further reductions were seldom practicable; so the retrenchers fell the more eagerly on civil expenditure.[1] The chronic indebtedness of the Civil List directed parliamentary attention to it, and one of the departments most frequently criticised in the early years of the Regency was that of the Lord Chamberlain.[2] The opposition had strongly criticised the lavish expenditure on the occasion of the visit of the allied sovereigns in 1814: temporary buildings, furniture and embellishments had been ordered without preliminary estimates—a proceeding already condemned by two successive committees on the Civil List.[3] During the years of war such prerogative revenues as the Droits of Admiralty vastly increased, and from them the Civil List was occasionally subsidized;[4] but with the return of peace it was essential to put the Civil List on a satisfactory footing, and to ensure Treasury control over public expenditure.[5] Accordingly not only was the Office of Works reorganized, and removed altogether from the Lord Chamberlain's control—so passing finally out of the Royal Household—but new arrangements were made to regulate its expenditure. The royal palaces were to remain a charge on the Civil List, but the other public buildings and works were to be provided for by annual parliamentary vote. In this way the Civil List would be freed of a heavy and increasing burden, and at the same time the responsibility for the upkeep of official buildings would be transferred to Parliament. When it was decided to place the buildings of the Office of Woods and Forests under the Office of Works, these formed a third category, the cost of whose maintenance was not voted by Parliament but discharged from the land revenues of the Crown. The Cashier was instructed to keep distinct accounts for each of these services, in which 'the receipts and disbursements . . . are not to be blended or inter-mixed'.[6]

Opposition, however, remained 'clamorous for economy, and fastened . . . on small extravagances . . . involving only a slight outlay'.[7] The Regent's building operations at Brighton and in Windsor Great Park were among its favourite and most vulnerable targets.[8] Liverpool, Vansittart and Castlereagh, as the ministers most immediately connected with the Treasury and government business in the Commons, presented a minute to the Regent shortly before the Civil List bill came under discussion, stating their belief that

---

[1] The 1828 select committee on public income and expenditure showed in their Fourth Report (*Parl. Pap.* 1828, v, 543 ff.) that charges of a fixed nature had absorbed £36 million out of an expenditure of £56 million in 1827, and the army and navy votes had taken £16 million. The comparable figures for 1824 were £37 million, £55 million and £15 million (to nearest million).

[2] See p. 95 above.   [3] *Parl. Deb.* xxviii, 696.

[4] £70,000 was allotted from the Droits of Admiralty for alterations to and furnishing of the Royal Pavilion, Brighton, by Treasury minute, 23 February 1816, printed *Parl. Deb.* xxiv, 272–3.

[5] An initial experiment was Bankes' Act of 1815, by which the Civil List accounts were to be made up to 5 January each year and reported to Parliament by 28 February following. It proved impossible for the Office of Works to comply with this and the Chancellor of the Exchequer explained, 4 March 1816, that 'the work in the department of the Board of Works, was to be re-measured and valued before the bills could be passed' (*Parl. Deb.* xxxii, 1080).   [6] Treasury instructions, art. xxxiv, printed in *Parl. Pap.* 1814–15 (158)x.

[7] S. Walpole, *History of England from the conclusion of the Great War in 1815*, i (1878), p. 411.

[8] *Parl. Deb.* xxx, 631; xxxiv, 868 ff.

no Administration can continue to carry on the Government of the country under present circumstances, which is not determined to enforce a system of economy & retrenchment in every department of the State, and especially to abstain from every new & additional expense which however expedient or desirable cannot be represented as indispensably necessary . . . no subject is viewed with more jealousy and suspicion than the personal expenses of the Sovereign or his representative at a time when most of the landed gentlemen of the country are obliged to submit to losses & privations as well as to retrenchment . . .

Your Royal Highness's servants humbly submit that the only means by which they [sic] can be a prospect of weathering the impending storm is by stating on the direct authority of your Royal Highness and by your command, if it should be necessary, that all new expenses for additions or alterations at Brighton or elsewhere will, under the present circumstances, be abandoned.[1]

The reforms were taken a step further by the Civil List Act of 1816, when the expense of maintaining the public buildings at the Tower, Whitehall, Westminster, and the private roads was transferred from the Civil List to the vote of Parliament: and expenditure on repairs and necessary alterations to the remaining royal palaces was limited to £40,000, a sum calculated on the average expenditure over the preceding three years.[2]

My Lords [wrote the Secretary of the Treasury to Stephenson] are persuaded that you will feel the necessity of the strictest attention to economy in the expenditure of the sum which has been assigned for your department, and that the same may in no case be exceeded. This sum is intended to cover the expense of the whole of the works at the several palaces and buildings referred to in the said estimate, both ordinary and extraordinary; and therefore if any applications whatever are made to you, or any applications are referred to you by this Board for works not immediately and indispensably necessary for the preservation of the buildings, My Lords desire you will always report whether the expense can be defrayed out of the sum appropriated for the particular quarter in which it may be to be incurred, after satisfying the expense of all the other works and repairs previously sanctioned or indispensably necessary in the same quarter.[3]

For the ordinary repairs and maintenance of the buildings provided for by annual parliamentary grant, another £40,000 was voted. The Woods and Forests continued to meet the expenditure on their buildings from their own revenues. Similarly, repairs to the Exchequer Offices were paid for out of the Exchequer Fee Fund. Special parliamentary grants for new works such as the rebuilding of the British Museum or the restoration of Westminster Hall formed another head of account, as did the reconstruction of Windsor Castle, while the rebuilding of Buckingham House was a charge on the Land Revenue.

Although the Act of 1814 had provided for the transfer to the Office of Works of the buildings belonging to departments 'concerned in the receipt or management

[1] *Letters of George IV*, ed. Aspinall ii, pp. 158–9, 15 March 1816. The possibility of building a new palace had been rejected by the Treasury on 14 July and 15 November 1814 (*Parl. Deb.* xxviii, 732; xxix. 212).
[2] *Parl. Deb.* xxxiv, 197, 214. The Civil List retained financial responsibility for Carlton House, the Mews, the Queen's Palace (Buckingham House), Kensington Palace and Gardens, St. James's Palace, Richmond, Kew House and its appendages, Hampton Court Palace and House Park, and Windsor Castle and Queen's Lodge.   [3] Works 1/7, pp. 181–3, 5 July 1816.

of the Public Revenue', no steps were taken to implement this clause, for the Treasury decided that such a general transfer 'at the present moment, might be productive of the most serious inconvenience and embarrassment' to the Office of Works. Special instructions would be issued when the Treasury might decide to entrust these buildings to the Surveyor General, or refer questions concerning them to him, but the additional burden of their regular maintenance could not be imposed on his department until its capabilities had been tested by experience.[1] Following Pittite principles, reform had to be carried out gradually and without incurring new expenses. In the conditions of financial stringency following the abolition of the property tax in March 1816 it was clearly hopeless to attempt an enlargement of the Office of Works. The staff proved hardly adequate to cope with their increased duties, yet the Treasury 'deemed it premature and inexpedient to enlarge the Establishment'.[2] A further burden was imposed in 1817, at a time of continuing financial depression, when in accordance with the recommendations of the select committee on Finance all the public offices and places previously under the super-intendence of the Surveyor to the Horse Guards, twenty-three in number, were placed under the Office of Works, without addition of staff.[3]

Driven by the select committee on Finance, the Treasury even proposed pruning the establishment. Stephenson replied 'that the duties of this Department furnish very ample Employment for all the Officers and Clerks belonging to the Establish-ment, and that it is sometimes even necessary to have extra Assistance, in order to prevent the Business of the Office from falling into arrear'.[4] From early in 1819 a temporary assistant was constantly employed in the office.[5] By April 1823 the pressure of new works was delaying the examination of accounts.[6] Finding it impossible to manage without more clerks, Stephenson sought Treasury permission in May 1823 to employ up to four more as necessary.[7] He renewed his application in February 1824, stating that he was obliged to hire two extra clerks to check the bills,[8] and that as the post of Labourer in Trust at Somerset House had been vacant nearly seven months, he had had to second an office clerk for that duty.[9] The Treasury, approving the additional four office assistants on 17 March 1824, promised to revise the establishment if necessary.[10] The labours of the Office continued to grow. Dissatisfied with long hours and inadequate pay, French, the second Exam-ining Clerk, resigned in April 1825.[11] The promised revision of establishment was never made. Arrears accumulated, and were blamed onto disobedient or negligent

---

[1] Treasury Instructions, Art. iii. The Inquiry Commissioners had recommended that all public works voted by Parliament should be placed under the Office of Works. The Act went beyond this, including those paid for by the revenue departments out of their gross receipts, which often escaped parliamentary scrutiny.

[2] Treasury Instructions, art. ii.

[3] Works 1/8, p. 107; 4/22, p. 411; *Parl. Pap.* 1817 (162) iv, Second Report of the Select Committee on Finance, p. 31.

[4] Works 1/8, p. 195, 29 August 1817. Davis and French were paid overtime in the first quarter of 1817 for checking accounts for extra works, principally at the Mint (Works 5/107).

[5] John Phipps was employed at 7s. 6d. a day from 1819 until appointed to a vacant clerkship in 1822; William Clifford Smith was then employed until 26 April 1823; and from 22 May 1823, Charles Hiort (Works 5/107, 108). [6] Works 1/11, p. 441. [7] *Ibid.* p. 513.

[8] Henry Joshua Robinson had been engaged early in 1824 in addition to Charles Hiort (Works 5/108).

[9] Works 1/12, p. 361.

[10] Works 1/12, p. 397. James R. S. Cox (from 5 April) and William Albon (from 3 May) were recruited, and Charles Hiort and Robinson retained (Works 5/108). [11] Works 1/13, p. 300.

officers.[1] In these circumstances there were limits to what even the most zealous administrator could accomplish. An active and efficient head could ensure that work ordered was done in a sound manner, and at reasonable prices: what he could not control were the arbitrary economies dictated by government policy.

In March 1821, in reply to a House of Commons interrogation about the growth of the civil service, Stephenson summed up the situation as follows:

> The present Office is placed under the immediate control of the Lords of the Treasury; and its duties extend to all public buildings the expenses of which are defrayed by the Civil List, from the Grants of Parliament, or out of the Revenues of His Majesty's Woods and Forests; . . . The payment of these expenses, with the salaries and disbursements of the department, are now made in the Office, by the Cashier, who pays by drafts on the Bank of England, and renders to the auditors an annual account of all his receipts and expenditures.

Such was the framework within which the department was meant to operate.

> An entire new Establishment has been formed, and a more enlarged and efficient system arranged for conducting this branch of the Public business; imposing many additional checks upon expenditure, and requiring a more minute and accurate examination of all estimates and building accounts. . . .[2]

How did the system work in practice? Basic to its operation was the maintenance of a schedule of prices. By article xxviii of the Treasury Instructions, a book of prices of materials and workmanship was to be kept in the Office and revised every quarter at least. The compilation of such a schedule was not of course a new idea; but previous schedules had not been kept up to date. Accordingly, one of the first duties of the new Office was to compile an up-to-date schedule. The prices were calculated on the prime cost of materials; Stephenson explained the procedure to the 1828 committee:

> The prices are regulated every month, if it is necessary; the mode of regulating them is by getting from the clerks of the works, from the architects occasionally, and from the merchants and dealers, the prime cost of the different materials, and upon these prime cost prices the tradesmen are allowed twelve and a half per cent profit. The office prices thus fixed, are submitted to the tradesmen, who are informed (I speak now of common repairs and alterations, not of new works) that these are the prices their works are to be charged at till a further alteration takes place. All accounts for works are delivered in blank, and the prices put in at the office. All works susceptible of measurement, are measured by the office clerks with the tradesmen. There are some articles of ornamental gilding, &c. the prices for which cannot be fixed by previous agreements; these must in a great measure depend as to their value upon the integrity of the tradesmen; but in such cases reference is always had to their own prime-cost books, and to the best further evidence that can be obtained.[3]

---

[1] West, the measurer, was blamed for the delay in settling accounts for Windsor Castle (Works 1/14, pp. 329–30), J. W. Hiort for absenting himself from the Office and thereby delaying the examination of accounts (Works 4/29, pp. 72–3; see p. 108 above).   [2] Works 1/10, p. 364.   [3] *1828 Report*, p. 15.

The three architects' first meeting for this purpose was on 31 August 1815, when they settled certain changes in practice. Plumber's pipe was no longer to be charged by measure, but by weight, though still checked by linear measure. More important, the attempt to impose a general price for bricks, sand and lime was abandoned; and out of central London these were directed to be charged at local prices, determined by the Clerks of the Works.[1] In 1816 the prices of day-work were reconsidered,[2] and in October–November a prolonged revision of prices was undertaken with the assistance of the Clerks.[3] It was then agreed that the architects should meet on the first Tuesday in March, June, September and December to regulate prices for the current quarter. Frequent changes were made in prices as prime costs fluctuated,[4] and so much work was involved that in November 1818 the architects decided to meet on the first Thursday of every month.[5]

The relationship between the Office, the merchants and the master tradesmen was close. In December 1817, for instance, the Clerks of Works were instructed to ask the tradesmen if there had been any recent price alterations;[6] in September and November 1818 the master plasterers and carpenters asked for an increase in the price allowed for labour.[7] After consultation with the master bricklayers it was decided in 1819 that, because of local variations, no fixed price could satisfactorily be established for measured brickwork. It was accordingly dropped from the schedule, prices being determined from time to time with reference to the locality.[8] Another conference with the bricklayers took place in December 1820, when prices for brickwork at the Fleet Prison and the new Stationery Office were compared.[9] A year later reductions in prices for slater's work could not be settled without further reference to the master slaters,[10] and the master tradesmen generally were asked if they were reducing wages to correspond with the great fall in prices of provisions. This initiative produced a number of proposals, and in February 1822 a general reduction of threepence per day was decreed.[11] The master painters were instructed to make out prices taking account of the reduced cost of white lead, oil, turpentine, etc.; but as the result was not considered satisfactory, the architects drew up a scale based on the prime cost returns, to operate from 10 October 1821. The painters then protested that the change should operate only from 5 January 1822, and were instructed to submit their prime costs for the earlier quarter before a decision was reached.[12] Again, in February 1827 prices in slater's and plumber's work were reduced, and founder's and glazier's were increased. After representations from the tradesmen, all except the glazier's were altered agreeably to their wishes.[13]

In 1824 the low prices secured by competitive tender for the new General Post Office and the British Museum led the architects to examine the better adjustment of prices for common repairs, and to consider the possibility of performing such work

---

[1] Works 4/21, p. 524. The actual prices are rarely given in the Minute Books at this period. The entire schedule of current prices was printed in *Parl. Pap.* 1824 (120) xvi.
    [2] Works 4/21, p. 819.   [3] Works 4/22, pp. 155 ff.
    [4] See Works 4/23, pp. 233, 270, 272, 458; 4/24, pp. 31, 139, 167, 286, 327, 375, 391; 4/25, p. 66 etc.
    [5] Works 4/23, p. 272.   [6] Works 1/8, p. 331.
    [7] Works 4/23, pp. 232–3, 241, 270, 272.   [8] Works 4/24, p. 31.
    [9] *Ibid.* p. 391. Prices per rod were £16 14s. 7¾d. and £16 7s. 2¼d. respectively.
    [10] Works 4/25, p. 157.   [11] *Ibid.* pp. 165, 170, 175, 201, 215.
    [12] Works 4/25, pp. 215 (23 February 1822), 228 (14 March), 236 (25 March).
    [13] Works 4/28, pp. 162, 179.

by tender—an idea rejected as impracticable, as it would open a door to tradesmen of inferior ability and doubtful integrity.[1] An investigation of prices revealed that the Clerks of the Works were obtaining their lists from the tradesmen, seldom from the merchants. In June a new plan for obtaining prices (of which no details survive) was proposed, but the architects dispersed for the summer with the subject still under their consideration. Nash reported to Stephenson on 10 August 1824,

> I have gone very deeply into the subject which you have so much at heart—namely the organization of Prices to be adopted by the Office of Works—it is no trifling task I have already bestowed three whole days on it and fragments of others and have scribbled many sheets of paper with remarks and figures but I am very far from the end . . .
>
> As soon as my revision of Prices is compleat . . . I shall enclose them to you with my sentiments on the subject generally when you will if you think proper communicate them to my colleagues . . .[2]

These prolonged deliberations did not, however, result in any great change. At the February meeting in 1825 the list of prices for timber submitted by the builders Baker and Son (Smirke's relations) was taken as the prime cost for carpenter's and joiner's work; but a form of tender was adopted for smith's work, in which the tradesmen had applied for an increase: blank specifications were to be sent to the smiths and founders holding warrants asking the lowest prices for which they would undertake the various items for ordinary works.[3] The July meeting was postponed for three weeks because the merchants' returns had not been received;[4] then a memorial was presented from the master carpenters for an increase in the rate of wages allowed. The repeal in 1824 of the Combination Acts had been followed by an upsurge of trade union activity, and the journeymen carpenters' society had some success in staging strikes and compelling masters to pay 5s. or 5s. 6d. a day.[5] On the understanding that the masters would report to the Office if they paid less than 5s. to any workmen during the quarter, 5s. 11d. for joiners and 5s. 8d. for carpenters were allowed. The prices for the Michaelmas quarter were adjusted on the basis of the merchants' returns on 25 November, when the plasterers too petitioned for an allowance on wages, 5s. being again taken as the average daily rate paid by the masters.[6] Similar treatment was accorded in April 1826 to tradesmen employed at the Board of Trade, Mint and General Post Office,[7] though Messrs. Lee's application was rejected as inconsistent with their contract for works at the Custom House. In 1826 it was December before the prices for the quarter ending 10 October were revised, but widespread fluctuations occurred at this period.[8] Some adjustment of

---

[1] Works 4/26, pp. 302, 329. The contracts for carpenter's, bricklayer's and mason's measured work averaged at the British Museum 9% lower than Nash's Buckingham House contracts, and those for the new Post Office 13% lower. Tendering was employed by the Ordnance, for ordinary as well as major works: competitive tenders were obtained in the several trades at a percentage below (or above) the scheduled prices, and contracts were then allocated for three-year periods. The Ordnance had tested this system in Ireland before adopting it generally. See 2nd report of select committee on public income and expenditure, *Parl. Pap.* 1828, v, pp. 271–2.

[2] Works 19/50.   [3] Works 4/27, p. 130.   [4] *Ibid.* pp. 234, 252.

[5] Works 4/27, p. 253. One such attempt at Buckingham House was interrupted by the guard picket, see p. 267 below.

[6] Works 4/27, p. 343.   [7] *Ibid.* pp. 387, 456.   [8] Works 4/28, p. 124.

prices after the quarter's close was perhaps inevitable, but when it was delayed or prolonged into a third quarter, although the public interest might be consulted, that of the tradesmen was not, and the whole work of examining and passing accounts was delayed. Wyatville commented out of his own experience as an appointed tradesman on this aspect of the system, and suggested that prices should be fixed during the quarter, so that tradesmen might enter correct prices on their bills, and escape the alterations in red ink which gave them a suspicious character.[1] Although Stephenson stated in 1828 that the tradesmen submitted bills in blank, for prices to be affixed in the Office, this was evidently not the invariable practice.

The Office schedule offered a criterion which was resorted to for pricing even private undertakings.[2] It also provided a basis for prices for new works or major alterations, tradesmen tendering at a percentage below the scheduled price. But the method was criticised by the builder Henry Rowles (Henry Holland's nephew) in 1828:

> The instructions with respect to getting at prices are clumsy, and leave no individual responsible; and the practice is even more clumsy than the instructions . . . The present practice is, I believe, that the Board endeavours to get at the prime cost of all articles, which is a very difficult point to attain; and they then proceed in this way: They take the prime cost . . . let us call it £100; they add a computed profit, of, I believe, fifteen per cent, that would make together £115. The Board then calls on the tradesman to work five per cent under the price, which, added to the Exchequer fees of two and a half per cent, amounts to seven and a half per cent altogether. Now seven and a half per cent on £115 makes £8 12s. 6d. and that subtracted from £115 leaves £106 7s. 6d.; of which £100 was the prime cost, and £6 7[s]. 6d. the nominal profit, which no man could afford to work for, the use of his capital, his premises, his clerks, and his own time considered. Therefore, as the Public Works are done on these terms, there must be other advantages, which are not apparent. This example shows why I said the manner of settling prices is very clumsy and confused; and it is capable of being simplified by settling a fair price at starting, and not leaving it subject to deductions.[3]

The discontinuance recommended in the 1813 Report of the ancient habit referred to by Rowles of making a two and a half per cent deduction from tradesmen's bills was considered by the Attached Architects in December 1827; and on 12 May 1828 its abolition as from 5 January (quarter day) was agreed upon, on the ground that it was 'attended with no one benefit to the public', but imposed 'unnecessary labour, and consequent delay in settling the accounts of the Office'. Thenceforward the tradesman's profit 'for common and ordinary works' was to be a clear twelve and a half per cent on the prime costs of the materials.[4]

The practice of the Office also established a set of rules for measuring, which otherwise was governed by the custom of the locality or trade,[5] and was open to

---

[1] Works 1/13, p. 503.   [2] *1831 Report*, p. 11.

[3] *1828 Report*, p. 102. Stephenson in fact denied during his examination on 25 March that any deduction was made from tradesmen's accounts (*ibid.* p. 33).

[4] Works 4/28, p. 431; 4/29, p. 51. That this custom survived so long was probably due to the deduction of fees from issues by the Exchequer, which amounted to nearly 3%; a different arrangement was adopted in 1827.

[5] See M. H. Port, 'The Office of Works and early nineteenth-century building contracts', *Econ. Hist. Rev.*, 2nd ser. xx (1967), pp. 94–110; F. M. L. Thompson, *Chartered Surveyors* (1968), chap. 4.

much quibbling. Tradesmen might dispute, 'as the method may produce less money than the methods of private trade', but as Wyatville assured the select committee in 1828, on this point the Office never gave way.[1] Stephenson himself was satisfied that the system was the best; replying to criticism from Nash, he stated in 1830 that:

> the system of measurement adopted by this Office has repeatedly been a subject of discussion at the periodical meetings of the attached Architects, and more particularly at the commencement of the present Establishment, when many alterations and improvements were at different times suggested and adopted, and some at the particular recommendation of Mr. Nash himself, who most frequently attended these meetings; and from the opinions of many professional men of eminence, I have every good reason for believing that the mode of measurement pursued by this Office is more advantageous to the Public and freer from abuses of every kind, than what is adopted generally in private business.[2]

When works had been measured, the tradesmen sent in their accounts as soon as possible after the end of every quarter (5 January, 5 April, 5 July, 10 October). Slackness by tradesmen in getting out bills had contributed to the previous confusion in the Office, and considerable stress was laid under the new organization on the timely rendering of accounts.[3] In April 1817 the tradesmen were warned to send in a full statement of outstanding demands—any omissions would 'not be suffered to be brought forward, or included in any subsequent account to be passed in this Office'.[4] Two years later the carpenter at St. James's Palace was warned that he must deliver his bills on time; in 1823 the Greenwich tradesmen were told that they would lose their positions if their accounts were not forthcoming.[5]

Ordinary accounts were delivered to the Clerk of the Works, who examined them against his own (or the Labourer in Trust's) notes, making any necessary corrections. Crocker, for example, refused to pass a charge by Henry Westmacott, mason at the King's Mews, for the purchase of extra scaffolding, and this item was reserved for the Surveyor General's decision.[6] Every item of account underwent 'three distinct and very minute examinations' in the Office, but it is not clear whether this included the initial scrutiny by the Clerk of the Works. They were not mere mathematical checks, as formerly: prices were examined to see that they agreed with contracts; and the quantities were checked against the measurements.[7] In 1815 the examination of bills for works at Warwick House (some of which had already been paid by the Lord Chamberlain) revealed over-charging;[8] and an exhaustive examination of plumbers' charges in 1817 disclosed irregularities in almost every article, the consequent revision achieving a reduction of rather more than ten per cent on two quarters' bills.[9] Some of the problems that might occur are referred to in a letter from Stephenson to Nash respecting his accounts for the King's Cottage, Windsor Great Park:

> The Cottage accounts are under examination, but the progress has been impeded for the want of some previous explanations from the Clerk of the Works, the dimension

---

[1] *1828 Report*, p. 97.   [2] Works 1/18, pp. 255–6.
[3] 'Great care is taken to prevent any arrears of accounts at the termination of every quarter' (Works 1/6, p. 439).   [4] Works 1/8, p. 20.   [5] Works 4/23, p. 400; 1/12, p. 188.
[6] Works 1/8, p. 421, 29 February 1816.   [7] *1831 Report*, pp. 147–8, Hiort's evidence.
[8] Works 1/6, p. 325.   [9] Works 1/8, pp. 215, 347–8.

books sent in with these accounts are all copies, and the Clerk of the Works says, he cannot give us his rough dimensions as they were only taken in pencil, and are in a large book containing a variety of private work; the Clerk of the Works will call here again early in the next week, to explain many errors that are found in the Books of Dimensions delivered here, such as wrong squaring of dimensions etc. The day notes are all without signature, but the Clerk of the Works admits them to be exact copies of those sent to the different tradesmen; it will also be necessary for him to separate the expences of the Stand at Ascot, from those of the Cottage, which are at present blended together, as the Treasury want to know the cost of this Stand.[1]

When the accounts had satisfied examination, they were certified by the Surveyor General, and the tradesmen were usually paid twice a year.[2]

The making of contracts was another important feature of the Surveyor General's work. Once a major building had been decided upon, and estimates approved by the Treasury, the Office had to obtain tenders from reputable tradesmen for the execution of the works.[3] Stephenson claimed that the Instructions bound him to seek competitive tenders, though they contained no specific requirement to that effect. There was, however, no question of open competition: tenders were sought only from those tradesmen known to the Office, or recommended by the architects. From experience it was found that 'it is only amongst persons who have a certain command of capital that the public can expect to obtain advantageous terms for the execution of any extensive works'.[4] Within these limits Stephenson was insistent on the importance of competition. When Soane wished to employ on the new Board of Trade those tradesmen whom he was employing at the new Law Courts—who, chosen by competition, had 'executed their several works in the most satisfactory manner with the greatest expedition and on very eligible terms'[5]—Stephenson replied:

> if these Buildings are to be conducted under the controul of this Department, it will not be in my power to allow a deviation from the Official Regulations, upon so material a point as that of declining all competition for so large an undertaking; particularly as no similar buildings have been erected by this Office, upon any other Terms than those of limited competition. The persons you have proposed for building the Board of Trade and Council Offices, are already largely concerned in extensive public works, and however great their respectability, it would be a positive dereliction of my Duty, and render me liable to serious responsibility, were I to authorize their undertaking the works in question, without previously calling for tenders from other respectable Tradesmen.—I have upon all occasions been most anxious to meet your wishes to the full extent of my power, and much regret I cannot accede to your present proposal, without some proper authority for that purpose.[6]

Soane believed that value for money was best obtained by employing workmen he could trust, and refused to make any selection from the list sent to him, declining 'to be considered responsible for the materials to be used or the soundness of the construction or for any delays that may occur in the execution of the several works'.[7]

---

[1] *Works* 1/11, p. 299.   [2] Stephenson's evidence, *1828 Report*, pp. 15, 33.
[3] Treasury Instructions, art. xxvii.
[4] *1831 Report*, p. 195, Stephenson to Treasury, 26 January 1826. It was for not selecting such men that he criticised Nash's Buckingham Palace contracts.   [5] Soane Mus. Corr. 2, xii, A. 30, 5 June 1824.
[6] *Ibid.* 23, 7 [June] 1824.   [7] *Ibid.* 32, 8 June 1824.

Competitive tenders created their own problems, as Soane did not fail to point out:

> On examining the tenders for the Carpenters and Joiners work if my recollection is correct it appeared that all Martyr's prices for the Carpenters work were under those of the other competitors: of course his tender was accepted:—On referring to the Joiners work—he offered to do all the Joiners work at thirteen per cent *only* under the Office of Works prices whilst Bennett and Hunt were ready to do the same at fifteen per cent—under these circumstances it would perhaps be more consistent with the *principles* laid down to give Martyr the Carpenters Work and Bennett and Hunt the Joiners Work. As to the Bricklayer I have only to state that in the works done under my direction, the work done by Stutely is worth at least twenty shillings per Rod more than that done by Whitehead.
>
> The execution of the exterior of the Board of Trade . . . is of such vital importance to the Office of Works that I most sincerely trust that a tried and faithful tradesman accustomed to such works, may not be passed by for the saving of a few pounds to make room for another who with the best intentions cannot be supposed equally competent to complete the works.[1]

The experienced architect was more likely to know how to get work done to the best advantage than the administrator whose great object was to keep down expenditure.

We find that upon occasion the rule of competition might be waived. Thus Kepp's tender for copper-covering the roof of the King's Library at the British Museum was 'after very mature consideration' accepted without competition, as the price was reasonable; Kepp had satisfactorily executed 'very extensive similar Works . . . at many different Buildings', and there were not 'any Persons sufficiently competent to compete with Mr. Kepp in Works of this particular description'.[2] Similarly the usual measure and prices contract might be departed from. Nash was in most circumstances keenly in favour of contracting in gross, i.e. for a lump sum, with a single contractor, and, 'against the decided opinions of Mr. Soane, Mr. Smirke, and Mr. Browne,' he insisted on this mode for the contract for the new Royal Mews at Pimlico, a building of that plain description usually thought most suitable for contracting in gross.[3] Nash's preference was again to be a source of disagreement with Stephenson during the building of Buckingham Palace.

In that great matter, however, the Surveyor General's jurisdiction was limited. The crisis of royal displeasure which nearly cost Stephenson his post in October 1823 had its consequences. Liverpool had promised the King that he would make 'arrangements as to the conduct of the Board of Works' that would relieve him 'from any further inconvenience'.[4] It was no doubt in accordance with this assurance that special arrangements were made for the restoration of Windsor Castle and the rebuilding of Buckingham House—arrangements that very largely withdrew the conduct of these important works from the purview of the Surveyor's staff. For Windsor, a commission was appointed, consisting of the Duke of Wellington, Lords Liverpool and Aberdeen, Sir Charles Long, Sir M. W. Ridley, Messrs. F. J. Robinson,

---

[1] *Ibid.* 37, draft to Stephenson, 21 June. [2] Works 4/27, p. 69.
[3] See p. 303.
[4] *Letters of George IV*, ed. Aspinall iii, p. 34. See p. 106 above.

Alexander Baring and Charles Arbuthnot, to whose management the £150,000 voted was entrusted.[1] The commissioners' superintendence was limited to 'the regulation of matters of *taste* with what connected itself with the fabric and improvements *immediately attaching* to it'.[2] They examined the plans submitted by Nash, Smirke and Jeffry Wyatt;[3] and they supervised Wyatt's operations. Their influence no doubt eased the voting of large additional sums for the completion of what in contrast to Buckingham House was a popular work.[4]

At Buckingham House, however, no such arrangement was contemplated. The work was done under the immediate authority of the Treasury, but in fact that was little exercised until 1829. Nash, working as the King's private architect, communicated directly with his royal client and acted on his personal instructions. The necessary funds were not derived from parliamentary grant, but from surplus funds of the Land Revenue specifically appropriated by the Act 5 George IV, c. 77. Buckingham House was, Nash claimed, 'taken entirely out of the Office of Works'.[5] But for Nash's refusal to be accountable for public money, the rebuilding would have been done under the aegis of the Commissioners of Woods and Forests. However, as Nash told the 1828 select committee, since 'the person that certified the expenditure of the money would be called upon by the auditors to show, not merely that it was expended but that it was providently expended . . . it became necessary for [the Office of Works] in some way to be mixed with the accounts'. The Office of Woods had no measurers or means of verifying the accounts, indeed its own building works were usually performed by the Office of Works. Thus it came about that the oversight of Nash's operations was restored to the Office of Works, with its professional staff.[6] The arrangements were defined in a Treasury minute of 5 August 1825,[7] which directed the Office of Works to measure the work and inspect the materials. The pricing of the bills and making out of the accounts was also done by the Office.[8] Nash's proposal that he should retain power to make contracts, but subject to Office of Works approval (which might be assumed if no comment were made within three weeks), was also incorporated in the minute. Until then, Nash had considered himself in this work 'totally independent of the Office of Works', and he continued to act as exclusive director of the undertaking, believing himself to be authorised (until Goulburn's order in 1829) to execute whatever the King ordered 'without the approbation of the Treasury'.[9] Stephenson duly appointed a measurer, but warned the Treasury that the architect was himself responsible for the quality of materials and workmanship, and that no inspector should therefore be appointed.[10]

---

[1] *Parl. Deb.* new ser. xi, 147. The idea of a committee of taste stemmed from that appointed in 1802 to superintend the erection of monuments to heroes of the revolutionary and Napoleonic wars. The concept became a favourite theme of parliamentary critics of public works.

[2] G. Harrison to Lord Liverpool, 23 April 1824, reporting Long's view (RA 34690).

[3] Works 4/26, p. 385. See below p. 384.

[4] *Parl. Deb.* new ser. xxi, 1578; 3rd ser. ii, 592.   [5] *1828 Report*, p. 46.

[6] *1828 Report*, pp. 46–7; *1831 Report*, pp. 13–14, 194; T. 1/3489, ii, f. 13226/26.

[7] *1831 Report*, pp. 196–7.

[8] Nash's evidence to the two select committees does not entirely accord, but it is possible that the procedure adopted (which echoes that suggested by Stephenson during the 1819 discussions about organisation, see p. 109) put more in the hands of the Office than Nash had purposed: he consistently argued that as he had no control over the bills, he could not be held responsible for the cost of the work (see *1828 Report*, pp. 45–7).

[9] *1828 Report*, pp. 46–7; *1831 Report*, p. 13.

[10] *1831 Report*, pp. 196–7.

The minute of 5 August 1825 also applied to the works at Windsor, which the Treasury declared to be 'in all respects analogous' to those at Buckingham Palace.[1] The Windsor works had hitherto been conducted by Wyatville on his own responsibility as to contracts and accounts, of which he sent an abstract to the Treasury, where the tradesmen were paid at the Commissariat department.[2] In submitting his contracts to the Treasury on 1 January 1825, he wrote:

> I considered myself as engaged upon the works at Windsor Castle, to conduct them in the same manner as I had found to answer in all my private works of magnitude, but afterwards feeling that your Lordships might justly consider it to be necessary to require the works to be carried on under your own sanction for the public security, I adopted the method followed by the Office of Works.
>
> I therefore applied to various Artificers for price lists and took the lowest, finding this method from the intricate nature of the work (in the mixture of materials) to involve great delay. I then pursued the second more simple mode of the Office of Works, by issuing a circular letter.[3]

To the 1828 select committee he further explained:

> I found afterwards it was better, instead of getting lists of prices, to resort to the method of the Office of Works, and to ascertain how much less than the Office of Works quarterly prices, persons would do the work for . . . I stated, that from the largeness of the work they should enter into the consideration of doing it at a much cheaper rate, the regular payment of the money having been voted by Parliament, so that there would be no risk on that point. In consequence of that, I think some of the trades, that would allow of it, deduct $7\frac{1}{2}$ per cent less than the Office of Works quarterly arranged prices, and the others, nearly all, 5 per cent, in consequence of such large quantities, which has reduced their profits to as little as they possibly could afford to do the work well for. I think if I had tried to procure less prices than these, by getting a competition among people who were not qualified, I should have had constant quarrels and bad work.[4]

On 3 January 1825 he wrote again to the Treasury, explaining his methods in greater detail:

> Each Workman that may be employed at day work receives a Tin Ticket upon which is the initials of his Master, and retains in his memory a number to distinguish himself, these tickets are delivered at the Gate by the man on coming to his work, and are immediately taken account of by the superior intendant, or one of the Assistant Clerks of the Works, the tickets are then fetched from the Office by the Tradesman or on his part, and given to the Workmen before the next meal, and each man again deposits it at the Gate, by this arrangement each quarter of the day undergoes a regular check.[5]
>
> A note of the materials delivered that are to be used independent of the works to be measured, accompanies each delivery, and at the end of each week two notes are formed, one of which is retained in the Office and the other given to the Tradesman.

---

[1] *1831 Report*, pp. 197–8.   [2] T. 1/4398, f. 18918/32.
[3] *Ibid.*, f. 359/25.   [4] *1828 Report*, p. 94.
[5] If a man 'did not keep his time to five minutes [the clerk] sent him back, and he lost a quarter of a day' (*1828 Report*, p. 98).

> From these notes a general abstract and Bill is formed for each artificers day work. In regard to the measured work . . . my instructions . . . are, that the whole measurement Abstracts and Bills shall be made out in the Office at the Castle, and open at all times to the investigation of every one authorised or being concerned therein.
>
> And the prices to be affixed to the accounts so made out, will be founded on those regulated every quarter (and which are generally very low) by the Office of Works.[1]

Having been engaged on the works for a year already, Wyatville was not pleased to have his arrangements disturbed, and protested against the view that the works at Buckingham Palace were analogous to those at the Castle, where there was

> a mixture of all sorts of materials in its walls, rough stone, smooth stone, chalk and brick, all shapes of angles to reconcile in walls from five to nine feet thick, upon foundations, in many instances very defective; and requiring two thirds of my active time deciding matters on the spot to keep the works moving with regularity.
>
> Whereas Buckingham Palace . . . might be carried on by an architect at a remote corner of the kingdom with an occasional visit of two or three times a year, on this point I speak from the experience of years at the Palaces, Longleat and Chatsworth etc.

Wyatville, like Stephenson, disliked the proposed office of inspector; as for a measurer he protested that he had wished to have someone from the Office of Works, but had now engaged Thomas West, a well-known and reliable man for the job, who had given up much of his usual work. The appointment of a stranger would increase the architect's difficulties. It would be enough, he suggested, if the inspector were to come at 'any or frequent unexpected times'.[2]

Invited by Stephenson to discuss the problem, Wyatville put forward his own proposals: the contracts, weekly notes and measuring books should go to the Office of Works with the bills when made out, instead of the bills going immediately to the Treasury. Abstracts should be made at Windsor, to facilitate reference 'and not oblige an artificer who may have a hundred men at the works to go to London and neglect them for two or three days'. Articles which could not be previously valued were best priced on the spot; West could be appointed official measurer. By this plan, Wyatville could certify the accounts; but if the bills were 'finished under superior authority my signature appears to be useless'. To prevent error and 'the mutilation of fair bills' he suggested that a quarter's prices should be fixed during its last week, so that the tradesman could make accurate bills. West was accordingly appointed official measurer, and the new régime commenced with the Christmas quarter of 1825.[3]

Windsor, however, gave the Office of Works less concern than did Nash's operations. On examining Nash's bills for the first four months' work at the palace, Stephenson found the contracts unsatisfactory: 'some are in writing, some merely verbal, but all are in my opinion more or less improvidently made, as compared with those . . . for similar works by this department'. Nash had also stipulated that the tradesmen should be paid within three months of each quarter's account, on pain of losing the beneficial prices—a proviso criticised by Stephenson and rejected by the

---

[1] T. 1/4398, f. 143/25.   [2] Works 1/13, pp. 457–8.   [3] *Ibid.* pp. 508–9.

Treasury in January 1826. Nash too had his own notions of competition; employing three or four tradesmen of a kind, he would obtain the lowest practicable price and refuse to allocate work to the others unless they agreed on the same price. Though the masons and bricklayers collusively predetermined their tenders, the mason Wood complained it had been a hard bargain.[1] Unfortunately Nash's specifications were sometimes so vague that the resulting tenders were not really comparable, like those for the important contract for ironwork, awarded to Crawshays.[2]

More explicit criticisms of Nash's dealings were made by Stephenson in January 1826.[3] Not only was there uncertainty about contracts,[4] but some of the tradesmen chosen were of doubtful standing; prices agreed were excessive compared with recent contracts for other public buildings; the advantage of competition was lost; the architect was himself supplying materials; and he was charging a five per cent commission instead of the three per cent allowed by the Office regulations. Eventually the Treasury approved Nash's conduct:[5] but its failure to act on the report that Nash was supplying materials was severely animadverted upon by the select committee of 1831.[6] The Chancellor of the Exchequer had already, on 18 January 1826, written to the King promising that Nash would 'have every facility which can be given him for the purpose of expediting the works . . . and Mr. Nash', he concluded optimistically, 'now quite understands and enters into the necessary forms and regulations connected with expenditure'.[7] On 27 June, the Treasury decided that Nash's responsibility was similar to Wyatville's at Windsor, 'differing greatly in character and degree from what is imposed upon the Architects who superintend the public buildings executed under the authority and directions of the Board of Works', and deserved five per cent. While employed on the Palace he was not to draw his salary as Attached Architect, though continuing to give advice;[8] but no deduction was to be made from his commission for the measuring and making up accounts done by the Office as Stephenson had suggested.[9] This put Nash on the same footing as Wyatville.[10]

It is difficult to say how far the charge of improvidence can be sustained against Nash's contracts. His timing was unlucky, for prices reached their maximum in mid 1825 and Stephenson was consequently able to point to other large works that had been contracted for at substantially lower rates only a year or two earlier.[11] Subsequently there was a fall in many prices, which left Nash's standing as high peaks. But where his prices were tied to those of the Office of Works, they of course would fall too. Nash strongly rebutted Stephenson's charge in a letter to the Treasury dated 7 July 1826: the Office of Works prices allowed only the minimum profit a tradesman could afford to accept, unless the merchant's and manufacturer's profits were

---

[1] *1831 Report*, pp. 55, 68, 70.

[2] *Ibid.* pp. 134–9. Crawshays were paid £17 a ton for iron girders, and sub-contracted the work at £12 10s. a ton (*1831 Report*, p. 4). But Crawshays' excessive profit was chiefly due to a rapid fall in iron prices.

[3] *1831 Report*, p. 197.

[4] When asked by the 1831 select committee if any loss to the public had arisen from contracts being verbal, Stephenson replied, 'I cannot state any loss, but great trouble in pricing the accounts' (*1831 Report*, p. 31). [5] Treasury Minute, 23 June 1826 (*1831 Report*, pp. 198–200). [6] *1831 Report*, p. 5. [7] B.M. Add. MS. 40862, f. 154. [8] Works 1/14, pp. 304–6; *1831 Report*, p. 196. [9] *1831 Report*, p. 196. [10] Wyatville did not charge for his journeys—an important item—but was given a residence in the Winchester Tower in Windsor Castle; Nash was not paid for his journeys to see the King at Windsor, and his salary as an Attached Architect was discontinued (*1828 Report*, p. 45). [11] See Appendix C.

sunk in the price of the worked article, and ready money were paid. Thus a deduction of ten per cent from Office of Works prices was a provident bargain for the public.[1] The masons, who received this rate, were thought by the stone merchant Freeman to have 'received a fair profit', and to have been 'introduced into a very good work'; but one of them, Launcelot Edward Wood, regarded it as a hard bargain 'attended with considerable expense' and would not 'accept a similar contract again'. James Firth, one of the carpenters and joiners employed on the same terms, claimed he did not make one and a half per cent profit out of it.[2] William Whitehead, a bricklayer, who received seven and a half per cent under the Office prices—the rate for his work at the House of Commons—obtained a better profit from his private clients. The palace, he thought, might possibly have been done for less if put out to competition, and he himself would have accepted ten per cent deduction if given the whole job.[3]

The comparison of prices for various buildings was a tricky business; Nash, after all, was building a palace, not public offices. There could not be any comparison, thought the carpenter George Harrison, between the carpenter's work of the new Post Office and that of the Palace. Not even that of York House was equal to what he had done at the Palace.[4] Stephenson sometimes complained that Nash did not furnish enough information to enable him to assess those tenders he did submit;[5] but for much of the work, as Nash justly pointed out, there was no precedent. 'It is really unfair to expect accurate estimates of such work where there are no precedents nor anything but my own judgement to guide me',[6] he told Spearman, the Treasury official charged with the business of the Palace.[7] Where that was so, he often devised means of arriving at a fair price for the job. The pedestal of the garden balustrade, for instance, was carved as rock-work. By getting an experienced mason to carve several styles, Nash obtained a model and ascertained the time taken, which enabled him to fix a price, whereas payment by the day would have provided no incentive to the mason.[8] Nash acted similarly over the inlaid floors of the state rooms, inviting tradesmen to construct samples. When he called for tenders for the marble staircase in November 1827, it was for steps only: 'knowing how very much the prices would be encreased had the columns and bases been included [as distinct items in the specification] I considered that I should make an advantageous bargain for the public if I could get the columns included in those prices'. The prices tendered by Joseph Browne were not all quite as low as those of Michael Crake, but Nash declared that Browne's were 'on the whole the most reasonable', and he preferred employing Browne if he would include the columns and bases at the same rate. But this competition was merely a façade: 'it was almost an imperial necessity to employ Mr.

---

[1] *1831 Report*, pp. 200–202.   [2] *Ibid.* pp. 37, 70, 82.
[3] *Ibid.* pp. 55–6. The automatic deduction of $2\frac{1}{2}$ per cent by the Office of Works is included in these percentages.
[4] *Ibid.* pp. 76–7. Thomas Martyr, another joiner of wide experience, said the work in the state apartments and connected rooms was 'very superior', both in materials and workmanship (*ibid.* p. 79).
[5] E.g. letters of 25 January, 13 February and 19 March 1827, printed in *1831 Report*, pp. 206–7.
[6] T. 1/3488, 19 August 1829. See also Hiort's evidence, *1831 Report*, p. 145.
[7] Sir Alexander Young Spearman (1793–1874), cr. Bart. 1840; auditor of the Civil List 1831; assistant Secretary of the Treasury 1836, resigned 1840; secretary and comptroller, National Debt Office, 1850–73. For his career, see Sir John Winnifrith's article in *Public Administration* vol. xxxviii (1960), pp. 311–20. Goulburn put him in charge of the palace correspondence at the beginning of 1829 (*1831 Report*, p. 124).
[8] Works 19/3, f. 239.

Browne', for it was he whom Nash had sent to Italy with the measurements and drawings to choose the blocks of marble, 'and in choosing the blocks he considered their conversion and designated part of one block for one purpose and part of it for another . . . how could any one but himself direct the conversion of the marble and I should have had no alternative but to have employed him to superintend the conversion'.[1]

Sometimes there was no pretence of competition, as with the large contract for excavator's work:

> The work was not offered to any person but Mr. McIntosh—his known probity, his great means of performing the work in the short time allowed him, and my own experience as to his means of executing great works on the most moderate terms were considered by the Board and myself as sufficient inducements to employ him without other competition, and his proposals were accepted seeing that they were within my Estimate.[2]

But even so Nash's methods do not appear to have excessively enriched many of the contractors. Profit margins were sufficiently narrow for the tradesmen to be seriously inconvenienced when the payments of accounts fell into arrears. Stephenson complained that some were men of inadequate capital, but the few who were bankrupted were warrant-holders under the Office.[3] Francis Bernasconi, contractor for the plastering, wrote to the Surveyor General on 12 March 1829, that if his contract were to be strictly abided by, he would lose heavily because of the extra labour and expense of the description of workmanship required, which he had not anticipated when the contract was made. Yet Bernasconi had been extensively employed by the Office of Works, and had a very large business as an ornamental plasterer; and his contract was typical of the Palace contracts.

It was true that some of the tradesmen Nash employed were not well-known in their business. Francis Read, nephew of an old Household officer, Benjamin Jutsham, was a newcomer among the master bricklayers. He had served his time, but never before executed a large work: he was allotted the north wing.[4] Wood, the mason, had never executed any extensive public works, though long employed by the Office of Works at Hampton Court and the Horse Guards; nor had he ever before worked in Bath stone: he built the east front.[5]

It was true, moreover, that Nash broke the code of the newly-emerging architectural profession by selling his own bricks and cement to the tradesmen. For these, he did sometimes receive more than the current price, but since the tradesmen's return was regulated not by what they had paid, but by the Office of Works' prices, the loss fell on them and not on the public. Nash himself appears to have kept this trade as far as possible distinct from his activities as an architect, and held it of no

---

[1] *Ibid.* ff. 256–7.　　[2] *Ibid.* f. 32.

[3] Joseph Barrett, painter, who was a warrant-holder (Works 4/29, 10 July 1829). Henry Warren, carpenter and joiner, another warrant-holder working at the Palace, fell into difficulties, and surrendered his warrant, 25 September 1829 (Works 1/17, p. 485), but was re-appointed 5 February 1830 (Works 1/18, p. 53). Michael Crake, whom Stephenson had wished to prefer to Browne for the marble staircase at Buckingham Palace, became bankrupt as a result of extensive building speculations (Works 1/18, p. 52, 8 February 1830).

[4] *1831 Report*, p. 63.　　[5] *Ibid.* p. 68.

account in his official dealing with tradesmen; but they confessedly and understandably could not distinguish the architect from the purveyor.[1]

The chief criticism of Nash's conduct that may fairly be made lies in the vagueness of his arrangements. A verbal contract may have been satisfactory where both parties agreed on what had been said—but Martyr declared he had undertaken his part of the carpentry without any contract, whereas Nash 'considered he had made some agreement with me, and that I had agreed to do the work at ten per cent under the Office of Works price, the same as some other men had done'.[2] Martyr had also expected to perform a larger portion of the work than he was given, as had his fellow-carpenter James Firth.[3] George Stratton, who installed his patent heating apparatus, believed Nash had instructed him to begin, whereas Nash consistently denied giving such an order.[4] It seems clear that Nash, with his multifarious activities elsewhere, relied too much on his subordinates, and failed to exercise a sufficiently close personal control over operations at the palace.

Criticisms of a similar nature were also levelled against Wyatville. Stephenson alleged that his contracts were at much higher prices than obtained for other public works, and pointed out that the architect was charging five per cent commission, besides the cost of measuring—an item that in private practice was normally included in the commission. On the other hand, he was not charging for travelling, which might be considered an equivalent.[5] Wyatville retorted that he was merely following the custom of his private practice in charging for measuring, but had omitted many other charges and 'rejected all the advantages that are to be obtained in private business', for, with the eyes of the nation on his work, 'I have considered the Honour and Glory of deserving the approbation of my King and Country as my greatest reward'. As for the contract prices, 'no person is getting more than a fair living profit'. Taking into account the lack of facilities, prices did not much differ from those in London. That the tradesmen were substantial enough was shown by their carrying on with the 'utmost vigour' though £60,000 was owing to them for three quarters' work. 'It is not necessary to enter into the variety of foolish reasons that induce many inferior offers for contracts,' he concluded, 'because I feel that both the time of their Lordships and myself has already been most unnecessarily employed on these topics'.[6]

But Stephenson found that several eminent architects included measuring in their five per cent, and prepared a table showing differences between the Windsor prices and those for recent works in London.[7] Wyatville argued in reply that the prices were made not by himself or the tradesmen, but by the Office of Works; that they were subject to a deduction of at least five per cent; that the tradesmen's

---

[1] *Ibid.* pp. 74, 82; *1828 Report*, p. 18. But considerable confusion about the role of an architect prevailed even among those whom one would expect to have clear ideas thereon, e.g. Peel in 1843 asked Lincoln to allow a young architect who had sought his patronage to 'enter into competition by Tender for the execution of any works under the Superintendence of your Department' (B.M. Add. MS. 40481, f. 112).
[2] *1831 Report*, p. 78.   [3] *Ibid.* pp. 80, 82.
[4] *Ibid.* pp. 121–3; Works 1/18, pp. 200–10; 1/19, p. 23. It appears from his examination by the 1831 Select Committee that Nash may have been deaf; if so, this may have caused misunderstanding.
[5] Works 1/13, pp. 520–1.   [6] T. 1/4398, f. 13084/26.
[7] Works 1/14, pp. 444, 491. Soane, Smirke and Pilkington agreed that five per cent included measuring, but the Treasury decided that as Wyatville did not charge for other things he should be allowed the measuring costs (*ibid.* p. 471).

expenses were five per cent higher than in London; and that their profit was ultimately only about five per cent.[1] He pointed out that Stephenson's table showed wide variations; 'It would perhaps prove on enquiry that the same tradesmen have different prices under the same Architect. And that the men employed under one Architect . . . do not succeed, or perhaps [do not] try to get contracts under another so that each have their followers'.[2] Of fifty-eight articles in the schedule only twenty-two were more expensive at Windsor, and the schedule contained 'proofs of speculation only equalled by the late Joint Stock Companies'. Some tradesmen had made tenders 'even at less than prime cost', hoping for an ultimate profit as warrant-holders. Thinking Bath stone too expensive, he had taken measures to obtain it at 2s. 6d. instead of 4s. the foot, so saving 'many thousand pounds'. 'I am perfectly justified in the conclusion, that such reductions having taken place at Windsor has operated upon all other works under Government.' After this, there was no further complaint about Windsor prices.

Castle and palace were the most notorious of the King's Works to be conducted outside the routine of the Office of Works, but even more anomalous were the works in the Royal Parks, conducted exclusively by the Office of Woods and Forests. The chief reason for this revival of independent activity, according to Charles Arbuthnot, Chief Commissioner of Woods and Forests, was that he had 'recommended Mr. Decimus Burton to undertake them, and as he was not one of the established architects of that department [the Office of Works] there were official difficulties against his being employed except under our own immediate direction'.[3] Arbuthnot stated that

> having seen in the Regent's Park, and elsewhere, works which pleased my eye, from their architectural beauty and correctness, I made inquiries as to the name of the architect, and I was informed that it was Mr. Decimus Burton. Feeling that it was open for my office to employ any architect who, in our opinion, would be likely to perform the work entrusted to him satisfactorily for the public, I sent for Mr. Burton, and desired that he would prepare designs for the erection of Lodges at the different entrances into Hyde Park . . . Mr. Burton showed great anxiety to meet the wishes of the Government, and most readily undertook to make such alterations as the noblemen and gentlemen, to whom they were shown, thought desirable.[4]

This explanation, however, is not entirely satisfactory, as Burton was soon afterwards employed to build the Parliamentary Mews, at Storey's Gate, under the direction of the Office of Works; it may be that jealousy of Nash's young protégé caused the initial difficulties. As for the bridge over the Serpentine, the Treasury selected Rennie 'as a very competent person for the undertaking',[5] and it seems to have been overlooked that the work (costing £45,000) ought to have been placed under Stephenson's direction. The method of contracting for these works, however, appears to have followed that of the Office of Works.[6]

---

[1] 5 January 1827, T. 1/4398, f. 472/27.
[2] There was truth in the suggestion that certain tradesmen were associated with particular architects. Thus Baker, Smirke's brother-in-law, was employed in many of his works.
[3] *1828 Report*, p. 130.   [4] *Ibid.* p. 123.   [5] *Ibid.*, p. 25.   [6] *Ibid.* pp. 126, 128.

Whatever room there may have been for stricter control of the major works at Windsor and Buckingham Palace, the evidence hardly justifies the sweeping denunciations of extravagance made by professed critics of public expenditure. Indeed, we have the unanimous evidence of the tradesmen questioned by select committees that the Office of Works habitually drove a hard bargain.[1] Of course they were not disinterested witnesses, but their testimony was supported by Wyatville, who explained to a select committee in 1828 that although an Office of Works contract offered less gain, it was still attractive because there was 'constancy of employment and certainty of payment'.[2] Moreover the steady flow of maintenance and repair work might enable a tradesman to hold together the nucleus of his work force in intervals between larger undertakings. It was not that there was much scope for a man to make a fortune from such work. As for the lower prices obtained in the limited competitions for major works, they were not a criticism of the Office schedule, but rather resulted from the desire to get government employment with its expectations of regular payment, and to secure work much in the public eye as an advertisement. Doubtless open competition would have attracted yet lower tenders, but whether this would have promoted efficiency is questionable. In the keener competition of the mid-Victorian period several government building contractors were bankrupted, to the detriment of the work in hand.[3] And as Soane pointed out, even in the prevailing narrowly limited competitions for tenders, the cheaper man might do less good work —not indeed such that the architect would be justified in condemning it: but posterity might have to bear the cost in repair bills.[4] Stephenson's system at any rate seems to have given value for money.

It is clear that Stephenson was a careful and conscientious administrator who achieved some measure of success in establishing sound building practice in the conduct of public works. But his discretion was strictly limited. On the one hand he was bound to defer to the Attached Architects on architectural matters; on the other he was subordinate to the Treasury in matters of policy and finance. It was the Treasury alone that could initiate, and which examined and approved the plans of all major undertakings. Finding his initiative thus restricted, and immediately responsible to the Treasury lords for the conduct of works that so easily became the subjects of public controversy, Stephenson wisely determined to live by the letter of his instructions. If he abided by the rules, and things went wrong, the responsibility could hardly be imputed to him.

The rules were laid down in the Code of Instructions issued by the Treasury in March 1815.[5] By articles xxii and xxiii the Treasury itself was the body that was empowered to sanction and approve plans, designs, elevations and estimates for any new buildings or major repairs or alterations, or any deviation from approved designs. Routine repairs were dealt with in articles xvi–xxi. The palaces and public buildings were to be surveyed annually, and only such alterations and repairs as were then found necessary were to be carried out, except for the repair of accidental

---

[1] See p. 138.

[2] *1828 Report*, pp. 95, 98–9. Wyatville had himself had experience as an appointed tradesman as well as an architect.

[3] E.g. The new Law Courts, Natural History Museum, and Burlington House forecourt.

[4] Soane Museum, corr. 2, xii, A. 37.   [5] Printed in *Parl. Pap.* 1814–15 (158) x.

damage, and trifling works required without delay 'for the necessary comfort, convenience or accommodation of the Queen or the Regent', which might be executed on the Surveyor General's authority if they could not stand over till the next survey, or until previous estimates could be submitted for Treasury approval. Details of all such works were to be reported to the Treasury within fifteen days of the end of the quarter. The Treasury might also approve special works on the Surveyor General's representation supported by estimates.[1] No private lodging might be repaired at public expense; but the occupants of 'grace and favour' residences in the royal palaces were not to undertake structural alterations without Treasury authority, and any such works done at their own expense were to be carried out by the Office tradesmen.[2] Requisitions for alterations and repairs were to be forwarded either to the Treasury or to the Office of Works by the officer in charge of the building.[3] Estimates of all these repairs and alterations were to be examined and passed by the Clerks of the Works at their weekly meeting with the Surveyor General, distinguishing between those executed under special authority, those resulting from the general survey, and those ordered by the Surveyor General.[4] Within fifteen days of the start of a quarter the Surveyor General was to receive an estimate of the probable amount of work to be executed during that quarter.[5] Armed with this information, he was to furnish the Treasury with both annual and quarterly estimates of money needed for the works due to be carried out under his direction.[6] Past experience should have warned the Treasury that such rules were rarely effective.[7] Unfortunately it was seldom possible to foresee all the works likely to be needed in the course of a year and embrace them in a comprehensive estimate. In 1816–17 expenditure exceeded the estimates for the year by £16,580, because of additional works ordered during the course of the year.[8] An attempt was made to include everything within the preliminary estimate, and to postpone anything subsequently requested until the succeeding year. Requisitions from other departments were referred to the Treasury on the ground that there was no money available. The responsibility of decision was then thrown onto the Treasury.[9]

Supplementary estimates were a common feature of the old system that Stephenson did his best to stamp out. He wanted the whole expense stated at the outset, rather than be faced with successive additions to an initially low—and misleading—estimate. In 1818 additions to the Stud House at Hampton Court were required for Sir Benjamin Bloomfield, the Regent's secretary. For this Nash submitted on 9 February an estimate of £300, some works having been already begun by Hardwick as Clerk of the Works. Stephenson thought the cost would be greater, 'but as I cannot be supposed competent to judge with much accuracy of a business of this nature', he asked for Nash's detailed estimate.[10] Nash replied that his estimate was for a 'modification' of the works begun by Hardwick, whose estimate was £800.[11]

[1] Art. xvii, xviii.   [2] Art. xxi.   [3] Works 1/6, p. 124.   [4] Art. xix.
[5] Art. xxii.   [6] Art. xxxi.   [7] Cp. above, pp. 33, 65.   [8] Works 1/7, pp. 373–5.
[9] E.g. the question whether to provide accommodation for an office keeper in 13 Downing Street when it became part of the Colonial Office (Works 1/16, pp. 141, 329). See also D. M. Young, *The Colonial Office in the Early Nineteenth Century* (1961), pp. 126–7.
[10] Works 1/8, pp. 404, 407.
[11] *Ibid.* pp. 408–9.

If Mr. Hardwick is to make a detailed estimate there cannot be the least necessity for my making one, as he is quite as capable as I am, I only say that I am confident the whole may be done for £1100—and I beg I may not be understood as wishing to interfere where I have no business, and that I have said what I did say, because I should be sorry the conveniences which I know are indispensable to receive the Prince should be beat to the ground by a heavy estimate.

Stephenson suggested that Nash ought to meet Hardwick, as

there appears to be much confusion and misunderstanding upon the subject of the alterations which have recently been done . . . as well of those now proposed to be done, by your plans, and which it will be very desirable to have cleared up with as little delay as possible . . . As to the estimate . . . being heavy the cause must I conceive lay in the plan alone as the calculations will be fairly and justly made to cover the work described but without leaving any part to be provided for by supplementary estimates, a practice I wish to avoid in this Department by every means in my power.[1]

Nash's reply is so characteristic of the problem Stephenson so often had to resolve with Nash—that of the architect's entirely *ad hoc* methods—that it is worth quoting *in extenso*:

Herewith I send you more correct plans of the alterations proposed at the Stud House, than those transmitted with my letter of the ninth, they in no way differ from those which accompanied that letter, than what arose from the inaccuracy of my plan of the present building, except that I have omitted the small back stairs, and substituted the stairs by the old kitchen; as will appear when the two plans are compared; for which purpose I return those originally sent—I must beg to correct an error in my letter of the ninth wherein I state £300 to be the expense between the plan I proposed and the alterations which were stated to me as previously intended—That sum of £300 was the difference of enlarging the two rooms proposed as a dining room, instead of laying the present two rooms together, and raising one of them, but the alterations of moving the stairs and converting the site of the present stairs, as additional space to the Drawing Room, and a Dressing Room, and Garret over; and making a back passage on the chamber floor; and the back stairs, were not included, and which I am of opinion would increase the £300 to £500; but these opinions I beg distinctly to state as my judgment only in considering the plans, and not the result of detailed estimates—I have accompanied these plans with a specification of the whole of the alterations proposed, including those intended to be done before I was consulted, which will enable a person to make a correct estimate of the whole, should such an estimate be required.[2]

Hardwick's estimate for the whole amounted to £2350, nearly twice Nash's rough estimate.[3] But at least the whole cost to be incurred was thus presented to the Treasury beforehand. Nash was not the only offender. In pressing Soane for full and accurate supplementary estimates for alterations at the House of Commons and the completion of the new Council Office in 1827, Stephenson remarked,

You will I hope my dear Sir, excuse the trouble I am thus occasioning you, but it really is on my part unavoidable; as the Treasury are very particular in requiring

---

[1] *Ibid.* p. 410.　　[2] *Ibid.* pp. 418–19.　　[3] *Ibid.* p. 441.

from me satisfactory estimates; and express upon every occasion great displeasure when authorised estimates are exceeded and I am certain that great reluctance will be felt, in making applications to Parliament for further sums to complete these buildings, and more particularly for the New Council Office.[1]

For ordinary works the Clerk of the Works' estimate would normally be fairly close to the actual cost. But for new buildings a detailed estimate, which could be based only on working drawings and full specifications, was rarely forthcoming: as Nash told the 1831 committee, 'Architects never make that sort of estimate in the first instance; I believe it is so much the contrary, that were an architect to be called on to deliver that sort of estimate . . . he must apply to professed measurers, unless he has measurers in his own office'.[2] He had told Stephenson much the same in 1825, when he estimated the rebuilding of Clarence House at £9000–£10,000: 'any Estimate formed without the aid of Working Plans and Specifications of the manner of the Work and Materials to be used and the parts of the Building severally measured must be vague and uncertain nor do I suppose such Estimates were in contemplation when our commission was reduced to three per cent well knowing the measurers employed to make such Estimates would expect from 1½ to 2½ per cent—all the working drawings being made for them'.[3] All too often, moreover, unforeseen circumstances would arise during the execution of works to increase the cost—whether it was the existence of unsuspected dry rot in an old building, a rise in prices of materials, or the discovery of bad ground on a site for a new building. Should this happen, the officer in charge was to report it immediately to the Surveyor General, who was to refer to the Treasury for a decision whether additional expenditure was to be incurred. On this issue the Treasury was unable to make an effective stand: in the repair and alteration of old buildings even the present day has not discovered a means of preventing estimates being exceeded,[4] nor are costing methods for new techniques always accurate. However efficient Stephenson might be, he could not prevent unascertainable defects in old buildings increasing expenditure. Called upon for an estimate of the ordinary and necessary alterations and repairs needed at the royal palaces for 1816–17, Stephenson reported to the Treasury that 'An Estimate of these works calculated upon the General Survey which has been made of most of the different Palaces, although taken with great care and attention could not be framed with any degree of correctness, from the nature of the Repairs required at the Buildings, many of which are in a very delapidated state.' He therefore suggested that a round sum might be allocated for this service.[5] The Treasury's reply regretted that 'any difficulty should arise in complying with so important an Article of your Instructions'. In the circumstances, however, the Treasury would be content with a report of the general condition of each palace, relying on the Surveyor General to conduct 'those Repairs which may be absolutely necessary' with the 'strictest attention to Economy'.[6] Similarly no preliminary estimate could be formed for the

[1] Works 1/15, p. 444, 29 September 1827.
[2] *1831 Report*, p. 20.   [3] Works 1/13, pp. 266–7, 2 April 1825.
[4] E.g. the restoration of nos. 10, 11 and 12 Downing St., in 1957–64, originally estimated at £400,000, cost over £1 million. 'One cannot regard an estimate for a job of this sort as anything but extremely provisional', Mr. Harding of the Treasury told a select committee (*Parl. Pap.* 1962–3, vi [cmnd. 295]; 1963–4, v [cmnd. 273]).   [5] Works 1/6, pp. 382–3, 2 February 1816.   [6] Works 1/7, pp. 23–4, 30 April 1816.

restoration of the north front of Westminster Hall; the whole front had first to be scaffolded and examined.[1] Stephenson afterwards recalled that even then:

> It was impossible to make any satisfactory estimate; there was a probable estimate of £20,000 sent to the Treasury; the stone was measured; but from the nature of the repair, it was deemed necessary to execute the remainder by day-work . . . Where there is much work in a building that must be done in day-work, it has generally been found impracticable to form any very correct previous estimate of the cost of a building.[2]

Works at the Ranger's Lodge, Greenwich Park, in 1816-17 exceeded the estimates because they were carried out in a severe winter which damaged plaster and brickwork; and the extent of the repairs needed could only be ascertained when the roof had been stripped and the floors taken up: to make a supplementary estimate was impossible as the works were 'so blended with what was estimated and what was daily occurring, that the extent of the mischief could never be known till the works were compleated'.[3] Similarly at the Regent's Cottage, Windsor Great Park, Matthew reported that dry rot was very extensive; 'in fact I do not know where it will end, or what sort of Estimate can be formed unless the whole is laid open wherever it is tainted'.[4] Commenting on excess expenditure in 1825, Stephenson said that none of the alterations which occasioned it had originated in the Office of Works, but that the Office had often remonstrated against them when demanded, 'and sometimes with success'.[5]

In repairing 10 Downing Street and the adjacent Foreign Office in 1825-6, Soane met man-made difficulties as well as problems of repair; 'from the manner in which these works were executed by night and by day', he reported, 'from the variety of directions from different persons and different authorities—no probable conjecture could be formed of the amount of such works (so often altered in progress) until the works were actually completed'.[6] When the Treasury criticised the excess incurred there, Stephenson replied that 'it was out of my power to procure any supplementary estimates which could be relied upon but I took frequent opportunities of verbally representing that the expences of the . . . repairs and alterations would necessarily exceed very considerably the sum originally authorised'.[7] Here then Stephenson was limited to barking: the Treasury's watch-dog could hardly bite the Chancellor of the Exchequer or even the Foreign Secretary.

That Treasury control was not as effective as had been hoped was due to the Treasury itself: it was too small a department to exercise a close supervision over the detailed activities of the Office of Works; and it lacked any technical staff competent to evaluate the proposals submitted to it. Liverpool and Vansittart (then Chancellor of the Exchequer) had approved the design of the new Law Courts that attracted such opprobrium in the Commons. Liverpool and Robinson saw the plans for Buckingham Palace before that much criticised building was begun. Even ministers regarded as amateurs of architecture were astounded at the appearance of rooms the plans of which they themselves had approved. Soane's characteristic ceiling for the

---

[1] Works 1/9, pp. 419-21.   [2] *1828 Report*, p. 17.   [3] Works 1/8. pp. 27-30.   [4] *Ibid*. p. 34.
[5] Works 1/14, p. 116.   [6] *Ibid*. p. 313, 30 June 1826.   [7] *Ibid*. pp. 313-4.

Privy Council Chamber erected in 1824–7 came in for much adverse comment, but, as he pointed out: 'The great features of the Council Room, the columns, the four arches from whence the groined ceiling springs, as well as the groined ceiling itself are to be traced in the different plans, and as such I conceived sanctioned'.[1] Yet this was a building that had occupied the close attention of several Cabinet ministers before receiving the Treasury *fiat*.[2]

This block of offices, indeed, shows just how unsatisfactory the operation of Treasury control could be in practice. It is a sorry tale of indecision in high places: of ministers uncertain how large a scheme they wanted, shifting the line of the front, obliging the architect to change the style of his architecture, and entering upon the minutiae of the design—what order to employ, whether columns should be free-standing, whether there should be a crowning balustrade—as well as altering the internal arrangements of the plan. Particularly prominent in this *ex officio* committee of taste were the lately-appointed Chancellor of the Exchequer, Frederick John Robinson, irresolute but finical, and J. C. Herries, the pedestrian Secretary of the Treasury. Lord Harrowby, President of the Council, also demanded a number of changes. After three years' work, Soane noted: 'I am in a fever about the Estimates. So many alterations and additions have been made at different times, and so many Estimates dovetailed into each other, that I am mortified at the result of such mixed calculations'.[3] When the Treasury complained of the increased cost of the building, Soane pointed out that 'When the plain example of the Corinthian Order in front of the Board of Trade and Council Offices was changed to the richest order in all the remains of Antiquity', the whole 'tone and character' of the building was altered in a manner which affected even 'the internal Finishings of [the] Offices'.[4] 'It is not possible for me [he told Stephenson] to pledge myself to any precise sum, more particularly as the estimates have been, in some instances, made under imperfect views of the alterations required'.[5]

Less idiosyncratic designs ran less risk of being altered during construction. Thus Smirke's innocuous Grecian was not much cavilled at in the 1820s. Moreover Smirke, unlike Soane, was an architect who usually kept within his estimates. He was also favoured by other factors. His buildings were less in the public eye than those of his colleagues—the King's Library at the British Museum was comparatively secluded, and the existence of a semi-public body, the Museum trustees,[6] discouraged interference by Treasury ministers. The new General Post Office was only entrusted to Smirke after years of indecision. Since October 1819 the Treasury had had before it numerous plans obtained by open competition. Rejecting all these, as well as that previously prepared by the Post Office architect, Joseph Kay, the Treasury at last instructed Smirke to draw up plans of which the elevation and general character should follow those pointed out to the Secretary of the Post Office at the Treasury Board—presumably one of the competition designs.[7] Smirke was required to attend

---

[1] Works 1/15, p. 91, Soane to Surveyor General, 7 February 1827.
[2] *1828 Report*, pp. 38–42, 147 ff. See below pp. 551–9.
[3] Soane Museum, Corr. 2, xii, A. 96, 6 November 1826. See also the whole of this file, and *1828 Report*, pp. 33–43.
[4] Soane Museum, Corr. 2, xii, A. 130.   [5] Works 1/16, pp. 72–4, 1 February 1828.
[6] Of whom Henry Bankes was himself one.   [7] See p. 432.

the Board with his plans in December 1823, but subsequently was left without interference from the Treasury, the Post Office itself meeting the cost.[1] In building new offices at Somerset House Smirke could do little other than follow Chambers' design, which was then commonly regarded as all that a public building ought to be. Careful with his estimates, Smirke gave no handle for criticism. But it cannot be said that the rule of the Treasury in matters of style was advantageous. Nor was it any more successful in questions of planning. The architect of government offices and public buildings was usually presented with an incomplete brief, and his works were consequently subject to frequent alterations which were bound to augment the cost.

Defects of personality apart, this failure of the Treasury ministers to think out clearly what they wanted and then to commission their technical advisers to produce an answer was probably conditioned by the prevailing political circumstances. Unable to control the House of Commons, Liverpool's government was never certain of obtaining funds for its projects, and was afraid that the legislature might impose its own architectural notions on public building.[2] This situation was exacerbated by the organisation of the Office of Works, whose head was neither architect nor politician. Between 1815 and 1828 the only architect in the full-time service of government was the Assistant Surveyor—until 1823 Robert Browne, a worthy man who had first entered the Office of Works under Chambers, and thereafter Henry Hake Seward— neither of whom was in any way comparable with such men as the Attached Architects. Indeed the role of the Office in respect of plans for new buildings was to act merely as a channel of communication between the Treasury and the architect; and as Soane's correspondence about the Board of Trade shows, even as such the Office was often by-passed. Thus in architectural matters government was entirely dependent upon the Attached Architects, men distracted by large private practices. Relations between ministers and these part-time public servants were to all intents and purposes the same as those between private patrons and their architects. Yet they formed part of an establishment of which the official head was the Surveyor General, a civil servant answerable to Parliament only through the Chancellor of the Exchequer. But the Office did not actually form part of the Treasury establishment, and as its funds were derived from the Civil List and the Land Revenues of the Crown as well as from Parliamentary votes, the Chancellor was able to disclaim responsibility for its actions. Robinson was only too ready to exonerate himself from blame. When assailed in the House with criticism of Soane's work on the House of Lords he

> confessed that he was not at all surprised that this subject should have attracted the attention of the House. He did think it necessary that some alteration should take place in the system upon which these works were carried on . . . the authority under which these alterations had taken place, was the Board of Works; and he thought it very desirable that henceforward the public responsibility for all works of this kind should be vested in the Treasury. The fact was, that at present the Treasury was not responsible for these matters, and of course could not control the high notions which the architect or the Board of Works might have formed of the taste in which

[1] Works 1/12, p. 150; T. 29/224, p. 327; Works 4/26, p. 237.
[2] The abortive General Post Office competition of 1819 was held in response to a demand of the 1817 Select Committee on the Post Office that henceforth designs for public works should be obtained by competition; a resolution confirmed in 1819 by the whole House (*Parl. Deb.* xl, 234, 1437).

buildings of this kind should be erected. He conceived the proper duty of the Board of Works to be to take care that the old public works should be kept in repair, and that proper materials should be provided for the new ones. He would endeavour to frame some system upon which there should be in that House some officer like himself, responsible for what occurred in his department, and upon which the whole power might be vested in the Treasury.[1]

Such a repudiation of responsibility was of course unjustified; the system of 1815, as Robinson should have known after a year at the Exchequer, was designed to ensure Treasury control. If Robinson was arguing that the system had not been properly applied, he was criticising his own as well as his predecessor's administration: moreover it was not true that the Treasury could not regulate architects' 'notions', for this is precisely what Robinson himself had already done in the General Post Office competition.

Nor did Robinson's evasions serve to disarm the critics. The assault on Soane's work on the House of Lords was led by the mischievous Henry Bankes.[2] His appetite whetted by Robinson's inaccurate revelations, he at once renewed his onslaught: the next object of his wrath was another work of Soane's, the new Courts of Law that were rising westward of Westminster Hall. He condemned the 'abominable taste in which new buildings of a different order of architecture had been grafted on to the old Gothic'. Robinson, floating with the tide,

> regretted quite as much as his hon. friend, the existence of the unpleasant excrescence of which he had so deservedly complained. He had seen it for the first time in the course of last year, when the foundations were already laid, and it was unfortunately too late to put a stop to the building. The only amends which could now be made was to take care that nothing else should be erected so unsightly.[3]

Bankes then moved for papers, and followed on 18 March 1824 with a motion for a select committee on the new Law Courts—an attack that Nash considered was aimed at the Office of Works as much as at Soane.[4] Robinson promised to suspend the work for two or three days if Bankes would defer his motion; but opposed a committee as unnecessary. When Bankes renewed his motion five days later, Robinson found that it was too late to stem the adverse tide. Though he declared that he could not, in the public interest, consent to a committee 'having for its object to consider the propriety of pulling down buildings which were now so near their completion'; though he feared the 'removal of one excrescence would only lead to the creation of another'; though he urged that till lately the House had displayed no interest in the adornment of the metropolis, that there was an urgent need for the new courts, and that 'Colonel Stephenson and Mr. Soane . . . had really acted with their hands tied', the appointment of a committee was carried by 43 votes to 30.[5] When the Committee reported in favour of demolishing the northern façade of the courts and rebuilding it further south in a Gothic style to assimilate to Westminster Hall, the government acquiesced, though the Commons were encroaching on one of the important features of its prerogative, the sole right to propose measures involving public expenditure. Thus

---

[1] *Parl. Deb.* new ser. x, 623 ff. [2] See pp. 102, 158. [3] *Parl. Deb.* new ser. x, 633.
[4] Works 19/50, 10 August 1824. [5] *Parl. Deb.* new ser. x, 1381.

M

another handicap was loaded on the Office of Works, the fitful interference of Parliament or more strictly, of parliamentary connoisseurs. It was probably to obviate such interference as well as to fulfil Liverpool's pledge to relieve the King from trouble with the Office of Works, that the restoration of Windsor Castle was placed under the direction of a commission of members of both Houses.[1]

Proposing a grant of £150,000 for the Windsor works, Robinson remarked on 5 April that formerly matters of taste had been left to the Board of Works; thus earlier repairs at the Castle had been entrusted to Chambers. 'At that time nobody suspected the Treasury of taste'. When Parliament had voted a sum for public monuments to the fallen heroes of the war in 1802, individuals had been appointed by a Treasury minute to consider designs; this he thought an effective system, and this was the precedent adopted.[2] This pleased the House, and a motion demanding to see the plans and estimate was defeated by 123 votes to 54.[3]

When the Office vote for 1825 was moved, on 28 March that year, the Custom House scandal had broken, and this intensified the call for 'a regular superintendant of public works' and for the closest scrutiny of building grants.[4] Soane again fell under criticism for his Board of Trade, which reminded Sir M. W. Ridley 'strongly of the stand on the racecourse at Doncaster'.[5] But there was evidently also a feeling that criticism had gone too far, given expression by William Smith, a prominent Dissenter, who

> animadverted on the extreme facility with which gentlemen had lately indulged in reflections upon the architects employed on the public buildings. Almost every member who had spoken on these subjects . . . seemed to believe that he had discovered some infallible rule of excellence, by the test of which all new edifices might be tried; and, if their proportions and aspects did not come up to this test, hon. gentlemen really loaded the parties with the severest censures, not to say the most opprobrious epithets, alike inconsistent with ordinary candour, and offensive to good manners. They spoke as if they themselves were intimately acquainted with all the rules received in the science of architecture; and as if everything was to be conceded to their opinions, and nothing to the technical skill, the knowledge, or the judgment of the architect whose works they reprobated.[6]

Certainly after this, criticism died down for a period, and the Office of Works was left to pursue the tenor of its way.

The House of Commons was not the only handicap the administration had to carry. Even more delicate problems arose in the reconstruction of the state apartments at St. James's Palace. This in any case would have been a difficult task:

> From the ruinous state of this old building [wrote Stephenson to the Treasury], these works required more than common care and attention; presenting many serious difficulties, and which were much encreased by the very limited time in which they were directed to be completed, so that the expences of them, excepting in a few instances, can only be satisfactorily ascertained after the bills have been examined and settled. I beg however at the same time to assure their Lordships, that every

---

[1] See p. 133.   [2] See M. Whinney, *Sculpture in Britain, 1530–1830* (1964), p. 199.
[3] *Parl. Deb.* new ser. xi, 147.   [4] *Parl. Deb.* new ser. xii, 1263–4.   [5] *Ibid.* 1258.   [6] *Ibid.* 1261.

exertion has been used here to check and controul this expenditure, as far as it was possible to do it, under the many difficulties I have had to encounter in carrying on these numerous and very complicated works.[1]

Stephenson found it impossible, even after £42,000 had been spent there, to 'venture naming any sum . . . that can be relied upon, as likely to cover the additional expenses'. The great difficulty evidently lay in the King: 'alterations are very frequently making in the decorations and fittings-up of the State Apartments; and also in the approaches to them, and in so many different directions, as to have occasion[ed] alterations in nearly every remaining part of this palace'.[2] Even the hope that the work might be completed without exceeding the year's appropriation proved illusory.[3] Stephenson, sending an estimate of £20,000 for gilding and reporting another of £6000 for works in progress since January 1824, remarked that it was impossible to state how much more might be required, 'nor do I conceive it possible for any economy or management to keep the expenditure of this department—at least for the present— within the sum' appropriated. On 30 March he forwarded an estimate of £1309 for altering old buildings in the palace for the German Office according to a plan signed by the King, 'which is very inaccurate, was not made by this Office, but appears to have been executed by some person not fully informed of the exact purposes for which these alterations were intended, nor much acquainted with the state and condition of the buildings'.[4]

This illustrates one of the fundamental weaknesses in the Surveyor General's position, and a major problem for the Treasury ministers. Restraining the King's appetite for 'improvement' was to prove beyond Stephenson's powers. With such a King as George IV, keenly interested in questions of taste, but constantly changing his mind, and with such an architect as John Nash, careless of detail and obsequious to the whims of his royal master, it was impossible for a comparatively insignificant official like Stephenson effectively to control expenditure. The restoration of St. James's Palace was a foretaste of the rebuilding of Buckingham House. After a struggle, culminating in an exhaustive parliamentary inquiry, Nash was brought to realize that he must not carry out the King's wishes without previous Treasury authorization. He then simply omitted to carry out the King's directions; and it was only the fact that the King died without discovering this that resolved an awkward situation. The immense difficulty of dealing with George IV and Nash in combination may be further illustrated from the history of the Cottage at Windsor.

A *cottage orné* on a large scale, the Windsor Cottage had been constructed under the original superintendence of the Office of Woods and Forests. When it was transferred to the Office of Works, Nash submitted an estimate for additional works to cost £5234, authorised by Treasury letter of 14 January 1815.[5] But on inquiry, Stephenson found that this sum 'was to cover what had been already completed, without any previous estimate'. The accounts that he submitted on 25 September 1816, totalling £30,074, were consequently for works no part of which was done

[1] Works 1/12, p. 350, 23 January 1824.   [2] *Ibid.*
[3] *Ibid.*, p. 394, 11 March 1824.   [4] *Ibid.* p. 416.
[5] Works 1/6, pp. 365–6; 1/7, p. 280. Nash's first estimate, £5851, included items that were also included in other estimates (Works 1/6, pp. 349–50).

under the Office of Works. 'After much time and pains had been taken by this Office in examining these accounts', Stephenson reported, 'it was discovered that many of the vouchers were mislaid, and could not be found. I therefore called upon Mr. Nash specially to certify, that all Dimensions, and day work, in these accounts were fair, and justly charged'.[1] 'The nature of the work', wrote Nash, 'and the manner in which it was done induced me to consolidate the estimates and make the accounts out as if the whole had been done under one estimate by which I avoided the possibility of the works of one estimate being included in another'—an error which had in fact occurred in 1815 when Nash had included the fitting-up of a farrier's shop and wash-house at Cumberland Lodge in distinct estimates for both the Cottage and the Lodge.[2] 'You have no conception how peremptory the King is on the subject', Nash remarked of further works at the Cottage in September 1820.[3] In December the Treasury refused to authorise another £10,000 estimate, but works on the Cottage in 1820–22 amounted to some £12,000 nevertheless. On examination the accounts were found to be full of errors and to be intermingled with works on the royal stand at Ascot.[4] When in December 1823 further works estimated by Jeffry Wyatt at £5000 were sanctioned, the Treasury directed that they should be under the 'sole superintendence and direction' of the Commissioners of Woods and Forests.[5] The Surveyor General summed up the difficulties of building for George IV in his report on the works at the Stud House, Hampton Court, stating:

> that it appeared during the progress of this work, that considerable and constant deviations were directed to be made from the original plan, and that from the great hurry and confusion in which these works were conducted, it seems to have been very difficult, if not almost impossible, to have provided additional estimates, that could have been depended upon; and that in carrying on works of this description, under such circumstances, and within such limited time, very great allowances are to be made; as I have found it upon many occasions of this kind, to be impossible strictly to adhere to official regulations. . . .[6]

Historical factors, too, served to diminish the degree of control over the sovereign's operations that his ministers might exercise. If it were question of a parliamentary grant, then their influence was at this period decisive.[7] But George IV also had the disposal of a considerable personal income (the Privy Purse) from his Civil List, and from the Duchies of Cornwall and Lancaster and the Irish hereditary revenues (surrendered to Parliament by William IV), which permitted him to undertake building on his own account, though such operations might require subsidy from other funds at a later stage: and for this purpose he had access to certain other prerogative and hereditary revenues free of parliamentary control.[8] Then the Crown Lands managed by the Office of Woods, Forests and Land Revenues, the estates surrendered by the monarch on his accession, were regarded as being still in some way at his disposal for purposes such as building and planting; and on this

---

[1] Works 1/7, p. 280.　　　[2] *Ibid.*, p. 168; 4/21, p. 361.
[3] Works 1/10, p. 220.　　　[4] *Ibid.* pp. 253, 274; 1/11, pp. 269, 299, 323.
[5] Works 1/12, p. 316.　　　[6] *Ibid.* pp. 319–22, 7 Jan. 1824.
[7] E.g. the proposed building of a new palace was countermanded by ministers in 1814, see p. 125. For the proposed rebuilding of Buckingham House, 1819–25, see pp. 263–7; the restoration of Windsor Castle. see pp. 383–4.　　　[8] In wartime the most important of these was the Droits of Admiralty.

department fell much of George IV's expenditure. Where such works involved building, the Office of Works was generally involved too, though as an agent possessing little power of decision. The Treasury, which could have exerted its authority, showed (as we have seen) little inclination under Lord Liverpool to restrict the King's minor extravagances; and it was not until Wellington's administration, when so many schemes were afoot that the government despaired of financing them, that the Treasury determined to restrain George IV.[1]

The other members of the royal family constituted a rather less serious problem. Until her death in 1818 Queen Charlotte continued to reside with her daughters at Buckingham House or Kew, demanding little of consequence. The Regent's sovereign position enabled him more readily to gratify his own enthusiasm for building; but he agreed with Liverpool in attempting to restrain the like propensity in his brothers. Yet so decrepit were the apartments allotted to them in the old palaces, such as Kensington and Hampton Court, that merely keeping them in good repair was costly. Under the Treasury Instructions for the Office, the younger members of the royal family were placed on the same footing as any other inhabitant of the royal palaces, article xxi forbidding 'repairs of any sort . . . in any apartments, houses, outhouses, stables, or other offices . . . which shall be occupied by any persons whomsoever, either by Royal Authority, by Warrant from the Lord Chamberlain, or in right of office, (excepting such as shall be necessary for the safety and preservation of the building,) unless express authority shall be given to the Surveyor General for such purpose by the Commissioners of the Treasury'; nor were any alterations to be made, even at the occupier's own expense, without the special authority of the Regent or the Treasury. The Duke of York's splendid mansion by St. James's, built largely at the expense of his tradesmen, lies outside the scope of this history.[2] The next heir, the Duke of Clarence, had Bushy House improved after his marriage in 1818, and his apartments at St. James's were rebuilt by Nash as Clarence House in 1825–9, at an estimate of £10,000 which grew into an ultimate charge of £22,000. The Duke of Cumberland's apartments at the same palace were improved in 1829 at a cost of £5550.[3] Most persistently bothersome of the royal brothers until his death in 1820 was the Duke of Kent, who had succeeded in bringing a large part of Kensington Palace into his occupation, and also enjoyed apartments at Hampton Court as Ranger of the Home Park. Other members of the family whose residences were maintained or restored at the expense of the Office of Works were the Duke of Gloucester (Bagshot Lodge), Princess Sophia Matilda (Brunswick House, Greenwich), the Princess of Wales, and her daughter Princess Charlotte. The Duke of Cambridge (with a house at Kew) spent most of his time in Hanover as Regent, and the Duke of Sussex, who lived at Kensington Palace, disagreed with his eldest brother's politics, and received little of the public bounty.[4] Expenditure on the junior branches of the

[1] *Letters of George IV*, ed. Aspinall iii, pp. 391, 402–3; *Wellington Despatches*, new ser. v, pp. 28, 337.
[2] See H. M. Colvin, 'The Architects of Stafford House', *Architectural History*, i (1958), pp. 17 *et seq.*
[3] See below p. 369.
[4] Goulburn MSS., Surrey R.O., Goulburn–Wellington correspondence 1829: Goulburn, 'The Duke of Sussex is very urgent about this room. The expence will fall on the Civil List. . . . The sum however is not considerable. . . .' Wellington's reply, 'We shall certainly have a discussion with the King, respecting all this Expenditure and His Majesty will immediately reproach us with constructing this new Room . . .'; see also *Letters of George IV*, ed. Aspinall ii. p. 186.

royal family was probably limited as effectively as the prevailing system of hereditary monarchy would permit, and the Office of Works provided a barrier behind which Treasury ministers might shelter.[1]

One further question that may be asked is how far the Office of Works promoted economical methods or proposed new arrangements by which economies might be realised. There is nothing to suggest that the Office of Works was a technical innovator: its position was one in which it did not dare to take risks that new techniques might involve. Occasional experiments were resorted to in response to outside suggestions,[2] but no consequences appear to have followed, and that was the extent of official involvement.[3] The real innovations came from the architects, pursuing ideas first tried out in their private practice. Thus Smirke explored the use of concrete in foundations,[4] and Nash and he developed the use of iron constructional members and of composition roofs.[5] Stephenson did, however, suggest minor improvements in organisation. In June 1817 he pointed out the drawbacks of the arrangements at Somerset House by which internal repairs were left to the several departments occupying the buildings, and his representation at length bore fruit.[6] Various changes in the customs of the department were also made: the Labourers in Trust were instructed to ensure that the plumbers kept the same hours as other workmen (instead of going for dinner one hour late);[7] only two coats of paint were normally to be applied in internal works;[8] and a new method of paying labourers' wages at the Office weekly was adopted in 1819.[9]

But however efficient the Office of Works might be in its limited functions, the real issues with which the department was faced were resolved not in Scotland Yard but in the Treasury. It was the Treasury which had to restrain the pressures for spending; the demands from other departments for works; the improving propensities of a numerous royal family; the grandiose notions of official architects; the interference of Members of Parliament. By and large, the control over non-revenue departments was effective. The greatest difficulty occurred no doubt when an important and resolute minister insisted on having improvements and alterations made in his office which were necessarily executed as a matter of urgency to prevent disruption of the public business. The only notable example of this was in 1825, when the enlargement and reconstruction of the Foreign Office and no. 10 Downing Street, already mentioned, involved a heavy charge for both works and furniture.[10] The one major disaster in the conduct of public works during this period—the

---

[1] An example of this is provided by the Duke of Kent's efforts to secure works at Kensington Palace in 1815 (Works 1/6, pp. 13, 31–2, 33, 223, 224–6, 229, 230, 231, 282–3, 288, 294, 296, 303–4, 381).

[2] E.g. with Worth stone and Carter's stone, see Works 1/6, pp. 490–1; 1/7, pp. 10–12, 17; 1/9, pp. 116–9. The Office was also called upon to investigate the feasibility of machinery to supersede climbing boys for sweeping chimneys (Works 1/9, pp. 178–81).

[3] Seward replied to an importunate inventor, 18 March 1842—and this is true of the earlier period too— '. . . In this Department the duties of it do not allow the individuals employed in the discharge of them sufficient time and opportunity to make the necessary experiments upon new schemes to work them out in all the nice details which are always attendant upon bringing such schemes to practical maturity . . .' (Works 1/25, p. 334).

[4] See pp. 415, 428; also J. Mordaunt Crook, 'Sir Robert Smirke; a Pioneer of Concrete Construction', *Trans. Newcomen Soc.* xxxviii (1965–6), pp. 5–22.

[5] *1831 Report*, pp. 272–4.   [6] Works 1/8, pp. 76–8; 1/11, p. 459.

[7] Works 1/8, p. 350, 31 December 1817.   [8] Works 4/23, p. 327, 21 January 1819.

[9] Works 1/9, p. 543.   [10] *1828 Report*, p. 10.

collapse of the newly-erected Custom House—could not be laid at the door of the Office of Works, for the Treasury had decided not to place the revenue departments' buildings under the Office, as had been provided for by the 1814 Act. Had this important work, already under way in 1814, been placed forthwith under the Office's supervision, the frauds perpetrated might well have been avoided or detected, the faults of construction corrected. The rebuilding, though entrusted to one of the Attached Architects, Smirke, was still not under the direction of the Office.[1] The 1828 select committee recommended that such buildings should be placed under the Office's control, a move the Treasury was then belatedly contemplating.[2] The building of the new General Post Office, another work of Smirke's, had already in 1824 been supervised by the Office of Works, as recommended by a select committee, the Post Office merely paying the bills after examination by the Works officials.[3] It was a retrograde step, however, when the Woods and Forests were given control of architectural works, as in Windsor Great Park and Hyde Park.[4]

The system established in 1815 was a moderately successful instrument for the economical maintenance and repair of public buildings, but in respect of new works it was ineffective if those works were of sufficient importance to command much attention (be it from ministers, Parliament, or public); and before the sovereign power most constraints melted. But as Wellington's administration took control, both the advantages and the defects of the system were about to be exposed to the searching light of a select committee.

[1] See pp. 422–30.   [2] See p. 157.
[3] Works 1/12, pp. 150, 163: see pp. 431–2. The real force of the 1815 select committee's recommendation (*Parl. Pap.* 1814–15 (235) iii, p. 9), however, was that the Surveyor-General of Works should conduct a competition for architectural designs for all major public works, the architect selected being remunerated by a fixed fee instead of a percentage commission. This was endorsed by resolution of the whole House in 1819 (*Commons' Jnls.*, lxxiv, p. 606).
[4] Above, p. 141.

Chapter VII

PARLIAMENTARY SCRUTINY AND TREASURY STRINGENCY, 1828–1831

As expenditure on public works mounted, so did concern about their management. The works in question were by no means all conducted by the Office of Works—indeed the most expensive fell under the Office of Woods and Forests. Thus the formation of Regent Street, which had originally been estimated by Nash at £385,000, a figure subsequently revised to some £517,000, was stated in the Commissioners' fifth Triennial Report of May 1826 to have cost ultimately over £1,533,000. The vast disparity between estimate and cost, however reasonably it might be explained, was enough to alarm the most enthusiastic metropolitan improver.[1] Rennie's new bridge over the Serpentine and the connected works were also known to have exceeded the estimate.[2] The revenue departments were spending heavily on new buildings: and the collapse of part of the Custom House in 1825 had focussed attention on their activities. The new General Post Office involved an outlay of £300,000 for site alone, another £520,000 for buildings, and a further sum for fitting-up. Under the Office of Works, the Parliamentary Mews near the Abbey had been erected at a cost more than half again that originally contemplated.[3] Expensive improvements had recently been made in offices and ministerial residences in Downing Street. Such mounting expenditure contrasted with a general depression in industry and commerce, and the prospect of a poor harvest for 1826. The Treasury determined to cut expenditure on public buildings, and Stephenson was ordered to confine work to unavoidable repairs; his funds for 1827 would be limited to £25,000 and any unexpended portion of the 1826 vote. Canning's administration proved even more severe, fixing the 1828 parliamentary vote at £20,000[4], but it was not to gain the credit it deserved. Had Canning lived, indeed, changes in the conduct of public works might have come earlier than they did. Shortly before his death, the Treasury called for a report from the Commissioners of Excise on the duties of their

---

[1] *1828 Report*, pp. 103, 144. The difference was explained by juries assessing 'goodwill' for trading properties compulsorily purchased at vastly greater sums than Nash had allowed; and the original plan had been greatly altered by the Treasury (*ibid.* p. 104).

[2] Rennie's original estimate for the bridge was £36,500. The cost was £45,464, and a further sum of £13,048 was spent on connected works (*1828 Report*, p.128).

[3] See p. 537. The government had intended to spend about £22,000, but a more decorative design which cost over £35,000 was insisted upon because of the situation.

[4] Works 1/14, p. 316, 30 June 1826 (see also *Annual Register 1826* (History), p. 172); 1/15, p. 314.

surveyor of buildings, with a view to placing him under the Office of Works. 'All buildings occupied as offices for Public Departments, should', thought the Treasury Lords, 'as far as it may be practicable, be subject to the superintendence of that Department'.[1] Towards the end of 1827, as the next weak administration, Lord Goderich's, crumbled, the deficiencies of the rebuilt Buckingham House became apparent to all. Low wings linking the main block to high terminal pavilions emphasised the design's lack of unity, and the awkwardness of the dome, half visible, half hidden from public view, was painfully obvious.

So many public works having thus aroused criticism on account of expense or defects of construction, planning, or style, comment became louder in press and in Parliament. On 5 February 1828 Henry Bankes, that self-appointed watchdog over public works, to whom Buckingham Palace was simply yet another tasteless failure of an official architect, moved for an account of the salaries and commission paid to the Attached Architects, expressing a hope that this would throw some light on the Board of Works.[2] 'Very large sums', he declared, 'were lavished upon works the most tasteless and the most inconveniently contrived, that it was possible to imagine, while there seemed to be no other control over the actions of the architect than his own whim or caprice'. He imputed no blame to Stephenson, 'a highly honourable man'; but 'the truth was, that not being a professional man, he knew nothing of the business of the office, and left the whole to the architects'.[3]

The more respectable opposition papers began to voice criticisms, the *Morning Chronicle* alleging that a Genoese ship which had brought marble for the new palace had taken back in payment a cargo of guns from the Ordnance store at Woolwich— a way of making costly palaces appear to have been built at little expense.[4] The same paper attacked the 'wasteful improvements' at the palace and in St. James's Park in a leading article on 21 March. Bankes followed this up that night, between midnight and one a.m. when few members were present, by moving for a select committee to inquire into the state of public buildings in the Office of Works and the application of part of the land revenue of the Crown.[5] Sir James Graham, an independent Whig, complained on 24 March that this would enable ministers to get off lightly: the subject ought to be examined by the Finance Committee which was then scrutinizing public expenditure.[6] Although Bankes had stated that his purpose was to inquire into the style of architecture employed for palaces and whether any trees in the Mall had improperly been cut down by Nash, Graham feared that the *bloc* of official members on the committee would force it to consider questions of expenditure as well, in order to avoid the more rigorous enquiry.[7] Bankes replied that the Finance Committee was already very busy, but there was no reason why it too should not investigate the Office of Works. His committee was intended to consider both taste and expenditure: major works had been undertaken without the knowledge of the House, as at the Custom House. 'It would be for the select commit-

[1] Customs 48/126, pp. 119, 262.   [2] *Parl. Deb.* new ser. xviii, 108.
[3] *Ibid.*   [4] *Morning Chronicle*, 2 March 1828.
[5] *Commons' Jnls.* lxxxiii (1828), p. 191.   [6] *Parl. Deb.* new ser. xviii, 1304.
[7] In addition to Bankes himself, the members of the committee were Lords Lowther,* Morpeth and Hotham, Sir Thomas Baring, and Messrs. Agar Ellis, G. Lamb, Ridley Colborne, Cust, Herries,* Arbuthnot,* Frankland Lewis,* Wilmot Horton, M. Fitzgerald and William Ward (*Commons' Jnls.* loc. cit). Members holding office are indicated by an asterisk.

tee to consider how far certain works had been proper and necessary, and how far it would be right to put a stop to any of the plans now in progress.' This alarmed Sir Joseph Yorke: why, he asked, should they take six members away from the busy Finance Committee? 'As to the public buildings, they were certainly a sort of hobby of his honourable friend, and no doubt he presided over the public taste very judiciously: but then his honourable friend had a manner which was directly against economy: for he was in the habit of saying, "I don't like the building you have erected here; take it down and put up another".' Ridley Colborne,[1] another of the parliamentary *cognoscenti*, commented that the Treasury Board had little time to consider such questions. A committee of some kind was absolutely necessary, 'under whose authority the matter might be fairly investigated, and who might be able to apply some timely check to the present extravagant proceedings'.[2]

The select committee, thus appointed, inquired into all those matters that had aroused comment. Nash was interrogated about his various activities: Regent Street, Carlton House Terrace, St. James's Park, and the palace. Wyatville was closely examined about his work at Windsor, and Decimus Burton about the Parliamentary Mews and his other official commissions in the Parks. Smirke was questioned about the Custom House and various general topics, and Soane was required to go into the fullest detail about the Board of Trade and Council Offices, a subject on which Lord Goderich (Frederick Robinson) himself gave evidence. Another minister to appear was Charles Arbuthnot, head of the Woods and Forests; and Stephenson described the workings of his own office. Other official witnesses were Spearman,[3] the parliamentary accounts clerk of the Treasury, and Mash, the permanent head of the Lord Chamberlain's Office. Criticisms of official procedure in respect of contracting and pricing had been made by Nash, so the committee took evidence also from two of the principal London general builders—Henry Rowles (Holland's nephew) and William Cubitt.

The immediate occasion of the committee had been disquiet about the proceedings at Buckingham Palace, and about these both Nash and Stephenson were examined; the whole truth, however, was not elicited until 1831. Stephenson's evidence was not particularly helpful: asked if Nash had given any reason for seeking to conduct the works on a special footing, he replied that he did 'not recollect . . . officially';[4] nor could he remember the sum expended. Sometimes he did not give information that must have been at his command. When asked why Nash's commission was five per cent instead of the usual three paid to the Attached Architects, he replied: 'I cannot answer that question',[5] though the reasons were set forth in a Treasury minute of 23 June 1826, communicated to the Office of Works on 27 June.[6] On other occasions he was obscure, or cautious, to the point of prevarication.[7] His evidence in general displayed the discretion of the civil servant.

---

[1] 1779–1854, cr. Lord Colborne 1839; brother of Sir M. W. Ridley; a trustee of the National Gallery.
[2] *Parl. Deb.* new ser. xviii, 1304–8, 24 March 1828.
[3] See p. 138 above.   [4] *1828 Report*, p. 31.   [5] *Ibid.* p. 29.
[6] Works 1/14, p. 304. The Treasury minute is printed in *1828 Report*, p. 164.
[7] Thus to the question whether an architect supplied any part of the materials himself, he answered: 'No, not if he does his duty'. The further enquiry, 'Does he do that in fact?' merely elicited: 'I have reason to suspect that this has been done; but it is contrary to the practice of the profession.' His interrogator then abandoned the search for the truth on this point (*1828 Report*, p. 18.)

Nash, on the other hand, was perfectly willing to talk—indeed, to overwhelm his questioner with information, though not necessarily quite to the point. Some of his evidence was equivocal. He stated: 'There are estimates before the Treasury of everything I have done' at the palace.[1] But no estimate was given to the Treasury of the increased expense required to carry alterations into effect, 'and none could be given, because they are alterations made as the work proceeds'. When asked what difference these extra works would make in the estimate he was unable to say, because 'many of those things that are ordered are not yet even begun . . . There are 104 capitals ordered; I do not know whether there are six, or sixteen, or sixty of them done'.[2] Yet, 'in the last estimate, I have given an estimate not only of the things that have occurred, but of the things that I imagined would occur.' 'Then you have presented to the Treasury', the Committee asked, 'an estimate of the increased expense that would be occasioned by the alterations made subsequently to that first estimate?'—'Yes, of the alterations made and to be made; because I have got the details of all the estimates'.[3] He was equally elusive when questioned about the total cost:

> 'The total amount of what I conceive will be required to complete the Palace as it originally was intended to be, and with the additions that have been already made to it, will come to 331,373 *l.*'[4]
> ' . . . you are not to consider 331,000 *l.*, as placing the King in the Palace, with it completely finished, because there are other things of which I have delivered estimates to the Treasury, and of course I wait the Treasury's orders to carry them into execution'.[5]
> 'What do these items amount to altogether?'—'£50,953'.[6]

But in addition to all this, there would be 'some incidental expenses', garden works, and £50,000 for alterations to the wings.

Given Nash's tendency to answer a question slightly different from that actually posed, we may read his evidence as meaning that he had estimated the total cost at £432,000 plus incidental and garden works, but that he could not estimate the value of what had actually been done (because he was not fully aware what had been completed); and he could not tell what relation there was between his estimate and the actual cost, for (as he explained) he had no control over the measuring of the work or the making up of the accounts. Since most of his contracts were fixed at a percentage under the Office prices, he could not directly control the price at which the work was executed: and he declared that the arrangement was not an economical one. But Nash was a past master at finding excuses for discrepancies between estimates and expenditure: in 1821 Robert Gray, the King's auditor, endorsed a statement of Nash's Brighton Pavilion accounts, with the comment: 'the states furnished by Mr. Nash . . . fully prove the fallacy of his occasional estimates, and the impossibility of his being deceived as to the general state of the concern (his present excuse), if he had ever compared the amount of his bills with his supplies'.[7] As at the Pavilion, so at Buckingham Palace: Nash failed (whether from burden of work or disinclination for the task) to keep a satisfactory check on the actual outgoings.

---

[1] *Ibid.* p. 47. [2] *Ibid.* pp. 48–9. [3] *Ibid.* p. 49. [4] *Ibid.* p. 50.
[5] *Ibid.* p. 52. [6] *Ibid.* p. 53. [7] RA 33972.

The other question was highly controversial, but highly complex also: that of the mode of agreement with tradesmen for the actual work of building. The contention basically was between those who favoured the traditional practice of making agreements with the various master tradesmen each to perform the work of his own trade at a price per unit, the works being measured in order to calculate the sum ultimately due; and those who preferred contracting in gross, i.e. agreeing with one tradesman to execute the whole for a predetermined lump sum. These basic systems were capable of considerable variations.[1] The former was said to call forth the better workmanship, but there were disputed customs in 'measure and value', as one method of pricing was termed, and contemporary opinion was beginning to favour the beautiful simplicity of contracting in gross, whereby the client knew beforehand how much his outlay would be. Opponents of that system claimed that it lent itself to fraudulent practices and bad workmanship and that its beauty was a snare and delusion. Nevertheless it was growing in popularity for several reasons. It was not a method that was practicable unless complete working drawings and specifications were prepared beforehand, so that the information was available on which the cost might be calculated. The growing professionalisation of architecture facilitated the preparation of such specifications and drawings. Then it was necessary to calculate the amounts of materials to be required. For this the emergence of the quantity surveyor as a professional man distinct from the architect provided the means. The builder could be sure of the data on which he calculated his expenses, so permitting him to name a safe price and obviating the risk of his being unable to make a contract pay except by scamping the work. The architect, too, was becoming altogether independent of the builder, and could be expected to see that justice was done to all parties. Finally, the emergence of a race of master builders with workmen of all trades in their constant employ reduced the dangers of bad or fraudulent workmanship through sub-contracting or inadequate resources. By the mid-1820s there were a number of such respectable master builders in London, of whom the Cubitts are the best known.[2] The practice of the Office of Works was, of course, to contract on terms of 'measure and prices' with individual master tradesmen for their own branches only of building; and not only were the contracts made by the Office rather than by the architect, but the measuring also was carried out by public officers. Nash argued that, unable to control the prices and make out the bills, the architect could not be answerable in any way for the accuracy of his estimate, and avowed 'his inability of judging how nearly the expense of the Palace has come to his estimate, because he has nothing to do with the measuring, or making out the accounts'. The committee's conclusion was that 'A mode of proceeding which affords so plausible an excuse or justification for excess and deviation, (unless some great counterpoise can be alleged in favour of its utility in some other point of view) is hardly to be maintained or continued with advantage to the Public'.[3]

Smirke's view was opposed to contracts in gross, and was in general support of official policy. As this was such a disputed issue—and one that had previously come

---

[1] See M. H. Port, 'The Office of Works and early 19th-century building contracts', *Econ. Hist. Review*, 2nd ser. xx (1967), pp. 94–110.
[2] See E. W. Cooney, *Econ. Hist. Review* 2nd ser. viii (1955–6) pp. 167 *et seq.*   [3] *1828 Report*, p. 5.

under the consideration of the 1812 Inquiry Commissioners[1]—the committee heard evidence from other architects and builders, including some not connected with the Office of Works. Wyatville, Decimus Burton and Henry Harrison supported the official view; but Rowles and William Cubitt defended contracts in gross as more advantageous to the employer. The committee pointed out that the certainty of a work being performed for a fixed sum was 'a powerful recommendation to contracts in gross'; but that if such works were, as alleged, more liable to be badly and fraudulently executed, and if such frauds and evasions were less easily detected than under contracts for prices, 'the latter mode would certainly be preferable, even at an increased charge'. But Nash's argument that the untiring eye of the architect was the employer's only real security perhaps strengthened a tendency, on Bankes's part at least, to favour contracts in gross. The committee's cautious conclusion was that

> with the superintendence of clerks of the works and other men bred to the profession, belonging to and dependent upon the Office, and with such accuracy in the specifications as the ability and experience of the attached Architects cannot fail to insure, Your Committee consider that the method which appears the most prudent and economical for individuals to adopt could not prove disadvantageous to the Public; and they are therefore inclined to think that with precise specification and careful superintendence, and where all deviations from the original plan are avoided, the system of Contracts in gross might be found to be the least expensive.[2]

The architect's responsibility should, the committee thought, be restored to him in the examination and making up of the accounts. But his commission was to be based on his own original estimate, not on the actual cost, 'for no mode of payment', they declared, 'can be more absurd or contrary to economy, that that of a per centage upon the ultimate charge, which makes it the interest of those who conduct extensive works to render them as expensive as they can, and affords to them a premium upon their own unrestrained inaccuracy and extravagance'.[3] For the world at large was not yet convinced of the professional integrity of the architect.

Another topic examined was the Attached Architects' alleged monopoly of public building. There was a strong body of opinion which favoured public competitions for architectural schemes, and the House of Commons, moved by Bankes, had in fact resolved in 1819 that competition should be resorted to for all major departmental undertakings.[4] The government had complied in the case of the new General Post Office, but so unsuccessfully that official opinion had hardened against the notion.[5] The feeling among the architects who gave evidence was that while competitions might be very well for young men seeking to make a name, those of proven ability and considerable employment would not be willing to expend their energies on so uncertain a trial. These opinions evidently impressed even Bankes, but the committee still felt need for a number of designs from which the government might choose. Their criticisms of the official monopoly show the strength of their belief in the

---

[1] *1813 Report*, p. 63.   [2] *1828 Report*, p. 5.   [3] *Ibid.* pp. 4–5.
[4] *Parl. Deb.* xl, 1437, 1 July 1819.   [5] *1828 Report*, p. 32. See p. 148 above.

judgement of the amateur and at the same time the considerable limitations of that judgement:

> . . . the effect of this system has been, and must continue to be, the narrowing and limiting the choice of those who are to determine upon the general taste and character of public Buildings, whose judgment ought to be assisted by some variety and diversity of design, and some increase in the power of selection.
>
> The faculty of originating and inventing what is excellent in Architecture, as in everything else, is undoubtedly confined to few; but many of those who are at all conversant in works of art, particularly if they have had opportunities of observing the best examples of ancient and modern architecture, are capable of forming a correct judgment upon designs or models which are placed before them, and will seldom fail to prefer the best to the worst. The inconvenience of this want of choice, supposing no more essential change to be made in the constitution of the Office, may certainly be obviated by directing each of the attached Architects to give a general notion or representation, or a slight sketch, of the style and character in which he would propose any public Building to be treated, which is either to be newly erected, or considerably enlarged or altered; and slight sketches might also be called for from other Architects of experience and reputation, so as to afford some opportunity of competition, without incurring the inconveniences attending unlimited tenders.[1]

The history of architectural competitions for public works in the nineteenth century was to show how unsatisfactory were even carefully-prepared, long considered and highly organized plans prepared on the basis of elaborate instructions; and it is quite certain that 'slight sketches' would have been entirely delusive.

Other matters relating to the Office of Works on which the committee commented included the construction of new buildings by the revenue departments. The scandal of the Custom House in particular called forth the recommendation that 'all works of this description should be carried on under the direction and management of the office specially appointed for the execution of such works; . . . in future no new buildings for any of these departments should be undertaken except under the authority of a grant of Parliament, upon an estimate to be laid before the House for that purpose . . . No Department should be allowed to order any thing beyond mere incidental repairs, without referring to and receiving directions from the Office of Works'.[2]

The committee also criticised the provision of residences for public officers at the public cost. Building and furnishing an official residence for the Foreign Secretary had cost over £42,000.[3] The public business did not require the constant residence of such officers; if the houses were considered part of their salary, 'the expense incurred by the Public very much exceeds the benefit received by the individuals'; and the provision of furniture opened 'a more unlimited field of extravagance'. The old arrangements for the provision of furniture for official buildings, hitherto managed by the Lord Chamberlain's department, were condemned as 'defective in many respects'; but this responsibility had in fact recently been transferred to the Office of Works under regulations the committee regarded as satisfactory.[4]

---

[1] *Ibid.* p. 4.   [2] *Ibid.* p. 9.   [3] *Ibid.* p. 10.
[4] *Ibid.* p. 10. The relevant Treasury minute of 22 February 1828 is printed on pp. 137–8.

The committee concluded their report by summing up the defects in the existing system, and suggesting some remedies:

> The Defects of the present system, under the Act of 1814, appear to be,
> 1st. Want of responsibility,
> 2d. Want of competency to decide,
> 3d. Want of choice and competition,
> from which three causes proceed the erection of buildings unsightly and unsatisfactory, much confusion and variation, both in the planning and executing of them, and the expenditure of larger sums than are necessary.
>
> 1st. The Surveyor General, according to the present constitution of that office, is solely the channel of communication between the Commissioners of His Majesty's Treasury and the Architect: he exercises no judgment nor control, nor gives any opinion as to the work to be done, or the mode of doing it; confining himself to fixing prices, and making contracts accordingly, and examining and checking the accounts after they have been made out by the clerks of the works, and the measurers belonging to the office.
>
> 2d. The Surveyor General having no duty to perform in judging of the propriety or sufficiency of the design or plan, that important business is imposed upon the Commissioners of the Treasury for the time being, who may not always be competent to decide upon such matters; and although it may happen frequently that there are among them persons eminently conversant with works of Art, it may also happen that a very efficient Board of Treasury for all other and more important purposes, may be unfit for this; and in such a case the Architect of the district, without any real control or useful supervision, may plan and execute whatever is to be done, according to his own pleasure and discretion.
>
> 3d. No sufficient choice is afforded to the Board of Treasury, who are to judge and decide, for they have not even taken advantage of having three Architects attached to the office and paid by it; nor does it appear that they have hitherto at all encouraged the competition of other professional men, or called for any variety of designs.
>
> This last inconvenience may undoubtedly be obviated (as has been before observed) without altering the Act of 1814; for the Board of Treasury may, if they think fit, require designs or slight sketches from each of the three Architects, before any considerable work is undertaken; and they may also increase their latitude of selection, by calling for designs from other professional men of known reputation and ability.
>
> The appointment of a professional architect to the office of Surveyor General having been tried, and abandoned, is not again to be recommended, although it possesses the advantage of placing at the head of this department a responsible person, which the present method does not.
>
> So much will always depend upon the qualifications of the persons who are placed at the head of any department, that it becomes extremely difficult to point out or contrive any regulations which can be confidently relied upon, under all circumstances; but Your Committee venture to suggest, that a considerable improvement may be effected in the existing system, without over-turning, or remodelling, or even disturbing it to any great extent; and their recommendation upon the whole matter is this:—
>
> That no public buildings should be hereafter erected, nor any considerable alterations in the structure of any of the existing buildings be adopted, except upon

directions given by the Lords of the Treasury, and founded upon Minutes of that Board; and that the plans and estimates for all such new buildings or alterations of existing buildings, should be signed by at least three Lords of the Treasury, and be preserved in the records of that office:

That a commission, consisting of five persons, two of whom at least should be Privy Councillors, and holding some responsible offices, should be appointed by His Majesty to act as a council without salary, to advise the Board of Treasury upon all designs and plans for the erection or considerable alteration of public buildings:

That previously to the decision of the Board of Treasury on any designs, plans or estimates, to be signed and recorded by them as before suggested, the opinions and recommendations of this council for public buildings to be so appointed, should be laid in writing before the Board, and should be annexed to the plans and estimates approved of and recorded at the Treasury.

It will be seen by a reference to Lord Goderich's evidence, that some such assistant council as is here recommended, would in his opinion be of great service in enabling the Commissioners of the Treasury to judge and determine upon the designs for buildings which are laid before them.

Your Committee cannot conclude this Report in which they have deemed it necessary to offer so many observations concerning the unsatisfactory manner in which the erection of the public buildings is at present directed and superintended, without recommending to the immediate attention of His Majesty's Government the expediency of a revision of the existing regulations by which the conduct of that department is governed.

There are many points in the evidence accompanying this Report, suggested by professional persons of experience and judgment, which are deserving of consideration; and it appears that some useful reforms might be introduced into the code of instructions now in force for the guidance of that office, if a careful inquiry were made into the subject.

In suggesting that such an inquiry should be forthwith instituted, they desire to be understood, as not intending to convey the imputation of any blame upon the officer now at the head of that department, of whose diligence, fidelity and zeal in the execution of his duties, according to the existing instructions, they have learned nothing in the course of their examination which could induce them to entertain the slightest doubt.[1]

The moderate tone of this report lends some substance to opposition criticisms that it was intended to whitewash rather than lay bare the inadequacies of the Office of Works. Probably it was influenced by its quota of official members, by a reluctance to offend the King, and perhaps also by a belief that the administration was now in command of the situation. The committee had been led by Nash to believe that the Treasury was fully informed of the expenses he contemplated; and the new regulation for the supply of furniture to public offices seemed to promise efficient and economical government.

The important select committee on public income and expenditure, the 'Finance Committee' which some M.P.s had suggested should investigate the Office of Works, also gave some consideration to the question of public works. Examining miscellaneous

---

[1] *Ibid.* pp. 11–12.

N

expenditure (which included special parliamentary grants for new public buildings), the Committee remarked in its Fourth Report:

> However desirable some of the objects may be to which the large sums expended have been applied, it is of the utmost importance in the present state of the Finances of the Country, to abstain from every expensive undertaking, that can, without positive detriment to the Public Service, be avoided.
>
> This remark, however, applies much more forcibly to the expenses which have been incurred under the head of MISCELLANEOUS GRANTS.
>
> A considerable proportion of these grants have been for works of general or local utility, not forming part of the necessary Expenditure of the Nation.[1]

This criticism doubtless strengthened the resolve of the Wellington administration to check the expenditure of the Office of Works.[2]

Called upon by the Treasury to satisfy the Bankes committee's demand for a review of the regulations adopted in 1815, Stephenson sought to rebut the criticisms of his department at almost every point.[3] He recommended, however, that the 'care, controul and Expences incurred for all Public Buildings, should be regulated by, and executed upon, one fixed and general principle of management which should extend over every department of Government'. But by this he did not mean a single public works service, for he suggested that the Woods and Forests should resume the management of its own buildings, 'for it may be presumed, that no advantage to the Public can be derived from divided responsibility between the two Departments in respect of the erection and repair of Buildings'. He acknowledged that certain details of the regulations could not be strictly complied with, but recommended an even more stringent application of the rule forbidding officers to be concerned in any contract.[4] The defects alleged by the select committee could only be remedied—'if necessary'—by additional instructions, as those in force were clear and explicit.

Some of the criticisms, Stephenson argued, were mistaken: for instance, neither 'choice' nor 'competition' had been wanting. Competition had been resorted to for Windsor Castle, while choice had been exercised for works in the Parks, 'none of which have been designed or executed by the Attached Architects or under the controul of the Office of Works—altho' the Buildings in these Parks, were considered by the Treasury Regulations as belonging to the Department of Works etc.' But competition had been tried for the Post Office without success, for all 33 sets of designs 'were rejected as wholly inapplicable in every respect'. The committee, he maintained, had been misled by the evidence they had heard from Nash and Rowles:

> the evidence of Professional Men when directed against the Regulation and Conduct of a Department Established for the almost exclusive purposes of imposing a check and controul, upon their proceedings ought to be received with some doubt, and acted upon with great caution; more especially so when it can be shewn, that in many and some important particulars, the correctness of such Evidence cannot safely be relied upon.

For instance, Rowles's remarks on the Surveyor General's lack of responsibility were inaccurate, for—as the Instructions showed—he was responsible for every official

---

[1] *Parl. Pap.* 1828, (519) v, p. 553. The grants referred to included those for the New Mint, New Law Courts and Houses of Parliament.   [2] See below, p. 169.   [3] Works 1/17, pp. 43–66.
[4] Hiort had been permitted to supply his patent fire-bricks for a number of public buildings, see p. 107.

act in his department 'and to an extent, much beyond the liability of his Predecessors'. This defence was hardly convincing, for what the Instructions gave the Surveyor General was a power of veto rather than of positive action, such as would have satisfied those critics who wanted a whipping boy when anything went wrong.[1] Stephenson himself had told the Duke of Kent in 1815 that 'the Treasury Instructions for the Regulation and Conduct of this Department leave no discretionary powers with me to alter an Estimate that has been once sanctioned by the Lords of the Treasury'; and again 'my powers are circumscribed by most positive Rules and Regulations'.[2] In 1819 he said that his authority did not go beyond sanctioning an estimate of £50.[3] Stephenson was right in arguing that the Surveyor General was responsible for all that went on in his department, the activity of the clerks of the works, the conduct of the labourers in trust, the proper observance of the regulations and so forth. What the critics alleged however was that he was not independent—that the major decisions were made by others, principally the Treasury, and that the Surveyor General was merely the agent transmitting their instructions to those who were to carry them out. They ignored the need for an officer who would ensure that those instructions were properly carried out. Both sides saw a truth, but not the whole truth.

Stephenson admitted that 'the approval of Plans and Designs for great Public Buildings certainly does not fall within the province of the Surveyor General', adding inaccurately, 'or ever did; and it may be very questionable how far it would be expedient, even for a professional Surveyor General, to have any such powers.' The final approval may be said, of course, always to have rested with the Crown, but Chambers and Wyatt had had a decisive voice in the design of many of their principal public undertakings. Stephenson, however, contended that an architect was not needed at the head of the Office:

> In respect to common and Ordinary Works in the Department extensive and impor-
> tant as they are; yet under the existing regulations, and with the Professional assis-
> tance they afford, a moderate share of Abilities, with well directed perseverance and
> Integrity will always enable a Surveyor General, though not a Professional Man
> (provided he is properly supported) to conduct the duties of his Department, with
> credit to himself and advantage to the Public Service. It may not be deemed
> irrelevant here to remark, that including the appointment of Inigo Jones, to the
> present period there appear upon record to have been thirteen Surveyors General
> out of whom four only were selected from amongst Professional Men.

The existing code of instructions was, he concluded, generally adequate to serve its purpose. One failure he did however admit: exceedings on estimates had 'too fre- quently been a source of Complaint and in some Instances with much reason'. For

[1] The limits of the Surveyor General's powers are perhaps illuminated by two incidents of April 1816: the temporary repair of the Home Office front 'with Brick in a substantial manner at an Expence of about 600 pounds', authorized by Stephenson without any official report to the Treasury, as he conceived 'this repair to have been of that extent, and particular discription, which I was empowered by the Treasury Instructions . . . to direct upon my own authority and responsibility'; and Stephenson's refusal of a request for fitting up a lodge at Somerset House as accommodation for a magistrate in an emergency: 'I can not undertake any alterations, or repairs, that are not necessary for the safety and preservation of that Building, without an express authority from the Treasury' (Works 1/6, pp. 481, 485; 1/7 p. 19).
[2] Works 1/6 p. 33, 24 July 1815; p. 231, 26 October 1815.   [3] Works 1/9, p. 436.

this he put forward a remedy which had for long been a favourite notion of his, as it had been of Bankes:

> In order therefore if possible to impose some check upon this serious irregularity it is suggested that in future no Architect be allowed a Commission or per Centage upon any Amount beyond his original approved Estimate; unless he can satisfactorily prove, that such exceedings arose from Alterations or Additions executed under a competent previous Authority during the progress of the Building. It is also further suggested, as a necessary security to the Public, that no Architect be allowed, directly or indirectly to be concerned in supplying Materials, which are to be used in any public Building where he is employed as an Architect; this tho' contrary to the rules, and general usage of the respectable part of the profession is nevertheless too frequently practised.

In Parliament the opposition seized on the select committee's criticism of the application to Buckingham House of £250,000 from the surplus funds of the Commissioners for French Claims.[1] Although Lord Liverpool had satisfied himself of the legality of this action, there was strong criticism in the House, and M. A. Taylor moved a motion of censure on 23 June 1828.[2] The government triumphed on this occasion by 181 votes to 102; but in 1834 the select committee on Crown Land revenues resolved that the loan had been improper.[3] The opposition press fully reported the debate. According to the *Morning Chronicle* it was a fraud by which ministers tricked the country into squandering the revenues of the Woods and Forests, while simultaneously spending vast sums on the new palace.[4] *The Globe* declared 'the transaction seems to have been one of the most mischievous of financial irregularities that has for some time been made public . . . It appears that while the new palace has been paid for out of the mis-appropriated fund, the revenue of the Woods and Forests has in its turn been diverted to other purposes'.[5] Though the government had won the day, belief was nourished that there had been chicanery over the King's Works, and in the next session Bankes continued his campaign.

In a debate on the Charing Cross Improvements (the responsibility of the New Street Commissioners, i.e. the Commissioners of Woods and Forests) on 7 April 1829 Bankes called for a 'more efficient control than that which at present existed over the expenditure of public money and improvements'; and in reply Goulburn

> admitted that it was very desirable that the actual cost should approach as near as possible to the estimate, and that the control argued for . . . should exist. The subject had been for some time under consideration of the government; but there had been no new undertaking to test the efficiency and practicability of definite rules, on the apportioning of the expenditure to the estimate.[6]

---

[1] These were funds supplied by the French government to compensate British subjects for losses in the wars. *The Globe* commented, 17 June 1828, 'The extravagant expenditure connected with the Woods and Forests department has for some time attracted notice; and some surprize has been excited how the funds were supplied. . . . We trust some other independent Member will urge the necessity of reforming the whole administration of the Woods and Forests. The present plan is evidently calculated to make it a cover for all sorts of extravagance and folly.'

[2] In the debate young Edward Stanley condemned the government's action as 'mean, shuffling and underhanded' (*Parl. Deb.* new ser. xix, 1495; see also 1476–94).

[3] *Parl. Pap.* 1834 (579), xv.   [4] 25 June.   [5] 24 June.   [6] *Parl. Deb.* new ser. xxi, 531.

On 12 May, on the committee stage of a Land Revenue Bill to meet the increased expenditure on Buckingham Palace, Bankes lamented the haste in which the whole had been begun.[1] Robert Gordon, an opposition Whig, wanted the business put on another footing. When a few days later Colonel Davies, an inveterate enemy of Nash, moved for a committee to inquire into his management of the New (i.e. Regent) Street, Bankes again mounted his hobby-horse:

> he was sure, if the House had imagined that the new palace, without a single article of furniture, would have cost nearly half a million of money, they would not have sanctioned such an estimate, nor have consented to place the residence of the sovereign at Pimlico, in the neighbourhood of shabby houses, breweries, factories, and steam-engines; with all the filth, and smoke and dirt which belonged to that part of the town. That proceeding had raised the price of all these dirty contemptible places at least five hundred per cent.[2]

But Bankes had never liked the site.[3]

The Wellington administration had not in fact waited for parliamentary advice or criticism before attempting to set matters in order. Wellington and Goulburn did not propose to make any increase in the low figure of £20,000 put forward by Canning's administration for expenditure in 1828 and persisted in this against Stephenson's strongest protests that 'though prudence and economy may do much, it cannot accomplish impossibilities', and that works necessary to preserve buildings must be deferred, at the cost of greater expenses in later years.[4] They had also realised the need to control the King's extravagance—something that previous administrations had shirked. On 17 February 1828 the Duke in a conversation with Knighton—the King's private secretary in all but name—agreed to provide £150,000 for Windsor and £100,000 for Buckingham Palace in 1828, with a similar amount for the palace in 1829, as well as a sum to cover improvements in the Parks.[5] Nash received directions to make a complete estimate for the palace,[6] and Knighton assured the King that the alterations proposed for the wings were to be 'acted upon without a moment's delay'.[7] On 11 March an account of Civil List expenditure for 1827 was delivered to the Duke and the following day the Treasury obtained an account of expenditure under grants of Parliament.[8] Knighton's expectations, however, were not realised, and the King wrote bitterly to him on 29 April that 'no one single step' had been taken to enable the royal works to proceed. Wyatville and Nash were both on the point of suspending their operations.[9] 'Poor little Nash' was to be further disappointed in the following year, when Wellington declined to gratify the King's inconvenient desire to bestow a baronetcy on his favourite architect.[10]

---

[1] *Ibid.* 1322.

[2] *Ibid.* 1585. Lord Lowther, then head of the Woods and Forests, was implicated in Davies' attack on Nash, according to C. Arbuthnot, in a letter to J. C. Herries, 30 December 1832 (B. M., Herries Papers, unsorted). Mrs. Arbuthnot also referred to this, 14 June 1829; 'Lord Lowther, who is a great blackguard, is attacking Mr. Nash, but he has totally failed in his object of proving Mr. Nash to have been a cheat' (*Journal*, ii, p. 283).

[3] See *Parl. Deb.* n.s. xiii, 1205, 16 June 1825.

[4] Works 1/16, pp. 98 (1 February), 136 (18 February), 239 (3 April 1828).

[5] *Letters of George IV*, ed. Aspinall, iii, pp. 391–2.   [6] *1831 Report*, p. 20.

[7] *Letters of George IV*, ed. Aspinall, iii, pp. 391–2.   [8] Works 4/28, pp. 514, 516.

[9] *Letters of George IV*, ed. Aspinall, iii, pp. 402–3.

[10] *Ibid.* iii, p. 460; *Journal of Mrs. Arbuthnot*, ed. F. Bamford and the Duke of Wellington (1956) ii, p. 289.

But if the King had cause to complain, so had his minister, who wrote to Knighton:

> It was settled that the whole revenue of the Woods and Forests this year should be applicable to finish the London Parks; which is all that it can do, and that next year it should be applicable solely to Buckingham Palace.
>
> This is an application for £1000 in advance for planting at Windsor.
>
> I assure you that we have not a shilling. Every farthing of money that can be scraped together has been applied to H.M.'s purposes; and if we don't adhere strictly to what has been settled respecting the future application of the money coming in, H.M. will be disappointed in that which must be more important than a few additional plantations in Windsor Park.[1]

In a letter in the Goulburn Papers referring to proposals for a new church in Edinburgh, of which the beginning is missing, but which was probably written early in 1828, Wellington remarked:

> We must make some rule about Buildings such as a Limit to the sum to be laid out in any year in the whole of the United Kingdom; and to place the whole of the Buildings under the Treasury in the whole Kingdom under the superintendence of one Board of Works.
>
> We shall then know what we are about; and should have responsible Persons for the due execution of our Works; and should be certain not to expend more money upon them than we originally intended.[2]

In the reconstruction of the ministry at the end of May, Arbuthnot was replaced by Lord Lowther as Chief Commissioner of Woods and Forests, presaging a stiffening in that department's attitude in accord with the ministry's general policy.[3] Thus in September an estimate of £975 for works at the Hampton Court paddocks was returned by the Treasury with the remark that the King had ordered that no new expenses were to be defrayed out of the Land Revenue, so that it might all be applied to Buckingham Palace.[4] There was also an estimate of £770 for repairing the Ranger's Lodge, Richmond Park. The King may perhaps have mooted yet other schemes. In these circumstances Wellington wrote to Goulburn:

> I return the enclosed paper, upon which I will speak to Sir William Knighton. Lord Lowther is quite right. He [the King] must undertake nothing until Buckingham Palace is finished.
>
> I will likewise speak to Knighton, and, if necessary, to the King, on the other points in your letter. We must put a stop to this expenditure.
>
> We have hanging over us a demand for finishing the Duke of Clarence's house in the stable-yard, and likewise the Duke of Cumberland's house in St. James's Palace.[5]

A few days later he recommended following the regular course with the estimate, and obtaining from Stephenson a balance sheet showing the state of his funds, including £10,000 promised for the King at Windsor, and the completion and putting in a

---

[1] *Letters of George IV.* ed. Aspinall, iii, pp. 403–4 (2 May 1828).
[2] Surrey Record Office, Goulburn MSS. 11/12 R.
[3] Charles Arbuthnot wrote to his wife, 13 July 1828, '. . . I cannot tell you how amused I am with the King not choosing to be approached by Lowther on money matters' (*Correspondence*, p. 105).
[4] Works 1/16, p. 510.   [5] *Wellington New Despatches*, v, p. 28, 6 September 1828. See pp. 325, 369.

habitable state of the Duke of Clarence's house.[1] Doubtless he hoped in this way to bring the whole issue before the King, and keep expenditure within the limits he had prescribed. Among other items that the Treasury refused to allow at this period were the repair of the Diana Fountain at Hampton Court, with painting and minor repairs to the Ranger's Lodge, Bushy Park,[2] and alterations at the Colonial Office.[3]

During 1828 the Treasury was collecting information and revising rules. In March Goulburn had called for a statement showing the annual cost of repairs to palaces since 1761.[4] A Treasury letter of 3 April directed that 'grace and favour' residences 'in the vicinity of the Royal Palaces, but not immediately connected therewith', should be repaired at the cost of their occupants.[5] Next the Treasury, on the initiative of the Commissioners of Woods and Forests, instructed the Surveyor General to send those commissioners even ordinary estimates of proposed works, so that they would know what expenses were anticipated and might advise on their practicability.[6] But Stephenson pointed out that no great improvement was to be expected from this procedure; of £31,000 expended on the Woods and Forests account in the previous year, three-quarters was for works executed under immediate directions from the commissioners or of which they had had due notice.[7]

In June, following rapidly upon the report of the select committee, came orders relating to the works at the palace. Nash was restricted to an expenditure of £10,000 a month, a figure fixed in relation both to the anticipated surplus income of the Woods and Forests and to the rate of expenditure in the preceding year. He was also to state on the first day of each month the expense incurred in the previous month, and give an estimate for that succeeding.[8] This, as Nash pointed out, was unrealistic.[9] The accounts were made up only quarterly, 'and even then a great portion of the several works must be paid for by advances on account, for they cannot be measured till they are finished and fixed, and much of the work cannot be finished and fixed till nearly the close of the building.' Nevertheless, he thought that he could restrict expenditure to the sum allowed. Stephenson commented to the Treasury that the regulation of monthly accounts would be difficult, but that the architect could supply sufficient reports and estimates to avoid exceeding the appropriations.[10] Referring to Nash's evidence before the committee, on the impossibility of being able to answer for an estimate where he did not control the prices and measuring, he suggested that Nash should be directed to measure the works at the palace and make up the accounts himself, thus leaving him no loophole by which he might wriggle out of his responsibility. This proposal found favour; and Stephenson at last realised his wish that Nash should pay for the measuring out of his five per cent commission.[11] But if he thought that placing the responsibility on Nash's shoulders would exonerate the Office of Works and secure it from criticism, he was mistaken, for its failure to control the operations at the palace was in itself a condemnation of the system, and Nash's inability to build within his estimates was to bring all down.

[1] *Ibid.* p. 33.
[2] Works 1/16, p. 264. This was the out-of-town seat of the heir to the throne, the Duke of Clarence.
[3] *Ibid.* p. 239.   [4] *Ibid.* p. 208. This statement is now in Works 19/25/1.
[5] Works 1/16, pp. 238–9.   [6] *Ibid.* pp. 242–5, 11 April 1828.
[7] *Ibid.* pp. 252–3, 16 April 1828.   [8] *1831 Report*, p. 153, Treasury minute of 17 June 1828.
[9] Works 1/16, pp. 411–13, 9 July.   [10] *Ibid.* pp. 437–41, 29 July.   [11] *1831 Report*, pp. 156–7.

The effect of the select committee's inquiries was a tightening of Treasury control, but its specific recommendations were ignored by the government. In October the Treasury announced that 'no expenditure should be incurred for any alteration whatever, or for any addition to any public building which is not unavoidably necessary, and even then not without their special sanction'; and asked Stephenson for his minimum estimate to put before Parliament.[1] Stephenson proposed a sum of no less than £66,924, including £13,000 for repairing the Banqueting House, £700 for ventilating the House of Lords, and £22,727 for purchasing and altering the Westminster Sessions House for a State Paper Office. Paving rates in Whitehall and Westminster came to £3020; furniture for the Horse Guards, oil and gas lights, and watching at Somerset House demanded another £4573; and necessary repairs were limited to £15,404.[2] The new arrangement under which the Office of Works instead of the Lord Chamberlain was to supply public offices with furniture was found to require £3490 more. The Treasury ruthlessly pared the programme: only £6000 were allowed for the Banqueting House, and the other works were all postponed, leaving a vote of £32,487.[3] The Civil List expenditure and that of the Woods and Forests were of course additional to the vote of Parliament. The Woods and Forests estimate Stephenson calculated at £16,952, exclusive of works done by Nash without authority from the Office of Works.[4]

The effect of this retrenchment was soon felt in the Office of Works itself. Lewis Wyatt, now Clerk at Hampton Court, was told that his estimate of nearly £2200 for repairing the Water Gallery made it necessary to obtain competitive tenders.[5] Soane, similarly, was told that for the repairs of Whitehall Chapel (the Banqueting House) fresh tenders must be obtained: it was not satisfactory merely to adopt those accepted for the works at the House of Lords.[6] The tradesmen were warned against making fictitious charges for labour, and the Clerks of the Works were called upon to check their returns and to keep the Labourers in Trust up to the mark.[7] Stephenson kept most rigidly within his official bounds. Thus when Freeling, the secretary of the Post Office, enquired if he had received any directions from the Treasury for taking charge of the fabric of the new General Post Office and suggested that if not, he should apply to the Treasury for instructions, Stephenson replied that he had received no official intimations on the subject, and 'I therefore apprehend that it will be considered an improper interference on my part were I to offer, uncalled for, any suggestions to Their Lordships upon this subject:'[8]—this though he had a duty to make proposals for the better administration of the Works. A week later we find the Treasury asking him to report on an inquiry from Freeling whether the General Post Office were to be placed under the Office of Works or the Post Office architect.[9] Stephenson replied that he saw no inconvenience in placing the General Post Office under the Post Office architect, who might receive assistance from the Office of Works as necessary.[10] Stephenson perhaps did not wish to become entangled with the revenue departments, which possessed a certain initiative in matters of

---

[1] Works 1/16, pp. 531–2.   [2] Works 1/17, pp. 23–5.   [3] *Ibid.* pp. 153–5, February 1829.
[4] *Ibid.* pp. 90–2, 31 December 1828.   [5] *Ibid.* p. 411, 11 July 1829; p. 450.
[6] Works 4/29, p. 411; Soane Mus. Corr. 2, xi, E. f. 10.
[7] Works 1/17, pp. 397–9, 7 July; p. 433, 30 July 1829.
[8] *Ibid.* p. 470, 12 September 1829.   [9] *Ibid.* p. 477.   [10] *Ibid.* p. 483, 24 September 1829.

building, for which they were able to pay from their receipts before those were handed to the Exchequer.[1] The Treasury decided that the post of architect to the Post Office should be abolished, and the new General Post Office be placed under the Office of Works.[2] It was ironical that very soon after this the cautious Stephenson should receive a Treasury reprimand. Mindful presumably of Liverpool's direction that he was to attend to the King's wishes, and not sufficiently sensitive to the subsequent change in climate, he had allowed Wyatville to construct by the King's command at Cumberland Lodge, Windsor Great Park, twenty temporary coachhouses costing £1015. The work was urgent and it was impossible to frame a previous estimate.[3] In authorising the expenditure the Treasury remarked on 'the irregularity and impropriety of the Execution of the same prior to an Estimate having been submitted for their approval', begging 'particularly to call your attention to the avoiding such a course on future occasions'.[4] Nevertheless a saving of some £7500 on the Civil List account for the preceding year was achieved.[5]

When the *6th Triennial Report of the Commissioners of Woods and Forests* was published, showing what funds had been provided for the palace and for the so-called Parliamentary Mews,[6] there was more adverse comment out of doors. 'We are amazed', remarked *The Times*, 'on looking back and considering some of the evidence before the committee [of 1828],—we are amazed at the freedom from salutary control which has been suffered so long to flourish'.[7] The cost of the stables and the palace was 'frightful'; 'an end must be put to this'. There ought to be a quarterly investigation

> to intercept each folly as it first takes wing, and to blight the budding mischiefs which, when full grown, it would appear that no wisdom or courage can disarm. Besides this exercise of especial vigilance in some appointed officers, we would urge most earnestly upon the acting chiefs of the Government themselves, an inflexible and inexorable disregard of every proposition which can be tendered to them for indulging wild propensities to extravagance in the charge of public revenue. The country cannot bear such weakness as has hitherto been displayed on the matters to which we have adverted.

For 1830, Stephenson prepared an estimate of £49,075 to be voted by Parliament; but the Treasury again reduced the figure for Whitehall Chapel from £10,500 to £6000 and allowed only £10,000 for the new works at the British Museum, where the Trustees were anxious to complete part of the west wing to accommodate the Grecian marbles.[8] The Woods and Forests' estimate, including Wyatville's works in Windsor Great Park, was calculated at £14,479.[9]

Nevertheless public opinion was such that the estimates ran into trouble. Robert Gordon voiced an opinion more general than merely that of the parliamentary Whig party when he complained of rising expenditure on public works.[10] Though Dawson, the Secretary of the Treasury, pointed out that since the administration had come into office, 'no public work had been undertaken of which an estimate was not

---

[1] See p. 157.   [2] Works 1/17, p. 502, 29 October 1829.
[3] *Ibid.* p. 497, 16 October 1829.   [4] *Ibid.* p. 506, 4 November 1829.   [5] *Ibid.* p. 450.
[6] *Parl. Pap.* 1829 (317) xiv. See p. 537.   [7] 6 January 1830.   [8] Works 1/18, pp. 33, 68, 73.
[9] *Ibid.* pp. 60–1.   [10] *Parl. Deb.* n.s. xxiv, 331, 3 May 1830.

previously made, in order to form a judgment as to the expenditure it was likely to induce', defeat was only narrowly averted.[1]

Ministers then brought forward a vote for £100,000 for continuing the works at Windsor Castle. Though this restoration was much more favourably regarded, there was opposition to such incessantly mounting estimates, and Goulburn was obliged reluctantly to agree to refer the vote to a committee which might ascertain the ultimate expense.[2] Wellington wrote the next day to Peel (who had been absent from the House), 'all these questions on the King's buildings are bad ones',[3] and to Knighton that 'We are in the wrong for bringing forward for the third or fourth time a vote for a fresh grant without an estimate of the whole expence'.[4] The committee's report, dated 9 July 1830, recommended the gradual expenditure of at least another £277,000 under Wyatville; but it criticised 'the course which has been followed, of expending large sums of money in anticipation of the Votes of the House of Commons'. Admitting that it might be impossible entirely to avoid such a practice, particularly in a lengthy work of restoration, they were anxious that it might be restrained as much as possible.

> In this view they suggest that in every public work which, from its extent, may require several years for completion, before any sum is voted on account, a statement ought, in the first instance, to be submitted to the House, showing the whole estimated charge of such work. And they observe, that with respect to several other considerable works now in progress, the rule appears to have been of late years generally observed; but it appears further desirable that, in every subsequent year, the estimate for that year should be accompanied with a statement showing: 1st, The actual expenditure settled and paid. 2dly, The amount of demands outstanding up to the date of such estimate: also a specification of the total amount (so far as the same can be ascertained) requisite for finishing such parts of the work as may be then in progress, and for the completion of the whole; together with a summary explanation of any circumstance which, in the progress of the work may have occasioned any considerable alteration in, or addition to the original plan and estimate.[5]

The death of George IV on 26 June 1830 marked the beginning of the end of an era in the King's Works, an era in which (as Stephenson wrote to Lewis Wyatt, Clerk of the Works at Hampton Court, immediately after the accession of William IV):

> You must obey whatever commands the King may be pleased to honour you with respecting the Buildings within your district; but taking care to communicate such commands to me, at your earliest convenience, transmitting at the same time an estimate of the probable expense of any works His Majesty may be pleased to direct being done.[6]

The wishes of the sovereign had henceforth to take their place as but one factor in the consideration of the ministers who ruled.

For the Office of Works the accession of William IV was also significant in other ways. The new King had no pretensions to taste, and his wife, who does appear to

---

[1] By 139 votes to 123 (*Parl. Deb.* n.s. xxiv, 339, 344).   [2] *Parl. Deb.* n.s. xxiv, 347–51, 3 May 1830.
[3] *Wellington New Despatches*, vii, p. 18.   [4] *Letters of George IV*, ed. Aspinall, iii, p. 475.
[5] *Parl. Pap.*, 1830 (656) ix.   [6] Works 1/18, pp. 160–2, 28 June 1830.

have taken some interest in artistic questions, regarded with distaste the dissipated habits of the late monarch. The Windsor Cottage, tainted by memories of royal indulgence and expensive to maintain, was accordingly doomed, and the King decided to reside only in the Castle. Cranbourne Lodge, empty since Princess Charlotte's marriage, was also largely demolished.[1] Alterations were required in other palaces to provide fitting accommodation for the Queen and her suite. Works were accordingly put in hand at Brighton and changes proposed at Buckingham Palace.[2] But that palace was by no means ready, so the new sovereign elected to stay at Clarence House, a communication being made with the adjoining State Apartments at St. James's.[3] Thus the works consequent on the change of monarch involved a not inconsiderable expenditure. However, the climate of the day and the King's own predilections severely pruned the coronation ceremonies, those in Westminster Hall being altogether omitted.[4]

The new King showed no wish to displace Wellington's administration. But the inevitable general election did nothing to improve the Duke's position; he refused to strengthen his ministry by taking in some of the rival groups; and his declaration against any reform of the parliamentary system sealed the doom of his government. Defeated unexpectedly on the question of a committee on the new Civil List, he resigned and the King commissioned the old Whig aristocrat Lord Grey to form a ministry which embraced all shades of parliamentary opinion except for supporters of the previous administration. If Lord Grey's ministry was to achieve striking economies, as its cry of 'retrenchment and reform' implied, it would have to exercise the tightest control over government expenditure, for Wellington had already cut expenditure from the £56,337,000 of 1827 to £52,019,000 in 1830. In the event, Althorp, the new Chancellor of the Exchequer, was able to reduce expenditure for 1831 by less than a third of a million.[5]

One third or more of that might be regarded as having been saved by the suspension of work on Buckingham Palace, ordered by the Treasury on 15 October 1830, shortly before Wellington's fall from power.[6] The discovery, so soon before the meeting of Parliament, that Nash's last estimate fell considerably short of what was required for the completion of the palace led immediately to the overthrow of the architect and ultimately to a revision of the old system. One of the first activities of the new ministry was to instigate a select committee to sift the palace affair thoroughly—investigating the provision of furniture for Windsor Castle at the same time. Had the Treasury had the personnel it might well have undertaken such an enquiry itself, but the resort to parliamentary means had the political advantage of bringing before Parliament any possible delinquencies of the late ministry, and was scarcely avoidable after the 1828 committee. A great mass of papers for examination was put before the House by Lord Althorp, who moved for them to be referred to a

---

[1] *Parl. Pap.* 1833 (677) xiv, *Report on the Land Revenues of the Crown*, q. 2730.

[2] See pp. 259–60, 280.   [3] See p. 325.

[4] The Works expenditure on the coronation was £12,086, compared with £52,095 for that of George IV (*Parl. Pap.* 1837–8 (350) xxxiv).

[5] 'Income and Expenditure of the United Kingdom,' *Parl. Pap.* 1841 (438) xiii. Althorp planned to reduce expenditure by a million (*Parl. Deb.* 3rd ser. ii, p. 405 and S. Walpole, *Hist. of England from . . . 1815*, ii, 1878, pp. 633–4).

[6] *1831 Report*, p. 187; Works 1/18, pp. 250–3. Work was suspended on 23 October.

select committee.[1] The estimates, he explained, had been so exceeded—£576,000 having been spent up to mid-summer 1830 on an estimate of £500,000—that there was no money left and the workmen were in great distress. Before the House voted further funds, they must find why the estimates had been exceeded. 'It was not fair to Mr. Nash to place this to his conduct, for many of the works were not calculated for by him'. A chorus of criticism rose up; and Hume wanted to impeach Goderich (actually a member of Grey's administration). Goulburn defended his own conduct, declaring that 'the moment it was known at the Treasury that the estimates had been exceeded, that moment were the works put a stop to'. Edward Cust, out to make a name for himself in these matters, contended 'that it was only by establishing an authority in the Government, whose business it should be to exercise a control [over architects of public buildings] that they could hope to avoid such extravagant expenditure for the future'. Hobhouse attacked the late ministers for pandering to royal commands: 'Was it made known that the demand for the grant was a mere farce, and was to be applied as might suit the absurd, extravagant, bizarre and ridiculous taste of any person who might have the superintendence of the work?' At the end of the debate Hughes Hughes raised a delicate point by asking if it were true that William IV had decided not to live in Buckingham Palace: Althorp refused an answer.[2]

The committee under Robert Gordon's chairmanship worked assiduously through the spring and summer, making its first report on 27 September 1831.[3] This referred only to the furnishing of Windsor Castle. The committee, unable themselves to value the furniture supplied, had referred the valuation to 'competent judges', who also found the task beyond them. A different approach was therefore tried: a Treasury accountant calculated the tradesmen's actual expenditure, and thereby reduced the claims by some £25,000, leaving an excess of about £5000 over the estimates. This work had not been supervised by the Office of Works, as a special committee had been appointed by the Treasury in 1826; and the select committee condemned this resort. Far from managing the business economically, it had led to 'an increased lavish expenditure', as the Treasury and the Lord Chamberlain's Office had regarded themselves as exonerated of responsibility, 'while the members of the Furnishing Committee did not supply any adequate check on this extravagant waste of Public Money'. The committee concluded their first report by strongly

---

[1] *Parl. Deb.* 3 ser. ii, 586, 15 February 1831. The following members were appointed: Lords Althorp, Lowther, Killeen, Granville Somerset and John Russell, Messrs. Goulburn, Pendarves, Herries, John Wood, William Bankes, Guest, Sturges Bourne, Littleton, Ellice, Sandford, Jones, Pusey, Warburton, Rumbold and Robert Gordon, Colonel Davies, Sir R. Vyvyan, Sir. J. Sebright (*Commons' Jnls.* lxxxvi, pt. i, p. 253). It is noteworthy that of these, only Lowther and Herries had sat on the 1828 committee. After the general election, the committee was re-appointed on 23 June 1831, consisting of the following: Lords Althorp, Killeen, Duncannon and Granville Somerset, Messrs. Goulburn, Pendarves, Herries, Wood, Bankes, Ellice, A. Sandford, Warburton, Robert Gordon, Croker, Bonham Carter, Calcraft, Protheroe, E. Denison, Kennedy, W. Ponsonby, Pollock, Harcourt, Frankland Lewis and P. Thompson, Col. Davies, Sir J. Sebright, Sir T. Fremantle, and Sir H. Bunbury (*Commons' Jnls.* lxxxvi, pt. ii, p. 550). On 24 June, Messrs. Miles and Strutt were added (*ibid.* p. 558). Robert Gordon served throughout as chairman.

[2] It was indeed true that William IV was not anxious to move into the new palace, and he discussed with his ministers the possibility of its being converted into a barracks (*Correspondence of Earl Grey with William IV*, ed. 2nd Earl Grey, 1867, i, p. 389). After the 1831 general election, when the government had a large majority, the committee was instructed to consider whether the palace might be more advantageously applied to some other public purposes (*Commons' Jnls.* lxxxvi, pt. ii, p. 670; *Parl. Deb.* 3 ser. iv, 1447–50, 18 July 1831).

[3] *Parl. Pap.* 1831 (272) iv.

deprecating 'the practice of establishing any irresponsible Boards, who thus relieve the proper authorities from the performance of duties which strictly belong to their official situations'.[1]

The committee's principal undertaking was their great investigation into the works at Buckingham Palace, on which they compiled a voluminous Second Report.[2] This naturally covered much of the ground already examined by the 1828 committee, but the examination was more probing. Many of the contracting tradesmen were called as witnesses, as well as Nash, Stephenson, and Spearman, the Treasury official who dealt with the palace accounts. The committee also studied a considerable quantity of official papers; and a committee of architects (Soane, Smirke and Seward) was called upon to examine the construction—a task in which they thought it wise to seek the assistance of engineers, the extensive use of cast-iron proving something of a puzzle to them. Finally, the committee asked Edward Blore[3] for an opinion on the feasibility of completing the palace as a royal residence. Apart from the examination of the stability of the building, the inquiry was chiefly directed to the nature of Nash's proceedings. In their second, final report, dated 14 October 1831, the committee censured Nash for failing to prepare his estimate of May 1829 with sufficient care, 'either by ascertaining from the different Tradesmen the amount of Balances then due to them, nor the probable amount of what would be so due when the Works by them to be executed should be completed'. They further censured him for making improvident contracts, particularly with Crawshay for ironwork; and for selling materials to the tradesmen, expressing 'in the strongest terms their marked disapprobation of such a practice'. Nash was 'chargeable with inexcusable irregularity and great negligence in his transactions relative to Buckingham Palace'. But they found no proof that he had 'wilfully concealed' the facts from the Treasury. Indeed, previous governments, they concluded, were to blame: they should have obtained more information before submitting estimates to Parliament: and despite the efforts of Wellington's administration, 'no adequate control on the execution of the Works was established during the reign of His late Majesty'. Stephenson had 'performed his duties strictly and impartially, and exerted himself to the utmost of the powers with which he was invested', but the Treasury had not given him adequate support. When he had pointed out Nash's 'improper proceedings', they were 'either slightly passed over, or insufficiently visited with the disapprobation of the Government'. A more strict examination of estimates by the House of Commons might, the committee thought, have 'perhaps in some degree' prevented the excessive expenditure of public money that had occurred.

With the results of the professional examination of the palace before them, the committee decided that 'apprehensions of security may be obviated, and that the other defects, which at present render the Building ineligible as a Royal residence,

---

[1] Wellington and Goulburn had directed their attention to this question in 1828–9. £74,000 more than the sum granted for Windsor had been incurred in the Lord Chamberlain's department. Wellington thought the commission should wind up its labours after the tradesmen's bills had been severely taxed; but remarked that the commission did 'relieve the Treasury from so much of their responsibility' (*Wellington New Despatches*, v, pp. 335, 417–8).   [2] *Parl. Pap.*, 1831 (329) iv.
[3] Described by Lady Gower in November 1830 as 'the *cheap* architect' (*Three Howard Sisters*, ed. Lady Leconfield and J. Gore, 1955, p. 156). He was then enlarging Lambeth Palace and had worked for Althorp's father, Lord Spencer.

may be remedied'. They accordingly advised that the building, 'which is not applicable to any other Public Service,' should be completed 'as a Royal Residence, and ultimately as a Palace for purposes of State', which would save any further expenditure on St. James's.[1] From Blore's plans they were 'inclined to believe' that £75,000 would suffice for the necessary alterations, though considerably more would be required to fit it up for the King's occupation; and its completion as a state palace—for the holding of courts, levees and all the royal ceremonial functions of the state—would require a further outlay.

Before submitting its final report to the House, however, the committee made a special report recommending the discharge of debts already incurred on the works.[2] The case of Stratton, inventor of the palace warming apparatus, was particularly remarked on. From being in respectable circumstances, he had 'actually had the bed sold from under him', and had been given £100 royal bounty to keep him from starving.[3] When the Secretary of the Treasury moved a vote of £163,670 9s. 2d. to defray expenses at the palace and at Windsor, there was again much criticism, but the general feeling was that the House was bound to pay the debts incurred on the palace, which Althorp stated at £104,704 3s. 4d. £63,000 were for the year's works at Windsor, and some £4000 of arrears were left unprovided for. Althorp also revealed that Blore, whose accurate estimating he commended, had calculated that the palace could be finished for about £70,000. Though a number of speakers wished to wait for the committee's report before voting any funds, the government's view prevailed.[4] That criticism had not been without effect was shown by the decision to raise the funds necessary for completion by sales of Crown property rather than from taxation.[5]

It was the end of the year before the 327 page report was published, when *The Times* commented:

> Mr. NASH and Buckingham Palace are again before the public today, and a sorry figure each of them makes. However, we must say that it would have been more honourable in the Lords of the Treasury, if they had stopped the chief offender in his career of extravagance. He is gone to render up his own account; and now those of his architect, poor NASH, are investigated with proper rigour, and his false estimates justly reprehended. Upon the whole, there is great meanness in pouring the stream of vengeance on NASH, now that the prime mover of the folly is no longer alive to protect him, or frighten his accusers.[6]

---

[1] Among those who advocated other uses for the palace was Col. F. W. Trench, M.P., who vehemently expounded its value as a National Gallery for sculpture and paintings, a public record office and accommodation for the King's College, a project dismissed by Robert Gordon as 'wild and fantastical' (*Parl. Deb.* 3rd ser. iv, 1447, 18 July 1831; xi, 957 ff. 27 March 1832).

[2] *Parl. Deb.* 3rd ser. vii, 722.

[3] *Parl. Deb.* 3rd ser. vii, 714, 722.   [4] *Ibid.* 711–22.

[5] *Ibid.* ix, 144, 9 December 1831. This decision was subsequently attacked by Goulburn (*ibid.* ix, 576–7, 17 January 1832), though it followed the original precedent of 1825.

[6] 30 December 1831.

Chapter VIII

RETRENCHMENT AND REFORM: THE OFFICE OF WOODS AND WORKS

ALTHOUGH the Office of Works bore no responsibility for the confusion at the palace it could not hope to escape odium. That it was not responsible was in itself a criticism of the existing system of public works; and the popular demand for re-trenchment spelt its doom. Already in the summer of 1830 the chill eye of Henry Goulburn, contemplating the new Civil List, had been cast on the Office: he wished to reduce the establishment and urged the merits of competition among tradesmen and of ready money payments.[1] Stephenson argued strenuously against any econ-omies: salaries had been fixed in 1815 only after 'very mature consideration'; the duties of the department and of its officers had been 'most accurately defined'. £40,000 a year was the minimum required for the maintenance of the royal palaces, for expenditure for this purpose had averaged £39,000 a year since 1820, and now there was the additional cost of looking after the Royal Pavilion at Brighton. Com-petition was already resorted to whenever practicable; and ready money payments offered little advantage, for payments for common repairs were made 'at a very short period' after the accounts had been examined and approved.[2] Goulburn, however, still pressed his inquiries;[3] and the defeat of the administration on the new Civil List only strengthened the prospect of change. The new Treasury ministers demanded returns of all houses and buildings in the royal palaces and parks occupied by Works personnel (December);[4] of persons occupying official houses, and of buildings occupied as public offices that might be dispensed with if the offices were transferred to Somerset House (February 1831);[5] of official accommodation and expenditure thereon over the last seven years (March).[6] The Office establishment and officers' retired pay were also investigated; all payments additional to salaries were to be stated.[7] All this was with a view to reduction. Stephenson defended his subordin-ates' competence, though admitting that with two exceptions their duties were 'strictly professional [i.e. technical]; and relatively speaking can not in the general

---

[1] Works 4/30, pp. 289–90, 11 August 1830. See also pp. 361, 385.
[2] Works 1/18, pp. 212–3, 217–9 (19, 20 August 1830).   [3] *Ibid.* pp. 232–3, 264–5.   [4] *Ibid.* p. 295.
[5] Works 4/30, p. 485. This led to the Stamp, Tax, and Audit Offices being transferred to commissioners Mitford's and Bates's houses in Somerset Place (*ibid.* pp. 524–5, Treasury minute, 29 March 1831).
[6] Works 1/18, pp. 384–8.   [7] *Ibid.* p. 326; 4/30, p. 465.

acceptation of the words be considered either as important, confidential or such as require a more than ordinary degree of capacity'.[1] One reform Stephenson did hint at: it was, he thought, a 'matter of great doubt' whether the Labourers in Trust should have been allowed to carry on private business. This led, in September 1831, to an inquisition into the private business activities of the Labourers in Trust, and to their being forbidden to engage in any without permission from the Clerk of the Works for their district, of which notice was to be sent to the Surveyor General or his assistant.[2]

An early economy of the new administration was to reduce the Office of Works in Scotland to a mere branch of the English office.[3] Another was a further reduction in the burden of the Civil List by transferring the upkeep of those palaces the sovereign no longer occupied to annual parliamentary vote, so belatedly implementing a recommendation of the Inquiry Commissioners of 1813. However, when Stephenson reported, for the new ministers' benefit, on the condition of the buildings in his care, he stressed the considerable expenditure still necessary:

> Many of the above buildings will require external painting in the course of the ensuing summer, as necessary for their preservation; independently of which, a considerable annual expenditure is required for the common and ordinary repairs to such numerous and extensive premises, exclusive of the many alterations which are in almost constant requisition for the better accommodation of His Majesty's household in the royal palaces, as also for that of the several officers, clerks, and others belonging to the different public departments in London and Westminster. The Prisons require to be whitewashed throughout every year; and a considerable sum is annually expended in painting and repairing the numerous forcing houses, hot houses, pine pits etc. in the several royal gardens.[4]

This led to a further request for an account of the Office's duties in respect of royal palaces and gardens. Stephenson detailed the procedure, remarking that the Treasury regulations, common to all public buildings, had 'in practice been generally found to answer the several purposes for which they were framed'. He followed this with a list of the buildings in his charge, and an account of the way in which the Office provided furniture for public offices under a Treasury minute of 15 January 1828: 'the charge of this supply of furniture etc. has necessarily occasioned considerable additional labor in correspondence etc., but the whole of this extra business has hitherto been satisfactorily conducted with the assistance only of one additional clerk and a common labourer to assist at the stores'.[5] Another matter to which he had to turn his mind was devising a means of registering attendance of the outdoor staff.[6] To satisfy the Treasury, the Clerks of Works were instructed to keep an account of each night's absence from their districts.[7]

Stephenson's position as a non-parliamentary official at the head of the Office of Works was not affected by Lord Grey's taking office. The Woods and Forests was

---

[1] Works 1/18, pp. 328 ff.   [2] *Ibid.* pp. 536–7, 28 September 1831.   [3] See p. 252.
[4] Works 1/18, pp. 404–16.   [5] *Ibid.* pp. 496–500, 502 ff.
[6] Works 4/31, pp. 116, 132 (12, 27 August 1831). In line with regulations observed at the Treasury Duncannon instituted attendance registers in the Office in May 1839 (Crest 25/46, 3 and 17 May).
[7] Works 1/18, pp. 536–7 (28 September 1831).

however a political office that the new Prime Minister gave to George Agar Ellis,[1] 'an eager political partisan' and party whip.[2] When the news was bruited, Ellis's wife wrote: 'He always used to say it was the only thing that would tempt him to take office, as he should feel equal to it . . . anything that is laborious would not have suited his health'.[3] Agreeable but conceited, he was not robust and possessed no talent for public speaking. He soon found that the burden even of attendance as a minister in the Commons was too great and vainly sought a peerage.[4] He therefore gave place at the end of January 1831 to the Chief Whip, Lord Duncannon.[5] Recuperating at Brighton he drew up a scheme to reform the Office of Works.[6] 'You will see', he wrote to his successor, 'that my scale of reductions is considerable; but not in my opinion larger than may be easily effected.' Ellis's plan was for nothing less than uniting the Offices of Works and of Woods, thus taking a stage further the process begun in 1810 with the amalgamation of the Woods and the Land Revenues.

Ellis distinguished three objections to the existing Office of Works: the expense of the establishment; the 'injurious and costly' system of Attached Architects which deprived the Office of proper control; and the 'unsightly appearance' of many of the public buildings recently erected, which incurred unpopularity for the Office and for the government. If all public works and buildings were placed under the Woods and Forests, Ellis thought the first two problems would be solved. The Office of Works building in Scotland Yard might be let, and the post of Surveyor General abolished. As the First Commissioner of Woods was a Member of Parliament, 'a greater responsibility in the person directing public works would thus be acquired'. The duties of the office might then be performed by a chief secretary, preferably 'a professional man, i.e. conversant with Architecture', four clerks and two messengers. As for the outdoor staff:

> The attached Architects are expensive and worse than useless, as they prevent competition and thereby occasion expensive as well as hideous buildings. The Clerks of the Works (who ought to be Architects of integrity) may be necessary, in order to examine and controul estimates etc.—but the Labourers in Trust who are only an inferior sort of Clerk of the Works may surely be dispensed with—as well as the other Officers at present belonging to the department. Some better plan of checking expense, and taking care that the works undertaken are executed in a substantial and workmanlike manner may also without difficulty be adopted.

'For suggestions of this nature' Ellis referred to the report of the 1828 committee (of which he had been a member), no doubt having in mind its proposals for competition among architects and for lump-sum contracts.[7] To support his third objection, Ellis cited the Privy Council Office and Board of Trade building only recently erected by

---

[1] 1797–1833, son of Lord Clifden and son-in-law of Lord Carlisle; cr. Lord Dover, 1831.
[2] See Greville, *Diary*, ii, pp. 388–91; *Three Howard Sisters* (1955), ed. Lady Leconfield and J. Gore, *passim*. In 1827, however, Ellis had described himself as having 'never been connected with any party' (A. Aspinall, *The Formation of Canning's Ministry*, Camden Soc. 3rd ser., lix, 1937, p. 94).
[3] *Three Howard Sisters*, p. 167.   [4] *Ibid.* pp. 173, 175, 180, 183–4.
[5] 1781–1847, called up to Lords 1834, suc. as 4th Earl of Bessborough 1844; First Commr. of Woods, etc. 1831–4, Home Secretary 1834, Lord Privy Seal and first Commr. of Woods, etc. 1835–41, Lord-Lt. of Ireland 1846–7.
[6] Works 6/413, Ellis to Duncannon, 24 February 1831.   [7] See p. 162 above.

O

Soane. The proposal of the 1828 committee for a council of taste to approve plans before they were passed by the Treasury, Ellis thought 'the only possible method of remedying these great evils'; but it would be sufficient to have a council of three, the First Commissioner being one. The other two must be unpaid, but their services might be rewarded by the exercise of patronage and by 'other little perquisites' of office.

Ellis's scheme would have reduced expenditure on salaries by over £5000 annually. In that finally adopted, the saving was not quite so great, because of different arrangements relating to the outdoor staff; but Ellis's proposals formed the basis of the changes. Duncannon discussed the question with the Chancellor of the Exchequer and submitted his recommendations to the Treasury on 25 November 1831.[1] The two Offices should be united under a board of three commissioners, of whom the chief would sit in Parliament. This arrangement was facilitated by the retirement of Commissioner Dawkins[2] from the Office of Woods, which made it possible to appoint Stephenson as Third Commissioner, though he would have to be compensated for a £300 reduction in salary.

In the method of conducting large works, whether repairs or new buildings, Duncannon proposed a fundamental change:

> to open the same generally to professional architects of eminence and experience who will be paid the usual commission, and who are to be held responsible, not merely for the designs, quality of materials and execution of workmanship, but are also to make out the bills and be immediately responsible for all measurements and to discharge generally all the duties of supervision and control which usually devolve upon architects in their private employment and according to the course adopted in the Department of Woods. . . .

Thus a considerable part of the professional establishment could be dispensed with, the 'duties of check' being performed by the architects engaged. But as the Board would require professional opinions on plans, estimates and tenders, as well as prices, and needed to be able to check any doubtful accounts, Duncannon recommended that Seward should be retained, relieved of his duties as cashier, 'and devote his whole time and attention to professional employment'. He would be assisted by four clerks for clerical duties and whatever examination of accounts might be necessary. The clerk of the furniture, Cox, should also be retained.

It was in the outdoor department that the principal departures from Ellis's suggestions were made. Duncannon proposed to dispense with the Clerks of the Works but retain several Labourers in Trust. He proposed that one Clerk of the Works should be kept to 'report directly to the Board upon all applications for repairs, alterations or other works required at the Palaces in the immediate occupation of His Majesty'; and that of the thirteen Labourers in Trust, six should be given charge of the other palaces and public buildings. They should report to the Itinerant Surveyor of the Parks, an official of the Woods, whose duties should be extended to public buildings and whose salary should accordingly be increased by £300 to £700. While this plan was still under consideration by the Treasury, Duncannon suggested

[1] Works 1/20, f. A.
[2] Henry Dawkins (d. 1852), M.P. 1806–8, 1812–14; Commissioner of Woods and Forests since 1810.

some modifications.[1] Instead of retaining a Clerk of the Works, he wished to appoint a full-time Assistant Surveyor, 'professionally educated and competent to estimate and superintend all ordinary and current repairs of buildings', at £500 per annum.

When the Letters Patent establishing the new united Office were issued, the Treasury asked that the new Board should reconsider Duncannon's proposals before a final decision was taken.[2] At the same time the Treasury claimed the right of appointing to all vacancies in the new department, overriding the commissioners' attempt to defend their patronage.[3] In subsequent practice, however, appointments continued to be made on the nomination of the commissioners.[4] Another Treasury stipulation was that the accounts of the new office, which as custodian of the Crown Lands was a revenue-collecting department, should show 'the whole of the pecuniary transactions in the simplest and clearest manner', and keep expenses chargeable on the Land Revenue distinct from those provided for by Parliament. They recommended that a Mr. Abbott, an accountant occasionally employed by the Treasury as an adviser, should be asked to devise a system of accounts and to superintend its working for twelve months, to be paid £300 if his system were successful.[5]

Duncannon's recommendations were endorsed by his colleagues with the rider that if, after fair trial, it was found necessary to have additional assistance, their position should not be prejudiced by their having now adopted a 'scale of the utmost practicable economy'.[6] This was only made possible by putting full responsibility on the architects employed, and by the intention 'as far as possible, to execute all Public Works by competition and under contract'. In a more detailed memorandum, Duncannon remarked that architects who might in future be employed

> in the erection or repairs of Public Buildings, are, as in cases of private Business, and in the case of Mr. Blore at Buckingham Palace, to be wholly responsible with regard to the prices and quality of all Materials and Workmanship, and the correctness of Day and Measured Accounts (under regulations and Instructions to be hereafter settled); and it being also intended, as far as possible, to execute all Public Works by Competition and under Contract, whereby a great portion of the Professional Duties of Check and Controul which have heretofore been performed in the Office of Works, will devolve upon the Architects. . . .[7]

He therefore proposed an establishment of a Surveyor of Works and Buildings, an Itinerant Surveyor of Works, an Assistant Surveyor of Works and Buildings, a Clerk of the Furniture, two professional clerks and two writing clerks. In addition, the buildings were to be placed in the care of seven Clerks of Works (i.e. Labourers in Trust given the more honourable designation).[8] Requisitions for repairs and

[1] Works 1/20, f. B. 30 January 1832. [2] *Ibid.* f. C, 27 February 1832.
[3] Works 6/413, Commissioners of Woods etc. to Treasury, 6 March 1832; T. 1/4383, f. 4422/32, Maule to Ellice, 3 April 1832. [4] Works 22/2/7.
[5] Works 1/20, f. C. P. H. Abbott was an official assignee of the Court of Bankruptcy, 1832–41.
[6] *Ibid.* f. E, 16 March 1832. [7] Works 6/413, n.d.
[8] These were arranged as follows: Windsor (Busher); Hampton Court, Kew and Richmond (Slade); St. James's Palace and Park, Buckingham Palace, Kensington Palace, Hyde Park, the King's and Queen's Mews (Morris); Horse Guards, Treasury, Council Office, Board of Trade, Secretaries of State Offices, Downing Street houses, State Paper Office and all other buildings west of Whitehall (Lee); Houses of Parliament and four official houses, Chapter House, Whitehall Chapel, Law Courts, Somerset House, and Fleet Prison (Whibley); British Museum, Tower, Mint, King's Bench and Marshalsea Prisons, National Debt Office, Rolls Buildings, Post Offices, Insolvent Debtors' Court, Greenwich Park and all other buildings east of Whitehall not otherwise mentioned (Pulman); Brighton (Tyrell) (Works 6/413).

furniture would be taken into consideration only quarterly, unless urgent. They were to be made in writing to the secretary of the Board, and such as the Board entertained would be referred to the Surveyor and his assistants, who would inspect and make a report with an estimate.

The new commissioners recommended that all the personnel of the former Office of Works should be retained until 5 April 1832, the next quarter day, after which the Chief Examiner (Hiort), First Copying Clerk (Leckenby) and one messenger might be discontinued. It was left to the Treasury to decide when to terminate the other officers' (including Attached Architects') employment; Stephenson was drawing up a list of services for compensation.[1]

Thus the old Office of Works came to an end on 5 April 1832. Of the Attached Architects, Nash was already suspended; Soane was instructed to complete the works already under his direction at the State Paper Office and Whitehall Chapel; and Smirke to continue the new buildings at the British Museum at a five per cent commission provided that the aggregate did not exceed his estimates.[2] Seward became Surveyor of Works and Buildings. The five Clerks of the Works were discharged, as were several of the Labourers in Trust. For them, the new arrangements involved hardship. Stephenson recommended three to the Treasury for further consideration: Molinix, Hudson and Peacock, 'who have been nearly worn out in the service, and who after many years faithful discharge of their . . . duties; from age and infirmities are no longer capable of earning a maintenance for themselves and families'.[3] The claims of efficiency and economy were hard to reconcile with those of equity. Hudson, aged 72, had since 1818 been Labourer in Trust at Buckingham House, the Mews, etc., and previously 'constant carpenter' at the Houses of Parliament and Speaker's House—but as that was not a warrant appointment, it did not count for superannuation, and he was finally allowed only £25 per annum despite a favourable recommendation from the King.[4] Similarly, Peacock's years of service from 1800 to 1819 did not count: it was hardly surprising that he clung to his official house at Kensington; peremptory official letters failed to move him, and he was still there in December 1834.[5] Molinix, at 65 considerably junior in years, had been fortunate enough to serve in a warrant appointment for 39 years: he was at first allowed £72 per annum, revised to £90.[6] William Evans, aged 54, had several years of unestablished service, but had served only four years as Labourer in Trust and obtained only a gratuity of £30.[7]

The Clerks of the Works were treated even more ungenerously, though they suffered less hardship. Three of them certainly had little claim, having less than three years' service; but although William Matthew had forty years and Lewis Wyatt thirty-three as a warrant officer, the Treasury took the view that officers whose situation 'did not occasion a hindrance to their continuing the business of their professions' were not entitled to a pension, 'any more than if they had been employed by the Public, and paid for each work performed'. This was the more unjust as Crocker and Kidd, who had retired from similar posts a few years earlier, were drawing £400 and

---

[1] Works 4/31, p. 344; 1/20, f. E.   [2] Works 1/20, pp. 1, 10.   [3] *Ibid.* p. 94, 26 October 1832.
[4] *Ibid.* pp. 121, 140, 162; T. 1/4378. Hudson's superannuation had at first been fixed at £20 p.a.
[5] Works 1/20, pp. 121, 140, 302; 1/21, pp. 83, 183, 211; T. 1/4378. For Peacock's career, see p. 121.
[6] Works 1/20, pp. 121, 140; T. 1/4378.   [7] *Ibid.*

£300 per annum respectively. There was no Sir William Chambers to fight for them: but Matthew was able to prove that he was 'under an express obligation to abandon all private business' on taking up his post at Windsor; he was therefore granted a pension, but died on 2 March 1833.[1]

There was a less drastic removal of the office staff. Hiort, now 60, was unable to carry out his threat of remaining at his post until infirmity should drive him out, but his 38 years' service and comparatively high salary qualified him for a pension of £450 per annum. William Leckenby, First Copying Clerk since 1815, received £75 per annum. Tempany, the messenger, was also pensioned, at £35 per annum.[2] Of the other clerks, John Phipps (*c.* 1796–1868), late Drawing and Examining Clerk—described in 1821 as 'active, zealous, and intelligent . . . an excellent draftsman'—was promoted to be Assistant Surveyor for London. William Bennett Barker (b. *c.* 1794), First Assistant Examining and Measuring Clerk, was appointed First Professional Clerk (ranking as a senior clerk and charged with measuring), and Henry Joshua Robinson (b.1800), Second Professional Clerk (as chief examiner of works accounts, with the standing of assistant clerk). J. R. S. Cox was retained as Clerk of the Furniture; and William Madox Wyatt and Charles Papendiek became writing clerks. The opportunity having been taken to superannuate two clerks from the Woods and Forests, in poor health and willing to retire, and a third having recently resigned, three 'intelligent and useful' clerks (W. S. Phipps, W. J. Smith and Joseph Bedder) were transferred from the Office of Works as junior clerks, at a saving of £353 6s. 3d. per annum.[3]

It was not to be expected that the old Office of Works should welcome its virtual extinction. The new arrangement was an implicit condemnation of the old, and was not accomplished without friction. The ill-feeling over superannuation was only one aspect. Stephenson's unusual acerbity in rebutting a complaint from Blore about lack of help over the Buckingham Palace accounts indicates his irritation at the transfer of control to the Woods and Forests.[4] Stephenson felt that as an old friend of King William he should have continued to exercise authority over the works at the palace. When he found that his entire department was to be submerged in the Woods and Forests, and that Buckingham Palace was to be kept out of his hands, he was angry; and as a member of the new Board he did not prove a co-operative colleague.[5]

Those Labourers in Trust fortunate enough to be retained on the new establishment were thenceforth designated Clerks of the Works. Placed under the Itinerant

---

[1] *Ibid.*; L.R.R.O. 54/14, p. 382.

[2] T. 1/4378. The pensions originally awarded were revised by two junior ministers after general complaints; these three being upgraded from £400, £66, and £30 respectively.

[3] Works 1/20, f. E; L.R.R.O. 54/14. Papendiek, a protégé of Soane, had succeeded Cox as a 'temporary clerk' in 1828 (Bolton, *Portrait of Sir John Soane*, 1927, p. 300; Works 4/29, pp. 13, 376).

[4] Works 19/4, ff. 592–3, 15 December 1831. 'It is to be regretted', Stephenson told the Commissioners of Woods, 'that the delay in proceeding with the works . . . should be imputed by Mr. Blore to the unsettled state of Mr Nash's accounts; more especially, as Mr Blore has already had access to the accounts in question, and has been furnished with every particular relative to Mr. Nash's contracts, as well as all other information, which he himself required, and which it was in the power of this Office to afford—Mr. Blore having been likewise apprized that he could still avail himself from time to time, of any further facilities in the possession of this Department, which he might consider necessary to further the progress of the Works. . . .'

[5] Nottingham University Library, Newcastle MS. 9073 c, memorandum by Lord Lincoln, May 1845.

or Assistant Surveyor, according to locality, they were personally to superintend all works ordered by the Board through the appropriate surveyor, and were directed to communicate with him on all questions relating to the buildings in their charge. They were forbidden to take on private work, except with the Board's sanction, and were subject to article xlix (setting out the Labourer in Trust's duties) of the Treasury Instructions of 1815, which remained in force.[1] In June 1832 the Board decided to extend regulations xli and xlii, to forbid any officer 'undertaking or having any pecuniary interest directly or indirectly' not only in public but in private works also, or receiving 'any fees, gratuity, gift or perquisite'.[2]

The reform of 1832 meant that the Office of Works became in effect a sub-department of the Woods and Forests. Although in theory the junior and assistant clerks were not allotted to any particular branch of the office, but were employed wherever their services were needed, the same individuals appear in practice to have formed the staff of the Works department, which continued to possess a clear identity of its own, receiving a distinct parliamentary vote and discharging distinct functions for which distinct accounts were rendered. Thus, for instance, works in the parks on 'woods, fences, plantations and drains' were executed under the Woods and Forests department, while those on 'buildings and external fences, where those fences are of iron railings or of brick' were executed by the Works department—precisely the demarcation that had existed prior to 1832.[3] The case for maintaining such a demarcation lay, of course, in the revenue-generating character of the Woods and Forests, the Works on the other hand being purely a spending department. Until all receipts were paid into the Exchequer and all expenses were the subject of parliamentary vote, the two had to be distinguished. The economies of organisation lay in the reduction of overheads—one office building the less, with its keeper and messengers; and in a smaller staff now exclusively engaged in the public service.

Other economies might be achieved by rigorous control of ordinary repairs, which constituted the bulk of normal expenditure. Close attention to these at every stage could reduce costs considerably. The key role in the new organisation was allotted to the surveyors. Seward, the principal, was relieved of his duties as cashier, so that he might consider 'all plans, estimates, specifications, and tenders for works intended to be undertaken, as to the prices charged for materials and wages, and in the re-examination of any works or accounts which may be delivered into the Office; but of the correctness of which any doubts may be entertained'.[4] The Itinerant Surveyor (Edward Jesse of the Woods and Forests) and Assistant Surveyor (John Phipps), replacing the old Clerks of the Works, would supervise the buildings; to them the Board would refer all applications for works. At three stages their watchful care could be decisive: in checking requisitions; in controlling expenditure when sanctioned; and in ensuring good workmanship. As all orders for services in the new department of works would fall into either Seward's section or that of Jesse and Phipps, the head of each would be separately responsible to the Board for the

---

[1] Works 1/20, pp. 2–4, 31 March 1832.   [2] *Ibid.* pp. 35–7, 13 June 1832.
[3] *Parl. Pap.* 1833 (677), xiv, qq. 947, 1067–8. The same workmen, however, were now employed under contract by both departments.
[4] Works 1/20, pp. 37–41, 19 June 1832.

execution of his duties.[1] Thus there was no single supervising officer at the head of the department; the Board alone would co-ordinate its activities.

An opportunity for achieving small economies was seen in the ordinary maintenance of the extensive properties at Kew and Hampton Court. Instead of appointing warrant-holding tradesmen for this purpose, direct labour was employed. At each palace one carpenter, one bricklayer and one painter and glazier were to be permanently employed on weekly wages. At Hampton Court there were in addition to be a plumber, a mason and mason's labourer to keep the stonework in order, and two labourers to clean the courts; the necessary materials were to be kept in store by the Clerks of the Works.[2] Thus the old system of 'constant' artisans was revived, but with a down-grading of status.

The commissioners' arrangements were confirmed by a Treasury minute of 3 July 1832, which recognised their experimental character.[3] It was soon discovered that the scale of the establishment had been drawn too small: it had been intended to place Kew under the officer at Hampton Court, but John Matthew's services had to be retained as Clerk of the Works 'in consequence of the very numerous buildings at Kew, many of them old and requiring daily inspection'. It was also necessary to retain John Fortune exclusively for the Post Office.[4] After rather more than a year's experience, the commissioners proposed some further changes in their arrangements.[5] Barker, who under the old system had examined accounts after they were delivered into the Office, was now working very long hours measuring buildings from Greenwich to Windsor, and the commissioners proposed he should receive an additional £50 salary (i.e. £360 per annum rising to £450 by annual increments of £10). The former Labourers in Trust, too, had had their labour and responsibility so much increased by the discontinuance of the former Clerks of the Works, that they deserved an increase from £100 per annum to £130, and £10 for journey money. The St. James's and Kensington Clerk was overburdened and a Clerk residing at Kensington was needed for that palace and Hyde Park.

As always, close supervision of the man on the job was essential. The old Labourers in Trust were not always adequate to the responsibility of their wider functions under the new system. The delinquency of George Slade at Hampton Court has been referred to above.[6] John Matthew, Clerk of Works at Kew, who was nominated to succeed him, had failed on a number of occasions to transmit promptly to the surveyor the tradesmen's weekly notes of day labour and materials. But it was his failure to report rising expenditure on the Orangery in Kew Gardens that caused his transference in December 1833, not to Hampton Court, but to Kensington, where a closer watch could be kept upon him.[7] Clearly the commissioners were determined to keep the closest check on officers' disbursements. Upon Slade's dismissal and Matthew's removal the Board called on the surveyors to frame

---

[1] *Ibid.* pp. 37–41, 127–8 (8 January 1833).   [2] *Ibid.* pp. 35–7.   [3] T. 1/4383, f. 11671/32.
[4] Works 1/20, p. 72, 24 October 1832.
[5] *Ibid.* pp. 223–6, 14 August 1833. These were approved with back-dating to the beginning of the quarter (T. 1/4383, f. 15834/33).   [6] Above p. 121.
[7] Works 1/20, pp. 67–8, 192–3, 245, 280, 289, 295; see below, p. 440, n. 14. Slade, Fortune (G.P.O.) and Busher (at Windsor) had also been carrying out works before delivering an estimate (*ibid.* pp. 132, 18 January; 269, 7 November 1833).

rules for the Clerks of Works, on the basis of the old Office of Works regulations.[1] 'Regulations for the Conduct of the Clerks of the Works . . . in the Discharge of their Official Duties' were accordingly promulgated in January 1834: combining the functions of the old Clerks of the Works and Labourers in Trust, they were to ensure efficient work and prevent waste or abuses and were explicitly placed under the immediate control of the appropriate surveyor.[2] Before the month was out, John Tyrell, Clerk of Works at Brighton, was dismissed in consequence of charges brought against him by a labourer.[3] It was particularly in the out-stations, less constantly watched by superior officers, that the resident officers were prone to malpractices. In July 1834 the new Clerk at Richmond was rebuked for exceeding his estimates.[4] Slade's successor at Hampton Court, Craib, was the object of accusations by tradesmen, and in September 1837 the Board after investigation declared his conduct 'most improper and highly reprehensible, and in direct violation of the Regulations'. He was warned that any similar offence would lead to his immediate dismissal and was ordered not to undertake any private repair work save with the written permission of the Board.[5]

Edward Jesse himself, the surveyor responsible for the out-districts, was not conspicuously fitted for his post. As a young man private secretary to Lord Dartmouth, he had obtained through his patron a valuable place at Court. Later Lord Glenbervie appointed him also Deputy Surveyor of the Woods and Forests. Retained in the united office as Itinerant Surveyor, his increased duties obliged him to resign his post at Court.[6] According to his daughter he possessed a 'constitution which was at no time remarkable for vigour', and he passed part of every winter at Brighton.[7] This habit may account for his frequent failures to prepare his annual estimates in due time.[8] A further handicap was a 'nervous temperament' which obliged him often 'to struggle against fits of impatience and irritability'.[9] Lord Lincoln described him to Peel as 'a very indiscreet man'.[10] Even his enthusiasm for restoring the 'original gorgeous and artistic beauty' of Hampton Court Palace led him into trouble because he overspent.[11] He was a man of an earlier age who lingered on in the public employ until 1851.[12]

Fortunately indolence and incompetence were not universal. John Phipps, the Assistant Surveyor for London, was a keen and intelligent officer who had worked his way up from temporary assistant clerk in the old Office of Works. He devised a form of abstracts to accompany his weekly estimates (probably showing totals expended and sums still available) which Jesse was recommended to adopt; and he clearly exercised a vigilant supervision over his Clerks of Works.[13] Even Craib lived down his misconduct, and, together with Thomas Pulman, Clerk for the Eastern District of London, was recommended in 1841 for a £25 per annum salary increase,

---

[1] *Ibid.* p. 298.   [2] Works 22/8/7, ff. 1–2.
[3] Works 1/20, p. 304, 15 January 1834.   [4] Works 1/21, p. 137
[5] Works 1/22, pp. 351, 361.   [6] T. 1/4383, f. 9024/32.
[7] 'M.C.' [Mrs. M. C. Houston] *Letters and Reminiscences of the Rev. John Mitford* (1891), pp. 6, 10, 15, 55, 105, 256, 279–83.
[8] See, e.g. Works 1/22, pp. 35, 41, 174, 187, 387; 1/23, p. 235; 1/25, p. 263.
[9] Houston, *op. cit.* p. 105.   [10] B.M. Add. MS. 40575, ff. 198–9.
[11] Works 1/27, pp. 96–7; Houston, *op. cit.* p. 55.
[12] He died in 1868 at the age of 88. A bust of him was placed in the Royal Pavilion at Brighton (F. Boase, *Modern English Biography* ii, 1897, p. 94).   [13] Works 1/21, pp. 435–6.

the commissioners having 'every reason to be satisfied with their zeal and activity'.[1] When John Busher was obliged to give up his Windsor clerkship on account of a paralytic stroke, the commissioners praised his 'zeal and unquestionable integrity'.[2]

Alterations in the Board came when Lord Melbourne succeeded Lord Grey as Prime Minister in July 1834. Duncannon was promoted Home Secretary; and William Dacres Adams,[3] the Second Commissioner, took the occasion to retire, prematurely worn out at fifty-eight. As commissioner dealing with the Woods, Forests and Land Revenue departments, he has little place in the history of the Office of Works, but his retirement facilitated changes which, Duncannon argued, would increase efficiency without involving additional expenditure. For the secretary of the board, Alexander Milne,[4] had injured his eyesight by constant attention to business, though he was 'sufficiently active both in mind and body to undertake any official Duties in which much writing is not required.' As he had hitherto super-intended all the plantations in the forests and knew the Crown estates thoroughly, he was particularly qualified to serve as a commissioner.[5] This recommendation was Duncannon's although implemented shortly after his departure to the Home Office.

His close relationship with Milne had facilitated Duncannon's domination of the Office.[6] Milne described his own work as

> a general supervision, under the orders of the Board, of all the business of the department, having to bring before the Board all letters and matters coming into the Office, to take their directions, to see that their orders are distributed to the heads of departments, and properly executed, to communicate personally with parties who have business with the Office, but who may not have occasion to see the members of the Board.[7]

He opened all letters and signed all those sent out except reports to the Treasury—between 100 and 150 a week.[8] Milne seems not to have relished parliamentary interference, and when the select committee of 1833 investigating the land revenues of the Crown inquired what improvements he could propose, he avoided the question. He was not even candid about the Board's procedure. He admitted that an arrangement was under consideration by which, instead of the secretary laying all letters before the Board in the order of receipt, he would distribute them immediately to heads of departments (senior clerks), whose draft replies would be brought before the Board with relevant papers by either Adams or Stephenson. But Milne did not

---

[1] Works 2/3, p. 103. The Treasury refused the increase. [2] Works 1/22, p. 405.

[3] 1775–1862; private secretary to Pitt 1804–6; to Duke of Portland 1807–9; Commissioner of Woods, etc. since 1810. After nearly 43 years in the public service, he could no longer 'bear fatigue of riding or any other strong exercise'; his sight was very defective, 'much more so than is usual at his age'; severe attacks of gout had weakened his limbs; and he suffered from other infirmities (T. 1/4383, ff. 15196/34 and 22170/34). For his career, see R. R. Nelson, *The Home Office* (1969), p. 161.

[4] *c.* 1781–1861; clerk in Woods and Forests, 1798; secretary to Surveyor General; joint secretary of Woods, Forests and Land Revenues, 1811, sole secretary 1822 (T. 1/4383, f. 15196/34). See also Lord Glenbervie, *Diaries* (ed. F. Blickley, 1928); *Parl. Pap.* 1833 (677), xiv, qq. 1128–9, 1896. As secretary of the Woods and Forests Milne received £1000 p.a.; but he was also secretary to the New Street Commissioners (£450) and the Holyhead Road Commissioners (£200); so that by his promotion to commissioner at £1200 p.a. he lost £450 p.a. Duncannon suggested that he should receive a compensation of £250 p.a. and continue to reside in his official house and that any future superannuation should be calculated on a salary of £1650 p.a.

[5] T. 1/4383, f. 15196/34.

[6] Nottingham University Library, Newcastle MS. 9072, Lord Lincoln to Peel, 9 June 1845.

[7] *Parl. Pap.* 1833 (677) xiv, Report of select committee on the Land Revenues of the Crown, q. 2108.

[8] *Ibid.* qq. 2109–10.

reveal that this system had already been adopted by a Board minute of 17 July 1832.[1] Its ostensible purpose was to provide the Board with the necessary data for its decisions, which hitherto it had too frequently lacked. It was an intelligent measure of devolution, giving the senior clerks a greater part in the process of decision-making; one that was, doubtless, a consequence of the additional business brought upon the Board by the annexation of the Office of Works. But it also affected the principle of corporate responsibility: instead of the junior commissioners sharing in decisions taken collectively at a Board, they acted as departmental heads in a relationship with the First Commissioner similar to that of the secretary, a subordinate officer, while the First Commissioner, thus relieved of some of his responsibilities, nevertheless retained the ultimate power of decision. A simultaneous development of this character in the Board of Control was formalised in a statute of 1833 which replaced the assistant commissioners by secretaries.[2] Duncannon, with his 'remarkably calm and unruffled temper', 'very good sound sense', and 'extreme liveliness and elasticity of spirits', found legislation unnecessary.[3] Politically, he was the most weighty First Commissioner of the united office; and when convenient he settled issues by direct conversations with the Treasury ministers instead of through the formal machinery of the Board.[4] Lowther, First Commissioner in 1828–30, had wished to dispense with the junior commissioners, conducting business through a president and his deputy, although he admitted that he had never experienced any opposition or impediment from his colleagues: he had not even found it necessary to attend Board meetings, the secretary transmitting his remarks or written opinions.[5] Duncannon, with a resentful and sometimes obstructive colleague in Stephenson, was no doubt encouraged to act in a similar fashion; and he tended to conduct departmental business directly through the secretary without even consulting his colleagues.[6] In theory the commissioners were collectively responsible for action taken in the Board's name. 'The Office may go on better under one responsible head,' said Lowther, 'but the view is, that they should be a check upon any extravagant act'.[7] 'In the terms of his appointment, no separate and distinct powers are given to the Chief Commissioner', Milne stated, adding 'but he has that control and authority over the whole proceedings which his situation in the Government and his responsibility in Parliament naturally give him'.[8] Duncannon exploited his advantages. 'Nothing', Milne told the select committee of 1833, 'nothing beyond the merely routine business is done' without consulting with the First Commissioner.[9] When Stephenson died in 1839

---

[1] *Ibid.* qq. 2111–13; Crest 25/36, 17 July 1832.

[2] By the Act 3 and 4 William IV, c. 85. See Sir W. Foster, *John Company* (1926), p. 259 and cf. J. R. Torrance, 'Sir George Harrison and the growth of bureaucracy in the early 19th century', *E. H. R.* lxxxiii (1968), p. 68.

[3] Greville, *Diary*, v, p. 447 (for a less flattering view see iii, p. 60). Duncannon's successor, Hobhouse, remarked that he 'was not to be deterred by scruples or trifles of any kind from steadily pursuing the object in view' (Lord Broughton, *Recollections of a Long Life*, vi, 1911, p. 192).

[4] T. 1/4383, f. 19841/38, 26 May 1838, Commissioners of Woods to Treasury, refers to a recent communication between Chief Commissioner and Chancellor of the Exchequer; and f. 19941/38 (Treasury minute, 21 September 1838) embodies the Chancellor's recommendations after discussion with the Chief Commissioner. Works 2/2, p. 250 (Treasury Minute 20 April 1838) states that no written reply has been received from the commissioners, but the First Commissioner has told the Prime Minister and Chancellor of the Exchequer that his department concurs.

[5] *Parl. Pap.* 1833 (677), xiv, q. 2157.   [6] Nottingham University Library, Newcastle MS. 9072.

[7] *Parl. Pap.* 1833 (677), xiv, qq. 2151–4, 2157–8.   [8] *Ibid.* qq. 1761, 1722.   [9] *Ibid.* q. 1761.

Duncannon designated as his successor his own acting private secretary, young Charles Alexander Gore (1811–97):[1] Duncannon wanted no more than an efficient, hard-working clerk as a colleague. And so long as Duncannon himself was in charge the system worked as he intended it to work.[2] Even as Home Secretary (July–November 1834) or out of office (November 1834–May 1835), he was still associated with the department through his continuing control of the Buckingham Palace works; and his abiding interest is shown by his resumption of it in May 1835, together with the more honourable but unlaborious post of Lord Privy Seal. This was the only occasion on which the first commissionership was held with another ministerial office. That Duncannon, standing high in cabinet rank, should have chosen to resume responsibility for his old department is remarkable. The changes made in the interim were but a continuation of his policy and when he resumed control he made little further alteration in organization for some years.

When Duncannon went to the Home Office in July 1834 his immediate successor was Sir John Cam Hobhouse,[3] whose tenure was brief, for William IV dismissed the Melbourne administration on 13 November. Hobhouse acted as caretaker until Lord Granville Somerset[4] took office on 31 December under Sir Robert Peel. Peel resigned in April 1835 and Duncannon resumed his old place on 7 May, retaining it until the final resignation of the Melbourne administration in September 1841. The Tory ministers regularised certain practices that had been adopted without formal authority, such as Duncannon's direction of the works at the palace,[5] and it is probably in this light that we should view a Board minute of 27 February 1835, which divided all business into departments under the two junior commissioners.[6] Milne was to supervise most of the old Woods and Land Revenue business; while Stephenson was charged with the works and buildings department, house estates in London and elsewhere and royal parks in or near London (except the Regent's Park under Milne). Under Stephenson were placed Seward and all officers of the Works Department, as well as Thomas Chawner and Henry Rhodes, the joint architects and surveyors employed on the Land Revenue side.[7] This was little more than a formal recognition of the existing division of labour, for Milne had stated in 1833 that the care of buildings in London was principally superintended by Stephenson. Adams, the Second Commissioner, confirmed this: 'Sir Benjamin Stephenson has the superintendence of all that which relates to Works and various public buildings, and my department is that of the Land Revenue and the Woods and Forests'; his duty being 'to superintend, generally, the department . . . to communicate with the Secretary

---

[1] Brother of the 4th Earl of Arran and nephew of the Duchess of Inverness. Clerk in the Pay Office, 1829; private secretary to Lord John Russell 1831–9, with rank as clerk in the Treasury from 1834; temporary private secretary to Lord Duncannon 1839; Commissioner of Woods, etc. 1839–51; Commissioner of Crown Lands 1851–85. Married Duncannon's daughter Augusta, Countess of Kerry, 1845. See J. Gore, *Charles Gore, Father and Son* (1932), pt. 1. I am grateful to Mr. Gore for his reply to my inquiries about his grandfather.
[2] Nottingham University Library, Newcastle MS. 9072.
[3] 1786–1869; suc. as Bt. 1831; cr. Lord Broughton, 1851. Friend of Byron, and something of a radical. See his own *Recollections of a Long Life*, ed. Lady Dorchester (6 vols. 1909–11), and *D.N.B.*
[4] 1792–1848. A junior Lord of the Treasury, 1819; Chancellor of the Duchy of Lancaster 1841–6. See *D.N.B.*   [5] See p. 194.   [6] Works 6/413.
[7] Thomas Chawner (1774–1851) and Henry Rhodes (c. 1778–1846) were appointed joint surveyors to the Woods, Forests and Land Revenues on the amalgamation of the two offices in 1810. Rhodes became subject to a series of 'very slight' paralytic attacks that resulted in 'severe depression of spirits' and 'extreme loss' of strength (T. 1/4383, f. 15112/40).

and the heads of the different branches on the business connected with it, and to bring the Papers on these several subjects before the Board'.[1] Yet the minute specifically stated that the division of work was to come into operation on 3 March 1835; its effect was further to diminish the collective responsibility of the commissioners as a Board, and emphasize the importance of the First Commissioner as the only man with an overall responsibility.

A change already made at Duncannon's behest was the abolition of the post of secretary: its duties were 'too great for one man'; they were divided between the two junior commissioners and the heads of departments. The work of the eight subordinate departments was reorganised into three main divisions: the Forests and Land Revenues in England and Accounts (under King, a chief clerk in the Land Revenue branch); the Irish and Scotch (under Weale, principal clerk in the Irish branch); and Works and Buildings (under Seward). The head of each received £800 per annum. Secretarial duties in connection with board meetings were to be performed by the secretary to the First Commissioner, with an allowance of £100 a year.[2] This left the secretarial work in a state of some confusion. Letters were signed and despatched by the heads of departments. Lord Granville Somerset found however that various other duties of the secretary had not been provided for and proposed appointing a Clerk to the Board to discharge most of the duties of the former secretary—but without holding a position of such dignity: he was to open all official letters and send them to the registrar; and was responsible for distributing material to the different departments.[3] As soon as possible after each meeting of the Board he was to send the minutes to the several departments for immediate action; the head clerks would then send them to the minute clerk.[4] There could be little doubt that a capable man as Clerk to the Board could exercise the same influence over proceedings as Milne had done. But he would be a junior officer more dependant upon the First Commissioner and not a potential rival. Somerset appointed to this post his own private secretary, whose 'known assiduity' would enable him to discharge both offices without increase of salary (£530). Since 1827 the position of private secretary to the First Commissioner had been held by Trenham Walshman Philipps (1795–1855), who made himself indispensable to successive First Commissioners.[5] He was constantly at hand: 'from the usual hour of attendance in the morning till all hours at night', seldom leaving the office before 7, more frequently 8 o'clock; and during the sitting of Parliament there till 10 'and sometimes later, but very rarely'. When the First Commissioner was away from London, he even looked in at the office on Sundays.[6] He described his work thus to the 1833 select committee:[7]

---

[1] *Parl. Pap.*, 1833 (677), xiv, qq. 1719, 2117–8, 2165–6, 2473, 2465.

[2] T. 1/4383, ff. 15196/34 and 15383/34. By these changes the amount of Adams' pension, £1000 p.a. was saved. Approved by the Treasury, the new arrangements came into effect on 3 March 1835 (Works 6/413).

[3] Works 6/413, Seward's memoranda, 29 February [sic] 1835; *Parl. Pap.*, 1847–8 (538), xxiv, App. pp. 539–40, Lord Granville Somerset's minute February 1835.

[4] *Ibid*. Board minute, 24 February 1835.

[5] Lord John Manners, as First Commissioner of Works, 'depended fearlessly upon the knowledge and loyalty of Philipps, the permanent Secretary' (C. Whibley, *Lord John Manners and his Friends* ii, p. 50). See also below, p. 217. Philipps was appointed an extra clerk in the Woods and Forests, December 1814; placed on the establishment in 1820 or 1821; appointed private secretary to the Chief Commissioner (Arbuthnot) 1827 (*Parl. Pap.*, 1833 (677) xiv, qq. 2748–52; 1847–8 (538) xxiv, app. Q. 21).

[6] *Parl. Pap.*, 1833 (677), xiv, qq. 2754, 2758–9.   [7] *Ibid*. qq. 2754.

The duties of private secretary are many of them necessarily confidential. Those, however, which occupy the principal portion of my time are strictly public and official. I am the medium of communication between the Chief Commissioner, the Secretary, and the heads of the different departments. I receive persons who have business with the Chief Commissioner in his absence from the Office, and I either furnish or procure such information as he may require while Parliament is sitting, or during his absence from town. I am partially engaged in drawing Reports to the Treasury, and preparing Returns to Parliament upon matters that do not strictly belong to the other departments of the Office.

To these, another duty was added by Lord Granville Somerset instituting a commissioner's letter book, 'for recording in a Book for the use of the Chief Commissioner and for the information of the Board, the Letters received and issued from day to day from the several Departments of this Office'. In August 1836 it was further ordered that

> all Letters issued in the names of the Commissioners and sent to them, or to any one of them for signature, shall be marked with the number of the Paper or Papers upon which the Proceeding shall have immediately originated and the date of the Board's Minute directing such proceeding.

The clerk to the Board was to see that these particulars were duly entered in the letter-book.[1]

There was one further appointment made by Duncannon which should perhaps be mentioned, though outside the Works Department proper. The united office had continued to employ the joint surveyors to the former Woods and Forests, Rhodes and Chawner. In June 1840 the commissioners decided to supersede Rhodes, whose persistent ill-health had left Chawner to sustain the whole duty. They appointed as successor James Pennethorne,[2] Nash's professional heir, who himself was greatly preoccupied with metropolitan improvements. To meet the difficulty consequent on this curious choice, a post of assistant surveyor to the House Estate department was created at an annual salary of £300 for the first five years; and Duncannon selected William James Smith, who had entered the Office of Works in 1830 as a professional assistant after 'many years' in private business.[3]

At the outset of the union with the Woods and Forests important alterations were made to promote economy in the Works Department. Reference has already been made to the device of placing full responsibility for a work upon a specially employed architect. This was first tried in October 1831, when Edward Blore was directed to take over the completion of Buckingham Palace. He was to receive a commission of five per cent upon his estimate only, and was to keep checks on day work and see to the measuring. 'This Board', wrote Duncannon, 'will have no

---

[1] Works 1/22, p. 107. One of these letter-books, that for 1845, has survived among Lord Lincoln's papers in Nottingham University Library (Newcastle MS. Ne. O.35). At the same time it was proposed, perhaps on Philipps's initiative, that all correspondence relating to particular subjects should be bound and indexed (Crest 25/43, 30 August 1836). But nothing came of this in the Works department at least.

[2] 1801–71. A relation of Mrs. Nash, brought up by her, to whom Nash transferred his practice in 1834. The secretary of the Office of Works in 1860 described Pennethorne's original engagement as 'somewhat obscure' (*Parl. Pap.* 1860 (483) ix, q. 1046). See also Works 22/8/1.

[3] Works 1/25, pp. 124–7; 22/8/1, f. 1; 5/111.

objections to undertake the superintendence of the payments which it may be necessary to make under the directions of Mr. Blore'.[1] This was similar to the system adopted in respect of Nash's work at the palace in 1828. But Nash had looked to the King as his only master. Now Duncannon was the director. Although the Board managed the receipt and issue of money and the examination of accounts, 'the services at the Palace were under Lord Duncannon's exclusive controul. Mr. Blore received all his authorities either direct from Lord Duncannon, or in his Lordship's name'.[2] When Duncannon moved to the Home Office he arranged, to avoid difficulties which might result from the friction between Stephenson and Milne, that he should retain control of the palace works.[3] Operations there were suspended when, after the fire at Westminster, William IV offered the building for Parliament's use. When it was decided to complete it according to the original intention, Duncannon suggested that he should continue to supervise the work, despite the change of administration that had occurred in the interval:

> As the Repairs and alterations have been from the first entirely under my control, and as all the contracts were made by my authority, and not more than two or three months are now required for its completion, and as it is totally unconnected with any political event that has taken place, I feel that it will be more conducive to His Majesty's comfort in an early occupation of the Building, and to the necessity of keeping the works within the original estimate that no change should take place in the arrangements . . .[4]

The arrangement by which Duncannon had kept the business in his hands was, however, a private one, which the new government regularised by a Treasury minute: the accounts for both building and furniture would be prepared on Blore's responsibility and certified by Duncannon, as hitherto, 'Their Lordships relying upon Lord Duncannon that no exceeding should take place'.[5] In May 1837, when he handed the completed palace to the Lord Chamberlain's care, Duncannon was able to record that 'no additional charge has been made on the Public' beyond the estimate.[6] Blore ascribed the success of the operation to the perfect confidence placed in him by the minister.[7]

Another work brought to a successful conclusion under a similar arrangement was Wyatville's reconstruction of Windsor Castle.[8] Meanwhile, the new buildings of the British Museum were rising year by year under Smirke's direction at a rate determined by the annual vote.[9] Less successful was Wilkins' commission at the National Gallery.[10] His proposal for converting the old State Mews at Charing Cross won the government's approval on grounds of economy, but, as so often happened, once the plan was adopted it acquired an independent momentum which carried it on to the erection of an entirely new building at a cost more than double the original estimate.

[1] T. 1/3489, f. 21403/31.
[2] Nottingham University Library, Newcastle MS. 9073c. The precise nature of Blore's authority was defined in an exhaustive series of questions by Blore and answers by Duncannon in May 1832 (Works 19/4, ff. 722–9).
[3] *Ibid.* 19/5, f. 1377.   [4] T. 1/3489, with f. 22973/34, 17 November 1834.
[5] *Ibid.* 28 November 1834.   [6] *Ibid.* f. 10619/37.   [7] Works 19/7, ff. 2305–6.
[8] See pp. 384–91.   [9] See pp. 412–4.   [10] See pp. 461–7.

The most important undertaking of the period was the building of new Houses of Parliament,[1] and the same policy of devolving responsibility on the architect was followed. This building presented peculiar difficulties, which call for a digression at this point. The Whig government felt itself unable to dictate to Parliament on the subject after Peel, during his brief ministry of 1834–5, had been defeated in proposing that the rebuilding should be entrusted to Sir Robert Smirke. Peel confidently referred to a select committee Smirke's proposals for simple Gothic-trimmed buildings of moderate size. Only Joseph Hume appeared to be critical until a popular agitation was whipped up, led by Sir Edward Cust, a courtier and man of taste who had been prominent as a critic of Soane's Law Courts. He did not sit in the reformed parliament, so missing the place on the select committee which otherwise would doubtless have been his. He made up for this exclusion by addressing to Peel an open letter dated 31 January 1835:

> A rumour is in circulation [Cust wrote] that an architect has been already directed to prepare plans,—that he has been, in fact, appointed to the duty of building a new House of Parliament. I hope this is not so. I will take the liberty of speaking of that eminent individual with the freedom that is permitted towards a known public character. I do not think the selection will give satisfaction. I doubt whether the poverty of his taste is counterbalanced even by his other professional acquirements and by the unimpeached respectability of his character. But my business is not with individuals. I object to any appointment that is not accompanied with some avowed responsibility in the party making the selection, and, further, to any appointment without some avowed control over the course of his proceeding.[2]

Cust condemned the old system of public works as producing feeble architecture at great expense, and suggested that instead of an architect being selected by government,

> something of a competition, not from among the mere tyros of the profession, but from the large class of its 'very first line' should be resorted to, in order that the best talent of the day may be elicited; and that the selection and control over the architect should vest in some authority who can be held responsible for what is done, and who may prevent the abuses to which the public have been exposed on these subjects, to the loss both of our money and our reputation.

Open competition he was decidedly against: 'it is necessary for every high station that a man should be first introduced to society by some evidences of his talent'. He named instead fourteen metropolitan architects[3] and suggested that to such a list others could easily be added, as well as provincial and Scottish practitioners. The whole business should be superintended by a royal commission—'a certain number of gentlemen known to take an interest in the art, in number not too many to divide responsibility, nor too few to create suspicion of abuse'. They would be

---

[1] See pp. 573–626.

[2] *A Letter to the Rt. Hon. Sir Robert Peel, Bart. M.P. on the expedience of a better system of control over buildings erected at the public expense; and on the subject of rebuilding the Houses of Parliament*, 1835.

[3] Barry, Blore, Cockerell, Cottingham, Deering, Hardwick, Hopper, Salvin, Shaw, Smirke, Vulliamy, Wilkins, [B.D.] Wyatt, and Wyatville.

unpaid, but the work would be 'accordant with the amusement of those who have the most leisure time at their disposal'. In brief, Cust's proposition was

> that to a commission of five gentlemen should be entrusted the mode and extent of competition; the selection of the architect; the consideration of the style of the building to be adopted, and the arrangement of all its details, leaving the business of finance to be controlled and checked by the office of Woods and Forests; a division of business not very dissimilar to that which exists between the Commander-in-chief and the Secretary-at-war in the government of the Army.

In building the Houses of Parliament it might be particularly desirable that one or two members of each House should be included, but as the commission would exercise no control over money there was no pretext for its becoming a parliamentary commission—the more so, as M.P.s were no longer all men of leisure. It is clear that Cust was designing this engine with an eye to driving it himself, and indeed he admitted as much. He thought that there would be no difficulty in finding persons willing to give their services,

> nor will I shrink from the frank avowal, that if I could be of any service in a matter to which I have directed much of my attention, I should be very ready to undertake those duties that I impose upon the commissioner, without fee or reward; and that principally because I am desirous that the opportunity of building the New Houses of Parliament should be taken to try the experiment of a better method of selection and control over the architect.

He hoped that the government would decide this question for itself without leaving it to the 'chance-medley' of a Commons debate.

In the upshot the select committee, stimulated by Hume, veered round in favour of a competition to be judged by a royal commission of five members (of whom Cust became one); but the competition was open, not select as Cust had proposed; and the style of the building was designated by the committee and not left to the discretion of the commission. The management and results of that competition are considered below.[1] In effect, public pressure had taken the decision out of the hands of the government. The consequence was that no government in the next twenty years ventured to impose its views in respect of the Houses of Parliament upon the legislature, and that the two Houses intervened from time to time to criticize and amend. The whole system of public works was, in the long run, again called in question.

The most persistent and vigorous critic of the arrangements for rebuilding was Joseph Hume, but he was so constant a critic of government, and particularly of measures involving expenditures he did not approve of, that the impact of his attacks in the House was somewhat diminished. He was seconded by the radical Member for Lambeth, Benjamin Hawes,[2] and in a series of debates during the

---

[1] *Parl. Pap.* 1835 (262) xviii. See pp. 575–88.

[2] 1797–1862. M.P. for Lambeth 1832–47, Kinsale 1848–52. Under-Secretary, Colonial Office 1846, War Office 1857–62. Once a soap manufacturer, married daughter of Sir Marc Isambard Brunel. Advocated appointment of Fine Art Commission (on which he served), and Sunday opening of the British Museum. See *D.N.B.*

session of 1836 they attempted to upset the decisions that were taken.[1] Hume favoured a different site, and feared the expense of Barry's design; a number of competitors were constituents of Hawes, and found him sympathetic to their complaints of unjust treatment. But with Peel's help, and moving with caution, the ministers were able to defeat hostile criticisms that, if successful, would seriously have jeopardised the starting of work on the new Houses. The judges' choice once endorsed by the Commons, Barry was instructed to prepare working drawings as a basis for a firm estimate, checked by the Works department with the help of specially engaged measurers before it was submitted for the Commons' approval.[2] When the employment of an expert on ventilation resulted in a large additional estimate, the Whig ministers declined to act without the approval of the House.[3]

Another example of the cautious official approach to this great undertaking is provided by the determination to pay the architect a lump sum instead of the usual percentage commission on outlay. This had long been an aim of the advocates of economy; one, furthermore, which had the persistent support of Stephenson.[4] On 20 February 1838 the Commissioners of Woods and Works recommended that Barry's remuneration should be a fixed amount: 'in consequence of the opinions expressed at different times in both Houses of Parliament against the principle of remunerating Architects by a Commission or per centage upon the amount of their Estimates', and having considered the extent and importance of the building, the probable duration of the works and the very large expenditure contemplated, they recommended £25,000 as a 'fair and liberal remuneration'.[5] On 28 February, the Treasury replied approving both this proposal and the general principle, but this letter was somehow lost, and not until a year later, when Treasury approval was again obtained, was Barry informed of the decision. His considered reply pointed out that the sum fell far short of the customary remuneration, and that he regarded it as very inadequate for the skill, labour and great responsibility involved. He therefore asked on what principle the sum had been calculated. This information was, for no good reason but in a manner characteristic of the contemporary civil service attitude towards professional men in government service, denied him, both then and subsequently. Barry's reply was ill-worded: that as he was prevented from questioning the data on which the decision was founded, he had 'no wish to do otherwise than bow' to the Board's decision. This phrase was seized upon by the government as a full justification for its stand, although Barry went on to express 'most decidedly' his view of the inadequacy of the sum, and his hope that, when this should become apparent on the completion of 'any considerable part' of the building 'that there will not be any indisposition on the part of the Board (especially if [my] work should prove to be satisfactory to the Public at large) to award to me the remainder of the remuneration which has hitherto been customary on similar occasions'.[6] To this there was no reply; and the next act opened with a letter from Barry dated 2 January 1841: the works had progressed to a point requiring some permanent arrangement relative to the measuring and making out of the accounts for works executed, and he sought

---

[1] *Parl. Deb.* 3rd ser. xxxi, 235 (9 February), 501 (17 February), 613 (19 February); xxxii, 327 (15 March); xxxiv, 672 (21 June); xxxv, 398 (21 July).
[2] Works 1/22, pp. 198, 249; 11/1/2, ff. 1–12.   [3] Works 1/25, pp. 94, 137, 148, 164, 182.
[4] See pp. 109, 168.   [5] Works 11/1/2, ff. 30–1.   [6] *Ibid.* ff. 32–9; Works 2/2, pp. 203, 315.

P

authority to make the necessary arrangements, the 'expense of which I conceive to be included in the Estimate for "Contingencies".'[1] He was thereupon informed that such expenses were included in his professional remuneration; he protested, but was merely referred to the Board's previous answer. Barry later produced a letter which he claimed was a copy of a further protest, dated 6 February 1841, declaring his future intention to renew his application. No such letter was registered in the office, but this is not proof that it was not received, as occasionally communications were not registered. At all events Duncannon determined that he could not recommend to the Treasury any revision of his former decision.[2]

There can be no doubt that in this he was mistaken. The basis on which Barry's fee had been determined was that of a three per cent commission on his estimate—the commission paid to the former Attached Architects of the Works for new buildings—plus the Attached Architects' salary of £500 a year for the seven years Barry had estimated would be required for building the new Houses. The resultant figure, £24,506, had then been rounded up to the nearest thousand.[3] The flaw in this was that the office staff had previously carried out the measuring and making up of accounts, which had been regarded as equivalent to the further two per cent making up the customary commission of five per cent to the architect. To allow Barry only three per cent and then require him to pay all expenses was decidedly ungenerous, even taking into account that he was not called upon, as the Attached Architects had been, to give advice when required. The basis of the calculation was misconceived. It was the work of Stephenson, and after his death it may perhaps have been misinterpreted, since there is no evidence to show whether the question of measuring and making up the accounts had ever been taken into consideration. Barry's subsequent attempts to secure additional remuneration belong to the next chapter. So also do the criticisms provoked by Barry's handling of the work, which led ultimately to the architect being deprived of his direct responsibility and placed under various controls.[4]

Another change to promote economy was one that had been recommended to the 1828 select committee and that Stephenson had rejected as impracticable:[5] the putting out of ordinary repairs and works to tender. Instead of employing warrant-holders, an invitation was sent out to selected tradesmen enquiring the rates at which they would carry out all works in their trade in a particular district.[6] The method of tendering was the old one of stipulating a percentage under (or, rarely, above) the Office schedule of prices. Those invited were known to the department's officers or recommended by the architects,[7] but any tradesman 'of

---

[1] Works 11/1/2, f. 44.   [2] *Ibid.* ff. 46–50, 52–4.
[3] *Ibid.* f. 45.   [4] See p. 233.   [5] *1828 Report*, pp. 83–4; Works 1/17, p. 53.
[6] Works 1/20, pp. 45, 56. The first competition was held in July 1832; those submitting the lowest tenders were: *London:* W. Whitehead, bricklayer; Jos. Griffiths, carpenter; Wood and Crake, masons; W. Holroyd, plumber, E. district; Estall and Robson, plasterers (West); J. Warmsley, slater (West); W. North, slater (East); J. Fowler, smith; Barron and son, ironmongers; J. and W. Johnson, paviours. *Hampton Court etc.:* as London, except: J. Carless, carpenter; G. Jones, plumber; R. Wilson, plasterer; Goldring and Son, smiths; no paviour. *Windsor:* J. and W. Hollis and G. H. Lawrence, bricklayers; R. Tebbott and Thomas Jenner, carpenters; P. Nowell, mason; W. Goddard and G. Cooper, plumbers; E. Foster, plasterer; W. Taylor, slater; W. Berridge, smith and ironmonger (*ibid.;* Crest 25/36, 18 and 24 July 1832).
[7] Works 1/20, p. 382. In September Phipps, Jesse and Good were asked for the names of tradesmen to be invited to tender for Hampton Court, Windsor and Brighton.

respectability in his particular branch', 'living in or near the district where the work is to be performed', was allowed to tender. By reserving the right to allow a tradesman to compete, the department committed itself to accepting the lowest tender. This was thought preferable to an open competition in which the Board would retain the right of rejecting the lowest tender.[1] A trial was made in October 1831 with a competition for painter's and glazier's works only in the London district, in consequence of differences 'impossible to reconcile' between the merchants' returns of prices and those obtained by tenders for contracts.[2] In most branches of trade between ten and fifteen tradesmen were invited to tender, though in fact the number was often less.[3] There were wide variations in the tenders received, ranging in 1832–3 from one to twenty-five per cent below the schedule prices.[4] The resulting contracts, determinable by either side on three months' notice, ran for a year. All works, however small, were done by the contract tradesmen. The same men were employed by the other branches of the Office in the Parks.[5] It was perhaps some measure of the success of this method in getting satisfactory work done at the cheapest rate that in April 1834 Holroyd and Tarte (plumbers) and Barron (ironmonger) declined to renew their contracts for the London district, and Tebbott (carpenter), Jenner (carpenter), Bedborough (mason), and Holroyd declined for Windsor.[6] In 1835 and 1836 it was found that most tradesmen continued their contracts,[7] so subsequently contracts were allowed generally to run for three years (and in fact often longer), though any exceptional change might lead to their revision within that period.[8] Thus because of an increase in the price of lead, new tenders for plumbers' work were called for in March 1839.[9]

The scale of prices itself would also be revised if tenders were consistently below it, or because of such a change as the repeal of the timber duties. Otherwise it was allowed to stand for several years.[10] A general revision was determined on in 1840. A circular to those architects connected with the Board remarked:

> A considerable number of years having elapsed since the Schedules of Prices were framed, upon which Tenders are obtained for the different Artificers Works executed under this Board, and as changes may have since taken place in the value of Materials or rate of Wages . . . I have . . . to request that you will confer with Mr. Seward with a view of revising the Prices, and that you will as early as convenient favour the Board with such observations and suggestions as may occur to you thereon.[11]

[1] *Parl. Pap.* 1833 (677) xiv, qq. 2016–9; 1847–8 (543) xviii, pt. 1 qq. 246–9, 259–60, 275.

[2] Works 4/31, p. 159; 1/19, p. 2. Pitt Cobbett of Bedford St. won the painter's contract and Richard Cobbett and Son of Northumberland St. the glazier's for one year.

[3] *Parl. Pap.* 1833 (677) xiv, q. 2022.   [4] *Ibid.* q. 2038.

[5] Works 1/20, pp. 263, 275–6, 23 October and 25 November 1833. There was some difficulty in enforcing the rule as to the employment of the contract tradesmen in the Parks, see, e.g. H. J. Robinson to Maslin, the Windsor parks superintendent, 26 November 1842 (Works 1/26, pp. 17–18), which refers to frequent irregularities since 1833.

[6] Works 1/21, p. 66.   [7] *Ibid.* pp. 322–8; 1/22, p. 43, 16 May 1836.

[8] *Parl. Pap.* 1847–8, (543) xviii, pt. 1 qq. 257, 482–3, 487–8. Lord Morpeth told a committee in May 1848 that there had not 'been any occasion for the appointment of any new tradesmen' since he had been at the Office (i.e. July 1846), (*ibid.* (538) xxiv, q. 191).   [9] Works 1/23, p. 305.

[10] *Parl. Pap.*, 1847–8 (543), xviii, pt. 1. qq. 482–3, 487–8. Although Milne stated that the scale of prices was revised 'about once in three years' (q. 482) there is no evidence of a full revision between 1832 and 1840.

[11] Works 1/24, p. 319, 3 August 1840.

Notice was given for terminating all contracts at Christmas 1840, and on 14 October the architects met to consider the new schedule.[1] The new prices appear still to have been quite ample, and some contractors offered a discount greater than twenty per cent.[2] For articles not specified in contracts the Office allowed $7\frac{1}{2}$ per cent on prime cost, or $2\frac{1}{2}$ per cent less than the old Office of Works.

At the same time, the official attitude towards contracts for major works was revised, again in line with the thinking of the 1828 select committee. Stephenson's marked distaste for contracts in gross was suppressed. 'I may venture to say', Blore had told Milne in January 1832, 'that it is my intention as far as practicable to proceed [at Buckingham Palace] upon Contracts in the Grose, and to avail myself of the advantage of fair competition, avoiding as far as possible day accounts with tradesmen; and only having recourse to measured prices in cases where I cannot advantageously obtain general contracts'. Thus in May 1832 he contracted with Clarke for the masonry of the new work on the garden front of the palace, Clarke's being the lowest of four tenders.[3]

Blore also tackled the problem of day-work. Where it had to be resorted to 'to any considerable extent', he employed direct labour at weekly wages under 'skillfull and active foremen'. Where day accounts with tradesmen were unavoidable he required a daily statement of the men's time and of the work on which they had been employed, with the quantity and quality of the materials used. These statements were to be certified at least weekly by the Clerk of Works. For measured works the accounts were to be made up at the shortest possible intervals; and accounts generally were to be submitted at stated periods, comprehending every claim up to that time.[4]

Accounts, though kept distinct after the annexation of the Works to the Woods, were handled according to the latter's procedure, which had remained unaltered since before 1804. The immediate effect of the junction was to increase 'very materially' the labours of the accounts department and throw it into great arrears. A new system of paying direct labour through the Clerks of the Works caused an increase in the number of cash payments that obliged the cashier to start work at nine o'clock. Demands for payment were presented to the Board together with drafts for the signature of two commissioners. Works accounts were transmitted with relevant vouchers to the chief accounts clerk, William Nash Round, who at the year's end had to make up a general account of receipt and expenditure for the auditors. His task

[1] *Ibid.* p. 421.
[2] *Ibid.* p. 508. The tenders accepted were *London:* Baker and Son, carpenters, $16\frac{1}{2}\%$ under Office schedule prices; W. Harrison, bricklayer, $12\frac{1}{2}\%$; J. Mowlem, mason, 22%; Cooper and Fores, slaters, 20%; Clark and Son, plumbers, 16%; J. Harrison, plasterer, $15\frac{1}{8}\%$; T. Horner, painter, 25%; Cobbett and Son, glaziers, $28\frac{1}{2}\%$; W. R. Gladwin, smith and founder, $13\frac{1}{4}\%$; J. Pike, ironmonger, $27\frac{3}{4}\%$; W. Johnson, paviour and labourer, 11%. *Hampton Court, Kew and Richmond:* J. Carless, carpenter, $7\frac{5}{8}\%$; W. Harrison, bricklayer, $11\frac{1}{8}\%$; J. Trigg, mason, 10%; Cooper and Fores, slaters, 15%; Clark and Son, plumbers, 8%; Goldring and Son, smiths $13\frac{3}{4}\%$; R. Wilson, plasterer, $5\frac{1}{4}\%$; J. Cain, painter, $17\frac{5}{8}\%$; Cobbett and Son, glaziers, 16%; P. Wood, paviour, $21\frac{1}{2}\%$; Goldring and Son, ironmongers, $10\frac{3}{4}\%$. *Windsor:* J. Bate, carpenter, $17\frac{1}{2}\%$; W. Stacey, bricklayer, 22%; Bedborough and Jenner, masons; G. H. Lawrence, slater, 14%; W. Goddard, plumber; J. Brown, smith and founder, 6%; T. and H. George, plasterer, 21%; Cooper and Son, painter; R. H. Butler, glazier, $10\frac{1}{2}\%$; W. Stacey, paviour and labourer, $17\frac{1}{2}\%$; J. Brown, ironmonger, 3%. *Brighton:* J. Fabian, carpenter, $16\frac{2}{3}\%$; Patching and Son, bricklayers, $17\frac{1}{2}\%$; E. Bruton, mason, 10%; T. Wisden, slater, $8\frac{1}{4}\%$; B. Wood, plumber, $7\frac{9}{13}\%$; Williams and Yearsley, smiths and founders, 18%; J. Fabian, plasterer, 12%; W. A. Field, painter, 26%; C. W. Vick, glazier, 16%; Williams and Yearsley, ironmongers, $12\frac{1}{2}\%$ (*ibid.* pp. 508, 518–21.) Where no percentage is stated, the tender was at the schedule price.
[3] Works 19/4, ff. 601–4, 721. [4] *Ibid.* ff. 601–4.

was complicated because the accounts of the deputy surveyors (like those of the receivers of Land Revenue) were not brought into the general ledger. Round was anxious to change this, telling the 1835 select committee that every 'receipt and payment of the monies of the department should be entered into the ledger'. The major reforms, however, were instituted by Abbott, the free-lance accountant employed at the Treasury's behest, who introduced double-entry book-keeping, and an 'audit cash book' containing the authority for every payment.[1]

Further difficulties were experienced by the auditors.[2] The accounts of the old Office of Works had been submitted in good order, details of work and labour and building charges that the Audit Commissioners were not competent to check being supported by certificates from Seward and Hiort as professional men and from Stephenson as the responsible directing officer. But before the accounts of the united office were presented for audit, there was a delay of at least two years; and when at last, in June 1838, the building accounts for 1832/3 came under scrutiny, the auditors discovered that 'the practice in the present Accounts is various and without any uniformity or system, even in cases which are similar to each other, and in general much less satisfactory than it was before.' Now that Stephenson was a member of the Board of Woods he could no longer give his certificate, and there was seldom any certificate of independent examination by the Chief Examining Clerk, who contented himself with a mere arithmetical check. The Audit Commissioners complained to the Treasury:

> We have now in some cases Accounts only signed by Mr. Seward who states he has examined the Accounts, in some instances we have Warrants of your Lordships for the payment, but which can scarcely be considered as satisfactory as to detail; in some cases we have still Certificates of Work and labor being done and properly charged, by Mr. Blore, Mr. Soane or other persons conversant, but in many instances we have no under Vouchers or independent Certificates whatever, nothing but receipts for payments and which receipts are sometimes only given by the Surveyors and Clerk of Works, Overseers, or others, who are themselves to pay the parties entitled to receive the money due; which receipts sometimes state 'as per bill delivered', the bill not accompanying the receipt. The consequence is that very numerous queries have been submitted to us by our Examiner on these points, but as we have considered that certificates granted at such a distance of time from the transactions, even if they could be obtained would be of little value and as the same defects will probably attend more or less all the arrear Accounts of this Service, we have deemed it most advisable to draw Your Lordships attention to the subject at once . . .[3]

They were anxious that the Treasury should decide what sort of vouchers should be submitted in future, and suggested that the Works officers should annex to the Treasury warrants such statements as would identify the charges in the accounts included in those warrants.

These views were forwarded by the Treasury to the Woods and Works, who after reflection proposed that a practice as similar as possible to that of the former Office

---

[1] *Parl. Pap.*, 1833 (677) xiv, qq. 947, 2262–4, 2558–9, 2655, 2567–70, 1852, 2570.
[2] Works 2/2, pp. 280–3, 31 July 1838. [3] *Ibid.*

of Works might remove the difficulty.[1] The inability of the auditors to undertake more than a mathematical check of detailed bills and measurements of artificers' works led the commissioners to suggest the re-introduction of Treasury 'approval warrants', as formerly used in the Office of Works, but not employed in the Woods and Forests on the grounds that 'the sanction of the Treasury to undertake the work is considered sufficient authority to make the payment'.[2]

> From the 31st of March 1839, all Accounts of Expenditure for Building Works etc. under the superintendence of this Department, shall be rendered to the Treasury for Approval Warrants with the following Certificates.
>
> The regular Quarterly Accounts for Ordinary Works and Buildings to be certified by the First Examining Clerk in the following manner. Vizt.
>
> 'I have carefully examined this Quarterly [Account] (or this Account) with the contracts, authorities and other proper Vouchers, and agreeably to the Rules and Regulations of this Board; and do hereby certify the same to be correct.'
>
> The account to be also certified by the Surveyor of Works and Buildings in the following form. Vizt.
>
> 'I do hereby certify that I have inspected this Quarterly Account (or this Account) that the Works therein specified were done under the Authority of this Board, that the same have been examined by the proper Officer of the Department, and that the Account is according to the best of my knowledge and belief just and true.'

Similarly the architects in charge of works were to certify that the works were done in 'a good and workmanlike manner' and that they had 'carefully examined the Account'. Where necessary the accounts should be accompanied by a pay list to identify the sums paid in each. Statements of disbursements and payments on account were to be made up at the end of each quarter and certified by the surveyor, accompanied by receipts and Treasury approval warrants. The commissioners themselves held the original bills, to which, they stated, reference was frequently made. On 5 August 1839 the commissioners informed the Treasury that steps had been taken to expedite the examination of accounts. Six weeks later Seward sent Jesse and Phipps copies of new regulations for the measurement of works and the delivery of quarterly accounts.[3]

Further moves to promote efficiency were initiated in 1837–8. The first was the result of the death of Soane, which vacated the clerkship of the works at Chelsea Hospital. This led the commissioners to propose bringing that building under the Works Department. The Hospital trustees disliked this idea, and the Treasury at first supported their preference for transfer to the Ordnance. But the Commissioners of Woods and Works wanted to extend their empire, and expressed their 'conviction of the expediency of vesting as far as possible the superintendence of all Buildings similarly circumstanced in the Department of Government especially constituted for that purpose'. The Treasury Board on reflection was 'so fully convinced' by the department's argument that Chelsea Hospital passed under Works control.[4] The primary responsibility for a second change appears to rest with the Treasury. A

---

[1] Works 1/23, p. 254. The Treasury reference was dated 19 September, the Woods' reply 29 December 1838.
[2] *Parl. Pap.*, 1833 (677) xiv, qq. 2040–2.   [3] Works 1/23, pp. 418, 471.
[4] Works 1/22, pp. 196–7, 239 (20 April), 278 (23 June); 2/2, pp. 111, 135 (9 March, 16 May 1837).

Treasury minute of 19 January 1838 drew attention to the confused responsibility for internal works in the palaces, some of which, whether charged on parliamentary votes or on the Civil List, were under the management not of the Works Department but of the Household.[1] To prevent conflicts between departments or cross-responsibility of officers, the minute proposed to make a distinction between palaces occupied by the sovereign and those not so occupied; the latter to be charged entirely on Works funds, and the former entirely on the Lord Chamberlain's, although alterations affecting the fabric must be under an architect appointed by the Works. This problem was one that Duncannon discussed personally with the Treasury ministers.[2] He recommended the analogy of the Post Office buildings: all expenses for Buckingham Palace and Windsor Castle should be transferred to the Lord Chamberlain, except for roofs and external walls; St. James's, Kensington, Hampton Court and Kew Palaces, together with the Stud House at Hampton Court, and Cumberland and Royal Lodges in Windsor Great Park, should be placed entirely under the Works Department for repairs, fittings and furniture. No change would be made in respect of the Royal Pavilion, Brighton. Thus a more sensible distribution of responsibilities between the departments would be effected, while the charges borne by each would remain approximately as before.[3] The details of these changes were studied without haste: after interdepartmental discussions in June, Seward submitted draft regulations in July; not till the following February did the commissioners notify the Lord Chamberlain that they were ready to make the exchange and it was in March that the Clerks of the Works received their directions.[4] They were to execute internal works on the Lord Chamberlain's written requisition, employing the contract tradesmen, provided that no danger to the safety or security of the building was involved, and send weekly accounts kept distinct from other works. If they considered the proposals involved any danger, they were to consult the Board. Prince Albert was to complain that the Woods and Forests cleaned the outside of the palace windows and the Lord Chamberlain the inside, so that both were never clean at once.[5] But some such clear division of function was necessary unless the palaces were to be maintained entirely either out of the Civil List or by parliamentary vote.

Then came a revision of the office establishment scale. This was in response to a recommendation from Duncannon and his colleagues, who urged particularly that there should be an increase in the number of clerks in the higher grades and a diminution of the number in lower grades (many officers had suffered by reductions in the salary scale existing when they entered; and most were at their maximum and could only benefit from a general improvement in the scale).[6] By 1838 three branches had been added to the eight existing in 1833: a cash-book, journal and ledger keeper, a register and minutes clerk, and a Clerk to the Board. There were in the various branches six men ranking as chief or principal clerks, six as senior clerks, seven as assistant clerks and fourteen as junior clerks. The revised establishment (not entirely in accord with the departmental proposals) by dispensing with a book-keeper and the clerk of quit rents in Ireland, and by providing that special allowances

---

[1] Works 2/2, pp. 188–9, printed with relevant correspondence in *Parl. Pap.* 1884 (233).   [2] *Ibid.*
[3] *Ibid.* pp. 250–3, 20 April 1838.   [4] Works 1/23, pp. 120, 283, 296, 308, 333–8.
[5] Elizabeth, Lady Longford, *Victoria R.I.* (1964), p. 209.
[6] T. 1/4383, f. 19841/38 (26 May 1838), printed in *Parl. Pap.*, 1847–8 (538), xxiv, App. pp. 540–3.

should be reduced by the amount of any increases in salary, provided more senior posts: an extra chief clerk (£700 per annum), a Clerk to the Board (£550–£700), and another assistant clerk. The number of junior clerks, however, was reduced by two.[1] Improvements were made in the salary scale, the increments being altered, and the maximum increased. But not only was a greater opportunity of promotion offered: that opportunity was afforded to merit rather than to mere seniority, as hitherto. The Treasury decreed that the senior was only to be promoted if he was 'also fully qualified to discharge with advantage to the public the duties of the higher office'.[2] There were so few promotions in the Works Department, and those sometimes demanding distinct professional qualifications, that no meaningful comparison can be made between the practice here and in other departments of the Civil Service. When Joseph Bedder (b. 1801) was promoted Chief Examiner of Works Accounts in 1843 in place of H. J. Robinson (promoted accountant), his senior on the list, William Wyatt (b. 1787) was given a special increment to raise him to the same salary.[3]

How successful were these new arrangements? The real test was, of course, whether they promoted efficiency and economy. The self-constituted guardians of the nation's purse in the House of Commons employed the simple criterion of a reduction in expense as a test of efficiency; but reductions were sometimes achieved at the cost only of an increased subsequent expenditure, or by injustice towards individuals. A more satisfactory criterion is value for money, but any straightforward comparison is vitiated by fluctuating prices, which in the 1830s were tending to fall.[4]

At first the enthusiasm of Duncannon and Ellis met the Treasury's annual autumnal demand that in the estimate for the coming year every practicable reduction should be made. The Treasury required estimates before the end of each year, itself under the pressure of a Commons' resolution that estimates had to be laid within ten days of supply. When the Treasury's call was heard, the Board's surveyors were instructed to survey all buildings in their care and submit an estimate of the smallest amount that would maintain each 'in such a state of repair as to prevent its being damaged or deteriorated during the coming year, avoiding every alteration or unnecessary expense'. The surveyors' estimates were 'gone into by every Member of the Board and pretty severely tested'; anything that could be postponed was struck out. Then, submitted to the Treasury, they were finally revised by the Chancellor of the Exchequer going through them with the First Commissioner.[5] The approved figures were submitted to the House of Commons under general heads: repairs and maintenance of palaces; of public buildings; of furniture; rates and lighting, etc. 'Additional works' were also specified with increasing frequency and precision from 1836 onwards.

---

[1] T. 1/4383, f. 19941/38 (Treasury minute, 21 September 1838), printed in *Parl. Pap.*, 1847–8 (538) xxiv App. pp. 543–4.

[2] *Parl. Pap.*, 1833 (677) xiv, q. 1907; 1847–8 (538) xxiv, App. p. 544.

[3] *Ibid.* 1847–8 (538), xxiv, App. pp. 547–8, Commissioners of Woods, etc. to Treasury, 5 March 1847. When the retirement of John King, First Chief Clerk, permitted a series of promotions in 1844, including Wyatt's to Assistant Clerk, the Board remarked that he, as First Junior Clerk, had 'most satisfactorily discharged the duties of an Assistant Clerk, and the Board would have been happy to have had an earlier opportunity of placing him in a position more consistent with the course of his Official Avocations' (Works 22/2/7).

[4] See B. R. Mitchell and P. Deane, *Abstract of British Historical Statistics* (1962) pp. 470–1.

[5] *Parl. Pap.* 1847–8 (543), xviii, pt. i, qq. 276–9, 289–90; Works 2/1, p. 202.

As a result of these rigorous measures the annual vote for public works and buildings shewed a remarkable reduction in 1833/4, and the estimates remained low in the two succeeding years; but there was a sharp increase in 1836/7, and thereafter an almost continuous yearly increase.[1] The mere votes however do not tell the full story. The Whigs' reduction in the Works estimates, approximately one-third, was accomplished over the period 1831–3. In 1831 the estimate for public buildings (including services, rates and furniture) had been cut by about £6500 to some £26,000, and that for palaces formerly on the Civil List by £4800 to £39,000.[2] The total of £73,800 did not reflect these reductions because of the transfer of Scottish works from the hereditary revenues (surrendered to Parliament by William IV) and provision for the restoration of Whitehall Chapel, in all amounting to £8300.[3] Then 1832/3 was a 'year' of five quarters, owing to Lord Althorp's decision that subsequent fiscal years should commence in April: so the estimate of £70,800 (the third prepared that year) represented a reduction of about fourteen per cent in a normal year, falling most heavily on the palaces (at a rate of about twenty-eight per cent). Reductions, in proportion nearly as great, were made the following year; at £20,000 the vote for palaces was brought down to half the sum fixed in 1816. The actual Works vote was further reduced by an unapplied balance of some £7000 from the previous year.[4] In 1834/5 and 1835/6 similar sums were carried over, so that while the approved estimates never fell below £50,000 per annum, the ordinary works executed in 1833/4 and 1834/5 cost only about £42,000 per annum, rising in 1835/6 to the full estimate.[5] The sharp rise in the following year was largely accounted for by the restoration of the Chapel Royal at St. James's, repairs at Marlborough House, and the reconstruction at Kew of the conservatory removed from Buckingham Palace. Even the increased estimate proved too little by some £6000.[6]

A further increase in 1837/8 called forth criticism from the Treasury.[7] Duncannon explained that the 'natural decay of the Buildings' required increased repairs; he cited particularly 'the Roofs, and External parts' of the Riding House at Buckingham Palace, of Kensington Palace, of the ornamental buildings at Kew, of those parts of Windsor Castle not included in the grant for Wyatville's restoration, and of the Brighton Pavilion. Other charges included repaving in front of St. James's Palace, maintaining the temporary Houses of Parliament, including their lighting, through very much lengthened sessions; repairs and furniture for parts of the Mint newly placed under the department; absolutely necessary repairs to secure the foundations of the Office of Works; and the cost of additional offices for the Registrar General,

---

[1] The Works Department votes were:

1832/3	£70,800	1837/8	£66,208 and £5851 supplementary for 1836/7
1833/4	43,370	1838/9	74,986
1834/5	42,721	1839/40	84,066
1835/6	41,200	1840/1	88,629
1836/7	64,450		

(*Parl. Pap.* 1831–2 (157) xxvii, 1833 (165) xxiv, 1834 (180) xlii, 1835 (140) xxxviii, 1836 (156) xxxviii, 1837 (145) xl, 1837/8 (310) xxxvii, 1839 (142) xxxi, 1840 (179) xxx).
[2] *Parl. Pap.* 1830–1 (228) vi; 1831 (27) xiii.
[3] *Ibid.* 1831–2 (157) xxvii; Works 1/19, pp. 37, 96–106, 112–3. The first estimate submitted by the Office of Works had exceeded £120,000 excluding works for the Woods and Forests, but this was reduced to £81,000, chiefly by a reduction of £19,000 in the provision for the British Museum and of £3650 for Whitehall Chapel.
[4] *Parl. Pap.* 1833 (165) xxiv.   [5] *Ibid.* 1834 (180) xlii; 1835 (140) xxxviii.
[6] *Ibid.* 1836 (156) xxxviii.   [7] *Ibid.* 1837 (145) xl.

the sale of parliamentary papers, and the Tithe Commission. There would also be a considerable charge for the accommodation of the Poor Law Commission. In addition the Treasury itself had directed the fitting up of a new office for the Judge-Advocate-General, the repair and redecoration of apartments at Somerset House for the School of Design and London University, and the completion of the restoration of the Banqueting House in Whitehall (Whitehall Chapel). Finally there was an application for providing temporary accommodation for the Lord Advocate.[1]

Duncannon's explanation convinced the Treasury: he expressed his readiness to accept the same sum as the previous year, but the increase was allowed; and a further increase in 1838 appears to have passed without criticism. By then the estimate for palaces had risen again to £30,000, and that for public buildings to £38,500, a figure however that included the Royal Military Asylum and Chelsea Hospital (formerly on the Army vote), parts of the Mint (previously maintained at its own expense), and several new offices such as the Tithe Commission's and Registrar General's, accommodated at Somerset House in former official residences.[2] An increase of £10,000 in the palaces vote for 1840/1 resulted from works at Buckingham Palace. These, and others at Windsor Castle, took the palaces vote for 1841/2 to nearly £50,000 out of a total of £103,000.[3] That for furniture and fittings for public buildings in 1839/40–1841/2 (excluding those at Chelsea and the Mint) was more than treble that in 1828–31.[4] As Lord Lincoln remarked to the select committee on miscellaneous expenditure (April 1848), repairs were 'of course casual in their nature', and could not be accurately estimated for at the start of the financial year.[5] If, towards the end of the year, it appeared that a surplus would be left on any estimate, it would be applied to the most urgent work so as to reduce the next year's estimates. But as the Treasury required estimates by the beginning of January, and the financial year did not end until 31 March, there was a considerable element of guess-work in these calculations. Balances were not transferred to a distinct vote, but only between items in the same vote. The detailed distribution between buildings, delivered to the Treasury but not to Parliament, was merely intended 'to show . . . the way in which the Board has arrived at the idea that such a sum [in total] will be required, rather than with a view to their being tied down to the exact distribution of that sum in its eventual appropriation.' According to Milne, there would be no transfer of 'any considerable portion' of an estimate from one building to another without prior reference to the Treasury. If the whole were not spent, it was carried on to the following year's service. The Treasury did not control the actual expenditure on repairs building by building, but only the sum total; the details however were submitted to the Treasury subsequently, before the accounts were finally sanctioned.[6]

From a purely financial point of view, the Whig reforms appeared to have failed. The expenses of the new Works Department had outstripped those of the old Office of Woods within ten years. But a detailed examination suggests that a moderate measure of success had in fact been achieved in respect of government offices in London, where the vigilance and zeal of John Phipps as Assistant Surveyor may well have been largely responsible for holding down expenses: excluding furniture, the

[1] Works 1/22, pp. 240–5.   [2] *Parl. Pap.* 1837–8 (310) xxxvii.   [3] *Ibid.* 1840 (179) xxx; 1841 (224) xiv.
[4] *Ibid.*   [5] *Ibid.* 1847–8 (543) xviii, pt. 1, q. 2651.   [6] *Ibid.* qq. 290–306, 2649.

relevant estimates for 1839/40–1841/2 averaged about £27,000, compared with £26,000 for 1828–30. In part this success may have been adventitious: the expensive old buildings of Parliament had been burned down, and several of the government offices had been recently rebuilt, thereby diminishing annual maintenance charges. The downward movement of prices was another favourable factor.

In the Office itself there had undoubtedly been beneficial changes. A saving on salaries and office expenditure had been achieved in the region of £5000 per annum. A smaller outside staff was able in the united office to carry out the duties of the old Office of Works with at least a comparable degree of efficiency because the officers were devoting their time fully to the public service and were not distracted by the importunities of private business. The local officers were supervised, too, by full-time public servants. Nor was the Works Department untouched by the higher standards of conduct in public life characteristic of Victorian England. We hear less of drunken officers or embezzlement of official stores after the early 'thirties. The age of Wyatt and Nash was over: in their place we find men perhaps of lesser stature, but certainly of greater integrity, servants now of the Crown rather than of the Queen, of the public rather than of the palace.

Chapter IX

THE FAILURE OF
AN EXPERIMENT

THE second decade of the Office of Woods and Works was one in which flaws in the system were exposed. With Duncannon's controlling hand removed, centrifugal tendencies were given play, and potential antagonisms came into evidence. The First Commissioner was a politician, changing at least as often as every ministry: his colleagues on the Board were to all intents and purposes irremovable. Yet his being in Parliament, and sometimes in the Cabinet, invested him with an authority they could not hope to rival; and he acquired functions which they did not share.[1] On the other hand, the Board was so constituted that the junior commissioners in accord could inhibit their chief's freedom of action and bring business to a standstill. And only with the greatest reluctance did a First Commissioner call the Treasury to his aid: he was expected to be capable of managing his department; an open confession of failure might damage his political future; and the Treasury's dispensation might not be precisely that which he desired. Nevertheless such an appeal was to be made.

The House of Commons, furthermore, goaded by vexatious delays and mounting expenditure on the new parliamentary buildings, subjected the Office to renewed scrutiny. After Peel, there was a revival of niggardliness; and the Commons' select committee on miscellaneous expenditure of 1848 devoted much of its attention to the department.[2] At the same period the vigorous prodding of one M.P., Lord Duncan,[3] brought about the appointment of another select committee, directing its inquiries to the Woods and Forests, where it revealed frauds and abuses.[4] All too evidently, further reforms were necessary. But their character was itself a subject of controversy: the critics of the New Houses of Parliament and the fraud-exposing radicals demanded a stricter accountability to Parliament. The Woods and Works was at once a revenue-producing department and a spending one. This was the most serious of the defects of the united Office, the different functions being sometimes confused and revenues applied to public works without parliamentary authority,

---

[1] Lord Morpeth, in evidence to the Duncan Committee, referred to the following duties he executed in addition to the first commissionership of Woods and Works: Council of Duchy of Cornwall, direction of geological surveys and museums; chairman, Buckingham Palace, Metropolitan Improvements, Metropolitan Sewers, and Commons Enclosure Commissions; supervision of sanitary measures in Parliament—this subsequently becoming chairmanship of the General Board of Health (*Parl. Pap.* 1847–8 (538) xxiv, qq. 87 ff.). In 1851, Lord Seymour was said to be on 18 boards (*Parl. Deb.* 3rd ser. cxviii, 602).

[2] *Parl. Pap.* 1847–8 (543) xviii, pts. I and II.

[3] Adam Duncan (1812–67), succeeded his father as 2nd Earl of Camperdown 1859.

[4] *Parl. Pap.* 1847–8 (538) xxiv; 1849 (513) xx.

just as had occurred in such other revenue departments as the Post Office and the Customs. The critics demanded that all revenues should be paid into the consolidated fund, and all expenditure receive the preliminary sanction of the Commons. Members with ministerial experience however preferred to allow the cost of managing the Crown estate as a first charge on its revenue as hitherto; their remedy was to place greater power in the First Commissioner's hands. There was a subsidiary problem that not only had the Crown estate been associated with public works, but that many other functions had been allotted to the First Commissioner or the Office. As Russell put it, 'too many offices have been heaped together'; or in Peel's blunter language, the department had been regarded as 'the Common Sewer of all the flotsam and jetsam of the offices'.[1] Prince Albert, too, in his capacity as guardian of the Crown's reversionary interest in the Land Revenues, urged a separation of management and of works.[2] So before the united office had lasted twenty years it was determined to unscramble it, attempting in the process to satisfy in some measure at least all shades of opinion.[3]

When Peel came to power in September 1841 he appointed as First Commissioner Lord Lincoln (1811–64).[4] One of a group of young Peelites which included Gladstone (who encouraged his political ambitions), Lincoln seemed well-qualified for the post: heir to a great estate, already active in county administration, a keen amateur of architecture. But Lincoln was beset by family cares,[5] and was in truth too inflexible and insufficiently tactful for an office which required close relationships with Parliament, the sovereign, and colleagues on the Board. 'He was a high and strong character', wrote Gladstone immediately after his death, and some years later he referred to his 'vigour of administration and breadth of view'; but he was aware of Lincoln's egotism. The worldly Greville found him 'rather priggish and solemn, with very little elasticity in him'. His 'grave dignified presence' impressed Roundell Palmer, who commented: 'He took great pains with himself . . . he was not, however, a good judge of men; his ambition was in excess of his powers'. Lord Blachford was another who noticed the same shortcoming, and thought that Lincoln's 'familiarity, friendly enough, was not such as invited response'.[6]

---

[1] RA, F 42/57; B.M. Add. MS. 40481, ff. 289–90.　　[2] RA, C 16/67 (17 December 1848).

[3] On the unpopularity of Boards after 1855, and the reasons for this development (of which the Board of Woods was one of the first examples) see F. M. G. Willson, 'Ministries and Boards: some aspects of administrative development since 1832', *Public Administration*, 33 (1955), pp. 43–58. H. Parris, *Constitutional Bureaucracy* (1969) appeared after the above was written.

[4] Suc. father as 5th Duke of Newcastle 1851. Irish secretary, February–June 1846; Sec. for War and Colonies 1852–4, for War 1854–5, for Colonies 1859–64. See J. Martineau, *Life of Henry Pelham, Fifth Duke of Newcastle* (1908).

[5] Lincoln's relationship with his arch-conservative father was uneasy, and after he joined Peel over the repeal of the Corn Laws there was an open rupture; his wife, after two reconciliations, left him finally in 1849 (occasioning a visit to Italy in her pursuit by W. E. Gladstone); he then divorced her. See J. Martineau, *op. cit.*; Morley, *Life of Gladstone*, i, p. 364; P. Magnus, *Gladstone* (1954), pp. 92–4; *The Times* 2 March, 4, 27 April, 2, 13 May 1846; B.M. Add. MS. 40481, ff. 291–4. Lincoln commented to Peel, 31 August 1842, that domestic affairs since the prorogation had prevented him attending to the Metropolitan Improvement Commission (B.M. Add. MS. 40481, f. 30).

[6] Morley, *Life of Gladstone*, i, p. 480 n. (3 January 1863); ii, pp. 193 (23 October 1864), 256 (29 January 1869); Greville, *Diary* (ed. Strachey and Fulford) v, p. 201 (30 January 1845—Greville then described Lincoln as 'more than useless', but within three years revised his opinion, remarking, 'So much for hasty judgements on untried or half-tried men', *ibid.* p. 201 n.—but that applies rather to his abilities than his character); Lord Selborne, *Memorials*, Pt. I, *Family and Personal 1766–1865* (1896), ii, pp. 256–7; Lord Blachford, *Letters* (1896), p. 225. See also Duke of Argyll, *Autobiography and Memoirs* (1906), i, p. 380.

In the Commons Lincoln was a 'business-like speaker' who represented his department creditably.[1] The royal family faced him with greater difficulties, and his departmental colleagues with ones even worse. The Queen and Prince Albert, anxious for a country retreat of their own, 'free from all Woods and Forests, and other charming Departments who really are the plague of one's life', were not content to rely exclusively on Lincoln's services as an estate agent.[2] And there were numerous royal dependants whose claims for their 'grace and favour' residences Lincoln was determined to resist as a burden on the Land Revenues. Other problems arose over the administration of the Duchies of Lancaster and Cornwall, with which Lincoln was also concerned.[3] Nevertheless Prince Albert appreciated his merits.[4] Milne and Gore did not. Milne, a man of twice his age, who had had all the business of the Woods and Forests at his finger-tips when Lincoln was still in the nursery, resented the younger man's determination to 'be the Head of the Office'.[5] With Gore, Lincoln may have had political as well as personal differences. Gore's closest connections were with the Whig aristocracy (in 1845 he married Duncannon's daughter) and Lincoln's use of the Office's influence for party electoral purposes may not have been to his liking.[6] At all events, Lincoln's self-assertion soon produced difficulties with the junior commissioners. His feelings about them underlie the humour of a correspondence with Peel in December 1843. A draft in the Newcastle papers (22 December) reads: 'You will see the new fire escape. I should think it would be the duty of Mr. Milne to try the efficacy of it by taking a jump after the manner of Edward Golding and of equal Height. He might then report to the Treasury upon the value of the discovery.' The version in the Peel papers (24 December): 'I quite approve of your suggestion that *a* Commissioner of Woods should make personal trial of the new Fire-escape,—but I request that Charles Gore may make the essay *first*. *Fiat experimentum* &c, & by all means, and if unfortunately the first attempt should end fatally I can supply from the Office of Woods 3 or 4 more *corpora vilia* for a further test'.[7]

The First Commissioner became convinced that some change would soon have to be made to ensure the 'regular and efficient conduct of the public business'. His admission to the Cabinet in January 1845 did not result in any greater deference on the part of his colleagues; but, anxious for harmony and not seeking to enhance his own position, Lincoln forbore to urge changes while he continued in the office.[8] But the crisis moved to a head. The Geological Survey, placed under the commissioners in 1843, was the occasion of one dispute. The Treasury's decision that payment and receipt of monies for this service should be entrusted to the Board had

---

[1] Selborne, *loc. cit.*
[2] *Letters of Queen Victoria 1837–61*, ii, p. 35; B.M. Add. MS. 40481, ff. 201–8, 217–8, 225–9, 234–7.
[3] B.M. Add. MS. 40481, ff. 9–10, 46, 52.
[4] As his appointment to the Councils of the Duchies of Cornwall and Lancaster bears witness.
[5] Nottingham University Library, Newcastle MS. 9072.
[6] Writing of the City of London election to Peel, 14 October 1843, Lincoln remarked, 'I . . . have sent out letters to all the tradesmen employed by the Office of Woods—of course so worded that I shall not care who sees them' (B.M. Add. MS. 40481, ff. 180–2); and in October 1845 he sent a trustworthy officer to Windsor to Crown tenants and Office tradesmen in support of Col. Reid (who was ultimately returned unopposed) (*ibid.* 40575, ff. 196, 198).
[7] Nottingham University Library, Newcastle MS. 11952; B.M. Add. MS. 40481, ff. 230–3.
[8] Newcastle MS. 9072 (9 June 1845).

given offence to the junior commissioners, who refused to sign any cheques concerning it (on the ground that the survey was not 'an act matter or thing required to be done' by the commissioners under the Act of 1810 which regulated their operations), thus obliging Lincoln to carry on the survey out of private funds. Bringing the matter before Peel, Lincoln pointed out that he himself signed cheques in confidence of the rectitude of other officers; that this was done in other departments; that the junior commissioners had signed blank cheques, and cheques for services conducted entirely under Duncannon, as at Buckingham Palace. 'The fact is—it is simply and solely a struggle on the part of my two Colleagues for nominally coordinate, and really paramount, power.' It must now be decided, he declared, whether the Chief Commissioner was the 'proper source of *all* control'. Of the 'transactions which have eventually led to the assertion of a perfect equality' Lincoln found the origin partly in Duncannon's choice of the former secretary, Milne, as a commissioner.

> As the immediate Patron of Mr. Milne and Mr. Gore [wrote Lincoln], it was not likely that he [Duncannon] would feel the effects of his arrangement, which by the abolition of the Secretaryship placed his Successor necessarily in a false position with his Colleagues if they should be inclined to avail themselves of the advantages given them in any question in which the powers of the Board should be brought into discussion.[1]

Another dispute had developed over Lincoln's nomination of the receiver of crown rents for Yorkshire to the receivership for the northernmost counties also, in which his colleagues refused to concur. The patronage of the Office was customarily divided among the commissioners, the First appointing receivers and deputy surveyors of forests, while all three nominated office clerks and messengers in rotation, 'a very inconvenient and improper practice'. If no appeal lay to the Treasury, Lincoln warned that the 'Chief Commissioner would become . . . a mere parliamentary cloak for their irresponsibility'. Unless his successor were to be a cipher, there must be a permanent settlement. 'The Constitution of the Office is radically bad—I have a very low opinion of all Boards as instruments of conducting real business,—but of all Boards, such an one as that of the Woods and Forests is the worst.' In Lincoln's view there were two possible solutions: either to revive the post of secretary 'in the person of some Gentleman of station . . . capable of taking a position with the Board and keeping it', which would be very unfair to the faithful private secretary and clerk to the Board, Philipps; or to reduce the junior commissioners to secretaries.[2]

His colleagues had opposed Lincoln's consolidation of receiverships on the ground that an experienced officer was being passed over for one with only eighteen months' service; that, at the least, the duties should be shared equally between the two. To this specious argument Goulburn, as Chancellor of the Exchequer, apparently lent an ear. Lincoln denounced it as 'really too transparent a humbug to allow me to argue it with common patience'. 'If the matter is to be settled at all, the two Junior Commissioners must knock under, I can consent to nothing else. If they hold out, then either they or I must go—the Government must decide which.' Philipps

---

[1] *Ibid.*   [2] *Ibid.*

supported him in sticking out for a settlement in principle which would formally recognise his authority.[1] A Treasury minute of 16 September 1845 attached the northern district to the Yorkshire receivership by Treasury authority, directing that the appointment itself should be made as was customary. As for the refusal to sign cheques for the Geological Survey,

> the necessities of the Public Service have, of late years especially, often required Departments of the State to undertake duties in some degree foreign to the immediate purposes for which they are constituted and the instances have been rare indeed in which reluctance has been expressed to conform in such a matter to the recommendation of my Lords.[2]

Should Milne and Gore continue recalcitrant, the Treasury would prescribe other means of providing for the Geological Survey which they had asked the Chief Commissioner to conduct. The two commissioners renewed their objection to being made responsible public accountants for monies applied to services of which they had no knowledge; so the Treasury placed the Survey and the Museums of Economic Geology in London and Dublin under the Chief Commissioner's sole authority. Thus a further step was taken towards placing a single political minister at the head of the department.[3] Nevertheless, this was a drawn encounter in the sense that the junior commissioners successfully sustained their objection to signing, which was a recognition of their authority. It was perhaps unlucky that Lincoln had little chance to exploit the strength of his position, as in the reconstruction of the government resulting from Peel's determination to repeal the Corn Laws he went to Ireland as Chief Secretary. He was succeeded by a peer, Viscount Canning,[4] who, when Peel fell in June 1846, was displaced by Lord John Russell's choice, the Whig Lord Morpeth (1802–64), afterwards 7th Earl of Carlisle.[5]

Morpeth, a man of moderate capabilities, lacked 'solidity', but was amiable and good-natured.[6] The impression one gains of him from contemporary comments is borne out by his evidence before the Duncan Committee in 1848. There he tended to minimize the distinction between the First Commissioner and his colleagues, remarking that 'perhaps the position of the First Commissioner attracts a greater notion of responsibility' and that 'from his being in Parliament, and being in the habit of more frequent communication with the Treasury, . . . he has necessarily insensibly more discretion vested in him, but the other Commissioners are not more responsible to him than they all are to the Treasury'.[7] Asked specifically whether all the patronage of the office should not be vested in the First Commissioner, instead of being

---

[1] *Ibid.* 9078–9, 9042a, b.   [2] *Ibid.* 9075.   [3] *Ibid.* 9087b, 9088.

[4] 1812–62. Third son of George Canning, 2nd Viscount 1837, cr. Earl 1859. Under-Secretary, Foreign Office 1841–6; Paymaster-general 1853; Governor-General of India 1855–62. See *D.N.B.* and M. Maclagan, *Clemency Canning* (1962).

[5] Irish secretary 1835–41; First Commissioner of Woods etc. 1846–50; Chancellor of the Duchy of Lancaster 1850–2; Ld.-Lt. of Ireland 1855–8 and 1859–64. See *D.N.B.*

[6] See Morley, *Gladstone* i, p. 222; *Creevey Papers*, ed. Maxwell (1904), ii, p. 307; Greville, *Diary*, iii, pp. 198–9, iv, pp. 77, 138; *Letters of Queen Victoria 1837–65*, iii, p. 452. Greville in 1835 had thought Morpeth 'ill-selected' for the Irish secretaryship, commenting, 'he has very fair ability of a showy kind, but I doubt the solidity and strength of his material for the rough work which is allotted him' (iii, pp. 198–9). Similarly, in 1851, the Queen questioned whether he was 'up to' the business of a ministerial committee to consider extension of the franchise (*Letters 1837–65*, ii, p. 324). Lord Aberdeen did not find him a place in the coalition of 1852.

[7] *Parl. Pap.* 1847–8 (538) xxiv, qq. 76, 71, 74.

Q

shared among the three, he replied that it was hardly a fair question to put to him, because he was likely to be biased. The furthest he would go was: 'As a general rule, I should say, that the head of a department had better be vested with the entire patronage belonging to the department; but I do not at all wish it to be understood that I am desirous of assuming any additional rights in that respect'.[1] He was similarly reluctant to acknowledge any limitation on his colleagues' independence. Asked how correspondence was conducted in his absence, he replied that he received a daily return of letters and that the other commissioners meanwhile acted on their own responsibility.

> q. 167 [Lord Duncan:] Without communication with the Chief Commissioner?— [Lord Carlisle:] They would communicate with him upon any subject which they thought admitted of doubt or consideration.
> q. 168. But is it their option to communicate or not?—The arrangements are made by mutual agreement.

He finally admitted that he would not allow the others to act independently of him 'in any matter at all involving responsibility or importance'. 'Occasionally matters of routine business may be done without communication with him, but I imagine that at any time he would consider himself entitled to require that nothing should be done without his cognizance.' He implied that no differences had arisen between him and his colleagues, though he had 'known instances in which one Commissioner did not feel inclined to concur with his colleagues, and therefore withheld his signature'. As to any improvement in the system, he would do no more than hint:

> I am not prepared to say whether, upon general grounds, a paramount head of the department would not be the most efficient mode of transacting its business; three persons with concurrent rights might occasionally run the risk of coming into conflict; when I state this, I ought to mention that the duties of the office are at present discharged by the other two Commissioners with singular industry and intelligence, and therefore my notion about the advantage of concentrating the jurisdiction in the head of the department is not founded upon any deficiencies of theirs.[2]

This was in May. At the end of August he wrote to the Prime Minister: 'I have long had a growing conviction that the Board is a faulty and bad-working system'.[3] His loyalty to his colleagues is an endearing feature of Morpeth's character; but he was a weak minister, who must share with Russell the principal responsibility for deferring for inadequate reasons reforms that all could clearly see were necessary. It is true that he was overburdened with duties: though the control of the Geological Survey and the chairmanship of the Buckingham Palace commission did not occupy much of his time, and the important work of the Metropolitan Improvements Commission was in 1848 suspended for want of funds, yet the Commons Inclosure Commission, the Metropolitan Sewers Commission, the Council of the Duchy of Cornwall, and the responsibility for sanitary legislation demanded, he said, more

---

[1] *Ibid.* qq. 162–3.   [2] *Ibid.* qq. 172–3, 224, 212, 189.
[3] P.R.O. 30/22/7C, f. 56. In May 1849 Lincoln told Prince Albert that the two junior Commissioners 'constantly voted in conjunction against the First Commissioner and thus rendered his Authority null—That Lord Carlisle had complained to him of this' (RA, C 81/9).

time 'than I feel can be devoted, in order to do justice to all the subjects connected with them'.[1] But this in itself was to concede the case for change.

That he was not happy at his post Morpeth admitted to Russell. In July 1848, when the Duncan Committee drew up its interim report, he wrote (though he did not then send) a letter to the Prime Minister in which he declared: 'I have never at any time felt myself suited to the office; it requires qualifications I have not; some I may have are not wanted in it'.[2] His real interest lay in public health, a question much to the fore at that time.[3] He commented that Duncan's committee had exposed 'inveterate abuses . . . and considerable laches', and the department needed overhaul, work 'for which I have neither inclination or aptitude'. He wished to give up the Woods but retain responsibility for public health questions; reforms in the Office 'would be better carried into effect by a new and disengaged hand'. Such were his views when 'rather over-whelmed and worried with the pressure of business'. Earlier in the session he had told the Commons that 'he had sometimes to give an opinion upon matters which required the education and acquirements of a land steward, of a practical farmer, of a builder, of an architect, of an inspector of mines, a valuer of timber, and of a practical engineer'; and remarked on 'his own radical deficiencies in these respects':[4] an old-fashioned view of a minister's duties, a misunderstanding of the function, as it was developing, of a political head of a department, but indicative of the inadequacy of his professional staff. When he succeeded in carrying his Public Health Act, his heart lightened, and he told Russell that he was prepared to soldier on; but by October he was again feeling anxious to escape.[5] In January 1849 on Auckland's death he asked for the Admiralty; the Woods did not suit him, and he did not suit it: 'it goes against the grain'.[6] But it was March 1850 before he escaped to the Duchy of Lancaster.

Successive First Commissioners' views of their department's deficiencies did not move governments to action. It was pressure from the Commons that produced changes in the system, and a major overhaul was only carried through when the Radicals' threat to make the entire expenditure of the Woods and Forests subject to a preliminary vote attracted widespread support.[7] Before turning to the circumstances that rekindled parliamentary interest in these matters, it will be convenient to examine the operation of the Works Department in the 1840s.

After the appointment of Gore, Duncannon had re-allocated duties between the commissioners.[8] Milne took over a great part of Stephenson's former responsibilities —public works and buildings, and the royal parks—retaining also the forests, and metropolitan improvements. Gore assumed Stephenson's supervision of house estates, and relieved Milne of all questions relating to the Crown as landlord, as well as the Scotch and Irish departments. The Chief Commissioner, as we have seen, had a number of functions peculiar to himself, and as Morpeth remarked, 'rather presides over the whole business than attends to any particular branch'.[9]

---

[1] *Parl. Pap.* 1847–8 (538) xxiv, qq. 87 ff.   [2] P.R.O. 30/22/7C, f. 55.
[3] See R. A. Lewis, *Edwin Chadwick and the Public Health Movement* (1952), and S. E. Finer, *Life and Times of Sir Edwin Chadwick* (1952).
[4] *Parl. Deb.* 3rd ser. xcvii, 142–4.   [5] P.R.O. 30/33/7E, ff. 1668–9.
[6] *Ibid.* ff. 1666–7.   [7] *Parl. Deb.* 3rd ser. cxiv, 1242 ff. (11 March 1851).
[8] *Parl. Pap.* 1849 (513) xx, q. 6.   [9] *Ibid.* 1847–8 (538) xxiv, q. 73.

Duncannon's arrangements were not seriously modified for several years. But the duties of the department grew steadily as government itself became more complex. Before 1841 there had appeared a registrar general of births, deaths and marriages, a registrar of designs (for copyright), permanent or continuing commissions on tithes, the Poor Law, the Church of England, factories and tidal harbours, and a prison inspectorate, for all of which offices had to be provided, as well as for the senate of London University and a paymaster of Polish refugees. To these the Conservatives added a school of design, a Fine Arts Commission, commissioners of enclosures, metropolitan commissioners in lunacy, a registrar of joint-stock companies and a registrar to administer the Metropolitan Buildings Acts. In addition there were occasional royal commissions and a periodic census commission.[1] The scope of legislation relating to insolvent debtors was broadened, bringing more business to that court; the institution of county courts required a department of the Treasury to handle their financial side; and the general increase of legal business required more judges and additional courts. And for those convicted the Home Office devised a new model prison on the separate principle.[2] Industrial and commercial developments were reflected in the creation of new departments by the Board of Trade, the railway department being a notably busy one.[3] Though sectarian problems inhibited the development of public education, the Committee of the Privy Council on Education set up a 'normal school' for training teachers for workhouses.[4] New learned societies sprang into being which looked to the precedent of the Royal and Geological Societies for accommodation at the public expense. Peel had called for a statement of accommodation in public offices soon after coming to power. By 1843 some further building of offices had become almost unavoidable. 'Hardly any Government Office has sufficient accommodation', Lincoln told him, ' . . . £3000 or £4000 a year are annually voted for apartments which are hired in various parts of the town. All the Government Buildings are full to repletion'.[5] But a year elapsed before Peel and Goulburn decided to enlarge the Board of Trade, a project which led to Barry's expensive reconstruction of Soane's building and of the adjoining Home Office.[6] When in June 1846 the needs of the Registrar General's office were brought urgently forward the Treasury refused to sanction any new public building; but Goulburn had previously admitted that 'Buildings for the custody of the public Records, State Papers, Inns of Court, Offices in Downing Street, for the Custody of Wills &c &c are urgently pressed and can not be long delayed'.[7] Meanwhile, more houses had to be hired, or official residences, as at Somerset Place, converted into

[1] These are taken from the list in *Parl. Pap.* 1847–8 (543) xviii, pt. II.
[2] See Holdsworth, *History of English Law* xvi (1967); *Parl. Deb.* 3rd ser. liii, 1188–9.
[3] See L. Brown, *The Board of Trade and the Free-Trade Movement, 1830–42* (1958), and H. Parris, *The Government and the Railways in Nineteenth-Century Britain* (1965).
[4] *Parl. Pap.* 1850 [1196], [1256] xliii. See p. 446 below.
[5] Works 2/3, p. 222 (15 November 1841); B.M. Add. MS. 40481, ff. 238–41 (28 December 1843).
[6] Nottingham University Library, Newcastle MS. 12057 (19 December [1844]). Peel remarked that the building estimates (including refuge harbours and dock defences) for the next session would be enormous, but he was 'not disposed to thwart Goulburn if he sanction Barry's plan for increasing the Board of Trade &c'. He thought the more complete plan was to be preferred, though doubting whether the estimate (£10,975) would cover the expense—nor did it. See pp. 239–41 below.
[7] B.M. Add. MS. 40570, ff. 44–6 [July 1845].

offices.[1] The taking over of such former private residences as Gwydyr House provoked criticism, and Morpeth remarked that 'he sometimes thought that the vacant space of ground near the Foreign Office would be well devoted to an edifice capable of accommodating in a simple and substantial manner these various offices and commissions'.[2] The growth of postal services as a result of the introduction of penny postage in 1840 also threw an increasing burden on the Works Department.[3] Another development pregnant with future consequences was Lord Lincoln's acceptance of responsibility for the repair of certain historic buildings.[4] The superintendence of works at ambassadorial residences overseas was extended from Paris to Madrid and Constantinople, and even stretched to the provision of carpets for the British minister's tents at Teheran.[5]

Lincoln had also called the Treasury's attention to the particular burdens of a First Commissioner:[6] the increased work of the Office fell on him as much as on the others, especially as regarded the Works Department, while he was without any official secretary except for matters concerning the Board as a whole. 'For the very onerous duties, however, both in and out of Parliament, devolving especially on the Chief Commissioner, no provision has been made whatever, beyond the assistance of which he has been enabled accidentally to avail himself, by having for his Private Secretary, a Gentleman [Philipps] who, in addition to his position as Clerk to the Board, has had more than thirty years' experience in the business of the department and seventeen years of confidential intercourse with successive Chief Commissioners.' But Philipps acted rather as official secretary to the head of the Board; pressure of official emergencies left the duties of private secretary unfulfilled. Lincoln therefore asked that a private secretary to the First Commissioner should be appointed at £300 per annum.

It was, however, probably the Clerk to the Board who carried the heaviest burden of duty. Under Duncannon Philipps had gradually accumulated more and more functions and responsibilities, and he became the mentor of succeeding First Commissioners. The authority that he acquired was recognised formally by his appointment in 1851 as secretary of the revived Office of Works. This authority may be illustrated in reference both to Lord Lincoln and to Lord Morpeth. Lincoln, at odds with his colleagues, was greatly dependant upon the secretary's support and advice, and accordingly anxious to strengthen Philipps's position: he therefore obtained Treasury sanction for appointing him 'Official Secretary to the Chief Commissioner,

---

[1] Between 1838 and 1848, the average annual vote for rent was nearly £2800; in 1847/8 the vote was £6305 and in 1848/9 £7781. The actual rent expected to be incurred for 1848/9 however was £4694 for 16 different offices; the remainder was to reimburse the Land Revenue for loss of rent resulting from the building of the Economic Geology Museum (£3412); and a credit of £325 was due from official houses let for rent (*Parl. Pap.* 1847–8 (543) xviii, pt. II). However, a subsequent return states expenditure on rents in 1848/9 at £6525 (*Parl. Pap.* 1849 (513) xx, app. p. 211). By 1855, apart from Crown property, 49 houses were rented for £16,758 (*ibid.* 1854–5 (340) liii). As an example of the problem one may cite the Registrar of Designs Office. In February 1848 the Treasury decided it could not be accommodated in the new Board of Trade; so the Office of Woods proposed a twenty-roomed house at 2 Parliament Street, at £350 p.a. The Treasury referred this back, asking whether no official building were available. In June it was decided to appropriate the Surveyor of the Navy's residence, no. 4 Somerset Place (Works 2/6, pp. 304, 327, 334, 351, 371).

[2] *Parl. Deb.* 3rd ser. ci, 98–9.
[3] Works 2/4, pp. 386–9; 2/8, pp. 15–20, 78, 125, 202, 210–12, 215, 218, 256, 442.
[4] Below, pp. 641–5.   [5] Works 2/8, pp. 14, 24, 60, 74; 2/9, p. 9; see pp. 633–9.
[6] *Parl. Pap.* 1847–8 (538) xxiv, pp. 544–6.

and Clerk to the Board'.[1] A few months later, laying before Peel the unhappy state of his relations with the two junior commissioners, Lincoln was concerned that the reforms he sought should not prejudice Philipps,

> of whose merits in every point of view I cannot speak too highly—Indeed I may truly say that without his able and judicious assistance and cooperation I never could have carried on the business of the Office for nearly four years without that appeal to you which I am now compelled to make.[2]

Morpeth relied on Philipps to at least an equal degree. During the enlargement of Buckingham Palace it was Philipps who settled with Blore the course to be pursued preparatory to starting the works; it was he who drafted the reply (endorsed by Morpeth 'entirely approved') to an uncandid letter of Blore's about delays, with a cautious eye to 'the use that may hereafter be made of this correspondence';[3] it was at his instigation that competitive tenders were obtained for warming the new wing— a work entrusted by Blore to the contractor, Cubitt, described by Morpeth as 'very acceptable at the Palace'—because he thought 'Mr. Cubitt may be conscious of his position at the Palace, and disposed, perhaps, to work upon it', so that 'some caution might be useful'.[4] Nor was Philipps's initiative solely intra-mural. It was he who 'hit upon' a site for a new Museum of Economic Geology, where Crown leases between Piccadilly and Jermyn Street were falling in; and he appears to have conducted the whole of this rather complicated affair.[5]

However able Philipps was, he was not in a position to oversee the entire office. The variety of accounts kept for the Board's different functions had led to confusion, and by 1848 they were not in a 'convenient state for immediate reference and explanation'. Partly for this reason there had been great delays in presenting the accounts for audit, and further problems were raised by the audit commissioners themselves. So in December 1847 the First Commissioner applied to the Treasury for expert advice, and the Assistant Paymaster General, W. G. Anderson, was subsequently instructed to place the accounts on a better footing. Anderson pointed out that so many changes and additions had been made since Abbott had overhauled the book-keeping in 1832 that his system was no longer applicable; and that the books having fallen into arrear the advantages of his system were lost. Anderson introduced the improved double-entry method adopted by Graham for the Navy in 1831; and under his supervision, by working extra time early and late and employing additional clerks, five years' arrears were cleared off beween July 1848 and June 1849.[6]

---

[1] *Ibid.*   [2] Nottingham University Library, Newcastle MS. 9072 (9 June 1845).

[3] Works 19/7, ff. 2352, 2356.

[4] Works 19/8, ff. 2556, 2559. 'Very well done—dear Mr. Philips' commented Morpeth.

[5] Works 17/17/1, *passim*, especially ff. 6 (29 August), 12–13 (16 September 1844) and 24–5 (29 August 1846).

[6] When the accounts for 1832/3 had been delivered at the Audit Office on 14 September 1835 the auditors returned 840 queries. A fair state was sent to the Treasury, 14 May 1840, and not returned until 22 February 1843, receiving its re-audit on 11 February 1845. By July 1848 no accounts had been finally audited beyond 1838/9, though those up to 31 March 1843 had been sent to the auditors (*Parl. Pap.* 1847–8 (538) xxiv, qq. 40–2, 5594–5617, pp. 311–13; 1849 (513) xx, qq. 1587–1640). The diminishing efficiency of the Office's account-keeping may be observed in the series of account books L.R.R.O. 24. A statute of 1848 (11 & 12 Vict. c. 102, s. viii–x) gave the Treasury full authority to make regulations governing the Commissioners' finances and accounts.

The Office relied to a great extent during the 1840s upon extra clerks to get through its ordinary business. Employed theoretically only to alleviate temporary pressures, their use became so habitual that they came to be regarded as probationary clerks. In 1844 Lincoln proposed that six should be transferred to the permanent establishment and that extra services should then be strictly limited to meet purely temporary needs.[1] A deeply pondered revision was brought into effect three years later. The incapable were, as far as possible, superannuated; temporary clerks whose services were considered to be permanently necessary were confirmed, and the establishment was increased by four assistant and three junior clerks. The officers were placed in two distinct categories, drawing salaries either from the Forests and Land Revenue or from the Public Works branch. Two appointments were removed from the usual classes altogether—the accountant and the librarian: for these, the usual procedure of progression from class to class would be set aside, and they might even be recruited from outside the department. As far as the Department of Works was concerned, four extra clerks were made permanent, viz. one assistant to the surveyors (junior), two to the Chief Examiner (one at assistant clerk grade, one at junior), and one (junior) to the Clerk of the Furniture. The Chief Examiner was promoted to a senior clerk's salary. Certain of the professional posts were to be regulated on a vacancy: the Assistant Surveyor of Works in London (who enjoyed £600 per annum and a house) was to receive £500 with increments of £50 after five and ten years; and the Itinerant Surveyor (£900, including £50 for a horse) was to be placed on the same scale, and to receive his travelling expenses.

Correspondence in the Works Department would still be written by clerks from the general establishment, but the salaries of that portion of the staff 'immediately and exclusively employed in the direction of these services' would come on a parliamentary vote instead of on the Land Revenue. Certain officers would be common to both divisions (accountant, book-keeper, librarian, registrar and assistant, office-keeper and messengers) and half their salary would be charged on the vote. The cashier's department would be reformed, receipt being entirely separated from payment of monies. At the same time Morpeth recommended that Philipps's salary should be raised to £1000 (from £950), and that his burden should be lightened by giving him a private secretary.

In approving this detailed scheme the Treasury emphasized again the principle that 'the property of every public servant in his time must be regulated by the exigencies of his department': officers must, if necessary, 'continue, without extra remuneration, their attendance beyond the usual hours of business'. This should enable law stationers (employed instead of copying clerks) to be dispensed with except at times of great and temporary pressure. No officer was to accept any private employment. Willingness to give up one's time was to be made a criterion for promotion. 'In no case should persons who show no zeal for the service, and give it only such portion of their time and attention as is enforced upon them, be promoted to a superior class'. A further step to professionalising the service was a requirement that henceforth any nominee for a junior clerkship must undergo a preliminary

---

[1] *Parl. Pap.* 1847–8 (538) xxiv, pp. 547–8.

examination of education and ability; if satisfactory, he would then serve a probationary year.[1]

A number of changes also occurred among the professional officers of the outdoor department. Henry Hake Seward, at the age of sixty-five, after nine months' 'continued severe illness', submitted his resignation in June 1844, fifty years since he had entered the profession as a pupil of Soane.[2] 'Held in the highest estimation' by Stephenson, Seward had been ill intermittently for some four years past, to the disturbance of the Board's affairs, an inconvenience not altogether remedied by the occasional employment of Joseph Gwilt or the increased exertions of the indefatigable Phipps.[3] In his place as surveyor was appointed William Southcote Inman (1798–1879), of whose earlier career little is known. He appears never to have acquired the same importance as Seward, and Sir Benjamin Hall in 1855 formed no high opinion of his abilities.[4] That his previous experience had not been wide may perhaps be inferred from a reference made by the Board in August 1845 to those we may term the 'official architects', habitually employed in public undertakings: Robert Smirke, Charles Barry, Edward Blore, Decimus Burton, Thomas Cubitt, Joseph Gwilt, and the official referees under the Metropolitan Buildings Act (W. Hosking, A. Poynter, and J. Shaw). This related to special works contracts put out to competition. The Board stated that:

> It has come to their Knowledge recently that it is the practice of the Competitors to add to each of their Tenders for the Work, the Sum which has been paid to a Surveyor employed on their behalf to take out the quantities. In the case which has brought this fact within their Knowledge the payment of this Sum was separately and substantially put forward as a condition in the making of the Tender. In the other cases connected with the same competition, it is not specifically mentioned but the Board have reason to believe that the Surveyor's charge is included in each of the Tenders.
>
> The Board are in ignorance of the practice pursued . . . in Building transactions in general, where Offers for Tenders are resorted to; and assuming the course above

---

[1] *Ibid.* pp. 552–4. The Treasury now directed that upon a vacancy the next senior should be promoted unless demonstrably inadequate. This change of emphasis was in line with the Board's practice: considering whom to promote in 1844, the Board remarked that 'looking only to considerations of *general* fitness, it is not imperative upon them to apply to the older Members of the Establishment—to those who have passed the greater portion of their Official Service under regulations less attentively directed than the present to the means by which such fitness is to be acquired—the same rule which it will not only be just but obviously indispensable to apply hereafter to their present Assistants and Juniors'. The Board would 'be not disposed to insist' on so wide a qualification for promotion to a senior clerkship; fitness for the charge of any one department would suffice (Works 22/2/7).

[2] Works 2/4, pp. 209–11.

[3] *Ibid.* pp. 170–3, 261, 457–9; see also 1/26, pp. 389, 518. In proposing that Phipps' salary should be raised from £500 to £650 p.a. the commissioners wrote to the Treasury, 7 June 1845, that because of Seward's ill-health, 'a Weight of Duty has devolved upon Mr. Phipps much beyond what could have been contemplated. He has not only had the supervision of all ordinary Works and repairs at all the Public Buildings and Offices, in London, in charge of this Board, but has, on numerous occasions furnished Designs, Working Drawings, detailed Specifications and Estimates for various Works, in the Windsor district and at Richmond Park. He has also in different parts of the Country inspected and reported upon the execution of Works on the Crown Farms, and in these multifarious and laborious Duties Mr. Phipps has manifested much zeal and great professional intelligence. He has not limited his Services to any ordinary hours of Office business, but has devoted himself at extra hours, early and late, to accomplish the objects entrusted to him' (Works 2/4, pp. 457–9).

[4] *Parl. Pap.* 1860 (483) ix, qq. 1337–8. For what is known of Inman's earlier career, see Colvin, *Dictionary*. He came second to Wilkins in 1823 in a competition for new buildings at King's College, Cambridge.

referred to, to be the practice, they have doubts as to the justice of their recognizing in Tenders for Public Works, the principle of including . . . a Sum for expenses already incurred, expenses incidental to the making of the Tender, not of executing the particular Service in reference to which it has been called for.[1]

The Board therefore sought both information and advice, whether they were justified in paying such a charge; and if not how they might obtain tenders divested of such a charge. Unfortunately no replies are extant, but general practice suggests that builders continued to recoup themselves for these expenses in their tenders. In July 1846 Blore recommended that the quantity surveyor should be paid by the Board 'instead of the Amount of his charge being added by the successful competitor to the amount of his contract as is usually done. In either case it will be paid by the Board: but in the one it is done openly and in the other clandestinely'.[2]

At this time the outdoor department can scarcely have been functioning at a high level of efficiency. Craib, Clerk of the Works at Hampton Court, had a severe stroke in the autumn of 1843; although nearly paralysed, he remained on the strength until March 1845, his duties being executed by Robinson, the Clerk at Kew, who himself resigned at the end of 1844.[3] Kew and Richmond were then placed under Craib's successor, Henry Riley Wilson.[4] After five years the commissioners again decided that the combined district was 'far too much for one Officer', and appointed the superintending foreman at Kew, Benjamin Gregory, as Labourer in Trust. But six months later, Wilson himself resigned. He had been promised an increased salary for the enlarged district, but the precise sum the commissioners wished to base on experience of the labour involved: thus it was August 1848, more than three years after Wilson's appointment, before they decided on an extra £35 per annum, with another £35 for a horse. The Treasury, however, refused to antedate this earlier than the beginning of the current financial year, so Wilson went unremunerated for three years' extra duty.[5]

Another district that can hardly have been receiving the proper attention from its Clerk of the Works was Chelsea, where Richard Hall (*c.* 1774–1853) was the victim of 'increasing infirmities' as well as of 'advanced age'.[6] He was superannuated in 1845, his successor being William Burnett,[7] who since 1840 had assisted at Windsor, where Whitman was kept busy by the 'almost daily requirements' of the royal household. In December 1845 it was decided to divide this district, Whitman taking charge of the numerous buildings in the royal domain of Windsor not immediately connected with the castle. For the castle itself a new clerkship of the works was created at an enhanced salary of £200 per annum to which John Robson Turnbull was appointed.[8]

---

[1] Works 1/28, pp. 313–4.   [2] Works 19/40/5, f. 6.
[3] Works 2/4, p. 409; 1/26, p. 343; 2/5, pp. 54–8.
[4] Son of Robert Wilson, plasterer, sometime Office of Woods contracting plasterer at Hampton Court (Works 1/35, p. 320).
[5] Works 2/6, pp. 434–6, 457; 1/36, pp. 19, 426.   [6] Works 2/4, p. 512.
[7] Burnett had been for a 'considerable time' employed by Messrs. Buller, extensive building contractors, who strongly recommended him. He gave up his apartments at Chelsea in May 1850. It is probably he who became architectural clerk to the Courts of Justice Commission, 1866 (Works 2/5, pp. 54–8; 1/36, p. 316. *Parl. Pap.* 1871, [C.290] xx.)
[8] Works 2/6, pp. 54–8; 1/29, p. 97.

Because of a fall in prices of building materials since 1843, the commissioners determined towards the end of 1848 to end the subsisting contracts and call for tenders on the basis of a new schedule of prices. Its preparation was entrusted to Phipps, who obtained returns of marketable building material prices from merchants, manufacturers, tradesmen and general builders in London. The schedule he prepared was referred to Barry, who praised it highly.[1] Similarly, the Scottish prices were revised by William Burn.[2] Jesse and Phipps were then asked for names of some six tradesmen in each branch and district to apply to for tenders.[3] The number of those actually tendering ranged from one (mason, Windsor Great Park District), to ten (smith, Hampton Court), averaging nearly five per trade per district. The result of the competition was a general displacement of most of the tradesmen previously employed. Higher discounts were generally obtained in the Windsor districts than at Hampton Court.[4] The new contracts ran from 1 April 1849. The districts covered by the contract tradesmen were re-arranged: Windsor was divided into two, the Castle and Frogmore constituting one, the Great Park the other.[5] Several alterations were also made in the terms. The Clerks of the Works were particularly warned against permitting anything to be done as day work that could be measured, and to be vigilant that the contractors worked satisfactorily:

> . . . if in any case the Contractors shall employ inefficient Workmen; or men, who in Day-work shall be found negligent, and improperly to waste their time, (of which many complaints have come under the notice of the Board), you are immediately to give notice to the Contractors, and desire that such men may be withdrawn, and replaced by Others who are efficient and unobjectionable, and in the event of your requisition to this effect not being attended to, you are immediately to report the circumstances to the Surveyor, or the Assistant Surveyor of Works in this Department.[6]

However stringent their rules, the Board had still to cope with problems of human weakness. In October 1846, for example, they had to reprimand Wilson, the Clerk at Kew, for departing from his estimates and substituting new work for repairs to old at the Duke of Cambridge's.

> He is not [wrote Milne to Jesse] to take upon himself authority to alter what has been ordered to be done, Or in any way to deviate from what has been approved by the Board, without previously reporting the circumstances through his Superior Officers for the information and consideration of the Board: nor is He then to proceed unless such alterations shall be sanctioned by the Board. It is obvious that Works being executed otherwise, must not only be subversive of the Regulations, and of proper inspection by the Superintending Officers under whom the local Clerks of the Works are placed, but in great measure renders nugatory the general control, exercised by the Department.[7]

Again, a brick tank built in the dairy farmyard at Frogmore by the contract bricklayer, Lawrence, proved defective in materials and workmanship: Whitman,

[1] Works 2/8, pp. 1–5; 1/33, p. 243.   [2] Works 1/33, p. 396.   [3] *Ibid.* p. 242.
[4] *Ibid.* pp. 379–81, 384–90.   [5] *Ibid.* pp. 380–1.   [6] *Ibid.* pp. 382–3.   [7] Works 1/30, pp. 272–3.

the resident clerk, was told: 'If you had paid that attention to the execution of these works, which the difficulties of the case demanded, the extremely unpleasant circumstances connected with this business would never have occurred'.[1] It might be said, in Whitman's favour, that he had a very laborious district to supervise, for this was before it was divided into two. The most serious case however was that discovered in 1847 of Whibley, Clerk of the Works at Brighton, who had sold old lead and brass, public property, for his own profit.[2] Such malfeasance was rare at this period.

* * * * * * * * * *

The growing interest of Parliament in the Office of Woods and Works was probably a consequence of increasing expenditure on public works coupled with a change of parliamentary climate. In July 1845, Goulburn wrote to Peel: 'I am quite aware that there is at the present moment in the House of Commons a general disposition to extravagant expenditure especially when connected with the encouragement of the fine arts or the gratification and improvement of the people by gratuitous exhibition'.[3] 'In 1845 profusion was popular', wrote Lord John Russell to the Queen in January 1850, 'in 1850 economy will be pushed to its uttermost limits'.[4]

After the great reform of 1832 and the reduction in the estimates of the succeeding years, the House of Commons had interfered little with the proceedings and projects of the department except for the Houses of Parliament, a matter of domestic concern. It was possible for Philipps to write in 1842,

> According to the practice which has hitherto prevailed in Parliament Government has been left very much to itself in the erection of its *Public buildings*. It is impossible to deny that Estimates have been proposed, and money voted, without any very jealous watchfulness as to the means to be employed, or the objects upon which this money was to be expended.[5]

Philipps probably would not recall the instances of parliamentary interference that had occurred when he was a young junior clerk in the Woods and Forests, not concerned with public buildings. For the immediately preceding decade his remarks are undoubtedly valid. And although in the succeeding decade parliamentary interference was to become more frequent again, we no longer find, as in the 1820s, the gentleman connoisseur imposing his own judgement on the architect. There was a growing feeling, no doubt reflecting the increasing professionalisation of architecture, that architectural design was something to be left to the expert. The M.P. might require Gothic or Italian, but he would not sketch in details with his own hand. In the 1850s and '60s, when practitioners as well as students of architecture appeared in the Commons, criticism might acquire a keener edge, but the effect was to strengthen the tendency towards giving the architect as much independence as possible. Members might seek to displace one architect in favour of another, knowing that X was the exponent of one style, Y of another; but they did not substitute their own 'slight sketches' for the designs of the professionals.

[1] Works 1/27, p. 140 (5 August 1844); 1/28, p. 90 (5 May 1845).
[2] Works 1/31, pp. 190, 208, 230, 233, 284.   [3] B.M. Add. MS. 40570, f. 44.
[4] P.R.O. 30/22/8C, f. 795.   [5] B.M. Add. MS. 40517, f. 211 ff.

It was with a view to cutting costs that the select committee on miscellaneous expenditure, forced on the government after the hostile reception of its original budget in 1848, regarded the Woods and Forests with a particularly critical eye:

> Of all Departments of the Public Service the Commission of Woods and Forests perhaps requires the most economical superintendence. The expenses of all the Public Offices and Public Grounds are entrusted to it, and it has to exercise a discretion upon the applications of all Public Functionaries, and to decide upon matters of reference from Architects and Artists; it should therefore be subject to the closest supervision of Parliament, and the special control of the Treasury.[1]

There can be little doubt that in creating this attitude the unhappy story of the building of the New Palace of Westminster played an important part.

Once the Commons had determined to implement Reid's scheme of ventilation (involving the construction of a central tower)[2] work should have proceeded rapidly. But there was a strike of masons, and difficulties were encountered with bad ground as well as in clearing the site for the new Houses themselves, for many of the old buildings were still in use for the current business of Parliament. By the spring of 1843, work was sadly behind schedule and the central parts of the palace were only about six feet above ground level.[3] The slow progress of the new building was most felt as a hardship by the Lords, whose accommodation was far smaller and less convenient than before the fire; the Commons, on the other hand, enjoyed the spaciousness of the old House of Lords conveniently altered to their requirements by Smirke and ventilated with surprising efficiency by Reid.[4] Thus the first serious criticisms of delay came from the Lords. Lord Clanricarde enquired on 21 February 1843 why the agreement that the new House of Lords should have priority had not been kept, and moved the appointment of a committee.[5] This heard evidence from Barry and Reid and, despite the architect's reluctance to undertake to have the House ready in under two years, reported that

> . . . the Architect be directed so to conduct his operations as to secure the occupation of the new House of Lords, with temporary fittings, at the commencement of the Session of 1844 . . .[6]

As this report was not officially communicated to the Treasury or the Office of Woods, no action was taken. Barry however proceeded more rapidly with the Lords' than the Commons' House, though by no means as rapidly as the peers desired. In the subsequent session another committee was therefore appointed to investigate the changes in plan made by Barry since 1836.[7] In their second report this committee recommended that the works 'should be advanced with the greatest possible speed', so that the working parts of the House of Lords might be ready for use by April 1845.[8]

---

[1] *Parl. Pap.* 1847–8 (543), xviii, pt. I, p. x.   [2] See pp. 603–5.   [3] See p. 608.
[4] Tributes to Reid's success were paid, e.g. by Lord Campbell, 21 February 1843 (*Parl. Deb.* 3rd ser. lxvi, 1035–6); 31 March 1846 (lxxxv, 975–6); 26 June 1846 (lxxxvii, 1035); and Lord Sudeley, 26 June 1846 (lxxxvii, 1033).
[5] *Parl. Deb.* 3rd ser. lxvi, 1033 ff.   [6] *Parl. Pap.* 1844 (381), vi, with minutes of 1843 committee.
[7] *Ibid.* 1844 (269) vi, qq. 82–98.   [8] *Ibid.* 1844 (629) vi.

In their first report they had criticised Barry for having made alterations without authority,[1] which provided a ground for Clanricarde's call for some overruling authority to direct the great work.[2] The Treasury he did not think suitable, and the Board of Works, he complained, would be guided by the government's wishes. The architect's difficulties would be increased by orders coming from different directions, so there should be either a committee of members of both Houses and some others, or a joint committee of both Houses. This is interesting as the first suggestion of the arrangement that was to be adopted four years later. Dissatisfaction expressed in the committee led Barry to suspend work on the Victoria Gallery, and alterations were decided upon.[3]

Lord Lincoln gave consistent support to Barry,[4] and a Commons' select committee was appointed under his chairmanship to seek to rob the Lords' criticism of its force. Their report declared:

> Your Committee have examined various parties, as to the course hitherto adopted by Mr. Barry, with reference to alterations of the interior arrangements shown in the Plan approved by Committees of both Houses in 1836. They impute no blame to Mr. Barry for that course, and have every reason to believe that all the alterations hitherto made have conduced to the convenience and general effect of the Building; but looking to the misapprehension that appears to have prevailed as to these proceedings hitherto, they are prepared to recommend that, in future, Mr. Barry should make a half-yearly Report of the progress of the works to the Commissioners of Woods and Forests; and should also submit to that Board any alterations which may hereafter be deemed advisable, and accompany such Report with Plans of the alterations proposed.[5]

Barry undertook to adopt various alterations proposed in the internal arrangements of the Commons by officers of the House, and he stated that committee rooms and other offices might be prepared for use in the 1846 session, though that might impede the final completion. The committee accordingly warned the House of this likelihood, and further observed that the ventilation system could not be completed until 1847.[6]

Difficulties over the ventilation, culminating in an open quarrel between Barry and Reid, further delayed the completion of the House, and in June 1845 Lord Brougham, after three stifling nights of debate on the Maynooth grant, fiercely attacked Barry.[7] Already in the previous year he had shown his antipathy, describing the new palace as 'a monument of barbarity'.[8] Now he declared,

> I don't regard the assurance of Mr. Barry as worth the value of the paper on which it is written. Mr. Barry is all but resisting the authority of this House; he is fencing with the House. He foolishly, short-sightedly—and, as he will find to his cost, most ignorantly—fancies that he has high protection out of this House. He will find himself mistaken, completely mistaken.

---

[1] *Ibid.* 1844 (269) vi.   [2] *Parl. Deb.* 3rd ser. lxxiv, 1249 (17 May 1844).
[3] *Parl. Pap.* 1844 (381) vi, q. 179.
[4] See *Parl. Deb.* 3rd ser. xcv, 1334 (16 December 1847); xcvi, 570–6 (14 February 1848); A. Barry, *Life of Sir C. Barry* (1867), pp. 162, 269.
[5] *Parl. Pap.* 1844 (448) vi.   [6] *Ibid.*   [7] *Parl. Deb.* 3rd ser. lxxxi, 120–2 (5 June 1845).
[8] *Ibid.* lxxiv, 1247–9 (17 May 1844).

When, a few days later, through Lord Wharncliffe, Barry denied these assertions, Brougham repeated them: 'Mr. Barry was not only a Gothic architect, not only was he a dilatory man, but the very name of delay itself'; he was trying to make the House of Lords subservient to the views of the Fine Arts Commission presided over by Prince Albert.[1] Lord Lincoln referred the matters in dispute between Barry and Reid to an arbitrator, Joseph Gwilt, who had been recommended to him in 1842 by Barry, and on whom Lincoln relied a good deal after Seward's retirement.[2] Gwilt reported on 28 September 1845 that the delay arose from having two independent 'directors of work' on the same building; and was scathing in his criticisms of Reid's incompetence.[3]

Further committees of both Houses were appointed in February 1846, and again a divergence appeared in their respective views. But now their own circumstances persuaded the peers to veer round in Barry's favour, while the Commons' committee without Lincoln's influence shewed itself less sympathetic to the architect. The first of the peers' four reports urged that their House should be completed in time for the 1847 session, with temporary arrangements for warmth and ventilation, and that the Commissioners of Woods should take steps to ensure a constant supervision of works under their charge;[4] but the government persuaded the Lords to await the deliberations of the Commons' committee. This contained only two official members, the Secretary of the Treasury and the Master of the Mint, and was composed of a majority of opponents of the government.[5] The first of their three reports recommended that Reid's plan for ventilation and warming should be carried out in the New Palace, but that any difference between Reid and Barry should be referred to a third party, whose decision should be final. This arbitrator was to consist of one person appointed by Barry and one by Reid, subject to the approval of the Chief Commissioner of Woods, who should name an umpire if necessary.[6] The Lords' reply was to interrogate a rival ventilator, Goldsworthy Gurney, as well as Reid, and recommend that further experiments should be conducted before any plan was adopted.[7] The Commons retorted that no evidence was forthcoming that Gurney's system had been applied to an existing public building.[8] In June the Lords heard further evidence from Barry, and reported that

the only impediment to the preparation of the new House of Lords, for the commencement of the Session of 1847, arises from a delay in the arrangement for warming and ventilating the apartment according to the views of Dr. Reid.

That the Architect has expressed his willingness to undertake the warming and ventilation of the new House upon a plan of his own, and on his own responsibility.

---

[1] *Ibid.* lxxxi, 203–6 (9 June 1845). It was ironical that this charge should be made against Barry, who tended as far as possible to ignore the commission (of which he was not a member), which had been appointed in 1841; see below p. 614.   [2] B.M. Add. MS. 40481, ff. 34–5.

[3] *Parl. Pap.* 1846 (719) xv, p. 19.   [4] *Parl. Pap.* 1846 (719) xv.

[5] The members were Cardwell (Treasury sec.), Sir G. Clerk (Master of the Mint), Sir H. Douglas, Viscount Duncan, Col. Fox, Gaskell, Lord R. Grosvenor, Hawes, Sir R. H. Inglis, Sir C. Lemon, Stafford O'Brien, Lord Palmerston, Pendarves, Lord J. Russell, Wyse.

[6] *Parl. Pap.* 1846 (177) xv.

[7] *Ibid.* 1846 (719), xv, pp. 24–36. Gurney (for whom, see *D.N.B.*) had been employed to light the Commons from 1839 to 1847 (*Parl. Pap.* 1852 (511, 481) xlii).

[8] *Ibid.* 1846 (349) xv.

That the Committee are convinced, that if this proposal of the Architect be not accepted, the occupation of their new House by the Peers will be postponed to an indefinite period.[1]

Reid promptly appealed to both Houses against such a verdict, but Lord Canning, Lincoln's successor, not convinced that one uniform system of ventilation for the entire new palace, as advocated by Reid, was either practicable or wise, called in three experts, Philip Hardwick, George Stephenson and Professor Thomas Graham. Waiting for their conclusions, the Commons' committee declined to interfere.[2]

The referees agreed that the only impediment to progress arose from the delay in making arrangements for ventilating and warming according to Reid's views; if the architect's proposal to undertake that task were not accepted, they thought the occupation of the new House would be indefinitely postponed.[3] Clanricarde thereupon moved an Address for acting on this report. He would have been willing to leave the matter to the First Commissioner's decision; but Canning, in view of the large expenditure already incurred on Reid's plan, wanted the opinion of Parliament to be taken on the subject. Despite some support for Reid, the peers, in order to get into their new House, voted the Address on 26 June.[4] The Commons' committee made its third and final report on 5 August, wisely leaving the question of ventilation in the hands of the Chief Commissioner and his experts, but adding the rider: 'The great improvement which Dr. Reid's system has effected in the atmosphere of the existing House of Commons can be appreciated by every Member of the House, and Your Committee entirely concur in what they consider to be the general opinion in its favour'.[5] The Lords on 14 August heard further evidence from both Barry and Reid. The ventilator's replies were little but a continuous complaint: 'I see nothing but unfair play at every step' (q. 26); 'were I assisted, instead of being opposed and thwarted and deceived as I have been, I believe there is no man who will not say [my plans] are as definite as any one in my position could wish to give' (q. 32); and (of Gwilt, and the committee of three experts) 'Both references were conducted with perfect unfairness' (q.50). It was not surprising that the Lords in their final, fourth report, approved Barry's plans, but left Reid's evidence to speak for itself.[6]

In June 1846 there was a change of administration. The new First Commissioner, Morpeth, when he had taken his bearings, wrote to the Prime Minister, with considerable sense but with obvious misgivings, that after 'personal communications' with both Barry and Reid,

> I came to the conclusion that it was hopeless to expect a satisfactory progress, or a termination within a reasonable period, of the remaining Works at the New Palace of Westminster, under the system of divided authority and responsibility, which has hitherto been established between them.
>
> It seems equally plain to me, that it is with Mr. Barry as the Architect, that the entire controul and responsibility, subject to such regulations as either the Houses of Parliament through their Committees or the Government may think proper to impose, ought henceforth to reside. I should therefore propose, if I obtain your

[1] *Ibid.* 1846 (719) xv, pp. 37 ff.   [2] *Ibid.* 1846 (574) xv.
[3] *Parl. Deb.* 3rd ser. lxxxvii, 1033 ff. (26 June 1846).   [4] *Ibid.* 1035.
[5] *Parl. Pap.* 1846 (574) xv.   [6] *Ibid.* 1846 (719) xv.

Lordship's sanction, to give directions that Mr. Barry should be at liberty to go on with all the Works remaining to be executed, without any check or obstacle from any person, without the express authority of the Government. It might at the same time be desirable that upon a subject so much controverted and so imperfectly ascertained in all its bearings as ventilation, some third person of experience and judgment, should be instructed by the Government, to inspect Mr. Barry's plans, from time to time, and report upon them.

Nevertheless, Reid's success in the temporary House of Commons discouraged Morpeth from 'any step, unnecessarily disrespectful, or injurious, to Dr. Reid'; he also reminded Russell of the terms of the agreement between Reid and the Treasury.[1]

So the government, with the indecision that was its chronic weakness, began the whole sorry cycle again: on 28 November 1846 Morpeth invited Reid to prepare plans for ventilating the Commons' part of the palace:[2] a minority administration dared not ignore the wide support he enjoyed in that House. Reid was also able to make play with his appointment in 1840 to superintend the ventilation of the new Houses until a session after completion, with right of appeal to the Board against Barry—'without which I should have declined accepting the honor of the apppointment'. Reid was as captious and evasive as ever, and the Board commented that it had had no success in inducing Barry and him to co-operate; 'we apprehend that their differences are of such a nature as to preclude our indulging in the hope of their mutually combining their Labours for the Public Service'. But Reid had 'a very numerously signed testimonial' approving his ventilation of the temporary House of Commons, and the Treasury accepted his estimate, though it was twice as expensive as Barry's plan.[3] It is noteworthy that the cheese-paring Chancellor of the Exchequer, Wood, was not a stronger contender for the cheaper system.

The reluctance of ministers, whether Whig or Tory, to give a clear lead on the various problems concerning the new palace is a marked feature in its history. Were governments then so weak that they dared not incur a little more unpopularity? Rather, they seem to have been guided by two feelings, not entirely compatible: that Parliament must decide for itself the vital questions about its home; and that the expenditure must be kept to a minimum. In 1841 Melbourne's government would not take upon itself responsibility for the great ventilating scheme, nor would Peel's that followed it. In 1846 Peel's ministry would not take the responsibility for abandoning it; nor would the Whigs who succeeded to office a few months later.

In the same way, faced with the need to make arrangements for a major extension to Buckingham Palace, Peel shuffled off responsibility onto a royal commission. He explained to Prince Albert on 10 June 1846,

> as I do not think Parliament with the present tendencies to architectural Criticism, could have been satisfied with the original design of Mr. Blore for the Additions to Buckingham Palace—the appointment of the Commission will in my opinion tend to obviate the delay—which might have been interposed had a vote been proposed without the intervention and Sanction of a Commission.[4]

---

[1] Works 2/5, pp. 288–90, 14 September 1846.   [2] Works 11/12, f. 246.
[3] *Ibid.* f. 236; 2/6, p. 246 (Commissioners of Woods to Treasury, 2 December 1847), 264 (Treasury to commissioners, 8 December 1847).   [4] RA, C26, f. 80.

Thus appointed 'for the purpose of considering the Plans and Estimates which may be submitted for effecting the improvement and enlargement of the Palace and of afterwards superintending the application of any Funds which may be provided for carrying them into effect', the commission consisted of the First Lord of the Treasury, the Chancellor of the Exchequer, the First Commissioner of Woods, Earl de Grey, Lord Lincoln and Lord Francis Egerton.[1] Although the commissioners held four meetings, no instrument of appointment was issued before the fall of Peel's ministry. Philipps then took up the question with Arbuthnot of the Treasury, who explained that the outgoing administration had thought nothing more than the Treasury letter was necessary, as the commissioners were 'only to help the taste of the Architect and to report upon plans'. But it was intended that they should also supervise expenditure, and Philipps was anxious to obviate parliamentary criticism of the procedure adopted. Further discussions led to the issue of a Treasury minute dated 15 September 1846, formally delegating authority to the palace commission. In this the precedent established in 1831 was followed, the commission being substituted for Duncannon. Blore was to report to and receive his directions from the commission, and to deliver his accounts with supporting vouchers to it for transmission with certificate of approval to the Treasury, which would order the Board of Woods to pay.[2]

Blore was less happy with the commission than he had been with Lord Duncannon. The principal reason for this was the active part played by Lord de Grey, a leading Conservative peer who was a noted amateur of architecture and President of the Institute of British Architects.[3] But to Blore he was 'the Dictator'. Having played a considerable part in modifying the architect's elevations in 1846–7,[4] he then sought to interfere with the planning, which had already been settled between Blore and Prince Albert. 'I shall', Blore wrote, 'be glad to know in case any member of the commission exercises individually an authority over the works, or the persons employed therein, in what position as to power and responsibility I shall professionally stand.' Unless he had 'entire and sole control over the Clerk of the Works, Tradesmen, and all other persons employed in the subordinate departments of the works', and they were 'kept free from interference from any other quarters', he could not be held liable for the usual responsibilities of an architect.[5] Nevertheless such interference continued, and the Master of the Household also bypassed the architect to deal directly with subordinates. Workmen not engaged by the architect entered the building to instal fixtures without his leave. To such a state had things come by June 1849 that Blore threatened to resign, demanding that 'my supremacy over the works must be established and acknowledged'.[6] No written undertaking was given, but interpreting the First Commissioner's silence as consent, Blore ordered a resumption of work,[7] and carried the east front to completion before retiring from his profession.

[1] Works 19/7, f. 2286, Treasury to Commissioners of Woods, 23 May 1846.
[2] *Ibid.* ff. 2295–9, 2318–24.
[3] For his responsibilities in connection with the new Houses of Parliament, see below p. 233.
[4] See pp. 290–1 below.   [5] Works 19/8, f. 2459, 10 January 1848.
[6] *Ibid.* ff. 2633–5, Blore to Lord Carlisle, 3 June 1849. Work had been suspended for several weeks until Parliament voted funds.
[7] *Ibid.* f. 2636, 9 June 1849; Carlisle summoned Blore to an interview about this, see RA M53, f. 130.

R

With Queen and Lords provided for, it was the turn of the Commons to grow restive. Their criticism, however, was far less concerned with moving into a new House—for they enjoyed considerable comfort where they were—than with the rising scale of expenditure. A question by Lord Duncan on 9 December 1847 referred to the expense incurred in rents as a result of the non-completion of the official residences and library.[1] A week later Sir R. H. Inglis, a member of many of the earlier committees, moved for a select committee on the present state of the new palace, 'with a view to the reception and accommodation of this House therein', and the opportunity was seized by a number of members to attack the 'extravagant expenditure' on the building,[2] stigmatised by Ralph Bernal Osborne[3] as a 'gross job': 'a more profligate and gross expenditure of the public money had', he said, 'never taken place'. Lincoln and Morpeth both rose to Barry's defence, but Osborne declared that he made no charge against Barry personally: 'his charge equally applied to the Government; and he was determined to do all in his power to show that no efficient control was exercised over matters of this nature'. On the following night he returned to the charge:[4] 'He was prepared to prove that the Commissioners [of Woods] had not discharged their duties, and that the office ought to be abolished'. Further debate was postponed for the laying of papers. When Barry returned an estimate of £1,400,000 for the entire work, Osborne asked whether the Woods considered themselves responsible for that amount. Morpeth's reply that he relied on the architect's assurance did not satisfy Osborne, who asked the Prime Minister if, considering the deficient and sinking revenue of the nation, he was prepared 'to check this enormous expenditure' and give an assurance that no more than £1,400,000 would be spent on the work. Russell refused to commit himself: 'as to being responsible for any architect, it was quite out of the question'.[5] Such replies did nothing to mollify Osborne, who remarked that the attitude of the two ministers reminded him of the Joe Miller dialogue: '"What are you doing, Jack?" "Nothing, Sir." "And what are you about, Tom?" "Helping of Jack, Sir."'[6] Further criticism came from Hume, who considered that he had fought since the beginning for an effective means of control: 'Mr. Barry should be put under curb and bridle, for he had had his own way too long'. Another member thought that 'Parliament might be more usefully employed in controlling public expenditure, and in legislating in accordance with the spirit of the age, than in founding magnificent palaces of Gothic architecture'.[7]

To these charges Morpeth replied not only with an eulogy of Barry and praise of the Fine Arts Commission, but also with a statement of the duties of his department as he, his colleagues and his predecessors understood them:

> All those gentlemen conceived that they acted ministerially, as a subordinate department of the Treasury, and that as such it was not their duty as a department to settle what annual amount of expenditure was to be incurred, any more than it was their

[1] *Parl. Deb.* 3rd ser. xcv, 858.   [2] *Ibid.* 1332–5.
[3] Ralph Bernal Osborne (1808–82), son of Ralph Bernal, M.P.; Liberal M.P. 1841–65, 1866–8, 1869–74; see *D.N.B.*
[4] *Parl. Deb.* 3rd ser. xcv, 1404.   [5] *Ibid.* xcvi, 290 (8 February 1848).
[6] *Ibid.* 543 (14 February 1848).   [7] *Ibid.* 543–64.

duty to settle the details of the architectural arrangements . . . the duty of this department was to exercise a control similar to that of an accountant—to see that the sums annually voted by Parliament were applied to the service for which they were voted, after having obtained the sanction of the Treasury—to see that the contracts were entered into with proper and responsible persons, and upon proper terms—to examine all the accounts—to see that the contracts were faithfully performed according to the rates of measurement, and to provide for the bills being paid accordingly. That office . . . was a very laborious one, and he was convinced that it was discharged with great zeal and ability by the officers of the department; and he might especially mention the name of a gentleman who, for a long period of the years, had been especially called upon to transact this business— . . . Mr. Milne. Further, it was certainly the duty of the Woods and Forests to report any deviation from the original design to the Treasury, for their sanction or disallowance; and this rule, he believed, had been regularly acted upon by that department.[1]

This of course had been the limited function of the Office of Works ever since the concept of a professional Surveyor General had been given up. Morpeth added that the government were reducing annual expenditure as much as possible, which would entail slower progress. Priority was being given to completing the new House of Commons and committee rooms. Inglis replied that it would be a truer economy to complete the building within the next two years. In a subsequent speech (2 March 1848) Morpeth declared his department had done its best to discharge the duties devolved on it either by Parliament or by the Treasury: but it was not a ministry of works. The government as represented by the Chancellor of the Exchequer were responsible for the estimates, and the Board of Works were willing to take the responsibility of 'fully inspecting all the accounts, and of forming the best judgment they could upon the points referred to their decision with regard to deviations from the original plan'.[2]

It was left to Peel to tell the House that it was itself much to blame for the state of affairs. When the House specified sums for public buildings the result was not satisfactory, as was shown by Buckingham Palace, the Treasury building and the National Gallery. 'First, you limit the architect to such an amount that his skill is fettered; and then you become so dissatisfied with the effects of your limitation of expense, that you pull down the whole front of a building, and employ another architect to supply a better one'.[3] Lord Lincoln fixed the blame even more specifically on the House. When alterations had been proposed for heating and ventilation, Duncannon had recommended that the estimates should be submitted to the House with a view to reducing the amount. But the result of the reference to select committees had been 'rather to increase than to diminish the expense'.[4] The radical M.P. Ewart agreed: 'Committees had been appointed—Committees had sat—and Committees had invariably added to the expense. It often happened that the Government was seized with a cold fit of economy; but Committees were more frequently visited by those warm excesses'.[5]

These discussions reached a climax on 2 March 1848 when Inglis again brought forward his motion for a select committee.[6] Ralph Bernal Osborne moved an

[1] *Ibid.* 552. [2] *Ibid.* xcvii, 142–4. [3] *Ibid.* xcvi, 564–9. [4] *Ibid.* 570–6.
[5] *Ibid.* 578. [6] *Ibid.* xcvii, 138 ff.

amendment for a royal commission to supervise the completion. He attacked Barry, Reid, Inglis, the Fine Arts Commission, and select committees. As guardian of the public purse, the House must call for a commission. His father, the experienced chairman of committees, Ralph Bernal, 'never recollected an instance in which any advantage had arisen from discussing matters of taste in the House . . . A Committee of the House of Commons was the most incompetent body in the world to decide on any matter of taste, or to control the expenditure of money on objects of taste'. Rather than a committee, he would prefer the First Commissioner and Chancellor of the Exchequer to settle the matter, or employ 'proper persons' to investigate and report. Lincoln had by this time slightly modified his view: despite Morpeth's opposition to a commission, Lincoln thought the proposal a good one if some 'competent authority' could be found. He agreed that the duties of the Woods and Works had become so burdensome that the department could not devote sufficient attention to such matters as the new Houses of Parliament; he therefore favoured the appointment of 'some functionary . . . who should have the superintendence of the New Houses of Parliament, and of any public buildings of a large character which the State might undertake'. Neither the Windsor Castle nor the Buckingham Palace commissions however were desirable precedents; and he did not see to whom authority should be delegated: so why not appoint a committee limited to investigating the best mode of controlling expenditure?

Judging the temper of the House, the Chancellor of the Exchequer declared in favour of a commission. Clearly the course of debate led the ministers to change their minds. Wood acknowledged his own responsibility merely to the extent of deciding how much money should be voted annually; he could not concern himself with the details of building. To a dilettante commission he was opposed, because it would only lead to expense.

> At the same time he was not prepared to say that it was not advisable to devise some means to control the expenditure. This, however, was out of the power of his hon. Friend and himself; and therefore if any body of persons could be constituted, with an adequate knowledge of the subject, who could effectually control the expenditure, he would not make the slightest objection. Probably then a Commission might be appointed with adequate powers to decide what would contribute to the economy and proper construction of the Houses of Parliament. They should not be allowed to recommend an increased expenditure. The amount of expenditure should be left to the Government and the Chancellor of the Exchequer, who should determine in each year. He was inclined to think that Government had better take on themselves the appointment of such [a] Commission. They should be a purely controlling body, in conformity with the plan sanctioned by the Commission of both Houses. He believed the noble Lord [Morpeth] would take on himself the responsibility of recommending the appointment of such a body.[1]

Inglis offering to withdraw his proposal, Morpeth concurred in the wishes of the House: if they wanted 'some means of closer and better control', he would propose a commission of a 'very few' persons.[2]

[1] *Ibid.* 151–2.   [2] *Ibid.* 152–3.

Thus it was that a royal commission was appointed in April 1848 to supervise the completion of the New Palace of Westminster. It was, according to Morpeth's wishes, a small body of only three members: one from each House, with an independent chairman. Earl de Grey was an obvious choice from the Lords. The Commons' representative was Thomas Greene,[1] ex-chairman of committees. The chairman was Sir John Fox Burgoyne,[2] Inspector-General of Fortifications and former Chairman of the Irish Board of Works. Their duties were defined by Treasury minute:

I. . . to superintend the completion of the New Palace of Westminster with reference to the Designs approved and the amount of the Estimates laid before Parliament.

II. They are to determine upon designs and propositions submitted for the decorations, furniture, fittings, Fixtures, Clocks, Bells &c. which are requisite to complete the Palace in a fit and becoming manner for occupation, subject however to the approval of the Treasury in regard to the cost to be incurred.

III. They are to decide upon all modifications or alterations of plan or Design which may be suggested by The Architect or other persons in authority connected with the Business of Parliament except when such modifications involve an increase of Expense in which case their decision is to be subject to the approval of This Board [i.e. Treasury].

IV. They are to control and finally decide upon all arrangements with reference to the Warming Ventilating and Lighting of the Building where such arrangements are at present undecided subject as above to the approval of This Board.

V. They will communicate to This Board Their recommendations on these various points in order that the necessary directions may be given to the Commissioners of Woods to make the arrangements for the execution of the same by Contract or otherwise.

VI. The Commissioners will have recourse to the assistance of the Commissioners of Woods &c. or Their Solicitors, when necessary.

VII. They will be governed by such further Instructions as may be conveyed to them from time to time by This Board.[3]

The appointment of the special commissioners did not however deprive the Office of Woods and Works of all cognizance of proceedings at the New Houses, for it continued to settle the accounts when certified by the commissioners and sanctioned by the Treasury. This merely interposed another link in the chain of communication, and thereby hindered rather than speeded business. 'Although their relations with the architect were of the most friendly character', wrote Alfred Barry of the special commissioners, 'I cannot find that their appointment greatly facilitated the progress of the work'.[4] Some improvement was made in October 1848, when the Treasury issued a general authority for the Office of Woods to pay sums certified by the special commissioners. This facility, however, was of but short duration, as the Woods ran out of funds, having in February 1849 only some £5500 in hand to meet Barry's certificates for over £11,000 as well as wages at the Thames Bank workshops and other incidentals. To meet this serious deficiency the Treasury authorised the use of

---

[1] 1794–1872; Cons. M.P. 1824–52, 1853–7; chairman of committees 1841–7; See Boase, *Modern English Biography.* [2] 1782–1871. See *D.N.B.*
[3] Works 2/6, p. 332; 11/9/5, ff. 1–3. [4] A. Barry, *Life of Sir C. Barry* (1867), p. 164.

other funds, and in March 1849 agreed to take an early vote on account of the 1849/50 estimate.[1]

Towards the close of the 1848 session the Commons had called for an estimate of the cost of completing the New Palace. This was at length submitted to the Treasury by the special commissioners on 27 February 1849. Barry's estimate was a further £1,025,000. This enormous sum caused the Treasury to ask the special commissioners how far the original estimate could be 'considered as having been a sufficient estimate of the Expence of the Buildings contemplated, what grounds there are for the excess which has taken place, and to what extent such Excess has been sanctioned by competent Authority'.[2]

Although the appointment of a commission satisfied the government, members of the Commons remained critical.[3] In August 1848 Henry Drummond wished to 'refuse to advance a farthing until a board had been appointed who should be responsible for expenditure'; and in July 1849 Sir H. Willoughby asked whether the Chancellor 'could not appoint some particular department of the Government to have an effective control over the expenses'. The commission, anxious to complete the useful parts of the building, sought to defer the completion of the towers, but Barry warned that this would violate existing contracts.[4] When the 1850 session opened members were still in their temporary accommodation, and Greene told them that although the new Chamber could be finished during the session, they would not be able to use it with comfort until the completion of the refreshment rooms and library.[5] Then difficulties arose about the number of M.P.s who might be accommodated. One gallery was put up and taken down, another put up—was it, demanded Osborne, intended as a gallery, or a shelf for *Hansard*? Cobden wanted a permanent committee of the House; Osborne, to remodel the commission, appointing Lord Sudeley, Sir Benjamin Hall (who 'had the power of saying no, and could shut his ears to the blandishments of Mr. Barry'), and two other M.P.s. He denied that the new Houses were built to encourage the fine arts, and Sir de Lacy Evans seized the opportunity to move a reduction of a thousand guineas in the vote—the sum paid Landseer for three paintings to hang in the obscurity of the Lords' refreshment room—which he carried by 94 to 75. Encouraged by this success, the attack then concentrated on the Fine Arts Commission, which Hume sought to supersede, demanding another select committee on the new palace. But the radicals were not united; Roebuck condemned members' pretensions as architectural critics; and Peel's authority helped defeat Hume's proposal.[6]

When members tried out their new quarters at long last they were no better pleased. Hall was called in, and a select committee determined to insert a lower ceiling in the new House, which Hume with some justice declared would 'destroy the appearance of the chamber'—though he could not forbear adding, 'any schoolboy would be flogged for designing such a place'. The irrepressible Colonel Sibthorp remarked that he would be sorry to employ any member of the committee in building a pigsty: the palace was not built for business, but 'much more fitted for a harem'.

[1] *Parl. Deb.* 3rd ser. cii, 567–8 (12 February 1849).   [2] *Works* 2/7, pp. 279–80 (28 April 1849).
[3] E.g. *Parl. Deb.* 3rd ser. cxi, 333–8.   [4] *Ibid.* ci, 136 (14 August 1848); cvii, 350, 352 (13 July 1849).
[5] *Ibid.* cviii, 270 (4 February 1850).
[6] *Ibid.* cx, 795–6, 1314; cxi, 328–32, 338–9, 341–2, 347–58, 981 ff.

'The only thing the House was fit for was to hold the Exhibition of 1851', said Osborne. In the ensuing debate the question of responsibility was again dominant, several urging that it should be placed on one man, though it was pointed out that the First Commissioner of Woods already had too much to do.[1]

Ultimately, having given little satisfaction to any of the disputants, the New Palace Commissioners recommended to the Prime Minister on 20 November 1851 that, as the general arrangements of the building had been completed in all essentials,

> the entire management and charge of this great and intricate undertaking revert to the Department of the Board of Works.
> In offering this suggestion we beg leave to assure your Lordship that we are not influenced by a sense of dissatisfaction at the conduct or proceedings of any party, or individuals, towards us, nor by a reluctance to continue in any such employment, if really useful to the Public Service; but solely by a strong impression that it is desirable to put an end, as early as convenient, to an organization that leads in some degree to a mixture of duties and responsibilities, by two independent bodies in the management of one concern.[2]

In this view the Treasury acquiesced, and the commission was relieved of its duties by a royal warrant of 19 December 1851.[3]

The attack on the New Palace of Westminster was only the prelude to a major offensive conducted on two fronts against the Office of Woods and Works. A select committee on miscellaneous expenditure proceeded to investigate works on palaces and public buildings;[4] and a committee obtained by Lord Duncan a month later, on 24 March 1848, devoted its labours particularly to the forests, though casting an eye also over the organisation of the Board.[5]

The dislike of the Commons for Wood's proposal to increase the income tax led not only to the appointment of the committee on miscellaneous expenditure but also to a revision of departmental estimates: those of the Works department were cut from £146,000 to £121,000 (still an increase on the previous year). The committee heard evidence from Milne and Gore, from Phipps and Cox among the officers, Barry and Blore among the architects, from Lord Lincoln, and from a number of civil servants who had dealings with the office, such as Trevelyan of the Treasury and Kay Shuttleworth of the education committee. The select committee's range of reference took it of course far beyond a single department, and we are only concerned here with a part of its investigations and conclusions. Much of the questioning was directed towards particular buildings though attention was also given to the methods and practices of the department. The committee called for 'the strictest inquiry . . . into the cost of all works before their commencement', and the greatest care that all estimates submitted to Parliament should 'include the entire and utmost possible expense that would cover their execution'. Further—Hume at last won his point—Parliament should be supplied with more information on the detail of the estimates: the amount to be voted for each item should be stated, instead of the lump totals as before. It is doubtful whether this, desirable as it might at first seem, was of

---

[1] *Ibid.* cxiii, 726–8, 731–2, 735, 738–9.   [2] Works 11/9/5, f. 31.
[3] *Ibid.* ff. 32, 35.   [4] *Parl. Pap.* 1847–8 (543) xviii.   [5] *Ibid.* 1847–8 (538) xxiv.

much value in enhancing parliamentary control: as with so much of the information furnished to it in the nineteenth century, the House of Commons might fuss if it were not on the Table, but did not bother to digest it. Moreover, the difficulties of calculating expenditure on old buildings, urged by the Office as a reason for presenting only sums total, were real and tended to turn the estimates into little more than guide-lines. But the difference between estimate and expenditure on a given building, the committee argued, showed 'the necessity of exercising every possible check over expenditure in this Department upon ordinary occasions'. The committee wisely commented, however, that though the utmost economy must be enforced, post-ponements of necessary work leading to an increased ultimate expenditure were 'delusive and inexpedient'.

The chairman of the committee, Vernon Smith, declared that 'in all the public departments there was wanting a proper financial check upon the expenditure'. He blamed the Treasury for lack of supervision before the estimates were submitted to Parliament, but confessed that the Treasury had 'a great deal too much to do'. Another problem was that a large part of the expenditure on public buildings was 'practically exempt from Parliamentary control'.[1] This and the devising of a proper financial check required consideration. Another member of the committee, John Bowring,[2] also pressed for more parliamentary control. Osborne pursued his vendetta, denouncing the estimate for the Works Department as 'the most disgraceful ever brought before the House . . . mixed up in most inextricable confusion . . . it was a fraudulent estimate'. Morpeth agreed to implement the select committee's proposal that estimates should be presented in detail,[3] and in the following year the commissioners duly submitted their estimates to the Treasury 'in the form recommended' by the select committee.[4]

The second arm of the parliamentary offensive was Lord Duncan's committee. The evidence of their prolonged investigations stretching over two sessions fills two whole volumes of parliamentary papers, but little of it relates to the King's Works.[5] After its first report had been presented, with evidence of irregularities in some of the forests (Milne's department), Hume had called on the government to reform the Office of Woods during the recess, putting an end to the Board and concentrating all power in the First Commissioner's hands.[6] Morpeth, informing Russell of his feelings about his office, was 'ready to do the best' he could in it if a commission of enquiry were authorised.[7] He had agreed with Wood that the best plan would be to employ the two Treasury members of the commission then investigating the Home Office, C. E. Trevelyan and Gibson Craig (a member of the Duncan committee), with himself as third member. He disclaimed 'any unkind feelings' towards his colleagues, but was sufficiently convinced that the outcome must be a change in line with Hume's ideas to suggest that in that event Milne should be superannuated, while 'equivalent employment and undiminished salary' should be provided for Gore, 'of whose ability and faithfulness in the discharge of his duty I have a very high opinion'. A month later he reported that it had been 'pretty well settled' with Wood

---

[1] *Parl. Deb.* 3rd ser. ci, 93 (11 August 1848).   [2] 1792–1872. See *D.N.B.*
[3] *Parl. Deb.* 3rd ser. ci, 94–100.   [4] Works 2/6, pp. 181–4; *Parl. Pap.* 1849 (268–I) xxxi.
[5] *Parl. Pap.* 1847–8 (538) xxiv; 1849 (513) xx.   [6] P.R.O. 30/22/7 C, f. 56.   [7] *Ibid.*

to hold such a Treasury inquiry. He preferred this 'conjoint inquiry', because all who had considered the subject concurred that 'more unity of authority and responsibility' must be given to the Chief Commissioner, so that 'it may be more seemly that such a proposal should not appear to emanate exclusively from himself'. Morpeth disclaimed any personal ambition in the matter, 'not being, as you must be aware, much enamoured of, or feeling myself well suited to, the Office'. The object sought was 'to deepen and concentrate responsibility'.[1] In the end, however, Duncan persuaded Carlisle (as Morpeth had become) not to make any changes until his committee had looked further into the problem.[2] Duncan's committee intensified its labours, but no final report was drawn up, as the committee was not appointed for a third session: the unfinished draft report dealt principally with the royal forests.[3] The chief interest of these monumental inquiries to an historian of the Works lies in their influence on the future of the department. The general feeling induced was that this rag-bag of administrative odds and ends must be emptied and re-sorted into some more sensible and efficient arrangement. Neither of the junior commissioners emerged with an undamaged reputation: a majority of the committee deleted from the draft report a comment that the evidence justified the belief that the commissioners had 'conscientiously and judiciously' performed their duties.[4] Milne after fifty years of public service was clearly ripe for superannuation. Gore, too, made an unfavourable impression in 1849 by having to correct some of his evidence before it was published.[5] These two had further given offence to their seniors by influencing William Hayter,[6] most assiduous of committee members, who in 1849 attended every one of the thirty-nine meetings: he had become as it were their counsel, receiving from them 'constant instructions as to the mode of Examination to be pursued, and facts to be elicited'.[7]

Clearly the climate was unpropitious for Barry to revive, as he did on 6 February 1849, the question of his remuneration. Asking the commissioners for the new Houses of Parliament for an early settlement of his claims, he argued that he was entitled to at least the customary rate of commission, for the work was more difficult and vexatious than a private work. He had also performed many special services, such as attending committees and commissions, preparing reports, and conferring with the law officers. His private practice, far from growing because of his celebrity, had suffered. Further, on all other contemporary public works, architects had received the full five per cent. Expenditure was a fair criterion of the amount of skill and labour required from the architect. His specific claims were five per cent on an outlay of £472,000 for works comprised in his estimate of £707,104 and executed to that date, and on extra works costing nearly £370,000, amounting in all to £42,081 10s.; and for special services, £5256.[8]

---

[1] *Ibid.* 7D, f. 62. [2] RA, F 42/57, Lord John Russell to Prince Albert, 11 December 1848.
[3] *Ibid.* C. 81/29, Lord Duncan to Prince Albert, 17 July 1849.
[4] *Parl. Pap.* 1849 (513) xx. [5] RA, C 81/51, 61.
[6] William Goodenough Hayter (1792–1878), barrister, Liberal M.P. 1837–65; Judge-Advocate-General 1847–9; Joint Secretary to the Treasury, 1850–8, cr. bart. 1858. See *D.N.B.*
[7] RA, C 81/9, minutes of conversation between Lord Lincoln and Prince Albert, 14 May 1849. Perhaps this accounts for the falling-off in Lincoln's once-regular attendance, though his domestic problems may also have been a factor.
[8] Works 11/1/2, ff. 61–9, printed in full. A. Barry, *Life*, app. C.

His claim having been forwarded to the Treasury, Barry asked in July 1849 for
£5000 on account, having received no commission for nearly two years past.[1] The
government agreed to this,[2] thereby acknowledging the inadequacy of the amount
fixed in 1839, of which Barry had received all save some £265. But the question took
a new turn when Barry declared that he could not bring the measuring up to date
unless more clerks were provided. He estimated that he was spending £587 a year
on measuring and making up the accounts, and valued his own time at an additional
£300. There were vast arrears which would clear only when the government would
make a fair arrangement: that is, to pay him one and a half per cent on the £220,000
of unmeasured works.[3] Philipps warned the Treasury that the question was not
whether the original fee was enough, but rather what services it was intended to
cover: the evidence of the previous ten years was that Barry had accepted it as
covering all his responsibilities; his objection had been that the amount in sum was
insufficient. 'Pertinacious as he was on that point, it never occurred to him', wrote
Philipps, 'to enter into the question of what services the remuneration was intended
to cover: we have not a line of remonstrance or even question on that point recorded
in the books of this Office'. The difficulty Barry found in calculating the expense of
measuring gave a clear inference, Philipps argued, that he had not regarded this as
a grievance.[4] Here Philipps did less than justice to Barry's case, for not only had
Barry raised the question who was to pay for measuring in 1841 (being then told,
admittedly, that his fee was to cover the whole), but the basis on which that fee had
been calculated was, as we have seen, a comparison with the fees paid to the Attached
Architects, for whom the measuring and making up accounts were done by the Office
of Works.[5]

Other objections were also brought forward by Philipps. Some of the measurers
were already employed full-time in the public service as clerks of works. Even if
Barry's claim for one and a half per cent on the £220,000 outstanding could be
supported, it did not follow that such a rate was appropriate on the total cost of the
building; for the unmeasured works, mostly joinery in the new chambers, were the
most ornamented, minute and difficult to measure in the entire edifice. The Office
could get measuring done more cheaply—and it might be 'reasonable' to relieve
Barry of measuring for the future: 'It is too much to expect that a Man should
provide liberally for the execution of other services out of a sum which he deems
barely sufficient for his own'. By May 1850, Philipps was making arrangements to
this end, engaging Caleb Norris, 'undoubtedly the best of the professional Measurers
employed in, or known to this Department', at a rate of three-quarters per cent on the
first £50,000 and half per cent thereafter. Under pressure, the question might be
disposed of, he thought, without raising the general issue of Barry's remuneration;
otherwise it was likely to incur trouble and public censure.[6] Yet nothing more was
done until April 1851 when Grissell, the contractor for the New Houses, anxious
about the delays in measuring and their effect on his own bills, offered to pay for an

---

[1] Works 11/1/2, ff. 76–7.   [2] *Ibid.* f. 110 (5 September 1850).
[3] *Ibid.* ff. 81–2 (22 November 1849). Alfred Barry in his account ignores the prolonged argument about
measuring, alleging that for five years government took no notice of Barry's 1849 claim (*Life*, p. 213).
[4] Works 11/1/2, ff. 84–9 (10 December 1849).
[5] See p. 197.   [6] Works 11/1/2, ff. 90, 92, 95–8.

additional measurer if the government would do likewise. Barry was reluctant to agree unless he was to be reimbursed. The New Palace Commissioners urged that the Treasury should meet Barry's wishes, as the arrears were increasing. The Commissioners of Woods, however, apparently misunderstanding Grissell's offer, argued that a measurer employed for the public should be exclusively accountable to the Board, and renewed the proposal that Norris should be so employed, to which the Treasury assented. Barry then protested that his own position as architect embraced the protection of the public interest. He would not have objected had the Woods' officers done the measuring from the early stages, but after nearly fourteen years sole control, he thought that the proposed change would be read as a slur on his character. Nor could he certify accounts not prepared under his own immediate control. If he were but provided with the money he would clear off all arrears in six or eight months, whereas the introduction of a stranger would merely increase the need for constant reference to him and the demands on his time. In face of this the New Palace Commissioners advised the Treasury not to persist in their proposal. But this complex chain of communication acted too slowly; the Works department had concluded its arrangement with Norris, with whom Barry refused to act. A conciliatory offer by the department led to a personal discussion between Barry and the First Commissioner, who agreed that if no greater expenditure resulted, Barry might himself engage a measurer instead of Norris. He accordingly selected H. A. Hunt.[1] Unfortunately the matter did not end here, for Lord Seymour then required Barry to discontinue using clerks of works, paid by the public, as measurers. Barry argued that they were the fittest persons, that he paid them an additional salary, and that as he would take on himself, as usual, the payment of Hunt's charges there would be no separate demand for that expense. Seizing this point, Seymour refused to pay for any persons engaged on measuring or making up accounts; and persisted that no clerks in the pay of the public should be so employed. The dispute was only resolved by Barry relieving his measurers of their duties as clerks of the works.[2]

The core of the problem lay in the government's refusal to bring the question of remuneration to a just conclusion. Had they conceded Barry his five per cent on outlay there would have been no great arrears of measuring. Although willing to concede him a larger sum than originally contemplated, government were not prepared to concede the principle, or even to state how far they would be willing to go. As Barry's biographer wrote, the real ground of the government's attitude was 'the great increase of expenditure on the building, the delay in its completion, and the unpopularity into which, from these and from other causes, it had been brought', the whole responsibility for which they sought to throw on the architect.[3]

This was not Barry's only controversy with government: a somewhat similar problem had arisen when he incurred an excess of nearly £10,000 on his estimate of £30,000 for rebuilding the Home Office and Soane's Privy Council Office and Board

---

[1] 1810–89. See Boase, *Modern English Biography.*

[2] Works 11/1/2, ff. 115–152, April–November 1851.

[3] A. Barry, *Life*, pp. 234–5. The end of the story, which may be followed in Works 11/1/2, lies outside the scope of this history. In 1855–6 the Treasury offered 3 per cent on outlay and one per cent for measurement on the whole of the works included in the outlay, as a final settlement. Barry published his case (*The Times*, 11 February 1856) but was eventually obliged to 'yield' under protest to the Treasury's terms. See A. Barry, *Life*, pp. 205–35.

of Trade. He claimed to have provided extra accommodation and argued that much more work had been necessary than he could have foreseen. With this assertion, Inman and Phipps disagreed; and the Commissioners of Woods advised the Treasury that the architect's commission should be paid only on the estimates sanctioned. Barry for his part denied that the surveyors could form an accurate opinion; there had been no extravagance, and departures from the original design had been effected principally for greater internal convenience. The surveyors stood their ground, and the Treasury reserved its decision until the accounts were settled.

In the meantime Barry protested vigorously against any limitation of his commission. There had been no such previous arrangement; he had honestly earned the usual rate; a reduction was derogatory to his character: '. . . all that can be said is, that in considering the contingencies, or rather possibilities, which must always be conjectural in altering extensively an old Building, I did not make sufficient allowance in my original Estimate', which 'was not and could not be founded upon minute and accurately detailed calculations'. Moreover, he had reported from time to time both verbally and in writing that extra works were necessary, and no objection had been made.[1]

Barry convinced the Commissioners, who recommended to the Treasury that 'a retrospective application of the principle' would be a hardship. The cost would have been no less if the original estimate had been more carefully formed, and the resulting work was 'very generally approved of'.[2] This however did not satisfy the Treasury. Pointing out in March 1847 that the excess related only to Barry's estimate of £13,771 for the Soane building, they calculated it at £11,658; they could 'not acquit him of negligence in the preparation of the Estimates, upon the faith of which the work was commenced'. Probable cost was a principal element in deciding on new works; and if the ultimate cost had been known at the outset, the Treasury might have hesitated to sanction it.

> The inaccuracy of Estimates for Architectural Works gives rise to just and well founded complaints in the House of Commons and My Lords feel it incumbent upon Them to pause before They agree to the payment of the Architect's Commission on the whole Expenditure in a case in which the practice, which is too common, of forming loose and imperfect Estimates appears to them to have been carried to so great a length.[3]

After further consideration of the circumstances, they declared:

> in this and in similar cases the proper course to be adopted is not to allow the Architect a Commission upon a larger sum than was comprised in the original Estimate sanctioned by This Board or any additions thereto subsequently authorized: with perhaps a reasonable allowance for contingent expenses, although My Lords are of opinion that an adequate sum for this purpose should, according to what they believe to be the practice of Architects, be included in the original Estimate.[4]

[1] Works 2/5, pp. 173–8, 207, 241–4, 281–3, 413–6, 418–21.
[2] *Ibid.* pp. 413–6.   [3] Works 2/6, pp. 47–9.
[4] *Ibid.* pp. 88 (Commissioners of Woods to Treasury, 29 April 1847), 124 (Treasury to Commissioners, 2 June 1847).

This principle had been laid down by the 1828 select committee.[1] The Woods were to state the utmost sum on which Barry could be allowed commission; the settlement might be held over until the completion of the Home Office, so that he might have the benefit of any savings there. The Woods calculated that Barry would be entitled to commission on £31,890 for the entire work, to which ten per cent might be added for contingencies.[2] After a glance at the legal position and remarking that 'the Work was designed with much ability, executed at fair prices, and in a satisfactory manner', the Commissioners recommended once again that the full commission should be paid. Barry had claimed that authorised estimates totalled £34,112 and that

> from the nature of the Extra works, mixed up as they were with the rest of the Work, the cost could not be ascertained until the Building was completed, and the whole of the Accounts made up, and that consequently they could not be reported . . . previously, although the Cost had been mentioned as likely to be considerable . . .

Barry further argued that five per cent had become part of the law of the land for works from an architect's designs erected under his direction. Moreover, where a considerable degree of artistic skill was required, it was a rate far from adequate. And to apply the principle of 1828 was to mistake entirely the character of the architect and his relation to his employer, as well as to ignore the fact that an unscrupulous architect could make much more through undetectable practices.[3] Barry's determination to fight for his full five per cent on outlay was doubtless the stronger because of his conditional acceptance of the fixed sum principle in respect of his far greater work at Westminster.

The Treasury reiterated its criticism of Barry's loose framing of estimates and in May 1848 posed two questions: could the principal extras not have been foreseen; and was there any reason why they were undertaken without the necessity having previously been reported? Barry and the Commissioners succeeded in convincing their masters that it had been impossible to ascertain the extent of works required until parts had been demolished, and that there had been difficulty in reporting the probable cost; but the Treasury insisted that Barry should have reported in general terms, and that no outlay of such a size should have been undertaken without prior sanction. Extras must be reported before the work was embarked upon. But as Barry 'appears to have proceeded in the manner usually practised by Architects' his claim would be allowed.[4]

But there the wider question could not be allowed to rest: the Treasury was convinced that the principle of remunerating architects recommended in 1828 was the best; it had been sanctioned in a Treasury letter of 24 February 1839 concurring in the Commissioners' suggestion of lump sum payments. They regretted that the principle had not been followed here. An additional allowance could be made for any necessary increased expenditure approved during the progress of a work. The salary of a clerk of the works together with incidentals should be included in the estimate.

---

[1] See p. 162 above.   [2] Works 2/6, pp. 266–73 (9 December 1847).
[3] *Ibid.* pp. 273–8 (Barry to Commissioners, 28 July 1847).
[4] *Ibid.* pp. 363–5 (Treasury to Commissioners, 16 May), 383–6 (Commissioners to Treasury, 24 June), 401–4 (Treasury to Commissioners, 11 July 1848).

My Lords therefore desire that in case of all public Buildings which may be here-after undertaken under your charge, the principle which is herein laid down may be adopted, and that it may be communicated to all Architects who are now or may be hereafter employed under your Department, as the condition upon which Works are to be undertaken by them.[1]

The building of the new Houses of Parliament was, however, almost the last major work undertaken strictly under the Office of Woods and Works. The enlarge-ment of Buckingham Palace was placed under a commission, and for years nothing came of the various schemes for rebuilding government offices, the National Gallery, or the Law Courts. The completion of Somerset House by Pennethorne was under the aegis of the Board of Inland Revenue; and although the Works Department was concerned in many other projects of the day—the model prison, the normal school, and suchlike—a building to house the public records was the only significant struc-ture begun under its auspices between 1848 and 1851.

When Lord Seymour (1804–85)[2] was appointed First Commissioner in March 1850, Russell had already introduced a bill to separate the Woods from the Works; but, 'adamant for drift', he abandoned it as soon as difficulties appeared. Seymour thus presided over the united Office for a year and a half. We may look at the character of his administration before considering the legislation that was to dissolve the union.

It is not unlikely that Lord Carlisle, who confessed his lack of interest in the Woods and Works aspects of his duties, left things a good deal to his colleagues and subordinates. His enthusiasm was for the sanitary legislation which, guided by Chadwick, he had promoted in Parliament, and by which the First Commissioner became in 1848 *ex officio* president of a General Board of Health. His evidence before the Duncan committee showed that after nearly a year in office he was not aware of the rules relating to the appointment of tradesmen;[3] and his dependence on Philipps has already been noticed. His successor has been sharply criticised by Dr. R. A. Lewis,[4] and by Professor S. E. Finer, who writes of 'his fantastic pride, his proverbial haughtiness, his icy nonchalance'.[5] Carlisle appears in contrast as a well-meaning and painstaking minister. Such verdicts from the historians of the General Board of Health underline the impossibility of a minister's doing justice both to that department and to the Woods and Works. Carlisle, avowedly more engaged by public health matters, was an indifferent First Commissioner; Seymour in two years attended only three meetings of the Board of Health, but was industrious at the Office of Woods, albeit his concept of administration was still that of the early nineteenth century. Indeed, he informed Shaftesbury that he would be unable to attend the Board of Health without neglecting his duties at the Woods and Forests.[6] To details, he gave a close personal attention. He noticed, for example, that Jesse

---

[1] *Ibid.* pp. 401–4.
[2] Lord of the Treasury, 1835; secretary, Board of Control, 1839; under-secretary, Home Office, 1841; suc. as 12th Duke of Somerset 1855 (*D.N.B.*). He had already been marked out by Russell and Wood for his new post in November 1849 (P.R.O. 30/22/8B, 9 November 1849).
[3] *Parl. Pap.* 1847–8 (538) xxiv, qq. 190–196.
[4] R. A. Lewis, *Edwin Chadwick and the Public Health Movement 1832–1854* (1952), pp. 245, 367–8.
[5] S. E. Finer, *Life and Times of Sir Edwin Chadwick* (1952), p. 387; see also pp. 397–400.
[6] *Parl. Deb.* 3rd ser. cxxxv, 1079–83 (cited by Lewis, pp. 368–9).

was submitting small estimates week by week for the same set of apartments at Hampton Court, kitchen offices one week, other rooms in another week; thus doubtless getting them passed where the larger total sum would have been queried. Seymour stamped out this practice. He laid down that every estimate was to have a 'leading title'; that each item should additionally be headed with the name of the place where the work was to be done; and that if additional work proved necessary, or an additional sum to meet the cost of work already sanctioned, the new estimate should be entitled in red ink: 'Supplementary Estimate for further Expenditure, in reference to an Estimate for   dated   day of 18   '. Another feature of Jesse's estimates that Seymour criticised was combining work of a single trade but on different services, for instance at a house and on a park wall, as a single item.[1] A requisition from Kew for a thousand cast-iron labels for naming plants, at a cost of £14, called forth his query whether it would not be preferable to have names enamelled on iron, or whether there was any other better way.[2] In Fincham's weekly estimates for the Houses of Parliament, Seymour noticed an item of charge for a carpenter employed under Reid, and inquired what services he performed and when they would cease to be necessary.[3] Seymour challenged the payment of two of the clerks of the works at the new Houses as measurers, an expense which was to be borne by Barry.[4] He also personally visited the iron-works making a railing to front Buckingham Palace in 1851 when the work was delayed.[5] Again, it was Seymour who set in motion an examination of the needs of the Stationery Office for extra accommodation, and directed the comptroller's attention to the Royal Westminster Mews as a possible cheaper alternative.[6] More important, he determined to introduce the principle of open competition that had from time to time been suggested,[7] and which had already been adopted by the Ordnance in respect of general works. Public advertisements were issued inviting tenders for ordinary repairs and maintenance works, for one year certain from 1 April 1851. The principle of three districts was reverted to, Windsor being reunited, but the castle itself was excluded, together with Buckingham Palace, the British Museum and Kew Gardens. The move was successful in that there was a considerable competition, and greater discounts were obtained than hitherto.[8] The most important new building undertaken while Seymour was in office was the Public Record Office. He required that those invited to tender should include all builders known to be fully competent to execute the work, except any who had failed in former contracts. He was also concerned that the stone for the building should be inspected on delivery, and that the iron girders should be satisfactorily tested; he called for an opinion from De la Beche, the geologist, on the use of newly-quarried stone; and contemplated altering the windows in order to save money.[9] Sir Benjamin Hall, a trenchant critic, remarked after Seymour had been in office for nearly a year, that 'He had never seen a public officer more anxious to prevent the continuance of the abuses which existed,

---

[1] Works 1/36, pp. 57–8 (7 December 1850).
[2] *Ibid.* p. 50 (6 December 1850).   [3] *Ibid.* p. 17 (19 November 1850).
[4] Works 1/37, pp. 19 (17 October), 168–71 (15 November 1851).
[5] RA, C 81/122, Seymour to Prince Albert, 8 February 1851.
[6] Works 1/37, pp. 27–8 (5 August 1851). See p. 537.
[7] E.g. by R. V. Smith, in the select committee on miscellaneous expenditure, 1848 (*Parl. Pap.* 1847–8 (543) xviii, pt. I, q. 275).   [8] Works 1/36, pp. 228–9.   [9] Works 12/64/3, ff. 62–3.

or more anxious to remedy them'.[1] But Hall was, like Seymour, a critic of Chadwick and the General Board of Health, and his evidence was not, perhaps, entirely impartial. Seymour was however appointed in the expectation that legislation pending would relieve him of health matters. We must now examine the course of that business.

When, after its second session, the Duncan committee proved unable to agree on a full report, ministers were left free to choose their own course. Without further inquiry they determined on a bill to separate the Woods from the Works.[2] The measure appears to have owed its shape to Hayter, from 1850 joint Secretary to the Treasury.[3] It provided for twin boards of three commissioners to preside over the two departments, but the First Commissioner of Woods was not to sit in Parliament, while the Board of Works was to have a parliamentary commissioner. Although both Boards were made subordinate to the Treasury, the problem of authority was not entirely resolved: the First Commissioner might act alone in certain cases, but so might two commissioners. Prince Albert's proposal for a larger board, to contain architects and artists as well as administrators, was rejected by Hayter.[4]

Thus the Whig experiment was confessed a failure. That experiment had been based on a notion of economy through fusion: that one set of men might discharge multitudinous functions more cheaply than a distinct set for each function. But fusion had degenerated into confusion. Improvements were charged on the Land Revenue, and to some extent escaped parliamentary observation. This ran counter to the strong tide for greater accountability to Parliament, and eventually had to yield to it. 'A large part of the expenditure . . . was practically exempt from parliamentary control', remarked the chairman of the miscellaneous expenditure committee of 1848.[5] No efficient control was exercised over public building, argued another; the Commissioners of Woods and Works had not discharged their duties and ought to be abolished.[6] 'Some functionary', thought the former First Commissioner, Lord Lincoln, might be appointed 'who should have the superintendence of the New Houses of Parliament, and of any public buildings of a large character which the State might undertake'.[7] To this clamour the government was ready to yield. In proposing his Woods and Works bill on 22 February 1850, Russell remarked that a First Commissioner of Works in Parliament would be able 'to exercise a control over public works which have of late years occasioned very considerable expense, and which certainly deserve being made a special object of attention on the part of a Minister of the Crown'; public works should not be paid for out of the Land Revenue but should be brought before Parliament, for they were 'large public questions' often leading to debate in the Commons.[8]

This remained a constant theme during that session. Persistent voices declared that the government must bear responsibility for expenditure on the New Houses of Parliament for instance: the work should be placed under one man. As O'Brien Stafford complained, 'If the blame was charged on Mr. Barry, he charged it upon a

[1] *Parl. Deb.* 3rd ser. cxvi, 1262.   [2] *Parl. Pap.* 1850 (77), viii.
[3] See RA, C 81/55, memorandum by Hayter.   [4] *Ibid.* C 81/52, 55.
[5] *Parl. Deb.* 3rd ser. ci, 93 (11 August 1848); similarly, Bowring (*ibid.* 95).
[6] *Ibid.* xcv, 1334, 1404 (B. Osborne, 16 and 17 December 1847).
[7] *Ibid.* xcvii, 146 (2 March 1848).   [8] *Ibid.* cviii, 1318.

Committee, the Committee charged it upon another Committee, both the Committees put it upon the Woods and Forests, the Woods and Forests charged it on the Government, and the Government upon [the] House'.[1] Hume declared that 'He did not wish to see any more public buildings, unless there was to be a responsible person to guard against any increase of expenditure'. Disraeli complained that no one defined what responsibility meant, but clouded a pertinent criticism with a flight of fancy in which he suggested that if the government would contemplate the possibility of hanging an architect, it would put a stop to blunders.[2]

The desire for a reform of the system under which public works were managed in England was widespread, even if the criticisms were not well-informed. William Archer Shee, writing in his diary about the Wellington Statue, for which the government were not really responsible, remarked: 'What a pity it is that every public work . . . is invariably a job, and that whatever precautions are apparently, or at least nominally, taken, whenever a monument is to be erected, to secure its being entrusted to skilful hands, the intrigues of would-be connoisseurs, or of the powerful friends of third-rate artists, are sure to triumph'.[3] *The Builder*, as one might expect, focussed its criticism rather on the cheese-paring spirit of the Commons:

> If some of our economical legislators would bestow more attention in securing to our national works the utmost completeness of design in the first instance, and then address themselves to reducing the estimates to the lowest cost compatible with the carrying out of this principle, the public would have less reason to complain of the misapplication of the funds devoted to such purposes.[4]

With the Duncan committee's report stimulating the movement for reform, *The Builder* remarked: 'It is morally impossible these works can be properly carried on by the present scheme of superintendence. The limited powers (to go no farther) of the Office of Woods, makes it wholly inefficient; it is quite sufficient that department should take charge of public buildings when completed.' *The Builder's* solution was to create a commission to supervise the erection of public buildings sanctioned by Parliament, financed by public loans to be repaid over a lengthy period.[5]

There were, then, two main lines of criticism: that there was a lack of a person or body on which responsibility might be fixed; that there was a lack of sufficient control by Parliament. The first arose more especially from the business of the New Houses, but as we have seen had been a cry of reformers and critics for many years under differing systems. There was, as Disraeli pointed out, confusion about the meaning of 'responsibility'. What disgruntled M.P.s called for was a minister who would be responsible for both the expense and design of public buildings and who would answer for any failure by the loss of his office. But this theory of ministerial responsibility was really rooted in a tradition of departmental independence older than that of the contemporary system of cabinet government. The Office of Works was a minor department more or less under the control of the Treasury. It was the

---

[1] *Ibid.* cxiii, 728–9 (2 August 1850).
[2] *Ibid.* 270, 738. See also the debate of 2 August 1850 generally.
[3] W. A. Shee, *My Contemporaries 1830–1870* (1893), p. 139. See p. 494 below.
[4] *Builder* viii (1850), pp. 258–9.   [5] *Builder*, viii (1850), p. 52.

Treasury that decided whether major works should be undertaken and how much money should be devoted to them. A minister of works could not make much headway against an unsympathetic Chancellor of the Exchequer; the scale of a work was not really for him to determine. Nor should he be accountable for disputatious questions of taste. These matters were, on the other hand, hardly of sufficient importance for a Chancellor of the Exchequer to stake his fate upon. So the experiment of a minister of works was not necessarily the best solution to the problem, and in the 1860s there were proposals for taking the Works out of politics by the appointment of a permanent commissioner, an expert in the arts; but this notion, too, was dropped after Layard's unsuccessful period in office. However, in the 1850s the demand for an aunt sally in Parliament was insistent and was provided for in the bills of 1850 and 1851. This accorded with the general tendency in the government as well as in the parliaments of this period to prefer individual responsibility to the security supposedly afforded by boards.[1] The advantages possessed by a board as a means of checking improper proceedings were now more conveniently supplied 'in the legislature, as to the principles of management; in the Treasury, as to the observance of these principles, and in the Audit Office, as to . . . expenditure'.[2]

The question of parliamentary control was more difficult: such control was largely an illusion, at any rate in the sense understood by Hume, Osborne and their associates. As Seymour, an experienced committee-man, put it: 'if there was one principle more clear than another . . . it was that the House might lay down rules, establish good principles, find out former difficulties, warn them from those difficulties in future, lay down a general guide for the conduct of any department, but could not exercise any effective control over the expenses'.[3] It would be fallacious if every minute expenditure for the repair of a farmhouse were submitted for Parliament's approval. The true principle that had to be established was that of accountability to Parliament, and this was asserted by the Act of 1851 with its provision for laying detailed accounts before the two Houses within a year.[4]

That lack of control over expenditure was due in some measure to confusion of functions was evident. But critics who, like Lord Duncan and Lord John Russell, ascribed the trouble to the consolidation of offices in 1832 were scoring no bull's-eye. The real error had been made in 1811, when the Commissioners of Woods and Forests became also the New Street Commissioners. For it was chiefly metropolitan improvements that had overwhelmed the Land Revenue. The building of palaces had been charged on the Land Revenue by Act even before the fusion of Works and Woods, which clearly made little difference in that respect.[5] Indeed the Department of Works discharged its limited functions with a high degree of success. The smaller post-1832 establishment was quite as efficient as Stephenson's independent régime; and this we may ascribe to private practice being thenceforth forbidden to government officers, the adoption of contracting in gross, and the employment of direct labour. Financial comparisons are particularly difficult because of the gradual removal of

---

[1] See *Parl. Pap.* 1860 (483) ix, evidence of W. C. Temple; and Willson, 'Ministries and Boards', *loc. cit.*
[2] *Parl. Pap.* 1847–8 (538) xxiv, q. 41.
[3] *Parl. Deb.* 3rd ser. cxiv, 1256–62 (11 March 1851).   [4] 14 & 15 Vict. cap. 42.
[5] E.g. the rebuilding of Buckingham Palace, 6 Geo. IV. cap. 77, 10 Geo. IV. cap. 50.

duties on building materials, as well as fluctuations in wages and prices.[1] But there can be little doubt that the Works Department gave Parliament value for money. The great failures of the day lay outside the department's competence: the real criticism of the 1832 annexation must be that it left the department too small to undertake the great public works of the 1830s and 40s, even had the climate of opinion favoured their being executed by government rather than by private architects.

During the summer of 1850 Milne, by then incapable of discharging his duty, retired in fulfilment of the wish he had expressed nearly two years before.[2] In his place Russell appointed an old friend, Thomas Francis Kennedy (1788–1879), an old Whig hack who had (like Phineas Finn) exchanged political office for the greater security of a permanent official post in Ireland.[3] Kennedy had already revealed a capacity for controversy, over the cultivation of potatoes in Phoenix Park,[4] a capacity that was to land him in trouble culminating in his dismissal in 1854.[5] When problems chiefly concerning the legal department induced Lord Seymour to ask the Treasury to institute a departmental inquiry in the late summer of 1850 only Gore among the commissioners had much experience, and was inevitably selected as the departmental representative to serve with Hayter and Spearman, a former assistant secretary of the Treasury who has appeared already in connection with the inquiries into Nash's work at Buckingham Palace.[6]

Given Gore's position and natural bias, and the known connection between him and Hayter, it was not surprising that Carlisle's forecast that any inquiry would recommend strengthening the First Commissioner's hand should be falsified. The committee, on the contrary, praised

> The arrangements of Lord Bessborough [Duncannon], by which an entire change was ultimately made . . . [in the conduct of the Office] and greater labour and more direct responsibility devolved upon the Junior Commissioners, by requiring each of them himself to superintend and direct an important branch of business specially assigned to each Commissioner, [which] placed the Board itself upon a far more advantageous footing for the public interest because it secured the direct consideration of all matters of business in the office by all those who are at the head of it, and who are responsible by law for the management of the department.[7]

---

[1] The duties on various building materials were affected by the tariffs of 1842 and 1845; the glass excise was abolished in 1845, and that on bricks in 1850.

[2] *Parl. Deb.* cxviii, 183–4. The delay had been so that he might 'bear any charge that might be made against him'. Prince Albert thought his retirement would be 'a great advantage' (RA, C 17/75, the Prince to Lord J. Russell, 7 July 1850).

[3] M.P., Ayr, 1818–34; junior lord of the Treasury 1832–4; paymaster of Irish Civil Services 1837–50; Commissioner of Woods etc. 1850–4. Russell referred to him in 1854 as 'a man whom I have known all my life— whose integrity and veracity I highly respect—& whom I placed in what I thought was a permanent office' (B.M. Add. MS. 44291, ff. 202–5, cited Conacher, *The Aberdeen Coalition 1852–1855*, 1968, pp. 377–82).

[4] B.M. Add. MS. 40519, ff. 118–159.

[5] See Conacher, *loc. cit.* and the references there given. Some idea of Kennedy's character is given in a letter from an old friend, Lord Dunfermline, to Lord John Russell, 31 October 1854: ' . . . He may have been too unbending in enforcing what he thought was right, he may have been too hasty in temper, his manner may not have been conciliatory, but that he has ever been activated by any other motives than an honest and earnest desire to do his duty to the public, I know to be impossible' (quoted, Conacher, *loc. cit.*).

[6] See p. 138 above. Spearman had retired on account of ill-health in 1840, but in 1850 returned to the public service as secretary and comptroller of the National Debt Office.

[7] *Parl. Pap.* 1852 (522) liii, p. 5.

This was a salvo aimed at the Lincoln–Carlisle doctrine that the parliamentary commissioner should control the office. Stressing the co-ordinate authority of the commissioners, the committee's report recommended that the collective responsibility of the board should be emphasized and strengthened by substituting a 'secretary to the board' for the 'anomalous' office of secretary to the Chief Commissioner held by Philipps. Indeed, much of the report may be read as an attack on that hitherto highly-praised officer. Because he was also secretary of the Metropolitan Improvements Commission, his attention, it was alleged, must, despite his assiduity, have been 'largely withdrawn' from the Office of Woods and Works. The endeavours to supply the want of a secretary had removed business from its proper channels and an anomalous and inconvenient course had been taken.[1]

As the bill for dividing the Woods from the Works had been withdrawn, the committee devised an establishment scale that could apply to either a united or a divided office. All payments and receipts relating to parliamentary grants should be transferred to the Paymaster-General's office. In this way, and by consolidation of departments and the abolition of the posts of accountant and librarian, ten out of a staff of 54 might be dispensed with, at a saving of about £3000 per annum. All staff would be expected to work such hours as necessary without extra pay, and the strictest control should be exercised over the use of temporary writing-clerks. Officers should never be promoted merely on grounds of length of service, and none had a title to continued employment if he were inefficient or incapable of giving the services for which he was paid. The report also examined the legal branch, and recommended that the Board's solicitors should be replaced by full-time salaried officers at a saving of about £1800 per annum.

It was late in March 1851 before the committee finished its task: meanwhile the government had been overtaken by events. Lord Duncan carried against it (by a single vote) on 11 March a motion that all expenses of the Woods and Forests should be submitted as preliminary estimates to the Commons.[2] 'If all the votes are to be submitted to Parliament', wrote Russell to the Queen, 'a Minister must be present to explain and defend them.'[3] The Queen replied forthrightly: 'It would never do to transfer the Administration of the Crown Property from 3 Commissioners who already are found too many for executive purposes, to 656 . . . The Queen had always regretted that the Bill introduced last year was not vigorously proceeded with.'[4] The following day Russell informed her that he was adopting her suggestion, and re-introducing the previous year's bill with some changes.[5] To the disappointment of those who would adduce this as an example of the Queen's political influence, it must be pointed out that Seymour himself had already moved, during the debate on Duncan's motion, an amendment to this effect, a step he would scarcely have taken without consulting his seniors.[6]

It was as if the Treasury committee had never sat: where the bill of 1850 was

---

[1] The implication is that the First Commissioner had conducted official business through a subordinate officer.
[2] *Parl. Deb.* 3rd ser. cxiv, 1242 ff. See Malmesbury, *Memoirs of an ex-Minister* (1884) i, p. 281.
[3] RA, C 81/127, Lord John Russell to the Queen, 12 March 1851.
[4] *Ibid.* 129, 12 March 1851.   [5] *Ibid.* 132, 13 March 1851.
[6] *Parl. Deb.* 3rd ser. cxiv, 1256–62 (11 March 1851).

changed, the trend was contrary to their report. Instead of three Commissioners of Woods, Forests and Land Revenues, and three of Public Works, the First Commissioner was to become First Commissioner of Works, unsaddled with other than ex-officio colleagues forming a nominal Board which might act during a vacancy.[1] The two junior commissioners were to take over the administration of Crown Lands, but the Treasury was empowered to assign them separate duties. Provision was even made for replacing them with a surveyor general and deputy surveyor general (when death or retirement should have relieved the Treasury of the possibility of a demand for compensation for loss of office).[2] Changes made during the bill's progress were to increase the responsibility of both departments to Parliament, though an attempt by Duncan to enforce on the government the principle of his resolution was defeated by 99 votes to 73.[3] The Act was to come into force on 10 October 1851.

Thus the Office of Works became a ministry, directly responsible to Parliament. Its expenditure continued to rise, its responsibilities to grow, and perhaps (one might venture to add) the power of its permanent officials to increase as First Commissioner after First Commissioner hastened up the ladder of ministerial promotion or was relegated to the back benches. The King's Works had truly come to an end. Their history presents a microcosm of the history of government in England: institutionalization, then escape from the royal household, accompanied by even wider responsibilities, under the suspicious gaze of a Parliament that finally insisted on taking full control for itself. But the final metamorphosis—from an office into a ministry—constitutes a change of nature that puts a term to this history.

[1] *Parl. Pap.* 1851 (307), (417), (501) vi; *Parl. Deb.* 3rd ser. cxviii, 179–80.
[2] *Parl. Deb.* 3rd ser. cxviii, 180–1.   [3] *Ibid.* 184–8.

Chapter X

THE OFFICE OF WORKS
IN SCOTLAND

PUBLIC buildings in Scotland in the eighteenth century were under the control of the Scottish Court of Exchequer. They included the Palace of Holyroodhouse and the great churches (some ruinous) which had passed to the Crown on the abolition of episcopacy in 1690.[1] The post of Master of Works, once held by Sir William Bruce, had long been a sinecure, and the old organisation of the royal works in Scotland had fallen into abeyance. But in 1808 a leading Edinburgh architect, Robert Reid (1776–1856), who was then engaged in building the Law Courts in Parliament Square, obtained a commission authorising him to use the title of 'King's Architect and Surveyor in Scotland'.[2] The appointment was purely honorary and conferred no salary on its holder. Reid was, however, determined to make it a reality, and when the English Surveyor General of Works, Col. Stephenson, was in Edinburgh in 1821 in connection with George IV's visit, Reid persuaded him that

> it would be attended with beneficial consequences if an Office of Works was established in Scotland on principles similar to the Office of Works in London, by which means one regular and efficient system of superintendence and control would be enforced in all matters of Building and Repair, not only of the Royal Palaces and other Buildings the property of the Crown in Scotland, but likewise of the several Buildings occupied by the Courts of Justice, and all the Buildings belonging to the Civil department connected with the receipt and management of the Public Revenue.[3]

No immediate action was taken, but when the titular Master of Works, James Brodie of Brodie, died in January 1824, Reid succeeded in getting that office merged with his own. As 'sole Master of our Works and General Inspector and Overseer and Architect and Surveyor of all our Palaces and Public Buildings of whatever kind in Scotland', he was to receive a salary of £200 a year.[4] Meanwhile, Stephenson had made a report to the Treasury which in 1827 resulted in the decision to put public works in Scotland on a new footing: the Treasury directed Stephenson to

---

[1] These included the cathedrals of St. Giles at Edinburgh, Glasgow, Kirkwall, Elgin and St. Andrew's, and the abbeys of Arbroath and Dunfermline, as well as some lesser churches.

[2] Register House, Edinburgh, Register of the Privy Seal, xiii, p. 313.

[3] Register House, E. 329/2, ff. 213–8.

[4] Register House, E. 313/15, p. 246. Reid had a rival in the person of the architect James Gillespie (Graham), for whose pretensions to the post see National Library of Scotland, MS. 351, ff. 102–3 and MS. 1056, f. 141.

draw up a code of instructions for a Scottish Office of Works, established by royal warrant in January 1827. Reid, 'a man of excellent character, and whose talents and professional qualifications are fully equal to a very efficient discharge of the several duties of [his] station', was to superintend and control all repairs to Crown property, the Register House, Courts of Justice and Exchequer Court in Edinburgh, and all premises occupied by the revenue or other public departments. His salary was fixed at £500 a year, back-dated to 1824. To assist him provision was made for two professional clerks and a junior clerk or messenger.[1] An office was provided in Parliament Square.

This establishment remained independent of the English Office of Works until January 1831, when Lord Grey's administration decided that, as the King had placed the hereditary revenues of the Crown in Scotland at Parliament's disposal, the expenses of the Scottish Works should be voted by Parliament. The Treasury accordingly placed Reid's department under Stephenson, directing him to provide for it in his annual estimates.[2] The consequential arrangements were still under consideration when the Office of Works was annexed to the Woods and Forests.[3] The problems involved in uniting these two important offices pushed consideration of Scottish affairs into the background. Although Reid's salary was scrutinized, no immediate changes were made.[4]

The new Scottish department inherited several major undertakings: a general repair of Holyroodhouse costing some £25,000 between 1824 and 1835; extensive additions to the Courts of Justice (£66,000, 1828–37); and the 'repairing and embellishing' of St. Giles' Cathedral (£10,000, 1829–32).[5] Edinburgh University having already received £130,000 from government, it did not share in the £30,000 granted from the hereditary revenues for buildings at the Scottish universities in 1826.[6] Glasgow had sufficient endowments, so it was understood that this grant was to be divided between St. Andrews, where Reid's additions and repairs in 1829–31 amounted to some £13,000, and Aberdeen, where discussions about uniting King's and Marischal Colleges deferred any action.[7] King's was repaired with a contribution from the Privy Purse, but Marischal was said by the royal commission on the universities that reported in 1831 to be 'in the most ruinous condition . . . even dangerous'. Yet not till 1834 was Reid sent to Aberdeen, where he produced estimates of £41,850 for rebuilding Marischal College. But his works at St. Andrews were said not to have increased his reputation, and as the Treasury was not inclined to insist on such expensive plans, those of a local architect, Archibald Simpson, were utilised instead. Simpson's Tudor Gothic buildings were erected in 1836–41, the

---

[1] Register House E. 329/1, ff. 1–5; P.R.O. Works 1/13, pp. 243–52, 283–6; 1/14, pp. 372, 479–90; 1/18, pp. 330 ff.; T. 1/4381, ff. 3007/25, 6733/25, 19400/26, 184787/32.

[2] Register House, E. 329/1, ff. 203–4; P.R.O. Works 1/18, pp. 330 ff.; Works 4/30, pp. 452, 458.

[3] Works 1/18, p. 502.

[4] Register House, E. 329/1, ff. 204, 213–18.

[5] T. 1/4381, f. 3935/33. The Courts of Justice were extended under the Act 6 Geo. IV cap. 86. Reid's additions to the Register House under the Acts 3 Geo. IV, cap. 62 and 7 and 8 Geo. IV cap. 46 were completed in 1830 at a cost of £38,000 paid from fees (*ibid.*). The restoration of Holyroodhouse was hampered by the hereditary interests of the Duke of Hamilton and Lord Haddington: see Lord Broughton, *Recollections of a long life*, v (1911) p. 13. For designs see P.R.O. MR 763 (Courts of Justice), MPD 193 (St. Giles').

[6] See D. B. Horn, 'The Building of the Old Quad, 1767–1841', *Univ. of Edinburgh Jnl.*, 1968, pp. 309–21; 1969. pp. 39–52; and Sir A. Grant, *The Story of the University of Edinburgh* (1884).

[7] *Parl. Pap.* 1835 (326) xxxviii; 1844 (484) xxxiii; Works 1/20, p. 281; 1/21, pp. 1–3.

government grant amounting with accumulated interest to nearly £21,000 out of a cost of £30,000.[1] In 1844 a further sum of £6000 was voted for completing the rebuilding of the United College at St. Andrews on the basis of Reid's plans, modified by William Nixon.[2]

In November 1832 Reid's complaints of the complexity of his accounts brought the matter under consideration. Although the buildings of the Scottish revenue departments had been placed in Reid's care in 1827 some of the boards in London had objected to control by the Scottish Barons of the Exchequer, so that repairs were only undertaken at the request of the local chief officers, authorised by the boards in London. Arrangements were now made with the Commissioners of Stamps and Taxes and the Postmaster General to put repairs in their Edinburgh departments under Reid's superintendence.[3]

Reid did not, however, get control of all public works in the Scottish capital. The building of the church known as Tolbooth St. John's is a case in point. The General Assembly of the Church of Scotland was customarily held in a part of St. Giles' Cathedral: in 1832-3 a hall was fitted up in the south aisle for sessions of the Assembly, which met meanwhile in the Tron Church. Although £3000 were spent on this adaptation, it proved unsatisfactory, and in 1834 it was suggested that a new church and sessions hall should be built in the city.[4] The government agreed to obtain a vote of £10,000, the city of Edinburgh finding whatever further sums might be necessary, and in 1839 plans by James Gillespie Graham (1777–1855) were accepted. The contract was awarded to David Lind at £12,896, and the building was completed in 1843. In its later stages the work ran into difficulties, and the corporation stubbornly refused to increase their contribution. The celebrated Dr. D. B. Reid was called in to design a heating and ventilating system.[5]

The *ad hoc* employment of an independent architect probably influenced a Treasury proposal for the abolition of Robert Reid's office. The ordinary work of the department could, it was claimed, be conducted by an 'active clerk of the works', while 'the services of the most eminent architects' could 'at all times be commanded for works that may render their aid necessary'. The Commissioners of Woods and Works urged that a man of superior professional training was needed at Edinburgh, but Melbourne's administration was in search of any savings it could devise and in 1837 had cast its eye on the Scottish Office: in May 1839 it determined, despite the Commissioners' opinion, to abolish the Scottish Office of Works from the end of the financial year. Reid, now aged 64, was retired on full pay and William Nixon was brought from Phoenix Park to head the reduced establishment.[6]

---

[1] *Parl. Pap.* 1831 (310) xii, p. 362; 1835 (326) xxxviii; 1844 (484) xxxiii; R. S. Rait, *The University of Aberdeen* (Aberdeen, 1895), pp. 314–16; Works 1/21, pp. 18, 97; 1/24, p. 558; 2/1, pp. 142, 165; 2/3, pp. 6, 39; P.R.O., MPD 190.

[2] *Parl. Pap.* 1844 (484) xxxiii; R. G. Cant, *The College of St. Salvator* (1950), pp. 216–19.

[3] Works 1/21, pp. 36–7, 71, 98, 110; T. 1/4381, f. 3935/33.

[4] T. 1/4381, f. 3935/33; T.1/3696; Works 1/21, pp. 87, 106, 158, 438, 458, 465.

[5] Works 1/24, pp. 1–2, 13, 127, 154, 211, 218–9, 337, 509, 555; 1/25, pp. 28, 467–8, 523–4; 1/26, pp. 42, 142, 152–3, 192–3, 214, 234, 240–6, 256, 282, 285, 291, 318, 326, 346, 354–6, 498, 501; 2/2, pp. 360, 362,423; 2/3, pp. 40, 50, 82–4, 96, 124, 127, 144, 226, 245, 264–5, 270, 280, 285, 290, 308, 353, 361, 399, 405.

[6] T. 1/4381, ff. 20630/37, 22718/37, 8035/39, 16925/39; Works 1/23, p. 322; 1/24, pp. 21, 175; 2/2, pp. 365, 350, 396; 2/6, pp. 347–9. Nixon was probably a son of William Nixon, clerk of works at Brighton, and later at Buckingham House under Nash (see p. 267).

His duties proved more extensive than the Treasury had anticipated, and in 1846 his salary was increased from £200 to £400 a year. He was called upon to give occasional supervision to the building of new post offices, to report on the works at Marischal College, to examine Glasgow Cathedral, and to take charge of the Parliament Square buildings at Edinburgh.[1] The law courts required additional accommodation; and although when the Queen stayed at Holyroodhouse in 1842 the furniture clerk, Cox, was sent from London to help in furnishing the state rooms, the 'progressive increase of business' in the department by then had made additional help essential. Nixon was permitted to employ an extra clerk at 30s. a week. He found it difficult to engage a professional man on such terms, and the Treasury was induced to improve the offer.[2] In 1843 the Glasgow Post Office was placed under Nixon, the Board approving the Post Master General's proposal 'as the Railway affords such facilities for travelling between Edinburgh and Glasgow'.[3] Meanwhile in the capital the nave of St. Giles' was fitted up as a parish church to designs by Thomas Brown at a cost of £1121.[4] Repairs were also required at most of the former cathedrals. At Glasgow some extensive works of restoration were carried out from 1840 onwards under the direction of Edward Blore.[5] Elgin required buttressing in 1843, and in 1845 the Duke of Sutherland effectually brought the claims of Kirkwall before the First Commissioner.[6] Although maintenance and repairs formed its staple, the Scottish branch also superintended occasional new works, such as the post office at Aberdeen, four additional court rooms for the Lords Ordinary at Edinburgh, and the prison at Perth.[7] When Nixon died in 1848, he was succeeded by Robert Matheson, who had started as a junior assistant to Reid in 1828, and who remained in charge at Edinburgh when the Office of Works recovered its independence in 1851.[8]

---

[1] Works 1/24, pp. 220, 296, 468, 560; 1/25, pp. 1, 27, 72, 101; 1/26, p. 433.
[2] Works 1/25, pp. 293, 356, 379, 415, 477, 490; 2/3, pp. 355, 386, 405, 462, 564, 608.
[3] Works 1/26, pp. 149–50.   [4] Works 2/3, pp. 258, 266, 269, 281, 417, 420, 434, 455, 519.
[5] Works 1/24, pp. 122, 160–1, 220, 296, 463, 467, 486, 512, 531, 560; 1/25, pp. 1, 27, 415, 422, 433; 1/26, pp. 427, 463, 512; 2/2, pp. 52, 69, 70–1, 83–7, 108, 122, 167; 2/3, pp. 79, 394. For further details of this complicated and controversial restoration, whose history goes back to 1835, see T. Bonnar, *Biographical Sketch of George Meikle Kemp* (1892), pp. 60–80, and E. L. G. Stones, 'Notes on Glasgow Cathedral', *Innes Review* xxxi (1970).
[6] Works 1/26, p. 198; B.M. Add. MS. 40568, ff. 390, 392, 394–5; 40572, f. 86.
[7] Crest 25/63; Works 1/26, p. 436; 2/3, p. 432.
[8] T. 1/4381, ff. 16925/39, 2168/40; *Royal Kalendar*, 1852; Works 1/24, pp. 390, 411.

PART II

WORKS IN PROGRESS
1782–1851

I. THE ROYAL PALACES AND OTHER RESIDENCES

ASCOT HEATH, ROYAL RACE-STAND

THE Ascot race-meeting was an annual event in George IV's calendar and the royal stand at the race course was built for him by Nash in 1822 at a cost to the Land Revenue of £5813.[1] It was 'so constructed as to enable every person in it to see the horses during the whole time of running'.[2] Repairs were soon needed, and in 1824–6 were mingled with alterations at a cost of nearly £1200. One roof was blown off by a storm; a floor for spectators was laid over a lead flat, making alterations necessary to the parapets and to the shutters which when raised formed a parapet.[3] Further alterations were carried out in 1828, including a ladies' room and a wider stair with a lower rise for the King.[4] For Queen Victoria a refreshment room and covered entrance were added in 1840, costing £487.[5] Further alterations were made in the 1860s and in 1873. A new stand was built for King Edward VII.[6]

Ascot Heath also accommodated George IV's hunting dogs. The royal kennels required frequent repair. In 1829 stone paving was substituted for wooden, which

Fig. 1. The Ascot Race Stand designed for George IV by John Nash
(from a contemporary engraving).

[1] Works 5/119, f. 2. See J. Summerson, *John Nash* (1935), pp. 231–2. [2] *Reading Mercury*, 3 June 1822.
[3] Works 1/12, pp. 331, 334, 339, 370; 1/14, pp. 159, 412, 431, 504, 508; 5/109.
[4] Works 1/16, pp. 165, 248, 317. Alterations in 1827 and 1828 cost some £2200 (Crest 35/5).
[5] Works 1/24, p. 206 (estimate £450), 440; 2/2, pp. 407, 445.
[6] Crest 35/14, 35/16 (with plans); MPE 1454.

was thought to make the dogs lame.[1] New kennels were built in the Home Park in 1840–1.[2] The stables on the Heath were rebuilt in 1840–2 at the expense of the Land Revenue.[3]

BAGSHOT PARK, SURREY

THE Duke of Gloucester held this house as Ranger of the park. 'The House is comfort itself', wrote his wife (a daughter of George III) a few weeks after her marriage in July 1816. 'Tho' not large, it is convenient', was Queen Charlotte's comment. But its smallness proved a drawback: 'From the Duke's appartments and mine being so compleat people who don't know the House run away with the idea that it is a larger house', the Duchess told the Regent. '*Now* the fact is barring *our rooms* there is not another place in the House fit to be seen and those Gentlemen who belong to the Duke are lodged in the garrets'. The Duke was unwilling to put the government to expense, so the Duchess entreated her brother to 'represent their *real situation* to Lord Liverpool'.[4]

To inconvenience were added defective drains and faltering foundations; water was standing under the floors of some of the lower rooms. Nash prepared a plan, improved by the Regent himself, to provide every comfort the Duchess could wish.[5] Alterations were authorised in June 1818 on an estimate of £4000. Matthew, the Windsor Clerk of the Works, was warned to give 'the most strict attention' to the works to ensure that 'nothing be done but what was comprised in the Estimate', which must 'be not on any Account exceeded'.[6] Despite such categorical instructions, 'unavoidable expense' was incurred, and further works ordered by the Duke to a total of £7523. The Duke agreed to contribute £1200, but for the remainder of the deficiency the tradesmen vainly petitioned the government in 1820, 1821 and 1822. Only when one of them began proceedings against Matthew in 1826 did the Treasury authorise paying some £2200.[7]

No further expenditure was incurred until 1836, when the widowed Duchess went to visit her relations in Germany, and Bagshot was put in repair at a cost of £3857.[8] In 1841 she offered to surrender it to the Duchess of Kent, who preferred Frogmore.[9] Only such repairs 'as are essentially necessary for keeping the premises wind and water tight' were allowed after the Duchess moved to White Lodge, Richmond Park, in 1847. In 1848 one of Prince Albert's equerries was allowed to live in the house, the principal rooms on the upper floor being retained for the Queen's use when accompanying the Prince for shooting or fishing. The equerry's family was attacked by fever, blamed on drains 'in a most imperfect state', which were accordingly reconstructed.[10] The house was demolished after the Prince's death.

---

[1] Works 1/9, p. 33; 1/17, pp. 248, 414; 5/108–111; 19/1/1.   [2] See p. 399.
[3] *Parl. Pap.* 1843 (343) xxx (£1200). Repairs and works on the Royal Stand and Kennels in the midsummer quarter, 1841, cost £1452 17s. 10d. (L.R.R.O. 2/10, p. 48).
[4] D. M. Stuart, *The Daughters of George III* (1939), pp. 240–2, quoting the Royal Archives.
[5] *Ibid.* p. 242; Works 1/7, p. 496.   [6] Works 1/9, p. 545 (3 November 1818).
[7] Works 1/10, pp. 89, 109, 134, 199, 512; 1/11, p. 132; 1/14, pp. 170–1, 200–1, 231–3, 251–2.
[8] Works 1/22, pp. 68, 100; 1/23, p. 164. The King had ordered some improvements in the course of the works, completed by August 1838, which caused a slight excess over the estimate.
[9] RA Z 480/83. See p. 326 below.
[10] Works 1/26, p. 25; 1/31, p. 437; 1/33, p. 330; 2/3, pp. 455, 475; 2/7, pp. 197–200, 204.

THE ROYAL PAVILION, BRIGHTON

GEORGE IV's most celebrated architectural extravaganza, the Royal Pavilion at Brighton, was begun long before his accession to the throne. It was moreover built almost entirely from his private funds, and under the direction of his own architects, first Holland, then Porden, followed by Nash and J. H. Good. Unlike Carlton House it was not even technically under Office of Works control until the accession of William IV. The construction and decoration of this 'marine pavilion', with its oriental domes and equally exotic interiors, therefore falls outside the scope of this *History*. However, in the confusion prevailing after Wyatt's death in 1813, Nash did in his official capacity carry out some alterations on the strength of an estimate of some £3000 submitted to the Treasury in April 1814, but never in fact approved. Protests by the unpaid workmen ultimately persuaded the Treasury to authorise payment in November 1817.[1] Although the King continued thereafter to bear the cost of maintaining the Pavilion, he insisted in 1823 that the stables should be repaired by the Office of Works.

> The stables [he told Lord Liverpool] must be immediately put into complete repair by the Board of Works. . . . The King desires that the whole of the repairs be completed in the space of ten weeks, which is quite practicable, and that no scaffolding of any kind be taken into the Lawn, because it is unnecessary. . . .
> The King again urges that there may be no delay in these repairs at the Stables and when once begun that it may be pressed on with the utmost expedition, as the King does not choose to have workmen for any time about the Palace.[2]

The work was entrusted to H. H. Seward, the Assistant Surveyor. He found that exterior and interior alike had suffered from not being painted, and that so much timber had been used in the construction that it was difficult to judge the extent of repairs necessary, but reported they would probably amount to £3500.[3] Seward supervised operations, assisted by Francis Edwards,[4] but as the buildings had not previously been under their charge they had to consult the royal clerk of the works, William Nixon, who provided a constant superintendence. The total cost, £7114, justified Seward's caution in putting forward his estimate.[5]

After his accession, William IV transferred the Pavilion to the care of the Office of Works.[6] Like others of his predecessor's palaces, it was not designed for a married sovereign, and the Queen's household immediately required additional accommodation. A first provision of £1000 was rapidly followed by a requisition for

---

[1] RA 33983, 34086; Works 1/7, pp. 477, 483. The history of the pavilion is told and the building described in H. D. Roberts, *History of the Royal Pavilion, Brighton* (1939), and C. Musgrave, *The Royal Pavilion* (1959).
[2] Works 1/12, p. 93 (3 Aug. 1823).   [3] *Ibid.* pp. 112–3, 120.
[4] 1784–1857; with Seward in Soane's office; see Colvin, *Dictionary*.   [5] Works 5/108.
[6] T. 1/3463, f. 12136/30, Treasury minute, 16 July 1830. This did not prevent his taking a close personal interest in additions and alterations to the building: his architect, Good, reported that 'during the whole of the reign of William the 4th, I had very frequent interviews with His Majesty . . . on the subject of various Plans, sometimes with Sir Benj: Stephenson, but most often alone' (Works 19/1/2, f. 520, 24 February 1851).

additional rooms for footmen over the larders (£450) and for stable servants over the stables (£150), as well as for reinstating fallen ceilings over the recesses in the music and dining rooms in wood instead of plaster (£160).[1] Expenditure on the Civil List account for 1830 amounted to nearly £2400.[2] More extensive works, chiefly to enlarge the stables and provide new north and south entrances, were estimated at £15,000, of which £7125 were required for 1831.[3] Designed by J. H. Good, employed as architect at the Pavilion by George IV since 1823, these were contracted to William Ranger at £2440 for the dormitories, built in 1831, and £3285 10s. for the south entrance lodge.[4] Ranger's further tender of £8998 for the north entrance, additional stable buildings and alterations at the house of Sir Herbert Taylor, the King's secretary, was accepted in April 1832.[5] These additions were mostly plain structures in brick and flint, except for the north lodge, which the King wanted to commemorate the foundation of the Pavilion by George IV, and which was therefore built in stone in an appropriate oriental style.[6] Current expenditure on the palace averaged over £2500 per annum between 1833 and 1839, falling to about £1600 per annum in 1839–47.[7] Queen Victoria, like George IV, found that it was excessively exposed to the populace, and in 1839 instructions were given that expenditure on the building was to be reduced: the outside should be merely kept in good repair and internal injury from dry rot be prevented.[8] Some additional expenditure was incurred for royal visits in 1842, principally by new ventilating arrangements contrived by Dr. D. B. Reid.[9]

Then the Queen found a more private marine retreat at Osborne, and it was determined to sell the pavilion in aid of the enlargement of Buckingham Palace. The furniture was removed in 1847 and the fixtures taken away in 1848, much of the material being applied to the fitting up of Blore's new east wing of Buckingham Palace.[10] Even George IV's marble baths were packed up, though the Lord Chamberlain's department failed to remove the cases before the Pavilion's sale to the Brighton

[1] Works 1/18, pp. 230 (2 September), 236 (20 September 1830); 19/1/2, f. 25 (21 September 1830).
[2] Works 5/111.   [3] Works 1/18, p. 272.
[4] Works 19/1/2, ff. 34, 35, 37; 1/18, pp. 511–12 (Ranger's account to 5 July 1831, including £2405 4s. for dormitories and £2064 for works on the south entrance lodge—carcass, roof, floors, plastering, mason's work, sashes, frames and plumber's work); 5/111 (total special expenditure to 10 October 1831, £6592 17s. 6d.). These were completed by 29 September 1831, when the Court returned (Roberts, *op. cit.* p. 163).
[5] Works 19/1/2, f. 50; 1/20, p. 13; Roberts, *op. cit.* p. 164. Additional special works in 1832 included alterations and repairs to Sir H. Taylor's house (£355), converting a mess kitchen to coach-houses (£151), and providing a carpenter's shop and engine house (£135) (Works 1/20, p. 15; L.R.R.O. 24/2, p. 35.)
[6] Good is said to have taken the design for this from a 'model prepared by the late Mr. Nash'; Good's original drawings were discovered in 1950 (Musgrave, p. 117). As early as August 1830 William IV had commanded that the Surveyor General should submit a design for an appropriate gateway 'bearing some emblematic or expressive Dedication thereof to His Late Majesty George the Fourth' (Works 19/1/2, f. 13). The total expenditure on these works is given by Roberts as £19,710 10s. (*op. cit.* p. 164); but the total payments to Ranger on his second contract recorded in the office accounts are £9930 15s. 8d. (L.R.R.O. 2/1–3), which with the sum paid on the first contract (n. 4 above) totals £16,523 13s. 2d. Fittings probably account for the difference. The Commissioners of Woods and Works submitted an estimate of £10,546 for completing the works on 10 April 1832, five days after the date of Ranger's tender of £8998, so it is clear that provision was made for some additional works, as well as architect's commission (Works 19/1/2, ff. 49, 50).
[7] L.R.R.O. 24/2–7; *Parl. Pap.* 1843 (343) xxx; 1851 (374) xxxi.
[8] Works 1/23, p. 419 (5 August 1839). See Musgrave, p. 122, on the lack of privacy.
[9] Reid's estimate was £300, to be shared between the Office of Woods and the Lord Chamberlain's department; his works cost £1097 18s. 1d. (Works 1/25, p. 534; 1/26, pp. 24, 74, 336). Another alteration at this time was in the flues to permit machine sweeping (Works 1/25, p. 506).
[10] See p. 291.

town commissioners for £50,000. The purchasers complained bitterly and with justice of the devastation wrought in the building.[1] The adjacent chapel royal, formed out of some assembly rooms, was as a consecrated building excluded from the sale, and was demolished in November–December 1848.[2]

BUCKINGHAM HOUSE

PURCHASED by George III in 1762 as a dower house for Queen Charlotte, Buckingham House became the London home of the royal family, and was considerably enlarged in the twenty years before 1782.[3] No major alterations were made in the following decade, during which expenditure on the palace averaged some £560 a year.[4] In 1792–9 this rose to £1760, partly because of the increasing domestic requirements of the royal family, partly because of the need for major repairs, such as the reconstruction of the roof of the north-east wing in 1799.[5] The principal alteration to the palace itself up to this time was the addition in 1791–2 of a building for a cold bath on the south front, under the direction of John Yenn, the official Clerk of Works.[6] In 1793 the colonnades were enclosed to form a 'commodious and dry' passage between the palace and its offices.[7]

More considerable alterations were made in the first years of the nineteenth century; for the eight years to 1807, expenditure averaged £3630 annually. The works began with the reconstruction of the great staircase. The old staircase, with its right-angled turns past two successive landings, gave way to a new one which rose in one flight from the centre of the hall and then divided for the second flight to the doorway of the Saloon. This, though the work of Wyatt, appears to have been based on an earlier project of Chambers.[8] The other internal alterations which followed included the provision in 1801 of a warm bath for the King and of a bedroom and library in 1805.[9] Additional offices and servants' rooms were constructed, of which the principal was a brick building for the accommodation of the pages, erected under Yenn's superintendence on the north side of the palace at a cost of over £1800 in 1801–2, and stuccoed in 1805.[10]

---

[1] Works 1/31, pp. 85, 277; 1/32, pp. 348, 358; 1/33, pp. 8, 32, 49, 145, 205, 272, 274, 339; 1/34, pp. 7, 310; 1/35, pp. 195, 281–3; 2/8, p. 76.
  [2] Works 1/34, pp. 1, 267; 1/35, pp. 416–8; 1/36, p. 16. £3000 was awarded to the Town Commissioners for this demolition, deducted from the previously agreed price of £53,000 for the Pavilion (Works 19/1/2, f. 554).   [3] See *History of the King's Works*, v.
  [4] The tradesmen's quarterly bills are bound up in yearly volumes, Works 5/72–103 (1783–1814). An abstract of totals of annual expenditure on the Queen's and other palaces is given in Works 19/25/1.
  [5] Works 5/78.
  [6] Works 5/81. Yenn was paid £20 for drawings, and for inspecting and measuring the work. A plan of the bath in Westminster Public Library (box 39, no. 28) differs in some respects from the description of the work executed.   [7] Works 6/22, f. 84.
  [8] Works 5/89; Pyne, *Royal Residences* (1819). A plan by Chambers in Westminster Public Library (box 39, no. 17), drawn prior to the building of the Prince of Wales's wing (1776), shows the staircase in the form executed by Wyatt.
  [9] Works 5/90, 94. In 1805 marble chimneypieces from the Great and Octagon Libraries were removed to Windsor.   [10] Works 5/91, 94; 6/23, ff. 155, 199v.

T

Although from 1808 to 1813 the only alterations were of a minor character, expenditure averaged £2260 annually. Writing to James Wyatt in 1813, John Yenn accounted for this on the grounds that

'repairs are always wanted and during the time of their [the Royal family] being in Town, continual orders are given for various works which must be done immediately, and which cannot be estimated for—viz. packing cases of all descriptions—occasional preparations and boxes for Her Majesty and Princesses—the Repairs in the Libraries and Bookbinders shop, the great expense in repairing and cleaning the windows of the royal apartments, the Libraries, Offices, Greenhouse, Riding House and stables, which on an average of three years amounts to £92 per annum—The expense attending the keeping the riding house, stables and greenhouse, and all the buildings and chain fence in the Garden, and the division of the flower garden for a Rick Yard, the garden, wall, gates and fences and garden seats have been very considerable; and I must observe a considerable repair has been done lately at the Stables and Offices at Pimlico now occupied by the Duke of York—Ordered by Mr. Stephenson. . . .'[1]

As much as £6287 was spent in 1814, when a general repair was undertaken. A timber girder over the saloon had to be trussed with iron plates, 'the end being quite rotted off the wall', and the roofs of the great staircase and of the library wing were similarly in need of repair. Externally, the upper cornice had to be renewed, and parts of the great cornice, work that continued into 1815.[2] Some of the old King's private rooms were fitted up as libraries at this time.[3]

Despite Soane's report in November 1816 that some of the outbuildings, 'originally formed in a temporary manner', were worn out and needed rebuilding 'in a more corrected plan',[4] no works of importance were undertaken until the general reconstruction of the palace in 1825. Maintenance and repairs however averaged over £1900 annually. In July 1821 it was reported that the roofs of the great staircase and drawing room were in a dangerous state, but after careful investigation Soane decided that no change had occurred since the repairs of 1814. 'No danger', he declared, 'exists from the state of the roof nor is any to be apprehended for years to come'.[5] At that point the palace was transferred to the charge of Nash,[6] who promptly reported that a new roof was needed, with new ceilings to the upstairs rooms. Furthermore, the timbers of the basement were rotten, the entablature of the Corinthian order had warped, the stone balustrade had decayed, and the roofs of the wings were in a bad state. Nash estimated the cost of repair at £15,000.[7] But by then George IV was contemplating a much more extensive rebuilding.

---

[1] Works 6/27, ff. 53ᵛ–55, Yenn to James Wyatt, 27 February 1813. The increased expenses also reflected rising prices, particularly that of timber. See pp. 86 ff. The annual totals given in Works 19/25/1 do not accurately indicate the work carried out 1810–13 because of delays in accounting and payment.
[2] Works 5/103; Soane Mus. Corr. xii G(2) 14.
[3] Works 5/103. In 1818–19 a small room next to the Great Library was fitted up for rare books (Works 1/7, pp. 345, 379); and in 1821 a gallery for the 'Library of the Great Room' was erected to Soane's design (Soane Mus. Corr. xii J. 13, and sketch, *ibid.* G(2) 4.).   [4] Soane Mus. Corr. xii. G(1) 1.
[5] *Ibid.* G(2) 6, 14, 15.   [6] See p. 112.   [7] Works 1/11, p. 97.

BUCKINGHAM PALACE

1. THE PALACE

SOON after Queen Charlotte's death in November 1818, the Prince Regent began to consider moving from Carlton House to the Queen's Palace, which was preferable both in situation and in condition. Lord Liverpool warned the Regent that building new state rooms would be unpopular, that Parliament could not be expected to grant any public money, and that funds could only come from the sale of the site of St. James's Palace. The sole hope of obtaining parliamentary approval would be for the Treasury to have complete control of the work.[1] The Prince complained that he had no fitting state residence, but agreed to defer any plan for enlarging Buckingham House. In June 1819, however, he reopened the matter. Lord Liverpool now declared that £150,000 was the 'utmost sum' that could be raised over a period of three years. If the estimate were more, application would have to be made to Parliament at the outset, for there would be 'insurmountable objection' to applying afterwards to Parliament to make good any deficiency: the choice lay between seeking parliamentary authority to sell Crown property to meet any expenditure above £150,000 and resolving 'to complete the whole arrangements (externally and internally) for that sum, without the interference of Parliament'.[2] A calculation of ways and means, evidently by Stephenson, allowed £150,000 and £50,000 for contingencies. The Office of Works was to supply £15,000 per annum for three years, the probable period of building, and the remainder was to be found by the sale of the site of St. James's, of the old materials of that and the Queen's Palace, and of the palace at Newmarket and Crown property in Scotland Yard and to the east of Carlton House.

The Regent told his advisers that £150,000 was 'altogether inadequate' for converting the Queen's House into a state palace. Nearly half a million would be needed—'for the Building from 150,000 to 200,000—for fitting up Fixtures and internal decorations the like sum—for Furniture £100,000. The whole expense may probably be kept within £400,000 but it will be safer to reckon upon £450,000.' He asked Lord Liverpool to settle in Cabinet the arrangements for bringing the subject before the Commons, regretting that this necessity would put off any improvement until the following year.[3] Nothing was in fact done for two years:[4] then, on 12 July 1821, the King commanded Stephenson to furnish Nash with all plans relating to the Queen's Palace.[5] Soane, directing repairs there,[6] wrote in alarm to Stephenson asking him to 'represent to the King' that it was in his department, and persistently

---

[1] C. D. Yonge, *Life and Administration of . . . 2nd Earl of Liverpool* (1868) ii, p. 402.
[2] Works 19/3, f. 15.   [3] Works 19/3, f. 12, 29 July 1819; B.M. Add. MS. 38760, f. 206.
[4] During this time the palace was used as a temporary residence for junior members of the royal family, and for the King's 'drawing rooms' (*Reading Mercury*, 12 March 1821; *Windsor & Eton Express*, 20 November 1824; Sir Owen Morshead's index, Royal Library, Windsor).
[5] Nash had reported on 7 June that those plans had been taken to Carlton House three years before and never returned; now they could not be found (Works 19/3, f. 218).
[6] The roofs of the staircase and great drawing room had appeared to be in a dangerous state (see p. 262).

urged this until on 21 July Stephenson notified Soane that he had received 'His Majesty's commands to put the Queen's Palace in charge of Mr. Nash'.[1]

According to Nash, the King's intention at this point was merely to 'convert Buckingham House into a private residence for himself'. Nash's first plan added only a few rooms, but George IV wanted more extensive alterations. When Nash proposed building a new palace on another site, the King 'persisted that he . . . would add to the present house'. A proposal to rebuild in Green Park in a line with Pall Mall was also rejected, the King saying that he was too old to build a palace, but that he 'must have a *pied à terre*', which must be at Buckingham House because of early associations which endeared him to the spot.[2] The alterations proposed were extensive enough for Nash to warn the Surveyor General that they would take 'a year at least'.[3]

In a letter dated 10 August 1822 Nash transmitted plans to the Surveyor General, including one showing 'what is absolutely necessary to be done to make the present House habitable for His Majesty without any alteration of the rooms on the principal floor or the Libraries or the approach'.[4] The King wanted the kitchen offices removed to the opposite wing; and rooms on the ground floor, intended for his private apartments, were to have their floors raised to lessen their height. This would also enable Nash to improve the basement rooms, low, damp, and occasionally flooded by the common sewer. Raising the ground floor three feet would permit him to raise the basement floors one foot and increase the headroom as well, so providing a useful suite of offices the whole length of the garden front.

This idea was developed by Nash when he at last came to begin his alterations. His rough estimate of 'the probable cost of the alterations and additions to the King's Palace in St. James's Park', dated 20 June 1825, provided for raising the ground floor five feet and the basement two feet six inches.[5] The wings of the old house were to be taken down and rebuilt with a colonnade on either side of an enlarged courtyard. A portico forming a porte-cochère was to be added to the entrance front; the hall and great staircase were to be reconstructed; galleries were planned on two floors; the library to the south, and the corresponding wing to the north were to be heightened, as was the old Prince of Wales's wing on the north front; and to the west was to be added a range of rooms flanked by pavilions or conservatories.[6] Various external offices, internal alterations, and a triumphal arch placed at the entrance to a railed forecourt brought Nash's estimate to £200,000, exclusive of sculpture, and allowing for the re-use of material from the old house and from Carlton House. A supplementary estimate of £30,400, dated 10 October 1825, included further domestic

---

[1] Soane Museum corresp. 2, xii, G(2), ff. 6, 8, 10, 12, 13. The only ground for the assertion that the change resulted from Soane's failure to carry out the Coronation preparations (Bolton, *Portrait of Sir John Soane*, p. 353) appears to be that both topics are referred to in letters of 20 and 21 July.

[2] *1831 Report*, p. 271. But Mrs. Arbuthnot recorded in October 1825 that the King was 'madly eager' for a plan of Col. Frederick Trench's for a vast palace in Hyde Park, but supposed that his 'd–d Ministers' would not allow it (*Journal of Mrs. Arbuthnot, 1820–32* ed. F. Bamford and the Duke of Wellington, 1950, i, p. 420). This was the plan by Philip Wyatt which Trench published in his *Collection of Papers relating to the Thames Quay with Hints for some further improvements in the Metropolis* (1827), pl. xvi. The Duchess of Rutland may have had a hand in it: see C. Hussey, *English Country Houses, Late Georgian 1800–1840* (1958), p. 123.

[3] Works 19/3, f. 217, 21 October 1821.

[4] *Ibid.* f. 219. Stephenson however wrote to Nash, 27 August 1822, asking for his report on the house by the end of the week (Works 1/11, pp. 241–2).

[5] T. 1/3488, f. 19080/30; *Parl. Pap.* 1826, xxi, p. 8.

[6] In which use was to be made of some of the Ionic columns from the screen of Carlton House.

offices on the Pimlico (southern) side, additions to the wings, and raising the private apartments another storey.[1] The building was to be of Bath stone, which if taken from the best quarries and properly bedded would, Nash thought, last 'infinitely longer' than Portland.[2]

Although commissioned to create a palace, Nash was required to achieve this by enlarging and remodelling the existing house rather than by building on new foundations. Thus his plan was basically that of the old house. Internally, the dimensions of the hall, staircase and adjoining rooms in the east front, as well as of the sculpture gallery, corresponded to divisions of the old 'Queen's House'. On the south side the octagonal library was to be converted into a chapel,[3] with kitchen under; the bow in the north front was to be retained and the old Prince of Wales's wing, of which it was part, formed into one of the five suites which were to be provided in the new palace. Nash planned the principal floor in such a way as to permit both a circuit of the state rooms and an axial approach to the Throne Room. This resulted from the ingenious arrangement of the grand stair, entirely different from what it replaced. In part, it resembled that of Carlton House, but was more complex, consisting of a first flight rising to a landing from which a second flight continued upwards in the same direction, while curving arms on either side returned to a balcony over the foot of the stair (Pl. 9). The balcony opened into a guardroom which led to a drawing room immediately preceding the Throne Room: this suite occupied the east front. The drawing room opened on the west into a sky-lighted picture gallery above the sculpture gallery, itself flanked by the three magnificent drawing rooms of the west front and to the south giving access to a music room over the ground-floor dining room. Beyond this lay the rooms of the south front, intended to be fitted up as armouries, from which one returned to the head of the stair.[4]

In the elevation (Pls. 6–7) Nash had a freer hand. It owed much to French neo-classic influences, shown especially in the external panels of sculpture, a feature of late eighteenth-century Parisian mansions found often enough in books of designs by English architects of that period but seldom in their executed work, and in similar trophies and statues breaking the skyline.[5] Rousseau's Hôtel de Salm (1786) in parti-cular exhibited several features found also in Nash's design: the colonnaded quadrangle, the Corinthian portico forming a *porte-cochère*—both features that may be traced back to Gondouin's Ecole de Chirurgie of 1769–75—the panels in relief, the columned bow in the centre of the garden front surmounted by a low dome and statues.[6] With such conspicuous buildings Nash's visits to Paris must have made him

[1] T. 1/3488, f. 19080/30; *Parl. Pap.* 1826, xxi, p. 8. Garden works brought the total to £252, 690. The additional offices were never built; and it is uncertain in which estimate (if either) the third, north-east, conservatory should be placed. There was never a fourth conservatory. [2] *1828 Report*, p. 52.

[3] Intended to be adorned with the Raphael Cartoons (*Fraser's Mag.* i, 1830, p. 386). It was subsequently proposed to use it as an armoury and it was not until after Queen Victoria's accession that it was finally fitted up as a chapel.

[4] No plan of the palace by Nash is known to survive, but his work may be reconstructed from a plan of the north wing in the Soane Museum (xxxix, 6, no. 2), Blore's plans, formerly in the Victoria and Albert Museum and now in the Royal Library at Windsor, details in the *1831 Report*, and a description in *Fraser's Magazine*, i (1830), pp. 385 ff.   [5] These of course also recalled the original Buckingham House.

[6] J-Ch. Kraft and N. Ransonnette, *Maisons et Hôtels construits à Paris . . . 1771–1802*, ed. J. Mayor and L. Derobert (Paris, 1909), ppl. 73, 74. An engraving by Middleton after Holland, 1788, shows a somewhat similar domed and bestatued bow in the east front of the Royal Pavilion, Brighton; see D. Stroud, *Henry Holland* (1966) p. 87.

familiar. The very form of an open quadrangle entered through a triumphal arch linked to the wings of the palace by railings had lately been employed at the Tuileries by Percier and Fontaine.[1] Though Nash had not hitherto had the chance to employ them in a palace, such features were of course already part of his architectural vocabulary: thus the dome of the garden front had precursors at Rockingham and Hillgrove.[2]

George IV's liking for French neo-classicism, long before exhibited in Holland's Carlton House, may perhaps have influenced Nash's designs. Internally George IV's predilections stamped themselves on the planning as well as the decoration of the palace: the comparative lowness of the ground floor rooms intended for his private apartments; the long rooms with a central bow found on the north, west and south fronts;[3] the basement offices which prevented servants observing the King on the terrace. The decoration was progressively enriched as the King and his artistic advisers, Sir Charles Long and Nash, developed their ideas. Notable features were the very extensive use of scagliola[4] and of sculptured panels in high relief,[5] and the remarkable ceilings of the state rooms, which may be seen as a continuation of the series designed by Nash for the Royal Pavilion, Brighton.[6]

Drawings were being prepared in Nash's office during March 1825,[7] and late in April the architect submitted 'general designs' signed by the King to Lord Liverpool and Robinson, the Chancellor of the Exchequer, who countersigned them. But although the designs were the fruit of long discussion George IV almost at once proposed 'material alterations', which Liverpool demanded to see before work began. Nash replied that the new plans would be, 'though not finished yet in an intelligible

---

[1] The same idea was adapted by Soane in his designs for a royal palace exhibited at the Royal Academy in 1821; see Soane, *Designs for Public and Private Buildings* (1828), and Bolton, *Works of Sir J. Soane*, p. 123.

[2] Illustrated by T. Davis, *John Nash* (1966), pls. 32, 42.

[3] Also found in the east front at Windsor Castle (see pp. 387–90); perhaps imitated from the Regent's Gallery at Belvoir by James Wyatt, 1812–13.

[4] The use of scagliola for walls as well as for columns on a scale exceeding anything known in England may have been inspired by Russian example: Princess Lieven wrote, 5 January 1829, that George IV 'seemed excessively pleased by the Emperor [Alexander I]'s attention in sending him the model of a salon in Scagliola. He has given it a place of honour in the Long Gallery' [at Windsor] (*Letters of Dorothea, Princess Lieven*, ed. L. G. Robinson, 1902, p. 169). Nash, giving evidence before the 1828 select committee, remarked of the proposed scagliola dadoes and walls, 'That is a composition, a sort of scagliola which they do the walls with in Russia' (*1828 Report*, p. 53). Holland, however, had executed scagliola work at Carlton House in 1784, employing Italian workmen, George IV had had further such work executed in 1809 and there is a reference in 1804 to a 'Large Room lined with Scagliola' (see p. 313. See also R. B. Wragg, 'History of Scagliola', *Country Life*, 10 October 1957; D. Stroud, *Henry Holland*, p. 72; RA 35185). Sir Charles Long also influenced the King's taste for scagliola, see below, p. 368.

[5] Referred to as a new development in internal decoration in *Fraser's Magazine*, i (1830), p. 386.

[6] The convex coving of the music room in the Pavilion is repeated in that of the north drawing room. *Fraser's Mag.* i (1830), p. 385, refers to the ceilings of the palace saloon and throne room: 'It is indeed, not easy to conceive anything more splendid than the designs for the ceilings which are to be finished in a style new in this country, partaking very much of the boldest style, in the Italian taste, of the fifteenth century, . . . They will present the effect of embossed gold ornaments, raised on a ground of colour suitable to the character and other decorations of the rooms.' That of the picture gallery was described as 'not only picturesque and splendid, but really curious; possessing all the richness and play of outline of Gothic architecture, produced by a most skilful combination of classic forms' (See pl. 8B showing this ceiling after the centre compartment had been altered by Blore). Mrs. Arbuthnot's comment (12 March 1830) was: 'The sub-divisions in the ceiling make the room look narrow, and the drops are not, I think, correct Grecian taste' (*Journal*, ii, p. 343). Although the similarity between this ceiling and that of the picture room at 14 Lincoln's Inn Fields (1823–4) suggests that Nash may have derived his design from Soane's, Nash himself had used Gothic pendants in the stair-well at Killymoon, *c.* 1802–3 (illustrated, p. 28, Davis, *John Nash*).

[7] R.I.B.A. Drawings Collection, 'Shide Ledger', f. 42, quoted by Summerson, *Nash*, p. 235.

state by Wednesday Evening'.[1] The designs approved, a bill was introduced on 13 June for 'the application of part of the Land Revenue of the Crown for a repair and improvement of Buckingham House'. Meanwhile Nash was hurridly preparing an estimate which he submitted on 20 June.[2]

Work began on 6 June,[3] before either bill or estimate was before Parliament, and a week later nearly 400 men were said to be employed on the premises.[4] In order to satisfy the King's demand for speed, Nash divided the site into three sections by boarded divisions, the centre and each wing being placed under a separate clerk of works, with William Nixon, the King's clerk of works from Brighton, as general superintendent. Different tradesmen were employed in each section for the major trades.[5] Labour disturbances then prevalent almost immediately affected operations. The Journeymen's Society attempted to induce the carpenters to strike but pickets were dispersed by the Coldstream Guards.[6] During the first four months the contractors were stripping the interior of the building, pulling down the old wings, dismantling the grand staircase, taking off the roofs, digging new foundations and preparing old material for re-use in the foundations or basement.[7] Demolition continued in the second full quarter, when the quoins, architrave and pilasters in the front were taken down. Rebuilding began with the fixing of numerous cast-iron girders, which Nash used in place of conventional timber framing for the interior.[8] By the end of December the walls on the garden front were twelve feet above the ground.[9] The Chancellor of the Exchequer reported to the King on 30 January 1826 that 'all parts of the work appear to be proceeding with the utmost expedition, compatible with so extensive an undertaking'.[10]

As the work proceeded, the King made frequent alterations seeking a much greater degree of opulence. This may well have followed from his decision, probably made in December 1826 after the building had been roofed in, to hold his courts there. Although Nash pointed out that he had designed a private residence, lacking

[1] B.M. Add. MS. 38300, ff. 39, 41. It was reported in the *Reading Mercury*, 2 May 1825, that Nash and Eversfield, the auctioneer, had surveyed the apartments the previous Monday and Tuesday; that notice had been given to the inmates to remove immediately; and that it was expected that the wings and outbuildings would shortly be pulled down.

[2] *Commons' Journals* lxxx (1825), p. 535; T. 1/3488, f. 19080/30. Nash's evidence to the 1831 Select Committee is so confused and inaccurate about his early estimates as to be worthless (*1831 Report*, p. 9).

[3] B.M. Add. MS. 27805, f. 369.

[4] *Morning Advertiser*, 15 June 1825. The principal tradesmen employed were: *Carpenter and joiner:* J. Firth, T. & G. Martyr, G. Harrison, H. Warren, G. Woolcott. *Bricklayer:* J. Palmer, W. & J. Whitehead, F. Read. *Excavator:* H. McIntosh. *Mason:* W. Manderson and W. B. Moore, T. Grundy, T. Rice, L. E. Wood. *Plasterer:* F. Bernasconi. *Painter:* J. Barret. *Glazier:* R. Cobbett. *Plumber:* J. Holroyd & Son. *Smith:* J. Mackell. *Coppersmith:* R. & E. Kepp. *Labourer:* F. Swinney. *Marble mason:* J. Browne. *Ornamental metalworker:* S. Parker. In addition, major suppliers of building materials were W. A. Harris, J. Marshall, and W. Rhodes (hollow pottery cones); R. & W. Crawshay and May & Morritt (iron founders); W. Croggon (artificial stone—the name is often spelled Croggan, but Croggon is that used on his vases and corbels at the palace); Froom & Cribb (plate glass); and Wainwright Bros. (engraved glass).

[5] T. 1/3489, pt. ii, f. 13226/26; *1828 Report*, p. 60; *1831 Report*, p. 200. Although Nash once claimed that he divided the work into four parts, Palmer and Whitehead (tradesmen) stated in their evidence that there were three; as indeed Nash confirmed, stating that the centre was divided from the wings by boards, forming 'as it were, three distinct Buildings' (*1831 Report*, p. 265).

[6] B.M. Add. MS. 27805, ff. 365–9.

[7] Works 5/125, pp. 333–45. The bricks and stone were re-used, but most of the timber was sold (*1828 Report*, p. 50).

[8] Works 5/125, pp. 351–66; *1831 Report*, pp. 77, 132–4, 136, 226, 273.

[9] *Windsor and Eton Express*, 31 December 1825 (Royal Library card index).

[10] B.M. Add. MS. 40862, f. 159.

provision for a queen or for the Lord Chamberlain's or Lord Steward's departments, George IV insisted that it would 'make an excellent palace'.[1] 'It was impossible to conform to the Estimates', Nash confessed in 1831: 'Whenever I saw him, it generally happened that he ordered some alteration'.[2]

By the end of January 1828 the shell of the palace, including the wings, was complete. The ceilings were ready for plastering, and some had been begun. The basement offices and the two houses at the ends of the wings were ready for fixtures and fitting-up; the attic storey was nearly finished; the three conservatories were about to be roofed.[3]

When Wellington became Prime Minister in January 1828, the new Chancellor, Henry Goulburn, called for estimates 'to know what the amount of work still to be done would be',[4] and Nash submitted those dated 12 February 1828, which not only listed works specifically excluded from previous estimates—sculpture, parquet floors and the like, to the amount of £79,283—but also revealed the greater richness in the decoration ordered by the King, which added a further £50,952. An estimate of £50,000 for alterations to the wings brought the total to £432,926.[5]

Nash's low wings with their high end pavilions (Pl. 6A) came in for much criticism: indeed the architect himself admitted he did not like them.[6] As additional rooms were wanted, he proposed to solve both problems by raising the wings to the height of the main block, so forming a further twenty-seven apartments.[7] In the revised design (Pl. 6B) the note of French neo-classicism was struck again, the eastern extremities of the wings, new-modelled with four Corinthian columns, recalling *l'aile Gabriel* at Versailles. According to Nash, Wellington thought the alteration 'a great improvement'; but Creevey reported that he had said, 'If you expect me to put my hand to any additional expense, I'll be damned if I will!'[8] However, Knighton, the King's secretary, informed his master on 17 February 1828 that Wellington had promised to find £100,000 for the palace in both that and the succeeding year, when the whole revenue of the Woods and Forests should be applied to it; Nash had received instructions to revise his estimates, 'and the proposed alterations in the front elevation are all to be acted upon without a moment's delay'.[9] Nevertheless, by 3 April Nash had still not received Treasury authority to proceed,[10] and on 29 April the King complained to Knighton that work was almost at a standstill for want of funds.[11] Expenditure for the first quarter of 1828 was £14,084, the lowest for any quarter until 1830.

Expenditure by the end of 1827 totalled £268,492, and by June 1828, £293,296. When a select committee of the House of Commons began in March 1828 to inquire into the expense of public buildings, the Pimlico palace inevitably came under their eye. But although their examination of Nash was close and prolonged, and showed that between May 1826 and February 1828 he had spent some £80,000 without reference to the Treasury, their report had little to say about the palace—perhaps from motives of delicacy, and perhaps also because they believed all was now under

[1] *1831 Report*, pp. 270–1.   [2] *1831 Report*, p. 22.   [3] Works 1/16, pp. 96–7.
[4] *1831 Report*, p. 20.   [5] *1828 Report*, p. 159.   [6] *Ibid.*, pp. 53, 61.
[7] *Ibid.*, pp. 53, 62, 147.   [8] *Creevey Papers*, ed. Maxwell (1904), ii, p. 156.
[9] *Letters of George IV*, ed. Aspinall, iii, pp. 392, 403.   [10] *1828 Report*, p. 53.
[11] *Letters of George IV*, iii, p. 403.

control. The report, dated 19 June 1828, commented on the regrettable necessity for altering the wings and on the unfortunate appearance of the dome over the centre of the garden front, which proved to be half visible from the park;[1] but with regard to the mounting expenditure they merely took notice that it had only been possible to continue the work by drawing on 'other resources than those which were by law appropriated to it'.[2] So far as the palace was concerned, the principal effect of the report was to transfer responsibility for the accounts from the Office of Works to Nash.[3] With the works entirely in his hands, he pursued his favourite method of contracting in gross.

On 3 May 1828 Nash presented the Chancellor by his direction with estimates for additional works at the palace, which seem to have been a repetition of those of February 1828.[4] Goulburn then took measures to obviate criticism by preventing 'any expenditure being incurred beyond what shall be ascertained to be . . . the certain surplus of the land revenue'.[5] It was because of the inadequacy of the Land Revenue that a Treasury minute of 17 June 1828 limited Nash to a monthly outlay

Fig. 2. The Dome of Buckingham Palace: a contemporary caricature showing George IV, the Duke of Wellington and John Nash on the scaffolding: from *This is the Palace that N—h built*, by I. Hume (Westminster City Library).

[1] Nash planned to conceal the dome by adding an attic to the central block, crowned with statues (*Fraser's Mag.* i, 1830, p. 384).

[2] *1828 Report*, pp. 7–8. The Treasury had instructed the Commissioners for French Claims to loan £250,000 to the Woods and Forests, whose surplus revenues had proved unexpectedly small and quite inadequate to supply the 'unexpected rapidity with which the alterations had proceeded at the Palace' (*ibid.*). This loan was repaid in ten instalments by 26 February 1833; interest totalling £34,822 10s. was also directed to be paid (Works 19/5, f. 926).

[3] See p. 171 above.   [4] T. 1/3489, f. 7974/28.   [5] *1828 Report*, p. 122.

of £10,000, which on the basis of past expenditure as well as of available funds must have seemed a reasonable limit.[1] The minute also directed Nash to make a monthly return of expenditure, and to take care not to exceed the total of his estimate. At the same time the raising of the wings and the works for the completion of the interior included in Nash's estimate of February 1828 were authorised.[2] On 9 July, Nash accepted these conditions, though pointing out the difficulty of restricting expenditure to a fixed sum per month when months elapsed before the accounts were made up.[3] Moreover, work done in one quarter was often not finished, so it did not appear in the accounts until the following quarter; and 'much of the work and that of the most costly sort although finished cannot be fixed until the completion of the building and the only care I can take is that the several quarters shall not in the aggregate exceed the limitation'.[4] The clerks of works, however, were able to report the probable cost of the amount measured and so avoid exceeding £10,000 per month.[5]

A verbal instruction given by the Chancellor 'not to execute any works without the express orders of the Treasury' probably also followed on the select committee's revelations; Nash's evidence on this point is less than coherent, but a memorandum by him states that the verbal communication was made some time before it was formally embodied in a Treasury minute on 25 November 1829.[6] From that time Nash, by his own account, simply failed to carry out the alterations the King ordered, though he ran 'great risk' in ignoring the royal commands.[7] The inlaid floors to the state rooms were among the items put off, only the lobby and bow and south drawing rooms having been finished.[8]

Progress in the early months of 1828 had been slowed down by shortage of funds. Although not yet formally authorised, the alteration of the wings was going on during April, but 'very slowly', only £1765 being spent on it.[9] During the second quarter of the year full-scale activity was resumed. By the end of 1828 the external rebuilding of the wings must have been largely complete: charges of £33,759 (exclusive of commission) had been incurred. The year from July 1827 saw a renewed expenditure on ironfounder's work of £5318, much of which must be accounted for by the girders required for the new floors in the heightened wings. This expenditure fell off sharply after July 1828, as did that on artificial stonework, for which Croggon's bills in the same period total £6003, and for the succeeding year, £176.[10] The 1827–8 figure

---

[1] On 28 June the Commissioners of Woods reported that for the rest of the year they had only £41,000 available. To augment this they were instructed to sell the ground rent of the new houses on the site of Carlton House (T. 1/3488, f. 11997/28).   [2] *1831 Report*, p. 153.   [3] *Ibid.* p. 155.
[4] *1831 Report*, p. 155. This difficulty led to the practice of paying sums on account, which confuses the quarterly accounts of the palace.
[5] *1831 Report*, p. 19.
[6] *Ibid.* p. 24; T. 1/3488, with f. 8522/29. Pennethorne told the Select Committee that the first communication was on 23 September 1829 (*1831 Report*, p. 13).
[7] *Ibid.* p. 24.   [8] *Ibid.* p. 27.
[9] *1828 Report*, p. 72; Works 5/110. In his evidence before the 1828 Select Committee, Nash admitted that the 'old library' of Buckingham House had been pulled down (*Report*, p. 49); this probably refers to the Great or West Library. In a pamphlet of 1829, *Hints and Observations respecting the Parks and Palaces* by a Householder of Queen Square, Westminster, the adjoining Octagon Library is described as 'at this moment, level with the ground' (p. 6). The Octagon was, however, retained, to accommodate the kitchen and, above, the private chapel.
[10] Works 5/110. For the year ending October 1826 Croggon was paid £4428, doubtless for the frieze and grotesque consoles of the main block.

includes £1890 for sculpture and payment for the garden balustrade (the base for which had been completed by October 1827[1]), but the charge of £2001 for the second quarter of 1828 must relate to the Coade stone frieze of the wings. By December 1828, on the east front the four military trophies were fixed, and the three sculptured tympana; on the west front the two reliefs by Westmacott and Rossi's six Virtues were all in place.[2] The trophies to decorate the entrances to the wings were in hand by 1829, as were the wind dial and clock turret groups, and the panels below the pediments.[3] Plastering was now for the first time a significant item, Bernasconi charging no less than £8102. Payments to Browne for marble work, totalling £9204, indicate progress with the marble flooring and columns. Since 1827 there had been a six months delay in settling accounts, and under Nash's control this period lengthened to over a year as the 1829 accounts were made up.[4] During 1829 the last three quarters of 1828 and the first of 1829 were paid off, amounting to £122,117—compared with £130,120 for the first 13 months of operations.

In May 1829 Goulburn, who had called in February for an account of expenditure on the palace, demanded, at four days' notice, a complete and final estimate for submission to Parliament. Nash presented this on 15 May 1829, when the Chancellor struck out works estimated at £48,700, leaving a total of £496,169.[5] This figure, authorised by a new statute,[6] not without trenchant criticism, was based purely on previous estimates, arrived at thus:

Estimate of 20 June 1825	£200,000
Supplementary estimate, 10 October 1825	52,690
Estimates laid before the Treasury, 12 February 1828:	
Sculpture and decoration excluded from original estimate	79,283
Enrichments directed by the King	50,953
Sculpture for Marble Arch	31,000
Raising the wings	50,000
Additional cost of Chantrey's equestrian statue	3450
Temporary hoards, etc.	2500
Commission and incidentals	26,293
	£496,169

Nash can have made little attempt to check his estimates against the total expenditure, then, exclusive of the arch, already £366,873. And he had omitted internal sculpture estimated at £7544, as well as scagliola pilasters and columns for the North and South Drawing Rooms, the contracts for which are dated February 1829, and other enrichments ordered by the King. Much of this was put in hand, unknown to the Treasury.[7]

---

[1] Richard Day, who carved it in rock-work, was paid £1146 for the preceding three quarters (Works 5/110).

[2] T. 1/3489, ff. 12835 and 22040/28. See p. 301 below.   [3] T. 1/3488, f. 2484/29.

[4] Works 5/120. It was not until 19 August 1829 that Nash sent to the Treasury the accounts for the first quarter of the year (T. 1/3488, f. 18263/29).   [5] *1831 Report*, p. 165.

[6] 10 Geo. IV cap. 50. The specific sum of £496,000 was inserted on 25 May 1829. See *Commons' Journals*, lxxxiv (1829), p. 339; *Parl. Deb.* new ser. xxi, 1578 ff.

[7] *1831 Report*, pp. 179–80, 'List C'; Works 19/3, f. 342.

Then on 29 August 1829 Nash announced that it was necessary to provide for bell-hanging, baths, frames and looking glasses for chimneypieces, and a system of ventilation. He also confessed that additional internal work, chiefly sculpture, had been ordered by the King and actually commenced: 'Some of these were so connected with the plastered ornaments then in hand that they could not be deferred without stopping the work. All those which could be deferred have not yet been ordered and for which I crave their Lordships authority or the other works with which they are connected must also stop'.[1] The King had also ordered Nash to prepare designs for various outside works of which he had as yet made no estimate; altering the shape of the dome,[2] eight groups of the royal arms to decorate the turrets, four trophies for the two entrances to the wings on the north and south sides of the quadrangle, and various items mentioned in the original plan of 1825, including fountains (one in the great court), an orangery, two temples in the garden, and an ice house. These revelations were made probably at the suggestion of Alexander Young Spearman, a Treasury official who had been appointed to handle the finances relating to the palace.[3] But the effect of Nash's budget was to rouse ministers' ire. Wellington wrote to Goulburn on 13 September:

> Since I saw you yesterday I have been considering this question of the Expenses at Buckingham House. It is obvious that some of them are necessary; such as Bell hanging, the Baths; and even heating the House. Others are Ornamental and unnecessary; and their commencement might have been postponed. But these have been commenced without Authority; and part of this unauthorized Expense has been paid. It must likewise be observed that Nash might have stated these additions to the Building particularly those of which he has incurred part of the Expense, at the time you called upon him for an Estimate to be laid before Parliament.
>
> What I recommend is that you should make a 'Hash of Nash' in a Minute of the Treasury, for having omitted to make these statements, and for having incurred these unauthorized expenses. Then call upon him for an Estimate for Bells Baths and Warming the House. This will put the case in a shape for me to deal with it with the King; and the Minute can go before Parliament with the Estimate of those Expenses which we shall find necessary and shall think proper to authorize.[4]

Goulburn's minute, dated 22 September 1829, directed the Lord Chamberlain to draw up estimates for the fittings, mentioned that there were no funds to provide for the sculpture, and expressed 'great suprize' that Nash had not stated the expense of the fittings, he being 'perfectly aware' of the purpose of his May estimate—'of adequately providing once for all, for the whole expenditure which might be necessary to complete it so far as to fit it for the reception of furniture'. Finally it ordered Nash to take no measures without the previous approval of the Treasury.[5] Nash admitted his omission of the internal sculpture: a fault he ascribed to the fact that the sculpture had always formed 'a branch of expense professedly separate from the rest'. But he declared that his total estimate would not be exceeded, and pointed out

[1] T. 1/3488, f. 18263/29; *1831 Report*, pp. 159–60.
[2] Apparently by adding ribbing and 'appropriate ornaments' (*Fraser's Magazine*, i, 1830, p. 382).
[3] See p. 138 above.   [4] Goulburn MSS, Surrey Record Office.
[5] *1831 Report*, p. 161. Wellington wrote, 19 September, 'I quite agree with your proposed Minute about Nash' (Goulburn MSS).

that Goulburn himself had struck out the estimate for fittings.[1] The Treasury could not continue its hashing. A minute of 17 November approved that sculpture which was closely connected with the plastering—the bas-reliefs in the North Drawing Room, the *altirelievi* for the South, and the *dessus des portes* for the state rooms, a total of £3510. But the minute concluded on a warning note. No deviation from the plans, or works which would retard completion or increase expense would be permitted; and for any such Nash would be held responsible.[2]

On the same day, the First Commissioner of Woods reported that funds must be nearly exhausted: with payment of the accounts for the first quarter of 1829, his department's total issues for the palace were £431,465, and there were two quarters' accounts outstanding.[3] Spearman must promptly have warned Nash, who as soon as he had totalled up the second quarter's account—'about £20,634'—replied:

> Your apprehensions have put me so much on the qui vive that I am going over the whole work from the midsummer quarter it is attended with the greatest difficulty that I can seperate the work of one quarter from that of the other—in revising the work done since the Lady day quarter I can see no mistake the difficulty I allude to is the seperation of the works—for example there has been five months work done since the midsummer quarter all which is work in hand and what it will cost to finish those works is the difficulty—I have ever had my fears respecting the carving of the marble in the arch—which could not be done by contract or measure—and also of the inlaid floors which baffles all estimates—three of these floors are not begun— nor will I begin them although the King has ordered them until I can ascertain by the finishing of the others what they will come to.[4]

When the accounts for the first six months of 1829 were at length completed, the total, including marble, came to £461,743—nearly £10,000 more than Nash had thought. The Treasury warned on 2 April 1830 that only £37,867 remained available.[5] Though from then until September Nash was incapacitated by illness,[6] he at once stopped those works 'ordered by His Majesty, in addition to the Estimates sanctioned by the Treasury', and began an investigation as soon as he was able.[7] On 29 September 1830 he admitted to an expenditure of £34,787 in excess of his estimates up to 5 July 1830, with further work to be done to the sum of £11,656.[8] In addition, £4043 had been paid for incidental expenses and £29,395 for works ordered by the King 'which formed no part of the original estimates'; there were also the works ordered by the King which Nash had stopped in April, which he now estimated at £25,767, not to mention others not yet begun, valued at £21,806. But for all these extras, Nash did not consider himself accountable. The £46,000 for which he admitted responsibility he explained by the impossibility of stating in August 1829, when the works of the first six months of the year had not even been measured, what their

[1] *1831 Report*, pp. 162–4.   [2] *1831 Report*, p. 166.   [3] T. 1/3488, f. 18125/29.
[4] *Ibid*. with f. 18263/29.   [5] *1831 Report*, p. 172.
[6] *Ibid*. 'A rush of blood to the head, occasioned as the physicians say, by standing on the marble pavement in St. Paul's cathedral, during the funeral of Sir Thomas Lawrence.'
[7] *Ibid*. p. 174. Some items figure in previous estimates, and it would appear that Nash's office was in great confusion.
[8] This shows the worthlessness of Nash's excuses for the inaccuracy of his estimate of May 1829; the truth was, he did not then have the time to work out reliable figures (*ibid*. pp. 172–4).

value would be, or 'what balances would be due to the tradesmen (whose works had been only in part measured and paid quarterly) when the whole of the works then in hand should be finished'. He was therefore obliged 'to take for granted that the works then done would be found to be verified by the original estimate'—as he had done all along.[1] The two quarters' bills came to some £15,000 more than Nash had expected; to which must be added the balances due for work not then brought to account, as well as the extra cost of more expensive designs adopted in the ornamental plastering, and the incalculable parquet flooring. Thus in general, said Nash, the excess might be accounted for, though to ascertain its several items was impossible. To spread the blame, Nash revived the argument that he had put before the 1828 select committee: that he could not be responsible for works measured and priced by others, and that no estimates could be relied on unless contracts were made in gross. By such contracts, made since he was given full control in August 1828, he calculated that he had saved 25 per cent. Thus works previous to that time, costing £308,000, might have been contracted for at some £77,000 less, which would have brought the whole within his estimate.[2] This ingenious claim was based however on the difference between the highest and lowest tenders obtained.[3] There can be no presumption that 'measure and prices' would have been equivalent to the highest tenders. The statement that the contracts in gross 'came to thirty per cent less than my estimate' appears to have no other foundation.[4]

With such a confession in its hands, the Treasury was now entirely justified in 'making a hash of Nash', as it proceeded to do in a minute of 15 October 1830.[5] It seems unlikely that even had George IV still been alive he would have been able to save his all-too complacent architect. Goulburn took the view that Nash had concealed the excess from the Treasury, a view criticised as too harsh by Spearman, who probably knew more of the business than the Chancellor, and by the select committee, who exonerated Nash of deceit; but a view that received every justification from Nash's own admission of works ordered in addition to the estimates sanctioned (however inaccurate those might be).[6] Not surprisingly, the Treasury thought it 'incumbent upon them to mark their sense of such conduct by every means in their power'.[7] Not merely were the works stopped,[8] save for securing the palace from injury, but Nash was suspended from his post of Attached Architect, and a case was referred to the law officers respecting his pecuniary liability for expense 'incurred in defiance of the orders of My Lords'. To meet the deficiency on the bills for the third quarter of 1829, a payment of £6710 from the Droits of Admiralty was ordered.[9]

The architect's further reply was again delayed by ill-health. When on 9 February 1831 he defended his conduct, it was largely a repetition of his old arguments. In any case, he declared, he could not be bound by his estimate of 1825, framed on a merely general plan, particularly as he was 'referred for all details of the execution to the personal commands of the King; my instructions, given verbally, being only that the

---

[1] The tradesmen were to declare, however, before the Select Committee, that they would have had little difficulty in stating approximately what was due, but this Nash denied (*ibid.* pp. 268–9).
[2] *Ibid.* pp. 172–4.   [3] *Ibid.* p. 192.   [4] *Ibid.* p. 15.   [5] *Ibid.* p. 187.
[6] *Ibid.* pp. 179–80.   [7] Treasury Minute, 15 October 1830 (*ibid.* pp. 187–8).
[8] A letter of 21 October ordered Stephenson to stop the works, which was done the following day (Works 4/30, pp. 366–7).   [9] *1831 Report*, pp. 187–8.

general outline of the plan should be adhered to'. Not until 22 September 1829 had he been instructed that no work was to be done without previous Treasury sanction, an order he had thereafter observed. Until then, although the King had asked for numerous alterations and additions, Nash had made no deviations 'except by those express commands', and George IV had signed every drawing as authority for proceeding.[1]

An 'accurate statement of the whole expenditure', made by the Surveyor General on 16 February 1831, showed that up to 10 October 1829 £501,530 had been paid, and that a further charge estimated at £104,717 had been incurred.[2] To complete the palace in accordance with the late King's wishes, a further £33,762 would be needed. But by this time a new ministry was in power. The Whig Chancellor of the Exchequer, Lord Althorp, decided to lay the state of affairs before Parliament, and on 15 February 1831 moved for a select committee to investigate the palace accounts. £576,353 had been expended on the palace to Midsummer 1830, he told the Commons. He was better-disposed towards Nash than his predecessor: 'It was not fair to Mr. Nash to place this to his conduct, for many of the works were not calculated for by him'.[3]

To assist their investigations, the select committee under the chairmanship of Robert Gordon sought expert advice, and on 18 March 1831 Wyatville, Soane, Smirke and Seward were directed to report on the expense, condition and security of the palace. This body of Nash's colleagues reported on 15 July,[4] estimating the cost of finishing the palace at nearly £77,000, with a further £12,000 for additional offices and the completion of the side entrances. The various Household officers reported that there was not room for them all, and considerable alterations were thought necessary even if the building were merely to be a residence for the King and Queen: more light and air were required in the basement rooms, and the south entrance and circular colonnade should be replaced by additional offices. A change in the roof of the picture gallery and those of the conservatories, and other arrangements for the collection of armour were also recommended.[5] The architects were doubtful of the permanency of the roofing made of Stanhope's composition. Rain had already penetrated the covering of the south-west tower,[6] and though fissures in the composition might readily be closed, there was no guarantee against their recurrence. The substitution of a more durable covering was therefore advised.

The advanced state of the internal decoration made it difficult for the investigators to judge the security of the palace. The 'extensive and very peculiar use of Iron' intensified the problem. The drawings were inadequate, so they laid open some of the ironwork, to find the castings very rough; considering 'the uncertainty that existed in regard to the strength of the Iron in many parts of the Building', and 'the manner in which many of [the castings] were applied for the support of the walls', the architects obtained the advice of several engineers.[7] Messrs Rennie, Rastrick and

---

[1] *Ibid.* pp. 190–1.   [2] *Ibid.* p. 193.   [3] *Parl. Deb.* 3rd ser. ii, 586.

[4] *1831 Report*, pp. 222 ff.   [5] *Ibid.* pp. 231–2.

[6] *Ibid.* pp. 272–3. In response to an enquiry from C. W. Pasley, Stephenson wrote, 19 February 1838, 'Upon the First Coat of this Cement, Tiles or Slates were bedded, which were covered by a second Coat, each of about one inch in thickness; and thus used, it has effectually resisted the weather, and may be considered a good and satisfactory covering' (B.M. Add. MS. 41964, f. 244).

[7] A proceeding scathingly commented on by Nash (*1831 Report*, p. 274).

Bramah delivered their own reports, which differed greatly in their assessment of the strength of the ironwork. Often they judged the strength of the components simply on appearances. Thus Rennie remarked of the Large Armoury, 'The actual strength of the Girder(s) is unknown, and it is impossible to say what weight they may have to sustain'.[1] Apart from his remarks on the testing of the two beams to the floor of the Bow Room, his observations appear to have been based on visual evidence unsupported by calculations. Bramah quoted safe loads for a variety of beams, but gave no dimensions by which the validity of his figures could be checked. Rastrick, the most exhaustive in his inquiries, and the severest in his criticism, appears to have been unable to calculate the weight of the beams and claimed that the strength of any beam was 'directly as the square of the depth and thickness, and inversely as the length'.[2] He based his tests on the assumption that a load applied at the centre of a beam produced the same deflection as one of twice the weight uniformly distributed over the beam.[3] He also believed that 'hard common iron did not begin to stretch' until eight or nine tenths of the breaking load was applied. These ideas may have been due to the inaccuracy with which 'practical men' were then able to measure deflections, but calculations so misfounded go far to rob criticism of its force. Rastrick did, however, make a number of sound points, such as those about the bad positioning of floor beams over windows without secondary beams to pass the reaction around the window opening, and about the weakness of iron arches or 'cradles' embracing brick arches.[4] He also urged that beams shown by calculation to be heavily loaded should be checked by load tests; if the beams were as badly cast as the examiners thought, this was a matter of importance.[5] Rennie thought that 'in general the brick and stone work are well executed',[6] and George Harrison, a builder who did much of the carpentry of the palace, declared that 'the Palace itself is on a different construction to any building I ever saw of the same nature; it is so strong that it must last for ever, or go all at once; it is all iron, brick and stone; it is tremendously strong'.[7] Yet William Whitehead, one of the bricklayers, thought that the walls, 'about three bricks thick', were not thick enough. On his observing to the clerk of works that the walls of the bow in the west front were too thin for the great weight they would have to support, certain works were done to strengthen them, and the dome was not covered with stone as at first proposed.[8]

To all this Nash replied that he was 'the principal user, and perhaps I may add, the introducer of cast-iron in the construction of the floors of buildings'. The architect, not the iron founder, should be the judge of the castings he required. As for those used in the palace, he could not doubt that Messrs. Crawshay had in their own interests taken all the usual precautions necessary; and nearly all the bearers and ironwork had been tried at the building by both weighting and hammering. He pointed out that 'not a single experiment' justified the apprehensions of the engineers; nevertheless he was not opposed to, indeed strongly urged, a further trial—that of filling the building with soldiers. He proceeded to criticize the engineers' evidence in detail.[9]

[1] *Ibid.* p. 235.   [2] *Ibid.* p. 239.   [3] *Ibid.* p. 241.   [4] *Ibid.* pp. 245, 246.
[5] *Ibid.* p. 237. I am indebted to my colleagues, Dr. J. Allen and Dr. E. Burley, of the Department of Civil Engineering, Queen Mary College, London, for assistance with this section.
[6] *Ibid.* p. 237.   [7] *Ibid.* p. 77.   [8] *Ibid.* p. 56.   [9] *Ibid.*, p. 274.

A further report from the examining architects, dated 28 July, related to three specific points on which the select committee sought further information—how the palace might be made more secure, whether the roofing of Stanhope's composition need be removed, and how the basement offices might be improved. The architects recommended the removal of the dome and of the north-east and south-west towers—which would of course involve the demolition of the corresponding towers on either front; the taking off of the roofing and the upper tier of brick arches below it, to relieve the walls of 1500 tons weight, and substituting a copper or lead roof of 200 or 300 tons; and the opening of a wide area between the offices and the terrace.[1]

The committee were incapable of deciding among these conflicting opinions, and merely reported that the defects of the building could be remedied.[2] They resolved that the Treasury should be asked to name an independent architect to prepare plans and estimates for completing the palace either as a private residence for the sovereign, or as a state palace. Nash agreed that in the circumstances this was an equitable decision 'calculated ultimately to give satisfaction to the Public'.[3] For the rest, the committee held Nash guilty of 'inexcusable irregularity and great negligence' —a verdict that is surely unchallengeable. They agreed with the Treasury Minute of 15 October 1830, except that they found no proof that Nash had deliberately concealed anything. They also censured successive governments for not using sufficient caution in obtaining information before submitting estimates. Nash had had to produce his all-embracing estimate of May 1829 in four days. Nor had the Treasury adequately supported the Surveyor General—who alone emerged creditably from the inquiry. Thus it is somewhat surprising that the committee did not recommend placing the completion of the palace under that officer. But ministers moved quickly to anticipate any advice from the committee on that point.[4]

After so much money had been spent, there could be little doubt that the only sensible course was to complete the building, either as a state palace or simply as a royal residence. But how much it would cost to complete and who was to direct the work were questions to which the answers were not so obvious. The committee having anticipated their report with a series of resolutions, ministers were able to consider these questions in August 1831 with some confidence that Parliament would vote the sums necessary. Lord Althorp, Chancellor of the Exchequer, and Lord Duncannon, First Commissioner of Woods, proposed Edward Blore (1787–1879) as an architect unconnected with Nash or those architects employed to report on the palace, whose rebuilding of Lambeth Palace gave 'fair grounds for supposing that he would discharge this duty in the most satisfactory manner'.[5] His appointment was effected by a Treasury Minute dated 9 August, and approved by William IV the following day.[6] Blore accordingly examined the situation, ascertaining the King's wishes, and seeking the advice of the Household departments.

In his report, dated 26 September 1831, Blore, who largely followed the recommendations of the examining architects, strongly advocated the completion of the

[1] *Ibid.*, pp. 278–80.   [2] *Ibid.* p. 6.   [3] *Ibid.* p. 289.
[4] Grey Papers, Durham University, Duncannon to Grey [8 August 1831].
[5] T. 1/3488. Blore had also worked at Althorp House, adding a Gothic library in 1820, and for the Duke of Bedford, whose son, Lord John Russell, was in the Cabinet.
[6] T. 1/3488, draft Treasury Minute; Works 19/4, f. 489.

U

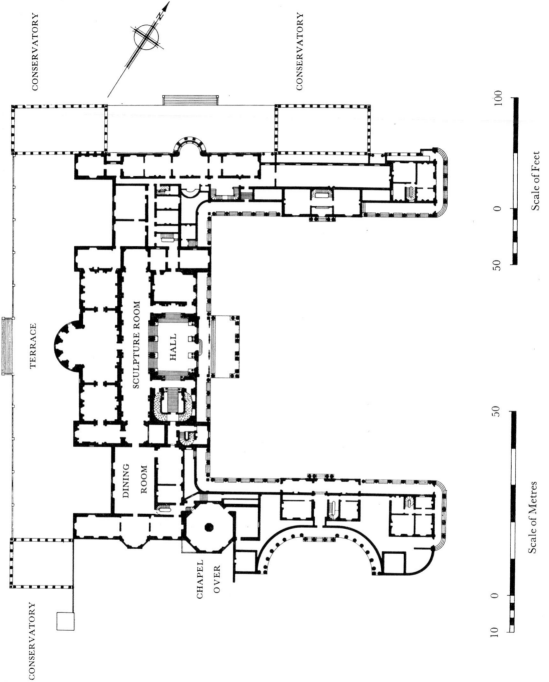

CONSERVATORY

CONSERVATORY

TERRACE

CONSERVATORY

CONSERVATORY

SCULPTURE ROOM

HALL

DINING ROOM

CHAPEL OVER

Scale of Feet

Scale of Metres

Fig. 3. Buckingham Palace as designed by John Nash: based on plans in Britton and Pugin's *Public Buildings of*

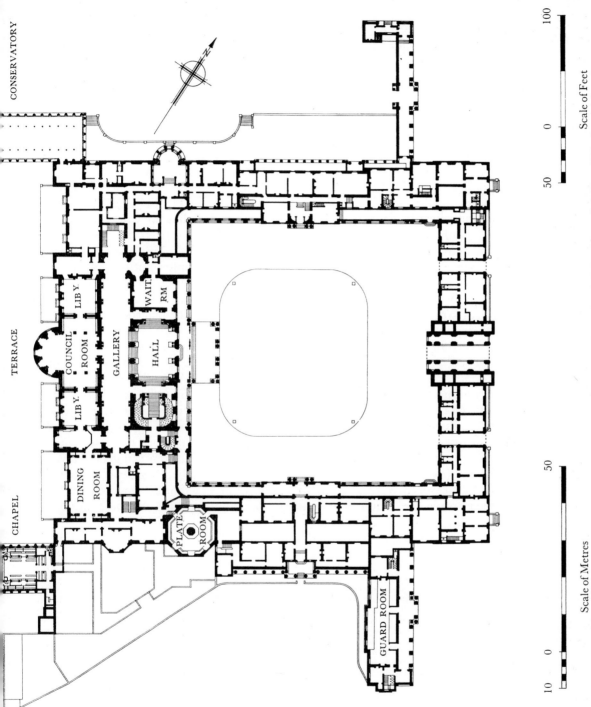

Scale of Metres

Scale of Feet

Fig. 4. Buckingham Palace in 1851: based on a plan in the Public Record Office (Works 34/1).

palace as a royal residence, praising the 'number, magnificence and excellent arrangement' of the principal apartments, compared with the merits of which the defects appeared trifling. If later required for state purposes, the palace could be enlarged. Its principal defects, Blore thought, were the inadequacy and inconvenience of the basement offices, and on the ground floor the lack of accommodation for the Queen, as well as generally some deficiencies of intercommunication. To rectify these, he proposed building a new service wing in place of the semi-circular colonnade on the south side; to advance the recessed parts of the west front and form internal areas,[1] improve communications between various rooms and different floors,[2] replace the north-west conservatory with apartments for the Queen (with a complementary block on the south-west), construct a private entrance on the north side, and demolish the north-east conservatory. To meet the King's wish for a dining room on the principal floor, he proposed converting the music room. His rough estimate for the whole was £73,777.[3] He suggested that the works commenced by Nash should be completed before any new work was started in order to avoid confusion, and agreed to accept a commission calculated on his estimate, provided there were no changes of plan.[4] The Treasury on 4 November authorised the completion of Nash's works, in accord with the system proposed on 26 October by Lord Duncannon. Superintendence of the payment of accounts was to be transferred from the Office of Works to Duncannon personally; Blore was to be placed in charge of the palace, to deposit copies of his contracts in the Office of Woods, and to be accountable (unlike Nash) for works under his direction, payment being made by the Office of Woods on receiving his quarterly accounts and certificates. Accordingly, the Office of Works handed over responsibility for the palace in mid-November 1831.[5]

Blore outlined his mode of operations in a report to the Office of Woods dated 4 January 1832.[6] As far as practicable he proposed employing competitive contracts in gross, avoiding day work and only allowing measured prices where he could not make advantageous general contracts. For unavoidable day work he would engage labour directly at weekly wages, thereby saving money and ensuring better work. Necessary day work done by master tradesmen would be very strictly checked. Accounts of measured work were to be made up at the shortest possible intervals. Tradesmen would be required to send in periodic accounts comprehending all claims, so that there could be no arrears, and he would be able to keep a proper check over all expenditure. He would himself spend the greater part of his time on

[1] Christopher Hussey (H. C. Smith, *Buckingham Palace*, p. 51) was under a misapprehension in stating that the east walls of the west block were brought forward to the colonnades, and that Blore filled in two wells 'contrived by Nash at the end of the main block for lighting purposes'. It was Blore who contrived these two internal areas, which permitted the Sculpture Gallery to be lighted by a window at its northern end; but in his subsequent alterations, Blore had to appropriate half his northern area to the Ministers' Staircase, so obliterating the window. Nash's small lighting well at the south-east end of the gallery was not touched, but the skylight over the north end was roofed in, and a room constructed above.

[2] Most important of those executed were doorways between the ground floor Dining Room and South Room (now divided into the Household Breakfast Room and '1844 Room'), and on the principal floor, between the State Dining Room and the South Drawing Room; this was made possible by the rebuilding of the dining rooms further to the west. On both floors, the communications between these rooms had previously been through the gallery (*1831 Report*, p. 325). Blore also enlarged the King's private stair by throwing in the adjacent back stair (*1831 Report*, p. 326). This was demolished when the Ministers' Stair was begun in 1838.

[3] *1831 Report*, pp. 323–7, 26 September 1831.   [4] 22 October 1831, T. 1/3489, f. 21403/31.

[5] Works 4/31, p. 215; T. 1/3489, f. 21403/31.   [6] Works 19/4, ff. 601–4.

the premises, so as immediately to 'explain and settle all doubtful and difficult points, and exercise a personal superintendence'. Still uncertain how far his own plans would modify Nash's, Blore proposed finishing off existing contracts, calculating on using any savings 'in aid of the expense of the alterations by which they will have been rendered unnecessary'. To this general principle the Commissioners of Woods were unwilling to commit themselves. The King in sanctioning further alterations insisted on 'positive certainty that the Expence will not be incurred beyond the Estimate'; and the Treasury urged the 'greatest caution and circumspection' in assenting to any alteration 'which could afford the slightest excuse or justification for an exceeding'.[1]

To the works he had previously advocated Blore specifically added on 13 January the removal of the dome and towers,[2] though after the report of the investigating architects this had been taken for granted. When he realised that this would adversely affect the appearance of the building, he suggested building an attic storey which would 'unquestionably greatly improve its appearance', would provide the bed-rooms that he had planned to build above the office wing and servants' hall on the south, and enable a more satisfactory roofing to be substituted for Stanhope's composition.[3] An early design for this attic is now in the British Museum, showing a central pediment and skyline figures on the garden front (Pl. 7B), but omitting the bas relief panels from the Marble Arch that Blore ultimately used.[4] The cost could be met by the saving on the south wing and other omissions, such as that of the inlaid parquet floors of the state rooms.[5]

Blore remarked that he was 'by no means desirous of departing from his [Nash's] plans where I find it practicable to adhere to them'[6] but the absence of drawings frequently left him uncertain as to Nash's intentions.[7] He also experienced consider-able difficulty in attempting to continue Nash's contracts, because of increased prices.[8] Further difficulties arose from the unreliability of the marble-mason, Browne, who was at length permitted to go on with his contracts while the old dis-putes about his accounts were still being fiercely argued between him, Nash, and the Office.[9]

During April 1832 Blore began to make contracts for his own alterations. Thomas Curtis & Son agreed to execute the brickwork at £11 14s. per rod in lime mortar, or £15 15s. in Roman cement; bricklayers to be charged at 5s. 6d. per day, labourers at 3s. Any day work was to be agreed previously, and accounted for daily.[10] The masonry contract for the attic and rebuilding the walls of the intervals between the centre block and wings on the garden front was awarded to William Clarke at £1294

---

[1] *Ibid.* ff. 628–9, 657.   [2] *Ibid.* f. 606.

[3] *Ibid.* ff. 624, 626. No one except Sir Frederick Trench seems to have remarked that the imposition of the attic would defeat the object of the removal of the towers—the lightening of the weight on the walls.

[4] B.M. Add. MS. 42047, ff. 12, 13.

[5] The decision whether or not to complete the parquet was one Blore declined to take on his own responsi-bility, 'as uniformity may be expected in a suite of rooms in all other respects of equal magnificence'. The floors of the Throne and Music (now Dining) Rooms and Saloon had not been begun; most of the others were finished or nearly so. The King displayed little interest, and it was left to Duncannon to choose the cheaper mode.

[6] Works 19/4, f. 681.

[7] A few of Nash's drawings, bequeathed with Blore's plans to the Victoria and Albert Museum, are now on loan to the Royal Library at Windsor; but the bulk has disappeared.

[8] Works 19/4, f. 699, 18 April 1832.   [9] Works 19/4, ff. 673, 682.   [10] Works 19/4, f. 720.

15s.[1] Holroyd once again obtained the plumber's contract (which included a new lead roof over most of the main block) though he was later to run into financial difficulties. That for plastering went to Bullock and Carter.[2]

But before these arrangements were complete, Blore had found it necessary to seek clarification of his powers. A correspondence with Duncannon established that Blore's plans were definitive, and could not be altered except by direction of the Treasury, but in other respects the architect was given almost a free hand, with full liberty to form contracts, and settle the 'degree of finish and ornament' to be given to the new part of the building, inside and out.[3] Provided no actual contract stood in the way, Blore might employ new tradesmen on unfinished work, which (he claimed) would 'greatly facilitate the progress of the works'. Any savings might be used in aid of the general expenditure, as might proceeds from sales of unwanted materials. The parliamentary grant for completing the palace was only £100,000, whereas £115,000 was needed in addition to the vote of £78,000 for Blore's own works. Savings from the two votes were expected to cover 'all the works required for the completion of the palace', but it was clearly understood that gilding, fixtures, baths, heating and papering were additional. Blore was guaranteed his commission of £3500 on the works embraced in his estimate.[4]

By 1 June 1832 demolition work had been completed except for the ironwork of the dome, to be removed within the week, and the ground had been cleared for the new building on the south side. Minor alterations in the north wing and at the north end of the picture gallery were nearly completed, and works in progress included the joinery of the state rooms (Martyr), the Bow Room parquet (Martyr), plastering of the state rooms (Bernasconi), iron work (Horseley Iron Company), masonry of the new attic and west walls, and plumber's and bricklayer's work. No item had exceeded Blore's estimates.[5]

A decision against completing the Marble Arch to its original design permitted Blore to make other use of the sculpture already executed for it. He proposed to employ the principal part in the decoration of the new attic.[6] Thirty feet of the 45 foot Waterloo frieze by Westmacott were applied to the southern section of the courtyard front of the new attic, balanced by two of the three sections of his Nelson frieze on the northern; and on the garden front were placed as a continuous frieze the military and naval bas-reliefs carved by Westmacott for the side-friezes of the Arch. But Blore found no use for the rest of the sculpture.[7]

The whole of the towers and dome had been removed and the roofs made good by 16 August 1832; in the west front, the intervals had been rebuilt as high as the principal floor. If the weather stayed fine, reported Blore, the attic would be roofed in about six weeks and the raised central portion about three weeks after that. Inside the palace, the floors had been laid in the two drawing rooms and the saloon; and most of that in the Throne Room was done. The parquet of the Bow Room would

[1] The drawing for this section signed by Clarke is now in the Victoria and Albert Museum, 8738/26.
[2] Works 19/4, ff. 741, 752.   [3] Works 19/4, ff. 722–9, 8 and 24 May 1832.
[4] Wrongly stated in a Treasury letter to Duncannon, 26 October 1831, as a maximum reducible if the works executed should cost less than the estimate (*ibid*. f. 724).
[5] *Ibid*. f. 740. The following week tenders for carpenter's work were received, John & S. Dixon being chosen (*ibid*. f. 767).
[6] *Ibid*. f. 762, 18 July.   [7] See Marble Arch, National Gallery, pp. 293, 461.

be finished in six or seven weeks. In the south drawing room the scagliola columns would be fixed by the end of September, as would the pilasters in the north drawing room. The King's stair and the adjoining back stairs had been reconstructed as one. In the north wing the long gallery on the ground floor had been divided into rooms, and other alterations had been made: improved communications between rooms and staircases, new passages, doorways and fireplaces. Work had begun on converting the north wing bow into the Queen's private entrance, and preparations were made for the Queen's private stair in the north-west angle.[1] As Blore was hoping for an extension of the site, the new kitchen buildings on the Pimlico side had not been started.

This hope was disappointed, and during 1833 the south side of the palace was the principal focus of activity: a new low office wing was begun to the south-west, and further east a new guard house, costing £3500 and commission, which Blore claimed would 'add much to the beauty of the palace by increasing the width of the wings and giving a greater degree of solidity to the building'.[2] To maintain uniformity with the existing colonnade of the courtyard and to retain the essential symmetry of the east front, twelve large Doric columns, ordered from the Horseley Iron Company at £47 10s. each,[3] were placed in front of the guard house and twelve more to form a corresponding screen in front of Nash's private entrance on the north flank. The royal arms over the two screens were provided by Croggon.[4]

Meanwhile, progress was made with the fixtures and fittings. Deficiencies discovered in the quantity of metal door ornaments supplied by Samuel Parker, now bankrupt, were made good by James De Ville. A 'considerable number' of the ornaments of the drawing room chimney pieces had never been cast, and Parker refused to give up the model—'the only authority we can get at for ascertaining what ornaments are wanting and how they are to be arranged'.[5] Important features of the decorations were commissioned from Pitts (three reliefs from his own designs for the South Drawing Room) and Croggon (a scagliola doorway for the Throne Room similar to those he had made for the picture gallery, but modified by Blore) in June and July.[6]

'I now conceive that by far the largest portion of the works comprehended in my estimate are completed', wrote Blore on 26 July 1833, 'besides other works which I never contemplated and which have during the last two years caused me a great deal of trouble'.[7] Blore had undoubtedly applied himself closely to the work, and a considerable part of the decoration evidently flowed from his pencil: what proportion was designed by Nash and what by Blore will probably never be precisely ascertained. The Throne Room ceiling, executed by Bullock and Carter, follows in general outline the description of the design given in *Fraser's Magazine* for May 1830.[8] That of the Bow Drawing Room was nearly finished at that time, though a later drawing

---

[1] Works 19/4, ff. 802–4.   [2] *Ibid.* 19/4, ff. 877, 885.   [3] Works 19/5, f. 920.

[4] *Ibid.* f. 1365 (18 April 1834, estimate £180 for achievements, plus £50 for lion and unicorn). See Victoria and Albert Museum, drawing 8738/40.

[5] *Ibid.* ff. 1071, 1019. These chimney pieces and overmantels appear to have been abandoned; a new one for the south drawing room was ordered from Browne, see p. 284.

[6] *Ibid.* ff. 952, 980. Pitts' reliefs, at 100 guineas each, were substituted for unexecuted designs by Stothard (*1831 Report*, p. 217; Works 19/5, f. 1154). Croggon charged the same price as for his earlier doorcases, £253.

[7] Works 19/5, f. 984.   [8] I, p. 385.

of it exists.[1] Another of Blore's drawings indicates the design for the frieze, a triangular motif, used in the west front rooms.[2] Several of the contracts of Browne, the marble mason, show him working from Blore's drawings for chimney pieces, pilasters, and trusses (as in the sculpture gallery).[3] The design of Nash's Music Room (in whose ceiling sculptural enrichments had already been fixed)[4] was completely altered when it was rebuilt further west as the Dining Room. The room below, designed by Nash as the State Dining Room and later known as the Household Dining Room,[5] was necessarily also rebuilt by Blore, Browne's tender of £362, dated 12 September 1833, being accepted for eight Ionic columns and capitals and antae in Ravaccioni marble.[6] Sometimes Blore re-arranged Nash's features, for instance by removing the third chimneypiece from the sculpture gallery to the new ante-room at the north end of the picture gallery.[7] Not all the alterations Blore had originally proposed were carried out—the conservatories flanking the garden front were not rebuilt as apartments, nor was the central door from the sculpture gallery into the ground floor bow room closed.

In September 1833 Blore successfully surmounted labour difficulties involving a strike of masons, and reported that 'everything . . . is going on as well as possible'.[8] His superior, Duncannon, sometimes wearied of his toil;[9] nevertheless he retained responsibility for the palace when in 1834 he moved to the Home Office, and he controlled the expenditure of £55,000 voted for furnishing the palace after the Commissioners of Woods and Works reported to the Treasury on 21 December 1833 that the alterations and repairs were nearly completed. The King was anxious that this money should not be 'diverted to the Decorations, which he considers to form part of the Architectural Estimate, especially as He has never calculated upon the Use of Buckingham Palace for any Purposes of State'.[10] The works at the new south wing offices and at the new guard house were reported on 21 January 1834 as completed externally.[11]

A good deal nevertheless had yet to be done to the palace. Faced with the problem of a damp kitchen, Blore proposed to raise the floor two feet.[12] A whole series of decorative works were commissioned in March—a statuary marble chimney-piece for the south drawing room (Browne), three engraved glass plates for the Dining Room clerestory (Wainwright), ornamental balustrading in hard white metal painted bronze for the King's and Queen's stairs (De Ville), and even external ornament in Bath stone to the tower on the south-west side of the offices (Clarke).[13] Not until July was the gilding of the rooms on the west front contracted for (Crace).[14]

Urged on by Duncannon to bring the palace to completion, Blore reported on 15 July 1834 that most of the rooms were finished, except for papering and painting, which was already commenced in the upper rooms and those on the principal floor of the north wing—where two chimney pieces from Carlton House were yet to be fixed. In the state rooms painting was in progress; they would then be gilded, and

[1] *Ibid.*; Victoria & Albert Museum, drawing 8738/61, Watermark 1835. [2] *Ibid.* 8738/66.
[3] E.g. Works 19/5, ff. 991, 1175. [4] *1831 Report*, p. 179.
[5] Described by Clifford Smith as 'of special interest as showing Nash's decoration unaltered by later additions' (*Buckingham Palace*, p. 198).
[6] Works 19/5, f. 1007. [7] Works 19/5, f. 1006. [8] *Ibid.* f. 1019.
[9] *Ibid.* f. 1021. [10] *Ibid.* f. 1080, Taylor to Duncannon, 27 December 1833.
[11] *Ibid.* f. 1091. [12] *Ibid.* ff. 1049, 1077. [13] *Ibid.* ff. 1162–80. [14] *Ibid.* ff. 1221, 1342.

finally hung with silk. The basement was generally complete, save for fixtures, but of the new offices on the south some still lacked floors, doors and windows. The workmen kept their materials there, and the work was 'so perfectly plain' that it could soon be finished when circumstances permitted. Four months should see the basement completed. The guardhouse was finished; but the conservatories were still in use for storing materials.[1]

But in October the destruction by fire of the Houses of Parliament brought an unexpected check to the works at the palace. William IV had never been anxious to occupy it, and now offered to hand the building over as a new home for Parliament.[2] All works were suspended while the offer was considered. Although Melbourne said the question must await the determination of Parliament, it was in effect decided by a Treasury minute of 24 October instructing Smirke to construct temporary accommodation at Westminster. The King agreed that work on the palace should be resumed under Duncannon, who retained this charge even when a Tory administration came into office in November 1834.[3]

To Blore 1835 was a year of vexation, with the work dragging on inconclusively. In May the old account with Browne was at last referred to arbitration. Blore reported that much of his work was unsatisfactory; the scagliola, wherever applied in large surfaces, was very defective; the pilasters in the north drawing room were 'by no means satisfactory'; and the marble paving of the sculpture gallery required relaying. The Commissioners accordingly claimed large deductions from Browne's account.[4] When in September it was proposed to move the north-east conservatory to Kew, Blore complained that it should have been sold to provide funds.[5]

The completion of the palace was bedevilled by uncertainty as to funds. The arbitrators' award to Browne of £14,799 was a larger sum than the Government had expected; it swallowed up the remainder of the grant of £100,000 from which Blore had expected to meet the cost of completing certain works begun by Nash, totalling £8537.[6] In December the King suddenly announced that he would move into the palace. Blore wrote 'in great anxiety' to Duncannon: the palace could not be occupied until the Treasury furnished funds. Work on the railing of the grand staircase was suspended until he knew that the Treasury would pay for its completion: the spectre of Nash must ever have been urging caution. Nor could the palace be used until the forecourt had been enclosed, which would require another two or three months.[7]

It was not, indeed, until 4 October 1836 that Blore was able to submit to Duncannon what he regarded as his final accounts, showing a surplus of about £728.

---

[1] *Ibid.* ff. 1241–6.

[2] Sir John Hobhouse, then First Commissioner of Woods, wrote in his journal for October 18: 'Went to St. James's and saw H.M. I cannot say he was much affected by the calamity, rather the reverse. He seemed delighted at having an opportunity of getting rid of Buckingham Palace; said he meant it as a permanent gift for Parliament Houses, and that it would be the finest thing in Europe'. Inspecting the ruins, 'The King looked gratified as if at a show, and perhaps by the prospect of getting rid of Buckingham Palace. Just before getting into his carriage he called the Speaker and me to him and said, "Mind, I mean Buckingham Palace as a permanent gift! mind that!"' (Lord Broughton, *Recollections of a Long Life*, 1911, v, 22–3). In 1831, before approving Blore's plans, William IV had considered turning the unfinished palace into a barracks (*Correspondence of Earl Grey and William IV*, i, 1867, pp. 389, 427; Works 19/3, f. 214).

[3] See p. 194 above.

[4] £1645 10s. for the pilasters, £5007 19s. 3d. for scagliola in the galleries, hall and staircase, and £185 for the marble paving (Works 19/5, f. 1424; 19/6, f. 1452).

[5] Works 19/6, f. 1475.   [6] *Ibid.* ff. 1499–1501.   [7] *Ibid.* f. 1505.

In January 1837 a further parliamentary grant of £6497 met the deficiency on the grant of £100,000 for Nash's works, of which £1069 was for repairing and repolishing marble and scagliola, and completing metal ornaments. The enclosure of the fore-court was then undertaken. As the fence was too weak to support side gates, Blore proposed stone gate piers:

> The great defect of the East front of the Palace is the want of an Architectural connexion between the Marble Arch and the wings: had the Fence instead of being of metal been constructed of stone with an Architectural character, the Arch would have appeared to belong to and form part of the building instead of being isolated and out of place. . . . The narrowness of the Wings is also a defect in the design of this front. Whatever therefore has a tendency to form a connexion between the Arch and the Wings and to give the appearance of a broader base to the Wings will as far as it goes be an improvement to the general design of the front: the latter object has been partly accomplished by the addition of the Guard House on the South and the New Screen on the North, and I feel quite confident that the Stone gate piers will to a certain extent by throwing out something of an Architectural abutment on the opposite sides still more aid the effect, besides forming the Architectural approxima-tion so much wanted between the Marble Arch and the Wings.

For his piers Blore recommended using Portland stone; it was only half the cost of the granite used for the kerb of the railing, and 'the colour holding an intermediate place between the white Marble of the Arch and the Bath Stone of the building will harmonize with both. They will also agree with the gate piers of the Lodge at the entrance of the Birdcage Walk and bring the whole of the buildings into connexion, an object not undeserving of attention'.[1]

Death spared William IV removal to his unwanted palace. After Queen Victoria took up residence on 13 July 1837[2] deficiencies became quickly apparent, and a stream of requisitions flowed from the officers of the Household during the early years of the reign. Apart from improvements in the offices, and in communications within the palace, greater privacy was required for the Queen in her own apartments. The history of these generally small alterations is confused; as the Queen was living in the palace, they could usually be carried out only during the autumn when she was away from London. Some were performed so hurriedly that they had to be done again at the next opportunity.[3] Others were soon outdated, for accommodation adapted for a young queen living with her mother was not always well suited to the needs of a married sovereign with a growing family, needs which could finally be met only by the construction of a new wing. Prior to the Queen's return to the palace in November, works estimated at £4167 were called for, including completing the entrance gates and gas-lighting the court;[4] and a lengthy list of works submitted by the Lord Chamberlain's office on 21 August included various rooms enlarged, stairs

---

[1] Works 19/6, ff. 1530–3; see also f. 1480; Works 3/5, ff. 55, 59, 75. To mark the completion of the palace, Duncannon applied for a knighthood for Blore, an honour the architect is said to have refused.
[2] *Letters of Queen Victoria 1837–1861*. ed. A. C. Benson and Viscount Esher (1908) i, pp. 84—5. Contempo-rary descriptions of the palace are given in Britton and Pugin, *Public Buildings*, ed. W. H. Leeds (1838), ii pp. 284–304, and J. C. Loudon, *Architectural Mag.* iii (1836), pp. 132–7.
[3] See Works 19/7, f. 1978.   [4] T. 1/3489, f. 20393/37, 28 September 1837.

altered or removed, doorways opened or stopped up, and the fitting up of the octagonal room as a chapel with a movable altar.[1]

Architecturally, the most important work done at this period was the removal of the 'King's private stair' of 1832, and the building of a new staircase (now called the 'Ministers' stair') at the northern end of the Marble Hall. This work was completed by February 1839.[2] At the same time the privacy of the Queen's apartments was improved, chiefly by providing a new stair to give access to the Duchess of Kent's apartments at the east end of the north wing.[3] Another of Blore's improvements was the formation of the Household Corridor on the principal floor of the south wing.[4]

Altogether some £20,000 were spent in 1837–9 on works designed to adapt the palace for the Queen's occupation. Of this, £10,000 was met from the Land Revenue, the rest from parliamentary votes.[5] From Michaelmas 1838 the Lord Chamberlain took over responsibility for all internal works,[6] but as the funds at his disposal for Buckingham Palace and Windsor Castle together amounted to only £3200 a year,[7] the Woods and Works had to be called in to help. In February 1840 the Queen's marriage resulted in consequential alterations costing nearly £9000, an excess of more than £1500 on the estimate because they had to be done in a 'very hurried manner ... a great part by candle-light'.[8] In the course of the same year a report by the physician Sir James Clark on the sanitary condition of the palace led to improvements in the heating, ventilation and drainage, and to the filling in of part of the lake in the garden.[9]

After this, few architectural works of any significance were carried out in the palace until the building of a new east wing in 1847. In addition to running repairs and minor alterations, a ventilating system was installed by Dr. D. B. Reid in 1842, and extended to the kitchen in 1843, after the failure of other attempts to improve ventilation and heating.[10] Blore's conversion of the south conservatory into a permanent chapel, to replace the makeshift arrangement in the octagonal room, was executed by Baker and Son in 1842–3.[11] The 'style and extent of the decoration' were decided by Prince Albert in December 1843 after the chapel had been in use for some months.[12] In the north wing alterations approved by the Prince were made in the nurseries; and a mezzanine floor for servants was inserted between the ground and principal floors.[13] In 1845 the Prince had the grand stair decoratively painted under

---

[1] T. 1/3489, f. 989/40.

[2] Works 19/7, f. 1922. Blore's drawings are in the Victoria & Albert Museum, 8738/34, 35, 45, 46, 51, 53, 56. A plan is in the Royal Library at Windsor. Clifford Smith, p. 193, misdates the Ministers' Stair to 1834, implying that it was the first to be constructed on that side of the palace.

[3] Works 19/6, ff. 1813–15.

[4] Incorrectly stated by Clifford Smith, p. 234, to be a work of Nash. Only the bay on either side of the stair from the Entree Corridor can owe anything to Nash. See Works 19/7, ff. 1952, 1956.

[5] Works 19/6, f. 1796. See also ff. 1826–7.   [6] Works 19/25/1, ff. 9–11.   [7] Works 19/6, f. 1822.

[8] T. 1/3489, f. 18183/40 (8 August 1840). The Queen wrote on 10 January 1840: 'It is all so changed, fresh painted and gilded, my rooms fresh painted and the doors altered, and the ceiling gilt ... it looks like a new house and so pretty' (*The Girlhood of Queen Victoria*, ed. Lord Esher, 1912, ii, p. 272).

[9] T. 1/3489, f. 26951/40; Works 19/6, ff. 1871–8. At high tide in rainy weather the kitchens were liable to flooding from the sewer (*ibid.* ff. 1854–67).

[10] Works 19/7, ff. 2119, 2125, 2128–9, 2152, 2154, 2160.

[11] The parliamentary grant for fitting up the conservatories was appropriated for providing a chapel therein (RA, C 26/34a, Peel to Prince Albert, 27 April 1842). See also Works 19/7, ff. 2135, 2144, 2148.

[12] *Ibid.* f. 2179; the further works were again entrusted to Baker (f. 2192).

[13] Works 19/7, ff. 2207–8 (July 1844); RA, C 26/82.

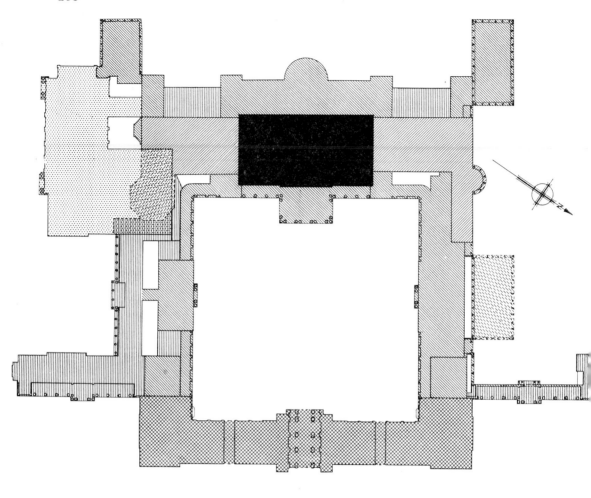

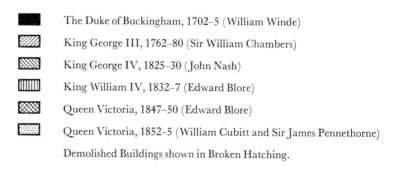

The Duke of Buckingham, 1702–5 (William Winde)

King George III, 1762–80 (Sir William Chambers)

King George IV, 1825–30 (John Nash)

King William IV, 1832–7 (Edward Blore)

Queen Victoria, 1847–50 (Edward Blore)

Queen Victoria, 1852–5 (William Cubitt and Sir James Pennethorne)

Demolished Buildings shown in Broken Hatching.

10   0   50   50   0   100

Scale of Metres   Scale of Feet

Fig. 5. The development of Buckingham Palace, showing the periods of construction.

the direction of Grüner;[1] and in the autumn more alterations were made in the north wing.[2] New store rooms and workshops were built in 1846–7 on the space between the palace and the riding school.[3]

The most interesting addition of this period was not to the palace itself, but in the grounds. In July 1842, after discussions with Blore, Lord Lincoln informed Prince Albert that 'by strict attention to economy in the completion of other necessary works', the Commissioners of Woods and Works would be able to provide £250 towards the erection of 'a place of Refuge' in the gardens.[4] Blore designed a Swiss cottage of three rooms and a kitchen: the principal room, an octagon, was decorated by eight Royal Academicians with frescoes illustrating Milton's *Comus*, and by Grüner with grotesques.[5]

Despite Prince Albert's improvements, the palace left much to be desired. Problems of heating and ventilation had not been mastered, the kitchens were unsatisfactory, the courtyard unfinished, and the whole building too small either for state purposes or as the residence of a sovereign with an increasing family.[6] After unsuccessful approaches by Prince Albert,[7] the Queen herself wrote to Peel of 'the urgent necessity of doing something to Buckingham Palace'.[8] Peel, though wishing to see the plans that were proposed, refused to make 'any immediate reference to the subject';[9] under the necessity of renewing the income tax he had no wish to be accused of courtly extravagance.

Blore had in January 1845 drawn up plans[10] for a new east wing to close the quadrangle, which were submitted to Sir James Clark, Sir Robert Smirke and Charles Barry to report how far such an addition might be made without inconvenience to existing arrangements and without depriving the palace of light and air. They advised that the new front should be erected not between but immediately to the east of the existing wings, and suggested removing the principal portico.[11] In order to spread the cost Blore proposed erecting only the carcass of the new wing, settling its internal arrangements subsequently.[12] Peel promised to do something the following year, and the government decided to finance works estimated at £99,500 by the sale of the Royal Pavilion at Brighton (valued at £60,000) and a parliamentary grant.[13] Blore prepared a model showing his proposals.[14] But the Corn Law crisis overrode the promise of early action. It was not till May 1846 that Peel set up a commission to control the extensions.[15] Until he had their report on Blore's plans he refused to bring

---

[1] Works 19/7, f. 2247; Crest 25/57, no. 5621 (26 August 1845). Lewis Grüner, Prince Albert's artistic adviser, was in England 1841–56.

[2] Works 19/7, f. 2255.   [3] Works 19/7, f. 2268.   [4] RA, C 26/38.

[5] See L. Grüner, *The Decoration of the Garden-Pavilion . . . Buckingham Palace* (1846); J. Steegman, *Consort of Taste* (1950), pp. 202–4.

[6] Plans of the palace at this period are Works 34/2–4, and Royal Library, Windsor (formerly Victoria & Albert Museum 8738/5).

[7] RA, C 44/25, 147/99.   [8] *Letters of Queen Victoria 1837–1861*, ii, pp. 33–4.

[9] Peel to the Queen, 11 February 1845, RA, A 17/26. The Queen replied that 'something must absolutely be done during this session. . . . A little blame and grumbling *must* be expected' (*Ibid.* 27).

[10] Works 34/7, 8; Victoria & Albert Museum, 8738/13, 15. See Works 19/7, f. 2300.

[11] RA, C 26/71, 18 March 1845.   [12] *Ibid.* C 26/76, May 1845.

[13] *Ibid.* C 44/25, memorandum by Lord Lincoln, Chief Commissioner of Woods &c., in expectation of going out of office, 9 December 1845.   [14] Works 19/7, f. 2273.

[15] *Ibid.* f. 2286. The members were the Prime Minister, Chancellor of the Exchequer, Chief Commissioner of Woods, Earls de Grey and Lincoln, and Lord Francis Egerton.

the matter before Parliament.[1] In the commission Earl de Grey[2] took the lead, and it is clear that the final design was the result of much interference on his part; Prince Albert's influence seems to have been concerned rather with planning and internal arrangements.[3] Prince Albert's requirements were, however, such as to make Blore's first proposals 'of no further use', and the commission directed Blore to prepare new plans and elevations according to de Grey's instructions.[4] These were not yet ready when on 28 June 1846 Peel resigned.

By August Blore was in a position to indicate that the cost would now be in the region of £150,000 He suggested that a start might be made that year on the basement of the east front and such part of the kitchen and adjoining offices as would not interfere with the occupation of the palace.[5] Prince Albert had told the new Whig Chancellor, Wood, that unless something was done the Queen would not be able to stay in London; she was 'worse off than any sovereign of Europe the small German Princes included'.[6] Blore set out the defects in a letter to the new Chief Commissioner, Lord Morpeth, which was then published in *The Times*,[7] and on 14 August the Commons voted £20,000 to start the works.[8] Authority to begin was given on 24 September, but nothing more than the foundation was to be built until the Commons had seen the proposed elevations.[9]

The contractor for the new buildings was Thomas Cubitt, who had already built Osborne for the Queen under the personal direction of Prince Albert. It was undoubtedly his proved reliability at Osborne that induced the commissioners to break with Office of Works tradition and make him the sole contractor at Buckingham Palace. Blore thought his prices, based on the Office schedules, 'perfectly fair and reasonable'—for smith's work, the Office price; and five per cent less for both carpenter's and bricklayer's. For day work he charged 5s. 9d. for 'mechanics of all descriptions'; for labourers, 3s. 6d. But he refused 'to enter into competition with other Tradesmen as to prices' and required an assurance that he would 'be allowed to carry out the whole Building to its completion'. 'Subject to these conditions', he

[1] RA, C 26/79. Peel said that he did not think Parliament 'with the present tendencies to architectural criticism, could have been satisfied with the original design of Mr. Blore' (*Ibid*. C. 26/80, 10 June 1846).

[2] Thomas Philip, Earl de Grey (1781–1859) and elder brother of F. J. Robinson (see p. 147), was a keen amateur of architecture who had rebuilt Wrest Park (Beds.) to his own designs. In 1834 he became the first President of the Institute of British Architects. In his unpublished memoirs (typescript in Beds. R.O. CRT 190/45/2) he records that it was 'At the conversazione which I gave to the Institute of Architects [in 1846 that] Prince Albert told me that the Queen wished I would form one of a committee to superintend various additions and improvements [at] Buckingham Palace. . . . I forgot who were also nominated, but I can say that during the ensuing two years that the works were in hand I never saw a colleague. Blore was the architect, and I thought him a very inefficient man. Thomas Cubitt of Belgravia was the builder, and I thought him a very superior intelligent person; and Oliver who had [been] my clerk of the works at Wrest was the clerk of the works under Blore'. Nevertheless, the MS. minutes of the Commission in Works 19/7 record some 15 meetings between 1846 and 1849.

[3] Works 19/7, ff. 2300–3, 2368–70, 2378–9, 2386–7, 2389–90, 2392; 19/8, ff. 2454, 2459—minutes and draft minutes of the commission.

[4] Works 19/7, ff. 2000–3. Various proposals for the centre are in B.M. Add. MS. 42047, ff. 13, 14, 16–19.
[5] Works 19/7, f. 2307.   [6] RA, C 26/82.   [7] 13 August 1846.
[8] *Parl. Deb.* 3rd ser. lxxxviii, 726–32. Hume argued, as did *The Times* (15 and 25 August), that Buckingham Palace was in an unhealthy position, and should be demolished, a new palace being built, perhaps at Kensington. Lord Lincoln wrote to Peel, 'You will see that the Buckingham Palace Vote was swallowed with great ease—Hume only wanting a later and a larger gulp. . . .' (B.M. Add. MS. 40481, f. 348).

[9] Lord John Russell to the Queen, 1 October 1846, RA, C 26/89. Blore's drawings were to go to Prince Albert before being submitted to the commissioners, and then to the Commons. Lithographs for Parliament are in *Parl. Pap.* 1847, lvii, 1–3. A ground floor plan dated 3 October 1846 is now in the Royal Library, Windsor (formerly Victoria & Albert Museum, 8738/17).

undertook to 'make such arrangements with regard to the other parts of my business as will enable me to do the work required in the very best manner, and also to ensure the greatest possible despatch'.[1] Blore recommended the acceptance of the terms, and they were duly approved by the commissioners. Cubitt began work in October 1846.

During the next nine months the commissioners made further alterations in the design, eliminating corner turrets, and reversing the arrangement of the sculpture crowning the centre of the front, so that it formed a triangular composition.[2] They also took a close interest in the internal arrangements, insisting in particular on the re-use of fittings removed from the Pavilion at Brighton. Blore, irritated by this interference, declined to take any responsibility for using fittings from the Pavilion, and warned Morpeth that unless given the 'entire and sole control over the Clerk of the Works, Tradesmen, and all other persons employed in the subordinate departments of the works' he would repudiate all responsibility.[3] Morpeth minuted that 'The Prince should be consulted. . . . The arrangements subsequently matured by Mr. Blore to be shewn to Lord de Grey before they are brought before the Commission. . . .'[4] But he asked Blore for an estimate for completing all the works originally proposed. This comprised £20,000 for finishing the east front, £2000 for the courtyard, £4800 for improving the arrangements of the north and south wings and their communication with the east front, and £53,200 for the proposed ball room and kitchens next Pimlico—figures 'merely conjectural', depending on the re-use of fittings from Brighton and on any alterations that might be made in the plans for the new south (ball room) wing, not yet considered by the commissioners.[5]

These larger schemes were shelved: in January 1849, when Blore calculated that the works in hand would total about £106,600,[6] the Chancellor refused to provide further funds that year for new works at the palace or for the removal of the Marble Arch, which stood uncomfortably close to the site of the proposed east front (Pl. 8A).[7] Blore then drew up estimates of £14,220 for finishing the east wing and its connected works, and the commissioners decided on their immediate completion.[8] But for lack of funds work had already been suspended and remained so until on 1 June Parliament voted £14,200. The Chief Commissioner at once instructed Blore to resume, but the architect's running battle with de Grey had reached its crisis: on 3 June he laid down conditions 'indispensably requisite for my own protection and the satisfactory progress and completion of the engagement'. The works were to be under his exclusive superintendence: de Grey must not play the dictator; and if Blore disagreed with the commissioners, he was to be free to resign.[9]

Work was resumed on 8 June, and by the autumn little was needed beyond finishing touches that Blore declined to direct, which were left to Hogg (permanent

---

[1] Works 19/7, ff. 2339–40, 22 September 1846.
[2] This was done at de Grey's behest. Works 19/7, ff. 2368, 2378–9, 2386–7, 2390. Blore's original arrangement of the sculpture is shown in Works 34/5, illustrated in *Builder*, 1847, p. 410, the lithograph reproduced in Harris, de Bellaigue and Millar, *Buckingham Palace*, pp. 32–3, and Pl. 10A below.
[3] Works 19/8, ff. 2454, 2459 (18 December 1847, 10 January 1848). [4] *Ibid.* f. 2461.
[5] *Ibid.* f. 2476 (22 February 1848). Alterations to the existing wings were approved by Morpeth, 6 September 1848—plans, formerly Victoria & Albert Museum 8738/12, 14, 19, now in Royal Library, Windsor.
[6] Of which £1200 resulted from the haste in November 1848–January 1849 to complete part required for occupation by the household on the Queen's return (Works 19/8, ff. 2579–80). [7] *Ibid.* f. 2577.
[8] *Ibid.* ff. 2614 (16 April 1849), 2628–9. [9] Works 19/8, ff. 2633–5; *Parl. Pap.* 1849, xxxi, p. 302.

clerk of the works) to complete early in 1850.[1] On 26 March Lord Carlisle expressed the commission's satisfaction at the manner in which Blore had carried out his duties, and especially with the saving on the sums voted.[2]

Despite this official approval, the new front cannot be deemed a success. As an architectural composition it has been criticised as provincial, retrograde and 'almost beneath the notice of posterity'.[3] Certainly its overcrowded centrepiece and rather vulgar ornamentation compared ill with the patrician assurance of such town palaces as Barry's Bridgewater House (1847–57), commissioned by Lord Francis Egerton, an active member of the palace commission.[4] The tentative mansard roofs over the pavilions of the new wing hinted at the growing French influence on English public architecture. Hardly characteristic of Blore (whose notions certainly ran to something grander, with domes or at least turrets)[5], they were in all probability due to Lord de Grey, who had himself chosen to rebuild his country house, Wrest Park, in a French style in 1834–40.

The result was not admired by contemporaries,[6] and survived for little more than sixty years before Sir Aston Webb was commissioned to replace it by the present anodyne façade. It was not, however, for aesthetic reasons alone that Blore's front was so soon condemned to destruction. What made its replacement inevitable was the imprudent use of Caen stone as a facing material. Although fine-grained and easy to carve, Caen stone deteriorates rapidly when exposed to the polluted atmosphere of an industrial city. The elaborately modelled surfaces of Blore's front soon began to demonstrate the corrosive action of carbonic acid carried by rainwater, and by 1853 pieces were already dropping off.[7] Thus by the end of Victoria's reign the principal front of her palace was once more a monument to architectural incompetence.

The front completed, and the Marble Arch at last removed, it still remained to lay out the forecourt. Designs for an elaborate Italian garden in the western portion of St. James's Park had been prepared by William Andrews Nesfield (1793–1881),[8] and it was planned to carry these out in conjunction with the forecourt enclosure, an architectural work entrusted to Decimus Burton. A joint estimate of £26,937 was submitted on 8 June 1850.[9] The plan however ran into opposition in Parliament, and the garden was given up.[10] On 17 September Burton sent in an estimate of £5591 for enclosing the forecourt, including £1016 for sculpture by John Thomas consisting principally of 'two large piers with four dolphins and four festoons of shells, etc. on the capitals' for the main entrance.[11] Burton also designed new railings (contracted for by H. and M. D. Grissell at £1864) and gates for the archway through the east front into the courtyard.[12] This contract was also

[1] Works 19/8, ff. 2636, 2659-63, 2684-5, 2705.   [2] *Ibid.* f. 2714. Blore then retired from practice.
[3] H. R. Hitchcock, *Early Victorian Architecture in Britain* (1954) i, pp. 9, 262–3.
[4] Egerton had, however, employed Blore to design his country house, Worsley Hall.
[5] B.M. Add. MS. 42047, ff. 15, 16b, 17–23, 27.
[6] E.g. *Builder* 18 August 1847; *Civil Engineer and Architect's Journal* September 1847, pp. 265–6.
[7] Works 19/8, ff. 3371, 3374–5.
[8] Works 19/8, f. 3492. Some plans and a MS. report by Nesfield are in the R.I.B.A. Drawings Collection.
[9] Works 19/8, f. 2752–3; of the total, £3000 was for removing the Marble Arch.
[10] *Parl. Deb.* 3rd ser. cxi, 323–8; RA, C 81/84.
[11] Works 19/8, ff. 2812, 2805. A considerable part of the carving was postponed.
[12] *Ibid.* ff. 2725, 2799, 2847.

given to Grissell's Regent's Canal Iron Works, who were unable to finish either on time but promised they should be completed for the opening of the Great Exhibition.[1] The works originally estimated for were completed at the end of May at a cost of £5122, together with further works amounting to £2504 to give greater privacy and convenience, such as setting back the palace railings and levelling the ground.[2]

The final task was the provision of new kitchens and of a ballroom large enough for the increasing numbers who expected invitations to the Queen's receptions. A necessary preliminary, the realignment of the great sewer, was made possible by the purchase of land in Pimlico.[3] The Chief Commissioner of Works informed Prince Albert that in the Office he had found only three plans by Blore, but that he would proceed with those and such information as he could obtain from Hogg.[4] It was probably on this basis that Cubitt prepared his specification and estimate of 3 September 1851 amounting to £45,800.[5] His specification refers to a building with towers and turrets; where visible from the road or gardens, Bath stone was to be used rather than the Caen stone preferred by the commissioners; where not, cement. Sculpture left by Blore was to be placed in a panel on the west front.[6] The staircase and servants' rooms were to be completed for occupation, but the ball and supper rooms with their corridors were to be finished externally only, 'the interior finishings and decorations not being determined'.[7] The Chief Commissioner was disappointed at the high estimate, which left 'a very small margin'; Prince Albert thought it even transgressed it: 'Still he is the safest and cheapest man we can deal with and the plan contains absolutely only what is wanted'.[8] Cubitt subsequently offered to execute the work on the basis of a seven per cent profit, but on no account exceeding his total estimate.[9] This remarkably favourable offer was promptly accepted, and the Chief Commissioner, anxious for an immediate start, authorised Cubitt to go ahead; but plans for a ventilation system in the ballroom roof caused delay in planning.[10] Cubitt was given permission to fence the ground for his operations in November,[11] but early in 1852 it was decided that the Office architect James Pennethorne should supply plans and elevations, and it was under his aegis that the new works—the last major addition to the palace—were carried on.[12]

2. THE MARBLE ARCH

The idea of embellishing the western approach to London by a triumphal arch went back to the reign of George III, when Robert Adam had produced an elaborate

---

[1] *Ibid.* ff. 2772, 2775, 2777, 2784, 2923–5. [2] *Ibid.* ff. 3025–8. [3] RA, P.P. Vic.
[4] *Ibid.* C 81/36. Some of Blore's plans, bequeathed to the Victoria & Albert Museum, are now in the Royal Library, Windsor.
[5] Works 19/9, f. 3094. Cubitt preferred to work to his own plans, and prepared at least the working drawings for these additions (*ibid.* f. 3065).
[6] Bas reliefs by Baily and Rossi from Nash's wings, withdrawn from sale in 1849; see pp. 300–1.
[7] Works 19/9, f. 3094. [8] RA, C 81/156, 158; see also 159. [9] Works 19/9, ff. 3098–9.
[10] *Ibid.* f. 3099; RA, C 81/156, 162. [11] Works 19/9, f. 3137.
[12] *Ibid.* ff. 3236–8. Some of his designs are Works 34/360–71. Cubitt was responsible for the parts not visible from the exterior (*ibid.* 19/9, f. 3262).

scheme for a gateway flanked by entrances to the two Royal Parks.[1] In 1796, as architect to the Woods and Forests, Soane was instructed by the King to draw up a scheme for an arch surmounted by an equestrian statue of the Prince of Wales, but his design (exhibited at the Royal Academy the same year) was postponed for lack of funds.[2] In 1813 William Kinnard published a design for a 'Triumphal Arch . . . commemorative of the victories achieved by the British Arms'.[3] In 1816 Parliament voted £300,000 for memorials to Waterloo and Trafalgar, and in the competition that followed, triumphal arches featured largely. Soane took up his old designs, exhibiting revisions in 1817 and again in 1826 and 1827.[4] In designs of 1823 for government offices in Whitehall he proposed placing triumphal arches at either end of Downing Street—one naval, the other military, with appropriate sculpture.[5] He used here the triple arch (after that of Constantine) instead of the single opening of the Arch of Titus as hitherto. The building of a new royal palace was under discussion at the time, and in 1821 Soane showed a design for one in Green Park, its quadrangle entered through a free-standing single arch surmounted by a quadriga.[6] Nash embodied this idea in his proposals for rebuilding Buckingham House in 1825, but he probably borrowed it directly from Percier and Fontaine's *Arc du Carrousel* of 1806 with which he would be familiar from his visits to Paris. The *Arc du Carrousel*, commemorating Napoleon's victories, formed the principal entrance to the Tuileries (with which it was connected only by a railing). Nash chose the same triple-arched form to celebrate British triumphs both naval and military, and provide a principal entrance to the palace.[7] A plaster model exists[8] showing the design worked out in collaboration with Flaxman.[9] An equestrian statue of George IV surmounted the attic, in front of which Nash originally contemplated a free-standing group of Wellington and his aides; as this proved unsatisfactory, a relief was substituted.[10] The King objected to trophies at the ends of the pedestal, so Nash proposed figures of Fame and Victory. Nash also suggested that the King should be dressed in a cloak rather than 'the square-cut coat and waistcoat' of the original design.[11]

Although Flaxman died before work was begun, the sculpture was largely executed from his designs.[12] Chantrey declined any share, but the King persuaded him to carry out the equestrian statue, at a price of 9000 guineas.[13] Sir Richard Westmacott undertook the frieze; two long sides in high relief, one a continuous panel of the battle of Waterloo, the other, three sections illustrating the life of Nelson,

[1] Dorothy Stroud, 'Hyde Park Corner', *Architectural Review* 106 (1949), p. 397. George III's set of the drawings is in B.M. King's Maps xxvii, 26 a–c. They are dated 1778.

[2] J. Soane, *Designs for Public and Private Buildings* (1828), pl. 1.

[3] B.M. King's Maps xxvii, 27, i; Bodleian, Douce Prints N8. For Kinnard see Colvin, *Dictionary*, pp. 347–8.

[4] J. Soane, *op. cit.* pl. 2, p. 2.   [5] *Ibid.* pl. 7, 8.   [6] *Ibid.* pl. 4.

[7] Writing to the Duke of Wellington, 2 July 1829, Nash called the arch 'a plagiarism of the Arch of Constantine' (*Wellington New Despatches*, vi 1878, p. 3). There are varying statements of the size of the Marble Arch compared with those of Constantine and the Carrousel, but it measures 55 ft. 6 ins. by 30 ft. 6 ins. and is 43 ft. 6 ins high (P.R.O. Works 34/9 and 19/8, f. 3001).

[8] In a store-room at the Victoria and Albert Museum; it is described and illustrated by H. Clifford Smith, *Country Life*, 4 July 1952.

[9] B.M. Add. MS. 39781, ff. 254–5, 312, 314; Flaxman's executors charged £30 for designs (*ibid.* 39783, f. 11).

[10] *Ibid.* 39781, ff. 254–5, Nash to Flaxman, 21 August 1826.

[11] *Ibid.* f. 312. A model was also carved in ivory by Richard Cockle Lucas (1800–83) under Flaxman's supervision (*ibid.* f. 314).

[12] *Fraser's Mag.* i (1830), p. 384.   [13] *1831 Report*, pp. 142, 158; T. 1/3489, f. 1682/29; Works 19/3, f. 17.

each side costing £3000; the shorter sides in low relief representing Fame displaying Britain's recent military and naval triumphs, £1000 each. On the east, or military face of the arch, Westmacott was to execute two reliefs, one 'representing the king's approbation of the plan of campaign' before Waterloo, and the other, his rewarding Wellington after the battle;[1] as well as two victories in the spandrels of the large arch at £200 each, and four in the spandrels of the smaller arches at £150, three keystones (£300), and four statues of warriors to surmount the columns (£3200). E. H. Baily undertook for the naval side four other statues (£3200), six victories in the spandrels (£900), two allegorical panels (£600); for the attic pedestal a relief of Britannia supporting a medallion of Nelson, and flanked by a lion and a unicorn (£2000); and four Victories at the corners of the pedestal (£1200). The corresponding pedestal relief on the military side—Europe and Asia, seated on a horse and a camel respectively, and supporting a medallion of Wellington—was executed by J. C. F. Rossi (£2500). Contracts were agreed on 12 June 1828.[2] Considerable changes in detail, however, were made subsequently. The original intention to place reliefs on the north and south flanks of the arch was abandoned: that intended for the north, 'the Genius of England showing to two youths of different ages the names of the heroes they should imitate', was placed, with a companion allegory doubtless once intended for the south flank, on the east face above the smaller arches, instead of the reliefs of the life of Wellington. For each of this pair Westmacott received £800. The design for the Waterloo frieze was altered 'immediately after' Wellington had inspected the model, and presumably therefore at his wish. Military and naval trophies were substituted for the intended heroes above the columns of the main faces: in July 1829 Nash wrote at the King's wish to Wellington for the names of officers who should be represented, but remarked that the King appeared to think that

> some other description of statues, such as Minerva, Mars, &c., would be preferable. His Majesty, however, did not decide; and I own I shall very much regret, as it will detract, as far as it goes, from the intention of its being altogether a national monument. But should it be determined otherwise, I should recommend that military trophies be substituted, as there is no classical authority for putting the gods of the ancients in such situations. On all triumphal columns the statue placed upon them is the person intended to be honoured.[3]

Wellington sensibly replied that the King must make up his own mind.

Originally intending to build the arch of Bath stone, Nash at an early date decided to face it with marble; and his agent Joseph Browne purchased Ravaccione marble for this purpose as well as for the palace on his visit to Italy.[4] The difference in cost, Nash estimated, was reduced to about £2000 thanks to the use of off-cuts of marble for other purposes. His original estimate was £8900; and the labour on the marble added another £5000; so that he estimated the total cost as £15,000 to £16,000 exclusive of sculpture (which cost £33,950).[5] In 1833, Blore calculated that the foundation, including brickwork, had cost £1120, and labour, from ground

---

[1] *Wellington New Despatches*, vi, pp. 3–4. The two reliefs are said by H. Clifford Smith to have been designed by Stothard, *loc. cit.*

[2] T. 1/3488, f. 19080/30; T. 1/3489, f. 1682/29; Works 19/3, f. 17.

[3] *Wellington New Despatches*, vi, pp. 3–4.   [4] *1828 Report*, pp, 48, 51.   [5] *Ibid.* p. 62.

level upwards, exclusive of marble, probably £13,317.[1] Duncannon told the Commons that the arch had cost £70,000.[2]

When work began on the structure, it was found that the Tyburn flowed beneath the site; the ground was a quicksand which had to be dug out and an artificial foundation formed of puddle work.[3] By February 1828 the foundations were complete and the marble plinth set. Nash gave Browne the contract for marble work,[4] but had to abandon his attempt to adapt the terms of the contract for the palace staircase, and asked for the assistance of the other Attached Architects in pricing the work.[5] A proposed compromise, that on account of the great size of the blocks hoisting should be allowed as an extra charge, proved unacceptable to Browne;[6] and the account remained contentious, ultimately being submitted to arbitration.[7] By October 1830, when work on the palace was stopped,[8] the body of the arch was almost complete; the upper plinth was set, only three cornice stones remaining to be fixed.[9] The six carved wreaths on the flanks were in place, and the sculpture nearly finished.[10] When Blore took charge he found himself handicapped by the lack of any drawing showing the disposition of the sculpture,[11] and by the difficulties concerning Browne, whom he thought of discharging.[12] Blore suggested that the arch should be finished 'without the Attic and equestrian statue': 'the lower it is kept the better it will look and the less it will interfere with the Palace'.[13] This was approved.[14] Reports in the papers stated that the King wanted the arch demolished altogether; Blore, officially called upon for his opinion, declared: 'the propriety of placing it in that position originally might have been a questionable matter'; but that no advantage would result from removing it.[15] In August 1832, a contract was made with Browne to execute all the marble, stone and brick work to complete the arch, 'commencing from the top of the plinth over the Corinthian Cornice', for £1275.[16] The 'mosaic gold' railing supplied by Parker to link the arch to the palace was found to be insufficient,[17] but its completion was left to the last stage of the works. Duncannon proposed on 13 January 1837 that the 'mosaic gold' should be replaced by iron, the railing completed and a low gate substituted 'in the centre opening of the Marble Arch in lieu of the unfinished gate prepared by Mr. Parker from Mr. Nash's design'. Blore then obtained a tender from Messrs. Bramah and Prestage for 'completing the centre gates . . . agreeably to the designs made by Mr. Nash, omitting the filling in of the Arch for which a great portion of the work has not been prepared, and the

---

[1] Works 19/5, f. 964.

[2] *Parl. Deb.* 3rd ser. xx, 537. This would appear to price the marble at about £22,000 which would be an excessively high proportion of the total marble account for arch and palace. Because of the contention over Browne's accounts, which was ultimately resolved by arbitration, it is impossible to arrive at the actual cost of the arch.

[3] Works 1/15, f. 331.   [4] *Ibid.* 19/3, ff. 256–7.   [5] Works 1/16, ff. 290, 375.

[6] *Ibid.* ff. 443, 458, 462–3, 468.   [7] T. 1/3489, pt. 1; *1831 Report*, pp. 296–323.

[8] See p. 175.   [9] *1831 Report*, p. 219.   [10] *1831 Report*, p. 216.

[11] Works 19/4, f. 688, Nash was in possession of a model however.   [12] *Ibid.* ff. 706–10, 734.

[13] *Ibid.* f. 742. Blore submitted two sketches, of which Works 34/19 is probably one.

[14] Works 19/4, ff. 759, 761. Of the discarded sculpture, two-thirds of Westmacott's Waterloo frieze and two-thirds of his Nelson frieze were placed in the east front, and the friezes of Fame displaying Britain's triumphs in the west front of Blore's new attic at Buckingham Palace. Wellington was expunged from Rossi's relief which was placed over the entrance to Wilkins' National Gallery, within the portico; Baily's Britannia, purged of Nelson, graces the east side, and his Victories, modified, adorn the facade of that building.

[15] Works 19/5, f. 1238.   [16] *Ibid.* f. 1009.

[17] *Ibid.* f. 1116; 19/6, ff. 1499–1500. Many of the shafts were too large for the holes in the curb.

omission whereof will in my opinion be a great improvement'.[1] This was adopted, with a further suggestion from Blore for giving the fencing of the side arches the 'character and appearance of gates'.[2]

The building of a new east wing to the palace in 1846–50 involved removing the arch,[3] which was now uncomfortably close to the principal front. The problem was to find an alternative site for it. Barry recommended extending Pall Mall to the Park, making the arch the entrance gate.[4] W. A. Nesfield designed gardens in front of the palace, moving the arch down the Mall.[5] Though his plan was approved officially, it was criticised in the Commons and given up;[6] when £11,000 was voted for a reduced scheme, the site of the arch was still undetermined.[7] On 19 August 1850 Thomas Cubitt estimated £700 for taking down the arch and enclosing part of Green Park in which to 'lay each course separately'; and on 12 November he tendered at £2900 for re-erecting it half a mile away, plus £60 for each additional mile.[8] In early December it was decided to re-erect it at Cumberland Gate, and Cubitt's tender was accepted on 20 December.[9] By March 1851 the work was done. Cubitt replaced the timber work of the roof by iron girders and brick arches. The rooms inside were altered, and the railing of the side arches converted into gates. The entire cost of demolition and rebuilding was £5386.[10]

3. THE SCULPTURE

Nash always treated the sculpture, executed by eminent artists of the day, as an element quite distinct from the ordinary building and decoration of the palace, and excluded it from his estimates. He had originally looked to Flaxman, the outstanding exponent of the neo-Grecian school, to assist him in this aspect, writing to him on 18 September 1826:

> . . . I take this opportunity also to remind you of the figures etc.—and of some Sculpture for the dial Turrets—one is for a wind dial the other for a Clock—all the sketches I have are the common place figure of time with his Scythe and hour glass and Lion and Unicorn at the base (as specimens I send you 2 of the Sketches) which you will say are common and bad enough. My wish is that they should be classically treated that is to say as the Antient Artists would have treated them—

[1] Works 19/6, ff. 1530–4, 1543. There is evidently no truth in the story recorded by Walford, *Old and New London*, iv, p. 68 and repeated by H. C. Smith, *Buckingham Palace*, p. 60, of the tympanum being broken on its way from the foundry.

[2] Works 19/6, f. 1540; Works 3/5, ff. 77, 82.

[3] Works 19/7, ff. 2218–9; 19/8, f. 2481. There were several offers to move it entire (Works 19/8, ff. 2485, 2656, 2745); and Browne, still in possession of the machinery used in its construction, offered to demolish it (*ibid.* 2496).

[4] Works 34/11.   [5] Works 19/8, f. 2535; 34/9, 10.

[6] *Parl. Deb.* 3rd ser. cxi. cols. 323–7, 24 May 1850.

[7] Works 19/8, ff. 2717, 2718, 2752–3, 2982–6.

[8] *Ibid.* ff. 2779, 2900. The assumption (H.C. Smith, *op. cit.*, p. 61) that the arch was demolished in 1847 and stored for several years is mistaken.

[9] Works 19/8, ff. 2905, 2917. Sundry connected works were to cost £1518.

[10] *Ibid.* ff. 2929, 2954, 2982–6, 3025–8; *Parl. Pap.* 1852, xxviii, p. 431. Rebuilding cost £3196, and connected works £1563.

avoiding Allegory as much as possible by which I mean the representation of the sentiment by symbols. I am aware they must in some measure be used but had better be avoided when the end can be accomplished without, however whether used or not I wish all the Sculpture to manifest the gusto Greco.

I mentioned to you that after setting down the Character for the 6 figures round the dome in the West front we were at a loss for subjects for the 16 others upon the columns of the four Turrets in the same front—our inventive faculties were at a stand—your fruitful mind will be more productive—If you should think of Trophies for them as was suggested for the other front—they should *all* of them be Trophies i.e. 8 trophies for the 4 Towers instead of 16 figures—for the Towers are symmetrical to each other forming a unity of the whole which would be disturbed were some of them to have figures and others trophies.[1]

Flaxman proposed 'Statues of Eölus and Time holding the Emblem of Eternity' for the turrets; and furnished sketches of Britannia Triumphant (for the central pediment of the east front), the Muses and Sciences (for the pediments of the wings), and of Alfred publishing the laws and King John signing Magna Carta (bas reliefs for the west front), as well as two 'small slight sketches' for military and naval trophies 'which one of the gentlemen in your office can draw correctly giving it the form you think most in harmony with the Architecture of the Tower by which it will be supported'.[2] The King highly approved of these designs 'with the exception only of the Basso relievo at the back of the colonade over the portico of the Entrance and part of the design of one of the pediments of the wings'; for the west front he chose 'the driving the Danes to their ships in preference to the Magna Charta subjects'.[3]

Compelled by Flaxman's death in December 1826 to find new assistance, Nash turned to the other sculptor academicians. Richard Westmacott executed Flaxman's designs for the west front reliefs in Malta stone,[4] and himself designed a panel (the Progress of Navigation) in place of that rejected by the King for the position over the entrance portico.[5] The rest of the external sculpture was largely shared between

---

[1] B.M. Add. MS. 39781, f. 258.

[2] Letter from Flaxman published in *The Times*, 30 November 1943, and then in the ownership of Gerald S. Hughes.

[3] B.M. Add. MS. 39781, f. 310, n.d. In July 1828 Flaxman's executrices submitted the following account to Nash:

	1826		
	'Nov. 20th	4 drawings of Pediments and 2 of Friezes for the Palace £20 each	120
		15 Statues for *do*	30
		2 Designs for the Towers	10
		2 Friezes from English History	40
		2 Pediments—Commerce and Agriculture	40
		Designs for the [Marble] Arch	30
		5 Statues, bas-reliefs etc etc [*cancelled*]	20 [*cancelled*]
			290 [*cancelled*]
			£270'

(B.M. Add. MS. 39783, f. 11).

[4] T. 1/3488, f. 21233/27. Hussey stated that these were of Coade stone (H. C. Smith, *Buckingham Palace*, p. 64) referring to the Department of Scientific and Industrial Research, *Building Research Special Report* no. 12, 1929, which describes the perfect state of preservation of the frieze at the palace: but it is clear that this relates to the continuous guilloche frieze, executed by Croggon in Coade stone. The weathered appearance of the reliefs bears out the contract specification for 'Malta stone'.

[5] *Fraser's Mag.* i (1830), p. 388. This was executed by one of Westmacott's pupils, John Edward Carew (T. 1/3488, f. 2484/29). Westmacott used the same theme on his Collingwood monument in St. Paul's (in five instead of seven roundels), and in the library at Woburn.

Charles Rossi and Edward Hodges Baily, though one group was executed by William Behnes, and the acroteria, of Coade stone, were supplied by William Croggon. The details are tabulated below, together with subsequent additions to the external sculpture.

The internal architectural sculpture consisted chiefly of plaster panels and friezes in low or high relief. Much of this was designed and executed by William Pitts (1790–1840), the rest taken from designs by Thomas Stothard, R.A. (1755–1824). Some of the projected work, chiefly over-door panels, was stopped by the government's intervention, and four executed by Pitts and Croggon appear to have been discarded.[1] Details of the internal sculpture are also tabulated below. Mention must however be made here of the magnificent marble chimney-pieces: that in the entrance hall by Joseph Theakston (1772–1842) cost £1000 (1829–32); and two in the armouries by Matthew Cotes Wyatt, £1050 (1829). Five for the Picture Gallery, embellished with portrait medallions of famous painters, were executed in Italy to Nash's designs at £250 each. Several of the notable sculptors of the day were employed on other chimney-pieces: Flaxman's brother-in-law, Thomas Denman (b. 1787) (six for £2460); R. W. Sievier (1794–1865) (two for £650); R. Westmacott, jnr. (1799–1872) (two for £900) and J. E. Carew (two for £800).[2]

---

[1] *1831 Report*, p. 217.   [2] Works 5/110 and 111; 19/4, ff. 557–65; T. 1/3489, f. 23417/34.

EXTERNAL SCULPTURE

Artist	Subject	Original position	Cost £	Date
BAILY, Edward Hodges 1788–1867	*Haut-relief: Britannia Triumphant (Roche Abbey Stone)	E. front, centre pediment	2500	1827–8
	*Nine Muses[1]	E. front, S. wing pediment	1500	1827–8
	Bas-relief: Britannia distributing rewards to Arts and Sciences[2]	E. front, S. wing, under portico[3]	800	1828–9
	Statues: *Æolus and the Seasons	E. front, S. wing, wind dial turret[4]	700	1829
	*Astronomy, Geography, History[8]	Surmounting S. wing pediment[5]	472	1827–8
	*Commerce, Neptune, Navigation[8]	Surmounting centre pediment[6]	472	1827–8
	*Painting, Sculpture, Architecture[8]	Surmounting N. wing pediment[7]	472	1827–8
BEHNES, William 1795–1864	Statues: Apollo, Morning and Night	E. front, N. wing, clock turret[9]	700	1828–9
CAREW, John Edward c. 1785–1868	Bas relief: Progress of Navigation (designed by R. Westmacott) (Roche Abbey stone)	Under centre portico	1300	1828–9

* Designed by Flaxman.

[1] Although this subject is one of those mentioned by Flaxman in his letter to Nash quoted above, and Nash refers to it among designs by Flaxman to be executed by Baily (T. 1/3488, f. 21233/27), the design of this tympanum is ascribed to Baily himself in the apparently authoritative account in *Fraser's Mag.* i (1830), p. 388. It was executed in Roche Abbey stone (T. 1/3488, f. 21233/27). Blore removed it to the inner face of his new East Front.

[2] These bas-reliefs were additions to the original design. For Rossi's, see *Gent's. Mag.* 1839, pt. i, p. 548.

[3] Displaced by Blore's new East Front, and re-erected on the garden front of the Ballroom by Pennethorne (B.M. Add. MS. 38678, ff. 128–9).

[4] Re-erected by Blore over the north wing of his East Front (*Illustrated London News*, 9 March 1850).

[5] Re-erected by Blore over the pediment on the inner face of his new East Front, and removed *c.* 1948.

[6] Removed as dangerous, with other statues, *c.* 1948; only fragments exist (*ex inf.* Palace Superintendent).

[7] *Sculpture* and *Architecture* were re-erected by Blore above the balustrade over the main entrance on the Park front, and removed when the palace was re-fronted in 1913; that of *Painting* was offered for sale in 1849 with other surplus displaced sculpture, all of which was struck out from the sale catalogue by the Chancellor of the Exchequer (Works 19/8, f. 2639). But by 1882 *Painting* had disappeared (B.M. Add. MS. 38678, f. 129).

[8] These nine figures in artificial stone were from designs by Flaxman (Works 19/3, ff. 285–6). Croggon was paid 150 guineas each for them, but according to J. Riddel, Baily's son-in-law (B.M. Add. MS. 38678, ff. 125, 126), and to the account in *Fraser's Mag.* i (1830), p. 388, they were executed by Baily, who (like Rossi) doubtless modelled for the firm of Coade, of which Croggon was the manager.

[9] Placed by Blore over the south wing of his new East Front (*Illustrated London News*, 9 March 1850).

Artist	Subject	Original position	Cost £	Date
CROGGON, William	Frieze[10]	Frieze of entablature around palace		1826–8
	Four military and four naval trophies	East front towers	1260	1828
	Royal arms	Guard house	230	1834
DAY, Richard	Wreaths	Pediments of conservatories	80	1828
	Rockwork base and balustrade	Garden terrace		1826–7
GRIMSLEY, Thomas	6 vases	Garden terrace	330	1828–30
ROSSI, John Charles Felix 1762–1839	Haut-relief: Arts, Sciences & Manufactures (Roche Abbey stone)	E. front, N. wing pediment[11]	1500	1827
	Bas-relief: The Seasons[2]	E. front, N. wing under portico[12]	800	1828–9
	Four military trophies (artificial stone)	W. front	630	1827–8
	Two military and two naval trophies	E. front, N. and S. wing entrances	693	1829
	Statues: Six Virtues (artificial stone)	W. front around bow[13]	1386	1827–8
TERNOUTH, John 1795–1849	Statues: St. George and Britannia	Centre of new E. front	600	1849
THEED, William Jnr. 1804–91	Relief: Hercules taming the Thracian horses	Riding school pediment	330	1859–60
WESTMACOTT, Richard 1775–1856	*Bas reliefs: Alfred driving the Danes to their ships; Alfred publishing the laws (Malta stone)	W. front	2200	1827–8
	Reliefs (intended for Marble Arch): { Death of Nelson, Battle of Waterloo	E. front attic	4000[14]	1828–32
	Fame displaying Britain's military and naval triumphs	W. front attic	2000	1828–32

[10] At Flaxman's death he 'left a considerable quantity of work on the stocks. Some of this, such as designs for a frieze on the exterior of Buckingham Palace, remained projects' (W. G. Constable, *John Flaxman*, 1927, p. 71).   [11] Offered for sale in 1849.
[12] Offered for sale in 1849; re-erected on the garden front of Pennethorne's west gallery.
[13] These figures of *Fortitude, Prudence, Temperance, Faith, Hope,* and *Charity* were modelled in artificial stone. Removed *c.* 1948 as unsafe, they now repose behind the Royal Mews. One is a later substitute by Doulton.
[14] Blore used only two-thirds of these two friezes, originally costing £6000 (T. 1/3489, f. 1682/29).

INTERNAL SCULPTURE

Artist	Work	Situation	Executant or tradesman	Cost £	Date
STOTHARD, Thomas	Reliefs: 4, cupids and birds	Cornice of Grand Stair	F. Bernasconi	500	1828
	4, the seasons	Grand Stair	A. J. Stothard	584	1828–9
	4, Wars of the Roses	Throne Room	E. H. Baily	1300	1828–9
PITTS, William	Reliefs: 12, The Origin and Progress of Pleasure (Sports of Boys)	N. Drawing Room	W. Pitts	720[1]	1829–32
	The Progress of Rhetoric	Bow Room	W. Pitts	450	1828–30
	Apotheoses of Shakespeare, Spenser and Milton	S. Drawing Room	W. Pitts	315	1833
—	3 Scagliola Doorcases with Terms and medallions of M. Angelo, Raphael and Titian	Picture Gallery	W. Croggon	660	1829
—	1 similar, with medallion of William IV	Throne Room	W. Croggon	253	1833
—	Victories in spandrels of screen to throne recess	Throne Room	Bernasconi		1829–30
THOMAS, John	Reliefs: War and Peace	Ante-room	J. Thomas		1853

[1] This is the figure given for the contract in Works 5/111; but only six of the reliefs had been executed when work was stopped (*1831 Report*, p. 217). Pitts completed this commission under Blore, receiving £850 in addition to £150 already paid on account. It is not clear, however, whether these sums relate exclusively to this work (T. 1/3489, f. 23417/34 and 1829–33 bundle of claims for payment).

4. THE ROYAL MEWS, PIMLICO

The proposals of the New Street Commission for opening up the view of St. Martin's Church from Pall Mall and forming a large open space extending to the end of Whitehall necessitated the removal of the old Royal Mews from Charing Cross.[1] The King approved the proposals in May 1820,[2] and on 29 June the Treasury directed the Surveyor General to prepare plans for new mews in consultation with the Master of the Horse. Nash's proposals to make use of the upper mews at Charing Cross were considered inadequate.[3] The ultimate decision to rebuild on the site of the Queen's stables adjoining Buckingham House gardens must be related to the King's wish to move to that palace.

On 22 June 1822 Nash submitted an estimate of £49,124 18s. 6d. for the new building.[4] His design comprised a great quadrangle, behind which lay irregularly shaped outer and Queen's mews.[5] To the east of the entrance gateway in Ward's Row were a porter's lodge and a house for the Clerk of the Stables and his clerk, and to the west, in Arabella Row, a pair of houses for the equerry of the crown stables and the veterinary surgeon. As the buildings were plain, Nash recommended making a contract in gross through a limited competition; he thought it might then be done for £35,000–£40,000; such care had been taken in the specification and drawing that there was little risk of omissions.[6] The other Attached Architects gave way to Nash's insistence on a contract in gross as 'most advantageous to the Public, for a Building of this description'[7]. Nineteen firms were invited to tender by 20 July,[8] but the tenders were not opened until 23 July, George Harrison having applied for extra time, 'in consequence of the very insufficient data to go from, in the Plans Elevations and Sections for several parts being wanting'.[9] Of the seven tenders submitted, Messrs. Want and Richardson's, at £48,565 the lowest, was accepted.[10] The Treasury authorised the work on 25 July, and Nash immediately instructed the contractors to lay in their materials.[11] Although there was a delay while the old stables were pulled down and trees cleared away,[12] by 27 August 'considerable progress' had been made in the building.[13] The contractors found that extra foundations were necessary beyond the three feet six inches specified,[14] but by 27 September the walls

[1] See p. 351.   [2] Works 1/10, p. 142.   [3] *Ibid.* pp. 170, 174, 175, 193.
[4] *Ibid.* 1/11, p. 165. Great Mews £31,787; Outer and Queen's Mews £9131; porter's lodge £291 2s.; two houses for clerk of stables, etc. £3454; two houses for surgeon and riding master £3031; commission and measuring at three per cent £1430 16s. 6d.
[5] Works 34/14, 18, 20, 527, 529.   [6] Works 1/11, p. 166.
[7] Works 4/25, p. 312; 'against the decided opinions of Mr. Soane, Mr. Smirke, and Mr. Browne' (Works 1/15, p. 486).
[8] Works 4/25, p. 314; 1/11, p. 200.   [9] Works 4/25, p. 332.
[10] *Ibid.* p. 334; 1/11, p. 206. The others were Baker £61,235, Joliffe and Banks £59,720, Bennett and Hunt £57,490, Whitehead £56,500, Harrison £55,700, Herbert £54,894. Thomas Want and John Richardson, who were associated with Nash in building the Regent Street Quadrant, were also contractors for the Royal Military College at Sandhurst, and several Commissioners' churches, and worked at Millbank Penitentiary and Covent Garden Theatre (R.I.B.A. Shide ledger, f. 130; A. Griffiths, *Memories of Millbank*, 1875; M. H. Port, *Six Hundred New Churches*, 1961).   [11] Works 19/50, 27 July 1822.
[12] Works 1/11, p. 497; 'The Building . . . is totally at a stand', complained Nash to Stephenson, 6 August (Works 4/25, p. 343).
[13] Works 1/11, p. 241.   [14] *Ibid.* p. 276. Nash valued the extra work at £828 10s. 9d.

were up to the level of the ground floor.[1] While work proceeded, the contract was still being drafted. Although Nash had spoken of the 'very great care' taken with the planning, the contract drawings he sent to the Office of Works on 13 August had to be taken back for finishing.[2] Completion of the draft was delayed by Nash's wish to alter the contract price to include the extras and various alterations. Stephenson, fearing any alterations would put him at the contractors' mercy, wished to conclude the contract immediately at the tender price,[3] and this was done late in October.[4]

Although Nash in forming his plans had 'most amply consulted' Parker,[5] the Clerk of the Stables, when the buildings began to go up the officers concerned began to discover all sorts of objections. For architectural effect the double state coach houses had doors only in the centre. These were two feet six inches wider than usual, but the royal coachman thought the planning awkward; and seeing the coach houses soon after they were begun, required them to be built deeper.[6] After further discussions with the Master of the Horse, the Duke of Dorset, some alterations were agreed upon in September at a cost of £240.[7] Despite the rebuilding involved, by 14 November the outer stables and buildings were up to the roof; the buildings around the quadrangle up to the sills of the circular windows; and the houses up to the first floor.[8] Nash's assistant, James Morgan, reported that 'The materials and workmanship are excellent—there are several bond stones through the walls not described in the plans or particulars, and the ashlaring is cramped at every joint with copper cramps';[9] and even Stephenson admitted that the contractors appeared 'very anxious to have the work well done'.[10] But Nash left supervision to subordinates.[11] This, and the indulgence of Nash's clerk of works, Day, permitted the use of unsatisfactory materials.[12] Stephenson employed the Labourer in Trust at the Queen's Palace as a check and disagreements arose between all the parties involved.[13] Day having been dismissed, there was no clerk of works when, after a very severe frost, the contractors recommenced the brickwork at the end of January 1823.[14] Another delay resulted from the refusal of the parochial road commissioners to allow the areas of the two houses designed for Mews' officers to encroach on the footway in Arabella Row.[15] By the beginning of February, when the buildings around the quadrangle were ready for the roofs, no further progress had been made on these houses.[16] But far greater problems were imminent. The Master of the Horse inspected the buildings and 'discovered so many objections' that he required the plans to be reconsidered.[17] After a conference between Dorset, Nash, Stephenson and Browne, the officers of the stables submitted twelve objections, some involving alterations of an architectural character, others relating only to the fitting up of the buildings.[18] Ultimately the Treasury on 11 March

[1] *Ibid.* pp. 169, 262, 323.   [2] Works 4/25, p. 347.   [3] Works 1/11, p. 253.
[4] *Ibid.* p. 314.   [5] *Ibid.* p. 465. For Parker see p. 350.
[6] Works 1/12, p. 1 ff.; cf. Works 34/14 for a plan showing the whole layout.
[7] Works 1/11, p. 258; 4/25, pp. 371, 373, 380. Arbuthnot of the Treasury blamed this 'sad blunder' entirely on Nash's inadvertence, *ibid.*, 1/11, p. 260.
[8] Works 4/25, pp. 419, 439; 1/13, p. 169.   [9] Works 1/11, p. 301, 23 October 1822.   [10] *Ibid.* p. 299.
[11] The Surveyor General remarked on Nash's neglect of the Mews on at least five occasions (Works 1/11, pp. 280, 299; 1/12, pp. 161, 340; 19/50, 9 October 1823).
[12] Works 1/11, pp. 280, 361; 4/25, p. 434; 19/50, 3 March and 9 October 1823.
[13] Works 1/11, p. 361; 19/50, 22, 23 January 1823.   [14] Works 1/11, p. 373.
[15] *Ibid.* pp. 381, 497.   [16] Works 1/13, p. 169.
[17] T. 1/3488, 24 February 1823.   [18] Works 1/11, p. 391–4.

referred the matter to the Attached Architects and the Assistant Surveyor General. Meanwhile, by 4 March Nash had stopped work on the parts objected to.[1]

The report of Browne, Soane and Smirke was completed, after long deliberations and an inspection of the buildings, on 29 March.[2] They reported what could be done to remedy the defects, taking the necessity for granted, but regretting that the objections had not been seen and remedied at an earlier stage, and blaming the faults on want of sufficient explanation at the time of planning, and the too hasty manner in which the building was undertaken. This did not put the entire responsibility on Nash; but the Treasury blamed him for not more accurately informing himself 'in an earlier stage of this proceeding'.[3] The principal alterations that he was obliged to make were to transpose the surgeon's offices and the equerry's house (respectively north and south of the surgeon's house) to give more light to the stables; rebuild these two houses so as to form their areas within Crown property; add a storey to the farrier's apartments; construct additional rooms for forage in the back mews; and alter the windows of the chambers facing the quadrangle, to make them only three feet from the floor instead of five feet six inches—an alteration which involved omitting the Bath stone frieze under the cornice.[4] These changes, with £300 worth of 'additional conveniences' for Parker's house that Nash promised to cover by saving in the external finishing,[5] cost £1700.[6] Unable at first to agree a price with the contractors, Nash had the alterations and additions done under the immediate supervision of the clerk of works.[7]

Want and Richardson's high price was no doubt a consequence of their financial difficulties. Already in February 1823 they had given to Messrs. Joliffe and Banks, another building firm, a power of attorney to receive their instalments on the mews.[8] Delayed by the long severe winter and by the alterations, they asked on 16 April 1823 for an extension of time and a payment on account. The contract provided for alterations, but they did not consider that this covered the taking down of work already done, which delayed the payment of their instalments, and put them in great difficulties. Although not technically entitled to their fourth instalment, they had done work valued at £19,000 beyond the sum of £8500 already received.[9] Nash thought that, though the number of men on the site had never been reduced, for the delay in starting and the subsequent suspension they might be allowed four months' grace, and recommended paying £10,000 on account.[10] Extensive employment of lead in September 1823 suggests that the roofs of the quadrangle buildings were being covered.[11] There were about 200 men working on the site in late October.[12] The contractors asked on 25 October for a further £10,000 on account.[13] Nash was informed

[1] Works 1/11, p. 389; T. 1/3488. Stephenson advised a general stoppage (Works 1/11, pp. 410, 414).
[2] Works 1/11, pp. 429–35; 4/26, pp. 10, 13, 14, 21, 23, 25. [3] Works 1/12, p. 37.
[4] *Ibid.* ff. 1–17, 234–43. Nash was reluctant to make changes, arguing that the buildings were what had been asked for (Works 1/11, ff. 465–7, 26 April 1823); and that 'it often happens in Architectural Buildings that sacrifices . . . are necessary to preserve Architectural symmetry' (Works 1/12, p. 17, 21 May 1823). The King, having considered the plans, gave certain directions on 14 June 1823 (Works 1/12, p. 35; 4/26, p. 97).
[5] Works 1/12, pp. 185, 195.
[6] *Ibid.* pp. 234–45. This specification and estimate were accepted by the contractors, 20 November 1823, when the alterations must have been nearly finished (*Ibid.* p. 226).
[7] *Ibid.* pp. 132–3. [8] Works 4/25, pp. 479, 481. [9] Works 1/11, p. 497.
[10] *Ibid.* pp. 509–10. On 1 December 1823 the contractors undertook to finish by Lady Day (*ibid.* 1/12, p. 244). [11] Works 1/12, pp. 161–3; 19/50, 26 September 1823. [12] Works 1/12, p. 190.
[13] Works 1/12, p. 215. Payment was authorised on 18 December 1823.

on 15 March 1824 that everything would be '*really* done by Wednesday';[1] but Parker then requested further improvements to his house.[2] On 10 August Nash again announced that the contract should be completed by the end of the week—indeed, Joliffe and Banks reported that it was already done.[3]

Although the buildings were completed structurally, there was a good deal of fitting up still to be done. Parker's list, estimated at £3203, was authorised by the Treasury on 11 November.[4] Want and Richardson's proposals for fixing stoves, ranges and coppers within three weeks were accepted on 24 November.[5] But in December the Duke of Dorset declared much was still lacking: paving was needed, and a supply of water to the various parts of the Mews. Nash recommended piping water from the Serpentine which cost £647.[6] Not until 17 March was he able to report satisfactory completion of the Mews.[7] In submitting his building accounts on 22 December 1824, Nash reported an extra charge of £120 for 'covering the interior of the gateways with mastic in imitation of the Bath stone work and forming the ceiling into groins, and which I considered in the progress of the works would be great improvements, but which did not occur in making the designs originally'.[8] A late addition, demanded by the Master of the Horse, was a clock turret.[9] Another list of desiderata was submitted by Parker on 10 May 1825. It consisted of fitments, the majority of which had been struck off his previous list by the Treasury[10], and he again demanded that water should be laid on by the Chelsea Water Company.[11] His requisition was approved, estimated by Nash at £571 for items previously rejected, and £692 for new ones.[12] In July Nash certified that the Mews had been constructed in a substantial and durable manner,[13] and that the contractors had remedied such defects as had appeared, except 'some trifling things' in the houses, that Parker and his colleagues wished deferred till their absence during the summer.[14] The final accounts totalled £65,078 11s. 9d.[15]

Once in use,[16] the Mews required almost constant common repairs, and by February 1828 several defects were evident.[17] Dry rot in the flooring was ascribed by Nash to failure to cleanse the sewers.[18] In the washhouses mastic floors had been worn

---

[1] Works 19/50.

[2] These included enlarging the area and wine cellar, and substituting boarded for stone floors, and cost £136 (Works 1/12, pp. 410–413, 440). 'It is quite shameful that the Public should incur daily expense to indulge the caprice of Parker', wrote Nash, 'and lamentable that the Master of the Horse should see through the eyes of such a fellow' (Works 19/50, 15 March 1824).

[3] It seems that the assignees had temporarily taken over the work.

[4] Works 1/13, pp. 77, 121.   [5] Works 4/27, p. 69.

[6] Works 1/12, pp. 513–5; 19/50, 10 August 1824; 1/13, pp. 110, 116–9, 128. The contract for paving was awarded to Swinney (Works 4/27, p. 74).

[7] Works 1/13, p. 255.   [8] *Ibid.* pp. 120–1. As a deduction there were omissions valued at £59.

[9] *Ibid.* f. 255. Nash's design is Works 34/528.

[10] Works 1/13, pp. 349, 358.   [11] *Ibid.* pp. 413, 429, 430.

[12] *Ibid.* pp. 377, 393.

[13] This was in accord with a regulation introduced by the Treasury in consequence of the collapse at the Customs House (Works 1/13, p. 393).   [14] Works 1/13, pp. 405, 410.

[15] Works 1/13, pp. 255, 387. Of this expense, £28,000 was met from the surplus fees of the abolished Transport Board, £500 from interest on Danish and Dutch loans; but these sums were recovered from money belonging to the Crown in the hands of the East India Company, arising from the sale of spices (Works 1/12, pp. 293, 336). In November 1828, however, Stephenson stated that the bills for the Mews totalled £61,062 (Works 1/17, p. 52).

[16] A reference to Nash's renting the Mews (H. C. Smith, *Buckingham Palace*, p. 67), is due to a misreading of Works 1/14, p. 57.   [17] Works 1/16, pp. 82, 348.   [18] *Ibid.* p. 393, 3 July 1828.

away by wet and women's pattens. Balconies had sagged, and a wall between two forage rooms had sunk because of inadequate foundations.[1] Stephenson thought the contractors should make good the defects, which Nash ascribed largely to wear and tear and a failure in maintenance.[2] Expenditure in 1833/4–37/8 averaged about £800 per annum rising in 1838/9–49/50 to nearly £1500 per annum.[3]

Additional coach-houses designed by John Phipps were erected in 1848 by Joseph Griffiths at a contract price of £685.[4] In the fifties, the construction of Victoria Road to the south and west of the Mews caused considerable changes: a house for the Crown equerry was built in 1857–8 to the west of the gateway corresponding to Nash's house to the east;[5] and in 1858–60 Chambers' riding school, untouched by Nash, but repaired by Blore in 1844,[6] was refronted, William Theed junior sculpting a relief of 'Hercules taming the horses of Diomedes' for the tympanum of its central pediment.[7] Considerable alterations to living quarters were made on several subsequent occasions.[8]

CARLTON HOUSE, PALL MALL

In 1783, when he came of age, the Prince of Wales took over Carlton House as his London residence. During the years that followed the interiors were remodelled and refurnished on a palatial scale. Several architects were involved: Chambers, Holland, Yenn, Porden, Hopper, Nash, and James, Lewis and Jeffry Wyatt; as well as several teams of craftsmen, interior decorators and furniture designers. During the later 1820s the whole of this ephemeral creation was dismantled. The story has been told several times.[9] To attempt to re-tell it in detail would be to exceed the scope of a *History of the King's Works*. Firstly because furniture and interior fittings were seldom the responsibility of the Office of Works. And secondly because in this case even the building itself came only intermittently, and often indirectly, within the orbit of the department.

Carlton House remained technically under Office of Works supervision throughout this period. But the effectiveness of departmental control varied according to the wishes of the Prince of Wales. On his coming of age in 1783 the Prince had hoped for

[1] Works 1/17, pp. 29–33, report of 15 December 1828.   [2] *Ibid.* pp. 145–7.
[3] L.R.R.O. 24/1–7; *Parl. Pap.* 1843 (343) xxx, 1851 (374) xxxi.
[4] Works 1/33, pp. 45–6; 19/50; 34/25–31.   [5] Works 19/176; 34/531–9.   [6] Works 2/3, p. 585.
[7] Works 19/9, ff. 3650–1; 19/10/2. This sculpture has often been wrongly ascribed to the elder Theed working under Nash.   [8] Works 19/50; 19/299.
[9] T. Rowlandson and A. C. Pugin, *Microcosm of London* (1808); R. Ackermann, *Repository of Arts* i (1809), pp. 398–400, vi (1811), pp. 167–8, 227 and vii (1812), pp. 29–30; W. H. Pyne, *Royal Residences* iii (1819); J. Britton and A. C. Pugin, *Public Buildings of London* ii (1828), pp. 193–201; *Survey of London* xx (1940), pp. 72–7; S. Sitwell, *British Architects and Craftsmen* (1960 ed.), pp. 283–8; D. Stroud, *Henry Holland* (1966), pp. 61 *et seq.*

£100,000 per annum. He had to be content with £50,000 per annum from the Civil List and £12–13,000 per annum from the Duchy of Cornwall, plus a lump sum of £60,000 for the settlement of immediate debts and the refurbishing of Carlton House.[1] The size of the project, as well as the Prince's personal preferences, meant that the Clerk of Works, John Yenn, was superseded first by Sir William Chambers and then by Henry Holland, Prinney's private architect. In this way Carlton House was removed from the sphere of Office of Works control between 1783 and 1796. Immediate repairs directed by Chambers to the tune of more than £6000 only whetted the Prince's appetite.[2] 'I am hard at work', he wrote to his brother the Duke of York in November 1783, 'and hope . . . you will not think me a bad architect'.[3] Recklessly mortaging his future income, he soon forgot the King's admonition to behave 'like a rational being'.[4] 'I owne I had hopes he was sincere', wrote George III in August 1784, 'as on my going to Carleton House he proposed . . . only painting it and putting handsome furniture where necessary; but in very few weeks this was forgot, and large additional buildings erected; and least these should not waste enough money, the most expensive Fêtes [were] given, and at this hour considerable additional [works] are begun'.[5] By October the debt stood at £147,293, of which £7743 was due for work under Holland and £8700 for work under the interior decorator cum clerk of works, Guillaume Gaubert. Holland's previous estimate of £18,000 had already jumped to £30,250 and Gaubert's to £35,000. 'It is with equal grief and vexation', complained the Prince's Treasurer and Secretary Col. Hotham, 'that I now see your Royal Highness . . . totally in the hands, and at the mercy of your builder, your upholsterer, your jeweller and your tailor. I say totally because these people act from your Royal Highness's pretended commands, and from their charges there is no appeal . . . [Holland and Gaubert] have undertaken and are carrying on works . . . to an enormous amount, without a single care or inquiry from whence money was to arise for their discharge; neither my advice, my expostulations, nor any representation of there being no fund whatever for this purpose, has been regarded.'[6] The stables alone cost £31,000 per annum. But when the King called for retrenchment, the Prince replied that 'it would be merely a drop of water in the sea'![7]

---

[1] Lord John Russell, *Charles James Fox* ii (1853), pp. 69–70; Lord Auckland, *Jnl. and Correspondence* i (1861), p. 53; Earl Stanhope, *Pitt* i (1861), pp. 123–4; N. Wraxall, *Memoirs*, ed. H. B. Wheatley, iii (1884), pp. 107–8; Hist. MSS. Comm. *15th Report, MSS. of the Earl of Dartmouth* iii (1896), pp. 668–9; *Correspondence of George, Prince of Wales* ed. Aspinall i (1963), pp. 98–9. The Chancellor of the Exchequer explained that 'the Prince was a young man and consequently it could not be expected that he should be a very great economist' (*Parl. Hist.* xxiii, 1782–3, cols. 1030–1, 25 June 1783).
[2] RA 35221–5 (disposal of £60,000 voted by Parliament, 1783–4); Works 4/16, 4 July 1783.
[3] *Correspondence of Prince of Wales* i, no. 100, 7 November 1783.
[4] *Ibid.* no. 119, 27 August 1784. See also *ibid.* nos. 79–80, 15–16 June 1783, George III to Col. G. Hotham and the Duke of Portland; *Correspondence of George III*, ed. Fortescue vi (1928), no. 4391, 17 June 1783, George III to Lord North.
[5] *Correspondence of Prince of Wales* i, no. 119, 27 August 1784.
[6] *Ibid.* no. 128, 27 October 1784. For examples of payments to tradesmen working at Carlton House 1783–6 cf. RA 35010–3 and 35043–7. For 'the prevalent disposition in all to take advantage of *The Prince*', at least as regards the sale of neighbouring property, cf. RA 35037–40, 35055, 35076 *et seq.*, 35090, 35106, 35108, 35119, 35129, 35146.
[7] *Correspondence of Prince of Wales* i, no. 122, 1 September 1784, Prince of Wales to Lord Southampton. He later declared 'that the screen alone had cost more than the Crown had allowed for the whole' (*Jnls. of Mrs. Papendiek*, ed. Mrs. V. D. Broughton i, 1887, pp. 256–7).

By the summer of 1786 creditors were becoming restive. The logical answer was a parliamentary grant based on an investigation by the Office of Works. But this was easier said than done. Both parliamentary grant and Office of Works certificate proved difficult to obtain. Expenditure under Chambers, Holland and Gaubert between 1783 and 1786 had totalled more than £71,000. Estimates prepared in June 1786 suggested £32,900 as the cost of concluding work already begun; and £69,700 as the cost of completion according to 'Mr. Holland's . . . Extended Plan.'[1] Less than a year later Holland's estimate had jumped to £80,200.[2] Gaubert protested that he had followed 'a plan of economy as clearly proved as it must be universally acknowledged'.[3] But with the Prince's debts standing at more than £250,000, the reputation of his tradesmen was naturally at a discount.[4] During the later months of 1786 the Prince temporarily dismissed his household and retired to Brighton with Mrs. Fitzherbert, leaving Carlton House 'dismantled' and 'shut up' and the settlement of his chaotic accounts in the hands of five trustees.[5] Parliament had to be propitiated: Fox even went so far as to deny publicly the fact of Prinney's secret marriage. Late one night at Carlton House, early in May 1787, the Prince at last persuaded Pitt's ministry to liquidate his debts. Dundas was the intermediary on this nocturnal occasion, and Wraxall assures us that 'this amicable conference was subsequently moistened with no ordinary quantity of wine'.[6] George III agreed to supply an extra £10,000 per annum from the Civil List; and the House of Commons voted £161,000 to the Prince's creditors (£60,000 being earmarked for Carlton House), plus another £20,000 for Carlton House 'as soon as an estimate shall be formed with sufficient accuracy of the whole expense for completing the same in a proper manner'.[7] This estimate was never presented. Holland had now decided that his previous estimates were 'merely . . . rough guesses'.[8] And the Office of Works declined to cooperate. 'It is impossible for us to form any judgment', wrote Chambers, Couse and Craig; 'exact estimates require such an insight into the intention of the Designer, and such a vast detail of Designs and explanations, as makes it scarcely practicable for one man to value another's Compositions, and we would not on any account mis-guide or deceive His Royal Highness by the usual guess Valuations'.[9] However Pitt managed to evade any further investigation by taking refuge in parliamentary phraseology: 'he imagined gentlemen would not think of instituting any

---

[1] RA 35053 (summary) and 35048 (details).

[2] *Correspondence of Prince of Wales* i, no. 235, 14 May 1787 (RA 38193–5).

[3] RA 35066, 2 May 1787, Gaubert to the Prince's Trustees.

[4] *Correspondence of Prince of Wales* i, no. 163, 15 June 1786 and no. 232 (abstract of debts 1783–7, including £55,000 owing to Holland and Gaubert for Carlton House).

[5] *Ibid.* no. 191, 16 July 1786 and no. 209, 28 December 1786; Wraxall *op. cit.* iv, p. 353. The Trustees were Lt. Col. Hotham, Henry Lyte, Lt. Col. Hulse and Lt. Col. Lake, plus Lord Southampton. In January 1787 Hotham resigned over the Prince's banking arrangements with Hammersley (*Correspondence of Prince of Wales* i, no. 211, 5 January 1787) and became the Duke of York's Secretary and Treasurer (*ibid.* no. 249, 10 August 1787).

[6] *Ibid.* no. 218, 2 May 1787; Wraxall *op. cit.* iv, pp. 463–4; *MSS. and Correspondence of James 1st Earl of Charlemont* (Hist. MSS. Comm. *12th Report*, 1891), ii, p. 53, 9 June 1787.

[7] *Commons Jnls.* xlii (1787), pp. 793, 798–9, 851–2; *Parl. Hist.* xxvi (1786–8), cols. 1010, 1048, 1064, 1207; *Gent's. Mag.* 1788, pt. i, p. 226 and 1788, pt. ii, p. 986; G. Tomline, *Life of Pitt* ii (1821), pp. 32–9; Auckland *op. cit.* i, pp. 416, 418.

[8] *Later Correspondence of George III*, ed. Aspinall i (1962), no. 805, 14 May 1787.

[9] Works 6/21, f. 116, 20 July 1787; Works 4/17, 13 July 1787, 20 July 1787, 27 July 1787; 'Accounts and Papers [relating to Carlton House]', *Parl. Pap.* 1790–91, xxxii (xc), nos. 708–9.

Y

very strict scrutiny into the state and nature of that account, not only out of personal respect to the exalted character whom it concerned, but because it was a circumstance which never could occur again'.[1]

The vagueness of these arrangements facilitated still further expenditure. Between August 1787 and November 1789 Holland paid out £50,374 8s. 9d., a sum which almost cancelled out Exchequer disbursements of £55,200 during the same period.[2] Another £38,700 was granted during the next three years.[3] But in December 1789 the Treasury refused to endorse an application to the Exchequer for £56,950 in furnishing bills: 'it does not appear to the Board that [this] additional estimate . . . comes within the *intention* of the [Commons] Resolution of 24 May 1787'. 'I did not *deal* unfairly', complained the Prince of Wales, 'with Your Majesty or the publick'. But his protests that Holland's 'guesses' had excluded furniture aroused little sympathy.[4] The Prince and his royal brothers had recourse to Dutch money-lenders.[5] And the tradesmen remained unpaid. In the summer of 1791 the Prince sent in yet another plea to George III: the King's generosity in 1787 had been 'unfortunately frustrated by the delay in forming the estimates then required by Parliament . . . the inadequacy of the sums since issued . . . [and] the inaccuracy of the short estimate delivered to Mr. Pitt by Mr. Holland. . . . Among those to whom large sums are due . . . are various respectable tradesmen who have represented that they are in the greatest distress and even in danger of ruin'.[6] An estimate produced in 1789 had actually been 'afterwards reduced nearly one half by H.R.H. himself'.[7] But by 1792 the Prince's debt stood at £370,000 and his Newmarket stud had to be auctioned at Tattersall's.[8] A few months later Lord Rawdon warned the Prime Minister that the bailiffs would soon be in attendance at Carlton House: the Prince is 'exposed to the daily hazard of public insult by an execution in Carlton House . . . at a time when there is but too much propensity to discredit every branch of monarchical establishment'.[9] In 1793 Thomas Coutts came to the rescue: a loan of £100,000 based on the security of the Duchy revenues and a deposit of the Prince's diamonds.[10]

An acceptable marriage held out the only prospect of a permanent solution. With his debts standing at £630,000 in 1795, the Prince could hardly afford to refuse. Caroline of Brunswick brought with her a generous marriage settlement. By the Establishment Act of 1795 the Prince's income was increased to £138,000 per

---

[1] *Parl. Hist.* xxvi (1786–8), col. 1207, 21–24 May 1787; Wraxall *op. cit.* v, pp. 24–5.
[2] RA 32001; *Later Correspondence of George III* i, p. 805.
[3] 'Accounts and Papers [relating to Carlton House]', *Parl. Pap.* 1790–91, xxxii (xc), nos. 708–9; Erskine May, *Constitutional History of England*, ed. F. Holland i (1912), pp. 168–70; Tomline *loc. cit.* For payments to the Prince in 1783–4, 1788–9 and 1796 cf. 'Public Expenditure and Income, 1688–1869', *Parl. Pap.* 1868–9, xxxv, pp. 181 *et. seq.*
[4] *Later Correspondence of George III* i, p. 805; *Diaries and Correspondence of George Rose* i (1860), pp. 100–4.
[5] *Correspondence of Prince of Wales* ii (1964), no. 486, pp. 48–9.
[6] *Ibid.* no. 589, pp. 158–9, 5 June 1791. In 1790 twenty-seven distressed tradesmen petitioned the Prince, who referred them to the Treasury officers, who referred them back to the Prince ('Accounts and Papers [relating to Carlton House]', *Parl. Pap.* 1790–91, xxxii (xc), nos. 708–9.
[7] 'Report from the committee . . . [on] Carlton House', *Parl. Pap.* 1790–92, ix (xxxix), no. 94.
[8] *Correspondence of Prince of Wales* ii, no. 653, p. 239, 9 February 1792; Lord Malmesbury, *Diaries and Correspondence* ii (1844), p. 450.
[9] *Correspondence of Prince of Wales* ii, no. 691, p. 280, 18 September 1792. What Prinney once called 'those damnable doctrines of the hell-begotten *Jacobines*' found an easy target in the 'vicious taste and unbounded expense' of Carlton House (*ibid.* no. 694, pp. 286–7).
[10] *Later Correspondence of George III* ii (1963), pp. xvii–xix; RA, box 3, nos. 170–71.

annum. Out of this sum £78,000 per annum (including £13,000 per annum from the Duchy of Cornwall) was set aside for the repayment of unpaid bills; five newly appointed Commissioners acting as financial guardians.[1] £27,500 seems to have gone immediately towards Carlton House, plus £5000 in preparing quarters for the ill-starred Princess of Wales.[2] Of course this financial settlement did not pass unopposed. Fox demanded the sale of the Duchy of Cornwall, Sheridan the disposal of Crown lands. Grey thought Parliament had 'a duty . . . to teach [the Prince] . . . that as his family were chosen to the throne for the good of the people, so . . . his situation was created not merely for luxury and indulgence'. Wilberforce called for wartime austerity: 'a certain chaste and dignified simplicity' instead of 'finery and tawdry decoration'.[3] Such language was less attractive to the Prince than Loughborough's statement that 'in these times of democratic frenzy it was necessary to support the splendour of Courts and Princes'; after all, 'the public would not wish that an English prince . . . should count over pounds, shillings and pence, with the minuteness of a petty tradesman'.[4] Still, as far as Carlton House was concerned, the Establishment Act supplied an immediate solution to the problem of unpaid tradesmen. Prinney's scheme to extend his residence eastwards over the site of Conway House was, however, 'completely knocked on the head'.[5] And the settlement embodied at least one provision designed as a permanent guarantee of future economy: Carlton House was brought back within the framework of the Office of Works.[6]

Thirteen years of princely spending, between 1783 and 1796, had imposed a coherent pattern upon an unplanned complex of buildings. Holland's famous Ionic screen, the great Corinthian *porte cochère*, the celebrated staircase and its attendant suite of exquisite rooms together constituted an architectural ensemble which Horace Walpole could proclaim 'the most perfect in Europe'.[7] The money for these operations had come from three chief sources: direct parliamentary grants; the revenue of the Duchy of Cornwall; and regular assignments out of that part of the Civil List Class I known as the Prince of Wales' Privy Purse. The Office of Works was accountable for none of this expenditure. Only in 1796, when the maintenance of Carlton House once more became a charge under Class IV of the Civil List, was the accountability of the Office of Works again confirmed. And even after that date the building accounts are confused by haphazard payments out of the Privy Purse which far outweigh the meagre sums advanced by the Office of Works.

The extra labour involved in maintaining Carlton House prompted first Chambers

---

[1] The Speaker of the House of Commons, the Chancellor of the Exchequer, the Master of the Rolls, the Master of the King's Household and the Surveyor of Crown Lands (35 G. III *c.* 129; *Correspondence of Prince of Wales* iii, 1965, pp. 4–5).

[2] RA 32466. For the Prince's will, 10 January 1796, leaving all the furniture in Carlton House as well as neighbouring property to 'my Maria Fitzherbert', and 'to her who is called the Princess of Wales . . . one shilling', cf. *Correspondence of Prince of Wales* iii, pp. 133–8.

[3] *Parl. Hist.* xxxi (1794–5), cols. 1464, 1490, 1493.

[4] *Ibid.* xxxii (1795–7), cols. 114, 118; *Correspondence of Prince of Wales* ii, no. 704, p. 303, 8 October 1792.

[5] Conway House had been previously adapted to accommodate officers of the Prince's Household (*Correspondence of Prince of Wales* iii, p. 273, 26 September 1796).

[6] Works 4/18, f. 166, 12 January 1796; L.C. 1/2, f. 20, 1 February 1796.

[7] H. Walpole, *Letters*, ed. Toynbee, xiii (1905), p. 320, 17 September 1785. For a detailed examination, plans etc. of the constructional sequence see Stroud *op. cit.* and *Survey of London op. cit.* pp. 71–3 (property plans 1699, 1761, 1794) and plates 55, 62 (house plans 1784, 1794, 1813). The two blocks of offices shown flanking the forecourt in the 1794 plan were never built.

and then Wyatt to press for higher salaries.[1] Neither request was well received. But at least Yenn was theoretically confirmed in office as Clerk of Works in 1796, having been 'dispensed with . . . for some years'.[2] One immediate problem involved the disentangling of a number of unsettled bills presented by Holland, Daguerre, Delabrière and Marsh and Bailey. The Office of Works informed the Treasury that out of a total of £17,612 15s. 8d. nearly half was 'for work employed in finishing only, but of which most of the articles are now hid, or so mixed with other articles in the Building, that they are totally incompetent to give them any examination upon which their Lordships could place the least reliance; and that the other part of the abstract . . . is principally for furniture, with the value of which articles they cannot be thought Competent Judges'. The Treasury replied laconically, expressing 'regret that the investigation proposed can be of no use'.[3]

After 1796 this financial confusion continued. It has sometimes been supposed that the next spate of building begins with Holland's death in 1806. His successor, the elusive Walsh Porter, is assumed to have begun the reconstruction of the low suite of rooms along the garden front, the operation being continued by Hopper in 1811 and concluded by Wyatt and Nash in 1812–14. In fact the chronology has to be pushed back several years, and the list of names involved must be lengthened to include several members of the Wyatt clan. In 1802 Holland finally withdrew from royal patronage.[4] And his dissociation from the work at Carlton House can perhaps be dated even as early as 1795. For in July of that year Prinney's sister Elizabeth, at James Wyatt's suggestion, made a point of recommending one of the younger Wyatts as successor to Holland, whose dismissal seems to have been common gossip.[5] Anyway, before long James, Jeffry, Lewis, Edward and Matthew Cotes Wyatt were all at work. Between 1796 and 1815 the Office of Works was responsible for running repairs, an average expenditure of about £2000 per annum.[6] On two occasions, however, the department went beyond these limits: James Wyatt's refurbishing of 1804–5 and Nash's festive additions of 1814–15. The bulk of the work, by Porter and Hopper between 1805 and 1812, was paid for out of the Privy Purse or out of the Duchy of Cornwall revenues.

In 1804 James Wyatt was directed by the Prince of Wales 'to repair, paint and whitewash the whole of Carlton House; to regild such parts as had been gilt before and to make some additions in the decorative part of the building'. As Wyatt put it, 'these repairs had certainly become very necessary, nothing of the kind ever having been done since the house was first fitted up'. But the order soon escalated. An initial estimate of £5000 was followed by another for £8500, and the total expenditure was probably higher still. In a letter to the Lord Chamberlain Wyatt explained this piece of irregularity: the first estimate 'I communicated to Mr. Addington and Mr. Vansittart one day when I had the honour of seeing them together at the White Lodge in Richmond Park. They gave me their verbal sanction to proceed . . . but

---

[1] Works 6/22, 19 February 1796 and 11 May 1796; Works 4/18, f. 167, 19 February 1796; T. 29/69, f. 305, 28 July 1796.
    [2] Works 6/22, 11 May 1796; Works 4/18, f. 175, 30 April 1796 and f. 177, 4 May 1796. The Prince suggested Groves.
    [3] T. 29/68, ff. 325–6, 23 October 1795; Works 6/22, 25 August 1795; Works 4/18, f. 139, 28 August 1795.
    [4] Stroud *op. cit.*, pp. 84, 148.   [5] *Correspondence of Prince of Wales* iii, no. 1014, p. 81, 28 July 1795.
    [6] Works 19/5/1, 'Statement of expenses at the royal palaces, 1761–1827'.

H.R.H. having expressed his intention of making some further alterations, upon which he had not yet finally decided, the estimate was not officially submitted to the Treasury but remained for the purpose of adding to it whatever might be the amount of the additional work which H.R.H. proposed to have executed'.[1] In this way a general redecoration of the basement rooms along the garden front was begun. Flitcroft's façade was refaced with Parker's cement. Work was set in hand 'to convert some rooms . . . into H.R.H.'s own apartments . . . with hot and cold baths. . . . To convert into a Drawing Room (to be ornamented with pictures) the Large Room lined with Scagliola, originally intended for a Dining Room, and . . . to substitute for the former Dining Room one which by making some new approaches to it will be much better suited to the purpose'. Westmacott supplied four chimneypieces, including two 'in very fine dove marble . . . from the designs of James Wyatt Esq.' Bernasconi was responsible for plastering; Edward Wyatt for carving and gilding. Matthew Cotes Wyatt received £507 3s. 0d. for 'eighteen bronzes' in the hall and octagon; 'four long panels in the ceiling with allegorical portraits of History, Painting, Architecture and Sculpture, two circles representing Poetry and Music [and] four small circles with Geniuses of Painting: two bas reliefs in the Dining Room [and] one large transparent window'.[2]

The next stage in the refurbishing of Carlton House was quite independent of the Office of Works. Between 1805 and 1812 Walsh Porter and Thomas Hopper were responsible for a good deal of decorative and structural alteration. Under their direction the total outlay from Duchy of Cornwall sources alone came to £22,685 1s. 0d.[3] 'Although Carlton House as finished by Holland was in a complete and new state', noticed Farington, the Prince 'has ordered the whole to be done again under the direction of Walsh Porter who has destroyed all that Holland has done and is substituting a finishing in a most expensive and motley taste'.[4] Once more Edward Wyatt appears as ornamental gilder. But this time Bartoli supplied scagliola and Fricker and Henderson were responsible for decorative painting.[5] Chief among the additions of this period was Hopper's celebrated Gothic conservatory, an exotic confection in cast iron and translucent coloured glass (Pls. 12, 13). It was constructed in 1807, and not for the Regency celebrations of 1811, as has sometimes been supposed.[6] Hopper's work at Carlton House constituted his first major commission and later formed the basis of a fashionable country house practice. It was his Gothic scheme for Walsh Porter at Craven Cottage, Fulham, in 1806 which had first attracted the Prince's notice.[7] Porter's position at Carlton House was that of decorative consultant. He was neither an architect nor a craftsman. He was a member of the Carlton House set, a picture dealer, a dandy, an impresario, a self-styled connoisseur who died heavily in debt in 1809.[8] Lord de Dunstanville dismissed him as a professional

---

[1] L.C. 1/40 ff. 4–5, 29 June 1804, 17 July 1804 and f. 11, 7 November 1804; Works 4/19, 8 February 1805.
[2] Works 5/94 (1804).
[3] RA 35214, Duchy of Cornwall accounts, wmk. 1823. For sundry payments (1806–8) to Walsh Porter out of the Prince's Privy Purse cf. RA 89441, 89443, 89445–9, 89452.
[4] Farington, p. 3258, 3 May 1806.   [5] RA 35185, tradesmen's bills, 12 September 1809.
[6] *The Times* 16 September 1807 p. 3, 24 September 1807 p. 3; Ackermann, *Repository* vi (1811), p. 167; J. B. Papworth, *Select Views in London* (1816).   [7] Colvin, *Dictionary*, p. 299.
[8] *Gent's. Mag.* 1809, pt. i, p. 485. He wrote a comic opera in 1797 called *In the Chimney Corner*. Despite his celebrity in the art world, he was snubbed by the R.A. and had to borrow 'much money of persons who insured his life' (Farington, p. 2628, 23 April 1804 and p. 4386, 16 June 1809).

flaneur, 'a very slight man'. Sir Francis Bourgeois agreed that he 'had not the least real knowledge of pictures', but had to admit that he 'was very eccentric and entertaining, and his society was much relished by the Prince of Wales . . . [for] in all that related to manner and fastidious delicacy in entertaining. . . . Walsh Porter far exceeded [the dandy] Mr. Skeffington'.[1] Under his influence the Prince exchanged Holland's gallic Neo-Classicism for the eclectic finery of Wyatt, Hopper and Nash.

Meanwhile Yenn still supervised some minor repairs, with Lewis Wyatt as nominal Labourer in Trust. Yenn also accounted for several small alterations to the Prince's adjacent property, notably work at Warwick House (ex Conway House) in 1807–11, directed by William Porden and executed by Carlton House tradesmen on behalf of Princess Charlotte.[2] But it was the work executed independently of the Office of Works which still attracted greatest attention. In April 1810 the Bishop of Salisbury told Farington that 'the apartments which were fitted up at a vast expense under the direction of the late Walsh Porter are now undergoing a complete alteration under the direction of a person appointed'.[3] This was probably mere rumour. But early in 1811 James Wyatt was certainly commissioned to direct elaborate preparations for a court fête held on 19 June. His own reward out of the Prince's Privy Purse was £1500. But the contracts obtained by Edward Wyatt for gilding and carving and by Tatham and Bailey for upholstering were very much larger, and extra payments via the Office of Works were still being disputed four years later.[4] More than 3000 guests thronged 'the grand circular dining-room . . . [with] its cupola supported by columns of porphyry'; the throne room 'hung with crimson velvet'; the 'four handsome marquees . . . pitched on the lawn . . . with a *chevaux de frize* to prevent all intrusion'; and, the climax of the display, Hopper's 'Gothic Green House' arranged as the royal supper room, its table decked out with cascades, waterfalls and artificial pools of live gudgeon—'Sadler's Wells business', as Tierney called it, to amuse '*grown* children'.[5] Several days later crowds were still clamouring for admission. Dance and Farington found themselves hurried from room to room by Yeomen of the Guard; 'several hundred ladies . . . were taken through a window . . . the men were let in at the door by degrees', and the Duke of Clarence held back the mob with a speech from 'the top of the wall which fronts the house'.[6]

A year later it was the tradesmen who were clamouring. Unpaid bills amounting

---

[1] 'He did what he could to get money by buying pictures and selling them. His expenses, however, were such that before his death his fortune was gone, and the collection now offered for sale [at Christie's] under his name, undoubtedly is the property of several persons' (Farington, p. 4488, 12 March 1810). For an amusing description of his eclectic style cf. Ackermann, *Repository* iii (1810), pp. 392–3.

[2] Works 6/24, ff. 126–7, 143, 153, 161, 193; Works 4/20, 8 April 1808, 16 September 1808; Works 6/25, ff. 192–3, 19–24 December 1811; T. 29/92, f. 663, 18 December 1807; T. 29/96, f. 416, 12 September 1808; T. 29/95, ff. 445–6, 22 July 1808; Works 5/98 (1809). For plans of the Prince's property around Carlton House cf. RA, box 3, nos. 156, 159 (1792). For a view of Warwick House cf. Ackermann, *Repository* vi, (1811), p. 350. Until the establishment of the Regency in 1812 (52 G. III c8, sect. 4) the Prince paid rent to the Crown for both Carlton House and Warwick House. After that date payment of rent ceased, but in 1820 the property, not being an official palace, was still subject to 'Land Tax, Property Tax, the House and Window Tax, and various parochial Rates' (RA 35201, 23 February 1820 and 13 March 1820).

[3] Farington, p. 4511, 8 April 1810.

[4] RA 42924, 42935; Works 4/21, 29 April 1814, 19 May 1815; Works 6/26, 5 April 1815 and f. 225, 19 May 1815; T. 29/135, f. 821, 20 June 1815. It was admitted that Wyatt 'did take a very active part in conducting and directing the works for the fête'; but Stephenson thought his charges 'very unreasonable'.

[5] *Gent's. Mag.* 1811, pt. i, pp. 586–7; Lord Colchester, *Diary and Correspondence* ii (1861) pp. 336–9; Farington, p. 5837, 15 June 1811 and p. 5841, 20 June 1811.

[6] Farington, pp. 5848–52, 26 June 1811 (sketch plans of layout).

to £20,000 had accumulated between 1807 and 1812. James Wyatt suggested an immediate payment of £15,000 while the 'great mass of accounts' was sorted out; after all two more members of his family were involved: Jeffry and Edward.[1] But Prinney pressed on. In September 1812 James Wyatt was directed 'to fit up a large room on the ground floor . . . adjoining the present Library as an additional Library, and in the same style; and also to fit up the Strong Room . . . as a Deposit for . . . Plate . . . with cases of Plate glass, in three lights, and sashes in front, to slide in brass grooves, on rollers, fronts supported by iron columns, shelves with brass columns and brackets, and the inside covered with Green Baize'. The estimates were £1053 9s. 0d. and £1393 0s. 0d.[2] Needless to say their presentation was administratively irregular. But with Wyatt's sudden death responsibility for Carlton House was transferred to John Nash.[3] It was he who completed Wyatt's work and he who undertook the next phase of building, the construction of the Gothic Dining Room (Pl. 12B) at the opposite extremity to the conservatory. The estimate submitted in 1814 was £8866 4s. 9d., of which the most expensive items were Bernasconi's Gothic plasterwork, Edward Wyatt's burnished gilding, Jeffry Wyatt's Gothic carpentry and the 'large chimney piece of statuary marble very richly inlaid and ornamented with ormolu' supplied by Westmacott and designed in the Gothic style by James Wyatt.[4]

Nash's arrival inevitably heralded further schemes and rumours of schemes. In 1803 the Prince of Wales had been granted an extra allowance of £60,000 per annum for three years towards the settlement of his accounts.[5] And in 1811 there was at last the prospect of an income appropriate to his status as Regent.[6] But with mounting expenditure at Brighton and London his debts continued to accumulate. By 1808 there were no fewer than 347 creditors whose total claims amounted to £259,964 19s. 2d. 'exclusive of the various tradesmen employed by the late Walsh Porter . . . at Carlton House'.[7] Nevertheless Prinney seems to have toyed with the idea of a complete rebuilding. Alternative designs by Nash have survived, one Gothic, the other classical (Pl. 11A), probably dating from this period.[8] But the Treasury decided that 'it was not intended that any steps whatever should be taken towards erecting a New Palace'.[9] Instead Nash became responsible for a series of elaborate temporary buildings erected for the festivities of 1813–15. In all there were five main celebrations: two fêtes to celebrate Peninsular victories in February and July 1813; the reception for the Allied Sovereigns in June 1814; the fête in honour of the Duke of Wellington in July; and the Grand National Jubilee commemorating the accession of the House of Brunswick in August.

---

[1] L.C. 1/5, 5 September 1812 and f. 270, 30 October 1812; L.C. 1/40, f. 299, 5 November 1812.
[2] L.C. 1/5, f. 287, 15 January 1813; Works 4/21, 10 September 1812, 20 August 1813.
[3] L.C. 1/6, f. 340, 23 December 1812.   [4] L.C. 1/6, f. 346, 18 March 1814.
[5] 43 G. III c. 26; *Parl. Hist.* xxxvi (1801–3), cols. 1197–1230; Stanhope, *Pitt* iv (1862), p. 13; Colchester, *Diary* i (1861), p. 413.
[6] For preliminary negotiations cf. Buckingham, *Memoirs of the Court of England during the Regency* i (1856), pp. 187 *et seq.* For payments out of the Prince's Privy Purse 1812–29 cf. RA 35468–35641.
[7] RA 89476 (1808). For sundry bills (1803–5) cf. RA 89418, 89420, 89422–6, 89433.
[8] Illustrated in H. Clifford Smith, *Buckingham Palace* (1931), p. 38. See also J. Summerson, *Nash* (1935), pp. 146–7. 'Rumour whispers—we hope untruly, that there is some notion of enlarging Carlton House, by adding buildings occupying the whole of the South side of Pall Mall' (*The Times* 28 July 1814 p. 3). For the construction of Waterloo Place cf. *The Times* 16 October 1813 p. 3; *Parl. Deb.* xxxii (1816), cols. 576–7, 15 February 1816.   [9] Works 4/21, f. 347.

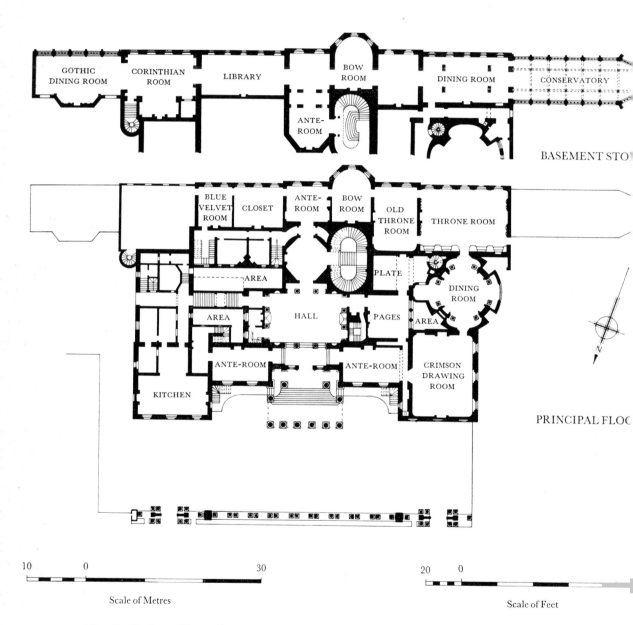

Fig. 6. Carlton House in about 1825: based on a plan in Britton and Pugin's *Public Buildings of London* (1825), with corrections.

These festive events were all public occasions, and the expenditure involved was therefore handled by the Office of Works. The fêtes of 1813 were fairly small affairs in the garden of Carlton House.[1] But the three celebrations in June, July and August 1814 were respectively grand, lavish and spectacular. In fact the London Summer of that year was spent in celebrations or preparations for celebrations which were almost continuous. At least two temporary supper rooms in the garden of Carlton House were available in time for the reception of the Allied Sovereigns in June.[2] But the full panoply of semi-permanent marquees was not ready until the following month. This was the occasion of the Prince Regent's ball in honour of the Duke of Wellington on 21 July 1814. The temporary buildings were spread out roughly in H formation to the South of Carlton House, with supper rooms at right angles to each other, a botanical arbour and a temple to Wellington at the main intersections and, as the centrepiece of the whole arrangement, a vast polygonal ballroom. If only because the polygonal room still survives—the sole constructional element in the whole Carlton House complex—at least one contemporary description of the general layout is worth repeating:

On this occasion the temporary erections in the gardens of Carlton House, which have been so long in preparation, were used for the first time. . . . The first of these was a tent, decorated with plate glass, and white and rose coloured draperies. This tent led to the large new polygon room, which measures 120 feet in diameter. Each side of this spacious room was groined and supported by fasces, ornamented with flowers: from these arose an elegant umbrella roof, terminating in a ventilator, decorated with large gilt cords, and painted to imitate white muslin, which produced a very light effect. The walls within the groins were decorated with muslin draperies and eight large plate glasses, round which the draperies were elegantly disposed. In the centre was a garland of artificial flowers in the shape of a temple, connected by a very large gilt rope from the roof; this was used as an orchestra for two bands. The floor was chalked with elegant devices in compartments for twelve sets of dancers, radiating from the centre to the pillars at the sides. This room was illuminated with twelve glass lustres with patent lamps. From the centre of each groin was suspended an antique alabaster lamp.

Immediately opposite . . . was a similar tent, in which were tables for tea, coffee, ices and fruits . . . from the royal gardens. To the west of the polygon room was a spacious covered promenade, decorated with white draperies, and ornamented with rose-coloured cords. In this were four recesses, lined with muslin draperies; at the end of this spacious apartment, a Corinthian temple presented itself, terminating with a large mirror, over which was a brilliant star, and the letter W in cut glass. In front of the mirror was a bust of the Duke of Wellington, executed in marble by Turnerelli. It was placed on a verde antique column, and formed an attractive and appropriate object from the polygon room. From each side of this temple, which terminated the promenade, extended a spacious supper room, ornamented with regimental silk colours belonging to the ordnance. . . . From the east of the polygon room extended another spacious promenade, decorated with green calico draperies.

---

[1] Accounts, Works 4/21, 22 October 1813, 12 November 1813, 22 April 1814.
[2] *Annual Register* 1814, Chronicle, p. 42; Summerson *op. cit.* The Lord Chamberlain's Department spent £2909 13s. 0d. 'for vocal and instrumental performers at Carlton House' on this occasion (L.C. 1/2, f. 98, 23 March 1815).

In this apartment were introduced allegorical transparencies. . . . Beyond [this] . . . was an arbour . . . decorated with rare and beautiful plants brought from Kew. . . . To the south of the arbour was a large temporary supper room for . . . three hundred persons. . . . Several tents, fitted up as supper rooms, communicated with this spacious apartment. All the temporary rooms were rendered pecularly comfortable from the floors being boarded, and great attention paid to their ventilation. An additional Gothic room erected at the end of the conservatory, calculated to accommodate one hundred persons at supper, added considerably to the splendour of the lower suit of rooms. . . . The royal party supped in the two rooms which were erected to receive the Emperor of Russia and King of Prussia.[1]

The dodecagonal room, as the ballroom was more specifically known, was in fact 116 feet in diameter and covered 10,600 square feet. Its design was probably the result of collaboration between Nash and Sir William Congreve, M.P. (1772–1828), inventor of the Congreve rocket.[2] But its execution was entrusted to J. W. Hiort and William Nixon.[3] The building's timber framing was conceived on a prefabricated principle, and from the start Congreve at least seems to have thought in terms of its eventual re-erection at Woolwich. Nash toyed with the idea of re-using the structure as a church.[4] But in August 1818 Stephenson was informed of the Prince Regent's wish that 'the grand circular room in the gardens of Carlton House should be removed from thence. It is H.R.H.'s desire that it should be transferred to Woolwich, there to be appropriated to the conservation of the trophies obtained in the last war, the Artillery models, and other military curiosities usually preserved in the Repository of the Royal Artillery'.[5] The Ordnance Department repaid to the Office of Works the cost of its removal—£210 10s. 4½d.;[6] and in 1819 the building was re-erected as an exhibition room, its permanence being guaranteed by the addition of external boarding and a single Doric column in the centre.[7]

Meanwhile the Grand National Jubilee had been celebrated and forgotten. Held on 1 August 1814 in Green Park, St. James's Park and Hyde Park, it marked the climax of months of festive preparation in and around Carlton House. The Allied Sovereigns had departed, but the buildings begun in their honour were not to be wasted. In Tierney's words, 'because it was intended to give an entertainment to the allied sovereigns, who had left town, it was [now] considered necessary to give a

---

[1] *Annual Register* 1814, Chronicle, pp. 63–5. For Lawrence's description, retailed to Farington and Smirke, cf. Farington, p. 6577, 22 July 1814.

[2] A favourite of the Prince Regent, Congreve succeeded his father as Comptroller of the Royal Laboratory at Woolwich and Superintendent of the Military Repository (*Gent's. Mag.* 1828, pt. ii, pp. 178–9). In June 1814 he also organised a rocket display for the Allied Sovereigns at Woolwich (*ibid.* 1814, pt. i, p. 615).

[3] 'Nixon . . . built it under my directions' (Works 19/11/5, f. 39, Nash to Stephenson 30 August 1818); T. F. Hunt, *Tudor Architecture* (1830), p. 97. Like other temporary buildings in 1811 and 1814 it was initially covered with oil cloth supplied by James Baker's Patent Floor Cloth Manufactory, Knightsbridge (Works 6/27, f. 146, 14 April 1814 and f. 240, 2 May 1815). Nash and Yenn were responsible for running repairs to these buildings in 1814–15 (Works 6/27, f. 200, 12 December 1814 and f. 247, 6 May 1815; Works 4/21, 3 May 1815, 6 May 1815). Some of the dismantled timbers were used by Nash for minor alterations at Warwick House (Works 6/27, f. 218, 21 March 1815; Works 19/11/5, f. 5, 21 March 1815).

[4] Works 19/11/5 f. 39, 30 August 1818. He also thought 'it would be a useful building in any of the dock-yards and other government establishments' (Works 19/11/5, f. 38, 26 August 1818).

[5] Works 19/11/5, ff. 36–7, 7–8 August 1815.

[6] Works 19/11/5, ff. 43–4, 29 October 1812 and 2 November 1818.

[7] J. P. Kaestlin, *Catalogue of the Museum of Artillery in the Rotunda at Woolwich* i (1963), pp. i–iv. For Nash's detailed description of its timber construction cf. Works 19/11/5, f. 38, 26 August 1818.

treat to somebody else'. Congreve justified the whole thing as 'a little harmless amusement'.[1] Despite press criticisms of its 'extravagance', its 'absurdity', its 'debauchery, drunkenness and mingled and various abominations', the occasion was wildly popular.[2] But its principal monuments were all ephemeral. Indeed, as one M.P. remarked, they were 'temporary in the strictest sense of the word' since they seemed to be 'made for the express purpose of being blown up'.[3] The funfair in Hyde Park lasted no more than a week, and the mock naval battle or 'naumachia' on the Serpentine no more than a day.[4] The Fortress cum Temple of Concord in Green Park, devised by Congreve with transparencies and classical trimming by Greenwood and Latilla, was dismantled within two months.[5] And the Pagoda and 'Rialto' Bridge in St. James's Park were largely destroyed by fireworks on the very night of the celebration, although the bridge was later restored by J. W. Hiort before being replaced by Nash in 1820.[6] Congreve was master of pyrotechnics on this occasion and supervised the technical side of all the buildings. Nash was responsible for the overall layout.[7] Congreve had predicted a bill of some £15,000, of which £4000 would cover the cost of fireworks.[8] But the total expenditure on buildings alone turned out to be £37,574 8s. 3d., of which Nash's percentage was £1767 16s. 7d., Hiort's fee as clerk of works was £450 and Jeffry Wyatt's bill for carpentry was £9874 9s. 10½d. When the Office of Works figures were queried by the Treasury Nash replied that his five per cent commission followed the system 'according to which my private and public practice has been regulated for thirty years without a single instance of deviation'. As for Hiort, 'he attended from five in the morning till eight at night, and afterwards at his office', so that by his 'very extraordinary exertions . . . he actually performed the duty of three Clerks of Works'. Nevertheless Hiort's fee was reduced to £350. Nash's claim was substantiated by Soane and Smirke, and Stephenson eventually agreed that the Grand National Jubilee had indeed been an occasion of 'extraordinary diligence'.[9] Admittedly there had been no initial estimate. But there was ample precedent for such irregularity in the festivities of 1749.[10]

---

[1] *Parl. Deb.* xxviii (1814), cols. 480–83, 30 June 1814.

[2] *The Times* 29 June 1814, p. 3, 4 July 1814, p. 3, 19 July, p. 3, 26 July 1814, p. 3, 28 July 1814, p. 3, 1 August 1814, p. 3, 4 August 1814, p. 3, 8 August 1814, p. 3, 9 August 1814, p. 3, 11 August 1814, p. 3.

[3] *Parl. Deb.* xxviii (1814), cols. 420–22, 29 June 1814.

[4] For a comic description see Peter Pindar's poem, *The Prince's Jubilee* (1814). The boats were built at Woolwich under Congreve's direction (*Parl. Deb.* xxviii, 1814, cols. 420–22, 29 June 1814).

[5] For contemporary views and descriptions cf. *The Times* 29 July 1814 p. 3; Ackermann, *Repository* xii (1814), pp. 236–8; *Gent's. Mag.* 1814, pt. ii, pp. 179–84. Part of its illumination was supplied by gas. The remains were auctioned on 10 October 1814 for £198 6s. 6d., 'to various brokers from Moorfields, the Mint and Seven Dials' (J. Larwood, *London Parks* ii [1872], pp. 52–7). See also Peter Pindar, *The Temple Knocked Down* (1814).

[6] Ackermann, *Repository* xii (1814), p. 225; Larwood *op. cit.*, pp. 261–5; Summerson *op. cit.*, p. 150; *Gent's. Mag.* 1814, pt. ii, pp. 179–84; Papworth, *Select Views* (1816), p. 13; *Annual Register* 1814, Chronicle, pp. 67–70; N. Braybrook, *London Green* (1959), p. 183; B. M. King's Maps xxvi, 7; B.M. Maps 33e 24(4).

[7] For a general plan cf. *The Times* 2 August 1814, pp. 2–3.

[8] *Parl. Deb.* xxviii (1814), cols. 480–83, 698–9, 837–9.

[9] Works 19/11/5, f. 1, 9 September 1814; Works 4/21, 10 February 1815, 17 February 1815, 2 March 1815, 6 March 1815, 4 April 1815, 31 May 1815, 29 July 1815, 23 August 1815; Works 6/26, ff. 161, 167, 189, 193, 233–5 (1814–15); Works 6/27, ff. 215, 224–5, 239, 254 (1815); T. 29/130, f. 971, 30 August 1814, T. 29/133, ff. 542–3, 3 February 1815. See also P. Fitzgerald, *Life of George IV* ii (1882), p. 157. Yenn was responsible for repairing damage to the parks, e.g. Works 4/21, 19 August 1814, 27 March 1815.

[10] *Parl. Deb.* xxviii (1814), col. 699.

In all these operations between 1813 and 1815 Nash relied on Hiort and Nixon rather than Yenn and Lewis Wyatt, the nominal Clerk of Works and Labourer in Trust.[1] Lewis Wyatt was a notorious absentee, and one of Stephenson's first actions as Surveyor General was to issue a temporary suspension order.[2] Yenn's inadequacy was rather less culpable. For over thirty years his responsibility for Carlton House had been more or less ignored. When called to account for excessive expenditure in April 1814 he justifiably replied that he was 'at a loss to proceed' since works were 'frequently commanded to be done without any previous communication to him'.[3] The need for an administrative reorganisation at Carlton House was obvious, a need retrospectively underlined in 1816 by the discovery that no less than £160,000 had been spent on this particular palace during the previous five years.[4]

Although in October 1815 there was no less than £20,000 outstanding for works done by Nash at Carlton House (exclusive of the grand fête), the Regent was still dissatisfied with his residence.[5] On 29 March 1816 Nash reported that

> as Carlton House is so destitute of the necessary and usual accommodation for Servants, both in respect of Offices, Bed rooms, and other conveniences, and the unfinished state of the East end of the Palace requiring consideration, it is the Prince Regent's pleasure, that nothing but the common repairs incident to the occupation of the building be done at present, but that the Sum intended to be laid out in more substantial repairs be reserved in aid of a general reparation and arrangement of Plan.[6]

The Treasury would not permit funds to be reserved from year to year, and only minor repairs were ever carried out.[7] When in 1817 the Regent wanted the old Eating Room on the basement floor to be made 'permanently secure and firm', Nash calculated the works necessary at £9000 at least; but nothing so expensive was permitted.[8] On the Queen's death in November 1818, the Regent planned a removal to the more secluded Buckingham House.[9] Some months later Nash described the condition of Carlton House as it had been for some years past: 'The whole of the ground floor towards the Garden is very weak, and on Levee and Court Days it is necessary to secure this floor by temporary supports. The floor of the Regent's Bedroom has sunk; and the ornamental work of the Conservatory requires considerable repair and

---

[1] 'In the beginning of the works I assembled the tradesmen, the Clerk of Works, Labourer in Trust and Mr. Lush the store keeper and informed [them] I should give my directions through the officers appointed by the Office of Works, not meaning to interfere with the regulations laid down by the Office. . . . In the course of the work I found it impracticable to communicate my directions through the Clerk of Works or Labourer in Trust, their other avocations allowing them very seldom to be there. I therefore availed myself of a very intelligent man (William Nixon) whom I found at Carlton House, placed there by the late Mr. Wyatt, and through whom I directed the works' (Works 6/27, f. 216, 4 March 1815).
[2] He was reinstated following an explanation by Yenn (Works 4/21, 14 December 1814, 3 January 1815, 7 February 1815, 9 February 1815, 7 March 1815).
[3] Works 4/21, 29 April 1814, 27 May 1814, 4 November 1814, 18 November 1814, 22–23 November 1814.
[4] *Survey of London* xx, p. 74; *Parl. Deb.* xxxiv (1816), col. 268.
[5] Works 5/107.   [6] Works 19/11/5, f. 32.
[7] Works 4/21, pp. 591 (4 November 1815), 753 (26 March 1816, estimates of £295 for a bath for the Regent on a platform on top of the house, with canvas and oil cloth sides and roof, see Works 19/11/5, f. 30); 1/6, p. 272; 1/7, pp. 497–8. Expenditure 1815–26 averaged about £2800 p.a. (Works 5/107–9).
[8] Works 19/11/5, f. 35. Nash recommended that brick arches should be turned under the floor; and that since the floor of the drawing room above was so thin because of the need to give height to the Eating room, that floor should be made of iron.
[9] Works 19/3, f. 12; B.M. Add. MS. 38275, ff. 78–9.

restoration'.[1] A few months later the Bow Room chimneypiece was sent to Brighton, and replaced by one in store.[2]

But the scale of the projected improvements at Buckingham House was too great to obtain ministerial sanction and in 1822 George IV still resided at Carlton House. Nash then prepared plans for a partial rebuilding, though he clearly preferred his design for Buckingham House: there would still remain, he wrote of Carlton House,

> the same unfinished appearance towards Pall Mall—the same dilapidated buildings at the East end of the entrance front and the side court exposed as it now is to the Entrance Court—there will be but one Entrance common to Noblemen's Carriages and waggons and carts—the necessary accommodation for servants of which Carlton Palace is so woefully deficient and which are now more than ever required will still be wanting.[3]

So when at last prosperity enabled the government to authorise the rebuilding of Buckingham House, the King's plate and wine were removed to St. James's (May 1826), the furniture and paintings stored in the Riding House and houses in Pall Mall, and the demolition of Carlton House was begun.[4] Several of the chimney-pieces were re-used by Wyatville at Windsor. The Corinthian columns of the great portico lay weathering for several years in St. James's Park, and Wilkins selected eight for the lesser porticoes of the National Gallery. The Ionic columns of the screen had already been utilised by Nash at Buckingham Palace.[5]

There remained however the Riding House and stables. The Riding House or 'Ride' consisted of one great room, 165 feet by 51 feet, and 30 feet high, with an ornamental porch in the middle of the garden side. The ground falling away to the east had permitted coach houses and harness rooms to be constructed below the Riding House, opposite the range of stables. These were used by Queen Adelaide. The Ride itself was turned into a store, first for furniture from Carlton House, then for the legal and other public records, which after the building of Soane's Law Courts had been temporarily accommodated in the Mews at Charing Cross.[6] When the royal furniture was finally removed in 1842 the entire Ride was taken for the records, and searching rooms, offices and workshops were erected along the west front. By December 1843 it was the largest of the record repositories, 'a very great convenience and advantage to the Public'; but Superintendent Braidwood of the London Fire Brigade reported that the risk of fire was 'very great and extraordinary': the building, of brick and timber, had walls slight for its size, 'in many parts intersected and bound by timber', and surmounted by a projecting wooden cornice. Windows opening into

---

[1] Works 1/9, p. 309. Cf. Works 19/11/5, f. 32 (29 March 1816); and 1/7, pp. 497–8 (3 March 1817).

[2] *Ibid.* 1/9, p. 465.

[3] Works 19/3, f. 220. See also Works 19/11/5, ff. 45–7, an estimate of £13,000 (16 March 1822) for repair of the main building and conservatory.

[4] Works 1/14, p. 264; an inventory of the fixtures is given on pp. 139 *et. seq.*

[5] Above p. 264; below p. 469. In 1827 the architect P. F. Robinson made designs (preserved in the Royal Library at Windsor, portfolio 58) for incorporating the columns in a temple intended to serve either as a monument to the Duke of York or as a building to house the books from George III's library.

[6] Works 1/14, p. 132 (23 February 1826, estimate for fitting up as furniture store, £1277); 4/28, p. 2 (4 July 1826); 1/21, pp. 214 (13 December 1834), 248 (6 February 1835); 2/1, p. 205 (3 January 1835); see also *Parl. Pap.* 1837 (60) xxxiv, pp. x–xi.

the new workshops were then bricked up and the most stringent precautions feasible taken against fire.[1] The entire cost of fitting up the record repository was calculated in May 1847 at nearly £3700.[2] In 1858 the records were removed to the new Public Record Office in Chancery Lane and the Ride was demolished in 1862.[3] Carlton House had finally disappeared.

CLAREMONT HOUSE, SURREY

When Princess Charlotte, daughter of the Prince Regent, married Prince Leopold of Saxe-Coburg in 1816, the task of finding a country residence for the royal couple devolved on the Commissioners of Woods and Forests, who purchased Claremont House, near Esher, for £66,000. The estate was then settled on the Prince and Princess for their lives.[4] Embellishments by Hiort and Papworth were made at the Princess's own cost, and after her death the estate was maintained by Prince Leopold from his parliamentary stipend of £50,000 a year.[5] After his accession to the Belgian throne in 1831, he placed this income under the control of trustees, and lent the mansion to Queen Victoria; until Osborne was ready, it afforded the royal family a private retreat.[6] In 1840 it was entrusted to the Works Department, the trustees continuing to discharge the expenses. The Board offered to continue the Esher tradesmen previously employed, if they would 'do the Work upon Tender the present contract prices in the Hampton Court district being fixed as a maximum'; otherwise, the Hampton Court contractors would be employed.[7] Chawner proposed alterations for the convenience of the Queen, executed in 1840 at a cost of £819; and in 1842 designed new stables, subsequently built under Pennethorne's direction.[8]

On Chawner's retirement, the Board in 1845 placed Claremont under the Clerk of the Works at Hampton Court: he made as many as twenty visits a quarter and received a guinea a visit from the trustees.[9] Works were executed only when an estimate was passed by the Board, all except urgent minor repairs being referred to the

---

[1] Works 2/3, pp. 298 (12 March 1842), 367; 2/4, pp. 88–91 (21 December 1843); *Parl. Pap.* 1846, xliii, 7th Report of the Deputy Keeper of the Public Records, pp. 32–5, App. pp. 42–4 (this report contains a plan of the building).

[2] *Parl. Pap.* 1847 (398) xxxiv. One small item of £75 8s. for the removal of rolls from the Treasury record office in January 1835 was justified thus by the keeper: 'When it is considered, that there are 2930 Rolls (most of them as much as two men can lift) first to be taken down from the Racks, and laid on the floors, from thence removed into Caravans, and from them into the Riding House, and then replaced in their proper Order on the racks now erecting, I am quite of opinion I have not taken too large a latitude for completing the work' (Works 2/1, p. 206). Between 1838 and 1847 a further £2613 was spent on fire precautions there and at the Rolls House. Annual maintenance, however, seldom rose above £100 (*Parl. Pap.* 1843 (343), xxx; 1847 (398) xxxiv; and 1851 (374) xxxi).

[3] Works 19/11/5, ff. 59, 95, 97. A plan *c.* 1850 of Riding House and stables is given in *Survey of London*, xx, p. 78.

[4] Statute 56 Geo. III, cap. 115; Works 19/12/1, f. 1. For an account of the house, rebuilt in 1770–2 by 'Capability' Brown and Henry Holland, see Dorothy Stroud, *Henry Holland* (1966), pp. 32–6.

[5] Colvin, *Dictionary*, s.v. 'Hiort'.

[6] *Letters of Queen Victoria 1837–61*, ii, pp. 5, 146; Peel's second administration was sworn in at Claremont (Morley, *Life of Gladstone*, i, p. 242).

[7] Works 19/12/1, ff. 6, 45, 110.   [8] *Ibid.* ff. 19–20; Works 1/24, p. 552; 1/26, pp. 5–6.

[9] Works 1/31, pp. 106, 129; 1/32, p. 208; 19/12/1, ff. 33–40.

trustees: they attended to the Queen's 'comfort and convenience', but deferred any major general repair.[1] The removal of cesspits and the provision of proper drains was necessary in 1846. Ordinary expenditure in 1847–51 averaged about a thousand pounds annually. This included the construction of stone steps from the saloon to the pleasure grounds (£368) in 1847, and repairs to Princess Charlotte's mausoleum the following year.[2]

When Louis Philippe was driven from the French throne in February 1848 King Leopold offered his father-in-law Claremont, where he lived as Comte de Neuilly.[3] Several of his family fell ill, from lead pipes contaminating the drinking water. A new water system with pure tin pipes and slate cisterns was therefore installed in 1848–9 by Easton and Amos at a cost of £1400.[4] Improved heating was also introduced, and plans for a new heating system were under consideration when the ex-King's death in August 1850 caused the trustees to discontinue all works at the mansion.[5] The house was subsequently occupied by his widow ex-Queen Marie-Amelie until her death in 1866, and then by Queen Victoria's fourth son the Duke of Albany. It was not until the death of the latter's widow in 1922 that it finally ceased to be a royal residence.

CLARENCE HOUSE, ST. JAMES'S

The rebuilding of Clarence House was a consequence of the Duke of Clarence's marriage in 1818 to Princess Adelaide of Saxe-Meiningen. The rooms that had satisfied Mrs. Jordan in 1809[6] no longer seemed adequate for the accommodation of a royal Duchess in the 1820s. In 1824 the Duke accordingly approached George IV for permission to alter Clarence House. 'His Majesty', he wrote to Sir William Knighton, 'is fully aware of the inconvenience and unfitness of our present apartments here. . . . I earnestly request, for the sake of the amiable and excellent Duchess, you will, when the King is quite recovered, represent the wretched state and dirt of our apartments'.[7]

Having obtained permission to extend his house at the expense of some rooms at the back hitherto earmarked for the Hanoverian Office, the Duke secured the services of John Nash, who was then engaged on extensive alterations to the adjoining palace of St. James's. Early in 1825 Nash's plans were officially submitted to the Board of Works. He proposed to convert the Duke's apartments into a plain three-storey house with attic and basement; the principal feature a two-storied portico (Doric and

---

[1] Works 19/12/1, ff. 39–40, 107–8; 1/30, pp. 28–30; 1/31, p. 327.
[2] Works 19/12/1, ff. 93, 117, 120, 123; 1/28 (7 July 1845); 1/29, pp. 204, 305–7; 1/30, pp. 28–30; 1/31, pp. 2, 49, 79, 327, 356, 379; 1/32, pp. 326, 381; 1/33, pp. 54–5, 179, 351.
[3] See *Letters of Queen Victoria 1837–61*, ii, pp. 160–5.
[4] Works 1/32, pp. 85, 106, 148, 157, 171, 183–5, 192, 206, 208, 221–3, 241, 253, 339; 19/12/1, ff. 93, 159 *et. seq.*; 2/7, pp. 137–9, 201.
[5] Works 1/32, pp. 182, 199–200; 1/35, pp. 36, 270–1, 337; 19/12/1, ff. 288, 319, 348.
[6] Below, p. 362.
[7] E. Sheppard, *Memorials of St. James's Palace* (1894), i, p. 104; quoted by C. Hussey, *Clarence House* (1949), which contains a detailed history of the house.

Corinthian) projecting over the footpath to Stable Yard.[1] Reluctant to give an estimate without working drawings and specifications, Nash suggested that his proposals would cost between nine and ten thousand pounds; and the works were approved at the larger sum.[2] When the work was put to tender, Nash's drawings and specifications were found inadequate, and some delay resulted.[3] The rebuilding of the Duke of York's house just opposite also proved a hindrance;[4] but by the end of September 1825 the necessary demolitions had been completed. The walls having proved worse than he expected, Nash proposed certain alterations. The wall next Princess Augusta's lodgings was 'mere partition brick and boards'; two walls of the Duke's room were rotten; and that to the east was merely a large open stack of chimneys, which he suggested should be thrown into the principal apartments to extend them three feet.[5] As the kitchen, with only a boarded ceiling, was under the Hanoverian record office, he suggested building a new kitchen in the area. The various changes would add £2000 to his estimate.[6] Approving the alterations, the Treasury deferred the question of the kitchen. In the following February Nash called for a decision on this point, alleging that the existing kitchen would need repair, was too small, and in an unsuitable position.[7] In the course of the subsequent sparring with the Treasury, Nash explained that when the state of the walls was discovered, so much ground had necessarily been excavated to permit underpinning that the expense of further excavations for a basement kitchen would be trifling.[8] Hardly had he obtained consent for a total expenditure of £12,000 when he suggested raising the new kitchen a storey to provide two additional rooms required by the Duke for his staff, an extra he estimated at £420. This was sanctioned provided it could be done within the sum already appropriated.[9]

Nash went on with the work in his usual carefree way, even when the Surveyor General informed him that £11,883 had already been spent. Pressed further, he declared that a careful revision of his estimate—that rough estimate which he had declared at the first was quite undependable—gave him no reason to change his mind; but that the execution of the works had been conducted by the Office of Works, and that he therefore could not be responsible for the actual expenditure.[10] But Hunt, the Labourer in Trust, then pointed out that Nash had ignored several

---

[1] Works 1/13, p. 262 (30 March 1825). Originals of some of these letters are in Works 19/24/1.

[2] Works 1/13, pp. 266–7 (2 April 1825).

[3] *Ibid.* pp. 419–20 (29 July); 4/27, p. 264 (1 August 1825). The contractors were: Stutely (bricklayer), Chadwick (mason), Warren (carpenter and joiner), Fowler and Jones (smith and founder), Warmsley (slater), M. Wyatt (painter), Bernasconi and Son (plasterer), Tarte and Son (plumber), R. Cobbett (glazier) (Works 4/27, pp. 264, 273, 276–82, 1–20 August 1825).   [4] Works 1/13, pp. 445–7.

[5] Hussey (*op. cit.* p. 65) supposed this wall to have been the north wall of the north wing of the old building; but as Nash described it as 'on the East side' it was more probably the eastern wall adjoining the room east of the entrance hall (shown solid on Soane's plan of 1792, Hussey, *op. cit.* p. 64), and the space accordingly taken into the great corridor or gallery.

[6] Works 1/13, pp. 457–8 (27 September 1825).

[7] *Ibid.* pp. 479–80 (15 October 1825), 1/14, p. 89 (15 February 1826).

[8] Works 1/14, pp. 218–9 (8 April), 246–7 (5 May 1826).

[9] *Ibid.* pp. 255 (15 May), 262 (18 May), 268 (27 May), 282 (30 May 1826). A plan of 1837 by Sir Robert Smirke of Princess Augusta's adjoining house (in T. 1/3904), shows a kitchen to the south-east of Clarence House, where a plan of 1841 (Works 34/129, reproduced by Hussey *op. cit.* p. 48, fig. 10), shows a carpenter's shop. However the 1841 survey shows a basement kitchen in the yard north of the carpenter's shop (Works 34/127–8). It is unlikely that any change was made between 1837 and 1841, so it appears that no upper storey was built over Nash's kitchen.

[10] Works 1/14, pp. 375 (28 July), 399 (16 August), 410 (29 August 1826).

material deviations from the original plans: the virtual demolition of the old house and the stacking of its materials for sale;[1] the excavation of the whole area behind the apartments; an increase of three feet in the height of the building; the construction and subsequent removal of dormers; the addition of two columns to support an iron bressumer; reinstating adjoining buildings; providing new drains—the list runs on. Had Nash surveyed the building since its commencement, remarked Hunt cuttingly, he would have seen how utterly inadequate were estimates of £12,420.[2] Nash denied that there were many additions; he had directed the inclusion of a passage (probably that on the north side) to extend the building by five feet—but the rooms (he remarked irrelevantly) were still small for such a tenant. Taking up the rotten ground floor had enabled him to raise the basement a foot in height, and he had raised the attics similarly. The only other alterations were substituting iron for Bath stone columns in the portico, as less liable to injury in the thoroughfare, and the introduction of Hiort's patent flues to prevent smoky chimneys.[3] As expenditure mounted, the Treasury censured the excess as 'not creditable to the Person by whom the estimate was prepared'.[4] The carcass of the house was finished by the end of 1827, at a cost of £20,869.[5] The Duke of Wellington as chief minister decided that the interior must be completed, and in November 1828 Hunt supplied an estimate of £1360 for fitting up the offices, providing a meat safe and game larder, setting stoves throughout the house, painting and whitewashing, installing new dormers, gilding the two drawing rooms and altering a window in one of them.[6] A final wrangle occurred over five smoky chimneys, which had not been carried as high as the roof ridge, which Hiort thought necessary.[7]

When the Duke of Clarence ascended the throne in June 1830 he continued to occupy Clarence House, a gallery of communication with the state apartments at St. James's being made on the first floor, under the direction of Sydney Smirke.[8] After the King's death, Princess Augusta moved into the house in 1838, but herself died two years later.[9] Queen Victoria then bestowed the house on her mother, the Duchess of Kent, for whom alterations and repairs were carried out at a cost of £1400, of which £500 was paid from the Queen's Privy Purse.[10] The alterations included the bringing of a porch from Ingestre House, the Duchess's former home in Belgrave Square.[11] A conservatory was erected at the south end of Nash's great corridor, Princess Augusta's old lodgings having been demolished; and the gallery made to the state apartments in 1830 was converted into the Duchess's wardrobe. In 1843 the carpenter's shop below that was made into a clerk's office, and part of the garden front (presumably exposed by the demolition already referred to) was stuccoed to

---

[1] There are however reasons for supposing that the three walls of the southern half of the breakfast room are 'structurally of the seventeenth century' (Hussey, *op. cit.* p. 65).
[2] Works 1/14, pp. 435 ff. (4 September 1826).   [3] *Ibid.* pp. 451, 516–24 (8 November 1826).
[4] Works 1/15, p. 491 (2 November 1827), see also 1/16, p. 33.   [5] Works 5/109, 110.
[6] Wellington, *New Despatches*, 2nd ser., v, pp. 28, 33 (6, 8 September 1828); Works 1/17, p. 16 (20 November 1828). Expenditure on these was £1363 10s. 6d. (Works 5/110), bringing the total Works expenditure on the house to £22,232 16s. 3d.   [7] Works 1/17, p. 286 (27 April 1829).
[8] Works 4/30, pp. 236 (28 June), 241 (30 June 1830, estimate £700–£800).
[9] RA, Add. Z 480/31, 46; Z. 501/18.
[10] Works 2/3, pp. 170, 211; 19/24/1, ff. 7, 13. The principal items were G. Baker (carpenter) £418, W. Harrison (bricklayer) £131, T. Horner (painter) £153, Huxley and Heriot (paper hanger) £166. See also RA. Add. Q 1049–86.   [11] RA, Add. Q 1050.

z

accord with the rest.[1] In 1874–5 the appearance and arrangement of the house were radically changed by alterations and additions for the Duke of Edinburgh.[2]

FROGMORE HOUSE, BERKSHIRE

Frogmore House had been a private residence of Queen Charlotte, who purchased a Crown lease in 1792 and employed James Wyatt to reconstruct the three-storied red-brick house in time for her birthday in May 1795.[3] Queen Charlotte bequeathed the lease to her daughters. After the death of Princess Augusta in September 1840, the reversionary interest was purchased by the Crown for £12,535, and the estate was annexed to Windsor Castle.[4] The Duchess of Kent, to whom the house was offered in May 1841, remarked that it was 'very large' and that 'if it was mine, and I could arrange it as I liked, it could be made very comfortable'.[5] The house, to be kept up by the Commissioners of Woods in the same manner as other royal palaces,[6] was forthwith put in repair on an estimate of £1888, and the Duchess continued to live there until her death in 1861.[7] Expenditure on the house and its grounds averaged about £1650 a year from 1842 to 1850.[8] A large part of the estate, however, was taken as the site for new royal kitchen gardens to replace those at Hampton Court, Kensington and elsewhere, under the Act 5 Vict. c. 1.[9] The estimate for forming the new gardens was £25,563.[10] Robert Abraham was consulted on plans for hot-houses, the contract for which went to Jones and Clark of Birmingham. The mason William Chadwick carried out extensive works, and the contract for gardeners' houses (in the Tudor style), entrance lodge, stable and sheds, designed by Phipps, was awarded in June 1842 to N. Winsland.[11] Expenditure on the gardens in 1842–3, when the bulk of the work was executed, was £21,415, charged on the Land Revenue.[12]

GREENWICH

During the later eighteenth century the Office of Works spent little or nothing on maintaining the fabric of the Queen's House, then the official residence of the Ranger of Greenwich Park. The Rangership of Lady Catherine Pelham, 1743–80, was marked by few alterations to the building, and from 1782 to 1806 the annual rate of expenditure seldom rose above £200.[13] The Rangership of the Duke of Clarence,

---

[1] *Ibid.* Q 1088; Works 2/3, p. 493.

[2] Works 19/24/1, ff. 58 *et. seq.*; elevation, Works 34/906. For these and subsequent changes, see Hussey, *op. cit.* pp. 82–6.

[3] It is illustrated in Ackermann's *Repository of Arts*, 3rd ser. i, pp. 125–8 and by J. Hakewill, *History of Windsor and its Neighbourhood* (1813), pp. 299–302. See also *V. C. H. Berkshire* iii (1924), p. 4.

[4] RA, Add. Q 963–73, 1462; Works 2/3, p. 154. I am indebted to Mr. R. Mackworth-Young for information about Frogmore.

[5] RA, Z 294, f. 27ᵛ, 12 October 1841.   [6] RA, C 26/16, 21 July 1841.

[7] RA, Z 294, f. 43, 19 April 1843; Works 2/3, pp. 323, 328.

[8] *Parl. Pap.* 1843 (343) xxx; 1851 (374) xxxi.   [9] Works 1/25, pp. 279, 282; 2/3, pp. 146 ff.

[10] L.R.R.O. 2/11.   [11] *Ibid.*; Works 1/25, pp. 286–7, 331, 391, 413, 479, 485; drawings in 34/187–205.

[12] *Parl. Pap.* 1843 (343) xxx.

[13] Works 5/72–96 (1782–1807). For views of Greenwich during this period cf. B.M. King's Maps xvii *passim*.

1794–7, was notable only for its brevity. Finally, in 1805, on the appointment of Caroline of Brunswick, the ill-starred Princess of Wales, opportunity was taken to rationalise the situation by removing Inigo Jones's building from the jurisdiction of the Office of Works altogether. Prior to that date the arrangements were far from satisfactory. Responsibility for the various buildings at Greenwich was divided as follows: the Board of Ordnance maintained the Royal Observatory, the Hospital Commissioners were responsible for all land and buildings between the London road and the river, the Queen's House fell to the Office of Works, and the Office of Woods and Forests maintained the rest of the park, gates, walls, lodges and railings. How the last two authorities discharged their responsibilities can be judged from the correspondence between John Robinson, the Surveyor General of Crown Lands, and Joseph Cawthorne, a Treasury clerk who had been pensioned off with the office of under-keeper of the park.[1] It appears that after the death of Lady Catherine Pelham the Rangership had been left vacant and the Ranger's house had fallen into bad hands. The Housekeeper, Mrs. Cooper, was only nominally under Office of Works jurisdiction. Cawthorne complained in vain that she and her husband 'make a Hog stye of the House and a Cow House of the Premises, . . . breaking the pailing and converting everything to their own use, and with £16 per annum they live as if they had £200'.[2] The Queen's House 'was most convenient for Smugglers. Wilkinson the Tavern keeper . . . [Joseph] Yates the Gardener, and Cooper . . . were connected and carried on a very profitable smuggling trade. Wilkinson found the money, Yates found the convenience and Cooper was Assistant. By this improper use of His Majesty's premises and abuse of the Gardener and Housekeeper's places, a great deal of money was made by Wilkinson and Yates until their man Cooper was detected and his cart seized. Cooper was sent to prison . . . until interest was made not only to release him but to restore him to the Park'.[3] In 1793 we find that Yates is thus able to pay £1600 for a neighbouring public house, and 'by converting the Garden [of the Queen's House] to the use of his Tavern, makes £100 per annum by it, without being of the smallest service to the Park'.[4] Successive Clerks of the Works, all non-resident, paid little attention to the situation: William Leach;[5] Robert Browne Snr., 'a savage';[6] and Edward Crocker, a careerist.[7] The Office of Woods and Forests even managed to outdo the negligence of the Office of Works. Cawthorne describes Soane (who had recently become Deputy Surveyor of Woods and Forests) as 'a man too wealthy to do his duty, and too indolent to employ others to do it for him'. When Cawthorne's lodge was eventually repaired in 1797, Soane 'condescended now and then to sneak

---

[1] Cawthorne succeeded Thomas Shord in 1788 and held office until his death in 1806. Appointed by Robinson at Pitt's request, 'through the goodness of Lord Walsingham' (Crest 8/2, f. 492, 28 June 1806; Works 16/40/3, f. 123, 17 November 1795), he described himself as the government's 'best Panegyrist' (*ibid.* f. 130, 22 September 1796). His publications include several anonymous and pseudonymous tracts against parliamentary reform and a pamphlet on *The Immediate Necessity of Building a Lazaretto* (1768).

[2] Works 16/40/3, f. 33, 25 July 1792. 'Is the keeping of Cows and Pigs, selling of milk and Pultry proper for a . . . place of dignity? Royal Premises should be almost *sacred* and not converted into Hog Styes, Hen roosts and Cow houses . . . the condition is a disgrace to that House and a reproach to the Board [of Works]' (*ibid.* f. 35, 27 July 1792). [3] *Ibid.* f. 85, 9 December 1793.

[4] *Ibid.* f. 148, 22 June 1796. Thanks to Chambers' recommendation, Yates was officially paid about £50 p.a. for looking after the Ranger's garden (T. 29/54, ff. 5–6, 15 April 1783; T. 29/56, f. 257, 3 February 1785; Works 5/72, 1783). [5] See p. 60.

[6] Works 16/40/3, f. 37, 30 July 1792. [7] Works 16/28/3, f. 3, 22 June 1801 and f. 5, 1 July 1801.

into the Park without deigning to consult or even speak with anybody'; instead he entrusted the work to a deputy, 'a stupid young fellow, . . . a drunken swab, . . . fitter for the Navy than the Park'.[1] In the hands of such men as Cawthorne's fellow under-keeper Eaglestone ('too much at Public Houses and too often in liquor'), Greenwich Park became 'an Asylum for the Riotous and a Receptacle for Whores and Rogues'.[2] Unpaid and unprotected, Cawthorne is bombarded with 'brickbats, stones and dead cats'.[3] During the day 'the College Men secure all the Benches to play at cards upon';[4] and by night the park becomes 'a seminary of vice', haunted by 'loose women and disorderly men, . . . sailors . . . watermen and fishermen . . . with their prostitutes'.[5]

Cawthorne's account is perhaps a little overcoloured. But his picture of Greenwich emphasises the neglected state of several 'out palaces' during the period prior to the reform of 1815. The logical remedy was to put the Queen's House to better use. In 1805 a suitable opportunity occurred. When Caroline of Brunswick became Ranger it was rumoured that £14,000 would be needed to make the Queen's House fit for occupation.[6] In fact Leverton's estimate was £2500–3000. Even so, the cost of repair seemed too high and a scheme to replace Inigo Jones's masterpiece by a new Ranger's lodge was very properly abandoned.[7] Instead Montagu House on Blackheath, leased from the Duke of Buccleuch, became the Ranger's Lodge and as such was extensively refitted by the Department of Woods and Forests.[8] The Queen's House was sold in 1806 for £7875 to the Royal Naval Asylum, an educational institution which had been founded in 1798 and had for some years been anxious to move from an inadequate site in Paddington.[9] Extensive alterations were soon put in hand, including one addition which substantially changed the appearance of Inigo Jones's composition: the construction of flanking colonnades in 1809–11, designed quite independently of the Office of Works by D. A. Alexander, architect to the Asylum Commissioners.[10] In 1825 the anomalous existence of two contiguous naval schools was eventually abolished by the amalgamation of the Royal Naval Asylum and the Royal Hospital School.[11] It was not until 1934 that both the Queen's House and the adjoining Hospital buildings were taken over by the Office of Works for maintenance as Historic Buildings.

---

[1] Works 16/40/3, f. 203, 14 October 1797 and f. 205, 19 November 1797. See also f. 187, 27 June 1797.
[2] *Ibid.* f. 24, 5 June 1792 and f. 30, 19 July 1792.
[3] *Ibid.* f. 8, 23 November 1790 and f. 142, 2 June 1796.   [4] *Ibid.* f. 172, 25 July 1796.
[5] *Ibid.* f. 37, 30 July 1792 and f. 48, 4 September 1792.
[6] *The Times*, 11 November 1805, p. 3.   [7] Crest 2/344, 17 June 1805.
[8] *Ibid.* 11 June 1806. Harvey's estimate was £13,500. In 1814 Montagu House was demolished and the nearby Brunswick House took its place as the Ranger's Lodge (*ibid.* 29 November 1814). Brunswick (formerly Chesterfield) House had been occupied since 1807 by the Princess of Wales's widowed mother, the Duchess of Brunswick, whose death in 1813 made it available as a substitute for Montagu House, by now in bad repair. The cost of refitting Brunswick House for the new Ranger, Princess Sophia Matilda of Gloucester (£6500) was partly met from the sale of the old materials of Montagu House (Works 1/6, pp. 46–57, 205–6, 211–14; Works 1/8, pp. 27–30, 285; Works 4/21, p. 495). There is a view of Brunswick House in Walford, *Old and New London* vi (1897), p. 211.   [9] G. H. Chettle, *The Queen's House, Greenwich* (1937), p. 55.
[10] For details see P.R.O. Adm. 80/111.   [11] Sir G. Callender, *The Queen's House, Greenwich* (1960), p. 39.

HAMPTON COURT PALACE

The later Hanoverians were not fond of Hampton Court. George III and George IV never lived in the palace; nor did the Dukes of York or Cumberland. On the other hand, in their capacity as Rangers of the parks, the Duke of Gloucester, the Duke of Kent and the Duke of Clarence spent a varying amount of time in their respective residences. Only one member of the royal family really admired Wolsey's palace, the Duke of Sussex. 'If I was King', he once remarked, 'I would certainly live there and soon rout out the present inhabitants in the only Palace in England'[1]. Instead Hampton Court became a labyrinth of at least fifty 'grace and favour' apartments, 'the quality poor house' as William IV called it.[2] Between 1782 and 1815 there was little in the way of significant alteration to the fabric except Wyatt's removal of the stage in the Great Hall;[3] the refurbishing of the 'Astronomical Clock';[4] the cleaning of Verrio's painting on the Great Staircase by Martin and Richards;[5] and the repair of the Tennis Court 'that any of the Royal Family may occasionally play at Tennis therein'.[6] Most of the architectural interest of this period is therefore concerned with the appurtenances to the palace: the Upper and Lower Lodges in Bushy Park; the Pavilions and Stud House in the Home Park; the roads and paddocks; the garden waterworks, canal, basin and Longford River; and the mews, barracks and houses surrounding Hampton Court Green. Some administrative interest also attaches to the fact that the Office of Works shared these various responsibilities with the Lord Chamberlain's Office, the Department of the Master of the Horse, the Barrack Office and the Office of Woods and Forests.

George III attempted to tighten up the regulations governing 'grace and favour' apartments. These rooms were in the gift of the Lord Chamberlain and under the direction of the Housekeeper.[7] The Office of Works was permitted to do no more than render these apartments 'wind and water tight'; internal alterations were executed by Office of Works tradesmen at the expense of the occupant.[8] 'As Hampton Court is so very full of Inhabitants', wrote Chambers, 'great difficulties have always been made about alterations of any Sort'.[9] As Surveyor General he often had to deal with personal complaints from impecunious but articulate tenants; George Ernst protesting about an unofficial privy outside his bedroom window; Mrs. Melliora Otway complaining about Lady Young's charcoal stove; or Mrs. Wright demanding that notice be taken of 'a very offensive Water Closet in the passage . . . the stench of which . . . obliges me to fumigate my rooms with francincense before I can go to bed'.[10] Among the less troublesome occupants during this period were two refugee rulers,

---

[1] R. Fulford, *Royal Dukes* (1933), p. 282.

[2] E. Law, *History of Hampton Court Palace* iii (1891), p. 332. For a detailed list of occupants see *ibid.* pp. 445-92.   [3] Works 3/3, 19 August 1796.   [4] Works 5/83, 1794.

[5] Works 5/72, 1783; *A Compendious Gazetteer to the Royal Palaces* (Windsor 1801), p. 3. The Raphael cartoons were returned from Windsor to Hampton Court in 1805 at the instance of George III (*The Times* 17 August 1804 p. 2, 20 August 1804 p. 2, 20 August 1805 p. 3, 29 August 1805 p. 3; W. H. Pyne, *History of the Royal Residences* ii, 1819, pp. 77-8).   [6] Works 3/3, ff. 25-6, 21, 29 August 1788; Works 4/17, 9 December 1785.

[7] Law, *op. cit.* iii, pp. 312, 444.

[8] Works 1/5, f. 50, 21 March, f. 64, 12 August 1783, ff. 78-9, 4 December 1784, 25 March 1785 and ff. 120-21, 10 February, 27 February, 18 March 1794; L.C. 1/5, f. 315, 4 June 1813.

[9] Works 1/5, f. 54, 11 April 1783.

[10] Works 3/3, 15 April, 28 July, 18 August 1786, 5 February, 8 February 1788.

William V of Orange and Gustavus IV of Sweden.[1] As to the Crown properties on Hampton Court Green, among which was the Clerk of the Works' house, it was not until after the reorganisation of 1815 that much was done in the way of sale and redevelopment on the lines laid down by Gilbert in 1783.[2]

Both the Royal Stud in Hampton Court Home Park and the King's Mews and barracks on Hampton Court Green brought the Office of Works into conflict with the Master of the Horse and the Barrack Office. It was from the Master of the Horse that permission had to be obtained for the demolition of a stable in 1786 and its reconstruction as a coach house in 1794.[3] And it was the Barrack Office not the Office of Works which was responsible for the conversion of the Mews into artillery and cavalry quarters in 1794–5.[4] Before long all three departments were at loggerheads over the maintenance of the stables and the state of the parade ground which was 'being made a perfect Slough' by dung-carts and private carriages.[5] Fourteen years later the soldiers were demanding reconstruction of their 'unfit and unhealthy quarter'; and in 1811 the barracks were rebuilt by the Barrack Office at a cost of £4400, despite Craig's protests on behalf of the Office of Works.[6] But in peacetime jurisdiction over the Mews reverted to the Master of the Horse, and this arrangement was confirmed by Thomas Hardwick in 1828.[7] As to the Royal Stud, the position was less confused. Stud house, paddocks and stud buildings were normally repaired by Office of Works tradesmen at the direction of the Master of the Horse.[8]

The maintenance of Longford River was a persistent irritant for the Office of Works. Variously known as the New River, New Cut, King's, Queen's or Cardinal's River, this channel had been constructed by Charles I in 1639 to supply Hampton Court gardens with water.[9] Eleven miles in length, it constituted an artificial tributary of the River Colne and flowed from Uxbridge across Hounslow Heath to Hampton Court and Bushy Park by way of Longford, Stanwell, Feltham, Hanworth and Hampton.[10] It cost the Office of Works up to £45 per annum in 'ploughing, harrowing with horses, and cutting the weeds by men from top to bottom' and 'draw-

---

[1] Law, *op. cit.* iii, pp. 319–21; *The Times* 23 January 1795, p. 3, 17 March 1795, p. 2, 8 June 1795, p. 2, 4 September 1795, p. 3, 10 October 1795, p. 3, 26 November 1795, p. 4, 16 June 1802, p. 2, 13 September 1802, p. 2. The Orange apartments were furnished by the Lord Chamberlain's Office at a cost of £5000. (T. 29/67, f. 434, 14 February 1795). In 1801 an application from the Comte D'Artois for the same apartments was refused. Five years later they were prepared for the Duchess of Brunswick (*The Times* 18 November 1801, p. 3, 22 December 1806, p. 3).

[2] See Gilbert's scheme (Works 6/20, ff. 103–8, 17 March 1783) and plan of 1783, copied 1796 (MPE 500). Compare MPEE 49 (1825).

[3] Works 4/17, 25 August 1786, Works 6/21, ff. 91–2, 25 August, 28 August, 1 September 1786; Works 1/5, f. 122, 11 April and f. 124, 7 May 1794; Works 4/17, f. 66, 17 April 1794; Works 5/83, 1794; T. 29/66, f. 400, 3 May 1794.

[4] Works 1/5, f. 122, 27–8 March and f. 124, 7 May 1794; *The Times* 4 April 1794, p. 3.

[5] Works 6/22, 16 December 1794.

[6] Works 4/20, 3 August 1810, 15 March, 24 May 1811; Works 6/25, f. 44, 13 October 1809; T. 29/110, f. 287, 20 March and f. 653, 23 April 1811; *The Times* 12 September 1811, p. 3. For plans showing the position of mews and barracks see B.M. Add. MS. 22875, f. 90 (1752) and P.R.O., MPE 329 (1799), MPE 773 (1800), MPEE 49 (1825), MPE 850 (1829) and MPE 779 (1835).

[7] Works 19/14/2, f. 10, 18 February 1828.

[8] E.g. Works 6/20, f. 274, 21 May 1784; Works 4/20, 1 March 1811, 19 June 1812; Works 4/21, 26 February 1813; L.C. 1/5, f. 263, 18 June and f. 331, 4 December 1812; Works 6/24, f. 54, 7 July 1806; Works 6/25, ff. 103, 8 January 1810, f. 115, 1 March and ff. 149–50, 17 June 1811; Works 1/5, f. 107, 4 October 1792; T. 29/55, f. 262, 27 May 1784; Works 4/18, f. 207, 4 November 1796 and f. 223, 17 February 1797.

[9] Law, *op. cit.* ii, p. 124. After 1876 the supply was used for drinking water (*ibid.* i, p. 23n.).

[10] See maps MPE 1340 (1805); MPE 1089; Crest 2/639; *Cary's . . . Survey . . . Ten Miles round Hampton Court and Richmond* (1786), B.M. Maps 3aa. 20.

ing the Grates and cleaning the Grating' at Longford.[1] After a severe frost the repair of the banks might cost as much as £200.[2] But it cost more in trouble with neighbouring landowners and business-men. In response to local pressure a new triple-arched bridge of brick and stone was built at Hampton in 1786,[3] another projected at Hanworth three years later,[4] a third erected at Stanwell in 1793,[5] and a fourth in Bushy Park in 1808.[6] Both Chambers and Wyatt regularly rejected applications to make use of the stream for water mills.[7] Nevertheless there were frequent complaints that the water supply had been depleted by the activity of mill owners or the officials of the Grand Junction Canal.[8] Chambers even had to cut off the supply to 'Mrs. Donaldson's Waterworks' when he discovered 'no less than six cocks playing in [her] house viz. two in the Scullery, one in the Servant's Hall, one in the Water-Closet, one in the Stable Yard, and one in the Gardens'.[9]

In 1782 the care of buildings in Bushy Park and Hampton Court Home Park was transferred from the Office of Woods and Forests to the Office of Works.[10] But under Chambers and Wyatt the position remained far from clear; and, anyway, little was spent on either of these parks or on Hampton Court Gardens.[11] During the Regency period there was only one major architectural project, and that came to nothing.

As Ranger of Bushy Park, the Duke of Clarence, later King William IV, lived happily at Bushy House between 1797 and 1830, first with Mrs. Jordan and their ten Fitzclarences and then with Princess Adelaide of Saxe-Meiningen.[12] He was not addicted to building, and such alterations as he required were generally paid for either by himself or else by the Office of Woods and Forests.[13] But the

---

[1] Works 6/21, f. 30, 20 April 1785. Chambers commented on the area's 'great number of Canals, water pipes, and water courses under ground . . . very intricate, and not to be managed by a stranger' (Works 6/22, f. 164, 24 July 1794).   [2] T. 29/127, f. 8, 18 February 1814; Works 4/21, 4, 11 February 1811.   [3] Chambers' estimate was £209 17s. 11d. (Works 6/21, f. 96, 24 November 1786 and f. 98, 9 February 1787).   [4] Works 6/21, f. 155, 22 April and f. 161, 10 July 1789.   [5] Under Tildesley's direction; cost £105 17s. 3½d. (Works 6/22, f. 16, 16 September 1791, f. 74, 23 November 1792 and f. 123, 13 August 1793; Works 4/17, 16 December 1791; Works 4/18, f. 31, 16 August 1793; Works 5/82, December 1793.)   [6] Thomas Rice's estimate was £198 10s. (Works 4/19, 15 April 1803; Works 4/20, 24 June, 26 August 1808; T. 29/97, f. 65, 5 October 1808).   [7] Works 4/17, 13, 24 August 1787; T. 29/56, f. 392, 21 May 1785; Works 6/21, f. 30, 20 April and f. 33, 4 May 1785; Works 1/5, ff. 104–5, 11 October 1791, and ff. 127–8, June 1794; Works 4/18, ff. 105, 130' 135, 145, 154, January–December 1795; Works 6/22, f. 177, 12 December 1794; T. 29/67, f. 334, 18 December 1794; Works 6/24, ff. 111, 115, August 1807 and f. 181, 3 May 1808.   [8] T. 29/65, f. 459, 12 April 1793; Works 6/23, f. 119, 20 April 1800 and f. 275, 8 February 1805.   [9] Works 1/5, f. 60, 17 May 1783 and f. 72, 5, 20 February 1784.   [10] T. 29/55, f. 209, 4 May 1784; Works 6/20, f. 234, 12 March 1784. For disputes over marginal items such as deer cribs and broken palings which allowed 'the deer to go out and the deer stealers to come in', cf. Works 6/23, f. 9, 17 November 1796; Works 4/18, ff. 210–11, 18–25 November, 1796; Works 4/17, 24 August 1792; Works 16/28/7, f. 8, 7 May 1803. For a general plan of the area cf. MR. 1454.   [11] Sizeable works included: new cherry house, 1811, £1100; new peach house, 1806–11, c. £2400 ('Inquiry into . . . the Office of Works', *Parl. Pap.* 1812–13, v, p. 409; 'Report . . . on the Civil List', 1812, *Parl. Pap.* 1830, ix, p. 199).   [12] ' . . . Bushey's lofty grove, Where Genius, Love, and raptured Clarence rove' (T. Maurice, *Richmond Hill*, 1807, p. 45). See also Fulford *op. cit.* pp. 105 *et. seq.*   [13] Minor alterations were made in 1801–2, 1808–10 (under Nash) and 1815–18 (under Hardwick). For details see T. 29/78, f. 251, 22 December 1801; Works 16/25/3, ff. 1–2, 4, 9, 19–24, 28, 31, 1802–18; T. 29/97, f. 307, 1 November 1808; T. 29/116, f. 61, 3 March 1812; T. 29/133, f. 329, 20 January 1815; Works 6/26, f. 184, 21 January 1815. Wyatt appointed Thomas Walker Clerk of Works at Bushy House in 1803 (Crest 8/1, f. 40, 9 April 1803). A plan of the house made in 1797 is in the Soane Museum (xxxix, set 9, 1). It had previously been occupied by Lord North, to whose wife George III had in 1771 presented the rangership. North lived at Bushy continuously between 1782 and his death in 1792, as did his widow, the Countess of Guilford, until her death in 1797 (Law, *op. cit.* iii, pp. 301–2). Extensive repairs were carried out at the house by the Office of Works in 1773–4 (Works 6/18, pp. 320–1; Works 5/142; *Parl. Hist.* xxiii, 952, 956).

Duke of Kent was less easily satisfied. When he succeeded the Duke of Gloucester as Ranger of Hampton Court Home Park in 1805, he found his official residence, the Pavilions, grossly inadequate. The four garden pavilions had been designed to surround the bowling green at the east end of the Long Walk alongside the Thames.[1] In 1792–3 two of the red brick pavilions had been connected by a flimsy stuccoed block designed for Gloucester by William Tyler and built under Tildesley's direction (Pl. 14A).[2] Further work ordered just before Gloucester's death had never been executed.[3] Within months of his appointment Kent therefore demanded complete reconstruction of pavilions, stables and stud house. Browne's estimate was £38,000.[4] In 1805 Gloucester had hoped to extend the central addition by erecting a conservatory at the rear.[5] But it was Kent's intention to turn the two unoccupied pavilions into gate-lodges, the bowling green into an oval carriageway and Gloucester's precarious central block into an elegant four-storey villa from designs by Thomas Hardwick.[6] With Kent's expenditure at Kensington in mind, the Treasury declined to co-operate and briefly informed the Ranger that 'there are not any Funds'.[7] When Kent complained that 'scarce a shilling had been laid out' to combat flooding, damp and dry rot, he was persuaded by the Treasury to 'forbear to press upon them for the present'.[8] In 1816 the Duke returned to the attack, appealing to Lord Liverpool against the refusal to carry out work on his residence. The minister was willing the premises should be re-examined, but declared that the expediency of any repair depended on their condition. Kent immediately begged Stephenson for a *'thorough repair of the Pavilions'*, especially as Liverpool had declared that 'he could not sanction (if they were pulled down) another Ranger's house being erected in their stead'.[9] But in November 1816 Soane (to whose charge the palace had fallen in 1815) reported that the basements of all four pavilions were damp and could never be habitable.[10] After the Duke's death in 1820 Soane recommended that the pavilions should be demolished, but the linked pair were left standing.[11]

In the main buildings Soane found that a good deal of stone and brick work needed repair. In the Great Hall he recommended the restoration of the centre of the roof, and the completion of the screen. The west wall was also considerably out of the vertical.[12] In the following year he recommended that the upper parts of the

---

[1] See Law, *op. cit.* iii, p. 211 for an early 18th-century engraving of the pavilions.

[2] Cost £985 (Works 6/22, f. 81, 11 January 1793; Works 4/17, 7 September 1792; Works 4/18, ff. 1–2, 1–4 January 1793. For a detailed description by Hardwick cf. Works 16/28/7, f. 2, 18 July 1816.

[3] Works 4/19, 26 April 1805; Works 6/25, f. 105, 18 August 1810.

[4] Works 6/24, f. 60, 14 August 1806; Works 4/19, 18 July, 15 August 1806. Robert Browne, jnr., the Clerk of Works at Richmond, was deputising *ad hoc* for the disordered Tildesley (see p. 42).

[5] Works 34/708 (1–4), wmk. 1803.   [6] Works 34/708 (5–12), 9 May 1811.

[7] T. 29/88, f. 47, 2 September 1806; Works 6/24, f. 60, 14 August 1806. Instead only minor repairs were executed (T. 29/92, f. 96, 11 September 1807).

[8] Works 6/25, ff. 103–5, 8, 18, 24 January 1810, f. 115, 1 March and ff. 149–50, 17 June 1811; T. 29/111, f. 794, 28 June 1811; T. 20/112, f. 348 6 August 1811.

[9] *Ibid.* pp. 226–7, 19 August 1816.

[10] *Ibid.* pp. 368 *et seq*. On the other hand the Duke's extensive stables, lying between the Pavilions and the Great Canal, were reported by Hardwick to be 'in general in a very good condition' (*ibid.* p. 191).

[11] Soane Museum, corr. 2, xii, G. 3, f. 1, 1822 survey. A plan of 1854 shows the building still standing; it was then proposed to demolish part and use the rest as a porter's lodge (B.M. Add. MS. 43200, ff. 30–7). It eventually became the residence of E. Law, the historian of the palace. See *Country Life*, 22 December 1900, p. 815 and *V. C. H. Middlesex* ii (1911) p. 384.

[12] Works 1/7, pp. 368 ff. A drawing of the screen by Hardwick (Soane Mus. 35/3/9, watermarked 1821) shows that it was not then surmounted by a gallery.

stonework of the octagon towers in the two main courts should be taken down and repaired.[1] The 1819 survey proposed the repair of the ceiling over the stairs to the Great Hall: the timbers being decayed, Soane suggested forming an arched ceiling to correspond in outline with that in the Great Hall, though without ornaments.[2] But this was never done, and others of his recommendations remained unexecuted at the time of the 1822 survey.[3] A general repair of the roofs was however carried out over a period of years.[4] In 1829 the water gallery was repaired after flood damage under the direction of Lewis Wyatt (who had succeeded as Clerk of Works on Hardwick's death in January).[5] In 1829–31, while the parish church was rebuilding, the Great Hall was used by the parishioners for worship.[6]

George IV visited Hampton Court only to see his horses in the royal stud, and despoiled the palace of statues and ornaments for his new garden at Windsor Castle.[7] William IV, himself a former Ranger of Bushy Park, showed more interest in the palace itself, sending there many pictures from other royal residences, 'to accommodate which several extra State Rooms were added to those already open to the inspection of sightseers';[8] and the King's Stair was restored in 1836 at the expense of the Lord Chamberlain's Department.[9] The following year a tower in the west front was found to be insecure, and was temporarily shored up until funds for underpinning could be obtained.[10] In 1835 the worn-out astronomical clock was removed from the gate-tower of Clock Court, a clock of 1799 from St. James's Palace being substituted.[11] After the accession of Queen Victoria the gardens and state apartments were opened to the public free of charge, and the necessary preparations included providing railings to keep spectators from the furnishings and pictures.[12]

The gradual restoration of the palace carried out during the reign of Victoria owed much to the enthusiasm of Edward Jesse, in charge of the district from 1832.[13] Expenditure rose from an average of some £2700 per annum in 1833–8 to over £7000 in 1838–50.[14] With Blore as consulting and Inman as executant architect many of the windows were restored to their original character, and the west front came to assume, in general, its present appearance.[15] The Queen's Stair was repaired;[16] dilapidated outbuildings were removed;[17] Wolsey's arms were discovered on the

[1] Soane Museum, corr. 2, xii, G. 1, ff. 5, 6. He also remarked on the good effect of works done as a result of the previous survey.　[2] *Ibid.* f. 7.　[3] *Ibid.* G. 3, f. 1.
[4] Works 1/12, p. 466. A piece of timber preserved in the Superintendent's office bears the following inscription: 'G. Smith of Hampton Carpenter. This Hall underwent a repair 1820 and 1821. George Slade Labourer in Trust. June 20th.'
[5] Works 1/17, pp. 408–14, 496, 504; 19/15/4. Wyatt's estimate of £2115 necessitated putting the work to tender, when H. McIntosh was successful at £785.　[6] Works 1/17, p. 516.
[7] A list in the Royal Library, Windsor, includes statues of Flora, Pomona, Ceres and Diana, removed from the south facade. All the lead urns were returned in 1955.
[8] Law, iii, pp. 342–3.　[9] Works 1/22, pp. 94, 120.　[10] *Ibid.* pp. 345, 357.
[11] Works 19/525. It was intended by William IV that the ancient clock should be restored, but while the Board haggled over Vulliamy's price, his drawings were lost, and it was not until 1881 that the greatly-restored clock was replaced. See also Law, iii, pp. 343–4.　[12] Works 1/23, pp. 181, 192, 205.
[13] In that year Seward had recommended that the progressive restoration of the fabric should continue (Works 19/25/1, pp. 7–8).
[14] L.R.R.O. 24/3–6; *Parl. Pap.* 1843 (343) xxx; 1851 (374) xxxi.
[15] Works 1/25, pp. 144, 159. For W.S. Inman's part see below. The Great Gatehouse was given its present turrets in 1882 (Hist. Mon. Comm. *Middlesex*, 1937, p. 32).
[16] Works 1/23, p. 201, 8 October 1838.
[17] Miss Secker's former apartments (Works 1/24, p. 115, 28 February 1840) and the late locksmith's (*ibid.* p. 231, 2 June 1840).

inner gatehouse; one of the celebrated medallions of the Caesars by Maiano was repaired, and two others were brought from Windsor and set in the west face of the outer gatehouse.[1] The windows of the Presence Chamber and of the Great Hall were gradually filled with stained glass by Willement between 1840 and 1847.[2] Jesse's enthusiasm led him into trouble on several occasions. In 1842 he exceeded the expenditure authorised on the Great Hall.[3] When a similar event occurred two years later the Treasury allowed the ornamental painting of the ceiling to proceed as the scaffolding had been put up.[4] The opportunity was taken to secure accurate drawings of the roof, 'specifying particularly any alteration made during this present repair, and the nature of the materials used therein, and of any which you may have rejected or substituted by others'.[5] The Clerk of Works was also instructed to ascertain 'whether there be any indication in the roof of there having been a l'ouvre or cupola over a central or other Fireplace in the Hall, and if so, . . . how it was framed and constructed'.[6] The year after, Jesse suggested that, to prevent accidents, the stone floor of the dais should be distinguished from that of the other portion of the Hall, by substituting encaustic tiles; but although the Board called for tenders, the project was not pursued.[7]

The restoration of the exterior of the palace (Pl. 14B) was a gradual process. The north-west front was restored under Blore's direction in or after 1841.[8] In 1844, windows in the upper storeys of the east side of Clock Court were directed to be restored 'in accord with the original style of the Building, that is, those looking into the Clock Court to have lattice quarries like some of the oldest specimens remaining in the two entrance Courts'. A stack of four chimneys near the west gable of the hall was to be rebuilt according to a figured outline drawing that had been taken.[9] The Lord Steward's department was urged to hand over for demolition vacant buildings near the Great Vine, as complaints were made of the 'disgraceful state of these wretched and ruinous Tenements'.[10] Another dilapidated residence, the surviving pavilion, was repaired largely at the expense of the occupier, Mrs. Moore, but the Board contributed £100.[11] When the repair of the 'Trophy Buildings' was proposed in 1846 the Commissioners demurred as this was a detached building of an inferior

[1] *Ibid.* p. 157; *Gent's. Mag.* 1845 ii, p. 594, where Jesse describes how Wolsey's arms in terracotta were discovered when those of Henry VIII were taken down for restoration; and states that two busts of Caesars found by him 'fixed in the front of keepers' cottages in Windsor Forest', were restored by Wilson, Clerk of Works at Hampton Court, and reset in 'the eastern [a mistake for the *western*] entrance'.

[2] Ten panels of the oriel of the Presence Chamber were directed to be filled with stained glass in 1841 (Works 1/25, p. 138, est. £105; the sketch for these is B.M. Add. MS. 34873, f. 224). The rest of the window was done later (*ibid.* f. 223). The first window in the Great Hall so treated was the west (E. Jesse, *A Summer's Day at Hampton Court*; 5th edition, 1842, p. 147). The sketch for this is B.M. Add. MS. 34873, f. 225. The sketch of the oriel of the Hall as first done is dated 1840 (*ibid.* f. 221). More glass was included in the 1842 estimate at £300 (Works 1/26, p. 262). That of 1845 allowed £1000 for stained glass windows in the Hall (Works 1/28, p. 202; also pp. 292, 320-1, 380), including the completion of the oriel; and a further £800 for 1846 (Works 1/29, p. 331). See B.M. Add. MS. 34873, ff. 222, 226-7, 231 for sketches. There is a description in *Gent's. Mag.* 1847, i, pp. 291-3.   [3] Works 1/25, p. 429.

[4] Works 1/27, pp. 96-7, 145 (estimate £400). In his guidebook Jesse justifies the extensive use of colour in the roof (*A Summer's Day*, p. 22). See also Law, iii, p. 369.

[5] Works 1/27, pp. 239-40, Inman to Robinson (Clerk of Works), 21 October 1844. The drawings are not among those in the P.R.O., Works 34.   [6] *Ibid.*   [7] Works 1/28, pp. 47, 48.

[8] Works 1/25, p. 144 (15 July 1841); p. 159 (24 July, estimate £535); Works 34/63, 69.

[9] Works 1/27, pp. 239-40.   [10] Works 1/28, p. 363 (29 September 1845); also 21 October 1841.

[11] *Ibid.* p. 273. The total estimate was £352.

description; only absolutely necessary works should be done there, so as 'to keep the roof Wind and Weather proof'.[1] Later in 1846 Blore was again consulted 'as to the most appropriate mode of restoring and renovating (so as to harmonize with the most ancient portion of the Building, and having due regard to those portions already renovated) the South West Wing'.[2] In June the Board ordered the immediate completion of this wing for Lady Emily Ponsonby. The work included six new windows in the west front, and two new ones in the north in place of two very small windows.[3] A two-storied oriel was eventually substituted for two of the mullioned windows proposed for the west front.[4] The parapet of the north return was to be renovated with 'Battlements, Stone Finials, Moldings and Gable with a Window on each side of its Finial and a roof to the Gable returned on to the main roof and with Armorial Figures, &c to correspond with Lady A. Paget's Parapet opposite [north west wing] and the Battlements on the other Parapets are to be reinstated and made good as they were originally'.[5]

The vote for 1846/7 for the Hampton Court district was £11,885, but a great part of this was for the park, gardens, and water-courses. This year saw work begin on the chapel, though not to the extent proposed by Jesse. A new external roof to the chapel was included in the estimates, together with further restoration of the roof of the Great Hall.[6] The following year about £660 were spent on repairing the internal woodwork of the chapel roof, which was then painted and gilded.[7] This work was completed during 1848. The restoration of the stone mullions of the windows to correspond with one that survived in the south-east corner of the chapel (concealed by a painted canvas) was deferred, together with under-draining and relaying on concrete the marble pavement of the ante-chapel.[8]

In 1847 Jesse was ordered to renovate the roof of the north side of the Base Court, and to restore the ancient mullioned windows in the south front of Sir George Seymour's apartments (in the north-west angle of the west front) to correspond with those of Lady Emily Ponsonby in the south-west wing, at an estimate of

[1] Works 1/29, p. 168, 9 March 1846. These buildings, formerly occupied by Lady Carnarvon, had in 1845 been allotted to Mrs. Heneage Finch, a relation of Jesse's (See M. C. Houston, *Letters and Reminiscences of the Rev. John Mitford*, 1891). They were eventually demolished in 1867.
[2] Works 1/29, p. 273, 11 May 1846; Works 34/60 appears to be the first proposals.
[3] Works 34/56–58. The first designs (by Inman) are dated June 1845. [4] Works 34/64, 66, 67.
[5] Works 1/29, p. 337, 11 June 1846; Works 34/63 is a drawing of the restored battlements, etc.
[6] Works 1/29, p. 331, 9 June 1846. Jesse was told to submit plans so that the Board could judge whether any works might be put out to competition. Wilson revised his estimate of £850 for the roof repair to £975, which earned him a reprimand from the Board, but he was directed to make the work fit and substantial, sending drawings and details first to Inman (Works 1/30, pp. 142–3, 24 August 1846; see also Works 19/302). Works 34/77–83 shew plans and sections.
[7] It was first proposed, as an economy measure, to omit the gilding, but Jesse appealed successfully to the Chief Commissioner, Morpeth. The estimate given by Edward Wyatt, £855, was regarded as too high, so Wyatt proposed omitting the 'angels in the round of the corbels', and merely painting the ante-chapel. Jesse again begged Morpeth to prevent such a display of bad taste, with the result that Blore's opinion was sought, the Board being 'unwilling to effect this saving of £231 at the expence of good taste'. Blore advised gilding the angels, but not the ribs of the staircase or the ceiling of the ante-chapel, where the wall was merely rough plaster whitened. But when specimens were prepared for completing the decoration of the roof, Morpeth in some doubt referred the matter to Pugin, who disapproved of the specimens, and gave his own ideas, which were carried out; gilded stars were set on the ground of the ceiling panels, and ten corbels and 16 panels were enriched with 'Scrolls and releif, and antient Writing', increasing the cost from £744 to £831 (Works 1/31, pp. 347, 367; 19/302).
[8] Works 1/31, pp. 156, 187. The windows were eventually restored in 1894 'on the Tudor lines' (Hist. Mon. Comm., *Middlesex*, p. 41).

£1499.[1] In 1848/9 the restoration of the Armoury roof and of Mrs. Ellice's apartments over the Guard Room and Presence Chamber, where a collapse had occurred, was undertaken (estimate £2451).[2] Work began on altering Lady Augusta Paget's windows in the north-west wing early in 1850.[3]

It was decided in 1847 to provide privies and urinals for the public, for whom none then existed. It was at Jesse's suggestion that the circular kitchen in Round Kitchen Court was converted for this purpose.[4]

Other problems that required the attention of the Board at this period included that of taxation, both national and local. Attempts to levy window tax on certain occupiers of 'grace and favour' residences were resisted in the courts,[5] but the Tax Commissioners persisted in their assault on the privilege of a royal palace. Similarly, the Hampton Guardians attempted to levy poor rates on the inhabitants of the palace, distraining when their demands were rejected. The courts were not enthusiastic to maintain the ancient privileges; and a collision of authorities was only averted by increasing the royal bounty to the parish from £50 to £450 a year.[6] Another source of anxiety was the condition of the Raphael Cartoons, then in the palace. The Keeper of the National Gallery, Uwins, called attention to their condition, but declined to incur sole responsibility for their restoration. The opinion of C. L. Eastlake was accordingly sought and a small committee of artists was appointed.[7]

The Board was also responsible for the maintenance of a number of detached buildings associated with the palace and its parks. The Banqueting House and the Mews were the closest. Little care seems to have been taken of the Banqueting House since repairs recommended by Soane in 1819 and the building was in a most dilapidated state when Sir James Reynett, the Duke of Cambridge's Secretary, obtained a grant of it in 1836.[8] Reynett claimed to have then spent over £1100 on it, adding a dining room and pantry.[9] Occasional repairs were made to the Mews, but nothing in the way of major works.[10] Ordinary expenditure on the palace gardens during the period 1815–31 averaged rather more than £2500 a year.[11] Part of this was for

---

[1] Works 1/31, p. 156. Some of this work, the restoration of roofs in the north range of the Base Court (Miss Copley's and Lady Montgomery's) was included in the 1848–9 estimates (*Parl. Pap.* 1847–8, xviii, pt. 2, p. 23). According to Hist. Mon. Comm., *Middlesex*, p. 33, the north range roofs are original. Additional garrets in the roofs of Miss Copley's and Lady Isabella St. John's apartments (south range of Base Court) had been proposed in 1845 (Works 34/76) where dormer windows exist today. Alterations to Sir George Seymour's apartments are shewn in Works 34/73 (5 July 1847), 74 and 75.

[2] Works 1/33, pp. 1, 13, 39; Law, iii, p. 463. [3] Works 1/34, pp. 379, 433.

[4] Works 1/32, p. 64; 1/34, pp. 48–9; 1/35, pp. 139, 231–2; 1/36, p. 2. Inman recommended that the w.c.s should be 'self acting by a lever Seat, or a foot board'. [5] Works 2/4, pp. 462–7, 481.

[6] The history of this long dispute with the parochial authorities is set forth in Works 2/5, pp. 37 *et seq.*, and 2/6, pp. 217–24. A summary is given in Law, iii, pp. 354–9, of the appeal by case stated, *Reg.* v. Lady Emily Ponsonby and others, 3 *Q.B.* 14. See also Works 1/34, pp. 87, 139, 214.

[7] Works 1/34, pp. 317, 335.

[8] Soane Mus. Corr. 2, xii, G. 1, f. 7. Law, iii, p. 347, gives an account of how Reynett obtained possession.

[9] Works 2/5, pp. 342–5, 397. Reynett in 1846 unsuccessfully sought permission to make further additions, asking the Woods and Works to pay the greater part of the cost, but the Commissioners were opposed even to allowing him to do the work at his own cost, on the ground that it would mean increased repairs in the future. The proposed addition is shewn in Works 34/71.

[10] Works 34/106; 19/14/2. Part occupied by troops was repaired by the Barrack Board 1811 –*c*. 1840; after George IV ceased to visit Hampton Court, it appears that the other parts were used by the inhabitants of the palace. In 1842 essential external repairs at a cost of £169 were approved, and the occupiers were instructed to keep the Mews in repair.

[11] Works 5/107–111.

greenhouses,[1] but it also included the maintenance of the Longford River. In 1838–47/8 the average was about £1600 a year, of which the bulk was for the river.[2] In 1851 vases in Portland stone, 'as near as possible a facsimile', were ordered to replace the old leaden ones on two gate-piers in the Wilderness that had been destroyed by a falling tree.[3]

The Royal Stud had been at Hampton Court since the reign of William III, but according to Ernest Law 'it was George IV who must be considered the real founder of the Hampton Court Stud' as it existed in the nineteenth century.[4] As Regent he revived the breeding of blood-stock in 1812, and in 1815 the stud buildings were placed under the Office of Works.[5] The consequential expenditure, including repairs to the Stud House and the formation and fencing of paddocks, amounted to £23,834.[6] On his accession in 1820 George IV handed the whole establishment over to his brother the Duke of York, but on the latter's death in 1827 he resumed possession. William IV maintained the stud, but after his death it was sold, to be re-established on a different footing in 1851.[7] In 1832–3 a house was erected for the principal stud groom, from plans by Lewis Wyatt, at a cost of some £850.[8] Estimates of £800 were authorised in 1850/1 for work on the stud buildings.[9]

The Stud House in the Park appears to have been a residence of the Master of the Horse; by 1815, however, it had been allotted by the Regent to his private secretary, Bloomfield, who as clerk marshall supervised the stud. After the death of the Duke of Kent, the Rangership of the Home Park was conferred on Lady Bloomfield, and the Stud House became her residence. In 1830, William IV persuaded her through Lord Duncannon to give up the house and place her Rangership in abeyance in return for financial compensation. The occupation of the house was transferred to the Master of the Horse, and Lord Albemarle resided there until about 1841. As his two immediate successors did not wish to do so, it was allotted to the Master of the Stag Hounds, and as such was occupied by Lords Rosslyn (to 1846) and Granville (1846–8).[10] During the period when Bloomfield was private secretary to George IV considerable works were done at the house. The first major alterations came in 1817–18.[11] The Treasury had scarcely approved an estimate of £490 for enlarging the kitchen and offices,[12] when a demand for further alterations costing £850 was presented, for the accommodation of the Regent's personal establishment. Deferred for lack of funds, these were begun early in the following year under Hardwick, the Clerk of Works.[13] At that point Bloomfield asked Nash to cast an eye over the

---

[1] E.g. Works 1/14, p. 515. Such works were sometimes paid for under a special authority, e.g. building three forcing houses 1816, £1277 15s. 2d. (Works 5/107; 19/13/15); repairs to the Great Vine House, 1826, £476 8s. 7d. (5/109).   [2] *Parl. Pap.* 1843 (343) xxx, 1851 (374) xxxi.

[3] Works 1/36, p. 292, 5 May 1851. The vases in question appear to be those on the piers of the gate between the Wilderness and the Broad Walk.   [4] E. Law, *op. cit.* iii, p. 335.

[5] By Treasury Letter of 4 November 1815, the stud establishment was placed under the Office of Works, and the Stud House works were defrayed out of the Civil List. But works on the paddocks and fences were distinguished by their character, brick and iron fencing only being done by the Office of Works. The resultant confusion led to the whole being placed under the Office of Works in June 1821 (Works 19/68; 1/10, pp. 406–7)

[6] Works 19/14/4, f. 7, 22 May 1815.   [7] Law, *op. cit.* iii, pp. 336–7.

[8] Works 1/20, pp. 78, 81; 2/1, p. 41. The working drawings appear to have been prepared by Phipps (Works 19/68).

[9] Works 1/36, p. 120, 21 January 1851.   [10] Works 19/44/4, ff. 2, 33, 40–1; T. 1/3905, f. 47/38.

[11] A Wine Cellar was constructed in 1815, estimate £310 (Works 19/14/4, ff. 1–5).

[12] Authorised 31 July 1817 (*ibid.* f. 10).   [13] Works 19/14/4, ff. 9–11.

alterations, and Nash advised some modifications that he estimated at not more than £300. He explained to the Surveyor General:

> The alteration which is now begun at the Stud House is to afford accommodation to the Prince Regent—In the present arrangement of the House this cannot be done without removing the family to the Offices, and [it] is principally owing to the impossibility of occupying the Bedrooms as most of them cannot be approached without passing through others which are occupied, nor is there any place for Genl Bloomfield to attend His Royal Highness which it is become more than formerly necessary for him to do.[1]

To provide accommodation 'indispensable to the occupation of His Royal Highness, even for the shortest time possible', Nash proposed moving the main stairs, constructing a new small stair and a passage to give access to all the bedrooms independently, and enlarging two of the ground floor rooms at the back, as well as rebuilding a stack of chimneys.[2] Nash claimed that all this could be done for a mere £300 more than Hardwick's estimate—a figure which, as usual, proved to be far below the real cost.[3] In August yet further additions were required: a 'living Room and sleeping Room over' were to be added to the offices for the Regent's footmen, who were 'obliged to be lodged in Tents'.[4] Hardwick's final estimates, totalling £4379, were slightly exceeded.[5]

A second wave of alterations for George IV's accommodation came in 1820–1. They cost nearly £3000, and once again Nash's estimate came to less than half the actual expenditure.[6] Blamed on 'constant deviations . . . from the original plan' and 'the great hurry and confusion in which these works were conducted', the excess led to such a prolonged examination of accounts that, although the unpaid tradesmen petitioned in the summer of 1822, Stephenson did not make his report until January 1824, and the Treasury authorised payment only in August 1824.[7] Bloomfield was dismissed from his secretaryship in 1822[8], and no further major works were carried out before George IV's death in 1830. Expenditure between 1838 and 1850 averaged £345 a year, the repairs before Lord Granville moved in in 1846 costing over £1300.[9]

The Woods and Forests bore the cost of maintaining the Ranger's House in Bushy Park, home of the Duke of Clarence since 1797, the works being undertaken by the Office of Works from 1815. Minor repairs were carried out from time to time, but a general overhaul became necessary when Clarence wished to live there after his

---

[1] *Ibid.* f. 11, 9 February 1818.

[2] Works 1/8, pp. 407–10, 18, 19 February 1818. Nash's specifications are given, pp. 419–23. The principal works were 'enlarging the two rooms proposed as a dining room, instead of laying the present two rooms together, and raising one of them'; building two first floor bedrooms with garrets over, with a hipped roof; moving the stairs and adding that site to the drawing room, with a dressing room on the first floor, and garret over; a communicating passage for first floor bedrooms; back stairs by the old kitchen; and covered ways linking the new kitchen and drawing room and bedrooms.

[3] Works 19/14/4, ff. 18, 19, 10 March 1818.

[4] *Ibid.* f. 25. The estimate of £689 included other minor alterations.

[5] Works 5/107. See also Works 19/14/4, f. 28.

[6] Works 1/12, pp. 319, 323. Bloomfield was at first to pay for certain works ordered by him costing £360 18s. 7d.   [7] *Ibid.*; 1/13, p. 10.   [8] *Letters of George IV*, ii, pp. 514–20.

[9] Works 19/68, 21 June 1834; *Parl. Pap.* 1843 (343) xxx; 1851 (374) xxxi. In 1846 £600 were allowed specifically for repairs before Lord Granville took possession (Works 2/5, pp. 287–298; 1/30, p. 434). See also 19/14/4, f. 34 *et seq.*

marriage to Adelaide of Saxe-Meiningen: 'Many parts of the Mansion House and the whole of the Stables [he informed the Treasury] have not been painted or repaired since the year 1772 and it is utterly impossible for me to reside in Bushey House with the Duchess without various repairs to the Mansion, and the Stables undergoing a complete arrangement'.[1] The house was accordingly repaired and improved under Hardwick's management at a cost of £4000.[2] In February 1821 Clarence urged that further works should be done, estimated at £1500; this probably related to the stables and outbuildings. But it was not until July 1823 that approval was given for these repairs, which cost some £1800.[3] Four years later, when the Duke had become heir presumptive, improvements costing over £2100 were executed;[4] but the over-burdening of the Woods and Forests' resources by the rebuilding of Buckingham House and works in the Parks limited any further outlay to what was 'absolutely necessary for the comfort and convenience of his Royal Highness', for which an estimate of £1118 was submitted.[5] The alterations were completed in the first half of 1828, but the cost formed part of the ordinary expenditure on the Park.[6] Further repairs were done in 1829, but again charged in the general account.[7]

After William IV's accession, Queen Adelaide was appointed Ranger, and occupied the house until her death in 1849. Bills for works at the Upper Lodge were ordered to be examined in the Office of Works, but to be defrayed by the Privy Purse.[8] In 1834, one room was fitted up as a library,[9] and in 1836 repairs estimated at £601 were ordered.[10] For her more frequent residence, after the King's death, some £2000 were spent in 1837–8, including a new conservatory and works in the gardens.[11] The agricultural buildings of the adjacent farm were demolished after the Queen's death.[12]

KENSINGTON PALACE

During the second half of the eighteenth century Kensington Palace became a royal backwater. Its architecture was out of fashion and its situation made it neither a country retreat nor a metropolitan court. Lysons calls it 'entirely forsaken';[13] Malcolm

[1] Works 1/10, p. 2, 6 January 1820; an account for new stables and repairs to the old, 1808–9 (Works 16/25/3, f. 4), suggests the Duke's word was not to be relied upon. Minor works done earlier include: drain and bakehouse, £186 8s., and laundry cupola, £93 11s. 10¾d. (spring of 1815); brewhouse, £23 16s. 4d. and iron water pipe, £642 16s. 8d. (early 1816) (Works 5/107).

[2] Works 1/10, pp. 50, 95; 5/108 (second and third quarters, 1820); 16/25/3, ff. 31–5.

[3] Works 1/10, p. 340; 1/12, p. 53; 5/108, third quarter, 1823.

[4] Works 1/15, pp. 233, 306–8 (Hardwick's estimate of £1883 dated 18 July 1827 was chiefly for additional offices, new stables, and improving the turn in at the Teddington Gate); 5/109.

[5] Works 1/15, p. 388, Treasury to Surveyor General, 27 August 1827; T. 1/3905, original and revised estimates.

[6] Works 1/15, p. 439; 1/16, pp. 23, 30–1, 349–50; 5/110. Building lodges at the Teddington gate was postponed till 1829–30, when they were executed under a gross contract for £350 (Works 5/111; also Works 1/16, pp. 186–96; 1/17, pp. 435, 473).

[7] Works 1/16, pp. 403, 488; 1/17, p. 414; 5/110–111.   [8] Works 4/31, p. 158 (22 September 1831)

[9] Works 1/21, pp. 81, 166 (estimate, £420).   [10] Works 1/22, p. 73.

[11] *Ibid.* pp. 392, 396; 1/23, pp. 29, 36; 16/25/3, ff. 43–8 (Carless's tender for conservatory, £1139 6s., f. 45). The house is now occupied by the Director of the National Physical Laboratory. A plan of the ground floor in the Royal Library at Windsor (Portfolio 58) signed by John Phipps shows the house as occupied by Queen Adelaide. It may be compared with one dated 1797 in the Soane Museum (xxxix, Set 9, 1). In the Royal Library there is also a bound volume containing elegantly drawn survey plans of the Bushy Park estate made by W. T. Warren in 1823.   [12] Works 1/36, p. 189.   [13] D. Lysons, *Environs of London* iii (1795), p. 185.

comments on its 'utter neglect';[1] and Pyne condemns it as 'a reproach to English taste'.[2] George III never cared for Kensington. And George IV's affection for the place cannot have been enhanced by the presence there of Caroline of Brunswick between 1808 and 1813. But the need to house George III's numerous children gave the palace a new lease of life. The Duke of Kent arrived in 1804, the Duke of Sussex in 1810. And in 1808 the ill-fated Princess Charlotte took possession of a set of rooms. Even so, the state apartments were never brought into regular use, and the various structural alterations produced little change in the architectural character of the palace.

The Duke of Kent (1767–1820), Queen Victoria's father, was a peppery martinet who shared with the Prince Regent and the Duke of York an obsessive interest in building.[3] What he lacked in vision he made up in intensity. His four houses at Hampton Court,[4] Knightsbridge, Ealing and Kensington, to say nothing of his temporary residences in Quebec, Gibraltar, Germany and Brussels, all reflected the hand of a perfectionist.[5] Plumbing was his speciality. For twenty years a running battle between the Duke of Kent and the Office of Works centred on the Duke's pernickety tastes and the way these tastes persistently conflicted with Wyatt's dilatory habits, Yenn's old age, the parsimony of the Treasury and the decaying fabric of Kensington Palace.

It was in December 1798 that the Duke of Kent was first allocated quarters at Kensington. But he did not move in 'for good' until January 1804.[6] At first orders were given for no more than a few 'trifling repairs'.[7] But this was the start of a cumulative process. The Duke's new accommodation was situated in the south-east corner of the palace, and consisted of the two floors below the state apartments now (1972) occupied by the London Museum. It was the basement floor which proved most troublesome. In addition he was given the use of the north-west stable block, built in 1740 for William, Duke of Cumberland. This was now altered under Yenn's direction and became known as the Ten Stall Stables.[8] At the same time the Duke of Kent's private apartments were reconstructed. Yenn's first estimate of £5980 for both operations was shelved during the summer of 1800.[9] This turned out to be doubly unfortunate. In May 1801 part of the proposed suite along the east front collapsed, and Kent felt justified in demanding a more extensive rebuilding. Yenn's second estimate of £9256 excluded the stables and dealt only with the reconstruction of the south, north and east fronts.[10] Even so, the figures proved much too low. Wyatt, unusually active, persuaded King and Treasury to authorise this sum, and even

[1] Malcolm, *Londinium Redivivum* iv (1807), p. 237.

[2] W. H. Pyne, *History of the Royal Residences* ii (1819), p. 74.

[3] For his career see *Gent's. Mag.* 1820, pt. i, p. 85; R. Fulford, *Royal Dukes* (1933), pp. 149–99; McKenzie Porter, *Overture to Victoria* (1962). He was a liberal in politics and a patron of many charities.

[4] See p. 332.

[5] For example, see his correspondence with the Board of Green Cloth on the subject of fruit and vegetables (Works 16/26/10).   [6] *Ibid.* 31 January 1804.

[7] Works 4/18, f. 319, 7 December 1798; Works 6/23, f. 71, 14 December 1798; L.C. 1/4, 21 February 1799.

[8] The stables were subsequently altered in 1873 for the Duchess of Argyll. In 1955 they were converted into a residence for Sir Alan Lascelles.

[9] Works 4/19, 6 June 1800, 1 August 1800; Works 6/23, f. 124, 7 June 1800.

[10] Works 4/19, 18 December 1801; Works 6/23, f. 155, 3 July, f. 156, 15 August and ff. 160–61, 15–18 December 1801.

prevailed upon the tradesmen to accept slow settlement.[1] Whereupon the Duke proceeded to demand further works estimated at another £3882 2s. 0d.[2] As the work progressed Kent's peremptory commands made a coherent building programme very difficult, and an overall rise of 20% in building costs soon made the estimates irrelevant.[3] Relations between Kent, Wyatt and Yenn rapidly deteriorated. In 1802 Kent had thanked the Surveyor General for his 'attention . . . in this, as well as in every other instance'.[4] But a year later he was demanding the immediate installation of a kitchen dresser, otherwise it would be 'impossible . . . to get even a Beef Steak cooked'.[5] And in 1804 Yenn received a curt note, couched in the third person, in which he was reminded that 'the Duke of Kent . . . is not fond of doing things by halves'.[6] When the Treasury tried to forbid all works except such as were 'absolutely and indespensably necessary for . . . preservation', Kent managed to circumvent the restriction by a personal interview with William Pitt.[7] In 1806 Yenn estimated future work on the stables at more than £10,000 and on Kent's apartments at more than £17,000.[8] When the Lord Chamberlain attempted to impose restrictions Kent forcibly reminded him of 'the real necessity of *every iota*'.[9] By the autumn of 1807 expenditure stood at £27,045 3s. 3¼d.[10] By the end of 1811 this figure had been approximately doubled.[11] And furniture supplied by the Lord Chamberlain's department between 1792 and 1812 added more than £30,000 to the bill.[12]

Kent's fastidiousness was not entirely to blame. Treasury attempts to inhibit expenditure by imposing contractual limits proved largely ineffective.[13] Building costs were rapidly increasing.[14] The structure of Kensington Palace had been neglected for half a century. Brickwork turned out to be decayed and woodwork infested with dry rot.[15] The construction of a new kitchen on the east front was

[1] 'The King has given to Prince Edward a suite of apartments in Kensington Palace. . . . The King ordered that they should be painted and whitewashed only; Prince Edward expressed a desire to Wyatt to have some new chimney pieces and other alterations—but did not choose to ask the King, saying *He had once been a bad boy, and would not be so again,* or subject himself to a refusal by asking what the King might not approve. Wyatt recommended that an estimate of any wished for alterations should be made out and he would lay it before His Majesty' (Farington, p. 1453, 26 January 1799).

[2] Works 4/19, 12 March 1802; Works 6/23, f. 173, 5 March 1802.

[3] Works 6/23, f. 238, 16 February and f. 240, 22 February 1804; Works 4/19, 19 November 1802, 27 January, 17 February 1804.   [4] Works 6/23, f. 171, 18 February 1802.

[5] Works 6/23, f. 234, 28 December 1803.   [6] Works 6/23, f. 260, 4 August 1804.

[7] Works 6/23, f. 253, 17 July 1804; L.C. 1/40, f. 9, 3 November 1804.

[8] L.C. 1/40, ff. 43–6, 29 November 1806; Works 6/24, f. 66, 24 October 1806. Expenditure on the stables was to be checked by the department of the Master of the Horse (*ibid.* ff. 49–50, 19–30 June and ff. 58–9, 26 July, 3 August 1806).   [9] Works 6/24, ff. 171–5, 12 March 1808.

[10] Works 4/18, 3 July, 10 July 1807; Works 6/24, f. 102, 17 July 1807. For estimates cf. Works 6/24, ff. 46–7, 17 June 1806.

[11] L.C. 1/5, f. 330, 17 September 1813; 'Report from the Select Committee on the Civil List' *Parl. Pap.* 1812, ii, p. 457 and 1830, ix, p. 199. For details of repairs to Kent's apartments on the east and north fronts see also L.C. 1/40, f. 9, 3 November 1804 and f. 96, 26 September 1807; Works 6/24, ff. 179–80, 29 April 1808; Works 6/25, f. 18, 6 October and f. 24, 2 November 1809; Works 6/24, ff. 129, 132, 136, 137, October, November 1807; 'Inquiry into . . . the Office of Works', *Parl. Pap.* 1812–13, v, p. 409.

[12] L.C. 1/40, ff. 243, 256, 278; L.C. 1/3, 23 December 1807.

[13] L.C. 1/4, 11 January 1810; T. 29/104, ff. 69–70, 9 January 1810.   [14] See p. 86.

[15] The building had been 'originally of bad construction, and of a composition of the worst and most inferior materials'; since then it had been 'decayed by mildews, damps and rottenness, chiefly arising from the various rooms and apartments on the basement floor of the Palace that had been long shut up containing old decayed furniture, and the level of the floor below the gardens which subjected the lower rooms to continual damps' (Yenn's explanation, L.C. 1/4, 19 July, 2 November 1809; see also Works 19/16/1, f. 7, 28 February 1806 and Works 6/24, f. 24, 2 November 1809).

delayed by the discovery of crumbling brickwork in the adjoining apartments which had once belonged to the Duchess of Manchester.[1] During 1810 and 1811 several sections of the Duke's apartments were in danger of collapse: the floor of the King's Council Chamber above his drawing room, and the hall and room adjoining his study.[2] Wyatt's response to the emergency was 'as dilatory as ever'.[3] At Windsor Kent looked in vain for the Surveyor General; but at Carlton House he ran him to earth during January 1811 and persuaded him to produce a report.[4] 'Not withstanding so much has been done', wrote Wyatt, 'the apartments are yet not only extremely uncomfortable but not habitable, partly owing to their never having been completely finished and in great measure to local circumstances. The Dry Rot . . . is certainly making its way in a very formidable manner. The soil on which Kensington Palace is built is of a nature which scarcely ever fails to produce the Evil complained of; and whenever the parts of a building so affected are uninhabited there is no check upon its progress'.[5] Five months later Kent sent the Treasury a further reminder: the King's State Bed Chamber and Drawing Room 'are still in the same unfinished state that they have been for the last eighteen years, without Doors, window shutters or linings, Dados, Plaster or Chimney Pieces, the want of all of which renders the Rooms below [the Duke's east drawing and dining rooms] scarcely habitable in severe weather'.[6]

By 1812 most of the work involved in fitting up the Duke of Kent's apartments had been completed. But after a moratorium imposed by the period of investigation he renewed his battle with the Office of Works. In December 1814 he complained to Stephenson: 'I cannot keep a single piece of meat in my larder [under the area at the southern end of the terrace on the north side], from the rain pouring through the ceiling at twenty different points, and I am literally perishing with cold in my Library'.[7] In the following June the sight of workmen repairing the gatepiers on the Kensington side of the palace roused him to anger: 'they are . . . colouring them like red oker and picking them out in white pointing as a Range of Stoves in a Kitchen', instead of using 'a coat of cement . . . drawn and coloured . . . like Portland or the Antique'.[8] Next he rediscovered dry rot and laid the blame on the 'obsequious . . . Mr. Yenn, whose lethargy and hatred of trouble was never more evident than in the present instance'.[9] Then followed a fusillade of letters from Kent 'expressing how much his feelings [had been] hurt by the manner in which his wishes [had] been thwarted by the Office of Works'.[10] In October 1815 the Treasury authorised such

---

[1] Works 4/19, 7 March 1806; Works 6/24, f. 29, 28 February 1806.
[2] L.C. 1/4, 2 July 1810, 13 April 1811; Works 19/16/1, f. 14, 18 April 1811; L.C. 1/40, f. 230, 19 June and f. 232, 28 June 1811.   [3] L.C. 1/4, 8 July 1811, 21 October 1811.
[4] L.C. 1/4, 27 September, 19 October, 25 November 1810, 7 January 1811, 9 January, 1 February, 4 February 1811.   [5] L.C. 1/4, 5 February 1811.
[6] L.C. 1/4, 8 July 1811. The estimate for fitting up these rooms (£1055) was later reduced to bare essentials (£250). See L.C. 1/5, f. 330, 17 September 1813; L.C. 1/40, f. 238, 10 July 1811. For further works see T. 29/108, f. 504, 11 February 1811.
[7] Works 6/27, f. 203, 29 December 1814.
[8] Works 6/27, f. 270, 15 June 1815. Kent's protest had no effect. Two years previously he had demanded a new gateway (estimate £254) at the Bayswater Road end of Palace Avenue (L.C. 1/5, f. 303, 8 April 1813; Works 4/21, 9 April, 15 April 1813).
[9] Works 4/21, 6 July 1815; Works 6/27, 26 June 1815; Works 19/16/1, f. 29, 30 July 1815. Stephenson defended Yenn's 'very long experience and very extensive practice as an Architect and Builder' (Works 19/16/1, f. 31, 3 August 1815).   [10] Works 19/16/1, ff. 32–5, 37, 41–3, 52, September–October 1815.

repairs as were 'absolutely necessary' to stables and apartments,[1] but such terminology was to Kent merely a fresh ground for contention.[2] Bricklayer's and mason's work costing over £300 was done 'in direct opposition to the Treasury instructions for the Regulation of this Department'.[3] But in general Stephenson effectively curbed the propensities of the Duke, who by May 1816 was complaining that his bedroom ceiling was 'all but tumbling down, in consequence of the continual leaking of pipes during the three preceeding winters'.[4] The staircase and entrance hall from Clock Court were still subject to damp, as were several rooms around White Court, including the chapel.[5] Another urgent need was for enclosing a passage between kitchen and dining room (promised by Wyatt years before), and making vaults for storing coal: 'for want of a place to stow the fuel away, [I] am debarred the advantage of purchasing it at the cheap season, and am exposed constantly to pay the most extravagant price of the Winter', he grumbled to the Chancellor of the Exchequer, who felt 'very much disposed' to assist.[6] But in the summer of 1816, overwhelmed with debt, Kent withdrew to Brussels.

Kent's younger brother, the Duke of Sussex (1773–1843), was rather less difficult to please. As a chronic asthmatic he followed William III and Prince George of Denmark in maintaining Kensington's tradition as a royal sanatorium.[7] As president first of the Society of Arts and then of the Royal Society his apartments were the scene of numerous *soirées*. And as a noted bibliophile his suite of rooms overflowed with a library of 30,000 volumes.[8] Sussex was first allocated quarters in August 1805.[9] But he did not take full possession until five years later.[10] His allocation consisted of the housekeeper's apartments in the south-west corner of the palace, plus stables in Housekeeper's Yard.[11] Sussex requested an extra floor. Yenn suggested complete rebuilding and put forward an estimate of £13,000 for the house and £500 for the stables.[12] But neither this, nor a later estimate of £10,423 for the house and £3260 for the stables which Yenn submitted in 1811[13] was accepted by the Treasury, and it was apparently not until the reign of William IV that the existing south-west block was built for the Duke's benefit. Meanwhile the library was enveloping more and more of the available space in the Duke's quarters. By the 1820s the books filled six

[1] Works 1/6, p. 223. [2] *Ibid.* pp. 229, 230, 231, 282–3, 288, 294, 296, 303–4.
[3] Works 1/10, p. 388. [4] Works 19/16/1, f. 60, 5 May 1816.
[5] The chapel seems to have been moved three times between the 1790s and the 1820s (Works 3/3, 16 February 1792; *The Times* 25 January 1810, p. 3; W. J. Loftie, *Kensington Palace and Gardens*, 1900, p. 79). A statement of apartments occupied by the Duke of Kent in August 1816 (B.M. Add. MS. 38263, f. 180) shows that he had 16 rooms and an entrance hall on the basement floor, 15 on the one-pair, and four on the state storey, as well as offices etc.
[6] Works 1/6, pp. 380, 381; 1/7, pp. 33–5.
[7] E.g. the installation of a warm bath 'from the delicate state of the health of His Royal Highness' (Works 19/16/1, f. 73, 4 November 1816). Kent described his brother as 'subject to daily severe attacks of an incurable asthmatic complaint' (*MSS. of the Earl of Dartmouth*, Hist. MSS. Comm. 15th Report, 1896, iii, p. 287, Kent to Dartmouth, 24 November 1804).
[8] *Gent's. Mag.* 1843, pt. i, pp. 645–9; Fulford, *Royal Dukes* (1933), pp. 253–84; T. J. Pettigrew, *Bibliotheca Sussexiana* (2 vols., 1827).
[9] Works 6/24, f. 11, 5 August and f. 13, 16 August 1805; Works 4/19, 2 August 1805.
[10] L.C. 1/40, f. 222, 8 March 1811. In the meantime he occupied 'one page's room at Carlton House' and temporary apartments at Windsor (*The Times* 19 October 1807, p. 2; *MSS. of the Earl of Dartmouth*, Hist. MSS. Comm. 15th Report, 1896, iii, p. 287, Kent to Dartmouth, 24 November 1804).
[11] L.C. 1/40, f. 185, 1 March 1810; L.C. 1/4, 26 July 1810.
[12] Works 4/19, 9 August, 16 August, 8 November 1805.
[13] L.C. 1/4, 21 October 1811.

rooms and eventually they had to be transferred to the Stone Gallery running along-side Clock Court.[1]

Both Princess Caroline of Brunswick (1768–1821) and her daughter Princess Charlotte (1796–1817) were given rooms at Kensington in 1804. Both sets were situated in the north-east section of the palace. The Duke of Kent informed the Lord Chamberlain that 'after giving the subject much consideration', George III had decided to present Charlotte with Lord Bute's rooms, 'as . . . he does not use them himself', and to give Caroline 'the Prince of Wales' apartments (those now occupied by Mrs. Wynyard) together with all the private rooms of the late Queen [Caroline of Anspach] which are understood to be those immediately at the back of the Queen's state drawing and dining room, and those behind the Queen's Gallery communicat-ing with Mrs. Meynell's (which also forms a part of them)'.[2] The alteration of these rooms, as well as those which had previously been occupied by the Duchess of Manchester, began in 1806 and continued for another six or eight years. By the autumn of 1811 £17,280 10s. 10½d. had been spent on the Princess of Wales' apart-ments, plus £18,415 13s. 1½d. on furniture.[3] Much of this work was structural in form: new chimneys and floors on the east front; iron supports for the Queen's Gallery; alterations to the Denmark Staircase; new dormers at the northern end and new railings along the east and north fronts.[4] At the same time a new stable (estimate £2000) was built at the back of the Cumberland (north-west) stables.[5] In 1808 the apartments were declared ready for occupation.[6] But in 1814 Yenn was still involved in 'putting up Raking shores to the outside . . . and underpinning and needling up the inner walls . . . to secure rotten and decayed brickwork'.[7] By that date, however, Caroline of Brunswick had already left Kensington and begun her unlucky career abroad.[8]

All in all, more than £60,000 was spent in making Kensington Palace fit for the reception of the Duke of Kent, the Duke of Sussex, the Princess of Wales and Princess Charlotte.[9] Internally, most of the new work is stylistically anonymous. Externally, the extent of the alterations can be traced by the slim glazing bars still visible along the lower storeys of the palace; also by four outside entrances to the private apart-ments: the two porches in Clock Court giving access to the apartments of the Dukes of Kent and Sussex, and the 'bridges' at first floor level on the north-east front linking the garden terrace with the rooms occupied by the Duke of Kent and the Princess of

[1] T. Faulkner, *History and Antiquities of Kensington* (1820), pp. 404–5; J. I. Sargeant, *Views in Kensington Gardens* (1831), p. 19; R. S. Rait (ed.), *Royal Palaces of England* (1911), p. 332.

[2] *MSS. of the Earl of Dartmouth* (Hist. MSS. Comm. 15th Report, 1896), iii, p. 284, Kent to Dartmouth, 17 July 1804.

[3] Works 4/20, 10 January 1812; L.C. 1/40, f. 243.

[4] Works 6/24, f. 183, 6 May and f. 184, 13 May 1808. See also L.C. 1/3, 17 March 1809.

[5] L.C. 1/4, 11 January 1810; L.C. 1/40, f. 174, 8 December 1809. For the Princess of Wales' wine cellar cf. L.C. 1/4, 5 April, 21 October 1811; L.C. 1/40, f. 231, 19 June 1811.

[6] *The Times* 19 November 1807 p. 2, 5 January 1808 p. 3, 2 June 1808 p. 3.

[7] Works 6/27, f. 123, 8 January and f. 124, 10 January 1814.

[8] While at Kensington she shocked the palace by 'keeping a sort of open house, receiving visitors in a dressing-gown, and sitting and talking about herself with strangers on the benches in the garden' (Leigh Hunt, *The Old Court Suburb*, ed. Austin Dobson ii, 1902, p. 166).

[9] 'Extra' works alone between 1800 and 1812 totalled £54,006 7s. 6¾d. ('Inquiry into . . . the Office of Works', *Parl. Pap.* 1812–13, v, pp. 503–4; Works 4/20, 24 July 1812).

Wales.[1] Whatever the criticisms of the cost, these works certainly rescued the building from its previous state of dilapidation.

Nevertheless, Kent's complaints of the state of the building were borne out by Nash, who, given charge of the palace, made his first survey in December 1816.[2] The 'general state of decay in which all the materials of the building are from time', he remarked, made inadvisable any major work of repair. He thought it preferable to continue the 'props supports and ties to the walls and floors as they shall from time to time require'. The basement floor throughout the building was 'exceedingly damp', so that adjacent woodwork was liable to rot. In many places slate skirting had been substituted, and stone door frames, and he suggested that this should be done generally. A surrounding drain should be constructed, as well as stink traps to cut off exhalations from the sewers. Some improvements had been effected in Kent's apartments, where the front hall, garden room and library had been hollow drained under the pavement, a system Nash wished to extend, most urgently to the chapel, which lay between the Grand Staircase and White Court. In the Queen's Apartments, leaking gutters had caused rot: and a heavy stack of chimneys in the dressing room had settled, causing a bulge in the front wall (held in by iron ties) and cracks in ceilings and cornices. In the State Apartments, the floor and chimney slab of the Cube Room had sunk and required support; the bedroom and dressing room beyond (south-east corner) were still unfinished, although doors, windows and floor had been installed; and the sashes and frames of the Grand Staircase were totally decayed— as indeed they were generally, except in 'Kent's and some other apartments where they are new'. For the decayed entrance portico Nash recommended 'the substitution of a more suitable and characteristic design, but not more expensive when it is rebuilt'. The present simple stuccoed *porte cochère* with incised decoration may date from 1823 or 1825, when expenditure on the palace was unusually high.[3]

When, early in 1819, Kent returned to England, a married man, he obtained the 'temporary use' of the apartments formerly occupied by Mrs. Meynell, 'which held the Princess [of Wales]'s Lady of the Bedchamber, and her House Steward; with the loan of the Kitchen and its appertaining Offices'.[4] It was not long before he was again laying complaints before Stephenson. The sashes in the south-east rooms of the State Apartments were letting in the rain, which penetrated the ceiling of the Duke's dining room, and that in which the Duchess was to be confined—'these identical sashes now complained of, were condemned by Mr. Wyatt, the year before he died' [i.e. 1812].[5] In June, it was the condition of the wooden stair from the Duke's dressing room to his wife's apartments, and the delay in paving the chapel after repairs

---

[1] The garden entrance to Kent's apartments was described as 'a Portland stone balcony leading to the Vestibule', plus 'a wrought iron Gallery in front of the Vestibule with a pair of folding Gates and returns for the Bridge way and an Iron Cradle for the Bridge'. The old entrance was 'totally decayed . . . ruinous . . . and dangerous' (L.C. 1/5, f. 330, 17 September 1813).

[2] Works 19/16/1, f. 74; 1/7, pp. 385–90.

[3] Works 5/108, 109. See Hist. Mon. Comm., *London*, ii, *West London*, pl. 65. The present portico may however be a twentieth-century reconstruction, as there is a story in the Royal Family that it was erected by Princess Beatrice. We are grateful to H.R.H. Princess Margaret for this information. The old portico was still standing in April 1819 (Works 19/16/1, f. 82). [4] Works 1/9, p. 263, 4 April 1819.

[5] *Ibid.* p. 338, 23 May 1819. Nash advised rebuilding the shored-up south end of the east front, as far as the middle of the corner room and buttressing the junction of new and old work (Works 19/16/1, f. 82, 24 April 1819).

necessitated by dry rot.[1] Nash was supervising these works, and proposed flooring the chapel with 'Dehls Mastic laid on Bricks'.[2] In September, Kent was proposing larger schemes, consequent upon the demolition of Cumberland House, but the Regent incorporated the site in the gardens.[3]

The voluble Duke died at Sidmouth in January 1820, and subsequent works for his widow must evidently have been of a routine character. The Duchess, her comptroller later claimed, was reluctant to impose any burden on public funds.[4] Stephenson ran foul of her by objecting to the conversion of a window into a doorway. Matters were smoothed over by Princess Sophia,[5] who had been granted the late Queen Caroline's apartment, to which in 1830 William IV added several of the Queen's Apartments immediately to the south.[6] The Duchess was reported in 1832 as already in possession of the Council Chamber on the first floor, and an expenditure of £4141 on the palace in 1825 may indicate the fitting up of this room, the decoration of which differs from that of the nearby rooms altered in 1835, referred to below.[7] In 1828 gas lighting was introduced into the palace.[8] In 1829 expenditure reached the exceptional amount of £4300; and the total from 1815 to the death of George IV was £41,000, or about £2700 per annum.[9]

Various improvements were also made in the Duke of Sussex's apartments. Nash had reported in 1816 that these were in need of general repair, and the offices of rebuilding.[10] Sussex returned to the palace in 1819, and like his brother, importuned the Surveyor General for repairs: 'a part, particularly the Staircase which his Royal Highness uses is *actually tottering*, being underproped, and . . . a considerable part of the West Side . . . is quite ruinous'.[11] In 1822 the Duke obtained three additional rooms, formerly offices, that he required to be converted into his private apartments;[12] and in 1827 the repair of the Long Gallery (leading to the State Apartments) was ordered.[13] Sussex was another beneficiary from the accession of William IV, extensive works costing £3900 being carried out in 1830–1.[14] The result of this expenditure appears to have been the erection of the plain brick block standing immediately to the south of the timber portico.[15]

Internal painting and the provision of double-hung sashes in the main rooms of

[1] Works 1/9, pp. 364–6, 436.   [2] *Ibid.* pp. 448–9.

[3] *Ibid.* pp. 461–3, 466. For a plan showing the Duke of Cumberland's house see vol. v of this *History*.

[4] T. 1/3898, Conroy to Spring Rice, 6 July 1836. Clearly, the Duchess benefited from the ordinary Civil List expenditure on the palace. The Clerk of Works, Hunt, wrote in 1830: 'Where Her Royal Highness' personal convenience was in the most remote degree concerned I have not even waited for the forms of office but have acted on my own responsibility' (Works 19/16/1, f. 128).

[5] *Ibid.* ff. 97–102. In fact wooden steps had merely been placed against a window to afford direct access to the terrace. It appears that the Duchess never forgave Stephenson; see Grey Papers, Durham University Library, correspondence of Lord Duncannon with Lord Grey, 1832.

[6] Works 1/10, p. 356; 19/16/1, f. 131.

[7] Works 5/109; portfolio NN in Royal Library, Windsor. This room was doubtless one of the four on the State Storey described as in Kent's occupation in August 1816 (B.M. Add. MS. 38263, f. 180).

[8] Works 19/16/1, f. 121; T. 1/3898, ff. 20061/28, 21093/28.

[9] Works 5/107–111.   [10] Works 19/16/1, f. 74.   [11] Works 1/9, pp. 358–9.

[12] Works 19/16/1, ff. 103–4. This may account for the unusually high expenditure of £3905 on the palace in 1823.   [13] *Ibid.* f. 117, estimate £241.

[14] T. 1/3898, f. 14458/30. Estimated at £3400, the works cost more because of alterations and repairs necessary in adjoining apartments (Works 5/111).

[15] Not yet built in 1826, when Buckler drew this side of the palace (B.M. Crace Coll. Views IX, 22), but shown on a steel engraving by Thomas Onwhyn published in 1839. For information about this block we are indebted to Dr. John Hayes, Director of the London Museum.

the Kent apartments were also ordered at the same time, estimated at £705.[1] The King, however, was 'very jealous' of any alterations, and kept the plans of the palace locked up.[2] The Duchess of Kent as mother of the heiress presumptive began to demand ampler accommodation, and in 1832 plans were drawn up by Wyatville for a general improvement of the Kent wing, and the possible completion of the east front by adding a new kitchen block.[3] Several of the State Rooms were to be taken into the apartments, the King's Gallery divided into three (a proposal given up by the Duchess to save time and money), and the State Bed and Dressing-Rooms, for many years in an unfinished state, completed. The total expense envisaged, £9150, was far beyond what Ministers would contemplate, and after communications between the Duchess and Lords Grey and Duncannon,[4] it was finally agreed to meet the urgent need for more accommodation in the least expensive way, by transferring the chapel to the old kitchen on the west side of Prince of Wales's Court, and using the former chapel (the room beneath the Presence Chamber) for other purposes. This, Wyatville estimated, would cost only £840:[5]

> The present Chapel to have a floor and become a Servants Waiting room. Leave all the Wainscot on the Walls—Take down the Gallery front but not the floors of the Galleries—Put in a new floor betwixt the present Galleries to be supported on Columns—To be framed and fitted so as to be put together with screws and without noise. . . . The fittings up of the Chapel to be used in the intended new Chapel now an old Kitchen.[6]

The work was executed early in 1833,[7] and Wyatville's plans suggest that the existing columns in the saloon (now the entrance hall of the London Museum) and adjoining dining room were inserted at this time. Some works had already been done in September 1832, but were interrupted by the return of the Duchess who required only two rooms close to her apartments to be completed at that time.[8] Creevey recorded that Duncannon had 'had the divel's own trouble with the Duchess of Kent, who bothers his and Lord Grey's and the King's life out with perpetual demands she makes for alterations, additions, furniture, &c. &c. on her Royal Residence'.[9] Another work of 1833 was the construction of an ice well on the west lawn, to Decimus Burton's design.[10]

A second instalment of Wyatville's plan, authorised at the end of 1835, was already under way: the King's Gallery was partitioned, and two fireplaces fixed there; the two south-east rooms (State Bed- and Dressing-Rooms) were repaired, and stoves installed; four iron columns cased in deal were placed in the garden room to

[1] Works 19/16/1, f. 132; T. 1/3898, f. 13826/30.
[2] Grey Papers, Durham University Library, Duncannon to Grey, 24 June 1832.
[3] Portfolio NN in Royal Library, Windsor.   [4] See Grey Papers, 22 June–16 September 1832.
[5] The expense appears to have been £767 8s., in addition to £60 paid to Wyatville for his unexecuted plans (L.R.R.O. 2/2). Screens were to be placed in the King's Gallery so that it might be used for summer apartments (Portfolio NN).
[6] *Ibid.* Note by Wyatville on plans. Plans for the new chapel are also in the portfolio.
[7] Works 2/1, p. 73, Treasury authority dated 22 January 1833.
[8] Grey Papers, Duchess of Kent to Lord Grey, 16 September 1832.
[9] *Creevey's Life and Times* ed. J. Gore (1937), p. 370, 30 October 1833.
[10] Works 19/16/1, ff. 150–4, estimate £395 9s. 7d.

carry a partition above; a glazed screen partitioned the servants' hall; and outside sashes were fitted to the King's Gallery and rooms in the east front.[1] Princess Victoria moved upstairs into her new apartments on her return to Kensington, 13 January 1836:[2]

> Our bedroom is very large and lofty . . . then comes a little room for the maid, and a dressing-room for Mamma; then comes the old gallery which is partitioned into 3 large, lofty, fine and cheerful rooms. Only one of these . . . is ready furnished; it is my sittingroom. . . . The next is my study, and the last is an anteroom; this last has no fireplace, but the two others have . . .

Between August 1834 and March 1836 Messrs. Snell refurnished and decorated the apartments at an expense of nearly £3900, which the Duchess succeeded in recovering from the government.[3] The King, however, was now less well-disposed towards his sister-in-law, and complained publicly that she had appropriated a suite of seventeen apartments, 'not only without his consent, but contrary to his commands'.[4] On the King's death, the Duchess moved into Buckingham Palace with the new Queen, though some of her furniture was still stored at Kensington in 1862.[5]

Princess Sophia's apartments were surveyed in 1838 by Seward, who estimated that to put them in fit condition for occupation would cost £10,500. The Woods and Works proposed that instead they should pay the Princess £800 for house rent, leaving the building as it was. A further report, in which Smirke and Wyatville were associated with Seward, confirmed the great dilapidation of the building, of which the external walls were supported by iron ties and timber shores. Repair would involve so much new work that the cost would be 'nearly as great as would be incurred by rebuilding it' entirely.[6] The Princess moved to York House, Kensington,[7] and her apartments were left shored up. About 1845 they were given to J. W. Croker, who was already in possession of some adjacent rooms in the north front.[8] It was not until 1898–9 that a thorough repair of this wing and the state rooms was carried out at a cost of some £32,000.[9]

The kitchen gardens at Kensington were an important branch of the Lord Steward's Department in the early nineteenth century. In 1817 a new mushroom house was provided, with rooms above for gardeners.[10] Between 1815 and 1832 expenditure on the gardens averaged nearly £1000 per annum.[11] The orangery, or 'Greenhouse' as it was then called, was repaired in 1816, when the 'battlements' were rebuilt, and the Doric cornice on the south front was repaired, the estimates totalling over £1400. In 1829 new sashes were fitted to its openings at a cost of £155.[12] Five

---

[1] T. 1/3898, 21 December 1835; building expenditure on the palace, July 1834—end 1836 was £9820, of which £3900 related to July–December 1836 (L.R.R.O. 24/3 and 4).
[2] *The Girlhood of Queen Victoria* ed. Lord Esher (1912), i, pp. 142–3, quoting the Princess's diary. Lord Esher states that the partitions in the King's Gallery were taken down after the accession of Edward VII.
[3] T. 1/3898, ff. 15078/37, 15757/37, 16824/37. The Treasury agreed to seek a vote in the 1838 session.
[4] *The Greville Diary*, ed. R. Fulford and L. Strachey (1938), iii, pp. 308–9.
[5] Works 19/16/1, f. 654.   [6] T. 1/3898, f. 19789/39; Works 2/2, p. 353.
[7] D. M. Stuart, *The Daughters of George III* (1939), p. 315.   [8] Works 19/16/1, f. 529.
[9] *Ibid.* ff. 749, 763.   [10] Works 19/16/2, ff. 4–6, estimate £1260.
[11] Works 5/107–111. Peak expenditures were in 1816 (£2400) and 1819 (£2100).
[12] Works 19/16/1, ff. 58, 72; 19/16/2, ff. 12–15. A late 18th-century drawing of the Orangery by Yenn is in the Royal Academy Library.

lodges were erected to Aiton's designs by Messrs. Baker in 1827.[1] In 1831 repairs to the hot houses were estimated at £1550.[2] The decision in 1841 to consolidate the royal kitchen gardens at Frogmore made available that at Kensington for disposal on building leases, Chawner acting as surveyor.[3] The road of detached houses known as Kensington Palace Gardens was subsequently built on the site.

MARLBOROUGH HOUSE, ST. JAMES'S

On the death of the 4th Duke of Marlborough in 1817 Marlborough House became the London home of Princess Charlotte and Prince Leopold. It was not, however, until 1835 that the Crown lease finally ran out, whereupon the house was designated by the statute 1 and 2 William IV *c.* 11 as a dower house for Queen Adelaide. A report by Seward and Chawner soon after the Crown obtained possession recommended the demolition of the stables and other low buildings east of the house.[4] More than £1800 spent on repairs and maintenance up to 30 June 1836 was covered by the sale of the old materials and the lessee's payment for dilapidations.[5] Expenditure for the following quarter was £2192; but only £325 were spent in the next half year.[6] William IV's death led to a parliamentary grant of £25,000 for putting the mansion into a fit state for the Queen Dowager's residence; but the 'much neglected' building required an expenditure of £30,385, of which £1785 was for alterations made during the course of the works. This repair was conducted by John Phipps of the Works Department, and completed early in 1839.[7] Whig ministers refused to make up the deficiency for a Queen who was considered politically hostile, and despite her Chamberlain's protests, the dowager was obliged herself to pay £5022, nearly the whole of the sum wanting.[8] Subsequently only small sums were paid for the external repairs of the building, until the Queen Dowager's death in 1849.[9]

The Act 13 and 14 Vic. c. lxxviii appropriated the mansion as the residence of the Prince of Wales, and allocated £5000 for building new stables. Accordingly Pennethorne made designs for these in 1850, and tenders were obtained in July 1851.[10] But the lowest was £8777, and although a reduction to the approved sum was negotiated, the work was deferred.[11] Not indeed until 1862 were stables built.[12] During the Prince's minority, the house provided accommodation for the Vernon and Sheepshanks collections of modern British paintings presented to the National Gallery.[13] It also housed the Government School of Design, when the state rooms were lined with deal and coloured cotton for exhibiting the productions of provincial schools.[14] Major alterations and additions were made for the Prince on his taking possession in 1860, and again in 1870, 1874, 1878 and 1885.[15]

---

[1] Works 4/21, pp. 218, 224, 250.   [2] Works 19/16/1, ff. 22, 23.
[3] Works 2/3, pp. 146–52, 163, 194, 208–10, 224; 19/16/1.   [4] Works 19/18/1, f. 5 (16 February 1836).
[5] *Ibid.* f. 6. The amount received was £1840 14s. 3d., the expenditure £1817 3s. 7d. But in L.R.R.O. 2/5, the expenditure is given as £1531 11s. 6d.   [6] L.R.R.O. 2/6. See also Works 1/22, p. 104.
[7] Works 19/18/1, ff. 16–17.   [8] *Ibid.* ff. 18–21, 33; Works 1/24, pp. 35, 118, 258.
[9] *Parl. Pap.* 1843 (343) xxx; 1851, (374) xxxi.   [10] Works 19/18/1, ff. 99–102 (plans for stables).
[11] *Ibid.* ff. 106–8 (tenders), 105, 112.   [12] *Ibid.* f. 270.
[13] Works 2/8, pp. 220–1 (24 April), 314 (8 June 1850).
[14] *Ibid.* p. 425 (11 February 1851).   [15] Works 19/18/1, *passim.*

THE ROYAL MEWS, CHARING CROSS

During the latter part of the eighteenth century the Royal Mews underwent no significant alteration. Only running repairs were called for, and for these a standard procedure was followed. Owners or occupiers of buildings sent applications for repairs to the Master of the Horse, who transmitted them to the Surveyor General, who then delegated responsibility to the Clerk of the Works. Between 1782 and 1815 there were five successive Masters of the Horse, but administrative continuity was maintained by the presence throughout this period of David Parker, Clerk of the Stables. And it was Parker to whom the Clerk of the Works, John Yenn, was in practice responsible. The position of Labourer in Trust was regarded, at least by Soane, as a sinecure.[1]

Only one new building added significantly to the architectural character of the area before 1815, Thomas Leverton's striking Phoenix Fire Station.[2] But for this intrusion into the Lower Mews both the Office of Works and the Office of Woods and Forests did no more than grant permission.[3] Yenn's activity was limited to repairs which he described as 'continual and constant'.[4] For example, in 1789 these included repairs to the King's Coach House, the stables of the Duke of Cumberland, the Duke of Clarence and the Prince of Wales, and stables used by the bedchamber women, the maids of honour and equerries like Colonels Goldsworthy, Gwynne and Garth, as well as premises occupied by Mr. Smith the riding master, Mr. Kerr the bitt maker, Mr. Shaw the farrier and Mr. Harrison the saddler.[5] In 1787 the old horse pond was filled in, being 'more of a nuisance than of any utility', and replaced by a new cistern for watering horses and washing carriages.[6] In 1794 Yenn put new doors on the farrier's shop to exclude 'the North Wind when horses are shod in the Winter, and [to prevent] persons from rendering the shop a Nuisance to the Mews and to the Workmen, by certain practices too filthy to be named'.[7] In 1803 alterations were undertaken for the accommodation of the Prince of Wales' Volunteers and the Royal Westminster Volunteers.[8] And in 1811 when the sword fell off Le Sueur's statue of Charles I outside the Mews, the Office of Works asserted its jurisdiction against claims by the Board of Green Cloth, recovered the sword from a schoolboy who had picked it up, and placed the trophy in the Board Room pending its restoration.[9] However the department responded less energetically to complaints by local inhabitants that the statue was cluttered up with 'Coaches, Carts . . . Caravans and . . . heaps of Gravel, Rubbish etc'. Instead of preventing 'the degradation of one of the finest specimens of art which adorns this great Metropolis', Wyatt procrastinated and Craig passed the problem on to the committee for paving, lighting and cleaning the Parish of St. Martin-in-the-Fields.[10]

[1] See p. 44.
[2] Plans and elevations 1793, MPE 380. See also MPE 560 and A. Stratton, 'The King's Mews at Charing Cross', *Architectural Rev.* xxxix (1916), pp. 119–26, for comparative plans of the mews area before 1725 and in 1796.   [3] T. 29/66, f. 91, 25 July 1793.
[4] Works 6/27, ff. 54–5, 27 February 1813.   [5] Works 5/78, 1789.
[6] Works 1/5, f. 92, 29 September 1787.   [7] Works 6/22, f. 181, 12 December 1794.
[8] Works 4/19, 2 and 23 September 1803.   [9] Works 6/25, f. 191, 3 December 1811.
[10] Works 4/21, 12 August 1814; Works 6/27, f. 174, 11 August 1814.

Yenn's repairs over a period of thirty years really constituted no more than a holding operation. By the start of the nineteenth century agreement had been reached as to the necessity for redevelopment when most of the leases fell in. By 1807 Leverton and Chawner were drawing up plans for a new road cutting across the Lower Mews and linking Pall Mall East with the portico of St. Martin's.[1] And when Nash produced a detailed survey of the condemned area in 1816 he remarked that 'all the wooden buildings which form the greater part of the Mews, are so old as not to be susceptible of permanent repair, and must shortly, in some shape or other, give place to new buildings. . . . The brick buildings, or the greater part of them, are in a similar state'.[2] Kent's Great Stables, on the other hand, were intended to be kept and had just undergone a 'solid, judicious, and economical' repair (as Nash declared) costing £6339. The first substantial repair for many years, this had been lamentably under-estimated by some £2000, 'which must be attributed entirely', reported Stephenson, 'to a want of proper attention and foresight in the Clerk of the Works who made out the estimate'.[3]

The King having approved the New Street Commissioners' plan for opening a road across the Mews to St. Martin's, the Surveyor General was directed in June 1820 to arrange with the Master of the Horse to provide accommodation in lieu of that to be given up. This led at length to the removal of the entire Mews establishment to Pimlico and the surrender of the Great Stables.[4] Milne, secretary of the New Street Commission, was pressing in April and May 1824 for the old Mews to be vacated, and writing of lawsuits threatened against the Commission for the delay.[5] But although the surrounding buildings were cleared away, the Great Stables were left standing, and were used for storage. In 1828 it was suggested that they should be converted into a national gallery, but a purpose-built structure on the site was preferred. Meanwhile, in 1831–5, the stables were requisitioned for the records removed from Westminster Hall.[6] With their demolition in 1835 disappeared the last feature of the Royal Mews at Charing Cross.

NEWMARKET PALACE, CAMBRIDGESHIRE

As the least of the 'out palaces', Newmarket was somewhat neglected during the second half of the eighteenth century. In 1784 Chambers noted that he and Couse 'went down to Newmarket on purpose to make a Survey of the House which we had never seen before'.[7] Only the fondness of the Prince of Wales and the Duke of

---

[1] Crest 2/543, 1807. The scheme was described as 'at once an ornament and an advantage to the Crown's estate'. See also Works 19/11/6, f. 40, 26 January 1818.   [2] Works 19/11/6, ff. 29 *et. seq.*
[3] *Ibid.* ff. 10, 14–18, 23–5, 31 (Bacon, the clerk of the works, had relied on the artificers' calculations for his estimate, and blamed the 'dilatory proceeding of the Mason which brought the work into the short days', *ibid.* ff. 23–5); Works 1/6, pp. 36, 76, 81, 440; 5/107.
[4] Works 1/10, pp. 142, 168, 174, 175, 193, 507; 1/11, p. 165. See p. 303 above
[5] Works 1/12, pp. 441, 461, 462.   [6] Works 12/68/2; 1/21, pp. 231, 248; *1828 Report*, p. 10.
[7] L.C. 1/39, 23 July 1784; Works 6/20 f. 324, 3 December 1784.

York for horse-racing prevented the palace from sinking into complete dilapidation. Until his quarrel with the Jockey Club in 1791 the Prince of Wales regularly attended the races. In particular the meetings in March and October were often preceded by frantic repairs and redecorations in preparation for the royal visit.[1] Such works were supervised by the resident Labourer in Trust and executed by local tradesmen, although workmen from London might occasionally be involved.[2] The Clerk of the Works had no more than a tenuous connection with the palace, which gradually took on the aspect of a racing stable. In 1812 the Duke of York took permanent possession of the southern section of the premises and, with the co-operation of the Master of the Horse, fitted up stables and coach houses at his own expense, employing his own workmen. And in 1818 he extended his holding on the western side of the site.[3] At the same time the lease of Hare Park Lodge and some neighbouring land to the Duke of Rutland was renewed. This was a long-standing lease stemming from a grant to the Marquess of Granby in the mid-eighteenth century.[4] The leasehold area changed hands after the death of the Duke of York in 1827. This dispersal by the Crown of the Newmarket estate was completed first by the leasing of large sections of land to the Duke of Bedford and the Jockey Club between 1808 and 1830,[5] and then by the sale of what remained of the palace in 1855.[6]

This slow process of disposal was largely arranged by the Office of Woods and Forests. For in 1815 responsibility for the palace was transferred to that department, and the Office of Works surrendered jurisdiction.[7] But for several years prior to that date the Office of Works had been involved in a clearance operation of some importance: the demolition of the old Lord Chamberlain's Office. The removal of this building was the only significant event in the architectural history of the palace between 1782 and 1815, and its passing occasioned a good deal of administrative confusion. Running alongside Newmarket High Street, to the west of Charles II's new building, the Lord Chamberlain's Office had long since lost all connection with its eponymous incumbent. In 1784 the Housekeeper, Mrs. M. Bonfoy, complained to Chambers that the building was 'a great disgrace to the Palace', being occupied by 'a set of Vagabonds' who made 'constant noises and disturbance'. The Surveyor General promised 'some speedy and effectual remedy'.[8] Seven years later nothing

[1] When 'the severe frost burst the pipes' in January 1785, the housekeeper told Chambers:'I expect His Royal Highness about 12th March, and if this inconvenience is not remedied before that time, I do not know what is to be done as the Water Closets will be useless' (Works 1/5, f. 79, 31 January 1785). See also Works 6/20, f. 330, 10 December 1784; Works 6/21, f. 6, 14 February 1785; T. 29/58, f. 386, 22 June 1787; Works 4/18, f. 251, 25 August 1797; Works 4/16, 3 December 1784.

[2] Before the October meeting in 1784 there was some redecoration of 'the Prince's Bedchamber . . . ten more Bedchambers . . . besides a Dining Room, Presence Chamber, Drawing Room, Breakfast Room and Dressing Room'. The housekeeper asked Chambers 'to get the same men who painted the Hall to do the rest . . . as I am very sure if a Country workman is employed the Rooms will not be finished this year' (Works 1/5, f. 74, 19 July 1784). See also Works 4/16, 20 August 1784; Works 5/74, Christmas 1785.

[3] Works 4/20, 21 August 1812; Works 4/21, 30 October, 18 December 1812, 13 and 18 May, 26 November, 10 December 1813; T. 29/123, f. 736, 22 June 1813; Crest 2/115. For the reconstruction of the King's Stand and weighing house cf. L.C. 1/6, f. 358, 24 May 1814. For Newmarket races see R. Mortimer, *The Jockey Club* (1958) and prints in B.M. King's Maps viii, 72–6.

[4] Crest 2/115, Rutland's lease, 1811.

[5] Crest 2/116.   [6] Crest 2/115, sale particulars and plan, 1855.

[7] L.C. 1/6, f. 390, 17 May 1815; Works 6/27, f. 253, 18 May 1815. The Housekeeper was awarded compensation and the Labourer in Trust was given an alternative post.   [8] Works 1/5, f. 74, 19 July 1784.

had been done. 'Two rich men', she informed Couse, 'one a Baker, the other a Carpenter, has got possession of it and look on it as their own property. The Baker has just made a Stable almost under one of the Windows in the Duke of York's Apartment, the Carpenter has built a Workshop under another. And when . . . [the Labourer in Trust] put a Padlock on the Door . . . the Baker . . . knocked off the lock and set everyone at defiance'.[1] Chambers therefore asked the Lord Chamberlain for a ruling: 'farther back than any information I have been able to obtain . . . some . . . persons . . . have clandestinely taken possession . . . and since the reform nothing has ever been done. . . . What I have now humbly to request is . . . whether or not I am to consider the Building under my Inspection'.[2] The Lord Chamberlain's reply must have been equivocal: for the next twenty years the building drifted towards collapse, occupied by vagrants who received exemption from rates and taxes since they resided on royal property. By 1810 Crocker and Arnold had convinced Wyatt of the need for action: 'the Buildings are frightful to look at . . . and if not taken down very soon . . . many lives may be lost'.[3] But demolition was averted by the pleas of the churchwardens and parish overseers who had nowhere else to put their thirty-five paupers.[4] 'The building', wrote Wyatt to the Lord Chamberlain, 'is in great danger of falling and perhaps the Parish Officers may think that an accident would be a short way of getting rid of some of their incumbrances'.[5] But the Prince Regent overruled the Office of Works, much to the Surveyor General's annoyance. 'I am perfectly aware', he complained, 'of the Prince Regent's humane disposition with respect to the poor wretches who occupy these buildings, but I cannot help thinking that the [cost of repairs] . . . might be employed in their behalf more to their advantage'.[6]

The dilemma was resolved by the reorganisation of the department. In 1814 the paupers were given notice to quit and the fabric of the Lord Chamberlain's Office was sold to a local master mason for £170.[7] During the next five years the Office of Woods and Forests produced detailed surveys of the site and auctioned off sections of the property, notably the White Building or Greyhound Inn facing Newmarket High Street and the Labourer in Trust's house known as the Nunnery, near All Saints Church.[8] A belated scheme by Nash for a general reconstruction on behalf of the Prince Regent came to nothing.[9] Sales of the property rented by the Duke of York and the Duke of Bedford followed in 1828, 1831 and 1855.[10] What little remained of the palace was incorporated in the house known as 'Palace House Mansion' still standing in Palace Street.

[1] Works 1/5, f. 99, 3 March 1791.   [2] Works 3/3, 18 March 1791.
[3] L.C. 1/4, 10 August 1810.   [4] L.C. 1/4, 23 April 1811; Works 6/25, f. 174, 26 September 1811.
[5] L.C. 1/4, 4 May 1811.
[6] Works 6/25, f. 175; 27 September 1811; Works 4/20, 27 September 1811; L.C. 1/40, f. 228, 24 May and f. 237, 10 August 1811.
[7] Works 4/21, 3 and 26 June, 2 and 16 September, 20 November 1814.
[8] For detailed plans see MPE 355 and 630 (1–6).
[9] *Gent's. Mag.* 1819, pt. i, p. 475. But some repairs were carried out in 1825 (Works 5/109).
[10] Crest 2/115; MPEE. 81.

RICHMOND AND KEW

Between the reforms of 1782 and 1815 there were several significant changes in the architectural character of Richmond and Kew; but they were changes in which the Office of Works played the role of spectator rather than participant. Topographically speaking, there were two chief areas of responsibility: Richmond New or Great Park; and Richmond and Kew Gardens, which were united after 1802,[1] and to which the various royal houses on Kew Green formed an appendage.[2] The Office of Works was usually responsible for running repairs at the White House (built by Frederick, Prince of Wales), the Dutch House, and the temples in Richmond and Kew Gardens. The department was also occasionally called in to repair the four principal lodges in Richmond Park: the Ranger's Lodge (Old Lodge), White Lodge (New Park Lodge), Thatched House Lodge (Aldrich's Lodge) and Lady Pembroke's lodge (Hill Lodge). But until 1815 alterations to these four lodges, as well as the upkeep of the park gate-houses, keepers' houses, walls, roads and palings, were normally dealt with by the Office of Woods and Forests. Major architectural works in either of the two areas were, however, frequently paid for not by the Office of Woods and Forests, nor out of the Civil List, but out of the Privy Purse. The principal architectural project of this period was in fact dealt with in this way, namely George III's Gothic Palace at Kew.

The various lodges in Richmond Park were normally used as official residences.[3] Between 1781 and 1813 Ranger's Lodge was occupied by four Deputy Rangers: Hon. James Stuart, son of the Earl of Bute; Hon. Stephen Digby; Capt. Leonard Smelt; and the Countess of Mansfield.[4] Such minor alterations as were required fell to the Office of Woods and Forests.[5] Between 1785 and 1841 Thatched House Lodge was privately occupied first by General Sir Charles Stuart, younger son of the Earl of Bute and conqueror of Minorca, and then by his widow Lady Stuart.[6] The Stuarts normally paid for their own repairs and alterations, but on occasion the Office of Woods and Forests was given Treasury permission to foot the bill.[7] The

---

[1] They had previously been separated by Kew or Love Lane.

[2] See a plan by Chawner and Rhodes, 1829, of George III's private estates at Richmond and Kew (MPEE 68; MPZ 19). For views of the houses on Kew Green see E. Walford, *Greater London* ii (1895), pp. 396, 408.

[3] For plans showing the positions of Ranger's Lodge, White Lodge, Thatched House Lodge and Lady Pembroke's Lodge, as well as neighbouring villas such as Asgill House (Whitshed Keene) and Lord Harrington's or Petersham Lodge (Duke of Clarence), demolished 1835, see Crest 2/639 and Works 16/211. Compare MPE 426 (*c.* 1755) with MR 296 (1771).

[4] For lists of Rangers and Deputy Rangers see C. L. Collenette, *History of Richmond Park* (1937), pp. 27–30.

[5] Works 16/2/4, f. 22, 16 June 1801. Between 1793 and 1795 £1100 were spent on repairs by the Woods and Forests (LR 4/15/30). Another £2000 was said to be required in 1807. But nothing was done and the Old Lodge was demolished in 1839–41 (Works 1/16, p. 488; 1/23, p. 391; 2/2, p. 352; Collenette *op. cit.* p. 47). There are plans of the building in the P.R.O. (MR 296) and the R.I.B.A. Drawings Collection (E 6/3³), and there is a drawing by Buckler in B.M. Add. MS. 36388, f. 274.

[6] Collenette *op. cit.* p. 50; *Country Life* cxxiv (1958), pp. 1240–1, cxxxiii (1963), pp. 974–5.

[7] Works 19/25/8, ff. 1–21, 1796–7 and f. 22, 13 March 1805 (John Harvey's estimate, £1204 8s. 6d.); Works 16/3/1A, f. 2, 22 March 1797. Between 1767 and 1810 £1430 16s. 9d. was spent on work at Thatched House Lodge (T. 29/108, f. 339, 6 December 1810). On Lady Stuart's death in 1841 the Lodge was given to Lt.-Gen. Sir Edward Bowater (d. 1861). Some repairs were then authorised (Works 1/25, pp. 177, 392; 2/3, pp. 309, 314, 331, 342, 454, 472). More may have been done, for Lincoln complained to Peel about the cost of 'Bowater Villa' (B.M. Add. MS. 40481, f. 9). In 1851 the drawing room was enlarged at Bowater's expense (Works 1/37, p. 32). There is a plan in the Soane Museum (xxxix, Set 9, 19) dated 1798.

same held good for Hill Lodge, for many years privately occupied by the Countess of Pembroke, and from 1831 to 1846 by William IV's daughter and son-in-law, Lord and Lady Erroll.[1]

Apart from the maintenance of park gates, walls, etc.,[2] White Lodge was the object of greatest expenditure in Richmond Park. Since 1761 the house had been an occasional residence of the Earl of Bute in his capacity as Ranger. When he died in 1792 George III declined to appoint a successor to his favourite. Instead he took the Rangership into his own keeping in order to effect certain agricultural improvements;[3] and it was not until 1814 that the Prince Regent presented the appointment to his sister, Princess Elizabeth. Meanwhile George III had granted White Lodge in 1801 to Henry Addington, later Viscount Sidmouth, then Prime Minister. Sidmouth lived there placidly until his death in 1844, being appointed Deputy Ranger in 1813.[4] George III was a frequent visitor and guests included Sheridan, Scott, Pitt and Nelson.[5] Alterations to the house between 1801 and 1816 transformed this Hanoverian hunting box into a self-contained country house. In the first place the lodge was insulated from the park by a grant of five acres of land personally allocated by the King and landscaped by Humphry Repton.[6] In the second place Stephen Wright's pavilions were united to Roger Morris's central villa by curved quadrant corridors, and the plain east front was dignified by the addition of a substantial *porte cochère*. These structural alterations, executed at the King's command, were begun by James Wyatt as Deputy Surveyor of Woods and Forests, and completed by Nash and Morgan as joint Surveyors to the same department. Robert Browne was Clerk of the Works and Office of Works tradesmen seem to have been employed. By 1806 nearly £20,000 had been spent.[7] Some confusion arose out of Wyatt's dual role in the operation as Surveyor General of the Office of Works and Deputy Surveyor of Woods and Forests. In the end payment was made by the Department of Woods and Forests and the same department was confirmed in its general jurisdiction over the house.[8] On Sidmouth's death in 1844, the first thought was to offer White Lodge

[1] Works 6/294, f. 19, 1811–12; T. 29/108, f. 399, 6 December 1810. Repairs estimated at £4475 were carried out for the Errols in 1831 (Works 1/18, pp. 450, 459; 4/31, p. 75; 1/21, p. 411; 1/22, p. 159; 2/2, p. 7) After Lord Erroll's death in 1846 Lady Erroll gave up the Lodge, which the Queen bestowed on Lord John Russell, then Prime Minister. Repairs executed on this change of occupancy cost £1058 (Works 2/6, pp. 62, 85, 216; 19/25/7, f. 1). Later alterations included the addition of a wing in 1859 (Works 32/67).

[2] Between 1764 and 1792 the Department of Woods and Forests spent £20,888 18s. 10½d. on Richmond Park (Works 19/25/8, f. 2, 1 July 1794). Richmond Gate, sometimes supposed to have been designed by Capability Brown (d. 1783), was built in 1798 under the jurisdiction of James Wyatt, if not from his own designs (Works 16/212; LR 4/17/118). From April 1817 the cost of maintaining the Park was transferred from the Civil List to the Woods and Forests account of the Office of Works.

[3] W. James and J. Malcolm, *Agriculture of Surrey* (1794), p. 82; D. Lysons, *Environs of London* i (1792), pp. 456–7.

[4] 'To Richmond high the sounding paeons swell,
    Where *Addington* and rural quiet dwell'.
    (T. Maurice, *Richmond Hill*, 1807, p. 26).   [5] Collenette, *op. cit.* p. 44.

[6] Repton found that 'the deer and cattle of the forest had access to the door and windows'. He claimed to have substituted 'the neatness and security of a gravel walk' for the 'uncleanly, pathless grass of a forest, filled with troublesome animals of every kind, and some occasionally dangerous' (H. Repton, *Fragments on the Theory and Practice of Landscape Gardening*, 1816, pp. 83–5, with view of west front). George III offered sixty acres; Addington was content with five. See also R.I.B.A. Drawings Collection E 6/3 (1–3); G. Pellew, *Life of Sidmouth* i (1847), pp. 408–10, ii p. 85.

[7] Works 19/25/9, ff. 1–27, 1803–4; T. 29/106, ff. 278–80, 10 July 1810. For Wyatt's designs, wmk. 1794/8, draughtsman Adam Lee, cf. R.I.B.A. Drawings Collection E 6/3 (4–12).

[8] T. 29/79, f. 536, 15 November 1802; T. 29/107, f. 63, 24 August 1810; T. 29/124, f. 983, 24 August 1813; T. 25/5, f. 97, 22 May 1810; T. 25/287, 16 November 1802.

to the Ranger, the Duke of Cambridge; but the Duchess considered that it was 'very dull from its seclusion'.[1] It was then offered to the Duchess of Gloucester, who demanded mains water, the removal of the stables from the left wing, and other improvements before she would give up Bagshot.[2] Phipps estimated necessary works at £3350, but the building proved more dilapidated than suspected, and Robinson, the Clerk of the Works, carried out additional, unauthorised works. Part of the main sewer had to be rebuilt, and the area walls; the slated timber roofs of the quadrant corridors were reconstructed and covered with lead, the walls plastered, and niches formed with stone cills; and the external stonework was repaired and cleaned. In all, £5529 were spent, to the wrath of the Treasury.[3] Further works were however authorised in November 1846: two servants' rooms were built on the site of the stabling, and new stables erected for 14 horses, with an incline from the stable yard to the carriage yard.[4] Subsequent occupants have made only one significant alteration to White Lodge, the construction of a balustraded perron on the west front.

While Wyatt was enlarging the Prime Minister's house he was also constructing a castle for the King. Despite the abortive projects of 1762 and 1770,[5] George III had never given up his ambition to erect a new palace by the Thames. By the 1770s the growing royal family had become too large even for the combined accommodation of the White House and the Dutch House. During the next twenty years George III paid regular but brief visits to Kew; twice, in 1788 and 1801, during bouts of insanity.[6] In 1802 the main body of the White House was demolished.[7] George III then moved into the Dutch House in order to watch over the construction of his new palace. The Gothic or Castellated Palace, as it was generally called, stood on the site of the present Nursery, a little to the west of the Dutch House, by the side of the Thames.[8] James Wyatt was awarded the commission in 1800, not as Surveyor General, nor as Deputy Surveyor, but as private architect to the King.[9] Work began in 1801, and the original estimate appears to have been £40,000.[10] But by 1806 at least £100,000 had been spent;[11] and by 1811 the half-finished carcass was reported to have cost more than £500,000 with maintenance bills standing at £500 per annum.[12]

---

[1] See p. 360 below. [2] Nottingham University Library, Newcastle MS. 9052, a, b (June 1844).
[3] Works 2/4, pp. 495, 502; 2/5, pp. 7–11, 32; 1/27, pp. 163, 188, 262.
[4] Works 2/5, pp. 312, 391 (estimate £1670). The new stables, to Phipps' design, were built by Winsland and Holland for £1156 (Works 1/31, p. 67, 23 March 1847).
[5] See vol. v of this *History*.
[6] N. Williams, *Royal Residences* (1960), pp. 78–83.
[7] O. Manning and W. Bray, *History and Antiquities of Surrey* i (1804), p. 447; *Journal of the Kew Guild* (1906), p. 297. The offices were left standing, and part of the kitchens still survives (J. Charlton, *Kew Palace*, 1956, p. 8).
[8] 'Yon Dome that soaring high in Gothic pride,
In majesty o'erlooks the wond'ring tide. . . .' (T. Maurice, *Richmond Hill*, 1807, p. 45). For views cf. Buckler Drawings, B.M. Add. MSS. 36388, ff. 244–9 and 36407, f. 48; D. Lysons, *Environs of London* i (1810), p. 150; J. Britton and E. W. Brayley, *Beauties of England and Wales* xiv (1813), p. 190; E. Walford, *Greater London* ii (1895), p. 390; W. L. Rutton, 'Royal Residences of Kew', *Home Counties Magazine* vii (1905), pp. 235–6; *Country Life* lxvii (1930), p. 537.
[9] In 1813 Benjamin Wyatt refused to surrender the plans to the Office of Works, 'the palace . . . being the King's Private Property, and my Father having received his Commission . . . in his private capacity as an architect' (Works 6/26, f. 106, 29 December 1813).
[10] *The Times* 12 September 1800, p. 2; *A Compendious Gazetteer to the Royal Palaces* (Windsor, 1801), p. 31.
[11] Farington, p. 3192, 26 March 1806.
[12] Architectural Publication Soc., *Dictionary of Architecture*, ed. W. Papworth (1848–92), s.v. 'James Wyatt'.

It was only the King's final attack of madness in 1811 which brought the building programme to a halt. Although the money came from the Privy Purse, Radical criticism of this Thames-side 'Bastille' was vehement and prolonged. Dance remarked to Soane in 1802 that 'the rascally Democrats have lately made it their stalking horse'.[1] Wraxall likened its 'bricky towers' to a Spenserian fantasy, a 'most singular monument of eccentricity and expense . . . [an] image of distempered reason'.[2] Others commented on the impracticality of its plan and the inconvenience of its site: 'the foundation is in a bog close to the Thames, and the principal object within its view is the dirty town of Brentford'.[3] Unfinished and unlamented, Kew Castle was eventually blown up in 1827–28. Some of the materials were re-used at St. James's Palace, Buckingham Palace and Windsor Castle. And one last fragment survives in the form of a window built into a garden shed in Kew Gardens.[4]

But in fact the Castellated Palace proved significant both structurally and stylistically. The weight of the building rested throughout on cast iron supports. The method employed probably followed Samuel Wyatt's 'incombustible' system, patented in 1800 and featured in his abortive scheme for rebuilding the Albion Mill, Blackfriars, in 1791, namely a combination of cast iron columns and supporting arches made up of cast iron plates.[5] In 1802 we find Dance questioning Soane as to the secret of Wyatt's technique; but Soane professed to be uninterested.[6] It seems unlikely that cast iron beams were used: that development was reserved for Smirke and Nash rather than Wyatt. But the early date of the palace (1801) makes the use of cast iron supports as well as cast iron tracery on this occasion something of a milestone in English domestic architecture. In style and plan the castle was equally interesting, if less novel. The layout was probably developed in two stages:[7] first the main body of the house with its corner turrets, imperial staircase and central keep, and then the spacious courtyard flanked by battlemented office wings (Fig. 7). It is just possible that George III personally influenced certain parts of this scheme.[8] The palace certainly marked an important stage in the development of Wyatt's Gothic style. Unlike his Sheffield Park, Sandleford and Lee Priory, Kew Castle was Picturesque rather than Rococo. Yet its plan was rigorously symmetrical on the lines of Mount Edgecombe or Inveraray, whereas Norris Castle had followed the tradition of calculated irregularity initiated at Downton and developed there and elsewhere

[1] A. T. Bolton, *Portrait of Sir John Soane* (1927), p. 94, Dance to Soane, 2 August 1802.
[2] Sir N. Wraxall, 'Reminiscences', *Historical and Posthumous Memoirs*, ed. H. B. Wheatley, v (1884), pp. 378–9. The palace appears to have been built of red brick (*The Times* 27 August 1805, p. 3), but Wyatt presumably intended to cover the walls with cement or stucco.
[3] Sir R. Phillips, *Morning Walk from London to Kew* (1820), pp. 380–81.
[4] 'Report . . . on the Office of Works', *Parl Pap.* 1828, iv, p. 479; J. Harris, 'Bicentenary of Kew Gardens', *Country Life* cxxv (1959), pp. 1182–4; J. Charlton, *Kew Palace* (1956), pp. 19—20. Plans survive in the Royal Library at Windsor, in the B.M. (King's Maps xli, 15e. 3, 4, entitled 'Richmond Lodge') and the Victoria & Albert Museum (Print Room E 1896. B–D–1948, entitled 'New Lodge, Richmond Gardens').
[5] British Patent No. 2410, 10 June 1800: 'a new . . . method of . . . constructing bridges, wharehouses, and other buildings, without the use of wood'. Wyatt Papworth first drew attention to the patent and its use at Kew, but mistakenly attributed it to James Wyatt (*Dictionary of Architecture*, s.v. 'James Wyatt'). For plans cf. MR 99 and MPD 128 and *Architectural History* xiv (1971), pls. 37 a–b.
[6] Bolton *op. cit.* pp. 56, 94, Dance to Soane 30 July, 2 August 1802.
[7] *The Times* 28 September 1803, p. 3, 27 August 1805, p. 3.
[8] *Ibid.* 22 June 1801 p. 2; *Civil Engineer and Architect's Journal* x (1847), p. 301; A. Dale, *James Wyatt* (1956), pp. 186–7.

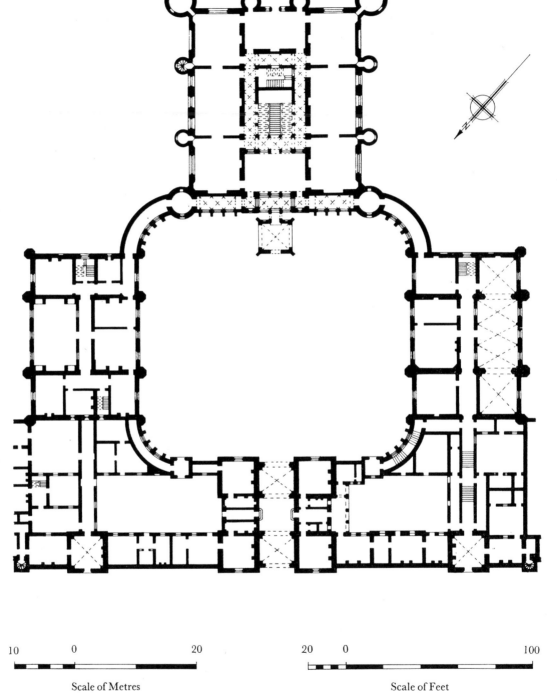

10 0   20   20 0   100

Scale of Metres   Scale of Feet

Fig. 7. Kew Palace: the Gothic palace designed by James Wyatt for George III: based on plans in the British Museum (King's Maps xli, 15e.) and the Royal Library at Windsor.

by John Nash. At Kew the decisive factor may well have been the need of the Court for two parallel suites of State Apartments, which could not so easily have been fitted into an asymmetrical layout. Fonthill, of course, had been *sui generis*; but from Kew stem Smirke's designs for Lowther and Eastnor as well as Wyatt's Gothic *finale*, Ashridge Park. Thus the memory of Wyatt's 'Bastille' lasted a good deal longer than the palace itself.

Meanwhile the 'Old' or 'Dutch' House remained the principal royal residence at Kew. During the Regency it was occasionally occupied by Queen Charlotte: the Dukes of Kent and Clarence were married there in her presence on 13 July 1818, and there she died four months later. Thereafter it was no longer inhabited save by caretakers and housekeepers. A general tidying-up was begun in 1845–6, when a large stack of chimneys was rebuilt. The ruins of the Gothic Palace were cleared away, new entrance gates were put up towards the river, and alterations made to the offices. Expenditure in 1847/8 mounted to £4790. The select committee on miscellaneous expenditure reported in 1848 that the Dutch House 'appears to be kept up without being put to any use for apartments or gratification of the sovereign'.[1] It was, however, not until 1890 that it was opened to the public as an Historic Building.

In 1818 the Regent purchased three adjoining houses on the north side of Kew Green as a 'summer residence'. Some £16,000 from his private funds were subsequently spent in repairs and consolidating them into a single mansion. In a valuation of the King's private property at Kew made in June 1823, the surveyor Chawner remarked: 'The house has very recently undergone a general repair and has been considerably enlarged, and attached thereto are a set of offices principally new built consisting of a large kitchen, confectionaries and other domestic accommodations, replete with useful fittings up, besides apartments adapted to the particular convenience of a part of the Royal Household upon His Majesty's occasional resort to Kew'.[2]

Ordinary expenditure upon the Dutch House and other buildings in the 1820s averaged about £3100 a year, except in 1825–6 when the pagoda was repaired at an expense probably exceeding £5000.[3] Works in 1824–7 in connection with the enclosure of Kew Green included new lodges by Thomas Hardwick, and a new gardener's cottage adjacent.[4] William IV had the lodges and railing moved nearer the palace, so restoring part of the Green to the parish. A new porter's lodge was

---

[1] Works 1/28, pp. 55, 158, 294; 1/30, pp. 13, 49, 78, 232; *Parl. Pap.* 1847–8 (543) xviii, pt. 1, p. x and qq. 2660–4. It is not clear in what circumstances Wyatville made a design for an extension to the Dutch House that is now in the R.I.B.A. Drawings Collection (J7/51).   [2] RA 34856–68, 34889, 34893, 34904.
[3] Works 5/107–111. The works on the pagoda form part of a general total of £11,718 for ordinary repairs of buildings at Kew in 1825 and 1826 (Works 5/109). For expenditure in the years 1832–50 see L.R.R.O. 24/1–7; *Parl. Pap.* 1843 (343) xxx; 1851 (374) xxxi.
[4] Works 1/12, pp. 146, 170, 172–3, 192; 1/13, pp. 267–8. Part of the enclosure was completed before the Office of Works assumed responsibility; but Works expenditure on a stone dwarf wall and entrance lodges was £1306, and the gardener's cottage £487 (Works 5/109–110). The position of the wall and lodges is shown by MS. additions dated 1859 to a plan of 1852 (Works 32/1081). The gateway was adorned with a lion and unicorn, now placed above gates in the Richmond Road wall of the Botanic Gardens (J. Smith, MS. History of the Royal Gardens at Kew in the Library of the Royal Botanic Gardens, p. 22; W. T. Thiselton-Dyer, 'Historical account of Kew to 1841', *Kew Bulletin* No. 60, 1891, p. 320).

consequently needed for the mansion north of the Green, now occupied by the Duke of Cumberland: this cost some £600, and works in the mansion £900 more.[1]

Round Kew Green were a number of houses and offices that were maintained for the accommodation of royal attendants: when not otherwise required, some were occupied in part by old royal servants, and later became 'grace and favour' residences.[2] From 1816 these, as part of the King's private property, were maintained from the Privy Purse, until in 1822 George IV transferred the Kew estate to the Office of Works (Civil List account).[3]

One of the houses on the south side of Kew Green was occupied for many years by George III's seventh son the Duke of Cambridge. Originally the property of Lord Bute, it had been acquired by George III and given to the Duke. From 1816 onwards the Duke was Viceroy of Hanover, but when his brother the Duke of Cumberland succeeded to the throne of Hanover on the death of William IV in 1837, he returned to Kew and made Cambridge Cottage his permanent residence. As Ranger of Richmond Park he was entitled to occupy the Old Lodge, but it was in a dilapidated condition, and as the Duke preferred to live at Kew it was agreed that the Old Lodge should be demolished and Cambridge Cottage repaired as his official residence.[4] Plans were prepared by Phipps,[5] but the Clerk of the Works for Kew, Robinson, drew up for the Duke a more grandiose scheme estimated at £8500. This was pared down to building a new east wing, providing a drawing room and additional bedrooms, and forming a library in the old house. Put to tender in June 1840,[6] that of Carless was accepted at £2724.[7] The sale of the materials of the old Ranger's Lodge produced £956 net, which with the Treasury grant of £3050 allowed the undertaking of further works. In 1840–1 additional contracts embraced the fitting-up and decoration of the new rooms, the addition of a Doric *porte-cochère*, the forming of a servants' hall, assimilating two adjoining small houses (one formerly the Clerk of the Works') and improving the offices. Completed by December 1841, the additions and alterations cost £4320 in all.[8] A verandah erected on the garden fronts in 1843 concluded the improvements.[9] When in 1844 Sidmouth's death left the White Lodge vacant, the Duke and Duchess were given the opportunity of removing to the seclusion of Richmond Park, but the Duchess preferred to remain on the Green, a place that was, she said, 'enlivened by the constant passage of omnibuses to and fro'.[10] The Duke died in 1850, but the Duchess lived on in Cambridge Cottage

---

[1] Works 5/111; the King's own alterations added between £500 and £600 to the total cost. This mansion is now the Herbarium. William IV's entrance was destroyed when the transfer of ground to the Botanic Gardens enabled Burton to construct a public entrance there (see p. 441), re-using vases from the former palace gateway (Smith, *op. cit.*, p. 42).

[2] Works 1/7, pp. 105 *et seq.* General Taylor, listing the King's private property at Kew (*ibid.*) referred to five houses: the Clerk of the Works' late house (Duke of Cambridge), that occupied by General Wynyard, the White House, the Equerry's House, the Ladies' House. For later works at these houses see T. 1/3903, f. 1198/25 and Works 2/6, p. 140.   [3] Works 1/11, pp. 163, 284, 305.

[4] Works 1/23, p. 391 (23 August 1839); 2/2, p. 352 (5 September 1839); *Parl. Pap.* 1847–8 (543) xviii, pt. 1, q. 4560.   [5] MPD 136, plans dated 23 August 1839.   [6] Works 16/29/1, ff. 1, 2 (plans), 3–5.
[7] *Ibid.* f. 7 (the highest tender, Hicks's, was £3700); 1/23, p. 460; 1/24, pp. 10–11, 124, 168, 246, 258.

[8] Works 1/24, p. 466; 1/25, pp. 86–7, 156–7, 238, 290, 485–6, 497; 16/29/1, ff. 13–27. The additions were designed by Robinson.

[9] Works 16/29/1, ff. 32–40 (Carless's tender, £398, was lowest of four). After a small fire in a bedroom, January 1846, repairs costing £153 were authorised, but the Clerk of Works built a new room instead (Works 1/29, pp. 85, 113, 134; 1/30, pp. 272–3; 1/31, p. 28). See also Works 32/1091.

[10] RA, A82/86, 6 March 1844, Peel to Prince Albert.

until 1889. The house was subsequently occupied by their son F. M. the Duke of Cambridge, but in 1910 it became a museum of forestry attached to the Royal Botanic Gardens.

ST. JAMES'S PALACE

During the reign of George III Buckingham House became the London home of the royal family. St. James's Palace was only used for ceremonial occasions: state balls, levees, drawing rooms, royal marriages and christenings. Until 1809 the palace contained seven principal courtyards: Green Cloth Court and Kitchen Court—united in 1823 as Ambassadors' Court; Engine Court, also known as Pump Court; Colour Court, formerly known as Chair or Great Court; and Paradise Court, which was united in 1821 with the adjacent areas known as Pheasant Court and Friary Passage under the title Friary Court. Around these courtyards unpretentious brick ranges still housed a number of 'grace and favour' apartments and a variety of traditional court offices: the Lord Chamberlain's Office, the Board of Green Cloth, the *London Gazette* office, the Central Chancery of the Orders of Knighthood, the Butter and Egg Office, the Lord Steward's department, the Spicery, the Ewry, the Jewel Office, the office of the Marshal of the Diplomatic Corps and many others. The picture was completed by a veritable warren of private rooms for minor functionaries, assistant housekeepers, ladies of the bedchamber etc., and by no fewer than four chapels: the German Chapel (the former Queen's Chapel), the Dutch Chapel, the French Chapel and the Chapel Royal. All these were maintained and repaired by the Office of Works. But as long as George III lived, maintenance and repairs were limited to essentials.[1] In 1793 Pennant admitted the convenience of the interior: 'the most commodious for royal parade of any in Europe'. But he also commented on the 'Uncreditable . . . outside' of the palace and remarked on the fact that Queen Caroline's Library was 'now a lumber room'.[2] Fourteen years later Malcolm was even more severe: Colour Court was infested with idlers who gave the place an 'air indicative of the worst streets'; the Ball Room was 'lighted by tapers placed in uncouth glazed sconces, and twelve chandeliers, too opaque to be termed lustres'; the Chapel Royal, was 'neither grand nor impressive'; and most of the state rooms served only as 'foils to the extreme richness of the Court dresses'.[3]

Altogether there were very few significant developments in the architectural history of St. James's Palace under George III: the fitting up of private apartments for the Dukes of Clarence, Cumberland and Cambridge; the construction of a colonnade on the south side of Colour Court to match that on the west in 1795;[4] the

---

[1] E.g. new matting in the German Chapel (Works 1/5, f. 77, 10 November 1784); painting and white-washing the rooms of the Queen's Bedchamber Women (Works 1/5, f. 93, 22 February 1788); or draught-proofing Col. Goldsworthy's apartments (Works 1/5, ff. 112, 117, August–September 1793; Works 4/18, f. 202 September 1796).   [2] T. Pennant, *Some Account of London* (1793), pp. 116, 118.
[3] J. P. Malcolm, *Londinium Redivivum* iv (1807), pp. 238, 240, 241.
[4] Cost: £1135 12s. 10d. (Works 5/85, 1795). See also Works 4/18, ff. 128, 132, 152, June–November 1795; Works 6/22, 13 November 1795; Works 3/3, f. 62, 20 June 1795. This colonnade still exists, but is now concealed from view from Colour Court by the present south wall of the court, built 18 feet forward of the colonnade in 1865. It is shown on Fig. 9.

redecoration of the state rooms in 1794 prior to the marriage of the Prince of Wales;[1] the construction of a new semi-circular guard room in Engine Court in 1795;[2] and the repair of the fabric following the fire of 1809.

On coming of age the Duke of Clarence had been given quarters situated between Vanbrugh's Great Kitchen and the Stable Yard.[3] As Clerk of the Works at St. James's the fitting up of these apartments fell to Soane, and under his direction at least £2000 was spent between 1791 and 1793.[4] These rooms were no more than a bachelor suite. But the Duke's mistress, Mrs. Jordan, successfully pressed for extension and redecoration between 1806 and 1809. The new furnishings were unexpectedly sumptuous. Groves's estimate of £4077 on behalf of the Office of Works was exceeded by more than £1600;[5] and by 1811 the Lord Chamberlain's Office had spent more than £13,000 in supplying new chimney pieces, elegant Grecian furniture and blue sarsnet hangings relieved by crimson panels.[6] In 1799 the Duke of Cumberland was allotted quarters overlooking Cleveland Row. These apartments he retained for more than half a century, although he lived in Berlin during the 1820s and resided permanently abroad after his accession to the throne of Hanover in 1837. Alterations again proved unexpectedly expensive: between 1799 and 1812 the Office of Works spent at least £12,000 and the Lord Chamberlain's Office another £9000.[7] Meanwhile £3450 had been spent on his house at Kew between 1790 and 1807.[8] Cumberland's unsavoury reputation lent colour to accusations of extravagance. It was in his rooms at St. James's in 1810 that the mysterious and fatal struggle with his valet took place; and the installation of a number of elaborate mirrors gave extra credibility to suspicions of secret orgies.[9] Such rumours strengthened the Treasury's hand in its campaign for economy. In 1810 the Office of Works' estimates for alterations were, for the first time in such a situation, tied to specific contracts with individual tradesmen.[10] But although 'each Tradesman was distinctly informed that he would not be paid beyond the amount . . . for which he had contracted', the contract was 'violated . . . [by] subsequent orders'. and the Chancellor of the Exchequer had to remind

---

[1] 'When the great rooms [Great Council Chamber, Drawing Room etc.] . . . were repaired, and ordered to be decorated for the reception of the new Tapestry [made for Charles II, lost, rediscovered and hung in the Tapestry Room, ex Presence Chamber], the rooms adjoining appeared so shabby, and ill prepared for a comparison with these great rooms, that the Lord Chamberlain . . . gave orders immediately to proceed on the decorations of the rooms and passages adjoining' (Works 6/22, ff. 184, 6 February 1795). See also Works 4/18, ff. 63–4, March–April 1794; Works 5/83 (1794); E. Walford, *Old and New London* iv (n.d.), p. 104.

[2] Cost: £1294 10s. 10¼d. (Works 5/82, 1792). Rebuilt on a semi-octagonal plan in 1875 (E. Sheppard, *Memorials of St. James's Palace*, i, 1894, pp. 393–4).

[3] C. Hussey, *Clarence House* (1949), pp. 41–2 and Soane's ground plan (1792), p. 64.

[4] Works 5/80, Christmas 1791; Works 4/18, ff. 33–4, 37, 42, 61, 1793–4; Works 3/3, f. 47, 29 August 1793; Works 5/83, 1794; Works 4/17, 29 July 1791; 23 November 1792, T. 29/63, f. 380, 6 August 1791; T. 29/65, f. 222, 21 December 1792.

[5] Works 6/24, f. 149, 28 November 1807; 'Inquiry into . . . the Office of Works', *Parl. Pap.* 1812–13, v, p. 503; 'Report on the Civil List, 1812', *Parl. Pap.* 1830, ix, p. 199.

[6] L.C. 9/368; L.C. 1/3, 23 December 1807, 2 February 1809; L.C. 1/40, ff. 119–20, 243, 13 October 1808, 5 November 1811; Hussey *op. cit.* pp. 42–9; R. Fulford, *Royal Dukes* (1933), p. 109; Liverpool Papers liv (1808–9), B.M. Add. MS. 38243, ff. 32–3, 13 October 1808.

[7] L.C. 1/3, 23 December 1807; L.C. 1/39, 2 and 6 May 1799; Works 6/23, ff. 83–4, 11 April and f. 89, 19 July 1799; Works 5/89 (1800), 91 (1802), 94 (1804); L.C. 1/4, 9 July and October 1811; L.C. 1/40, ff. 207, 226, 230, 233, 239, 260, 269, 1810–11; Works 4/20, 10 January 1812; T. 29/112, f. 356, 30 July 1811; 'Inquiry into . . . the Office of Works', *Parl. Pap.* 1812–13, v, p. 503.

[8] Works 6/24, f. 102, 17 July 1807.

[9] R. Fulford, *Royal Dukes* (1933), p. 205; J. M. Jesse, *Life of George III* (1867), pp. 545–6; *Gent's. Mag.* 1852, pt. i, pp. 85–8.   [10] L.C. 1/40, f. 207, 5 September 1810.

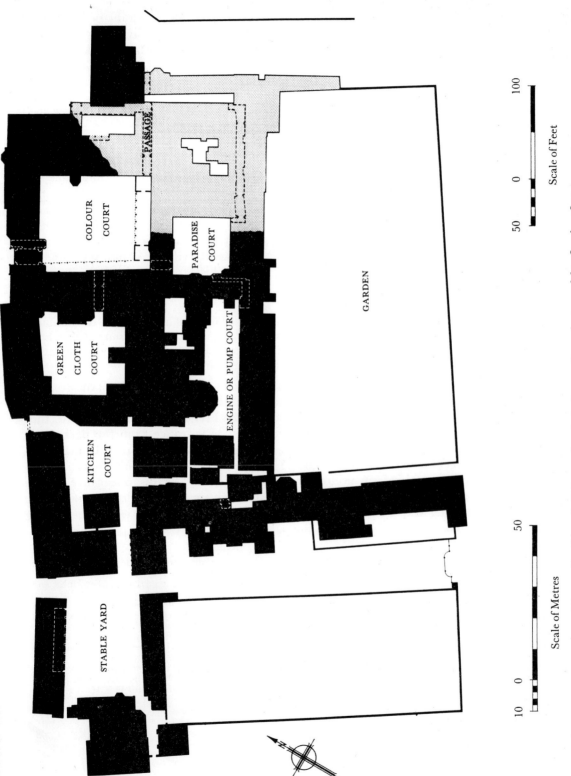

STABLE YARD

KITCHEN COURT

GREEN CLOTH COURT

COLOUR COURT

PASSAGE

PARADISE COURT

ENGINE OR PUMP COURT

GARDEN

Scale of Metres

10 0 50

Scale of Feet

50 0 100

Fig. 9. St. James's Palace, showing the portions destroyed by fire in 1809.

Cumberland that 'similar deviations and excesses . . . cannot again occur'.[1] The Duke of Cambridge's apartments were only slightly less expensive. The favourite and youngest surviving son of George III, he was granted quarters overlooking St. James's Park in 1801. During the next six years the Lord Chamberlain's Office spent £5000 and the Office of Works nearly £4000 on their improvement.[2] And just as further works, estimated at £6300, had been arranged,[3] the 'great fire' of 1809 destroyed a considerable portion of these apartments, forcing the Duke himself into temporary quarters in Grosvenor Street.[4]

On 21 January 1809, at 2 o' clock in the morning, the Duke of Cambridge returned home to find his rooms on fire. As the flames increased 'the inhabitants of the Palace were seen issuing in all directions from their apartments, half-naked'.[5] Water had to be pumped from the canal in St. James's Park one thousand yards away, and Westminster schoolboys handled buckets throughout the night. 'The Prince of Wales, and the Dukes of York, Kent, Cumberland, Sussex and Cambridge, attended, and remained until a late hour, encouraging the firemen'.[6] That night James Wyatt was staying with the Earl of Pembroke at Wilton. At half past nine in the morning Craig addressed the following letter to his superior:

> I am just returned from . . . a most dreadful fire . . . [it began] in a Court next St. James's Street (and is supposed through a Servant of Miss Price's, leaving a Candle in her sleeping room, whom I believe has perished in the flames), thence it continued in its destructive course to the front next the Park, and totally consumed the whole of the Duke of Cambridge's and part of the Queen's apartments. The walls are standing and the great part of the Paintings and Furniture are saved.[7]

In effect the fire destroyed the south-east angle of St. James's Palace: the greater part of Friary Passage, Paradise Court and Pheasant Court, containing the King's and Queen's private apartments, the Armoury, the French and Dutch chapels, the Duke of Cambridge's apartments, the King's private entrance from the park, and all the rooms behind the new colonnade on the south side of Great Court. The estimate for reconstruction was £100,000.[8] Needless to say nothing like that sum was spent.[9] Since the palace was no longer a royal residence, the disappearance of the private royal apartments was not regretted. Although the King of Prussia and Marshal Blücher lodged at the palace in 1814, no material alterations were effected for their accommodation.[10] Nevertheless the palace was still an essential part of the royal

---

[1] T. 29/112, f. 356, 30 July 1811.

[2] Works 4/19, 31 July 1801, 5 September 1806; L.C. 1/3, 23 December 1807; L.C. 1/40, f. 243; 'Inquiry into . . . the Office of Works', *Parl. Pap.* 1812–13, v, p. 503.

[3] Works 6/24, f. 223, 5 September 1808; Works 4/20, 25 November 1808; T. 29/97, f. 9, 29 September and f. 379, 8 November 1808.

[4] *The Times* 24 January 1809, p. 3. But when Clarence applied in 1808 for temporary accommodation while his apartments were being repaired, the Treasury refused: 'the apartment . . . being allotted not in Virtue of any obligation to provide a Residence, but as a Matter of Royal Favour' (L.C. 1/3, 18 March 1808).

[5] *The Times* 23 January 1809, p. 3.   [6] *Gent's. Mag.* 1809, pt. i, pp. 82–3; Sheppard. *op. cit.* pp. 404–6.

[7] Works 6/24, f. 245, 21 January 1809. A sketch by John Carter made 'two or three days after the fire', is at Westminster Public Library.   [8] *The Times*, 30 January 1809, p. 3; L.C. 1/4, 25 May 1810.

[9] Claims for damages and rewards totalled £1425 14s. 9d. (L.C. 1/40, 19 April 1809, 20 October 1809). Immediate repairs cost £484 2s. 1¼d. ('Inquiry into . . . the Office of Works', *Parl. Pap.* 1812–13, v, p. 409).

[10] *Morning Chronicle*, 8 June 1814. In 1813 further alterations were forbidden 'until H.R.H. the Prince Regent shall be pleased to signify his pleasure . . . as to the future appropriation of the Palace' (L.C. 1/6, 8 November 1813). Consequently the Board of Green Cloth was temporarily housed in the Chapel Royal (L.C. 1/40, f. 12, 9 July 1814).

establishment in London, not only providing town houses for members of the royal family, but also accommodating the Lord Chamberlain's and Lord Steward's departments. A new state palace had often been mooted but no steps were taken towards realising this project until the mid-1820s. The Commissioners of Woods, however, had layouts prepared by Leverton and Chawner for building houses on the site, and elevations were drawn for at least one of these schemes.[1] Meanwhile nothing was done to restore the royal apartments and in June 1816 the site of the fire was still 'covered with the heaps of ruins'.[2] Nash, keen to show his mettle as a palace architect, reported year after year that St. James's was ripe for demolition:[3] 'the Walls, Floors, Windows, Roofs and Doors are worn out and any sum laid out with a view to put them in a state proper for occupation would be money wasted'.[4] With time he grew more emphatic: 'I consider every shilling laid out on the buildings as money thrown away' he declared in 1821.[5] But the surviving buildings were kept weathertight[6] and in the end the old palace was given a new lease of life.

Despite its defects St. James's was retained as the official seat of the monarchy because there was no other palace capable of taking its place on state occasions. Carlton House was 'decayed' and 'destitute of the necessary and usual accommodation for servants';[7] the Queen's Palace (Buckingham House) in need of thorough repair and also too small; and Kensington likewise in no fit state.[8] The revenue was not flourishing and the ministry could not rely on its supporters in questions of royal finance. It therefore appeared the most feasible solution, because the cheapest, to refurbish the state rooms at St. James's while putting one of the other palaces in a fit state for the sovereign's private occupation. This decision appears to have been taken in 1821, and by the end of the year some £8000 had been spent on works at St. James's.[9] The usual story of George IV's building activities was repeated here: changes of mind, alterations of plan, and a steadily mounting bill of costs. Plans were submitted to the King in March and April 1822, and in July he ordered 'the immediate execution of certain extensive arrangements . . . for the necessary accommodation of the company attending . . . levees, and Drawing Rooms which are in future to be held at this Palace'.[10] Stephenson could obtain no accurate estimate, and reported that it would 'require very great exertions, and management to confine [the cost] within the sum limited . . . for the annual expences of the Royal Palaces'.[11] By the end of 1822 some £25,000 had been spent, and the work was substantially

[1] Works 34/138 (1–5, plans), 139–141 (elevations), dated 1815.
[2] Works 19/19/1, ff. 23–28, Leverton and Chawner's schedule of rooms and occupants. The extent of the destruction is shown on T. F. Hunt's plan dated 8 February 1816 (Works 34/127).
[3] Works 19/19/1, ff. 42 (10 April 1816), 49 (26 January 1818), 56 (11 April 1821); 1/9, pp. 346–7 (4 April 1819).
[4] Works 19/19/1, f. 42. His was not a solitary voice; see *The Times* 1 April 1818, for a proposal for a Grecian palace.   [5] Works 19/19/1, f. 56.
[6] E.g. Works 1/6, pp. 145, 265; 19/19/1, ff. 1, 19, 39–41, 46, 50, 52; 19/21/1, f. 1.
[7] Works 1/7, p. 417 (29 December 1816).   [8] See pp. 263, 345 above.
[9] Works 5/108 shows expenditures of £528, £1126, £2616 and £5152 for the four consecutive quarters of 1821. Previous expenditure on the palace averaged about £490 per quarter. However a report by the Assistant Surveyor General (Works 1/11, p. 370, 29 January 1823) records expenditure on the alterations and additions only from the third quarter of 1821, and gives a total of £7465 for that and the fourth quarter. The latter account may omit ordinary current repairs included in the former.
[10] Works 4/25, pp. 225, 247; 1/11, p. 171; 34/126 (plan).
[11] Works 1/11, p. 192.

completed by mid 1824 at a total cost of £60,000.[1] A maze of old buildings in Engine Court next to the Guard Room was demolished, as well as offices at the north-east corner of the palace (where Marlborough Road now runs); the courts were re-paved and apartments fitted up for the King and the household officials. The south front facing the gardens was extended eastwards in a style externally indistinguishable from the existing range of State Apartments. Internally a new Drawing Room (now misleadingly known as 'Queen Anne's Room') was added to the suite of reception rooms. To give access to it a corridor was built on arcading along the east side of Engine Court. A new entrance hall and staircase were formed in the south-west corner of Great Court, with a new approach from the east through the colonnade across the south side of Great Court.[2] The new Drawing Room was economically furnished with a fine eighteenth-century chimneypiece from the Drawing Room at Kensington, while the second drawing room and the Throne Room were provided with chimneypieces by Kent removed from Queen Caroline's Library.[3] Further alterations ordered in December 1823 included the remodelling of the interior of the old Ball Room on the south side of Green Cloth Court as a supper room; the demolition of the buildings separating Green Cloth and Kitchen Courts (thus forming Ambassador's Court); the blocking of the archway from Cleveland Row, and the cutting of a new one immediately to the west of the Chapel Royal.[4] 'Alterations', complained Stephenson, 'are very frequently making in the decorations and fittings-up of the State Apartments; and also in the approaches to them, and in so many different directions, as to have occasion[ed] alterations in nearly every remaining part of this palace'.[5] The Hanoverian office was altered at an estimated cost of £1300; changes to the kitchen under the Supper Room made that too small, so 'a different view of the subject was now taken,' involving the rebuilding of the stairs and the addition of a confectionary at a cost of £3837—works executed early in 1825.[6] The influence of George IV's principal artistic adviser is seen in the direction for painting the walls of the principal stair in imitation of veined marble, and the columns, pilasters and pedestals in imitation of grey granite, 'similar to those in the house of Sir Charles Long at Bromley'.[7]

Meanwhile Buckingham House was being transformed, and by the end of 1826 the King had made up his mind to use it not merely as his private residence but as a

---

[1] *Ibid.* p. 370. Rather different figures in Works 5/108 give approximately the same total for 1822. In 1823 expenditure was about £17,000 and in 1824 nearly £20,000. It is not clear whether a credit of £3648 for the sale of old materials in July 1823 (Works 1/12, p. 51) is to be added to the figure already given for 1823.

[2] Works 1/11, p. 192; 34/126 and 127. The intended demolition of the guard room in Engine Court, and the conversion of the Duke of Cumberland's apartments into guard rooms and an officers' mess were not carried out. Pyne, *History of the Royal Residences* iii (1819) shews the north front and several interiors before the restoration.

[3] Works 4/25, p. 181, 7 February 1822. The Library, an insulated building in Stable Yard, was demolished in 1825 (Works 19/19/1, ff. 73, 78).

[4] Works 4/26, p. 248; 1/12, p. 284. The effect of these changes can be seen by comparing the plan of 1793 (Fig. 8) with the plan of 1894 reproduced by E. Sheppard, *Memorials of St. James's Palace* i (1894), p. 410.

[5] Works 1/12, p. 349 (23 January 1824). An example of this is in the gilding of the state apartments, which were progressively enriched at a cost of over £2000, even the sash bars of the Throne and supper rooms being at last gilded (*ibid.* pp. 259, 283, 383, 406–7, 432, 437). Stephenson quarrelled with the Lord Steward's department about alterations and expense (Works 19/19/1, ff. 58–60, 90–3).

[6] Works 1/12, pp. 363, 416, 458; 1/13, pp. 139, 213; 4/26, pp. 314, 401. A 'Hot Table with Hot Closet to be heated by Steam' were among the desiderata (Works 4/27, p. 122).

[7] Works 1/12, pp. 406–7. Bromley Hill House, Kent, was Long's country seat.

state palace in which to hold his courts. St. James's would therefore become redundant, and the King and his architect saw no reason why, like Carlton House, it should not be demolished in order to build terraces of houses along the whole length of the Mall facing St. James's Park. Lord Liverpool, however, thought otherwise.

> There would [he rightly considered] be a strong public feeling against the demolition of the State Rooms so recently completed at a considerable expence: &, what is of more importance, he feels that until the King is completely established in His Majesty's new residence, and until His Majesty shall have had some experience of the fitness of that new building for the purposes of State as well as for his domestic comfort, it would be both unwise & unbecoming to deprive His Majesty of the only apartments in which he can at present hold his Court in London.[1]

So St. James's was once more reprieved, and as Carlton House was demolished and Buckingham Palace not yet finished, the King was temporarily resident there. Early in 1827 urgent provision was made for his personal accommodation, including a 'bath douche' and shower bath, and double sashes and doors to keep out the cold.[2] Major works were also carried out for his brothers, the Dukes of Clarence and Cumberland. Those at Clarence House, almost entirely rebuilt, are described above. In 1826 Nash had rashly promised to enlarge Cumberland's apartments, but found that they were hemmed in between 'the street on the north, the court-yard on the south, the Lord Chamberlain's office on the west, and the new wing fitting up for his Majesty on the east'. 'Where', he asked Knighton, 'can I propose to put the building unless I place the foundations in the clouds?—and castles built in the air will not afford His Royal Highness the accommodation he requires'.[3] At length an estimate of £5700 was approved in 1828 and the job nearly completed by the time of the Duke's return to England in February 1829.[4] Towards the year's end it was found necessary to repair the roof of the Chapel Royal and to instal a new water supply throughout the palace.[5]

When William IV succeeded to the throne he showed a strong disinclination to move to Buckingham Palace. What he would have preferred to do was to live in Marlborough House, where he thought 'he and the Queen could live . . . very comfortably indeed . . . if he might have a passage made to unite this house with St. James's'.[6] In March 1831 Soane, Smirke, Seward and Wyatville were asked 'to consider the expediency of preserving St. James's Palace, and of enlarging it by means of a connection with Marlborough House'.[7] Wyatville at least prepared a design on this basis. Marlborough House was to be linked to the east range by a raised gallery, but the private apartments were to be accommodated in a wing projecting

---

[1] *Letters of George IV*, ed. Aspinall iii, p. 191.

[2] Works 1/15, pp. 174, 180–1. The baths had to be provided within eight days. Between £2000 and £3000 were spent for the King's comfort at this period (Works 5/109, 110: special works are not distinguished from ordinary maintenance costs here).   [3] Lady Knighton, *Memoirs of Sir W. Knighton* (1838) ii, p. 54.

[4] The estimate included substituting a new lighter roof for the heavy decayed one, underpinning foundations, reinstating rooms at the east end demolished in the palace alterations, providing accommodation at the west for the Duchess and a suite, with new stair, for Prince George (Works 19/19/1, f. 108). See also Works 1/14, pp. 6, 91, 94, 99; 1/16, pp. 489, 523; Wellington to Goulburn 4 September 1828 (Goulburn MSS. Surrey Record Office); R. Fulford *Royal Dukes*, p. 225.

[5] Works 19/19/1, f. 121. About £4000 were spent in the latter half of 1829 (Works 5/111).

[6] *The Creevey Papers*, ed. Maxwell (1904) ii, p. 224.

[7] *1831 Report*, p. 222: Works 1/18, pp. 363–4 (16 March 1831).

southwards from Clarence House towards the Park. Its elevations were to be treated in the Tudor Gothic style. The exterior of the State Apartments was to be remodelled in the same style, and a new Ball Room was to be built in the area left vacant by the fire of 1809. Another wing containing a Picture Gallery was to extend southwards to balance the Private Apartments. In this way Wyatville proposed to give the palace a degree of architectural consequence while at the same time preserving its picturesque character.[1]

In the end very little was done. William IV remained at Clarence House, and had George IV's apartments united with his own by means of a gallery overlooking Engine Court. To this was soon added a private entrance for the Queen, with an octagonal back staircase and a pages' room, designed by Sydney Smirke as official Clerk of the Works.[2] Wyatville was subsequently commissioned to design a permanent gallery along the north side of the State Apartments, but in the end this was not built.[3]

In 1832 the roof of the great gateway was restored, together with the clock.[4] Sir Robert Smirke undertook the restoration of the Chapel Royal in 1836; the building was entirely refitted, the royal closet reconstructed with a new ceiling to match the Tudor work, a new roof constructed, and the internal walls on the north and east rebuilt (Pl. 17). The cost of these works, largely executed by Messrs. Piper, was £7606.[5] In this restored chapel, Queen Victoria's wedding was celebrated with some magnificence in February 1840, galleries for spectators being erected in Colour Court.[6]

William IV's indulgence to his brothers and sisters allowed Cumberland to add the Ewry office to his apartments,[7] and promised Princess Augusta improvements in her inconvenient lodging in the Stable Yard Road between Clarence House on the north and Harrington House on the south. Harrington House was an old structure let on a Crown lease expiring in 1837. Plans for pulling it down and enlarging the Princess's residence were obtained from Sir Robert Smirke, but the Treasury was unwilling 'to lay out money in enlarging an old House'.[8] So when Queen Adelaide left Clarence House, Princess Augusta asked for that house instead:[9] her own was demolished with Harrington House in 1838, and a new lodge was built to Smirke's designs at the Stable Yard entrance to the Park.[10]

---

[1] R.I.B.A. Drawings Collection J7/4, reproduced by H. M. Colvin, *Royal Buildings* (R.I.B.A. Drawings Series 1968), pp. 52–3. This was no doubt the 'design formerly approved for adding to St. James's Palace' which Wyatville exhibited at the Royal Academy in 1838. There are related drawings in the Royal Library at Windsor dated 1831 and 1834 (ref. VR. NN).

[2] Works 19/19/1, ff. 132, 140 (plan). The work was done by S. Baker, tender £383.

[3] *Ibid.* ff. 167, 169, 175; 1/21, pp. 138, 140.

[4] Works 19/19/1, ff. 145, 154. See also Walford, *Old and New London* iv, p. 101.

[5] Works 19/21/1, ff. 8 (Smirke's estimate, detailing works necessary), 10–16 (tenders, June 1836), 19–21 (tenders for painting and gilding ceiling), 22 (final account, 3 November 1837); see 1/22, pp. 59, 75.

[6] Works 1/24, pp. 57–8; 2/2, pp. 381, 385, 407. Total Works expenditure on the wedding, including illuminations, was £5323 5s. (Works 1/24, p. 195).

[7] Works 19/19/1, ff. 137–8. The Ewry occupied the rooms formed by blocking the old archway to Cleveland Row, which Cumberland had wanted for himself (Works 19/19/1, f. 79).

[8] Works 19/19/1, ff. 207, 210; 1/22, p. 314; 1/23, p. 171; 34/129–30; T. 1/3904, f. 17547/37 (containing Smirke's plans); RA, Add. Z 501, f. 18.   [9] RA, Add. Z 480, f. 46.

[10] Works 1/23, pp. 171, 192 (Baker's tender, 17 September 1838, £730), 202 (new gates, Stable Yard £480, 10 October 1838); 34/144–5 (Smirke's plan and elevation). Other tidyings-up included in 1840 the demolition of the Guards' suttling house next the gateway in Cleveland Row, and some alterations the next year to the northern side of Colour Court (Works 19/19/1, f. 243; *Gent's. Mag.* 1841, pt. i, pp. 86–7).

The future of St. James's Palace was again thrown into jeopardy by the completion of Buckingham Palace. In 1831 the general view of the select committee had been that St. James's should ultimately be used for some other public purpose.[1] When, soon after Queen Victoria's accession, Buckingham Palace at last became the sovereign's residence, calls for the demolition of St. James's were revived.[2] But it was still required for state functions, levees and Drawing Rooms, for which there was no adequate provision at the new palace until the late 1850s.[3] Faced in 1845 with the need to enlarge Buckingham Palace, Peel contemplated adding state apartments and using the site of St. James's for a new national gallery: but Goulburn killed the notion as unnecessarily expensive and likely to bring odium upon the government.[4] Expenditure on St. James's in the twelve years from 1838, when the Works Department took over the entire charge, formerly shared with the Household, averaged over £5500 a year. In 1843/4, when the supper room was repaired, £11,800 were spent.[5] Thereafter no major alterations were made till the 1860s.[6]

WINCHESTER PALACE

Throughout the second half of the eighteenth century Winchester Palace remained, in Chambers' words, 'little more than a carcass of a house',[7] used in turn as a camp for prisoners of war, a haven for religious refugees, and a military barracks. Expenditure on its fabric by the Office of Works continued to be slight,[8] but some considerable sums were spent by the Commissioners for Sick and Wounded Seamen who were entrusted with the custody of the prisoners.[9] After the American war they were anxious that this outlay (amounting to £2700) should not be wasted by peacetime neglect as they claimed it had been after the Seven Years' War. In 1783, therefore, it was suggested that the palace should be permanently maintained by the Commissioners of Sick and Wounded, 'in readiness for the Reception of Prisoners in case of a future war'.[10] Chambers loyally defended the vigilance of his Clerks of the Works: Thomas Dubisson (1725–75) and William Leach (1775–90). But he admitted the wisdom of transferring responsibility: 'as this Palace neither is, nor probably ever will be, of use to the Royal Family, and as from its age and unfinished state it always

[1] *Parl. Deb.* 3rd ser. ix, 144–6. The actual report of the committee made no recommendation about St. James's Palace, except that the completion of Buckingham Palace for purposes of state would ultimately obviate the need for further expenditure on the old palace (*1831 Report*, p. 6).
[2] Some M.P.s wanted to apply the site to the erection of Barry's Houses of Parliament (*Parl. Deb.* 3rd ser. xliii, 695–705).
[3] See p. 289 above. The move to Buckingham Palace did not mean that the Lord Chamberlain's and Lord Steward's departments evacuated St. James's, and when the chaplain sought better rooms in 1840–1, there were none available (Works 19/19/1, f. 264 *et seq.*).   [4] B.M. Add. MS. 40570, ff. 39–46.
[5] *Parl. Pap.* 1843, (343) xxx; 1851, (374) xxxi; Works 19/19/1, ff. 303–4.
[6] Alterations were made in the rooms to the east of the state apartments for the Duke of Cambridge in 1850 at the Duke's own expense (RA, C. 81, f. 89; Works 19/19/1, f. 333); and in the same year the palace was supplied with water from the government works in Orange Street (Works 19/19/1, f. 327). It was also in 1850 that the architect Alfred Beaumont put forward a scheme of his own for reconstructing the palace of which there is a copy in the Royal Library at Windsor.   [7] Works 6/20, f. 314, 13 November 1784.
[8] Between 1787 and 1796 only £800 were spent on its maintenance (Works 5/76–85).
[9] See vol. v of this *History*.
[10] Works 6/20, f. 263 26 December 1783 and f. 265, 21 January 1784; T. 29/55, ff. 307–8, 12 June 1784.

must be an expence to the Crown . . . [it might, he thought, be expedient] to sell it to the publick, at whose expence it might be compleatly finished and fitted up for a Prison in time of War'.[1] However, George III thought otherwise. He did not 'approve of the House being made over to any body'.[2] So in 1785, after a good deal of inter-departmental wrangling, the palace reverted to the care of William Leach, who 'generally . . . visited the place once a year', and of his nominal Labourer in Trust, a local carpenter employed to guard the site 'with no other reward than the liberty of occupying a small house contiguous to the Palace which formerly belonged to the Clerk of the Works'.[3]

During the Napoleonic Wars Winchester Palace was not used for prisoners of war.[4] Instead, between 1792 and 1796, the building became a place of asylum for nearly 700 French refugee clergy. The government showed its sympathy to the royalist cause by allowing them to occupy the palace. At the same time a semblance of neutrality was maintained by delaying parliamentary grants until 1794 and leaving the whole of the financial side to an independent Relief Committee.[5] During the Autumn of 1792 preparations were made by the Office of Works. Soane was given the task of accelerating the arrangements. On 23 November he showed Chambers a Treasury message 'saying the work went on very slowly and directing Mr. Soane to proceed thither with all dispatch in order to expedite the business'. In reply Chambers was able to promise that 'Mr. Soane would go to Winchester tomorrow morning and call at Windsor in his way and take Mr. Leach with him . . . as he is an entire stranger to the place and people there'.[6] The cost of fitting up bedrooms, dining room, kitchen and chapel was well over £2000.[7] These bills, as well as subsequent allowances of up to £1000 per month, were eventually dealt with by the Relief Committee.[8] In the course of the alterations it was discovered, much to Chambers' surprise, that some rooms in the palace had for years been secretly occupied by the families of an ex-Labourer in Trust and an ex-porter to the prison. But it was decided not to eject them in favour of French clergy, since their removal might 'tend in a great degree to create Disturbances' and might 'beget in the Mind

---

[1] Works 6/20, ff. 276–8, 21 May 1784. [2] Works 6/20, f. 268, 12 May 1784.

[3] Works 6/20, ff. 292–3, 5–9 July 1784 and f. 300, 3 August 1784. The cottage was also a store-room (Works 6/20, ff. 16–17, 15 March 1782). Despite pressure from Treasury and Lord Chamberlain, Chambers successfully defended Leach's supplementary allowance, the rent of an adjoining field: its loss would be 'a grievance which must affect his spirits, and render him unfit for the laborious task he has to fulfil. . . . He must appear decently and live so, to be respected by the tradesmen' (Works 6/21, ff. 3, 4, 9, 56–8, 64, 74, 1785–6; Works 1/5, f. 43, 31 January and f. 51, 28 March 1783; Works 6/20, ff. 328–9, 10 December 1784; T. 29/56, ff. 198, 237, 255, 274, 312, 553, 1784–5; T. 29/57, ff. 212–3, 14 February 1786; Works 4/16, 10 July, 10 December 1784, 28 January, 4 February 1785).

[4] For Napoleonic prisoners in England cf. 'Report on the Treatment of Prisoners of War', *Parl. Pap.* 1797–8, xx (i), p. 143 *et seq.*; *Gent's. Mag.* 1800, pt. i, p. 270 and 1808 pt. i, p. 168; M. Lewis, *Napoleon and his British Captives* (1962), p. 172 n.i.

[5] The 'Fund for the Relief of the Suffering Clergy of France in the British Dominions' was organised by J. E. Wilmot, M.P. and supported by Burke, Portland, Sheffield, Auckland, Buckingham and Bridgewater. It later became the Emigrant Office, a 'para-governmental department' (M. Weiner, *The French Exiles, 1789–1815*, 1960, *passim.*) See also *Gent's. Mag.* 1792, pt. ii, pp. 1166–7.

[6] Works 4/17, 28 September, 19 October, 23 November 1792; Works 6/22, f. 74, 23 November, 30 November 1792.

[7] Works 1/5, ff. 108–9, 18–19 October 1792; Works 4/18, ff. 5, 7, 11–13, 37, 40, 46, February–December 1793; Works 6/22, f. 97, 20 March and f. 101, 9 June 1793; T. 29/65, ff. 223, 332, 372, 452, 457, December 1792–March 1793; T. 29/66, f. 246, 12 December 1793; Works 3/3, f. 48, 26 September 1792.

[8] For detailed lists of clerical personnel, tradesmen's bills etc., cf. T. 93/46, pts. i (1792–3), ii (1794–5), iii (1795–6); T. 93/47, A and B, pts. i–xi; T. 93/48.

of the lower Order of people at least, that the Objects of Charity amongst those of our own nation are to be subservient to the administration of Charity to foreigners'.[1]

By the end of 1793 the refugee clergy had mostly been transferred from Forton Hospital near Gosport to their new home at Winchester. 'They were wont to chaunt their office together . . . and . . . their voices could be heard as a mighty wave of sound all over the city'.[2] 'Their deportment in general was peacable, humble'; and before departing for Reading and Thame in 1796 they set up a marble tablet in their temporary chapel recording their gratitude to the King.[3] 'Intended as the abode of royalty', Winchester had 'become a seat of royal benevolence'.[4]

Until 1797 the barracks at Winchester were situated in St. John's Street. But in 1790 Major Hart of the Inniskilling Dragoons had applied for permission to use part of the palace as a military gaol, otherwise recalcitrant soldiers might have to be confined in the city prison where they would be 'subjected to the inconvenience of meeting . . . Vagabonds and other disorderly persons'.[5] In 1793 the Treasury directed that the entire palace should be handed over to the soldiery.[6] Three years later the transfer was accomplished.[7] In 1810 the three stories were converted into four at a cost of £100,000, 'not however by increasing the height of the pile, but by making the rooms less lofty'.[8] Sixty years later further alterations were effected by T. H. Wyatt.[9] And in December 1894 the last recognisable portions of Winchester Palace were destroyed by fire.[10]

WINDSOR CASTLE AND LODGES

1. The Castle

Although never quite abandoned, Windsor Castle was little used by the earlier Hanoverian Kings, and remained in the latter part of the eighteenth century much as it had been left by Charles II: a huge medieval fortress with some superb state apartments but very little in the way of domestic convenience. In 1776, when he gave Queen Charlotte the old Garden House by the South Terrace once occupied by Queen Anne, George III took the first step that was to reinstate Windsor as one of

---

[1] Works 6/22, f. 66, 4 October and f. 69, 23 October 1792.

[2] Sermon by Abbot Gasquet, 1908, quoted in *V. C. H. Hampshire* v (1912), p. 12. See also *The Times* 24 September 1792, p. 2, 27 September 1792, p. 2, 3–4 October 1792, pp. 4, 3 November 1792, p. 2 and 9 February 1793, p. 2.

[3] Milner, *History of Winchester* ii [1798], pp. 179–80; A. R. Bramston and A. C. Leroy, *Historic Winchester* (1884), p. 354. The tablet was later removed to the Roman Catholic chapel in Winchester.

[4] N. Warren, *The Antiquities of Winchester* (n.d.), p. 182.

[5] T. 29/62, f. 252, 26 October 1790; Works 6/21, f. 174, 16 July 1790.

[6] L.C. 1/2, f. 10, 18 October 1793; Works 3/3, 7 November 1793.

[7] Works 4/18, f. 225, 24 February 1797; 'Inquiry into . . . the Office of Works', *Parl. Pap.* 1812–13, v, p. 439.

[8] Milner, *op. cit.* p. 208. See also Milner, *Guide to Winchester* (1825), pp. 48–9; *T. Prouten's Winchester Guide* (1875?), p. 28; *An Historical and Descriptive Guide to . . . Winchester* (1825), p. 51.

[9] W. Papworth (ed.), *Dictionary of Architecture*: 'Winchester'; *R.I.B.A. Sessional Papers* 1873–4, pp. 157–69.

[10] *V. C. H. Hampshire*, v (1912), p. 12.

the principal royal palaces of England. The Garden House, known henceforth as the Queen's Lodge, was sufficiently enlarged to become the regular summer residence of the royal family. At first the King had envisaged nothing more than a convenient *pied à terre*, but he had (as Farington reported) been 'led on from little to more' until by 1793 he was reputed (probably correctly) to have spent £70,000 'in building and in various expenses attending the making that place what it at present is'. As he said himself, 'if he could have foreseen that Windsor would be their chosen residence he would have prepared the Castle and resided in it'.[1]

But the castle was not entirely neglected. As the elder princes grew up they were given apartments on the south side of the Upper Ward, and from time to time the state apartments were brought into use for ceremonial occasions. In the 1780s they were handsomely fitted up. The 'Audience Room' (i.e. the Presence Chamber) was hung with garter blue, the cornice and mouldings were gilded, and a new canopy and chair of state were provided. A marble chimney-piece was installed in 1786, and the walls were decorated with paintings on canvas by Benjamin West illustrating the triumphs of Edward III. The King's closet, dressing room and drawing room were also hung with blue silk in 1788.[2] Some of the private apartments on the north side of the Upper Ward were repaired, and in 1789, when he recovered from his illness, George III proposed to live in the Castle. Grates were fixed in the Presence Chamber, the ballroom and the Guard Chamber, and sentry boxes at the 'palace gates'.[3] But by October the plan was 'quite given up'.[4] Nevertheless, expenditure on the castle began to mount. The roof of St. George's Hall was strengthened in 1791 (and again in 1799) and the upper windows were provided with 'slide casements' in 1792, when the stair in Horn Court leading to the King's Guard Chamber was repaired and newly stuccoed and its dome was given a plaster entablature and soffit ornamented with roses.[5] During the 1790s expenditure on castle and lodges averaged some £3200 per annum. Minor improvements were made in the state apartments; the south-east tower was fitted up for the Prince of Wales in 1795, and stripped of ivy and repointed in 1796, when improvements were also made for the benefit of his brothers of York and Clarence.[6] In 1794 new Gothic windows were inserted in the picture gallery in the Tudor wing and the Christmas survey of 1797 ordered new 'munnions' for the windows of the Beauty Room and the blank bow adjoining.[7] The principal work of this period, however, does not appear in the Office of Works accounts, but must have been paid for out of the Privy Purse: the construction by

[1] Farington, p. 53, 22 November 1793. For details of the works at the Queen's Lodge see vol. v of this *History*.

[2] Works 5/74; *Les Délices des Châteaux Royaux* (1790), pp. 25, 30; Pyne, *Royal Residences*: Windsor, p. 166 (the canopy was 'wrought under the direction of Mrs. Pawsey, from designs by Miss Mozer [*sic*] . . . the chair of state is the work of Mr. Campbell; and the paintings which ornament the gold columns, were executed by Rebecca, under the direction of Mr. West, who painted the medallion [on the columns] with profiles of their Majesties').   [3] Works 5/78.

[4] *The Harcourt Papers* (13 vols. 1876–1903), ed. E. W. Harcourt xi, p. 109, quoted by O. Morshead, *Windsor Castle* (1957), p. 77.   [5] Works 5/80, 81.

[6] Works 19/25/1, ff. 3–4; Works 5/83–85. New floors were laid in the Queen's Drawing Room, and the King's Bedchamber and Public Dining Room; a new stair was made to the north terrace. But no great sums were spent. William Martin, 'History Painter', repaired and repainted the privy staircase at the back of the grand stair in 1797 (Works 5/86). Martin also offered to repaint the great stair in 1798, commenting, 'the figures &c (the Ornaments, excepted) are done without much Study' (Works 6/25, ff. 57ᵛ–58). For painting a picture between the two stairs and repairing the ceiling of the Queen's Audience Chamber in 1798 he received £199 10s. (Works 5/87, 88).   [7] Works 5/83, 86 (Christmas surveys).

Yenn of a music room and a dining room in the east front.[1] This marks the beginning of the transformation of the east range into royal apartments, a development culminating in the next reign, when the sovereign abandoned the north range where his private apartments had been since the twelfth century.

The most important of George III's works at Windsor came in the following decade, when over £133,000 passed through the Office of Works and in all probability much more was paid by the King from his Privy Purse.[2] This was the transformation of the state apartments into a Gothic palace. James Wyatt, whom the King considered 'perfect in that style',[3] was put in charge, and under his direction the works were still in progress at the time of the King's final illness in 1811.

Wyatt designed a new Gothic stair and lantern over the site of the old grand and privy stairs, rising in a straight line of two flights from a new entrance hall and porch up to the King's Drawing Room (Pl. 23A). The lack of any ante-room between the top of the stairs and the Drawing Room was awkward, but Wyatt's plans were never fully realised, and it is possible that he intended to create a new sequence of state rooms round Horn Court, to which the existing Drawing Room would have served as a Guard or Presence Chamber. According to the *Windsor Guide* of 1800 the chapel was to be converted into a saloon and a new chapel built in Horn Court.[4] Although the chapel was not built in that court, the King's stair was demolished and a gallery continued all round the court, improving communications within the palace (Fig. 10). Besides a general conversion of the windows to Gothic forms, Wyatt planned to relieve the monotony of the north front by erecting octagonal towers at the corners of the Star Building and a new rectangular tower in the middle of the long stretch of walling further east, to form an extension of the King's Guard Chamber. Private accommodation was arranged for the King in the lower rooms along the north front, with libraries to the west, and for the Queen in the east front and the south-east tower previously allotted to the Prince of Wales.[5]

The most striking feature of Wyatt's work, the grand stair and lantern (1800–04), was among the first put in hand. The entrance to the palace was rebuilt from 1802 as a battlemented, machicolated feature with semi-octagonal towers enriched in Bernasconi's patent stucco (Pl. 22A). Excavating the quadrangle two feet and introducing a flight of steps to the doorway gave the porch elevation.[6] Within, an aisled Gothic entrance hall led to the stairs, from the head of which galleries were returned to the Queen's Guard Chamber, entered by doorways on either side of a new Gothic window overlooking the stair, and lighted by windows above the porch and in its

---

[1] Drawings in the Royal Library (VR.NN.E, dated 1794). In March 1795 Yenn showed Farington 'his designs for completing two rooms in Windsor Castle' (Diary, p. 310, 6 March 1795), and in 1796 he exhibited drawings of the rooms at the Royal Academy 'as executed in the east front of Windsor Castle'.

[2] The detailed accounts in Works 5/89–98 do not, as Hope pointed out, appear to include all the works known to have been done. The annual totals given in Works 19/25/1, ff. 3–4 were presumably abstracted from the Works accounts only.   [3] *Later Correspondence of George III*, ed. Aspinall iv, p. 135.

[4] Knight, the author of the guide, was a Windsor bookseller patronised by the King.

[5] Works 5/89–103. The Prince of Wales seems to have been given apartments in the Queen's Lodge instead (5/94 and 98).

[6] Works 5/92. Curiously, the steps are not shown in Wyatville's drawing of this front before alteration (Royal Library, reproduced by Hope, pl. xliv), but then Wyatville's drawing of the old north front (Hope pl. xlvi) does not show Wyatt's Blenheim Tower, though it appears in Smirke's contemporary sketch (R.I.B.A. Drawings Collection J. 11/29/3).

2C

flanking towers.[1] The rich plasterwork was Bernasconi's.[2] Above the stair rose a high octagonal lantern, visible externally. 'The Great Staircase is finished and very magnificent', Mrs. Kennedy, a resident in the castle, noted in January 1804.[3] The King, she reported, was intending to reside 'constantly' at the castle. 'His Majesty plans all the alterations himself: it is his great amusement'.

The gothicising of the windows began in 1800 with those of the Queen's Audience and Presence Chambers, progressively working round to the west front of the Star Building and its return.[4] During the royal family's summer visit to Weymouth in 1804 strenuous efforts were made to complete their private accommodation. 'Mr. Wyatt has promised the whole to be ready to receive them on their return', wrote Mrs. Kennedy in July. 'He has engaged about 200 workmen of different sorts, and the uproar the whole place is in is surprising'. Wyatt was now gothicising the windows of the north face of the Star Building, and constructing an octagonal tower 83 feet high at its north-east corner.[5] Internally, extensive alterations were in progress: the King's Closet was enlarged by the addition of an ante-room to the south; a new Gothic doorway was made at the southern end of the King's Drawing Room;[6] the Queen's State Bedroom was extended over a former staircase; and in the Tudor wing adjoining to the west the Beauty Room and Queen's State Dressing Room were thrown together.[7] The rooms below were reconstructed on a similar plan as libraries.[8] Other works were done on the east front in the Queen's private apartments.[9] On 4 September 1804 Wyatt sent an estimate to the Treasury for 'about Five Thousand Pounds', remarking that the King had ordered 'all the despatch

---

[1] The stair is illustrated by Pyne, *Royal Residences*: Windsor, opp. p. 87. The description in *Gent's. Mag.* 1805, i, p. 67 of the stair branching off right and left 'upon the geometrical principle' is oddly inaccurate.

[2] The other principal tradesmen employed at this period were Obadiah (d. *c.* 1801) and Robert Tebbott, carpenters; Lawrence and Hollis, bricklayers; Slingsby, mason; Jenner and Kelsey, joiners (Kelsey being employed principally in the libraries); Cutler, plumber and glazier; Cooper, painter; Hutchinson, ornamental painter; Davis, smith; Ould, slater; Allwright, labour. In 1804–5 John Perry (who was also employed at Carlton House at this time) appears as a joiner specialising in Gothic work, and Edward Wyatt as carver and gilder.   [3] MS. Diary, Typescript in Royal Library.

[4] Works 5/89–93. These large two-light transomed windows may, as Carter thought (*Gent's. Mag.* 1805 ii, p. 631), have been based on those shown in Hollar's or Langley's engravings of the castle, but Wyatt had used similar windows at Fonthill (cf. J. Britton, *Illustrations of Fonthill Abbey*, 1823, pls. vi, ix and x). The use of white Portland stone easily distinguishes those of James Wyatt's windows that survive from those designed by his nephew Wyatville.   [5] Works 5/93; *Gent's. Mag.* 1805, ii, p. 632.

[6] This doorway is described in the mason's accounts for the Lady Day Quarter, 1804, as 'at the entrance of the Queenes Drawing Room' (Works 5/93, quoted by Hope, p. 367, n. 33). But from Pyne's illustrations of 1816 (opp. p. 106) it appears that the doorway of the Queen's Drawing Room had never been altered. It was probably for this doorway that Perry supplied a 'very rich Gothic right Wainscot folding door 5″ thick, 13 ft. high, 5 ft. & 6 ft. [*sic*] wide on on [*sic*] side, extremely rich Gothic work on one side and on the other large bolexion molded and rais'd pannels' at £668 17s. (Works 5/94, 'extra' quarter Xmas, 1804). If so the doorway must have stood in a wall between a Gothic room and one that had not been altered. The King's Drawing Room fulfils this requirement, since it was not altered internally, but opened onto the Gothic grand staircase.

[7] Works 5/93. Hope, who says that the Queen's Bedroom was extended to the west (p. 350), appears to have confused the old State Bedroom (which became the Dressing Room) and the new one formed out of the Beauty Room and the Old Dressing Room; a more logical sequence of rooms was thus formed.

[8] Works 5/93–6.

[9] RA, Add. 2/13 (printed, *Later Correspondence of George III*, iv, p. 228), King George III to James Wyatt, 5 September 1804: '. . . He feels the reasons are conclusive why the opening cannot be made in the middle of the Musick Room, and approves of Handel's bust being placed in that pannel on a bracket as was intended over the chimney, but sufficiently high that the harpsichord may remain in its present place; the chimney in this case need not be altered. The door into the old Confectionary from the Withdrawing to it must now be executed as well as a passage at the back of that side of the room from whence the communication will come to Mrs. Egerton's Tower' (i.e. probably the Board of Green Cloth, now Prince of Wales's Tower, but possibly the Chester Tower).

possible in preparing Windsor Castle fit for the reception' of the royal family on their return.[1] To the King he wrote on 7 October 1804:

> I have forborne to trouble your Majesty on the subject of the works going on at Windsor Castle, during the state of confusion in which everything has been for the last three weeks, supposing that it would be much more satisfactory to your Majesty to recieve my report, after the works should be in such a state of forwardness, as to enable me to form a decided judgement on the time of their completion.
>
> I assure your Majesty that the difficulties with which we have, in several instances, had to contend, have been very great; and could not have been surmounted but by the most strenuous exertions. The prodigious thickness of many of the walls, through which it has been necessary to cut; the difficulty of procuring, at a short notice, so large a number of good workmen, as were indispensible to this undertaking; and the greater difficulty of confining them closely to their duty, have been unavoidable impediments to the rapid progress of the work; I have however now the satisfaction to inform your Majesty, that the work is in such a state as to enable me to decide, that the Castle will be ready for the reception of the Royal Family by the end of this month, although there are still those appearances of confusion which might perhaps induce anyone, less accustomed than myself to similar scenes, to doubt the possibility of its completion.[2]

The royal family returned to Windsor on 2 November, and on 25 February following gave a house-warming of great magnificence. Silver chandeliers from Hanover were hung in the ballroom, and silver tables and pier glasses set up.[3] In April 1805 the King revived the installation ceremonies for Knights of the Garter, and elaborate preparations were made for the occasion: the chapel was turned into a concert hall, St. George's Hall was fitted with an organ and music gallery; and accommodation was created in and over the Star Building for officers of state and their attendants.[4] The cost was nearly £11,000.[5] The Queen's Guard Chamber was fitted up at considerable expense as a temporary chapel;[6] the old-fashioned angle-chimneys in

---

[1] Works 6/23, f. 265; see also f. 265ᵛ.

[2] RA 11397–8 (printed, *Later Correspondence of George III*, iv, p. 238).

[3] *Gent's. Mag.* 1805, i, pp. 262–3. The embellishments included a floor in the ballroom painted 'by an eminent artist', instead of the commoner chalked designs. An example of such a design to be executed in distemper for the King's Guard Room dated 8 August 1792 exists among the Yenn drawings at the Royal Academy. On that occasion the painting cost £43 8s. 0¼d. (Works 5/81).

[4] Works 5/94; 6/24. Estimates for works ordered by the King at various times, all to be completed by 23 April, were sent to the Lord Chamberlain's secretary on 14 March 1805:

> Erect a scaffold in St. George's Hall for the installation of the Knights of the Garter, build a music gallery at the end with a Staircase . . ., remove and refix the Giants Gallery and put up another gallery in His Majesty's private Chapel, . . . repair and restore the paintings on the walls of the Hall, remove and make good the marble Haut-paux, fit up five temporary kitchens, etc. . . .   £3500.
>
> Take down partitions angle chimnies &c. in the Star Building and put new floors and partitions in part of Queen Elizabeths Tower, divide and fit up 26 Bedrooms in the same and build 4 new ones for the accommodation of the Officers of State and their attendants, put new Skylights, w.c.s. &c. and alter the Lead flats, take down the angle chimnies in 8 of His Majesty's State and private apartments and put them in the middle of the rooms and make a new State Bed room, put up 30 new Marble Chimney Pieces, make good the wainscotting, floors, doors &c. put up 2 new w.c.s. for the use of his Majesty, put new Ceilings where necessary and repair and white others Staine and Varnish the Wainscotting and Paint the other woodwork.   £5525

(Works 6/24, ff. 2ᵛ–3)   £9025

[5] Works 6/26, pp. 5–6.

[6] £1971 17s. 10d. to the carpenter alone (Works 5/94, extra Christmas qtr. 1804). The result is illustrated by Pyne, opp. p. 88.

eight of the royal apartments were removed, new ones being placed centrally in the walls.[1] One costly item was Gothic joinery—doors and sash frames—and library fittings were another.[2] Alterations were altered again, as in the taking out in 1805 of windows fixed in the southern face of the return from the west front in 1803.[3]

Operations on the North Terrace continued during 1806: the old windows and decayed wall of the library were taken down and rebuilt with new Gothic windows; work began on an octagonal tower at the north-west corner of the Star Building, on a porch in its centre, and on a new Blenheim Tower in the centre of the range further east contiguous with the King's Guard Chamber. This last tower was never completed, though window-framing was fixed in the lower stages in 1809; among the works subsequently charged for were the cornice and cordon, with seven heads carved in Portland stone.[4] Another work begun in 1806, but ultimately left incomplete, was the transformation of Horn Court, where a communication all round on two levels was planned. Plastering and glazing charged for in 1807 doubtless relate to the ground floor passages. Windows and frames were painted early in 1809. During 1810–14 Gothic frames for the galleries were provided. A staircase tower was also built in the court.[5]

Other parts of the castle in which Wyatt was active included the south terrace (where some windows were gothicised in 1805), the Queen's apartments in the centre of the east front (1807, 1811) and Princess Amelia's adjoining (1807); Princess Sophia's (1810), and the Duke of York's (1813), both on the south front. Expenditure in 1810 and 1811 exceeded £15,000; nor, it appears, did works cease with the King's illness: in 1812–14 about £20,000 were spent.[6] Some of this was for the completion of the Queen's State Apartments. In 1805–6 Francis Rigaud (1742–1810) painted the ceiling over the extension to her State Bedroom with 'Jupiter presenting a bow to Diana', to match the existing ceiling painting of Diana by Verrio.[7] Matthew Cotes Wyatt (1777–1862), James's youngest son, was employed to execute a further series of paintings. He was responsible for decorating the octagonal ceiling of the lantern of the Guard Chamber with 'Juno appeasing the wrath of Jupiter against the

[1] Works 5/94 (midsummer qtr. 1805); 6/24, ff. 2ᵛ–3 (ordered to be completed by 23 April 1805). Five new chimney pieces of red marble in the King's apartments were charged at 18 guineas each. As may be seen from Pyne's illustrations, they were of the simplest character.

[2] Perry charged £213 for a 2-light Wainscot Gothic sash frame (Works 5/94).

[3] The evidence of the Works accounts as to the gothicising of three windows on both the ground and principal floors in the return of the west front of the Star Building (Works 5/93) is supported by Carter's description (*Gent's. Mag.* 1805, ii, p. 723). But neither Lysons' plan (*Berkshire*, p. 421) nor Wyatville's drawings show windows here, and the mason's account for the midsummer quarter 1805 refers to taking out windows from the return of the west front and fixing three in the attic (Works 5/94). There are now only two windows on the principal floor there. Heath stone for the work was supplied from Chobham (Works 6/24, f. 7ᵛ).

[4] Works 5/103. Hope's statement that the tower was finished in 1807 (p. 352) is clearly incorrect. The porch appears to have been completed in 1808 (Hope, pp. 348, 367 n. 18, citing Works 5/96–7). A drawing of it by Smirke is in the R.I.B.A. Drawings Collection, J. 11/29/3. The bricklayer for the N.W. octagon tower was Hollis, whereas Lawrence had done the N.E. one (Works 5/93, 95, cited by Hope, p. 366, notes 16, 17). M. C. Wyatt designed an unexecuted ceiling for the tower for which, with models, he charged £52 10s. (Works 5/103).

[5] Works 5/95–103. Tebbott's bills for 1805 include 'taking down old Roof, Galleries, Stair case, &c.', which may refer to clearing Horn Court (Works 5/94, 'extra' Michaelmas quarter).

[6] Works 5/94–103.

[7] Works 5/95 ('Extra' Lady Day). According to Pyne (p. 116) the King thought that Rigaud, who had been trained to paint in the baroque style, 'could best accommodate his style to the old painting, . . . having been formerly employed upon the Continent as a painter of ceilings'. See also E. Croft-Murray, *Decorative Painting in England* ii (1970), p. 268.

Greeks' (1806–7, £210). More important, he provided a series of paintings of the story of St. George, commencing with 'St. George and the Dragon' in the enlarged King's Closet (1807, £787 10s.); next, 'the nursing of St. George', in the adjoining King's State Dressing Room (1808, £525), and culminating with further scenes in the enlarged Queen's State Dressing Room in the Henry VII wing (from 1809).[1]

Another sector of James Wyatt's restoration was the Tomb House. Between 1782 and 1792 the King had spent nearly £14,000 from his Privy Purse in 'improvements' to St. George's Chapel which included a new organ-screen of Coade Stone and the removal of the Perpendicular tracery of the east window to make way for painted glass representing 'the Resurrection' after designs by Benjamin West.[2] He then turned to the dilapidated chapel immediately east of St. George's, known as the Tomb House, intending to convert it into a chapter-house for the Order of the Garter with a royal burial vault below: the windows, pinnacles and battlements were renewed in 1800–4, and in 1804–10 an extensive burial vault was formed beneath the floor. A new Gothic plaster ceiling by Forster was then put up in 1811–12 with armorial decorations by Henry Milbourne, and Matthew Wyatt embarked on a series of 28 full-length paintings of the founder-members of the Order.[3] Here, as elsewhere in the castle, the work was left unfinished after the death of James Wyatt in 1813, which seems to have been the determining factor in halting the restoration.

During the fifteen years of George III's major works at Windsor, 1800–1814, some £150,000 had been spent.[4] Considerable alterations had been made both externally, to create a more varied, more Gothic appearance, and internally to achieve greater convenience, comfort and splendour. But St. George's Hall was left in an unsatisfactory condition; the quadrangle presented a strange mixture of windows, some by Wyatt with pointed heads and Gothic tracery, others with round heads and bold reveals still dating from May's work in the seventeenth century; and communication between the State Apartments and the private apartments on the east and south was possible only through the Queen's rooms (Fig. 10). Taste, moreover, was changing. What had seemed to a foreign visitor in 1811 'like a castle of Sir Walter Scott's own building'[5] would not long satisfy an increasingly sophisticated public. Wyatt's Gothic detailing was already condemned in antiquarian circles, and the want of a dominant feature to unite the whole composition was evident. The idea of achieving this by heightening the Round Tower was already 'whispered' in 1805,[6] but even if Wyatt seriously contemplated the operation he lacked the funds to carry it into effect.

---

[1] A charge in 1811 by Forster, the ornamental plasterer, for a rich ornamental ceiling with enriched cornice described as 'now executing' in the State Dressing Room led Hope (p. 352) to suggest that the work begun in 1809 may have been undone and renewed on a more elaborate scale. But Matthew Wyatt's 1814 account, summarising the whole of his work at Windsor, gives no indication of such reconstruction, describing the Queen's Dressing Room ceiling as the story of St. George in eleven pictures with nearly a hundred figures, whereas both Matthew Wyatt and Forster charged for work on the State Dressing Room ceiling in the Lady Day quarter of 1811. So it seems that Matthew Wyatt's work proceeded simultaneously with that of the ornamental plasterer (Works 5/94–103; RA Add. 17, containing M. C. Wyatt's bills).

[2] Hope, pp. 388–94. Henry Emlyn was the architect employed.

[3] *Ibid.* pp. 485–7, quoting Works 5/89–93 and 103.

[4] Works 19/25/1, ff. 3–4. This sum excludes Queen's Lodge, but includes the Tomb House.

[5] L. Simond, *Journal of a Tour and residence in Great Britain during the years 1810–11* (1815) ii, p. 115.

[6] J. Carter in *Gent's. Mag.* 1805 (ii), p. 819.

After James Wyatt's works there was an interlude. Under the new organization of the Office of Works the castle fell under the care of Robert Smirke, who had made something of a name for himself as a castle architect and naturally felt considerable pleasure that Windsor should be in his charge.[1] Under his aegis King John's Tower was in 1819 repaired and fronted 'with stone and windows corresponding with the adjoining buildings'.[2] The ancient east wall of the stairs to the Round Tower, exposed by the clearing away of old store buildings, was also repaired and cased; and the west wall of the stairway between the Round and Devil's Towers, having fallen in the winter, was likewise repaired.[3] Another important work carried out by Smirke was the reconstruction of the roof of St. George's Hall, executed early in 1824 at a cost of nearly £3000.[4]

Almost as soon as his father was dead, George IV began preparations for establishing himself in the castle. He acquired the Lower Lodge, with its stabling, from Princess Sophia; and there was in 1820 'a general belief amongst well-informed persons that a parliamentary grant would be applied for, for the repairs of Windsor Castle upon a large scale'. But then delay interposed. In November 1822 the Surveyor General mentioned that the King had given instructions for fitting up apartments in the castle for 'his future occasional residence'; but only on 1 October 1823 did George IV enter into occupation, staying for two months.[5] The demolition of the Queen's Lodge was ordered forthwith, but the King found that the castle, despite his father's operations, required further alterations if it were to become a state residence again. He at once began to plan improvements, and Sir Charles Long, his chief artistic adviser, summoned Soane (an old acquaintance) to discuss the problem as early as 23 November 1823. About this time it was determined to hold a competition, and Long drew up a brief:

> Questions particularly referred to the Consideration of the Architects who have been desired to furnish Plans for the Improvement of Windsor Castle.
> 1. The Entrance to the Great Court and the Entrance Gate to State Apartments.
> 2. The best Communication to the State Apartments either by the Horn Court, or the Brick Court, and Hall and Stairs forming such communication.
> 3. The building a Room next the King's Guard Chamber, to communicate the King's Apartments with the State Apartments.
> 4. The Application of such Room or any other in the Castle, for the purpose of a Picture Gallery, to be called the Waterloo Gallery, and to contain the Portraits painted for his Majesty by Sir T. Lawrence.
> 5. Any alteration of the Rooms over and under the State Apartments, so as to accommodate them to the reception of visitors.
> 6. To make communications between the Apartments to the East and South, either by Corridor or otherwise.

[1] Farington, p. 6741.
[2] Works 1/9, pp. 304 ff. The accounts for 1800 (Works 5/89) include two windows in King John's Tower. The effect of Smirke's alteration can be seen by comparing the plate published by Lysons in *Additional Plates to the first volume of Magna Britannia* (1813), reproduced by Hope, pl. xliii, with Wyatville's drawing of the Upper Ward before his reconstruction (Hope, pl. xliv). 'King John's Tower' is the 14th-century La Rose Tower.
[3] Works 1/9, pp. 304 ff. (general survey report). Smirke sent a sketch for alterations to the tower at the entrance to the keep, for the guidance of Matthew, the Clerk of the Works, who was supervising the alterations (Works 4/23, p. 369).   [4] Works 5/108.
[5] Works 1/11, p. 321; O. Morshead, *Windsor Castle* (1957), pp. 84–5; *Windsor Guide* (1825), p. 34.

7. To make elevations of the North East and South Fronts, and the same in the Interior of the great Court.

8. To make a distant view of the South front from the long Walk, shewing the general effect of the Designs when finished.

The Consideration of these Questions is not to preclude any other Suggestions which the Architects are disposed to make.[1]

Thus the main features of the future plan of the palace were sketched by Long. The architects invited to submit designs were the three Attached Architects, Nash, Soane and Smirke, and Jeffry Wyatt (1766–1840), nephew and sometime pupil of James Wyatt. As the architect appointed in December 1823 to carry out alterations to the Royal Lodge in the Great Park Wyatt was clearly a strong candidate for the greater commission, and probably the one favoured by the King himself, as well as by Long.[2] Not content with drawing up the brief, Long elaborated his ideas in a memorandum which he submitted to Lord Liverpool on 13 February 1824. This so exactly anticipates the alterations made that it must be quoted at length:

> If, as is supposed, any considerable Improvements of Windsor Castle are con-templated, it is probable there will be a great variety of Opinions as to the particular Improvements which are to be adopted—I will state shortly and generally what has occurred to me upon the subject.
>
> *Approach*
> It is almost obvious that the principal Approach to the Castle should be by continuing a direct Line from the magnificent Avenue called the long Walk to the Court of the Castle itself. It would be desirable that the Court should be entered through a Gothic Arch; and the continuance of the same line would lead directly to the doors of Entrance to the State Apartments; for this purpose the Garden of the late Queen's Lodge should be thrown into the little Park.
>
> Two Lodges in the Character of the Castle should be built at the Entrance into this part of the little Park, leaving the Road separating it from the long Walk as at present—this Approach should be considered as the Approach only of the Royal Family, or such Visitors as had special permission. From this Lodge there should be an Avenue of Clumps of Trees, continued to the Castle, so planted that from the Lodge the whole South front of the Castle might be seen from the Keep on the West to the Eastern extremity. The Clumps to the West would partially conceal the Town.
>
> The common Approach and Entrance into the Castle would be through the Town, and by what is called the lower Ward.

[1] Soane Museum corresp. 2, xii, B. 2, ff. 1–4.

[2] This is borne out by the evidence he gave to the Select Committee in 1830. When asked to recall the circumstances of his appointment, he stated that he had 'received most unexpectedly a message from His Majesty to attend him, to receive his instructions for making designs for the alteration of the Castle'. Subse-quently he 'received a notice to attend at Lord Liverpool's; and there, in the presence of two other architects that were there, we received similar instructions to what His Majesty had pointed out to me as his notions when I attended him' (*Parl. Pap.* 1830 (656) ix, qq. 251–2). Dr. D. Linstrum has suggested that 'it was undoubtedly the recommendation of . . . the Duke of Devonshire (for whom Wyatt was altering Chatsworth) . . . that led to his inclusion in the contest' ('Sir Jeffry Wyatville at Windsor', *Victorian Society Annual*, 1969–70, p. 43). This may have been the case, although Wyatt, who had long been employed as a 'master tradesman' at Carlton House and probably at the Royal Pavilion, Brighton, must have been well-known to others in the royal circle as well as to the Duke. He himself stated in 1830 that though 'personally known' to George IV and once 'in some favour', he had not been near the King for 25 years when he received the Windsor commission (*Parl. Pap.* 1830 (656) ix, q. 251). There is evidence that he was acquainted with Sir Charles Long, for when the latter spoke in favour of ranging the law courts like 'chapels' round Westminster Hall (*Parl. Deb.* new ser. x, 1384–5, 23 March 1824), Soane noted that the idea 'came to Sir Ch. thro Jeff' (Soane Museum 53/3/60ᵛ).

External Appearance

The Character of this Castle should be that of simplicity and grandeur, and as well from its History, as from the imposing style of Building belonging to that period, I should say the period of Edward the 3rd is that which should generally predominate, not however excluding the Edifices of earlier periods, where we find anything of grand or picturesque effect—Conway, Carnarvon, Harlech, Ragland, Bodiham, Haddon, and many others, will furnish most useful Examples. In considering Windsor in this point of view, the Architect will find as much to restore as to invent; for the Castle has so much in it which belongs to these times, that it may be considered even now as its principal Character. The Alterations which have been since adopted have been generally made in periods less favorable to Castle Architecture. The considerable Alterations which were made during the Reign of Charles the 2d. very much destroyed its Character; those which were made in the late reign were not more fortunate —and here I must observe, that the style of Alteration which I should most dread is that of *modern gothic Architecture*. By modern gothic Architecture I mean that which has been adopted in some of the most costly Mansions which have recently been erected—in which the repetition of small Towers appears to me to destroy the grandeur of the Edifice without adding at all to its beauty; this Style which has been called gothic is in a great degree fanciful, and does not belong to any period of Castle Architecture that I am acquainted with.

I am fully aware when I speak of the Architecture of the Reign of Edward the 3d. that it might be necessary to relax in some degree from the strict severity of this Style, in some parts of the Building—the South front however, might be kept entirely to the Character of this period. But as Castles afterwards became less important as places of defence, the external Appearance gradually changed . . . the stern grandeur of the Castle Character yielded in some degree to the more elegant and decorative style of the inhabited Mansion. Among the best specimens of the mixed Character are Raby, Lumley, Thornbury, Warwick, Oxburgh, Wingfield Manor, Brancepeth, Hampton Court in Herefordshire etc. I would recommend that the style of some of these Examples should be applied in any Alterations that may be made in the East and North fronts of the Castle, which consist of the State Apartments and those inhabited by His Majesty.

With respect to particular external Alterations, I will point out one or two which I think would be desirable. In an old Castle there should be some predominant feature, and the Keep seems to furnish such feature in Windsor Castle. At present there are small Towers rising from the Castle as high as the principal Tower of the Keep. I would add to this tower 20 or 30 feet, carrying it up of the same dimensions as the present tower—a smaller Tower rising out of the present would destroy its dignity and grandeur. This elevated Tower seen from a distance would much improve the general Effect of the whole Building. The other parts of the Castle should be kept comparatively low, and the outline as little disturbed as possible by small Towers.

I would recommend also, both with a view to external appearance and internal Comfort, that there should be a Corridor in the interior Court on the South and East sides. This would afford the opportunity of improving the exterior by the introduction of Windows more analogous to the Character of the Building than those of Charles 2d; and as this Corridor would not require to be more than 10 or 12 feet wide, it would diminish very little the dimensions of the interior Court.

Another Improvement in the Appearance of the interior Court would be the Alteration of the Windows of St. George's Hall—the upper square Windows should be taken away, and the lower Windows heightened, and their form made to accord with the general Character of the Castle; it should have a Hall-like appearance without as well as within.

If it were decided that the entrance should be in a continuation of the long Walk, the Archway might be made between two advanced battlemented Towers, in the style of those of Lancaster Castle. It appears to me that these towers, as well as the heightening the Tower of the Keep would improve the general Appearance, but neither of these Alterations is absolutely necessary to the grandeur of the Building.[1]

Interior Arrangement

The Corridor above suggested would essentially contribute to render the Apartments conveniently habitable, by restoring the passages to many of the rooms from which they have been cut off, and by affording a Communication to others instead of leaving them passage Rooms as at present. The Entrance to the State Apartments should be through a Gothic Hall to be built in what is called the Horn Court to the right of the present stairs—in which there might be a Gothic Staircase leading to the Guard Room, which should be the first room entered of all [the] State Apartments— the present Stairs lead, contrary to all precedent, directly into the Drawing Room. A Room of Communication should be made so as to connect the East side where His Majesty resides, with the State Apartments. This Room should be built in part of the space now occupied by the great Kitchen, and should communicate with the Guard Chamber. There are many other Arrangements which would add both to the Convenience and to the Magnificence of the Interior. . . .

General Observations

The outline of the square Towers of the Castle should not be altered—except perhaps in one or two in which the projecting of the battlement might give them picturesque effect, and at the same time preserve the Character of the period. What-ever alterations or additions may be made should be executed in rough Heath Stone, of which the Castle has been generally built, and which very soon will acquire the Colour, and will not be distinguishable from, the old parts of the Building. The brick Work which now disfigures parts of the Building should every where be re-moved.

It would be desirable that there should be a new public Entrance to the Terrace, which should be at the Western extremity of the North Terrace, near what is called the Winchester Tower. This North Terrace might then be always open to the public without inconvenience, as might also the East Terrace, when His Majesty was not resident, or at such other times as he might permit.[2]

C. LONG

Here the programme shortly to be entrusted to Jeffry Wyatt is clearly envisaged— from the extension of the Long Walk to the heightening of the Round Tower. But no architect had as yet been appointed, so to Long must be given the credit for laying down the lines of the transformation that gives Windsor its present architectural character.[3]

With the country prosperous and a surprise repayment by Austria of a British loan made to her in the Napoleonic wars, ministers had no difficulty in obtaining

---

[1] This sentence is a marginal addition.   [2] B.M. Add. MS.38371, ff. 1–8.

[3] Long's views on the restoration of Windsor Castle were subsequently repeated in the pamphlet entitled *Short Remarks and Suggestions upon Improvements now carrying on or under consideration* which he published anonymously in 1826.

parliamentary sanction for a vote of £150,000 towards the restoration of Windsor Castle.[1] In face of criticism of Soane's new Law Courts, then erecting, the government decided however that a 'committee of taste' should supervise the alterations, following the precedent of 1802 relating to public monuments for war heroes.[2] A Treasury minute of 13 April directed that all the plans and estimates for the repair and improvement of the castle should be submitted to commissioners appointed by the King, viz. the First Lord of The Treasury, the Chancellor of the Exchequer, and the First Commissioner of Woods, *ex officio*; and the Duke of Wellington, Lord Aberdeen,[3] Sir Charles Long, Sir Matthew White Ridley[4] and Alexander Baring:[5] three M.P.s and a peer noted for their connoisseurship. The omission of the Surveyor General is noteworthy: it may be recalled that the previous October he had been severely reprimanded by the King, who had demanded a different organisation of the Office of Works under the control of Arbuthnot, then First Commissioner of Woods. There can be little doubt that these arrangements for Windsor were one of the consequences of the King's dissatisfaction with the conduct of the Works in the recent past.[6]

The first meeting of this commission was called for 4 May 1824, when the competitors' plans were to be submitted. Soane, hastening the rebuilding of the Royal Entrance to the House of Lords and wrestling with a parliamentary committee over the design of the Law Courts, had nothing to offer.[7] Nash's plans are not extant,[8] but those of Jeffry Wyatt and Smirke show that Long's influence was predominant. Smirke's royal entrance was precisely that suggested by Long: 'between two advanced battlemented Towers, in the style of . . . Lancaster Castle' (Pl. 18).[9] Jeffry Wyatt accompanied his clever, attractively-shaded and coloured designs with an explanation:

> These designs have been made under a most ardent impression to add to the magnificence of the Castle, and at the same time it has been considered as the best feeling not to entertain any vain notions of destroying the existing parts merely for the

[1] *Parl. Deb.* new ser. xi, 147 (5 April 1824; see also 22 February 1824).

[2] *Ibid.* See p. 150 above; also M. Whinney, *Sculpture in Britain 1530 to 1830* (1964), p. 199 and references there cited.

[3] 1784–1860, 4th Earl. Travelled in Greece in early life; president of Society of Antiquaries 1812–46. See *D.N.B.*   [4] 1778–1836. Bart., of Blagdon, Northumberland.

[5] 1774–1848, cr. Lord Ashburton, 1835. Owner of The Grange, Hants.

[6] See p. 106 above. In June 1827 J. C. Herries, Secretary of the Treasury, was added to the commisson by the King's command (T. 1/4398, f. 8035/28). In a letter to Lord Liverpool, 23 April 1824, the assistant secretary of the Treasury, George Harrison, explained the extent of the commissioners' functions by reference to Long's view 'that the superintendence of the Commissioners was considered as resorted to more for the regulation of matters of *taste* with reference to what connected itself with the fabric and improvements *immediately attaching* to it. . . .' (RA 34690).

[7] Soane Museum, corresp. 2, xii, B. 2, ff. 7–11. Soane had had plans of the castle copied in January–February 1824. It is a commentary on James Wyatt's methods that the plans furnished by the Office to Soane were pre-1800, showing nothing of Wyatt's alterations (Soane Museum, xxxix, 7).

[8] They appear to have been bound up in a book, for after George IV's death Nash wrote to Knighton to ask for the return of 'my book of the alterations which I proposed for Windsor' (Lady Knighton, *Memoirs of Sir William Knighton*, 1838 ii, p. 161).

[9] R.I.B.A. Drawings Collection, J. 11/29/1–33 and a perspective belonging to the Arts Club, London. Long's brief imposed on Smirke's designs a certain basic resemblance to Wyatville's, but for the quadrangle fronts Smirke preferred triple lancets and four-centred arches, giving a somewhat ecclesiastical character. His royal entrance in the south front was preceded by a bridge and free-standing gatehouse closely modelled on that of Lancaster Castle. A further massive towered gateway at right angles to Henry VIII's Gate closed off the royal precinct from the town.

purpose of shewing a presumed ability to make better, but in such few changes as are made to have in view the original character of its construction, though it would be perfectly ridiculous to restore the whole to the appearance of a dungeon like residence.

Though Windsor Castle is altogether an imposing and grand mass of building, it does not abound with picturesque parts, and those who have made such buildings their study will not think it any great stretch of vanity in the declaration that no great difficulty would occur in designing a building of the same magnitude, possessing both qualities in a superior degree.

It will be found on inspecting the drawings, that both the instructions of His Majesty and those given by Government have been followed, in paying attention to those points in the first instance which are almost indispensible, and upon such only have the calculations of expence been made to embrace the allotted sum of one hundred and fifty thousand pounds.

As some of the designs were formed before the sum to be expended was known it is hoped that no impropriety is committed by leaving them for inspection, though being excluded from the Estimate their execution is not under consideration.

The parts not expected to be carried into execution though shewn in the designs, are, the raising of the Round Tower, the reopening of the Fosse, the Gateway seperating the upper and lower Ward, and the extention of the Terrace towards the East, and the alteration of Queen Elizabeth's buildings. The parts Estimated according to the instructions given, are the repairs and alterations of His Majesty's apartments, the new corridor on two sides of the Court, the new entrance to the Quadrangle from the South, the construction of a new Staircase to the State apartments, and the improvement of the North front, and these are visibly distinct in the Drawings from the parts that are not Estimated. As each Drawing contains the necessary description it is quite unnecessary to waste any readers time by further remarks . . . the Drawings are intended rather to explain than to fascinate by superior execution.[1]

Jeffry Wyatt in fact submitted three alternative schemes. The most expensive, at £155,500, included a new octagonal tower at the proposed south gateway, a new tower to the King's Drawing Room on the north front, a tower-flanked grand entrance to the State Apartments, a staircase in Horn Court and a Waterloo Gallery on the site of the old kitchen. The other schemes represented various modifications of this, the cheapest (£147,000) placing the grand stairs in Brick Court and making the Guard Room into a Waterloo Gallery.[2] After several meetings of the commissioners, Lord Liverpool directed Wyatt to proceed only with the south and east fronts, together with the kitchen 'and everything necessary for the King's residence and convenience'.[3]

A partner since 1799 with John Armstrong in one of the largest London firms of building contractors, Jeffry Wyatt was well known also as a country house architect specialising in 'oldentime' mansions, his most notable works, perhaps, being the reconstruction of Longleat for Lord Bath in 1801–11, and the completion after the death of his uncle James Wyatt of Ashridge for Lord Bridgewater. He had also shown his capabilities in another form of 'picturesque' architecture: the *cottage orné* at Endsleigh in Devon for the Duke of Bedford that perhaps led to his being chosen to

---

[1] Royal Library, 'Designs for Windsor Castle by Jeffry Wyatt'.
[2] *Ibid.* no. 22.   [3] *Parl. Pap.* 1830 (656) ix, qq. 25, 45.

succeed Nash at Royal Lodge.[1] His designs approved, he set about making his arrangements: in July he wrote to various tradesmen already known to him, including Philip Nowell, a Warminster mason whom he had employed at Longleat, Robert Todd (bricklayer), and G. H. Lawrence, the Office of Works' bricklayer at the castle, who had worked there under his uncle.[2] Finding this a slow method, he sent out circular letters to the building trade inviting tenders at a percentage under the Office of Works' prices. Thus the principal contracts were settled,[3] and on his birthday, 12 August 1824, the King laid the first stone and sanctioned the 'honourable augmentation' of Jeffry Wyatt's name to Wyatville.

At first, Wyatville's accounts were sent direct to the Treasury, but when the rebuilding of Buckingham House began, that department decided that the accounts for both should be made up in the Office of Works. But when they were sent for examination, the Surveyor General reported that he was unable to carry out more than an arithmetical check, as he had no knowledge of the contracts or the amount of work done. A different arrangement was therefore made by which the architect's measurer, West, was employed by the Office of Works.[4] Stephenson complained that the contract prices were too high, an accusation Wyatville vigorously rebutted. He explained measures he had taken to reduce costs, and declared:

> I am perfectly justified in the conclusion, that such reductions having taken place at Windsor has operated upon all other works under Government. . . . So far from endeavouring to allow of overcharges, or of entering into useless expences, I have forborne to commence many of the works which I am authorised to perform, being unwilling to incur a charge of endeavouring from interested motives to prolong my employment, and also being unwilling to involve Government in an additional expence without due orders, as the completion of what is in hand will expend the allowed money . . .[5]

The first £150,000 was, indeed, soon exhausted. When Wyatville stripped the walls of the south and east fronts he found the timbers rotten, so that the whole of the floors had to be removed; he renewed them with iron joists and brick arches. The roofs, in an equally bad state, had also to be taken off; so he took the opportunity to add an extra storey, providing sufficient rooms for the royal servants.[6] The walls were found to be often cracked or mutilated by later alterations, and the foundations

---

[1] For Longleat, see *Country Life*, cv (1951), pp. 798, 862, 926, 990; Ashridge, *ibid*. iv, pp. 560, 592; Endsleigh ('the outstanding and probably most nearly perfect surviving instance of a romantic *cottage orné*'), *ibid*. cxxx (1961), pp. 246, 296.

[2] T. 1/4398, f. 359/25; for Nowell, see R. Gunnis, *Dictionary of British Sculptors*.

[3] The principal contractors and their rates below Office of Works prices were: Ambrose Oliver, excavator; Philip Nowell, Bath stone mason; Robert Todd, G. H. Lawrence, bricklayers; James Bedborough, mason; Thos. Jenner, Robert Tebbott, carpenters and joiners 5%; J. Foster, plasterer, 5%; F. Bernasconi, ornamental plasterer, 5%; G. Cooper, painter 5%; W. H. Cutler, plumber, 7½%; G. Spicer, glazier, 5%; Davis and Berridge, smiths, 7½% ; W. Hollis, labourer, 3% (T.1/4398, f. 359/29). To these were soon added Armstrong and Siddon, 'Gothic joiners'; T. George, plasterer; Jos. Bramah and Sons, ironfounders; W. & C. Adron, marble masons; and Edward Wyatt, carver and gilder (Works 5/109, 110).

[4] T1/4398, f. 18918/32; see above, pp. 135–6. Wyatville continued to receive a 5% commission on outlay, but did not charge for his journeys.

[5] T. 1/4398, f. 472/27, Wyatville to Treasury, 5 January 1827. He was able to show that he had obtained (e.g.) Bath stone at prices substantially below the 'common current price' (T. 1/4398, f. 359/25, 2 c).

[6] Works 34/233.

so bad that Wyatville had in some parts to go down 25 or 30 feet. When the commissioners saw the condition of the building, they added £100,000 (voted in May 1826) to the authorised expenditure and £27,500 for a new Tower, the Brunswick, in place of the shattered one of Henry II's time at the east end of the north terrace.[1] Additional estimates for these works and a new entrance tower to the state apartments, 40 feet square and 73 feet high, brought up the total to £388,000.[2] With these works rapidly approaching completion—more than 700 men were at work[3]—a further programme was authorised in 1828, embracing a Ballroom to be formed out of the King's Guard Chamber and Wyatt's Blenheim Tower,[4] the remodelling of St. George's Hall, the Royal Chapel, the Queen's Guard Chamber, and the 'north entrance' (Kitchen Court gateway), the restoration of the Devil's (now Edward III's) Tower, and the building of a new 'St. George's Gate' between the Devil's Tower and the foot of the motte. An orangery under the north-east terrace completed the works then authorised at an estimate of £106,000, which in May 1829 Wyatville found it necessary to increase by £16,000. The commissioners had been reluctant to include St. George's Hall in their programme: 'I had to show the state of the ceiling . . . in order to convince the Commissioners that it was much better to take it down than to keep it up', said Wyatville.[5] The commissioners recorded in a minute that in the opinion of the artists consulted, restoring the hall and chapel in the old style of decoration would cost more than the alterations proposed by Wyatville.[6] Their caution as to expense was justified: on 29 April 1828 the King complained bitterly to Knighton that Wyatville had been brought to a standstill by lack of funds, 'and was on the point of dismissing the greater part of that immense body of workmen'. But Wellington promised to find the means, and the work was able to continue.[7]

King George IV resumed possession of his castle on 8 December 1828, and on the following day knighted the architect.[8] He had a magnificent and comfortable residence which, as Long had insisted, retained all the external characteristics of a castle. His private apartments on the east front contained a spacious suite consisting of a library (now the Green Drawing Room) flanked by two drawing rooms (Crimson and White), each of which presented a variation on his favourite plan of a long room

[1] *Parl. Pap.* 1830 (656) ix, q. 112; Works 34/297 (designs for cast-iron joists and cap for [principal] floor over confectionary, Brunswick Tower, 1 March 1826: 'N.B. Great truth must be used in making the pattern and casting the cap that no day work may be necessary in fitting in the joists'), 295 (design for wrought iron ties for cast-iron floor joists, principal floor, October 1825), 296 (roof timbers, 28 August 1826), 298 (design for cast-iron girder, 7 February 1827, 'wanted immediately').

[2] *Parl. Pap.* 1830 (656) ix, p. 31: 4 January 1827, £50,000; 21 February 1828, £88,000; expenditure to the end of 1827 was £358,000 (T. 1/4398, f. 8035/28).

[3] On 10 August 1826 Wyatville told Knighton that 709 workmen were employed at the castle, 50 joiners were making sashes, etc., and 20 plasterers preparing ornaments; another 36 workmen in Windsor were occasionally employed at the castle (RA 23570–1). By 5 August 1828, the number of workmen at the castle had fallen to 520 (*ibid.* 24546).

[4] This is not shown in Wyatville's drawing of the north front before alteration, but it is incorporated in his plan.

[5] *Parl. Pap.* 1830 (656) ix, q. 262. Poynter, in his introductory essay to *Illustrations of Windsor Castle*, refers to a report by Wyatville, remarking, 'The old body of the plastering [of the ceiling] had in fact lost its *key*, and was ready to fall in patches on the slightest disturbance'. Earlier, there had evidently been some notion of adopting M.C. Wyatt's painting of St. George and the Dragon for St. George's Hall, see RA 30657–8 (October–November 1828).

[6] T. 1/4398, f. 8035/28; Works 34/284 (5 June 1828), 285, drawings of St. George's Hall roof.

[7] *Letters of George IV*, ed. Aspinall iii, pp. 402–3.

[8] *Gent's. Mag.* 1828 ii. p. 557; *Companion to the Almanac* 1829, p. 216.

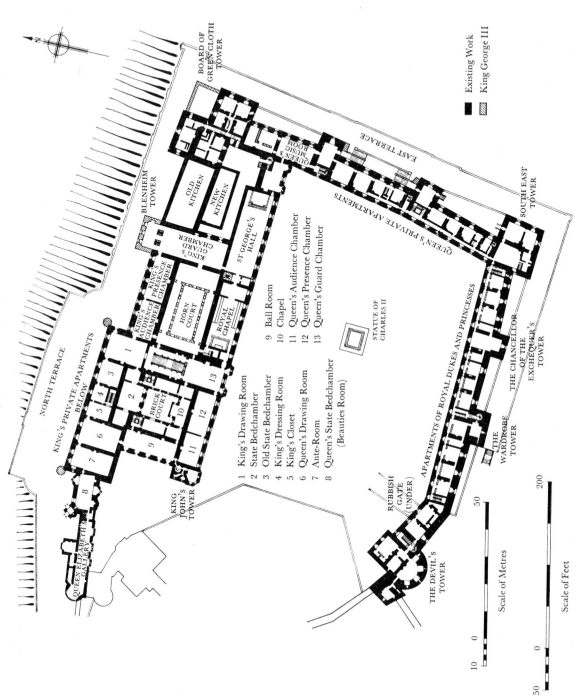

N

BOARD OF
GREEN CLOTH
TOWER

■ ▨ Existing Work

King George III

NORTH TERRACE

KING'S PRIVATE APARTMENTS
BELOW

BLENHEIM
TOWER

OLD
KITCHEN

NEW
KITCHEN

ST GEORGE'S
HALL

QUEEN'S
MUSIC
ROOM

EAST TERRACE

KING'S
GUARD
CHAMBER

KING'S
PRESENCE
CHAMBER

KING'S
AUDIENCE
CHAMBER

HORN
COURT

ROYAL
CHAPEL

QUEEN'S PRIVATE APARTMENTS

SOUTH EAST
TOWER

1
3
5 4
6
7
8

2

BRICK
COURT

9

10

11 12 13

QUEEN ELIZABETH'S
GALLERY

KING
JOHN'S
TOWER

9 Ball Room
10 Chapel
11 Queen's Audience Chamber
12 Queen's Presence Chamber
13 Queen's Guard Chamber

1 King's Drawing Room
2 State Bedchamber
3 Old State Bedchamber
4 King's Dressing Room
5 King's Closet
6 Queen's Drawing Room
7 Ante-Room
8 Queen's State Bedchamber
    (Beauties Room)

STATUE OF
CHARLES II

APARTMENTS OF ROYAL DUKES AND PRINCESSES

THE CHANCELLOR
OF THE
EXCHEQUER'S
TOWER

THE
WARDROBE
TOWER

RUBBISH
GATE
(UNDER)

THE DEVIL'S
TOWER

Scale of Metres

10   0   50

Scale of Feet

0   200

50

Fig. 10. Windsor Castle: the Upper Ward as occupied by George III; based on a plan in

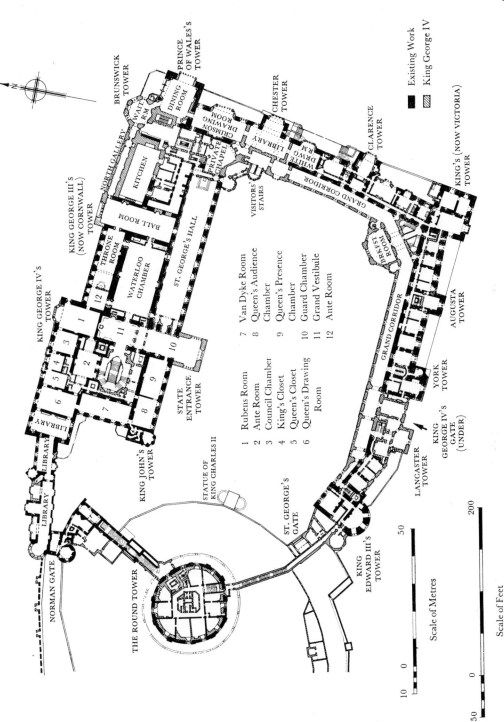

Fig. 11. Windsor Castle: the Upper Ward as remodelled by Wyatville for George IV and William IV: based on a plan in W. H. St. John Hope, *Windsor Castle* (1913) and a plan in the Public Record Office (Works 34/922). The Private Chapel was formed in 1843.

with a bow in the centre of one side.[1] All three rooms were adorned with fittings from Carlton House, notably doors and chimney-pieces.[2] The dining room was equipped with Gothic furniture designed by the 15-year old Welby Pugin.[3] The new Ballroom made out of the former King's Guard Chamber, 'a remarkably early case of neo-Rococo', perhaps owed something to the Elizabeth Saloon at Belvoir (dating from 1824).[4]

Authorised in 1829 to extend his operations to the remainder of the north front, Wyatville remodelled the Throne Room and Presence Chamber, putting new windows there and in the adjoining State Drawing Room, above which he constructed a tower,[5] demolishing his uncle's octagonal towers. The construction of the long-planned Waterloo Chamber in Horn Court was ordered, as well as that of a breakfast room (nearly completed by mid-1830) across the south-east corner of the quadrangle, balancing the Kitchen Court gateway on the north-east. Parliament had already voted £527,500, but expenses incurred amounted to some £34,000 more:[6] when the government asked for a further £100,000 the Commons turned hostile and forced ministers to postpone the vote and accept a select committee.[7] Under the chairmanship of a ministerialist, Calcraft, this reported in favour of completing the restoration at a cost of £148,796, which with the sum required for works in hand made a total of £277,000 to be voted. Windsor was more popular than the Pimlico palace, and Wyatville more fortunate, deservedly, than Nash: the committee exonerated him from 'any want of due precaution' in forming his estimates, blaming the increase on 'the nature of the undertaking itself'. But though recognising that expenditure in anticipation of votes of the House could not be wholly avoided, they recommended that it should be checked as much as possible. Among the further works approved was what is probably the most celebrated feature of all Wyatville's work, the heightening of the Round Tower, carried out in 1830–1.[8] After the coming to power of Lord Grey's administration a further select committee enquired into both Buckingham Palace and the castle, but limited its Windsor inquiries to the provision

---

[1] At Buckingham Palace he required this plan to be duplicated. A notable example of such a room, with which he was familiar, was the Regent's Gallery at Belvoir (James Wyatt, *c.* 1813); see C. Hussey, *English Country Houses: Late Georgian* (1958), p. 135. The window bay in the White Drawing Room at Windsor appears to have been added at a late stage of the planning (Works 34/249).

[2] The chimney-pieces in the White Drawing Room came from the Dining Room at Carlton House; those in the Crimson Drawing Room and the Green Drawing Room or Library from the Crimson Drawing Room and the Lower Vestibule; that in the Queen's sitting room (illustrated, Morshead, pl. 59) from the anteroom to the Throne Room, Carlton House. The doors came from the anteroom to the state apartments and from the Rose-Satin Drawing Room. RA 35217, 26 September 1826, lists 23 Carlton House chimneypieces for use at Windsor, as well as the parquet floors of the great drawing room, circular dining room and ballroom. The King also persuaded Wyatville to use Parrache's stained glass from Carlton House (placed in the Equerries' stair), see Morshead, p. 92; Lord Chamberlain's Office, Jutsham's MS. book of deliveries, iii, f. 100.

[3] B. Ferrey, *Recollections of A. N. Welby Pugin* (1861), p. 53.

[4] N. Pevsner, *Buildings of England: Berkshire*, pp. 39–40; Hussey, *loc. cit.* But Poynter in his introductory essay to *Illustrations of Windsor Castle* refers to 'the introduction . . . of old French boiserie of the age of Louis XV' as something 'which would never have appeared in the Castle had the architect been solely guided by his own judgment'.

[5] Works 34/311–313, roof to additional storey over George IV Tower, October–November 1832. The ceiling of the State Drawing Room was replaced in 1832, the old joists being '*decidedly too Rotten to Remain*' (Works 34/314, 7 December 1832).

[6] By mid-1830, £29,438 had been spent on purchases of land and houses, £471,656 paid for artisans' works, and bills under examination totalled £60,000.

[7] *Parl. Deb.* new ser. xxiv, 347–51; *Parl. Pap.* 1830 (656) ix.

[8] Works 34/327–30, 331–33. Works 34/330 shows how Wyatville constructed an inner skin to reinforce the old wall as a foundation for his superstructure.

of furniture under the Lord Chamberlain's department, for which bills of £294,000 had been submitted.[1]

The accession of William IV and his consort made 'numerous accommodations' necessary, involving an additional £35,000 by Wyatville's calculation.[2] During this reign he filled in Horn Court with his Waterloo Gallery, and Brick Court with his new oval State Staircase. Wyatt's stairs he demolished, forming on the site a lobby linking the quadrangle with the north terrace, opening to the west on the new stair. This rose in a single ascent to a landing from which twin flights returned to a vestibule over the lobby, so enabling the state apartments to be conveniently entered from the Queen's Guard Chamber (Pl. 23B).[3] The restoration of the state apartments he also completed, lengthening the Throne Room at the expense of the King's Audience Room, changing the chimney-pieces and putting new ceilings in the whole range of rooms to the west and in the Queen's Ballroom.[4] A parliamentary vote of £37,000 in 1834/5 completed the sum of £771,000 sanctioned by the Calcraft committee. In December 1835 Wyatville warned the Treasury that the bills for the Michaelmas quarter left a balance of only £3500, and that a further £20,000 over two or three years would be required.[5] Instead of special votes being obtained, however, Wyatville's works were continued slowly under the ordinary estimates, some £8700 (of which part was for the Tomb House) being spent under his direction in 1836–1838/9.[6] He had formed more extensive plans for a new private chapel between the Round Tower and the palace, for the restoration of the Lower Ward, and the provision of adequate stabling: he was permitted to embark only on the last, described separately below.[7]

When Wyatville died on 10 February 1840 he left the Upper Ward transformed into a palace worthy of the British monarchy. In place of what Queen Charlotte called 'the coldest house, rooms and passages that ever existed', he left 'a warm, dry, comfortable, well-appointed house'.[8] Nor did it lack a degree of magnificence appropriate to its function. Wyatville's work is naturally of its own time. What he was required to do—and what he did so effectively—was not to restore the castle with any degree of historical accuracy, but to carry out the programme of picturesque grandeur allied to internal convenience and comfort that Long had sketched out. The result was a masterpiece of Picturesque architecture that composes magnificently from almost any point of view, but does not bear inspection at close quarters, when Wyatville's coarse detailing and ubiquitous black ash mortar show a marked insensitivity to those variations in texture and profile that give life and interest to an

[1] *Parl. Pap.* 1831 (272) iv.   [2] T. 1/4398, f. 9838/35.
[3] See Hope, p. 369. The new staircase is shown in *Illustrated London News*, 1844, p. 232.
[4] Thus removing the work of his cousin M. C. Wyatt from several rooms, and leaving only the Queen's Audience and Presence Chambers with ceilings by Verrio; it was probably only shortage of funds that saved these, as the ends of the principals of the roof of the Audience ('Throne') Room were rotten. 'Flitches' were inserted to secure them (Works 34/294, May 1834). The chimney-piece in the Queen's Ballroom appears to have been removed from the Queen's State Bedroom (Cf. Pyne, *Windsor Castle*, opp. p. 116). Other chimney-pieces came from Buckingham House: that in the King's Bedchamber from the second drawing room (cf. Zoffany's 'The Prince of Wales and Prince Frederick', illustrated, J. Harris, G. de Bellaigue and O. Millar, *Buckingham Palace*, 1968, p. 226); that in the Queen's Chamber (by Bacon) from the Saloon (illustrated *ibid.* pp. 27, 29); that in the King's Closet from the Japanned Room (illustrated *ibid.* p. 105).
[5] T.1/4398, f. 25138/35.   [6] L.R.R.O. 24/4–7.   [7] See pp. 393–4.
[8] O. Morshead, *op. cit.*, p. 96, quoting a letter of Queen Charlotte to Lady Harcourt dated 6 November 1804, from *Harcourt Papers* (13 vols. 1876–1903), ed. E. W. Harcourt, vi, p. 83.

ancient building. Windsor Castle today is to all intents and purposes a nineteenth-century creation, and it stands as the image of what the early nineteenth century thought a castle should be (Pls. 19–22).[1]

When Queen Victoria required further improvements Blore was called in to superintend. During 1841 further repairs to the exterior of the Tomb House were carried out; and a general external and internal repair and painting of the Upper Ward begun.[2] The following year alterations were made to improve the accommodation of the now increasing royal family, a new heating system was installed, and additional water services provided as security against fire.[3] Blore contrived a private chapel out of the polygonal band room above the Visitors' Entrance.[4] His ingenuity was again called into play in 1846 to devise a private communication between the Queen's apartments and the orangery:[5] an underground passage was built with stucco mouldings to decorate its barrel vault.[6] A new arrangement of rooms took place about this time; and in 1848 further improvements in the heating apparatus were introduced to raise the temperature to 60°F.[7] Expenditure from 1838 to 1850 averaged close on £10,000 per annum.[8]

This large sum included, however, works in the Lower Ward as well. The houses of the Military Knights on the Upper Foundation, between the Henry VIII Gateway and the Henry III Tower, had had their brick chimneys and garden walls replaced by stone under Wyatville, who had received a vote of £7000 for this in 1830. From 1840 further external renovations were carried out by Blore, and a number of additional windows made.[9] In 1844–5 Blore carried out repairs to the Salisbury Tower, and in May 1845 Messrs. Locke and Nesham's tender of £4995 was accepted for converting that Tower and adjoining buildings, including the Henry VIII Gateway, as residences for the Poor Knights of Windsor on the Lower Foundation, retired officers hitherto accommodated in the seventeenth-century 'Crane's Building', between the Salisbury and Garter Towers. When the alterations were completed at a cost of some £6000, the old buildings were demolished in the spring of 1847.[10] The appointment of an additional clerk of the works for the castle in 1846 necessitated

---

[1] For assessments of Wyatville's work see Morshead, *op. cit.*, and D. Linstrum, 'Sir Jeffry Wyatville at Windsor', *Victorian Society's Annual*, 1969–70, pp. 41–50. Wyatville's work was described and amply illustrated in *Illustrations of Windsor Castle by the late Sir Jeffry Wyatville, R.A.*, ed. H. Ashton (Wyatville's assistant), 1841, with introductory essay on the history by A. Poynter (extensively quoted by Hope, pp. 361 ff.); and a rival publication by two others from Wyatville's office, M. Gandy and B. Baud, *Architectural Illustrations of Windsor Castle* (1842), with historical account by J. Britton. More than 200 drawings by Wyatville and others for the interiors of the east front, many initialled by the King, were sold at Sotheby's on 9 April 1970 (see illustrated catalogue). A number are now in the Royal Library and the Victoria & Albert Museum.

[2] Works 1/24, pp. 266, 281, 284, 537; 1/25, p. 113; 2/3, p. 429; 19/250.

[3] Works 1/25, pp. 338, 344, 353, 362, 370, 430, 482; 19/7, f. 2110.

[4] Estimates for Windsor Castle by Blore for 1843 totalling £6800 included £500 for alterations in the bandroom then used as a royal chapel in order to complete the adaptation. Transmitting the figures, Lord Lincoln requested Prince Albert to select works to the total value proposed, which he would order without delay. A memorandum by the Prince marks sums of £500 and £850 for the chapel (RA, C 26/48–9). The chapel was consecrated on 17 December 1843 (RA, Y 147/82).   [5] Works 19/40/6.

[6] Blore used the same mouldings in some of his corridors at Buckingham Palace. Henry Harley was the contractor at Windsor.

[7] Works 1/32, pp. 305, 342; 2/6, p. 392; RA, George V, CC 48/619.

[8] *Parl. Pap.* 1843 (343) xxx; 1851 (374) xxxi.

[9] Works 1/25, p. 113; 2/3, p. 429; 19/7, f. 2151; Crest 25/38, no. 1758; 25/50, no. 3720.

[10] Works 1/27, pp. 222, 278; 1/28, pp. 73, 103, 122, 421; 1/29, p. 20; 1/30, pp. 259, 371; 1/31, p. 58; 2/3, p. 553; 2/4, pp. 277, 284. Blore reported that the old houses were incapable of repair, and his first idea was to rebuild on the same site, see Works 34/234–9. For the history of these houses, see Hope, p. 531.

converting the architect's office into a residence for him.[1] In St. George's Chapel the ironwork of Edward IV's tomb was repaired and minor repairs executed to Princess Charlotte's memorial in 1844.[2] In 1846 £3000 were provided for the drainage of the castle, 'then in a state of the greatest filth', and further improvements were made in the years following; a new system of sewerage installed in the town facilitated the more efficient drainage of the castle by 'earthernware pipes of 9 inches and 6 inches diameter carefully jointed and cemented', flushed for five minutes daily. This entailed an improved water supply, and at least £11,500 (of which the Queen paid £1500) were spent on this in 1849–51.[3] Large sums were also spent by the Land Revenue in a town improvement scheme conducted by Pennethorne, clearing away houses from the castle ditch, widening adjacent streets, easing the ascent, and reforming the slopes of the castle.[4] Blore resigned his position at the castle at the end of 1847, and ordinary works were thereafter supervised by Phipps.[5] It was not until the 1860s that the restoration of the Lower Ward was completed under Salvin, who also reconstructed Wyatville's state staircase.[6]

2. THE STABLES

The stabling at Windsor had never been satisfactory.

> So great formerly was the want, at the Castle, not only of fit and commodious stabling, but of any stabling at all, that the horses and carriages of the Royal establishment and of the Sovereign's guests, could be accommodated only by dispersion in different parts of the town of Windsor, and the additions made to the mews of late years, were far from meeting the deficiency.[7]

Wyatville had accordingly provided for new stables on a long narrow site marked out by George IV on the south side of the castle hill, and the Calcraft committee had agreed that these were necessary. When the Clerk of the Works submitted an estimate of £1750 for repairs to the old stables in March 1835 Wyatville advised that it would be unwise to spend so much on ruinous buildings. Two years later he urged the need for new stables on Duncannon: 'It is not in idea to have external finery, but such substantial work as the situation merits'. Erected in parts, they might cost £80,000 over three or four years. The site itself clearly required the buildings to be spread out in several courts on various levels, precluding either an economical arrangement or 'grandeur of effect'.[8]

---

[1] Works 19/40/5. Jenner's tender of £704 was accepted, 7 September 1846.
[2] Crest 25/54, nos. 6652, 6835.
[3] Works 1/32, pp. 9, 148, 158, 368, 431; 1/33, pp. 55, 76; 1/35, pp. 44, 143, 146, 160, 256, 293–5, 312, 328, 341, 358, 397, 422; Crest 25/63, 9 November 1849; *Parl. Pap.* 1847–8 (656) xviii, pt. i, q. 2667.
[4] Works 19/30/2; 19/30/4; 34/183; Crest 2/62. When a railway station was projected in 1848, Pennethorne designed a bridge from it to the castle over Thames Street, to provide a private way for the Queen, Works 34/251. For an account of the improvements, see R. R. Tighe and J. E. Davis, *Annals of Windsor* (1858) ii, p. 370.
[5] Works 1/32, p. 451; 19/250, ff. 25–6; Crest 25/63, 10 April 1849.   [6] Hope, p. 370.
[7] H. Ashton, *Illustrations of Windsor Castle* (1841), p. 20.   [8] Works 19/40/2, ff. 1, 9, 11, 135.

The proposal was rapidly approved and a bill drawn for applying the arbitrary sum of £70,000 out of the Land Revenues;[1] but William IV's death deferred action. Some criticism was voiced in Parliament in 1838 of the failure to complete Wyatville's great works by building suitable stables, but the bill introduced in June 1839 nevertheless ran into opposition; Goulburn demanded production of the estimate.[2] It was not until 24 June, when the bill was safely through, that the Woods instructed Wyatville to prepare plans. The immediate object was now the construction of a riding house for the young Queen. Conversations between ministers and the architect determined the character of his design: a brick structure 'excepting such parts as will be seen in connection with the Views of the Castle'.[3] These parts were accordingly designed by Wyatville in a castellated style intended to harmonise with the Castle. Nowell's tender for a concrete foundation was accepted in August, and in December Grissell and Peto with a tender of £16,902 won the first contract against eight competitors.[4]

Work was progressing rapidly when Wyatville died in 1840; his assistant, Henry Ashton, was appointed in his place, receiving a fee of £2500, which with £1100 already paid made up the architect's five per cent commission.[5] With the Riding House up, the flanking stable courts were begun: by midsummer 1841, £35,000 had been spent; by Michaelmas, another £8800.[6] On 17 October 1842 Ashton announced that the stables, accommodating about 110 horses, were ready for Her Majesty's service. The total expense was £70,510, which included the conversion of the Lower Lodge for married quarters for about 30 stablemen, its external appearance made Gothic to accord with its surroundings.[7]

The hasty fitting-up (against Ashton's advice) of the Riding House for the Queen's recreation proved unwise: in 1846 dry rot was discovered. A patent cork and india-rubber composition, kamptulicon, was therefore substituted for the wall-boarding.[8] A projected tennis-court was abandoned, but Wyatville's proposal of a house for the clerk of the stables was executed in 1845-7 by the local firm of Jenner and Bedborough on a tender of £2040. Two years after its completion Prince Albert had the upper storey raised 18 inches and the parapet along the front towards the Mews raised four feet, work executed for £160 by Smith and Appleford.[9]

3. CRANBOURNE LODGE

Cranbourne Lodge in Windsor Forest had been the residence of George III's brother, the Duke of Gloucester, as Lord Warden. After his death in 1805 it was granted to the Hon. George Villiers. Between 1804 and 1808 it was 'completely

---

[1] *Ibid.* ff. 2, 3, 5, 6, 13, 14.   [2] *Parl. Deb.* 3rd ser. xlvii, 1401; xlviii, 30, 576.
[3] Works 19/40/2, ff. 15-16, 24; 34/265-70, designs by Wyatville.
[4] Works 19/40/2, ff. 18, 20, 26, 31-8. Even the highest tender, Tebbott's, was well within Wyatville's estimate of £19,081.
[5] *Ibid.* f. 49.   [6] *Ibid.* ff. 64, 87-8, 95-6, 104.
[7] *Ibid.* ff. 122, 132, 135-6. This is the building now known as 'Burford Lodge'. A proposal to repair old stables in St. Albans Street, intended to be demolished on completion of the new, was strongly resisted in 1842 by Lord Lincoln (B.M. Add. MS. 40481, ff. 42, 46, 52-4).
[8] Works 19/40/2, ff. 160-8.   [9] Works 19/40/4.

repaired and fitted up' by James Wyatt. The east front was rebuilt, the north-east, south-east and south wings were demolished, and instead a large octangular and a smaller square tower were erected to flank its plain classical façade.[1] In December 1809 the Queen and her daughters were reported to be 'in the continual habit of coming to the new apartments'.[2] Though at least £24,000 had been laid out, when in 1814 the house was required as a residence for Princess Charlotte the roof was found to leak, and repairs by Nash and the reinstatement of fittings removed by Villiers cost £2000.[3] When the Princess married in 1816 it was calculated that it would cost £10,000–£15,000 to make the house suitable for her enlarged establishment. Instead, Claremont was bought for her, and it was proposed that either Cranbourne should be demolished, or that it should be adapted for use by the royal hunt.[4] Eventually the Regent ordered its demolition, save for the larger tower, directing that the materials should be used in constructing new accommodation for the hunt.[5] It was Nash's responsibility to make the necessary plans, but owing to his dilatoriness nothing was done.[6] By 1830 the lodge was 'in a very ruinous state', at least £10,000 being required to make it habitable, so William IV ordered that it should be demolished, except for the octangular tower and staircase which were to be converted into a dwelling for a park-keeper. The operation was carried out by Wyatville at a cost of £782.[7]

4. THE GREAT PARK

The Great Park had been embellished by Thomas Sandby for George II's son, William Augustus, Duke of Cumberland, who was succeeded as Ranger by his nephew Henry Frederick, also Duke of Cumberland, on whose death in 1790 George III took the office into his own hands.[8] Thus the Great Lodge, or Cumberland Lodge, formerly the Ranger's residence, became part of the royal establishment. George III proceeded to enlarge it, probably creating the Gothic façade with Wyatt's help. But his works were left unfinished.[9] A general repair was necessary in 1814 when the Regent wished to accommodate his guests there while he resided in the former deputy ranger's lodge, rebuilt as a *cottage orné*.[10] The King's trustees in removing his property took from the new rooms bookcases for which the walls had been cut

[1] *Parl. Pap.* 1809, iv, pp. 286–7; Crest 2/47B (with detailed estimates of repairs and additions, 1805); R. Ackermann, *Repository of Arts . . . etc.* 3rd ser. 1823, i, pp. 63–4.

[2] Crest 2/47B, Nash to Surveyor-General of Woods and Forests, 19 December 1809.

[3] *Ibid. passim*; Works 19/44/14, ff. 1–4; 1/6, p. 453. In 1813 the tradesmen's outstanding claims amounted to £18,543 (Crest 2/47B, Nash to Commissioners of Woods, 18 December 1813). Nash himself briefly succeeded Villiers in occupation (*ibid.* 9 September 1814).

[4] Works 19/44/14, f. 7.   [5] Works 1/9, p. 37.   [6] *Ibid.* pp. 33–5, 245, 348, 422, 463.

[7] Works 1/18, p. 192; 5/111; *Parl. Pap.* 1833 (677) xiv, q. 2731. The sale of the old materials brought £1187 5s. 10d. (Works 5/111).

[8] See Colvin, *Dictionary*, s.v. 'Sandby, Thomas', and the sources there mentioned.

[9] Works 6/26, ff. 206, 209–10, 243. These works under George III do not appear in the Works accounts: a total of £1130 spent in 1806 related to new stables and outbuildings (Works 5/95; 6/26, f. 5 *et seq.*). George III went to Cumberland Lodge on 3 November 1804 'to see the great improvements making there' (*Gent's. Mag.* 1805, i, p. 67). In the *Windsor Guide* (1815) the Lodge is described as 'a large substantial building, but not possessing any architectural beauties', and so likely to be rebuilt (p. 181); the 1827 edition (p. 108) describes it as of stuccoed brick. A drawing of the Lodge forms part of a survey of the Great Park made by John Vardy for the Duke of Cumberland in 1750 (MR 280).   [10] See p. 399 below.

back, thereby imperilling the rooms above. Nash, living on the spot, undertook immediate repairs, and the Treasury approved estimates of £2547 in January 1815; but Stephenson, finding that further, unauthorised alterations had been carried out, stopped the works in February and they were not resumed until May.[1] In 1823 George IV ordered the old chapel to be converted into a kitchen for the stable establishment: its place was taken by a new private chapel at Royal Lodge. In the following year an orangery was authorised on Wyatville's estimate of £1020.[2] An ice-house was approved in 1826; and a series of alterations in the stables and offices were called for in May 1827. Forwarding estimates for £2051 to the Woods and Forests, the Surveyor General complained that 'the works are ordered in such rapid succession and are liable to so many variations in their progress that it is very difficult to obtain any satisfactory account of their cost until the works are nearly completed'. In November, sending to the Treasury a £500 estimate for alterations already begun by the King's command, he pointed out that the sum was indefinite as the plans were not even then finally settled. A royal proposal for new stables and coach houses costing £12,000 was deferred, but 20 temporary coach-houses were run up in the summer of 1829 at a cost of £1015, a proceeding criticised by the Treasury.[3] The lodge gardens, which included forcing pits and hot houses, were a constant source of additional expense.[4]

After George IV's death, the Lodge was conferred on the Duke of Sussex, and subsequently was inhabited by courtiers and younger members of the royal family. The stables, disused for many years and 'in a most dilapidated state', were repaired in 1840 for Prince Albert's hunters; and in 1847 the orangery was fitted up as loose boxes.[5] Schools were built near the stables at the Queen's desire for 123 children from the estate in 1844. Phipps' designs for schoolrooms for boys and girls and living accommodation for a master and mistress were estimated at £1350, an expense the Treasury thought 'beyond what the necessity of the case required'. Nevertheless a further sum of £400 was conceded for dining and washing rooms for the children, many of whom came 'great distances'.[6] The Lodge itself was largely rebuilt in 1869 (after a fire) and in 1912.[7]

George IV had also embellished the Park. The bridge over the artificial lake called Virginia Water, built by Sandby about 1785, was reported to be in a 'very bad state indeed' in November 1817, but it was not until 1826 that rebuilding was begun on Wyatville's estimate of £8600.[8] The estimate was exceeded, as the King had the walls at each end of the bridge extended to meet his new plantations, and much of the old stone was used in building a dry arch, hermitage and stone wall at the pond head, and forming foundations and walls for Roman ruins from Lepcis Magna in North Africa which had been presented to the King in 1816 by the Bashaw of

[1] Works 6/26, ff. 209–11, 244ᵛ–6, 257; 5/107.   [2] Works 1/12, pp. 90–1, 508–11; 1/13, pp. 43–5.
[3] Works 1/14, pp. 407, 498; 1/15, pp. 37, 233, 489; 1/16, pp. 64, 528; 1/17, pp. 104, 497, 506–7; 4/29, p. 435.   [4] Works 5/107–111.
[5] Works 1/18, p. 172; 1/24, p. 385; 1/29, p. 230; 1/31, pp. 197, 230, 270–1; *V. C. H. Berkshire*, iii (1923), p. 81; Princess Marie-Louise, *Memories of Six Reigns* (1959 edn.), p. 26.
[6] Works 2/4, pp. 504, 520, 526–9, 531, 536; 2/6, p. 117. Plans and elevations, MPE 615.   [7] See MPE 586.
[8] *Les Délices des Châteaux Royaux* (1785 edn.) (1790 edn. p. 119 n.); Works 19/44/13, f. 11; Works 1/13, pp. 57, 441–3; 1/14, pp. 209–11. Nash in 1817 had wanted to build a bridge 'of a lighter form and infinitely more ornamental . . . than the ugly clumsy Bridge in question' (Works 19/44/13, f. 12). For the Virginia Water see G. M. Hughes, *History of Windsor Forest* (1890), p. 293.

Tripoli; over £12,000 were spent in 1826–7.[1] The columns themselves, which had been reposing in the courtyard of the British Museum since their arrival from Africa in 1818, were conveyed to Virginia Water in 1826 by the Royal Engineers and set up under Wyatville's direction so as to form a landscape feature known as 'The Temple of Augustus'. Soon afterwards the King began to enlarge the Belvedere, a triangular Gothic tower built by Duke William Augustus in the reign of George II.[2] In submitting an estimate of £4000 for this building, dated 26 January 1828, Wyatville remarked on 'the anxiety that is entertained to begin'. Though Treasury approval was not accorded until 7 January 1829 the works were started; and in February 1829 Wyatville put in another estimate of £3300 for additional rooms and enlarging the battery of guns, works nearly completed by the end of April.[3] On 12 August 1829 the royal birthday was celebrated by a dinner party in the new rooms and by a salute from the enlarged battery.

Another of George IV's fancies was a 'fishing temple', for 'His Majesty frequently enjoys the recreation of Fishing upon the Virginia Water'. Wyatville's estimate of £3285 for repairing the boat house and boat-keeper's lodge on the island there, and building a small but ornamental structure for the King's comfort was in October 1825 given 'a due preference over other services not so immediately connected with the personal accommodation of His Majesty' charged on the Civil List.[4] The project rapidly grew in scope: within a year, £6595 had been incurred; the following year £2071 more.[5] In all by mid-1828 more than £15,000 had been spent on this wooden-framed building in the Chinese style, richly decorated by Frederick Crace with carved ornament, gilding and painting.[6] Its extension and decoration had proceeded without preliminary estimates, and the Windsor Clerk of the Works lamented that the best estimate 'must fall far short' for he had 'no Idea where they mean to stop'.[7] Greville described the finished structure in 1830 as 'one large room and a dressing-room on each side; the kitchen and offices are in a garden full of flowers, shut out from everything'. He also described tents on the shore, 'communicating together in separate apartments and forming a very good house, a dining-room, drawing room, and several other small rooms, very well furnished'. These tents, four large and four small, were supplied and erected at the charge of the Ordnance, which recovered the sum of £3170 from the King's executors.[8]

---

[1] Works 1/16, pp. 126–7; 5/109–110.

[2] Works 5/110. For the Roman ruins, see G. E. Chambers, 'The Ruins at Virginia Water', *Berkshire Archaeological Journal*, liv (1954–5). For Fort Belvedere see C. Hussey in *Country Life*, cxxvi (1959), pp. 898 and 960.

[3] Works 1/16, pp. 62–3; 1/17, pp. 165, 437; 19/44/15, f. 61. Expenditure on the Belvedere was charged against the Civil List and in 1829 amounted to £4825 (Works 5/110). See also Works 1/20, p. 218; 1/25, p. 551; Crest 25/50, nos. 4178, 4421, for subsequent repairs.

[4] T. 1/4398, f. 18971/25; Works 1/14, p. 407; 19/44/13, f. 14.

[5] Works 5/109–110. This also was charged on the Civil List, £6892 12s. 11d. in 1826 (Works 1/15, pp. 244–5).

[6] Works 5/109–110. Sketches, probably by Wyatville, of the boathouse, entrance to the Temple, and the scullery are in the Crace drawings at the Cooper Union Museum, New York, no. 1948-40-7. Drawings of the Fishing Temple are in the same collection, nos. 1948-40-96A and 96B, the latter a fine water-colour probably by Crace. Possibly the King was inspired by the fanciful Chinese hut built by the Duke of Cumberland in 1759 on 'China Island' in Virginia Water (see Hughes, *History of Windsor Forest*).

[7] Works 1/15, p. 405; 1/16, pp. 38, 214, 238, 282, 316, 354, 405; 19/44/13, ff. 16, 20, 21. Crace, in expectation of speedy payment, had reduced his prices between 15 and 25% (*ibid*. f. 23).

[8] Greville, *Diary*, ii, p. 30; *The Creevey Papers*, ed. Maxwell, ii, p. 233.

Last of George IV's works in the Great Park was a colossal equestrian statue of his father, designed to close the vista down the Long Walk from the castle. The statue, about 27 feet high and weighing about 25 tons, was commissioned from Richard Westmacott in 1824, and he was supplied with old brass cannon from the Ordnance.[1] Wyatville designed a granite pedestal 27 feet high, measuring 36 feet by 28 feet at the base, standing on a foundation of brickwork 16 feet high, of which half would be sunk into the ground and the remainder piled with earth to form a mound. His estimate for this 'immense work' was £16,000, subsequently reduced to £10,000 by using a cheaper granite from Haytor, and by specifying a cheaper form of brickwork.[2] Westmacott's statue, the horse's head detached from its body, and the king from his mount, was transported by wagon from London in August 1831,[3] and set up in October.

Little was added to the Great Park after George IV's death save keepers' lodges.[4] A private house called Holly Grove, built by Sandby for Col. Deacon, was added to the Park in 1829, reduced in size and made into a residence for the Deputy Ranger, Sir William Fremantle. It was repaired in 1842 and again in 1848.[5] William IV ordered repairs and alterations to the bridge and the Culloden Obelisk in 1833, and the Virginia Water itself required repair in 1834, when a serious leakage occurred at the sluice plugs, and again in 1849.[6] The fishing temple was repaired in 1841, though Jesse, who remarked that its good taste had been 'much questioned', would clearly have liked to demolish it. The deputy ranger, Fremantle, had already 'improved it' by removing some of the ornament in 1833. The adjacent cottage was enlarged in 1843, and a new boat house and store rooms were built in 1847 to Phipps' designs.[7]

5. THE HOME PARK

The old ranger's lodge was demolished in 1815. Some of the materials were re-used in building a thatched double lodge at the gates.[8] The head keeper's lodge formed the basis of Adelaide Cottage, the small *cottage orné* constructed by Wyatville for Queen

---

[1] Works 19/44/17, f. 25; *Letters of George IV*, iii, pp. 458, 484. The cost of the statue, £18,712, fell on the Privy Purse.

[2] Works 1/17, p. 444; 1/18, pp. 57, 88, 281; 5/111; 19/44/17. Tenders were accepted from Edward Turner for granite work at 4s. 4½d. per cu. ft., and C. and J. Oades for brickwork at £11 18s. per rod (*ibid.* ff. 3–6).

[3] Works 19/44/17, ff. 23–9; the cost was £113 16s. 3d.

[4] In 1834–5 a new lodge was built on High Standing Hill by Tebbott to Wyatville's design, to replace one burned down (Works 1/21, pp. 139, 155, 244–5). Wyatville also designed a woodman's cottage at St. Leonard's Hill in 1839, as well as two keeper's lodges in 1835 (Works 1/21, p. 388; 1/23, p. 335). Blore designed one at Flying Barn, built by Bedborough and Jenner in 1845, and enlarged another near Cumberland Lodge in 1846 (Works 1/28, pp. 214, 259; 1/29, p. 292). The Queen wished the gardener's cottage at Cumberland Lodge to have external additions 'of a Rustic character', carried out by the clerk of works, Whitman, in 1847 (Works 1/31, p. 203; 1/32, pp. 114–5; 2/6, p. 117).

[5] *Parl. Pap.* 1833 (677), xiv, q. 2731; Works 1/18, p. 478; 1/32, p. 141; 1/36, p. 199; 2/3, pp. 141, 318; 19/44/16, ff. 5–7; 34/260

[6] Works 19/44/13, ff. 34–5, 56, 119–20; 1/20, pp. 166, 182; 1/21, p. 22; 2/2, pp. 18, 27.

[7] Works 1/24, p. 508; 1/31, pp. 126, 167; 19/44/13, ff. 27, 90, 114, 116; L.R.R.O. 24/11, 24/16. See also Crest 25/38, no. 1328.

[8] Works 1/7, pp. 355, 486; 19/44/16, ff. 1–4.

Adelaide in 1831, partly out of materials from Royal Lodge.[1] Fenced with an iron railing,[2] it formed a private retreat for the Queen in a park then open to the public.

Dog kennels with a keeper's house were built in Home Park in 1840–1 to the designs of Henry Ashton. The original estimate of £1039 was increased to £1240, but additions were made in the course of building, £261 being paid from the Privy Purse.[3]

6. ROYAL LODGE

One of the most extravagant of the Prince Regent's architectural fancies was his Cottage in Windsor Great Park.[4] Intended at first as a temporary *pied à terre*, it soon developed into an expensive and fashionable *cottage orné*, complete with thatched roof, verandahs and other picturesque appurtenances. Although ingeniously designed by Nash to look as small as possible, it was constantly being enlarged, and though 'called a cottage, because it was thatched', it was still a very comfortable residence.[5]

The nucleus of this royal retreat was the former Lower Lodge or Dairy, a modest brick house once inhabited by Thomas Sandby in his capacity as Deputy Ranger of Windsor Great Park. Its conversion into the Prince Regent's Cottage was accomplished by Nash in 1813–14 under the Office of Woods and Forests at a cost of some £22,600.[6] When Nash on 28 November 1814 submitted a further estimate of £5851 the work was transferred to the management of the reconstructed Office of Works.[7] It transpired however that the new estimate was for

> Alterations, changes, and additions making in Work contained in former Estimates then in progress, and incomplete—that the same materials contained in other Estimates were taken down and parts used in other Estimates promiscuously so that it was impossible for the Accounts of the works of the several Estimates to be kept separate and distinct from each other. . . . [8]

This resulted in all the Cottage accounts being transferred to the Office of Works for examination, but no part of the works of 1813–16 costing £30,074 was executed under that Office.[9]

---

[1] Works 1/18, p. 404. O. Morshead, *George IV and Royal Lodge* (Brighton, 1965), pp. 43–4; R. R. Tighe and J. E. Davis, *Annals of Windsor* (1858) ii, p. 369, n.2. Works 19/508 contains a plan, and Works 34/954 elevations. Edward VII renamed it 'Adelaide Lodge', and the adjacent gardener's cottage became 'Adelaide Cottage'.

[2] Works 1/20, pp. 98, 144, 153, 156; 19/44/4.

[3] Works 1/24, pp. 392, 298, 406, 425; 1/25, pp. 56, 257; 2/2, pp. 435, 444; 2/3, pp. 122, 125, 421.

[4] The history of the Lodge has been elegantly recounted by Sir Owen Morshead, *George IV and Royal Lodge* (Brighton, 1965).

[5] This remark was first made by Castlereagh in the course of a Commons' debate on the Regent's debts (R. Huish, *Memoirs of the reign of George IV*, 1831, ii, p. 220). Another version is given in *Parl. Deb.* xxxi, 209.

[6] Works 1/6, pp. 365–6; abstract of tradesmen's accounts (Works 19/44/15, ff. 9, 14).

[7] *Ibid.* ff. 1, 2; 1/6, p. 334.   [8] Works 1/6, pp. 344–5.

[9] *Ibid.* pp. 350, 365, 431, 437, 450–2; 1/7, pp. 168, 280.

The first task for which the Office of Works was directly responsible was the construction of a ha-ha wall. This simple work offers a good example of Nash's careless methods of business. The wall was ordered in October 1817, tenders being obtained from four Windsor bricklayers.[1] Charles Dolby's bid, calculated at £1118 10s. 1¼d., was the lowest; but his bill, still unpaid in December 1818, was for £1733 2s. 10d., the difference being 'extras ordered by Mr. Nash'.[2] Invited to report on this bill, Nash remarked: 'I did not order any extras—the works were not executed under my directions though I felt myself entitled to find fault occasionally with the execution of the work'.[3] But Nash's specification of 4 October 1816 differed from one dated 24 October, delivered after the contract had been made,[4] and Dolby naturally regarded the additional requirements as 'extras.'[5]

In the same year urgent repairs were authorised to deal with dry rot in the middle drawing room before the Regent's visit for Ascot races, more extensive repairs being deferred until after his stay.[6] In September 1820 George IV, now King, peremptorily demanded that two guard rooms should be constructed.[7] This was merely a prelude to much more extensive additions at the east end (estimated at £6800), together with an entrance lodge (£1600) and improvements to the ha-ha, new drains, etc. (£1742) demanded in November. Although the Treasury declared no funds were available, the work went on under Nash, and in 1822–3 timber from the Great Park had to be cut to pay the tradesmen's bills, totalling £12,000.[8] Despite this expenditure, the conservatory was in a bad state,[9] and further works were required at the end of 1823, estimated at £5000. But these the King had determined to place under Jeffry Wyatt, soon to embark on his restoration of the castle;[10] and to avoid the irritation aroused in the King by Stephenson's adherence to official formalities,[11] they were to be done under the exclusive superintendence of the Office of Woods.[12] But when in 1827 a bath was to be constructed, and alterations made by Wyatville to the private chapel, the Office of Works was in charge once more—and indeed fell again under royal displeasure for failure to complete the bath in time for the King's Ascot week visit.[13]

Another wave of building began with an estimate of £1500 from Wyatville in February 1829. In April he told the Surveyor General that though without Treasury authority he had felt under an absolute necessity to proceed with these works, then nearly completed, 'His Majesty wishing it to be ready for him to go into at almost a

---

[1] Works 1/7, p. 292.   [2] Works 19/44/15, ff. 46, 50.   [3] *Ibid.* f. 48. Cp. 1/7, pp. 323–4.
[4] Works 19/44/15, ff. 48–9.   [5] *Ibid.* f. 54.
[6] *Ibid.* ff. 34, 36, 37, 40, 43 (£250 authorised immediately, of provisional estimate of £953).
[7] Works 1/10, pp. 220, 242 (estimate £680). Expenditure on the Lodge, 1813–21, was stated at £41,378 7s. 4d. (Works 1/13, p. 310).
[8] Works 1/10, pp. 253, 274; 1/11, p. 129; 1/12, p. 311; *Reading Mercury*, 2 April 1821, quoted by Morshead *op. cit.* p. 15. The principal tradesmen engaged on the Royal Lodge were Tebbott (carpenter), Dolby (brick-layer, discharged for using rotten bricks in making a well in 1821, Works 1/10, p. 345, and replaced by Hollis), Slark and Son (iron work), Bedborough (mason), and George (plasterer).   [9] Works 1/11, p. 251.
[10] Works 1/12, p. 316, 31 December 1823.   [11] See p. 106 above.
[12] See Morshead, p. 20, where a sum of £500 is referred to. In 1824–5 the thatched roof was replaced by slate (*ibid.* and *Windsor and Eton Express*, 8 June 1825).
[13] Morshead, p. 31. The bath was evidently not put in hand till the autumn of 1827 (Works 1/15, p. 449; 1/16, pp. 13–14). Other alterations were in progress in December 1827 (*ibid.* p. 38). Expenditure in the second half of 1827 and first half of 1828 on King's Lodge and Cumberland Lodge and gardens, etc. amounted to £4740 (Works 5/110).

day's notice'.[1] In January 1830 Wyatville gave in an estimate of £1350 for a new staircase and other works to be ready by May. Stephenson's annual estimates on the Woods and Forests account, dated 12 February 1830, included £5480 for the Royal Lodge; and on 10 March there came yet another estimate of £1130. The works embraced alteration of the conservatory and building the great dining room (the principal part of the Lodge to survive) which was not completed until after George IV's death.[2]

Despite the large sums spent on it, amounting in all to well over £60,000, the Royal Lodge was in need of extensive repair. William IV determined to demolish all except the conservatory, new dining room and adjacent chapel. As the Deputy Ranger explained to the Chancellor of the Exchequer in November 1830:

> The additions which his late Majesty made at this place were always rapidly constructed, for temporary convenience; the building had no vaulted foundation, and was consequently, in winter, hardly habitable from its dampness; the roof, raised only one storey in height, was so extended and varied, as to require constant and increasing expense; the buildings had no lodgments for the necessary attendants on a royal establishment, and was in every way unfit for such a purpose. When His present Majesty made a personal survey of this building, he could not but observe these defects; and having determined to reside in his Palace of Windsor, he no longer wished to impose on the public the burthen of maintaining the Royal Lodge, at an expense of at least 5000 *l.* p.a. With this view, His Majesty ordered the principal part of the building and paled inclosure to be taken down; the materials of the building . . . to go in aid of the building . . . of Windsor Castle; the paling, extending around these premises nearly two miles, to be applied in repair of the outward fences of the Park; and the ground immediately adjoining Cumberland Lodge, together with the conservatory and chapel, to be added to the lawn and garden belonging to Cumberland Lodge.[3]

Some fragments were reconstructed as Adelaide Cottage, a retreat in the Park for the Queen,[4] who also had a 'tent room' fitted up between the conservatory and the dining room.[5] These surviving rooms were saved from destruction in 1840 by Prince Albert, who installed his secretary there. To make them habitable works costing £485 were carried out in 1840, and an addition estimated at £300 was constructed the following summer by Whitman, the Clerk of Works.[6] After 1843 the Lodge was not regularly occupied for many years, but in the present century it has once more become a royal retreat in the privacy of the Great Park.[7]

[1] Works 1/17, pp. 165–6, 289; expenditure in the third quarter of 1829 added another £500 (Works 5/110–111).

[2] Morshead, pp. 38–42. The projected dining room was discussed by the King with Wyatville in September 1829 (RA. 24745); it was paid for from Duchy of Cornwall revenues and cost £8500. The three estimates referred to above, totalling £7960, correspond to the sum of the tradesmen's contracts, £7959 (incidentals, contingencies and commission brought the total to £8500) but this may be coincidental, as the new staircase 'etc.' were charged in the usual way on the Woods and Forests account of the Office of Works, payments in the first half of 1830 totalling £3906 (Works 5/111). The tradesmen employed on the dining room were Tebbott, Hollis, Bedborough, George, Cooper (painter, plumber), Butler (glazier) and Berridge (smith and ironmonger) (RA. 34634).

[3] *Parl. Pap.* 1833 (677) xiv, q. 2730.   [4] Above, p. 398.

[5] Morshead, p. 45; RA, Add. Q 3285. This probably relates to works by Wyatville costing £688 in the third quarter of 1831 (Works 5/111).

[6] Morshead, p. 45; Works 1/24, pp. 333, 342; 1/25, p. 69; 2/2, p. 430; 2/3, p. 30.

[7] For its subsequent history, see Morshead, pp. 45–6, and *Country Life*, lxxxv (1939), p. 706.

7. SWINLEY LODGE

The official residence of the Master of the Buckhounds, Swinley Lodge was sufficiently dilapidated in 1814 for its demolition to be proposed. Plans for the transfer of the hunt establishment to Cranbourne Lodge were still under consideration in 1818 when Lord Cornwallis, the Master, called attention to the nearly uninhabitable state of the building, particularly the bedrooms (of which there were twelve). Small sums were expended in 1821–3. In 1824 the house was said to be no longer habitable. It was not, however, demolished until 1831.[1]

[1] J. P. Hore, *History of the Royal Buckhounds* (1895), pp. 387–8 (engraving of 1795, p. 382); Works 1/7, p. 468; 1/8, p. 93; 1/9, pp. 33–5, 37; 19/44/14, f. 7; 5/108; Crest 2/56. Swinley Lodge and the Dog Kennels *c.* 1800 are illustrated, *V. C. H. Berkshire*, iii, opp. p. 77.

II. PUBLIC BUILDINGS

THE BRITISH MUSEUM

THE reorganisation of 1815 brought the British Museum within the jurisdiction of the Office of Works and, more immediately, within the purview of Robert Smirke. The building had previously been the responsibility of George Saunders, the Trustees' architect. Saunders had investigated the Office of Works and produced recommendations for its reorganisation and extension. He performed this task so efficiently that his own post at the museum became redundant. When Smirke took office schemes for extension or reconstruction had been in the air for more than a decade; so rapid was the museum's expansion that work continued unabated long after his retirement in 1846. Smirke's responsibility for the rebuilding of the British Museum must therefore be understood as part of a continuous historical process. Such an organic approach helps to resolve an initial difficulty with regard to the museum's architectural history. For at the outset historians are faced with a problem of chronology. What relation, if any, does the design of the museum bear to the designs of contemporary Continental museums? What was the date of its conception? Is it a precedent, a copy or an independent production? Attempts have been made to place the design more exactly in its European context, and these attempts have meant the postdating of Smirke's design by no less than thirteen years. In brief, it is supposed that the dramatic conception of the entrance front dates not from 1823 when the original plans were officially approved, nor from 1833 when these plans were modified for the sake of economy, but from 1836 when they were first published in diagrammatic form.[1] Now the British Museum certainly formed part of a general European movement, that alliance between the cult of the antique and the fashion for organised *kultur*, which engendered a rash of museum-building during the post-Napoleonic period. But a strict examination of the genesis and chronology of Smirke's scheme reveals that the design was almost certainly conceived with no more than indirect reference to its Continental counterparts, Klenze's Glyptothek in Munich (1816–30) and Schinkel's Altes Museum in Berlin (designed 1823, built 1825–28).

Since their establishment in 1753 the various collections which formed the basis of the British Museum had been housed in Montagu House, designed in a French style by Robert Hooke in 1676, reconstructed after a fire in 1686 and purchased by

---

[1] N. Pevsner, 'The British Museum, 1753–1953', *Architectural Review* cxiii (1953), p. 179. 'Begun 19 years after Schinkel's Altes Museum had been engraved. . . . Smirke must have known Schinkel's uninterrupted phalanx of Ionic columns. . . . Both Schinkel and Smirke . . . were no doubt familiar with Durand's design for a vast museum, published in 1808' (N. Pevsner, *The Buildings of England: London except the cities of London and Westminster*, 1952, p. 209). 'Built between 1841 and 1847 and there is no need to suppose that it was conceived much earlier' (Sir John Summerson, *Architecture in Britain, 1530–1830*, 1963 edn., p. 305). 'Probably not decided on until the thirties; such a redundancy of columns seems to belong well into the second quarter of the century' (H.–R. Hitchcock, *Architecture: 19th and 20th centuries*, 1958, p. 68). Hitchcock's earlier judgment does less violence to the evidence: 'Through most of the 1840s Sir Robert Smirke was proceeding with the British Museum, but with no stylistic modification of his original Grecian design of the early 1820s' (H.–R. Hitchcock, *Early Victorian Architecture in Britain* i, 1954, p. 294).

the Trustees for £10,250 in 1754. By the early nineteenth century this 'disgraceful place', as John Wilson Croker called it, 'known by the name of the British Museum', with its bizarre gateway, colonnaded forecourt, great staircase and painted ceilings, appeared increasingly unsuitable: 'a strange "Mismach" of works of art, natural curiosities, books and models, preserved in a miserable building'.[1] In 1802 George III's presentation of the Egyptian antiquities captured at Alexandria prompted the Trustees to set up a buildings committee consisting of Sir Joseph Banks, Sir William Hamilton, Thomas Astle and Charles Townley.[2] Their report, presented in the following year, laid down the pattern of the museum's future growth. They recommended a programme of staggered expansion with galleries running northwards from the main building first to the west and then to the east of the garden behind Montagu House. It was this programme which was begun by Saunders in 1804 and more than fully implemented by Smirke from 1816 onwards. Saunders produced several alternative proposals: two Palladian and one in the style of Montagu House. One of the Palladian versions was chosen. From the beginning, therefore, no attempt was made to imitate the architecture of the original building. Saunders' Townley Gallery (1804–8) survived as a Palladian anachronism surrounded by Smirke's new Grecian work until 1846.[3]

The purchase of the Phigaleian and Elgin Marbles in 1815–16 reinforced the wisdom of the Trustees' programme and coincided with the prospect of additional finance afforded by absorption into the Office of Works. Immediate problems of accommodation were solved by a temporary expedient. Since Lord Elgin's return to England in 1806 his priceless collection had been stored in the houses of the Duchess of Portland and the Duke of Richmond and then exhibited to the cognoscenti of the metropolis 'in a damp dirty penthouse' at No. 6 Park Lane. In 1812 another eighty cases of marbles arrived in London. After prevarication by the government and opposition from the egregious Payne Knight, who believed most of them Hadrianic, the marbles were bought in 1816 for £35,000.[4] Meanwhile, as an interim measure

[1] *Parl. Deb.* N.S. ix (1823), p. 1123, 20 June 1823; E. M. Butler (ed.) *A Regency Visitor*, letters of Prince Puckler–Muskau, trans. S. Austin (1957), p. 53, 15 October 1826. For Montagu House cf. Buckler architectural drawings, B.M. Add. MS. 36370, ff. 31–5; R. Wilkinson, *Londinia Illustrata* (1819); *Gent's. Mag.* 1814, pt. i, pp. 458, 557; 1845, pt. ii, p. 517; S. and R. Percy, *London* iii (1824), p. 286; *The Builder* ii (1844), pp. 324, 432; vii (1849), p. 199; *Illustrated London News* viii (1845), p. 199; E. Walford, *Old and New London* iv (1883–4), pp. 492, 511; M. Batten, 'The Architecture of Robert Hooke', *Walpole Society* xxv (1936–7); I. Dunlop, 'The First Home of the British Museum', *Country Life* 14 September 1951.

[2] Sir Edward Maunde Thompson, MS. History of the British Museum (c. 1898), B.M. Add. MS. 52292, Buildings section, ff. 1–6.

[3] Townley told the Principal Librarian, Sir Joseph Planta, that the new buildings should be 'a pattern to be followed in this improved age . . . without pretensions to expensive magnificence or fantastic novelty', (B.M. Add. MS. 36524, f. 33, 3 May 1803). The Townley Gallery, containing the Alexandrian, Hamilton and Townley collections, was linked to Montagu House by two passages, top-lit by circular tribunes, and cost some £28,000 (*Gent's. Mag.* 1810, pt. ii, p. 209, exterior; R. Ackermann, *Repository of Arts* iii, 1810, Plate 23, interior; *The Athenaeum* 1846, p. 1301). Saunders may have drawn up plans for further extensions dated 1803 and 1810 (Sir F. Madden, Collections relating to the British Museum, B.M. Add. MS. 38791, f. 55; B.M. Archives, 'Plans of the B.M. Premises' and 'B.M. Plans', i; *The Athenaeum* 1847, p. 573). He received commission, but no salary ('Report from the Select Committee on the . . . British Museum', *Parl. Pap.* 1835, vii, p. 301);

[4] This was far less than Elgin had spent in obtaining them, and little more that he already owed the government in taxes. The Phigaleian marbles had cost the government £19,000 ('Report from the Select Committee on the Earl of Elgin's Collection, 1816', *Parl. Pap.* 1816, iii, pp. 49–225; Diary of Sir Henry Ellis, B.M. Add. MS. 36653, i, 29 June 1816; A. H. Smith, 'Lord Elgin and his Collection', *Journal of Hellenic Studies* 1916; Sir Henry Ellis, *Elgin and Phigaleian Marbles* 2 vols., 1833). Among the early visitors to Park Lane were Haydon, Lawrence, West, Flaxman, Fuseli, Hamilton, Knight and Smirke.

Royal Academy students were permitted to gaze upon them in Burlington House. With the help of Flaxman, Westmacott and a marble cutter named Pistell, Smirke designed two prefabricated rooms to the west of the Townley Gallery. 'Constructed of frame work with fir timber and single bricks', they cost £2500.[1] Despite the risk of fire and its increasingly 'decaying state', this structure, visited by Keats and Severn and indeed by every contemporary aesthete, enshrined the Elgin and Phigaleian marbles until 1831. In that year part was demolished and part prepared as a temporary depot for architectural casts.[2]

Repairs to Montagu House between 1810 and 1815 had cost as much as £20,000; and during his first few years Smirke supervised alterations to the library and saloon which involved the use of cast iron supports and cost another £5000.[3] In 1819 it was suggested that the building be demolished and a new museum be erected as a national monument in Waterloo Place.[4] But in the following year the Trustees revived their programme of 1803 and directed Smirke to begin collecting information as to the museum's requirements. For this purpose he went to Sir Henry Ellis, Sir Joseph Planta, Taylor Combe and Edward Hawkins, as well as the Trustees' advisory committee: Sir Joseph Banks, Sir Charles Long (later Lord Farnborough), 'Athenian' Aberdeen, Lord Spencer, Lord Seymour and Richard Payne Knight. In February 1821, on behalf of the Trustees, he recommended to the Treasury the erection of two parallel wings and began to prepare detailed estimates.[5] For nearly two years plans were held up by litigation with the neighbouring landowner, the Duke of Bedford.[6] Just as permission was secured the project assumed a new importance: in January 1823 George IV formally offered his father's library to the nation and the British Museum accepted responsibility for the 'gift'.[7] The projected east wing became the King's Library and the first stage of Smirke's grand design.

While still a student at the Royal Academy, Smirke had worked on monumental schemes in the French *Grand Prix* tradition, adapted from designs by George Dance and incorporating the use of columnar screens, twelve years before Durand published similar projects in his seminal *Leçons d'Architecture* (1809).[8] In 1797 he produced 'designs for a Square and a Palace proposed to be built in Hyde Park'.[9] In 1799 he won the R.A. Gold Medal with a 'Design for a National Museum'.[10] Both schemes reflect the Parisian influence transmitted via Dance, and both anticipate some

---

[1] Works 1/10, f. 337; Works 1/7, ff. 213–4, 9 August and ff. 348–9, 9 December 1816. For Smirke's plans cf. Works 33/3 and 33/563–4. The Elgin Room cost £1697 17s. 6d. ('Report from the Select Committee on the . . . British Museum', *Parl. Pap.* 1835, vii, p. 309).

[2] Works 17/1/2, f. 165, 30 November 1831.

[3] Works 1/10, f. 78, 6 April 1820; Works 1/6, 13 September 1815; Works 1/10, ff. 76–7, 6 April and ff, 107–8, 11 May 1820. Smirke's plans and cross-sections are Works 33/1, 21 September 1815, 5 January 1816.

[4] *Gent's. Mag.* 1819, pt. i, p. 6.   [5] Works 1/10, f. 336, 13 February and f. 339, 19 February 1821.

[6] Duke of Bedford v. Trustees of the British Museum, before Lord Eldon, Chancellor, and Sir T. Plumer, Master of the Rolls, 6 July 1822 (Thompson MS., B.M. Add. MS. 52292).

[7] Lord Liverpool's government is said to have paid the King some £180,000 out of the Droits of Admiralty in order to prevent the library being sold to the Emperor of Russia (*Quarterly Review* lxxxviii, 1850, p. 143). The story was subsequently denied (*ibid.* xcii, 1852, p. 179 n.). For the Prime Minister's letter of acknowledgement to George IV cf. Liverpool Papers clxxxi, B.M. Add. MSS., 38370, f. 144, 16 January 1823.

[8] R.I.B.A. Drawings Collection J 11/1–2; B.M. Print Room, B.M. Portfolio, Case 243.

[9] R.I.B.A. Drawings Collection J 11/5. The designs were 'delivered to Mr. Tyrwit, the Prince of Wales' Secretary' (Farington, p. 1070, 19 July 1797).

[10] B.M. Print Room, B.M. Portfolio, Case 243. George III thought this design 'very neat and creditable'; but he longed for the Palladian grandeur of the 'Old School' (Farington, p. 1691, 10 December 1799, p. 1737, 16 January 1800).

columnar characteristics of Smirke's elevations for the British Museum. Thus the museum's decoration bears the characteristic imprint of European Neo-Classicism. But its composition, the projecting wings, the 'centre and ends' arrangement, rests firmly on the traditions of British Palladianism. And here a convincing source has been suggested: Sir Edward Lovett Pearce's Parliament House in Dublin, now the Bank of Ireland, begun in 1729 and engraved by Malton with figures by Robert Smirke Snr. in 1792.[1] But suggestions that Smirke's great entrance front was designed not in 1823 but in 1836, and was therefore susceptible to a number of intermediary precedents, can only be substantiated by making light of contemporary evidence and by leaning heavily on the suspect reporting of a dubious magazine for dilettanti.[2]

In 1824 this periodical had published a rumour that the new museum was to follow the precedent of Somerset House: a quadrangle pierced by a vaulted entrance carriageway, a quotation borrowed by Chambers from the Farnese Palace in Rome and hardly palatable to a Greek Revivalist like Smirke. *The Times* printed the story, but followed it a few weeks later with Smirke's official statement, itemising a piece-meal quadrangular plan, an elaboration of the programmes of 1803 and 1821.[3] It was this scheme for progressive reconstruction which was presented to the Treasury in July 1823, and to the members of a select parliamentary committee at about the same time, before being lodged with the Trustees.[4] Tenders for the first stage were accepted during the autumn. Despite changes in 1833, this general plan remained unpublished until 1836.[5] The entrance elevation was not published until 1844.[6] Even official access was limited to a specially prepared scale model, located from about 1830 onwards in the old Trustees' room at Montagu House, surrounded by gems from the library of Clayton Mordaunt Cracherode.[7] Smirke considered that the entrance front could not be 'very satisfactorily shown in a drawing', and preferred

---

[1] Cf. a note by Maurice Craig, *Architectural Review* cxiv (1953), p. 282.

[2] *The Somerset House Gazette and Literary Museum; or weekly miscellany of fine arts, antiquities and Literary Chit Chat*, ed. Ephraim Hardcastle [W. H. Pyne], i (1824), p. 242, 24 January 1824.

[3] *The Times*, 28 January and 20 February 1824. It was also rumoured that Montagu House 'is not to be pulled down, but repaired and beautified, so as to correspond as nearly as possible with the new work' (*Gent's. Mag.* 1822, pt. ii, p. 260).

[4] Works 1/14, f. 282, 30 May 1826. 'The three sides of the quadrangle might be built and occupied while the central apartments of the present house and the wings containing the apartments of the officers continue to stand, and the quadrangle could be completed according to the designs, when it became desirable or necessary to take down these old buildings' (Works 1/12, f. 219, 27 November 1823; Works 4/26, f. 118, 11 July 1823; Sir John Soane's Museum, Soane Correspondence xii C, January 1824; 'Estimates and Accounts', *Parl. Pap.* 1824, pp. 215–7). The King's Library 'should evidently form part of an entire plan, for the present edifice . . . is in a decaying state . . . the existing building would not interfere with such a general design; it would be appropriated to its present uses until the various objects contained in it were gradually removed into the new edifice' ('Report from the Committee on Papers relating to the Royal Library', *Parl. Pap.* 1823, iv, pp. 48–9).

[5] 'Report of the Select Committee on the British Museum', *Parl. Pap.* 1836, x, p. 1; R.I.B.A. Drawings Collection J 11/41 (1–2).

[6] The secret appears to have leaked out, and in March 1844 Smirke sent prints of the entrance front, lithographed by Mackenzie, to several of his patrons, including the Earl of Lonsdale, the Archbishop of Canterbury and Sir Robert Peel. 'I did not make it to gratify any feeling of pride in the architectural display', he told Peel, 'but I was induced to make this having lately seen some very bad engraved representation of it' (Peel Papers cclxi, B.M. Add. MS. 40541, f. 218. 14 March 1844; letters to Smirke in the possession of Sir Edward Malet, Bt.).

[7] Memoranda by Sir F. Madden, Collections relating to the British Museum, B.M. Add. MS. 38791, f. 55. 'About 1803 a large volume of drawn plans and sections of the museum by Mr. George Saunders, Archt., was kept in a corner of the Cracherode room, behind an upright mahogany case. In the same room, in 1830 or afterwards, used to stand the model of the new museum by Sir Robert Smirke'.

'reference to be made to the model'.[1] In the spring of 1844, in order to kill speculation and uninformed criticism, Sir Robert Peel assured the House of Commons that
the entrance front, then in process of construction, had never been altered, but
exactly followed the design originally authorised twenty years previously.[2] Six years
later Sir Robert Inglis repeated this statement in his evidence before a Parliamentary
Commission.[3] Peel had been Home Secretary in 1823 and both he and Inglis were
Trustees of the museum, sitting on the parliamentary committee of 1838 which
investigated the building programme. Inglis was also for some years a member of
the Trustees' sub-committee on buildings. But apart from their authors' experience,
there are good reasons for accepting these statements. We know that a provisional
masterplan was drawn up and authorised in 1823. Several variant proposals for the
entrance may well have been submitted. However, no drawings or specifications
survive to substantiate the rumour of a plan derived from Somerset House. Instead
we have a number of drawings by Smirke in several different collections. One set
of plans dated June 1827 shows the colonnade in its final form.[4] Others, variously
watermarked 1822, 1823 and 1825, show preliminary schemes for the entrance and
quadrangle elevations.[5] The date (1823) of one undated drawing for the interior
of the quadrangle (Plate 24A) is beyond dispute: the design follows another
dated '8th July 1823' and a third which is dated 1836 but inscribed 'according to the
arrangement of the general plan made in 1823'.[6] Another undated drawing—one of
a pair (cf. Pl. 24B)—showing a scheme similar to the final entrance front is almost
certainly datable to the year of its watermark, 1822. There is no stylistic reason for
doubting that this columnar project is in fact part of the provisional scheme presented
to the Treasury in 1823. The elements of the final entrance front are clearly visible in
Smirke's unexecuted design for the north side of the courtyard and in his variant
elevations for the exactly contemporary General Post Office.[7] The final form of the
entrance front can be traced to these experiments with colonnades and porticoes in
1821–3, which in turn derive from the architect's early training under Dance
and perhaps from a visit to Dublin in 1817. Similarly, the quadrangular plan,
rectangular rather than square, can be traced to *ad hoc* decisions by the Trustees
dating back to 1803 and to the advice of museum officials in the period 1821–3. In
particular, according to W. R. Hamilton, it was Sir Joseph Banks who demanded 'a
simple quadrangle, with four rooms below and four rooms above, large oblong
galleries'.[8] Finally, one crucial item of evidence clinches the argument. In August

[1] Peel papers cclxi, B.M. Add. MS. 40541, f. 218, 14 March 1844.

[2] 'In 1822 a resolution was passed that any plan pursued in the construction of the façade should be referred to the Lords of the Treasury, and in 1823 they approved of the plan. That plan had subsequently been laid before the two committees in 1836 and 1838, and received the sanction of those committees' (*Parl. Deb.* N.S. ix, 1823, p. 1358. 1 July 1823; lxxiv, 1844, p. 355, 29 April 1844; *The Athenaeum* 1844 p. 434; *The Times* 30 April 1844, p. 2).

[3] 'The plan of the South façade of the British Museum . . . was adopted by Lord Liverpool's government twenty six years ago' ('Report of the Commissioners appointed to inquire into the . . . British Museum', *Parl. Pap.* xxiv, 1850, p. 783).   [4] B.M. Archives.

[5] B.M. Print Room, B.M. Portfolio, Case 243; R.I.B.A. Drawings Collection J 11/41 (4); B.M. Archives, 'B.M. Plans', i, fo. lv–lvii; author's collection.

[6] MPD 38.   [7] Victoria and Albert Museum, Print Room, A. 173.

[8] 'Report of the Commissioners appointed to inquire into the . . . British Museum', *Parl. Pap.* 1850, xxiv. p 833. In 1754 Cornelius Johnston had published a quadrangular plan for a new museum (B.M. King's Maps xxiv, 17a); cf. *Apollo* August 1969.

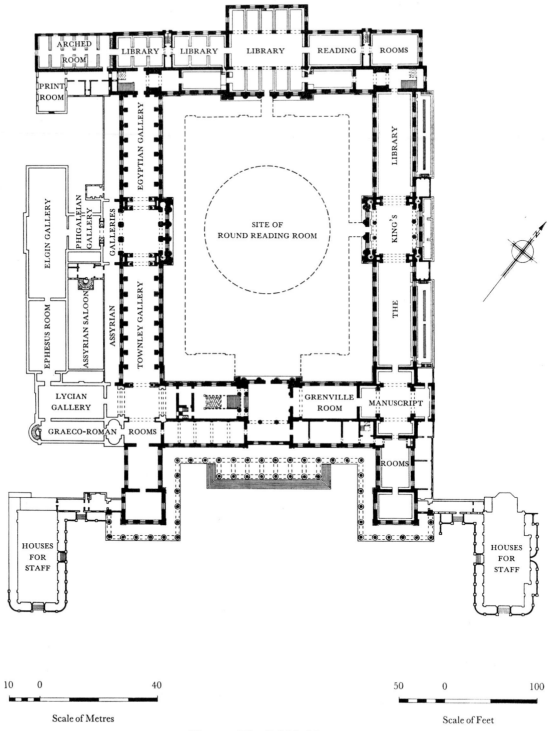

ARCHED ROOM

LIBRARY LIBRARY LIBRARY READING ROOMS

PRINT ROOM

EGYPTIAN GALLERY

LIBRARY

THE KING'S

ELGIN GALLERY

PHIGALEIAN GALLERY

GALLERIES

ASSYRIAN

SITE OF
ROUND READING ROOM

EPHESUS ROOM

ASSYRIAN SALOON

TOWNLEY GALLERY

LYCIAN GALLERY

GRAECO-ROMAN ROOMS

GRENVILLE ROOM

MANUSCRIPT

ROOMS

HOUSES
FOR
STAFF

HOUSES
FOR
STAFF

10   0   40

Scale of Metres

50   0   100

Scale of Feet

Fig. 12. The British Museum.

1823, Smirke took advice as to the design of the façade from his ablest pupil, C. R. Cockerell. Cockerell made a note of the meeting in his diary, and obligingly inserted a sketch plan of the colonnade.[1]

All in all, the evidence indicates firstly that in 1821 work began on a general plan which was finished early in 1823; secondly that this took the form of a closed quadrangle variously embellished with internal and external colonnades; and thirdly that in its essentials this scheme remained unaltered. As for the suggestion of plagiarism, Smirke answered this question, slightly equivocally, before the parliamentary committee of 1836. He admitted examining the designs of other museums and libraries during the preparation of his own plans in 1821–3. 'But there are none of the same description . . . in regard to the extent and variety of the collections . . ., and some of the best were not then built. The great buildings at Berlin and Munich were not then erected. . . . The only Library I had seen possessing any character of architectural importance was the Imperial Library at Vienna, which is a room about 230 ft. long and more expressive and magnificent in its decoration than any room in the museum here'.[2] Now Klenze's Durandesque Glyptothek at Munich was certainly begun before the British Museum. But it lacks the columnar characteristics of Smirke's design, and even its quadrangular plan can have been no more significant in the genesis of its English equivalent than the circumstances of the Bloomsbury site.[3] Years later W. R. Hamilton complained that not too much but too little attention had been paid to contemporary Continental museums.[4]

Although Smirke's plan remained substantially unaltered, the elevations underwent two important changes. Until 1833 he intended two of the internal façades to carry elaborate porticoes.[5] Visitors would enter the giant entrance colonnade, pass through the entrance hall and emerge from a second portico facing into the open quadrangle. To enter the northern wing they might then cross the quadrangle, mount an imposing flight of steps and pass through another portico, the third. Smirke surrendered his original scheme 'with great regret', but he 'had the satisfaction to hear that both Lord Grey and . . . [Lord Cottenham] expressed the same regret'.[6] Economy and lack of space reduced the two internal porticoes from majestic to decorative proportions. The same reasons ruled out the possibility of a linking corridor along the north wing, despite arguments based on coherence and convenience. The central area proved useless for botanical purposes, and so far from stimulating 'a free circulation of air', could be described as 'a mere well of malaria, a pestilent congregation of vapours'.[7] Indeed conditions both financial and climatic rapidly reduced Smirke's great quadrangle to the status of an enormous white elephant. Thus, at a parliamentary committee:[8]

---

[1] Diary of C. R. Cockerell, 7–8 August 1823.

[2] 'Report of the Select Committee on the British Museum', *Parl. Pap.* 1836, x, pp. 444, 448.

[3] For the quadrangular plan of Klenze's Glyptothek cf. O. Hederer, *Leo Von Klenze* (München, 1964), p. 193, and a drawing by C. G. Crace, R.I.B.A. Drawings Collection U 11/5.

[4] 'Report of the Commissioners appointed to inquire into the . . . British Museum', *Parl. Pap.* 1850, xxiv, 834.

[5] For Smirke's original proposals for the quadrangle see MPD 38; B.M. Print Room, B.M. Portfolio, Case 243; R.I.B.A. Drawings Collection J 11/41/(4).

[6] 'Report of the Select Committee on the British Museum', *Parl. Pap.* 1836, x, p. 458.

[7] *Mechanic's Mag.* xxvi (1837), pp. 457, 459 n. For the quadrangle as executed, see Smirke's drawings, Works 33/401, 409, 520 and C. Knight, *London* vi (1871), p. 164.

[8] 'Report of the Select Committee on the British Museum', *Parl. Pap.* 1836, x, p. 445.

> Mr. Hawes: 'When will the public have a view of the architecture of the inner quadrangle?'.
> Sir Robert Smirke: 'When they are in the quadrangle'.

Unfortunately few visitors shared the architect's confidence in the English weather. The quadrangle remained closed, visible only through the glazed panel of a subsidiary door in the entrance hall, and in 1852 it was agreed that the area be filled in to form the Round Reading Room.

The other point of departure from Smirke's original elevations was the alteration of the entrance front during the early 1840s. It originally echoed the General Post Office in that it lacked ornamental sculpture and possessed a continuous plain parapet.[1] There was even some intention to place the royal arms, a little incongruously, over the main doorway. But as the emphasis on the quadrangle diminished in 1833, so that on the entrance front proportionately increased. Moreover, popular criticism, blindly speculating on the unpublished elevation, may well have persuaded Smirke during 1842–44 to bend a little before the early Victorian demand for additional decoration. Earlier severity was tempered by several new proposals: the modification of the string course, the enrichment of the central entrance, the inflection of the parapet and the inclusion of sculpture within the pediment and upon its apex and corners, the addition of sculptured groups flanking the steps, and sculptured friezes adorning the centre and wings[2] (Pl. 25). However, of these proposals, which T. L. Donaldson later claimed would have set the seal on 'one of the finest compositions of modern times', only three were effected: the alteration of the doorway and string course, the rhythmic variation of the parapet and the insertion of Richard Westmacott's pedimental sculpture *The Progress of Civilisation*.[3] Economy prevented the completion of Smirke's grand design. Worse still, the great colonnade has never been seen to full advantage, although one of Nash's unfinished schemes for the Trafalgar Square area included an avenue linking Charing Cross with Bloomsbury, a tremendous vista aligned on the axis of the British Museum.[4]

Working drawings for the east wing of the new museum were available in 1823, for part of the west wing in 1826, for the north wing in 1831–3 and for the southern

---

[1] R.I.B.A. Drawings Collection J 11/41 (3).

[2] For different stages in the development of the South front compare R.I.B.A. Drawings Collection J 11/41 (3 and 6); Works 33/400 and 414, 12 July 1841; *Illustrated London News* iv (1844), p. 28 and vii (1845), p. 357; *The Builder* vii (1849), p. 187. For criticism of the central door cf. *Civil Engineer and Architect's Journal* xii (1849), p. 289; *The Builder* vii (1849), p. 188. Smirke's formal proposals for decorative sculpture were made at the time of his retirement in 1846. His estimate was £5800 (B.M. Add. MS. 52292, 15 August 1846).

[3] *Journal of the R.I.B.A.* 1867, p. 206. Westmacott had 'a horror of appearing in print' but agreed to produce a description of his sculpture which was later expanded by Sir Henry Ellis: 'Commencing at the Eastern end . . . man is represented as emerging from a rude savage state through the influence of religion. He is next personified as a hunter and a tiller of the earth. . . . Patriarchal simplicity then becomes invaded and the worship of the true God defiled. Paganism prevails and becomes diffused by means of the Arts. The worship of the heavenly bodies . . . led the Egyptians, Chaldeans and other nations to study Astronomy, typified by the centre statues, the keystone of the composition. Civilisation is now presumed to have made considerable progress. Descending towards the Western angle of the pediment, is Mathematics. . . . The Drama, Poetry and Music balance the group of the Fine Arts on the Eastern side, the whole composition terminating with Natural History' (B.M. Add. MS. 38626, ff. 198–202). The sculpture cost £3750 (Sir F. Kenyon, *The Buildings of the British Museum*, 1914, p. 5). The scheme was one of Westmacott's last, and indulged in a touch of polychromy: the tympanum was tinted blue and the ornaments were gilded.

[4] MR 1575 (1825) and MR 1483 (1825). One opportunity of reopening this vista was lost in 1946; another presents itself in connection with the construction of a new national library opposite Smirke's museum.

entrance front in 1841–4. 'There was a general arrangement considered and sanctioned . . . but each part successively, as it was ordered, underwent a detailed consideration'.[1] Between 1823 and 1852 the vast quadrangular structure slowly enveloped first the garden to the north of the old museum, and then the site and forecourt of the old building itself. The new courtyard was larger than Hanover Square. 'And strange it was to see the lofty pitched roof, balustraded attic and large-windowed front of "the French manner" giving way to the Grecian architecture of Sir Robert Smirke's new design'.[2] It was not until June 1847 that the 'decayed and dangerous' clock turret of Montagu House was finally removed.[3]

The east wing was finished within five years, at a cost of £130,000.[4] On the ground floor the King's Library, above it the Natural History Collection; at the southern end manuscript rooms and at the northern end an entrance from Montagu Place and a substantial single return staircase to the first floor. The Angerstein Collection of paintings, which was to have occupied the first floor, became instead the nucleus of the National Gallery. During the summer of 1829, George III's library was transported in vans from Kensington Palace to its new home, resplendent with oaken bookcases, inlaid mahogany flooring, and galleries of burnished brass.[5] It was a setting worthy of a collection once housed in Chambers' octagonal library at Buckingham House, and for which no less a repository had been proposed than Inigo Jones' Banqueting House in Whitehall.[6] The King's Library (300 ft. × 41 ft. × 30 ft. high with a central compartment 58 ft. wide) is almost certainly Smirke's finest interior design. Yet its spatial rhythms remain sluggish, and the general effect of its decoration is one of ponderous grandeur. The introduction of circular panels into the mass of plaster coffering is slightly anomalous; and the abrupt divisions created by the galleries detract from the room's lofty effect. The high cost of polishing the columns of Aberdeen granite with their Corinthian capitals of Derbyshire alabaster precluded the originally planned, and more effective, demarcation of the central area by eight additional columns.[7] As it is, the yellow scagliola pilasters seem insufficiently substantial, unlike the doors at either end, heavily framed with architrave and console. Stylistically hybrid and spatially dull, the King's Library is fully redeemed by the integrity and magnificence of its decoration. In particular,

[1] 'Report of the Select Committee on the British Museum', *Parl. Pap.* 1836, x, p. 445.

[2] J. Timbs, *Romance of London* (1865), iii, 177.

[3] Works 17/1/2, f. 171, 9 January 1834; Works 17/2/1, f. 442, 8 June 1847.

[4] Works 4/26, f. 231, 27 November 1823; Works 1/16, ff. 234–5, 1 April 1827. Smirke's estimate had been £129,200 (Works 1/16, ff. 234–5). For separate estimates and tenders 1823–6 cf. Works 4/26, ff. 130, 146, 150, 168, 231, 308; Works 4/27, f. 66, 133, 378, 502. The banking crisis of 1825–6 caused temporary difficulties in payment (Works 4/27, ff. 351, 363). The following tradesmen contracted: James McIntosh, excavating; Messrs. Baker, brickwork, carpentry, joinery; Mr. Freeman, masonry; Messrs. Jukes, Coulson & Co., ironwork; Mr. Kepp, copper roofing; Mr. Cobbett, glazing; Messrs. Palmer, plastering; Messrs. Dixon, painting; Messrs. Forster, ironwork.

[5] Works 17/1/2, f. 104, 24 August 1829; Works 4/29, f. 75. The cost of transport was £222 7s. 1d. For reasons of 'domestick feeling', George IV retained at Windsor about thirty valuable volumes. Nautical charts were sent to the Admiralty (Peel Papers cxx, B.M. Add. MS. 40300, ff. 246–54; Sir F. Barnard, MS. List of volumes retained by the King, B.M. Pressmark 11912 b55).

[6] Peel privately deprecated the library's disposal and agreed with those who suggested the Banqueting House (Peel Papers ccxiii, B.M. Add. MS. 40393, ff. 52–9; *Parl. Deb.* N.S. ix, 1823, p. 1112, 20 June 1823).

[7] *Gent's. Mag.* 1834, pt. i, p. 21. The columns were cheaply obtained, ready worked, for £15 apiece but their polishing raised their total expense to £2400. Had the original plan been executed, the layout would have corresponded with that of the parallel Egyptian Gallery. For Smirke's plans and working drawings of the east wing, cf. Works 33/4–163.

the details of the entablature show Smirke at his most fastidious. Alone among his works the King's Library proved almost immune to criticism.[1]

While rooms at the southern end of the east wing were being fitted up as manuscript and reading rooms (now the Middle and South MSS. Rooms),[2] work was progressing on the west wing. This block was needed primarily to rehouse the Elgin Marbles, whose accommodation was by 1825 in a state of 'impending ruin'.[3] Nevertheless its erection proved dilatory. By 1830 only the shell had been constructed, but thenceforward the Treasury proved more liberal and authorised the transference of the marbles and their 'fixing . . . in the manner proposed by Mr. Westmacott'.[4] By 1831, therefore, both floors of the east wing had been completed, as had the new Elgin Room; of the west wing, continuing Saunders' block northwards and joining the new Elgin room by means of the Phigaleian (now Nereid) Room, only the interior of the upper floor remained incomplete. Two sides of the great quadrangle, faced with Portland stone, with mouldings modelled on the Erechtheion, a single row of windows and attached Ionic porticoes, confronted each other across the garden of Montagu House, shaming its old colonnade which had 'long been observed to be in a deplorable state'.[5]

The reorganisation of the Office of Works in 1832 in no way diminished Smirke's position as architect of the British Museum. In fact he profited from the new arrangements. Besides receiving a compensatory knighthood he retained responsibility for the museum, but as an independent architect, with commission increased from 3% to 5%.[6] The Office of Woods and Works continued to be responsible for the execution of works designed by Smirke and approved by the Trustees.

The cost of running repairs at Montagu House, which between 1821 and 1833 totalled £14,566 13s. 7d., annually emphasised the necessity for further rebuilding, and in the latter year work began on the north wing of the new museum.[7] Five years later two new reading rooms (later the Music and Catalogue Rooms) were opened at its eastern end, with a separate entrance from Montagu Place. Printed

[1] E.g. *Library of the Fine Arts* ii (1831), p. 269 *et seq.*; *Foreign Quarterly Rev.* vii (1831), p. 455; *Polytechnic Journal* iii (1840) p. 53. Some critics preferred the decoration of Klenze's Glyptothek on stylistic grounds (*Gent's. Mag.* 1835, pt. i, p. 362). For a view of the exterior soon after completion cf. Buckler drawings, B.M. Add. MS. 36370, f. 36.

[2] These supplemented the old reading rooms in Montagu House (*Penny Mag.* iv, 1835, p. 487; v, 1836, p. 365). 'The reading room is . . . situated in an obscure corner of the premises, and approached by a labyrinth, leading along a gutter and over two drains' (H. S. Peacock, *Remarks on the Present State of the British Museum*, 1835, p. 7).

[3] Works 17/1/2, f. 84. Four years previously Smirke had warned the Treasury that in case of fire the marbles 'would inevitably be reduced to lime, as their weight would preclude the possibility of removing them on any such sudden emergency' (Works 1/10, ff. 336–9, 13 February 1821).

[4] Works 1/18, ff. 314–7, 6 December 1830; Works 1/2, f. 155, 12 August 1831. Westmacott thought the Elgin Room 'one of the finest rooms in the world; and . . . as finely lighted as any room I know' ('Report from the Select Committee on the . . . British Museum', *Parl. Pap.* 1835, vii, p. 289). As originally planned in 1826 it was to have projected westward at right angles to the west wing, instead of running parallel to it.

[5] Works 17/1/2, f. 84. In 1834 minimal external repairs were executed. Smirke did 'not provide for any other expenditure upon the turret over the gateway in the centre of the colonnade than what is necessary to preserve it from falling—the timber of which it is built being altogether in so decayed a state that it cannot be repaired' (*ibid.* f. 171).

[6] Between 1815 and 1832 Smirke's 3% commission on the British Museum totalled £5427 17s. 1d. (Works 1/16, ff. 104–7, 7 February 1828; Works 1/19, f. 21).

[7] Smirke's estimate for the structure was £70,000 (Works 17/1/2, f. 171, 1 August 1834; *Gent's. Mag.* 1834, pt. i, p. 423). Messrs. Henry and John Lee contracted for bricklayers', masons' and carpenters' work (Works 1/20, f. 243, 11 September 1835).

Books and Manuscripts were now distributed at either end of the King's Library. Some praise was bestowed at first on the reading rooms' heating and ventilating systems: four 'great sort of chests of hot water pipes' covered with marble slabs to appear 'exceedingly classical and ornamental',[1] and metal tubes conveying foul air into flues emerging from openings in the ceiling. But the Museum Headache and 'Museum Megrims', like the Long Room Fever at the Custom House, and perhaps even the death of Mr. Smith, Curator of the Print Room, were signs of the inadequacy of such ephemeral patent processes.[2] The adjoining Large Room,[3] (rebuilt as the North Library 1936–38) was still unfinished when in 1838 the number of visitors, 'increasing beyond precedent or expectation',[4] prompted the Trustees to press the Treasury for additional grants, and a parliamentary committee, headed by Sir Robert Peel, began an investigation of all accounts.

In his evidence before the committee Smirke estimated the cost of finishing the structural parts of his great scheme within six years at £250,000. 'Should the progress of the buildings', he warned, 'be continued in the same slow and uncertain manner as it hath hitherto been (having to the present time occupied a period of fourteen years since the commencement), I cannot give any assurance that my estimates will . . . be found correct'.[5] Although Smirke's estimates proved fairly accurate, the museum's expansion demanded still greater expenditure. As a precaution against overspending, annual Treasury grants were generally prefaced with demands for 'the utmost retrenchment' or 'the most rigid and severe economy'.[6] But between 1823 and 1849 expenditure totalled £696,995 and by the time the new museum had been completed, in 1852, the total had soared to about £800,000. Even as the building neared completion schemes were in preparation for the circular reading room, which was to add another £150,000 to this sum. Further extensions, notably the White Wing (by Sir John Taylor, 1884),[7] the Edward VII Galleries ('Greek re-Revival' by Sir J. J. Burnet, 1914) and the Duveen Gallery (the Elgin Marbles' latest home, opened 1961) have been made by each succeeding generation. Between

---

[1] *The Times* 10 September 1838, p. 6; *The British Almanac and Companion* 1838, p. 242; G. F. Barwick, *The Reading Room of the British Museum* (1829), pp. 81–4. Alterations were made in 1850 (*The Builder* viii, 1850, p. 440). Smirke's plans, Works 33/259, 271; plans and working drawings of the north wing, Works 33/189–319.

[2] Smirke used Perkins' system in the Museum Print Room, Bird Room and Reading Rooms, in the Custom House Long Room, in his own office at 5, Stratford Place and in his temporary Houses of Parliament. He used Price and Manby's system in the Elgin and Egyptian Galleries, and Stratton and Oldham's at the General Post Office. See Works 4/26, f. 290; Works 1/23, f. 398; Works 1/24, f. 197; *Architectural Mag.* ii (1835), p. 137, iii (1836), p. 91 and iv (1837), pp. 161, 263; C. J. Richardson, *Warming and Ventilation* (1837), dedicated to Smirke. The British Museum was contrasted with the Bibliothèque du Roi, Paris, where readers 'must keep themselves warm as well as they can' (Report of the Select Committee of the British Museum, *Parl. Pap.* 1836, x, p. 451).

[3] *Illustrated London News* xviii (1851), 507 (interior).

[4] For comparative statistics of visitors and receipts cf. *Gent's. Mag.* 1833, pt. i, p. 351; 1834, pt. i, p. 424 and 1836, pt. ii, p. 81; *The Athenaeum* 1836, p. 452 and 1844, p. 68; *The Builder* ii (1844), pp. 70, 84, iv (1846), p. 165, v (1847), p. 145 and vi (1848), p. 146; *Illustrated London News* x (1847), p. 269 and xiv (1849), p. 207. On Monday, 2 January 1843, 'no less than 30,000 persons visited this National Establishment! The conduct of all was orderly, and there was not one single instance of drunkenness or indecorum' (*The Athenaeum* 1843, p. 22).

[5] 'Report from the Select Committee on the British Museum', *Parl. Pap.* 1837–8, xxiii, p. 9; *Civil Engineer and Architect's Journal* i (1838), p. 346. 'The delay in the building which has so often been attributed to [Smirke's] inaction and inattention proceeds, in reality, from the parsimony of Government, who have seldom granted more to the annual building-fund of the Museum than half what was applied for' (*Mechanics' Mag.* xxvi, 1837, p. 459 n.).

[6] E.g. Works 1/23, f. 232, 7 December 1838; Works 1/25, ff. 224 and 542, 19 August 1841 and 1 November 1842.   [7] Cf. Taylor's plans, Works 33/1159–64.

1823 and 1860, when the Office of Works handed back responsibility for the structure to the Trustees, £1,090,274 13s. 6d., had been spent on rebuilding, £113,367 on repairs and £44,924 on the purchase of land.[1]

The decade 1839–49 was occupied by the construction of the Arched Room (1840–41), the Lycian [later Archaic Greek Sculpture] Gallery (1845), the Phigaleian Gallery (1847), the Long Room parallel to the King's Library (1846–50) and the great southern entrance façade (1841–48). As the entrance front grew so Montagu House was demolished in three stages, and the sites for two blocks of keepers' houses were prepared on either side of the forecourt.[2] Several houses belonging to the Duke of Bedford and occupying sites contiguous to the proposed forecourt were purchased in 1840 for £28,000.[3] During this period of transition the Principal Librarian, Sir Henry Ellis, resided at 70 Great Russell Street, which had been specially fitted up by Smirke at a cost of £530.[4] Between 1844 and 1849 the keepers' houses were constructed, first the western block and then the eastern. Messrs. Jeakes supplied firegrates; Messrs. Barron & Co. were responsible for paperhanging in accordance with Smirke's instructions that 'the drawing rooms are to have satin papers with a lining paper under them', and the other rooms 'plain suitable figured papers'.[5]

1840 was a crucial year in the architectural history of the museum. In that year a deputation headed by Sir Robert Peel persuaded the Treasury to sanction a higher rate of expenditure, and plans were put in hand for the construction of the entrance façade.[6] Messrs. Grissell & Peto, who had submitted the lowest tender for the south front, began work in September 1841, but in the following July transferred their contract to Messrs. Baker & Sons, the builders of the other three wings and contractors for the majority of Smirke's London works.[7] Smirke's sister Sarah had married the head of the firm, Samuel Baker of Rochester, and this special relationship between architect and builder did not escape the notice of Smirke's more malicious critics. The architect's specification stipulated 'hard, sound, grey stock bricks . . . mortar of Dorking, Halling or other stone lime . . . ground to a fine powder and mixed . . . with clean sand taken from the river above Blackfriars Bridge'; iron cramps for the stonework of Portland and Yorkshire stone; 'the best Memel, Riga and Danzig timber'; Craigleith and Gazeby stone for the steps and paving of the portico, and for the main staircase, 'steps and landings of stone from Elland Edge or other of the hardest and most compact quality of Yorkshire stone'.[8] By 1842 the walls had reached roof level, and Messrs. Kepp were employed to cover the roof with copper. No competition was held for this particular contract. 'The material is so rarely used', Smirke informed the Commissioners of Woods and Works, 'that I do not know of any other tradesmen employed in such work except upon a very small

[1] For tables of estimates, expenditure and parliamentary grants cf. Thompson MS., B.M. Add. MS. 52292; Works 2/5, f. 449; Sir F. Kenyon, *The Buildings of the British Museum* (1914), pp. 2–3; *Gent's. Mag.* xxxii (1849) p. 402; 'Accounts and Papers', *Parl. Pap.* 1860, xxxix, p. 295.
[2] For the sectional demolition of Montagu House cf. B.M. Add. MS. 52292 ff. 18–20; Auction catalogue 1843, B.M. press mark 1044 c. 35 (2–3). In 1845 it was decided that the painted ceilings could not be preserved.
[3] Works 17/1/3, 30 June 1840.   [4] Works 1/25, f. 509, 15 September 1842 and f. 549, 3 November 1842.
[5] Works 17/2/1, ff. 330, 337, 459. For plans and working drawings of the keepers' houses cf. Works 33/788 *et seq.*
[6] 'Communications . . . respecting the Enlargement of the British Museum', *Parl. Pap.* 1852, xxviii, p. 235.
[7] Works 17/2/1, ff. 177, 179.
[8] Works 17/2/1, f. 20. Plans and working drawings of the south front, Works 33/390 *et seq.*

scale'. Messrs. Robson and Estall were chosen as plasterers: 'all ceilings are to be lathed with double laths made of sound fir, nailed with nails of wrought or cast iron . . . with Keene's cement for the plastering of the walls of the principal rooms'.[1] Messrs. Collman and Davis were responsible for interior decoration. Glazing was supplied by Messrs. Cobbett and Son.

The entrance front, indeed the whole museum, gave Smirke a chance to display both the Grecian style and his mastery of constructional techniques upon the largest possible scale. The spacious, box-like galleries, his whole conception of a modernised Grecian architecture, rational, austere and economical, depended upon concrete and cast iron. At Millbank Penitentiary in 1817, he had been the first English architect to demonstrate the value of concrete foundations.[2] There is no evidence that concrete was used for the foundations of the King's Library in 1823 or for the first section of the west wing in 1825. The ground was presumably strong enough to support brick footings set in cement. But numerous working drawings survive to show that a concrete base between 2 ft. 6 in. and 6 ft. thick was used for the later wings, that is for all work after 1833.[3] The concrete raft supporting the colonnade is in places more than 6 feet thick. Fire-proofing was supplied in the form of slate flooring by William North. Besides traditional decorative materials such as marble, mahogany and bronze, much use was made of scagliola, papiermâché, Keene's cement and encaustic polychromy in hypothetically Grecian hues. Cast iron, usually disguised by plaster coffering, supported the ceiling and roof of every room, from the joists of the prefabricated Elgin Room (1816) to the beams (made by Foster, Raistrick & Co. of Stourbridge, 1824) of the King's Library, where Smirke even considered replacing the central pillars of polished granite by exposed cast iron columns.[4] Messrs. Dewar, who contracted for most of the later ironwork, including that supporting the great entrance front, were told to use 'castings made from pigs of the best English iron . . . all perfectly sound and smooth', tested by weights in the foundry under the architect's supervision, and 'secured from rust by two coats of lithic or other oil paint'. 'Considering the very unusual size of the beams required', added Smirke, 'I am anxious to have the castings made by founders upon whom . . . I may rely'.[5] The cast iron beams supporting the entrance front were in places more than 43 ft. long, and were tested to bear a weight of thirty tons. As in the rest of the building, the huge facing slabs of Portland stone were tied to a brick core with iron cramps. In 1850, soon after the completion of the colonnade, C. R. Cockerell was able to say that 'since the days of Hadrian no such stones have been used . . . the front . . . is formed by 800 stones, each from 5 to 9 tons in weight. Even St. Paul's contains no approach to these magnitudes'.[6]

It was the King's Library which set up structural standards for the rest of the

[1] Works 17/2/1, f. 216, 11 November 1842; Works 17/2/1, f. 230, 24 August 1843.
[2] J. Mordaunt Crook, 'Sir Robert Smirke: a Pioneer of Concrete Construction', *Trans. of the Newcomen Society* xxxviii (1965–6).   [3] Smirke's drawings of concrete foundations, Works 33/3–6, 150, 204, 325, 495, 786.
[4] 'Report of the Select Committee on the British Museum', *Parl. Pap.* 1836, x, p. 448; *Trans. of the Newcomen Society* xxi (1940–41), p. 145. Smirke's drawings of cast iron beams, Works 33/3–6, 105, 330, 423, 477, 530, 712, 769.
[5] Smirke's specification, Works 17/2/1, f. 187. For proof testing and iron cramping techniques cf. Smirke's plans, Works 33/423, 424, 432, 477.
[6] C. R. Cockerell's R.A. Lectures as Professor of Architecture, quoted by E. Walford, *Old and New London* iv (1883–4), p. 502.

museum. The room's unusual length (300 ft.) required brickwork of extra strength and thickness. Its unusual width (41 ft. overall; 58 ft. in the centre) required cast iron beams of exceptional span. Commenting on the 'massy' nature of the walls, C. W. Pasley noticed that they were from $5\frac{1}{2}$ to 6 bricks thick, built with mortar composed of one part Dorking lime to only 3 parts Thames sand, grouted externally with liquified cement and surrounded by a false area as a precaution against damp.[1] Smirke's use of cast iron in the ceiling of the King's Library constituted something of a revolution in metropolitan architecture. Much of the credit belongs to John Raistrick. In 1810 Smirke had used built-in cast iron bearers at Cirencester Park which were over 30 ft. in length.[2] But in 1823 he hesitated to span the width of the King's Library with beams cast in one section more than 40 ft. long. Instead he proposed to make use of a trussed girder composed of sections of cast and wrought iron. Two years previously Raistrick had laid a report before Parliament on the cast iron beams, 35 ft.–36 ft. long, used by Nash at Buckingham Palace. He now assured Smirke that in 1821 he had personally directed the use of beams no less than 90 ft. long for the Stourport Bridge over the Severn. Raistrick's beams for the King's Library had a flanged section and mostly measured 41 ft. long. Some were more than 50 ft. in length. Their depth varied according to an elliptical curve from 3 ft. at mid-span to 1 ft. 9 ins. near the ends, finishing with a quadrant. The ceilings were of arched plates of iron $\frac{1}{8}$ in. thick, stiffened by light angle bars, carried on the bottom flanges of the beams. He later informed a parliamentary committee that they were 'the first beams that were ever introduced into London of so great a length and with large openings through the web of the beam'. They were tested in 1824 with a dead weight of 40 tons.[3] Raistrick complained that he made no profit on this important contract because of the rising cost of pig iron.

When the Egyptian rooms were being altered in the early 1930s, several girders were removed and subjected to rigorous investigation. The results showed that Smirke had been ingenious rather than scientific. By perforating the web of the girders with long oval voids he reduced their weight and made handling easier. At the same time these 'Vierendeel' perforations set up secondary stresses, and effectively converted a single deep girder into two shallow beams, each susceptible to lateral buckling. The thickness of the flange thus became quite inadequate, and the whole girder was therefore at least partly dependent on the lateral support of secondary wooden beams. Still, there was nothing unusual in that. Most of the girders employed in early 19th-century building were similarly used in conjunction with wooden beams, or else were built in with brick jack-arches, the thrust of which was taken by iron tie rods.

---

[1] C. W. Pasley, *Course of Practical Architecture* (lithographed notes, Chatham, 1826), pp. 18, 248–9, 288; *Observations on Limes, Calcareous Cements, Mortars, Stuccoes and Concrete* (1838), pp. 25–6.

[2] *Journal of the R.I.B.A.* 1867, p. 207; Wyatt Papworth (ed.), *Dictionary of Architecture* (1852–92), 'Iron'.

[3] The apparatus used in this process had been constructed for Raistrick's previous commission, the Stratford and Moreton Railway, in the course of which (1823) he had made use of 'the first malleable iron rails ... South of Darlington' ('Report on the Application of Iron to Railway Structures', *Parl. Pap.* 1849, xxix, pp. 286–8, 404–5; W. Humber, *A Practical Treatise on Cast and Wrought Iron Bridges and Girders*, 1857, p. 102. For Raistrick's career cf. H. W. Dickinson, 'The Raistricks: Civil Engineers', *Trans. of the Newcomen Society* iv, 1923–4; J. Simmons 'The Raistrick Collection', *Locomotion* x, 1939, p. 33. For a recent analysis of the girders used in the British Museum, see S. B. Hamilton, 'Old Cast-Iron Structures', *The Structural Engineer* xxvii, 1949, 173–91 and xxviii (1950), 79–81; H. J. Gough, 'Tests on Cast Iron Girders Removed from the British Museum', *Institution of Civil Engineers Selected Engineering Papers*, no. 161 (1934).

As his greatest commission, under his immediate supervision for over twenty years, the British Museum made considerable demands on Smirke's professional ability, particularly during the closing stages of his career. After 1842 he was frequently unwell and occupied an office within the remaining portion of Montagu House in order to direct the work more effectively. As the great colonnade rose higher, the museum alone retained his personal superintendence, other commissions being delegated to his younger brother, Sydney Smirke. But within four months of his father's death in May 1845, ill health forced Smirke himself to take a holiday in Nice. In the following year he retired from practice altogether.[1] Thenceforward Sydney Smirke was permanently responsible for all the unfinished work, notably the forecourt and lodges (1849–53),[2] the Ephesus Room (1850–51),[3] the new Graeco–Roman Rooms (1852–3)[4] and the Record Repository (1851–3).[5] His eldest son Sydney Smirke Jnr. (1838–1912), who designed the lion water-basins in the portico, was the last of the family to be associated with the museum.[6]

The fine railings at the entrance, cast by John Walker & Co., were also designed by Sydney Smirke. He intended the massive gatepiers to act as plinths for decorative sculpture—Bacon, Newton, Milton and Shakespeare were the luminaries suggested.[7] Protests from Resident Keepers almost caused the new design for a dwarf wall and palisade to be replaced by a solid wall twelve feet high, thus giving the museum 'the aspect of a prison'. But an announcement in the House of Commons that this barricade would cost £24,100 proved 'a pleasantry beyond the digestion of members. . . . Think of walling up the work of a quarter of a century and the representative of a sum that would buy a small kingdom, in order that some officer of the establishment might not be looked in on at his dinner!'[8] Until 1896 the entrance lodges were guarded on the Great Russell Street side by a quaint anachronism: a low railing which marked the boundary of the museum and at the same time prevented 'nuisances'. Four of the little bronze lions which once embellished this curious survival now decorate the marble chimney-pieces of the Trustees' Boardroom; others surround the Wellington monument in St. Paul's Cathedral. They were modelled by Alfred Stevens from Sydney Smirke's drawing of the lion at the foot of the staircase of the Bargello, Florence.[9]

---

[1] Letters from Smirke to the Commissioners of Woods and Works, Works 17/2/1, ff. 179, 385, 400; Works 1/30, f. 37, 2 July 1846. [2] Sydney Smirke's plans of lodges, Works 33/554, 560–1.

[3] This connected the Elgin and Lycian Galleries. It was originally planned for the reception of Assyrian sculptures, cf. correspondence and drawings, Peel Papers ccccxxii–iii, B.M. Add. MSS. 40602, f. 280, 29 November 1849 and 40603, f. 28, 7 January 1850. [4] B.M. Add. MS. 52292, ff. 20–21.

[5] Its construction followed that of other rooms: wrought iron bearers and cast iron beams (Works 17/2/1, f. 542, 15 April 1851). [6] *Journal of the R.I.B.A.* xix (1912), p. 609.

[7] *The Times* 17 February 1851; A. Groves, *Royal Academy Exhibitors 1769–1904*, vii, 1906, p. 164. The legend that the present railings were designed by Alfred Stevens is disposed of by Sir Walter Armstrong, *Alfred Stevens* (1891), p. 15. The charge for gilding, in accordance with Sydney Smirke's designs, was £385 (Works 17/2/1, ff. 553, 572).

[8] *The Builder* viii (1850), p. 464; *The Athenaeum* 1850, pp. 769, 1049; *Civil Engineer and Architect's Journal* xi (1848), p. 291 and xii (1850), p. 337. Letters of protest, *The Times* 1–4 October 1850. Alternative suggestions were the use of Nash's Doric colonnade from the Regent Street Quadrant or the use of railings from St. Paul's Cathedral (*Civil Engineer and Architect's Journal* xi, 1848, p. 291; *The Athenaeum* 1850, p. 769).

[9] *Middlesex and Hertfordshire Notes and Queries* ii (1896), p. 91; letter from Alfred Cates to *The Times*, 17 January 1896. Smirke's plans of the Trustees' Room (1841), Works 33/696–7, 672, 727. Casts of Stevens' celebrated lion can be seen on railings outside Ely House, London; the Law Society, Chancery Lane; and the Leicester Museum (J. Gloag and D. Bridgewater, *Cast Iron in Architecture*, 1948, pp. 119, 216–7).

Among the works for which Sydney Smirke was responsible, the Round Reading
Room deserves particular mention. Sydney Smirke claimed credit only for its
architectural form, its decoration and its cast iron construction. He readily acknowledged the conception to be that of Sir Anthony Panizzi, the 'Napoleon of Librarians',
whose bust presides over the entrance today. But building in the quadrangle was
such an obvious solution to the problem of storing books that it had already been
formulated by Thomas Watts in 1836,[1] by Edward Hawkins in 1842,[2] by Edward
Edwards in 1847,[3] by William Hosking in 1848[4] and by James Fergusson in 1849.[5]
Another suggestion, in 1850, followed the pattern of the Regent's Park Colosseum.[6]
Henri Labrouste's Salle de Travaille des Imprimés in the Bibliothèque Nationale,
Paris, is a similar contemporary scheme with echoes of earlier projects by Delessert
(1835) and Durand (1808). As Panizzi put it, 'schemes for covering over, or building
in the quadrangle were numberless',[7] and most of them involved the construction
of a circular apartment for antiquities or printed books. His own plans began in
1848. In that year the Grenville bequest prompted him to produce a scheme for
an additional quadrangle alongside the north-east sector of the museum.[8] On this
occasion, and again in 1851, the Treasury refused to countenance the purchase of
additional land.[9] Panizzi therefore turned his attention to the central quadrangle.
In April 1852 he prepared a sketch which was drawn out by a draughtsman named

---

[1] Watts' pseudonymous article in the *Mechanics' Mag.* xxvi (1837), pp. 454–9, took the form of a commentary on the 'Report of the Select Committee on the British Museum, 1836'. As a member of the Printed Books
Department from 1838 onwards he assisted Panizzi's reorganisation, and became first Superintendent of the
Reading Room and Keeper of Printed Books (obituary, *The Standard* 10 September 1869).
[2] E. Hawkins, *Observations on the Reading Room* (1858). 'My colleague Mr. Hawkins [Keeper of Antiquities],
had often suggested long before a communication by corridors across the quadrangle, . . . with a central building for the Trustees' Meeting Room and offices standing round it': Panizzi to Hosking, 1 May 1857 (L. Fagan,
Life of Panizzi i, 1830, pp. 370–1).
[3] E. Edwards, *Public Libraries in London and Paris* (1847); *Lives of the Founders of the British Museum* ii (1870),
p. 555 *et seq.*
[4] *The Builder* vii (1850), 295, 307, 320, 550; *The Architect* 13 July 1850. Hosking, Professor of Architecture
at King's College, London, presented his plans to Lord Ellesmere's Commission of Inquiry in 1848. They
were laid before the Trustees in November 1849 and rejected. 'His proposal is to build in the middle of the
quadrangle court, a kind of modified copy of the Pantheon . . . and to do away with our present staircase'.
This 'would alter and revolutionise much which Sir Robert and Mr. Smirke have already done. . . . Mr.
Hosking, although somewhat advanced in life, has never been the architect of any public or great building'
(Ellis to Peel, Peel Papers, ccccxxiii, B.M. Add. MS. 40603, ff. 26–7, 7 January 1850). 'I recollect seeing your
plans at a meeting of the Trustees. . . . When, long subsequently, Mr. Panizzi showed me his sketch I
confess it did not remind me of yours' (Sydney Smirke to Hosking, in Edwards, *Founders* ii, 1870, p. 587).
[5] J. Fergusson, *Observations on the British Museum, National Gallery and National Record Office* (1849).
[6] *Civil Engineer and Architect's Jnl.* xiii (1850), p. 264.
[7] Fagan *op. cit.* i, pp. 370–1, Panizzi to Hosking 1 May 1859.
[8] This Panizzi–Sydney Smirke scheme envisaged 'an elongation of the North Front . . . carried eastwards
. . . the building should then be drawn southward to the point of intersection with the present façade. . . . A
square should be formed, not architecturally equal to the square of the present Museum, but for working
purposes sufficient . . . for 100 years' ('Report of the Commissioners appointed to inquire into the . . . British
Museum', *Parl. Pap.* 1850, xxiv, pp. 801, 783, 849).
[9] 'Communications . . . respecting the Enlargement of the British Museum', *Parl. Pap.* 1852, xxviii, pp.
202, 217; *Literary Gazette* 1852, pp. 739–41. Further plans prepared by Sydney Smirke in 1853 and 1857 were
similarly vetoed by the Treasury, along with variations submitted by Edmund Oldfield and Nevil Maskelyne
of the Archaeological and Mineralogical Departments. The problem was solved by removing Natural History
to South Kensington, the only alternative to Sydney Smirke's final suggestion of a third storey around the
quadrangle ('Papers relating to the Enlargement of the British Museum', *Parl. Pap.* 1857–58, xxxiii, pp. 473–7,
873 *et seq.*; 'Report from the Select Committee on the British Museum', *Parl. Pap.* 1860, xvi, pp. 185, 199,
365, 453–65, 475–91; 'Accounts and Papers', *Parl. Pap.* 1860, xxxix, pp. 282–3; *The Times* 27 August 1860, p.
9).

Charles Cannon and laid before the Trustees in May.[1] Sydney Smirke transformed the idea into a concrete project which met with an initial rejection from the Treasury. Meanwhile a rival scheme had been proposed by Sir Charles Barry and indirectly sponsored by John Wilson Croker.[2] Besides altering the north wing, this aimed at preserving the quadrangle by glazing over the entire central area and seems to have owed a good deal to the publicity surrounding Paxton's Crystal Palace. It was rejected by the Trustees in 1853 as gloomy, impractical and expensive. In May 1854 work began at last on Sydney Smirke's new building, the structure still in use today: a circular reading room set in an insulated rectangle and connected by corridors to the old north and south wings.[3]

Sir Robert Smirke's reputation suffered greatly from the museum's slow construction. If his original design had been published in 1823 it would probably have been hailed as a masterpiece. Instead his efforts provoked contemporary abuse and post-humous condescension. Conceived as the choicest product of the English Greek Revival, the building was finished amid mounting Victorian hostility, a generation too late. 'The building progresses like the Sinking Fund, by fits . . . no doubt our great Doric architect builds, as Zeuxis painted, for posterity'.[4] This tardy rate of progress was unfavourably contrasted with the rapid erection of public buildings at Munich.[5] But apart from its dilatory construction, both the planning and the style of the museum earned strong criticism. The planning of the galleries was formal rather than convenient and practical rather than scientific. Function had been sacrificed to grandeur in the shape of courtyard and colonnade. The lighting of both the north and west wings was impeded by 'a wretched pseudo-portico of three quarter columns', the vestigial relic of Smirke's grandiose quadrangular scheme. The Roman Gallery, which apart from the Lycian Room was alone aligned on that east-west axis which provided the most suitable light, was shaded by the colonnade; and the finest situation for any sculpture gallery was occupied by the main staircase. James Fergusson, an early and articulate apostle of functionalism, published a damning catalogue of errors. Even so, the original plan, shorn of its post 1852 accretions, struck an even balance between convenience and beauty. The quadrangular theme was thought worthy of repetition in the Victoria and Albert Museum. Fergusson had to admit that neither 'the Berlin Museum, nor the Munich [Regensburg] Walhalla, or Glyptothek, nor the Paris Madeleine, or Bourse . . ., considering the difficulties of

---

[1] Panizzi's first rough sketch is reproduced in J. Winter Jones, *List of the Reference Books in the British Museum* (1859), p. xvii. For alternative projects by Panizzi and Sydney Smirke, cf. 'Communications . . . respecting the Enlargement of the British Museum', *Parl. Pap.* 1852, xxviii, pp. 226–8, 234–5, 251–7. Panizzi's contribution is summarised in E. Miller, *Prince of Librarians* (1968), pp. 209–12.

[2] Barry's plans, R.I.B.A. Drawings Collection C4/25 (1–5); B.M. Portfolio, B.M. pressmark, Maps 151, f. 2; Sydney Smirke's letter to Sir F. Madden, criticising Barry's scheme, Madden cuttings, 'Views', B.M. press mark C. 55, 1. See also Fagan *op. cit.* i, pp. 356–7, A. Barry, *Life and Works of Sir Charles Barry* (1870), 277–9. Croker wished to lower and glaze over the courtyard, thus preserving the grandeur of the quadrangle 'in its naked severity'. He dismissed the first proposal by Panizzi and Sydney Smirke for a 'panopticon reading room' as a 'monstrous scheme . . . a gigantic birdcage' (*Quarterly Rev.* xcii, 1852, pp. 170–3). To Grenville the quadrangle was 'the finest mason's yard in Europe'; to others 'one of the grandest things in London' (*ibid.* lxxxviii, 1850, p. 153; *The Times* 29 September 1852, p. 4).

[3] For details of the Round Reading Room's construction, and for an account of the controversy which surrounded its completion, see J. Mordaunt Crook, *The British Museum* (1972), ch. v.

[4] *The Athenaeum* 1843, p. 947.

[5] *Foreign Quarterly Rev.* xix (1837), pp. 114–5.

the subject, . . . show more taste or knowledge of the style'.[1] But in the final analysis, the British Museum, like the General Post Office, symbolises the dilemma of the early 19th-century architect torn between reverence for classical models and the needs of urbanised society.

To many critics of the 1840s the mode of decoration seemed as out-dated as the system by which Smirke had obtained the commission. Having 'lived over the period for which he was so well adapted and run into another',[2] the idol of the Regency became a whipping boy for Victorian aesthetes. 'What if a "morning star", as Pugin calls it, be rising at Westminster', urged the most vitriolic of Smirke's accusers, 'all is Cimmerian darkness at Bloomsbury, where Smirkean night—or knight-hood—is suffered to reign supreme . . . all . . . stand in awe of the prime minister and his pet. . . It is impossible for any one to say of Sir Robert Smirke that he is a temporising or time-serving man, since instead of at all bending to the spirit of the present time . . . he shows himself a staunch conservative in maintaining that system of monopoly and irresponsibility under which he has flourished. The public is to him the same ignoramus, insignificant public as it was some thirty years ago'. The museum will be 'doubly *Bobbified* . . . Sir Robert Peel may be a very good *Cabinet*-maker, Sir Robert Smirke an excellent warehouse-builder, but let them stick to those trades, and not foist upon the country such a dowdy design as the one concocted for the British Museum out of the Post Office and the Custom House. . . . Something more than Sir Robert's formal stereotype Ionic is here required'.[3] Although Ruskin admitted the nobility of Smirke's design, others demanded his resignation. Abuse was showered upon the 'formalised deformity, shrivelled precision, and starved accuracy' of this 'miserable abortion'. 'Infinitely better would it have been to have kicked out Sir Robert at once, and plaistered him with a good round pension. . . . Poor Smirke! how greatly he is to be pitied!, and for the very reason that many now envy him, to wit, because he has had so many opportunities of manifesting his imbecility. Barry–Smirke, they are so far asunder as two poles . . . . Mr. Barry's ideas are so elastic—he has such a superabundance of imagination and invention that we wish he would out of charity's sake bestow a little of it, some of the mere crumbs and sweepings, upon Sir Robert Smirke, they would surely be acceptable to an architectural Lazarus'.[4]

Such abuse—and Soane, Nash and Wilkins were all similarly vilified in their turn—stemmed principally from two sources: political opposition and the vagaries of fashion.[5]

[1] J. Fergusson, *Observations on the British Museum, National Gallery and National Record Office* (1849), pp. 11–13, 27, 30–32; *History of Modern Architecture* ii (ed. Kerr, 1891), pp. 78–9; reviews of Fergusson's theories in *Civil Engineer and Architect's Jnl.* xii (1849), p. 197; *Quarterly Rev.* xcii (1852), p. 157 *et seq*. Fergusson's ghost has had its revenge: the Roman Gallery has recently become a bookstall.   [2] *The Builder* i (1843), p. 405.
[3] *Civil Engineer and Architect's Jnl.* vi (1843), pp. 216, 262, 411. See *The Athenaeum* 1844, p. 434 and *The Spectator* 25 September 1843.
[4] *Civil Engineer and Architect's Jnl.* iv (1840), p. 370; vi (1843), pp. 194, 262, 373, 375, 411, 416; vii (1844), pp. 141, 183; xii (1849), pp. 146, 161. 'Resign and abdicate. . . .' (*The Spectator* 3 October 1843). Ruskin tempered his praise with criticism of the use of artificial materials (J. Ruskin, *The Seven Lamps of Architecture, Works*, ed. E. T. Cook and A. Wedderburn, 1903, viii, p. 76).
[5] 'When a re-action begins to take place, it generally goes on at a "crescendo" rate. Sir Robert Smirke's fame is in that predicament, is getting "fine by degrees and beautifully less" ' (*Surveyor, Engineer and Architect* i, 1840, p. 219). 'James Wyatt is now beginning to be . . . rated at his actual worth, which is exceedingly low indeed. Nash's reputation is now scarcely worth a bawbee; nor would we give much for the reversion of that of Sir Robert Smirke' (*Civil Engineer and Architect's Jnl.* iii, 1840, p. 352). 'To have said or even hinted as much, many years ago, would have been considered, if not exactly high treason, little less than deplorable architectural heresy' (*Surveyor, Engineer and Architect* iii, 1842, pp. 135–6).

In 1815 Smirke had taken office as a Tory nominee. A decade of Whig government during the 1830s had left his position unimpaired. Sir Robert Peel had remained a staunch supporter although in Opposition. Now Smirke was paying the penalty for his political allegiance. Peel returned to power in 1841, the year in which work began on the great colonnade, and the fury of his opponents is reflected in the bitterness of their architectural criticism. As Conservative papers *The Times* remained silent and *The Builder* prevaricated. Other periodicals were less inhibited. Pugin's Gothic churches and Barry's Italianate palazzos produced a popular craving for ornament and a veritable avalanche of criticism for Sir Robert Smirke.[1]

In fact the British Museum is a magnificent essay in the adaptation and integration of antique sources: the columns themselves derive from the Temple of Athena Polias at Priene and the Temple of Dionysus at Teos; details can be traced to The Erechtheion, the Ilissus Temple, the Theseion, the Propylaea and the Thrasyllus Monument. Until the construction of the new Houses of Parliament it was the largest secular building in London. Its completion fully merited the award of the R.I.B.A. Gold Medal in 1853. The mouldings which adorn the façades of the entrance front and quadrangle are impeccably finished, and the side—or top-lit—galleries, articulated by Doric columns and *antae* and diversified only by the cool polychromy of their trabeated and coffered ceilings, form a splendid, if perhaps insufficiently anonymous, backcloth for the display of antiquities.[2] The solemn counterpoint of portico, wings and enveloping colonnade, massive stylobate and inflected parapet, extorted even from the giddiest of critics a grudging recognition of the composition's kinetic power. Smirke's serene design fused the Grecian combination of surface modelling and complementary planes with the spatial dynamics of Palladian tradition. In Covent Garden Theatre (1809; burnt 1856) and the British Museum he gave London the first and last of its great buildings in the Grecian style. His monumental creation in a Bloomsbury backstreet constituted the high water-mark of the English Greek Revival, and furnished the movement with a ponderous *finale*.

CHELSEA, THE ROYAL HOSPITAL

This extensive establishment was placed under the Office of Woods and Works after the death of its Clerk of the Works, Sir John Soane, in 1837.[3] The Board of Woods and the Trustees of the Hospital each interpreted the arrangement differently; a Treasury letter of October 1838 to decide the issue left each side maintaining its own interpretation, and the relationship was not a very happy one. It was not, however, until the 1870s that an open clash occurred.[4]

---

[1] E.g. *Illustrated London News* vii (1845)p. 357; *Civil Engineer and Architect's Jnl.* xii (1849), pp. 158, 179, 290; *The Times* 30 October 1850.

[2] Smirke's Greek Revival ornament, moulded cornices, string courses, etc., are perhaps too assertive for the display of statuary, cf. Hope Bagenal, 'Architectural Detail in Museum Design', *Jnl. of the R.I.B.A.* xl (1933), pp. 789–95.

[3] Works 2/2, pp. 111, 135; 14/93; see p. 202 above.   [4] See Works 14/93, *passim*.

No major improvements were undertaken by the Office of Woods and Works, but additional security against fire was obtained in 1842 by increasing the water supply.[1] Annual estimates for maintenance averaged about £3700 between 1838 and 1848.[2]

CHELSEA, THE ROYAL MILITARY ASYLUM

This institution for soldiers' orphans, founded by the Duke of York and built in 1801–3 to the designs of John Sanders,[3] was placed under the Works Department by Treasury letter dated 21 February 1833.[4] Maintenance averaged rather more than £1000 a year between 1837 and 1848.[5] In 1846 the Secretary at War proposed improving education in the army, and the Treasury called for plans and estimates for adapting the asylum as a model school. Phipps prepared plans for an extensive internal reconstruction costing £8500–£9000.[6] Action was delayed in order to secure the freehold of the entire site, a great part of which belonged to Lord Cadogan. In November 1847, however, the Treasury ordered the works to be put in train, expenditure being met from unclaimed monies in the Army Prize Fund.[7] Works under Phipps estimated at £4110 were authorised in September 1850, and in the following January he estimated additions and alterations for accommodating more students at £1321.[8] Since 1910 (when the school moved to Dover) the buildings have been used as barracks, under the name of the Duke of York's Headquarters.

THE CUSTOM HOUSE, LONDON

Office of Works responsibility for the London Custom House began in 1815 on an advisory and accidental basis. Unlike the Royal Mint, the British Museum and the General Post Office, the Custom House remained under the jurisdiction of the Customs Commissioners. It was only the building's unfortunate history which drew it into the orbit of the Office of Works.[9]

In 1671 Sir Christopher Wren's Custom House had replaced an Elizabethan building destroyed in the Great Fire.[10] Wren's work was in turn damaged by fire and reconstructed by Thomas Ripley between 1718 and 1725. It was the inadequacy

[1] Works 1/25, p. 507 (Easton and Amos' tender, £1434 1s. 6d.).
[2] *Parl. Pap.* 1847–8 (643), xviii, pt. ii; Works 1/34, p. 151; 1/36, p. 182; 2/7, pp. 436–40.
[3] Plans and elevations are given by G. Richardson, *New Vitruvius Britannicus* ii (1808), pls. 39–42.
[4] Crest 25/37.   [5] *Parl. Pap.* 1843 (343) xxx; 1851 (374) xxxi.
[6] Works 2/5, pp. 190, 262–9, 394; 1/30, pp. 65, 178–9; MPD 149.
[7] Works 1/31, pp. 34–5, 382; 1/34, pp. 142, 206–7, 413; 2/6, pp. 22–4, 58–9, 65, 90–4, 144–7, 243–4; 6/357/2–4. The Act 11 and 12 Vict. *c.* 103 provided for the purchase of the site, as well as improving the buildings.   [8] Works 1/35, p. 348; 1/36, p. 148.
[9] For further details see R. C. Jarvis, 'Laing's Custom House', *Trans. of the London and Middlesex Archaeol. Soc.* xxx (1961); J. Mordaunt Crook, 'The Custom House Scandal', *Architectural History* vi (1963), pp. 91–102.
[10] For Wren's building see vol. v of this *History*.

of this building to cope with an increasing volume of trade and an expanding administrative system which prompted plans for rebuilding during the Napoleonic Wars.[1] The designs of David Laing, an ex-pupil of Soane and Surveyor to the Customs since the resignation of W. Pilkington in 1810, were accepted by the Treasury in May 1812.[2] The foundations were begun, to the west of the old site, in the following year. On 12 February 1814 Ripley's 'old but useful pile' was gutted by fire and destroyed by an explosion of gunpowder.[3] Laing's building programme continued undisturbed and, as it turned out, unchecked.

Laing's original scheme for a Custom House situated to the north of Thames Street and approached by two new docks on either side of the quay was never realised. Instead he produced a simpler design for a building immediately adjoining Billingsgate.[4] Wings containing four storeys of offices built around an open area and raised on a vaulted basement were to flank the central portion of the plan occupied by the King's Warehouse and the Long Room. The architect's estimate was £209,000, plus £12,000 for piling, sleepers and planking, and £7000 for contingencies. Messrs. Miles and Peto[5] produced the lowest tender and contracted for £165,000 (carcass and foundations) plus £2050 for additional stone dressings on the three subsidiary fronts, as stipulated by Treasury order.[6] In 1812 the elder Rennie had warned Laing that the subsoil was treacherous and the use of piles essential.[7] But the execution of the piling left both architect and contractor open to accusations of negligence, conspiracy and fraud. Indeed Peto's profiteering, Laing's ineptitude and Smirke's eventual reconstruction produced a total expenditure of £435,000 between 1813 and 1829. As a result the Office of Works was involved in three consecutive investigations, commencing in 1815, beginning again in 1817 and culminating in 1825. The first disclosed unnecessary delay, the second unprofessional conduct and the third defective construction. All in all the Custom House scandal supplied a cogent argument for tighter Treasury control over departmental building.

Nine years before its collapse in 1824–5 the Custom House had already become an object of scandal in professional circles. Delays in excavation during the icy winter of 1813–14 had been followed by dilatory and irregular construction. By the spring of 1815 questions were being asked in Parliament; Laing's salary was held over as an incentive to speedier action; and in the following July, in response to a Treasury command, Hiort and Hardwick were called in to examine the progress of work on behalf of the Office of Works.[8] Laing's excuses were hardly acceptable. He explained that 'although Mr. Peto has made great personal exertions, the arrangements for providing and preparing materials also for employing sufficient workmen have not

---

[1] *Monthly Mag.* xxxviii (1811), p. 491.

[2] D. Laing, *Plans, Elevations and Sections of Buildings Public and Private including the Custom House* (1818), p. 2. For preliminary drawings probably prepared by Laing *c.* 1810, but unsigned, undated and variously watermarked, see Works 30/47–87 and 91–114.

[3] *Gent's. Mag.* 1814, pt. i, p. 191.

[4] For the original and subsequent design compare Laing *op. cit.* plate I and *Gent's. Mag.* 1817, pt. ii, p. 360.

[5] John Miles of College Hill and Henry Peto of 31 Little Britain.

[6] 'Estimates and Accounts', *Parl. Pap.* 1813–14, xi, p. 207; Report from the Select Committee on intended Improvements in the Post Office, *Parl. Pap.* 1814–15, iii, pp. 5–7.

[7] Rennie's report was referred to in 1825 by George and Sir John Rennie during their investigations, and again in 1829 during the legal proceedings which followed collapse (Institution of Civil Engineers, Rennie MSS., Reports 1st Series vii, ff. 52–3, 17 February 1812; 2nd Series ii, f. 127, 18 April 1825).

[8] Records of H.M. Customs, 'Rebuilding of Custom House' MSS., i, 14 March 1815, 20 July 1815.

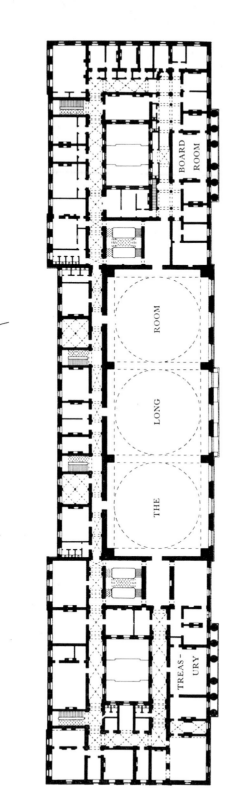

BOARD ROOM

THE LONG ROOM

TREAS-URY

Scale of Metres

Scale of Feet

10 0   30

0   50   100

Fig. 13. The Custom House, as originally built to the design of David Laing: from Britton and Pugin's *Public Buildings of London* (1825).

been commensurate to the desired object of dispatch'. Miles had died in February 1814 'and prior to his decease Mr. Peto could derive from him no assistance (excepting pecuniary aid) being totally unacquainted with building and consequently . . . a very unfit person to enter into such an undertaking'.[1] During the following year, the carpenters ceased work for a fortnight 'in consequence of their resisting the intention of the contractor to reduce their wages', and Messrs. Middleton and Bailey the upholsterers threatened Peto with prosecution for failing to cover the cost of their original estimate.[2]

But by the autumn of 1817 the building was approaching completion together with a new wharf designed by Rennie and constructed by Joliffe and Banks.[3] As a preliminary to the final payment of Peto and Laing the Customs Commissioners requested a second examination by the Office of Works. Reports were therefore produced by Robert Browne, the Assistant Surveyor General and Cashier, and by Nash, Soane and Smirke, all of whom had subscribed to Laing's description of the Custom House published in 1818. This official quartet limited Laing's claims to the customary 5 per cent, but agreed that this commission was payable on the full £255,000 expended, and even added with unconscious irony that the Custom House 'does Mr. Laing great credit'.[4] Browne and Smirke judged that Peto deserved payment of the seventh and final instalment of the £165,000 for which he had originally contracted, but significantly added that payment for all extra-contractual works would have to be settled separately.[5] As the inquiry progressed it became very evident that the work had been conducted in a haphazard and unprofessional manner. For the central dome of Laing's original design a straight roof had been substituted and a rectangular attic added to the front enriched with Coade Stone panels designed by J. G. Bubb (Pl. 26A). However this alteration had been authorised by the Customs Commissioners and involved no extra cost. The foundations had been increased in depth and thus made more expensive, but the specification had allowed a certain amount of latitude. But the lead and ironwork had been 'increased to an enormous and unprecedented degree'; the gutters had been covered with an iron grating which was 'unnecessary and injudicious'; the size of the timbers had been 'unnecessarily enlarged and a great number of others introduced in the walls not mentioned in the specification, uncalled for by the construction and injurious in some degree to the durability of the walls'. The accounts were therefore deemed to 'have no reference to the Contract', and the prices to be greatly in excess of those allowed. Worst of all, it was discovered that Askew, Laing's measuring clerk, 'was expressly directed by Mr. Laing not to make any separate measurement of the extra works as they occurred but to measure the whole as if there were no extras'.[6]

The architect thus stood accused of directing unauthorised and unrecorded alterations to the original specification, and the contractor of knowingly executing

---

[1] *Ibid.* i, 4 June 1815.   [2] *Ibid.* i, 1 March 1816, 9 December 1816.

[3] Built of Derbyshire stone, Aberdeen granite and beechwood piles, the wharf cost £72,747 18s. 4d. Rennie's design defeated a scheme produced by Ralph Dodd for a cast iron wharf raised on 'a range of iron pipes placed close together . . . having the appearance of reeds'. Peto's tender was narrowly defeated by that of Joliffe and Banks, Rennie acting as referee (Institution of Civil Engineers, Rennie MSS., Reports, 1st Series, ix, ff. 22, 39, 42, 62, 70, 82, 87, 230, 388 and x, ff. 93–102).

[4] *Ibid.* 18 December 1817; Works 1/8, f. 345.

[5] Custom House MSS. i, 22 November 1817; Works 12/100/2, f. 40.   [6] Works 12/100/2, ff. 1–41.

such work. In June 1821, before an Office of Works 'tribunal' composed of Stephenson, Browne, Nash, Soane and Smirke, Laing countered by claiming that he possessed power to direct alterations independently, and Peto that the contract had been invalidated from the beginning by reason of the general nature of the alterations. The architect's conduct was censured as being 'in the highest degree improper and reprehensible', and the contractor's as being 'inconsistent with the character of a fair and respectable tradesman'.[1] At this stage, however, it was unauthorised extravagance rather than incompetence, and irregular conduct rather than actual fraud, which were the objects of censure. 'The system that has been assumed', wrote Stephenson, 'is destructive of all fair competition for public contracts, for if an architect . . . can be allowed by mere sanction of his own authority to make such deviations from an agreement . . . as will render all conditions of it void and nugatory, leaving the contractor at liberty to make his own terms, the preference given to the lowest tender by public competition will under these circumstances be only a matter of deception'.[2] As for Peto, 'his endeavour evidently was, from the very commencement of this transaction, to set aside the original Contract and substitute for it an account of the whole building by measure and value: a practice not infrequently attempted, when large buildings are undertaken under contracts of this description . . . the architect must have known that it is upon a reliance on extras in the undertaking of a great work under such contracts, that speculators are induced to give in very low tenders, even such as appear scarcely to leave a profit upon the work'. Laing's duty was to have 'prevented as much as possible by proper plans and ample specifications, an accumulation of extra charges . . . and to have kept a distinct and accurate account of every extra charge as it appeared'.[3]

Cracks appeared in the vaulting of the King's Warehouse in the spring of 1820. Laing claimed 'no insecurity need be apprehended therefrom' and recommended that the 'fissures be caulked and stopt with tow and oakum, and then pointed with hard cement'.[4] He remedied signs of further subsidence in following years without even an official report.[5] Part of the Long Room and river facade collapsed in December 1824, and this was followed less than a month later by the collapse of the Long Room floor. Peto's action against Roe, the Customs Commissioner who alone of the four signatories to the Contract still survived, was due to be heard in January 1825, as he had refused all offers of arbitration based on the suggestions of Nash, Soane and Smirke.[6] The Treasury now suspected 'the most culpable negligence' and demanded the exposure of 'the persons who ought to be held responsible'.[7] Smirke was made responsible for investigation and reconstruction. During the next two years he produced a series of reports more damning even to the reputations of Laing and Peto than were those he produced on the conduct of D. A. Alexander at Maidstone Gaol in 1819 and on that of James Savage at the Temple Church in 1841.[8] The beechwood piling had rapidly decayed owing to the fact that the surround-

---

[1] Works 12/100/2, ff. 69–71. [2] Custom House MSS. ii, 7 June 1821. [3] *Ibid.* 19 July 1822.
[4] *Ibid.* 27 April 1820. [5] *Ibid.* iii, 12 January 1825. [6] *Ibid.* 9 June 1823.
[7] *Ibid.* 10 January 1825. Laing proposed to call the following architects to give evidence in his favour: Gwilt, Roper, I'Anson, Taylor, Abraham, Fowler and Montague, plus his own assistants, Bellamy and Anderson (*ibid.* 18 February 1825).
[8] J. Mordaunt Crook, 'The Restoration of the Temple Church: Ecclesiology and Recrimination' *Architectural History* viii (1965), pp. 39–51.

ing earth had been alternately damp and dry, but Smirke decided that the work had been so incompetently executed that the foundations would have failed even if oak had been used. Laing's drawings, he reported, 'represent nine piles under each of the twelve piers that supported the Long Room floor; but . . . there are under some only four, under others three piles, and under two of the piers only two piles, although a permanent weight of upwards of 150 tons was charged upon the base of every pier.[1] . . . The piles are of small round beech timber averaging little more than 7 in. in diameter and many of them so crooked that to drive them straight was impracticable, and they stand crossing each other in the most irregular manner.[2] . . . The average length of piles driven 21 ft. into the gravel as required by the specification [and as recommended by Rennie] would have been 13 ft. 3 in.,' but of the 2378 piles removed by 1827 'only 194 are of that length: the average length proves to be 10 ft. 1 in., their average thickness only $7\frac{1}{2}$ in. diameter instead of the 9 in. square as directed'.[3] Peto 'charged . . . for the workmen's labour in driving these piles at the rate of 1s. 0d. for what he paid no more than $3\frac{1}{2}$d.; the total length of all the piles was only 53,300 ft. but Peto had charged for 104,000 ft.'.[4] 'It seems highly probable', the Commissioners maintained, 'that of the sum of £24,931 paid to Mr. Peto on the amount of his bill for the piling certified by Mr. Laing, more than half will prove to be a charge so grossly unjust as to warrant the strongest suspicion of fraudulent collusion between the parties'.[5]

Other parts of the construction proved equally fraudulent. 'On taking away the wood flooring which covered the arches under the King's Warehouse it was seen that the spandrils of the arches had all been filled in with a mass of chalk lime and stone rubbish', costing 'little more than the labour of conveying it there'.[6] Yet Peto had charged £1600 for 'brickwork' spandrils, although he later professed his ignorance of the claim.[7] 'We have found masses of the same sort of rubbish', wrote Smirke, 'consolidated to form the foundations of large flights of steps on the South front . . . and other parts, all charged as solid brickwork. We have found some stone paving charged as 6 in. thick to the amount of about £3600, the great part of which proved to be little more than $4\frac{1}{2}$ in. in average thickness, the fair value of which must have been less than £2500. . . .[8] The boarding upon which the slates were laid and fastened is of the most improper description; it consists entirely of wood that had been used for other purposes, the great part of it of small irregular pieces . . . some boards were obviously pieces of a hoard fencing, for the remains of notice bills were seen upon them. . . . The whole is charged . . . at the price of new and the best materials'.[9] The water closets leaked, uneven surfaces had been disguised with plaster, and the lead required frequent repair.[10] Moreover it appeared that for small repairs Peto had charged 17 per cent more than contemporary Office of Works prices which were in turn 10–15 per cent higher than the rates officially charged for 'great new buildings'—an excess therefore of about 30 per cent. Well might Smirke invite Soane to visit the Custom House and examine 'the very extraordinary manner

[1] Works 1/3, f. 194, 26 January 1825.   [2] Works 1/13, f. 293, 16 April 1825.
[3] Custom House MSS. iii, 25 January 1827.   [4] *Ibid.* 13 February 1828.
[5] *Ibid.* 1827, notes for trial annotated with Smirke's comments.
[6] Works 1/3, f. 194, 26 January 1825.   [7] Custom House MSS. iii, 25 January 1827.
[8] *Ibid.*   [9] Works 1/13, ff. 370–1, 14 June 1825.   [10] Custom House MSS. iii, 13 February 1828.

in which the work was done . . . as it may be the subject of public remark'.[1] Questions were raised in Parliament.[2] The Chancellor of the Exchequer stated that 'the most scandalous frauds had been practised'.[3] Legal proceedings were begun against Peto; Askew was temporarily and Laing permanently suspended by the Customs Commissioners.[4] Smirke himself had no doubt as to where the blame should be laid: 'the neglect of those appointed to see that Mr. Peto fulfilled his engagement, will afford no justification whatever for neglect or misconduct on his part', particularly as the defects were such as 'an architect (although he should have seen that they did not exist) might reasonably expect a good builder would carefully have avoided'.[5]

After Smirke had directed preliminary shoring and centering, it was decided to rebuild the central portion of the river front at an estimated cost of £75,000.[6] This estimate excluded the cost of new concrete foundations and internal fittings which, together with the alterations effected in the northern entrance and the offices of the east wing, raised the cost of reconstruction to £177,219 18s. 3d., even allowing for the £4332 14s. 9d., produced by the sale of old materials.[7]

Smirke's reconstruction of the Custom House consolidated his reputation as 'the best constructor of his day'.[8] Almost alone among contemporary architects, his practice measured up to the highest standards of machine engineering.[9] Eight years previously, at Millbank Penitentiary, he had been the first English architect to make use of concrete foundations.[10] Since that celebrated occasion in 1817 he had displayed his mastery of the new material in several commissions, notably at Lancaster Place in the Savoy Precinct (1820–32) and at Sir Robert Peel's town house, No. 4, Whitehall Gardens (1822–24). The Custom House scandal endowed his new technique with the maximum publicity.

Smirke employed his usual method of laying concrete and his usual contractor, Samuel Baker of Rochester.[11] The piers and walls were underbuilt 'with a solid artificial stratum of gravel grouted with hot stone lime'.[12] While the building was shored up with timber supports, underpinning proceeded in sections 10 ft. long.

---

[1] Sir John Soane's Museum, Soane Correspondence, xii, C.
[2] *Hansard's Parl. Debates* N.S. xii (1825), p. 1354. [3] J. Britton, *Picture of London* (1825), p. 143.
[4] Custom House MSS. iii, 1 February 1825, 1 March 1825.
[5] *Ibid.* 25 January 1827, 13 February 1828.
[6] Works 1/13, f. 293, 16 April 1825. Smirke also suggested two cheaper alternatives involving a casing wall and/or intermediate supporting walls.
[7] Works 1/15, f. 422, 20 September 1827.
[8] Sir John Summerson, *Georgian London* (1945), p. 190. 'Mr. Smirke is pre-eminent in construction: in this respect he has not his superior in the United Kingdom' (*The Athenaeum*, 1828, p. 29). However his use of central heating in the Long Room was less successful and caused considerable controversy (*Architectural Mag.* iv, 1837, pp. 161 *et seq.*).
[9] Most architects were said to labour under 'a prejudice against . . . undertaking "construction" work, or anything in reference to *water*, as if they were suffering under hydrophobia' (J. Noble, *The Professional Practice of Architects*, 1836, p. 23).
[10] J. Mordaunt Crook, 'Sir Robert Smirke: A Pioneer of Concrete Construction', *Trans. of the Newcomen Society* xxxviii (1965–6), pp. 5–22.
[11] Baker married Smirke's sister Sarah in 1816. The Bakers had 'large dealings in land and timber . . . and the principal management of the Borough of Rochester for the [Tory] Government' (Farington, pp. 6680, 17 June 1815 and p. 6944, 3 June 1818). The partnership 'Baker and Son' consisted of Samuel Baker of Rochester and George Baker of Montagu Place, London. For a while Samuel Baker was in partnership with Nicholson of Rochester. Together they contracted for the Ordnance Barracks at Chatham. Nicholson later joined with Joliffe and Banks in contracting for the Sheerness Dock Yard (C. W. Pasley, *Outline of a Course of Practical Architecture*, lithographed notes, Chatham 1826; reprinted Chatham 1862, p. 185). Sir Herbert Baker F.R.I.B.A. (1892–1946) was the grandson of Sarah's brother-in-law, Thomas Baker.
[12] Works 1/13, f. 141, 7 January 1825.

'The operation is difficult', wrote Smirke to Stephenson, 'and very distressing to the workmen, many of whom are unavoidably kept engaged in deep excavations where they cannot long remain on account of the impurity of the air. I trust you will sanction the extra allowance which I have desired to be given to the men employed in this particular service'.[1] The new foundation consisted of three layers. Firstly, there was a platform of concrete mixed in the proportions of one part pulverised Dorking quicklime to seven or eight parts Thames ballast. Above this was placed a course of Yorkshire landing stones each measuring 5 ft. × 5 ft. × 5 in. thick. The final level consisted of twelve courses of brickwork laid in cement wedged close to the original brickwork with pieces of slate. These three layers served to equalise the pressure placed upon the lime concrete stratum.[2] For the sections begun *de novo*, where no underpinning was required, Smirke refined upon the system adopted at Lancaster Place. Above the concrete and Yorkshire landings were laid 'two chain timbers of scantling 9 in. wide and 12 in. deep . . . firmly bedded in the brick footing of the walls, without resting on sleepers in the usual manner'. It was claimed that 'this judicious arrangement possesses the advantages of a continued wooden platform without its disadvantages'.[3]

If the Custom House gained in solidity, however, it lost in architectural interest. The Parisian flavour of Laing's triple-domed Long Room lit by a series of round-arched windows gave way to a plain pilastered design with a coved ceiling (Pl. 27). For Laing's novel façade Smirke substituted a composition based on a conventionally quintuple division in which the wings were echoed too precisely by the inelegant Ionic portico in the centre (Pl. 26). 'Mr. Smirke's "rifacciamento" . . . may be appreciated at a glance', decided one critic. 'He has so far rendered it all of-a-piece, that the centre is now of no more importance than the wings . . . it is now as insipid and flat a pile of stone and mortar as can be imagined'.[4] A later commentator, having grudgingly praised Laing's design for 'some novelty of physiognomy', complained that 'the specimen [Smirke] has given here of architectural reform is enough to make us sicken at the very name. Not content with removing what was good, he substituted a host of incongruities', substituting 'littleness for continuity and grandeur'.[5]

Such judgments were too harsh. Smirke's reconstruction of the Custom House was a professional *tour de force*. Nor did his connection with the case end with the completion of rescue operations. Litigation dragged on for another ten years. While the rebuilding continued, Peto was still contending 'not merely for the hard earnings of an industrious life, but for what is more dear to me, for that character I have endeavoured to maintain through life'.[6] At the Middlesex sittings in May 1826 the Attorney-General failed to convince the jury that Peto had not executed the contract in accordance with his instructions and must therefore forfeit the £33,000 stipulated by the bond of 1812. However Peto's defence, that he had merely acted on Laing's instructions, was overruled by a judgment in the Exchequer Court '*non obstante veredicto*'.[7] In the following year he filed a bill for equitable relief, and the protracted

---

[1] Works 1/13, f. 353, 23 May 1825.
[2] C. W. Pasley, *Observations on Limes, Calcareous Cements, Mortars, Stuccoes and Concrete* (2nd ed. 1847), pp. 267–9. [3] *Ibid.* [4] *Library of the Fine Arts* ii (1831), p. 273.
[5] *Civil Engineer and Architect's Jnl.* i (1838), pp. 187–8. [6] Custom House MSS. iii, 2 January 1827.
[7] *Gent's. Mag.* 1826, pt. i, p. 460; *The Times* 18 May 1826, p. 4.

negotiations over the actual sums involved were intensified, with Peto's property at Furnival's Inn standing security for his eventual payment of the bond. By 1827 Peto's claims had been limited to £70,000 and by 1830 to half this sum. Against this the Crown claimed not only the £33,000 but also a total of £20,000 fraudently obtained by Peto. An Exchequer ruling of November 1829 appointed a further hearing upon interrogatories. But in the months before his death on 15 September 1830, Peto continued to press his case in Equity, even writing to the Duke of Wellington. The principal beneficiaries by his will were two nephews, Thomas Grissell and Samuel Morton Peto, later famous as building and railway contractors. Although it was maintained that Henry Peto had 'sacrificed his life in his legal contests with the Crown', his executors astutely consented to a compromise formulated by Lord Henley at the behest of the Court of Chancery.[1] £10,000 compensation, costs amounting to £4423 10s. 8d., and interest totalling £1079 8s. 10d., were to be paid by the executors before the end of 1836—fully twenty-four years after the original contract had been signed.

As for Laing, he ended by accepting charity from the Artists' General Benevolent Institution, the Fund for Distressed Architects, and the Surveyors' Club, a society over which he had once presided.[2] Professionally ruined, he lived until 1856, 'a beacon of warning to the young architect in particular, not to trust *to others* in matters of serious moment; . . . still . . . if one architect failed in this work, the *quid pro quo* can be adduced, in favour of another who succeeded, and *Smirked at the job!*'.[3]

THE GENERAL POST OFFICE

Like the British Museum, the General Post Office was already ripe for reconstruction when it entered the jurisdiction of the Office of Works in 1815. Its removal from Lombard Street had been envisaged as early as 1789.[4] By 1813 negotiations were in train for a new site in St. Martin's le Grand. Removal was justified on three grounds: postal convenience, urban improvement and social conscience. By moving 700 yards westwards to a more 'centrical' site, it was argued that 'the Letter Carriers might be despatched earlier, the Receiving Houses kept open longer, and the whole Metropolis have additional time to answer letters . . . both Houses of Parliament [having] half an hour longer to send their letters to the Office'.[5] As a metropolitan improvement the new arrangement would open up the area surrounding the junction of St.

---

[1] Custom House MSS. iv, passim.   [2] Colvin, *Dictionary*, p. 353, note 1.
[3] J. Noble, *The Professional Practice of Architects* (1836), p. 22.
[4] The new site originally canvassed was Blackwell Hall in Basinghall Street ('Report from the Committee on Petitions relating to the General Post Office', *Parl. Pap.* 1813–14, iii, p. 162). Another suggestion was the site of Smithfield market, which would involve 'the immediate annihilation of that abominable nuisance and scandal of the City, Bartholomew Fair' (B.M. Add. MS. 38379, f. 140, 1 December 1814).
[5] Liverpool Papers clxxxi, B.M. Add. MS. 38370, ff. 1–7, 31 January 1821; 'Report from the Committee on Petitions relating to the General Post Office', *Parl. Pap.* 1813–14, iii, p. 168.

Martin's le Grand and Newgate Street. As a piece of slum clearance the redevelopment plan would sweep away 'one of the greatest nuisances about the City' by demolishing 'all the alleys and back courts' infested by 'loose persons . . . bad women . . . and houses of ill fame.'[1] The Corporation of the City of London was therefore in favour of the move, first suggesting the new site and then offering to bear one third of the cost of purchase out of money made available from the Orphans Fund.[2] But it was the condition of the premises in Lombard Street which made some sort of change essential. They consisted of several 17th-century buildings 'obtained at different times, and laid together as circumstances would admit . . . disjointed . . . unconnected . . . and inconvenient'. Besides the danger of fire, the old Post Office was 'crowded to excess', requiring the employment of 'constables to prevent confusion and . . . depredations'.[3]

Since the death of J. T. Groves in 1811, Joseph Kay (1775–1847) had been Architect to the Post Office at a salary of £250 per annum.[4] While still a pupil of S. P. Cockerell he had acted as Smirke's travelling companion on the Continent in 1804–5.[5] Ironically it was Smirke who secured the commission which might well have been the logical climax to Kay's career. In 1814 Kay prepared preliminary plans for rebuilding the General Post Office, the 'general idea' being approved by the Postmaster General.[6] These plans formed the basis of negotiations for a new site and for the purchase of private property. With the assistance of S. P. Cockerell and William Montague, it was Kay who organised the detailed surveys which these arrangements involved.[7] But in 1815 a parliamentary committee advocated an open competition for fresh designs, to be judged by the newly-appointed Surveyor General. Particular attention should be paid to simplicity and economy: a Post Office 'concealed behind a Front fit for a Palace, and flanked by triumphal arches, would present an incongruity no less offensive to good taste, than inconsistent with rational economy'.[8]

For four years this recommendation hung fire. In the spring of 1819 the Treasury decided to examine Kay's proposals. His plans were referred to the Office of Works and tracings were made for the use of Nash, Soane and Smirke in preparing their

---

[1] 'Report from the Select Committee on intended Improvements in the Post Office', *Parl. Pap.* 1814–15 iii, pp. 194, 212. For the history of the site and Smirke's redevelopment plan see *Illustrations of the Site and Neighbourhood of the New Post Office, St. Martin's-le-Grand* (Smales and Tuck, 1830).

[2] The City also stood to gain because 'The effect of this plan . . . would be to "annihilate the present jurisdiction of Westminster over this district, and to bring it within the jurisdiction of the City" ' (*Parl. Pap.* 1814–15, iii, p. 194).

[3] 'Report from the Committee on Petitions relating to the General Post Office', *Parl. Pap.* 1813–14, iii, pp. 165–7. For the cost of alterations and repairs 1789–1814 cf. *ibid.* pp. 189–90. The cost of future repairs was estimated at £4–5000 per annum (*ibid.* pp. 176–7).

[4] 'Accounts relating to the Establishment and Expences of the General Post Office', *Parl. Pap.* 1822, xviii, p. 159. In this capacity he designed the Post Office at Edinburgh (Works 1/13). In 1807 he became Surveyor to the Foundling Hospital and in 1823 Surveyor to Greenwich Hospital (Colvin, *Dictionary*, p. 332).

[5] Smirke MSS. in the possession of Sir Edward Malet, Bt.

[6] 'Report from the Committee on Petitions relating to the General Post Office', *Parl. Pap.* 1813–14, iii, pp. 178–9, 181, 183.

[7] Houses were purchased in accordance with 55 G. iii *c.* 91: 'An Act for enlarging and improving the West end of Cheapside, . . . also St. Martin's le Grand, Aldergate Street, St. Anne's Lane and Foster Lane, and for providing a site for a new Post Office'. For details cf 'Report of the Progress made in . . . providing a Site for a New Post Office', *Parl. Pap.* 1816, vi, p. 407; 'Report from the Select Committee appointed to consider . . . a site for a new Post Office', *Parl. Pap.* 1820, ii, p. 254. Montague was Clerk of the Works to the Corporation of London and S. P. Cockerell was Surveyor to the See of London (Colvin, *Dictionary*, pp. 148, 398).

[8] 'Report from the Select Committee on intended Improvements in the Post Office', *Parl. Pap.* 1814–15, iii, pp. 187–8.

report. The report was made but not submitted. For on 1 July the Treasury at last decided to organise an open competition, after first making sure that Kay's designs were still secret.[1] During December 89 competitors entered nearly 100 designs. These were first sifted by a 'committee of taste' and then examined by 'the principal officers of the Post Office'.[2] In the following May Vansittart despatched to the Office of Works a 'sealed parcel, endorsed: "New Post Office: sealed addresses of the architects who have sent in plans", with a letter from the Postmaster General'.[3] The Attached Architects considered 'thirty three sets of drawings . . . from different professional men all of which upon examination were rejected as wholly inapplicable in every respect'. Nevertheless 'premiums were given for the most approved of these designs'. Among those which were rejected were designs by Thomas Hopper, John Goldicutt and J. B. Papworth.[4]

At this point it seemed to Post Office officials that the whole project was in jeopardy, although £240,000 had already been advanced for purchasing the site in St. Martin's le Grand.[5] In August, 1823, therefore, the Treasury resurrected Kay's designs and called for the Attached Architects' original report. Kay had proposed a building 'of the most solid construction, and with the exception of the internal fittings, to be entirely incombustible'. It was to be in 'a plain massive style, . . . as most appropriate to a public building of utility', with two entrance porticoes, 'Bassi Relievi . . . allegorical of the Inland and Foreign Commerce of the country', and a colonnaded courtyard dominated by 'an obelisk, or a column . . . from which the principal roads in the kingdom might be measured'.[6] Nash, Soane and Smirke found the result unimpressive. They considered the planning, communications, lighting and ventilation quite impractical; besides which there were 'too many false bearings, by which the strength of the walls would be much weakened, and the walls in general appear too thin'.[7] More important, 'however plain and devoid of ornamentation . . . it will cost a much larger sum' than the estimated £150,000.[8] Smirke, within whose area the building was to be erected, was thereupon commissioned by the Treasury to prepare plans after consultation with departmental officials.[9] Such were the events which many architects, including Hopper if not Kay, never ceased to regard as a conspicuous example of official corruption.[10]

---

[1] Works 12/104/1; Works 1/9, 9 March 1819.

[2] Sydney Smirke's account, in J. Britton and A. C. Pugin, *Public Buildings of London* (ed. W. H. Leeds, 1838), ii pp. 82–3.

[3] Works 4/24, f. 73, 10 December 1819 and f. 193, 11 May 1820.

[4] Works 1/17, f. 59, 18 December 1828. The designs for which John Goldicutt was awarded third prize are now in the R.I.B.A. Drawings Collection (J 11/303–5).

[5] Liverpool Papers clxxxi, B.M. Add. MS. 38370, ff. 1–7, 31 January 1821.

[6] Works 1/9, 9 March 1819. Kay's plans are in Sir John Soane's Museum, Drawer 38/6. Works 30/414–5 are copies made c. 1819.

[7] Works 1/12, ff. 100–110, report dated 30 June 1819.

[8] Sir John Soane's Museum, Soane Correspondence xii, F.

[9] Works 1/12, f. 163–4, 4 September 1823, f. 210, 12 November 1823 and f. 295, 18 December 1823.

[10] 'I applied to the friend who had induced me to [compete] . . . and was informed by him that a Committee of Taste had selected an elevation, and desired Mr. Smirke to apply it, omitting some of the columns; but he said the design was taken from the Vitruvius Britannicus. . . . Although our designs so nearly agree, it does not follow, because mine was first made, that Sir Robert Smirke copied it; but it is apparent that it was not rejected for the reasons stated' (T. Hopper, *A Letter to Lord Viscount Melbourne on the Rebuilding of the Royal Exchange*, 1839, pp. 8, 13n. See also W. Papworth, *J. B. Papworth*, 1879, pp. 118–9). In 1826, as Secretary to the Architect's Club, Kay formally exonerated Smirke from any imputation of unprofessional conduct with regard to the G.P.O. (H. M. Colvin, 'The Architects of Stafford House', *Architectural History*, i, 1958, p. 23).

Smirke's plans were soon prepared. His surviving drawings illustrate experiments with tetrastyle and dystyle porticoes which evidently preceded the final entrance façade with its giant central portico, hexastyle prostyle after the Ionic Temple of Minerva at Priene in Asia Minor, flanked by tetrastyle versions of the same design emphasising the wings (Pl. 28A).[1] Despite the columns, the main emphasis in the composition was horizontal: a ponderous stylobate of granite, a heavily moulded cornice, and two rows of windows along the Portland stone façade, those on the ground floor having ears, those above having plain architraves and sills forming a continuous string-course. The recessed entrance, which effectively increased the depth of the main portico, gave access to the main hall divided in basilican fashion by rows of Ionic columns. The hall separated the two wings of the building and led directly to the rear entrance adjoining which was the main staircase where Doric balusters of brass regularly progressed around the four sides of the well.[2] Both wings were subdivided into a multiplicity of offices with their attendant staircases and corridors. All in all the insulated building measured 389 ft. × 130 ft. × 64 ft. high.

The fact that Smirke's estimate of £200,000[3] was not exceeded in the erection of so large a building speaks well for the accuracy of the system of contracts for prices. To this sum must be added the £299,359[4] absorbed by the purchase of the St. Martin's le Grand site and the payment of compensation for the demolition of 131 houses, beginning in 1814.[5] Finally, £25,781 was spent on furnishings and £3855 on the gas lighting provided by the City Gas Co.[6]

Smirke was directing the arrangement of the site by November 1823.[7] The foundation stone was laid in May 1824,[8] and by December 1825 he could report: 'the walls are all raised to the level of the upper floor and some of the internal walls are at the level of the roof; the principal part of the roof is prepared, and workmen will begin to fix it early in the Spring'.[9] In March 1827 he wrote, 'the exterior is nearly finished except at the portico in the centre of the principal front. Every part of the interior of the hall is prepared to receive plaistering, which will be commenced in the course of the present month. The windows, doors, flooring and other parts of the joiners' work are prepared. I calculate on having the plaisterer's work finished this year and the joiners' work fixed immediately afterwards'.[10] By July £118,347 had been spent.[11] 'The exterior walls of the building, portico etc. are completed', he reported in the following January, 'and as soon as the season permits a proper railed enclosure will be fixed round the building and the pavements formed on those sides where the old houses have been purchased and cleared away. The North and South fronts however remain still encumbered with several other houses which must be purchased and taken down before convenient approaches can be made. The principal part of the interior will also be soon finished in all respects except the

[1] Victoria and Albert Museum, Print Room, A. 173.
[2] *Gent's. Mag.* 1829, pt. ii, p. 297. [3] Works 1/15, f. 170, 15 March 1827.
[4] Works 12/104/1, f. 27, 5 May 1828 (of this, £97,352 was borne by the City).
[5] *Gent's. Mag.* 1833, pt. ii, p. 351; G. Clinch, *Modern History of the City of London* (1896), p. 164.
[6] Works 12/104/1, ff. 1–62. Gas was supplied by two of Crossley's patent gasometers capable of registering 4000 cubic feet of gas per hour for the 1000 burners in the building (*Gent's. Mag.* 1829, pt. ii, p. 298).
[7] Works 1/12, f. 210, 12 November 1823. [8] C. Knight, *London* iii (1876), p. 281.
[9] Works 12/62/3, 12 December 1825. [10] Works 1/15, f. 170, 15 March 1827.
[11] 'Report from the Select Committee on the Office of Works', *Parl. Pap.* 1828, iv, p. 478.

painting, which I shall defer until a more favourable season. I am in the mean time engaged in working out with the principal officers of the Establishment an account of the desks, presses and other fittings required. . . . These may be made and the building prepared for public service, before Winter of the present year'.[1]

Tenders submitted by the following tradesmen were accepted during the course of construction:

Mr. Swinney:	excavating[2] and foundations.[3]
Mr. Lee:	brickwork.[4]
Mr. Paynter:	carpenter's and joiner's work.[5]
Mr. Mallcott:	Portland, Bath and Yorkshire stonework.[6]
Messrs. Johnson:	granite stonework.[7]
Messrs. Coulson & Co.: Messrs. Fowler & Jones:	ironwork.[8]
Mr. Good:	plumbing.[9]
Mr. Struther:	'best Bangor rag slates'.[10]

J. W. Hiort's patent bricks and chimney pots were employed,[11] as also Stratton's Patent Calorific Ventilators,[12] although Oldham's system of ventilation was installed in the Inland Department in 1840.[13] Messrs. Bramah were employed to alter the gates and railings which had been held responsible for a fatal accident in 1833.[14] It was Vulliamy who designed the double-faced clock over the entrance, criticised at the time as being 'one of the most harmless pieces of insipidity ever perpetrated by Mr. Smirke'.[15]

On the whole Smirke's design was well received. 'As a *city improvement*', it was remarked, the building 'marks an epoch, and promises to prove the commencement of a new era; while as a public building, its vastness, solidity and pretensions to architecture rank it among the most important edifices of the metropolis. . . . The masterly and substantial manner in which all the works have been executed . . . is equally creditable to the Government, the architect and the contractors'. The hall (80 ft. × 64 ft. × 53 ft. high), lit by windows above and below the iron balcony surrounding its walls, was deemed 'worthy of the first Post Office in the world'.[16] Waagen commended the structure's 'noble effect'.[17] The various offices, with their cast iron galleries, simply compartmented ceilings and walls divided by plain pilasters, required little alteration for over half a century. To the north of the hall, on the ground floor, lay rooms for the receipt of newspapers, inland, ship and foreign letters, and the comptrollers' and mail-coach offices. On the southern side were

---

[1] Works 12/62, f. 3, 10 January 1828.　　[2] Works 4/26, f. 258, 22 December 1823.
[3] *Ibid.* f. 302, 5 February 1824.　　[4] *Ibid.* f. 261, 24 December 1823.
[5] *Ibid.* f. 271, 3 January 1824.　　[6] *Ibid.* f. 292, 24 January 1824.
[7] *Ibid.* f. 296, 29 January 1824.　　[8] *Ibid.* 348, 22 March 1824.
[9] Works 4/27, f. 431, 15 March 1826.　　[10] *Ibid.* f. 438, 23 March 1826.
[11] Works 1/14, f. 52, 31 January 1826.　　[12] Works 4/26, f. 290, 22 January 1824.
[13] Works 1/24, f. 197, 14 May 1840.　　[14] Works 1/20, ff. 133, 141, 145.
[15] Works 12/104/1, 19 April 1828; *The Athenaeum* 1829, p. 617.
[16] *The Athenaeum*, 1829, pp. 616–7. For illustrations and descriptions of the various offices cf. *Illustrated London News.* ii (1843), pp. 146, 319; iv (1844), p. 401; vi (1845), p. 140; vii (1845) pp. 45, 313; *Penny Mag.* 1834, p. 32; *London Interiors* i (1841), p. 65; C. Knight, *London* iii (1876), p. 288.
[17] G. F. Waagen, *Works of Art and Artists in England* i (1838), p. 22.

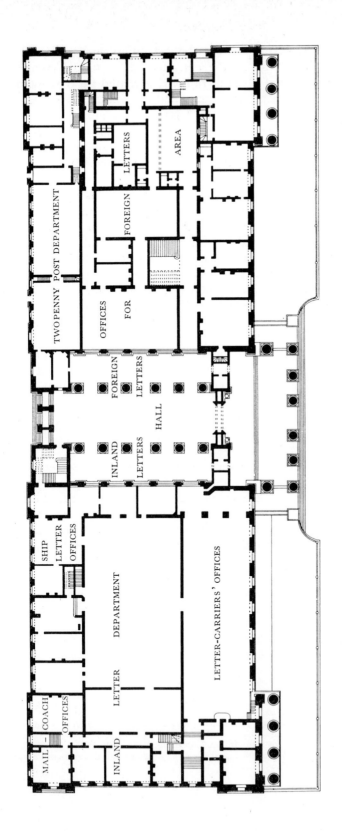

Fig. 14. The General Post Office: from Britton and Pugin's *Public Buildings of London* (1825).

situated the money-order, receiver-general, and accountant-general's offices, and the London district Post Office. Below the entrance hall a tunnel connected the different departments by means of a small 'railway' invented by Barrow. The first storey, with its flooring of American oak, contained administrative offices and the letter-bill, dead, mis-sent, and returned-letter offices. Machinery conveyed coal to every floor; two steam engines supplied ventilation; and fireproofing arrangements included water supplies, cast iron beams, metal plates and hollow bricks turned in flat arches and closely cemented together.[1] As late as 1844 it could be stated that 'for utility, strength and beauty, this is, perhaps, the finest structure in the metropolis'.[2]

Despite the ample accommodation provided by 190 rooms on five floors, an enormous expansion of Post Office business very soon necessitated the erection of additional offices.[3] In 1837–8 Smirke enlarged the Twopenny Post Office and improved the ventilation of the Inland Sorting Office at a total of £1715.[4] Plans for the expansion of the Money Order Office were mooted in 1841 and authorised in 1843.[5] But in the following year it was decided to erect a separate building for this purpose, opposite the main building, between St. Botolph's and the French Protestant Church. The office Smirke designed comprised three stories with floor space amounting to 6500 superficial feet, plus an attic and basement for records; the estimate was £7500.[6] It was built in 1845–6. At the same time he designed two additional rooms for the Sorting and Letter Carrier's Offices in the main building, and estimated the cost at £13,500. The execution of all these works was left to Sydney Smirke owing to Robert's ill health.[7] Erected as part of an additional storey and lit by skylights, the use of cast iron on this occasion struck contemporaries as 'novel and ingenious'. The roof of the Letter Carrier's Office (105 ft. × 33 ft) was merely carried by iron-arched trusses set in two pieces, but that of the Sorting Office (90 ft. × 50 ft.) was supported by seven iron arches, each cast in three sections, which also supported the floor by means of iron suspension rods. Two of these rods, $2\frac{1}{2}$ in. in diameter, 'of the best Crawshays iron . . . tested to bear 35 tons', depended from each arch. To each rod were bolted iron bearers, forming the tie, or chord, of the arches, and sockets 'to enable them to lay hold of all the timbers of the floor and of the old ceiling of the inland-office beneath'. These operations were executed without disturbing either the cradling of the old ceiling or the transaction of business below. The heavy ironwork, supplied by Messrs. Dewer and finished with their new steam planing-machine, was 'carried over the ridges of the intervening roofs . . . by that ingenious modern contrivance, the flying windlass'. The wrought iron bolts were 'of the best fagotted S.C. iron . . . heated towards the middle and head, and shrunk after the nuts were tightened'.[8]

Enthusiasm for the General Post Office lasted little longer than the cult of Greek Revivalism. Early criticism of specific details soon broadened into general abuse. So

[1] J. Britton and A. C. Pugin, *Public Buildings of London* (ed. Leeds, 1838), ii, pp. 82–9.
[2] *Illustrated Evening News* x (1844), p. xi.
[3] For the expansion of Post Office business cf. J. Grant, *Travels in Town* ii (1839), pp. 1–65.
[4] Works 1/22, f. 269, 10 June 1837; Works 1/23, f. 113, 12 June 1838.
[5] Works 1/25, f. 16, 3 March 1841 (estimate £1300); Works 1/26, f. 210, 7 June 1843 (estimate £3200).
[6] Works 2/4, f. 387, 21 February 1845 and f. 446, 9 May 1845; Works 1/27, ff. 253, 387, 410.
[7] Sydney Smirke was also responsible for some internal rearrangement of the offices in 1844 (*Illustrated London News* iv, 1844, p. 401).   [8] *The Builder*, iv (1846), pp. 13, 37, 42, full descriptions and diagrams.

far were the earlier critics from desiring exuberance of decoration, that Smirke was censured in 1829 for using so delicate an order as the Ionic on such an obviously utilitarian structure. 'Mr. Smirke . . . presents us a Theatre with a senatorial physiognomy, a martial clubhouse with a reverential aspect, and now a . . . . Post Office with a front suited by its richness and ornament to form a court residence.[1] Mr. Smirke seems a very sphinx in architecture, and to delight in propounding riddles to the gaping multitude'.[2] But sixteen years later the portico was claimed as the sole redeeming feature in a building which appeared like 'a jackdaw with a solitary peacock's feather in its tail. All the rest . . . can be described only by negatives . . . although every side is to be seen . . . the architect seems to have relied upon obtaining for them the loan of Gyges' ring, and accordingly gave himself no further concern about their nakedness'.[3] The Northern side seemed particularly bald: 'it partakes more of a Quaker's drab bonnet than of Athene's helmet'.[4] Constantly criticised were the unadorned tympanum and the meagre coffering of the portico;[5] 'those three insignificant, odd-looking arched doorways, with the clumsy gallery above them' at the east end of the hall, and 'those miserable windows fit only for a kitchen or stable' in the triforium;[6] the third storey windows—mere 'perforations of necessity'—which broke the frieze of the northern and southern fronts; and the 'miserable' railing in St. Martin's le Grand. As for the rear façade, with its mixture of round-arched and square-headed windows, it was claimed to be 'beneath criticism. The design has evidently been left to the taste of the clerk of the works. . . . Excepting always such parts of the monstrous edifice at Pimlico, we should pronounce the centre *break* to be one of the most glaring deformities to be found in any building ancient or modern. . . .'[7] The console-dressed windows are exactly the same in *pattern* as those of the new buildings at the British Museum and the Equitable Assurance Office. . . . Mr. Smirke is only classical when he copies columns'.[8]

These criticisms of the General Post Office, 'talked of and looked up to as the *beau ideal* of a public building' and as influential in its own way as Gibbs' St. Martin-in-the-Fields,[9] may be summarised in a single phrase: the lowering of neoclassical ideals to the level of mass-production. But as a piece of purposive design it was superb. Its rational planning and formidable structure stood the strain of public business for the best part of a century. An extra storey was added in 1892[10] and demolition followed in 1912.[11] Today some of Smirke's Ionic capitals serve as flower pots in the garden of Hyde Hall, Hertfordshire.[12]

[1] 'Ecod, if thot's on'y a Poast-office, I'd loike to see where the Lord Mayor o' Lunnon lives', remarks a visiting Yorkshireman in a contemporary novel, quoted by F. G. Kay, *Royal Mail* (1951), p. 54.
[2] *The Athenaeum* 1828, p. 30 and 1829, p. 616.
[3] *Civil Engineer and Architect's Jnl.* viii (1845), p. 34; *Surveyor, Engineer and Architect* iii (1842), pp. 136–7.
[4] *Civil Engineer and Architect's Jnl.* i (1838), p. 243.
[5] *The Athenaeum* 1829, p. 616. Its decoration with the imperial arms of the United Kingdom appears to have been contemplated (J. Elmes, *Metropolitan Improvements* ii, 1827–9, p. 158).
[6] *Library of the Fine Arts* i (1831), pp. 310–11; ii (1832), pp. 270–1; *Foreign Quarterly Rev.* vii (1831) p. 455.
[7] *The Athenaeum* 1829, p. 617.   [8] *Library of the Fine Arts* i (1831), pp. 310–11.
[9] *Architectural Mag.* ii (1835), p. 327.   [10] Designed by Anderson at a cost of £27,000 (Works 12/104/2).
[11] For a sketch of the demolition cf. *Manchester Guardian* 27 November 1912. Schemes for the re-erection of the 'dignified if dirty pediment and pillars' at St. Chad's College, Durham, or at Calton Hill, Edinburgh, or in the Edward VII Memorial Park, Shadwell, London, all failed. The portico was even offered to the R.I.B.A. (Works 12/104/2; *Architect's and Builder's Jnl.* xxxv, 1912, p. 626 and xxxvi, 1912, pp. 163, 618). Redevelopment of the site did not begin until 1924 (H. Clunn, *London Rebuilt*, 1927, pp. 40–1).
[12] N. Pevsner, *Buildings of England: Hertfordshire* (1959), p. 144.

THE INSOLVENT DEBTORS' COURT, LINCOLN'S INN FIELDS

Increasing business in the Insolvent Debtors' Court set up under an Act of 1813 demanded accommodation additional to that in the dilapidated house it occupied in Essex Street, Strand; and for that purpose in January 1821 the Treasury called on the Surveyor General for a report on Mr. Justice Park's house, 33 Lincoln's Inn Fields, comprising two back and two front rooms on three floors, with attics, and backing on to Portugal Street.[1] The Treasury authorised the purchase of the house for £4500 and Stephenson instructed Soane to call on the commissioner of the court for the information necessary for fitting up the house itself and for building a new court room on the premises.[2] Soane estimated repairs and alterations at £1200, and building a new court at a further £6000.[3] The Treasury wanted the expense kept within £5000, but Soane replied that the premises were 'so very inapplicable to the purpose for which they are stated to have been purchased by Government' that he would recommend reselling them.[4] Although he revised his plans,[5] he concluded that the premises could not be made satisfactory at a smaller cost. After discussions between the officers of the court and the Chancellor of the Exchequer, directions were given to Soane on 20 August to start immediately on the alterations only. In the July quarter of 1822 there was charged for fitting up the house £1403;[6] an attic was added, and the front modernised.[7]

Barely a term had passed however before the officers of the court complained of inconvenience from the want of a suitable courtroom. The Treasury then directed plans to be drawn up as cheaply as possible. On 24 January 1823 Soane sent his design[8] to the Surveyor General, with an estimate of £5300, which he thought might be reduced ten per cent by competitive tenders. On 21 February Stephenson directed him to start as soon as possible.[9] But in April Herries, the new Secretary of the Treasury, called for the plans; and authority to begin work was not obtained until the end of May.[10] Fronting on Portugal Street, the public entrance and offices formed the ground floor; behind rose the upper part of the court-room, another variation on Soane's 'Law Courts' theme, lighted on two sides by a clerestory and from above by a lantern (concealed externally by stone arcading linking two chimney

---

[1] Works 1/10, pp. 305–6, 308. For an account of Park's house, erected in 1659, see *Survey of London*, iii (1912), p. 3.

[2] Works 1/10, pp. 317–8, 8 February 1821; Soane Mus. corr. 2, xi, B. 1, 7 March 1821.

[3] Soane Mus. corr. 2, xi, B, 6, 9, 13; Works 1/10, p. 417, 4 June 1821.

[4] Soane Mus. corr. 2, xi, B, 15–18.

[5] Plans, elevations and sections, Soane Mus. 30/3/16–22, May 1821 (with a semicircular front to Portugal Street).

[6] Soane Mus. corr. 2, ix, B, 19, 26, 29; Works 1/10, p. 507; Works 5/108.

[7] *Survey of London*, iii, p. 3. 'One peculiar feature of the additional storey was that the queen-post roof trusses were left in position, the tie beams showing above the floor level'.

[8] Plans and elevation, Soane Mus. 30/3/6, 13–15, 31.

[9] Soane Mus. corr. 2, xi, B. 30, 32, 33; Works 1/11, pp. 357, 367.

[10] Soane Mus. corr. 2, i. B. 34, 40. Slightly revised plans dated June 1823 are Soane Mus. 30/3/10–12, 30; and a figured elevation, 30/3/27, is dated 27 August 1823.

stacks). Inside, the four semi-circular arches rising from piers without imposts closely resembled the Five per Cent Office at the Bank. The profiles of the round-headed windows were defined by recessed jambs like those on the first floor of New Bank Buildings (1807). The channelled quoins of the exterior looked forward to Soane's State Paper Office (1829),[1] and the whole building looked back to Vanbrugh's house in Whitehall.[2]

Tenders were accepted from Mallcott for mason's work, and from James Firth at 8 per cent under the office prices for carpenter's and joiner's.[3] On 12 February 1824 Firth stated that the roof and floors were fixed in the principal part, which had 'been nearly at a stand for some time'.[4] This delay, already complained of by Soane in August, resulted from the insecure state of the party wall on the east side, officially condemned on 7 November 1823. But the owner of the adjoining property was a minor; prolonged legal wranglings caused months of delay, making Soane the butt of 'peevish reflections and silly jokes'.[5] At length part of the wall was rebuilt by Office of Works tradesmen, and after further delay completed by those employed by the owner of the property.[6] The First Commissioner in Bankruptcy informed Soane that he was 'extremely satisfied with the Court, and its general accommodations, internal structure and appearance'.[7] It had cost nearly £8000.[8]

In 1831 additional accommodation for books and records was provided at a cost of £170.[9] A further enlargement was obtained by building an additional storey: in 1838–9 £850 were spent, and the following year a further £2800.[10] In May 1840 Dr. Reid was called in to improve the ventilation.[11]

Business so increased that accommodation was insufficient by 1847, when the Act 10/11 Vic. c. 102 greatly enlarged the court's activities. Accordingly, the debtors' commissioners proposed the purchase of the adjoining house, no. 34, formerly belonging to the late Mr. Baron Gurney,[12] on which they had already cast covetous eyes. Pennethorne having reported favourably, he negotiated the purchase for £14,600, and superintended the necessary alterations, fitting up three courts and offices,

---

[1] See illustrations and description in D. Stroud, *The Architecture of Sir John Soane* (1961), pp. 132–3, pls. 196–7. See also Dickens' account in *Pickwick Papers*.

[2] The resemblance is the more marked in an alternative design with two-storey wings (Soane Museum 30/3/32). In his Royal Academy *Lectures on Architecture* (ed. A. T. Bolton, 1929, p. 175) Soane wrote of Vanbrugh's house: 'The front, however small, contains the same number of general divisions, and at least as much Variety of Outline [as Burlington House] . . .The straight line, which terminates each of these buildings, accords most admirably with the general style and features of the Architecture, and this indication of a flat roof or terrace will always succeed, wherever Quietness of Character is aimed at, and the building is viewed at a small distance, or confined with projecting wings.' The arcaded chimneys were, of course, another Vanbrughian feature.

[3] Soane Mus. corr. 2, xi, B. 39, 46, 64.   [4] *Ibid.* 64.

[5] Works 1/12, p. 500, 28 June 1824. See also Soane Mus. corr. 2, xi, B. 44, 58, 68, 107.

[6] Soane Mus. corr. 2, xi, B. 107, Soane to Stephenson, 1 February 1825.

[7] *Ibid.* 93, 1 December 1824. Elevation, sections and plans drawn by C. J. Richardson are Soane Mus. 30/4.

[8] Works 5/109. In the six quarters ending 5 January 1825, £7234 14s. 7d. had been paid out, and a further £257 8s. 3d. credited for sale of old materials. In the last quarter of 1824, there was additionally £278 11s. 7d. for offices; and a year later £750 14s. 9d. for fitting up the vault and making a passage. The total expense of the new court itself was stated to the Treasury in November 1825 as £7943 8s. 8d. (Works 1/14, p. 113).

[9] Works 5/111.

[10] Works 2/6, pp. 187–191; *Parl. Pap.* 1847–8, xviii, pt. ii, p. 10.

[11] Works 1/24, p. 203; *Parl. Pap.* 1846 (574), xv, q. 1036.

[12] Works 2/6, pp. 150–2, 22 June 1847. The house had been purchased a year since by the Holborn Estate Charity for £12,699. In 1843 government had contemplated buying it, and Pennethorne and Chawner valued it at £11,000, which Gurney thought inadequate (*ibid.* pp. 187–91).

carried out by Messrs. I'Anson at the Office contract prices.[1] A delay occurred early in 1848 because the Office received insufficient funds,[2] the estimated total expenditure of £21,300 being defrayed under a special Act (11/12 Vic. c. 77) from unclaimed monies in the court.[3] In 1861 the court was abolished by the Bankruptcy Act. The buildings were used to house the Land Transfer Office, and demolished in 1911.[4]

KEW GARDENS

In the reigns of George III and George IV the gardens at Kew consisted of four parts—those immediately adjacent to the White and Dutch Houses, the Botanic Garden (about 11 acres), the royal kitchen garden (some 14 acres between the Botanic Garden and the Richmond Road) and the pleasure ground to the south between the road and the river (270 acres).[5] All were under the direction successively of two eminent botanists, William Aiton (1731–1793) and his son William Townsend Aiton (1766–1849).[6] Their salaries were paid from the Privy Purse, but the maintenance of the buildings was the responsibility of the Office of Works. Repairs were normally trifling. For example: repainting and re-roofing the Pagoda with copper, 1783–4;[7] building a new guard room in 1792;[8] painting 'the letters on the Flower sticks at . . . 3d. per dozen, three Dotts to be allowed equal to a Letter'[9]; 'spunging off Pencil writing in the Alcove Seats' and 'building a Shed for the Kangerous at the Cottage';[10] or mending '13,000 squares of Glass . . . broken . . . in consequence of an Hail storm on the Evening of 28 June 1813'.[11] In 1824 the locks of the Botanic Garden had to be changed because 'marauders of botany' had 'violated' the plants, 'through the intervention of keys, counterfeited for this purpose'.[12] In 1825 a new entrance was constructed to the south of the west end of Kew Green.[13] The 'great greenhouse' (presumably the orangery designed by Sir William Chambers for the Dowager Princess of Wales in 1761) was extensively repaired in 1833.[14]

[1] *Ibid.* pp. 187–91, 28 August 1847, Pennethorne to Commissioners; pp. 184–7, 9 September 1847; 191–2, 11 September; 204, 16 October 1847. Works 1/31, pp. 398–9, 16 September; 418–9, 16 October 1847.
[2] Works 1/32, pp. 207, 283.
[3] *Parl. Pap.* 1847–8, xviii, pt. i, p. xi; xl, p. 299; 1848, xxx, pp. 608–9. There was an excess of £63 7s. 10d. in the expenditure, the actual works costing £4901 18s. 7d. and furniture £1299 2s. 1d. (Works 2/7, pp. 34–7).
[4] B.M. Add. MS. 44337, f. 199; *Survey of London,* iii, p. 4. Plans of the buildings prior to demolition are given therein, pls. 19, 20; and plans of each floor made in 1871 are Works 30/5280–4. Works 30/5279 shows part of the ground floor in 1865.
[5] Walford, *Greater London,* ii, p. 411. For plans, see Works 32/101; Chawner's 1837–9 plan, Surrey R.O., Goulburn MS. III/10.
[6] See *D.N.B.*   [7] Works 4/16, 1 August 1783, 10 July 1784; Works 5/73, 1784.
[8] Works 4/17, 10 August 1792; Works 4/18, f. 6, 8 February 1793; Works 5/81, 1792; T. 29/65, f. 124, 11 October 1792.
[9] Works 4/17, 7 April 1786.   [10] Works 5/81, 1792.   [11] Works 4/21, 2 July 1813.
[12] Works 1/12, p. 375, Aiton to Stephenson.   [13] Works 5/109; this entailed a special expenditure of £1339.
[14] Works 1/20, p. 280. The Clerk of Works' failure to report expenditure in excess of the estimate led to his removal (*ibid.* p. 295). The building was further embellished in 1842, when the royal arms and cartouches bearing the letter A (for Princess Augusta, the builder of the Orangery) were placed in the pediments (J. Smith, MS. History of the Royal Gardens, Kew, in the library of the Royal Botanic Gardens, pp. 30–1).

William IV took some interest in the gardens, himself choosing the site for the re-erection in 1836 of one of Nash's Grecian conservatories removed from Buckingham Palace.[1] In the following year another temple was constructed by Wyatville at a cost of some £1800. This double-portico'd Doric temple formerly contained busts by Chantrey, now at Buckingham Palace, of George III, George IV, William IV and the Duke of Wellington. Set in the walls are a series of cast-iron panels commemorating British military victories from Minden to Waterloo. Originally called the Pantheon, it is now known as King William's Temple.[2]

In 1838 criticisms of W. T. Aiton's management led the Treasury to investigate the cost of the gardens, and a ministerial committee was appointed, which sought the technical and professional advice of Dr. Lindley, Professor of Botany at London University, and of two well-known gardeners, Messrs. Paxton and Wilson.[3] Lindley recommended that the Botanic Garden should be removed from the Lord Steward's control and either be abandoned or else established as a national Botanic Garden, for which purpose it should be enlarged by at least 30 acres.[4] No action was taken, but when in 1840 the Lord Steward proposed to convert the botanic into a kitchen garden there was an outcry in the press. The garden was transferred on 31 March 1840 to the Commissioners of Woods, and in 1841 Sir William Jackson Hooker was appointed Director.[5] Under Hooker, the gardens attained their world-wide reputation. In 1843 some 45 acres were added, on Aiton's retirement in 1845 the remainder of the pleasure ground, and in 1846 the kitchen gardens.[6] Works expenditure, only £1200 a year in the 1830s, averaged nearly £4000 in the 1840s.[7] Hooker's plans necessitated the construction of new greenhouses and buildings for study collections, work in which Decimus Burton was consistently employed as architect.[8] He also contributed to the embellishment of the grounds, replacing in 1845 'the decaying temple of Æolus . . . by a very chaste structure of a similar kind, in stone, from the original design of Sir William Chambers',[9] and designing new entrance gates from Kew Green in 1845–6.[10] At the same time new avenues and flower-beds were planned

[1] This was the north-eastern conservatory, removed by Blore (see p. 285) and re-erected at a cost of £3498 (L.R.R.O. 24/5): for William IV's interest see R. G. C. Desmond, 'John Smith, Kew's First Curator', *Kew Guild Journal*, viii (70), 1966, p. 578. We are grateful to Mr. Desmond for a copy of this article and for information about the archives of the Royal Botanic Gardens.

[2] E. W. Brayley, *History of Surrey* (1841–4) iii, p. 146; L.R.R.O. 24/6. The busts are illustrated by John Harris, G. de Bellaigue and O. Millar, *Buckingham Palace* (1968), pp. 184–5.

[3] Works 1/23, pp. 42, 331–4. The members of the committee were Lord Surrey (the Lord Steward), Robert Gordon and Edward Ellice. John Wilson was Lord Surrey's gardener.

[4] *Parl. Pap.* 1840, (292) xxix, 'Report made to the Committee appointed by the Lords of the Treasury in January 1838 to inquire into the Management, etc. of the ROYAL GARDENS, by Dr. *Lindley*. . . .'

[5] M. Allan, *The Hookers of Kew* (1967), pp. 105–6; *Parl. Deb.* 3rd ser. lii, 846–8, 3 March 1840.

[6] *Parl. Pap.* 1845 (280) xlv; 1846 (345) xxv—reports by Hooker to Commissioners of Woods, etc.

[7] L.R.R.O. 24/1–7; *Parl. Pap.* 1843, (343) xxx; 1851, (374) xxxi.

[8] Ten stoves and greenhouses, the orangery, and the conservatory from Buckingham Palace existed in 1840. One was rebuilt and several additions made to others, 1841–5 (*Parl. Pap.* 1840 (292) xxix; 1845 (280) xlv; 1846 (345) xxv). In 1846–7 Burton converted a fruit-store into a herbarium or museum of economic botany (Works 1/30, pp. 194 (14 September), 222–3 (29 September), 245 (8 October 1846, Harrison's tender, £627)). See W. B. Turrill, *The Royal Botanic Gardens, Kew: Past and Present* (1959), p. 20; illustrated, M. Allan, *The Hookers*, opp. p. 176.

[9] *Parl. Pap.* 1846 (345) xxv. See J. Harris, *Country Life* cxxv (1959), p. 1184. A working drawing by Burton is in the Library of the Royal Botanic Gardens. The Chinese temple and that of Pan were demolished in 1844 (Works 1/26, pp. 277–8, 494).

[10] Works 1/27, pp. 343, 428 (Burton's estimate, £1805); 1/29, p. 121. The iron gates cost the contractor, Walker of York (as he claimed) upwards of £100 more than the contract price of £500 (Works 1/29, p. 190). The vases were re-used from earlier gates to the Dutch House (J. Smith, *op. cit.*, p. 42).

by the landscape-gardener W. A. Nesfield.[1] The focal point of his axial layout was the new Palm House built in 1845–8.

The Palm House was by far the most important of the early Victorian works at Kew. Such a building had been contemplated since George III's reign; Wyatville had made plans, as had Robinson, the Clerk of Works. Hooker's first idea was that the new 'stove', as such buildings were termed, should be built over and around the old; but after two years as director he realised that neither the size nor the situation of the projected house would be satisfactory. The extension of the gardens offered a better site, on which Hooker proposed the gradual construction of a new building to form a complete department for tropical plants. Between 1842/3 and 1844/5 Parliament voted £5500 for this, but the project was discarded as impracticable because of the danger to the plants unless the whole were glazed at once. A more ambitious scheme was then decided upon.[2] Burton, who had already designed several large greenhouses, and with Paxton had recently constructed the great Palm House at Chatsworth,[3] was consulted as an architect experienced in the handling of large glazed structures.

Burton's role in this undertaking has been called in question.[4] The contracting iron-founder, Richard Turner, of the Hammersmith Foundry, Dublin, asserted in 1880 that 'the palm-house was not only erected by him, but was solely his design, although carried out under the supervision of Mr. Decimus Burton'.[5] He claimed to have submitted a design that was approved by Hooker, but said the Commissioners of Woods called in Burton, who consulted an un-named civil engineer in producing 'a most absurd set of plans'. 'I had nothing for it', related Turner, ' . . . but to tender for it, hoping that if my tender was accepted I could prevail in convincing the parties how discreditable and unwise it would be to carry it out'. At length, having erected a full-size portion at his own risk, he convinced the authorities, including Burton, and was allowed to carry out his design. 'Anything more foreign from Mr. Burton's design it would be difficult to imagine'. John Smith, former curator at Kew, corroborated this story, describing Turner sketching the Palm House 'as it was afterwards erected', without the numerous pillars that he said were a feature of Burton's original design.[6]

One may question the value of such accounts recorded thirty-five years after the event. Moreover, Smith seems to have been a man nursing a grievance; and Turner

---

[1] *Parl. Pap.* 1846, (345) xxv. Hooker wrote to Lord Lincoln, 1 February 1844, that he was 'gratified with [Nesfield's] intelligence. . . . He perhaps favors too much the formal or what he calls the "geometrical" arrangement, which to a certain extent, with so noble a piece of ground may be desirable. But I trust he is [sic] too much good sense to carry it too far. . . .' (Nottingham University Library, Newcastle MS. 8969). Some of Nesfield's designs are in the Library of the Royal Botanic Gardens.

[2] See Hooker's report, *Parl. Pap.* 1845, (280) xlv; and Commissioners of Woods to Treasury (Works 2/4, pp. 187–90, 7 June 1844).

[3] H. R. Hitchcock, *Early Victorian Architecture*, i, pp. 512–4; G. F. Chadwick, *The Works of Sir Joseph Paxton* (1961), p. 78 *et seq.*; G. F. Chadwick, 'Paxton and the Great Stove', *Architectural History* iv (1961), pp. 77–91.

[4] For an earlier account of the controversy see P. Ferriday, *Architectural Review*, cxxi (1957), pp. 127–8; Hitchcock, *loc. cit.* M. Allan, *op. cit.* pp. 148–9, suggests that Hooker himself had a hand in the design, quoting Sir J. D. Hooker's sketch of his father's life: 'the great Palm House was commenced in 1844 from the designs of Decimus Burton, F.R.S., and the Director' (*Annals of Botany*, xvi, 1902, no. lxiv, pp. lviii–lix).

[5] *Building News*, xxxviii (1880), p. 355, letter from Thomas Drew.

[6] *Ibid.* p. 385. See also Desmond, art. cit. p. 582, quoting from a MS. by Smith at Kew.

possessed no false modesty about his own abilities.[1] A series of letters addressed to the Commissioners severally and collectively bears witness to his extreme anxiety to obtain the contract; an anxiety which drove him to reduce his tender by £2400 at the last moment, leaving him doubtful whether he would cover his prime costs; and which sprang not only from a desire to make a name for himself in England and abroad, but also from a reluctance to return to Dublin without the prize that he had confidently asserted would be his.[2] For his part, Burton was no tyro in greenhouse design; and though the character of the Kew Temperate House (or Winter Garden) of 1860, which is undoubtedly Burton's, is different, it is unsafe to argue on that ground that the Palm House cannot have been his conception. The great conservatories with which Burton was associated at this period, at Chatsworth and Regent's Park, do resemble Kew; and certainly Burton is the common factor between them.[3]

The true facts appear to be almost diametrically opposite to those alleged by Turner. The minutes of the Office of Woods and Works show that Turner submitted a design for a palm house early in 1844. The Commissioners referred it to Burton as one 'who has acquired considerable experience in constructions of this nature'.[4] From Burton's report, dated 7 March 1844, it appears that Turner's designs were of 'the Ecclesiastical or Gothic style', with 'numerous ornamental details in fret work, crockets, perforated parapets, etc'.[5] Such details Burton considered 'out of place and tending uselessly to increase the amount of the Estimate'. Hooker agreed, writing after a meeting with Burton: 'I am quite delighted with his views of the *simple* form that ought to be adopted in our new Stove'.[6] Burton accompanied his report with a 'Sketch Design' of his own, affording a third more cubic capacity.[7]

[1] Drew recalled Turner 'in his vigorous days when he was ubiquitous, with a stock of daring and original projects always on hand, remarkable for his rough-and-ready powers of illustration of them, and sanguine belief in them, and his eloquent, plausible, and humorous advocacy of them' (*loc. cit.*).

[2] Works 16/29/8, ff. 13–17, Turner to Gore (9 May), to Commissioners of Woods (14 May), and to Milne (14 May 1844). To Gore, whom he begged that the competition should not be decided against him even if his tender were the higher, he wrote of his anxiety to erect the palm house,

thus Earning for myself a Name for the Erection of *Horticultural Buildings in this* C[ountr]y and that Foreigners, also may Employ *me*, and I *wish* to build my *Fame* upon this Structure at *Kew*, which *will be* unequalled as *yet*, by very *far* and not likely to be surpassed, I have *been* most anxiously solicitous, *and* ambitious, to *obtain* this *order* and particularly now after my absence from home being so long prolonged and the numerous Enquiries for *me* at home, was informed of my object here, so that, in fact, I w[oul]d now feel quite *ashamed*, not to take home with me the order, which I so confidently expected, *and* almost fully calculated upon, that, I have spoken with *great* certainty almost, upon my success . . .

To these beseechings Turner added hints of the interest that great personages (e.g. Lord Aberdeen, the Foreign Secretary) took in his success, and its importance in softening the feelings of the Dublin mechanics towards the government.

[3] The Regent's Park conservatory is described and illustrated in J. C. Loudon's *Encyclopaedia of Gardening* (new edition, 1850), pp. 279–80, 1213–5. Turner was again the contractor. The building was erected in 1845–6 and is therefore subsequent to Kew, though completed first.

[4] Works 1/26, p. 468, 19 February 1844. See also Nottingham University Library, Newcastle MS. 8969, Hooker to Lord Lincoln, 1 February 1844.

[5] Works 16/29/8, ff. 2–9, 7 March 1844.

[6] Newcastle MS. 8971, 20 February 1844.

[7] Works 16/29/8, ff. 2–9. The comparative dimensions were:

	Turner	Burton
Length of centre portion	140 ft.	137 ft. 6 ins.
Width	80 ft.	100 ft.
Height	50 ft.	54 ft.
		(exclusive of the ventilating lanthorn)
Superficies	11,200 sq. ft.	13,750 sq. ft.
Volume	300,000 cu. ft.	400,000 cu. ft.

A conventional style [he wrote] suitable for horticultural purposes is adopted and the classic and Ecclesiastical is avoided. Appropriateness, with as pleasing an outline as the case will admit of, are the objects aimed at, and all extraneous ornaments are dispensed with.

The introduction of the upper or lanthorn roof will be advantageous in facilitating ventilation, and on each side of this it is proposed that a portion of the glazed roof shall be moveable, to afford a ready mode of uncovering at periods a large extent of the house, a circumstance much desired by Horticulturists.

To afford greater extent of clear space for the larger trees than is proposed by Mr. Turner's plan, the internal range of pillars is omitted and the situation of the remaining perpendicular supports is changed so as to render them more available.

It seems clear, therefore, that Burton's designs represented an improvement on those submitted by Turner, rather than the reverse.

Turner was not the only contractor in the field: John Jones of Jones and Clark, a Birmingham firm, submitted a design and estimate for a circular building that could be constructed in either copper or iron.[1] This however did not meet Hooker's requirements, though it led Burton to suggest that the iron used should be galvanised. In a postscript to his report he recommended that after working drawings and specifications had been prepared both Turner and Jones should be invited to tender; and he was thereupon instructed to prepare the necessary drawings.[2] When the tenders were examined in May, Turner's was found to be considerably the lower.[3] But in his extreme eagerness to obtain the contract, Turner had over-reached himself: his capital resources were inadequate, and he had difficulty in finding the necessary two sureties. At length it was settled that Messrs. Grissell and Peto (who had been proposed as one of his sureties) should take the contract, the iron-work being sub-contracted to Turner.[4] Meanwhile, Hooker had suggested moving the site of the Palm House from the north to the west side of the pond, and Burton staked it out accordingly.[5]

Turner's principal contribution was still to come: towards the end of the year he proposed that the newly-invented wrought iron deck-beam should be substituted for the cast iron ribs of the frame. A conference in December between Burton, Turner, Grissell and Malins, the manufacturer of the new product, settled that one bay should be erected in wrought iron as a test. The trials were carried out at Grissell's yard on 12 and 13 June 1845. Turner had had to overcome the difficulty of welding together the pieces to form each rib, which he achieved by means of a new, more powerful blasting furnace, and 'expensive and ingenious machinery' which he constructed for bending the ribs.[6] In recommending this improvement, Turner had stated that the diminished quantity of metal required would compensate for the

[1] Works 16/29/8, ff. 6–9; 1/26, pp. 493–4, 16 March 1844. D. and E. Bailey, contractors for the Horticultural Society's conservatory at Chiswick, also enquired (Works 16/29/8, f. 12).
[2] Works 1/26, p. 506; 16/29/8, ff. 6–9. Working drawings are in Works 32/105–6, 109–112, in addition to the contract drawings in Works 13/3.
[3] Turner's tender was £18,500. Even the figure he had at first calculated, £20,900, was well below Jones and Clark's £25,067. Turner explicitly stated that his tender was to cover all the works specified by Burton (Works 16/29/8, f. 19).
[4] *Ibid.* ff. 41, 49, 178; 13/3 (contract, dated 27 August 1844).
[5] Works 16/29/8, ff. 47–8, Burton to Commissioners of Woods, 23 August 1844.
[6] *Ibid.* ff. 51–3, 68–71.

greater cost of the material, but he had not allowed for the difficulties of the undertaking, and according to his subsequent statements this was the principal cause of
his heavy losses on the contract.[1]

This alteration is clearly the basis of Turner's later claim to have revised the
design of the Palm House. Burton himself was in favour of the change, providing that
it was structurally sound, because it gave a 'stronger material with *reduced* size ribs'.
The cast iron columns, too, could be made proportionately slimmer, 'similar to
those I designed', wrote Burton, 'for the Great Stove House at Chatsworth'.[2] It
was, Turner claimed in 1848, an 'alteration which is the greatest possible improvement to the structure, as regards utility, beauty, and stability'.[3]

Turner's enthusiastic but unbusinesslike approach to this work is again shown
in the negotiations for the contract for the wings. When the frame of the central
portion was up, in the summer of 1846, it was determined to go on immediately
with the wings.[4] Turner told Burton that he had actually proceeded with the works
'in hope they would be ordered and that I could establish my reputation . . . for
punctuality'. Although the price of iron had increased nearly thirty per cent, he
would take the contract for the wings on his tender of 1844. The Board nevertheless
insisted, against Burton's advice, that Jones should also be invited to tender, but he
refused. Turner, declaring that his tender had been 'only a wholesale kind of conjecture, of my own, without entering into the *details*', and that another £2000 would
'only sufficiently remunerate' him, begged to have the opportunity of completing
the work 'upon any Terms almost'. He admitted to Burton that he was 'totally
inexperienced then, in the Manufacture of a Structure of such Magnitude as this has
proved to be'; and, pointing out that the wings were now each to be 112 ft. 6 ins.
long, instead of 100 ft., he raised his tender to £10,900. The contract for the wings
was then concluded with Turner personally at his especial request, the foundation
works being sub-contracted to Grissell. The wings were completed in 1848.[5]

Various other improvements were introduced as the Palm House went up. A
lightly-tinted glass was adopted after experiments, undertaken in response to proposals from Turner, who advocated plate instead of sheet glass.[6] Experience in the
Regent's Park Winter Garden, another work by Burton and Turner, showed that a
perforated flooring would be necessary for under-floor heating to be adequate.[7]
Turner also put up one larger spiral iron stair to the gallery in place of two smaller
ones originally proposed by Burton.[8] Ground works to create a suitable setting for
the house were designed by Burton,[9] as well as a tower in the form of an Italian
Romanesque campanile to house water tanks and provide a chimney for the Palm

[1] *Ibid.* ff. 178–9.   [2] *Ibid.* ff. 51–3.   [3] *Ibid.* ff. 178–9.
[4] Works 1/30, p. 136 (20 August 1846). Hooker argued that the plants would suffer from exposure if the
wings were added later. As this was an obvious risk under the proposed arrangements of 1844 (and had been
put forward as a reason for adopting a larger project than that originally adumbrated), this looks like Hooker's
way of obtaining the necessary funds from the Treasury. Turner's original price for the wings was £8500.
[5] Works 16/29/8, ff. 68–71, 74, 76, 80, 82–3, 85–6; 1/30, pp. 46, 59, 136, 168.
[6] *Ibid.* pp. 47, 402; 16/29/8, ff. 56, 58, 60–5, 90–2, 95–6, 102. The glass was referred to Hooker for its effect
on the plants, and to Burton for its appearance before being adopted (Works 1/30, pp. 47–8, 402–3). Smith
claimed that this adoption of tinted glass, such as had habitually been employed by Aiton, was his suggestion
(Smith, MS. History, p. 62).   [7] Works 16/29/8, f. 118.   [8] *Ibid.*, ff. 93–4, 97–8.
[9] These included excavation and in filling of ponds, building a wall and path between the palm house
and the pond, and constructing flights of steps to the water (Works 1/31, pp. 127, 205–6; 1/32, pp. 141, 432,
448, 1/33, pp. 11–12, 40, 104; 16/29/8, f. 175).

House, with which it was connected by subterranean flues. This was built by Grissell in 1847 for £988.[1]

The total expenditure on the Palm House and connected works to 31 March 1849 was nearly £35,600.[2] Turner alleged that he had lost £7000 on his contract, but the Commissioners of Woods pointed to his numerous pleas to be awarded it and criticised his 'considerable want of Method and regularity in conducting the Works'.[3] It was not surprising that he was not again employed under government. Nevertheless it is clear that he made a decided technical and aesthetic contribution to the Palm House, though a smaller one than he and his advocates were to claim.[4] Although it did not realise Turner's hopes of making his fortune, the Palm House at Kew was an important pioneer in the development of iron and glass structures, not only for greenhouses but also for the great mid-Victorian railway station 'sheds'.[5]

KNELLER HALL SCHOOL, MIDDLESEX

A minute of the Committee of the Privy Council on Education, dated 21 December 1846, directed that a training school should be established for teachers for workhouse schools and similar institutions. In 1847 the Kneller Hall estate at Whitton in Middlesex was purchased for this purpose.[6] To the old house built about 1709 by the artist Kneller for himself, Philip Hardwick had recently added two wings. Plans for adapting the building, adding additional storeys to provide accommodation for a hundred pupils, with apartments for three masters and a separate residence for the principal, were obtained from George Mair (1810–89). These were referred to the Department of Works, which pronounced them to be inadequate; iron girders

---

[1] Works 1/31, pp. 173, 223, 278. Burton's design of April 1847 was altered in June by increasing the tower's height by 10 ft. (Works 16/29/8, f. 120; see also ff. 123–4). Working drawings and a perspective of the tower are in the library of the Royal Botanic Gardens, Kew.

[2] Works 2/7, pp. 276–9. Special votes for the Palm House totalled £35,910. The two contracts totalled £29,400; extras and omissions amounted to a net addition of £1350 11s. 7d. The tinted glass had cost an extra £350 (Works 16/29/8, f. 110).

[3] Works 16/29/8, ff. 177–9, 190; 2/7, pp. 47–9, 120–1, 127–8; 1/33, pp. 161, 173. Drew, *loc. cit.*, ascribes the loss to the unexpected need for concrete foundations, but Turner himself was not explicit on this point. He remarked in 1846 that the Portland stone and building works for the centre had amounted to nearly double what he had supposed (Works 16/29/8, f. 76); but an early estimate (f. 22) allowed only £1800 for the subterranean works, whereas by his agreement with Grissell and Peto he allowed them £6600 for foundations and mason's work (ff. 178–9). Turner laid stress on the introduction of the wrought iron deck-beam as a principal cause of his loss; and also referred to the difficulty of estimating for a structure outside his experience, and the need to increase the wages of workmen brought from Dublin (ff. 178–9). Extras valued at £528 2s. 2d. were finally allowed him (iron doors and plate glass £443 7s. 6d., vertical rods at the staircase, £21 8s. 6d., and extra weight of iron in gallery railing, £63 6s. 2d., ff. 163–5, 177).

[4] Burton told the Board that the deck beam was 'a material improvement to the appearance of the building' (*ibid.* ff. 190–1). Smith ascribed to Turner the invention of the machinery for ventilating the Palm House: 'upright sashes round the Gallery and lantern, made to open simultaneously by a continuous lever and the roof lights by winding' (MS. History, p. 61). Description and illustrations of the Palm House and its structure are given in *Building News*, xxxviii (1880), p. 97, and Hitchcock, *Early Victorian Architecture*, ii, xv, 31–3.

[5] Turner was contractor for the shed of the second station built at Lime Street, Liverpool, in 1849, with a roof span of 153 ft. 6 ins., in which the combination of wrought iron and plate glass is again found. See Hitchcock, *Early Victorian Architecture* i, pp. 498–9.

[6] *Parl. Pap.* 1850 [1196], [1256] xliii. The purchase price was £10,557 10s. 6d.

for the new floors were too few and too weak.[1] When works began, the old house was found to be so dilapidated that it had to be demolished. The walls of Hardwick's new wings were, however, retained and incorporated in the new building. John Kelk's contract amounted to £17,336.[2] Mair's neo-Jacobean design was illustrated in *The Builder* for 1850.[3]

During construction, the advice of the Works officers was frequently sought,[4] and in August 1849 the Treasury empowered that department to accept tenders for the school, although the direction of the works was left to Mair. The school opened in January 1850. The total cost of rebuilding and enlargement was £19,544, with fittings, furnishings and incidental charges which brought the total to some £28,700.[5] On the initiative of the Committee on Education it was agreed in March 1851 that the Works Department should direct casual repairs and supply furniture on a written requisition from the principal, but that estimates should fall on the vote for public education.[6]

THE LAZARETTO AT CHETNEY HILL, KENT

Among the projects for which the Office of Works was indirectly responsible the Lazaretto at Chetney Hill was certainly the most bizarre. It took fifty years to prepare, fifteen years to construct and cost at least £170,000. But the combined efforts of Sir John Soane, James Wyatt and John Rennie merely produced a building which was not only never used but was pulled down before it was finished.

The idea of a land lazaretto, or permanent quarantine establishment, had its origin in a series of attempts to modify the stringent quarantine regulations governing trade between Britain and the Levant. A succession of Acts passed in 1710, 1721, 1733, 1743, 1752 and 1788 made it necessary for British ships returning from plague-infested ports to perform quarantine in the lazarettos of Malta, Venice, Messina, Leghorn, Genoa or Marseilles.[7] This meant that delays of up to seven months were occasionally involved. Dutch traders transporting Levantine cotton and silk were thus able to take advantage of their own easier regulations and undercut their British competitors. Pressure from the Levantine interest in Parliament was therefore directed towards the establishment of a lazaretto in the Thames estuary where goods might be deposited for the performance of a briefer period of quarantine.[8] The suggestion was first brought up in 1743 and a site was suggested in 1752, namely 'Chetney Hill, near the upper part of Standgate Creek, in the river Medway'.[9]

[1] Works 6/184/7, ff. 3 (6 November 1847), 8–9 (4 January 1848); 1/31, p. 408; 1/32, pp. 1, 96.
[2] Works 6/184/7, f. 15 (18 July 1848); *Parl. Pap.* 1847–8 (543) xviii, qq. 6221–3.
[3] *Builder*, viii (1850), p. 68, with plan and illustration.
[4] Works 1/33, pp. 103, 255, 264, 348, 415, 424, 437, 440; 1/34, pp. 108, 149; 6/184/7, *passim*.
[5] *Parl. Pap.* 1850 [1256] xliii, p. xii.   [6] Works 1/34, p. 338; 1/35, p. 267; 1/36, pp. 39, 183–4.
[7] For details see 'Papers relating to Quarantine', *Parl. Pap.* 1861, lxviii, p. 263, *et seq.*
[8] 'Petition of the Turkey Company', 1792, B.T. 6/149. There were also medical doubts as to the efficacy of quarantine in cases of plague, e.g. *Gent's. Mag.* 1799, pt. i, pp. 42–3.
[9] *Commons Jnls.* xxvi (1750–54), p. 478, 5 March 1752. For detailed maps showing the later location of the Lazaretto cf. D. Steel, 'Survey of the Rivers Thames and Medway, 1802', B.M. Maps 1240 (20) and S. Hemmans, 'Survey of the River Medway 1803', B.M. Maps 1240 (82).

Plans were prepared in 1764 and a grant of £5000 was obtained in 1765, but not until 1772 was an Act obtained enabling the Crown to purchase the site.[1] Agitation continued during the 1780s and intensified in the 1790s. Negotiations between the Committee of Council for Trade and Plantations, the Customs Commissioners, the Turkey Company, the Treasury and the authorities in Rochester were complicated by the obstinacy of a local landowner named Wildman.[2] In 1793 and 1795, as Surveyor to the Turkey Company, Soane produced a series of alternative designs for a land lazaretto at Chetney Hill: a rectangle fenced in by canals; a hexagon surrounded by a circular boundary wall; a double quadrangle with continuous colonnades; and a utility version with sheds on both sides of the creek.[3] None of these was adopted. Only in 1800 was the principle of internal quarantine accepted and a decision taken to begin building on the basis of a Treasury grant and under the direction of the Office of Works. The initial Treasury grant stood at £65,000. This was increased by £30,000 in 1804 and by £21,000 in 1810. After that date another £55,000 was disbursed by the Customs Commissioners.[5] Works continued intermittently until 1816 and further bills were incurred. Four years later the unfinished structure was dismantled.

John Howard once remarked that 'a lazaretto should have the most cheerful aspect'.[6] Another pundit claimed that 'the situation should be dry, healthy and airy'.[7] On each of these counts the choice of Chetney Hill was a mistake. Its sole advantage lay in its proximity to Standgate Creek where since the 1750s ex-naval hulks had acted as floating warehouses for the cargoes of Levantine ships bearing 'clean' bills of health.[8] Apart from transport difficulties and the shortage of fresh water, the site turned out to be marshy and inhospitable. Chetney Hill was composed of soft clay surrounded by 'small creeks and stagnant pools of water'.[9] One doctor called it 'the most unhealthy spot in England'.[10] And the subsoil proved inadequate even for the timber warehouses designed by James Wyatt and the canal, dock, and boundary wall added by John Rennie.

The construction of the lazaretto was based on two principles: isolation and ventilation. The 'floating lazarettos' had been 'old men of war, with houses built upon them like an ark . . . open like a brewhouse, with shutters, and the floors . . . all open gratings'. Their design, and the fact that they could 'swing with the tide . . . every six hours', made the ventilating force 'greater than the North West winds on

[1] 12 G. III *c*. 37, 'An Act to explain and amend. . . .' the 'Act (26 G. II *c*. 6), to enable Ships more effectually to perform their Quarantine'; *Commons Jnls.* xxix (1761–64), p. 1041, 9 April 1764, p. 1050, 13 April 1764 and xxx (1765–66), p. 309, 26 March 1765. [2] E.g. B.T. 5/9–12 and B.T. 6/149.

[3] Soane Museum, Vol. 5, pp. 105–9 and Drawer 24, set 4; B.M. Add. MS. 38230 f. 147; 3 March 1795; B.T. 5/8, f. 356, 21 January 1793. Soane received £40 3s. od. payment in 1798 (Soane Museum, Ledger C).

[4] 39 G. III *c*. 99, 'An Act to encourage the Trade into the Levant Seas'; 40 G. III *c*. 80, 'An Act for Erecting a Lazaret on Chetney Hill'.

[5] 'Second Report from the Select Committee on Foreign Trade, Quarantine', *Parl. Pap.* 1824, vi, p. 165, By 45 G. III c. 10 tonnage duties were imposed to pay for the land lazaretto at Chetney Hill and the floating lazarettos elsewhere (*ibid.* p. 169; B.T. 5/15, f. 28, 5 February 1805).

[6] J. Howard, *An Account of the Principal Lazarettos in Europe* (1779).

[7] P. Russell, *A Treatise of the Plague* (1791).

[8] I.e. Ships trading with the Levant but coming from ports where there was no plague or 'Contagious Distempers of an ambiguous kind' (B.T. 6/149). See also T. 29/75, f. 38, 8 August 1799.

[9] Institution of Civil Engineers, Rennie MSS. 1st Series iv, f. 80, 17 June 1806.

[10] 'Second Report from the Select Committee on Foreign Trade, Quarantine', *Parl. Pap.* 1824, vi, p. 232.

the coast of America'.[1] Wyatt's warehouses therefore followed this arrangement and at the same time imitated the 'land lazarettos' at Malta and Minorca: 'pavilions . . . built of wood and jalousied, where a current of air passes through'.[2] 'Each building above the foundation', wrote the architect, 'is an entire framing of timber from bottom to top, requiring the whole to be framed and put up together'.[3] Eight of these warehouses appear to have been constructed. Ten more remained unbuilt. Their cost presented George Saunders with one of his most difficult tasks in unravelling the Surveyor General's accounts.

In the first place Wyatt's brother Samuel had been given the carpentry contract and another relation held the contract for tinned copper.[4] In the second place the methods of payment differed markedly from normal Office of Works practice. And in this respect the lazaretto resembled several Office of Works projects which were not covered by the Civil List. Wyatt's commission stood at 5 per cent. The absence of the normal 3 per cent deduction made tradesmen's prices 3 per cent higher than usual. In addition Wyatt allowed an extra $9\frac{1}{2}$ per cent to cover extraordinary expenses: 'freight . . . travelling . . ., water, coals, and medical attendance . . ., cookery, fitting up a frigate for the lodging of the workmen, making wharfs, building sheds, . . . and beds and furniture for the men etc.'. Saunders was prepared to accept these charges, considering 'the inconvenient circumstances under which the work was carried on, being several miles from any habitation, and [without] fresh water . . . except what was brought from a distance'.[5] But the methods of accounting were disturbingly inaccurate. Bills had been mislaid and payments misdated, and the whole process of construction had been so dilatory that reconciling final charges with interim fluctuations in price proved extremely difficult. After ten years' work Wyatt's account stood at £111,897 5s. 5d. Saunders made it £109,778 3s. 11d.[6]

While Saunders was discharging Wyatt's unpaid bills,[7] the work organised by the Customs Commissioners and directed by John Rennie was running into serious trouble. In 1800 the Customs Commissioners had necessarily looked to the Surveyor General.[8] By 1806 they were delighted to transfer their patronage to an engineer. In conception Rennie's scheme was simple: a canal surrounding the Lazaretto 'to answer the double purpose of drainage and navigation'; a wet dock (about 75 yards × 25 yards) for barges transferring goods from ship to warehouse; a boundary wall to prevent 'pilferage'; a well for the supply of fresh water; six cranes to unload the barges; a system of surface drainage (gravel plus brick drains) designed 'to prevent

---

[1] 'Report from the Select Committee on the Doctrine of Contagion in the Plague', *Parl. Pap.* 1819, ii, p. 575.
[2] 'Second Report from the Select Committee on Foreign Trade, Quarantine', *Parl. Pap.* 1824, vi, p. 254.
[3] 'Inquiry into . . . the Office of Works', *Parl. Pap.* 1812–13, v, p. 507.
[4] *Ibid.* p. 77 *of report*. Charles Wyatt also tendered a gravel contract in 1806 (Rennie MSS. 1st Series iv, ff. 97–103, 7 August 1806).   [5] *Ibid.* p. 509.
[6] *Ibid.* p. 510; 'Seventh Report from the Committee on Public Expenditure, Buildings, Civil and Military', *Parl. Pap.* 1810, ii, p. 524.
[7] E.g. T. 29/111, f. 283, 26 September 1811. For issues of money to Wyatt and Treasury attempts to speed up completion cf. T. 29/78, f. 141, 21 October 1801 and f. 503, 2 April 1802; T. 29/80, f. 75, 14 December 1802; T. 29/82, f. 117, 23 December 1803; T. 29/84, f. 311, 12 February and f. 453, 1 April 1805; T. 29/86, f. 186, 25 February 1806; 'Second Report from the Select Committee on Foreign Trade, Quarantine', *Parl. Pap.* 1824, vi, p. 274.
[8] Works 4/19, 2 and 16 May, 6 June 1800; Works 6/23, f. 120, 13 May, f. 121, 16 May and f. 124, 6 June 1800.

men, horses, animals or carriages from sinking into the ground'; and 'on each side of the dock double iron railways . . . with proper branches to the different buildings'.[1] But from the start the project went badly. Rennie's first estimate was £40,670. Ten years later this had risen by nearly £20,000. The official Surveyor to the Customs Board, William Pilkington, refused to supervise the work, 'considering it out of his line'. Instead Rennie nominated John Temperley on the basis of his experience at London Docks.[2] Temperley proved competent enough, but the odds were against him. Wildman's opportunism with regard to the purchase of extra land for the boundary wall slowed down progress by three years.[3] In digging the canal the soil turned out to be too muddy and 'the sides slipped into the bottom'; when its course was replotted a new danger emerged, that 'the buildings themselves might tumble into the canal'.[4] During the summer of 1807 the labourers were struck down by a violent fever. Several died and none would take their place.[5] And on 1 October, while the surviviors lay sick in their half-built warehouses, the highest tide for twenty-three years smashed the canal banks and flooded the unfinished dock.[6] Not until two years later was the flood water drawn off 'by the means of Archimedean screws'.[7] By the autumn of 1808 the well on top of the hill had been bored to a depth of 132 ft. But on 3 November 'water burst in and rose 100 ft. in one night'.[8] During most of 1809 and 1810 work was at a standstill. Wyatt's legacy of unsettled bills made progressive accounting difficult.[9] And in 1811, just as a new set of contracts had been arranged, the principal contractor (Hugh McIntosh) fell ill, a sub-contractor (Enoch King) went bankrupt, and Rennie himself 'met with a severe accident'.[10] Two years later, as the ill-fated dock neared completion, another failure occurred and Joliffe and Banks had to be called in to make good inadequate piling.[11]

Having survived flood and pestilence Rennie prepared to face fire. £2430 was spent on a steam engine attached to the newly constructed well.[12] Another £5850 was allocated to an extension of the railway arrangements, partly on the advice of Pilkington's successor, David Laing.[13] Not until the spring of 1818 did the last labourer leave the site.[14] However construction had stopped in 1815,[15] not because the Lazaretto was complete, but because all parties concerned had lost faith in the value of the project. Until their modification in 1825 and 1847 the quarantine laws

---

[1] Rennie MSS., 1st Series iv ff. 80–83, 17 June and ff. 110–11, 6 September 1806.

[2] *Ibid.* ff. 120–21, 15 September 1806. For an undated plan of the dock, warehouses and railway cf. MPD. 14, 'A Plan of the Intended Iron Railways'.

[3] Wildman was paid £5250 in 1797 for the original piece of land (T. 29/71, f. 379, 21 November 1797). Between 1806 and 1809 the sale of eight extra acres was the subject of acrimonious negotiation (Rennie MSS. 1st Series iv, f. 169, 10 September 1806, f. 274 18 February, f. 348 20 June 1807, f. 391 7 September 1807; v, ff. 219–21, 16 July and ff. 294–5, 27 October 1808).

[4] Rennie MSS. iv, f. 348, 20 June 1807.

[5] Despite offers of 7s. od. per day and a guinea to the 'Gangs Men . . . for every man they brought to the work' (Rennie MSS. 1st Series vi, f. 423, *et seq.*, 23 December 1811). 'Those that did recover were a long time in a very weak and feeble state and unfit for work, and. . . a great many died after lingering two or three more years' (*ibid.* viii, ff. 383–4, 18 June 1816). Accounts include payments for three doctors, one surgeon, 'nurses and attendants, several funeral expenses . . . coffins . . . medicine . . . milk, wine, tea, sugar, fruit, eggs and . . . fresh meat' (*ibid.* viii, ff. 391–2, 2 July 1816).

[6] *Ibid.* v, ff. 24–7, 19 December 1807.   [7] *Ibid.* vi, f. 421, 1 October 1809.   [8] *Ibid.*

[9] Rennie complained that 'to Mr. Wyatt it is vain to make any application' (*Ibid.* v, f. 363, 7 February 1809).

[10] *Ibid.* vi, f. 423, *et seq.* 23 December 1811.   [11] *Ibid.* vii, f. 314, 13 September 1813.

[12] *Ibid.* vii, ff. 329–30, 6 October 1813.   [13] *Ibid.* vii, ff. 362–3, 8 December 1813.

[14] *Ibid.* ix, ff. 391–2, 3 July and f. 400, 14 July 1818.   [15] *Ibid.* viii, f. 324, 31 May 1815.

were satisfied by the 'Floating Lazarets' moored in Standgate Creek and elsewhere.[1] In 1820 the Lazaretto was demolished and its materials auctioned for £15,058 5s. 7d.[2] Among the purchasers of timber was Henry Peto, contractor for the London Custom House. In this way the relics of one government building scandal survived to form the basis of another.[3] Soon afterwards some of the hulks may have been converted into powder magazines, and before long all that remained of the Lazaretto was a few speculative houses, unoccupied and unsold.[4]

THE ISLE OF MAN

In 1841/2 Parliament voted £2244 for works to government buildings in the Isle of Man, the Home Office having referred the state of the court-houses and gaols there to the Office of Woods and Works.[5] Small sums were voted in succeeding years.

In 1846–7 the inhabitants of Douglas petitioned for an improved court-house. The Works Department engaged Ewan Christian (1814–95), then building a church in Douglas, to report. He drew up plans for enlarging the building at an estimate of £2500.[6] This sum was voted in 1848, but revised proposals were then put forward for a building on a new site.[7] No action was taken, however, until 1857–8, when St. George's Hall, Douglas, was purchased and subsequently converted into a court-house.[8]

Minor improvements and repairs were also carried out at Castle Rushen in 1847 and 1849.[9]

THE MILITARY DEPOT, TOOLEY STREET, SOUTHWARK

Among the minor projects for which the Office of Works took responsibility was the new Military Depot in Bridge Yard, off Tooley Street. Smirke was the chosen architect. His plans were prepared early in 1821: 'I have proposed the erection of two houses, one for the store keeper and the other containing . . . rooms for three

---

[1] Quarantine was finally abolished by the Public Health Acts of 1875 and 1896. The other quarantine stations were at Portsmouth, Liverpool, Milford, Hull, Falmouth, Bristol, Holy Loch and Inverkeithing, plus thirteen smaller stations in Ireland ('Papers relating to Quarantine', *Parl. Pap.* 1861, lxviii, 263, *et seq.*; 'Second Report from the Select Committee on Foreign Trade, Quarantine', *Parl. Pap.* 1824, vi, pp. 276–82).

[2] 'Select Report from the Select Committee on Foreign Trade, Quarantine', *Parl. Pap.* 1824, vi, pp. 222, 277.   [3] See p. 422 *et seq.*

[4] T. Nicholls, *The Steam-Boat Companion* (1823), pp. 172–5; J. W. Norie, *Sailing Directions for the River Thames* (1826), p. 8; G. H. Davidson, *The Thames and Thanet Guide* (1838?), p. 31.

[5] Works 1/25, p. 456; 1/26, p. 264; 2/3, pp. 112, 118.

[6] Works 1/31, pp. 39, 353; 2/5, pp. 441–5; 2/6, pp. 114–6, 177. The petition and correspondence are printed in *Parl. Pap.* 1847–8 (543) xviii, pt. ii, app. pp. 40–3.

[7] Works 1/32, pp. 432, 440; 1/33, pp. 97–9; 2/7, pp. 40–2.

[8] *Parl. Pap.* 1852 (238–I) xxix; 1852–3 (892) lvii, p. 6; 1857 (sess. I) (132) xiii, p. 12; 1859 (sess. I) (61) xiv, p. 19; 1860 (101) xl, p. 17.   [9] Works 1/33, p. 450; 2/6, pp. 158–60.

resident clerks and for the day porter', plus accommodation for 'military and other goods'.[1] However the Treasury preferred a plan incorporating two dwelling houses to a plan involving one house plus rooms for clerks.[2] These alterations added £700 to the original estimate of £6000.[3] By March 1823, when the buildings were handed over to the Board of Ordnance for completion, £4638 13s. 6d. had been expended. The apartments for storekeeper, clerk, porters, nightwatchmen and guards were arranged round an open courtyard in front of the military storeroom. The plain Tooley Street elevation, four storeys high and five bays wide, was relieved only by round-arched windows at first floor level.

THE ROYAL MINT, LONDON

The absorption of the Royal Mint into the jurisdiction of the Office of Works was only one stage in a lengthy process of reorganisation and reconstruction which began in 1787 and continued until 1823. In 1787 a Committee of the Privy Council was set up to deal with the parlous state of the coinage. In 1823 William Wellesley Pole, after nine energetic years as Master of the Mint, was 'sent to the dogs' as Master of the King's Buckhounds.[5] During the thirty-six intervening years the department had been purged of a number of sinecures, its headquarters had been moved from the Tower of London to Tower Hill, new machinery had largely re-minted the coinage of the realm and the maintenance of the new buildings had been transferred to the Office of Works.

Established in 1787 and reconstituted in 1798, the Committee on Coin was dominated by two men: Charles Jenkinson, 1st Earl of Liverpool and his friend Sir Thomas Banks.[6] Together they prepared to overhaul the antiquated establishment of the Mint, its staff, its machinery and its buildings. Plans were made for the reduction of redundant personnel.[7] Reports by Samuel and Francis Garbett urged the necessity of recoinage.[8] Investigations by Matthew Boulton, Charles Hatchett and John Rennie exposed the inadequacy of hand-operated, horse-powered machinery

---

[1] Works 1/10, ff. 314–5, 6 February 1821.

[2] *Ibid.* f. 403, 10 May 1821. For these alternative plans cf. MPD. 85 (1–3). MPD 85(4) is the one adopted.

[3] Works 1/10, f. 410, 16 May 1821.

[4] Works 1/11, ff. 247–8, 2 September 1822 and ff. 420–21, 24 March 1823.

[5] William Wellesley Pole, later 1st Lord Maryborough and 3rd Earl of Mornington (1763–1845), elder brother to the Duke of Wellington, Tory M.P. for Trim (1783–90), East Looe (1790–95) and Queen's County (1801–21). His initials W. W. P. decorated many examples of Pistrucci's new coinage (*Gent's. Mag.* 1845, pt. i, pp. 426–8; W. J. Hocking, *Catalogue of . . . the Museum of the Royal Mint* ii, 1910, p. 236).

[6] For the committee's membership and work cf. Liverpool Papers ccxxxiv, B.M. Add. MS. 38423, f. 95; 25th Report of the Select Committee on Finance 26 June 1798; 'Report of the . . . Committee of Council [on] . . . the state of the coins of this Kingdom, and the present Establishment and Constitution of H.M.'s Mint', *Parl. Pap.* 1816, vi, p. 403; 'Report of the Commissioners appointed to inquire into . . . the Royal Mint', *Parl. Pap.* 1849, xxviii, pp. 367, 398.

[7] E.g. 33 G. III *c.* 94 and 57 G. III *c.* 67. For the corrupt state of Mint administration cf. Royal Mint Registry, Mint Record Books xvi, f. 174, 15 April 1807, ff. 180–1, 28 April 1807, f. 184, 6 May 1807 ff. 225–9, 12 January 1808 and f. 354, 28 March 1808.

[8] For Messrs. Garbett's report of 1782 cf. 'Report from the Select Committee on the Royal Mint', *Parl. Pap.* 1837, xvi, p. 413, *et seq.*

dating from 1662.[1] And negotiations with the Ordnance and Barrack Offices emphasised the wisdom of removing staff, machinery and buildings alike outside the confines of the Tower.[2] Between 1770 and 1781 as much as £26,170 had been spent on repairs to the structure of the old Mint.[3] Rennie's reports in 1798 and 1805 indicated expansion as well as reconstruction: a new Mint on a new site.[4]

During this period there were three Surveyors to the Mint: Samuel Wyatt, James Johnson and Robert Smirke. Of these only Smirke reaped the reward of the department's expansionist policy. Wyatt was dismissed for negligence in 1794 and Johnson died in 1807 leaving his designs for the great rebuilding to be altered and completed by his successor. Smirke's appointment was a piece of political good fortune. The power of nomination was vested in the Master of the Mint. And between 1799 and 1807 the shifts of party politics dictated that the Mastership should change hands seven times: Robert Jenkinson, son of Lord Liverpool (1799–1801); Baron Arden (1801–2); the Rt. Hon. John Smyth, M.P., (1802–4); Henry 3rd Earl Bathurst (1804–6); Lord Charles Spencer (1806); Charles Bathurst (1806–7); Earl Bathurst (1807–12). The reappointment of Earl Bathurst, Smirke's Tory patron, neatly coincided with Johnson's death.[5] The Surveyor's salary had long been fixed at £21 per annum plus 5 per cent commission on all new buildings.[6] Joseph Farington's estimate of £80,000 as the value of the works that his young friend was to have the benefit of supervising was to prove almost absurdly low.[7] Work continued for another decade, expenditure rose to nearly £300,000 and even after 1815 Smirke's responsibility as Attached Architect entitled him to receive half the commission he had previously drawn as departmental Surveyor.

Plans for reconstructing the Mint were drawn up in the spring of 1805 and contracts signed in the autumn. Johnson supplied the architectural designs, Boulton most of the machinery and Rennie the rest of the machinery plus advice on the subject of installation and maintenance. General estimates were first fixed at £86,510 for reconstruction on the old site, and £126,490 for building *de novo*, minus £15,000

---

[1] 'There are only four kinds of power which could be applied, namely, Men, Horses, Water and Steam. . . . Manual Labour . . . is not only expensive and tedious, but also very imperfect. . . . Water . . . not only expensive, but very inconvenient', whereas Boulton's steam presses at Soho near Birmingham 'coin faster and with fewer persons, and make more beautiful money, than anything I have seen'. As for the danger of fire, 'I never knew an instance of fire happening from a Steam Engine' (Institution of Civil Engineers, Rennie MSS., Reports 1st Series iii, ff. 287–98, 8 January 1805). For Boulton's reports of 1788–9 also advocating steam, cf. Liverpool Papers ccxxxii–iii, B.M. Add. MSS. 38241, f. 238, 38422, ff. 1–6.

[2] 'Not only no further space within the Tower can be spared for the purposes of the Mint, but a part of the ground on which the building now stands is absolutely wanted for the defence of the Tower, and to secure the Ordnance stores in the garrison' (T. 29/85, f. 352, 19 August 1805).

[3] 'Report from the Select Committee on the Royal Mint', *Parl. Pap.* 1837, xvi, p. 413.

[4] T. 1/3997; Rennie MSS., Reports 1st Series ii, ff. 81–3, 10 July 1798, iii, ff. 278–98, 6 May and ff. 421–30, 19 November 1805; Mint Record Books xvi, ff. 27–32, 9 August 1804, f. 84, 10 October and ff. 104–5, 19 November 1805.

[5] Bathurst was gazetted in March, Johnson died in June and Smirke was appointed in July 1807 (Mint Record Books xvi, f. 195, 14 July 1807). 'Robert Smirke called and showed me a letter . . . from Lord Lonsdale. It was received by his Lordship from Lord Bathurst promising to his Lordship the appointment of the Architect of the Mint to Robert Smirke' (Farington, pp. 3766–7, 4 July 1807).

[6] Mint Record Books xvi (1804–10), ff. 60–61, 162–3, 340; 'Inquiry into the . . . Office of Works', *Parl. Pap.* 1812–13, v, p. 483; 'Report from the Select Committee on the Royal Mint', *Parl. Pap.* 1837, xvi, p. 415. The Surveyor's salary was subject to property tax. The Clerk of the Works received a separate stipend of £120 per annum plus £60 in perquisites.

[7] Farington, p. 4026, 2 April 1808. Farington had composed Smirke's letter of application to Bathurst (*ibid.* p. 3765, 30 June 1807).

from the sale of the old buildings as barracks or offices.[1] These figures proved sadly inadequate. Less than two months later the estimate for building afresh had jumped to £128,000 plus £7000 for a Portland stone facing 'instead of Bernasconi's Composition as at present proposed'.[2] The site chosen for the new Mint was that of the old Tobacco Warehouses on Little Tower Hill.[3] Its insulation required the purchase of surrounding houses in Swedeland Court, Rosemary Lane and Bailey Place. So expenditure jumped another £6000.[4] The officers' houses proved surprisingly numerous and costly.[5] Besides this, the installation of machinery cost a good deal more than the £32,000 originally suggested and arrangements for supplying water from the Tower Ditch added another £2596 to the bill.[6] Even the sale of old materials from the site involved Smirke in legal difficulties with a bankrupt auctioneer.[7] Instead of a contract in gross the size and complexity of the project, and the fluctuating cost of materials, encouraged a system of separate contracts with individual tradesmen. This system of 'measure and value' (labour plus materials plus 15 per cent profit) provoked considerable criticism as expenditure mounted. More important, these contracts were not the result of competitive tendering but the product of long-standing monopolies. All in all the soaring expenditure at the Mint, so carefully investigated by George Saunders, constituted a strong argument in favour of extending Office of Works jurisdiction to cover the whole of government building.[8] Between 1809 and 1812 several inquiries were made in Parliament as to the increased cost.[9] A statement by Smirke was made public in 1811 to the effect that £236,920 had been expended, leaving £9000 still necessary to complete the works provided no further additions were made.[10] But additions did prove necessary, despite stricter control over demands by senior Mint officers.[11] The bulk of the machinery was ready in July 1807, but not the buildings.[12] Work continued for some

---

[1] Rennie MSS., Reports 1st Series iii, ff. 323–7, 26 June 1805.

[2] T. 29/85, f. 352, 19 August 1805.

[3] A site previously occupied by the Cistercian Abbey of St. Mary Graces (1350–1539) and the Royal Navy Victualling Yard (1562–1784). Its proximity to the Tower guaranteed security (H. G. Stride, *The Royal Mint*, 1951, p. 12; Sir J. Craig, *The Mint*, 1953, pp. 270–1).

[4] T. 29/85, f. 503, 13 November 1805; T. 1/3997, 21 February 1810; Mint Record Books xvi, ff. 170–2, 31 March 1807, ff. 185–6, 30 December 1806 and f. 460, 13 February 1810. 'I have obeyed your instructions relative to secrecy, and have every reason to believe the neighbourhood are not yet apprized of any part of the premises being wanted for Government. . . . The back part of the Cloths Exchange, and the Fourteen Stars Public House, both of which you want, are all a part of one estate, which I find exceedingly involved; still I believe it is to be got at' (T. 1/3997, Henry Rowles to James Johnson, 5 August 1805).

[5] For lists and criticisms of residential quarters cf. Mint Record Books xviii, f. 117, 28 April 1815, xxix, ff. 90–4, 23 April 1831; 'Inquiry into the . . . Office of Works', *Parl. Pap.* 1812–13, v, p. 485; 'Seventh Report from the Committee on Public Expenditure, Buildings, Civil and Military', *Parl. Pap.* 1810, ii, p. 526.

[6] T. 1/3997, 24 January, 16 April 1807, 14 March, 24 April 1809; Mint Record Books xvi, ff. 104–8, 19 November 1805, 3 April 1806, ff. 456–8, 29 January, 12 February 1810; Rennie MSS., Reports 1st Series iii, f. 419, 4 November 1805, iv, f. 1, 4 December 1805.

[7] A Mr. Biggs, employed by the East India Company, by the Commissioners for the Improvement of Westminster and by Smirke at Covent Garden Theatre (T. 1/3997, 12 May 1809, 20 June 1809).

[8] T. 1/3997, 6 August 1812; 'Seventh Report from the Committee on Public Expenditure, Buildings, Civil and Military', *Parl. Pap.* 1810, ii, p. 526; 'Inquiry into the . . . Office of Works', *Parl. Pap.* 1812–13, v, p. 483; 'Report from the Select Committee on the Office of Works', *Parl. Pap.* 1828, iv, p. 323.

[9] E.g. Mint Record Books xvi, ff. 456, 31 January 1810, xvii, f. 34, 4 February 1811.

[10] 'Eleventh Report from the Committee on Public Expenditure', *Parl. Pap.* 1810–11, iii, p. 1063.

[11] T. 1/3997, 16 November 1810; Mint Record Books xvi, f. 477, 22 January, f. 480, 28 March 1810, xvii, ff. 156–7, 18 March 1811; 'Estimates and Accounts', *Parl. Pap.* 1812, ix, p. 301; 'Inquiry into the . . . Office of Works', *Parl. Pap.* 1812–13, v, p. 483.

[12] Mint Record Books xvi, ff. 199–201, 8 July 1807, f. 379, 21 April and f. 392, 23 May 1808.

time after the department moved into its new headquarters in the summer of 1811.[1] And in July 1812 'Smirke complained of the conduct of Mr. Wharton, Secretary to the Treasury, who having the last year expressed to the Commons that no more money would be required . . . and now having a further sum to move for was disposed to lay the blame on Robert Smirke'.[2] Most of the workmen had been dismissed in March 1812, but the bills continued to flow in. By the end of 1814 the total had reached £285,336 14s. 0¾d.[3]:

September 1805–January 1807	69,209 3s. 8 d.	⎱ under
January 1807–August 1807	28,164 5s. 4 d.	⎰ Johnson.
August–December 1807	26,308 18s. 5¾d.	⎫
23rd December 1807–31st December 1808	46,947 16s. 6¾d.	⎪ under
January–December 1809	27,895 12s. 0 d.	⎬ Smirke.
January–December 1810	27,338 16s. 5¼d.	⎪
January 1811–December 1814	59,472 1s. 7 d.	⎭

£285,336 14s. 0¾d.

At this point responsibility for operations was transferred to the Office of Works and Smirke began to perform as Attached Architect the duties he had previously executed as Surveyor to the Mint. Edward Crocker became Clerk of the Works in place of Thomas Pope who retired on a pension of £60 per annum.[4] Final figures revealed that £288,656 had been spent on the structure alone, excluding the purchase and installation of machinery.[5] But scarcely had the new building been completed when a minor disaster occurred. Early one morning in October 1815 a fire broke out causing damage wildly valued at £60–80,000. About 10 a.m. 'the flames were first seen to issue from the shaking-machine room, on the south side of the building. They soon communicated to the gold-room, from thence to some counting-houses, and eventually to the silver or rolling-room, on the eastern side; and in a short time the eastern and southern wings of the building were completely unroofed, and the interior totally destroyed. In these were contained the great machinery of the works, including the 10, 15 and 30 horse power engines'.[6] 'As all the Mint officers and workmen were at their posts at the time . . . every exertion was immediately made to extinguish it. The fire engine at the Mint began to play upon the roof, in the course of three minutes, and no time was lost in sending to the different fire offices who, very soon after, collected their engines at the Mint, and about 12 o'clock the fire was stopped'.[7] Some months previously, 'as the building happened to be finished

[1] Mint Record Books xvii, f. 61, 11 May 1811 and ff. 83–4, 7 November 1811. The keys of the old Mint were formally handed over to the Barrack Office in August 1812 (*ibid*. f. 200, 8 August 1812).

[2] 'Lord Bathurst and Mr. Rose etc., were much displeased at Mr. Wharton's statement and Lord Bathurst condemned his conduct in conversation with Lord Lonsdale who had patronised Wharton' (Farington, p. 6136, 28 July 1812). See also *Commons Jnls.* lxvii (1812), pp. 507, 653, 6 July 1812 and Appendix 3.

[3] Figures compiled from general building accounts, A.O. 1/2500.

[4] One third of his salary plus perquisites, in accordance with 50 G. III *c.* 117 (Mint Record Books, xvii, f. 53, 25 March 1811 and f. 234, 27 November 1815).

[5] Report from the Select Committee on Intended Improvements in the Post Office', *Parl. Pap.* 1814–15, iii, p. 186. The machinery itself, as supplied by Boulton, Rennie and Coxen, cost £38,907 12s. 6d. (Mint Record Books xviii, f. 119, 28 April 1815).   [6] *Gent's. Mag.* 1815, pt. ii, p. 458.

[7] Mint Record Books xviii, f. 211, 31 October 1815, Wellesley Pole's report to the Treasury.

just at the time when . . . all specie had disappeared, and also at the time when the new Custom House was planned, it was wittily observed . . . that we had a new Mint when we had no money, and a new Custom House when we had no trade'.[1] Jocular critics now claimed that the government had ended by blowing up the Mint itself.[2] The Ordnance Office rushed to the rescue: guards, labourers, tarpaulins, barrows and shovels were hurried across from the Tower.[3] Within a few days Smirke verbally estimated the cost of repair at £9–10,000.[4] But Stephenson's report 'that the most probable cause of this fire was some original defect in the construction', was followed by a decision to render all vulnerable portions of the building fireproof by means of party walls and iron roofs and doors.[5] For this purpose Smirke made an estimate of £13,000 in February 1816.[6] To this sum were later added those of £2100 for boilers, £180 for iron doors and £600 for interior decorations.[7] The cost of altering the Office of Receipt was estimated at £150.[8]

Smirke's directions for fire precautions also indicate the extent of his own responsibility for the buildings. He told Stephenson that he had

> considered attentively whether the principal building occupied by several officers of the Mint . . . may be rendered secure from total destruction in the event of a partial fire taking place within it. The walls of this, as well as of all those recently burnt down, were built and roofed before the works were placed under my superintendance, but I remember to have examined several of them with a view to this subject before they were plaistered, and I found so many pieces of timber connected with them, that it was impossible to make any very effectual separation by party walls. It is not however probable that the whole of this building would be consumed by a fire taking place in any one part, but a further security against its possible extension might be obtained at a small expence by making some partial additional separations within it. Of the other dwellings . . . those on the North side of the front area were also built and were completed before I went to the Mint, but as far as I can ascertain it they appear to be perfectly separated by party walls, except in the upper storey where three were united and formed into a range of work rooms for die-engravers; as these are no longer all used for that purpose, the separation in them may be now made complete at a trifling expence. The three buildings at the South side of the area were built by myself and have party walls separating each of them.[9]

The main façade of the Mint, and indeed the basic plan must be credited to Johnson.[10] As engineer to the firm of Boulton and Watt and co-ordinating adviser in London, John Rennie claims credit for the technical arrangements relating to the construction, installation and maintenance of the celebrated machinery.[11] Smirke's

---

[1] *Monthly Mag.* xxxvii (1814), p. 198. [2] Sir J. Craig, *The Mint* (1953), p. 277.
[3] Mint Record Books xviii, f. 216, 1 November, f. 220, 10 November 1815 and f. 292, 20 February 1816.
[4] Works 4/21, f. 593, 7 November 1815.
[5] Works 4/21, f. 588, 1 November 1815; Mint Record Books xviii, f. 225, 15 November 1815.
[6] Works 12/59/1, f. 13, 1 February 1816. Smirke's plans for the reconstruction, dated 1815–16, are Works 30/225–253.
[7] *Ibid.* 9 July 1816, 1 August 1816.
[8] Works 1/6, f. 351, 5 January 1816. [9] Works 12/59/1, f. 13, 1 February 1816.
[10] Johnson's Plans, cross-sections and elevations, R.I.B.A. Drawings Collection E 6/4 (1–8).
[11] Matthew Boulton died in 1809, James Watt in 1819. Their business at Soho near Birmingham was carried on by M. R. Boulton and James Watt Jnr. For technical details see *Encyclopaedia Britannica* (1823 ed.), 'Coinage'; C. Knight (ed.), *London* iii (1842), pp. 46–7; W. Thornbury and E. Walford, *Old and New London* ii (1874), pp. 105–7; Sir J. Craig, *The Mint* (1953), *passim*.

1.	Copper Foundry	9.	Shaking	17	Boiler Houses
2	Gold Melting House	10.	Coining Press Room	18.	Engine Room
3.	Silver Melting House	11.	Moneyer's Hall	19.	Grinding Room
4.	Rolling Mill Room	12.	Refinery	20.	Copper Store Room
5.	Adjusting Rolls	13.	Press Room	21.	Gasometer
6.	Cutting Out Room	14.	Lathes	22.	Retort House
7.	Milling Room	15.	Dies	23.	Pyx Office
8.	Annealing Room	16.	Smith	24.	Bullion
				25.	Mint Office

10   0   50

Scale of Metres

50   0   100

Scale of Feet

Fig. 15. The Royal Mint: from *Parliamentary Papers* 1849, xxviii, 665.

responsibility is less easy to define. When he succeeded Johnson in July 1807 the exterior and roof of the principal block had been largely completed, likewise the Adjusting Rooms, Engine Houses, Rolling Mills, Cutting Out Room, Coining Room and the houses of the three Engravers, the Warden and the Comptroller.[1] On the other hand Johnson's ground plan of 1805[2] differs markedly from Smirke's.[3] The first scheme suggests lateral entrances to the principal block; the second shows the final arrangement of central entrance, lobby and staircase. And indeed Smirke's hand is indicated in the Doric piers, the Ionic columns and the *antae* which decorate and punctuate the entrance hall, the first floor landing and the Master's suite. Again, Johnson envisaged a courtyard centrally entered by a single gateway. For this Smirke substituted a more appropriate arrangement: a pair of gate lodges which open up the forecourt and neatly frame the majestic view across the battlements of the Tower (Pl. 28B).[4] Finally, Smirke was responsible for all the interior decoration, for completing the officers' houses and workshops and for reconstructing the boundary wall which surrounded the whole property and incorporated the Military Way.[5]

Unlike most Office of Works buildings, the upkeep of the Mint required unusual technical skill. From the start there was a division of responsibility. The new Mint had been built by departmental contractors.[6] The Office of Works inherited a number of these tradesmen. Others were brought from Boulton's Soho works near Birmingham and installed in houses built to Smirke's designs and costing £3900.[7] In general the cost of new machinery came from the public purse, and the repair of old machinery was dealt with and paid for by the Provost and Company of Moneyers.[8] As for structural repairs, it was reported that 'the exterior of the dwelling houses is done, under estimates, by the Board of Works, as well as the whole inside and outside of the offices and workshops. The interior of the houses, in the painting, papering etc., is defrayed out of the funds in the hands of the Master of the Mint arising from the grants for the established service, coinage, or profits on coinage, conformably to the ancient usage of the office'.[9]

[1] T. 1/3997, Johnson's interim report 24 January 1807.

[2] MR 1093 (ex LRRO. 1/1009), ground plan signed and dated 8 January 1805.

[3] R.I.B.A. Drawings Collection E 6/4 (I), ground plan, inscribed 'received from Mr. Smirke Aug. 4, 1812'; presented by Arthur Cates 14 November 1898.

[4] Unfortunately the construction of the Central Stores in 1925–6 involved blocking up the guardroom entrance, thus spoiling the symmetry of Smirke's design.

[5] Rebuilding part of the boundary wall cost £650 and involved an exchange of land with the Commissioners for the Improvement of East Smithfield (Mint Record Books xviii, f. 4, 12 April 1814, f. 98, 22 February 1815 and f. 115, 19 April 1815; MR 10903 (ex LRRO. 1/1009), plans dated 15 June 1812). For the final plan (1842) cf. 'Report of the Commissioners appointed to enquire into . . . the Royal Mint', *Parl. Pap.* 1849, xxviii, p. 665.

[6] Henry Rowles: bricklaying, masonry, carpentry. Thomas Moorman; James Cruickshank: smithswork. Messrs. Buzzard and Dennis: glazing. John Coventry; C. Dixon & Sons: painting. William Tarte; John Wardell (executor to J. Jourdon): plumbing. John Thwaite: clockmaking. F. Bernasconi; William Thorogood & Sons: plastering. Messrs. Duppa, Robson and Hailes: paper hanging. E. Rigby: carving. Messrs. Fenton and Esden: slating. Messrs. Meredith and Hammerton: paving. C. Rossi: modelling. M. Boulton, J. Watt, J. Coxen and J. Rennie: machinery (list compiled from A.O. 1/2500 and Mint Record Books xvii, f. 188, 3 June 1812).

[7] Mint Record Books xvii, ff. 64–5, 13 April 1811; xviii, f. 4, 12 April 1815, f. 115, 19 April 1815, f. 264, 12 December 1815 and f. 293, 26 February 1816; Rennie MSS., Reports 1st Series vi, f. 308, 30 January 1811; 'Estimates, Accounts etc.', *Parl. Pap.* 1814–15, ix, p. 204.

[8] 'Report from the Select Committee on the Royal Mint', *Parl. Pap.* 1837, xvi, pp. 15, 38.

[9] *Ibid.* p. 225. These arrangements were little altered by the reorganisation of 1832 (Mint Record Books xviii, f. 157, 7 July 1815, xxix ff. 90–94, 23 April 1831, xxx, f. 101, 19 March 1832).

In fact few alterations were required during the next half century, and fewer still were executed. In 1815 Smirke designed 'a rail way or smooth path for the trucks to run upon, in conveying the bullion to and from the Office of Receipt, Melting House, Rolling and Coining Rooms'. This was renewed and extended in 1829.[1] In 1816 £3800 was spent on the installation of 'a gas light apparatus to furnish light equal to 250 or 300 Argand Lamps, for six months in the year, and six hours in each day'.[2] For this project Smirke co-operated with a chemist named Frederick Accum. One critic noted that 'the effect of the new lights, scattered upon so extensive a scale, over the beautiful machinery of the coining processes, is uncommonly striking; and the new Royal Mint now exhibits the most elegant establishment of the kind in the world'.[3] In the 1820s and 1830s minor alterations to workshops, houses and stabling were supervised by Smirke and by Crocker's successor, Lewis Wyatt.[4] It was not until the Coinage Act of 1870 that the need for reconstruction became acute, nor until 1880 that agreement was reached as to what form of reconstruction was most desirable. Schemes for removal to a new Thameside site at Whitefriars or the Savoy were abandoned.[5] Instead the principal building was retained, the workshops reconstructed and the machinery replaced.[6]

As a piece of metropolitan improvement, the New Mint opened up the periphery of the Tower, turning unrelated clutter into viable townscape.[7] At governmental level Wellesley Pole's unusual efficiency and Boulton's novel machinery represented tangible symbols of administrative and economic revival. As an architectural entity, however, the New Mint was less successful. Ackermann was probably thinking of its mechanical side when he called it 'the most perfect establishment of its kind in the world'.[8] Johnson's Tuscan semi-columns and Smirke's Doric *antae* made an unhappy combination. This mixture of late Palladian and ponderous Grecian struck contemporaries as incongruous; similarly the conjunction of crisp ashlar and dismal stock brick. 'It will probably strike every curious observer', commented one writer, 'that the houses on each side of this truly elegant building . . . would have been much more correctly assimilated with the fabric, if they had been fronted with the new *stucca*, and ornamented in the same style'.[9] Some condemned the whole composition as 'common-place . . . and humdrum'.[10] Others praised only the skill with which the

[1] Works 1/30, f. 47, 23 November 1829; Mint Record Books xviii, f. 192, 22 September 1815, xix, f. 251 14 June 1817 and xxvi, f. 242, 13 November 1829.

[2] Mint Record Books xix, ff. 33–5, 14 August, ff. 46–7, 7 August 1816 and xxi, f. 71, 11 May 1820.

[3] *Gent's. Mag.* 1817, pt. ii, p. 552.

[4] E.g. Works 4/27, f. 260, 28 July 1825; Mint Record Books xxi, f. 116, 22 July 1820, xxii, f. 11, 18 June 1821, xxvi, f. 13, 25 July 1827, f. 299, 12 September 1828, xxvii, f. 5, 15 October 1828, f. 102, 24 March and f. 136, 27 May 1829.

[5] 'Report from the Select Committee on the New Mint Building Site Bill', *Parl. Pap.* 1871, xi, p. 359; 'Accounts and Papers', *Parl. Pap.* 1871, xxxvii, p. 311; 'Annual Reports of the Deputy Master of the Mint', *Parl. Pap.* 1872, xviii, pp. 425–6; 1875, xxi, pp. 141–2; 1876, xxi, p. 45; 1877, xxvii, p. 144, 1881, xxix, p. 544; 'Report from the Select Committee on the London City Lands (Thames Embankment) Bill', *Parl. Pap.* 1881, ix, pp. 537, 627–35.

[6] For details and plans of the new buildings see 'Annual Report of the Deputy Master of the Mint', *Parl. Pap.* 1882, xxi, pp. 411–7. For the replacement of machinery see *The Engineer* 19 January 1883.

[7] 'The New Mint and the extensive offices belonging to it, having occasioned the removal of all the old houses on the left hand side of East Smithfield down to Norwich Court and Butcher Row, the street, which was before narrow and dangerous, is now rendered commodious and broad, and the improvement has added considerably to the good appearance of the neighbourhood' (J. Nightingale, *London and Middlesex* iii, 1815, p. 136). [8] R. Ackermann, *The Microcosm of London* ii (1809), p. 205.

[9] Nightingale *loc. cit.* [10] *Civil Engineer and Architect's Jnl.* ii (1839), p. 37; viii (1845), p. 33.

interior planning had been arranged.[1] Perhaps the building's highest claim was indeed that it combined 'a modest grandeur with the convenience of being admirably suited to business'.[2]

THE MUSEUM OF ECONOMIC GEOLOGY

In 1837 a museum of economic or practical geology was established in a vacant Crown house, No. 5 Craig's Court, Whitehall, as a result of a suggestion by Sir Henry De la Beche of the Geological Survey for forming a collection of mineral specimens under the care of the Department of Works.[3] The inquiry into stone for building the new Houses of Parliament brought additions to the collection which in 1839 was permitted to take over the adjoining house, No. 6; and by 1844 was in need of yet more room.[4] Philipps, Clerk to the Board of Woods and Works, suggested that Crown property lying between Piccadilly and Jermyn Street, of which the leases were then falling in, would provide a convenient site; and Pennethorne endorsed this proposal. De la Beche seized the opportunity thus offered to bring the Geological Survey and the museum together in a single building under the aegis of the First Commissioner of Woods, an arrangement approved by Lord Lincoln and Sir Robert Peel.[5]

Pennethorne's first design, for the museum and six houses with shops and vaults, estimated at £28,860, was submitted in November 1844.[6] De la Beche was hostile to shops on the ground floor of the museum, fearing their 'frizzling us out'; and Pennethorne produced a revised scheme with fewer shops (March 1845).[7] Various elevations were considered late in 1845, and a complete set of plans was signed by Lincoln on 2 March 1846. But the estimate for this scheme, £40,000, proved to be too high. The First Commissioner then ordered that buildings of a less expensive character should be designed, with only two storeys instead of three. The estimate for Pennethorne's third scheme came to nearly £30,000, including compensation to leaseholders' interests. There was, however, some parliamentary criticism of shops and wine vaults being constructed in juxtaposition to the museum, and on 2 September 1846 Lord Morpeth, the new Whig First Commissioner, called for fresh plans appropriating the entire site for the museum and its related services, though the façades and estimate of the third scheme were to be retained.[8] Three weeks later he ordered a start to be made on the basement, for which a contract on a schedule of prices was made with Messrs. Herbert and Kelk: this amounted to nearly

[1] C. Ollier and T. S. Boys, *Views of London as it is* (1842).

[2] S. and R. Percy, *London* iii (1824), p. 55. For favourable judgements see J. Elmes, *Metropolitan Improvements* ii (1827/9) p. 50, and *Dictionary of London* (1831).

[3] T. 1/3776; Works 17/7/1, f. 1, 13 July 1835, De la Beche to Chancellor of the Exchequer (*Survey of London* xvi, p. 219). See also Sir John Smith Flett, *First Hundred Years of the Geological Survey of Great Britain* (1937).

[4] No. 6 (hitherto the Earl Marshal's office) was altered by Herbert, under Chawner's directions, at a cost of £1288 18s. 6d. (T. 1/3776, f. 24046/39). After the museum's removal to Jermyn Street, the two houses were used to accommodate the 1851 Census (Works 2/8, pp. 300, 311).

[5] Works 17/7/1, ff. 6, 8, 12, 24; Nottingham University Library, Newcastle MS. 11952 (19 December 1844).   [6] Works 17/7/1, ff. 72–4.   [7] *Ibid.* ff. 14–18, 72–4.   [8] *Ibid.* ff. 75–80.

£3000. Morpeth was anxious to push the work on, and was impatient of interdepartmental formalities that were delaying it.[1]

Pennethorne completed his new design in October 1846, substituting a large central room with two galleries, skylighted, for an open area, and proposing certain changes in elevation. Difficulties then arose with the official referees under the Metropolitan Buildings Act. It was May 1847 before a second contract, for the superstructure, was given to Kelk on his tender of £24,520.[2] Last minute alterations were made in the elevations, and additional works on the museum and adjoining houses amounted to £1500. Consequential works brought the grand total for artificers' works to a little over £30,000.[3] The building was completed by the end of 1848.[4] Anston Stone as in the Houses of Parliament was used for the Piccadilly front (Pl. 29A) and for dressings on the Jermyn Street front.[5] The museum gallery with its semi-elliptical roof carried on plastered cast-iron beams was interesting for its 'remarkably frank articulation of interior structure', a compromise, as Professor H.-R. Hitchcock points, out, between the 'iron and glass court of Bunning's contemporary Coal Exchange . . . [and] the heavy trabeated interiors of Smirke's British Museum'.[6] The fitting-up was a lengthy business; the Craig's Court premises were closed in January 1850, and the museum re-opened in Jermyn Street on 12 May 1851.[7] Total expenditure, including fittings, to 1 January 1851 was £43,633, of which at least £17,000 were taken from the Land Revenue without prior parliamentary authority.[8] The building was demolished in 1935. It is described and illustrated in Volume xxix of the *Survey of London*.

THE NATIONAL GALLERY

The National Gallery was founded in 1824, when the collection of paintings formed by John Julius Angerstein was acquired by the nation.[9] Angerstein's house, 99 Pall Mall,[10] was purchased at the same time as a home for the collection, and some £400 were spent on works to improve the rooms for exhibition purposes.[11] The house opened to the public on 10 May 1824.[12] Early in 1826 a further £421 were spent on improving

---

[1] *Ibid.* ff. 21, 26, 81, 85; P.R.O. 30/22/5 C, Morpeth to Russell, 23 September [1846]. For an account of some of the problems relating to the site which caused delay, see *Survey of London*, xxix (1960), pp. 272–4.

[2] Of this sum £750 were for a stone front to Jermyn Street (Works 17/7/1, ff. 68–9, 82). The partnership of Herbert and Kelk was dissolved about this time (f. 83).   [3] *Ibid.* ff. 83–5.

[4] So it appears from Pennethorne's account, *ibid.* ff. 83–5. Doors commissioned from Alfred Stevens were never completed (V. and A. Museum, Dept. of Engraving, Illustration and Design, No. 8068).

[5] Works 12/64/14, ff. 56–9.   [6] Hitchcock, *Early Victorian Architecture*, i, p. 295 and figs. ix, 28 and 29.

[7] *Parl. Pap.* 1854–5 (21) liii, p. 10.   [8] *Ibid.* 1851 (374), xxxi, pp. 371–4; 1849 (513) xx, qq. 853–5.

[9] Parliament voted £60,000 on 2 April 1824 for the purchase, preservation and exhibition of the pictures (*Parl. Deb.* new ser. xi, 101–3).

[10] There was some variation in the numbering of this and adjacent houses. Angerstein's is numbered 99 Pall Mall in the Office of Works records, but in the January 1819 edition of *Boyle's Court Guide*, it is numbered 102, and in the January 1824 edition, 100, by which number subsequent literature generally describes it.

[11] Works 1/12, p. 427; 5/109, 5 July 1824.

[12] C. Holmes and C. H. Collins Baker, *The Making of the National Gallery, 1824–1924* (1924), p. 3.

the lighting of the exhibition rooms, and it may well have been on this occasion that a skylight was inserted above the principal room.[1]

By 1828 further gifts and purchases of paintings had absorbed all available hanging space. When an offer from the directors of the British Institution of £4000 for building an additional gallery was not accepted by the Treasury, the National Gallery Trustees, headed by Lord Aberdeen, proposed that part of the King's Mews at Charing Cross 'might be made suitable for the purpose of displaying the National Collection to great advantage and at no considerable expense'.[2] This site had already been proposed for the building of a new gallery by John Nash as a part of his improvements under the Office of Woods and Forests: instructed to re-plan the site of the Lower Mews, he designed a square of which the north side was to be formed by a columned gallery 460 feet long with domes and central Corinthian portico; opposite, in the centre of the square, was to be a new Royal Academy building copied from the Parthenon.[3] In August 1828, the *Gentleman's Magazine* announced incorrectly that this scheme had been approved by the authorities.[4] Nothing further was done until it was desired to construct a road from Pall Mall to Carlton House Gardens which would involve the demolition of Angerstein's house.[5] Then the Office of Works began to look for a new home for the collection. The Trustees suggested in December 1830 that the best site for a new gallery would be the portion of St. James's Palace cleared after the fire of 1809.[6]

Among the advocates of a new building was the then First Commissioner of Woods, G. A. Ellis; but the Prime Minister dreaded 'unnecessary expense', and no decision had been taken when in August 1831 the architect William Wilkins, Treasurer of the Royal Academy, proposed that the King's Mews should be adapted to accommodate both the Gallery and the Academy.[7] The Trustees recommended this plan to Lord Grey, as 'the most practicable that has hitherto been offered to them, and well adapted to that purpose'.[8] But ministers preferred the cheaper expedient of converting the adjoining house in Pall Mall, lately Lady Dysart's, at a cost of about £1500.[9] Swayed by Sir Robert Peel, himself a Trustee, opinion in the Commons declared in favour of building a new gallery; Lord Althorp at the Exchequer

---

[1] Works 5/109, 5 April 1826. A water-colour by F. Mackenzie in the Victoria and Albert Museum, reproduced by W. T. Whitley, *Art in England 1821–1837* (1930), opp. p. 268, shows the principal room with skylight.

[2] Works 17/10/1, ff. 1–2; National Gallery, MS. minutes of Board meetings of Trustees, i, f. 8. See also *Survey of London*, xxix (1960), pt. i, p. 350.

[3] *Fifth Report of H.M. Commissioners of Woods, Forests and Land Revenue*, Parl. Pap. 1826, xiv, p. 12. Appendix 23 is a plan of the proposals.

[4] *Gent's. Mag.* 1828, ii, p. 161.

[5] T. 1/4028, f. 13870/30. The pictures were moved from Angerstein's house into 105 Pall Mall in February 1834, and the old Gallery was then demolished (*Survey of London*, xxix, 1960, p. 351, citing Crown Estate Office files 10068, 12204).

[6] T. 1/4028, f. 21416/30; National Gallery, minutes of Trustees, i, ff. 9–17.

[7] Grey Papers, Durham University, Grey to Ellis, 30 November 1830; National Gallery, minutes of Trustees, i, ff. 19–20; evidence of W. Wilkins before select committee on Arts and Manufactures, *Parl. Pap.* 1836, ix, qq. 1392, 1430; W. Wilkins, *Letter to Lord Viscount Goderich on the patronage of the arts by the English government* (privately printed, 1832); *Library of the Fine Arts*, iv (1832), pp. 61–3; *Athenaeum*, 1833, pp. 104–6; Whitley, *op. cit.* pp. 237–8. One advantage of this proposal was that the removal of the Academy from Somerset House would release rooms needed for government offices.

[8] National Gallery, minutes of Trustees, i, ff. 19–22.

[9] J. H. Barrow (ed.) *Mirror of Parliament*, 1831–2, ii, 1820. Lady Dysart's, 104 Pall Mall, was used to house the King's pictures, 1831–6, see *Survey of London*, xxix, pt. i, p. 350.

was persuaded to change his views; and the government hastily considered designs for a new building.[1] Nash's project was revived; C. R. Cockerell proposed a gallery 400 feet long above a row of shops, a scheme he estimated at £60,000;[2] and Lord Grey told Wilkins to submit his own design 'with the least possible delay'.[3]

Lord Duncannon as Chief Commissioner of Woods and Works set up a committee consisting of himself, Lords Goderich, Farnborough and Dover (G. A. Ellis), Sir Robert Peel, and Messrs. Hume and Samuel Rogers, to consider the whole question of providing buildings for the paintings, the public records and various learned bodies.[4] In May 1832 this committee decided that Wilkins' project, retaining and extending the old Mews, would provide sufficient room for the pictures and for the public records.[5] Their decision that 'the objects sought for cannot be obtained by the public on terms more economical' than Wilkins' estimate of £33,000 practically settled the choice of architect.[6] After further deliberations, however, the committee on 14 June recommended that a new building should be erected, which Wilkins declared 'with the greatest confidence' could be done for £41,000 if he were entrusted with all the arrangements. This was for a brick structure, cemented, the use of stone being 'confined to the basis, the water tables and the portico; the latter to be constructed from the columns and entablature which formerly decorated Carlton House'. To face the principal parts with stone would cost another £10,000; or brick with stone dressings, £5000 more.[7] Finally the Treasury agreed to a building of Portland stone, to cost £50,000, and £15,000 on account were voted by the Commons on 23 July, 1832.[8]

Wilkins' proposals were for a long, low classical building, 461 feet from east to west, and 56 feet in width, consisting of a centre and two wings. In the long façade the central portico formed the only significant projection and the small dome and two turrets the only breaks in the skyline. The west wing was to provide on the ground floor rooms for the public records, and a vaulted passageway through it gave

---

[1] *Mirror of Parliament* 1831–2, ii, 1820–22; iv, 3306. The importance of so improving national taste as to make textile design competitive with that of France was strongly urged in support.

[2] Works 17/10/1, f. 10. Cockerell stated that Herbert, a builder, would carry out the project if he received the ground at a peppercorn rent for 99 years and could let the shops.

[3] *Ibid.* f. 11, Wilkins to Lord Duncannon, 18 May 1832. Mitford's story (recounted by Whitley, *op. cit.* pp. 268–9) that Samuel Rogers persuaded Wilkins to sit up all night in order to send in a design appears to be *ben trovato.*

[4] T. 1/4028, f. 9238/32. The Geological Society and the Naval and Military Museum were willing to pay for buildings.

[5] *Ibid.* f. 9302/32, 13 May 1832.

[6] Nash, who offered two plans (*Parl. Pap.* 1836, ix, Report of select committee on Arts and Manufactures, q. 1389), appears still to have been considering the matter at the end of May: see Pennethorne's Diary, quoted by Summerson, *Nash*, p. 270, n. 4.

[7] Works 17/10/1, ff. 13–14, 16. The Secretary of the Treasury told the Commons that a building entirely of stone (which would cost only £3000 more than a brick one faced with stone) had been decided upon as it was 'desirable that this edifice should not only be worthy of the pictorial treasures . . . but also afford honorable evidence of the progress of architecture in this country' (*Mirror of Parliament*, 1831–2, iv, 3306).

[8] T. 1/4028, f. 13193/32; *Mirror of Parliament*, 1831–2, iv, 3306. The appointment of Wilkins was attacked as a job, and his designs (as far as they were known) were harshly criticised, notably in a broadsheet by Sir Edward Cust (who employed Charles Barry to make an etching); in the *Spectator*, 15 February 1834 (for which, see Whitley, *op. cit.* pp. 267–8); and in the *Literary Gazette* 1833, pp. 122, 154, 169–71, 586, 618; 1834, pp. 138, 175–6. Wilkins did not exhibit his design publicly until early 1834. 'From its first conception to the present time no building, perhaps, has been the subject of more lively criticism' (Walford, *Old and New London*, 1873, iii, p. 145). Other contemporary appraisals are to be found in *Architectural Mag.* (1834), i, pp. 138–9, 319; *Gent.'s Mag.* 1835, ii, p. 181; *Civil Engineer and Architect's Jnl.* July, 1838, and J. Britton and A. Pugin, *Public Buildings of London*, ed. W. H. Leeds (1838), ii, pp. 190–209.

access to the barrack-yard immediately north of the site. On the first floor were rooms for pictures, and for the keeper. The floors were to be fireproof. The east wing, housing the Royal Academy, was similar, but possessed a basement; it too was penetrated by a passage which furnished a right-of-way for the inhabitants of Castle Street. The centre block was to contain halls, vestibules and staircases for both establishments, 'distinct and detached but so brought together as to form one grand object both externally and internally'.[1] The columns of the portico of Carlton House were to 'be preserved in the external decoration of this part of the building' if 'found to be entire and applicable to the purpose'.[2]

Considerable modifications were made to this design, some imposed on the architect, some willingly embraced by him. Public opinion insisted that the building line should be set back so as to give a view of St. Martin's portico from Pall Mall.[3] Although Wilkins obtained a change in the line of front so that his portico faced down Whitehall, he had to place it 50 feet further north than he wished,[4] and to set back the ends of the façade; at the end next the church he thought the effect better, but at the other 'decidedly worse'.[5] In order to relieve the long line of the façade, he brought forward the tetrastyle gateways marking the two passages (originally arched),[6] and to range the cornice with that of St. Martin's he raised the height five feet.[7] Other alterations were the addition of a semicircular gallery at the back; a re-arrangement of the ground floor of the west wing following the decision not to house the records there; and to meet criticism in the Commons a modification of the staircase to permit of subsequent enlargement.[8] Save for the addition in height, these changes had been decided upon by 12 January 1833, when they were approved at a meeting between Lords Grey and Duncannon and the architect, whose revised estimate was for £66,000, less £4000 for the value of old materials.[9] Wilkins' final design nicely illustrates the dilemma that confronted the

---

[1] T. 1/4028, f. 12786/32. A drawing in the R.I.B.A. Collection by G. Aitchison, dated '6.4.91', entitled 'The National Gallery from Wilkins' Drawings. Restoration of the supposed original design by Wilkins', shows hexastyle porticoes at either end of the south front; but there is no evidence to suggest that Wilkins ever officially put forward such a project, which appears to be based on his University College design.

[2] They had been stored in St. James's Park since the demolition of Carlton House in 1826. There is no reason to suppose, as do the authors of *The Survey of London*, xx (1940), p. 15, that 'In his treatment of the façade Wilkins was handicapped by having to utilise the columns and capitals from Carlton House'. If Wilkins did not originate the proposal, he adopted it readily (see Works 17/10/1, ff. 56–7) and modified it when he found it did not suit his purpose. See p. 467 below.

[3] Wilkins did not share popular enthusiasm for that portico. 'I should have passed a great many years of useless study' he declared 'if I could not design something very superior to that of St. Martin's Church' (*Athenaeum* 1833, p. 106).

[4] T. 1/4028, Commissioners of Woods &c. to Treasury, 2 April 1833; Works 17/10/1, ff. 256–8; *Parl. Pap.* 1836, ix, Report of select committee on Arts and Manufactures, q. 1207. See *Athenaeum* 1833, pp. 104–6, 135–6; 1834, p. 408, for Wilkins' views; for the opposition, J. Gwilt, *Observations on the communication of Mr. Wilkins to the Editor of the Athenaeum, relative to the National Gallery* (1833).   [5] Works 17/10/1, f. 4.

[6] T. 1/4028, Wilkins to Duncannon, 5 February 1833. An elevation, Works 33/927, dated 1833, shows the arches by which the passages were at first to be entered, and also a different form of turret over the wings. Both that form, and that finally adopted, are shown in Works 33/951.

[7] Works 17/10/1, ff. 71–3. For a more detailed account of these alterations see G. Martin, 'Wilkins and the National Gallery', *Burlington Magazine* cxiii (1971), pp. 318–29. which appeared while this volume was in the press.

[8] Works 17/10/1, f. 27. The drum of the dome may also be an afterthought, if one may accept the evidence of an illustration in the *Literary Gazette*, 1833, p. 122 (showing a dome resembling that of University College, London), and a remark of 'Candidus', *Architectural Mag.* i, 1834, p. 319. But the illustration is inaccurate in several respects and was repudiated by Wilkins (*Athenaeum*, 1833, pp. 104–6).

[9] T. 1/4028, Commissioners of Woods &c. to Treasury, 2 April 1833 (printed in *Parl. Pap.* 1833, xxiv, p. 559). As Wilkins' previous estimates had not included commission and incidentals, the real increase was £8525.

465

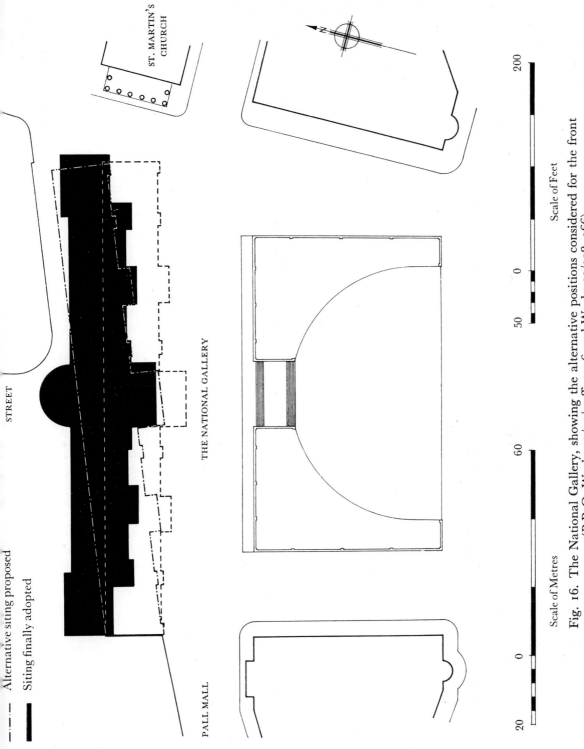

Alternative siting proposed

Siting finally adopted

STREET

PALL MALL

THE NATIONAL GALLERY

ST. MARTIN'S CHURCH

Scale of Metres

Scale of Feet

Fig. 16. The National Gallery, showing the alternative positions considered for the front
(P.R.O. Works 17/10/1, ff. 35–6 and Works 33/908, 966).

neo-classical architect in the age of Romanticism. Having designed an ostensibly Greek building, he sought constantly to relieve its severity, and enhance its picturesqueness (see Pl. 30). Advocating the enrichment of the exterior with sculpture, he stated that 'by breaking the horizontal *skyline* [it would] greatly improve the general effect'; Minerva placed between two trophies on the east front would 'break the horizontal line of the top of the ballustrade, so as to make the center *culminate* . . . in a triangular form so much desired by the lovers of picturesque effect'.[1] Arguing for the construction of a fountain in Trafalgar Square, he remarked, 'although it may seem objectionable as interfering with the portico in the approach from Whitehall to Charing Cross, [it] will add to the picturesque effect by making a new combination at almost every pace as we advance from the South. I am not at all in favour of viewing the portico under the same aspect for a long extent of distance'.[2]

An essential feature of Wilkins' scheme was the raising of the building twelve feet above the square in front, thus giving it an importance its own height did not.[3] For its height was governed not only by its relationship with St. Martin's Church, but also by its function—Lord Farnborough laying it down that the public would not care to see works of art where it was necessary to descend into cellars or mount up to garrets.[4] Its function was indicated by the elevation: 'the absence of windows in the upper story plainly denotes that the whole of the upper part can only be lighted by skylights, and this leads to the inference that the building before us is a picture gallery.'[5]

Once Parliament had voted funds for the new buildings, a Treasury minute desired that no time should be lost in taking the necessary steps 'according to the plans of Mr. Wilkins under the direction and *superintendence* of the Commissioners of Woods',[6] but the summer was wasted because of the difficulty of gathering the Gallery's Trustees to give their approval.[7] The various alterations decided upon obliged Wilkins to prepare an entire new set of plans,[8] and not until January 1833 were tenders invited.[9] With commission and incidentals, the sum of the lowest tenders amounted to £76,867.[10] This excess over the estimate threw the whole plan in jeopardy, and the alternative possibility of adapting the Banqueting House was considered.[11] Wilkins made the excuse that the building was 'of very peculiar and very unusual construction; and thus . . . analogy misleads us'.[12] Duncannon's committee reported that the excess was due to various alterations and the difficulty of forming a reliable estimate until the specifications were made out.[13] The Treasury accepted this and authorised a start, but required Wilkins to arrange the work so

[1] Works 17/13/6, ff. 1–2.   [2] Works 17/10/1, f. 244.   [3] *Ibid*. ff. 256–8.   [4] *Ibid*. ff. 59–60.
[5] *Athenaeum* 1834, p. 408.   [6] T. 1/4028, f. 14505/32.   [7] Works 17/10/1, ff. 27, 32–33.
[8] Many of these are now in Works 33/908–966.
[9] Works 17/10/1, ff. 32–3, 41–4, 46. Six general builders, and several bricklayers, masons and founders were invited to tender, being allowed until 14 March. This was extended to 19 April because of the time taken by the quantity surveyors in abstracting the quantities (*ibid*. ff. 71–3).
[10] *Ibid*.   [11] *Ibid*. ff. 3ᵛ, 82–3.
[12] *Ibid*. ff. 72–3. Wilkins sought to design a fireproof gallery employing cast iron instead of wood framing. But by 1833 this was scarcely a novelty. Cf. pp. 275, 416 above. Details of the iron floors and girders are shown in Works 33/935 and 953–5.
[13] T. 1/4028, 10 July 1833 (printed in *Parl. Pap.* 1833, xxiv, pp. 559–67).

that the Mews building housing the records should remain undisturbed for the time being.[1] Amended tenders were accordingly obtained, making the final estimate £75,883.[2]

Building began in the autumn. It was hampered by the continued presence of the public records occupying the centre of the site. The wings had to be commenced separately and the centre fitted in later. This made it difficult to sustain levels throughout the structure,[3] and great care was necessary in forming the foundations. Moreover, the nature of the site required additional foundations. At a considerable depth below the surface was discovered an ancient mill-race; deposits of soft mud had to be excavated and concrete substituted of an average thickness of four feet six inches.[4] By July 1834, however, the east wing was ready for its roof. Difficulties about the barracks delayed a start on the west wing. From August to October work was hampered by a builders' strike, though the preparation of stonework continued.[5] Not until early in 1835 were the records removed to Carlton Ride, and the centre of the site thus made available.[6] During that year the east wing was completed, the greater part of the west wing roofed, and the remainder, together with the centre, carried up about thirty feet.[7] But by the end of 1836, the dome and roof over the portico were still uncompleted, thanks to heavy rains that caused a two-months interruption in outside work.[8]

From an early stage, Wilkins had been an enthusiast for the introduction of sculpture into his design, and an opportunity arose in 1834 when it was decided not to use at Buckingham Palace all the sculpture originally designed for the Marble Arch.[9] Westmacott's frieze, thought Wilkins, might be applied over the two gateways, with trophies above; other trophies might flank Baily's Britannia (transformed into Minerva) on the east front; victories might flank the gateways; and Rossi's 'so very beautiful' group of 'Europe and Asia exalting Wellington' might, if the hero were expunged, be placed over the central door.[10] Duncannon's committee approved and the sculpture was placed in position. But Wilkins was disappointed in the effect of the frieze over the gateway and it was removed; the trophies too were discarded, the Treasury having criticised the unauthorised expenditure of some £800 already incurred by the adaptation and erection of the sculpture.[11]

One other change was made in the progress of the work, affecting the columns from the portico of Carlton House. Wilkins decided they were too small for the centre portico, in which he used entirely new columns of greater radius with less ornamented capitals. The Carlton House material was thus available for the side gateways, but

---

[1] *Ibid.* 30 August 1833; Works 17/10/1, ff. 84–5. For protests from the Commissioners of the Public Records, see *Parl. Pap.* 1833, xxiv, pp. 559–67.
[2] Works 17/10/1, ff. 86–8, 98, 101–2. The accepted tenders were

S. Baker and Son, general builders	£30,163
J. Mallcott and Son, masons	£18,492
F. Harrison and Son, bricklayers	£14,583
J. J. Bramah, ironfounders	£6395

Fixtures (£1000), conversion of Carlton House columns (£1000), and incidentals and commission brought the total up to £75,883.

[3] *Ibid.* ff. 216–9.   [4] *Ibid.* ff. 113–4.   [5] *Ibid.* ff. 143–4, 147–50.   [6] *Ibid.* ff. 160–1.
[7] *Ibid.* ff. 216–9.   [8] *Ibid.* f. 258.   [9] *Ibid.* 124–5, see p. 282.   [10] Works 17/13/6; ff. 3–4.
[11] *Ibid.* ff. 8, 11, 15–21; 17/10/1, ff. 187–8, 216–9.

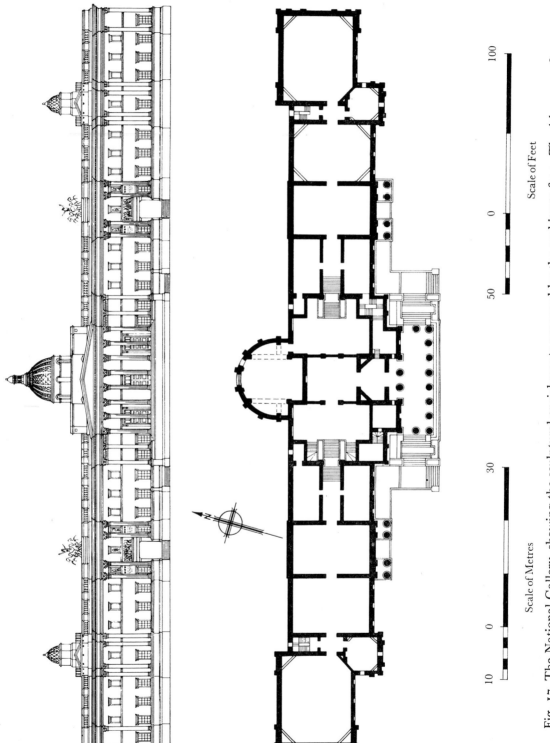

Scale of Metres

Scale of Feet

Fig. 17. The National Gallery, showing the sculptural enrichments proposed by the architect: from *The Athenaeum*, 1834. The east wing was to be occupied by the Royal Academy.

Wilkins determined that there too larger columns were necessary. He informed Duncannon on 14 July 1834, that

> by a subsequent agreement with the mason he has engaged to erect both [gateways] of entirely new materials except the capitals of the columns, which have been wrought anew and have been made, by the removal of some of their ornamental foliage, to correspond with the greater simplicity of those intended to be introduced in the center portico of the buildings. By this arrangement I have been enabled to give a greater substance, as well as height, to the columns insomuch that the difference in bulk between them and the columns for the center portico will be imperceptible.[1]

But we cannot say whether he carried out this intention to discard altogether the Carlton House columns (as distinct from their capitals and bases, which are undoubtedly those used in the side gateways): indeed there is evidence which suggests he did not. Wilkins certainly made all his columns larger than he had originally intended: those of the side gateways have a radius at the foot of 1 ft. 5.65 ins. as against the 1 ft. 2.8 ins. indicated on a plan dated 1832;[2] but he once wrote that the Carlton House columns were '*precisely* the same diameter and height' as those of the so-called Poihele Stoa—the radius of which is given by Stuart and Revett as 1 ft. 5.65 ins.[3]

The galleries in the east or Academy wing were brought into use in 1836, when the public exhibition of designs for the new Houses of Parliament was staged there, before the Academy took possession.[4] In the west wing more accommodation had to be provided for the keeper, but Wilkins retained some small ground floor rooms for 'the highly finished productions' of the Dutch and Flemish schools that must, he thought, some day be added to the collection.[5] Finally, before the pictures were moved in, greater security against fire had to be given, at a cost of over a thousand pounds.[6] The total expenditure on the building (without fire-proofing) was £81,793.[7]

As the gallery neared completion, Wilkins urged the importance of laying out the square in front in such a way as to give height and effect to the building. Believing the Treasury had decided against his project, he informed the Commissioners of Woods on 26 May 1837 that the decision was 'fraught with destruction to the general

---

[1] Works 17/10/1, ff. 143–4. In a plan dated 1833 (Works 33/912) Wilkins shows the columns of the central portico with a diameter of three feet, approximately that of the Carlton House columns (see below). The new capitals were carved by Charles Harriott Smith (*Parl. Pap.* 1835, v, report of select committee on Arts and Manufactures, qq. 622–3).   [2] Works 33/941.
[3] Works 17/10/1, ff. 37–8 (8 December 1832); J. Stuart and N. Revett, *The Antiquities of Athens*, i (1762), chap. v, pl. vii. The columns of the central portico, measured by the Ministry of Public Building and Works in 1968, have a radius immediately below the capital of 1 ft. 3.39 ins., those of the lateral porticoes a radius of 1 ft. 3.55 ins.; the Poihele Stoa being 1 ft. 3.325 ins.
[4] Works 17/10/1, ff. 240–1.
[5] T. 1/4028, Wilkins to Commissioners of Woods, &c. 5 August 1837.
[6] *Ibid.* Estimate of fireproofing works, July 1837. These, relating chiefly to the Academy's wing, included closing windows in the central hall and constructing a skylight, so as to seal off the hall from the wings, and were done on the advice of Chawner and Seward, having been recommended by the select committee on Arts and Manufactures (*Parl. Pap.* 1836, ix, report, p. ix).
[7] Works 17/10/1, f. 286; 1/23, pp. 16–17. Wilkins' final accounts (omitting the fireproofing) showed an excess of £681 over the parliamentary grants, the result of certain delays and changes costing £742 (*ibid.* f. 285).

effect', but he must let things take their course, for he had 'already suffered [him]self to be agitated to a degree prejudicial to [his] health if further prolonged'.[1] A scheme for Trafalgar Square similar to Wilkins' was eventually carried out by Charles Barry in 1842–5.[2] The gallery was opened to the public on 9 April 1838.[3]

It was not many years before additions were required: in 1844 the Chief Commissioner instructed Pennethorne to prepare plans providing more room for the Academy's sculpture exhibits; in 1847 the Trustees asked him to design an additional gallery. Next it was proposed that a large sculpture gallery should be provided on the ground floor and a picture gallery above. Pennethorne's design, estimated at £7000 or £8000, involved the internal reconstruction of the centre block, with steps either down to the sculpture room, or up to the picture gallery. Neither the Academy nor the Trustees were willing to accept such inconvenience, and the scheme was postponed by the Treasury.[4] In 1848 Robert Vernon's gift of the bulk of his collection of modern British paintings made the need for more room acute. A select committee of the Commons on providing more room for works of art examined the problem in June, and after hearing evidence from Pennethorne, Charles Barry and C. L. Eastlake, recommended that an 'enlarged and improved National Gallery should be constructed on the site of the present Gallery'. The Vernon collection was temporarily exhibited in the donor's house, but the Trustees urged the construction of a fire-proof gallery, and removed the bulk of their acquisition to the basement at Trafalgar Square. Another select committee which sat in June 1850 reported in favour of a larger building, but declined to recommend either enlargement on the existing site or removal of the gallery elsewhere.[5] This gave the government an excuse for inaction, particularly as the death of Queen Adelaide had made Marlborough House available for the Vernon pictures. When that house was required for the Prince of Wales in 1859 temporary buildings were erected at South Kensington which were used until 1876. Schemes to house either the Gallery or the Academy at Burlington House were thwarted until 1867 when the Academy made the move; but the great project for rebuilding the Gallery in Trafalgar Square, for which a major architectural competition was mounted, fizzled out; and the architect appointed, Edward Barry, merely added some rooms behind Wilkins' at the east end in 1872–6. Further additions by Sir John Taylor in 1884–7 involved the internal remodelling of the centre block and the closing of the western passage; and in 1907–11 five new galleries were added to the west.[6]

---

[1] *Ibid.* ff. 256–8, 267–8. Wilkins died 31 August 1839.

[2] Works 1/26, 27. See pp. 491–3 below.

[3] Holmes and Baker, *op. cit.* p. 10. Some account of the internal appearance is given in Whitley, *op. cit.* pp. 346–8.

[4] Works 17/13/7, ff. 1–8; 17/13/8, f. 5. See also *Parl. Pap.* 1850, xv, 1 ff. Pennethorne's scheme was carried out in 1860 (Holmes and Baker, pp. 37, 60 n.).

[5] *Parl. Pap.* 1847–8, xvi, 651 ff. 'Report of the select committee on works of art'; *Parl. Pap.* 1850, xv, 1 ff, 'Report of the select committee on the National Gallery'. The minutes of evidence of the 1848 committee are printed as an appendix to the 1850 report. Barry prepared a scheme for the 1848 committee, placing a new three-storied building in front of Wilkins', and proposing courts behind it over the barrack-yard and workhouse site (block plan and block elevation are appended to the 1850 report, and Barry's design is illustrated in *The Builder*, xviii, 1860, p. 416). By 1850 Ashton and Cockerell had also made designs (q. 456). Eastlake insisted on the need for a new building, urging that the removal of the Academy would not solve the problem.

[6] Holmes and Baker, pp. 55, 58, 60, 63. Many plans relating to these as well as to unexecuted schemes are in Works 33.

THE ORDNANCE OFFICE, PALL MALL

Plans for the consolidation of the various branches of the Ordnance, hitherto scattered in Westminster and at the Tower, were drawn up by Pennethorne in 1846. He proposed rebuilding the Ordnance premises in 83 and 84 Pall Mall and at the back of No. 85 at a cost of £15,000. No action was then taken, but in 1849 the Treasury called for a revised plan at an expense below £12,500. Pennethorne found that the Ordnance required in all 34 rooms to accommodate 109 persons; 12 rooms more than in 1846 were required for the Storekeeper and the Examiner of Accounts. He proposed to convert the former house of the secretary at 85 Pall Mall, raising the attic storey to give ten rooms, dividing the large drawing room, and forming a communication with the main office. This would cost £800. For a further £700 the south terrace might be excavated and the basement be made usable. Thus his estimate was increased to £17,000, and commission, contingencies and fittings brought the total to £22,000, a sum the Treasury authorised for the 1850/1 estimates.[1]

On 31 August 1850 the site was said to be covered with rubbish from the demolished buildings. Executed under the Works Department by William Holland, the reconstruction was largely complete by September 1851.[2] The façade, designed in a bold Florentine Renaissance style, was illustrated in *The Builder*, ix (1851), p. 515. The building was demolished in 1911–12.[3]

THE PUBLIC RECORD OFFICE, LONDON

The care of the public records became a matter of active public concern in the first quarter of the nineteenth century. The Chancery records were divided between the Tower of London and the Rolls Chapel; some of the many groups of Exchequer records were at Westminster (including Domesday Book in the Chapter House), some in the vaults of Somerset House; those of the King's Bench were at the Law Courts; and the Common Pleas (after 1822) were in a large wooden shed in Westminster Hall. All these were, under varying regulations, available to the public, unlike the State Papers, for which a new repository (the State Paper Office) was begun in 1829. The parliamentary records, also at Westminster, formed another major category, while in Whitehall there were various and extensive departmental records.[4]

---

[1] Works 2/8, pp. 12, 50–9, 66, 102–4, 130.
[2] Works 2/9, p. 45; G.L.C. Record Office, Metropolitan Buildings Office, vol. 87, pp. 181–9.
[3] For further details see *Survey of London* xxix (1960), pt. i, pp. 367–8 and pl. 271.
[4] See *Parl. Pap.* 1840 [251] xxviii, 'First Report of the Deputy Keeper of the Public Records', pp. 5, 7, 8. Sixteen distinct repositories are listed there. For the history of early nineteenth-century work on the public records, see P. Walne, 'The Record Commissions, 1800–37', *Jnl. of Society of Archivists*, ii (1960), pp. 8–16; R. B. Pugh, 'Charles Abbot and the public records: the first phase', *Bulletin of Institute of Historical Research*, xxxix (1966), pp. 69–85.

The desirability of concentrating the records in a single building and making them readily available for public inspection was acknowledged by the authorities. Nash's scheme for redeveloping the site of the Mews at Charing Cross accordingly provided for a record office as well as a national gallery. Wilkins' proposals also included provision for the public records, but in the end the Royal Academy was given the space.[1] The Common Pleas records were actually transferred to the old state stables at Charing Cross in 1831 in order to clear Westminster Hall, the Exchequer records following them in 1832, but they were a hindrance to completing the National Gallery. Meanwhile the increase of King's Bench and Chancery records compelled the fitting-up of the Rolls House as a repository in 1832.[2] In these circumstances the Commissioners for the Public Records recommended in 1833 that a new record repository should be constructed, and obtained plans from Gandy Deering.[3] The Master of the Rolls agreed to provide a site on the Rolls estate; and a bill was prepared for meeting the cost out of the Chancery suitors' fund. Such an application however was objected to by the law officers and the plans foundered.[4] Nor did anything come of the King's Remembrancer's proposal for taking over the Royal Academy's rooms in Somerset House when they should be vacated.[5]

The Treasury had referred proposals for a general repository made by the Record Commissioners in July 1831 and May 1832 to the Office of Woods and Works, without eliciting any response.[6] In February 1835 the new Master of the Rolls, Lord Langdale, inquired whether the Treasury planned to build such a repository, as he wanted the Rolls House fitted up as his residence.[7] The Record Commissioners, subjected to parliamentary criticism, recommended in their general report of 1836 that the 'most important portion of the public records should be removed to some one or more new depositories', expressing their preference for a single building.[8] A Commons' select committee on the Records Commission suggested a single repository as 'the first and perhaps most essential step for the improvement of the present system', and pointed out the Rolls estate as the most eligible site.[9] The estate was vested in the Crown in 1838, to be managed by the Commissioners of Woods with power to appropriate any part to the purposes of any courts of law or equity or for a record repository;[10] and a subsequent statute of the same year authorised the Treasury to provide a suitable building or buildings for the public records.[11] The Record Commission, not being renewed, expired six months after the death of William IV, and the Home Secretary committed its business and property to the care of the Master of the Rolls, who in January 1839 urged that a general record depository must be provided, and that a public record office should be opened in the Rolls House. The deputy keeper and his staff were accordingly fitted up with accommodation there,[12]

---

[1] *Parl. Pap.* 1829, (317), xiv, Sixth triennial Report of the Commissioners of H. M. Woods, Forests and Land Revenues. MPE 1287 (1–5) show various proposals for the site.   [2] Works 12/67/1, ff. 4–5, 10–14.
[3] Works 1/24, p. 159. Deering's plans were published in *Proceedings of the Record Commissioners*, ed. C. P. Cooper (1833), pp. 226–7.
[4] *Parl. Pap.* 1837 (60) xxxiv, pt. ii, p. xv; Works 12/64/1, ff. 1–10, 20. The proposed bill was never introduced in the Commons.   [5] Works 12/68/2, ff. 2–6, 3 December 1833.
[6] Works 12/67/1, f. 26ᵛ; *Parl. Pap.* 1847 [861] xvi, p. 43.   [7] Works 12/67/1, ff. 25–26.
[8] *Parl. Pap.* 1837 (60) xxxiv, pt. ii, pp. xiii–xiv. For the record commissioners, see P. Walne, *Journal of the Society of Archivists*, ii (1960), pp. 8–16.
[9] *Parl. Pap.* 1836 (565), xvi.   [10] 7 Will. IV and 1 Vict. c. 46.   [11] 1 and 2 Vict. c. 94.
[12] *Parl. Pap.* 1840 [251] xxviii, 'First Report of the Deputy Keeper', pp. 6–7, 67.

but the Treasury sought an economical way out by suggesting that the Victoria Tower of the new Houses of Parliament might be suitably adapted as a depository. Chawner and Barry were accordingly ordered to make surveys of the space required and also prepare an estimate for building on the Rolls site.[1] Fifteen months later Barry offered accommodation for records in the upper parts of the Victoria Tower, in part of the south front adjoining and all the basement between the wings of the river front, sufficient, he thought—if the records were weeded—for several centuries to come.[2] But Langdale adhered to his view that the Rolls estate was the best site, and Chawner drew up a scheme for a repository to be erected in stages. The first block was to be built across the Rolls garden in line with the chapel. It was then to be extended eastwards along the frontage of Fetter Lane and ultimately westwards over the Rolls buildings and the Chancery Lane frontage.[3] In October 1842 Langdale vainly urged the Treasury to abandon their plan to house the judicial records in the Victoria Tower.[4]

Meanwhile, some attempt was made to concentrate and arrange the records at Carlton Ride, to which those previously in the Mews had been transferred in 1835, 'a very great convenience and advantage to the Public'.[5] But alarming reports of grave fire risks there and at other depositories caused Langdale to urge immediate action on the government. Barry reported optimistically that parts of the new Houses of Parliament could be made available in 1844. The Victoria Tower appearing inadequate, he proposed using the roof spaces, rejected as wholly unfit by Langdale, who again urged on Peel the need for building a new repository (20 May 1845).[6] The Treasury firmly adhered to the Victoria Tower project, arguing that it would be ready before anything else could be built, and that, given the rapid increase of records, the hope of providing really adequate accommodation was chimerical. Restating his objections, Langdale nevertheless reluctantly acquiesced in this decision in order to obtain a fire-proof repository as early as possible.[7]

Sir Francis Palgrave, the deputy keeper of the records, was as earnest as Lord Langdale in seeking a satisfactory repository; his *Sixth Report* (1845) gave prominence to the dangers of fire in the existing offices, and attracted the attention of Graham, the Home Secretary, who requested the Office of Woods to take immediate action. In August the Treasury ordered the Woods to take the necessary steps to protect the Rolls House from fire.[8] Braidwood, superintendent of the London Fire Brigade, then made a series of inspections, and drew up a specification for a 'fireproof' record office of brick and iron. Recognising the danger of iron girders melting, he was concerned to prevent any fire from reaching the necessary temperature; he therefore advocated rooms no larger than 27 ft. by 17 ft. by 15 ft., having girders with a maximum span of 17 ft.[9] This proposal was printed as an appendix to the *Sixth Report of*

[1] *Ibid.* p. 71; Works 12/68/4, f. 1; 1/23, p. 325.

[2] Barry's calculation was based on an annual increase of 2000 cu. ft. (Works 12/64/1, ff. 21–4; *Parl. Pap.* 1841 (Sess. 2) [336] i, 'Second Report of the Deputy Keeper', App. I, p. 19).

[3] Works 12/64/1, ff. 33, 35, 37–41.

[4] *Parl. Pap.* 1843 [474] xlvii, 'Fourth Report of the Deputy Keeper', pp. 37, 39.

[5] Works 12/68/8, ff. 11, 25.

[6] *Ibid.* ff. 1–4, 33, 36–8; 2/4, pp. 87–91; 1/26, p. 424; *Parl. Pap.* 1846 (676) xliii, pp. 1–7.

[7] *Ibid.* pp. 8–11.

[8] *Ibid.* 1845 [625] xlviii, 'Sixth Report of the Deputy Keeper'; Works 12/68/8, f. 53; 2/4, p. 491.

[9] Works 12/68/8, ff. 56–9, 74–90, 95–101, 108–111.

the Metropolitan Improvement Commissioners[1] (1847), a body under the chairmanship of the First Commissioner of Woods, which recommended that if the government built a record office on the Rolls estate, part of a proposed road parallel to the Strand and Fleet Street should be laid out, passing immediately north of the office. With this report was printed also evidence by Pennethorne, as Surveyor to the Woods and Forests, and by a senior assistant keeper in the Record Office, the enterprising Henry Cole, whom Langdale had instructed to confer with the architect.[2] Pennethorne had designed a structure extending eastwards over Fetter Lane affording 1,054,350 cu. ft. of record accommodation, entirely fireproof, with 71 rooms on each of two floors, none larger than 7000 cu. ft., and separated by fireproof doors from an entrance hall, search room and library which were large and lofty: he argued with foresight that business might be expected to increase almost immediately on completion of the building. He envisaged a brick building in an Elizabethan style featuring a succession of bay windows, one to each room to accommodate record searchers if necessary, and affording the opportunity of eventually adding a third storey. For this his estimate was £175,000.

However, the decision to fit up the Jewel Tower at Westminster as a fireproof repository in 1847 showed that the government was not yet convinced of the need for a general record office.[3] In 1849 the deputy keeper made a further push.[4] He sketched out general principles: the repository to be erected entirely on the Rolls estate, fireproof, of three storeys, with capacity for those records then in the custody of the Master of the Rolls, the State Papers, and the accessions expected in the course of the next 50 years. He consulted Milne and Inman, who drew up a plan for a building to cost some £50,000. Palgrave suggested that the plain Georgian style of the Rolls House might be taken as a model that would be cheap but architecturally respectable. Such a building could be completed by the end of 1851. Langdale urged the Treasury to give this plan 'great consideration';[5] it was accordingly referred to the Works Department, and so to Pennethorne, who, directed to have 'regard to the strictest economy, excluding Decoration and Ornament', recommended a larger scheme that would serve for perhaps the next century. Again, his was a proposal for building in successive stages, much on the lines of Chawner's of 1840. Approved by Langdale and Palgrave, this was recommended by Lord Seymour as First Commissioner of Woods and Works to the Treasury, which promptly approved the first stage, estimated by Pennethorne at £45,320 (including fittings and fixtures), and obtained a vote of £30,000 for 1850/1.[6]

In his plan for a two-storeyed building Pennethorne adopted Braidwood's criteria of fireproofing. There was little to be found in the way of a model, for the only existing fireproof record office was that of the Duke of Bedford's estates in Russell Square. Pennethorne proposed that the floors should be of wrought iron beams protected below and above from fire, the spaces between being filled with

[1] *Parl. Pap.* 1847[861] xvi, App. p. 28.   [2] *Ibid.* For Cole, see *D.N.B.*
[3] Works 12/68/4, f. 4; 1/31, p. 201. Phipps's estimate was £3000.
[4] Works 12/64/2, ff. 2–9, 14 December 1849. Possibly Palgrave was stimulated by a fire at Lincoln's Inn, see *Builder*, vii (1849), p. 35.
[5] Works 12/64/2, f. 1, 8 January 1850.
[6] *Ibid.* ff. 9–14; 12/64/14 ff. 14. 25, 26, 42-8, 50; 1/34, p. 430.

brick arches, and nearly the whole weight being thrown on party walls. The record rooms were to be 25 ft. by 17 ft.[1]

> Two windows [his report continued] are provided for each Room, and as the Rooms are 15 ft. high divided by a Gallery or iron floor—it follows that the windows must be unusually lofty to light both floors, and to throw the light 25 ft. down the passages between the Records—these circumstances render the front a mass of window, they preclude any plain surfaces and render the ordinary forms, and proportions of Windows and piers inapplicable.
>
> Again—the enormous weight to be carried and the necessity thereby occasioned for stiffening the front wall, weakened as it would be by many and lofty windows, has induced the adoption of deep Buttresses.
>
> These two circumstances together—the mass of window and the adoption of deep buttresses, would produce in execution a bolder and better effect than on paper,— and with these, and its large scale, the Building though totally devoid of ornament could not fail to be rich and imposing provided the details be also bold and correct.
>
> Under these circumstances, it is, also, as it appears to me almost impossible satisfactorily to have recourse to any other than what are called Gothic forms if an Ecclesiastical feeling be at the same time avoided.

The principal front of this design (Pl. 29B) would have been to the north, on the proposed new street, with a 'round' or, more precisely, an octagon reading room projecting to the south. This disappeared as an external feature in the final plan.[2]

Palgrave, who feared riot as well as fire, wanted iron window shutters as a safeguard. Pennethorne suggested that if the mullions were filled with strong iron gratings, the apertures not more than seven inches across, and glass about half an inch thick, it would be as effective and cheaper. Lord Seymour proposed to substitute plate glass three feet across in the upper windows, to improve the appearance and give more light; but Palgrave insisted that 'a bright light, such as is thrown in a shop or dwelling house is not required for the consultation of the Records in a Repository'; and Pennethorne objected to larger panes as not accordant with the style: he suggested that cast-iron grilles would be little more expensive than Seymour's panes, and won his point.[3]

A tender of £1160 was accepted from Edmund Reddin for excavating the site in October 1850;[4] and on 2 December Pennethorne submitted his specification to Seymour, with 29 working drawings, 'according to the general Plan and Elevation submitted with my Report of the 10th of May last—and the Model of the Elevation which has been made upon a larger scale, since that date'.[5] He proposed that Anston stone (as used in his Museum of Geology and in the Houses of Parliament) should be employed for the external trim as the best obtainable in London at a reasonable price. Wrought iron girders should be used for the floors as the difference

---

[1] Works 12/64/2, ff. 14–28. The record rooms were reduced from the length proposed by Braidwood of 27 ft. to 25 ft. as the maximum to which light would travel well down the passages between the records; the weight of records was another factor in keeping the rooms small (*Builder* ix, 1851, p. 635).

[2] Works 12/64/2, ff. 30–41; 12/64/3, f. 10.

[3] Works 12/64/14, ff. 52, 56–9, 62–3; 1/35, p. 431.

[4] Works 12/64/3, ff. 8, 11; 1/35, pp. 374, 384, 404; 1/36, p. 4.

[5] Works 12/64/14, ff. 56–9; 30/201–24 (plans and drawings).

in cost from cast iron was 'almost nominal'. The four leading ironfounders whom he had asked if they could roll girders of the required depth with a net bearing of 17 feet all lacked sufficiently powerful machinery;[1] he therefore recommended girders 'built with plates and Angle iron in the manner now adopted for Railway Bridges and the formulae for which are now satisfactorily established'. He had consulted Mare of Blackwall as well as Fox and Henderson on the strength of girder necessary: this depended so much on the quality of both materials and workmanship that he suggested a special contract should be concluded after a competition between three leading ironfounders.[2]

After discussions with Lord Seymour, tenders from eleven builders and six ironfounders were called for on 21 January 1851.[3] The lowest, those of Messrs. Lee & Son for the building (£34,300), and Messrs. Robinson and Son for the ironwork (£2150), together with the excavation (£1160) came to some £5000 more than the architect's estimate. He therefore suggested working over the moneyed bill of quantities with Lee to ascertain the works that might be reduced and the amount that should be deducted from the tender. Revised working drawings completed in March provided for a first stage 'rather larger than before contemplated', being extended by a passage to a proposed eastern gateway, with a temporary building to connect it with the Rolls House; but reduced by various omissions to £32,722, at which Lee's tender was accepted.[4] A further economy was the substitution of cast for wrought iron girders. A new competition was won by Messrs. H. and M. D. Grissell at £1689 for 289 such girders.[5]

The walls of the Public Record Office had risen only to the middle of the ground floor when the Office of Woods and Works reached the end of its existence in October 1851. Completed in 1858 at a cost of some £77,000, it represents a characteristic Victorian achievement: a new type of building of essentially functional design, to which were applied techniques pioneered in works of pure engineering, devised in collaboration between architect, ironfounder and building contractor.[6]

THE ROLLS HOUSE AND CHAPEL, LONDON

None of the buildings on the Rolls estate came within the formal jurisdiction of the Office of Works. They did not constitute a charge on the Civil List; they were, however, a drain on the public purse. Repairs and alterations were executed by the Office of Works and paid for out of specific parliamentary grants. Such works formed part of the department's extraordinary responsibilities.

[1] Cf. the construction of special machinery by Turner, the contractor, for making wrought iron beams of the requisite size for the Palm House at Kew in 1846 (p. 444 above).
[2] Robert Stephenson and Co. was the third named by Pennethorne; but Stephenson as M.P. could not be a government contractor. Mare was contractor for the Britannia Bridge over the Menai Straits; Fox and Henderson for the Crystal Palace.   [3] Works 12/64/14, ff. 59, 61–4, 66–67.
[4] *Ibid.* ff. 68–9, 88; 8/78/2 (contract, with optional reduction of £414 if plain panelled parapet substituted for perforated battlement); 1/36, pp. 118–9, 126, 186–7.   [5] Works 1/36, pp. 204, 294–5.
[6] See *Builder*, ix (1851), p. 635 (illustrations, pp. 642–3). For further details see R. H. Ellis, 'The Building of the Public Record Office', in A. E. J. Hollaender (ed.), *Essays in Memory of Sir Hilary Jenkinson* (1962), pp. 9–30.

By the later eighteenth century the Rolls Chapel had become a record repository rather than a place of worship, the ancestor of the Public Record Office. The Master of the Rolls still lived in Colen Campbell's Rolls House. And the Rolls Court continued to function. But the chapel was crammed full with Chancery records, the 'presses ranged along the walls, . . . under the seats of the pews and even behind the altar'.[1] In 1772 a committee of the House of Commons had investigated the condition of the records deposited at the Rolls. They found 'very many . . . in the body of the chapel . . . much decayed, and partly obliterated, and the rest in danger of destruction'. As for the floor, it was 'scarce able to support the weight'. Repairs had therefore been put in hand on the basis of parliamentary grants totalling £1184 15s. od.[2] These secured the records while 'leaving a sufficient space for the celebration of divine service'.[3] At the same time a nearby house in Chancery Lane had been fitted up as an office for the transcription of documents. This was no more than a temporary measure. In 1784 another committee therefore recommended the purchase of land adjoining the chapel and the construction of an office for the Clerk of the Records with an apartment for the Secretary to the Master of the Rolls.[4] Chambers' first estimate was £1500.[5] But by the time the new arcaded office had been completed to the Clerk's own specifications the cost had risen to £1846 12s. 6½d.[6] Repairs to the chapel and Master's house were also executed at this time (1784–5), and again in 1788–9, 1793, 1799–1800, 1802–3, 1806, 1810 and 1814.[7]

In 1818 Sir Thomas Plumer, a newly-appointed Master of the Rolls, applied for a general repair of the neglected house, which had then been unoccupied for about sixteen years. Robert Smirke prepared a list of works and Crocker an estimate: some £3000 for repairs and £1680 for alterations to make the house more convenient for a family. The total cost was £4972.[8] His house made fit for his dinners to the Bar, Plumer then urged the needs of the chapel: repairs executed in 1819–20 came just within the £4750 estimated.[9] Further works, on the pews and the chapel record office, cost £360 in 1822.[10] On Plumer's death in 1824 the house was again repaired

---

[1] H. B. Wheatley and J. P. Cunningham, *London Past and Present* iii (1891), p. 166. For details of the chapel see T. Pennant, *Some Account of London* (1793), p. 173 *et seq.*; T. Allen, *History and Antiquities of London, Westminster and Southwark* iv (1829), pp. 431–3; D. Hughson, *London* iv (1807), pp. 127–8, and *57th Report of the Deputy Keeper of the Public Records* (1896), pp. 19–47.

[2] 'Public Income and Expenditure', *Parl. Pap.* 1868–9, xxxv, pp. 446–54 (1775–6).

[3] *Commons Jnls.* xxxiii (1770–72), p. 791; J. P. Malcolm, *Londinium Redivivum* ii (1803), p. 279.

[4] *Ibid.* xl (1784–5), pp. 419, 427.

[5] T. 29/54, f. 533, 17 January 1784; T. 29/55, f. 46, 10 February and f. 272, 28 May 1784; Works 4/16, 23 and 30 January 1784; Works 4/16, 23 April, 6 and 27 August 1784; Works 6/21, f. 13, 26 January 1785.

[6] Works 6/21, f. 70, 25 November 1785; Works 4/17, 23 December 1785, 10 and 17 February 1786; T. 29/57, f. 228, 25 February and f. 459, 8 July 1786; Works 5/74 (1785); 'Reports . . . on Public Records', *Parl. Pap.* 1st Series xv (1800), p. 9; 'Public Income and Expenditure', *Parl. Pap.* 1868–9, xxxv, pp. 446–54 (1786).

[7] T. 29/55, f. 199, 30 April 1784; Works 5/73 (1784); Works 4/17, 29 August 1788; Works 5/78 (1789); T. 29/59, f. 438, 9 August and f. 484, 11 October 1788; Works 4/18, f. 24, 5 July 1793; Works 5/82 (1793); Works 4/18, f. 351, 17 July 1799; Works 6/23, f. 87, 12 July 1799; Works 4/19, 3 October 1800; Works 5/89 (1800); Works 5/91–2 (1802–3); Works 4/19, 13 June 1806; Works 5/99 (1810); Works 4/21, 2 September 1814.

[8] Works 1/8, pp. 377 (14 January), 445 (4 April 1818); 1/10, p. 323; 5/107; 12/67/2, ff. 15–17 (Smirke's report 27 January), 18–21 (Crocker's estimates, March 1818—a reduction of nearly £200 was subsequently made in that for repairs). A rough plan of the basement and 'principal' floor in 1818 (*ibid*. f. 26; see also f. 9) may be compared with Campbell's plan, *Vitruvius Britannicus*, iii, pl. 44. Apparently Sir William Grant, M.R. 1801–17, did not reside in the Rolls House, *pace* Thornbury, *Old and New London*, i, p. 79.

[9] Works 1/9, pp. 410 (22 July 1819), 456, 458; 5/107; *Parl. Pap.* 1846 [703] xliii, 7th Report of the Deputy Keeper of the Public Records, pp. 27–8.   [10] Works 5/108.

and altered for his successor at a cost of £1060.[1] There was at this period a rapid succession of masters: Copley (1826–7) did not reside in the house; for Sir John Leach in 1827 only essential works were approved.[2] Apart from these special services, current repairs after 1815 were an insignificant occasional charge on the parliamentary grant.[3]

Leach remarked in 1831 that the house had ceased to be a desirable residence 'from the change of times and the habits of Society'; but he had fitted up the principal rooms 'for the purposes of that reception of Society . . . suitable to his Office'. He was not unwilling to surrender the residence for storing Chancery records, as the chapel was overflowing. It was then proposed to transfer the Rolls Court to Westminster, bringing the King's Bench records (also overflowing) from thence to the Rolls House, which was suitably fitted up at a cost of £1000 early in 1832.[4]

The various proposals for building a public record office on the Rolls estate are referred to in the account of that building. Lord Langdale, Master of the Rolls from 1834, who at first thought of residing in the house, was a strenuous advocate for such a record office on this site, and in 1838 surrendered the estate to the Crown for the use of a record office or for courts of law and equity. For years he continued to urge action on successive administrations.[5] Meanwhile, the stables were fitted up in 1839 as a depository for non-parochial registers, and the following year the gallery of the court was prepared for the Pells records from Westminster.[6] By 1846 house, chapel and chapel record office could hold few more.[7]

The Rolls garden was sufficiently large for the south side, next Serjeants' Inn, to be taken in 1836, despite the prospective record repository, for a new block of judges' chambers, the existing chambers being dilapidated and inadequate for the increased number of judges. Governmental expenditure was limited to £10,000, Serjeants' Inn undertaking to pay the rest of Sir Robert Smirke's estimate of £13,000.[8] Smirke carried through a reconstruction of the Inn itself in 1838, when the opportunity was taken of converting the dining hall into an equity court. The Treasury agreed to contribute £2000 out of the surplus fees of the Court of the Exchequer. New offices for the Common Pleas were also obtained under this arrangement.[9] West of the judges' chambers and south-west of the chapel record office stood the Petty Bag Office, a substantial brick building of four storeys, with the Subpoena Office adjoining to the south. A temporary office for the Clerk of the Crown was erected by Phipps in 1844.[10] More extensive projects for new offices for the courts of Common Law had to await a decision—not made finally until 1870—on the siting of the

---

[1] Works 1/12, p. 540; 5/109.
[2] Works 1/15, p. 284 (estimate £650); 5/110 (expenditure £520 4s. 7d.). Lewis Wyatt's scheme for altering the dining room (Works 12/67/2, ff. 9, 29) was not carried out.
[3] Works 5/107–111.   [4] Works 12/67/1, ff. 4–5, 10–14; 12/68/5, ff. 1, 2, 7.
[5] Works 12/67/1, ff. 25–6; *Parl. Pap.* 1837 (60) xxxiv, pt. ii; 1846 (676) xliii; see pp. 472–3 above. Fittingly, Langdale's bust overlooks the entrance hall of the Public Record Office.
[6] Works 1/24, pp. 45, 226, 306–8, 367, 465; 2/2, pp. 63, 177, 186, 436; 12/67/1, ff. 30, 34.
[7] *Parl. Pap.* 1846 [703] xliii, 7th Report of the Deputy keeper (which contains a description of the several structures and a graphic account of the difficulties of finding records there). The cost of fitting up these repositories since 1831 was stated in 1847 as £5938 14s. 9d. (*Parl. Pap.* 1847 (398) xxxiv). For plans of the estate see *ibid.* xvi, 6th Report of the Metropolitan Improvement Commissioners; Works 12/64/1, f. 37 (Chawner's plan, 1840); Works 30/197–200 (dated 1842–1850).
[8] Works 1/22 pp. 1 (2 March 1836), 14; 2/2, p. 29 (25 February 1836); 12/67/3.
[9] Works 1/23, pp. 15, 42, 50, 53, 115, 220, 244, 337 (29 April 1839, cost of fittings and furnishings, £1327 15s.), 355; 12/49/4.
[10] *Parl. Pap.* 1846 [703] xliii, 7th Report of the Deputy Keeper, p. 43; Works 1/27, p. 170.

courts themselves.[1] But in 1851 work began in the Rolls garden on Pennethorne's Public Record Office, and the progressive extension of this swept away the Rolls House and Chapel in 1895.[2]

ST. KATHARINE'S ROYAL HOSPITAL, LONDON

The construction of the St. Katharine Docks, to the east of the Tower of London, was made possible only through the co-operation of Sir Herbert Taylor, Master of the Royal Hospital of St. Katharine, an institution under the patronage of successive queens consort.[3] The dock company agreed to pay £125,000 for the foundation's estate; but as the company was unwilling to pay the £55,000 claimed by Taylor for buildings, the issue was referred to the Surveyor General of Works.[4] On the basis of estimates for new buildings made by himself and the Assistant Surveyor General, Stephenson in August 1825 awarded £36,600 to the foundation, in addition to the £2000 the company agreed to pay for a new site.[5]

Taylor had already secured a site on the perimeter of Regent's Park, at length conferred as a free gift.[6] His architect, Ambrose Poynter (1796–1886) had grandiose ideas and put forward an estimate of £72,300. The King and the Lord Chancellor were also anxious that there should be 'great Liberality in the Building', and Taylor himself, who resisted proposals for extravagant buildings, desired that the new church should, to sustain the character of a royal foundation, be 'more handsome and more ornamented than the Edifices built by the Church Committee' (i.e. Church Building Commission). He was willing to sacrifice size to 'a certain degree of Beauty and such ornaments as may distinguish it from the Common Class', but thought 'that Solidity is the chief desideratum and that Beauty may be found in Simplicity of Style and ornaments'.[7] As the buildings were to be in the Gothic style, he persuaded the Treasury to waive the stipulation that buildings in the Park must be of stone—'a useless expence'—or of stucco, to which he had a 'decided objection': he suggested white bricks with stone dressings.[8] Poynter's estimate was approved at £41,521 for church, master's house, three houses for brothers and three for sisters, a school and a porter's lodge. King's College Chapel and Winchester Cathedral were the models for the principal (west) façade, and the school was ingeniously fitted into the design as an aisle. Work began early in 1826 and was completed in the summer of 1828.[9] Thanks to his close relationship with ministers, Taylor was able to obtain the

---

[1] Works 2/3, pp. 63, 74, 358; 2/4, pp. 43–6, 58–9, 168, 170–6, 205–7, 261. See also M. H. Port, 'The New Law Courts Competition 1866–67', *Architectural History* xi (1968). New Exchequer Court offices were hired in Stone Buildings, Lincoln's Inn, when the lease of those in Old Buildings expired; the move cost £2325 6s., Works 2/5, p. 163.   [2] Works 12/67/2, ff. 78–9.

[3] For the history of the foundation see C. Jamison, *History of the Royal Hospital of St. Katharine* (1952).

[4] Works 16/33/1, ff. 6–11.   [5] *Ibid.* ff. 44, 49, 72–3.   [6] *Ibid.* ff. 18–19, 65; Works 1/17, p. 447.

[7] Works 16/33/1, ff. 8–11, 22–8.   [8] Works 1/13, pp. 492–6.

[9] Works 16/33/1, f. 3; T. 1/3905; Works 5/109, 5/119–20. The principal contractors were J. Seabrook (bricklayer), W. Chadwick (mason), Bennett and Hunt (carpenter, joiner), Gostling and Huxley (smiths), Wainwright (glazier), W. Struthers (slater), W. Good (plumber), R. Mott (plasterer), J. Barrett (painter) (Works 5/119–20). The buildings are illustrated in *Gent's. Mag.* 1828, pt. ii, opp. p. 9; there is a critical description by Carlos on pp. 9–10.

services of the Office of Works in making the contracts and controlling operations as for ordinary public works, while at the same time employing his own architect.[1] The total expenditure was £47,139.[2]

The buildings were subsequently maintained independently of the Office of Works.

SOMERSET HOUSE

When Sir William Chambers died in 1796 his masterpiece was substantially complete. In anticipation of his death, he had attempted to set up a permanent establishment for the completion and maintenance of the building, headed by his faithful assistants Browne and Yenn. His wishes were partly fulfilled and partly ignored. George III insisted on installing James Wyatt as Surveyor to Somerset House and opportunity was taken to annex the post to the Surveyor Generalship.[3] On the other hand Chambers had his way with regard to the subsidiary establishment and the responsibility for running repairs, for Wyatt inherited the assistance of both Browne and Yenn as joint Clerks of the Works. Under their direction building operations were completed between 1796 and 1801. Thereafter Chambers' scheme for the permanent care of the building came into operation. The Surveyor General's salary was augmented by £200 a year, while Browne remained as sole Clerk of the Works, assisted by a Labourer in Trust. The cost of their salaries and of minor repairs, heating, lighting and cleaning was apportioned between the various occupants: the Navy Office, Navy Pay Office, Victualling Office, Sick and Hurt Office, Stamp Office, Salt Office, Tax Office, Auditor's Office, Hackney Coach Office, Lottery Office, Hawkers' Office, the Treasurer of the Navy, and the Naval Commissioners' houses, the Royal Academy, the Royal Society and the Society of Antiquaries. These running costs averaged about £1000 per annum and were checked and authorised by the Treasury. Of the departments involved the Navy Office paid most and the learned societies least.[4] In fact the naval departments seem not only to have shouldered most of the burden but, like the Royal Academy and the Society of Antiquaries, to have employed their own surveyor. This came close to making Browne's private apartment and his £100 per annum (to say nothing of Wyatt's £200 per annum) the perquisites of a sinecurist.[5] Only in 1815 was the system reorganised and the building placed under the care of one of the Attached Architects, Robert Smirke.

[1] Works 1/13, p. 490; 16/33/1, ff. 56, 69.
[2] Works 5/120. During the progress of the works, additional estimates of £376 12s. 10d. and £2630 were submitted; and after completion Poynter reported extras amounting to £2550, including stone crosses on the chapel gables (T. 1/3905, Works 16/33/1, f. 85).
[3] T. 29/69, f. 304, 28 July 1796; Farington, p. 1088, 27–8 August 1797.
[4] T. 29/68, f. 144, 7 July 1795; T. 29/70, ff. 32–3, 10 December 1796; Farington, p. 843, 30 November, 1796.
[5] 'Inquiry into . . . the Office of Works', *Parl. Pap.* 1812–13, v, p. 339. As Treasurer of the R.A. Yenn was responsible for internal alterations and only tenuously supervised by Wyatt. Farington hoped in vain that Wyatt might use his position to obtain a strip of ground on the western side adjoining the Hawkers' Office as the site of an R.A. Deposit Gallery (Farington, pp. 845–6, 3 December 1796 and p. 1117, 2 November 1797).

Thanks to the friendship of Samuel Lysons, Smirke had already been responsible for some work at Somerset House: the construction of a gallery for the library of the Society of Antiquaries in 1807–8.[1] One of his first jobs as Attached Architect was the reconstruction of the arches under the east end of Somerset Place terrace in 1816.[2] This was followed first by his work on the Legacy Duty Office (1817–22) which completed Chambers' great quadrangle; and then by the building of King's College (1829–35) which completed the eastern section of Chambers' river façade. The Legacy Duty Office stemmed from his duties as an Attached Architect. But King's College was an independent commission.

The Legacy Duty Office was designed to occupy a vacant plot of ground in the north-west corner of the quadrangle. It was built in two stages, 1817–19 and 1821–22. The first section took the form of a narrow oblong, nine bays wide on the quadrangle side, and comprised a series of small rooms on three floors grouped round a rectangular staircase and an entrance hall with an apsidal end.[3] Its façade exactly reproduces Chambers' Palladian motifs and effectively completes the northern side of the quadrangle. The second section, overlooking the row of residences allocated to Admiralty officials, is merely a utilitarian structure of yellow stock brick in which the overarches and pediments to the windows form the only concession to decoration. A number of legal difficulties delayed the completion of the project. One adjacent property-owner named Perry forced the Crown to pay £8000 for a piece of ground valued by Smirke at a quarter of the price.[4] In the end the total expenditure was £24,805 and Smirke's commission £739 16s. 9d.[5]

Smirke's qualifications as the most suitable architect for King's College rested principally on his earlier employment at Somerset House and his long-standing connections with the Tory-High Church elements supporting this new educational project. As early as 1825 he had begun work on plans to complete the riverside frontage which had so long offended 'every eye of taste by its incomplete appearance'.[6] In 1829 a bargain was struck between the College and the Treasury: the Office of Works building yard to the east of Somerset House was freely surrendered in exchange for a guarantee that the extension of the river front should be completed according to Chambers' original design within five years, and the rest of the buildings not later than five years after that.[7] In the event King's College fulfilled its obligations in reverse order. The main body of the college was finished in 1831 and the river front in 1835. Chambers' original design for a row of houses on the east of Somerset House to match those on the west had never been executed. The only portion of his work which had to be demolished, therefore, seems to have been the small Privy Seal and Signet Office which abutted on the King's College site. This office was temporarily transferred under Smirke's supervision to a house in Abingdon Street.[8]

[1] Joan Evans, *History of the Society of Antiquaries* (1956), p. 216, citing Council minutes and correspondence.
[2] Works 1/7, f. 332, 16 November 1816.   [3] Works 1/8, ff. 270–2, 5 November 1817 (ground plan).
[4] Works 1/9, 3 and 7 October 1818, 9 February, 10 and 27 May 1819, 19 November 1820 (ground plan). For compensation to Mrs. Williams of the Holyland Coffee House cf. Works 12/99/2, ff. 1–21, 4 March 1819.
[5] Works 1/16, ff. 234–5, 1 April 1827; Works 1/10, f. 373, 27 March 1821; Works 1/19, f. 21; 'Report on . . . the Office of Works', *Parl. Pap.* 1828, iv, pp. 338–9.
[6] Works 1/13, f. 383, 21 June 1825; *Gent's. Mag.* 1823, pt. ii, p. 194; J. W. Croker, *Letter to the Earl of Liverpool proposing to finish the East Wing of Somerset House for National Galleries* (1823).
[7] F. J. C. Hearnshaw, *Centenary History of King's College London* (1929), p. 61, *et seq.*, citing founders' minutes.
[8] The cost was £597 13s. 5d. (Works 1/20, f. 123, 22 December 1832).

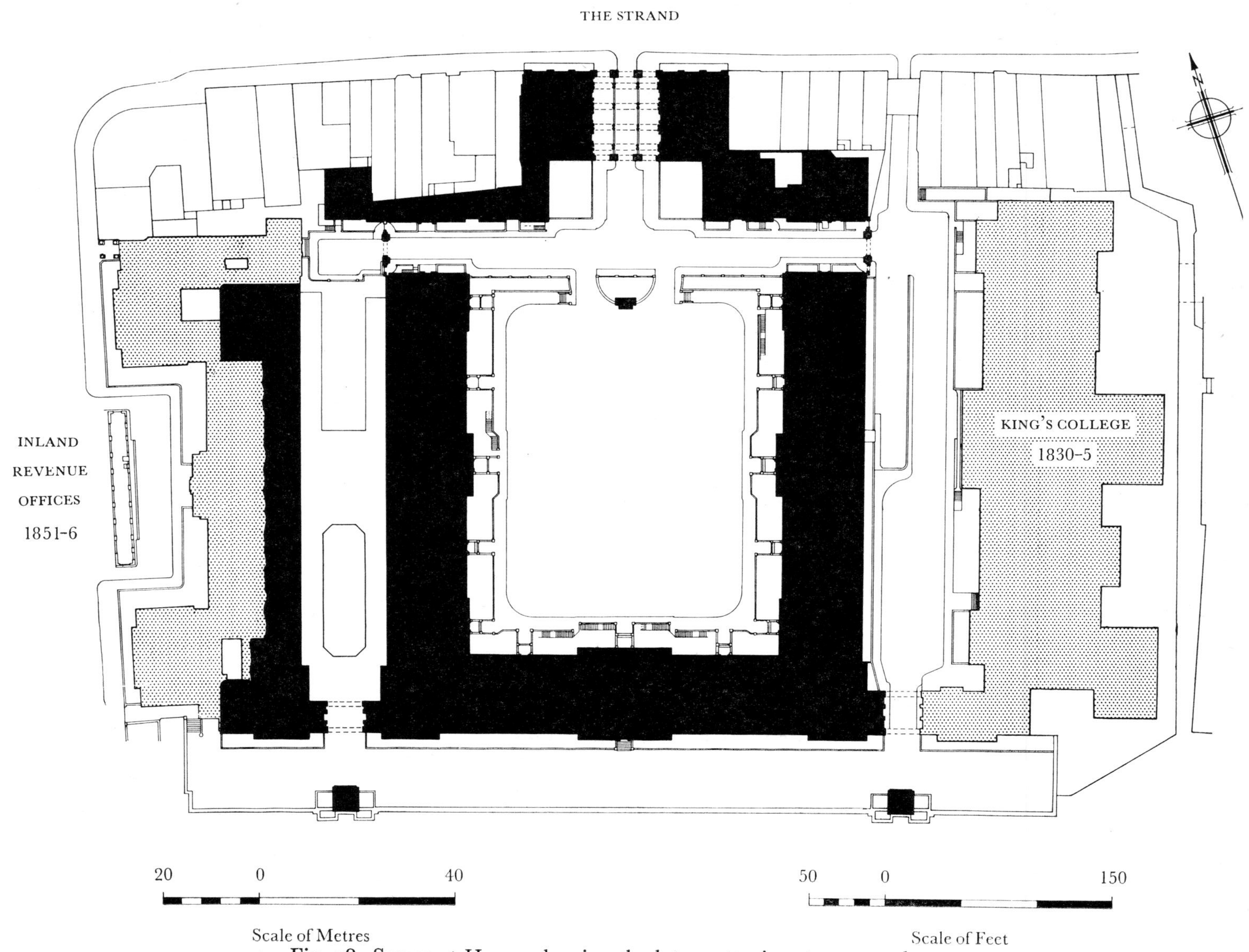
THE STRAND
N
INLAND
REVENUE
OFFICES
1851-6
KING'S COLLEGE
1830-5
20
0
40
Scale of Metres
50
0
150
Scale of Feet

Fig. 18. Somerset House, showing the later extensions to east and west

In May 1829 Smirke estimated the cost of the new college at £140,000 with £10,000 for furniture.[1] But by the spring of 1830 it had been decided to delay the non-essential portions of the plan. For £80,000 Smirke reported that it would be possible 'to erect the carcass . . . except the river front; to . . . finish the anatomical theatre and dissecting rooms . . . the South wing [providing] four lecture rooms capable of holding together about 1100 students . . . two rooms for the chemical laboratory . . . two rooms for the museum and two for the library . . . schoolrooms in the North wing . . . for the Lower Department, sufficient to receive 300–350 boys; and to finish the entrance hall and chapel in the centre of the building'.[2] In February 1831 Smirke's plans for the Strand gateway were passed. Six months later, almost on the eve of the formal opening of the College, £85,889 had been expended and much internal work was still unfinished. During its first academic year (1831–2) the college only managed to cover current expenses with profits from the junior school. For the completion of the river front and principal's house in accordance with the Treasury's requirements the college possessed in 1832 only £6000 towards the £16,500 originally estimated by Smirke.[3] And on 26 April 1833 operations were suspended after £6339 had been spent in finishing only half the Thames frontage. But after frenzied efforts to raise funds the work was restarted in June and finished in April 1835 at the low cost of roughly £7100.[4]

Smirke's design for King's College comprised a three storey block, with basement and sub-basement, 304 ft. long and 120 ft. deep. The central part of the plan was occupied at ground floor level by the entrance hall, balustraded staircases to left and right, and examination room supported by concealed cast iron supports. Above lay the chapel, with seating for 800, later transformed by Sir G. G. Scott into an apsed 'basilican' church divided by decorated columns and bedizened with Byzantine motifs.[5] On either side of this central portion were ranged the ten principal lecture rooms designed to accommodate over 2000 students, laboratories, class rooms, library and museum. The top floor was designed largely for professorial apartments, the basement for King's College School, and the sub-basement for stores. Arched corridors, tall and lengthy, provided access to the rooms on each floor.

Smirke's comprehensive scheme has been improved neither by Banister Fletcher's addition of an attic storey over the entrance and of mansard roofs crowning the wings (1886–8), nor by the erection in the 1890s of an ugly block at the south-east corner of the site. Nevertheless some of the contemporary criticisms were justified. Grinding economy produced a design wholly lacking in richness or vigour. Smirke's work certainly compares unfavourably with both Chambers' quadrangle and Pennethorne's westward addition of 1851–6. 'He is less Italian than his predecessor', remarked one critic, 'without being a whit more Grecian'.[6] Pugin found an easy, if unfair, target in

---

[1] Hearnshaw *op. cit.* Thomas Martin of Osnaburgh Street contracted for the carcass at £63,947. It was calculated that a saving of five per cent was effected by the availability of water transport for the building stone: Scottish granite, Portland and Yorkshire stone (*ibid.* p. 66).

[2] *Ibid.* p. 77.　　[3] *Ibid.* pp. 62, 78, 118.

[4] *Gent's. Mag.* 1833, pt. i, p. 450; 1835, pt. i, p. 644.

[5] R Needham and A. Webster, *Somerset House* (1905), pp. 277–8; Hearnshaw *op. cit.* pp. 159, 226–8.

[6] *Library of the Fine Arts* ii (1831), p. 275. See also *Civil Engineer and Architect's Journal* vi (1843), p. 193. Compare *Literary Gazette* 1830, p. 306.

contrasting the Strand gateway with Wren's Tom Tower at Oxford.[1] Smirke's reproduction of Chambers' 'Palladian bridge' at the opposite end of the vista appears all the more elegant by comparison. Still, another step had been taken towards the completion of Chambers' grand design; and, in a sense, the college had merely paid the penalty of its territorial bargain with the Treasury.[2]

THE STATIONERY OFFICE, BUCKINGHAM GATE

Improvements in Scotland Yard required the clearing away of the old Stationery Office, and the Treasury called for plans for a new office in October 1819.[3] Lord Liverpool, however, 'particularly objected to the Building of a new Office', presumably on grounds of economy, and so Lord Milford's former house on Crown land in James Street, Buckingham Gate, was selected for conversion. This had five bays flanked by slightly projecting wings, giving a total frontage of 74 feet.[4] Undertaken by Soane, the alterations, including the addition of warehouses, were executed in 1820–1 at a cost of over £10,000.[5] Soane suggested that several thousand pounds might have been saved by selling the house, which he thought unsuitable; but Stephenson stated that it was thought 'rather an Economical Arrangement' to adapt Milford's house, obtained without either rent or purchase.[6] In 1823 apartments were fitted up for a storekeeper, and in 1824 further alterations were made.[7] The business of the Office steadily increased with the growth of government departments and official publications. The Treasury directed in January 1832 that all stationery used by departments was in future to be supplied by the Office.[8] In 1837 the comptroller applied for additional warehousing, that built in 1821 being allegedly not strong enough. The unsatisfactory nature of the existing arrangements was pointed out by Chawner and Pennethorne in January 1843. The Treasury declined their proposal for erecting a new warehouse, arguing that there would be plenty of storage space when the Houses of Parliament were completed.[9] In November 1846 the comptroller suggested that, business having doubled in the past seven years, the east wing of the office should be extended two storeys in height, at a cost of about £2000, but the Treasury again rejected the plan.[10] When in 1850 the Ordnance wished to enlarge Wellington Barracks, the Office of Woods proposed that the Stationery Office site should be made available, and this led ultimately to the transfer of the Stationery Office to the Parliamentary Mews.[11]

[1] A. W. Pugin, *Contrasts* (1841), frontispiece; *The Athenaeum* 1831, p. 649. Smirke's gateway was demolished in 1969.
[2] For plans and illustrations of Somerset House and King's College cf. Needham and Webster *op. cit.*, pp. 271–2; *Architectural Association Sketch Book* 3rd series ix (1905).   [3] Works 1/9, pp. 475, 479. See p. 543.
[4] Plans, Works 30/2886–8. Soane considered a site near Westminster Abbey, next to the Middlesex Sessions House (Soane Museum corresp. 2, xii, H (3)).
[5] Soane Museum, corresp. 2, xi, B. 19; Works 5/108. Soane's estimate was £4888 for alterations and £3020 for additions (Works 1/10, p. 208, 19 August 1820); £2458 18s. 7d. more were expended (Works 1/11, pp. 118–20).
[6] Soane Museum, corresp. 2, xi, B. 17, 19. The tradesmen employed included H. Westmacott (mason), Stutely (bricklayer), Firth (carpenter), Mears (plasterer), Warmsley (slater), Cobbett (glazier), Holroyd (plumber) and Barret (painter) (Works 5/119, f. 32).   [7] Works 5/108.   [8] Works 4/31, p. 287.
[9] Works 12/102/1, ff. 1–8; 1/22, p. 305; 2/2, p. 123.   [10] Works 12/102/1, ff. 9–12.
[11] *Ibid.* ff. 14 *et seq.*; Works 1/37, pp. 15, 27–8. See below, p. 536.

THE TOWER OF LONDON

During the later eighteenth century the fabric of the Tower of London (Pl. 66) underwent little alteration. The greater part of the site was still shared between the Royal Mint and the Ordnance Office. The Office of Works was merely responsible for the maintenance of an assortment of civil buildings, notably the Governor's House, the Fort Major's house, the Master Gaoler's house, the Warders' houses, the Chapel and chaplain's house, the Jewel Office, the Record Office, the Menagerie and several taverns.[1] The Clerk of the Works therefore had few responsibilities. When in 1810 Crocker was replaced by the aged and infirm Leach, James Wyatt reassured the Treasury in the following words: 'although advanced in life, and unequal to the duties of any active situation . . . he is certainly . . . adequate to all the duties he would have to perform as Clerk of the Works at the Tower where there is little else to attend to than the ordinary repairs of the menagerie and of houses occupied by warders'.[2]

On the reorganisation of the Office of Works in 1814, a Labourer in Trust, William Lush, was placed in charge of the civil department of the Tower. On his death in 1818 the post was combined with that at the Mint.[3] After 1815 few repairs were done to Warders' houses, the greater number being rented out by Warders for their own profit. Attempted improvements were blocked by their proprietary interests until the 1840s.[4] Smirke reported in 1818 that there were several very old decayed buildings, and that repairs should be limited solely to those necessary to 'uphold' them.[5] The following year he recommended the gradual repair of the chapel windows.[6] The Clerk of the Works for the eastern district, Lewis Wyatt, reported in 1825 that parts of the base of the White Tower were being cut away for the Horse Armoury that the Ordnance Department was erecting on its south side.[7] But the White Tower, though its upper floors housed records, was the responsibility of the Ordnance, on which the upkeep of the fortress principally fell.[8] Works expenditure, transferred in 1816 from the Civil List to vote of Parliament, averaged about £1350 a year between 1815 and 1825, falling to about £520 in 1826–32. By 1838–48 the estimates had risen again to some £1100 a year.[9]

The major works carried out in the Tower during the first half of the nineteenth century—the building of the Waterloo Barracks on the site of the Great Storehouse (destroyed by fire in October 1841), the draining of the moat and the construction of the North Bastion after the Chartist agitation of 1839–42—were the responsibility

---

[1] 'Inquiry into . . . the Office of Works', *Parl. Pap.* 1812–13, v, p. 439.

[2] Works 6/25, f. 53, 25 April 1810.

[3] Works 4/23, p. 256. Thomas March, Labourer in Trust from 1818, absconded on 17 May 1825 when charged with embezzling stores from the Tower (Works 1/18, p. 302; 5/109).

[4] See Works 2/5, pp. 201–2, 251 ff.

[5] Works 1/8, p. 464.   [6] Works 1/9, pp. 304 ff.   [7] Works 1/13, p. 343.

[8] Works 1/9, p. 281. The buildings under the civil department are shown on a plan dated 13 January 1834 (Works 31/42).

[9] Works 2/3, p. 469; 5/107–111; *Parl. Pap.* 1847–8 (543) xviii, pt. ii.

of the military, not of the civil department. A plan for the military improvement of the fortress put forward by the commanding Royal Engineer in September 1843 involved the demolition of a considerable number of old buildings, some of which belonged to the civil department. Over the next four or five years this plan was carried out, and Warders' houses (some let as public houses) were removed at the south-east corner, alongside the east and north walls, and close to the Beauchamp Tower, as well as those running north from the Record (Wakefield) Tower.[1] The Chapel of St. Peter was improved in 1842, when, with the removal of adjoining Ordnance workshops, a window was opened in the north wall.[2] Further repairs were made in 1850 but the chapel's present appearance largely dates from a major restoration in 1876–7.[3]

1. The King's House and Other Lodgings

By the end of the eighteenth century the principal officers of the Tower of London— the Constable, Lieutenant and Gentleman Porter, had become non-resident dignitaries. But the other officers—the Deputy Lieutenant, Major Yeoman Porter, Yeomen Warders, Chaplain, Keepers of Records and Jewels, etc., were all normally in residence and possessed official houses maintained by the Office of Works. Repairs were usually trivial: refitting one Warder's house in 1793, ruined by water seeping through the roof;[4] or repairing another in 1794, 'much damaged by the firing of guns from the platform'.[5] The chaplain's house, like the adjoining Chapel of St. Peter ad Vincula, required no more than running repairs during this period.[6] At much the same level were repairs to the guard officers' mess, once the Master Gunner's house, executed by the Office of Works in 1796 and paid for by the Ordnance Office.[7] More important were improvements to the King's House or Lieutenant's Lodgings, known in the early nineteenth century as the Governor's House. Repairs in 1786 cost only £126 4s. 10½d.[8] But in 1794 the Deputy Lieutenant, Major John Gore, complained that his house was 'totally unfit to be tenanted', and that the stables under his kitchen were a constant source of 'offensive smells'. On this occasion the bill came to more than £1500.[9] In 1812 further repairs estimated at £855 13s. 6d. were delayed by the Treasury, pending the reorganisation of the Office of Works.[10] The Governor's House was again repaired and altered in 1817.[11]

---

[1] See annotated plans, Works 31/44–47.
[2] Works 1/25, p. 499. The Ordnance were called upon to repair the north wall, in which they had made flues and recesses (*ibid.*). A scheme to convert the pews into open seats was not executed (*ibid.* p. 341).
[3] Works 1/35, p. 251; D. C. Bell, *The Chapel of St. Peter ad Vincula in the Tower of London* (1877).
[4] Works 1/5, f. 110, 12 September, 1793.
[5] *Ibid.* f. 127, 9 May 1794. 'On a large platform before the Tower, on the Thames' side, 61 pieces of cannon used to be planted, and fired on rejoicing days; but these were removed in 1814, and those on the ramparts are used in their stead' (D. Hughson, *Walks Through London*, 1817, p. 22).
[6] For a view of chapel and chaplain's house in 1817 see Lord R. S. Gower, *The Tower of London* ii (1902), p. 175.   [7] Works 4/18, ff. 117–8, 155–6, 181, 185, 191.
[8] Works 5/75 (1786); Works 4/17, 16 June, 7 July 1786; T. 29/57, ff. 405–6, 27 June 1786.
[9] Works 4/18, f. 68, 25 April and f. 95, 31 October 1794; T. 29/67, f. 158, 19 August 1794; Works 5/84 (1795).
[10] T. 29/120, f. 485, 1 December 1812.   [11] Works 1/7, pp. 43–5, 215, 375; 1/9, pp. 304 ff.

But the Tower official who gave the Office of Works most trouble between the reforms of 1782 and 1815 turned out to be the Gentleman Porter. As an absentee sinecurist his income was made up of rents drawn from property held by him in right of office. In particular he received £80 per annum from a tavern on Tower Hill known as the Suttling House or 'Bunch of Grapes', plus £52 10s. od. in rent for the adjoining bar. The 'Bunch of Grapes' was situated over the principal outer gateway, in Chambers' words, 'the only entrance to the Tower'. When in 1787 the Gentleman Porter applied for repairs, Chambers' estimate was £1038 18s. od.[1] Although General Vernon considered such a place of refreshment 'absolutely necessary for the garrison', the Treasury rejected his claim as militarily irrelevant.[2] Five years later the gateway was described as 'ruinous', and Chambers warned the Treasury that 'the inhabitants . . . are under apprehension of its falling'.[3] Chambers' estimate had now increased to £1100. The Treasury therefore pressed for demolition. Four years later nothing had been done, and coachmen continued to be struck down as they passed beneath the archway's sagging beams. 'What is still more dreadful', wrote one petitioner, 'is the apprehension that some persons will be buried under its ruins'.[4] But even Chambers' 'known humane character' was unable to reconcile Treasury and military. It was only after his death that a compromise was reached. In April 1797 the inhabitants of Great Tower Hill petitioned the Constable of the Tower, Lord Cornwallis, for the repair or removal of the Suttling House and toll bar, since they had 'entered into a liberal subscription for carrying into execution a plan drawn by Mr. Samuel Wyatt for improving' the area.[5] Three months later the 'Bunch of Grapes' was at last demolished; and the Gentleman Porter, who happened to be the Bishop of Lichfield and Coventry, was fully compensated by means of an annual pension from the Lord Chamberlain.[6]

2. THE MENAGERIE

Towards the end of the eighteenth century the menagerie at the Tower was allowed to decline. Little was spent on the maintenance of buildings, and less on the purchase of animals. By 1815 the stock had sunk to 'one lion, two lionesses, one panther, one hyena, one tygress, one jackall, one mountain cow and one large bear'.[7] And the cost of feeding stood at little more than a guinea a month. By 1822 'the whole stock . . . consisted of the grizzly bear, an elephant, and one or two birds'.[8] But in that year Alfred Cops became Keeper and instituted a dramatic revival which continued until the transference of the animals to Regent's Park in 1834.

Prior to that date the beasts at the Tower were kept in 'a range of dens in the form of a half-moon . . . twelve or thirteen feet high, divided into three apartments, a

---

[1] T. 29/58, f. 274, 22 March 1787; Works 6/21, f. 99, 16 March 1787.
[2] T. 29/58, f. 418, 21 July and f. 488, 15 August 1787.
[3] Works 4/17, 10 February 1792; T. 29/64, f. 228, 25 February and f. 301, 11 April 1792.
[4] Works 6/21, f. 38, 6 February 1792; Works 6/21, f. 37, 10 February 1792; Works 6/23, f. 7, 3 November 1796; Works 4/18, ff. 207–8, 4 November 1796.   [5] Works 6/23, f. 32, 10 April 1797.
[6] Works 6/23, f. 33, 26 May 1707; Works 4/18, ff. 213, 215, 236, 242, 244, 257, 1796–8.
[7] T. 29/135, ff. 653–4, 3 August 1815.   [8] E. T. Barrett, *The Tower Menagerie* (1829), p. xv.

large one above and two below'. 'In the upper apartment', it was reported, 'the beasts generally live in the day, and at night retire to the lower to rest. You view them through large iron grates, like those below the windows of a prison; so that you may see them with the utmost safety, be they ever so ferocious'.[1] The only significant repairs by the Office of Works came in 1802 and 1810 when the Keeper Joseph Bullock demanded alterations 'for the security and comfort of the animals'.[2] In 1802 the cages had been improved by substituting 'stone and iron fronts instead of wood which, from the urine of the animals was always decaying'.[3] In 1810 Crocker directed alterations to the walls and Keeper's house as well as the installation of 'moving dens in each of the apartments of the several beasts'. This meant, as Crocker assured Wyatt, that 'the animals cannot possibly escape, or get at each other'.[4]

From 1817 there was a progressive repair of the dens,[5] and Alfred Cops formed 'one of the finest collections in the universe'.[6] It stood, however, 'so much in the way of the restoration of the entrance towers and gates, and appeared such an unnecessary appendage' that in 1831 the Duke of Wellington as Constable of the Tower obtained the King's permission to remove it and 'clear away the unsightly dens and sheds with which the entrance was encumbered and disfigured'.[7] In 1834 the animals were accordingly taken to the new Zoological Gardens in Regent's Park, and the dens sold in 1835. The buildings however remained until 1853, despite an Ordnance application in 1838 for the site as 'most desirable . . . for a Bastion to improve the outer defences of the Tower'.[8]

3. THE RECORD OFFICE

Records deposited in the Tower of London were kept in two places, the White Tower and the Wakefield Tower. Between 1783 and 1819 both depositories were reorganised and extended, thanks to the efforts of two notable Keepers, Thomas Astle and Samuel Lysons. Patient, learned and industrious, Astle succeeded Sir John Shelley in 1783.[9] He began by improving the security of the Wakefield Tower depository, then proceeded to direct the indexing of manuscripts in the White Tower, and ended by co-operating in Speaker Abbot's mammoth survey of national records.[10] But his death in 1803 left the implementation of that project to Samuel Lysons.[11] As Keeper between 1804 and 1819 Lysons turned his enormous learning

[1] T. North, *The Tower of London* (1806 ed.), p. 13. For views of the interior and exterior of the menagerie cf. E. W. Thornbury, *Old and New London* ii (1873), p. 85; Lord R. S. Gower, *The Tower of London* ii (1902), p. 138.
[2] Works 6/25, f. 49, 23 March 1810.   [3] *Ibid.* f. 52, 25 April 1810; Works 4/19, 19 June 1802.
[4] Works 6/25, f. 52. 25 April 1810.   [5] Works 1/9, pp. 304 ff.
[6] J. Bayley, *History and Antiquities of the Tower of London* (1830), p. 266.
[7] Lord de Ros, *Memorials of the Tower of London* (1866), p. 272.
[8] Works 2/2, p. 289; Thornbury, *Old and New London*, ii, p. 89. The keeper's house at the southern end of the half moon, was demolished in 1850 (Works 2/8, pp. 20–2). For plans of the area see Works 31/44–8; J. H. Harvey, 'The Western Entrance of the Tower', *London and Middlesex Archaeological Soc. Trans.* N.S. ix, pp. 31, 34.
[9] For Astle see *Gent's. Mag.* 1803, pt. ii, pp. 1190–1 and 1804, pt. i, p. 84.
[10] R. B. Pugh, 'Charles Abbot and the Public Records: the First Phase', *Bulletin of the Institute of Historical Research* xxxix (1966), pp. 69–85; P. Walne, 'The Record Commissions, 1800–37', *Jnl. of the Society of Archivists* ii (1960), pp. 8–16.   [11] *Gent's. Mag.* 1819, pt. ii, pp. 90, 273–5.

and practical good sense to the calendaring of his collection and the extension of the White Tower depository. Astle had one assistant; Lysons employed six.

It was the destruction of the Ordnance Office in 1788 which prompted Astle to strengthen the security of the Wakefield Tower and its adjacent Record Office.[1] Manuscripts were removed from the Record Office and consolidated in the octagonal room of the Wakefield Tower. Under Chambers' direction, 'the staircase, which was of wood, and the wainscot, were removed; an iron door was placed at the entrance into the room; the inside of the roof was plated with iron, as were the insides of the window shutters'. Chambers' estimate was £466 12s. 8d.;[3] the cost was only 13s. more.[4]

During Astle's tenure of office records in the White Tower were distributed between the chapel, an adjoining room and corridor and an upper gallery containing 'several lockers' for 'parchments of a very miscellaneous nature'. He found 'the records in Caesar's Chapel . . . covered with dust, and the tickets of references so obliterated, that many of them were not legible; in . . . 1795 these records were arranged, and had near three thousand new tickets of references put on them, by the zeal and perseverance of . . . Mr. Robert Lemon'.[5] As soon as he took office Lysons ordered new furniture.[6] He 'found a great portion of the records . . . lying in total disorder, and their consequence almost wholly unknown; but by obtaining a competent establishment, and by directing attention to these neglected treasures, a vast collection of royal letters, state papers and parliamentary and other documents . . . were rescued from a state of filth and decay, and the whole arranged and methodised, in a manner essential to their preservation'.[7] At the same time Lysons managed to expand his department by obtaining possession of the watch room and turrets above the chapel. In 1811–12 these rooms were vacated by the Ordnance Office and fitted up for the Record Office by the Office of Works. Crocker's first set of estimates totalled £2979 16s. 6d.[8] This the Treasury dismissed as 'exorbitant'; and alternative estimates were produced totalling £1987 5s. 9d.[9] Lit by skylights, these extra rooms housed the newly calendared records of Chancery Proceedings.[10]

The Treasury also suggested that the buildings of the old Mint might be made use of. Three houses were to be given up to the Keeper of the Records, to be exchanged for three Warders' lodgings: one in the Bloody Tower and two others adjacent to the Record (i.e. Wakefield) Tower. One Warder's refusal spoiled this project; but the house north of the Record Tower was obtained and partly occupied by the office

[1] 'At the time of the late alarming fire . . . the records in the Wakefield Tower, and in the rooms adjoining were in imminent danger of being destroyed, and had the wind been in the East . . . the danger would have been greatly increased' (Works 6/21, ff. 157–8, 17 October 1788). For descriptions of depository and contents cf. J. Bayley, *History and Antiquities of the Tower of London* (1830 ed.), pp. 213–57; J. Britton and E. W. Brayley, *Memoirs of the Tower of London* (1830), pp. 335–46.

[2] 'Reports . . . on Public Records', *Parl. Pap.* 1st series xv (1800), pp. 52–5.

[3] Works 6/21, f. 160, 23 May 1789; Works 4/17, 12 August 1789; T. 29/60, f. 373, 27 May 1789.

[4] Works 5/78 (1789).

[5] 'Reports . . . on Public Records', *Parl. Pap.* 1st Series xv (1800), pp. 52–6.

[6] Nothing had been supplied 'since the beginning of the last century. . . . The business of the office cannot be conveniently carried on, unless there be at least one desk in each room, and one long table covered with cloth for unrolling the Rolls, which at present are frequently in danger of being injured, by laying on the floor; a few chairs are also wanted' (Works 6/23, f. 242, 27 February 1804). See also Works 5/94 (1805).

[7] Bayley, *op. cit.* p. 252.

[8] Works 4/20, 7 June, 5 July, 9 August 1811, 17 January, 14 February 1812.

[9] *Ibid.* 10 April, 1 May 1812.   [10] Bayley, *op. cit.* p. 111.

keeper.[1] Lysons sought in 1816 to extend the office northwards over Ordnance land, and Smirke furnished plans and an estimate of £500, but nothing came of this proposal.[2] In 1825 works costing £367 were carried out for the accommodation of the person employed on the new edition of the Rolls of Parliament.[3] The Commissioners of the Public Records asked in 1832 that the ammunition stored in the vaults of the White Tower should be removed, but the Ordnance suggested that the records should go instead. The Commissioners would have been delighted to remove them had a general repository existed: Joseph Braidwood of the London fire brigade reported that the White Tower was in 'extreme and imminent danger' of fire.[4] When in 1846 a large quantity of Admiralty records was brought from Deptford dockyard,[5] the Master of the Rolls applied for the Bloody Tower; but the Duke of Wellington, the Constable, urged decisive objections: state prisoners were still sent there occasionally (the last in 1820) and the Bloody Tower was the 'best, if not the only good place of security . . . in which such prisoners can be placed'; any alterations should be concerted with the Royal Engineers; and the portcullis should be preserved as the only one in England capable of use.[6] With some cogency he argued that it would be both more economical and more convenient to build a proper record office, a solution which was finally adopted five years later with the building of the Public Record Office in Chancery Lane.

4. The Jewel Office

During the later eighteenth century the Crown Jewels continued to be kept in the Jewel Office, that is the Martin Tower at the north-east angle of the Inner Ward. Between the reforms of 1782 and 1815 the Office of Works was responsible for only one significant alteration. In 1796 George Hoare, Keeper of the Regalia, complained that although his office was 'ancient, necessary and respectable', yet his house was 'one of the worst within the walls of the Tower', being 'so exceedingly circumscribed, as to consist of only one small incommodious sitting room and two smaller bedchambers for a numerous family'.[7] An extra bedroom was therefore added, the estimate being £120.[8] Nevertheless during the early nineteenth century the Jewel Office remained fairly cramped with the regalia displayed in a vaulted ground floor

---

[1] Works 2/5, pp. 201–2, 253–7. The proposed alterations required the removal of the portcullis of the Bloody Tower and of a weight-bearing internal wall, so that the Warders were not the only obstacles (Works 14/1/19).
    [2] Works 1/7, p. 356; 2/2, pp. 258–9.   [3] Works 5/109.
    [4] 'No merchant of ordinary prudence', said Mr. Braidwood, 'would keep his books of accounts in the same situation in which the Records are placed in the White Tower' (*Parl. Pap.* 1846, xliii, '7th Report of the Deputy Keeper of the Public Records', pp. 29–32). In their general report, the Record Commissioners had drawn attention to the existence of the magazine, remarking: 'as the explosion . . . (should such a disaster ever occur), would occasion not the destruction of the records only, but of the whole edifice of the Tower, of every person within its precincts, and of the surrounding neighbourhood to a very considerable distance, we are persuaded that every precaution will always be taken to avert so dire a calamity' (*Parl. Pap.* 1837 (60) xxxiv, pt. ii, p. x).
    [5] Works 2/5, pp. 201–2 (30 June 1846).
    [6] *Ibid.* pp. 330–3 (17 October), 337 (10 November 1846).   [7] Works 6/22, 11 August 1796.
    [8] Works 6/23, 2 September 1796; T. 29/69, f. 431, 10 October 1796.

room, 'arranged on shelves, as in a large beaufet, or closet', and lit by six Argand lamps.[1]

Hoare's successor, E.L. Swifte, complained forcefully about the inconveniences of the Regalia Office, and in 1816 repairs were authorised on an estimate of £730, which actually cost £966.[2] These were not to Swifte's satisfaction: he wanted more room for his family, and better facilities for showing the regalia. Further improvements were made in 1817–18.[3]

The Commissioners of Woods suggested in 1840 that a new Jewel House should be built, and a structure in the Tudor style was erected by the Ordnance, to which the regalia were transferred after the great fire of 30 October 1841, when the old building was damaged and the iron grille had to be broken to rescue its contents.[4] The new Jewel House, which stood against the outside of the inner curtain wall, immediately to the south of the Martin Tower, was transferred to the care of the Woods and Works in December 1842.[5] In 1849 an Ordnance request was approved for demolishing the dilapidated part of the keeper's residence built on the ballium wall; the old jewel room was converted into a kitchen; and a workshop in the basement under the new jewel room was converted into a military prison.[6] In 1870, when the regalia were transferred to the former Record Tower, the Jewel House was handed over to the military, and demolished.[7]

TRAFALGAR SQUARE

In extending Pall Mall eastwards to St. Martin's Church, the New Street Commissioners realised that 'a much larger space, than was at first designed, ought to be left open' in front of the Great Stables. Nash prepared a new plan for a large square, with provision for a Royal Academy and a National Gallery on the site of the stables; and this was authorised under an Act of 1826.[8] The area was then cleared, but no specific layout was adopted.[9] The existing National Gallery was eventually built on the northern part of the site in 1833–38. Its architect, William Wilkins, proposed in 1837 that the open space to the south of the Gallery, already called Trafalgar Square,[10] should be levelled, and a terrace formed to support the road immediately

[1] J. Britton and E. W. Brayley, *Memoirs of the Tower of London* (1830), p. 297. For an illustration of the interior see C. Knight (ed.), *London* ii (1842), p. 232.

[2] Works 1/6, pp. 123, 156–7, 357, 359; 1/7, pp. 27, 45, 51, 169; 5/107.

[3] Works 1/7, pp. 329, 338; 1/8, pp. 10, 114, 426.

[4] Works 14/1/18, ff. 1, 7; 1/24, p. 92; 2/3, pp. 445, 469; J. Hewitt, *The Tower: its history, armories, and antiquities*, 2nd edn., n.d., p. 129. An account of this dramatic episode, illustrated by Cruikshank, is given by Lord R. S. Gower, *op. cit.* ii, pp. 142–3.

[5] Works 14/1/18, ff. 11, 12; Crest 25/50, no 5163. There are plans in MPHH 605. The Jewel House is shown on several plans of the Tower dating from the 1840s (Works 31/44, 47, 50, 137).

[6] Works 1/34, pp. 195, 257–8, 263, 368.

[7] Works 14/1/18, f. 31; E. H. Carkeet James, *His Majesty's Tower of London* (1950), p. 39.

[8] *Parl. Pap.* 1826 (368) xiv, 'Fifth Triennial Report of the Commissioners of Woods and Forests, etc.' (contains plan); Act 7 Geo. IV, *c.* 77.

[9] A number of projects for the area exist, cf. MPE 1163, 1164, 1179, 1254, 1274, 1287, 1293; MPEE 124.

[10] *Survey of London*, xx, p. 16. Pevsner, *The Buildings of England: London* i (1957), p. 326, says the name was given in 1830. G. L. Taylor, in his *Auto-Biography of an Octogenarian Architect* (1870–2), claimed that it was he who persuaded the King to change the name from 'William IV Square' to 'Trafalgar Square'.

in front of the Gallery, thus giving it a greater elevation (Pl. 30.)[1] When a vote of £7600 to lay out the square brought the project to public notice, a committee of subscribers for a monument to Nelson urged that the site should be made available to them. The government agreed in April 1838, and the square was temporarily enclosed with a post and rail fence while the committee held a competition for designs. They chose that of William Railton, fourth prizewinner in the Houses of Parliament competition, for a Corinthian column surmounted by a statue of the hero; a choice endorsed after a second competition. The Works Department referred this design to Smirke, and to Walker, the engineer employed for the river terrace of the new Houses of Parliament. They considered that, on grounds of safety, the proposed height of 203 feet should be reduced by 30 feet. They also recommended that the column should be of solid stone with a bronze capital, and that it should be increased in diameter at the base.[2]

When Wilkins died in 1839, the layout was referred to Barry, who in April 1840 was instructed to prepare detailed plans—being warned, however, that only £6000 were available.[3] Similar in principle to Wilkins', especially in relating the terrace wall to the National Gallery, Barry's proposal embraced a much larger area, for which he submitted an estimate of £11,794.[4] This increase instigated a select committee to examine the project, which backed Barry's plan, so that a further £5000 was voted.[5] Meanwhile Grissell and Peto had won the contract for excavating the site.[6] In September 1841 Barry proposed that the space between the terrace wall and the column should be adorned with fountains.[7] The new government's approval led to yet another scheme, the construction of an artesian well in Orange Street (north of the National Gallery), not only to feed the fountains, but also to obtain an independent supply of water for the Houses of Parliament and other public buildings. The experienced firm of Easton and Amos was employed on this operation, which did not at first satisfy all the government's expectations.[8] After prolonged consideration the Board of Woods approved Barry's proposals and accepted, in August 1843, Messrs. McDonald and Leslie's tender of £840 for two red granite fountains 9 ft. 6 ins. in diameter, on the understanding that Barry would not exceed the vote for the entire works.[9]

[1] Works 2/2, p. 161.

[2] Works 1/24, pp. 24, 45, 232–4; 1/23, pp. 435, 482, 506; Crest 25/46, nos. 15900, 16876. Peel warned the Commons that 'it would be extremely inconvenient should the monument fall in that crowded part of the metropolis' (*Parl. Deb.* 3rd ser. lxxvi, 1252). The correspondence with the subscribers' committee (Works 6/119) is printed as an appendix to the report of the select committee on Trafalgar Square, *Parl. Pap.* 1840 (548) xii. Spring Rice, Chancellor of the Exchequer, was also a member of the subscribers' committee. Works 35/40 and 41 show alternative plans by Railton dated 2 August 1839 and 2 March 1840.

[3] Works 1/24, p. 172.   [4] Works 1/24, pp. 232–4, 1 June 1840; 35/45–50 (plans).

[5] *Parl. Pap.* 1840 (548), xii.

[6] Works 1/24, pp. 188, 350, 390. Ten firms were invited to tender.

[7] Works 35/43–4; MPE 1359 (plans).

[8] Works 1/26, pp. 145–6, 289, 310; 1/34, pp. 196, 384, 426; 1/35, p. 29; 1/36, pp. 149–52 (7 February 1851), 152–4 (list of places to be supplied from the Orange Street waterworks, including 260,000 gallons every 24 hours for the Houses of Parliament), 170 (15 February), 172 (24 February), 402–3 (11 July), 427–8 (24 July 1851); 2/3, pp. 172–7 (21 September 1841, with plans), 178, 248. Almost at the outset Easton and Amos incurred the wrath of one local notability, the Rector of St. Martin's, for allowing men to sink the wells on Sundays (Works 1/27, p. 27, 16 May 1844). See also Works 35/57–64 (plans and elevation, 24 January 1844, approved by Barry 27 January 1844); Works 6/358A/1.

[9] Works 1/26, p. 289; 1/30, p. 302. Works 35/51 is a plan signed by Barry, dated May 1843; 35/43 is similar, and 44 and 46 show a slightly different design of fountain; see also MPE 1359.

Barry's plan provided for a granite pedestal at either end of the terrace wall to accommodate a statue (Pl. 31). After Sir Francis Chantrey's death in 1841, his executors were anxious to be relieved of the great equestrian bronze statue of George IV designed to surmount Nash's Marble Arch. Prince Albert proposed placing it within the forecourt of Buckingham Palace, but Lord Lincoln, then Chief Commissioner of Woods, opposed hiding 'this fine work of art' from the public who had paid £9000 for it, and commented on the additional expenditure that would be required for a pedestal. Peel in discussion with the Prince then reconciled him to the statue's 'temporary occupation' of one of the vacant pedestals in Trafalgar Square. Barry was authorised in September 1843 to set up the statue, which has remained on the north-east pedestal ever since.[1] Soon after this, the levels of the surrounding roads were aligned with the square, and in December the Bastinne Bitumen Company's tender of £1435 was accepted for asphalting the surface. But it was another twelve months before the works were finished, at a total expense (including the waterworks) of £32,667.[2]

The Nelson Monument, however, was by no means completed. The column itself had been erected, and Baily's statue hoisted to the top in November 1843 (Pl. 32).[3] This had been the responsibility of the subscribers' committee, but having almost exhausted their funds, some £20,000, they appealed to the government to complete the design: £12,000 more were needed for the granite steps, bas-reliefs, and lions. The government had already assisted by casting the bronze ornaments of the capital at the Woolwich Arsenal, and at length agreed to finish the job.[4] Although the work continued under the committee's architect, Railton, the government selected the sculptors and laid down the general conditions they were to observe. In September 1844, to judge the effect of the lions, Railton had wooden steps and platforms set up round the base of the Column. To meet Lord Lincoln's criticisms the steps on the west were doubled in depth and width. Lincoln also wanted the lions brought three feet closer to the column. Barry's opinion was invited and his views were accepted by Peel.[5] Grissell and Peto's tender of £5140 secured the contract for the stylobate in April 1845.[6]

Lincoln then turned to C. L. Eastlake for advice about sculptors, selecting J. E. Carew and W. F. Woodington for two of the bas-reliefs. Peel endorsed this choice, as well as Eastlake's recommendation of J. G. Lough for the lions, adding M. L. Watson and John Ternouth for the remaining bas-reliefs. Lincoln stated that the results of the exhibition of models in Westminster Hall (for the decoration of the Houses of Parliament) had influenced this selection.[7] Eastlake's advice was also taken regarding the conditions to be prescribed.[8] An eight-inch border to the top and sides

[1] B.M. Add. MS. 40481, ff. 119–24, 10–21 April 1843; Works 1/26, pp. 318–9; 2/3, pp. 266, 273. The other pedestal is still empty.   [2] Works 1/26, pp. 333, 338; 1/28, p. 431; 2/5, pp. 397–8.
[3] For an illustrated account of the foundations and column, see *Builder*, viii (1850), p. 169; also *Illustrated London News*, 1843, pp. 311–2.
[4] Further correspondence between the Treasury and the subscribers' committee is printed, *Parl. Pap.* 1847–8, (543), xviii, pt. ii, pp. 232–4.
[5] Nottingham University Library, Newcastle MSS. 12044 (23 September), 12052 (23 November 1844). Railton's original design is shown in *Illustrated London News*, 1843, p. 265, his revised design for the stylobate, dated 29 March 1845, in Works 35/1.   [6] Works 2/4, pp. 181–4, 264; 1/27, p. 438; 1/28, pp. 24, 66.
[7] *Parl. Pap.* 1847–8 (543), xviii, pt. i, q. 4664. For biographies of these sculptors, see Gunnis, *Dictionary of British Sculptors, 1660–1851*.
[8] Newcastle MSS. 9107 (3 October), 12095 (13 October), 9108 (18 October), 9109 (26 November), 9110 (28 November 1845).

of each relief was to be designed by Railton; the composition as a mass was to occupy only the lower two-thirds of the panel (which measured 13 ft. 7¾ ins. by 14 ft. 3½ ins. high); the costume of the period was to be observed, the introduction of smoke—for these were battle-scenes—to be avoided. The government provided the bronze and the apparatus for the casting, but the artist was to execute it, receiving £1000 for his labours.[1] Votes of £2000 were obtained in 1847 and 1848; a further £2800 in 1849 brought the total public subsidy to £14,800.[2] The first relief (Carew's) was fixed in position in December 1849; two more were placed in position in March and December 1850; and the monument was completed in 1852—save for the lions, eventually to be designed by Landseer and executed by Marochetti.[3]

THE WELLINGTON STATUE

A statue of the Duke of Wellington to be erected within sight of his house at Hyde Park Corner was first projected in the 1820s: he told Croker, 'I don't think that the gateway into the Park was constructed when the idea of the statue was first mentioned to me by the Duke of Rutland'.[4] It was not until 1838, however, when £14,000 had been raised, that a committee of subscribers determined that an equestrian statue should be commissioned from Matthew Cotes Wyatt to surmount Decimus Burton's unfinished triumphal arch in the Green Park opposite Apsley House.[5] The Prime Minister, Lord Melbourne, agreed after discussions with Duncannon and Spring Rice, the Chancellor of the Exchequer. Some opposition from subscribers who regarded the selection of Wyatt as a 'gross job' induced Melbourne to suspend his consent until they should reach agreement. Duncannon, probably instigated by Spring Rice, set up a wooden silhouette of the figure on the arch in order to burlesque it. However the general committee of subscribers gave its approval in July 1839, and the government then advised the Queen to grant permission.

Controversy revived as the statue approached completion. In May 1845 Rutland asked the First Commissioner of Woods, Lord Lincoln, to make the arch ready; Burton, as its architect, was opposed to the scheme, arguing that 'the relative proportions of the Building and of the Statue . . . are entirely inharmonious'. Twenty-seven feet high, the statue would crush the architecture of the Arch, yet would be too far from the ground to be clearly seen, and would appear too small: only the pyramidal form of a quadriga would provide a fitting termination. Impressed by such arguments, Lincoln told Rutland that he thought the proposed position for the statue 'particularly ineligible', suggesting better sites might be found. But when Rutland and his sub-committee insisted, Lincoln did not feel he could withdraw the

---

[1] Works 1/29, pp. 121–3, (9 February 1846). The subjects were allocated thus: Watson—Battle of St. Vincent; Woodington—the Nile; Ternouth—Copenhagen; Carew (whose talents Eastlake had praised)—Trafalgar (*ibid.* pp. 124–7).

[2] *Parl. Deb.* 3rd ser. xcii (31 May 1847); *Parl. Pap.* 1847–8 [327] xl; 1849 [268] xxxi; 1850 [256] xxxiv.

[3] Works 1/34, pp. 155, 178, 191; 2/7, p. 419; *Illustrated London News*, 1849, p. 392; 1850, pp. 176, 444.

[4] *The Croker Papers*, ed. L. J. Jennings (1885), iii, p. 124.

[5] Resolutions of the subscribers and Rutland's correspondence are among the papers printed in *Parl. Pap.* 1846 (446) and (553) xliii. Many of the original letters are in Works 20/4/2. The following account is based on these sources, unless otherwise indicated. The contemporary debate can be followed in *The Times*, 1846–7.

permission previously granted, a view shared by Peel.[1] In December Wyatt applied for possession of the arch; but Burton urged that a plaster model should first be tried; and pointed out that the building accommodated a gate-keeper and police constables who would be displaced by the operations, and that the necessary internal buttressing could permanently interfere with its occupation. Wyatt contrived arrangements for raising the statue which, he claimed, should not interfere with the use of the Arch. Lord Canning (who had succeeded Lincoln) vainly attempted to dissuade Rutland from his course in April 1846, even suggesting that the government would pay the extra cost of a granite pedestal in Waterloo Place or Horse Guards Parade.[2]

This offer was repeated by Lord Morpeth, Canning's Whig successor, in August 1846 after a discussion in the Commons.[3] Rutland protested, but offered to remove the statue if it should prove unsuccessful, once set up. Morpeth replied that the government had advised the Queen to rescind her consent, but he yielded to pressure from Lord George Bentinck and Disraeli—'Nothing like *squeezing*', remarked Lincoln to Peel.[4] So up the statue went, and some of the scaffolding was removed towards the end of October 1846.[5] Morpeth circularised the Royal Academicians for their opinions, though 'a forest of scaffolding' still effectively prevented 'forming a judgment of the general effect of the whole'.[6] Morpeth, arguing that sufficient had been removed 'to give a just idea of the general appearance', condemned the effect, and called on Rutland to honour his pledge. Rutland, protesting, played for time. The statue had been up for six months when Morpeth told a questioner in the Commons that he believed men were that day employed in removing it.[7] But the sub-committee refused to have anything more to do with the statue if they had to take it down.[8] The Government, with the prospect of having to hold a twenty-seven foot high statue of the nation's hero, undertook that a pedestal on a suitable site would be provided before the statue was taken down.[9] However, Wellington, who had hitherto resolutely refused to give any opinion, was persuaded to express privately his displeasure at the 'disgrace' and 'ridicule' that would thus be inflicted upon him.[10] Lord George Bentinck, thus armed, took up the issue in the Commons, supported by the radicals, and the Prime Minister agreed to find out Wellington's views. On 12 July 1847 he announced that as Wellington thought the statue's removal might be construed as a mark of royal disapprobation towards him, the government would not persist in its demand.[11] The statue remained on the Arch until 1884, when it was removed to Aldershot.[12]

[1] *Parl. Deb.* 3rd ser. lxxxvi, 960 (21 May 1846).

[2] Instructions for giving possession of the arch to the subscribers' sub-committee were issued on 23 June 1846 (Works 1/30, p. 277).   [3] *Parl. Deb.* lxxxvii, 1408–17 (24 July); lxxxviii, 372 (7 Aug. 1846).

[4] B.M. Add. MS. 40481, f. 325, 17 August 1846. See also C. Berkeley's remarks, *Parl. Deb.* 3rd ser. lxxxviii, 755–7 (17 August 1846).

[5] The erection of the statue was recorded graphically in the *Illustrated London News*, ix (1846), pp. 21, 105, 209, 213, 216–7, 224, 329. Burton not only had to suffer the statue on his arch, but had the greatest difficulty in obtaining reimbursement from government for the considerable amount of work it had caused him between 1845 and 1847 (Works 2/7, pp. 78–83; 2/8, pp. 333, 337, 434, 441; 20/4/2).

[6] *Croker Papers*, iii, pp. 124–5.   [7] *Parl. Deb.* 3rd ser. xc, 1341 (15 March 1847).

[8] *Ibid.* xci, 148 (18 March 1847).   [9] *Ibid.* xciii, 125–6 (4 June 1847).

[10] *Croker Papers*, iii, p. 128, Wellington to Croker, 14 June 1847. See also Greville, *Diary*, v, pp. 458–9.

[11] *Croker Papers*, iii, pp. 129–31; *Parl. Deb.* 3rd ser. xciii, 1079–80; xciv, 102–3, 183.

[12] For illustrations of the statue and details of its removal from the Arch see J. Physick, *The Wellington Monument* (1970). The existing quadriga by Adrian Jones dates from 1912.

WESTMINSTER

The general appearance of Westminster changed considerably between the 1780s and the 1820s. The House of Lords moved from the Parliament House to the Court of Requests. The Speaker was given a spacious new residence, the various Clerks were freshly accommodated, St. Stephen's Chapel was extended and re-styled to meet the needs of a larger House of Commons. In New Palace Yard the old buildings running along the east side were progressively demolished and Westminster Hall was cleared of the out-buildings clinging to its northern front (Pl. 41A). In Old Palace Yard the changes were still more drastic. The whole area from Abingdon Street to Parliament Street was opened up. St. Margaret's Lane became St. Margaret's Street linking New and Old Palace Yard. Westminster Abbey was cleared of surrounding houses and Henry VII's Chapel re-faced. St. Margaret's Church became an insulated monument flanked on one side by its own churchyard and on the other by a new 'Garden Square', the ancestor of Parliament Square. A vista was opened up from the Banqueting House to the precinct of the Abbey. And the architectural patchwork of Britain's legislative and legal centre was concealed by the addition of irregular battlemented fronts overlooking the river on one side and St. Margaret's Street on the other.

Few of these alterations were due to the Office of Works. The maintenance of the Palace of Westminster fell within the department's jurisdiction. But large-scale alterations or additions were not paid for out of the Civil List. Instead they were covered by specific parliamentary grants. Minor works were normally entrusted to the Clerk of the Works and his resident Labourer in Trust. But larger works at Westminster easily took on a national significance; royal influence was enlisted and political factors became involved. In this way the designs made by Soane as Clerk of the Works were easily defeated by those made by Wyatt—not as Surveyor General, but as architect to George III. The situation was also complicated by administrative factors. Wyatt was responsible for the restoration of Westminster Abbey, but as Surveyor to the Dean and Chapter, not as Surveyor General. J. T. Groves executed much of the new work in St. Margaret's Street, but as Surveyor to the Commissioners for Westminster Improvements, not as Soane's successor as Clerk of the Works. Such complications made for a good deal of confusion.[1] The Commissioners of Military Inquiry made it their business to disentangle these arrangements. They discovered that Adam Lee, Groves's successor as Labourer in Trust at Whitehall and Westminster, was responsible for ordinary repairs at the following buildings: the Houses of Lords and Commons; Westminster Hall and the Courts of Chancery, King's Bench and Common Pleas, with their attendant offices and record depositories; the Stone Building containing the Commons' Committee Rooms and Clerk's House; the Parliament, Journal and Record Offices adjoining Westminster Abbey; and the various official houses and apartments belonging to clerks, housekeepers and minor

---

[1] For examples cf. Works 1/5, f. 112, 9 August 1793; Works 4/18, f. 30, 9 August and f. 33, 30 August 1793; Works 6/22, ff. 130–1, 4 October 1793; T. 29/66, ff. 57–9, 11 July and f. 131 16 August 1793; T. 29/103, f. 518, 22 December 1809; Works 4/19, 5 December 1806; Works 6/24, f. 77, 3 December 1806.

parliamentary officers. As Clerks of the Works at St. James's, Whitehall and Westminster, Soane, Groves and Bacon were in turn generally responsible for extra works, unless superseded by Wyatt. But several buildings remained peripheral to the department's normal responsibilities. Repairs at the Court of the Exchequer were dealt with by the officers of that court. The two coffee houses beneath the Exchequer fell to Groves in his capacity as Surveyor to the Commissioners for Westminster Improvements. The coffee house at the northern end of Westminster Hall came under the jurisdiction of the Westminster Bridge Commissioners. Repairs at the Exchequer Offices were dealt with by the Office of Works but paid for by the Exchequer. And from 1805 onwards a separate Labourer in Trust, first Bacon and then Crocker, looked after the houses belonging to the Speaker, Serjeant at Arms and Clerk Assistant, as well as the Exchequer Offices, under Wyatt's direction and Groves's supervision.[1]

The reforms of 1814–15 placed the Palace of Westminster in the care of an 'Attached Architect', Soane, with Crocker as Clerk of Works and Adam Lee as Labourer in Trust. The Exchequer Offices, Speaker's House and Law Courts remained financially distinct from the Houses of Parliament. In 1832 Attached Architect and Clerk of Works were swept away, and the buildings entrusted to a Labourer in Trust, newly designated 'Clerk of the Works'; for major alterations an architect—until 1835 invariably Smirke—was specially engaged. Smirke arranged the temporary accommodation after the fire of 1834, but the new buildings were, after competition, awarded to Barry; while the Law Courts and other surviving parts of the old palace (progressively demolished) remained under the Clerk of Works.

1. WESTMINSTER HALL

It was not until the 1820s that the transformation of Westminster Hall was complete, its exterior fully restored and its court rooms removed from the interior of the hall to chambers outside sheltering between its buttresses. But between the reforms of 1782 and 1815 the Office of Works co-operated in several important alterations and repairs and in the gradual demolition of surrounding buildings. For a description of the whole area during the 1780s we need look no further than a report produced in 1789 at the behest of the House of Commons and signed by no less than fourteen architects: Robert Adam, Dance, S. P. Cockerell, Holland, Yenn, Soane, Browne, Tildesley, Woolfe Snr. and Jnr., Milne, Fulling, Craig and James Wyatt.

> The Buildings East of Westminster Hall, between it and the river, are the Pell Office and Chambers over it in the East Tower, and the Offices of the Exchequer, contiguous and connected with the Hall, and situate between New Palace Yard and St. Stephen's Court; those of the Four Tellers are most inconveniently arranged, and liable to immediate Destruction in case of Fire, being placed in the upper Story, without any Walls of Division or Arched Floors; are separated only by Timber Partitions, surrounded by combustible Buildings, Stables, Coach Houses, Hay Lofts,

[1] 'Inquiry into . . . the Office of Works', *Parl. Pap.* 1812–13, v, pp. 471–2.

Servants Lodging Rooms, and Kitchens; the Dutchy Court of Lancaster, a slight Building of one Room, and over it the Dutchy Chamber, with Garrets above; the Kitchen of the Clerk to the Deputy Usher of the Exchequer, a low Shed, between these Rooms and the Easternmost Tower, and immediately connected with them. The house inhabited by the Usher of the Exchequer, in New Palace Yard, Eastward of the Dutchy Court of Lancaster, has a Brick Front, and its rear is entirely of Timber, Lathed and Plaistered, forming two Sides of a narrow Court, from which it receives Light, and which communicates with the Windows of the Tellers' Offices, Cash Rooms, and of the Dutchy Court; and most of the Kitchen Offices belonging to the Deputy Usher and his Clerk are immediately under those Offices, and the small wood Staircase in the Center of them and leading thereto.

The Buildings on the East side of New Palace Yard, from the King's Bridge or Water Gate, to the House in Possession of Mr. Roberts, Tenant to the Marquess of Buckingham, as a Teller of the Exchequer, contain the late Cofferer's Office, the Office of the Auditor of the Land Revenue, the Lottery Office, the Examiner's Office, the Tellers for the Payment of American Claims, the Pells American Office, the Exchequer Bill Bookbinder's Office, the Office of the Auditor of the Principality of Wales, the Annuity Pell Office, the first and second Annuity Offices, and the 14 per cent Annuity Office, which are principally constructed with Timber, Lath and Plaistered, or Weather-boarded; in many places prop't up, and in others contiguous to low Sheds, equally combustible. The adjoining Building Southward is Mr. Roberts's House, which with the Garden occupies all the Space from St. Stephen's Court to the River, and is immediately connected with the last-mentioned Offices; it has been lately repaired, and some additional small Buildings erected thereto. The next house, adjoining Southward to the last-mentioned, belongs to Lord Viscount Bayham, as Teller of the Exchequer; the Buildings and Garden likewise extend to the Thames, and are at present unoccupied, being in a very dilapidated State.

On the West side of St. Stephen's Court, against the East Wall of Westminster Hall, are the Coach Houses and Stables of the Auditor of the Exchequer, having Hay Lofts and Servants Lodging Rooms over them, which adjoin to and come close under the Windows of the Office and Cash Room of one of the Tellers. On the South of this Court is the Auditor of the Exchequer's House, extending Southward to the House of Commons, and under Part of it; the Garden extends to the River. The Buildings are substantial, and extend under two of the Committee Rooms of the House of Commons.

The Court of Exchequer and Exchequer Chamber, contiguous to, and connected with, Westminster Hall, are very old, but not in a State of actual Ruin. On the Ground Floor, under the Court of Exchequer, is the Custos Brevium of the Court of Common Pleas, and Treasurer's Office belonging; the Ceiling and Walls of them are lined with Deal, are insecure from Fire, and very damp. Adjoining Westward to these, and projecting into the Street, to the great Obstruction and imminent Danger of Persons and Carriages passing to and from the Houses of Parliament, is situated an old Brick Building, occupied on the Ground Floor by the Deputy Usher of the Court of Exchequer, most of his Rooms containing a Fire Place, and the Ceilings are flat and low; over these, on the one Pair of Stairs, is the King's Remembrancer's Office, and over that the Augmentation Office. . . . The Public Houses and Coffee Houses on the South side of New Palace Yard immediately adjoin the Custos Brevium of the Court of Common Pleas, and are particularly dangerous, as they have several Chimneys and Coppers; the Roofs are under and close to the Windows of the Custos Brevium, and some of them covered with Sail Cloth pitched . . .

Next to St. Margaret's Street, and adjoining Southward to the old Brick Buildings before-mentioned, is a Building of the same Kind, containing the Tally Office, being a Depository for the Tallies belonging to the Exchequer. Adjoining Southward thereto is the Coach House for the Judges, a slight Timber Building, covered with Tiles.

The Stone Building next St. Margaret's Street, comprising Committee Rooms, and other Apartments occupied by Officers of the House of Commons, Custos Brevium of the Court of King's Bench, and the Exchequer Bill Office, is of recent Date, and very substantial. Behind that Building and contiguous to Westminster Hall, are the Court of Common Pleas, Judges Chambers, and Record Office, which are in tolerable good Condition; to them are annexed sundry Excrescences, mostly of Timber, which should be removed, as they increase the Danger of Fire and its Communication.[1]

Together with Soane's ground plan of 1793 (Fig. 19), this description graphically illustrates the conglomeration of legal and administrative buildings surrounding Westminster Hall. Writing in 1800 John Carter called for drastic changes: 'Away with these usurping excrescences, of sheds, hovels, taverns, and alehouses, that blot out and disfigure the walls of old English splendour and old English hospitality!' As for the inside of the Hall, he found Kent's Courts of King's Bench and Chancery particularly obnoxious: 'what a farrago of pinnacles and pineapples, pointed compartments and ogee arches, buttresses and balusters, a Grecian entablature and French ornaments!'[2] During the 1780s and 1790s a number of alterations were begun: the enclosing of the Court of Common Pleas with a wooden screen; the addition of a record depository for the same Court; and the demolition of several buildings to the north, east and west of Westminster Hall, notably in 1793 most of the former Augmentation Office which cut off St. Margaret's Street from New Palace Yard.[3] In 1805 it was at last agreed that the Courts of Chancery and King's Bench should be removed and rebuilt 'in the same manner as the Common Pleas'.[4] At the same time it was announced that 'all the sheds which now disgrace that venerable pile are to be pulled down and the entrances to the Hall repaired and beautified'.[5] Part of the Exchequer buildings on the east side of New Palace Yard were pulled down in 1808, and in the same year Wyatt prepared designs for a new range of Exchequer Offices abutting on the north-west tower of the Great Hall.[6] Before long Carter

---

[1] *Commons Jnls.* xliv (1788–9), pp. 548–9. See also *ibid.* xliii (1787–8), p. 531; *Gent's. Mag.* 1788, pt. i, pp. 549–50 and 1790, pt. i, pp. 175–6.

[2] *Gent's. Mag.* 1800, pt. i, pp. 36, 215–6.

[3] Works 1/5, f. 75, 7 October 1784 and f. 120, 21 February 1794; Works 4/16, 25 March 1785; Works 4/18, ff. 58, 129, 135, 137, 150, 153, 192 (1794–6); Works 5/74, December 1785; Works 5/84–5 (1795–6); Works 6/20, ff. 26–7, 2 and 11 April 1785; T. 29/53, f. 4, 7 December 1782; T. 29/56, f. 353, 20 April 1785; T. 29/69, f. 384, 10 August 1796; T. 29/68, f. 279, 13 October 1795. For a view of the buildings demolished 1793 cf. *Gent's. Mag.* 1806, pt. ii, p. 1184. For the progressive truncation of the Exchequer and Augmentation Office buildings cf. H. M. Colvin, 'Views of the Old Palace of Westminster', *Architectural History* ix (1966), pp. 30–31, 33 and pls. 11–13, 31–2; O. C. Williams, 'Topography of the Old House of Commons' (1953, Dept. of Environment Library photostat), p. 2.

[4] *The Times* 23 July 1805, p. 3; 11 August 1806, p. 2.   [5] *Universal Mag.* vi (1805), pp. 71, 175.

[6] His Tudor Gothic design is Works 29/14. Another surviving set of unexecuted plans (Works 29/10–11, unsigned and undated) for new Exchequer offices in the Gothic style provides for a turretted octagonal central block, built round a central stairwell and flanked by canted bays. It probably dates from the late 1790s.

was protesting that restoration in this area had gone too far: the new mouldings on the north front were inaccurate; adjoining windows were 'bastard copyings of the Tudor'; the new doorways were inappropriate; and the Hall itself seemed to be endangered by 'myriads of compo and masonic harpies . . . waiting to catch the *job of restoration*!'[1] 'All the shabby taverns, ale-houses etc', it was reported, 'are to be removed, and the whole is to assume the appearance of a large Gothic edifice, in the center of the North front of which will be Westminster Hall. The old Star Chamber, and other offices between Palace Yard and the river, will be thrown down, and all the space will be laid open between Great George Street and Henry VII's Chapel; so that the utmost degree of convenience of access will be gained, and the finest possible picturesque architectural effect produced, by the grouping of such an assemblage of edifices, laid open to the public view. Some years, however, will elapse, before the whole plan can be completed'.[2] This prediction as to delay was amply fulfilled: Carter did not live to see the final restoration of Westminster Hall by Gayfere, Soane and Smirke.

Meanwhile Westminster Hall was, for the last time, the scene of two historic state trials; the impeachments of Warren Hastings and Lord Melville. On both occasions the Office of Works constructed temporary scaffolding, the Lord Chamberlain's Office supplied soft furnishings and the Lord Great Chamberlain directed ceremonial. During this period the office of Lord Great Chamberlain was vested in the Burrell family. Horace Walpole commented on the 'deluge of wealth and honours' which fell their way by marriage.[3] In 1779 Peter Burrell, later first Lord Gwydir (1754–1820), won the hand of Lady Priscilla Bertie, co-heiress of the third Duke of Ancaster, hereditary Great Chamberlain of England. Through his wife he inherited ceremonial responsibility for the Palace of Westminster. It was he who organized the trail of Warren Hastings; his son directed the coronation of George IV; and both co-operated in the arrangements for the trial of Lord Melville.

Hastings' trial must rank as one of the most extraordinary legal proceedings on record. 'Twenty volumes of parliamentary reports, eleven folio volumes of evidence, . . . three thousand pages of oratory . . . twenty years of agitation', memorable performances by Burke, Fox and Sheridan, all resulting in an acquittal seven years after the start of the trial.[4] Westminster Hall became 'a vast improvised theatre. Red-covered seats for all but the Commons, whose seats were green; at the far end, the throne and the royal boxes, with the Chancellor, judges, and heralds beneath them. To the left were the peers, to the right the Commons; over the heads of each, galleries for peeresses and all the ticket-holders favoured by peers, or the great officers of the Palace of Westminster'. And for Hastings a place to face his accusers, 'a little box near the door, divided only by the witness-box from the Commons' managers'.[5] The cost of fitting up and furnishing the court came to £3758 19s. 4½d.[6] But the cost of heating, lighting and maintenance throughout the trial added more

---

[1] *Gent's. Mag.* 1807, pt. i, pp. 133–5, 322–4; 1807, pt. ii, pp. 623–5; 1808, pt. ii, p. 977 (with plate).
[2] *The Times* 23 October 1806, p. 3. For a detailed plan dated 1807 showing the half-completed improvements cf. J. T. Smith, *Antiquities of Westminster* (1837) p. 125.
[3] Cf. J. H. Round, *Peerage and Pedigree* i (1910), pp. 51–4; *Gent's. Mag.* 1820, pt. i, p. 637.
[4] Cf. Sir K. G. Feiling, *Warren Hastings* (1954), pp. 352, 367.
[5] *Ibid.* dp. 394–50.
[6] *Gent's. Mag.* 1788, pt. i, p. 457; 1788, pt. ii, pp. 1082, 1084, 1140, 1142, 1145.

than £2500 to this total.[1] The usual Office of Works tradesmen were employed, Samuel Wyatt holding the principal contract for carpentry.[2] Chambers, Couse and Woolfe were the officers chiefly concerned in the original preparations; Soane was responsible for maintenance during the later years of the trial. The work was executed at great speed, and a detailed timetable (December 1787–February 1788) survives to illustrate the methods employed.[3] Precedents existed in the arrangements for the trials of Dr. Sacheverell (1709), the Duchess of Kingston (1776) and Lord Lovat (1746), as well as in what Chambers called 'the plan of John Gaudet Anno 1698' and 'a plan of Sir Christopher Wren, executed upon some occasion, but we know not when'.[4] Boxes were therefore arranged according to custom for the various grades of spectator, as well as for privileged individuals ranging from the Prince of Wales to the Surveyor General himself. 'Every body appeared to approve of what had been done in general, but great Complaint was made about the Cold'.[5] It was not until 1792 that J. W. Oldham supplied 'a very capital dome Warming Machine with large Pillars and Capitals, brass festoons and ornaments and a fluted Crown top, the whole made very strong and of large Dimentions'.[6]

Arrangements for the impeachment of Lord Melville in 1806 were less dramatic but equally lavish. The cost of scaffolding and furnishing for the seventeen day trial was £8188 4s. 6d., of which the bills incurred by the Office of Works came to £6695 6s. 0½d.[7] 'I never knew what earthly magnificence was', wrote Lord Campbell, 'till yesterday when I was present at Lord Melville's trial. Ye Gods! the Peeresses' box! A glory seemed to play round their countenances, and to shoot in vivid flashes to the extremities of the Hall'.[8] On the other hand, Wellesley declined to attend because he 'could not bear the cold of the Hall'.[9] The recent precedent of Hastings' trial simplified most of the arrangements. But Gwydir's illness left temporary responsibility for ceremonial in the hands of Pitt's 'man-manager', William Eden, Lord Auckland. And Auckland's inexperience was hardly assisted by Wyatt's absence at Fonthill.[10] On 5 April 1806 we find Auckland writing to Prime Minister Grenville: 'Before I left Palace Yard, I settled with Lord Dartmouth, Mr. Groves, and a Mr. Craig of the Board of Works . . . that the preparing of Westminster Hall shall be pushed forwards with all possible despatch . . . Wyatt *non est inventus*'.[11] But by 21 April the Surveyor General had been found in time to announce at the bar of the House of Lords that Westminster Hall would be ready by the end of the week.[12]

After clearance of New Palace Yard the façade of the Hall itself had emerged in

[1] Works 4/18, f. 175, 30 April 1796; Works 3/3, f. 44, 17 December 1792 and f. 68, 25 April 1796. The figures recorded in 'Public Income and Expenditure, 1688–1869', *Parl. Pap.* 1868–9, xxxv, pp. 445–54, include legal charges etc.

[2] Annual accounts: Works 1/5, f. 97, 9 December 1790; T. 29/62, f. 387, 18 December 1790; Works 5/77, 1788; Works 5/79, 1790; Works 5/81, 1792; Works 5/82, 1793; Works 5/83, 1794; Works 5/84, 1795.

[3] Works 11/24/6.

[4] Works 6/21, ff. 127–133, 28–29 December 1877; Works 11/24/6, 3 January 1788. For a plan of the arrangements at Hastings' trial see B. M. King's Maps xxiv, 24.

[5] Works 11/24/6, 16 February 1788.   [6] Works 5/82, Midsummer Quarter 1793.

[7] L.C. 1/1, 4 February 1807; L.C. 2/40; Works 4/20, 10 January 1807.

[8] Quoted by C. Matheson, *Henry Dundas, Viscount Melville* (1933), p. 366. For details of the trial cf. *Gent's. Mag.* 1806, pt. i, pp. 462–4, 560–67; *Parl. Pap.* 1805, ii, pp. 817–27, 829–41 and 1806, ii, pp. 63–141. For a plan of the seating arrangements see B. M. King's Maps xxiv, 24 lm and R.I.B.A. Drawings Collection J7/34, 1–4.

[9] Hist. MSS. Comm. *Fortescue MSS.* viii (1912), p. 123, 29 April 1806.   [10] *Ibid.* p. 87, 9 April 1806.

[11] *Ibid.* p. 79, 5 April 1806. See also pp. 85, 125, 182.   [12] *Parl. Deb.* vi (1806), pp. 794, 1808.

a somewhat battered condition.[1] Although some repairs had been carried out to the entrance in 1807–8, the upper part of the front was left to be dealt with later. In May 1818 Soane found it 'in a most dangerous state'; had the winter been severe the gable must have fallen. But it was April of the following year before the Surveyor General asked him how the north front might be secured from endangering the public, and August before the Treasury was informed that it must be rebuilt. Soane intended to 'strictly adhere to the original style of architecture, wherever the same is practicable'.[2] Thomas Gayfere (1775–1827), the experienced master-mason of Westminster Abbey, who for some years past had been engaged on the restoration of Henry VII's Chapel, carried out the work in Bath stone under Soane's superintendence, with some assistance from Hiort and Browne of the Office of Works. All four were involved, for instance, in the renewal of missing ornaments: Hiort reported in May 1820 that Gayfere's people had clay-modelled another crocket, which did not agree with the idea that Browne had given of it; it seemed much larger than was required, and Browne wished Soane to see it.[3] Other features of the restoration included the replacement of battlements on the flanking towers, of crockets on the gable, and of a quatrefoil cresting over the porch. Despite Soane's assurances, one deviation from the original design was made: one of the two courses of cusped panelling above the lower niches was omitted in order to increase the height of the niches. As all the surviving statues were removed and not replaced, the result was to emphasise the vacancy of the empty niches.[4]

'When the new front was in progress', say Brayley and Britton, 'an additional tier of windows was inserted in the slope of the roof on each side of the Hall, and the lantern upon the roof was renewed and glazed'.[5] This was in accordance with Soane's recommendation that the skylights, many made at the time of Lord Melville's impeachment, should be converted into 'dormant windows'.[6] The restoration of the roof itself involved the use of 'forty loads of well-seasoned oak' from broken-up ships. The carved angels were repaired by Edward Wyatt, and the roof was completed at the north end where it had originally been left unfinished.[7] The decayed medieval lantern on the ridge of the roof was taken down and replaced by an approximate replica with cast-iron tracery.[8] Some £4000 for repairs of roof and lantern were

[1] See drawings by Capon and Buckler reproduced in Colvin, 'Views of the Old Palace of Westminster,' *Architectural History* ix (1966), figs. 32–4.

[2] Works 1/8, p. 463; 1/9, pp. 283, 304–20, 419–21.   [3] Soane Museum corresp. 2, xii, J. 1, f. 16.

[4] Compare Buckler's drawings reproduced by Colvin, *op. cit.* figs. 33–4, with Britton and Pugin, *Public Buildings of London* ed. Leeds i (1838), p. 258, pl. 2. For the fate of the statues see vol. i of this *History* p. 528, n. 4.   [5] E. W. Brayley and J. Britton, *History of the Ancient Palace . . . at Westminster* (1836), p. 440.

[6] Works 1/9, pp. 304 ff.   [7] Brayley and Britton, pp. 440–1; Works 4/24, p. 242.

[8] Britton and Pugin *op. cit.* p. 257 and plate. Many years later Hiort stated in his *Autobiography* (privately printed 1861) that nothing remained of the old lantern, whose position was marked only by a leaded flat, and that the new lantern was made to resemble the original 'so far as could be gathered from the indications given by the remains of the framing, from the relics found among the timbers of the roof, and from a collation of old views and documents'. It is difficult to reconcile this account with drawings by Buckler inscribed 'Frame work of the original Louver of Westminster Hall, sketched and measured immediately after its removal from the roof. Apl: 10. 1821' (B.M. Add. MS. 36436, f. 431, reproduced by Colvin, *op. cit.* fig. 47). The old louver is moreover clearly shown in place in Buckler's view of the Hall drawn in 1814 (B.M. Add. MS. 36370, f. 211, reproduced by Colvin, *op. cit.* fig. 33). Hiort's recollections may have been confused by the fact that originally there were two louvers (cf. Wyngaerde's view reproduced in vol. i of this *History*, pl. 24), only the southern of which remained by the mid-seventeenth century (cf. Hollar's view of 1647 reproduced by Colvin, *op. cit.* fig. 5). No doubt it was the destroyed northern louver whose vestiges Hiort and his colleagues discovered in 1821, but it was the surviving southern louver that they took down and replaced.

charged on the ordinary parliamentary grant in addition to nearly £26,000 for the other works (estimated by Soane at £18,000–20,000), which were completed in the spring of 1823.[1]

Soane never had the opportunity to complete the interior restoration of the hall; even after the removal of the Courts of King's Bench and Chancery to their new quarters part of the space was used for storing official records; but in 1834 this work was entrusted to Smirke on his estimate of £17,000.[2] Robert Johnson won the mason's contract.[3] 'The old facings of the walls were cut away', reported Brayley and Britton, 'and their place is supplied by a beautiful ashlaring of Huddlestone stone, six inches in thickness'. The cornice and corbels were restored 'in exact correspond-ence with the original work', and the great south window and those on the long sides were also restored.[4] The floor was repaved with York stone.[5] The hall was saved from the conflagration of October 1834[6] and the restoration went on, some £5400 being expended in 1834/5, some £7250 in 1835/6, and £4200 in 1836/7.[7] Sydney Smirke described discoveries made during the operations to the Society of Anti-quaries.[8]

Meanwhile the hall had witnessed in 1821 the last coronation banquet of an English king.[9] In 1843 it was used to exhibit the cartoons for the decorations of the new Houses of Parliament resulting from a competition conducted by the Fine Arts Commission; when this was repeated in 1846, eight of the dormer windows were specially glazed with sheet glass.[10] Barry conceived a grandiose scheme for raising the roof to give greater external importance to the structure, somewhat overshadowed by his New Palace, and for an avenue of statues of statesmen within the hall to form a magnificent public approach to the Houses of Parliament, but the only part of his projects to be realised was the southward prolongation of the hall into St. Stephen's Porch.[11] Thereafter the fabric remained undisturbed until J. L. Pearson's restoration consequent upon the demolition of Soane's Law Courts in 1883.

[1] Works 1/9, p. 446; 5/108, 109.
[2] Works 1/15, p. 132; 1/21, pp. 73–4; 11/28/8, f. 10.
[3] Works 1/21, pp. 120, 134.
[4] Brayley and Britton, *loc. cit.*
[5] According to Brayley and Britton the ground was lowered about twelve inches; but an officer of the Woods and Forests, J. W. Adams, who had some connection with the work, wrote to Charles Barry jnr. in 1884: '. . . I recollect Sir Robert Smirke being employed for some repairs there, and he laid the present stone floor, raising it some two or three or four feet, for the special purpose of keeping it above the tide, which used some-times to flow into it, so that the barristers had to get to the courts in boats. . . .' (*Parl. Pap.* 1884–5 (166) xiii, q. 2094). These differing accounts may be reconciled by Sydney Smirke's explanation that the floor was excavated four or five feet below the late 18th-century Yorkshire paving; a Purbeck stone floor *temp.* Richard II was discovered 1 ft. 4 ins. below the paving, and the floor restored to that level (*Archaeologia*, xxvi, 1836, pp. 415–6).
[6] Ministers joined in working the pumps, Campbell, the Attorney-General, injuring his knee in so doing (*Life of John, Lord Campbell*, ed. Mrs. Hardcastle, 1881, ii, p. 54).
[7] L.R.R.O. 2/4–6.
[8] *Archaeologia*, xxvi (1836) pp. 406–21. For the rebuilding of the pinnacle on the southern gable see *Gent's. Mag.* 1836 (ii), pp. 268–70. The original pinnacle housed two statues of kings for which replacements were carved. It is possible that the original statues were those that were secured in September 1836 by Sir Charles Tennyson d'Eyncourt for his new Gothic house at Bayons Manor, Lincs., and were recently recovered by the former Ministry of Public Building and Works (Tennyson d'Eyncourt Papers, Lincs. R.O. See also *Country Life* 1960, pp. 430–3, and *The Times*, February 1963).
[9] See p. 647.
[10] Works 1/26, p. 115; 2/5, pp. 250–1.   [11] See p. 587, n. 1.

2. THE LAW COURTS

For centuries Westminster Hall had been England's legal forum. In the eighteenth century Gothick enclosures had been erected at its south end for the Courts of Chancery and King's Bench, while the Court of Common Pleas had been rehoused in a new room on the west side of the Hall, close to the Exchequer Court and other buildings. But these arrangements were still far from ideal, and the burden of judicial business continued to grow. In 1817 an additional Chancery judge, the Vice-Chancellor, was appointed, and had to be provided with a court. But it seems to have been the restoration of Westminster Hall and the inconvenience caused by having to remove the courts for the first coronation banquet for sixty years that in 1820 determined the government to erect new courts to the west of the Hall.[1] Soane, being in charge of the Westminster district, was called upon for plans, which were ready for the judges by the year's end.[2] In June 1821 Soane transmitted his designs to the Treasury. Except for the Court of Exchequer, the old buildings on the site were too dilapidated to be preserved; the eighteenth-century 'Stone Building' in St. Margaret's Street, however, which had never been completed towards the north, was a substantial structure that could be conveniently adapted, the more so as part of it fell vacant in 1821. Soane determined 'to dovetail into my Design as many parts of the old Buildings as were capable of alteration and useful repair'—not, he added, 'from any apprehension of the plaints of a Gayfere, the ravings of a Carter, or the lamentations of a Capon—but from a much more important consideration—a due regard to the economical expenditure of the public money'.[3] On the north side facing New Palace Yard he proposed to retain the existing Tudor Gothic elevation as far west as the octagonal stair-turret, and 'to continue in the same style of architecture' round the corner in St. Margaret's Street as far as the Stone Building, which he intended to complete in accordance with the original Palladian design (Pl. 38A).[4] But on a drawing marked 'App[rove]d 27 July 1821', the whole of the western elevation is annotated 'Proposed to make the front correspond with B', i.e. the Stone Building.[5] Had this proposal been executed the octagonal turret would no doubt have served to separate the Tudor work from the Palladian.[6] But soon afterwards part of the Exchequer Court was demolished in order to expose the western face of the adjoining tower of Westminster Hall (then under restoration), and Soane accordingly abandoned the idea of preserving any of the old work. In considering the character of the new elevation that was to take its place he was confronted with a major aesthetic problem, created by the proximity of the newly-restored façade of West-

---

[1] Soane Museum, New Law Courts corr. (hereafter N.L.C.), 20, Stephenson to Soane, 12 July 1820. This was a proposal that went back at least to 1805, see above, p. 499.

[2] N.L.C. 7, 10. A sketch plan, Soane Museum 53/1/15, is dated 18 October 1820.

[3] *Designs for Public and Private Buildings* (1828), p. 10.

[4] Soane Museum 53/8/1. This version is illustrated in Soane's *Designs for Public and Private Buildings* (1828), pl. 10c.   [5] Soane Museum 53/8/2.

[6] *Ibid.* 53/1/13, a plan produced by Soane at the Treasury on 27 July 1821 and 'ordered to be submitted to the different judges'.

minster Hall. His solution was one much favoured by present-day opinion, the use of a contrasting style in his own idiom:

> After mature deliberation, I judged that the magnificence and unique character of Westminster Hall would be most effectually preserved by connecting the new building as little as possible with that venerable structure, and by making the exterior of the Court of King's Bench in a character entirely different from the Northern Entrance into Westminster Hall.[1]

He accordingly composed an elevation of Palladian character to match the Stone Building.[2] The problems presented by the commission were not only stylistic: for it was only with difficulty that the various courts and the necessary service accommodation could be fitted into the very restricted site available between the Hall and St. Margaret's Street. However, by December 1821 Soane was ready to submit a scheme to the Chancellor of the Exchequer which he estimated would cost £80,000–£100,0000.[3]

The Treasury in January 1822 ordered the Surveyor General to make the necessary preparations for the new buildings, and the King's approval some weeks later was the signal for an immediate start.[4] But before anything further could be done it was necessary to erect a temporary building in Westminster Hall to house the legal records displaced by the demolition of the old buildings.[5] In June the Treasury urged that there should be no further delay; by August the Exchequer Court had been cleared, but it was not until October that the bricklayers began work at the south end of the site, on the Chancery and Vice-Chancellor's Courts.[6] Yet Soane had by no means determined their final appearance, which was still under consideration in May 1823.[7] The proximity of the projected works to those on the Royal Entrance of the House of Lords led Soane to employ the same contractors.[8] The plans for the remainder of the site were still the subject of consideration, and Soane's meeting with the Lord Chief Baron on 5 March 1823 produced alterations in that judge's quarters.[9] On 15 March Soane offered at least three Palladian designs to the ministers at a meeting attended by Robinson as Chancellor of the

---

[1] *A brief Statement of the proceedings respecting the new Law Courts at Westminster . . .* etc. (1828), p. 2.

[2] *Ibid.* pp. 2–3.

[3] Works 1/11, p. 47; Soane Museum N.L.C. 30–36; 53/1/20 (plan): cf. 53/8/6–7 (elevations).

[4] Works 1/11, pp. 56, 70; Soane Museum N.L.C. 51.

[5] Soane Museum, N.L.C. 53, 54; Works 1/11, p. 149; *Gent's. Mag.* 1822 pt. i, p. 637.

[6] Soane Museum N.L.C. 57, 52; B.M. Add. MS. 36370, f. 223 dated 26 August 1822 (reproduced by Colvin, 'Old Palace of Westminster', fig. 67); Soane Mus. plans dated October–November 1822, 53/1/3–5, 8.

[7] *Ibid.* 53/2/46–54, plans and elevations of the Vice-Chancellor's Court, dated October–November 1822. One version consists of an elongated octagon with doubled columns at the angles. A plan and section, close to the executed design, is dated 26 May 1823, but the lantern differs (No. 57). The elongated octagon is transferred to the Chancery Court in another design, 26 November 1822 (No. 69). See also Nos. 60–78. The plan of Chancery Court as executed, No. 65, is dated 13 May 1823.

[8] The contractors were: Johnson and Brien (diggers), Stutely (bricklayer), T. Martyr (carpenter), T. Grundy (mason), T. Palmer (plasterer), May and Morritt (smith), Mackell (smith), Watson (painter and glazier)—as Watson did not proceed fast enough, Cobbett was called in—Good (plumber), Holroyd (plumber). Soane went to considerable lengths to enable Jeffry Wyatt (for so many years an Office tradesman) to be employed as joint carpenter, a contract taken over by his partner Armstrong when he withdrew into solely professional practice on his appointment as architect for the restoration of Windsor Castle (Soane Museum N.C.L.). The royal arms in Coade Stone for the King's Bench were supplied by Croggon; those in the other courts carved in wood by William Warne (*ibid.* ff. 42, 43, 46).　　　[9] *Ibid.* 53/1/22.

Exchequer, Sir Robert Gifford (Attorney General), Sir Charles Long and J. C. Herries (financial secretary to the Treasury).[1] One was selected (Pl. 38B). Sir Charles Long, however, 'expressed a wish that as much as possible of West[minster] Hall might be seen',[2] which induced Soane to round the corners of this north front (Pl. 39A).[3] The plan then approved was much altered after a further meeting in or before September,[4] by which time all the foundations of the courts had been laid.[5] Soane also produced a number of variant designs for the north front. Temporary courts for the Exchequer and Common Pleas were erected in Westminster Hall; the Exchequer Court and Exchequer Coffee House were pulled down in May, and the old Common Pleas Court was taken down in July.[6]

The planning of the new courts was highly ingenious. Five of them—the Bail Court, the Court of Exchequer, the Court of Common Pleas, the Vice-Chancellor's Court and the High Court of Chancery—were fitted into the spaces between the great buttresses of Westminster Hall. For the remaining courts—of Equity and King's Bench—Soane found room beyond the buttresses in the area of the former Exchequer buildings. The courts were linked by the two north-south lines of communication: one for the judges and officers, the other, alongside the Hall, for those with business in the courts; both joining to provide access to the Commons' committee rooms. Every other available space was filled up with retiring rooms, robing rooms and offices. There was no room for windows, so the new courts were necessarily lighted by clerestory and lantern. Soane accordingly composed a remarkable series of variations on the theme of a top-lighted room, a theme that had attracted him from the time of his earliest work at the Bank of England (Pls. 42–3). 'Here', writes Summerson,

> we find him expanding old ideas in the most intrepid manner. Thus the Court of Chancery . . . was, in essence, an enormously expanded version of the 'tribune' at Tyringham, the lower arch-lines drawn out into a mere camber, the lantern rising from a ceiling whose hanging arches remind us of the dining-room in the [Soane] Museum. There is no new invention here, only an incredible determination to stretch the old themes as far as they would go, and perhaps even a little further.[7]

Again, the Lord Chancellor's retiring room, of three domed bays, with oculi (Pl. 43B), closely resembles Dance's Council Chamber at Guildhall (1777).[8]

Progress was rapid, and by March 1824 the outlines of the design were apparent. They did not please the mischievous Henry Bankes, M.P., who, residing in Old Palace Yard, frequently passed by. He opened an attack in the Commons when, on 1 March, the vote of £30,000 for the works to be done in 1824 was moved,[9] objecting to the 'abominable taste in which new buildings of a different order of architecture had been grafted onto the old Gothic'. Robinson, who already that evening had repudiated Treasury responsibility for Soane's works on the Royal Entrance, now

---

[1] *Ibid.* 53/8/4, 6, 7 (elevations); 53/1/21 (plan). [2] *Ibid.* 53/8/7.
[3] *Ibid.* 53/2/34, 35 (plans); 53/8/8 (elevation). [4] *Ibid.* 53/1/23; N.L.C. 97. [5] *Ibid.* N.L.C. 52.
[6] *Ibid.* 89, 101; *Gent.'s Mag.* 1823, pt. i, p. 390.
[7] J. Summerson, *Architecture in Britain 1530–1830* (2nd ed. 1955), pp. 287–8. The hanging arches can indeed be traced back to Soane's early work at the Bank, cf. Summerson, *Sir John Soane* (1952), p. 30. See also p. 438 above.
[8] Summerson, *Sir John Soane*, pl. 17. [9] *Parl. Deb.* new ser. x, 632 ff.

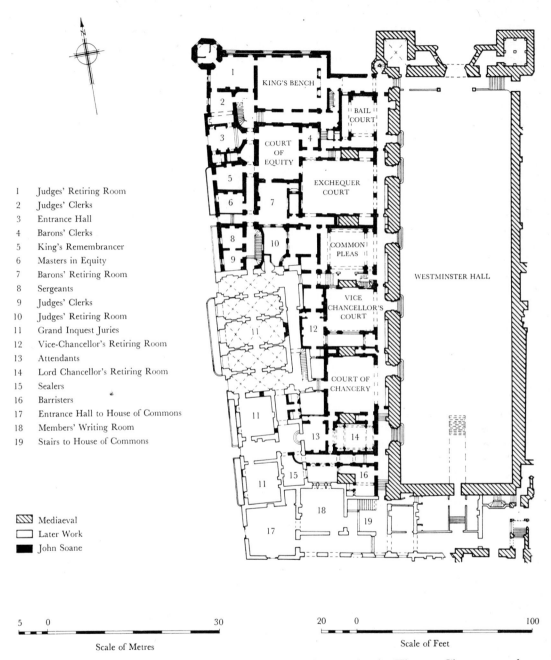

1   Judges' Retiring Room
2   Judges' Clerks
3   Entrance Hall
4   Barons' Clerks
5   King's Remembrancer
6   Masters in Equity
7   Barons' Retiring Room
8   Sergeants
9   Judges' Clerks
10 Judges' Retiring Room
11 Grand Inquest Juries
12 Vice-Chancellor's Retiring Room
13 Attendants
14 Lord Chancellor's Retiring Room
15 Sealers
16 Barristers
17 Entrance Hall to House of Commons
18 Members' Writing Room
19 Stairs to House of Commons

Mediaeval
Later Work
John Soane

Scale of Metres
5   0   30

Scale of Feet
20 0   100

Fig. 20. Westminster Palace, Soane's Law Courts: from a plan by Thomas Chawner made
in 1834 (Works 29/20).

lied blatantly. He regretted, he said, 'the existence of the unpleasant excrescence' of which Bankes 'so deservedly complained'. Although he had on 15 March 1823 approved Soane's plans and visited the site, he declared that 'he had seen it [the "excrescence"] for the first time in the course of last year, when the foundations were already laid, and it was unfortunately too late to put a stop to the building'. Bankes next moved for a select committee,[1] which was resisted by Robinson, belatedly aware of the danger of running with the pack: he could not in the public interest consent to a committee 'having for its object to consider the propriety of pulling down buildings which were now so near their completion'. In a thin house, Government was defeated by 43 votes to 30.

The committee included Bankes, Robinson, Sir Charles Long, Col. Trench, Edward Cust and Agar Ellis.[2] It lost no time: on 25 March it summoned Soane and ordered him to prepare a plan confining the courts 'within a straight line drawn from the North angle of the uniform elevation of the Stone Building, to the wall of Westminster Hall'.[3] When Soane demonstrated that this was insufficient, he was allowed a little more, but still inadequate, space.[4] He was then permitted to go as far north as the north wall of the Court of King's Bench, and instructed to 'Gothicise' the fronts next Old Palace Yard and in St. Margaret's Street up to the Palladian façade of the Stone Building.[5] The committee then began to polish his design: they determined on an octagonal tower for records of the Common Pleas at the north-west corner. It was to be of 20 feet diameter and show only five sides; then it was reduced to eighteen feet diameter, lowered seven feet, and orientated differently (Pl. 40)[6]. Alterations were also made in the fenestration. When Soane submitted an estimate of over £9000 for the alterations, Col. Trench produced a scheme of his own which he claimed was 'far more beautiful and extensive'.[7] Moreover, a 'distinguished artist' had said that it could be built for half the sum mentioned by Soane. When that artist, Philip Wyatt, called on Soane the following day to explain that his estimate had been 'merely an off-hand affair' for Trench, his 'intimate friend', Soane showed him the door.[8]

In order to obtain the authority of the House for their decision, the select committee drew up a hasty and unfinished report which declared that the north entrance of Westminster Hall was 'so beautiful in itself, and has been lately so admirably restored' that 'any new structure to be raised in its vicinity should be kept entirely subordinate, both in height and alignment'.

[1] *Ibid.* 1283 (18 March), 1381 (23 March 1824).
[2] *Commons Jnls.* lxxix (1824), p. 206.
[3] Soane Museum 53/3/30–1.
[4] *Ibid.* Soane's plans are 53/3/51, 53, 54, 58, 59; elevations, 53/3/34–6 (various dates in April).
[5] *Ibid.* 53/3/30–1; plans Nos. 44, 48, 56; models 2 SC and 30 MR (Nos. 79 and 80 in J. Wilton-Ely, 'Catalogue', *Architectural History* xii, 1969, p. 32). Mr. Wilton-Ely is mistaken in regarding No. 80 as the executed design, which incorporated a corner tower, see *Gent's. Mag.* 1824 pt. ii, p. 608, and Brayley and Britton, *Ancient Palace . . . at Westminster* (1836), pl. ii.
[6] Soane Museum, 53/3/59 (1 April), 35 (6 April), 51 and 58 (9 April), 33 (12 April), 43 (14 April with alterations of 5 May), 42 (30 April with alterations of 6 May), 41 (5 May with alterations of 6 May), 37 (13 May with alterations of 24 May).
[7] Trench published this in *A Collection of Papers relating to the Thames Quay with Hints for some further improvements in the Metropolis* (1827), pl. 7 (signed 'Philip Wyatt, Archt.'). Ogival caps copied from Henry VII's Chapel were introduced to flank the central gable of a Gothicised Stone Building.
[8] Soane Museum N.L.C. Select Committee papers, 9; *A brief Statement*, pp. 6–7.

The completion of the stone building . . . was necessarily connected with the formation of the new Courts which are placed within it; but this building, which was left unfinished on one side of its centre, required, as far as symmetry and good effect were concerned, nothing beyond an addition of the same length, with a square turret, towards the North, similar to that which it presented to the South of the centre. . . . The rendering this building again irregular, by making that side of the centre too long, which was antecedently too short, and the effecting of this irregularity by the addition of two Venetian windows, with one rectangular window interposed, and another placed at the curvilinear extremity, obviously called for revision and correction . . . [as did] the great projection of this excrescent part into New Palace-yard, and the incongruous style of architecture which thus comes into immediate contact with that magnificent and enriched specimen of Gothic architecture . . .[1]

The committee accepted the inviolability of the dimensions of the courts; the communications appeared 'perfectly satisfactory', and keeping all the courts on one side of the Hall was 'deemed expedient, to prevent any further procrastination in completing them'. The committee therefore recommended that the 'front towards New Palace Yard, containing the three Venetian windows' should be 'set back as far as the boundary wall of the Court of King's Bench, so as to sacrifice only some small rooms'.

The alteration in fact involved the demolition of a law library, of rooms for attorneys, barristers and judges, and of their separate entrances. Bankes argued that because such accommodation had not existed in the old courts, its loss was immaterial: 'it was all nonsense, nothing of the kind was in the old Court, nor was it necessary'.[2] But the Metropolitan Law Society had vainly sought accommodation in 1822, and the Bar found the loss of rooms a serious inconvenience. The courts themselves, the dimensions of which had been settled with the judges to be only slightly larger than the old courts, and which the select committee had thought too large, proved to be too small: 'Formerly the Courts sat for shorter periods and with longer intervals . . . and the Evil was not felt so severely but now [1825] when the Profession almost pass their lives in Court the grievance is very serious'.[3]

The Commons accepted the report, though the lawyers were soon to experience the inconvenience that resulted. The government abdicated its responsibility and failed to oppose the report, which was completed so hastily that Bankes had to append a memorandum:

The lower windows are to be rectangular, not pointed, nor rounded at the top: let this alteration be made upon the drawing annexed to their report. Let the battlements be made larger upon a strip of paper to the scale of that drawing, and try the effect: the Committee were of opinion that it would be better larger, and only left the drawing as it was, that no further delay might occur in presenting their Report.

The objectionable chimneys, which are built up like a wall, must be altered: this part also of Mr. Soane's drawing was left by the Committee, without sufficient alteration, for the reason above given. Let Sir C. Long see the battlements when drawn.[4]

[1] *Parl. Pap.* 1824, vi, p. 487; *A brief Statement*, p. 10.   [2] *A brief Statement*, pp. 8–9; Soane Mus. N.L.C. 128.
[3] *A brief Statement*, p. 13; Soane Mus. N.L.C., 64, 128, 137.   [4] *Works* 1/12, p. 495 (14 June 1824).

Soane submitted various sizes of battlements, of which those of the dimensions of the battlements of Westminster Hall were approved by Long as 'best corresponding with the large masses of the building'.[1]

Soane felt humiliated and angry. For the design evolved by the committee he had nothing but contempt: 'I believe it will be found impossible to make anything less analogous to Westminster Hall, more clumsy, puerile, and disgraceful to the 19th Century than the exterior of the Court of King's Bench'. He subsequently wrote at considerable length by way of protest and self-justification a pamphlet entitled *A brief statement of proceedings respecting the New Law Courts at Westminster . . . etc.*, which he published in 1828. It is a somewhat confused and repetitive narrative which does not entirely coincide with the documentary evidence. To the Chancellor of the Exchequer Soane observed that a Gothic façade in New Palace Yard would 'enter into competition with the Front of Westminster Hall, and like a Pigmy compared with a Giant, both will suffer by the comparison—If on the contrary the exterior is made to correspond with the Old Stone Building, the Front of Westminster Hall rising majestically above the surrounding objects will retain its imposing aspect'. If however it were determined to gothicise the front and have a corner tower, that tower should not be octangular but rectangular to correspond with those of the Hall.[2] He even prepared drawings to show how easily his Palladian north front could be gothicised (Pl. 39B).[3]

Bankes's interference delayed completion of the courts by nearly a year, and the alterations added nearly £9000 to the cost. They brought one amusing incident: Edward Cust, M.P., told Cook, the labourer in trust, that he wanted to see the foundation stone of the octagon tower laid. Cust was allowed to spread the mortar; when the stone was in place he asked Cook to affix a brass plate inscribed to the effect that the stone had been laid by Cust. Cook referred this request to the Surveyor General, who refused it and reprimanded him for allowing Cust to interfere. The brass plate, handed to Soane, is now in the Soane Museum.[4]

The courts were fitted up in the course of 1825.[5] In April 1825 the Attorney General inspected the new courts, but thought the King's Bench too small, a view endorsed by the Bar.[6] When the judges viewed that court towards the year's end they found the changes resulting from Bankes's operations made it 'wholly unfit for use, without very material alterations, to supply the want of the rooms lately pulled down'.[7] After modifications had been made, the court was brought into use on 3 February 1826, two months before the Chancery Court. Lord Chief Justice Abbott approved the 'taste' and accommodation, but declared that the court was generally too dark, and alterations were made in the summer vacation to improve the lighting.[8]

[1] Soane Museum 53/3/39 (approved 18 January 1825), 46, 47. The battlements were those constructed during Soane's restoration of the Hall.
[2] Soane Museum 53/3/29 (26 May 1824), the draft for a printed letter to the Chancellor of the Exchequer.
[3] *A brief Statement*, p. 7; Soane, *Designs for Public Improvements*, pl. 11. This is the design illustrated by Wilton-Ely, *op. cit.*, fig. 20b (No. 80).
[4] Soane Museum N.L.C., select committee papers 26, statement by Cook. This varies from Soane's account in *A brief Statement*, p. 11, which avoids any mention of Cook and presents Cust's proceedings as even more surreptitious than they were.
[5] Soane Mus. 53/2/41, 42, 44, 55; 53/3/1, 4, 9. The Vice-Chancellor's Court was temporarily occupied by that of Common Pleas (*Civil Architecture*, p. 4).   [6] Soane Museum N.L.C., 133, 137.
[7] *A brief Statement*, pp. 11–12.   [8] Soane Museum N.L.C. 151, 159, 162, 203, 205; 53/5/7, 16.

Alterations were also made in the Chancery Court, taking the passage next the Hall into the court by the formation of a great arch.[1] Soane was faced with further complaints and demands, for, as the Surveyor General put it, 'every one expects to be accommodated in Westminster Hall, in the same manner as in their own Houses'.[2] Most of these complaints were in fact due to lack of space resulting from the setting back of the front.[3] The care with which Soane attempted to meet the reasonable requirements of the lawyers is shown by his construction of models of the King's Bench with the alterations proposed.[4]

There still remained certain works to be executed: the alteration of the centre of the old Stone Building to accommodate the Common Pleas records, and the completion of the restoration of the adjoining Hall, whose interior now demanded attention. Soane thought that the unexpended portion of the vote of £100,000 plus that of £8612 for the committee's alterations, making some £12,000 in all, would be available and would nearly cover the cost.[5] But this view was not accepted by a hard-pressed Treasury. Work on the courts was effectively finished by the end of 1827: they had cost nearly £100,000.[6]

In February 1829 Soane submitted two designs to provide additional accommodation for the Court of King's Bench, as well as space for the records which were still in Westminster Hall.[7] He envisaged the construction of a Gothic building to the east of the Hall corresponding to the Courts on the west, on which side the portion demolished by the select committee would have been reinstated (cf. Pl. 41B).[8] His estimate was £21,000 for the east wing and £13,000 for the west, which, deducting the balance he calculated on the votes, left some £23,000 to be provided.[9] Nothing came of this project, despite a campaign by the Metropolitan Law Society, supported by such friendly M.P.s as Ewart. The Treasury refused to bear the expense of altering an already-altered building.[10]

All too soon the inadequacy of the site for all the superior courts of law and equity was revealed. When the Master of the Rolls decided to move to Westminster in 1831, the King's Bench record rooms had to be fitted up as a court for him.[11] The need for a new Bankruptcy Court in 1834 was met by a decision to convert the old Tally Office. It was the disposal of the latter's contents which led to the burning down of the Houses of Parliament.[12] The Law Courts, like the Hall, survived the fire. The courts of equity found additional accommodation in Lincoln's Inn; but wooden courts for two additional vice-chancellors were put up by Barry in New Palace Yard in 1845.[13]

---

[1] Soane Museum N.L.C. 216, 218 (Cook's reports, September 1826). £2100 were expended in the second half of 1826, presumably on alterations (Works 5/109). Stroud, *The Architecture of Sir John Soane* (1961) pl. 207, shows the court before the alterations: Summerson, *Sir John Soane* (1952) pl. 58, after.

[2] Soane Museum N.L.C. 222 (30 October 1826).

[3] Works 1/14, pp. 257. 265–6, 320–4; 1/15, 38–9.

[4] Soane Museum N.L.C. 234; Wilton-Ely, *op. cit.*, nos. 79, 80. See also Works 4/28, pp. 47, 110, 433, 437.

[5] Works 1/15, pp. 132–3, 2 March 1827.

[6] Works 5/108–111. In the autumn of 1828 another £200 were spent; in addition credit was given during the building for old materials valued at some £2400.

[7] Works 1/17, p. 168 (14 February 1829).   [8] Soane Museum 53/6/1 and 7; 53/3/19, 20.

[9] Works 1/17, pp. 187 (28 February 1829), 189 (2 March 1829).

[10] Soane Museum corr. 2, xi, C. 18–46. Soane told Col. Davies, M.P., that he himself was prepared to pay for alterations, evidently those calculated at £13,000 (*ibid.* 26, 28 May 1829).

[11] Works 4/31, pp. 75, 248; 12/49/5, ff. 23–4.   [12] Crest 25/39, No. 3702; Works 11/26/5; see p. 532.

[13] Works 2/4, pp. 337 (estimate £1831), 355; 12/49/5, ff. 32, 43. These wooden buildings were demolished in 1851 for the construction of a new entrance to the House of Commons.

Before Soane's courts had been in use a dozen years, need for new ones had become a topic of discussion in legal circles, and as overcrowding grew and offices and judges' chambers were scattered almost at random over London, so the campaign for new law courts gathered strength. In 1842 Barry made designs for a building in the Grecian style to stand in Lincoln's Inn Fields, but the proposal foundered in Parliament. After a series of false starts, enabling legislation was passed in 1865, and steps were taken towards the erection of a great legal complex in the Strand.[1] The New Law Courts designed by G. E. Street were completed in 1883, and Soane's courts were demolished soon afterwards.

3. The House of Lords and Old Palace Yard

In 1789 the architects' report on Westminster Palace stated that 'the House of Lords, Princes Chamber and Painted Chamber, are Buildings of great Antiquity, in many Parts defective, and have been altered and repaired so very much . . . that though they may stand many Years, are incapable of useful Repair and Improvement; and [of their] Cellars . . . only One is secured by Arches from the Communication of Fire. All Buildings East of the House of Lords are in so bad a State, that many of them are in immediate Danger of falling down, and are therefore unoccupied and shut up; and the others would cost more to repair than re-build them. The Building West of the House of Lords, containing the Entrance thereto, and the Staircase and Committee Room, is a substantial modern Building; and the other Buildings adjoining, comprising the Passages, Black Rod and Privy Seal Rooms, are in part built with Timber, liable to rapid Decay, and Accidents from Fire; and the Remainder extremely old and ruinous'.[2] It is the piecemeal alteration and replacement of these buildings, together with the opening up of Old Palace Yard, which constitutes the principal theme in the architectural history of Westminster Palace between the 1790s and the 1820s.

Soane had been working on various schemes for a great senate house ever since his days in the office of George Dance. While in Rome in 1779 he produced at least one scheme 'without regard to expense, or limits as to space, in the gay morning of youthful fancy'.[3] With his appointment in 1790 as Clerk of the Works at St. James's, Whitehall and Westminster his ambition must have seemed appreciably nearer fulfilment. In 1789 he had done no more than join in the condemnation of Westminster Palace as dangerous and combustible. But in the autumn of 1792 Chambers was officially asked to 'consider whether something could not be contrived to temper the air of the House of Lords'; and if not whether 'the Court of Requests might not be fitted up as the House of Lords, and the air therein tempered'.[4] The cheaper course

[1] See M. H. Port, 'The New Law Courts Competition 1866–7', *Architectural History* xi (1968) and John Summerson, *Victorian Architecture: Four Studies in Evaluation* (Columbia, 1970), chap. iv. It was perhaps overcrowding that caused Dr. D. B. Reid to be called in to ventilate the Common Pleas in 1841; his system proving inefficacious, the Treasury in 1850 adopted Gurney's plan (Works 1/34, pp. 340, 388–90; 1/35, pp. 301, 306; 1/36, pp. 180, 193).   [2] *Commons Jnls.* xliv (1788–9), pp. 548–9.
[3] J. Soane, *Three Designs for the Two Houses of Parliament* (1835), p. 71; *Lectures on Architecture by Sir John Soane* (1929), ed. A. T. Bolton, pl. 49.   [4] Works 4/17, 26 October 1792.

was taken, under Soane's direction as Clerk of the Works. The ventilation in the Lords' Chamber was improved, and the cost came to less than £500.[1] But more elaborate plans were in the air. In August 1793 Soane was asked to supply plans of Westminster Palace to the following architects with a view to their submitting designs for reconstruction: Holland, Groves jnr., Mylne, White, Samuel and James Wyatt, S. P. Cockerell, Brettingham, James Adam, Dance, Jupp and Johnson.[2] Little seems to have come of this. For in the following year it was Soane alone who was asked by a House of Lords committee to consider schemes for improving their accommodation.[3] This decision represented a personal blow to Chambers. In July 1794 he was compelled, by Treasury directive, to supply plans and drawings of Westminster Palace to Soane, an architect he had 'disciplined' for negligence only a few months previously.[4] Between June 1794 and February 1795 Soane's office was 'almost wholly occupied . . . in the combination and construction of plans [and] . . . estimates'. These were shown to the Lord Chancellor (Loughborough), Lord Grenville, the Prince of Wales, the Dukes of York, Clarence, Gloucester and Leeds, the Marquesses of Buckingham, Lansdowne and Abercorn, the Earls of Hardwicke and Carnarvon and Lord Gwydir, the deputy Lord Great Chamberlain.[5] At first Soane seems to have toyed with a Gothic design.[6] But his final scheme (Pl. 51B) eventually consisted of an imposing neo-classical edifice with two principal façades, one facing west, the other overlooking the Thames, and both sporting terminal domes and giant Corinthian colonnades. 'The new House of Lords was to be situated to the South of the Painted Chamber, and the new House of Commons to the North of St. Stephen's Chapel. The Painted Chamber was to be reinstated, as near as possible, in its ancient character. The modern alterations in St. Stephen's Chapel were to be removed, and that superb Structure restored to its ancient magnificence, as a church for the use of Members of both Houses of Parliament'.[7] Soane estimated that the scheme would cost £124,600 and take five years to complete.[8] George III examined the

[1] Works 4/17, 9 November, 7 December, 28 December 1792; Works 4/18, f. 20, 7 June 1793 and f. 31, 16 August 1793. For a cross section (1808) showing a ventilator in the roof of the House of Lords cf. R.I.B.A. Drawings Collection J 7/37; for heating arrangements ('a plan of the Stoke Hole under the Robing Room') cf. R.I.B.A. J 7/45.

[2] J. Soane, *A Statement of Facts respecting the Designs of a New House of Lords* (1799), p. 7. The plan prepared by Soane was presumably MPE 327. See also A. T. Bolton, *Architecture of Robert and James Adam* i (1922), p. 129.

[3] Soane, *Statement op. cit.*, p. 11; *Lords Jnls.* xl (1794–6) p. 253, 23 and 30 June 1794. Soane also executed minor alterations to the heating system of the House of Lords at this time. Groves informed Chambers: 'It is with the fullest conviction that Mr. Soane is acting under the highest authority that I nevertheless conceive it is my duty to acquaint you workmen are introduced by him into the Chamber of the House of Lords. What they are about or may be the extent of their operations I have yet to learn. I shall not fail to communicate it to you as soon as I am acquainted with it' (Works 1/5, f. 131, 11 August 1794).

[4] Works 4/18, f. 81, 25 July 1794; Works 6/22, f. 165, 24 July 1794. For Chambers' dispute with Soane see above pp. 43–5. In answer to Soane's request for all available plans Chambers replied: 'We have found a set of Plans of a House of Lords and Commons designed I believe by Mr. Kent, but I can hear of none designed by Mr. Benson, nor any so far back as King James. As these plans are loose I have ordered an inventory to be taken . . ., and on Monday next you may see them in the Office . . . and take copys . . . it being contrary to the established practice to deliver any drawing out of the Office' (Works 1/5, f. 129, 25 July 1794).

[5] Soane, *Statement, op. cit.*, p. 14.

[6] 'The idea was relinquished chiefly in consideration of the unfitness of that manner of building for the purposes of public speaking, and the enormous expense and great delay that would have attended its execution'. (Soane, *Three Designs, loc. cit.*).

[7] Soane, *Designs for Public and Private Buildings* (1828), pp. 19–20; *Lectures on Architecture by Sir John Soane* (1929), ed. A. T. Bolton, plate 50.

[8] Soane, *Statement, op. cit.*, p. 28. His private estimate to Dance was four years (Farington, p. 278, 3 January 1795).

plans at Windsor and gave his 'entire approbation, and was particularly pleased with the idea of appropriating the two great rooms [Court of Requests and Painted Chamber] leading into the proposed new House of Lords as a depôt for Sculpture, commemorating great public actions . . . [and] with the idea of the Great Scala Regia, to be decorated with Statues of our Kings'.[1]

Two factors defeated Soane's ambition: the economic situation and the influence of James Wyatt. 'On my return from Windsor', Soane recalled, 'Lord Grenville . . . again examined the plans, and expressed his approval', but 'regretted that in the present state of the country it would be inexpedient to commence the works. This postponement was . . . a severe disappointment . . . but . . . I [later] composed another design [for the Law Courts], embodying the former, in which the same line of front, next New Palace Yard, is preserved as traced out by the buildings erected in the time of Queen Elizabeth'.[2] In December 1798 and January 1799 Soane's final designs, as exhibited at the Royal Academy, were twice submitted to Grenville. Grenville passed them on to Wyatt. And on 11 July 1799 Soane read in the *Morning Herald* that his rival had been given the job of 'making plans for a new House of Lords'.[3] Since his succession to the Surveyor Generalship three years previously, Wyatt's influence over George III had continued to increase. Thanks to the indefatigable Farington, we can trace the steps by which Wyatt ousted Soane: parliamentary opinion moved in favour of a cheaper plan in the Gothic style;[4] George III was conditioned to reject Soane's idiosyncratic manner;[5] and Dundas poisoned Pitt's mind against Soane.[6] One final card probably clinched the intrigue: the influence of Lady Grenville. Anne Pitt, daughter of Thomas Pitt, first Baron Camelford, had married the future Prime Minister in 1792. She seems to have shared some of her husband's scholarly interests and little of his *hauteur*.[7] Bibliophile, horticulturalist and amateur architect, Lady Grenville had already encountered the Wyatts at Cleveland Row, St. James's, and was to do so again at Dropmore.[8] By 1805 it was

---

[1] Soane, *Statement, op. cit.*, p. 15. The idea of a national gallery of sculpture and painting, either at Westminster or on the future Trafalgar Square site, was much discussed at this time and contemplated by Wyatt as well as Soane. Cf. Farington, pp. 1401, 1442–3, 1445, 1449, 1451–2, 1461, 1469, December 1798–January 1799.

[2] Soane, *Three Designs, op. cit.*, p. 72. [3] Soane, *Statement, op. cit.*, pp. 19–20.

[4] 'Wyatt told us it is now in agitation to have all the new buildings including the House of Lords of Gothic Architecture, so as to make a whole mass of that kind of building. The King and others approve this idea' (Farington, p. 1591, 5 July 1799).

[5] 'Wyatt said the King had observed on [Soane's] designs [for a new House of Lords] and on Soane's gates in the [Green] Park and knew his peculiarities well. If so there can be no apprehension of future works being trusted to a bad taste' (*ibid.* p. 1443, 20 January 1799).

[6] Wyatt had originally feared Pitt's partiality towards Soane: 'Soane being employed by Mr. Pitt might be an awkward circumstance especially as he had undertaken to make designs for a House of Lords &c. which were exhibited' (*ibid.*). But by getting involved in a dispute with Dundas over the Nabob of Arcot's debts, Soane lost not only the Westminster project to Wyatt but the East India Company Surveyorship to Holland: 'Soane has lost all footing with Pitt, who wishes to see the lines on the "Modern Goth" ' (*ibid.* p. 1569, 29 May 1799). See also *ibid.* p. 1536, 23 April 1799 and p. 1625, 27 August 1799.

[7] Thomas Grenville refers to her as a 'dear little wife'. She interested herself in Grenville's celebrated library and in his appointment as Chancellor of Oxford University (Hist. MSS. Comm. *Fortescue MSS.* ix, 1915, pp. 394, 412–4).

[8] Samuel Wyatt designed the Grenville house in Cleveland Row in 1794 (Colvin, *Dictionary* p. 735). He was probably also responsible for Dropmore, Bucks. (G. Nares, 'Dropmore', *Country Life* cxx, 1956, pp. 772–5, 834–5, 1011, 1068). Lady Grenville designed the garden buildings at Dropmore and advised Auckland upon the layout of his estate at Eden Farm, near Beckenham, Kent (*Fortescue MSS.* ix, 1915, p. 164, 1 January 1808; *Architectural Mag.* i, 1834, p. 121).

common gossip that she actually had a hand in Wyatt's design.[1] This must remain a matter for speculation. But she may well have been instrumental in securing him the commission. Anyway, the result was a mortifying set-back for Soane. It was only by petitioning the House of Lords and by submitting the testimony of his clerk, H. H. Seward, that Soane managed to secure some compensation for his considerable labour and expense.[2] In May 1799 the Lord Great Chamberlain informed the Lord Chamberlain of the King's wish that James Wyatt should prepare 'plans for rendering the Buildings of the House of Lords more commodious'.[3]

Whatever long-term plans Wyatt may have had in mind, additional accommodation was made urgently necessary by the Union with Ireland in 1800. This was met by moving the Lords from the constricted Parliament Chamber to the larger Court of Requests. Intended at first as a temporary expedient, this arrangement lasted in fact until the fire of 1834. The Parliament Chamber and the Painted Chamber were fitted up as conference rooms. A new royal entrance and new offices for the House of Lords were erected in Old Palace Yard, fronting the Court of Requests. The Speaker's House was rebuilt and extended into St. Stephen's Cloister. And the House of Commons found itself in an enlarged and refurbished version of St. Stephen's Chapel. Finally, the whole complex of buildings was given a semblance of coherence by the addition of two battlemented façades, one overlooking the Thames, the other facing Old Palace Yard.

These changes in the topography of Westminster Palace formed part of a much wider movement, the redevelopment of Westminster. The Westminster Improvements Commission traced its origin from two earlier bodies: the parliamentary committee set up in 1792 to improve the approaches to both Houses of Parliament;[4] and the Commission appointed in 1777, and strengthened in 1799 and 1804, for the purpose of erecting a new Westminster Sessions House.[5] Seven Acts of Parliament between 1800 and 1814 consolidated its membership and fortified its powers of land purchase.[6] The nine Commissioners represented most of the interests involved: the Speaker of the House of Commons, the Lord Chief Baron of the Exchequer, the Dean of Westminster, the High Steward of Westminster, the Clerk of the Parliaments,

[1] *Universal Mag.* vi (1805), p. 376; *Gent's. Mag.* 1807, pt. i, p. 324; *The Times* 23 October 1806, p. 3. 'The plaster screen of the House of Lords, . . . when first finished, was so ridiculously like a Lancashire cotton factory, that a charitable Peeress, in 1806, had to supply a central tower front, studded with oriel windows and a Saintly niche, garnished with Watch Turrets, round and square, crenellated but inaccessible (unless by monkeys) from their slender size' (*History and Description of Westminster Hall*, printed for G. Dreton, 1829, pp. 23–4).
[2] Soane submitted 217 drawings, and spent £445 15s. 10½d. in paying 'surveyors, measurers and draughtsmen' (Soane's petition, 23 February 1801, Liverpool Papers clxvii, 1800–8, B.M. Add. MS. 38356, ff. 66–21). In 1801 Farington noted that 'Soane has had no remuneration for his laborious designs' (Farington, p. 1935, 29 March 1801). In Carter's words, Wyatt, 'superior in patronage to our Grecian', defeated Soane who 'dutifully bowed the head, and retired with all his documents' (*Gent's. Mag.* 1807, pt. i, pp. 133–5; see also 1807, pt. ii, p. 800). When the Marquess of Buckingham, Grenville's relative, sent his apologies, Soane endorsed the letter 'So much for Buckingham!' (A. T. Bolton, *Portrait of Sir John Soane*, 1927, p. 89, 27 July 1800). For later correspondence see *ibid.* pp. 161, 164.
[3] L.C. 1/39, 4 May 1799; Farington, p. 1569, 29 May 1799. For Soane's retrospective account of his defeat cf. Works 11/28/10, Soane to Stephenson, 1816.
[4] *Commons Jnls.* xlviii (1792–3), pp. 848–58; 'Public Income and Expenditure', *Parl. Pap.* 1868–9, xxxv, pp. 181–95.
[5] 18 G. III *c.* 72; 39 G. III *c.* 82; 44 G. III *c.* 6.
[6] 41 G. III *c.* 13; 44 G. III *c.* 6; 45 G. III *c.* 115; 46 G. III *c.* 89; 48 G. III *c.* 137; 50 G. III *c.* 119; 54 G. III *c.* 154. For meetings of the Commissioners cf. *Fortescue MSS.* viii (1912), pp. 143, 145, 181, 204; ix (1915), pp. 142, 194; x (1927), pp. 6, 181, 240.

the Lord Chancellor, the Lord Great Chamberlain, and two professed politicians, Earl Spencer and Lord Auckland. The improvements effected followed the precedents set in opening up Parliament Street during the early 1750s. Over a period of twelve years the Commissioners opened up the Westminster precinct, demolishing large numbers of houses and isolating the major monuments, Westminster Hall, Westminster Abbey and St. Margaret's Church. In the process both New and Old Palace Yard were stripped of post-medieval work; a riverside embankment was formed to the east of Old Palace Yard; the west side of St. Margaret's Street, including the Ordnance Office, was demolished; the area surrounding St. Margaret's churchyard, Broad Sanctuary and the Westminster Sessions House was cleared and redeveloped; and the buildings between St. Margaret's Street, Bridge Street and King Street were replaced by a 'Garden Square', so that travellers across Westminster Bridge were faced with 'a striking and magnificent view of Westminster Abbey in its whole extent from Henry VII's Chapel eastward, to the great Towers of its western entrance'. The amount of public money involved must have been well over £250,000.[1] As Surveyor to the Commissioners, Groves supervised the complicated process of planning, valuation, purchase and compensation. In this he was assisted by five other surveyors: Spiller, Montagu, Robinson, Inwood and Thompson. Land purchased by the Commissioners became Crown property; and in 1826, when the Commission was wound up, all responsibility was formally transferred to the Commissioners of Woods, Forests and Land Revenues.[2] At the same time St. Margaret's Church and Westminster Abbey were undergoing extensive restoration, in part at public expense. Between 1799 and 1813 the House of Commons contributed a total of £14,280 to successive restorations of the church officially attended by its Members,[3] while even larger sums were voted for the repair of the Abbey Church. In 1807 Wyatt informed a parliamentary committee that apart from five parliamentary grants of £4000 received between 1733 and 1738, the Dean and Chapter had spent £28,749 on maintenance and restoration during the previous twenty years; for the period 1800–19 the figure was £39,120 3s. 3d., excluding parliamentary grants for the restoration of Henry VII's Chapel.[4] These figures presumably excluded

---

[1] £228,497 had been spent by 1810 (*Gent's. Mag.* 1810, pt. ii, p. 280; *The Times* 3 September 1810, p. 3). For topographical plans and accounts cf. *The Times* 27 July 1811, p. 3, and 6 September 1814, p. 3; *Monthly Mag.* xxvii (1809), p. 144; 'Report . . . of Commissioners for . . . improvement of streets . . . near to Westminster Hall', *Parl. Pap.* 1808, iii, p. 1, *et seq.* 1810, ii, 83 *et seq.*; 1810–11, ii, p. 225 *et seq.*; 1813–14, iii, p. 151 *et seq.*; 'Report . . . on Improvements in Westminster', *Parl. Pap.* 1809, iii, p. 381; 'Report . . . respecting Improvements in Westminster', *Parl. Pap.* 1810, ii, pp. 158–9. For views of Westminster before and after improvement see J. T. Smith, *Antiquities of Westminster* (1807), scene from roof of Banqueting House; B.M. King's Maps, xxiv 4g (1753) and 4 q. 1. (1812). For rumours of further improvements cf. *The Times* 11 August 1806, p. 2 and 29 December 1807, p. 3.
[2] 7 G. IV *c.* 78. For details of improvement schemes 1809–10 cf. 'Report . . . of Commissioners for . . . improvements of streets . . . near to Westminster Hall', *Parl. Pap.* 1810, ii, pp. 114, 117, 120–22, 124–6, 1810–11, ii, p. 343 and 1813–14, ii, p. 82; Farington, p. 4206, 21 April 1809 and p. 4218, 3 May 1809.
[3] H. F. Westlake, *St. Margaret, Westminster* (1914), p. 115; 'Public Income and Expenditure'. *Parl. Pap.* 1868–9, xxxv, pp. 181–95; 'Report . . . of Commissioners for . . . improvement of Streets . . . near to Westminster Hall', *Parl. Pap.* 1808, iii, pp. 75–7; *The Times* 20 September 1808, p. 3. Carter was particularly critical of S. P. Cockerell's restoration (1799–1802): 'from what ancient or modern buildings, either in Rome, France, Egypt, China, Lapland or elsewhere [were] the peculiar parts . . . selected?' (*Gent's. Mag.* 1802, pt. i, p. 128 and 1806, pt. i, p. 496).
[4] 'Report on the Westminster Abbey Petition', *Parl. Pap.* 1807, ii, p. 27; Liverpool Papers xcvii (1820), B.M. Add. MS. 38286, f. 268.

expenditure on ceremonial occasions, such as the Handel Commemoration in 1784 when Wyatt designed the Abbey's elaborate seating arrangements, including a Gothick royal box.[1] As surveyor of the Abbey's fabric he was responsible for two concurrent tasks of restoration on each of which he drew five per cent commission. He directed the repair of the central lantern following a fire in 1803, a work costing £3848.[2] Under the supervision of the Parliamentary Committee for Superintending Public Monuments, commonly known as the Committee of Taste, he was also responsible for the restoration of Henry VII's Chapel.[3] Begun in 1793, this renewal of the fabric was completed by the mason Gayfere in 1822 at a cost of more than £42,000.[4] Despite all Carter's fears and alarms the work was meticulously executed, not in stucco, but in Bath stone and Kentish rag, and represents something of a milestone in the revival of Gothic techniques.[5]

Of all these Westminster Improvements it was Wyatt's House of Lords buildings in Old Palace Yard which were the most conspicuous and attracted the greatest volume of criticism (Pl. 37B). Writing to Grenville in June 1806, Auckland remarked: 'Wyatt's plan for the *façade* of the House of Lords is on my table to be shown to you; it looks well on paper, and the expense will be very inconsiderable'.[6] But Auckland knew more about politics than he did about architecture. Wyatt's brick and stucco battlements, his cast-iron window-frames and lath and plaster oriels, were an unqualified disaster. Dance refused to have anything to do with the project and remarked on its 'beastly . . . bad taste'.[7] The intention was to give Westminster's 'shapeless pile of buildings a regular form . . . worthy of the first people, and the greatest assemblies in the world', with 'the utmost degree of convenience and access . . . and the finest possible picturesque architectural effect'.[8] But the finished product had 'more the appearance of a *cotton-mill*, than of offices for the public business of the Nation'.[9] Carter was not alone in denouncing the 'cement influenza' of 'that august pile of brick bats and stucco', with its debased windows 'constructed by the united efforts of the Smith, Bricklayer, and Compo-ist . . . Judicious triumvirate of modern

[1] *European Mag.* v (1784), pp. 323–5; Publishers' MSS. i (1703–1810), B.M. Add. MS. 38728, ff. 73b, 81b.
[2] For Carter's account of the fire cf. *Gent's. Mag.* 1803, pt. ii, pp. 636, 1128. See also *The Times* 11 July 1803, p. 3, 16 July 1803, p. 3, 20 August 1803, p. 3, 25 August 1803, p. 3, 28 March 1805, p. 3; J. P. Neale and E. W. Brayley, *History and Antiquities of Westminster Abbey* (1856), p. 10.
[3] The committee consisted of Sir Charles Long, the Marquesses of Stafford and Buckingham, Lord Aberdeen, Sir George Beaumont, Thomas Hope, Payne Knight, Flaxman, Banks and Westmacott. For details cf. *The Times* 9 September 1807, p. 3, 20 September 1808, p. 3 and 11 December 1810, p. 3; E. Carpenter (ed.), *A House of Kings, the History of Westminster Abbey* (1966), pp. 233–6.
[4] Wyatt's first estimate was £25,200 ('Report on the Westminster Abbey Petition', *Parl. Pap.* 1807, ii, p. 27). For later figures see *Gent's. Mag.* 1811, pt. ii, p. 82 and 1812, pt. i, p. 166; 'Report . . . on the Westminster Abbey Petition', *Parl. Pap.* 1810, ii, pp. 131–44; 'Report . . . on . . . the Repair of King Henry VII's Chapel', *Parl. Pap.* 1810–11, ii, pp. 209–10; 'Inquiry into . . . the Office of Works', *Parl. Pap.* 1812–13, v, pp. 424–5; For the payment of masons cf. T. 29/129, f. 240, 17 May 1814 and T. 29/133, f. 921, 28 February 1815.
[5] For a detailed account of the restoration see L. N. Cottingham, *Plans etc. of Henry VII's Chapel*, 2 vols. 1822–9. For Carter on Henry VII's Chapel see *Gent's. Mag.* 1803–1813, *passim*. For views of the exterior during (1811) and after restoration (1813) see R. Ackermann and W. Combe, *History of the Abbey Church of St. Peter's Westminster*, ii (1812), pl. 4 and Hawkins' measured drawings, B.M. King's Maps xxiv, 4bb.
[6] *Fortescue MSS.* viii (1912), p. 178, 5 June 1806.
[7] Farington adds laconically, 'very sad' (Farington, pp. 3524, 3548, 3737, 1806–7). Works 29/19 (1808) is Wyatt's design for the south front (old Prince's Chamber, House of Lords, etc.).
[8] *The Times*, 23 July 1805, p. 3, 26 July 1805, p. 2, 23 October 1806, p. 3; *Universal Mag.* vi (1805), p. 468.
[9] *Gent's. Mag.* 1806, pt. ii, p. 1127. It was supposed to be 'in the pointed style of Henry VIII . . . in a new lime, which is moulded and congeals instantaneously' (D. Hughson, *Walks Through London*, 1817, p. 230). For working drawings by Adam Lee (?) cf. R.I.B.A. Drawings Collection J 7/43–44.

art!'[1] Soane scornfully recalled how Wyatt's Gothic scheme had been expected to 'produce a burst of Architectural Scenery . . . unparalleled in any part of Europe'.[2] Samuel Lysons explained the stucco in terms of profit: 'it is said Wyatt has a *concern in the Patent* and therefore urges the use of it'.[3] Indeed it was the financial side of the project which aroused the greatest resentment. Whatever Groves's powers as executant, whatever the supervisory capacity of the Westminster Commissioners, and whatever Lady Grenville's shadowy role, Wyatt must bear the chief burden of blame. To the Office of Works it was merely one of those 'extra-Civil List' embarrassments subsequently investigated by Saunders.

   Wyatt's idea of re-facing Westminster to 'create a piece of scenery', was justifiable only as a wartime economy. But between 1800 and 1812 parliamentary grants towards his reconstruction of the Houses of Parliament and Speaker's House totalled £180,229 12s. 4d. On all of this Wyatt or his executors received five per cent commission.[4] By 1815 the final bill must have been over £200,000.[5] And throughout this operation the Treasury accountants found Wyatt more than a little elusive. At one point in 1806 the Treasury discovered that work had been abandoned because of Wyatt's failure to file the imprest necessary to turn a parliamentary grant into an issue. The Treasury therefore imprested the money direct to Groves, 'to mark the sense they entertain of Mr. Wyatt's neglect in leaving the money granted by Parliament so long unapplied, and . . . also to ensure a quick and short payment to all the persons who have suffered by this delay'.[6] When three years later the House of Commons demanded a statement of accounts and no answer was received, Huskisson informed Wyatt, on behalf of the Treasury, of his 'very great surprize'. Craig was directed to send out a reminder 'by express', and four copies were prepared: 'three of them to as many places in the Country where Mr. Wyatt was likely to be, and the fourth . . . to his town residence'. On this occasion, however, Craig took the opportunity to remind Huskisson that 'the Houses of Parliament are not under the cognizance of this Office either as to receiving orders for repairs and alterations, expenditure in consequence thereof, or of any monies received or paid'.[7] But when Wyatt pleaded ignorance of certain items of expenditure, the Treasury took a very firm line, expressing 'great surprize that any works whatever at the Houses of Parliament or Speaker's House should have been undertaken without his authority' at a time when he was expected to observe 'the utmost economy'. He was strongly urged to put his house in order, 'it being the intention of my Lords to mark such conduct in a very special manner'.[8]

   The result certainly bore no relation to the expenditure. Responsibility for the new House of Lords with its 'piazza or Gothic arcade embattled on the top'[9] was

---

   [1] 'As the Bricklayers elevate themselves, the *Compoists* follow, hand to fist, trowel to trowel, rubbish to rubbish. And thus the work is perfected; smeared over at the same time with the Housepainter's brush, by way of *pencilling* mock masonry joints, and mock tints of perforated stone-work' (*Gent's. Mag.* 1806, pt. i, p. 422; pt. ii, p. 1005; 1807, pt i, pp. 432, 534; 1809, pt. ii, pp. 827–9).
   [2] *Lectures on Architecture by Sir John Soane* (1929) ed. Bolton, p. 104.
   [3] Farington, p. 3514, 1 December 1806.   [4] T. 29/127, ff. 762–3, 15 February 1814.
   [5] E.g. Bacon's bills as Groves's successor, T. 29/130, f. 319, 22 July 1814.
   [6] T. 29/86, f. 506, 8 May 1806.   [7] Works 6/24, f. 196, 29 June 1808, and f. 246, 2 February 1809.
   [8] T. 29/102, f. 257, 29 August 1809.
   [9] *The Times* 23 October 1806, p. 3; 19 September 1807, p. 3.

denied by every leading politician in or out of office. Lord Auckland and Speaker Abbot were undoubtedly cognizant of the design. But Auckland unfairly blamed the Office of Works and Abbot dared to claim that 'nobody knew anything of the plan till the building exhibited itself in its present form'.[1] During a debate in 1808 Whitbread, Sheridan and Rose called for immediate demolition. But the advice of Petty, Long and Perceval carried the day: they 'preferred the eyesore of the present building to the expense of pulling it down'. William Windham likened Wyatt's design to a prison; 'Mad Jack' Fuller compared it to a gentlemen's lavatory.[2]

These criticisms were directed against the exterior of Wyatt's House of Lords, for there was little or no interior work to criticise. His object had been to Gothicise Old Palace Yard, and in the process supply additional entrances and office accommodation. When the Lords moved into the Court of Requests, they took over what was basically an 18th-century interior, with plaster-vaulted ceiling and clerestory lunettes (Pl. 35A). Externally such classical features were carefully screened from view by Wyatt's battlemented offices. It was not long before the great fire revealed the flimsiness of this Gothic disguise.[3] Indeed, as Soane remarked in his general survey report of 1816, Wyatt's alterations to adapt the Court of Requests for the 'temporary' House of Lords had been made chiefly with combustible materials; the much dilapidated wooden royal entrance was covered only with oil cloth, and a temporary platform was required when the sovereign went in state. No more money should be spent on these buildings, he thought, than would suffice to keep them in repair.[4] In his next report, dated 30 January 1817, Soane stated: 'some considerable repairs must necessarily be done, to several parts of the House of Lords . . . in the course of the present year to preserve them in a proper state of safety'.[5] The principal alteration of this period was the provision of a new room for the journals, at a cost of some £380.[6] In December 1817, Black Rod asked for a door to be made from the House into the Long Gallery, and for new doors like those at the Peers' Entrance to be provided for the bishops, who complained that their apartments were much exposed to the cold.[7] Soane's general survey of September–October 1817 reported, among some minor defects, that the dormer windows of the old House of Lords needed repair,[8] and the year following the roof of the Painted Chamber was found to require immediate attention.[9] A new roof and ceiling were constructed in 1819 at an estimated cost of £1276.[10]

When George IV at last ascended the throne, he called for immediate alterations in the House. These included a new throne and an alteration to the steps; making a new door at the lower end of the House to correspond with the upper one; widening the entrance of the Painted Chamber; and replacing broken marble slabs in the

---

[1] *Parl. Debates* xi (1808), pp. 863–5. [2] *Ibid.*
[3] 'It was', wrote A. W. N. Pugin, who witnessed the fire in person, 'a glorious sight to see [Wyatt's] composition mullions and cement pinnacles and battlements flying and cracking, while his two and sixpenny turrets were smoking like so many manufactory chimneys till the heat shivered them into a thousand pieces. The old walls stood triumphantly amidst the scene of ruin while brick walls, framed sashes, slate roofs fell faster than a pack of cards . . .' (unpublished letter in possession of the Editor).
[4] Soane Mus. corr. 2, xii, G. 1, no. 2. [5] Works 1/7, pp. 468–9. [6] Works 1/7, p. 160; 5/107.
[7] Works 1/8, p. 349. [8] Soane Mus. corr. xii, G. 1, no. 5. [9] *Ibid.* no. 6.
[10] Works 1/107; 11/28/10, f. 20. The specification provided for a 'new plaster ceiling and cornice with ornaments to match the old'.

2M

fireplaces with cast-iron ground ones.[1] At the end of 1820 he directed that the throne should be fixed to the wall and another step made.[2]

The proceedings in connection with the King's divorce necessitated considerable works in the House: a temporary gallery was erected at a cost of £921 11s. 3d., and works to improve the ventilation cost nearly £600 more. Not ordered by the House until 31 July, the works were completed in about a fortnight by Soane's 'daily and almost constant attention'.[3] The galleries were admired by the Peers as 'highly ornamental'.[4]

It was not, however, until 1822 that Soane received his chance to leave his characteristic imprint on the Lords. His work here was carried out in four stages: a new royal entrance and stair (1822–3); a royal gallery, with committee rooms and offices (1823–4); a library (1824–6); and more committee rooms, this time in Gothic, towards the river (1826–7). When George IV approved Soane's designs for the new Law Courts, he told the Surveyor General that the royal entrance must be improved, and commanded that Soane should prepare a plan.[5] Approved by Lord Liverpool and Sir Charles Long, the plan was then submitted to the King.[6] Soane estimated for works on different scales of expense, and on 21 April a project costing £8000 was selected as the first stage of a larger scheme.[7] Sir Herbert Taylor and the Duke of York were among those consulted before work was begun on 10 August.[8] The carriage-entrance was Perpendicular in style, with fan-vaulting (Pl. 42B), but the staircase rising from it in three flights to the Prince's Chamber (with the later ante-room and royal gallery) was a characteristic Soanic exercise in the grand manner (Pl. 44).[9] A. T. Bolton remarked:

> The Scala Regia was, perhaps, the best of all Soane's designs, and even if it was possibly somewhat gaudy in detail, . . . it is undoubtedly a fine and characteristic composition. The very haste and urgency of the work may have been beneficial to an architect of Soane's temperament. He was precluded from the hesitation and fluctuation which too often clouded and marred in execution his first instinctive conception. . . . . Though in part, as in the Royal Gallery . . . Soane was only reproducing what he had done before on a smaller scale in some of the Bank interiors, yet as a whole this latest of his works was a fresh and spontaneous creation.[10]

Summerson however justly stresses the retrospective character of these works, remarking that 'Soane returned to a neo-classicism, which, although mixed with

[1] Works 1/10, pp. 46, 53, 56; 4/24, p. 122; *Journal of Mrs. Arbuthnot 1820–32*, ed. F. Bamford and the Duke of Wellington, i, p. 15.   [2] Works 1/10, p. 268.
[3] Soane Mus. corr. 2, xi, D, f. 1; plan and elevations, 51/3/55, 56, 63.
[4] *Ibid.* corr. 2, xi, D, f. 2, Stephenson to Soane, 22 August 1820. These galleries were re-erected as occasion required, see below.   [5] Soane Mus. New Law Courts corr. f. 51, Stephenson to Soane, 28 February 1822.
[6] Soane Mus. 14/7/72, a sketch of the Scala Regia, dated February 1822, is marked 'Submitted to His Majesty by Col. Stephenson and approved'.
[7] Soane Mus. corr. 2, xi, H. 1; 14/7/84 (a plan dated July 1822, including the later buildings of the royal approach 'to be decorated with Paintings, Bassi-relievi and statues to perpetuate the glorious achievements of British valour'); Works 1/10, p. 124.
[8] Soane Mus. corr. 2, xi, H. 1. Soane proposed three lines for the Scala Regia, at differing angles to the Prince's Chamber, Soane Mus. 14/7/58v, 80, 81. This last is inscribed 'This plan was submitted to the Earl of Liverpool on the 21st July 1822 at Fife House & approved & directed to be carried into execution as soon as poss.'
[9] The doorway through which the transition was made, Gothic on one side, classical on the other, is shewn in Soane Mus. 51/2/13, dated December 1823.
[10] A. T. Bolton, *The Works of Sir John Soane* (1924), pp. 112–13.

"Soanic" details, is no advance on his very earliest studies'.[1] Undoubtedly they draw heavily on the designs for new Houses of Parliament of 1794–6,[2] though they have become more linear and more mannered.[3] The Gothic *porte cochère,* set in a curved extension to Wyatt's arcade, was an after-thought. Soane later wrote, 'In the Design for the New Carriage Entrance approved by His MAJESTY, the Entrance into the Circular Corridor was under a temporary awning. The Building, as it now is, was an alteration made during the progress of the Works'.[4] A schedule of drawings contains the entry, 'no. 6. Plan of the New Entrance, shewing the Porte Cochère added to the original design by command of His Majesty communicated by Coll. Stephenson after the Entrance was far advanced (September 1822)'.[5] This feature presented some difficulty, and the King required it to be 'more enriched'; in November and December there were further consultations about it with Long, Stephenson and the Duke of York.[6] By 5 February 1823 the new entrance, including the grand stair and carriage porch, was complete.[7]

In July 1823 the more extensive works of the royal approach to the House, consisting of an ante-room, roughly square in plan, at the head of the staircase, and a three-bay gallery connecting it with the Painted Chamber, came under consideration, and a Lords' Committee directed them to be modified by the addition of rooms for records, journals and committees.[8] These were to be placed to the east of the royal gallery, enclosing a court.[9] For this larger plan Soane submitted an estimate of £21,800 which was forthwith approved by the Lords and immediately authorised. Within a week the rooms were cleared ready for work to begin. The demolition of the old House of Lords and the Prince's Chamber was a necessary preliminary, and met with some criticism in the Commons.[10] The building, begun on 3 October 1823, was carried on with great speed, and the Royal Gallery was completed by 3 February 1824, £3550 being charged in the accounts of the third quarter of 1823, no less than £13,595 in the last quarter, and in the following two quarters £5786 and £1596 successively, a total of some £24,527.[11] Soane blamed the excess over his estimate on having to take the foundations four feet deeper, put a new floor in the Painted Chamber, and use hot air apparatus for drying plaster.[12] In March 1824 Soane announced that 'The approach for His Majesty to the House of Lords is completed,

---

[1] John Summerson, *Sir John Soane* (1952), p. 20.

[2] Cf. Soane Mus. Folio D. 67–71, sketches of interiors of 1794–6 designs.

[3] The Royal Approach is described by Britton and Pugin, *Public Buildings of London,* ed. W. H. Leeds i (1838), pp. 269–73.

[4] *Designs for Public Improvements* (1827).   [5] Soane Mus. corr. 2, xi, H. 1.   [6] *Ibid.*

[7] Works 1/12, p. 388. The cost was £7232 1s. 2d., the principal contractors being W. and J. Whitehead (bricklayer) at 5% under Office prices, T. Martyr (carpenter and joiner) 12½% under, T. Grundy (mason), 12½% under, and May and Morritt (smith) 12½% under. These were selected from a limited competition of three in each trade (Soane Mus. corr. 2, xi, H. 1.).

[8] Soane Mus. corr. 2, xi, H. 1.   [9] Soane Mus. 14/7/85.

[10] As did the new buildings erected in their place. See debate of 1 March 1824, *Parl. Deb.* x, 623 ff., initiated by Bankes who attacked the 'strange and anomalous building . . . a thing of such strange and absurd proportions that it was impossible to look at it without a feeling of disgust'. Grey Bennett wanted to know who was the architect in order to know whom to avoid, Tennyson spoke of 'modern additions of mongrel architecture'; and Sir J. Mackintosh thought it 'almost sacrilegious' to pull down the buildings where 'the constitution of this country was finally settled'.

[11] Soane Mus. New Law Courts (select committee) papers, f. 31; Works 1/12, pp. 388–90; 5/108. Further works to the end of 1824 bring to total to some £25,441.

[12] Soane Mus. corr, 2, xi, D. 22.

522

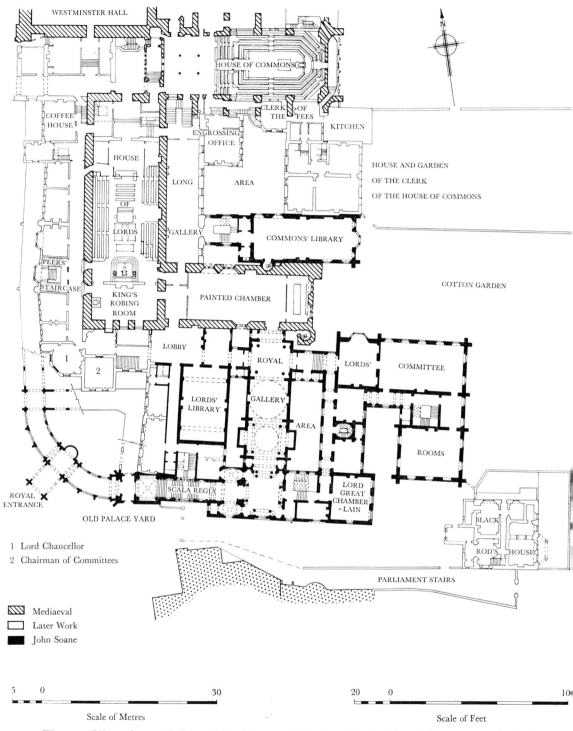

Fig. 21. Westminster Palace: The House of Lords with the Royal Entrance rebuilt by Soane: from a plan by Thomas Chawner made in 1834 (Works 29/20).

and the Record Rooms, Committee Rooms, and Journal Rooms are in a progressive state of finishing and will be completed in the course of three Months'.[1] The work was carried on by night as well as by day; and the contractors, having tendered at very low prices, being thus 'called on to proceed with extraordinary expedition . . . thereby sustained considerable loss'.[2]

In July, as a result of a select committee's report, the Treasury called for plans for an additional committee room and a record room on the level of the Painted Chamber. In November instructions were given that the new rooms should be begun immediately, to be ready for the meeting of Parliament about two months later; but temporary committee rooms had to be provided, as well as a new bishops' entrance at basement level.[3] The new committee room, which occupied the space between the Scala Regia and the Painted Chamber, was separated from the royal gallery by a narrow court, and was of similar classical character. The works did not proceed far before the reassembly of Parliament, and only some £1700 were expended between October 1824 and April 1825.[4] In July of that year a select committee inspected both the works in progress and the plans prepared for further accommodation,[5] reporting that

> The new Committee Room which was directed to be built, and is now in Progress, will be more conveniently appropriated to the Purpose of keeping the Journals and other Books belonging to the House; that the Plan now submitted to them by Mr. Soane [for building towards the river] will afford Two Committee Rooms of large Dimensions, and a Third of a smaller Size; and that the upper and lower Stories of the same Building will provide a sufficient Space for the placing and safe keeping of the increasing Mass of Records, Papers, and Writings, which cannot now for want of Room be deposited in the Parliament Office, and at the same time, for the necessary Accommodation of some of the Officers and Servants of the House.[6]

Major works were resumed in July 1825, once again having to be fitted in during the recess—no wonder Soane lamented, 'it is the rage at present to do things so quick. It ought to take a considerable time'.[7] From July 1825 to March 1826 work on the committee room now designated as a library and on its connected rooms cost more than £9000.[8] Soane stated on 27 April 1826 that the Lords' rooms were in use, though not quite finished; the Library was fitted up 'in a temporary way for their Lordships to see what my idea of the accommodation there would be'.[9] In May the Lords decided to fit up the Library (Pl. 45) and a fireproof room for printed papers,

[1] Soane Mus. corr. 2, xi, D, 8. Soane gave the workmen a dinner, for which he was reprimanded by Stephenson, see Bolton, *Portrait*, pp. 370–1.

[2] Soane Mus. corr. 2, xi, H. 4; D. 17. Martyr claimed some £500 extra, and Palmer a similar sum on a bill of £2145. Croggon, who supplied the scagliola, had asked 5 guineas for Ionic capitals measuring 1' 6", but remarked that if 4½ guineas were all Soane could allow, he would accept that, being 'willing to make a Sacrifice rather than lose the order' (*ibid.* H. 5).

[3] Works 1/13, pp. 65, 66, 68; *Lords' Jnls.* lvi (1824), p. 468.   [4] Works 5/109.

[5] Soane Mus. 51/3 contains plans and elevations for a large Gothic block eastwards of the existing buildings, see nos. 2, 4–6, 17–19, 29, 30.   [6] *Parl. Pap. H.L.* 1825 (206).

[7] *Parl. Pap.* 1826 (403), iii, p. 10.

[8] Works 5/109. Expenditure in the following three quarters brought the total to £10,150.

[9] *Parl. Pap.* 1826 (403), iii, p. 9.

but rejected Soane's proposals of 1825 for a large block in favour of a smaller one providing two large rooms, estimated at £14,000.[1]

This new block, to the east of and connected with that erected next to the Royal Gallery in 1824, was Gothic to correspond with the Painted Chamber and Soane's own Commons' library. Once begun, work went on rapidly, £3244 being spent in the July–October quarter of 1826.[2] Over the next nine months expenditure ran steadily at an average of about £1650 a quarter, but in the summer recess of 1827 the work was hastened almost to its conclusion, at a cost of £7600.[3] After that only comparatively trifling works remained to be done.[4] Soane, when asked for a final estimate, replied that he could not pledge himself to any precise sum: the grant for 1827 was founded on his estimate of £14,000, 'in which was not included certain works that I had calculated would have been paid for out of the usual annual grant to the Office of Works for Public Buildings; but which it appears could not be so provided for, the annual grant having been so much reduced'; namely, fitting up the library, the fireproof repository and a room in the Stone (i.e. the Jewel) Tower, at a cost of £2200. Additional works would bring his estimates to £16,543 10s.; and the total cost would probably amount to £2000 more, including Treasury and Exchequer fees (£500) and extra foundations.[5] Another £4500 would therefore be required for the House of Lords.

In 1828 the Parliament Office was transferred to the new buildings, and the house in Abingdon Street given up, separate access being provided to the Jewel Tower in which the Rolls of Parliament were still stored.[6] At the end of the 1828 session the Peers called for better heating and ventilation of their own chamber; Stephenson reported however that the machinery was sufficient if properly managed.[7] For the battles over the Great Reform Bill they resolved in September 1831 that the galleries put up in 1820 should be re-erected; but in October called for those to be removed, and a new one built across the lower end of the House on a plan of Smirke's. The old central fireplace, too, was to make way for additional benches.[8] Some alarm was felt in the summer of 1832 because of a sinking of the library roof.[9]

[1] *Parl. Pap. H.L.* 1826–7 (58); Works 1/14, pp. 280–1, 285. Soane reduced the extent of his new block on the east, but proposed extending Black Rod's house westward (Soane Mus. 51/3/7, 8); but the extension was not built (*ibid*. nos. 9–12, the last being signed and dated by Soane, 21 March 1827). It is not clear when this house became Black Rod's; an Office of Works report of 1828 refers to his apartments having been taken down in consequence of 'the late alterations' (Works 12/62/9).

[2] Works 5/109; see also Works 5/126 and 127. Among the alterations, a bay window was thrown out from the room nearest the Painted Chamber, part of Soane's additions in 1823–4.

[3] *Ibid.* The largest sum, £5013, was paid to Martyr for the third quarter of 1827, but included work on the Abingdon Street Journals Office, and alterations and fittings costing nearly £900 to Soane's earlier building adjoining the new block to the west. Joinery for the new building included 16 'wainscot Gothic molded cased frames in 2 compartments with plain molded pointed heads to 2 upper Do on both faces of frame with eye and corner spandrills on inside face, eye only on outside face', with double hung sashes, 6 ft. 11 ins. by 5 ft. 5½ ins. at £20 17s. each; and 15 similar frames 'in four compartments with tracery cinquefoil heads, points and eyes, to 2 upper compts—large eye perforated compartment and side perforated spandrills filled in with sashes; solid corner spandrills on inside face', and open framed transoms for sashes to pass through, 8 ft. 9 ins. by 5ft. 5 ins. at £41 8s. each (Works 5/127, f. 288ᵛ.).

[4] Works 5/109, 110. About £1300 were spent in the five quarters, October 1827 to the end of 1828, and of this £591 appears to be for converting a room under the Painted Chamber for the Journal Office (Soane Mus. corr. 2, xi, E. 2).

[5] Works 1/16, pp. 72–4, 112 ff.   [6] Works 11/28/12, ff. 4–6; *Parl. Pap. H.L.* 1828 (181), 1829 (105).
[7] Works 4/29, p. 108; 1/17, p. 150; *Parl. Pap. H.L.* 1828 (181).
[8] Works 1/19, pp. 17, 20; *Parl. Pap. H.L.* 1831 (126); *Lords' Jnls.* lxiii (1831), pp. 1003, 1100. The new north gallery cost £1990 (Works 5/111).   [9] Works 1/20, p. 65; Soane Mus. corr. 2, xi, G. 1.

The Lords, like the Commons, soon found that their new facilities were inadequate. Smirke was asked in 1834 for an estimate for enlarging the library. His plan was approved at £3700, but the tender for works on the library accepted from Grissell and Peto at the end of the Session amounted to only £1300 (and extras at 7½ per cent below the schedule price), presumably for the carcass.[1] Most of Soane's work escaped the fire that devastated the Lords' House itself, and Smirke's estimate of £1500 for enlarging the library was authorised in August 1837; by October the works were in an advanced state.[2] The bulk of these buildings appears to have been demolished in the autumn of 1851.[3]

4. THE HOUSE OF COMMONS

During the second half of the eighteenth century St. Stephen's Chapel was criticised as the home of the House of Commons on three grounds: lack of space, inefficient ventilation and inadequate protection against fire. The architects' report of 1789 noted that surrounding buildings, such as the house and offices of the Auditor of the Exchequer, tended 'to expose the Whole to a general Conflagration'. But the report also added that 'the House of Commons, though an ancient Building, has been so continuously repaired, that it is in a State to remain a great many Years'.[4]

In April 1791 a Commons committee was set up to deal with the perennial problem of heating and ventilation. Henry Holland was the architect employed, and the cost was ultimately covered by a special parliamentary grant. But the Office of Works was responsible for the execution of the work, much to Chambers' annoyance. When Holland demanded plans and sections of St. Stephen's Chapel, its vaults, roof, parapet and turrets, Chambers replied: 'there are no such designs in the Office, nor, were there, has [the Surveyor General] any person to copy them, as both the draughtsman and Clerk Itinerant were suppressed at the reform [of 1782]. Mr. Soane, Clerk of the Works at Westminster, has directions to attend the Committee . . . and be ready to give Mr. Holland every assistance his leisure may permit after discharging the duties of his place in His Majesty's service'.[5] The cost of 'bettering and regulating the air and its temperature' eventually came to £1349 19s. 10½d. Out of this sum Holland received £105 5s. 0d. and Soane £26 5s. 0d. The contractors were Messrs. Bramah, Moyser, White and Walker and their supplies included ventilators in the roof, a Patent Air Machine and 'two new large pieces of foliage for ventilation in the ceiling'.[6]

For the next alteration to the House of Commons the Office of Works was in no way responsible. By the Act of Union one hundred new Irish M.P.s were added to the House of Commons. James Wyatt was given the task of extending the chamber, as part of the general reconstruction of Westminster Palace. Work began

---

[1] Works 1/21, pp. 58, 73, 134; 2/1, pp. 153, 154.   [2] Works 1/22, pp. 315, 327, 352.
[3] Works 11/10/2, ff. 76, 81.   [4] *Commons Jnls.* xliv (1788–9), pp. 548–9.
[5] Works 1/5, f. 100, 6–8 April 1791. See also Works 4/17, 29 April 1791, 25 May 1791.
[6] Works 1/5, f. 101, 20 April and f. 102, 22 April 1791; Works 4/17, 22 June 1792; T. 29/65, f. 113, 11 November 1792 and f. 290, 20 January 1793.

on the Commons in August 1800 and finished soon after the opening of the first Imperial Parliament in January 1801.[1] During the winter months the oak wainscoting covering the walls was removed, revealing medieval wall-paintings 'as fresh and vivid as if they could only boast a twelvemonth's date'. During Wyatt's absence these were carefully recorded by J. T. Smith; after Wyatt's return the paintings were recorded once more on behalf of the Society of Antiquaries by Richard Smirke.[2] Then the walls were cut back to make way for additional benches, thus destroying the paintings. In Carter's words, the wall-paintings had been destroyed merely for the sake of adding 'a bench, one poor solitary bench run in between the opening of each window'.[3] Apart from John Carter, most contemporary commentators seem to have been more worried by the reduction of the Strangers' Gallery than by this piece of wanton vandalism.[4] It was only after Wyatt's death that his desecration of St. Stephen's was generally condemned.[5] Having altered the interior of St. Stephen's Chapel, Wyatt next proceeded to transform the exterior in accordance with his over-all Gothick plan. In 1805–6 Wren's round-arched windows at the east end were given a spurious fourteenth-century finish with Gothic tracery tricked out in brick and stucco (Pl. 36).[6]

Wyatt's work did not suffice for long; and after his death Soane at last had his chance to make a substantial impact on the Houses of Parliament, though this never extended to the complete rebuilding he had envisaged. Within a year of the buildings being placed in his charge, he had drawn up a report in which he revenged himself on the late Surveyor General. Few of the defects pointed out in the architects' report of 1789 had, he declared, been remedied: Wyatt's alterations were insubstantial. 'To restore St. Stephen's chapel to its original splendour and thereby render it suitable to be used as a chapel for the Members of both Houses of Parliament, with a new House of Lords on one side, and a new House of Commons on the other . . . are important objects humbly offered for consideration'.[7]

Even the mere keeping in repair of this heterogeneous collection of buildings required a considerable expenditure, averaging about £3360 annually from April 1815 to April 1832.[8] In addition, special repairs were undertaken: Hatsell, the Clerk of the House of Commons since 1768, who had not executed his duties in person since 1797, remained in possession of his house in Cotton Garden, which was repaired in the autumn of 1816 at a cost of some £362. The house of the Clerk Assistant, John Henry Ley, in the Stone Building, was also repaired at the same time for over £200.[9]

[1] *Gent's. Mag.* 1800, pt. ii, p. 998; *The Times* 20 August 1800, p. 3, 17 January 1801, p. 2.

[2] *The Times* 16 October 1800, p. 3; J. T. Smith, *Antiquities of Westminster* (1807); J. Topham, J. Carter, Sir H. C. Englefield and R. Smirke, *Some Account of the Collegiate Chapel of St. Stephen, Westminster* (1795–1811); H. M. Colvin, 'Views of the Old Palace of Westminster' *Architectural History* ix (1966), pp. 25–7.

[3] *Gent's. Mag.* 1807, pt. ii, pp. 799–800.

[4] *The Times* 6 March 1800, p. 3, 21 January 1801, p. 3; M. Hastings, *Parliament House* (1950), pp. 110, 111, 115.

[5] E.g. E. W. Brayley and J. Britton, *The Ancient Palace and Late Houses of Parliament at Westminster* (1836), pp. 400–401, 455–6.

[6] Compare Colvin, 'Palace of Westminster', *op. cit.*, plates 93 and 94. For Carter's detailed criticism cf. *Gent's. Mag.* 1806, pt. i, pp. 495–6; 1807, pt. i, pp. 531–4. For a plan and section of the staircase to the House of Commons, probably by Adam Lee, dated 17 September 1811, cf. R.I.B.A. Drawings Collection J 7/38.

[7] Works 11/28/10; Soane Mus. corr. 2, xii, G. 1, no. 2.

[8] Works 5/107–111: Houses of Parliament (excluding Speaker's house). The quarterly figures given in these accounts evidently include some expenditure on alterations, which is not distinguished; the parliamentary votes for specific works are additional.   [9] Works 5/107.

Further repairs were made to Ley's house a year later. In 1820 Hatsell died, and Ley moved into his house, succeeding him as Clerk of the House of Commons. Over £450 were then spent on his new residence.[1] Late in 1821 nearly £500 more were spent on the 'official houses'[2] and two years later more than £900 on the 'Clerks in Parliament's Houses', i.e. those of Sir George Rose and Mr. Cowper. These works appear to have been brought to a conclusion with the £75 5s. 4d. charged in the accounts for the third quarter of 1824 for the Clerk of the House of Commons' [i.e. Ley's] house. No wonder he was so reluctant to give up his residence.[3]

This refusal impeded a project to meet the pressing needs of the Commons for additional offices and committee rooms. The gradual but relentless increase in parliamentary business made the problem chronic. In 1815 new presses for the printed journals costing nearly £1000 provided relief for a period.[4] In 1818, committee room 3, occupied for several years by S. R. Gunnell, a committee clerk and parliamentary agent to the Irish secretary, was taken over for the growing library of the House, formerly kept at the Journal Warehouse in Abingdon Street.[5] By 1820 pressure was evidently being felt on committee rooms.[6] The growth of general parliamentary business and especially of private business (i.e. such matters as paving and lighting, docks, canal and turnpike bills), which meant heavy pressure on committee rooms,[7] led in 1824 to the appointment of a select committee. In its second report[8] this committee drew attention to the lack of suitable committee rooms: of the ten available, excluding the smoking room and the Long Gallery, three on the west side (i.e. probably nos. 12, 13 and 14, on St. Margaret's Street) were so exposed to the noise of the street as to be scarcely suitable for business. So many committees, on both public and private business, were contending for the rooms available that some were obliged to sit in the body of the House.

In the following session a select committee on committee rooms and printed papers heard evidence from Soane and others.[9] Although another committee room had been made available,[10] the situation was deteriorating: on one occasion four public and 30 private bill committees had met on the same day, 19 being appointed to meet in the same room. Not only the Chamber itself, but even the Court of Exchequer had been pressed into service, as well as the Long Gallery and Members' waiting rooms. Six of the committee rooms were too small for contentious private business involving many parties. Ten more rooms were needed urgently. The library, too, was inadequate, and could not take the sessional papers of another two sessions. The committee therefore recommended that a new library should be built on the site of the court bounded by the Thames, the Long Gallery, the Painted Chamber and

---

[1] Works 5/108.   [2] This may refer to residences of the Serjeant at Arms or Black Rod.
[3] See O. C. Williams, 'The Topography of the Old House of Commons' (1953, D. of E. Library).
[4] Works 5/107.   [5] *Parl. Pap.* 1826 (403), iii, p. 49.
[6] See Soane Mus. corr. 2, xii, J, f. 22, 6 November 1820 for Stephenson's proposal for using rooms in Ley's former house.
[7] Not only was there a considerable increase just at this time in the number of bills, but they were of a more important character, with more M.P.s discussing them for longer periods.
[8] *Parl. Pap.* 1824 (468), vi.
[9] *Parl. Pap.* 1825 (496), v.
[10] The smoking room had become committee room no. 3 as the dimensions given in the committee's report show (*Parl. Pap.* 1825 (496), v, p. 19).

the House, which Soane declared to be 'the only spot on which the plan can be carried into effect'.

> Plans [stated the report, 28 June 1825] have been prepared under the inspection of Your Committee by the officers of the Board of Works, affording ample space for the public offices belonging to the House in a basement and entresol Story, and for the Library, Librarian's apartment, Committee and Witnesses Rooms, in the entresol and upper parts of the Building.

This involved the removal of Ley's house,[1] and the committee suggested that a new residence should be built for him between the north entrance of Westminster Hall and the river. It would also be necessary to remove the Clerk of the Fees' Office. Soane promised that apartments to replace them could be completed before the next session. The existing library and rooms 6 and 7 over committee rooms 1 and 2 (above the Speaker's Gallery), currently used to store papers of the Vote Office, could then be returned to the use of the House, the Vote Office being provided with accommodation in the basement of the new building. Although stressing the need for despatch, the committee was careful to emphasize also the need for solidity of construction, and making the new building fireproof. It was to be designed with reference to 'the site and character of the adjoining buildings'—for this was just after the committee of taste had condemned the north side of Soane's Law Courts— and with a general view to subsequent additions or improvements.

The building that Soane designed in accordance with the committee's instructions would have filled the east side of the space between the House of Commons and the Painted Chamber.[2] The east end of the Painted Chamber would have been reconstructed to match Wyatt's east end of St. Stephen's, and the Commons' needs would have been supplied in a building linking the two, of four storeys disguised externally as three. On the other side of the Painted Chamber Soane planned new committee rooms for the House of Lords in a three-storey block. But as so often at this period, rights granted by letters patent presented an obstacle to improvement: Ley refused to give up his newly repaired house. All that could be done for the moment was to convert into temporary committee rooms two rooms over Bellamy's old dining room in Old Palace Yard.[3] Meanwhile the Speaker had urged the provision of a new record room because of the danger of fire to that in use, which appears to have been over a coffee room; and the Labourer in Trust's rooms under the Long Gallery were pointed out as suitable.[4]

Ley however put forward a compromise: a sketch plan in the Soane Museum, as the late Orlo Williams pointed out,[5] is annotated by Soane: 'a design by Mr. Ley to remove all the inconveniences of the plan ordered to be carried into execution immediately by the House of Coms—The Lords of the Treas[ury] etc. Recd. of Mr. Ley 9 Aug: 1825 in the Speakers House'.[6] This left Ley's house intact, using the entire space between it and the Painted Chamber for a library on a level with the floor of the Long Gallery and supported on pillars or arches so as to leave open the communication between Westminster Hall and Cotton Garden. It was to be lighted 'in a beautiful manner from the cieling—and by windows to the river' (at its narrow

---

[1] This had been proposed in some plans drawn up by the Clerk of Works, Adam Lee, in June 1821 (Soane Mus. 51/4/5–7).   [2] Soane Mus. 51/5/24–30, June 1825.   [3] *Parl. Pap.* 1826 (403), iii, 39–66.   [4] Works 1/13, pp. 80–2, 3 and 4 December 1824.   [5] *Op. cit.*, p. 24.   [6] Soane Mus. 51/4/1.

east end). A further reason for making this building of a single storey was that the offices adjoining the Long Gallery might have light and air.[1] The library might be made as long or short from east to west as might be thought desirable. This sketch also provided for a new room for the Clerk of the Fees, to be erected over the single-storey kitchen of Ley's house, and for alternative enlargements of the offices in the corner formed by the Long Gallery and the Commons' Lobby.[2] When another committee on committee rooms sat in April 1826, Soane produced designs based on this proposal, but for a block of three or four storeys.[3]

The committee of 1826 preferred Soane's original proposals, but reluctantly accepted the inevitable, and sanctioned a reduced plan 'much less complete' for library and five committee rooms (based on Ley's proposal)which could be completed by the beginning of the 1827 session. The rooms over committee rooms 1 and 2 had already been cleared of papers. The inconvenience of the nearer room on either floor being a passage to the further room would be removed by the construction of an outer passage,[4] and Col. Trench's suggestion that the level of the floors of rooms 15 and 16 in the Stone Building should be altered, and access by the stair improved, was to be carried out.[5]

With agreement thus secured, the work was put in train forthwith. The Treasury directed Stephenson on 14 July 1826 to send an estimate and begin the work on the library and five committee rooms, to be completed by 1 February 1827. Soane's estimate was £10,560.[6] The new block comprised on the ground floor an entrance and stair, and two rooms, one semi-circular, the other rectangular (committee room 22). The library itself formed a room 55 ft. by 23 ft., and 13 ft. 6 ins. high, on the first floor, with an eastern oriel, Gothic fenestration and a low vault (Pl. 45). Creevey thought it 'the best and most agreeable room in London'.[7] On two floors above were four committee rooms, nos. 18–21.[8] The work appears to have been executed to schedule, but there was an excess over the estimate, which Soane ascribed to having had to carry the foundations 4 ft. 6 ins. deeper in order to underpin Ley's house and the Painted Chamber.[9] Nor had the library been fitted up. The Treasury had thought that this was included in the original estimate, but Soane stated that with the fitting up and finishing there would be a probable excess of £2500.[10] Over £1000 were spent in the third quarter of 1827, and some £600 in the first quarter of 1828.[11]

[1] Williams was clearly mistaken in thinking this building could have contained committee rooms also (*op. cit.* p. 24).
[2] None of these projects was carried out. Cf. Works 29/20–27, plans of the Houses of Parliament drawn in August 1834; and proposals similar to Soane's by B. Wyatt (*Parl. Pap.* 1831, iv, pp. 166–7).
[3] Soane Mus. 51/5/7, 14–17, 35; *Parl. Pap.* 1826 (403), iii.
[4] An angled corridor giving access to the further room without passing through the nearer was constructed (Works 29/20).
[5] *Parl. Pap.* 1826 (403), iii, p. 18. A comparison of Soane's plans of May 1826 with Works 29/20 (1834) shows that the stairs were modified, and the height of room 14 was reduced from 18′ 6″ to 14′ 10″.
[6] Works 1/14, p. 297.　　[7] *Creevey's Life and Times*, ed. J. Gore (1937), p. 347.
[8] Soane Mus. 51/5/11–13, 19–21.
[9] Works 1/15, p. 427, 21 September 1827. The cost was £11,888 10s. 2d. (Works 5/109, 110).
[10] Works 1/15, pp. 352, 444; 1/16, p. 112. The additional foundations accounted for £939 6s. 2d.; fittings to the library £450; and fees on the issues for the works £350 (Works 1/16, pp. 72–4).
[11] Works 5/109, 110. The total cost, as far as these works are separately distinguished in the accounts, was £13,789 8s. 11d. The principal contractors were the carpenters and joiners, Martyr, who received £4528 7s. 4d. for the last quarter of 1826; Whitehead, bricklayer (£2151 17s. 6d.); Grundy, mason (£1295 19s. 8d.); and Palmer and Son, plasterers (£909 16s. 2d. and in the following quarter £197 18s. 4d.) (Works 5/126 and 127).

Even so ample an increase of space did not for long meet the needs of the library, and a select committee again investigated the matter in 1830.[1] It recommended that committee rooms 18 and 19 on the floor above should be added to the library, and that the Augmentations Office in Stone Building should be moved upstairs in order to provide space for additional committee rooms. Soane accordingly prepared a design for removing part of the library ceiling, leaving the rest as a gallery reached by a stair, and for the conversions in the Stone Building, at an estimate of £3000.[2] These alterations were not executed and a committee further considered the position in 1832, when Smirke was called in. He proposed lengthening the library towards the east at a cost of £4000;[3] but, although no other rooms were then available for committees, the easiest way was taken and rooms 18 and 19 were used for library purposes, neither Soane's nor Smirke's proposals being followed. The alterations were conducted by Smirke, whose estimate of £1600 for a small spiral stair, a messenger's lobby and the fitting up of the two rooms, was forwarded by the Treasury to the Office of Works on 16 November 1832 with directions for the work to be done quickly.[4] The provision of committee rooms in the library building appears to have released some of the less satisfactory older ones for other purposes: a list supplied to the 1832 committee shows that no. 8 had become a kitchen (at the corner of the Stone Building): no. 9, on a mezzanine at the south-east corner of the Stone Building, accommodated the Chairman of Ways and Means and a store for the Journal Office; no. 10 had recently been demolished; no. 16 was used for the Poor Returns; no. 12 had lately housed the Court of Reviews; and nos. 13 and 14 had been used as equity courts.[5]

The Commons Chamber itself (Pl. 34A) underwent no significant architectural change during this period. But the perennial problem of warming and ventilation received much consideration. Works in the recess of 1816 included, as well as the relaying of the floor of the House, the erection of a partition on the stair from the Stone Lobby 'to prevent the dust rising to the upper rooms', improving the ventilation of some committee rooms, and replacing the fireplace in the House Lobby with a stove 'so as to diffuse a more regular heat generally through the House'.[6] The most obvious change was made in 1818, when an additional stair and two doors were erected to facilitate egress from the gallery for divisions.[7] Early in the following session the Marquis de Chabannes was called in to provide a system for heating and ventilating the House; he was authorised to start in March, on an estimate of £1100, the carpenter's and bricklayer's work being done by the Board's tradesmen; and he was not to receive payment until the success of his method had been demonstrated. He reported on 21 April that all was ready, but members were not satisfied with the results.[8] Expenditure amounted to £1678 4s. 4d.[9] A year later Chabannes was claiming £256 for his ventilating machine constructed by the Speaker's order, but

[1] *Parl. Pap.* 1830 (496) iv.
[2] Soane Mus. corr. 2, xi G. 2, f. 13, 18 May 1830. The estimate of £2500 is altered in pencil to £3000.
[3] *Parl. Deb.* 3rd ser. xiv, 1130, 4 August 1832; Soane Mus. 51/5/1, 4, 41.
[4] Works 2/1, p. 52.   [5] *Parl. Pap.* 1831–2, (600) v, p. 245 ff.
[6] Works 1/7, p. 197. Estimated at £784 19s. these works were executed for £780 12s. 3d. (*ibid.* p. 237; 5/107).
[7] Works 1/8, p. 524.   [8] Works 1/9, pp. 247–50, 252–4, 256, 284, 353.   [9] Works 5/107.

Fig. 22. The burning of the Houses of Parliament in 1834: from a contemporary print (Westminster City Library).

finally accepted £200.[1] In 1826 Feetham, a stove manufacturer, was consulted on the heating, and in 1829 R. Howden.[2] Any improvements in the ventilation however appear to have been negligible.

A select committee on 'the possibility of making the House of Commons more commodious and less unwholesome' which reported in October 1831, after hearing evidence from Benjamin Wyatt, Smirke and Wyatville, decided that there was no satisfactory way of enlarging the existing House and that a new one was necessary.[3] The same conclusion was drawn by a similar select committee in the 1833 session, which appended to its report designs by George Allen, George Basevi, Edward Blore, Decimus Burton, John Deering, Francis Goodwin, James Savage, John Soane, Jeffry Wyatville, Adam Lee (the former Labourer in Trust at Westminster) and three M.P.s, J. W. Croker, Rigby Wason[4] and Charles Hanbury Tracy.[5] Joseph Hume, the economical radical, who was leading the agitation for improved accommodation, found, however, that the Treasury was as unwilling to listen to his plea for expenditure as to those he made for economy.

The solution was provided by the Clerk of the Works, Richard Whibley. Instructed by Milne to destroy a great number of wooden tallies, rendered useless by the reform of accounting in 1826, Phipps, the Assistant Surveyor, consulted Whibley, who suggested burning them in the Lords' furnaces. By about 6 p.m. on 16 October 1834 the over-heated flues had begun the conflagration which swept away Wyatt's work and reduced the two chambers and the Commons' library to smouldering shells. 'Mr. Hume's motion for a new house is carried without a division', remarked a bystander.[6]

5. THE SPEAKER'S HOUSE AND PARLIAMENTARY OFFICES

Wyatt's improvements to the Houses of Parliament involved remodelling the Speaker's House and several adjoining offices which, together with St. Stephen's Chapel, made up the heterogeneous river front of Westminster Palace. His work consisted 'simply in repairing or rebuilding the Offices towards the river in an irregular Gothic manner, and finishing them in plaister'.[7] 'This', it was hoped, 'will add extremely to the effect of the Speaker's House, and give it entirely the air of a grand old dwelling, of which the House of Commons will appear to be the chapel' (Pl. 36B).[8] Besides the Speaker's House, the following were the principal parliamentary buildings which were also subject to alteration between 1782 and 1815: the Clerk Assistant's House,

[1] Works 1/10, pp. 166–8; 5/108. [2] Soane Mus. corr. 2, xi, D, 38.
[3] *Parl. Pap.* 1831 (308), iv. Benjamin Wyatt was a pet architect of that strenuous improver, Sir Frederick Trench, who vainly attempted to secure him reimbursement for his labour (T. 1/4068, 1971/32).
[4] The plans submitted by Wason were actually by the architect William Bardwell, who occupied in relation to Wason a position similar to that of Wyatt to Trench.
[5] *Parl. Pap.* 1833 (487), xii, with 22 plates. The committee also heard evidence from Sir Robert Smirke and Thomas Hopper. A further result of its activities was a detailed survey of the existing House to a large scale, now Works 29/30. The drawings made by Wyatville for this committee are in the R.I.B.A. Drawings Collection (J 7/2), those by Soane in the Soane Museum, 51/6/20–30.
[6] *The Times* 18 October 1834, p. 5. [7] *The Times* 26 July 1805, p. 2. [8] *Ibid.* 28 March 1805, p. 3.

the Serjeant at Arms' House, the Stationery Office, the Parliament Office, the Parliamentary Committee Rooms, the Journal Office and the Private Bill Office.

The reconstruction of the Speaker's House, like that of several other parliamentary buildings, was due largely to the energy and ambition of Speaker Abbot.[1] His predecessor, Addington, had been the first Speaker of the House of Commons to occupy a separate residence at Westminster. In 1794 Addington had moved into the rambling house, previously occupied by the Auditor of the Exchequer, which extended from St. Stephen's Court to the House of Commons and incorporated most of St. Stephen's Cloister.[2] During the next four years upwards of £1000 was spent on fittings and alterations.[3] At the same time a house previously occupied by Lord Bayham as Teller of the Exchequer, with an entrance in St. Stephen's Court and a garden running down to the river, was made over to the Serjeant at Arms and suitably fitted up.[4] But soon after his election in the spring of 1802 Abbot took over the Serjeant at Arms' house so that his own quarters could be rebuilt.[5] 'I represented to the Treasury', he wrote, 'the damp insecure state of the Speaker's house, in consequence of which the family part of it was pulled down . . . and new foundations laid in a manner to secure the building from any risk of damp in future'.[6] Wyatt's promise to finish work by the winter was soon forgotten, and what began as an alteration developed into a general reconstruction. It was not until January 1808 that operations were completed.[7] Though 'spacious and replete with conveniences', it had taken 'wanton and reckless alterations' to make it so. Britton and Brayley commented on Wyatt's 'insipid plastered walls, with squared holes for windows', and noted that St. Stephen's Cloister had been 'fitted up for the appendages of a kitchen, for servants' offices, and the most menial purposes'; its central area was 'occupied by a large shed-like kitchen; part of the exquisite lower Oratory was converted into a scullery; and chimneys, sinks, and closets were cut into, or patched up against its florid windows and tracery. The upper Cloister was divided into numerous small apartments and offices'.[8]

These alterations were all financed by parliamentary grants, and it was not until 1815 that the Speaker's house was formally placed in the care of the Office of Works. Thereafter little was done for a number of years. Annual expenditure on maintenance averaged £346 from 1816 to 1832.[9] In 1816 all that was required were repairs to the wash house and laundry totalling nearly £500.[10] When preparations were under way for the coronation of George IV a new fire engine was provided.[11] In June 1824

---

[1] For Abbot's contribution to the development of parliamentary procedures and the preservation of parliamentary records, see *Gent's. Mag.* 1829, pt. i, pp. 463–6.

[2] Works 6/22, f. 162, 20 June 1794; Works 4/18, 20 June 1794. For Groves's plan (1794), now in the Soane Museum, cf. O. C. Williams, Topography of the Old House of Commons (1953, photostat in D. of E. Library), pl. 21.   [3] Works 4/18, ff. 76, 203, 238, 255, 301; T. 29/69, ff. 161–2, 384, 396.

[4] Works 4/18, ff. 74–5, 6–13 June 1794; Works 6/22, f. 162, 13 June 1794. The estimate was £1985.

[5] Coleman, the Serjeant at Arms, was given £300 p.a. compensation (Works 4/19, 15 April 1802). For alterations to quarters occupied by Clementson, Deputy Serjeant at Arms, including the Commons' Prison House, cf. Works 4/16, 1 August 1783; Works 6/20, ff. 23–4, 29–30, 151–2; Works 1/5, ff. 115, 117; T. 29/66, f. 62; Works 5/72 (1783); T. 29/52, ff. 442, 480; T. 29/54, ff. 186, 243.

[6] *Diary of Charles Abbot, Lord Colchester,* ed. Lord Colchester i (1861), p. 285.

[7] *Ibid.* i, p. 412, ii, p. 137.

[8] E. W. Brayley and J. Britton, *The Ancient Palace at Westminster* (1836), pp. 455–6.

[9] Works 5/107–111.   [10] Works 1/7, p. 150; Works 5/107.

[11] Works 5/108. £507 11s. 9d. were charged in the accounts for the quarter ending 5 January 1821 for fire engine etc.

Soane drew up a list of alterations required by the Speaker, including a new stair from the principal floor to the upper rooms, separating the best stair from the library by a lobby, taking down and reversing the stair from the dining room into the state apartments, removing the low arch on the landing, and alterations to the rooms above. Soane reported that it was impossible to form a correct estimate, but that the alterations could probably be done for £2000.[1] In the upshot they cost £2646.[2] Crocker informed Soane that the excess arose 'in pulling down the Cross partition running over the Levee Room which upon a minute examination (which could not before be got at) proved to be defective, was obliged to be taken down and a wall carried up in its stead'. Weak timbers had to be trussed with iron, and new floor framing put in.[3]

During the recess of 1826, the Speaker's kitchen was moved, involving an expense of £680.[4] No other major work is recorded before the fire of 1834, when the state dining room in the under chapel of St. Stephen's was burned, but the main body of the house suffered comparatively little damage. Smirke reported that the rooms preserved included

> three in the Attic Story, four in the Chamber Story, two on the first floor, the large Library and the private Library, besides the three Levee rooms, and on the Ground floor the private Dining room.
>
> These Rooms have received no injury from the fire and require no other repair than the refixing of some Chimney pieces hastily taken down, the repair of several doors injured in the confusion of the night, the mending of broken windows, and cleaning of the rooms and passages.[5]

Speaker Manners Sutton declared that this would suffice for his family; but he was not re-elected when the new parliament met. Speaker Abercromby did not reside in the house, which was used for the examination of entries in the Houses of Parliament competition,[6] and subsequently provided Commons' committee rooms[7] until demolished in the late summer of 1842 to make way for the new House of Commons.[8]

Like the rebuilding of the Speaker's house, major alterations to minor parliamentary offices were seldom Civil List projects before the reforms of 1815. They were only incidentally directed by Office of Works personnel and were paid for by (or repaid out of) specific parliamentary grants.[9] This was the case with the Journal Office, established in 1800 at No. 1 Abingdon Street, a house belonging to the Westminster Bridge Commissioners which had previously served as the residence of J. T. Groves, Clerk of the Works for Westminster until 1811.[10] Similarly the Private Bill

---

[1] Soane Mus. corr. 2, xi, E. 1, ff. 3, 7.　　　[2] Works 5/109.　　　[3] Soane Mus. corr. 2, xi, D. f. 15.
[4] Works 1/14, p. 409; 5/109.　　　[5] Works 11/10/2, f. 4, 28 October 1834.
[6] The Levee room was so used (Works 11/10/1, ff. 17–20).
[7] Works 2/2, p. 157. Treasury authority for converting rooms to committee rooms at Barry's estimate of £3419 2s. 11d., 25 August 1837.
[8] *Parl. Pap.* 1846 (574), xv, qq. 113, 237.　　　[9] E.g. L.C. 1/40, f. 224, 1 April 1811.
[10] Alterations cost £1281 4s. 0¼d. (Works 6/23, f. 237, 17 February 1804; Works 4/19, 22 April 1803; *Commons Jnls.* lviii, 1802–3, p. 525). See also T. 27/51, f. 528; T. 29/50, f. 145; T. 29/75, ff. 211–12, 307; Works 1/5, 23 December 1799; Works 4/16, 24 December 1779; T. 29/80, f. 486, 24 April 1783; Williams, Topography of Commons, p. 20. For additions to the Journal Office, see designs by Adam Lee, 26 March 1808, R.I.B.A. Drawings Collection J 7/36.

Office established by Abbot in 1810 at the south end of the floor over the Long Gallery;[1] and the Stationery Office in New Palace Yard, reconstructed under Groves's direction in 1799–1800.[2] The refitting of the Clerk Assistant's House followed the same administrative pattern. Until 1807 the Clerk Assistant to the House of Commons, Jeremiah Dyson, resided in St. Margaret's Street.[3] When in that year his apartments were demolished by the Improvements Commissioners he moved to a red brick house north-east of Westminster Hall, approached from New Palace Yard and backing on to St. Stephen's [Speaker's] Court.[4] This house had been fitted up in 1802 for an Usher of the Exchequer named Roberts,[5] and was refitted once more in time for Dyson's arrival.[6] This period also saw improvements to the house in Old Palace Yard belonging to Henry Cowper, Clerk of the House of Lords;[7] the rehousing of the Parliament Office in nearby Abingdon Street;[8] and some slight improvements to the Parliamentary Committee Rooms.[9]

By the beginning of the nineteenth century the dependencies of the House of Commons had expanded northwards until all available space on the east side of Westminster Hall had been occupied. But agitation for extra space in the years after 1807 did not become urgent until 1824. And nothing permanent was built on the vacant site south of the House of Commons until 1826.

6. THE CHAPTER HOUSE

The ancient Chapter House of Westminster Abbey had since the late Tudor period been used as a repository for the records of the Law Courts and the Exchequer. In

---

[1] T. 29/106, 17 July 1810; Williams, *Topography of Commons*, p. 22.

[2] Estimate £2126 (Works 6/23, ff. 62, 67, 72, 74, 79, 82, 83). See also Works 4/17, 16 December 1791, 23 December 1791, 17 August 1792; T. 29/64, ff. 301, 417; Works 4/18, ff. 186, 192, 194, 205, 284, 319, 336, 337, 348; Works 4/19, 4 April 1800.

[3] John Hatsell, Clerk of the House of Commons, retired in 1797 but lived on in his house in Cotton Garden until his death in 1820. As Deputy Clerk from 1797 onwards, John Ley (previously Clerk Assistant) also had apartments in St. Margaret's Street. Dyson remained in the same house when he succeeded Ley as Deputy Clerk in 1814. In that year Ley's apartments were inherited by his nephew J. H. Ley who became Clerk Assistant. For details of ownership see Williams, *Topography of Commons*, p. 21. For minor repairs to Hatsell's house and Ley's apartments cf. Works 1/5, f. 130; T. 29/58, f. 441; T. 29/64, f. 282; T. 29/61, f. 83; Works 6/21, 28 August 1789.

[4] For views see B.M. Crace Colln. xv, No. 85 and O. C. Williams (ed.), *Life and Letters of John Rickman* (1912), pp. 77, 123. For Bacon's plan, dated 21 February 1816, cf. Soane Museum, Drawer 35, set. 5, no. 22.

[5] Estimate, £1432 10s. 0d. (T. 29/80, ff. 105, 260); Works 4/19, 2 August 1805).

[6] Estimate, £860 (T. 27/60, 7, 12 and 25 November 1807; T. 29/92, f. 373).

[7] T. 29/66, f. 142, 16 August 1793; Works 5/84 (1795); Works 4/19, 30 May 1806; T. 29/59, f. 459; T. 29/61, f. 51; Works 5/78 (£2153 spent in 1789); T. 29/58, f. 425; Works 4/17, 29 September 1785, 12 and 19 August, 26 September 1788; T. 29/56, f. 530; Works 5/74 (1785); Works 4/18, ff. 27, 33.

[8] Works 4/18, ff. 49–50, 73 (1793–4); Works 1/5, f. 103, 30 July and 10 August 1791; T. 29/64, ff. 109, 303, 354; Works 5/82 (1793); Works 5/83 (1794); Works 4/17, 5 and 13 August 1791; 9 and 23 November, 28 December 1792; T. 29/65, f. 209.

[9] Works 4/17, 1 September 1786; *Commons Jnls.* lvii (1801–2), pp. 647–8. Four small committee rooms were fitted up in 1802 to deal with controverted elections (*The Times* 23 October 1802, p. 2). Two committee rooms were added in 1809 above the Fees Office; and some committees may have been held in a first-floor room over Alice's Coffee House. See Williams, *Topography of Commons*, p. 20. For undated designs for new committee rooms cf. R.I.B.A. Drawings Collection, J 7/39.

1751–2 the vaulting had been removed, an upper floor inserted resting on beams radiating from the central pillar, and the windows altered (Pl. 33).[1] At the recommendation of the Records Commission in 1800, Wyatt added two rooms for the office clerks, but they proved damp and unsatisfactory.[2] Complaints from George Rose and John Caley (secretary of the Records Commission) achieved little.[3] But the greatest concern of those responsible for the building was the high risk of fire. Soane, in a survey made in 1818, recommended iron doors and shutters to the record office. A number of outhouses and sheds had been built against the walls to serve the prebendal houses, and it was with the greatest difficulty that the Office of Works secured the demolition of the most dangerous.[4] In 1832 Sydney Smirke, as Office of Works Clerk, was involved in an argument with Edward Blore, as Surveyor to the Abbey, who described the encroaching buildings as 'essential appendages' to the Chapter House. The Records Commissioners were still protesting in 1836 that the kitchen of a prebendal house abutted on the record office.[5] A survey in 1846 showed that the external stonework was very decayed; but Scott's restoration was not carried out for several years after the removal of the records in 1859.[6]

7. THE PARLIAMENTARY MEWS

The problem of accommodating one's means of private transport was as acute for the early nineteenth-century Londoner as it is today. Robinson when Chancellor of the Exchequer directed the Commissioners of Woods and Forests to initiate inquiries on the need for stabling in Westminster.[7] Having done so, they decided to erect stables and coach houses, partly for official use, partly for letting to private individuals. A site was selected between Great George Street and the Abbey. A design, obtained from Decimus Burton, and approved by the Treasury, was submitted early in 1825 to the Westminster Improvements Commissioners, who required various changes.[8] The main entrance was to be moved from the south side (facing the Abbey) to the west, and replaced by a 'handsome Architectural Front, without either doors or Windows'; the space adjoining was to be laid out in an ornamental manner.[9] Burton's 'pure Doric' structure was described and illustrated by Elmes and Shepherd in their *Metropolitan Improvements* (1827–9).

---

[1] See vol. v of this *History*.

[2] Works 14/4/1, f. 4. In 1815 outstanding bills for Wyatt's works at the Chapter House amounted to some £724 (*ibid.* ff. 1–2).   [3] *Ibid.* ff. 3–7.

[4] Soane Museum, corresp. 2, xii, G(1) 6. A plan made by Soane's office (xxxv, set 5, no. 19) shows the encroachments.

[5] Works 1/11, p. 520; 1/13, pp. 345, 348; 14/4/1, ff. 8–13; *Parl. Pap.* 1837 (60) xxxiv, pt. ii, p. x.

[6] *Parl. Pap.* 1846, xliii, 7th Report of the Deputy Keeper of the Public Records, pp. 26–7, 42. Scott, *Gleanings from Westminster Abbey* (1863), p. 40, illustrates the unrestored Chapter House before the removal of the records, and Thornbury and Walford, *Old and New London* (1873–8) iii, p. 451, afterwards. See also the plan and section in the P.R.O. (MPB 2/99) and a drawing in the R.I.B.A. Drawings Collection (J 7/48).

[7] *1828 Report*, p. 128, Arbuthnot's evidence. 'Numbers', he said, 'applied for stabling and to such an extent that I thought it would be absolutely impossible to make a mews sufficiently extensive to meet the numerous applications.'

[8] Great difficulties were experienced, according to Arbuthnot, from the Dean of Westminster as well as the Improvement Commissioners, *ibid.*

[9] Works 12/63/7, ff. 1–3; Works 4/27, p. 289; 4/28, p. 236; 4/30, p. 189.

Although the building was placed under the care of the Office of Works, the Treasury directed that Burton should be appointed superintending architect, as he had been employed by the Woods and Forests to prepare the original plans.[1] His original estimate of £22,000 was increased to £34,288 for the revised design. Late in 1825 the *Gentleman's Magazine* reported that workmen were preparing the foundation, 'by lining the excavations with lime, in order to insure its dryness and durability'.[2] When it was decided to let the various sets of stabling on long leases the District Surveyor required the party walls to be carried through the roof and coped with stone. This brought the total expenditure to £35,264.[3]

The Mews were to be kept in repair by the tenants; but they were not the success that had been expected, and the appropriation of some stabling by Government reduced potential receipts. When the Ordnance sought to enlarge the Wellington Barracks in 1850, the Office of Woods suggested that the Stationery Office building in James Street might be handed over for the purpose, the Office being accommodated in the 'Royal Westminster Mews', as they were then called.[4] In September 1851 Pennethorne submitted a plan for adding a storey to the structure, and building a warehouse in the centre of the courtyard, at a cost of £9900.[5] The Treasury approved the transfer and Pennethorne's proposals, but the Comptroller of the Stationery Office decided that the warehouse should be omitted and the height of the rooms in the main building increased. Pennethorne estimated the total cost at about £20,000, and the alterations were carried out in 1853–4 by Messrs. Piper.[6] They included the removal of Burton's Doric façade and the remodelling of the principal elevations in a plain late Georgian manner. After serving its new purpose for nearly a century, the building was demolished in 1950.[7]

WHITEHALL

The Whitehall area constituted one of the heaviest responsibilities of the Office of Works, in terms of trouble and expenditure. The number and variety of buildings was considerable: the Treasury, the India Board, the Privy Council Office and the Board of Trade; the offices of the three Secretaries of State; the Downing Street accommodation of the First Lord of the Treasury and the Chancellor of the Exchequer; Whitehall Chapel, that is the Banqueting House; and the various offices and official houses in the three Scotland Yards. After 1832 reforms involving a consolidation of offices led to a number being moved to Somerset House, but the growth of official machinery was inexorable and more and more space was required for public purposes. Much office accommodation was hired, often from Crown lessees, and rent

---

[1] Works 12/63/7, f. 5, 7 October 1825.   [2] *Gent's. Mag.* 1825, ii, p. 638.
[3] *1828 Report*, pp. 129, 132. The stalls were let at 10 guineas, and carriage-standing at 12 guineas p.a. (*ibid.* p. 133).   [4] Works 1/37, pp. 15, 4 August 1851; 27–8, 5 August 1851; 41–2.
[5] Works 12/102/1, ff. 18–21. The estimate included alterations to the Mews, £2500; raising a storey, £4500; erecting colonnades on two sides of the courtyard, £500; and erecting a fireproof warehouse in the centre, £1500.
[6] *Ibid.* ff. 47–50, 53–4, 115, 131. Piper's two contracts totalled £19,884.
[7] There are photographs in the National Monuments Record and partial plans in the Public Record Office (Works 30/2886–2891).

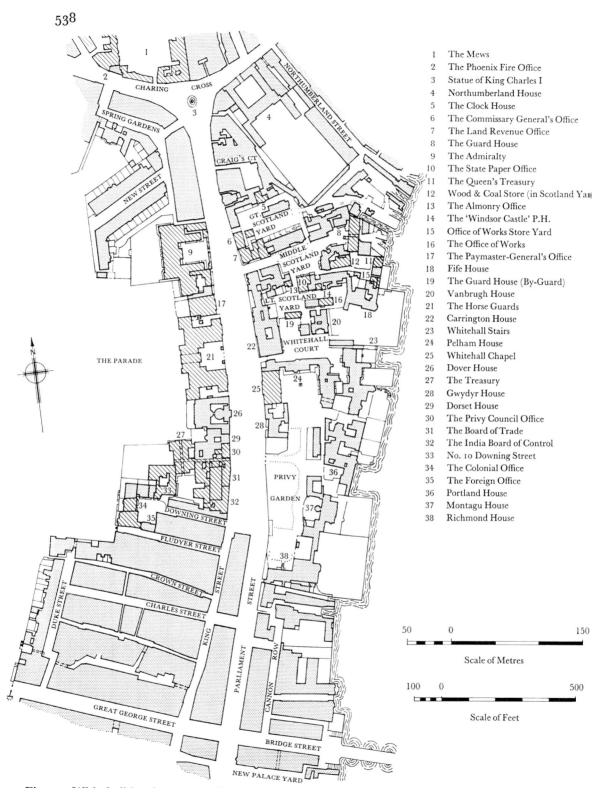

1   The Mews
2   The Phoenix Fire Office
3   Statue of King Charles I
4   Northumberland House
5   The Clock House
6   The Commissary General's Office
7   The Land Revenue Office
8   The Guard House
9   The Admiralty
10 The State Paper Office
11 The Queen's Treasury
12 Wood & Coal Store (in Scotland Yard)
13 The Almonry Office
14 The 'Windsor Castle' P.H.
15 Office of Works Store Yard
16 The Office of Works
17 The Paymaster-General's Office
18 Fife House
19 The Guard House (By-Guard)
20 Vanbrugh House
21 The Horse Guards
22 Carrington House
23 Whitehall Stairs
24 Pelham House
25 Whitehall Chapel
26 Dover House
27 The Treasury
28 Gwydyr House
29 Dorset House
30 The Privy Council Office
31 The Board of Trade
32 The India Board of Control
33 No. 10 Downing Street
34 The Colonial Office
35 The Foreign Office
36 Portland House
37 Montagu House
38 Richmond House

50   0   150

Scale of Metres

100   0   500

Scale of Feet

Fig. 23. Whitehall in about 1800: from a survey by Marquand and Leverton in the Public Record Office (MPZ 10). Public property is hatched.

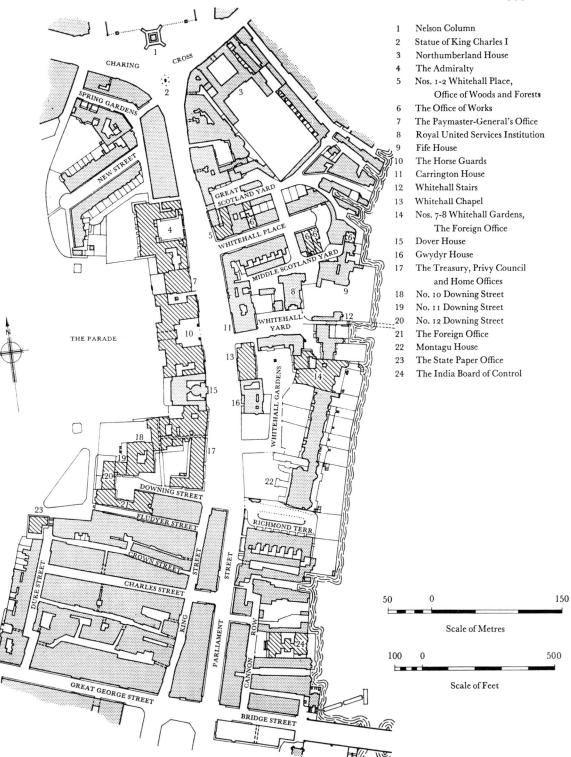

1 Nelson Column
2 Statue of King Charles I
3 Northumberland House
4 The Admiralty
5 Nos. 1-2 Whitehall Place,
     Office of Woods and Forests
6 The Office of Works
7 The Paymaster-General's Office
8 Royal United Services Institution
9 Fife House
10 The Horse Guards
11 Carrington House
12 Whitehall Stairs
13 Whitehall Chapel
14 Nos. 7-8 Whitehall Gardens,
     The Foreign Office
15 Dover House
16 Gwydyr House
17 The Treasury, Privy Council
     and Home Offices
18 No. 10 Downing Street
19 No. 11 Downing Street
20 No. 12 Downing Street
21 The Foreign Office
22 Montagu House
23 The State Paper Office
24 The India Board of Control

Fig. 24. Whitehall in about 1860: based on a plan in *Parliamentary Papers* 1864, xxxii.
Public buildings are hatched.

became a considerable charge on the parliamentary vote in the 1840s.[1] Between 1815 and 1832 current repairs and maintenance for the Whitehall district averaged about £3200 a year; and in the 1840s estimates rose to over £3800 a year.[2] In Whitehall itself the Horse Guards buildings, hitherto a separate department, were finally placed under the Office of Works in 1817.[3] Thereafter only the Admiralty retained its independence, employing its own surveyor throughout this period.

In general, two phases of activity altered the face of Whitehall between the 1780s and the 1850s: the Whitehall Improvements of the Napoleonic period, corresponding to the Westminster Improvements of the same date; and the extensive rebuilding of government offices by Soane and Barry, beginning in 1823. Of these two phases only the second was strictly the responsibility of the Office of Works. The first was sponsored by the Office of Woods, Forests and Land Revenues. But since the Office of Works was so closely related to its sister department, the redevelopment of the Whitehall area which began in the 1790s, notably in Whitehall Place, Whitehall Gardens and Richmond Terrace, merits at least passing reference in a history of the King's Works.

1. SCOTLAND YARD

Co-operation between the Office of Works and the Office of Woods, Forests and Land Revenues was particularly close in the Scotland Yard district. For here the offices of both departments were situated, and here the territorial claims of the Office of Works had to be harmonised with the redevelopment of Crown property by the Office of Woods, Forests and Land Revenues. One of the by-products of Burke's Act had been Gilbert's scheme to dispose of official houses made redundant by the abolition of sinecures. But Gilbert was outmanoeuvred, the homogeneity of Crown property was preserved, and the Acts of 1783 and 1787 authorising sales were first quietly ignored and then formally repealed in 1794.[4] The various houses attached to the old Office of Works in Great, Middle and Little Scotland Yards were therefore under suspended sentence of death for twelve years before they were at last involved in a comprehensive scheme for the improvement of Whitehall. The process of redevelopment was necessarily slow. 'Certain of the leaseholds', it was remarked in 1812, 'are enjoyed by persons of high rank, and others by individuals variously circumstanced . . . some of the lessees would entirely refuse to enter into any treaty . . . and others would expect terms so high that it would be inexpedient to accede to them'.[5] As late as 1815 a number of properties scheduled for demolition in 1782 were still standing, although 'in a state of considerable dilapidation and occupied in a manner very injurious to the interests of the Crown'.[6]

Early in 1795 John Fordyce, Surveyor General of Land Revenues, was authorised by the Treasury to 'lay before architects eminent in their profession' plans of the old palace area, and to offer £200 reward for the best 'plans and elevations for new

[1] See p. 216 above.　　[2] *Works* 5/107–111; *Parl. Pap.* 1847–8, xviii, pt. ii.　　[3] See p. 126 above.
[4] See p. 73 above. For a plan of Scotland Yard properties scheduled for sale in 1782 cf. MPE 1131.
[5] T. 29/118, f. 297, 21 July 1812.
[6] Crest 2/808, 28 February 1815, report giving full details of sixty-four properties.

Streets and Buildings in Whitehall and Scotland Yards'. Dance, Soane, Holland, Brettingham, S. P. Cockerell and James Wyatt were all approached, and all declined to participate in such a nebulous competition.[1] George Byfield and John Robertson, with more to gain and little to lose, did in fact submit detailed schemes.[2] As might have been expected, however, the project ended up safely in the hands of Leverton, Marquand, Chawner and Rhodes, the architects attached to the Land Revenue Office. During the next thirty years their overall plan gradually took shape as individual leases fell in, and by the 1820s the stretch of land between Whitehall and the Thames had taken on a very different appearance.

These developments are best illustrated by comparing three plans dating from *c.* 1780, 1804 (Fig. 23) and *c.* 1815.[3] As Charles Bacon remarked in 1812, there is otherwise an inherent 'impossibility in describing without innumerable words' the topography of Privy Gardens and the three Scotland Yards.[4] In 1795 each competing architect had been instructed 'not to restrain himself too much by the desire of preserving the present buildings, or any part of them which may interfere with what he shall think an eligible plan'. The following offices were, however, to be re-accommodated in the redesigned Scotland Yard area: the Land Revenue Office, the Office of Works, the State Paper Office, the Wardrobe Office, the Queen's Treasury, the Almonry Office, the Transport Office and the two Orderly Rooms for foot guards.[5] A beginning was made in 1796 by building a new Land Revenue Office on the site of the old Office of Works building, opposite the Admiralty, at the corner of Caddick's Row and Whitehall. The Office of Works itself was transferred to a house previously leased by Mr. Bownas in Little Scotland Yard. The other Office of Works properties along the decrepit peninsula between Great and Middle Scotland Yard were then gradually demolished as Caddick's Row became Whitehall Place, 'a fine wide street . . . open to the river, giving a grand view from Whitehall of St. Paul's Church and Blackfriars Bridge'.[6] The experiments with squares and crescents which had preceded Leverton's Whitehall Place during the 1790s were then multiplied during the early 1820s by the various schemes which preceded Smirke's Whitehall Gardens and Harrison's Richmond Terrace.[7] By the end of George IV's reign the new layout on the eastern side of Whitehall was practically complete. Whitehall Place had replaced Middle Scotland Yard, and Whitehall Gardens and Richmond Terrace were together filling up both Privy Gardens and the Richmond House site, just as Horse Guards Avenue was eventually to replace Whitehall Court (Fig. 24).

In all these arrangements the Office of Works played a fairly passive role. Craig protested vigorously against the department's removal to Little Scotland Yard. He

[1] Crest 2/918, March 1795.

[2] *Ibid.* 9 November 1795 (Byfield to Fordyce); MR 1453 (Robertson's designs).

[3] MR 1452 (*c.* 1780); MPZ 10 (1804), survey by Leverton and Marquand; MPEE 105/9 (*c.* 1815), proposed layout by Leverton and Chawner. See also *Survey of London* xvi (1935), pl. 93.

[4] Works 6/27, ff. 22–3, 29 June 1812.   [5] Crest 2/918, 16 March 1795.   [6] Crest 2/907, 13 June 1808.

[7] For the genesis of Whitehall Place cf. Crest 2/828, Crest 2/918 and MPEE 105, and *Survey of London* xvi (1935), pp. 193 *et seq.*; for Whitehall Gardens cf. T. 55/28, pp. 243 *et seq.*; L.R.R.O. 60/925, 28 July 1824; Peel Papers, B.M. Add. MSS. 40605–9, *passim*; *Survey of London* xiii (1930), pp. 204–13; for Richmond Terrace see *Survey of London* xiii (1930), pp. 249–50. But it is clear from the *1828 Report*, p. 86, that Richmond Terrace was designed by the architect Henry Harrison and not by T. Chawner of the Woods and Forests as suggested by the authors of the *London Survey*.

was quite content with the old office, used 'above a century', and 'though perhaps not quite as convenient nor roomy as might be wished, yet it is quite sufficient to transact the business in and to lodge the office keeper and family'.[1] Apart from the cost, he complained that 'the inconveniency of the [new] situation is great, it standing opposite to an alehouse frequented by noisy low people, draymen and others, and there being behind it a long narrow passage, frequented by prostitutes etc. besides all which there is very scanty room for the purposes of our office'.[2] The location was certainly insalubrious. Close by, in Privy Gardens, the nightly 'concourse of disorderly women' had in 1792 prompted Chambers to suggest the appointment of 'a stout watchman or two, at the expense of the inhabitants, to patrol about, and keep the place clear till the hours of meeting are over'.[3] The local night watchman seems to have been fairly frequently employed in 'removing persons lurking about' the new Office of Works.[4]

The cost of fitting up the department's new quarters came to £795 5s. 2d., of which £12 5s. 11d. went to John Spence for 'moving books, papers, desks etc.'.[5] The new premises were ready in March 1796, fitted up to the designs of J. T. Groves. In the new Board Room the principal officers of the Office of Works held their weekly meetings, sitting at a table covered with 'a green cloth eleven feet long and five feet wide with a silk fringe three and a half inches deep'.[6] During the troubled years of Wyatt's surveyorship the room also contained reminders of the department's better traditions: a portrait and a bust of Sir William Chambers.[7] Here the Office of Works remained until 1832, when, on amalgamation with the Office of Woods, Forests and Land Revenues, it moved to the two houses, Nos. 1 and 2, Whitehall Place, which that department had occupied since 1810. Hitherto No. 1 had been the residence of the First Commissioner, while No. 2 had been used as offices. In 1832 the First Commissioner moved out to make way for the Works officials, but Milne, the secretary, continued to live in part of the building. The old Office of Works in Little Scotland Yard was then granted, rent free, to the United Service Institution.[8]

The difficulties involved in the distribution of the department's official houses are best discussed elsewhere.[9] By comparison the changes effected in the tenure and appearance of other Scotland Yard properties during the Napoleonic period are relatively simple. Fife House was enlarged by the acquisition of adjacent property in 1803. At least until the arrival of Lord Liverpool in 1809 part of the premises continued to be used for the storage of Office of Works building materials.[10] Vanbrugh House and Carrington House were both enlarged by private tenants.[11] In 1788 the State Paper Office moved into premises opposite the Office of Works, between Middle and Little Scotland Yards, and during the next few years various minor alterations

---

[1] Works 6/22, 7 August 1795.   [2] Works 6/22, 2 October 1795.
[3] Works 1/5, f. 106, 13 January 1792; Works 4/17, 13 January 1792.
[4] Works 6/27, 1 October 1813; Works 4/21, 1 October 1813.
[5] Works 4/18, f. 153, 27 November 1795 and f. 182, 4 August 1796; T. 29/69, f. 207, 14 June 1796; Works 5/85.
[6] Works 3/3, 6 February 1796.
[7] Works 4/18, f. 170, 24 March 1796; Works 4/19, 25 September 1801; Works 4/20, 19 February 1811.
[8] *Survey of London* xvi, p. 188.
[9] See p. 73 above.   [10] *Survey of London* xvi (1935), p. 167.
[11] *Ibid.* pp. 170, 177. For plans and views of Vanbrugh House, Whitehall Court, etc., *c.* 1803, cf. also MPE 1109 and MPE 1106.

were executed by the Office of Works in the usual way.[1] The adjoining public house, known as the 'Windsor Castle', was sublet by the turncock of the Office of Works, and survived until 1819 when it was demolished as part of the development of Whitehall Place.[2] Further towards the Thames the Queen's Treasury remained in the building which had been partly rebuilt in 1760, being joined by the Almonry Office in 1819 when the quarters of the latter department were demolished along with the old Wardrobe Office.[3] On the north side of Great Scotland Yard the Old Clockhouse was demolished in 1812 to make way for a new Marshalsea Court House 'on a scale of the strictest economy', care being taken to replace the clock and weathervane on top of the new building.[4] Finally, among the minor responsibilities of the Office of Works throughout this period, such as the paving and watering of Whitehall, was the repair of Whitehall Stairs and the maintenance of the causeway between Whitehall and the Thames.[5]

One building which linked both the Westminster and Whitehall Improvements as well as affecting the organisation of the Office of Works was the new Stationery Office in Little Scotland Yard. In effect this was no more than a refitting of two small houses adjoining the Office of Works. But the process of transferring the Stationery Office from New Palace Yard to Whitehall neatly exposed two Office of Works skeletons: the inaccuracy of Wyatt's accounting and the irregularity of departmental house tenures.[6] When Wyatt submitted an estimate of £5451 8s. 3d., of which £4775 15s. 0d. represented bricklaying and carpentry, the Treasury claimed to be 'at a loss to conceive how the cost of bricklayers and carpenters work can amount to so large a sum as that . . . considering that the quantity of new building . . . is extremely small and for the most part of the coarsest kind'.[7] The estimate was thereupon reduced to £3369. At this the Treasury expressed 'extreme surprize and displeasure at the inaccuracy manifested by the Board of Works'. Forbearing 'to make any further observations upon this extraordinary transaction', the Treasury merely administered the following warning to Wyatt 'for his information and guidance': 'it is quite impossible to deny that an estimate of £4775 15s. 0d. which on Reconsideration is capable of being reduced to £3369 must have been formed with a want of precision and of vigilance on the part of the Surveyor General and with a want of integrity on the part of the artizans . . . which calls for the most marked

---

[1] *Survey of London* xvi (1935), p. 189; Works 4/17, 3 February 1792; Works 1/5, f. 62, 24 July 1783 and f. 88, 11 August 1786; Works 4/16, 25 July 1783; Works 4/17, 4, 12 and 18 August 1786; Works 5/75–6 (1786–7).

[2] *Survey of London* xvi (1935), pp. 189–90.

[3] *Ibid.* pp. 191–2 (view dated 1882, just prior to demolition). In 1786 it was remarked that 'this house and office have always been repaired at His Majesty's expense' (T. 29/57, f. 500, 15 August 1786; Works 4/17, 18 August 1786). In 1791 the house was saved from fire by 'the exertions of Mr. Matthias, Treasurer's Clerk', who, 'having laboured almost naked is very much hurt and confined to his bed' (T. 29/63, f. 523, 19 March 1791; Works 4/17, 11 February 1791). The Almonry Office was transferred to a building between the Queen's Treasury and a Stationery Office warehouse demolished in 1822.

[4] T. 29/117, f. 560, 9 June 1812; T. 29/118, f. 300, 21 July and f. 933, 28 August 1812; T. 29/121, f. 122. 12 January 1813; *Survey of London* xvi (1935), p. 208 (plan of Marshalsea Court House, 1850).

[5] Works 6/21, f. 107–8, 21 and 25 May 1787; Works 4/17, 15 June 1787; T. 29/58, f. 344, 31 May 1787; Works 5/76. The watering contract was a perennial problem: in 1784 Chambers even suggested that 'a trial might be made of trusting to the weather for waterage' (Works 6/20, f. 258, 14 May 1784). In 1813 expenditure estimated at £1770 was authorised in response to Lord Melbourne's complaint of 'the badness of the foot paving . . . at Whitehall' (Works 4/21, 11 January 1813, 3 September 1813).

[6] See p. 72 *et seq.* above.

[7] T. 29/115, f. 467, 18 February 1812.

reprehension'.[1] Three years after its completion in 1812 the building had once more to be altered, but this time to designs less ambitious, and very much less expensive, than those of James Wyatt.[2]

Meanwhile more offices had been accommodated in and around Whitehall Place. No. 5, built in 1814 on a 99-year lease by John Holroyd, a master-plumber employed by the Office of Works,[3] was occupied by the commissioners for auditing the public accounts; subsequently it housed the Auditor of the Civil List (to 1823), and then the Colonial Audit Office until 1832; in 1833 it was refitted for the commissioners for French and Danish claims and those enquiring into the excise.[4] When their labours were concluded, the Ecclesiastical Commissioners obtained part of the house in 1840. Although the claims' commissioners' records were removed in November 1843, the increasing business of the Ecclesiastical Commission required yet more space; but despite complicated negotiations the Ecclesiastical Commissioners were still at No. 5 in May 1851, only moving to No. 11 in 1855.[5]

When Peel's Metropolitan Police Force was established in 1829, No. 4 Whitehall Place (built in 1814) was taken for offices and fitted up at a cost of nearly £1600.[6] This was another body that expanded rapidly. An extra room was made available for it at No. 5, and by 1840 the incorporation of the Horse Patrol and the Thames Police, and the addition of 140 parishes to the Metropolitan Police District necessitated building more rooms at the rear of No. 5 by Harrison and Son at a cost of £800 to plans by Phipps. But soon these too proved inadequate.[7]

The Poor Law Commissioners established under the 1834 Act were accommodated on the other side of Whitehall Place, in No. 20, but as early as 25 August 1834 complained that the space was inadequate; they moved to Somerset House in 1836.[8] Nearby, the old State Paper Office partially collapsed in March 1819, necessitating removal of the papers to Great George Street.[9]

The next group of offices stood in Whitehall Yard, behind the Banqueting House. No. 1 (Pelham House) was occupied between 1812 and 1835 by the Comptroller of Army Accounts, who had moved from No. 2, which then became the Exchequer Seal Office. When the Army Accounts were consolidated with the Audit Office and moved to Somerset House, No. 1 was selected for the Comptroller of the Exchequer and Paymasters of Exchequer bills, whose offices at Westminster were to be demolished for the new Houses of Parliament. As the Exchequer Seal Office was now too small, its business having 'prodigiously increased' since the opening of the Exchequer Court to all attorneys, it was moved and No. 2 was added to No. 1.[10]

[1] T. 29/116, f. 105, 6 March 1812. See also T. 29/117, f. 75, 5 May 1812. Wyatt's plan and elevation, dated March 1812, are Works 30/5160.
[2] T. 29/124, f. 427, 27 July 1813; Works 4/21, 6 December 1814, 9 January 1815.
[3] *Survey of London*, xvi, p. 198.
[4] Works 1/17, pp. 394, 400; 2/1, p. 92; 5/108; Crest 25/36 (29 May 1832), 37 (15 February, 12 April, 30 April 1833); *Parl. Pap.* 1819, ii, p. 122; 1831–2, xxvi, p. 611.
[5] Works 1/24, pp. 458, 506; 1/27, pp. 113–5; 2/3, pp. 131, 161, 165; 2/4, pp. 16, 37, 369; 2/5, pp. 422–5; 2/9, p. 1; G. Best, *Temporal Pillars* (1964), pp. 424–5. Cf. plans, Works 30/399–404.
[6] Works 1/17, p. 449; 4/29, p. 449; 5/110. This house, of course, backed on to Great Scotland Yard.
[7] P.R.O. Mepol. 2/2, memorandum of 11 February 1840, and draft of 22 July 1844; Works 1/24, p. 513; 1/27, pp. 113–5.   [8] Works 2/1, pp. 175, 179, 181; 2/2, pp. 47, 104; 1/22, p. 98.
[9] Works 1/9, p. 257. The building in Great George Street was not much better, see p. 567 below.
[10] Works 2/1, pp. 231, 237, 240, 242–3; *Survey of London*, xiii, pp. 142–3, 150 (plates 47–9 show these buildings).

The expense of fitting up the two houses anew, £1120, incurred strong Treasury criticism.[1] Evacuated by the Exchequer officials in 1842, No. 1 later became the home of the secretary to the Chief Commissioner of Woods, T. W. Philipps, who died there in 1855.[2] No. 3 Whitehall Yard became the office of the Auditor of the Civil List in 1826; and in 1831 was fitted up to receive the records of the Common Pleas and Custos Brevium.[3]

South of the Banqueting House, Gwydyr House was hired for offices in 1842.[4] In Cannon Row, the building occupied by the Transport Office, erected in 1816 to the designs of William Pilkington, the District Surveyor, had been taken over for the India Board of Control in 1817. Works costing about £5700 were then executed there, paid out of that Board's own funds.[5] A temporary office, used during Soane's rebuilding of the Privy Council Offices, cost some £500 to fit up in 1825.[6] The new Stationery Office in James Street is noticed separately; also removed to James Street in 1832 was the Colonial Audit Office.[7]

In Whitehall and at Charing Cross gas street lighting was introduced in 1821.[8] An iron pump was substituted in 1816 for the wooden one by Charles I's statue,[9] which itself was made more secure under Chantrey's supervision in 1836.[10] Away on the further side of Charing Cross, in Spring Gardens, the Office for Military Boards occupied No. 29, and No. 11 was fitted up at a cost of £800 in 1819 for the Auditors of Land Revenue.[11]

2. THE BANQUETING HOUSE

Inigo Jones's masterpiece was treated with a good deal of reverence during the eighteenth and nineteenth centuries. But this did not prevent its being subjected to considerable alteration. Between the 1780s and the 1830s there were no less than four sets of alterations: by Chambers in 1785; by Wyatt and Groves in 1809; by Charles Bacon in 1815; and by Soane and Smirke in 1829–37.

In 1785 Chambers followed up his earlier refacing of the basement storey with a renewal of the original balustrade.[12] This was merely a pious piece of restoration. But in 1808 it was decided to convert the Banqueting House from a chapel royal into a

---

[1] Works 1/21, p. 453; 1/22, p. 37; 2/2, pp. 19, 36.
[2] *Survey of London*, xiii, p. 143.   [3] *Ibid.* p. 150; Works 5/111.
[4] Rooms were then fitted up for the Treasury Solicitor (Works 2/3, p. 315).
[5] Works 1/7, p. 535; 1/8, pp. 95, 121, 156, 359; 4/22, p. 263; 4/23, p. 73; 5/112; *Parl. Pap.* 1857, xli; Sir W. Foster, *John Company* (1926), p. 263.
[6] Works 5/109.   [7] Works 5/108; 5/119, f. 35 (expenditure £1060 13s. 11d.).
[8] Works 5/108 (lamp-posts cost £372). The Office of Woods was gas-lighted about mid-1816 (Works 1/7, p. 55). The gas-lighting of Whitehall was under active consideration from that time, and the Admiralty had been equipped by 1819 (Works 1/7, pp. 302, 391, 393, 427; 1/9, pp. 403–5).
[9] Works 1/6, p. 487; 1/7, p. 30; 5/107 (cost £81 5s. 3d.).   [10] Works 1/21, p. 490.
[11] Works 1/9, p. 484; 5/108; *Parl. Pap.* 1831–2, xxvi, p. 612. See *Survey of London* xx (1940), p. 78 (plan of Spring Gardens *c.* 1850). The Land Revenue Office is not to be confused with No. 11 (new numbering) Spring Gardens, described and illustrated in *Survey of London* xiv, pp. 128–9.
[12] The estimate was £269 18s. 0d. (T. 29/56, f. 500, 20 July 1785). Cf. also Works 4/16, 3 June 1785; Works 4/17, 22 July 1785; Works 6/21, f. 51, 15 July 1785; Works 5/74 (1785).

military chapel. With Groves as executant, Wyatt set out to provide seating for 2131 soldiers 'without interfering with the architectural beauty of the building'. At the same time he produced designs for the reconstruction of the northern annexe to the Banqueting House, those 'old and shabby buildings', as he put it, 'which at present disgrace the Chapel'. His estimate for the first part of the programme was £3000, and for the second £1500.[1] But the total expenditure turned out to be something in the region of £16,000, of which £7000 had to be taken out of the Army Extraordinaries.[2] Naturally enough, the Treasury expressed their 'very great surprise', especially as the original estimate had never been delivered to the Lord Chamberlain in the customary way.[3] The whole affair was obviously a suitable subject for investigation by the Commissioners of Military Inquiry. Wyatt's main excuse was the wartime cost of building materials, particularly timber.[4] But he also instanced 'the decayed state of certain parts . . . which had not been foreseen', as well as 'alterations to the original plan during the progress of the work'.[5] These arguments were substantiated by the testimony of Adam Lee.[6] There is also some evidence to show that Wyatt's original designs were altered at the personal intervention of John Fordyce, the conscientious Surveyor General of Land Revenues. Feeling personally involved in the improvement of Westminster and Whitehall, Fordyce wrote to Huskisson at the Treasury on behalf of the Banqueting House, 'that fine old Building . . . though not in my Department'. Complaining that Wyatt's northern additions 'must have a bad effect', he submitted a plan of his own which was then passed on to the Office of Works.[7] Replying to Fordyce on behalf of the Treasury, Chinnery assured him: 'you were just in time to enable me to stop the work going on without causing much derangement in the plan. If I had had the good fortune ever to have seen your plan of Scotland Yard etc. I would not have forgotten the idea of widening the entrance of Whitehall Chapel and have mentioned it accordingly to Mr. Wyatt—as it is you are *now safe*'.[8]

Wyatt's reconstruction of the northern annexe was certainly an improvement, even though Carter objected to its finish as 'an olio of stone, brick and compo'.[9] By recessing the additional bay he avoided compromising the Whitehall front; and by extending the balustrade he effectively linked the new work to the original composition. The interior alterations were less successful. Apart from the organ on the west side, the fittings of the chapel royal had not greatly injured the appearance of the room.[10] But the wainscot pews, galleries and spiral staircases required for the accommodation of chapel-going guardsmen cruelly camouflaged the beauties of Inigo Jones's design.[11] Carter itemised the outrage as follows: 'Centre doorway cut

[1] T. 29/95, ff. 311–2, 4 July 1808; Works 4/20, 29 July 1808.

[2] Works 4/20, 5 May 1809; L.C. 1/40, f. 194, 28 June 1810; T. 29/108, ff. 35–6, 26 October 1810.

[3] T. 29/106, f. 640, 17 August 1810; L.C. 1/40, f. 224, 1 April 1811.

[4] Works 6/24, f. 233, 1 December 1808.

[5] 'Inquiry into . . . the Office of Works', *Parl. Pap.* 1812–13, v, pp. 422–3.

[6] *Ibid.* p. 472.   [7] Crest 2/907, 16 November 1808.

[8] *Ibid.* 23 November 1808. From the start the Treasury had been concerned about the building 'and . . . desirous of preserving as far as may be possible its Architecture' (Works 6/24, f. 168, 18 March 1808).

[9] *Gent.'s Mag.* 1812, pt. ii, p. 440.

[10] See Groves's plan dated 1796, showing the chapel fitted up for the christening of Princess Charlotte (B.M. King's Maps xxvi, 5c.); and a late eighteenth-century view, *Survey of London* xiii (1930), p. 123.

[11] *Survey of London* xiii (1930), p. 124.

down to the height of the side [doorway]; its opening is now a perfect square; a novelty at least; the open pediment cut away, bronze busto removed, and the openings of the side doors filled in with niches. The lines of the first tier of columns etc. nearly obliterated by a common pew gallery; the second tier of pilasters, etc. in the same predicament, by the obtrusion of another pew gallery; and the original balustrade gallery . . . utterly annihilated'.[1] The chapel was further encumbered in 1811–12 when the French eagles captured in Spain were ceremonially exposed there;[2] and again in 1814–15 when Bacon supervised extensive alterations, including a new organ by Elliot and the installation of furniture and fittings in preparation for a series of music concerts held in aid of German war refugees.[3]

By 1828 the building was in need of thorough repair. Britton and Pugin's *Illustrations of the Public Buildings of London*, published in that year, remarked 'that this invaluable pile is fast mouldering to dust, the festoons in the third story are entirely destroyed, and the pediments and cornices of the windows are in a most dilapidated state'.[4] In September 'a piece of the Architrave of one of the upper windows in the West [Whitehall] front fell on the footpath, and of course created considerable apprehension'.[5]

Soane was instructed to take steps for repairing the chapel. Scaffolding was erected to permit a close examination of the building's condition, and when part of the balustrading was removed, Soane found that the masonry was in a bad state, the brickwork behind it 'much decayed, and so loose that constant attention and great care was necessary' to prevent its falling down. A new roof was needed: 'some of the Beams have sunk nine inches in the centre, . . . one of them is broken, and the ends of the whole of them are entirely decayed, as are likewise all the original plates on which they rested. The principal Rafters and other parts are so much worm eaten that the Strength of the Timber is in a great degree destroyed'.[6] Soane estimated that the repair of the stonework would cost about £13,000, and that of the roof £3500 beyond what the sale of the old materials might produce. No progress could be made with the work until Rubens' paintings had been removed from the ceiling.[7]

Meanwhile Soane instructed his mason, Thomas Grundy, to lose no time in 'preparing the Upper Cornice and the Dressings of the Upper Tier of Windows in the Front next Whitehall of New Portland Stone, and likewise with reworking the two Plinths under the Base of the Balustrade, making good such parts as are absolutely requisite with New Stone, and of which parts I should wish to be apprized previously'.[8] But the Surveyor General, mindful of the report of the 1828 Select Committee, stressed to Soane the need for inviting tenders from 'as many respectable competitors as possible'.[9] The tenders received, he complained that the prices were

[1] *Gent.'s Mag.* 1812, pt. ii, p. 440.

[2] The ceremony was described as 'one of the finest ever witnessed' (*Gent.'s Mag.* 1811, pt. i, p. 488; 1812, pt. ii, p. 286; *The Times* 1 October 1812, p. 3 and 20 October 1812, p. 3).

[3] L.C. 1/6, f. 353, 30 April 1814 and f. 355, 13 May 1815; Works 19/24/2, f. 6, 5 January 1816; Works 1/6, ff. 214–5, 253, 372–3, 397; T. 29/130, f. 505, 5 August 1814; *The Times* 6 March 1815, p. 3.

[4] Vol. ii, p. 117.

[5] Soane Mus. corr. 2, xii. E. 1 (Soane to Stephenson, 23 February 1829), E. 33; Works 1/16, p. 502.

[6] Soane Mus. corr. 2, xii. E. 1, 21 February 1829.

[7] *Ibid.* ff. 1, 7 (23 February and 18 April 1829); Works 19/24/2, ff. 10 (18 April 1829), 12 (5 May 1829) and 13 (25 July 1829, reporting that the scaffolding was erected for removing the paintings).

[8] Soane Mus. corr. 2, xii. E, f. 5, 11 March 1829. [9] *Ibid.* f. 10, 4 June 1829.

too high, and that 'with the exception of the Smith, there does not seem to have been any competition': he insisted that more tenders must be obtained.[1]

The condition of the building was yet worse than the preliminary examination had revealed: the clerk of the works, William Craib, informed Soane on 2 July that

> having examined minutely the masons work I find the Ketten [i.e. Ketton] stone rustic ashler throughout the building to be in so bad a state that it is not possable to make a good job by refacing the said stone, as it requires at least $\frac{3}{4}$ of an Inch to bring it regular leaving a back Joint behind pilaster at least $\frac{3}{4}$ or $\frac{7}{8}$ of an Inch. the rusticks consequently would be considerably enlarged to what they originaly were— and as the portland Cornices are all to be taken down in consequence of their being so very much decayed with good management I might venture to say little if any New Stone would be wanted provided you will alow me to have the same converted in ashlering as a substitute of the Ketten Stone.[2]

When the Banqueting House was first built, the basement had been differentiated from the upper storey by the use of brown Oxfordshire stone. As this had already been replaced by Portland in 1774,[3] the refacing of the remainder in the same material now gave to the masonry a uniformity that was new and perhaps unfortunate.[4]

During 1829, some £5500 were spent on the repairs, and the following year another £9000. The new roof was completed during the summer of 1831, some of the windows on the Whitehall side that had been blocked up were opened, and by November little remained to be done: but a decision to restore the paintings before they were replaced delayed the completion of the works.[5] Soane submitted an estimate of £3650 for finishing the south front in stucco like the north, and for painting and gilding the ceiling and other minor interior works,[6] but the Treasury decided 'not to incur any expense on account of the Whitehall Chapel in 1832 beyond the amount already sanctioned for restoring the Pictures'; £16,550 had already been expended.[7] The works were brought to a close on 20 November 1833, £18,204 9s. 2d. having been spent.[8]

Orders were given in 1834 for the restoration of the interior, some of the old fittings serving to furnish a new Guards' chapel in Birdcage Walk.[9] The work was

---

[1] *Ibid.* f. 12, 10 June 1829; Works 4/29, p. 411. It was 'deemed prudent', however, to employ Grundy as mason, but his prices were to be revised. Martyr's tender was accepted for the carpenter's works, Holroyd's for the plumber's, and Gostling and Huxley's for the smith's; while the small quantity of brickwork required was to be executed by Whitehead at the Office prices (Works 4/29, pp. 490, 499–500).

[2] Soane Museum corr. 2, xii, E, f. 13.   [3] See *History of the King's Works*, vol. v.

[4] 'Soane, however,' remarks Sir John Summerson, 'reproduced the original details with scrupulous care and the façade may even have gained a little from two centuries of practice in the cutting of classical ornaments' (*Inigo Jones*, 1966, p. 56).

[5] Soane Mus. corr. 2, xii. E. 20, 33; Works 4/29, p. 370; 4/31, p. 170. According to the *Survey of London*, xiii, pt. ii (1930), p. 131, the form of the roof may have been altered in this restoration, but the original structure and Soane's strengthening are shown in models in the Soane Museum; see J. Wilton-Ely, 'The Architectural Models of Sir John Soane: a Catalogue', *Architectural History*, xii (1969), nos. 91–3. 'Mr. Sieguer' (i.e. Seguier) was the artist employed to clean the paintings.   [6] Works 19/24/7, ff. 35–6 (1 December 1831).

[7] Works 4/31, p. 293; 5/110; 5/111. £450 were allocated for restoring the pictures and £400 for replacing them (Works 19/24/2). Soane undertook to confine his 1832 expenditure within the total sum already voted, except for the work on the pictures (Works 19/24/2, f. 36).

[8] *Ibid.* B.M. Add. MS. 40415, f. 20; Works 1/22, p. 96. The figure of £17,819 9s. 2¼d. is given in Soane's papers (xii. E, 33). This does not include £560 spent by the Lord Chamberlain's Office in protecting the paintings, but charged to the Works' vote (Works 19/24/2, f. 23); and was evidently reduced in the final examination.

[9] Works 1/21, p. 167, 30 August 1834; *Commons' Jnls.* xc, p. 361.

now entrusted to Smirke.[1] Tenders were invited in December, and that of Messrs. Baker for £1794 was accepted.[2] Smirke's various alterations were finished in 1838 at a cost of £10,816 3s. 3d.[3] They comprised: the removal of Wyatt's gallery and the reconstruction of Inigo Jones's gallery as originally conceived except that the centre of the northern gallery was brought forward as an organ loft over coupled Ionic columns;[4] the repair of 'Father' Smith's organ;[5] the renewal of the doors and window reveals; complete interior furnishing;[6] and iron railings around the outside of the building.[7] Oak flooring and pews were installed: 'fourty-four pews for families, each with five convenient sittings and thirty-six pews for servants, of the same size, re-serving at the same time ample space for the royal pew'.[8] The gilding of 'the en-tablatures of the Corinthian pillars which beautify and support the walls' and the addition of a 'splendid altar-piece', hot water heating and red hangings for the walls completed the work.[9]

Most of Smirke's interior fittings vanished with the transfer of the building in 1891 to the Royal United Service Institution. Sir Aston Webb added a southern gallery and central doorway; the organ was transferred to the Tower Chapel of St. Peter-ad-Vincula; and the panelling and altar-rails were sold.[10] Only in 1963–4, as a result of a decision taken during the Ministry of Lord John Hope, was Inigo Jones's master-piece finally cleared of all the bric-à-brac, first ecclesiastical and then military, which had encumbered the interior since the great fire of 1698.

3. THE TREASURY OFFICES

In the topographical history of the Treasury the reign of George III represents a lull between the construction of Kent's Treasury Buildings and those of Soane and Barry. The tennis court area was obviously ripe for redevelopment, and in about 1793 Chambers prepared a scheme for new Board of Trade and Privy Council Offices on the site.[11] The tennis court itself was eventually demolished in 1809, but nothing was done with the site until the 1820s.[12] Instead several expanding depart-ments were obliged to make do with a series of inadequate offices. One example of

[1] Works 1/21, p. 259, 23 February 1835.
[2] *Ibid.* pp. 447, 476. At an advanced stage of these proceedings, 29 December 1835, the Treasury required that no arrangements were to be adopted without their previous sanction (Works 19/46/1, f. 1).
[3] Works 1/23, p. 56.
[4] Mr. Palme has commented on the character of the restoration. The carving of the gallery brackets is 'somewhat dry in execution, but definitely magnificent. The moulded front to the gallery floor . . . is much poorer, and so are the symmetrically turned balusters above with their moulded handrail. It is difficult to know if this is in accordance with the prototype, or due to the restorers. The same doubt applies to the door-ways. They conform to a late Renaissance type favoured by Inigo Jones, but the mouldings appear, by their dry precision, rather neo-classical in character. They were probably redrawn by Soane or Smirke' (*Triumph of Peace*, 1957, p. 227).   [5] Works 1/22, f. 226. Estimate £114.
[6] *Ibid.* f. 271 (estimate £1600), f. 369 (cost £1589 19s. 0d.).   [7] *Ibid.* f. 237 (estimate £390 11s. 6d.).
[8] B.M. Add. MS. 40415, f. 20, Smirke to Lord Granville Somerset.
[9] *Gent.'s Mag.* 1836, ii, p. 644; E. and W. Young, *Old London Churches* (1956), p. 159.
[10] Much of the woodwork was incorporated in the residence of Mr. Edgar Horne of Shackleford, Surrey (*Survey of London*, xiii, p. 125 n.).   [11] Soane Museum, Drawer 50/2/1–2.
[12] MPEE 94 (plan of Treasury 1794); *Survey of London* xiv (1931), p. 43 and plate 36 (plan of 1793). For minor repairs to the tennis court see Works 4/18, ff. 76, 80, 82 (1794).

piecemeal adaptation was that portion of the old palace situated between the Treasury Passage and Dover House. Usually known as the Old Tennis Court, this Gothic building dating from Henry VIII's time survived as a visible relic of the Tudor palace until 1846. But it did not survive unaltered (Pl. 46). A classical doorway had been inserted in the reign of Charles II. This formed the entrance to the northern section of the building, eventually known as Dorset House. In the 1770s the battlements had disappeared, the tall traceried windows had been replaced by plain openings arranged in three tiers and the Gothic finials had been replaced by 'common masonic conic caps.' In 1804 Wyatt inserted a second entrance from Whitehall, this time in 'a tolerable imitation of the Tudor style', but ornamented with what Carter called 'frightful irrelevant bustos of an Assassin and a Queen, of no ancient authority of any kind'.[1] This and various other alterations between 1802 and 1805 cost more than £4000.[2] A few years later Wyatt also altered the Dorset House section of the premises for use as offices for the Secretary of State for the Home Department and the India Board of Control.[3] The India Board moved into their new quarters in 1810, leaving their old rooms further south along Whitehall for the occupation of the Privy Council.[4] The old Privy Council Offices, situated between the tennis court and Kent's Treasury, had occasionally been known as the Cockpit, in distinction from other buildings on the Cockpit site. Towards the end of the eighteenth century these offices are frequently described as chilly and decayed, and the officials of the department were more than ready to take over the quarters of the India Board.[5] Meanwhile the rest of this block of buildings facing Whitehall remained, almost continuously, in the possession of the Board of Trade.[6]

The winter of 1815–6 brought large stones down from the front of the Old Tennis Court, now the Home Office, described by Soane as 'a compound at best of strange parts'.[7] To protect the passers-by scaffolding had to be erected. Partial repair was found to be impracticable; to refront the building in stone was estimated at not less than £3000. 'After much deliberation', Stephenson had the front re-cased in brick— intended to be colour-washed to harmonize with the rest of the building—to secure it at a moderate expense (£600) while leaving open the possibility of a future restoration (Pl. 46). But this roused the ire of the antiquaries; questions were asked in the Commons, and Bankes complained of 'buttresses of yellow brick', 'not very creditable' to the judgment of the new Board of Works. So work was suspended.[8] Although a number of offers were made to case the front in stone, the Treasury finally authorised Stephenson to proceed. The building remained unimproved until

[1] *Gent.'s Mag.* 1816, pt. i, p. 423–4; 1816, pt. ii. p. 489, Carter's engraving of the Old Tennis Court in three stages: in Wolsey's time, in 1815 and in 1816; *Survey of London* xiv (1931), pp. 76–7 and plates 58–9.
[2] Works 4/19, 8 February 1805; Works 5/93–4.
[3] Works 6/24, f. 234, 1 December 1808; Works 6/25, f. 23, October 1809. The alterations appear to have cost over £11,000 (Works 1/7, p. 354).   [4] *Survey of London* xiv (1931), pp. 75, 91.
[5] *Ibid.* pp. 77–8 and plate 60 (plan of 1824); P.R.O., P.C. 2/184 pp. 198–9; Works 6/23, f. 68; Works 4/17, 19 and 26 August 1791, 20 July 1792; Works 4/18, f. 146, 16 October 1795 and f. 305, 31 August 1798; Works 6/21, ff. 72–3, 16 December 1785. Groves's estimate for fitting up the India Board rooms as quarters for the Privy Council Office was £2676 (L.C. 1/5, f. 330, 15 January 1811). At the same time the old Privy Council Office was repaired: estimate £1803 16s. 6d. (Works 4/20, 6 September 1811, 20 September 1811).
[6] *Survey of London* xiv (1931), pp. 79–80, plates 61 (plan of 1793) and 62–5 (views of 1809–23). The Board was abolished in 1782 and reconstituted in 1786. For minor repairs see Works 1/5, f. 71, 25 January 1784; Works 4/17, 22 September 1786; 30 October 1789.   [7] Soane Museum corr. 2, xii, G. 1, f. 3.
[8] *Ibid.*; *Parl. Deb.* xxxiii, 985–6 (5 April), 1031–2 (8 April 1816); Works 1/6, pp. 480–1, 484–5.

Barry in 1845–7 demolished the front in order to rebuild it in conformity with his remodelling of the Council Office.[1]

The Board of Control left Whitehall in 1817 for Cannon Row, giving place to the Commissariat Department. The necessary alterations to Dorset House cost £1843, and in 1818 a further £619 were spent in making a new staircase and altering doorways to improve its communications with the Treasury.[2] Minor works apart, there is little more to record about the Treasury. Gas lighting was installed in 1835, but not by the Works Department, 'from the necessity', as the Treasury Secretary explained with some embarrassment, 'of adopting great caution before their [lordships'] determination to introduce Gas within the Treasury, and their having therefore been obliged to communicate with the Tradesmen themselves ere they resolved upon the mode of lighting the Lobbies and Passages of this Office, but my Lords [he concluded] are nevertheless of opinion that the charge ought to be defrayed from the Funds voted by Parliament', i.e. for maintenance of public buildings.[3] A small three-storied structure containing six rooms, made necessary by the increase of business resulting from the County Courts Act of 1846, was added in the court at the back of the Treasury Chambers in 1848, at an estimated cost of £1440 exclusive of furniture.[4]

4. The Privy Council Office and Board of Trade

'The building of a new office for the Board of Trade originated in a representation made by that department, of the great dilapidation of the building, its great insecurity, and its entire inadequacy, from want of accommodation, for the ordinary business of the office'.[5] As early as the summer of 1819 the chief clerk, Lack, gave Soane a note of accommodation required.[6] But Soane's next memoranda are dated April 1823. At the end of May his plans were sufficiently advanced to be shewn to Huskisson, the President of the Board, who was urging the scheme on.[7] Two or three designs were produced, 'to all of which' said Robinson, the Chancellor of the Exchequer, 'I thought there were considerable objections; but I think there was one of them which appeared to be less objectionable than the rest, and it was intended to give the necessary orders for the execution of that design'.[8] Soane's estimate was some £14,222 for a building of brick, with stone ornaments, with a frontage on Whitehall of 82 feet, a depth of 46 feet, and a height of 60 feet.[9] A meeting of Treasury ministers in July 1823 decided that the front rooms should be made two feet larger, and the whole of the street front of stone. This increased the estimate to £17,200.[10]

[1] Works 1/6, p. 490; 1/7, pp. 10–13, 17–18, 72. See below, p. 560.
[2] Works 1/8, p. 359; 5/107; Soane Museum corresp. 2, xii, J. ff. 3, 5 (estimate £349).
[3] Works 2/1, p. 247 (8 October 1835).
[4] Works 2/6, pp. 214–5 (4 November), 279–80 (Phipps' estimate of £1040 for two storeys, 12 November), 287 (21 December, additional £400 for third storey), 290–1 (29 December 1847).
[5] *1828 Report*, p. 147. The old buildings are illustrated, *Survey of London*, xiv (1931), pls. 62, 64.
[6] Soane Mus. corr. 2, xii, A, 1.
[7] *Ibid.* ff. 2–6; 50/1/11, 12 (plans); 49/3/1, 2 (elevation).   [8] *1828 Report*, p. 147.
[9] *Ibid.* p. 36; Soane Mus. corr. 2, xii, A. f. 7. The Board Room was placed in the Whitehall front (Soane Mus. 50/1/10) but Lord Harrowby objected to this, and Huskisson ordered that it should be placed at the back (*1828 Report*, p. 36).   [10] Works 1/12, p. 140, 29 August 1823, Soane to Stephenson; Soane Mus. 50/1/12.

When the old building was delivered over to the Surveyor General for demolition on 15 September 1823, Soane made arrangements to preserve the ceiling of the old Board Room (a relic of the old palace bearing the initials of the Duke and Duchess of Monmouth),[1] but it did not prove possible to save the cornice.[2] In October came a Treasury order to begin the work immediately; but in the next few months it was decided also to rebuild the dilapidated Privy Council Office, which adjoined the Board of Trade to the south.[3] In December 1823 Soane designed a façade from Downing Street to the Treasury Passage, involving the demolition of a 'very shabby alehouse' next Downing Street, giving a frontage along Whitehall of some 150–160 feet, of which the Board of Trade would occupy the northern part.[4] Soane's first designs were strongly neo-Grecian in character: some with Ionic pavilions at either end, and a central feature articulated by various combinations of columns, with or without a low dome, recalling his projects for the Houses of Parliament (Pl. 51B). These are dated December 1823 or February 1824 (Pl. 47B).[5] Subsequently Soane designed a continuous columnar façade, with Ionic or Corinthian (Tivoli) orders as alternatives,[6] which had resemblances to his Threadneedle Street façade of the Bank of England (1823) (Pl. 47A).[7]

> Various meetings were held at Fife House [Lord Liverpool's residence] upon the subject, [Robinson told the 1828 select committee] and there was much discussion as to what ought to be the character of the façade; and I perfectly remember representing to Mr. Soane, that I very much wished that in forming his plan he would have reference to the opposite building of Whitehall Chapel [the Banqueting House], and the general designs of Inigo Jones for a new palace at Whitehall, which notwithstanding some defects in the details, was nevertheless so grand in its proportions and so harmonious in its general effect, that it appeared to me it might furnish suggestions very applicable to those new buildings about to be erected in the immediate neighbourhood of Whitehall Chapel. The design which Mr. Soane first produced in consequence of this communication, did not appear to be founded upon this suggestion.[8]

In May 1824 there were several meetings between the architect and ministers; and a meeting at Fife House on 5 June[9] approved the Corinthian version of the unbroken columnar design, and directed an immediate commencement so that it might be roofed in by Christmas.[10] Soane proposed using the same contractors as were engaged on his works at the House of Lords; but the Surveyor General was

---

[1] See Soane, *Designs for Public and Private Buildings* (1828), p. 8. The old Board Room is illustrated in Ackermann, *Microcosm of London* (1809), reproduced in *Survey of London*, xiv, pl. 63A; pls. 64–5 reproduce drawings made by Soane in September 1823, prior to its demolition. Pl. 63B, a drawing probably by T. H. Shepherd, is dated 1821, but corresponds to the plan of the new Board Room as built by Soane (Works 30/321). This being so, the drawing may simply be mis-dated; and the complexities of the argument of the authors of the *Survey of London*, xiv, pp. 81–2 and n., disappear.   [2] Soane Mus. corr. 2, xii, A, ff. 10, 11.
[3] Soane prepared plans for a building on the site of the old Council Chamber (to the west of the Board of Trade, near the Treasury) which had been vacated as unsafe in 1811 (see *Survey of London*, xiv, p. 78) (Soane Mus. 50/2/26, 32–5).   [4] *1828 Report*, p. 147; Soane Mus. 49/3/21–3, 50/1/5.
[5] Soane Mus. 49/3/27–31 (elevation), 50/1/13, 14 (plans).
[6] *Ibid.* nos. 3, 4 (May), 25, 26, 41 (June); 49/4/7, 8.
[7] Bolton, *Works*, pp. 39, 66–7.   [8] *1828 Report*, pp. 147–8.
[9] Attended by Lords Liverpool and Harrowby, Sir Charles Long, Robinson and Huskisson. Liverpool insisted on the Corinthian version.
[10] Soane Mus. corr. 2, xii, A. ff. 24–6, 28, 30; 49/3/41; 49/4/7, 8; 50/1/1, 2.

unwilling either to anticipate Treasury orders for starting the work, or to authorise a departure from the rule requiring competitive tenders.[1] Soane replied with characteristic petulance that: 'Under all the circumstances I trust not to be considered responsible for the materials to be used or the soundness of the construction or for any delays that may occur in the execution of the several works'.[2] But although authority for the work was sent on 11 June, the details of the façade were still subject to interference by the officious amateurs at the Treasury. The design approved on 5 June had a continuous colonnade of Soane's favourite Tivoli order, but the centre receded, leaving the majority of the columns insulated, those on the projecting flank being three-quarter columns.[3] On 11 June, Soane told the Select Committee in 1828,

> this plan . . . was again examined by Mr. Herries and the Chancellor of the Exchequer [Robinson]; Mr. Herries for some time preferred the insulated columns, and fortified his opinion by referring to the effect of the columns in the Chancellor of the Exchequer's room; the Chancellor of the Exchequer disapproved of the insulated columns, however, and wished to have three-quarter columns through the centre front,[4] to which ultimately Mr. Herries acceded. On the 12th of June I had again the honour to attend the Chancellor of the Exchequer with the drawings, when Mr. Robinson expressed himself less satisfied with the three-quarter columns; but although a very large drawing of the front was produced, the Chancellor did not think he could determine satisfactorily without a model of the whole front, which I was directed to have made, and in the meantime to proceed with the works.[5]

The reason for Robinson's objection to the original design is sufficiently interesting to repeat: he remarked that although the columns were insulated,

> and having therefore the advantage of a play of light and shade, they were still intended to be so near to [the wall] that there would be scarcely room for any one to pass between the columns and the wall; so that it would have had the appearance only but not the reality of a colonnade; and I thought, and others thought also, that it would be better to make them all three-quarter columns throughout, than by separating a part of them to aim at producing an effect which after all would only be a deception.[6]

Another change that Robinson suggested was in the order, that of Tivoli 'being universally deemed extremely defective from the dwarfish proportions of its capital'. Instead, he proposed that of the temple of Jupiter Stator at Rome, 'allowed to be amongst the finest specimens of the Corinthian order'.[7] This had consequences that Robinson did not appreciate: 'When the plain example of the Corinthian order . . . was changed to the richest order in all the remains of Antiquity, a [different] tone and character was thereby given to the internal finishings of those Offices,

---

[1] *Ibid.* corr. 2, xii, A. f. 23, dated 7 May, but avowedly in reply to Soane's of 5 June.
[2] *Ibid.* f. 32.   [3] Soane Mus. 49/4/8.
[4] A drawing showing this elevation, with a plan of the front showing the alternative arrangements, is reproduced in *Survey of London*, xiv, pl. 69.
[5] *1828 Report*, p. 37. There is a note to the same effect written by Soane on a plan, Soane Mus. 50/1/1. Two models in the Soane Museum relate to this period, see J. Wilton-Ely, 'The Architectural Models of Sir John Soane: a Catalogue', nos. 84, 85, *Architectural History*, xii (1969), p. 34.
[6] *1828 Report*, p. 148.   [7] *Ibid.* See Works 30/319 for Soane's comparative sketch of the orders.

more particular[ly] as far as relates to the Board Room of the Board of Trade and the Council Room in the Council Offices'.[1]

Nor did Robinson's intervention end there. Enlarged by the area occupied by the Privy Council Offices, the site was ample enough for all the accommodation asked for without a third storey on the street front, and Soane accordingly eliminated it from his design.[2] Robinson was struck by the consequent lack of height, and stating his feelings 'very decidedly' to Soane, proposed two modes of remedying the fault: either by raising the basement, 'which being partly underground was not intended to be more than three feet above the ground', to correspond with that of the Banqueting House, some 10 or 12 feet high; or to make the windows of the two storeys behind the columns of equal height, so increasing the height of both the columns and the building.[3] Soane objected to the first that it was 'contrary to good principle and good taste' so much to elevate the base of three-quarter columns (despite the example of the Banqueting House); and to the second, that 'there was no example to be found in the works of the best Italian architects, particularly Palladio'. He 'maintained his own opinion', and the utmost that Robinson could persuade him to was 'to raise the basement story . . . to its present elevation of about four or five feet'. But as the building progressed, 'the defect in point of height became apparent, and the upper part [a wall linking the chimneys and concealing skylights] . . . so visible from the opposite side of the street, as to constitute a great disfigurement to the whole design'.[4] A balustrade was suggested to crown the wall.[5] Someone else then suggested that the only remedy was to construct pavilions at either end of the building, 'whereby the wall connecting the chimnies would have at least the appearance of some utility, as connecting together the two flanks of the building'. After much consideration, it was determined to adopt this scheme,[6] breaking forward the colonnade and raising an attic to form one pavilion on the Downing Street corner, and a corresponding one by extending the design in front of the Home Office, the next building to the north.[7] This, it was subsequently realised, would bring the Home Office twelve feet in advance of the adjoining Melbourne House; a feature to which great exception was taken.[8] Soane's own alternative was to construct a triumphal arch across Downing

---

[1] Works 1/15, p. 91, Soane to Stephenson, 7 February 1827. Soane Mus. 49/3/34 (22 July 1824) compares the two orders in a bay of the building; and 49/3/7 (20 September 1824) shows the revised elevation.

[2] *1828 Report*, p. 38. This occurred at an early stage.

[3] Both these changes were subsequently made by Barry, see below, pp. 560–1.

[4] *1828 Report*, pp. 148–9. Yet when Westmacott dined with Robinson, Canning and others, 'all expressed their fullest pleasure at your Board of Trade' (R. Westmacott to Soane, 18 March 1825, printed in Bolton, *Portrait of Sir John Soane*, pp. 372–3). A few days later, Sir M. W. Ridley attacked the design in Parliament: 'with its one tier of building so strangely heaped upon the top of the other, it resembled a double stand on a race-course' (*Parl. Deb.*, n.s. xii, 1257).

[5] 'Tuesday 13 July [1824]. Attended at Fife House when I was directed to put an Iron Balustrade over the Attic of the Corridor . . .' (note by Soane on Soane Mus. 49/3/8).

[6] According to Soane the reason for forming pavilions was that the unbroken front of the two offices was thought to be monotonous (*1828 Report*, p. 39; Soane, *Designs for Public and Private Buildings*, 1828, p. 8 and pl. ix).

[7] In March 1825 Soane made designs incorporating the Home Office. Soane Mus. 49/4/5 shows that approved by a meeting at Fife House on 12 March (Lord Liverpool, Robinson, Peel, Long, Herries, Arbuthnot, Croker) in which the columnar façade is unbroken. See also 49/3/19, 20; 50/1/21.

[8] The original line of front was thrown back several feet at Lord Harrowby's suggestion, to prevent any southern continuation cutting through King St. Soane's attitude in these controversial matters seems never to have been to express an explicit opinion, but to leave the politicians to discover the truth for themselves from his plans. See *1828 Report*, pp. 38 ff.; and for plans, Soane Mus. 49/5/2, 4.

Street, and build a similar block to the south, so forming a symmetrical composition without interfering with the Home Office.[1] Neither project was adopted. The rather curious rear façade (Pl. 48B) appears to have been accepted without comment.[2]

From this account of the evolution of the design, we may return to follow the progress of the works, which were as bothersome to Soane as was the irresolution of the politicians. A contract for the excavation had been made with Johnson and Co. in January 1824, and work began in February. By June the ground had been excavated between 10 and 15 feet to a stratum of hard solid gravel.[3] According to Britton, a sort of concrete foundation was then made.[4] Soane was not happy about the tradesmen selected for the works by competitive tender,[5] and in particular sought authority to employ a second master mason. Chadwick, who had won the contract, reported that there was no granite in London suitable for the plinth of the new building; could Soane wait a month for a supply?[6] Bricklaying began on 2 July; work went on apace,[7] so that by November the Board of Trade was ready for roofing, to the discomfiture of the master slater, John Weston, who complained that others had cornered the supply of Westmorland slates.[8]

Arrangements for the Council Chamber and Offices, at the Downing Street end of the design, were under consideration in February 1825, and were approved on 1 March.[9] Soane had notions of building as far as No. 10 in Downing Street, but Robinson on 15 August decided on a less extensive scheme, and ordered an immediate start.[10] But it was not until December that work began on the foundations in Downing Street, a delay that Soane (who had been staying in Bath and was about to be couched for cataract) blamed on Chadwick, using it as a pretext to call in his favourite mason, Grundy.[11] Chadwick promised to have the building up to the roof by the last day of February, urging the shortage of large blocks of Portland Stone as an excuse for the delay.[12] Chadwick was allowed to continue, and an interesting report on his activities

[1] See Soane, *Designs for Public and Private Buildings* (1828), plates vii–ix; *1828 Report*, pp. 39–42, 149–150; Soane Mus. 49/5. Another version, Works 30/139, includes the Home Office but sets it at an angle to link the Board of Trade and Melbourne House. There is also a model in the Soane Museum (Wilton-Ely, 'Catalogue', no. 87).
[2] Soane Mus. 49/6/3, 5. Works 30/319–322 are copies of Soane's plans, signed by him and dated April–May 1833.   [3] Soane Mus. corr. 2, xii, A, f. 27.
[4] 'A stratum of broken granite and Kentish rag, three inches thick, was closely rammed; and three other similar layers were made; each of which was grouted with strong Dorking lime and sand. On the top of this was laid a series of six-inch York landings, bedded in solid mortar' (Britton and Pugin, *Public Buildings of London*, ii, 1828, p. 238). George Bailey, one of Soane's assistants, gives the specification in a letter to T. L. Donaldson dated 14 January 1836; the stone was to be 'broken to the size of an ordinary hen's egg'; and the lime and sand to be used in the proportion of 2:1 (R.I.B.A. MS. S.P. 6, II).
[5] See p. 132 above. The principal contractors were T. and G. Martyr (carpenter and joiner); W. White-head (bricklayer); W. Chadwick (mason); W. Good (plumber); T. Palmer and Son (plasterer); W. Watson (painter and glazier); J. Weston (slater); J. Mackell (smith); T. and J. Moorman (iron); R. and E. Kepp (coppersmith).   [6] Soane Mus. corr. 2, xii, A. ff. 38, 40, 41.
[7] Bolton, *Portrait of Sir J. Soane*, p. 451. Mrs. Conduit reported to Soane, 20 October 1824, that a few days earlier the men were 'getting very forward with the Board of Trade, the capitals are finished, and they were putting on the cornice'. 'I am told everyone speaks of it in terms of admiration', she added (Bolton, *Portrait*, p. 382).   [8] Soane Mus. corr. 2, xii, A. ff. 46, 49.
[9] Robinson was anxious that the plan should be so arranged as to allow space at the back for the construction of stabling for the First Lord of the Treasury's official house (then inhabited by Robinson) (*ibid*. ff. 52–6). In the debate on the Office of Works vote, 28 March 1825, Robinson said that a plan was under consideration for 'uniting under one façade, the Council-office, the office of the Board of Trade, and the Home-office.' The space to the rear, overlooked by these offices, would not be suitable (as had been suggested) for ministerial residences, but might be used for Exchequer offices (*Parl. Deb.* n.s. xii, 1257).
[10] Soane Mus. 49/5/35.
[11] Soane Mus. corr. 2, xii, A. ff. 68, 70–2; (plans) 50/1/24, 27, 34–40.   [12] *Ibid.* corr. 2, xii, A. ff. 69, 75.

556

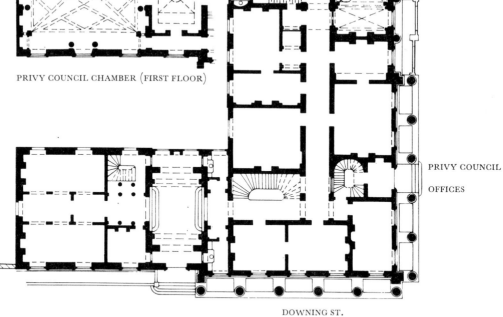

THE HOME OFFICE

TREASURY PASSAGE

BOARD OF TRADE

OFFICES

WHITEHALL

PRIVY COUNCIL

OFFICES

PRIVY COUNCIL CHAMBER (FIRST FLOOR)

DOWNING ST.

5   0   10

Scale of Metres

10 0   30

Scale of Feet

Fig. 25. Whitehall: the Privy Council Office and Board of Trade designed by Soane:
from a survey in the Public Record Office (Works 30/319–323).

was delivered to Soane on the last day of the year by Walter Payne, his trustworthy clerk of works at the Bank:[1]

[On the Parliament Street front,] the columns and caps all sett, I saw part of the archatrave that was finished and part upon the masons bankers they where cutting the joggles in part of them, Mr. Chadwicks man the foreman of the masons told me it would be all sett on Wedensday next 4 January 1826 I made him no answer, but thought it impossible, I believe there had been no order for setting the wood horses, to support the archatrave, I found by examining the cornice for Parliment Street front about 55 feet in hand some pieces turnd of the bankers, and some the masons was at work upon. There is about 30 feet of the cornice the carver have finished. I find it take one carver about three weeks to compleat one stone with three modillion and two pannels, make me verry doubtfull this will delay the buisness, if there are not more carvers imployed, . . .[2]

Next there was difficulty with the slater. Weston—'one of the most troublesome men I ever had to deal with, as well as the most unreasonable', wrote Stephenson—was discharged, and replaced by Struther.[3]

However, by September 1826 the work was nearing completion: the Board of Trade's rooms were being grained and varnished; and in the Council Offices the joiners were at work.[4] But in November Soane was harried with another problem: that of the upper balustrade surmounting the attic, which a recent meeting at Fife House had condemned as objectionable. Soane had not understood that it was to be removed, and had replaced it after an alteration to take account of the corner pavilion on Downing Street and the proposed refronting of the Home Office.[5] The Treasury authority for extending the work over the Treasury Passage, however, was accompanied by an order for the removal of this balustrade.[6]

By this time Soane was quite agitated about the works: in a private memorandum, he noted:

I am in a fever about the Estimates. So many alterations and additions have been made at different times, and so many Estimates dovetailed into each other, that I am mortified at the result of such mixed calculations.

The fact is, it has never been clear to me what part of the work remained un-finished:—Even now unless the work is *stopped*, or somewhat like it, I shall not *see* my way with any reasonable hope of success.

Entablature—Modillions fully enriched.

The Entablature, twice the quantity of the same as the estimated Entablature.

The Capitals almost double in expense.

Six detached columns in each of the two Pavillions instead of columns merely detached from the walls.

The Order changed from the most simple to the most enriched, at a considerable expense.[7]

---

[1] See A. T. Bolton, *The Works of Sir John Soane*, p. 61.   [2] Soane Mus. corr. 2, xii, A. f. 76.
[3] *Ibid.* ff. 77–9, 85.   [4] *Ibid.* f. 91. See also 92, 94.
[5] *Ibid.* ff. 96, 99. This upper balustrade may be seen in Soane's elevation, G.L.C. collection, reproduced in *Survey of London*, xiv, pl. 70, and in Higham's engraving, *ibid.* pl. 71. Pl. 72 shows it removed. Alternative versions, dated 25 November 1826, and inscribed by Soane, 'Elevations as (last) approved with the order of the three Columns in the Campo Vaccino & the balustrade over the Attic of the Corridor removed', are Soane Mus. 49/3/43.   [6] *Ibid.* corr. 2, xii, A. f. 102, 15 November 1826.   [7] *Ibid.* f. 96.

Further trouble arose in the shape of allegations made by a discharged labourer, one Tippett, against the clerk of works, William Evans.[1] More serious was the financial situation: Soane had formed a revised estimate of £61,990 14s. 9d. in March 1826; he now added £10,350 for a southern pavilion and for fittings and £3850 for extending the front northward to include the Treasury Passage (in other words the width of the Treasury Passage was incorporated to form a bay of the main front).[2] At the end of 1826 only some £5600 were left out of the parliamentary grant for paying the tradesmen; the Treasury insisted that there would be no further issue till a further vote should have been obtained from Parliament.[3] Stephenson suggested that in the circumstances the only alternatives were to stop the works or ask the tradesmen if they would continue to allow protracted credit and carry on. Work appears to have gone on. The front was extended over the Treasury passage; but the Home Office was not included.[4] In September 1827 the Surveyor General ordered works at the Council Offices to be stopped on account of an excess expense beyond even Soane's supplementary estimate; but it was resumed when Charles Greville, the Clerk of the Council, urged on him the need for moving the clerks into the new offices as soon as possible.[5]

Greville had already crossed Soane's path, for it was apparently at his instigation that in September 1827 the Privy Council asked for the removal of the four pairs of Ionic columns which ornamented the Council Chamber (Pl. 50),[6] and it was he who demanded the substitution of a flat ceiling for Soane's groined elliptical dome suspended between skylights.[7] These skylights were only introduced 'when the works were nearly completed'. Soane originally intended the room to be lit by windows overlooking Downing Street, but these were objected to (either because they would expose the Council to public gaze, or because of street noises), and to take their place Soane introduced the skylights. Although the Treasury finally decided that the columns and domed ceiling might be left for the time being, they criticised Soane's actions:

> My Lords take this opportunity of expressing their regret that in the execution of this work, a course should have been pursued, whereby an apartment of so much importance on account of the public purpose for which it is designed, has been finished without any plans of it having been submitted either to the Treasury, or to the heads of the Department for whose use it has been constructed.[8]

Soane had already pointed out to Stephenson that 'the great features of the Council Room, the columns, the four arches from whence the groined ceiling springs, as well

---

[1] See p. 122 above.   [2] Works 1/15, pp. 9–11, Soane to Stephenson, 14 November 1826.
[3] Soane Mus. corr. 2, xii, A. ff. 123, 124.   [4] Works 1/15, pp. 29–31.   [5] *Ibid.* p. 444.
[6] 'I am directed by the Lords of His Majesty's Most Honourable Privy Council to desire that you will give orders for the removal of the Eight Columns in the New Council Chamber at Whitehall. Their Lordships being of opinion that these Columns interfere with the Arrangements which will be necessary for the transaction of Business in that Apartment' (Greville to the Surveyor General, 6 September 1827, Works 1/15, p. 400). These columns were of yellow scagliola, supplied and fixed by Croggon for £249 (Works 5/126, f. 213).
[7] Works 1/15, p. 413. A drawing in the Soane Museum shows the Chamber 'before' and 'after' the destruction of its Soanic features. It is mockingly inscribed 'To the Rt. Hon[b] Lord Harrowby; Mr. C. Greville and Mr. Amyott' (Soane Mus. 49/3/16). Harrowby was Lord President of the Council, Amyott an official who was also Treasurer of the Society of Antiquaries. For his rôle see Soane's *Brief Statement of the Proceedings respecting the New Law Courts, the Board of Trade, and the New Privy Council Office* (1828), p. 31.
[8] Works 1/15, p. 504, 12 November 1827.

as the groined ceiling itself are to be traced in the different plans, and as such I conceived sanctioned'.[1] But the Treasury's ill-founded complaint was typical of Robinson, now Lord Goderich, and First Lord.[2]

For 1828, Soane thought that about £4000 in addition to the previous votes would be needed.[3] Reporting on the excess over his estimate, he pointed out that the alteration of the order had necessitated an increased richness throughout, 'particularly to the front next Downing Street, which in the original design was intended to have been of brick, with stone dressings to the door and windows'. His supplementary estimate (November 1826) had brought the total to £76,190 14s. 9d., but the total cost was not likely to exceed £80,000.[4]

The 1828 Select Committee animadverted on

> the unsatisfactory state in which this large and costly Structure stands, from being begun without a plan which had been maturely considered, from injudicious alterations and changes having been made during its progress, and contrary, as it appears by his own statement, to the opinion of the Architect . . . and although your Committee cannot clearly ascertain to whom the blame attaches, the system cannot be good which has produced such a result.

'It therefore now remains a question', the Committee concluded, 'how it can either be left as it is, or how it can be completed on the end towards the North'; for any balancing block on the other side of Downing Street they regarded as neither necessary nor desirable.[5] Nothing of consequence was, in fact, done until the 1840s.

The Board of Trade was one of the most active departments of government in the 'thirties and 'forties, producing among other offshoots statistical and railway branches. In 1835 for the Statistical Department the Lords of Trade sought the return of two rooms Soane had never received directions to fit up, which had been used as a store for Treasury papers.[6] In 1841 the Statistical Department required more room, as did the Railway Department.[7] The Treasury did not encourage suggestions for altering the building, so the Board proposed that the Railway Department should be moved out, as the Corn Department was.[8] Some alleviation was obtained by converting into a room an unfinished passageway next to the Treasury entrance.[9]

Thus by 1844 the new buildings erected by Soane were too small for the department; the office for the registration of joint-stock companies in particular made serious demands on space and the Railway Act of that year brought matters to a head: the 'extreme inconvenience and impediments to the despatch of railway business by the limited offices assigned to the Department in the Board of Trade, and of the increasing interruptions and delays in the Office of the Privy Council particularly on days appointed for hearing appeals', compelled action,[10] and in September

[1] *Ibid.* p. 91, 7 February 1827. Stephenson had inquired, 26 January 1827, whether the design had been approved, as 'there has been some dissatisfaction expressed, as to the decorations, and expence of this room' (Soane Mus. corr. 2, xii, A. f. 128).

[2] Another criticism was that the room was cold, but Soane ascribed that to a broken window. He provided for heating the room by hot air flues, as well as four fireplaces, but after the fire at the Houses of Parliament heating by flues was abandoned by order of the Office of Woods (Works 2/5, pp. 21–3).

[3] Works 1/16, p. 72.   [4] *Ibid.* pp. 112 ff.   [5] *1828 Report*, pp. 6–7.

[6] T. 1/3574, 4 May 1835.   [7] Works 2/3, p. 190, 7 October 1841.

[8] *Ibid.* p. 420, 18 July 1842.   [9] *Ibid.* p. 477, 15 December 1842.   [10] Works 2/4, pp. 384–5.

1844 Phipps prepared a plan for building offices for the Railway Department at the rear of the main building.[1] Lord Lincoln, then Chief Commissioner of Woods, thought this 'so objectionable in all respects' that he asked Barry to form a plan 'for giving *all* the accommodation required both by the Board of Trade and the Council Office and at the same time if possible improve the Architectural appearance of the Building'.[2] Peel approved a scheme estimated by Barry at £10,975, remarking 'I doubt whether the estimate will cover the Expense'.[3] Barry's designs,[4] involving an additional storey, and providing 25 new rooms in the Board of Trade, 5 in the Council Office and 16 in the Home Office, which was also included in the scheme, were transmitted to the Board of Trade for approval in April 1845, and tenders were called for in July. Only three of the six firms invited returned tenders, William Cubitt being successful,[5] and work began promptly.[6]

Soane had employed the 'richest order of antiquity' for his building, but Barry's biographer contrasts 'the strict classicism of the original' with 'the growing taste for richness and vigour of effect' exhibited in Barry's alterations.[7] Barry had to work to a narrowly drawn brief, preserving the floor levels and fenestration of the original building, and

> he was obliged also to keep and work in the Corinthian order of the original building, in spite of his objection to engaged columns. The original design, with many points of excellence, yet seemed to him to want symmetry, force, and grandeur. To remedy these defects, he raised the order on a basement story, did away with the super-structure, which seemed to oppress it, and, removing the colonnades, which by their shadows and projection cut up the wings, he gave the great flanking masses their full effect.[8]

Obliged to keep the engaged columns that had been forced on Soane, Barry pondered how best to alleviate the impropriety:

> He had begun to think of breaking entablatures (which in days of classical purism would have shocked him), partly from the example of Inigo Jones's Banqueting-house, partly from his Gothic studies, and the tendency to vertical lines which they fostered. He conceived that, when this step was taken, the engaged column changed its character; it no longer affected to support the entablature, but became avowedly an adjunct. This feeling, joined to the desire of greater variety and richness, carried the day . . . he felt that, from the necessary position of the columns, the breaks were somewhat overcrowded; and he rather regretted that he had not carried out an idea, which had occurred to him in studying his design, of crowning the principal windows with pediments to relieve the appearance of squareness.[9]

[1] Works 30/323, reproduced in *Survey of London*, xiv, pl. 74.
[2] Nottingham University, Newcastle MSS. Ne C 12053, Lincoln to Peel, 13 December 1844. The registry of designs was among the new departments to be accommodated (Works 1/27, p. 324).
[3] Newcastle MSS. Ne C 12057, 19 December 1844.
[4] Works 30/324–9, signed by Barry and dated 1 January 1845. Works 328 and 329 are elevations to White-hall and Downing Street respectively. They differ from the executed design principally in the character of the pavilion attics, which have round-headed windows with caryatids between, and the smaller size of the second floor windows. These elevations are reproduced in *Survey of London*, xiv, pl. 75 and 76; pl. 77 is somewhat simplified from Works 30/324–5.
[5] Works 1/28, pp. 23, 75, 224, 253, 256. The other firms tendering were Grissell and Peto, and Baker.
[6] Works 2/5, pp. 173 ff.   [7] Alfred Barry, *The Life and Works of Sir Charles Barry* (1867), p. 111.
[8] *Ibid.*   [9] *Ibid.* p. 112.

The works at the Board of Trade and Council Office were altered during their progress.[1] Barry's estimate of £13,516 was exceeded by no less than £13,352,[2] largely accounted for by extras; the construction of a new roof instead of raising the old one, and rebuilding of almost an entire storey.[3] Barry explained that 'owing to the unusual and unlooked for construction of the Attic Story of the privy council office, it was necessary to take down the external wall . . . to the level of the ceiling of the one pair floor,—that it was necessary to alter nearly the whole of the flues . . . that in consequence of the work and arrangement adopted in the original construction of the Building, in order to ensure the permanent safety of the structure it was necessary . . . to take down and reconstruct . . . also the Ceilings of the one pair [floor] throughout the Building, whereby two new Stories have been added to the Council office. . . .'[4] A large additional quantity of facing stone was also required, including 'a large amount of elaborate carving in consequence of the old Stone being found to consist of smaller Blocks, and to be more decomposed than was anticipated'.[5] Inman and Phipps, reporting on Barry's statement, remarked that works had been carried out that were not shown on the original drawings: balconies put to the first floor windows, the second floor windows enlarged, and carved panels introduced in the attic.[6] The completion of the Board of Trade's new rooms was reported on 18 June 1846,[7] and those for the Education Department on the second floor of the Council Office were directed to be furnished on 30 June.[8]

For the rebuilding of the Home Office, which was to be entirely taken down,[9] Cubitt submitted an additional tender of £11,745, which together with £2809 16s. spent on the entrance to the Treasury and the Home Office was narrowly within Barry's estimate of £14,721.[10] Soane's Council Chamber was remodelled at a cost of £255, the roof and columns so disliked by Greville being removed.[11] The total expenditure on the entire works (including Barry's commission) was £44,976 18s. 9d., as against the original estimate of £28,237.[12] The 22 additional rooms formed in the new Home Office alone, however, accommodated departments hitherto spending £2247 10s. per annum in rent.[13]

---

[1] Traced working drawings, Works 30/330–1, are dated 19 June 1846.

[2] Works 2/5, pp. 413–6, 11 January 1847. Barry's estimate for the Council Office and Board of Trade was increased by the alteration of the Council Chamber (£255) and installation of a warming system (£1442) to £15,213. The warming system actually cost £1445 11s. 9d.; but expenditure on the rebuilding was £28,268 3s. 6d. Barry's commission and incidentals brought the total expenditure to £31,374 18s.; but Barry stated that £2809 16s. was chargeable to the Home Office account for the entrance to that building and the Treasury. The reason for the excess was investigated by Inman and Phipps, and their report led to some sharp exchanges with Barry, and to the suggestion that his commission should be limited to that on the estimate—against which he successfully protested (*ibid.* pp. 413–6; 2/6, pp. 47–9, 88, 124, 266, 273–8, 363–5, 383–6, 401–4).

[3] Works 1/30, pp. 254–6; 1/32, pp. 293–4.   [4] Works 2/5, pp. 173 ff.   [5] *Ibid.*

[6] *Ibid.* Traced working drawings dated 19 June 1846 show the revised design with first floor balconies and enlarged second floor windows (Works 30/331).

[7] Works 1/30, p. 35.   [8] Works 2/5, p. 169.

[9] Inman and Phipps recommended that a contract in gross would be suitable for this work, though it had not been for the complicated remodelling of the adjacent buildings (Works 2/5, pp. 173–8).

[10] Works 1/29, pp. 57, 342–3; 1/30, pp. 291–2; 2/5, p. 173. Works 30/336, showing the proposed reconstruction of the Home Office, is dated 4 Feb. 1846.

[11] Works 1/30, pp. 254–6. Greville said that changes in the ceiling had long been wanted for improving hearing and warmth, and 'removing some existing encumbrances which now disfigure the Room' (Works 2/5, pp. 75–7, 9 March 1846). Barry's specification for the alteration is given in Works 2/5, pp. 77–8.

[12] Works 2/6, pp. 266–73 (9 Dec. 1847), 444 (29 Aug. 1848).

[13] *Ibid.* pp. 134–6.

Soane's work was thus almost entirely destroyed or remodelled.[1] A characteristic design was lost, and replaced by one of less distinction. But in the process the problems that had vexed Soane and his critics were solved: the giving additional height to the building, and its completion so as to form a symmetrical composition. The problem of the line of the front of the Home Office, forming an awkward angle with Melbourne House to the north, was made less acute by removing the colonnade of the southern pavilion, so that the entire façade stands on a single line. Barry's designs doubtless met with the approval of Lord Ripon, who, as Frederick Robinson, had sketched out its principal features twenty years before.

5. Downing Street

During the late eighteenth and early nineteenth centuries Downing Street became increasingly occupied for official purposes. Number 10, a house much larger than it appeared from the street, was a residence 'attached to the Treasury as a Part of the Office', and occupied by the senior Treasury minister who might desire to live there.[2] From 1783 to 1801 the younger Pitt lived there, as did his successors as First Lord until 1812.[3] During Lord Liverpool's administration it was occupied by the Chancellor of the Exchequer, Robinson returning as First Lord after Canning's brief occupancy in 1827. Wellington resided there during the reconstruction of Apsley House in 1828, but in 1830 Lord Bathurst was in occupation. Lord Grey lived in the house, but after his resignation it was used as offices and sometimes occupied by the minister's private secretaries.[4]

The adjoining house, then known as No. 11, was privately occupied until 1824, when it was thrown together with No. 12. That house had been purchased in 1805 with the intention of combining it with No. 13 as the Home Office: but the Chancellor of the Exchequer moved in instead. During Liverpool's ministry successive Secretaries to the Treasury resided there; in 1828 the Chancellor resumed possession, and except for a reversion to the Secretary in 1834–8, it remained the Chancellor's official residence.[5] The house further west, next to the Park, No. 13 (later No. 12) was acquired in 1803 as a residence for the Judge-Advocate-General; in 1827 it was added to the Colonial Office, situated at No. 14 since 1798.[6] No. 15, Sir Robert Preston's, was added to the Foreign Office (No. 16, formerly Sir Samuel Fludyer's) in 1825. All these overlooked the Park. The next two houses on the south-western return of the street were absorbed into the Foreign Office by 1825, and smaller

---

[1] The western part of the Downing Street front remains, and several of the lobbies. The Council Committee room or Second Court also appears to have been little altered, but the Board of Trade board room was divided by Barry and re-ceiled. See *Survey of London*, xiv, pp. 94–6, and pl. 87–93.

[2] B.M. Add. MS. 38292, f. 11, Lord Liverpool to C. Ellis, 22 January 1823, printed in *Survey of London*, xiv, p. 127, n. A number of books have been written about No. 10 (e.g. by C. E. Pascoe, 1908, B. Fuller and J. Cornes, 1936, H. Bolitho, 1957 and R. J. Minney, 1963) but none adds anything significant to the *Survey of London's* history of the building itself.

[3] Except in 1807–9, when Spencer Perceval, Chancellor of the Exchequer, lived there instead of the Duke of Portland, who had his own town house.

[4] *Survey of London*, xiv, pp. 127, 137.   [5] *Ibid.* p. 146.   [6] *Ibid.* p. 154–9; see below.

houses still farther west were used for various official purposes.[1] Those opposite, on the northern side of the street as far as No. 10, were demolished in 1825 to make way for the new Privy Council Office.[2] Thus the whole street had become an official precinct.

At this point it may be convenient to refer to the schemes for rebuilding the Foreign and other public offices which were not realised until Scott began the construction of his great block in 1863. Soane had put forward various proposals for rebuilding Downing Street, which had been officially ignored.[3] Nevertheless, the Treasury was contemplating providing more accommodation for some of the public offices already in Downing Street and also moving the Exchequer there from its semi-ruinous buildings in New Palace Yard.[4] Under the Act 7 Geo. IV cap. 77 all the freeholds and some of the leaseholds in Downing Street and the north side of Fludyer Street were purchased for £61,496. In May 1833 the Commissioners of Woods submitted a plan by Seward to rebuild Downing Street in continuation of the line marked out by Soane, but without any appropriation of the sites. The Treasury approved the line for the south side only. A further report suggested offices should be provided there for the Auditors of the Exchequer, Judge-Advocate-General, Army Medical Board, Army Arrears Accounts and any department of the Treasury, or alternatively for parliamentary commissions. The Treasury, declaring that public offices had the first claim, told the Office of Woods to consult heads of departments. The Commissioners then turned to Decimus Burton, who in 1836 was instructed to design offices with an 'elevation of a more economical character' than Soane's Board of Trade. He suggested that Fludyer Street should either be swept away or realigned parallel to Downing Street, and estimated his main building, of 27,700 square feet, at £106,000, with £40,000 for land purchase. This would accommodate the Judge-Advocate-General, the Poor Law Commissioners, and the Comptroller General of the Exchequer, as well as the Foreign Office. Directed to confine himself to the existing site, he produced a hybrid plan, incorporating the western houses in a narrow elongated structure. When its awkward shape and extreme length of 250 feet were objected to, Burton suggested using a corner of the Park west of Downing Street, and in February 1839 designed a structure about 107 by 225 feet to house both the Foreign and the Colonial Offices, at a cost of some £80,000. After discussions, ministers decided to introduce a bill for purchasing the south side of Fludyer Street, and Burton prepared a more extensive plan, incorporating the Fludyer estate, repeating Soane's Council Office westward, and forming a 'Downing Square'.[5] Several of his plans were printed with the report of the 1839 select committee, which recommended building new Foreign and Colonial Offices as part of a general plan for the construction of public offices in Downing Street and on the Fludyer estate.[6] It was doubtless lack of money that caused Melbourne's administration to shelve

---

[1] No. 18 housed the West India Department in 1824, and its imminent demolition was reported in 1826 (D. M. Young, *The Colonial Office in the early nineteenth century*, 1961, pp. 124–5). In 1836, No. 20 was offered to the Tithe Commission (Works 1/22, pp. 110, 112, 123–5, 140, 195, 304, 330). Some houses were taken down in 1838 in preparation for redevelopment (Works 1/23, p. 211), and all these houses had been demolished by 1857 (Westminster Public Library, Print Collection 13/19).

[2] *Survey of London*, xiv, pp. 92–3.   [3] See, e.g. his *Designs for Public and Private Buildings* (1828).

[4] The following section is based on the 'long paper' on Downing Street Improvements, T. 1/3668.

[5] *Parl. Pap.* 1839, (466) xiii, qq. 264–397.   [6] *Ibid.* p. 235 and appendix.

this report. The idea was not taken up again until 1853, when Sir William Molesworth as First Commissioner of Works directed Pennethorne to prepare a new plan,[1] a step that led eventually to the building of Scott's government offices.

Turning to the details of works at these various houses, we find that at No. 10 after the extensive alterations of 1781–3 comparatively little was done for many years. Minor alterations in 1796 conducted by Groves, costing nearly £800, included the removal of the partitions between the library and dining room, four Corinthian columns being inserted to support the wall above.[2] Further alterations were effected under Wyatt in 1806 and 1812.[3] The roofs of Nos. 10 and 12, together with that of the Foreign Office, were repaired in 1820 at a cost of nearly £1000.[4]

A much more considerable expenditure followed the ministerial reshuffle of 1823. F. J. Robinson became Chancellor of the Exchequer, occupying No. 10, and the new Secretary of the Treasury, S. R. Lushington, displaced Arbuthnot at No. 12.[5] That autumn extensive renovations were carried out on both houses.[6] To satisfy Robinson's pretensions, Soane adapted the rooms above the kitchens at No. 10 in 1825, constructing an anteroom and a state dining room with a ceiling of 'star-fish' pattern.[7] His estimate of £1800–£2000 for this 'great improvement' proved inadequate, the total expense being £4649.[8] At the same time, No. 11 having reverted to the Crown in August 1824, that house was taken over by the Treasury and communications formed with No. 12. At the back of No. 11 Soane built out a new dining room for Lushington with a domical ceiling lit by narrow skylights on two sides, in the manner of the breakfast room at 13 Lincoln's Inn Fields and of the Privy Council Chamber. Alterations were also made to the entrance hall, and in No. 12 to the large back room.[9] Again, estimates (£2670) proved fallacious: it was found necessary to 'spread the footings of the walls by putting stone landings and stone steps to give them a broader foot; they were in a very rickety state'; in the end some £5800 was spent, the bulk of the work being completed by the summer of 1826.[10] Six years later, No. 10 was put in tenantable condition for Lord Grey at an expense of over £1200.[11] Subsequently, little was spent on the house. Despite these frequent repairs, Seward declared in 1839 that these houses were 'nearly worn out'.[12]

When Sir Charles Wood became Chancellor of the Exchequer in July 1846 he decided that his house (Nos. 11 and 12) should be made 'more convenient both for

[1] Works 12/84/1.

[2] Works 12/62/11, ff. 1, 2; 4/18, ff. 137 (21 August 1795), 153 (27 November 1795); 6/23, f. 4 (30 September 1796); 5/85; T. 29/69, f. 459 (15 October 1796).

[3] Works 4/19 (18 April 1806); T. 29/119, f. 499 (9 October 1812); T. 29/120, f. 48 (3 November 1812).

[4] Works 5/108; 1/10, p. 190.

[5] It had at first been suggested that Arbuthnot should keep his house though giving up his office, and Canning as Leader of the House of Commons had hoped to occupy No. 10; but it was found that both houses pertained legally to the Treasury ministers. See *Corr. of Charles Arbuthnot*, ed. A. Aspinall, Camden Soc. 3rd ser. lxv (1941), pp. 38, 42, 44; B.M. Add. MS. 38292, f. 11; *The Diary of Henry Hobhouse*, ed. A. Aspinall (1947), pp. 101–2.

[6] Estimates for repairs: No. 10, £1732, 29 August 1823; No. 12, £1456, 1 September, Works 1/12, pp. 139, 142. Expenditure £2068 and £1356 respectively (Works 5/108).

[7] Works 1/14, p. 25; Soane Mus. 50/4/11–21 (plans and perspectives); D. Stroud, *Architecture of Sir John Soane*, pp. 134–5, pls. 217–9. The plasterer was T. Palmer, and the dining room was first used on 4 April 1826.

[8] Works 1/13, p. 415 (27 July 1825); 5/109. [9] Soane Mus. 50/4/1–6 (plans).

[10] Works 1/13, p. 471; 1/14, p. 113; *Parl. Pap.* 1839, (466) xiii, Report of select committee on Public Offices, q. 66; Works 12/62/9; 5/109.

[11] Works 1/20, p. 80, estimate £2261; *Parl. Pap.* 1854, (219) xlvii, p. 389.

[12] *Parl. Pap.* 1839, xiii, Report *cit.* q. 61.

Official purposes and for the residence of a Family, by allotting separate portions for each object, instead of continuing the mixed occupation which has existed'.[1] Phipps drew up plans for moving the staircase of No. 11 further back and concentrating the office accommodation on the ground floor of the two houses, the upper floors becoming entirely residential. The additions and alterations were estimated at £1400 in addition to works incidental to a change of occupier (£750); but weaknesses in the garden front necessitated its rebuilding at an additional cost of £300.[2] The total cost of the works executed in 1847 was nearly £3800.[3]

The next house towards the Park, No. 13, housed the Judge-Advocate-General from 1803 onwards. When John Beckett was appointed in 1817, the house was thoroughly repaired at a cost of about £750 (excluding furniture) after its long occupation by Charles Manners Sutton. On Beckett's resignation in 1827 a new office was fitted up for the Judge-Advocate-General in Crown Street, and 13 Downing Street was added to the Colonial Office, which adjoined it to the south.[4] It survived that building, but the upper floors were demolished in 1879 after it had been gutted by fire.[5]

Since 1798 the Department of War and the Colonies had been accommodated at 14 Downing Street. Repairs costing £562 were executed in 1824, and further works estimated at £286 were done in 1827–8.[6] These, however, were insignificant compared with those at the Foreign Office at this period. Of the houses in Downing Street occupied by the Foreign Office, the principal was that built for Sir Samuel Fludyer, No. 16, on the south side. Two other houses projecting into Downing Street, with two more behind, fronting on Fludyer Street, had also been acquired by 1825, when Sir Robert Preston's (between Fludyer's and the Colonial Office) was purchased as a residence for the Foreign Secretary, Canning, who had no house of his own in central London.[7] Soane gave an estimate of £1600 for opening communications between Preston's house and the Office, with concomitant alterations, including a new façade with tetrastyle portico, and throwing together the two south-west rooms of Fludyer's house on both the ground and first floors.[8] Considerable modifications were also planned in the two houses projecting into Downing Street, forming a new Cabinet Room, and rebuilding the west return wall. In October Soane reported that Canning and Planta, his under-secretary, had altered the plans, involving an additional charge of £2000. Soane's final estimates totalled £4173, but by the end of 1825 expenditure rose to £4691 more, and in 1826 a further £4811 was spent, making a total of £13,675.[9] The Treasury strongly

[1] Works 12/62/11, ff. 29–31 (11 August 1846).

[2] *Ibid.* ff. 26–7, 28. Plans of the alterations are Works 30/311–15.

[3] *Parl. Pap.* 1854, (219) xlvii, p. 389. With this exception, expenditure on the Chancellor of the Exchequer's house between 1832 and 1852 rarely exceeded £200 p.a.

[4] *Survey of London*, xiv (1931), pp. 154–9; Works 12/62/11, f. 15 (3 October 1817); D. M. Young, *The Colonial Office in the early nineteenth century* (1961), pp. 124–6. The Colonial department had vainly attempted to obtain Beckett's house in 1826 (P.R.O. C.O. 324/75, f. 272, quoted by Young, p. 126).

[5] *Parl. Pap.* 1957–58, x (Cmnd. 457), Report of the committee on the preservation of Downing Street. See also Works 30/5015–18.

[6] Works 5/108–110. Expenditure from 1832 to 1852 averaged about £250 p.a., never exceeding £400 in a year (*Parl. Pap.* 1854, (219) xlvii, p. 389).   [7] Works 1/13, p. 425.

[8] *Ibid.* p. 422; 4/27, p. 241; Soane Mus. 50/5/1–22 (plans and elevations, July–Oct. 1825); MPD 69 (1–4), plans by Soane, 30 July 1825.

[9] Works 1/14, pp. 113, 307; 12/62/9. The totals in the quarterly abstracts of accounts, Works 5/109, amount to only £13,500. A further £9350 were spent on furniture and fixtures, which, with the purchase price of Preston's house, brought the total expenditure to £42,147 (*1828 Report*, p. 10).

criticised the excess over estimates, and the failure to submit supplementaries. Soane replied that 'from the manner in which these works were executed by night and by day, from the variety of directions from different persons and different authorities— no probable conjecture could be formed of the amount of such works (so often altered in progress) until the works were actually completed'.[1] A view of Downing Street in 1827 shows a plain façade to the Foreign Office: the portico planned by Soane was not executed.[2]

Canning was the only Foreign Secretary to reside in the Office, and Soane's alterations provided for little more than the immediate needs of the day. The librarian, Lewis Hertslet, complained in 1839 of books and manuscripts being 'placed in the most irregular and inconvenient manner possible; some of them are stored away in obscure rooms and passages, . . . on two floors, or rather on three floors, and these are distributed in the four or five houses'.[3] The increase of business in the Foreign Office (almost doubled by the recent establishment of relations with South America) and the Colonial Office (where business also doubled between 1824 and 1839) led the government to contemplate the construction of new offices,[4] and the problem was in 1839 referred to a Commons select committee. In his evidence Seward described the poor condition of the greater part of the Foreign Office, and the unfortunate effect of some of Soane's alterations.[5] Great alarm had been caused some eight years previously by the bulging of a wall of the 'great room' in Fludyer's house. Investigations showed that the main beams, running east-west, rested on a cross beam where Soane had removed a wall; the weight had caused the cross beam to sag dangerously.

> I directed [said Seward] a very strong beam to be placed above it in the upper story (the bed-room story), trussed with very strong iron work, which was likewise bolted through the front and the back wall, so that they should not be forced out by the weight. I caused that floor to be suspended by iron rods, and have thus hung up two floors to the upper part of the building; the consequence is, that at those points of bearing the walls are very much weighted, having to carry the weight of a very large portion of the building, resting only on a small space.

It also became necessary to shore up the wall in Downing Street; but in March 1845 rents 'of a very formidable nature' appeared there, and the officers of the Works Department reported that the eastern part of the office must be rebuilt.[6] Works expenditure on the Foreign Office that year at some £900 was twice the annual average over the period 1832–1852,[7] and continued high in the following year. The old buildings were eventually demolished about 1864 to give place to Scott's new offices.[8]

[1] Works 1/14, p. 313.
[2] Water colour by J. C. Buckler, Crace Collection, B.M., reproduced in *Survey of London*, xiv, pl. 142.
[3] *Parl. Pap.* 1839, (466) xiii, Report of select committee on Public Offices.
[4] *Ibid.* qq. 412, 209. The growth of these departments may be followed in Sir J. Tilley and S. Gaselee, *The Foreign Office* (1933) and Sir G. V. Fiddes, *The Dominions and Colonial Offices* (1926).
[5] *Parl. Pap.* 1839, (466), xiii, qq. 2–36. An ancient sewer ran east-west near the centre of the buildings; and the party wall between the projecting houses in Downing Street had sunk, distorting the floors. Preston's house was the best part, having smaller rooms and fewer alterations, though originally Fludyer's had been better built.   [6] Works 2/4, pp. 401, 436.   [7] *Parl. Pap.* 1854, (219) xlvii, p. 389.
[8] Walford, *Old and New London*, iii, p. 392.

6. THE STATE PAPER OFFICE

The records of the secretaries of state when no longer retained by the departments were entrusted to the care of the State Paper Office, housed since 1788 in a building between Middle and Little Scotland Yards.[1] In 1797 the select committee on finance had recommended that a new building should be constructed for the War Office and Board of Control, with provision in the lower part for the public archives, but no action had been taken. When part of the Scotland Yard building gave way early in 1819, the records from 1688 to 1783 were deposited in a corner house in Great George Street formerly the Agent-General's;[2] those from Henry VIII to Charles II were kept in the Middle Treasury Gallery. In December 1824 Peel, then Home Secretary, urged on the Treasury the need to provide a fit depository with the 'least practicable delay', for the Great George Street office was damp, not fireproof, and unable to bear the weight of more papers. In consequence, the Treasury ordered that one of the Attached Architects should see the keepers and make a plan for a new building.[3] Nothing, however, came of this, and eighteen months later, Henry Hobhouse, as Keeper of the Records, reported to Peel that the office had settled towards the east. In March 1828, newly appointed Keeper of the State Papers, Hobhouse informed the Surveyor General of the requirements for a new State Paper Office.[4] In July he reported a further settlement towards the street, whereupon Peel called the 'serious and immediate attention' of the Treasury to his previous reports. Various possibilities were considered. One was to take over the Westminster Sessions House; but the magistrates would require a new one, which the Surveyor General said would cost not less than £50,000.[5] Another alternative was Lady Suffolk's house, insulated on the corner of Duke and Delahay Streets, of which the lease had just fallen in to the Crown, but this proved to be old and unsuitable.[6] The Treasury therefore decided to erect a new State Paper Office on that site, and Soane was asked for a design.[7] His estimate was £12,850,[8] for a brick building of two principal floors, an attic storey surmounted by an entablature ornamented with Greek fret pattern in the frieze, and channelled quoins in the manner of the Insolvent Debtors' Court.[9] After consideration, the Treasury, probably influenced by the report of the select committee of 1828, invited both the other Attached Architects to submit a plan and estimate for a similar brick building with stone dressings containing a large library with a gallery on the upper floor, lighted from the roof if necessary.[10]

[1] See above, p. 542.

[2] Works 1/9, p. 257. Plans (dated 1829) of the Great George Street house, which had three storeys, attic and basement, are in Soane Mus. Portfolio 6, C. Works were executed costing £890 9s. 1d. (Works 5/107).

[3] Works 1/13, p. 114, 27 December 1824.   [4] Works 1/16, p. 188.

[5] T. 1/4257 is a 'long paper' or collection of documents relating entirely to the State Paper Office from 1824 onwards, from which all references are taken unless otherwise indicated.

[6] Works 1/17, pp. 218–9, report by S. Smirke. Plans of the house are in Soane Mus. portfolio 6, D.

[7] Works 1/17, p. 266, 18 April 1829.   [8] *Ibid.* p. 323, 16 May 1829.   [9] Soane Mus. Portfolio 6, A.

[10] Works 1/17, p. 339, 1 June 1829. Soane also was instructed that there was to be a single large room on the upper floor. (*Ibid.* p. 340).

Except at Windsor Castle in 1824, this was the only occasion on which the Attached Architects were required to compete against each other. Smirke's estimate was £26,000 and £3000–£4000 for cases for papers. Nash, whose estimate was £16,000 if the old materials of the house were re-used, or £18,500 with new materials, stressed the fireproof character of his construction:

> . . . No Timber whatever to be laid in the Walls but the Bond and some lintels to be of Yorkshire Stone—the floors to be formed of Iron girders with brick arches between them—the Basement floor throughout to be paved with Yorkshire Stone—the Roofs to be flat formed of Iron girders and brick arches between them and covered with slates laid in Stanhope Composition with lead gutters and water pipes—the Staircases and landings—the floor of the great Library and the Galleries within to be of Portland Stone—the Clerks Offices, the Reading Rooms, the waiting room, the Keeper's and Deputy Keepers apartments and the private apartments of the Resident Keeper to have deal floors laid on the Brick arches and deal Base and surbase mouldings . . . the Bookcases to be formed of Bath Stone—and the Shelves and doors of wrought Iron[1] formed in open framings to circulate the air—the Skirtings of the Rooms to be of Mastic . . .

The library would be in the centre of the building, with two stone galleries and clerestory lighting. Heating would be by a hot air stove situated in the stairwell of the basement. The domestic apartments were to be as separate as possible.[2]

It was perhaps some compensation to Soane for earlier disappointments that here he was the successful competitor. In his revised design, which he estimated at £17,600, the end bays of each front (except the re-entrant east front) were rusticated and marked off by pilasters, the bracketted cornice emphasized, and the attic storey concealed.[3] In September, however, Goulburn, the Chancellor of the Exchequer, called for alterations: he 'disapproved of the Rusticated Quoins' and wished two orders of pilasters to grace the elevation, something after the style of the Banqueting House.[4] Soane thought this 'a very absurd alteration', and drew the Banqueting House and Goulburn's proposal to the same scale to show how Jones's decorative features on the smaller building would appear 'trivial in character and defective in the relative proportions of the parts to the whole and the parts among themselves'.[5] Another drawing shows half the proposed Office to Soane's design, half to Goulburn's 'according to the dilettanti Architecture of the present day'.[6] Despite his views, Soane followed Goulburn's instructions in a design which he sent to the Office of Works on 19 November 1829. A month later he submitted an estimate of £900 for stone ashlar to all the fronts; and on 29 December the Treasury Board selected Soane's as the 'most appropriate design'. As Goulburn's alterations added another £3000 to the estimate, thus raising it above Nash's, and as no attempt was made (as far as

---

[1] He also suggested using copper plates framed in panels, filled with thinner perforated plates.
[2] T. 1/4257, f. 16430/29 (22 September 1829).
[3] Soane Mus. Portfolio 6/A/17–22, plans, elevations and perspective, dated 20 June 1829. Copies by John Phipps of the Office of Works are in T. 1/4257.
[4] Soane Mus. Portfolio 6/A/21. He also directed: 'No fire places to be between the Windows where it can be avoided. Library to be Fireproof'.
[5] Quoted by Bolton, *Works of Sir John Soane* (1926), p. 128, and illustrated, D. Stroud, *The Architecture of Sir John Soane* (1961), fig. 222.   [6] Soane Mus. Portfolio 6/A/4.

is known) to persuade Nash or Smirke to render their designs 'appropriate', it would seem that the intention all along had been to give the building to Soane, and that the competition was arranged merely to satisfy the House of Commons.[1]

Soane continued to ponder the design, and drawings of various dates in May 1830 show alternative treatments of the attic windows, either as a distinct half-storey, or nestling between the brackets of the cornice.[2] The egregious Bankes proposed raising the height of the attics from eight feet to 11 feet 6 inches, an alteration which appears to have decided Soane to put the windows in the metopes, in order to keep down the total height of the building.[3] Bankes also advocated a rusticated treatment of the end bays instead of Goulburn's pilasters.[4] Goulburn rejected Bankes's alterations, and his own preferred version was approved by the Treasury Board on 24 June 1830.[5] Difficulties with the foundations delayed the building, and on 1 December 1830, after the appointment of Grey's ministry, Soane submitted two elevations 'for further consideration', which Stephenson promptly refused, although Soane claimed that one would save £2000 at least.[6] Nevertheless, Goulburn's alterations were not in the end carried out, and the completed Office more closely resembled Bankes's version.

Features of the design (Pl. 51A) derive, as Miss Stroud has pointed out, from 'Vignola's Villa Farnese at Caprarola, a work which had made a deep impression on [Soane] when he had visited it some fifty years before; and of which a number of engravings were in his library'.[7] The

> most obvious debt to the Villa was the bracket cornice with wide eaves, creating the illusion of a pantiled roof. In fact they merely screened the flat roof behind, in which were set a number of glazed lanterns. From the same source came the rusticated treatment of the end bays of the west elevation [to the Park], and the main entrance in Duke Street, which was Soane's version of Vignola's famous doorway.

Perhaps, however, the dominant feature of the composition is its astylar character. This originated with the instruction to design a brick building, with dressings only of stone. Moreover Soane much disliked engaged columns in conjunction with two storeys of windows of equal height, as was the case here.[8] Some of the window architraves were taken from the upper storey of the Banqueting House, of which Soane was then superintending the restoration. Channelled quoins, as in his first design, Soane had employed in the Insolvent Debtors' Court, but in his final version he followed the Caprarola model of long and short alternating.[9] Given Soane's instructions and principles, we can perhaps in some measure account for this late development of Soane's style, which, contemporaneously with Barry's

[1] See above, p. 164. Soane's revised estimate of £23,300, dated 7 January 1830, included £1800 for presses, stoves and fittings, and was approved by Treasury letter of 27 January 1830 (Works 1/18, pp. 23, 40).
[2] Soane Mus. Portfolio 6/A/33, 40, 45.   [3] *Ibid.* nos. 41 (31 May), 42 (2 June 1830).
[4] *Ibid.* no. 41, an elevation 'altered as suggested by Mr. Bankes'.
[5] *Ibid.* no. 15 and letter, Stephenson to Soane of 26 June, with no. 6; Works 1/18, p. 151, Stephenson to Soane, 19 June 1830.   [6] Works 4/30, f. 413; 1/18, p. 283; 12/67/7, f. 15.
[7] D. Stroud, *op. cit.*, pp. 135–6. In his Royal Academy *Lectures on Architecture* (edited A. T. Bolton, 1929, p. 87) Soane remarked, 'The beautiful plans and exterior of the Papa Giulio at Rome and the Farnese Palace at Caprarola, can never be sufficiently admired or too much studied'. (We owe this reference to Miss Stroud.)
[8] Soane refused to have two equal storeys in the Board of Trade and Council Offices, see p. 554 above.
[9] There are models of differing treatments of the corner bays in the Soane Museum; see J. Wilton-Ely, 'The architectural models of Sir John Soane: a catalogue', *Architectural History* xii (1969), fig. 21c.

Travellers' Clubhouse, introduced the Italian palazzo style to London. Soane himself described the building as 'imitated from the Architecture of Vignola, Palladio, Inigo Jones, Sir C. Wren, &c.'.[1] It appears to be unnecessary to postulate Barry's influence in turning Soane to a Roman model he so much admired.[2] It is interesting to notice how the designs gradually became more Vignolan, the doorway, for instance, only appearing in May 1830.[3] This was modified in the working drawings dated May 1831; and Soane restored the Greek fret frieze to the cornice in June 1831.[4] He continued to modify details, producing a number of alternative designs for chimneys in February and April 1834.[5]

Progress was at first very slow, owing to difficulties with the foundations, only resolved in August 1830.[6] Up to the end of the year only £4575 had been expended out of a vote of £12,000;[7] and in the quarter following, £77 3s. Thereafter, work went on faster; the fourth course of the basement was finished on 28 May; and nearly £9000 were spent in the remainder of 1831.[8] The girders for the fireproof floors were ordered in May (ground) and July (upper floors). Soane's construction of these floors as arches of hollow bricks springing from girders governed the triple-arched form of the ceilings throughout the building.[9] In September 1833 Soane was designing presses for the library; and in the summer of 1834 the carcass was completed by the construction of the chimneys.[10] By November 1834, the total expenditure (including fittings) was £23,593.[11] One alteration in design proved to have been a false economy: a reduction in the proposed height of the stone chimney shafts. The chimneys smoked, and modifications by Feethams, the stove-makers, produced no satisfactory improvement, so that Soane had to raise his stone shafts to the height originally intended.

Soane's last important official work was entirely demolished in 1862 to make way for Scott's new Foreign Office, but short-lived as it was it had a considerable influence on London's architecture, providing (together with Barry's club-houses) a formula for Victorian architecture which satisfied the growing demand for greater richness in elevational treatment.

[1] Soane Mus. Portfolio 6/A/4.   [2] As does Bolton, *Works*, p. 130.

[3] Soane Mus. Portfolio 6/A/49, 50. Soane, in fact, did not like this first version, commenting: 'This door etc. is in its proportions like Vignola's book. Here is another example that a design originally on a large scale cannot be copied on small scale—The door in the present case would not be more than about 7 feet high, which would be preposterously low.' (no. 50). That Soane was at this time experimenting considerably is shewn by another drawing, dated 3 May 1830, with busts flanking the windows in the metopes, with a note by Soane (6 May), 'Query Busts in Cornice—If shields—Trophies etc. are admissible in the Metopes of the Doric Order why not have busts of illustrious persons whose labours are supposed to be deposited within the walls of this Edifice?' (Soane Mus. Portfolio 6/A/35).   [4] *Ibid.* B/21, 13.   [5] *Ibid.* nos. 1, 28, 29.

[6] *Ibid.* A/90, 'Foundations . . . as settled by Mr. Soane 7th April 1830' shews a foundation to a total depth of about ten feet. A/96 (13 August 1830) shews one of about 20 feet. Soane told the select committee on House of Commons buildings, 13 May 1833, 'it was necessary to sink below the level of the street at least 20 feet, to the bed of gravel, to remove the loose earth and mud, and to form foundations for the walls of solid materials' (*Parl. Pap.* 1833 (269) xii, q. 119). Broken granite, laid in layers and grouted, formed the bottom three feet of foundation.

[7] Old materials were sold for £861 11s. 6d., correspondingly diminishing the net expense (Works 5/111). The principal contractors were McIntosh (excavator), Martin Stutely (bricklayer), W. Whitehead (bricklayer), Jane Grundy (mason), T. & G. Martyr (carpenter), Geo. Woolcot (joiner), W. R. Holroyd (plumber), J. Mackell (smith), Robson & Estall (plasterer), Wm. Watson (glazier) (Works 5/119, pp. 65, 94–5).

[8] *Ibid.*; Soane Mus. Portfolio 6/A/55.

[9] Soane Mus. Portfolio 6/A/68, B/62; Folio VI, 101; 26/3/3 (showing how the iron girders were bolted on either side of wooden joists, hardly a convincing fireproof design).

[10] *Ibid.* Portfolio 6/B/38, 56 (July 1834). A drawing for an octagonal lantern for the principal stair is Works 12/62/7, f. 25.   [11] Bolton, *Works*, p. 128, n.

7. THE HORSE GUARDS DEPARTMENT

The Horse Guards department was placed under the Office of Works in July 1817.[1] Besides Kent's Horse Guards building itself the department included some sixteen other buildings used for military purposes.[2] Annual expenditure averaged nearly £4400 during the years 1818–31, but fell to about £2000 a year during the 1830s.[3] The adjoining Paymaster-General's house was repaired at a cost of nearly £2400 (including furniture), on Sir Charles Long giving up that office in 1826.[4] The Horse Guards building itself had been enlarged about twenty years previously by its surveyor Thomas Rice, whose designs for raising the blocks that linked the wings to the main building were approved by James Wyatt before being put into effect.[5] By 1845 additional accommodation had to be found for the out-pensioner department of the War Office, and for the Adjutant-General's department. A preliminary suggestion for closing the entrance to the Tiltyard from Whitehall, building two rooms on the space and adapting the Guards' suttling house did not find favour,[6] and Phipps stated that space could not be gained

> by any other means than by heightening the present Buildings, a measure which from the firm and substantial character of the existing Buildings, [the Commissioners] are inclined to believe might be adopted with great advantage, and so as to afford not only the additional accommodation now so urgently required for the out Pension and Adjutant-General's Departments, but also for various other Offices connected with the Military Establishments, now occupying separate and detached Buildings inconveniently dispersed in different parts of the Town at Rents and other expenses very disproportioned to accommodation afforded.[7]

Barry was commissioned to provide 'much Additional Accommodation combined with improved Architectural Appearance' by heightening the old buildings as Phipps had suggested.[8] The grandiose scheme which 'floated before his mind' is described by his biographer[9] and represented by a set of drawings in the Public Record Office.[10] It included a new central tower and other alterations which were estimated at £131,631.[11] But, like the projects of William Wilkins and Alfred Beaumont for creating a 'triumphal entrance' to the building,[12] it was never seriously considered.

[1] Works 4/22, p. 411; Works 6/357/6, no. 7. Kidd, the Surveyor to the Horse Guards, retained his post until 1819.
[2] Including Paymaster-General's house, Army Pay Office, Office for Military Boards, Chaplain-General's office, Comptroller's Office, Judge-Advocate-General's house, Recruiting Department (Duke Street), Department of Accounts (Duke and Crown Streets), Army Medical Board Office, and Army Prison Ship (Works 1/10, p. 400).   [3] Works 5/107–111; L.R.R.O. 24/1–8.
[4] Works 1/14, p. 428 (7 September 1826); 1/15, p. 160; Works 5/109; Soane Museum corresp. New Law Courts, pt. ii, f. 206. For this house see *Survey of London*, xvi (1935), Chap. 3, and pp. 1, 32–44.
[5] *Later Correspondence of George III*, iv, no. 2796, Secretary at War to the King, 15 September 1803. For Rice's accounts see *Parl. Pap.* 1812–13, v, pp. 478 and 512 and T. 1/1218, no. 13276, T. 1/1224, no. 4271, etc.
[6] Works 2/4, pp. 426, 454, 500; Works 2/5, p. 24.   [7] Works 2/5, pp. 33–5, 17 December 1845.
[8] Works 1/29, p. 45, 2 January 1846.   [9] A. Barry, *Life and Works of Sir Charles Barry* (1867), p. 276.
[10] Works 30/183, 185–196 (dated 18 January 1847). Works 30/184 is a later scheme (on paper watermarked 1850) to raise the height of the blocks on the street front.   [11] Works 11/1/2, f. 159.
[12] Wilkins' design for a 'Triumphal entrance to the Horse Guards, designed to commemorate the services of a deceased Field Marshal, and approved by his late Majesty George IV' was exhibited at the Royal Academy in 1837. Beaumont's design forms part of a scheme for the improvement of St. James's Park dated 1850 and preserved in the Royal Library at Windsor.

III. THE NEW HOUSES OF
PARLIAMENT

THE destruction of the Houses of Parliament by fire on 16 October 1834 provided English architects with their greatest opportunity of the century. There was now no government architect to whom the work of reconstruction might be entrusted, but Melbourne turned, as if instinctively, to Robert Smirke, the only active survivor of the old trinity of the Office of Works. William IV offered Buckingham Palace as a home for Parliament, and Westminster Hall, St. James's Palace and Guildhall were also suggested,[1] but after hesitating briefly the ministers placed the ruins in Smirke's charge, directing him to construct temporary Houses on the site and to prepare plans for a rebuilding on a 'moderate and suitable scale of magnitude'.[2]

Smirke's report of 21 October, which determined the government's course, stated that the walls of the House of Lords and the Painted Chamber, when partially repaired, would be 'in a condition to receive a Roof and the fittings necessary for their temporary use with perfect safety'.

> If the Painted Chamber [he wrote] were fitted up for the reception of the Peers, convenient access may be given to it through the Kings Entrance Gallery making a temporary connection between it and the Gallery the end of which next the Painted Chamber is destroyed.
>
> The Peers would then also have immediate communication made with their Committee Rooms, Library & other rooms & offices to which the fire has not extended, or where it has but partially injured them.
>
> The Walls of the House of Lords which are standing and enclose an area nearly 40 feet wide & 120 feet long, would afford sufficient space for the convenient temporary accommodation of the House of Commons, giving access to it by a wide passage that may be made from the Arcade next the Approach hitherto used by the Members.
>
> Another approach may be readily given thro[ugh] Westminster Hall as soon as the Works in progress for the restoration of the Hall are completed.
>
> A communication may also be made with the Committee rooms which are partially destroyed so that they may be used as soon as they are repaired, and it is probable that some of the rooms adjoining, in that part of the Building occupied by the Courts of Law may be used without material inconvenience to the business of the Courts.
>
> Observing that these arrangements may be so well made, leaving the extensive area between Westminster Hall and the River clear for future disposal I have little to state in favor of [the] Plan for fitting up the interior of the Hall [for the two Houses].[3]

[1] *The Times*, 18 October, p. 5; 27 October, p. 3; 5 November 1834, p. 2.
[2] Spencer Walpole, *History of England from . . . 1815*, iii (1880), pp. 286–7; Works 11/10/2, ff. 1–2, 24 October 1834, Treasury to Commissioners of Woods and Works; Works 1/11/1, f. 61–2.
[3] Works 2/1, pp. 189–90.

Three days later, he submitted detailed proposals, remarking:

> By their connection with the extensive building that is preserved, a better opportunity is afforded of providing for the convenience of the two Houses than by any other Plan, and it would leave the whole Area between Westminster Hall and the River, a space exceeding four hundred feet in length and more than 250 feet in width, clear for the arrangement and erection of any Buildings that may be required for the permanent reception of the Houses of Parliament or other purposes.[1]

An accurate estimate could not be formed, but the cost, including the repair of partly damaged rooms required for immediate use, would be about £25,000 or £30,000; the work might be completed for the reception of both Houses by the first week in February. A further estimate for furniture amounted to £7500.[2]

The Painted Chamber, measuring about 26 feet by 80 feet, was fitted up with the throne against the east wall, three rows of seats on either side and a space reserved below the bar at the west for the Commons. A narrow gallery was constructed on either side with a single row of seats for peers (Pl. 35B). Soane's King's Stair and gallery provided a peers' entrance and connected with the offices of the House.[3] The former House of Lords accommodated a Commons' Chamber 38 feet by 80 feet (larger than the old), with members' galleries on either side, a public one at the north end, and a small gallery above the Speaker's chair for reporters (Pl. 34B).[4]

The temporary Houses were ready by 17 February 1835, the works being executed by S. Baker and Son and T. and G. Martyr.[5] The rapidity of the work was facilitated by the prefabrication of the timbering and iron girders,[6] and the use of papiermâché by Charles F. Bielefeld for the ornamental features, principally in the House of Lords.[7] More than half the labour of preparing boards for ceiling linings, for parts of the walls and for slating was carried out by night.[8]

By the end of July 1835, out of a vote of £44,085, some £39,500 had been expended on the Temporary Houses[9]—for accommodation that was far from adequate. Additional committee rooms had to be hired for the Commons,[10] rooms built for the Speaker's chaplain and for members' cloaks and hats,[11] and alterations made for the Speaker.[12] A division lobby at the south end of the House was wanted,[13] and in accordance with a select committee's report, the Strangers' Gallery was partitioned to provide 24 seats for ladies, 'screened in front by an open trellis work'

[1] *Ibid.* pp. 192–4.   [2] *Ibid.* p. 201.

[3] I.e. committee rooms, library etc., 'being nearly all that has hitherto been used except the Apartments for the accommodation of the Officers of the House' (Works 11/10/2, f. 3).

[4] *The Times*, 9 and 23 December 1834. This gallery may be seen in pl. xxxix of Brayley and Britton, *History of the Ancient Palace . . . of Westminster* (1836). Greville noted its significance: 'For the first time there is a gallery in the House of Commons reserved for reporters, which is quite inconsistent with their standing orders, and the prohibition which still in form exists against publishing the debates. It is a sort of public and avowed homage to opinion, and a recognition of the right of the people to know through the medium of the press all that passes within those walls' (*Memoirs* 1874, ed. iii, p. 205).

[5] E. W. Brayley and J. Britton, *The Ancient Palace . . . at Westminster* (1836), p. 464; Works 11/10/2, f. 10.

[6] *The Times*, 1 November and 3 November 1834.

[7] *Gent.'s Mag.* 1835, i, pp. 45, 312; *Architectural Mag.* ii (1835) p. 41. A plate of the interior of the temporary House of Lords is given in C. F. Bielefeld's publication, *On the Use of the Improved Papier-Mâché* (1850).

[8] Works 11/10/2, f. 10.   [9] Works 1/21, p. 565.   [10] *Ibid.* pp. 229, 249, 268.

[11] Works 11/10/2, f. 6, estimate £290.

[12] Works 1/21, p. 304, 30 April 1835.

[13] Works 11/10/2, f. 20, 13 July 1835.

and reached by a separate stair.[1] The Lords complained of the narrowness of their chamber, claiming that it was 'impossible to conduct the business of the country in a manner that is consistent with the dignity of the highest branch of the legislature'.[2] The fact was that, as Lord Duncannon told the Chancellor of the Exchequer, 'the space between the side walls will scarcely admit, even on ordinary occasions, of a passage from the Woolsack to the Bar, and when the House is full the communication from one part of the House to the other is almost impossible'.[3] Smirke reported that the walls of the Painted Chamber, though from $4\frac{1}{2}$ to 5 feet thick, were of 'rough materials, chalk and rubble stone loosely held together, and in some parts so much fractured that it would be impossible to increase the width of the room by cutting away any portion of their thickness'. Instead he suggested that a room of 38 by 70 feet might be built in the space between St. Stephen's Chapel and the Painted Chamber.[4] Although the government called for an estimate for all these works, to be laid before the Commons before the end of the session,[5] only the Commons' needs were provided for, a new lobby being erected by Messrs. H. and J. Lee for £1106.[6]

Meanwhile Smirke had been preparing designs for rebuilding. Completed by February 1835,[7] they were submitted to the King, 'who directed that they should be given with his approval' to the new Prime Minister, Sir Robert Peel.[8] As the architect's known patron and friend,[9] Peel laid himself open to the charge of favouritism, while Smirke appeared to his professional colleagues to be quietly converting a rescue operation into a major commission. The monopoly of the Office of Works in a matter of such importance was also criticised. The agitation was led by the prominent amateur Sir Edward Cust,[10] who addressed an open letter to Peel attacking the poverty of Smirke's taste, and urging that a limited competition should be held under the auspices of a royal commission, of which he offered to serve as a member.[11] This pamphlet struck home. A select committee appointed by the Commons on 2 March 1835 to 'consider and report on such Plan as may be most fitting and convenient for the permanent Accommodation of the Houses of Parliament',[12] at first favoured Smirke's plan and rejected Hume's proposal for a competition. But opinion soon began to harden against the old ways.[13] The committee changed its mind and, although not accepting Cust's suggestions in their entirety, reported on 3 June 1835 that it was 'expedient that the designs for the rebuilding of

---

[1] *Parl. Pap.* 1835 (437), xviii, with Smirke's plan and estimate of £280.   [2] Works 11/10/2, f. 13.
[3] *Ibid.* f. 13, Smirke to Duncannon, 25 June; f. 16, Duncannon to Chancellor of the Exchequer, 16 July 1835.   [4] *Ibid.* f. 13.   [5] *Ibid.* f. 19, 29 July 1835.   [6] *Ibid.* f. 21, 25 August 1835.
[7] R.I.B.A. Drawings Collection J 11/37/1–5.
[8] Works 11/1/1, ff. 61–2. William IV favoured Smirke's designs on grounds of economy and speed. 'The great object', he told Stephenson, 'is to have the plans complete *before* the legislature *can* proceed to business . . . the most extravagant ideas are otherwise likely to be brought forward which must impede the business of the session' (MS. in possession of Sir Edward Malet Bt., 8 February 1835).
[9] For the relationship between Sir Robert Peel and Smirke ('the Prime Minister and his Pet') see J. Mordaunt Crook, 'Sir Robert Peel: Patron of the Arts', *History Today* xvi (1966) i, pp. 3–11.   [10] See p. 195.
[11] Sir E. Cust, *A letter to the Right Hon. Sir Robert Peel, Bart., M.P., on the expedience of a better system of control over buildings erected at the public expense; and on the subject of rebuilding the Houses of Parliament,* 31 January 1835. Peel replied to Cust, 8 February 1835, that 'The Report you have heard that an "Architect has been appointed to the duty of building a new House of Parliament" that is of course new, as distinguished from the present provisional arrangement, is without foundation'. This was strictly true, but the implication was misleading. Peel also pointed out that Cust had ignored the vital question of who was to pay for the new building, and commented: 'I think you will find the House disposed to claim a much greater share in the deliberation, as to the extent and plan, and every detail of the Building than you are willing to assign to them' (B.M. Add. MS. 40413, f. 134).   [12] *Commons' Jnls.* xc (1835), p. 38.   [13] *Mirror of Parliament*, 1836, iii, 2489, Sir John Hobhouse.

the Houses of Parliament be left open to general competition,' and that 'the style of the buildings be either Gothic or Elizabethan',[1] a requirement inspired by belief in the Englishness of these styles and their propriety in juxtaposition to Westminster Hall and Abbey.[2] The Committee also laid down various detailed requirements for the new House of Commons: which should be nearly square, and large enough (including galleries) to seat all 658 members. Accommodation was also to be provided for peers and visitors. Competitors were to be supplied with a lithographic plan showing the space available for building, including that to be gained by embanking the river. Certain other conditions were imposed: all designs were to be on a uniform scale of 20 feet to one inch; no coloured drawings would be received, and perspectives only from view-points to be specified. Designs were to be submitted by 1 November. To save time and expense, no estimate would be required initially. A royal commission of five persons was proposed to examine the plans, and select and classify not less than three nor more than five as most worthy the attention of the committee, reporting by 20 January 1836. The selected competitors would each receive £500, the winner, who 'shall not be considered as having necessarily a Claim to be entrusted with the Execution of the Work', receiving if not so employed an additional £1000. These resolutions were adopted also by the corresponding committee of the Lords, which added details of the requirements of the Upper House.[3] Thus the commissioners were not given the free hand proposed by Cust: the parliamentary committees (more especially that of the Commons) kept control over the proceedings, and, though allotting to the commissioners the invidious labour of selection, retained the final choice.

Cust, although his scheme had been mauled, did not decline an invitation to serve on the royal commission. Lord Duncannon, the First Commissioner of Woods and Works, also invited two celebrated noble connoisseurs, the 'Athenian Thane', Lord Aberdeen, and Lord de Grey, but both refused.[4] The four commissioners finally selected with Cust—'gentlemen who have devoted much of their time to the study of Architecture', as Duncannon informed the King[5]—were Charles Hanbury Tracy (the chairman), Thomas Liddell, George Vivian, and Samuel Rogers (who declined to act).[6]

---

[1] *Parl. Pap.* 1835 (262) xviii.

[2] On the brief vogue of 'Elizabethan', see M. Girouard, 'Attitudes to Elizabethan Architecture, 1600–1900', *Concerning Architecture* (1968), ed. Sir John Summerson, pp. 13–28. The competition judges had little idea how to define the term (*Parl. Pap.* 1836 (245), xxi, qq. 62–3).

[3] *Parl. Pap.* 1835 (262) xviii; *Parl. Pap. H.L.* 1835 (73) xxviii, 609.

[4] Works 11/1/1, ff. 14, 16. De Grey, who was at this time rebuilding Wrest, remarked that he had 'so much business of a private nature'.   [5] *Ibid.* f. 19.

[6] Hanbury Tracy, 1777–1858, cr. Baron Sudeley of Toddington 1838, designed the great Gothic house of Toddington, Glos., from 1819, and reconstructed Hampton Court, Herefs. 1834–9. See M. J. McCarthy, 'Charles Hanbury Tracy, Amateur Architect of the Gothic Revival', B.A. (Fine Art) thesis, Cambridge 1964. I am grateful to the present Lord Sudeley for lending me his copy. For Toddington see C. Hussey, *Late Georgian Country Houses* (1958), pp. 161–7. The Hon. Thomas Liddell, 1800–56, a son of the 1st Lord Ravensworth, and brother-in-law of Lords Mulgrave and Hardwicke, is said to have designed a gatehouse at Ravensworth Castle (J. C. Loudon, *Encyclopaedia of Cottage, Farm and Villa Architecture*, 1st additional supplement, p. 1162), and the principal front of the Castle itself (*Illustrated London News* 1846, p. 45). In 1834 the north side was still unfinished, and further additions were made in the 1840s (N. Pevsner, *Buildings of England, Durham*, 1953, p. 196). In 1832 Lady Wharncliffe described it as 'really beautiful (in Queen Elizabeth's style) as well as comfortable' (*The First Lady Wharncliffe and her family, 1779–1856*, 1927, ed. C. Grosvenor and Lord Stuart of Wortley). George Vivian, 1800–73, of Claverton Manor, Bath, who sat on the Fine Arts Commission throughout its existence (1841–63), published works on Iberian and Roman scenery, as well as *Some Illustrations of the Architecture of Claverton, etc.* (1837) (F. Boase, *Modern English Biography*, suppl. iii, 1921).

There was some delay before the final instructions were issued to competitors. Notices were issued in the *London Gazette* on 21, 24 and 28 July, inviting architects to apply for instructions at the Office of Woods, and on 18 August they were informed that a plan of the site would be available from 24 August. This plan, signed on 2 June by Lord Granville Somerset as chairman of the select committee, showed that part of the river which might be embanked, and also the ground in New Palace Yard, 'now occupied by Buildings, but hereafter to be left vacant to complete the façade of Palace Yard', a stipulation which invited a symmetrical treatment of the north front on the axis of Westminster Hall.[1] On 3 November a warning was issued that non-compliance with the instructions would cause rejection of entries: there had been some misunderstanding of the requirement that entries should be under a 'figure, motto, or other device', and some had been received with name and address affixed. The closing date, at first 1 November, was extended to 1 December 1835.

Even before the closing date some dissatisfaction with the arrangements was being expressed. James Savage, one of the better-known competitors, wrote to the radical M.P. Henry Warburton, a member of the select committee, on 21 November, complaining of the shortness of the time allowed, which was further diminished by the Board of Woods' delay in making the complete instructions available—a delay which had given rise to suspicion that some competitors were favoured with prior information. Believing he could not finish in time, Savage sought Warburton's advice.[2] In forwarding his letter to Duncannon, Warburton remarked that complaint was very general among architects.[3] A 'lawyer' wrote to Sir John Hobhouse, former Whig Chief Commissioner of Woods and Works, about a common rumour that Cust had 'lent himself in rather an extraordinary manner to the support of one Architect'— namely Barry, who had been associated with Cust in criticism of Wilkins' National Gallery.[4] Duncannon replied that he had had fifty such letters, and could pay no attention to them; the commissioners might each have a favourite architect, but the final selection lay in the hands of Parliament.[5]

Certainly Barry was tipped to win. J. F. Goodchild, an assistant of C. R. Cockerell, years later recalled how

> Mr. Cockerell with his brother-in-law Geo Penrice the sculptor, were looking at a pencil sketch view of the River Front . . . when master Freddey came running in, and placing himself between his Father and his Uncle with his hands in his pockets, and with his clear full voice, 'Well, Papa, and do you think Barry will beat that!' he had heard us talking of the reports which were being made, that Mr. Barry was going to send a design that would surprise every body, and some of the know-all ones went so far as to say that the carriage of one of the Commissioners appointed for the selection of the Designs, had been seen at Mr. Barry's door.[6]

---

[1] MR 1050. For further details see *Parl. Pap.* 1835 (262) xviii, p. 35.

[2] Works 11/1/1, ff. 30–1. See also Savage's letter in *The Times* 3 May 1836. Savage, with George and Joseph Gwilt and L. N. Cottingham, petitioned the House of Commons about the delay (Works 11/1/1, f. 37).

[3] *Ibid.* f. 58, 26 November. See also T. Hopper, *A Letter to the Rt. Hon. Lord Viscount Duncannon* (1837).

[4] Works 11/1/1, ff. 32–3; W. Wilkins, *An Apology for the Design of the Houses of Parliament, marked* 'Phil-Archimedes' . . . (1836); *Builder* 1860, pp. 416–7. Barry had also designed an addition to Cust's house in Spring Gardens (MPE 1285). [5] Works 11/1/1, 1 Dec. 1835.

[6] MS Reminiscences, from Sir Albert Richardson's Library, on loan to R.I.B.A. Library.

Hanbury Tracy himself admitted that he had heard so much about the beauty of Barry's design that when he saw no. 64 he guessed it must be his.[1] Loudon, writing in his *Architectural Magazine* a year after the competition, remarked:

> With respect to the subject of the plans having been seen by the commissioners;[2] we have no doubt some of them were, and we believe, among others, that of Mr. Barry, for which we attach no blame to that gentleman, who, in common with all the other architects, had a right to exhibit his plans if he thought proper, to all the world. That most of the competing architects did exhibit their plans to their friends, we believe, is generally known. We saw some, and we know one gentleman who saw seven or eight, and described the leading features of each. The magnificence of Mr. Barry's design, and the grandeur of his idea of a central [sic] tower as a royal entrance, were matters of conversation, among those interested in the subject, for weeks before it was announced that he had obtained the prize.[3]

Ninety-seven entries were received, and the commissioners were faced with the formidable task of examining some 1400 drawings. On 15 January they themselves asked for an extension of time to make their report.[4] Hanbury Tracy declared that he spent nearly two months from morning to night examining the plans.[5] The report was finally presented to Parliament on 29 February 1836.[6]

The commissioners selected only four designs, declaring they were unable to give a preference to a fifth: those of Barry (no. 64, marked with a portcullis);[7] John Chessell Buckler[8] (no. 14, marked, according to the commissioners, with an R; but in fact, as rivals commented, with an obvious rebus, an R inside a buckle), David Hamilton[9] (no. 13, 'King, Lords and Commons'), and William Railton[10] (no. 42, a winged orb).

Barry's design (Pls. 52, 55A), the commissioners agreed unanimously,

> bears throughout such evident marks of genius and superiority of talent, as fully to entitle it to the preference we have given it. . . . The Elevations are of an order so superior, and display so much taste and knowledge of Gothic Architecture, as to leave no doubt whatever in our minds of the Author's ability to carry into effect Your Majesty's Commands, should you be pleased to honour him with your confidence.

Buckler's elevations deserved 'much commendation', though it was more difficult to judge the effect, 'from the number of projections and recesses, which give a broken character to all the River front' (Pl. 54A). Criticisms of the ground plan affected the placing of this design, as also of Hamilton's, who, unlike Buckler, cleared away

---

[1] *Parl. Pap.* 1836 (245) xxxi, q. 14.

[2] As Hume had alleged in Parliament (*Parl. Deb.* 3rd ser. xxxi, 503).   [3] *Op. cit.* iii (1836), p. 107.

[4] Works 11/1/1, f. 38.   [5] *Parl. Pap.* 1836 (245) xxi, q. 78.   [6] *Parl. Pap.* 1836 (66) xxxvi.

[7] It is perhaps noteworthy that the two designs with which Pugin is associated were indicated by Tudor royal badges—Barry's, the portcullis; and Gillespie Graham's, H.R. with the rose and coronet (*Catalogue of the Designs offered for the New Houses of Parliament now exhibiting in the National Gallery* 1836, p. 19).

[8] 1793–1894, designed Costessy Hall, Norf. 1826. For his Westminster designs, see Works 29/38–48.

[9] 1768–1843, designed Glasgow Exchange 1837 and many other public and commercial buildings in Glasgow, as well as country houses. See R. Chambers, *Biographic Dictionary of Eminent Scotsmen* (edition by T. Thompson, 1869). His designs for the Houses of Parliament are Works 29/49–58.

[10] *c.* 1801–77, later to win the competition for the Nelson Memorial, Trafalgar Square, see p. 492. His Westminster designs are Works 29/59–74.

St. Stephen's Chapel and cloister. Hamilton's Elizabethan design (Pl. 54B) possessed, they thought, 'sufficient of the characteristics of the Style'. Being aware, they remarked, 'of the difference of opinion that exists as to the date which affixes the limits to the Style termed Elizabethan even amongst the Profession, we determined to give it the greatest latitude of which it can possibly admit'. Railton was particularly commended for his plan.

The commissioners commented that whether a plan preserved 'those venerable and beautiful remains of antiquity', St. Stephen's Chapel and cloisters, had not been a factor in their choice.[1] But from the the plans submitted, they were sure that preservation need not hamper the new building. They made two further suggestions. The chosen plan needed revision before execution, and they were confident that the architect would be able to remove objections, so that his work would throw lustre on the era in which it was built. But, they remarked (strangely, in view of their expressed confidence in Barry's 'ability to carry into effect' the work), 'as the beauty of this Style depends upon the attention to detail, for which the Architect has no rule to guide him, ... we humbly, yet strongly recommend ... that his Drawings shall be submitted from time to time to competent judges of their effect; lest from over confidence, negligence or inattention in the execution of the Work, we fail to obtain that result to which our just expectations have been raised'. The design should not, however, be altered in such a way as to change its character or impair its unity.

Their other suggestion was that, though it had been prudent not to put competitors to the expense of making an estimate, the successful competitor should be called upon to furnish a specification 'of the style in which he intends to finish the interior, and the particular parts requiring, in his opinion, extra decoration, previous to his being called upon for any Estimate'. This was suggested by the 'profuse and unnecessary ornament introduced by many', which would be a waste of public money. Aware that this criticism might be levelled equally at Barry, they stated:

> the enriched appearance of the several Elevations will naturally excite suspicion that it cannot be carried into effect but at an enormous expense. In the absence of the detail of any portion of the Work, we can form no perfect idea of the Architect's intentions; but even with the minute Drawings before us, we have sufficient evidence to lead us to the belief, that from the unbroken character and general uniformity of the different Fronts, and external decoration being wholly unnecessary in any of the Courts, no Design worthy of the Country of equal magnitude can offer greater facilities for economy in the execution.[2]

Such a report, so vague, with so much of what seems special pleading, was hardly likely to assuage all the doubts and suspicions and animosities that had been excited. On 9 March the House of Commons re-appointed the last session's select committee, 'to consider and report on such Plan as may be most fitting and convenient for the

---

[1] Hanbury Tracy had wished preservation to be insisted upon (*Parl. Pap.* 1836 (245) xxi, q. 79).

[2] A drawing in the collection of the Society of Antiquaries is labelled 'Elevation of a portion of the King's Tower and of the Elevation towards Old Palace Yard prepared since the decision of His Majesty's Commissioners to shew the nature of the Details of the proposed exterior of the Building towards Old Palace Yard and New Palace Yard'. It corresponds in character with the drawing of the North Front (Works 29/3205), a copy of Barry's competition design (Plate 52), but is less ornamented.

permanent Accommodation of the Houses of Parliament'—Peel being added to the number. The following day, the committee examined the commissioners. They sought to discover the basis on which Barry's design had been selected. It was, they were told, the 'superior merit of the internal arrangements, and of the beauty of the external architecture'. The ground plan was not so decidedly superior, but taking plan and general design together, Barry's was 'far superior to any other plan'.[1]

Barry's original plan (Fig. 26)[2] was for a building of irregular shape with a central spine, containing the Houses of Lords and Commons, running roughly north-south, parallel to Westminster Hall, and extending nearly 300 feet further southwards. The river front, some 780 feet long, containing offices, libraries and committee rooms, lay at right angles to Westminster Bridge and at an acute angle therefore to the Hall and the central spine. At the north end of this front was placed the Speaker's House, which was linked with the central block by officers' apartments, facing New Palace Yard. Two towers rose from Old and New Palace Yards, the one a massive structure 80 feet square providing a royal entrance, the other some 50 feet square containing a state dining room for the Speaker. The two Houses were placed back to back on either side of a central hall with lateral lobbies.[3] The House of Commons was approached by a stair to the north, behind the Speaker's chair; and the Lords' Chamber by a stair to the west. From the royal entrance a long flight of steps interrupted by a landing rose to the King's Hall, connected by the King's Gallery with the King's Robing Room, immediately adjoining the House of Lords behind the Throne. Barry's original designs have disappeared, but copies of some of the drawings are to be found in the Public Record Office, where tracings of the original plans also exist.[4] From these, from drawings in the House of Lords,[5] and from contemporary references we can determine the character of the original designs. The whole complex of the palace buildings, including the law courts, was wrapped in a Perpendicular fabric. Above a high unadorned basement rose two unequal storeys of windows linked vertically by panelling and topped by elaborate panelled battlements. Much sculpture enlivened the façades. The towers at either extremity, though massive, were elaborately decorated with buttresses and finials, achieving an effect recalling the richest of Somerset church towers. But despite the angels with which the upper string-courses were plentifully graced, the elevations were not too ecclesiastical in character, while on the other hand the dullness of extensive surfaces of regularly-cut ashlar characteristic of much contemporary Gothic Revival building was avoided (Pl. 52). In the heart of the complex the two Houses soared up. Committee rooms and

[1] *Parl. Pap.* 1836 (245) xxi   [2] Works 29/81, a tracing, with room designations in Barry's hand.
[3] In the sectional drawings an octagonal lantern 145 ft. high crowned the central hall; but this did not appear on the elevations or perspective drawings (Hopper, *Letter to . . . Viscount Duncannon*, p. 58; Works 29/3204).
[4] The plans (Works 29/81–3) are not those signed by Tracy, referred to in evidence before the select committee of 1844, but tracings with writing in Barry's hand. A large sheet of sections (Works 29/3204) carrying the portcullis symbol used by Barry, is watermarked however 1844; and a drawing of the north front elevation (Works 29/3205) is watermarked 1843. Nevertheless, these tally with the plan and with descriptions of the sections and elevations, and they may have been prepared for the Lords' committees of 1843 and 1844 (see pp. 224–5 above).
[5] The Moulton–Barrett album in the House of Lords Library contains a tracing (p. 339) of the south front of Westminster Hall and the Law Courts which appears to relate to the premiated design; as well as an early proposal (p. 326, water-marked 1835), perhaps drawn by Pugin, for flanking the south end of the Hall with towers similar to those at the north end, but with the addition of semi-octangular turrets.

libraries essential to their efficient functioning were ranged along the river front, distant from the noises of the street, but with ample light.

Tracy told the select committee (q. 10) that he had laid down certain rules as a guide in determining the merits of each plan: 'the general disposition and convenience of the several entrances, and of the different communications of the interior; the situation of the different offices; the situation of the Houses with respect to each other; the communications to them, private and public; the situation of the libraries, committee and refreshment-rooms, and the various conveniences required'. 'After examining a plan', he explained, 'and weighing the objections to it, we decided upon its general merits as a design compared with those of other competitors' (q. 12). Expense was not taken into account (q. 13), any more than questions of ventilation and acoustics (q. 15).[1] Asked by Hume where the superior merits of Barry's plan lay, Tracy was evasive: 'It is very difficult in a matter of taste to enter into descriptions; I would refer to the plans themselves, conceiving it impossible for any one to look at that of Mr. Barry, and not to feel what it is difficult to describe, the great superiority of it over every other that has been submitted to the Commissioners' (q. 20). The commissioners preferred it on account of its superior beauty as a Gothic building, though not solely on that ground (q. 22), nor merely from its regularity of form, 'but its general beauty and excellence also as a design' (q. 23). Another great merit was its simplicity (q. 37): a design 'simple and easy to be executed'. Pressed more closely, he referred to the river front, 'which owes much of its grandeur and beauty to the solidity of its basement', to its unity of design, and to its general proportions (q. 21). That 'the embankment from the river forms in appearance the basement, and is an integral part of the elevation' was yet another beauty; and the unique feature of the river front being at a right angle to Westminster Bridge was praised as producing 'a most happy effect' (q. 66). Hume persisted in asking in what the superior advantages of Barry's arrangement consisted, but Tracy refused to be pressed further: 'I wish the hon. Member would spare me the necessity of making comparisons between the several designs' (q. 46). Hume then attacked features of Barry's plan—the triangular courts lying behind the river front, the towers of great height, which would impair light and air, the lack of durability of Gothic ornament as exemplified in Henry VII's chapel opposite. He suggested that the river front should be made parallel to Westminster Hall (q. 51), but none of the commissioners would accept his criticisms.

Their indeterminate defence of the premiated design might have stimulated suspicions of collusion, but the commissioners firmly denied any connexion with Barry. Tracy declared,

> I never had the pleasure of seeing but one design of Mr. Barry's in my life; I knew nothing of his style, and was not even personally acquainted with him; but I had

[1] Although Tracy had been appointed to the committee of the previous session on sound and ventilation, he had not taken much interest in it, not having even read its report (q. 16), though he had discussed ventilation with Reid (q. 17). The commissioners took the view, perhaps not unreasonably, that knowledge of these subjects was too imperfect for them to be allowed to affect their decisions (*Parl. Pap.* 1836 (66) xxxvi, and (245) xxi, qq. 15–18); also Report of the select committee on ventilation, *Parl. Pap.* 1835, (583) xviii, quoted below, p. 603). Lord Seymour, however, though not a member of the ventilation committee, was convinced by Reid's arguments, and thought that the new Houses should be built in accord with his ideas (*Letters, Remains, and Memoirs of . . . Twelfth Duke of Somerset, K.G.*, ed. W. H. Mallock and Lady G. Ramsden, 1893, pp. 67–8).

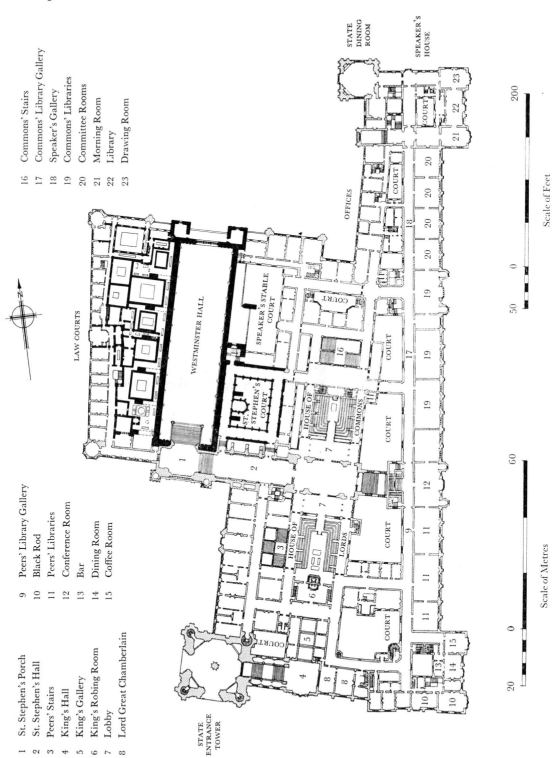

1	St. Stephen's Porch	9	Peers' Library Gallery
2	St. Stephen's Hall	10	Black Rod
3	Peers' Stairs	11	Peers' Libraries
4	King's Hall	12	Conference Room
5	King's Gallery	13	Bar
6	King's Robing Room	14	Dining Room
7	Lobby	15	Coffee Room
8	Lord Great Chamberlain		

16	Commons' Stairs
17	Commons' Library Gallery
18	Speaker's Gallery
19	Commons' Libraries
20	Committee Rooms
21	Morning Room
22	Library
23	Drawing Room

Scale of Metres

Scale of Feet

Fig. 26. The Houses of Parliament: Barry's Competition design of 1835: from a tracing of the lost original (P.R.O., Works 29/81). Existing buildings are marked in solid black.

heard so much of the merits of his plan, when No. 64 [Barry's] passed in review, which was not till I had seen the greater number of those which were submitted to us, I certainly had a strong suspicion from the beauty of it that it could be no other than Mr. Barry's; but I had nothing in the world to lead me to this belief excepting the superiority of the design. Neither had I a knowledge, from looking at the plans of the authors, of any of them; I made a guess, it is true, at one or two; but in each conjecture I was mistaken (q. 14).

Cust added that, as the only commissioner who knew Barry personally, he had warned him that they must not communicate or discuss the plans, and denied having even the 'glimpse of a sketch or slightest hint' which would have led him to infer that no. 64 was Barry's (q. 14)—not quite the same thing as denying that he too had guessed its authorship.

The commissioners had no fear that Barry's design might prove too expensive in execution. In view of rumours that it would cost up to £2 million, Tracy had studied the subject carefully (q. 13), and thought the cost would be about half a million.

> One main feature in Mr. Barry's plan is, that there are no projections serving to increase the girth of the building. Another main feature . . . is, that, except the front-ages themselves, there is no extraordinary expense whatever to be incurred; no external decorations being required for any of the interior courts. Considering the magnitude of the building, it is impossible to conceive a design equally magnificent, and at the same time less expensive than that proposed by Mr. Barry (q. 109).

The question of expense was, however, further examined on 29 April when Hume interrogated Barry's quantity surveyor, H. A. Hunt,[1] who had prepared an estimate for the select committee, and who admitted the possibility of an error of the order of 4–5 per cent (qq. 211–44).

The committee, reporting on 9 May 1836 in favour of adopting Barry's plan, observed that 'subsequently to the Award, some alterations in the Plan have been made, at the suggestion of the Commissioners and of the Architect himself, which, in the opinion of Your Committee, are calculated materially to improve the Plan'. When examined before a joint select committee of both Houses on 22 April, Barry stated:

> the principal alterations are,—a Removal of the entire Building from Westminster Bridge; to the extent of 150 feet, instead of being, as in the original Design, sixty feet; an Extension of the River Front, which has enabled me to enlarge the whole of the internal Courts for the Purposes of increased Light and Ventilation; a Removal of the Two Houses to a greater Distance from each other, and certain Modifications in the Arrangement of the Offices, Residences, &c. The Plan in all other respects remains much the same, except in being more square, and upon a Parallel with Westminster Hall, in consequence of a late Alteration in the line of Embankment towards the River. The Composition and Character of the Design remain nearly the same.[2]

---

[1] 1810–89. See Boase, *Modern English Biography*.

[2] *Parl. Pap.* 1836 (245) xxi, p. 14. Barry's revision of his original design is p. 2 of the Moulton–Barrett album in the House of Lords Library. It shows traces of an intermediate stage in which the river front would not have been advanced so far east.

In other words, Hume's criticisms in the select committee had made their impact. Barry also admitted altering the smaller (northern) tower 'to improve the external Character of the Design'[1] and omitting generally 'Niches, Statues, panelling of Parapets &c.', omissions which would reduce the cost by £50,000, though the 50 feet increase in length would cost about £60,000 more. An additional width of four feet had been obtained for the river terrace by setting the building back.

The alterations were however more extensive than Barry was willing to admit. As he had stated, the building was removed nearly 90 feet further southwards from the Bridge, but the 'extension' amounted to about 100 feet.[2] The re-alignment of the river front with Westminster Hall was also achieved by advancing the north-east corner into the river so that the distance from the angle to the clock tower was increased from 130 feet to slightly less than 160 feet. The effect of this upon the elevation was to increase the number of bays in the river front from 37 to 41, arranged 5–10–1–9–1–10–5, instead of 5–8–1–9–1–8–5; and on the return to repeat the angle turret, so creating at each end of the front a block with turrets at its three external corners. This is shown in drawings of the north front in the R.I.B.A. Drawings Collection,[3] and in an engraving published in *The Athenaeum*[4] (Pls. 53, 55B). The style of the building was changed, as Barry admitted (q. 234), to accord with that of the Birmingham School which he had lately erected with assistance from Pugin. Much of the beauty of the original design vanished with the decorative features, and the revised design recalled rather the east front of Wyatville's Windsor Castle. A conspicuous feature of the river front was a heavy parapet with stepped battlements, concealing the roof, and marked off by a continuous string-course above the upper range of windows. To break the monotony of the extended front, the whole central feature was given an attic storey with a continuous range of windows;[5] and the great oriels at the ends of these nine central bays were flanked by battlemented octagonal turrets. The upper windows of the entire front were, as at Birmingham, larger than the lower, but were linked with them by a common moulding into a single sunken panel with a wide traceried transom (recalling Barry's church of All Saints, Stand, of 1822). The five-bay terminal blocks at either end of the front were somewhat simplified, being uniformly brought forward to the river bank, and without the buttresses which demarcated the bays generally, though retaining the pinnacles to the parapet which in the rest of the front formed the termination of those buttresses. Drawings of the other three sides of this design, signed 'Charles Barry Archt 21 April 1836'. exist in the collection of the R.I.B.A.[6] That of the north front (Pl. 53) may be compared with the copy of the competition design in the Public Record Office (Pl. 52).[7]

[1] It was reduced in area, and given a spire; see also an account of Barry's alterations in *The Times* 11 July 1836.

[2] As Barry admitted to the Lords' select committee of 1844 (*Parl. Pap.* 1844 (269) vi, q. 128). His statement that the original plan had a river front of 780 ft. is borne out by the tracing, Works 29/81 (which has no scale, but is figured with dimensions). The plan published by Barry's critics states the length of the revised front at 870 ft., 100 ft. more than the original; the revision published in Barry's mouthpiece, *The Athenaeum*, however, indicates only 860 ft.: it seems that Barry in 1836 was anxious to minimise the extent of his alterations.

[3] RAN 2/A/2, 2/A/5(e).   [4] 1836, opp. p. 360.   [5] A. Barry, *Life* pp. 251–2.

[6] R.I.B.A., RAN 2/A/2. These are what Professor Hitchcock mistakenly terms 'the competition designs' (*Early Victorian Architecture in Britain*, 1954, i, p. 48; illustrated ii, II, 22–4).

[7] Works 29/3205.

The greatest change here was in the tower. In the revised plan, it was made free-standing on three sides, instead of being rather awkwardly connected with the building on parts of two sides. Somewhat increased in height, and crowned with an ornate spire, it was given a specific function as a clock tower. The entire surface was now panelled, the fenestration greatly altered, and the double buttresses at the angles (which rose to form corner turrets) became single buttresses rising to pinnacles at parapet level. Although it was long before this tower assumed its final appearance, the spired clock tower was to become a cliché of Victorian architecture. In addition to those changes consequent upon the alterations in plan, such as the doubling of the corner turret on the return, the other principal alterations on the north front were the omission of the trefoil panelling of the parapet, and the introduction of pinnacles on the battlements marking off pairs of windows. The windows remained of the same character; but the two storeys were made equal instead of the lower being of greater height. The arcading immediately east of Westminster Hall was replaced by a basement, as in the river front.

At the other extremity of the building, the changes made in the King's Tower were similarly towards a character of greater simplicity. 'The great tower', remarked Barry to the Commons select committee, 'is more ornamented than any other portion of the building, and there are some panels there between the windows; but it is by no means panelled all over like Henry the Seventh's chapel'.[1] In the revision, the tower was enlarged to 100 feet square.[2] A drawing of the lower stages belonging to the Society of Antiquaries, marked 'prepared since the decision of His Majesty's Commissioners to shew the nature of the Details of the proposed Exterior', is of a simpler character than the competition designs, with twin pairs of windows linked vertically by panelling set in plain ashlar. According to Hume the tower was 178 feet high, presumably to the parapet.[3] It was suggested that by increasing its distance from Westminster Bridge its intended effect of giving elevation to the building would be diminished, but Barry denied this.[4] As a store for public records, it was intended to serve a functional as well as an aesthetic purpose.[5] The drawing at the R.I.B.A. shows six tiers of windows, topped with a continuous arcade and embattled parapet. The corner turrets terminated in large crowns.[6] The central pillar of the gigantic porte-cochère of the ground storey, a feature that had been criticised, was omitted.

There were also important internal changes upon which Barry had not seen fit to dwell. An outer lobby or corridor was inserted between the central hall and each House, so that the tight-knit unity of design (one of the features liked by the commissioners) vanished. The Commons' stair was moved from north of the chamber (behind the Speaker's chair) to the south-west, facilitating ingress at the bar end; and the royal approach, too, was considerably modified. The royal stairs originally rose direct from the King's Tower entrance, running east-west; but in the revised design a lobby was inserted, from which they now rose (in three flights instead of two)

---

[1] *Parl. Pap.* 1836 (245) xxi, q. 269.
[2] The alteration in the area of the tower led to confusion in the select committee, *Parl. Pap.* 1836 (245) xxi, q. 31. See also *The Times*, 11 July 1836.
[3] *Parl. Pap.* 1836 (245) xxi, q. 24.   [4] *Ibid.* q. 309.   [5] *Ibid.* qq. 320–1.
[6] RAN 2/A/2, reproduced by H.-R. Hitchcock, *Early Victorian Architecture in Britain* ii, II 22.

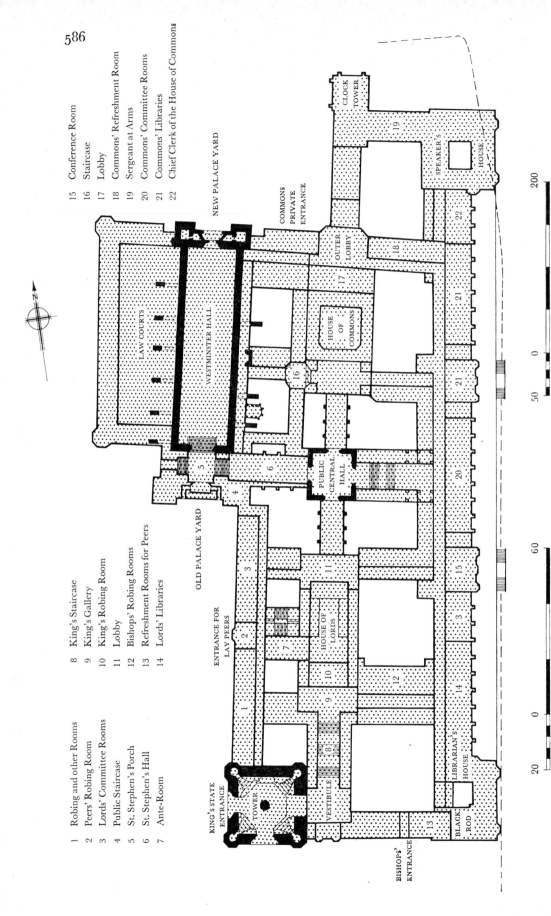

1 Robing and other Rooms
2 Peers' Robing Room
3 Lords' Committee Rooms
4 Public Staircase
5 St. Stephen's Porch
6 St. Stephen's Hall
7 Ante-Room

8 King's Staircase
9 King's Gallery
10 King's Robing Room
11 Lobby
12 Bishops' Robing Rooms
13 Refreshment Rooms for Peers
14 Lords' Libraries

15 Conference Room
16 Staircase
17 Lobby
18 Commons' Refreshment Room
19 Sergeant at Arms
20 Commons' Committee Rooms
21 Commons' Libraries
22 Chief Clerk of the House of Commons

OLD PALACE YARD

NEW PALACE YARD

ENTRANCE FOR LAY PEERS

KING'S STATE ENTRANCE

BISHOPS' ENTRANCE

COMMONS PRIVATE ENTRANCE

LAW COURTS

WESTMINSTER HALL

PUBLIC CENTRAL HALL

HOUSE OF LORDS

HOUSE OF COMMONS

VESTIBULE

OUTER LOBBY

LIBRARIAN'S HOUSE

BLACK ROD

SPEAKER'S HOUSE

CLOCK TOWER

TOWER

Scale of Metres

Scale of Feet

Fig. 27. The Houses of Parliament: Barry's design as revised in 1836: from a lithograph in the Public Record Office (Works 29/85). The broken line marks the authorised line of embankment.

north-south, in line with the House of Lords, the King's Robing Room lying as before immediately behind the throne. Another modification was an alteration of the south end of the law courts to open a public entrance to St. Stephen's porch from St. Margaret's Street in addition to the entrance contrived through Westminster Hall.[1]

The mutterings against Barry swelled into open discontent when the publication of the select committee's report and the exhibition of Barry's competition design made these alterations more generally known. It was pointed out that Barry's plan did not satisfy all the desiderata listed by the two Houses' committees. Worse still, it was alleged that the revised design incorporated some hints from the plans of Barry's disappointed rivals. Had the government commissioned a limited number of architects to prepare plans at its expense, it might have been acceptable for the one finally adopted to incorporate good features from rejected plans; but when the competing architects received no recompense unless winning a prize, it seemed hard that the plan adopted should incorporate features which had not been present in the winner's but were to be found in others submitted.[2]

To upset the decision, the critics tried to show that Barry's plan was unduly expensive. On 17 February 1836 Hawes, the radical M.P. for Lambeth, proposed that the select committee should be instructed to obtain estimates from all the competitors. Several M.P.s supported the idea then mooted of exhibiting all the designs. Two days later, the Chancellor of the Exchequer said that the government would not object to such an exhibition, but would not on that account delay proceeding.[3] Accordingly an exhibition was organised, the government lending the newly completed Academy wing of the National Gallery. The premiated designs were not at first displayed. Duncannon explained that they were required by the select committee.[4] But on 22 April the committee resolved that they should be exhibited with the rest.[5]

The discontented architects formed themselves into a committee, and 34 of them petitioned Parliament, where the disgruntled Joseph Hume was ready to air their grievances. On 21 June they presented a petition complaining that no sum had been stated in the instructions, though the necessity of economy was implied, and that professional knowledge was necessary in the judging. Hanbury Tracy in reply declared that save for Hume the committee had been unanimous.[6] Hume resumed his attack on 21 July, when he moved for a new competition, criticising the failure to set a limit for expense, the restriction as to style, the naming the judges before the designs were delivered, the shortness of time allowed and the judges' error in accepting

---

[1] Alfred Barry wrote of the setting back of the great south window of Westminster Hall and the 'grand idea of St. Stephen's porch' as an alteration from Barry's original plan in which he 'proposed merely to enlarge the existing entrance under the great south window' (*Life*, p. 244). But the competition plan tracing (Works 29/81) and the April 1836 elevation (R.I.B.A., RAN 2/A/2) alike show the extension of the hall, with the window further south. The new public entrance was in the west side of this extension.

[2] Cottingham, for instance, argued that Barry had in his revision stolen his own plan for disposing the two Houses (Works 11/1/1, f. 34). In reply it was naively contended that the idea was to be found in other plans also.

[3] *Mirror of Parliament*, 1836, i, 184-5.   [4] *Ibid.* 11 April 1836, 890-1.

[5] *Ibid.* 1125. There is a printed *Catalogue of the Designs offered for the New Houses of Parliament now exhibiting in the National Gallery*, of which several editions were published.

[6] *Parl. Deb.* 3 ser. xxxiv, 672-4; *Mirror of Parliament*, 1836, ii, 1986-7 (prints petition).

plans that departed from the instructions laid down as to the accommodation to be provided.[1] Tracy again defended the commissioners:

> To have examined whether or not each apartment was according to the specifications would have been out of their power within the period allotted for making their award;—even had—(which was not the case in numerous instances)—the dimensions of the apartments been figured. But the Commissioners, too, were of opinion that it was not for them to reject a plan distinguished for its beauty as a design, on account of a few unimportant omissions in the detail readily provided for, or a few inaccuracies readily corrected. . . . The Commissioners never presumed that what they had approved might not be improved.

Hawes had told him that Barry's design was not Gothic. 'To my perception', Tracy pontificated, 'it possesses all the characteristics of Gothic architecture, without its defects. It is true, it is less varied in its outline, and has more simplicity than Gothic structures usually have; but to me these circumstances, instead of constituting an objection, are a recommendation in its favour.' He agreed with criticism of the detail, particularly the continuous band of Perpendicular tracery which looked like a Grecian entablature, but that had now been altered.

Peel ensured the defeat of Hume's motion: declaring that he retained his opinion that it would have been better to employ 'the most eminent architect of the day' rather than rely on the uncertain results of an open competition, which the more eminent would not enter, he nevertheless insisted that to quash the proceedings would strike a fatal blow against the principles of competition and adjudication by impartial commissioners, would indefinitely postpone the execution of the work, and injure the character of the architectural profession.[2] A fitting note was struck by the final speaker, Thomas Wyse,[3] who thought Barry's design a most magnificent structure, and declared that the first object of such a work should be to express the national dignity. Competition was the best means of achieving this end, and should be made the rule.[4] A war of pamphlets ensued, but Parliament took little notice and endorsed the decision of commissioners and committee. But before examining the further history of the building it is necessary to consider how far Charles Barry may be given sole credit for the approved design.

This question was posed by Edward Welby Pugin, the son of Augustus Welby Northmore Pugin, in 1867. An article in the *Westminster Gazette* of 2 March 1867, reviewing the designs for the new Law Courts, remarked that the 'lamentable gables on the North side of the Palace [of Westminster] were arranged after Sir C. Barry lost the vigorous guiding hand of Pugin'. This was noticed in other papers, and ultimately in November 1867 the younger Pugin compiled a pamphlet of some 60

---

[1] *Ibid.* iii, 2485–7. The debate that followed is reported *ibid.* 2487–92.

[2] The importance of Peel's support was acknowledged by Tracy in subsequent correspondence (B.M. Add. MS. 40543, f. 357), and as Prime Minister in the 1840s he continued firmly to rebut parliamentary criticism of Barry's work, as the architect on one occasion gratefully acknowledged (B.M. Add. MS. 40600, f. 68).

[3] 1791–1862. Lord of the Treasury 1839–41; member of Royal Fine Arts Commission. He had travelled with Barry in Egypt, Palestine and Syria (A. Barry, *Life* p. 15). Dr. P. Stanton suggests that it may have been Wyse, a friend of Lord Shrewsbury, who was the means of introducing Pugin to Barry ('Welby Pugin and the Gothic Revival', London Ph.D. thesis 1952, pp. 57–8).

[4] *Parl. Deb.* 3 ser. xxxv, 398–417; *Mirror of Parliament* 1836, iii, 2485–92.

pages entitled *Who was the Art Architect of the Houses of Parliament?* He claimed that his father had

> actually originated and designed the whole of the elevations of the Palace—that he made the sections and working drawings for every portion of the building—and that, generally, every detail, both externally and internally, was his work. In admitting— as I fully do—that the ground plan and general arrangements of the building were Sir C. Barry's, as my father often assured me, it is impossible to suppose that the details of the plan were not greatly influenced and modified by the elevations. As a matter of course I also cede to Sir C. Barry the natural authority and advantages of his position as the publicly appointed and recognised architect of the Houses, whose decision was final in all questions, and upon whom devolved an overwhelming amount of forethought, labour, difficulty, and responsibility.[1]

Edward Pugin was an irascible man and a violent polemicist, and the very terms of his question betray a certain remoteness from reality: what is an 'art architect'? He also failed to account satisfactorily for his extraordinary delay in bringing forward his father's claims. He alleged however that A. W. Pugin had drawn the designs, which Barry either traced or re-drew, before destroying them. Barry then gave his own handiwork out to his office for working up. 'This scheme effectually blinded all but the principals.'[2] His father, he suggested, had had a free hand in style and design.[3] Once Barry had acquired sufficient material from Pugin, he entrusted the execution to John Thomas, whom Pugin had trained at the building of the Birmingham Grammar School. Pugin 'felt Sir Charles's ungenerous treatment so acutely, that for many years he refused all intercourse with him, and it was not until the year 1844 that my father again consented to work for him'.[4] He had then insisted on the arrangement being placed on an official footing. Barry had, however, compelled him to publish a denial that the designs of the Palace were in reality his.[5] The conspiracy of silence was carried to its ultimate point by Barry after Pugin's death. Securing from Edward Pugin letters he had written to his collaborator, and which he had discovered with surprise to be still in existence, he had failed to return them, and they had vanished altogether.

There was much in Edward Pugin's account that seemed improbable, if not specifically inaccurate. But there was sufficient weight in his claims for Barry's sons to reply at twice the length.[6] Alfred Barry, his father's biographer, had stated their view in *The Life and Works of Sir Charles Barry*, already in the press when the controversy broke. 'Such a work could not', they conceded, 'be carried out by the unaided exertions of a single man' (p. 194). Foremost among Barry's collaborators was Pugin.

> As soon as he was appointed architect to the New Palace, he [Barry] immediately thought of his friend, and resolved to invite him to his aid. Convinced that Mr. Pugin was at that time unrivalled in his knowledge of Gothic detail, admiring his extraordinary powers as a draughtsman, carried away by sympathy with his burning artistic enthusiasm, he could wish for no other coadjutor. The invitation was accepted,

---

[1] *Art Architect*, p. 3.   [2] *Ibid.* p. 22.   [3] *Ibid.* p. 25.   [4] *Ibid.* p. 32.   [5] *Builder*, 6 Sept. 1845.
[6] *The Architect of the New Palace at Westminster. A reply to the statements of Mr. E. Pugin* (1868).

and a connection was established equally honourable to both artists. No man was more original than Mr. Pugin. . . . Yet for the furtherance of his art he was willing to accept a distinctly subordinate position, and to work under the superintendence and control of another. . . . Nor, on the other hand, could Mr. Barry be unaware of the danger of calling in a too powerful coadjutor. He knew the almost inevitable risk which he incurred of being supposed to wear other men's laurels, of having all that was good or spirited in the details attributed to Mr. Pugin, and of finding it difficult or impossible to control an enthusiasm, which might work in what seemed to him undesirable methods. But these things he resolutely put aside for the sake of an aid, which he thought likely to improve his great building, and which he knew to be genial and inspiriting to himself. That Mr. Pugin was the last man in the world to encroach on another man's authority or credit he knew, and that this confidence in his friend's character was not misplaced is shown by the strong disclaimer which he put out, when an attempt was made to attribute to him more than he felt to be his due. The misapprehensions of others he could afford to disregard.

The first aid which he received from Mr. Pugin was under the pressure of shortness of time in making the original design. Working under Mr. Barry's own eye and direction, Mr. Pugin sketched for him in pencil a complete set of details, in a style perhaps bolder, less carefully proportioned and less purely English, than would have been adopted by himself. In the design they differed *toto cælo*. Mr. Pugin would have recommended irregular and picturesque grouping of parts, utterly at variance with the regularity and symmetry actually adopted. Except in details, he neither had, nor could have had, any influence whatever, and those who compare the details of his own buildings with those of the New Palace will readily see that even here his influence, however valuable, was chiefly indirect.

After Mr. Barry's appointment as architect, he still received the same aid in preparing detailed drawings for the estimate, most of which however, by changes in design, were afterwards set aside. Finally, at his recommendation, Mr. Pugin was formally appointed superintendent of the wood carving, and in that capacity he directed, first the formation of a valuable collection of plaster casts of the most famous examples at home and abroad, and next the execution of the wood-work, ornamental metal-work, stained glass, and encaustic tiles throughout the whole building. But in all cases it was thoroughly understood between them, that the architect's supremacy was to be unimpaired. Every drawing passed under his eye in all cases for supervision, in very many for alteration.[1]

Such was the Barrys' answer to Edward Pugin's allegations. Among the evidence they brought forward was a statement by Barry's close friend J. L. Wolfe, who told how, as soon as the competition was announced, Barry took a rapid tour in Belgium with him. After discussions between them, Barry had made his first sketches,

which comprehended the entire design and contained the germs of all that followed.

Long before Barry sought Pugin's assistance, the entire design had been not only worked out in his own mind, but committed to paper in a series of plans, elevations, and sections, all drawn by his own hand, in his well-known and admired style of pencilling. These drawings, though on a small scale, were so minute, intelligible, and expressive, that any able assistant could, under Barry's eye, have worked out the details.

[1] *Op. cit.* pp. 195–7.

In general character the elevations differed little from those in the competition design, but they were somewhat less ornate; indeed, those for New Palace Yard were in harmony with the entrance front of Westminster Hall. . . .

Barry had already made considerable progress with a set of drawings on a larger scale, and had even sketched many specimens of detail, which he felt himself fully competent to design, when he began to fear time would run short; and it was then, and mainly for that reason, that he determined to seek the assistance of Pugin. But this was at so late a date that, had not the designs, in plan and elevation, been definitely settled, it would have been impossible, even with Pugin's assistance, to complete the competition drawings by the time fixed for their reception—and as it was, they were not delivered till within a few minutes of the last hour.

The first work Pugin was set to do was this. Barry laid before him his own drawings, explained his views as to character and style, gave him the requisite dimensions, and left him to work out the details. Thereupon, Pugin prepared a complete set of drawings, or rather of rough but masterly sketches in pencil, showing on a large scale the details of every part of the building, inside and out. . . .

But, before these drawings were completed, Barry had begun to have misgivings as to the use he could make of them, and after discussions with me, his 'fresh-eye' and critic, he determined to lay them aside, and he did so for these reasons. The details appeared to him so large, and even coarse, that he feared they might lessen the scale of his work; they were—in Barry's eye a great fault—ill-proportioned; and he perceived in them a tinge of foreign Gothic, sufficient to destroy the purely English character he wished his building to exhibit.

Wolfe also believed that Barry was influenced by these drawings not being his own.

So, when Barry came to prepare his finished drawings, he adopted details of his own, smaller in scale than those proposed by Pugin, and more purely English.

This first set of drawings by Pugin having been completed and laid aside, Barry engaged him to assist in preparing the finished drawings to be sent in for competition; and, accordingly, he made several drawings, mostly perspective views, of the important parts of the interior, such as the Houses of Lords and Commons, the Royal entrance and staircase, and others. All these drawings were made from Barry's own designs, and under his direction, but were drawn and finished by Pugin in his usual etching-like style, and they were sent in as they came from his hand, without any attempt having been made . . . to conceal the fact that he was the draughtsman. . . . All persons who worked under Barry knew, to their cost, that he could never re-draw a design, even his own, without altering it, to suit his almost fastidious taste, again and again. . . .[1]

This account appears to cram a very considerable amount of activity into the last few weeks. The select committee had reported on 3 June, and if Barry's visit to Belgium followed immediately, as Wolfe stated, it was presumably over by early July. Barry could not, however, have worked out his plans in detail until the instructions (published in the *London Gazette*, 21 July) and the site plan (sold at the Office of Woods, 27 July–29 August) were available. On 6 August 1835, little more than a week after the site plan could have been obtained, Pugin's diary records 'saw

[1] A. Barry, *The Architect . . . A Reply*, pp. 22–4.

Mr. Barry, working drawings £15'; and subsequent entries from 10 August show Pugin busily engaged with Barry and on 'composition' and 'drawings' for him. On 27 September appears for the first time the entry 'Parliament House', and subsequent entries refer to 'central portion' (30 September), 'S. E. view' (5 October) and 'Elevations' (6, 7 and 8 October). Then:

October	10	left [for] London
	11 to 18	Drew at Mr. B[1]
	18	Returned to Sarum
November	2	Mr Barry arrived
	3	on river front. 5 compartments
	8	Mr Barry left paid £99[2]
	9	The present condition of Architecture is deplorable. Truth reduced to the position of an interesting but rare & curious relic.
	19	Left Sarum
	20	began at Mr. Barrys
	22	at Mr. Barry's on working drawg
	23	ditto ditto
	24	ditto
	25	ditto
	26	At Mr. B on views
	27	£10 Mr. Barry
	28	finished at Mr. Barry
	29	ditto ditto £50[3]

It is clear that Pugin was doing a good deal of work for Barry, though it is not until 27 September that it becomes indisputable that Pugin was working on the Houses of Parliament. This would fit in with Wolfe's thesis; but it is to ignore the earlier entries in the diary. It is possible that those for early August may refer to the Birmingham Grammar School then under construction, upon which Pugin was also working for Barry.[4] But the entries referring to 'composition' cannot refer to that building. They must relate to something new. It may also be significant that 24 August, when Pugin 'began Mr. Barry's drawings', was the date from which a revised site plan was to be made available.[5] Thus it appears probable that Pugin was consulted earlier, and played a more considerable role than Wolfe allowed. Though it does not necessarily follow that Pugin's share in the formulation of the competition design was decisive, the existence of a series of drawings made by him in 1833 for an imaginary 'St. Marie's College' argues in favour of his having contributed more, albeit in detail, than the Barrys conceded. For these drawings, as Edward Pugin pointed out[6]

[1] This is written sideways across the ruled compartments for the dates and apparently extends to 20 October.

[2] From other such financial notes in the diary it appears that this payment is not necessarily connected with Barry.

[3] Pugin's diary (now at the Victoria and Albert Museum). The entries printed in Ferrey's *Recollections of A. W. N. Pugin*, pp. 242–4 are not reliable.

[4] A. Barry, *Life*, pp. 131–2. That Pugin was in 1835 working on more than one building for Barry has naturally bedevilled the investigation of the problem, from the publication of *Who was the Art Architect* to the present day. Dr. Stanton remarks that the notations of Pugin's diary 'seem to indicate that Pugin was working [for Barry] on Trentham Chapel, the domestic interiors for Mr. Currie's house, and King Edward's Grammar School' (*op. cit.*, p. 94).   [5] *London Gazette*, 18 August.   [6] *Art Architect*, pp. 3–4.

and as Robert Dell was to argue at some length,[1] show an 'extraordinary resemblance' to the Westminster designs. Dell came to the conclusion that

> Pugin not only drew the elevations which were sent in to the competition by Mr. Barry, as he then was, but was in fact their actual designer; that when, after Mr. Barry's appointment as architect, considerable alterations were made, Pugin made the designs for nearly every detailed part of the building, and that practically all the details of the building as it now stands—everything, that is, beyond the shell—are really Pugin's.[2]

Dr. Stanton admits that examination 'certainly confirms the assertion that these drawings had something to do with the Parliament designs',[3] but ascribes their derivation to Belgium and France, confirming Wolfe's description of Pugin's work as being too continental in character. The copy of Barry's competition design in the Public Record Office (Works 29/3204) includes sections of the central tower, showing large windows of a Perpendicular design very similar to those of the chapel of 'St. Marie's College';[4] and the very considerable use of sculpture in the central tower or hall is also paralleled in the drawings. Drawings of the King's Tower at the Society of Antiquaries are of a very similar character (Pl. 56). It is difficult to do other than agree with Dr. Stanton's conclusion that the exact nature of the collaboration between Barry and Pugin cannot now be sorted out in detail.[5]

> Pugin collaborated with Barry and produced the skeleton of Barry's plans and sections, the network of ornament which gave character to the building and pleased the commissioners. Barry and Pugin worked together at Salisbury [where Pugin was then living] in November and finished off the details, and the final rendering of the drawings and the perspectives were done in London in Barry's office, because time was getting short and they required the assistance of Barry's staff.[6]
>
> The arrangement was not discreditable to either of the men. Pugin was well paid[7] and Barry was busy and had done a share of the design and supervised the realisation of it. . . . Had Barry meant to keep his relationship with Pugin a dark secret he would never have submitted those 'minute' drawings which Tracy admired.[8]

Barry's critics were quick to seize upon discrepancies between the plans and the elevations of his design; and Dr. Stanton suggests that these may have occurred because one man did the plans and the other did the elevations: Barry was meticulous but Pugin careless when preoccupied with the look of a building, as can be shown by his designs for a 'Deanery'.[9]

Despite the difficulties of the problem, however, we can perhaps point out features of the design that may be ascribed to Barry on stylistic grounds. J. L. Wolfe provided Alfred Barry with notes on the aesthetic views expressed by Barry during

---

[1] *Burlington Magazine* viii (1905–6), pp. 403–20.   [2] *Op. cit.* pp. 403–4.
[3] *Loc. cit.* p. 87.   [4] Dell, *loc. cit*, pls. I and III.   [5] Thesis, p. 150.
[6] *Ibid.* p. 142. Dr. Stanton's 'skeleton' would seem to refer to 'the network of ornament'.
[7] He received £271 12s. from Barry between 1 August and 1 December, the closing date of the competition (Stanton, p. 143).   [8] *Ibid.* p. 151.
[9] *Ibid.* pp. 153–4; P. Stanton, 'Pugin at twenty-one', *Architectural Review* 110 (1951), pp. 187–90.

the Italian tour they had undertaken together in their youth. From these we learn that Barry admired the imposing effect of vast mass, as in the principal front of the Farnese Palace, 'greatly enhanced by the unbroken lines of the entablature and string-courses, the number and relative smallness of the windows, the complete subordination of all horizontal divisions to the crowning cornice, and the consequent full effect of the entire height'.[1] To balance the great cornice, he required 'an important basement':

> Even in the river-front of his new Palace at Westminster he rejected the idea (once entertained) of introducing a cloister; and was so jealous of the solidity and plainness of his basement, that he grudged every window and would hardly enrich a gateway.[2]

He acquired a taste for 'luxuriance of ornament' and 'boldness of outline', and favoured continuous vertical lines to unite the two storeys of a building, as by breaking the entablatures when using superimposed orders.[3] Visible roofs satisfied his aesthetic theory—'being essential features, they ought not to be concealed'.[4] He 'never willingly employed a Tudor arch; but where cramped for height, he preferred the arch formed by two flat segments of circles, making an angle with the jambs (as seen in certain windows at Winchester).'[5] In the competition design such windows occur in the internal courts and in the north tower, and the windows of the two upper (principal) storeys are linked vertically with panelling, each vertical pair forming a single unit separated from its neighbour by a strip of unrelieved walling (Pl. 52).[6] Furthermore this structure rises, except for the portions immediately adjoining the Hall (where there is an arcade), from a basement broken only by small, single-light windows. Above, a string-course and panelled battlements form a sort of heavy cornice, the panelling being continued across the towers.

Other stylistic preferences are described by his son. He was fond of 'a central mass with two slightly elevated angles',[7] a characteristic of the river front of the new palace. In the Birmingham School he was 'inclined to raise these wings into towers', but the confined situation prevented this, so he proposed a clock tower at one end of the front, and a central lantern to 'relieve the flatness of the skyline'[8]— ideas also used at Westminster. To give more prominence to the main entrance of the school, he thought of advancing the centre and raising a gable over it; but 'he could never make up his mind to advance the centre of an architectural composition', because this would destroy in its perspective effect the apparent size of the building.[9]

> 'In composing, he always began with the simplest forms, and never made a break, till he felt it absolutely necessary. If the length of a front was too great for its height he admitted flanking towers. These did not destroy the unity of the mass. But to raise the centre was to cut the mass into three separate parts—a decomposition which he abhorred.' In the river front 'the excessive length compelled him to raise the centre, but nothing would induce him to advance it.' MS. Note *W*[olfe].[10]

[1] A. Barry, *Life*, p. 49.   [2] *Ibid*. p. 52.   [3] *Ibid*. p. 50.   [4] *Ibid*. p. 53.   [5] *Ibid*. p. 59.
[6] Works 29/3205. Windows and arches of a similar character occur in Pugin's work at St. Giles' Cheadle (1841–6) and St. John's Hospital at Alton Castle (from 1841), as well as the 'Deanery' designs of 1833.
[7] *Life*, pp. 121–2.   [8] *Ibid*. p. 130.   [9] *Ibid*.   [10] *Ibid*. p. 242.

While Pugin's aid must have been invaluable in working out the ornamental features, as well as in executing the drawings, it is undeniable that 'the principles of symmetry, regularity, and unity, so dear to his [Barry's] artistic taste'[1] governed the design, and that those were, as Alfred Barry pointed out, scarcely the principles for which Pugin contended. It would thus appear that Barry's control over the building was tighter than some modern studies have allowed. In any case, it was Barry who had to bear the labour of the organization of the greatest building work of the nineteenth century. It was a particularly burdensome task because of the number of masters whom Barry had to serve. He had to attend numerous select committees of both Lords and Commons, especially in 1843–51, to win their approval as well as that of the full Houses; to deal with the government through the Board of Woods, and in 1848–51 through specially appointed commissioners as well; to contend perpetually with the insatiable and slippery 'ventilator', Reid; and to struggle with the Treasury over his remuneration. Small wonder that he should make changes without consulting these manifold authorities; or if he should seek to arrogate the credit for the achievement.

So large a work as the New Palace of Westminster, as contemporaries began to term it, extending over eight acres of ground and giving employment to 1200 or 1400 workmen, could in any case only have been conducted by an architect controlling a large office. The names or initials of at least seventeen assistants occur on tracings and drawings in the Public Record Office, apart from such architects as Barry's sons Charles and Edward, R. R. Banks, John Gibson and Somers Clarke, all of whom are known by their own statements to have worked on the project.[2]

Having determined on Perpendicular as lending itself 'most easily to the requirements of the building, and to the principle of regularity, which he intended to introduce into his design',[3] Barry set to work.

> The character of the building was, of course, to be palatial. There were however but fragments of Gothic palaces to be found in England. Italian Gothic had not yet attracted much observation. The town-halls of Belgium occurred to him, and he went over to that country. . . . They recurred to him afterwards, as examples of visible roofs, and general enrichment. But at the time they did not affect his design, which was mainly 'castellated' with embattled parapets, concealed roofs, and an absence of all spires. The great tower, one hundred feet square, was to be treated as a 'keep'; the clock-tower differed little, except in size, from the same general character. With his great love of unity and regularity he might have desired a central tower,[4] but it must have been over the central hall, and there it would have been too far back to form a centre to the great river front, and half its height would have been concealed. He always thought that great towers should be seen from their parapet to their base; accordingly, he was content to place his towers in positions where they would form natural and prominent features, without interfering with each other, or with the great river front. . . . He made countless variations, drawings literally by hundreds,

---

[1] *Ibid.* p. 241.

[2] Edward Barry listed 19 assistants whose work he had recognised in the Houses of Parliament drawings, other than his brother and himself (*The Architect . . . a reply*, p. 101).   [3] *Life*, p. 238.

[4] A. Barry's own footnote reads: 'The present central tower was not a feature of the original design. It was added to meet the requirements of Dr. Reid.' Nevertheless, an impressive octagon lantern crowned the central hall in the Competition Design (Works 29/3204).

as studies of its prominent features, in the course of its formation; but the main principles were deeply fixed in his mind, and to them he always returned.[1]

It is the survival of some of these essays that makes it difficult to work out the precise history of the design. However, certain developments are reasonably clear.

The evolution of the design may be followed in drawings in the R.I.B.A. collection. One has been subsequently inscribed: 'Some of the studies by Sir Charles Barry made in 1836 from which the estimate drawings which were completed in Jany. 1837 were prepared by Mr. Pugin Mr. Wright Mr. Banks Mr. Gibson and others.'[2] This drawing of part of the river curtain shews the earlier octagonal turrets flanking the end bays of the centre developed into more massive turrets; and in the centre bays the tracery of the lower windows merges into the decoration of the transom. The next stage was to give yet greater variety to the elevation by forming towers at each end of the central feature; these with their angle turrets were only about a third wider than the ordinary bay, whereas the great oriels and flanking turrets that they replaced were more than two bays wide. This resulted in a change in the articulation of the front from 5–10–1–9–1–10–5 to 5–12–1–11–1–12–5.[3]

A further important change, the introduction of visible roofs throughout the river front, save on the towers, is found in a group of contract drawings in the Public Record Office, dated 5 February 1840 (Pl. 58A). Alfred Barry explained that in this way his father sought to obtain a 'variation in outline' by means other than advancing the centre, to which he was 'strongly averse at all times'.[4] Professor Hitchcock, while noting that the high roofs 'give plastic depth to the long front', suggests that Barry's reasons 'may well have been more largely technical than stylistic', and states that 'their all-iron construction was one of the greatest innovations Barry introduced in attempting to make the New Palace fire resistant'.[5] But the introduction of high roofs in the design antedates both Reid's proposals for ventilation channels in the roof and those for accommodating public records there, which stimulated the endeavour to construct a fireproof building.[6] As Barry employed iron for flat as well as sloping roofs,[7] it may be doubted whether constructional reasons were paramount in the choice of high roofs at Westminster. The development of the windows, too, was taken a stage further by equalizing the height of the two storeys;[8] and the horizontal division between the two was obliterated by continuing the mullions over the intervening transom, much as Barry had done at Stand church in 1822, so forming one continuous vertical feature. A third important change was to replace the buttresses by small polygonal turrets with ogee caps:[9] 'the "castel-

[1] *Life*, pp. 242–3.   [2] R.I.B.A., RAN 2/B/1. Watermarked 1836.   [3] R.I.B.A., RAN 2/A/4.
[4] Works 29/1814–56; A. Barry, *Life*, p. 251.
[5] H.-R. Hitchcock, *Early Victorian Architecture*, i, pp. 274–5. For a description of the roofs (quoted by Hitchcock) see J. Weale, *Quarterly Papers on Engineering*, no. 5 (1844), reprinted in *Builder* ii (1844), p. 581.
[6] See p. 605 and Works 1/24, p. 327, 7 August 1840.   [7] *Parl. Pap.* 1844 (448), q. 149.
[8] This change Barry apparently did not approve of in theory, as jarring with his dominant principle of unity. See note by Wolfe, *Life*, p. 253.
[9] The buttresses, wrote Alfred Barry, 'had no thrust to sustain, they interrupted the cornice and string courses, and interfered with the panelling. For these reasons Mr. Barry himself disliked them, and, external criticism coinciding with his own feeling, he resolved to change them into turrets, which were free from all these objections, and which would tend at once to elevate and break the skyline, and by their greater projection to relieve the flatness of the front. These turrets, once introduced, must of course prevail throughout; they made their appearance accordingly in the prominent masses of the wings'. Their tops 'after many trials, and with some reluctance, were made of the ogee form' (*ibid.* pp. 251–2).

lated" form necessarily disappeared at once', wrote Alfred Barry, 'the parapet became subordinate . . . an upward tendency was given to the whole'.[1] The space between the turrets and the window moulding was filled with panelling; the continuous arcading of the central attic was broken up into groups of three windows, echoing the three-light pattern of the windows below; and the panelled parapet of the competition designs reappeared. Thus the vertical lines of the composition were emphasised, and the hitherto dominant horizontals weakened, only the string courses above the basement and over the main windows forming continuous horizontal lines.

By January 1841 yet further changes had been evolved (Pl. 58B).[2] The most significant was the reintroduction of a horizontal emphasis by breaking up the unity of the window bay; the transom became a band of panelling extending across the whole façade, turrets as well as bays, with coats of arms between upper and lower windows. Narrower continuous bands of gothic lettering ran immediately above and below the windows. There were also changes in the windows: the lower range was made square-headed, and the four-centred arch of the upper range was somewhat depressed; the two-light basement windows were given quatrefoil instead of trefoil heads. On the turrets the panelling was simplified and made accordant with the window tracery. For the elaborately crocketed finials simpler forms were substituted; but the earlier form was ultimately adopted. The wings, too, were modified.[3] Finally further alterations were made in the fenestration, so that the spandrels to the upper windows were eliminated, and the windows themselves became square-headed. The parapets were elaborated, in accord with Barry's theory that richness should increase with elevation.[4]

This account of the evolution of the design of the river front is in itself enough to dispose of the belief that 'every visible foot of the Houses of Parliament is the work of Pugin'.[5] Between 1838 and 1844 Pugin was not working for Barry, though there appears to have been no such quarrel between them as was suggested by Edward Pugin, and some of the details supplied by Pugin in 1835–7 may still have served Barry several years later.[6] Professor Hitchcock has, moreover, drawn attention to the resemblance between 'the general handling of the river front' and 'the wall treatment of Highclere Castle' designed by Barry before 1840: 'the [stylistic] vocabulary may be different but the syntax is the same'.[7]

Corresponding changes were made in the other elevations and in the two great towers: but the towers were far from complete in 1851, and in part therefore lie outside the scope of this *History*. The early changes in the design of the King's Tower, later re-named Victoria Tower, have already been referred to. Although the basic features of the lower stages, the great arches and the surmounting row of niches, were retained in the executed design, the arches were greatly increased in size, so facilitating the admission of a state coach, for this was the royal entrance. The final

---

[1] *Ibid.*
[2] Works 29/1898–1901, dated between 5 and 13 January 1841. An intermediate stage appears to be represented by drawings in the House of Lords (Moulton–Barrett Album, pp. 27, 29).
[3] Soc. of Antiquaries' drawing.   [4] Works 29/3203. See *Life*, p. 252.
[5] Kenneth Clark, *The Gothic Revival* (revised edn. 1950), p. 175. Cf. also p. 179.
[6] *Art Architect*, p. 76. Cf. Stanton, Thesis.   [7] *Early Victorian Architecture*, i, p. 273.

arrangement of two tiers of three great windows[1] emphasizes the vertical axis more strongly than do the early designs; the upper tier, to the distant eye the third stage of the tower, is made 'somewhat more important', so according with Barry's aesthetic theory.[2] According to Alfred Barry the tower was arranged with 'two lofty internal stories' to contain 'such of the public records as were not frequently in use'. When the government decided it should form a general record repository, numerous floors had to be inserted 'not without great inconvenience, but with much ingenuity'. Another alteration springing from the same cause was an increase in height from 200 ft. to 250 ft. to the top of the battlements.[3] Professor Hitchcock has remarked on the structural interest of the tower, the internal metal skeleton of the upper stages anticipating the structure of the skyscraper.[4] But the extensive use of iron in the form of dowels and iron bands round the turrets tended to disintegrate the stonework.[5]

While Pugin may have had a hand in designing the upper stages of the Victoria Tower after 1844, there can be no reasonable doubt that the famous Clock Tower in its most significant feature is his. The overhanging clock stage, perhaps an echo of Flemish town halls, is found in Pugin's designs of 1837 and 1839 for Scarisbrick Hall.[6] This was adopted at Westminster about 1846 only after many tentative designs had been drafted; and the shape of the terminal feature was similarly subject to much revision (Pl. 60).[7] A tendency in the development of both these towers was to greater height: the Clock Tower, in the approved design, was to be 200 ft. to the top of the roof, but eventually gained nearly half as much again.[8] The third or Central Tower, added essentially for purposes of ventilation, was conceived as a spire by Barry in order to provide a contrast with the other towers, but, like them, it underwent numerous revisions of design. An early version, in 1842, rose to a height of 210 ft. above the ground; one of 1846 to 253 ft.; but in 1847 Barry reduced it to 149 ft. (Pls. 61, 63). At this time, work had only reached the groining of the central hall, so there remained ample opportunity for further alterations.[9]

Yet another important change in the elevation was the creation of St. Stephen's Porch. Originally conceived merely as providing a communication between Westminster Hall and St. Stephen's Hall, the porch was in the plan of 1843[10] pushed out to provide a major entrance from Old Palace Yard on the south as well as a lesser one to the west, each approached by an external flight of steps. The Old Palace Yard entrance was subsequently abandoned, and from 1846 to 1850 numerous revisions of the upper parts of the porch were made (Pl. 59).[11] A drawing dated

---

[1] Works 29/3203 shows this scheme, though not exactly as executed. This drawing cannot be later than early 1845 as the uppermost windows of the river front towers differ from those executing at that time.
[2] The development of the design of the tower between 1840 and 1855 may be studied in Works 29/631–760 and R.I.B.A. Drawings Collection RAN 2A/3, E/3. [3] *Life*, p. 255; Works 11/9/7, f. 50.
[4] *Early Victorian Architecture*, i. p. 292. For a description of the construction see E. N. Holmes, *Illustrations of the New Palace of Westminster*, 2nd ser. (1865). See also M. Bond, 'New Life for the Record Tower', *The Times*, 3 July 1963, and references cited p. 625, n. 1 below. [5] See Works 29/3371.
[6] H.-R. Hitchcock, *Early Victorian Architecture*, i, p. 291; ii, VIII, 2.
[7] Works 29/1735–96, 3222, 3280–1; Soc. of Antiquaries, no. 11; R.I.B.A., Drawings Collection RAN 2C/1–4, D/1–6, E/1. See A. Barry, *Life*, p. 255, '. . . at last an example was remembered in which the whole clock-story was made to project beyond the body of the tower'.
[8] Works 11/10/1, f. 2. [9] Works 29/1601–36, 3049, 3052, 3203.
[10] As published in *Illustrated London News*, 30 September 1843, p. 224.
[11] Works 29/887–964; 11/6/4, f. 16.

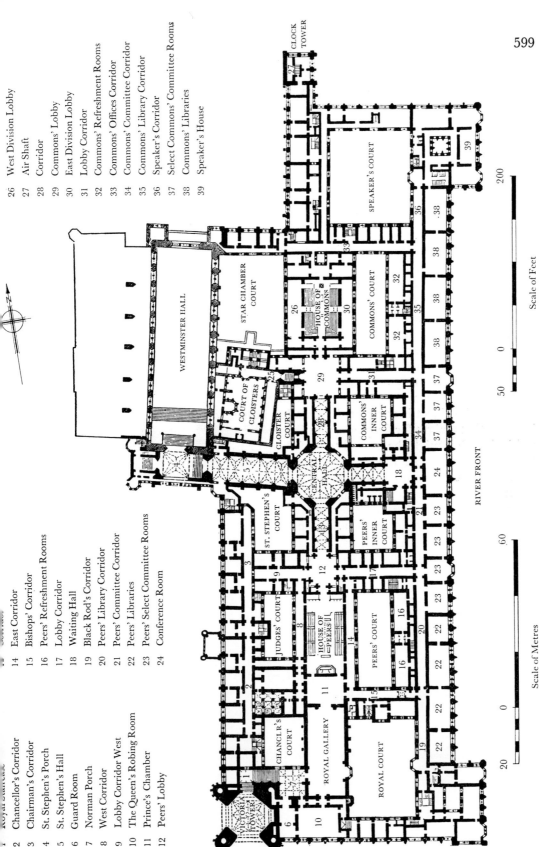

1 Royal Staircase
2 Chancellor's Corridor
3 Chairman's Corridor
4 St. Stephen's Porch
5 St. Stephen's Hall
6 Guard Room
7 Norman Porch
8 West Corridor
9 Lobby Corridor West
10 The Queen's Robing Room
11 Prince's Chamber
12 Peers' Lobby
13 Content
14 East Corridor
15 Bishops' Corridor
16 Peers' Refreshment Rooms
17 Lobby Corridor
18 Waiting Hall
19 Black Rod's Corridor
20 Peers' Library Corridor
21 Peers' Committee Corridor
22 Peers' Libraries
23 Peers' Select Committee Rooms
24 Conference Room

26 West Division Lobby
27 Air Shaft
28 Corridor
29 Commons' Lobby
30 East Division Lobby
31 Lobby Corridor
32 Commons' Refreshment Rooms
33 Commons' Offices Corridor
34 Commons' Committee Corridor
35 Commons' Library Corridor
36 Speaker's Corridor
37 Select Commons' Committee Rooms
38 Commons' Libraries
39 Speaker's House

Fig. 28. The Houses of Parliament, as finally completed: from A. Barry, *Life and Works of Sir Charles Barry* (1867).

2R

22 June 1848 refers to the use of the north-west turret as an air intake for Reid's scheme for ventilating the House of Commons.[1] Professor Hitchcock has written of the 'plasticity and . . . confusion' of the turrets and gables of the porch, 'turgidly picturesque', in contrast to the mechanical regularity of the rest of the New Palace Yard façade, and suggests that its architect may have been 'seeking to emulate the bolder and more irregular handling of Gothic forms in Butterfield's first London churches'.[2] This seems to introduce an unnecessary further complication into the story. The composition is a symmetrical response to the requirements of the plan, and though the ogee caps of the turrets overwhelm their neighbouring prototypes on Henry VII's chapel, they are no more 'turgidly picturesque' than many of Barry's sketches for, say, the Central Tower. Once again, they accord with Barry's aesthetic of elaboration increasing with height.

At this point one may revert from the design to the course of events. The select committee having asked for a detailed estimate before giving formal approval, Barry had in the summer of 1836 to prepare working drawings as the basis for his estimate, a work completed at the end of January 1837.[3] Once again he turned to Pugin to help him get the work done. Barry's letter to Pugin of 23 September 1836, printed by Edward Pugin in his *Art Architect*, shows the degree of his dependence on Pugin at this stage. It accompanied a parcel of tracings from which Pugin was to prepare 'a large batch of internal details, including the two Houses complete, the King's Robing Room, Gallery and Staircase, and the Entrance Vestibule, all of which I shall be obliged to you to set about immediately and send them to me from time to time as each subject is completed'. Detailed instructions follow, Barry observing for instance that designs for fireplaces that Pugin had already sent would do 'exceedingly well', though it might be as well to have 'one or two more *rather* richer for Speaker's House, but remember the motto "*simplex* &c." '[4] Acknowledging on 22 October the receipt of the required drawings of the House of Lords and King's Stairs, Barry informed Pugin that he was sending tracings 'of the Grand Public Entrance, and approach to the Houses and Committee Rooms', which though 'wretchedly made by a youngster', should afford all the necessary data.[5]

> The groining [he continued] and interior generally of the King's or Record Tower entrance you may make of any design you think proper: you need not to be shackled as to height, but the groin should, I think, be concentric with the arch of the opening to the vestibule at the foot of the King's Stairs, which you already have. The design of this part of the building should, I think, be of a simple and massive character, and a pillar in the centre of the tower must be avoided.

R. R. Banks (partner of the younger Charles Barry) recalled in 1868 how for much of the period from August 1836 to January 1837 Pugin had been employed with himself and others 'in preparing a complete set of drawings under the incessant direction of Sir C. Barry. . . . Mr. Pugin of course, from his knowledge of matters of

---

[1] *Ibid.* 29/2910.   [2] *Early Victorian Architecture*, i, p. 288.
[3] Works 11/1/2, f. 4.   [4] *Art Architect*, pp. 23–4.
[5] B. Ferrey, *Recollections of A. Welby Pugin* (1861), pp. 245–6. A tracing of designs for the King's Stair (with an open timber roof) is in the House of Lords' Library, Moulton–Barrett album, p. 328 (Pl. 57).

Gothic detail, was requested to confine himself to getting out sheets of details of portions of the elevation and various internal fittings, such as doors, panelling, fireplaces, etc., whilst others, whose talents lay more in structural matters, made details of roofs, floors, etc., the general staff being occupied in the more mechanical labour of making out the entire set of drawings'.[1] These were then handed to H. A. Hunt, Barry's surveyor, for taking out the quantities. Pugin's 'sheets of details' were not intended, said Banks, 'as drawings from which to execute the works, their object being only to show the surveyor the relative costliness of the various parts of the work, and to insure the provision by him in the estimate of a sufficient amount to carry out works with a similar amount of elaboration. Accordingly the work was never executed from them'.

Seward and Chawner then officially examined Barry's measurements; working with the help of several quantity surveyors they were able to make their report on 17 April.[2] The detailed bills were finally calculated at £642,822, compared with Barry's own estimate of £635,951.[3] The addition of a conventional ten per cent for contingencies brought the estimate to £707,104, and this became the official figure. The surveyors however pointed out other expenses in their report: embankments and steps, £44,000; additional land, £70,000; foot and carriage ways, £3000; and unascertained sums for fittings, for warming, lighting, ventilating, and for the great clock. No mention was made of furnishings.[4] There could be no doubt that expenditure would exceed a million. The estimates having been approved, the Treasury directed that the greatest care must be taken to settle the basis upon which the works were to be conducted before they began.[5] But the proposal for a commission to direct them was dropped, the building being placed, like other official undertakings, entirely in the architect's hands under the supervision of the Commissioners of Woods and Works.[6] And so was begun the greatest building of the century.

Meanwhile on 25 July Barry had reported the dangerous state of the ruins of St. Stephen's Chapel, whereupon the Board empowered him to direct the 'immediate taking down the Ruins of the superstructure . . . and also for covering . . . the Crypt, and Cloisters proposed to be retained'. So, amidst the groans of the antiquaries, the ancient structure was finally demolished.[7]

---

[1] Banks to Alfred Barry, 10 January 1868, *The Architect . . . A reply*, pp. 37–8.

[2] Works 11/1/2, ff. 11–14; draft report by Seward, 14 March 1837, Works 11/10/1, f. 5. The month intervening was spent on settling many questions with the architect. Barry's calculations had produced a figure of £654,710, to which Seward and Chawner wished to add £38,000 for works they considered to be essential, most of which were disputed by the architect: more substantial scantlings, additional bonding stones and iron girders, were among the principal. A suggested £500 for gas lighting in dark seasons called forth the comment: 'Not any work will be allowed to be performed in the Building after dark: It involves a great responsibility which in a large public Work, no Contractor would take upon himself, and I consider the practice at best extremely objectionable' (Works 11/10/1, ff. 9, 7 April 1837, 10). An extra £13,000 for wood ceilings Barry met by a reduction in the prices for wood and stone carving, which he considered excessive, and by the substitution of deal for oak in the joinery of the servants' rooms and offices in the residences (*ibid.* f. 13, 12 April 1837).

[3] *Ibid.* ff. 214, 220 (12 April 1837).

[4] Works 11/1/2, f. 1. The failure of government to submit an all-inclusive estimate is extraordinary after the parliamentary inquiries of 1828 and 1831.

[5] Works 2/2, p. 147 (11 July 1837).   [6] See above, pp. 182, 197.

[7] Works 2/2, p. 296; *Parl. Pap. H.L.* 1835 (119), B.M. vol. 36, 'Reports from Architects relative to the Condition of the Walls of St. Stephen's Chapel'.

An embankment had to be constructed before the new palace could be begun and in this Barry was associated with an eminent engineer, James Walker.[1] Walker was directed to communicate with the City Navigation Committee on a change of line proposed by Barry, building further into the river at the north end.[2] On 5 August 1837 tenders were invited from ten London firms for the coffer dam, river wall, and part of the foundations; and the contract was signed on 11 September with Messrs. Henry and John Lee of Lambeth.[3] In November Barry recommended that the Lees should proceed with a further part of the foundations, on a contract for prices, as the depth of excavation and concrete foundations required was uncertain.[4]

Progress at first was slow, the work difficult, and Messrs. Lee not especially adept.[5] But by June 1839 the foundations were sufficiently advanced for Barry to recommend letting a contract for part of the superstructure.[6] He was evidently anxious that work should begin that summer, but Treasury permission was not obtained until 10 July, and the measurements required to form an accurate estimate were so laborious that although the builders employed 'twice the usual number of surveyors' their bills of quantities could not be ready so as to deliver tenders before 26 September—instead of 8 August as Barry had intended.[7] The choice of stone not yet having been determined, they had to give prices for various alternatives. The lowest tender was that of Messrs. Grissell and Peto, averaged at £159,718, some £11,000 more than Barry's original calculation.[8] He decided that the contract should be taken at the price for Bolsover stone, to allow using that in the plinth, string courses, copings, pinnacles and other exposed parts of the building at the prices of the contract schedule; the rest might be of the cheaper Steetley. The ultimate cost would then probably accord very nearly with his original estimate.[9] The principal part of the site was to have been given up to the new contractors by 1 January 1840, but as Lee had not then finished, Grissell and Peto took over portions successively during the month, arranging to complete that part of the second contract that Lee had failed to finish.[10] Contract number 3 (the river front) was to be completed by 31 March 1843.[11]

The question of the choice of stone had been raised by Barry in a letter of 5 July 1838 to the Commissioners of Woods. He was anxious to avoid criticism for using unsatisfactory stone, and suggested that he should, in the company of some 'scientific gentlemen', tour the country's quarries, inspect old buildings of stone, and collect

---

[1] 1781–1862; see F. Boase, *Modern English Biography*, iii (Truro, 1901).

[2] Works 11/1/1, ff. 47–8 (25 March 1836).

[3] Works 1/22, pp. 302, 327–8 (29 August 1837). For plans see Works 29/3112–20. The unsuccessful tenders were Baker & Son £74,450, W. Cubitt £77,500, H. Mackintosh £82,000, Grissell & Peto £83,900, Geo. Mundy £93,800 (Works 11/5/17, f. 13).   [4] Works 11/5/18.

[5] Seward recommended extending their contract to part of the foundation, 15 November 1837 (Works 1/22, p. 379); but in 1839 Barry and Walker complained of 'a want of proper management and the non-employment of a sufficient number of hands' (Works 11/5/17, f. 22).

[6] Works 11/6/1, f. 1 (18 June 1839).

[7] *Ibid.* ff. 1–5; Works 1/23, pp. 372, 379, 385, 393, 401, 414, 483. The builders expressed their willingness to tender on assumed quantities, or by a schedule of prices only, by the earlier date; 'but we should very much prefer to deliver our tenders upon the actual ascertained quantities' (Works 11/6/1, f. 4).

[8] Works 11/6/1, ff. 8 (26 September 1839), 11 (10 October 1839). Lee's tender was not opened because it was not accompanied by the required schedule of prices (*ibid.* f. 13a).

[9] Works 11/6/1, f. 12 (10 October 1839). In fact, Bolsover (or rather Anston) stone was used for the entire exterior, the additional cost being estimated at £22,000, *Parl. Pap.* 1844 (448) vi, qq. 31, 36–41.

[10] Works 11/6/1, f. 16 (7 January 1840).   [11] *Ibid.* f. 22.

all necessary data.[1] Accordingly Sir Henry De la Beche of the Geological Survey,[2] Dr. William Smith,[3] geologist and engineer, and Charles Harriott Smith,[4] a master mason who had carved the new capitals for the National Gallery portico, were appointed to accompany Barry on a six-weeks tour. Some £1300 were spent on the inquiry, including a second visit by Barry to ascertain the supply of stone at Bolsover, which was selected as the most suitable.[5] It is ironical that after so much effort had been expended, supplies of the selected stone proved inadequate, and the neighbouring Anston stone which was substituted should turn out a disappointment.[6]

The superstructure was begun in February 1840, the 'first stone' being laid by Mrs. Barry on 27 April 1840.[7] The question of heating and ventilation now became urgent.[8] The ventilation of the old House of Commons had been a perennial problem, and in 1835 a select committee had inquired into the question of ventilation with a view to discovering the best mode for the new buildings. Their end-of-session researches, however, were terminated too quickly for them to come to any decision; but they urged that some plan might 'be systematically adopted for this purpose, before the commencement of the new Buildings . . . whatever Plan shall be hereafter selected, provision should be made for its adoption in the first instance by the Architect, so as not only to insure its success, but to prevent needless expense and inconvenience. . . . The whole space immediately below the Two Houses of Parliament, as well as that between the Ceiling and the Roof, should be prepared and altogether reserved for such arrangements as may be necessary. . . .'[9] Among the experts called in evidence, with Michael Faraday and W. T. Brande, was a Scotch teacher of chemistry, David Boswell Reid (1805–63). Unlike nearly everyone else, he had a definite system to propose: one that he had already tried with success in his Edinburgh classroom. He suggested that fresh air should be admitted to the House of Commons through many small holes, and be drawn out through a single aperture: 'If there be one great chimney or ventilator through which every thing is to pass, by opening or shutting a valve in every individual room or apartment, be it what it may, any degree of ventilation can be commanded that is required'.[10] He was eventually given charge of the ventilation of the temporary House of Commons, where he achieved a considerable measure of success, triumphantly demonstrated in November 1836 with the aid of smoke, ether, oranges and an audience of obedient guardsmen. The concomitant works included a new ceiling of 'entirely novel construction'[11] (Pl. 34B). In the temporary House of Lords the improvement was less marked, a fact that Reid ascribed to the inadequate sum allowed, and to the failure of their lordships to give to the operator sufficient information as to their requirements. Thus a situation arose in which, as a rule, the Commons had faith in Reid, while the Lords did not.[12]

[1] T. 1/4068, f. 16677/38.   [2] See p. 460 above.
[3] 1769–1839, 'the real founder of stratigraphical geology' (*D.N.B.*)   [4] 1792–1864, see *D.N.B.*
[5] T. 1/4068, f. 16677/38; *Parl. Pap.* 1839 (574) xxx.
[6] For an explanation, see C. H. Smith, 'On Stone for Building', *I.B.A. Transactions*, 30 May 1853, p. 6.
[7] A. Barry, *Life*, p. 160; *Parl. Pap.* 1846 (349) xv, app. 16.   [8] Works 1/23, p. 494 (19 October 1839).
[9] *Parl. Pap.* 1835 (583) xviii.   [10] *Ibid.* q. 409.
[11] *The Times*, 20 October 1836, p. 3 and 5 November 1836, p. 3. See also *Architectural Mag.* ii (1835) pp. 136–7 and v (1838), pp. 87, 134. On a later occasion Reid exploded gunpowder in the roof cavity (*Parl. Pap.* 1837–8 (358), xxxvi).   [12] See above, p. 226.

Reid's success in the Commons made him the obvious person for Barry to turn to for advice, though he wanted the further assistance of one Manby to superintend the installation.[1] But Duncannon forthwith concluded an agreement with Reid to supervise the ventilation of the new House.[2] While Barry was instructed to give Reid every assistance, there was impressed on Reid 'the expediency from time to time of making such arrangements with Mr. Barry on points involving any interference with the structure of the Building as shall at the same time secure the best means for giving effect to your Plans, and render any recourse to alterations and extra works unnecessary'.[3] On 24 January 1840 Reid was given charge of the warming and ventilation of the new Houses from 1 April following until the end of the first session after the completion and occupation of the building, at a salary of £500 per annum.[4]

> It is scarcely necessary for the Board to suggest to you that the authority for, and the direction of your proceedings will at all times emanate from this Board; but that the reservation of this control is intended to apply to cases only in which a difference of opinion may arise between yourself and Mr. Barry, and that, as a general principle, without appealing to the Board, you must defer to him upon all points affecting either the Solidity or the Architectural character of his Building.

Problems put by Reid before the Board were referred to Barry, who recommended that Reid should submit a detailed report with plans to elucidate his system. To assist him in this, he was allowed one of Barry's clerks. By the end of April 1841 Reid had submitted to the architect 'a series of Plans and Sections shewing the leading Air Channels and the general arrangements' that he proposed. Barry then drew up a 'conjectural estimate' of £62,000 for the system.[5]

The principal feature and expense was a central tower costing £20,000 to act as a unique vent for the entire palace.[6] Reid proposed that the fresh air that he would draw in from a great height, through either the Victoria Tower or the Clock Tower,

---

[1] Barry wrote to Duncannon, 3 October 1839, that Reid and John Oldham (1779–1840), engineer to the Banks of England and Ireland, were 'in all respects . . . eminently qualified to be employed upon this business; but as Dr. Reid is a resident of Edinburgh, and does not profess to be thoroughly acquainted with the practical details of building and machinery, and as Mr. Oldham's official appointment . . . would prevent him from giving up much of his time . . . I should wish also to have the further assistance of a practical engineer who has specially turned his attention to the subject, and whose duty should be to direct, superintend, and be responsible for the proper execution of all the works that may be requisite in carrying out the details of the system that may be agreed upon'; and for this he proposed Manby, the agent for Price's patent hot-water heating system (*Parl. Pap.* 1846 (349) xv, q. 258). Though putting this letter in evidence, Barry told the Commons' committee of 1846 that the appointment of Reid was contrary to his recommendation (*ibid.* q. 257); but he had so phrased it that Duncannon's obvious response would be to consult Reid, see Works 1/23, p. 494 (19 Oct. 1839). Reid proved willing to leave Edinburgh.
[2] Works 2/2, p. 383.   [3] Works 1/24, pp. 80–1.
[4] *Ibid.* pp. 88–9.   [5] *Ibid.* p. 358; 1/25, pp. 71, 80, 90, 94 (estimate, 20 May 1841).
[6] Barry's revised estimate (26 May 1841) was:

New ventilating tower over octagon saloon	£20,000
Fireproof floor under the whole of the various roofs of the building	£20,680
Air and chimney flues, in the walls, under all the floors and roofs; vaulting of the basement story; and various alterations of the building	£12,320
Apparatus—about	£12,000
	£65,000

He also recommended that the whole fabric should be rendered fireproof, 'as far as any Building can be made so, by adding a Brick floor on Iron Beams, between the Principal and upper Floors', estimated at £21,000 (Works 2/3, pp. 99–100).

according to the direction of the wind, should be heated to any desired temperature and admitted by channels into the two Chambers and the various rooms; but that local fires should be retained for cheerful appearance and individual warming.[1] Smoke and vitiated air alike would pass into great ducts in the roofs leading to the central tower, and so into the outside air.[2] The addition of an extra tower the Board at first sought to avoid, enquiring whether the Victoria Tower might not serve the purpose. As the formal communications between architect and expert, conducted through the Board, were time-consuming, the Board called for a joint report, which Barry was reluctant to make, presumably being unwilling to admit Reid on an equal footing with himself.[3] But all efforts of the Board to speed matters were thwarted by the Treasury, which in the last days of Melbourne's shaky administration would not commit itself to such a major alteration as a third tower without reference to Parliament.[4] In the short session after the 1841 general election a select committee considered the question.[5] Reid was still experimenting, and Barry reported that no expense was necessary in the next six months beyond strengthening the foundations then in progress for the central hall; so the committee reported that it was 'unnecessary to come to any final decision upon the matter . . . at the present moment'. The foundations should be strengthened to permit the erection of a tower if subsequently that were to be decided upon.

In the following session a committee reported in favour of Reid's scheme, and approved a central tower. This, suggests Professor Collins, marks 'the first occasion when mechanical services had a real influence on architectural design'.[6] But this influence was limited to the mere provision of a central tower, and it was Barry, not Reid, who decided the character, appearance, and even height of that tower (Pl. 63). The other ventilation shafts were built later because of the ultimate rejection of Reid's notion of making the tower the unique vent, on which the select committee refused to express 'any decided opinion'. 'Serious doubts', they went on, 'may fairly be entertained as to the success of such an experiment'. But not wishing to preclude the adoption of the plan if it should be found desirable, the committee suggested that 'a double provision of flues should be made', i.e. of ordinary chimneys and of Reid's channels. The committee also recommended adopting Barry's proposal for making the building as fireproof as possible at an additional cost of £21,000. This involved constructing the ceiling of the principal storey of brick arches on iron girders.[7]

By the autumn of 1840, Barry was recommending that Grissell and Peto should be allowed to proceed with the foundations of the Central Hall, the Royal Staircase, and the remainder of the south flank; as he was

> perfectly satisfied with the manner in which they have hitherto performed the Works undertaken by them, as well as with their despatch, and the excellent arrangements

[1] *Parl. Pap.* 1842 (536) xiv, qq. 19, 20, 29. Reid hoped to find a smokeless but cheerful fuel for the fires (q. 2).   [2] *Ibid.* qq. 5, 6, 30, 31, 69.

[3] Works 1/25, pp. 102–3 (1 June 1840), 164 (28 July), 169 (3 August); 2/2, pp. 99–100; 11/12, f. 75.

[4] Works 1/25, p. 182 (17 August 1840); 2/2, pp. 114, 119, 131, 142, 145, 186, 220, 229.

[5] *Parl. Pap.* 1841, sess. 2 (51) i.

[6] *Parl. Pap.* 1842 (536) xiv; P. Collins, *Changing Ideals in Modern Architecture 1750–1950* (1965), p. 238.

[7] A practice pioneered in factory construction. Cf. Nash's work at Buckingham Palace, and Soane's at the State Paper Office (*1831 Report*, p. 77 and p. 570 above).

they have made for their future proceedings, as well as that . . . the employment of another Builder or Builders would produce much confusion and consequent delay and further that the prices recommended are those of the lowest tender by competition for such works under the first Contract, and are such as are not only reasonable but probably lower than would be obtained by a new Competition.[1]

In November, a little more than a month later, this was authorised to the extent of £163,350.[2] The Victoria Tower (as the King's Tower was now termed) was excluded under Treasury instructions of 11 April 1839 reserving the question of this tower for further consideration.[3] But Barry urged that its foundations would be 'so intimately connected with the Works to be performed . . . as to render it of the greatest importance that they should be carried up simultaneously',[4] and gained his point in February 1841.[5] Excavations then revealed quicksands and springs, so they dug deeper, driving a tier of sheet piling into a clay stratum below the gravel on which the foundations were laid. Barry also prescribed hydraulic lime and metallic sand in the concrete under the footings of the walls—in all, an addition of £10,000 on the estimate.[6]

The principal contractors, Grissell and Peto,[7] proved to possess remarkable powers of organisation. In recommending them for the third contract in 1842 Barry praised the extent of their preparations.[8] *The Times* commented in September 1844 on 'the regularity and precision which prevail in every department, and . . . the numerous novel and ingenious devices' devised to save labour and perfect construction, among them Dr. Spurgin's patent hoist for bricks and mortar (thus dispensing with mortar-carriers). Allan, the foreman, was credited with the 'introduction of zinc plates or moulds in lieu of the old wooden templets', and with improvements in the use of the travelling crane and in the newly-introduced system of framed timber for scaffolding (instead of poles tied with rope). With the crane on the scaffolding's summit, 'one mason . . . can set as much work in one day as was formerly done in three days; whilst at least six labourers are dispensed with'.[9] It also offered a

---

[1] Works 11/6/2, ff. 1 (23 October), 2 (2 November 1840).

[2] Works 2/2, p. 456 (28 November 1840). The contract was signed by Grissell and Peto on 9 December 1840, the specification directing that the whole excavated area was to be covered with a bed of concrete (of a thickness to be directed), 6 measures gravel or clean ballast to 1 of fresh ground Dorking lime mixed dry and then well worked together with water, and in that state teemed and thrown into the work from a height of at least 10 feet. The brick foundation walls were to be laid in English bond, no four courses exceeding 11¾ ins.; the mortar of 3 of sand to 1 of best burnt Merstham or Dorking lime, well compounded together in a proper pugmill (Works 11/6/2, f. 7).

[3] Works 1/24, p. 491 (3 December 1840); 2/2, pp. 321–2 (11 April 1839).

[4] Works 11/6/2, f. 8 (11 December); 1/24, pp. 515–6 (19 December 1840).

[5] Works 11/6/2, f. 10 (6 February 1841).

[6] *Ibid.* f. 12 (8 November 1841); 2/3 p. 223 (15 November 1841); 1/25, p. 259.

[7] Samuel Morton Peto (1809–1889, cr. bart. 1855) retired in 1846 from his partnership with Thomas Grissell in order to enter Parliament (Works 1/29, pp. 281, 308; Works 1/30, pp. 11–13). See also *D.N.B.*

[8] Works 11/6/3, f. 1.

[9] *Times*, 10 September 1844, quoted *Builder*, ii (1844), p. 465; T. Grissell, 'On Timber Scaffolding for Buildings', *Proceedings of Institution of Civil Engineers* iii, 1844 pp. 203–17 quoted *Builder*, iii (1845), p. 33. Grissell claimed to have introduced such scaffolding (employed in Northern England) on the Reform Club, and then on Nelson's Column (see Plate 32); in the discussion that followed, earlier examples were referred to. For illustration and description of revolving scaffolding used in erecting the Central Tower at Westminster, see *Builder* iii (1845), p. 41. As well as Spurgin's patent, a hoist devised by one Pierre Journet was employed, consisting of a continuous chain on which hods and buckets could be hooked and winched up, capable of raising 900 bricks an hour to a height of 60 feet. Grissell declared that for the Victoria Tower he intended to apply steam power to this device (*Proceedings of Institution of Civil Engineers*, iii, 1844, pp. 218–22, with illustration).

means whereby 'heavy worked blocks might be raised without any chance of injury, and adjusted in their places with the same precision and facility as a brick could be laid by hand', so obviating the need to finish elaborate decorations *in situ*.[1]

On the building site Grissell and Peto employed on average about 500 men between March 1842 and November 1845, and thereafter 600 or 700; as well as large numbers in the Thames Bank workshops opened at Millbank in January 1845 specially for the finishings of the New Palace (222 men at work there by July 1845, 335 in December 1847, and 246 six months later); and at the quarries (128 in July 1840, 292 in November 1843, 147 in June 1847); with often over a hundred engaged elsewhere on miscellaneous activities. In the three years from autumn 1845 there were constantly over 1100 men in their employ working on the Houses of Parliament; in December 1846 as many as 1470.[2] Yet this was by no means the only public building being built at this time by the firm, which must have been one of the largest employers of labour in London. The difficulties of the confined site were met in part by establishing the Millbank workshops already mentioned, further extended in 1845, and partly by utilising the coffer dam, not removed until 1848, for workshops.[3] Nevertheless their arrangements did not always run smoothly: progress was hindered in September 1841 by a strike of the masons employed on the river front, seeking to induce the contractors to dismiss the zealous Allan who had complained in too vigorous language of 'want of exertion on the part of some of the Workmen'. The contractors, however, backed their foreman, secured the support of the Office, and found other labour.[4] It was May 1843 before the strikers resumed work.[5]

Several temporary works and obstructions having been removed, the opportunity was afforded to extend the foundations towards New Palace Yard and Little Abingdon Street. This was included in Grissell and Peto's contract in December 1841.[6] But after a further addition of £450 for foundations under the corridor of the House of Commons, Barry was instructed that there must be no more such extensions of existing agreements, but a new contract for new works.[7]

In March 1842 Barry made the first of a series of progress reports: the river front and a considerable part of the flanks were about 23 feet above the level of the principal floor or 43 feet above Trinity Standard. The foundations of the royal approach, the two Houses, and the Clock Tower were in a forward state, part being already at the surface, but delays had been caused by the bad nature of the ground and the need to secure the surrounding buildings. The Anston stone was in plentiful supply and of 'excellent quality', and the same was true of the Painswick stone used for internal masonry. There were 588 men engaged on the works.[8]

It was clear that the next stage, the superstructure of this vast spinal range, would have to form a separate contract; but Barry again urged that Grissell and Peto

[1] *R.I.B.A. Transactions*, 1856–7, p. 156. Charles Barry junior therein claimed the merit for his father and his assistants Meeson and Quarm.

[2] Works 11/9/7; *Parl. Pap.* 1846 (349) xv, app. 16: Return of men employed.

[3] Works 11/9/3; 2/4, pp. 522–5. Barry designed a house for the manager at Thames Bank, and a gate-keeper's lodge (Works 1/27, pp. 424, 431; 1/28, p. 14).

[4] Works 1/25, p. 203 (17 September 1841); R. W. Postgate, *The Builders' History* (1923), pp. 129–30.

[5] *Parl. Pap.* 1844 (448) vi, qq. 504–6.

[6] Works 11/6/2, f. 18 (3 December 1841); 2/3, p. 244; 1/25, pp. 270, 296.

[7] Works 11/6/2, ff. 25 (31 May), 26 (6 June 1842); 2/3, p. 382 (15 June 1842).

[8] Works 11/9/7, f. 3.

should be continued as the contractors, on grounds of efficiency and economy; and also because it would enable them to recoup somewhat 'the burthensome cost of their preparatory arrangements'. Instead, however, of a lump sum contract, Barry proposed that the work should be measured as it proceeded, and paid quarterly, holding back a percentage for the security of the public. It would, he thought, cost about £212,249 and take about two and a quarter years.[1] This contract (number 5) for the principal part of the palace, including the Victoria Tower to a height of 83 feet and the Central Tower to 86 feet, required a decision on the system of heating and ventilation; but the Treasury followed the 1842 select committee's report, and directed a double provision of flues to be made, so as to leave the choice open until Reid had completed his experiments for making the Central Tower the outlet for all the flues.[2] The contract was given to Grissell and Peto in August 1842 at the old prices, but subject to a periodic revision of timber prices, affected by Peel's reduction of customs duty.[3]

By this time the lower portions of the river front as well as a considerable part of the flanks were ready for roofing. The central part of the river front and the wings were rather higher, and expected to reach their full height by mid-December. The west part of the south front, the Victoria and Central Towers, the Royal Gallery, House of Lords, and west front towards New Palace Yard averaged about 15 feet above Trinity Standard. Anston stone was still abundant, nor was there then any deficiency of Caen stone, which had recently been employed for internal masonry. The contractors had increased the number of workmen at the Anston quarry to about 300, with additional tackle and horses, to ensure the adequacy of supplies in the future.[4] By April 1843, the central part and wing towers of the river front were 66 feet above high water mark, and the central and southern parts of the palace about 6 feet above ground level. There were 548 employed on the works.[5] In July the Board criticised the recent slow pace of progress, not commensurate with the sums voted; according to contract number 3 the river front and returns should have been completed by Lady Day 1843, but no part of the roof was in progress, nor was all the stone-work finished. Similarly, they remarked, considering the facility for employing large numbers of workmen afforded by the extent of the works, progress on contract number 5 was not satisfactory. But operations were hampered by the continuing needs of the two Houses: the site was not a clear one. The masons' strike had caused delay. The arrangements for fireproofing were complex. Reid's prescriptions for ventilation were 'a continual source of difficulty'. And much time had been required for carving stone before fixing it.[6]

Work on the roofs of the river front had begun by the New Year of 1844, when 614 men were employed on the site: a year later, although the roofs of the centre and linking portions had been finished, the towers of this front were not yet structurally complete. Similarly, much of the north and south flanks was up to roof level in January 1844, but the south flank containing Lords' committee rooms was still

[1] Works 11/6/3, f. 1 (14 June 1842). This contract was extended by Barry to include the Commons' private entrance, and by 1851 when that part was under construction the prices tended considerably in Grissell's favour (*ibid*. ff. 42–5).   [2] *Ibid*. f. 7 (6 August); 2/3, p. 427 (30 August 1842).
[3] Works 1/25, p. 484 (11 August 1842); 2/3, pp. 395, 412–3.   [4] Works 11/9/7, f. 4.
[5] *Ibid*. f. 5.   [6] Works 1/26, pp. 269–70; 11/6/1, f. 27.

without a roof in April 1845. The House of Lords was roofed about August 1844. Between January 1844 and April 1845 the Victoria and Clock Towers rose from 22 and 12 feet above ground to 38 and 36 feet, respectively, but during the same period the remaining parts of the new buildings rose only some 12 feet (from 18 to 30 feet).[1] The great quantities of Caen stone needed for the interior had caused delay in 1843; and the following year the unsettled state of the iron trade and difficulties with the workmen interrupted the fixing of the ironwork of the roofs.[2] By March 1845 Barry had cleared sufficient of the site to propose that a contract (number 6) for the St. Stephen's Hall that was to replace the old chapel should be concluded with Grissell and Peto on the same terms as contract number 5, except for glass, on which the duty had recently been reduced.[3] To enable the work of Parliament to go on as the works extended, ten new temporary committee rooms were erected in New Palace Yard, and the opportunity was taken to provide at the same time two new courts for the homeless new equity judges, the vice-chancellors.[4]

This slow progress was particularly galling to the Lords, who had never been reconciled to their temporary chamber, the discomforts of which neither Smirke nor Reid had overcome.[5] A Lords' committee examined the situation in March 1843 and questioned Barry closely.[6] He argued that it was unwise to build up the chamber alone, or faster than the adjacent parts of the palace, that it was not safe to erect it in less than a year, and that it was not prudent to work on plastering or finishings in winter. But by using a wooden instead of a plaster ceiling, the House might be got up and the ceiling completed, the walls fitted up in a temporary manner, and temporary seats provided, by the session of 1844. Reid stated that the new House could be ventilated independently of the central tower; and made suggestions for improving the existing House. The committee recommended that the new House should be prepared for occupation at the start of the 1844 session, and that no expensive alterations should be made in the ventilation of the temporary chamber.

Barry made no effort to comply with the Lords' demands as the committee's report was not notified to the government.[7] No special efforts were made to hurry on the Lords' buildings, so that when the peers assembled for the session of 1844 they found themselves once again in their cramped quarters in the Painted Chamber. They consequently appointed a new select committee,[8] which met in March, April and May, and reported

> That it appears from the Evidence of Charles Barry, Esquire, that during the Progress of the building of the Houses of Parliament certain departures have taken place from

---

[1] Works 11/9/7, ff. 7, 13, 16; 2/4, pp. 433–5; *Parl. Pap.* 1846 (719) xv, q. 6.

[2] For landing of Caen stone, see Works 1/26, p. 163; 2/3, pp. 545, 556. Grissell undertook the contract for the iron roof over the Royal Gallery and House of Commons in April 1845 for £8500; although this was £21 11s. a ton, compared with a tender of £17 a ton from Boydell of Dudley, Barry argued that 'the acknowledged superiority of London over country castings', the ease of superintendence, and avoidance of delays and other workmen coming onto the site, justified giving the contract to Grissell, whose profit would be only 10 per cent (Works 11/7/3).   [3] Works 2/4, p. 433; 1/28, p. 120.

[4] Works 1/27, pp. 246 (26 October 1844), 280 (23 November, estimate for ten committee rooms, £4725), 314 (11 December); 2/4, pp. 310–14, 324. Barry's estimate, which varied slightly from letter to letter, but included £585 for warming and ventilating, specified timber rooms 18 ft. high, roofed with asphalted felt; walls lined with deal to height of five ft.; interior lined with canvas and paper; boarded floors (Works 2/4, pp. 313–14, 23 and 29 October 1844).   [5] Works 11/10/2, ff. 13–16, 19–20; *Parl. Pap. H.L.* 1835 (96).

[6] *Parl. Pap. H.L.* 1843 (40); the evidence is printed in *Parl. Pap.* 1844 (381) vi.

[7] *Ibid.* 1844 (629) vi, q. 580.   [8] *Ibid.* 1844 (269) vi.

the original Plans approved by the Committees of the Two Houses of Parliament, and ordered to be carried into Execution under the Direction of the Boards of Treasury and Works, from which Alterations have been made by Mr. Barry without authority from either of those Boards; to which Circumstance they think it right to call the particular Attention of this House.

The communication of this report to the House of Commons created sufficient stir to oblige the government to agree to the appointment of a Commons' select committee, which under the chairmanship of the Chief Commissioner, Lord Lincoln, traversed much the same ground as the Lords.[1] From May to August the Lords resumed their inquiries, concluding that a temporary manner of finishing would be undesirable, but that the Lords' buildings 'should be advanced with the greatest possible speed'.[2] Much of what came then under discussion belongs rather to the administrative history of the Office of Works than to the building of the Houses of Parliament, but the inquiries of the select committees of 1844 provide a convenient point from which to embark on an examination of the development of the plan up to that time.

The censure of Barry turned on the nature of the architect's authority. Barry himself considered that, subject to keeping within his estimate and maintaining the general principles of his design, he had a free hand to determine the details of plan as of elevation; that for any change involving extra expenditure he was bound to obtain the authority of the Woods and Forests, but that he was then at liberty to decide the mode of the change.[3] In this view he was supported by Lord Lincoln. But Duncannon (now Earl of Bessborough) and the weight of opinion on the two committees considered that he must submit plans of any change whatsoever to the Board of Woods.[4] The changes Barry had made to the plan of 1836 were of two types: those consequent upon an official instruction; and those made of his own initiative to improve the design without incurring any additional expense. At the wish of the government or of the Houses a number of small additions had been made over the years. During the sitting of the committee of both Houses before the competition entries had been submitted, Hume urged that a house for the sergeant-at-arms must be added, and forced his view on a reluctant Board of Woods.[5] In August 1837 the Metropolitan Police sought accommodation in the palace; additional accommodation was provided for attorneys at the request of the Law Society (estimate £5000); a residence for the Commons' Librarian (£1250), and one for the Clerk of the House (£2000) were placed on the west side of Speaker's Court, between the Commons and the clock tower.[6] The requirements of the ventilation had of course necessitated much detailed modification of the plans, particularly in the lateral towers and the introduction of a central tower.[7] Another problem, for which Barry had then produced no solution, was that of the public records. It had originally been proposed to store only certain classes of the records in the Victoria Tower, but the Treasury had subsequently asked that provision might be made for all the

[1] *Ibid.* 1844 (448) vi.   [2] *Ibid.* 1844 (629) vi.
[3] *Ibid.* 1844 (269) pp. 20–1.   [4] *Ibid.* 1844 (448) vi, qq. 457–9, 473, 475.
[5] *Ibid.* qq. 460–8; Stephenson told Duncannon 'that if we once consented to alterations in a work of that magnitude, all sorts of difficulties would occur' (*ibid.* q. 464).
[6] *Ibid.* qq. 31, 48–50.   [7] *Ibid.* 1844 (269) vi, p. 31.

public records; basement rooms and roof spaces were alternatives considered as well as raising the Tower fifty feet.[1]

Rather more important were Barry's own changes.[2] The most obvious was the alteration in the alignment of the spine of the palace, or 'centre line through Houses of Lords and Commons', so as 'to equalise the Size of the adjoining Courts, obtaining Carriage Access to every Court'. This meant that the principal axis was no longer parallel to Westminster Hall, but to the river front. This enlarged the eastern range of courts, enabling Barry to fit the Peers' and Commons' refreshment rooms into the two courts adjoining their respective Houses. And—perhaps most important—he had altered the royal approach. In the plan of 1836 the sovereign would pass under the King's Tower into an entrance hall in which he would alight at the foot of a stair rising in three tiers of steps straight to the royal Robing Room immediately behind the throne in the House of Lords.

> But on consideration [Alfred Barry tells us] Mr. Barry grudged the great sacrifice of space, and the interruption of communication on the principal floor, for a staircase, which could be used only twice a year. He conceived the notion of the Royal gallery, as a hall for the use of the House of Lords, for the viewing of the royal procession, and for the display of architectural effect, unrestrained by the encumbrances which business renders necessary in the Houses of Lords and Commons. To these considerations he sacrificed the greater magnificence of the original staircase, and on his own responsibility proceeded with the work.[3]

The alteration made in or after 1840 provided for a flight of steps on the north side of the great tower, rising to a landing from which, at a right angle, an unbroken flight of 36 steps gave access to a guard room and robing room overlooking Old Palace Yard, from which the Royal Gallery or great hall extended right up to the House of Lords.[4] The height of the hall was increased in order to form a level ventilating duct from the House of Lords across the building. Barry used this factor as an argument for not reverting to that insulated House of Lords which had been an admired feature of his original design, and therein was supported by Reid.[5] Lord Sudeley (the former Hanbury Tracy) was particularly critical of this change when he discovered it in 1844, and he used the select committee to attack it.[6] The unbroken flight of steps withstood the critics, but the practical inconvenience of placing the robing room so far from the Lords obliged Barry to truncate his great hall to create what is now known as the Prince's Chamber immediately adjacent to the House.[7]

The result of the select committee of 1844 was that Barry was instructed to render half-yearly progress reports to the Woods and Forests, and to make no alteration

---

[1] *Ibid.* qq. 217–220.   [2] *Ibid.* pp. 20, 31.

[3] *Life*, pp. 245–6. Barry stated some practical objections leading to the change in *Parl. Pap.* 1844 (269) vi, q. 136.

[4] See Works 29/3004, four drawings by Reid of different stages of this plan, dating the first change to 1840; also *Parl. Pap.* 1844 (269) vi, qq. 137–8, in which Barry dates his alterations to 1842. The robing room or 'inner hall' was moved because it needed a lantern light, which became an impossibility when the ventilating system was placed in the roof.

[5] *Parl. Pap.* 1844 (269) vi, qq. 132–6, 141, 192–202, 255, 266.

[6] B.M. Add. MS. 40543, ff. 360–4. He also put forward a plan of his own.

[7] Works 2/4, pp. 196–7 (10 June 1844, Barry to Lord Lincoln). Barry at the same time enlarged the robing room; *ibid.* pp. 200–1 (20 June, Treasury to Commissioners of Woods).

whatever without authority; and that it was decided to push on with the House of Lords as fast as possible. Barry recommended that Grissell and Peto should immediately proceed with the works for the roofs and ceilings, at an estimate of £7500.[1] Although it would be possible to fit up the new House in a temporary manner for the 1845 session, it would not be advisable, he reported, and no such attempt was made. Barry was, however, instructed 'to advance the Buildings . . . with the greatest speed compatible with the due execution of the Work'.[2]

Pressed to complete the House of Lords, and evidently determined to retain control of the decorative scheme, to which the Fine Arts Commission[3] was a threat, Barry turned again to Pugin, who replied in June 1844 that the way in which he could be of most help to Barry would be to adapt 'the best examples' and get them executed.[4] This he subsequently did by collecting examples of medieval carving which were used as models for the craftsmen. However, he also helped Barry with drawings, and on 3 September Barry wrote again urgently for his assistance with the 'working drawings for the fittings and decorations of the House of Lords'.[5] Finally Barry evolved a scheme for the carving and ornamental woodwork to be executed under Pugin's superintendence in special government workshops, a proposal that

[1] *Ibid.* pp. 201 (22 June 1844), 208 (1 July).
[2] *Ibid.* pp. 243 (1 August 1844), 263 (14 August), 277 (10 September 1844).
[3] See p. 226 above; 614 below.
[4] Pugin to Barry 'Nottingham, Thursday', endorsed 16 June 1844:
'. . . I am sure I can never do you real service except in absolute detail; you should fully make up your mind as to every arrangement and then turn the small work over to me. It is next to impossible for me to design any abstract portion of a great whole in the same spirit as you have conceived the rest, and I know it is only a waste of time in me to attempt it. . . . I can do you far more service by adapting the best examples and getting them carried out in execution than by making a lot of drawings which could never be worked from. Remember, I never made a drawing which was of any real use to you yet, and it is a dreadful loss of time to me, incessantly occupied as I am with Church work, to attempt it; as I said before, I can do you no good except in actual detail, and in that more by ferreting out the fine things that exist than by composing new ones. . . .' (A. Barry, *The Architect . . . A reply*, p. 53).
It seems to me folly to try to distort these words from their natural meaning.
[5] This letter, printed by A. Barry, *The Architect . . . A Reply*, p. 39, is important enough to reproduce:

                                                                    3 Marine Parade, Brighton.
                                                                    September 3rd 1844.
Dear Pugin,
    I am in a regular fix respecting the working drawings for the fittings and decorations of the House of Lords, which it is of vital importance to me should now be finished with the utmost possible dispatch. Although I have now made up my mind as to the principles, and, generally, as to the details of the design for them, including a new design for the throne, which is at last perfectly satisfactory to me, I am unfortunately unable to get the general drawings into such a definite shape, as is requisite for preparing the working details, owing to a lameness in one of my legs, which has laid me on my back, either in bed or on the sofa, for the last ten days, and is, I fear, likely to keep me in the same position for some days, or, perhaps, weeks to come, at this place, where I have been advised to take up my quarters for the advantage of change, sea air, bathing, &c, &c. Now, as I know of no one who can render me such valuable and efficient assistance, or can so thoroughly relieve me of my present troubles of mind in respect of these said drawings as yourself, I am induced to write to you in the hope that you may be both able and willing to pass two or three days, or even a week, with me for the purpose of making out the drawings in question, and of enabling me to consult you generally, and enter into some permanent arrangement that will be satisfactory to you, as to occasional assistance for the future in the completion of the great work, as well as for the discharge of my obligations to you for what you have already done. I feel quite sure, that, if we were here together quietly for a few days, we should be able to make out definitively every portion of the design of the House of Lords' fittings, &c, in general drawings, so that you might be able to supply me with the details subsequently, from time to time, according to your leisure and convenience. I earnestly hope you will give me a line, by return of post, expressive of your consent to fall into the arrangement which I have proposed, and to name a time when I may expect to have the pleasure of seeing you.
    I have all the requisite drawings with me, together with a good supply of drawing-paper, tackle, &c. It would really do me good, both in body as well as in mind, to have you with me; therefore, pray do not disappoint me if you can in any way help it.

was approved in December 1844.[1] In reality Pugin appears to have had little to do with the workshops, but the appointment was a means of officially recognising his position as Barry's consultant 'interior decorator'.[2] Pugin accordingly directed 'the execution of the wood-work, ornamental metal-work, stained glass, and encaustic tiles throughout the building'.[3] According to Pugin's own letter to *The Builder* dated 3 September 1845, he did nothing on his own responsibility, 'all models and working drawings being prepared from Mr. Barry's designs, and submitted to him for his approval or alteration previous to their being carried into effect',[4] but 'designs' may not signify more than indications of a general character.[5] Pugin's influence may be seen in the elaboration of the decorative work during 1845.[6]

The contract for 'finishings' was let to Grissell and Peto in December 1844, for three years, determinable earlier at the option of either party. This was a contract for prices, Grissell and Peto offering percentage reductions from the Office schedule of prices on the whole comparable to those then obtaining for the contracts for ordinary repairs. Barry thought the tender 'much below the amount, at which any other respectable and competent Building firms in London, would be inclined to propose', but his opinion was not put to the test.[7] To save time and labour Barry had suggested that newly-invented machinery might be used to prepare the joinery.[8] After examining two types of machine he recommended the hire of Messrs. Taylor, Williams and Jordan's carving and copying machines at £100 per annum each.[9] Jordan himself was engaged in March 1845, when Barry represented that he needed a skilful and experienced manager to superintend under his directions the moulding and carving of the wood fittings.[10] In October Grissell gave notice of termination as the joiners' work was proving 'so entirely unsatisfactory in point of remuneration'.

[1] Works 1/27, p. 318 (16 December 1844). Pugin was to receive £200 p.a. The workshops themselves were placed under the superintendence of Richard Bayne, at the same salary (*ibid.* p. 362, 27 January 1845).

[2] An anonymous correspondent recalled for Edward Pugin how his father had told him 'that, after all, they could not do without employing him *publicly*, but, said he, "I now work for the Government, and Barry shall no longer get the credit of my plans." ' (*Art-Architect*, p. 11).   [3] A. Barry, *Life*, p. 197.

[4] *Builder*, iii (1845), p. 426. Edward Pugin suggested that this was a smokescreen put up at Barry's direction.

[5] The character of Pugin's collaboration with Barry may be observed in drawings in the P.R.O.: ornamental features have been pencilled in upon outline drawings of walls, arches, etc, and include both wood & stone work. I am indebted to Professor P. B. Stanton for pointing out to me drawings in which she had identified Pugin's hand, the subject of a forthcoming article by her.

[6] Barry calculated his original estimate for the Lords' ceiling at £3490; in September 1845 the Treasury authorised an additional £1300 for decorative painting and gilding 'absolutely necessary to ensure a proper degree of harmony and consistency with the proposed fresco paintings'. In November a further estimate of £10,629 was submitted for extra oak carvings, enrichments of wall framings and fittings, heraldic and other decorations of walls, metal screen doors, etc. (Works 11/9/4, ff. 12, 18, 21; 1/30, pp. 80–1).

[7] Works 2/4, pp. 341–5.   [8] *Ibid.*

[9] Works 1/28, p. 32; 11/8/4. Barry described the machine as consisting of: 'an Iron table which has two rectilinear motions at right angles to each other; over this table is a fixed horizontal support furnished with a vertical slide, and to this slide is attached several rotating mandrils carrying the cutters, and one fixed tracing point. The original Carving to be copied, serves as the guide for the tracing point, and is placed on the centre of the rolling table, with the work to be executed on each side of it. The Cutters are made to spin round many thousand times per minute, the workman bringing every point of the original Carving successively under the tracer, while the cutters are simultaneously producing from one to eight copies of it according to the size of the work. The Tracer is guided with the utmost facility over every variety of surface, by the Workman's foot, and the cutters being attached to the same slide, necessarily follow exactly its varied motions and ultimately produce perfect copies of the work required to be imitated' (Works 11/8/4, f. 5, Barry to Milne, 3 April 1845).

[10] Works 1/27, pp. 434–5 (18 March 1845). Jordan's salary was discontinued from 30 June 1848, because of the very limited attendance then required, and of his being a partner in Taylor & Co., the contractors for the woodcarving (Works 1/32, pp. 255, 291).

Barry, subjecting Grissell's expenditure to 'a very close investigation', recommended increased prices, but Grissell wanted them to apply to everything done since February 1845 as the work was 'of a much more expensive and elaborate nature than was contemplated ... a considerable amount of work has been executed by hand labour, which was . . . contemplated to be done by machinery'. The negotiations were inordinately prolonged, however, first over the question of responsibility for fire damage, which Grissell repudiated save on a basis of further price increases, and then over that of determining what works should be included in the contract and what allotted to other tradesmen. Work continued, but the new contract was not concluded until October 1850: in September 1851 Barry advised that the contract should be terminated, as other arrangements might be made more cheaply.[1] Previously, in July 1845, Grissell had already in a limited competition lost the contract for glazing to John Foord and Sons.[2] The metal railing for the House of Lords' galleries was commissioned from Hardman, the only 'manufactory . . . in the Kingdom where such work is properly executed'.[3] And a year later Barry chose Frederick Crace and Son to execute all the painting and gilding.[4] Another subcontractor was Deville, who supplied the metal frames and sashes for the windows.[5]

Another of the architect's problems that now impinges upon the story of the building was the existence of the Royal Fine Arts Commission. Appointed in November 1841 under the chairmanship of Prince Albert, and with C. L. Eastlake as secretary, to consider rather than superintend the decoration of the palace, this body (of which Barry was not a member) in 1844 conducted competitions to discover the best talent, exhibiting the entries in Westminster Hall and Crockford's Bazaar. Barry told the Commons' 1844 committee that no alteration had been made in the building at the suggestion of the Commission;

> but where any alteration has taken place with reference to the accomplishment of the objects they have in view, that alteration has originated with myself as a suggestion ... wherever I imagine it may be the wish of the Commissioners to decorate the walls of the building with painting, I am making such provision as will allow of a ground for such paintings of any kind that may be thought most favourable to the species of painting that may be adopted.[6]

Called upon, early in 1843, to report on the general character of decorations that he conceived best adapted to realise his intentions, Barry drew up a report, favourably received, from which Alfred Barry printed extracts.[7] Barry later submitted his designs for the decoration of the House of Lords, which were approved.[8] In June and July 1843 the Commissioners invited competitions for wood carving, stained

---

[1] Works 1/31, pp. 5–6, 45, 210; 1/32, pp. 11, 143; 1/35, pp. 133, 174; 1/36, pp. 86–7, 205; 11/6/5 *passim*. A new competition for tenders was won in June 1852 by John Jay (Works 11/6/6, f. 1).

[2] Works 11/7/11. Foord was 'in an extensive way of Business particularly in connection with Messrs Baker and Sons Builders' (*ibid.* f. 3). [3] Works 11/7/9.

[4] Works 1/30, pp. 144, 169; 11/7/6. Plain painting was to be at 10 per cent under the Office price; 'superior artists' to be paid 21s. a day and 'artists' 12s., compared with 5s. 5d. for 'painters' (*ibid.* f. 1).

[5] Works 1/28, pp. 163, 233, 251; 1/31, p. 362.

[6] *Parl. Pap.* 1844 (448) vi, qq. 86, 87; see also 88–94.   [7] *Life*, pp. 184–7.

[8] Works 11/9/4, f. 42, Barry to Milne, 23 June 1846, on which the rest of this and part of the next paragraph are based.

glass, arabesque painting, ornamental metal-work and ornamental pavements. The Commissioners selected certain of the entries, and sent the names to Barry with a view to their being employed; and in February 1845 asked Barry to report on the extent and probable cost of the Lords' decorations, and also as to the way in which the selected artists, especially the woodcarvers, might be employed. Barry replied that 'as the Wood Carvings must be of an Architectonic character, to be in harmony with the general design, I conceived that they should be executed under the direction and control of the Architect on the premises . . . at Thames Bank'. The Commissioners then referred the chosen craftsmen to him, but as master carvers they declined to work in a subordinate capacity at Thames Bank, and were consequently not employed.

Barry was next asked for a detailed design for stained glass windows for the Lords, in consequence of which Messrs. Ballantyne and Allan were commissioned to prepare cartoons. In June and July 1845 the Commissioners relinquished control over the artists to Barry, declaring that they were unable to recommend other descriptions of decoration than those within their special province and that as regards the Lords' decorations Barry should apply for sanction to the Woods. To avoid delay Barry therefore with Lord Lincoln's authority gave detailed instructions for the works to be carried out. But in June 1846 Eastlake complained to the Treasury that the Commission had found that

> The Architect has undertaken upon his own responsibility the whole of the decorative Work in reference to the several objects comprehended in the said Notices [of 1843 to artists], with the exception of Stained Glass, though even in this branch the Artist recommended by the Comm[issio]n has been instructed by the Architect to adopt his designs instead of following his own conceptions.[1]

Under the circumstances the Commission had abstained from any further interference with the works in question 'and think it their duty to state . . . that they do not hold themselves responsible for the taste or for the Expenditure of the decorations already adopted . . . and that unless otherwise required by Her Majesty's Government they do not propose to adopt any other course in reference to the decorations not yet commenced of the descriptions already referred to.' The Office of Woods suggested to the Treasury that in future the Fine Arts Commissioners should communicate with the architect only through the Treasury, which could decide whether their suggestions were to be carried out.[2] 'The Commission [in Alfred Barry's words] accordingly confined their attention to "works of art", and decided that (generally speaking) the painting and sculpture should be historical and that their subjects should be chosen from English history and literature'.[3] The artistic consequences of this decision need not be described here, as the Commission's place in the history of English painting and sculpture has been authoritatively studied by Mr. T. S. R. Boase.[4]

[1] Works 11/9/4, ff. 37–8, 6 June 1846.   [2] *Ibid.* ff. 44–5, 11 July 1846.   [3] *Life*, p. 188.
[4] T. S. R. Boase, 'The Decoration of the New Palace of Westminster, 1841–1863', *Jnl. of the Warburg and Courtauld Institutes*, xvii (1954), pp. 319–58. See also A. Barry, *Life*, pp. 188–92; T. S. R. Boase, *Oxford History of English Art 1800–1870* (1959) pp. 208–18; J. Steegman, *Consort of Taste 1830–70* (1950), ch. vi; W. Ames, *Prince Albert and Victorian Taste* (1967), ch. 4.

Despite such activity on the House of Lords, progress in general remained slow, and a large balance remained unexpended from the previous year in May, when £85,000 was voted for the works in 1845/6.[1] Much of the delay was caused by the smouldering disagreement between architect and 'ventilator' that burst into open flame in 1845. Relations were already tense in March;[2] but in April Barry threw a bombshell: 'it is only now upon being made acquainted for the first time with the method in which you propose to complete the unfinished arrangements hitherto made, that I consider it my duty . . . to object to them as interfering with the fire proof principle of the Building'.[3] After acerbated correspondence Barry declared that, as they were distinctly at variance over facts and inferences, 'a competent tribunal must shortly decide between us'.[4] For lack of information from Reid the finishings in the river front were at a stand, and 14 carpenters had been discharged.[5] The Board of Woods decided to refer first the dispute over fireproofing, and then the whole question of the ventilating to Joseph Gwilt, as an independent arbitrator.[6] Reid wanted a ventilation expert associated with Gwilt, and when this was refused nursed his grievance. Gwilt, indeed, scarcely proved sympathetic to his case, informing the Commissioners of Woods and Works on 28 September 1845 that Reid's scheme had disrupted the fireproofing; and that the delay in the work sprang from the 'impolicy . . . of having two separate directors of works independent of each other, on the same building'. Reid's

> total unacquaintance, as he himself admits, with all matters connected with design and construction, was of itself, even though he were assisted by competent persons, sufficient to cause delay and create confusion in the works. . . . For want of detailed drawings, such as are usually furnished by ventilators, an extraordinary number of flues has been introduced into the building, whereby it has been rendered less solid. . . . I am not aware of any mode for better carrying on the works, and preventing a recurrence of delay, than that of leaving the whole arrangement of the warming and ventilating works in the hands and entirely under the control of the architect, and empowering him to select a person conversant with the construction of the building, and of experience in that particular branch.[7]

---

[1] Works 1/28, p. 95.

[2] Reid's letter to Barry of 5 March 1845 is a good example of his tone:
'After the remarks you made to me this morning, and the complaining statement which you also thought proper to advance as to alterations in plans made by me for the Ventilation of the Committee Rooms, which are quite in unison with what has been hinted to me elsewhere, I can not allow this matter to pass without addressing this letter to you, and forwarding a copy of it to the Office of Woods.

I protest as I did this morning to yourself, against your telling me that I have altered my plans, or that any addition has ever been asked for, in the nine new apartments (Committee Rooms and Courts,) until I found out that *some* of the workmen had poured water from the foundations into some of the air flues, and until *other* workmen had rubbed the roof over in many places with Coal tar, instead of cementing defects with asphalte pitch. . . .

. . . I have difficulties enough to contend with in the popular prejudices I have to meet with in the application of my plans, and cannot afford also to be charged with alterations for which I am not responsible. I can only answer your statements, and hints, I receive elsewhere in unison with them, by saying, that I am prepared to substantiate what I have mentioned, and that if you dont think it advisable to have any inquiry before an impartial tribunal, you must at least consider that I shall not acquiesce in views and statements which I am prepared to refute' (Works 11/12, f. 113–14).

[3] Works 11/12, f. 130 (24 April 1845).   [4] *Ibid.* f. 136 (5 May 1845).   [5] *Ibid.*

[6] *Parl. Pap.* 1846 (719) xv, q. 77. Joseph Gwilt (1784–1863) was the author of *Encyclopaedia of Architecture, Historical, Theoretical and Practical* (1842) and other works, as well as a practising architect (see Colvin, *Dictionary*).

[7] *Parl. Pap.* 1846 (719) xv, p. 19.

The Board took some time to digest Gwilt's report with its 'very voluminous' evidence, but at last formed the opinion that Reid's plan should be carried out through the appointment of an intermediary between architect and ventilator.[1] The general delay in the whole of the works, and the practical suspension of those on the House of Lords resulting from this situation led to the early appointment of committees of each House in the session of 1846. Barry appeared before the Lords on 23 February, when he declared that 'under the circumstances in which I am placed, and the interference of Dr. Reid with my control and authority in this building' he could give no date for the completion of their House.[2] Reid's activities had 'most seriously obstructed' the works for some time past; 'indeed I might say throughout the whole progress of the work it has been a continued drag upon it', to a considerable extent from specific alterations in Reid's arrangements, 'but principally owing to indefinite instructions'. Reid was 'always very unwilling to commit himself to any thing definite upon paper'. For five months they had had no personal communication, Barry requiring Reid 'to put on paper everything that he required'. Reid had, for instance, proposed eight different ways of ventilating the House: consequently nothing had been done about the floor, and it was impossible to fix the wall framing or joinery. 'Matters are now in a perfect state of stagnation, as to proceeding with the finishings of any portion of the building'.[3] The theory of the system, he told the committee, was simple and well-known;[4] to effectuate it in the palace required in the person employed 'great mechanical skill, a thorough knowledge of the arts of construction, sound judgment and decision, and in fact the method and habits of a man of business; in all which attainments and qualities of mind Dr. Reid is, in my opinion, most certainly deficient'.

Reid's evidence only goes to confirm the impression that Barry's summary was accurate—though doubtless Barry's own faults of character contributed to the *impasse*. Reid alleged that minutes of conversations with Barry were fraudulent; that his 'specific and connected' scheme of 1841 had been 'altered indefinitely with the architecture, which has been altered to a great extent'; and that as for the floor of the House, 'I am not aware of any alterations, because there was no final adjustment.' He was a slippery witness giving replies often off the point.[5]

The committee, perhaps unable to decide between 'ventilator' and architect, called on the government to secure the opening of the House for the next session, displaying its irritation with all the parties involved, not omitting the Board of Woods.[6] But a second report, made after examining a rival ventilator, Gurney,[7] advised that the Woods should make further experiments before finally adopting

---

[1] *Ibid.* qq. 78, 93.   [2] *Ibid.* q. 1.   [3] *Ibid*, qq. 3–5, 11, 12, 15, 23.
[4] *Ibid.* q. 26. Barry told the committee:
'I believe I understand the theory of the system, which has nothing whatever that is new in it. It is perfectly simple and intelligible to the meanest understanding, and is adopted by all scientific persons engaged in the practice of warming and ventilating buildings. The only novelty, and a startling one it is, consists in the mode of applying it to such a vast and important pile of building as the new palace at Westminster. The novelty alluded to is in receiving the fresh air from either the one or the other extremity of the building, according, I believe, to the direction of the wind, causing it to pervade and pass through every portion of the interior, and to pass out of the building by one central discharge tower; also in conducting the smoke from all the ordinary fires throughout the building by smoke flues, either separately or conjointly with air flues, according to circumstances, and passing off the whole of the products of combustion through the central discharge tower . . .'
[5] *Ibid.* qq. 29–75.   [6] *Ibid.* p. 3.   [7] Goldsworthy Gurney (1793–1875), kt. 1863; see *D.N.B.*

any plan hitherto proposed.[1] By the end of a further interrogation of Barry on 23 June, the committee had become hostile to Reid, reporting that his scheme was 'the only impediment to the preparation of the new House of Lords, for the commencement of the session of 1847', and recommending that the architect's offer 'to undertake the warming and ventilation of the new House upon a plan of his own' should be accepted.[2] As a consequence the warming and ventilation of the House of Lords were placed officially in Barry's hands.[3] Reid promptly accused him of giving false evidence to the committee and to the Commissioners of Woods.[4] This secured Reid (as well as Barry) another hearing before the committee, in which he was more contentious than ever.[5] The effect was to confirm the committee in its views, and in a fourth report it approved Barry's plans for accommodating the peers in their new chamber at the opening of the 1847 session.[6]

Meanwhile the Commons had been conducting their own inquest: a committee was appointed on 16 February 1846, including such familiar figures as Sir R. H. Inglis, Hawes, Wyse, and a new star, Viscount Duncan. This met ten times before making its first report.[7] Barry, examined on 3 March, made much the same charges against Reid as he had earlier made to the Lords' committee. He said the most serious problem presented by Reid's apparatus was the amount of space required. Reid demanded the whole space of the roofs, which would 'afford good available space for other purposes', as well as the 'whole of the basement story of the entire building, with one or two trifling exceptions as regards the residences . . . and in addition he has a very large proportion of the space in the ground story'. The openings for ventilation left in the walls 'have from time to time been so much enlarged, and so many and long discussions have taken place upon their constant enlargement, as to have impeded the progress of the works most seriously'.[8]

The Commons' committee, with its tenderness for the ventilator, recommended in its first report (1 April) that differences of any sort between Reid and Barry should be referred to a third party, consisting of one person nominated by Barry and one by Reid, subject to governmental approval; if they could not agree, an umpire should be appointed by the Chief Commissioner of Woods. The decision made by this third party should be carried into effect by Barry.[9] A second report (29 May)[10] merely recommended that Gurney's plan of ventilating might be put before a committee of three experts appointed by the Chief Commissioner, for Lord Lincoln, in the hope of resolving the matters in dispute, had nominated Messrs. Hardwick, Stephenson and Graham as a third party: but Reid thought they treated him as unfairly as Gwilt had done.[11] The Commons' committee met on a further nine occasions, and concluded its labours with a third report (5 August)[12] recalling the recommendation of its first report, and adding—for the benefit of the Lords—

---

[1] *Parl. Pap.* 1846 (719) xv, p. 23.   [2] *Ibid.* p. 37.   [3] Works 2/5, pp. 237, 269.
[4] Works 11/12, f. 199 (13 August 1846).
[5] *Parl. Pap.* 1846 (719) xv, 4th Report, qq. 21–51. Told that the effect of his evidence had been to 'induce the Committee to think you had no very decided plans', Reid replied: 'I most distinctly assert that that cannot be the case. It has been Mr. Barry's attempt to induce that belief; but my plans were distinct and definite, and the quantities in my drawings in 1841; and were I assisted, instead of being opposed and thwarted and deceived as I have been, I believe there is no man who will not say they are as definite as any one in my position could wish to give' (q. 32).   [6] *Ibid.* p. 41.
[7] *Parl. Pap.* 1846 (177), xv.   [8] *Ibid.* (574), qq. 128–31, 162.   [9] *Ibid. loc. cit.*   [10] *Ibid.* (349).
[11] *Ibid.* (719), Lords' 4th Report, q. 50. For the referees, see above, p. 227.   [12] *Ibid.* (574).

that though the problem of ventilation was best left to the 'eminent scientific persons' called in to advise the Board of Woods, Reid's work in the Commons had effected a 'great improvement'.

Barry was not anxious to expose himself to 'the cavils of Dr. Reid', and accordingly declined to state officially how he now intended to proceed, though offering to give the Commissioners any private explanation they might desire.[1] His estimate for warming and ventilating the House of Lords, Victoria Hall, public lobby and private corridor was nearly £6200.[2] The new Whig Chief Commissioner, Lord Morpeth, tested the ground, but decided that to prolong the former diarchy would be to prolong chaos; he therefore entrusted the ventilation of the House of Lords to Barry, advising that 'upon a subject so much controverted and so imperfectly ascertained in all its bearings' an expert should occasionally inspect Barry's plans. He proposed this course without reference either to the merits of the Reid–Barry controversy or to Reid's ability, simply as a means to the completion of the building, and as such it was approved by Lord John Russell.[3] Barry immediately excluded Reid and his assistants from the works, thereby occasioning long and clamant protests.[4] His plans were submitted to Faraday and approved as far as the theory went.[5]

Unfortunately the government then began the whole sorry cycle again: on 28 November 1846 Morpeth invited Reid to prepare plans for ventilating the Commons' part of the palace.[6] Reid's success in the temporary House of Commons had won him much support in that quarter[7] and he was also able to make play with the terms of his appointment of 1840.[8] He of course complained of obstruction, demanded independent architectural assistance, and sought to evade giving precise particulars.[9] At length, on 31 July 1847 Barry reported that he had obtained the necessary information from Reid to enable him to pronounce the plan practicable, but that the cost, exclusive of apparatus, would be very considerable.[10] He subsequently made out an estimate of over £11,000 for constructional works and over £9000 for apparatus—figures that Reid promptly disputed—compared with some £6500 total cost for his own system of ventilating the Commons.[11] Finally, on 2 December, the Woods submitted three estimates to the Treasury for the warming and ventilating of the Commons' wing: Reid's own (£14,368); Barry's calculation of

---

[1] Works 11/12, f. 308 (31 August 1846).   [2] *Ibid.* f. 309.   [3] Works 1/30, pp. 71–2; 2/5, pp. 288–90.

[4] Works 11/12, ff. 227 (Reid to Board of Woods, 30 September 1846 with copy of Barry's letter of the same date—'. . . I [Barry] have to request that the visits of yourself and your assistants to the works, may for the future be discontinued. I have given orders to close the doorway by which you have lately been in the habit of obtaining access to them.'), 236 (Reid to Lord Morpeth, 15 October 1846), 237 (Reid to Milne, 15 October 1846—'the attempt made by the Architect to confuse and disguise the real questions at issue').

[5] *Ibid.* ff. 244 (18 November), 247 (30 November 1846).

[6] *Ibid.* f. 246.   [7] *Parl. Pap.* 1846 (177) xv, para. 54.   [8] Works 11/12, f. 236.

[9] *Ibid.* ff. 249–50 (8 December), 252 (14 December.—'the most audacious effrontery has been practised by the Architect in representations addressed to the Commissioners'), 253 (17 December), 254 (23 December 1846), 260 (6 February—respecting which Barry replied 'The personalities and insinuations which pervade this letter are unwarranted and in bad taste but are beneath Mr. Barry's farther notice.' f. 262), 265 (22 February), 267 (25 February 1847), 273 (5 April—'the unmitigated oppression to which I am subjected by present proceedings'), etc.

[10] Works 11/12, f. 313.

[11] *Ibid.* f. 317 (30 August 1847), 327 (25 September). Reid insisted that some £3300 should be deducted from Barry's calculations; controversy particularly centred on a figure of £1537 11s. 6d.—according to Inman Reid could not grasp that this sum, variously placed under 'structure' (Barry) and 'apparatus' (Reid) might be deducted from one or the other, but still formed part of the total (ff. 325, 336, 338, 341, 342, September–November 1847).

Reid's plan (£17,491); and Barry's own (£6472). For the ventilation and warming of the entire building, Barry's estimate was nearly £39,000, Reid's £62,000.[1] The Board commented that it had had no success in inducing the two men to co-operate, and 'we apprehend that their differences are of such a nature as to preclude our indulging in the hope of their mutually combining their Labours for the Public Service'.[2]

In view of Reid's backing in the House of Commons, the Treasury Board quickly decided in his favour despite the greater expenditure involved.[3] Barry had lost his great support, Lord Lincoln, in the change of administration, but the decision is difficult to explain except against the background of Commons' support for Reid and the weakness of the ministry even after the general election of 1847. The Treasury's decision produced much further correspondence between Reid and Barry (conducted through the Board of Woods) which became violently heated over the use of the central tower, calling forth an official rebuke to Reid.[4] The sympathies of the Board indeed seem to have inclined towards the architect. Wearying of their role as transmitter, the Board told Barry: 'as the continuous misapprehension as to the mode of proceeding is such an entire obstruction to the progress of the Works the Board consider that if you afford Dr. Reid the information he asks as regards the Central Tower, it may be the means of enabling him to reply to your general requirements'.[5] But to Reid they said:

> as this continuous vacillating mode of proceeding is extremely inconvenient to this Department as well as detrimental to the Public Service inasmuch as the Works in preparing the Structural arrangements are much impeded; I have to convey to you the Board's urgent desire that you will forthwith submit a perspicuous Statement written as Questions in half margin (so as Mr. Barry may attach his Answers in juxtaposition) explaining fully every point on which you require information, and which in your opinion it rests with the Architect to afford.[6]

Finally Reid alleged that Barry, 'mistaking the whole spirit and scope' of his design, had 'actually blocked up by Brick work the principal Channels of Supply of fresh Air from the Clock Tower to the New House of Commons' and so rendered his plans 'utterly impracticable'.[7]

With the problem of ventilation became entangled that of drainage, and Barry was again in the thick of controversy. The sewer constructed for the New Houses in 1838–9 by J. and J. Bennett, contractors to the Westminster Court of Sewers, had been of the normal character for its day, large and brick-built. By 1848 the development of sanitary engineering had produced a glazed earthenware pipe that could be efficiently flushed. Henry Austin, consulting engineer to the Metropolitan Sewers Commission, criticised the earlier work at Westminster and advocated a nine-inch pipe. Barry crustily rebutted the criticism, throwing blame on Reid. The controversy

---

[1] Works 2/6, f. 246.   [2] *Ibid.*
[3] *Ibid.* pp. 246, 264 (8 December 1847); Works 1/32, pp. 58–9 (9 December 1847).
[4] Milne told Reid that as it was 'extremely objectionable that the Official correspondence with Them should be made the medium of indulging in personal invectives, I have to suggest to you the omission, in your future Official letters to This Board of matters wholly personal between yourself and Mr. Barry' (Works 1/32, p. 176; see also pp. 62, 92, 104, 116, 121, 132, 146, 156, 169 and 175).
[5] *Ibid.* p. 186, 6 March 1848.   [6] *Ibid.* p. 190, 11 March 1848.   [7] *Ibid.* p. 213, 30 March 1848.

broke into print and came before Parliament. In 1850 the main sewer was altered to direct the entire drainage to a single outfall on the north side of the abutment of Westminster Bridge.[1]

Of the controversy over the great clock, little need be said here: it is principally a story of the 1850s, though it began in March 1844 when Barry, wanting the specifications so that the walls of the tower might be 'carried up in accordance with the necessary arrangements for the weights and machinery', applied to Vulliamy, leading clockmaker of the day, for a specification and working drawings. In November 1845 E. J. Dent, a maker of marine chronometers of great accuracy, sought to compete for 'the large clock, and such others as may be required for the new Houses of Parliament', submitting testimonials, including one from G. B. Airy, the Astronomer Royal. Dent was informed that when the drawings and specifications were ready, he would be admitted a competitor. Then in June 1846 Lord Canning, the First Commissioner, wrote to Airy for his advice, without consulting Barry, who wished to obtain tenders on a common specification. Airy specified certain desiderata, and recommended that Dent should be employed. This enraged Vulliamy, who refused to enter any competition. Barry, who agreed that he had not been fairly treated, was meanwhile employing him to make the small clocks required. In July 1847 Dent complained that unless he could tender for those also, he would not compete for the great clock, and won his point. Airy declared Vulliamy's specification merely 'a village clock of very superior character'; and in his advocacy of Dent was joined by E. B. Denison, an amateur clockmaker of great knowledge and ability. When Lord Seymour raised the matter anew in 1851, Airy asked that Denison should be associated with him, and they prepared a design which Dent was employed to execute. It was then that the controversy rose to its height.[2]

The House of Lords, 'a hall worthy of this advanced age and this opulent empire', was completed for the Peers' occupation in April 1847 (Pl. 64), although only one of the murals and one of the stained glass windows were then in place.[3] But the House of Commons was at a standstill, partly because of the dispute between Reid and Barry, partly for financial reasons. In the hope of getting it finished, the government, yielding to strong pressure in the Commons, agreed to appoint a royal commission. A Treasury minute of 17 March 1848, implemented by royal warrant dated 7 April, appointed Lord de Grey, Sir John Fox Burgoyne, and Thomas Greene, M.P., as such special commissioners, to superintend the completion of the New Palace, determine upon designs for decorations, fittings and furnishings, and settle all relevant problems, subject to the financial control of the Treasury.[4] The Office

---

[1] Works 11/8/11; 1/33, pp. 31, 169; *Parl. Pap.* 1850 (482) xxxiii.

[2] Works 1/27, p. 4; 1/28, pp. 428–9, 459; 1/30, pp. 8–9, 19, 38–42, 52–4, 112, 137, 185, 223, 266, 306, 339–40, 413, 418–9, 422, 432, 438; 1/31, pp. 18–19, 87, 183, 254–5, 263–4, 335, 352, 392; 1/33, pp. 8, 448; 1/34, p. 9; 1/37, p. 71; 11/8/7; 11/134 (original correspondence); *Parl. Pap.* 1852 (415, 500, 500–1) xlii (in which is printed all correspondence to that time). For the personalities see *D.N.B.* and for more detailed accounts of the entire controversy see A. Barry, *Life*, and P. Ferriday, *Lord Grimthorpe* (1957).

[3] For a description of the new House see *Builder* v (1847), pp. 177, 189, 303.

[4] Works 11/12, ff. 332, 339–41. For de Grey, see p. 229. Fox Burgoyne (1782–1871) had been chairman of the Irish Public Works Board, 1831–45; and Inspector-General of fortifications since 1845 (see *D.N.B.*). Greene was chairman of committees, and had sat on several select committees concerned with public works and the new Houses, see p. 233. In February 1851 John Wilson Patten, M.P. was appointed an additional commissioner during the absence of Greene (Works 11/9/5, f. 27).

of Woods and Works, however, continued to pay accounts when certified by the commissioners. This system, interposing another link in the chain of communication, hardly speeded business.[1]

Whereas in the earlier stages of the work Barry had found himself unable to use the whole of his annual votes of money, by 1848 shortage of funds was proving an impediment. The estimates of 1848/9 having been reduced to permit an increased expenditure on defence, a particular difficulty arose in June 1848, when Barry proposed a smoking room and offices for the Commons on the ground floor, in a part formerly intended for fireproof record repositories, at an extra cost of nearly £5000. In recommending this change, the special commissioners remarked to the Treasury that 'the delay which has taken place in the progress of the Building has already caused serious embarrassment to the contractors'; and the Board of Woods sought a supplementary grant. This was refused. Barry replied that for the occupation of the Commons' chamber in 1850 it was essential the proposed alterations should be carried out immediately; 'but . . . in consequence of the proposed Vote for the present Year being so much below the amount of my Estimate, the cost of such alterations can not be defrayed out of the amount of the vote, without occasioning a Stoppage of other Works equally important to the fulfilment of the expectations which have been held out, as to an early occupation of the Building'. The Treasury retorted that it would be for the special commissioners to decide what works should be done, but that the vote for the year must not be exceeded.[2] Despite all the pressures for completion of the building the Treasury insisted that progress should be regulated by the sums it chose to make available: the result was that the number of men employed had to be reduced.[3] Further delays resulted from a dispute between the architect and the government about the payment of measurers, a question related to the whole issue of Barry's remuneration, originally fixed at £25,000 on an undisclosed principle that officialdom refused to abandon explicitly. In presenting Barry with the gold medal of the Institute of British Architects in May 1850, Lord de Grey declared: 'the means have been withheld, and difficulties have been unnecessarily created'.[4]

One of the questions left for the decision of the special commissioners was that of the mode of lighting the Commons. The Treasury on the recommendation of the Office of Woods had placed this under Reid, with an addition of £250 to his salary. The lighting of the new House of Lords had been carried out under Barry's directions, together with all the other works in that part, and the special commissioners determined to entrust him with that of the new House of Commons. This led the Commissioners of Woods to query the amount of Reid's salary, and the Treasury replied in January 1849 that a 'conclusive arrangement' should be made with Reid as to his future duties and salary. By November 1849 Reid was complaining of his 'extreme pecuniary difficulties, arising out of the state of my case at the Houses of Parliament; and the suspension for the last ten years of the principal part of my profession'.[5]

Reid was however able to go ahead with his principal project at Westminster, and

[1] Works 1/32, pp. 319, 338, 402, 406; A. Barry, *Life*, p. 164.
[2] Works 1/33, pp. 81, 292, 331, 350; 2/7, pp. 46–9, 196, 240–3. For other financial problems, see Works 2/6, pp. 381–3, 398, 409, 415.   [3] Works 1/32, p. 167; 11/11/3, ff. 55–7.
[4] *Builder*, viii (1850), p. 253. For the remuneration controversy, see above, p. 237.
[5] Works 2/7, pp. 449–50.

had matured his plans ready to go to tender by the end of 1849. In January 1850 it was settled that Messrs. Turner should make the ventilating and warming apparatus, and Nasmyth Gaskell and Company the requisite steam engine and boilers; to speed the work Collinge and Company were allowed to carry out a small part of the ventilating apparatus.[1] Meanwhile Messrs. Jeakes had been at work on the apparatus for the House of Lords, under the directions of Barry, whose estimate of nearly £35,000 for warming and ventilating the palace (excepting the House of Commons) was approved in April 1850. Barry proposed in November that a permanent establishment should be settled for operating this, but Lord Seymour, the new Chief Commissioner, deferred any such arrangement until both Houses had been fully completed and occupied.[2]

Towards the close of the 1848 session the Commons had called for an estimate of the cost of completing the New Palace. This was at length submitted to the Treasury by the special commissioners on 27 February 1849. Barry's estimate was £1,025,000. This enormous sum caused the Treasury to ask the special commissioners how far the original estimate could be 'considered as having been a sufficient estimate of the Expence of the Buildings contemplated, what grounds there are for the excess which has taken place, and to what extent such Excess has been sanctioned by competent Authority'. A more detailed report was then prepared, and laid before Parliament in May.[3]

At the time of the appointment of the special commissioners, the carcass of the central part of the palace had been completed, St. Stephen's Hall nearly roofed in, the porch raised to a height of 65 feet, and the three towers to 100 feet. The southwest block between the Victoria Tower and St. Stephen's Hall, and the Members' Entrance, closing Star Chamber Court from New Palace Yard, had not been begun, the sites being occupied by old or temporary buildings. Inside, the wooden ceilings along the royal approach were generally complete. Some of the stained glass had been fixed in the windows of the House of Lords; and in the Commons, the wooden ceiling was partly fixed, and the iron floor ordered. The rooms in the river front generally were complete, except for painting and decorating.[4] A year later, the towers were 121 feet high, the carving of the roof of St. Stephen's Hall nearly finished, the roof over the porch completed and the gables and turrets far advanced. The groining of the three great corridors from the Central Hall was completed, and all external windows glazed. The foundation for the Members' Entrance had been formed, and 481 men were working at the palace.[5] Shortly after, Barry applied for authority to begin works at the south end of Westminster Hall to form the public approach to the Central Hall.[6] In May 1850 the Commons' chamber (Pl. 65A) was temporarily fitted up for experimental sittings. Some changes had been made earlier: a gallery for 120 M.P.s behind the Speaker's chair had been objected to and accordingly removed. Other changes were now demanded and as a result a select committee was appointed in June.[7] The high roof was blamed for the poor acoustic qualities of the chamber, though experts told the committee that it

[1] Works 1/35, pp. 54, 87–8; 11/7/15.   [2] Works 1/35, pp. 89–91, 126; 1/36, p. 23.
[3] Works 2/7, pp. 279–80; *Parl. Deb.* 3rd. ser. civ, 156–7; cv, 494–5.
[4] Works 11/9/7, f. 33 (7 April 1848).   [5] *Ibid.* f. 35 (31 March 1849).   [6] Works 1/35, p. 101.
[7] *Ibid.* pp. 140, 202; *Parl. Deb.* 3rd. ser. cxi, 328–57, 456–60, 981–1008.

was impossible to build a room in which one could predict that the hearing would be equally good in all parts. The committee therefore experimented with a boarded roof. The division lobbies were said to be too small, and seating for members inadequate. Sir Benjamin Hall, long a critic of Barry, put forward a plan of his own. Barry suggested lengthening the House instead, but the committee preferred the squarer form of 1836 to the traditional shape of St. Stephen's Chapel, and Barry revised Hall's proposals. The galleries were to be widened, permitting a second row of benches on each side; an oriel was to be added to each of the division lobbies. These and other minor improvements were estimated at £8600. A new ceiling, costing £6200, was installed with sloping sides terminating level with the transom of the windows, of which only the lower half remained visible (Pl. 62)—though Hume declared that 'any schoolboy would be flogged for designing such a place'.[1] These works had largely been effected by the end of March 1851, when the carcass of the Members' Entrance and the restored cloisters and offices above were so far completed as to be ready for their roofs. The warming and ventilation system of the river front was in operation, and the smoke arrangements for the whole building had been completed. A force of 742 men was at work; and the towers rose to nearly 150 feet.[2]

The erection of towers of such height involved constructional problems to which answers of some ingenuity were devised by Barry and his assistants. The scaffolding for the Clock Tower was entirely internal, carrying a steam engine used to operate a hoist. This arrangement enabled a setter to work faster than did the ordinary framed scaffold and traveller: here 40 men were required below to keep one setter supplied instead of the usual 25. The Victoria Tower, of larger dimensions and having a groined roof to its lowest storey, required a different arrangement: a strong trussed frame constructed to carry machinery and stiff enough to be raised in one piece by screw power was placed over the whole area of the tower. A circular iron rail was then laid on the frame, on which ran one hoisting and two setting travellers. The central tower was at first built internally, materials for the cone being raised through a central orifice in the groining; but the needs of Parliament obliged Barry to clear the central hall and construct an external hoist in the Peers' Inner Court to take materials to the platform level of the upper rim of the cone where they were deposited on trucks running on a tramway over the roofs to the centre of the platform over the cone. Above this, the lantern was built by a system of framed scaffolding with platforms at various levels, the stone being raised in the centre. Barry's son claimed that these details were to prove that 'architects are equal, when called upon, to devise and carry out works of construction requiring *originality and daring* as successfully as . . . engineers'.[3] Daring indeed was exhibited in the internal construction of the Victoria Tower: eight iron columns, of between 8 and 14 inches diameter, supported eight floors

[1] *Parl. Pap.* 1850 (650, 650–II) xv (with plan); *Parl. Deb.* 3rd. ser. cxiii, 726–39; *Builder* viii (1850), pp. 370, 392; Works 1/35, p. 394.
[2] Works 11/9/7, f. 36 (21 March 1851); *Builder* viii (1850), p. 442; ix (1851), pp. 255, 433, 460.
[3] C. Barry junior, 'Some description of the mechanical scaffolding used at the New Palace at Westminster, particularly in reference to the three main towers of the Building', *R.I.B.A. Transactions*, 1856–7, pp. 156–64. Barry junior acknowledged that Meeson and Quarm had been materially concerned in devising and executing the scaffolding. The steam-powered hoist for the Victoria Tower was presumably that referred to by Grissell in 1844 (see p. 606, n. 9 and references there cited). Drawings for the hoists are Works 29/699, 700 (Victoria Tower); House of Lords, Moulton–Barrett album, p. 176 (Clock Tower); and Work s29/1621–2 (Central Tower).

of Hopton-Wood stone, as well as top-hamper weighing 726 tons. These columns rested on four massive iron girders, 4 ft. 6 ins. deep and 2 ft. broad, held in iron templates over the apex of the great arches of the sovereign's entrance, which were enclosed by walls 6 ft. thick. At the level of the first arcade the floor was supported by girders considerably stronger than those for the other floors; fixed into the piers of the wall and resting on the columns, these were intended to assist the lowest girders in supporting the weight. Access to each floor was obtained from a large spiral stair of iron in the centre of the tower. When this whole structure was examined in 1952, several parts were found to be over-stressed and a major rescue operation had to be carried out.[1]

In June 1851 Barry proposed putting in hand the last major part of the new palace, with the demolition at the end of the session of the temporary House of Commons and its adjuncts, and the whole of the Parliament Office with its repositories and officers' rooms.[2] Thus disappeared the last elements of Soane's royal approach, as well as the ancient Court of Requests which during the nineteenth century had successively housed both Lords and Commons. Demolition began early in September.[3] The special commissioners insisted that a new contract must be made for the new buildings.[4] That settled, they wrote to the Prime Minister, 20 November 1851,[5]

> The general arrangements for the New Houses of Parliament, to facilitate which, the Commission of which we are members, was chiefly appointed, being now decided upon, in all essential matters; we beg leave to submit to your Lordship that the time seems to have arrived when the Commission may be dissolved, and the entire management and charge of the great and intricate undertaking revert to the Department of the Board of Works.
>
> In offering this suggestion we beg leave to assure your Lordship that we are not influenced by a sense of dissatisfaction at the conduct or proceedings of any party, or individual, towards us, nor by a reluctance to continue in any such employment, if really useful to the Public Service; but solely by a strong impression that it is desirable to put an end, as early as convenient, to an organisation that leads in some degree to a mixture of duties and responsibilities by two independent bodies in the management of one concern.

In this view the Treasury acquiesced, and the commission was relieved of its duties by a royal warrant of 19 December 1851.[6]

The subsequent history of what de Grey called 'the most difficult and most magnificent work ever attempted,'[7] falls outside the purview of this volume. It is a story as complex as that which has been related above, and can only be sketched in outline here. The Royal Approach was used for the first time when Queen Victoria opened Parliament in February 1852, and a few days later she knighted the

[1] E. N. Holmes, *Illustrations of the New Palace of Westminster, 2nd series*, (1865); R. W. Frost, 'Reconstruction of Floors in Victoria Tower', *Structural Engineer*, 1961, pp. 107–110; House of Lords Record Office file 381–58 (memorandum by J. W. Worricker, architect of the reconstruction, November 1961). I am indebted to Mr. M. F. Bond for pointing out and supplying copies of the last two mentioned. For an historical assessment of the framing, see H.-R. Hitchcock, *Early Victorian Architecture*, i, p. 292.

[2] Works 11/10/2, f. 76 (26 June 1851).   [3] *Ibid.* f. 81.   [4] *Ibid.* f. 80 (28 August 1851).
[5] Works 11/9/5, f. 31.   [6] *Ibid.* ff. 32, 35.   [7] *Builder*, viii (1850), p. 253.

architect. His great coadjutor, Augustus Welby Pugin, died later that same year. But although both Chambers were now in full use, much remained to be done. The upper parts of the towers, the Speaker's and Serjeant at Arms' residences, the Lords' offices looking over Old Palace Yard, had still to be completed (Pl. 65B). Progress was not accelerated by a change of contractor in 1852.[1] Controversy did not diminish. The battle over the great clock reached its climax.[2] The dispute over Barry's remuneration wore on.[3] The problems of ventilation caused more head-aches: Reid was dismissed in 1852 and obtained (as the Works officials had so long feared) damages for the government's breach of agreement. Meeson was entrusted with his apparatus, but in 1854 Gurney took over and drastically simplified the whole system.[4] Expenditure continued to climb beyond the estimates.[5] When Barry died on 12 May 1860, leaving the New Palace substantially complete, the total outlay amounted to some £2,400,000.[6] In the course of the following decade many finishing touches were contributed by his son, Edward Middleton Barry, including approaches, railings, internal decoration and the 'restoration' of St. Stephen's Crypt as a chapel. The dismissal of E. M. Barry by First Commissioner Ayrton in 1870 and the transfer of the fabric to the care of the Office of Works may be taken as marking the formal completion of a building that succeeding generations have continued to alter and adorn.

[1] Grissell's contract was terminated as too expensive, and a new competition was won by John Jay (Works 11/6/6).
[2] See p. 621 above.   [3] Works 11/1/2; see p. 239 above.
[4] *Parl. Pap.* 1852 (237) (252) (371) xlii; 1852–3 (570) xxxiv; 1854 (149) (270) (384) (403) ix; 1866, lvi, p. 747. Gurney's methods were later improved by Dr. Percy, F.R.S.
[5] Works 11/9/6. f. 76, 24 September 1860.
[6] Total expenditure for building, furnishing, lighting and ventilating the New Palace from the commencement to 31 December 1859 was £2,198,099 2s. 11d. That excluded the following, accounts for which were made up to 31 March 1860:

Frescoes	19,828	10s.	6d.
Statuary	22,010	5s.	0d.
Maintenance and repairs	65,210	9s.	4d.
Current expenses of lighting and ventilating since those services placed under the Office of Works.	87,068	2s.	1d.
Grand Total	£2,392,216	9s.	10d

(*Parl. Pap.* 1860 (32) (223) xl.)

IV. PRISONS

1. The King's Bench, Marshalsea and Fleet Prisons

THE maintenance of the King's Bench, Marshalsea and Fleet prisons was not normally the responsibility of the Office of Works. In fact at this period the Office of Works was never responsible for major penal building works: the Millbank Penitentiary, for example, was not built under the Office's direction. From time to time, however, the officers of the Works were called in to supervise structural work at the King's Bench, Marshalsea and Fleet Prisons. On such occasions expenditure was nearly always covered by specific parliamentary grants, independent of the Civil List allocation.[1] The King's Bench, or the Prison of the Marshalsea of the Court of King's Bench, to give it its full title, was populated by debtors and those guilty of contempt of the Court of King's Bench. The Marshalsea, officially the Prison of the Marshalsea of his Majesty's Household, was for debtors and those guilty of contempt of the Court of the Marshalsea, the Court of the King's Palace at Westminster and the High Court of Admiralty, as well as for Admiralty prisoners sentenced by courts-martial. The Fleet was reserved for debtors and bankrupts and those guilty of contempt of the Courts of Chancery, Exchequer and Common Pleas. All three were of course primarily debtors' gaols. Charles Dickens immortalised the Fleet in *Pickwick Papers* (1836–7), the Marshalsea in *Little Dorrit* (1855–7) and the King's Bench in *Nicholas Nickleby* (1838–9), *David Copperfield* (1849–50) and *The Uncommercial Traveller* (1860).[2] During the early nineteenth century the legal position of debtors was gradually ameliorated by humanitarian legislation. And so the three prisons, notoriously run for private profit rather than public advantage, gradually went out of business. Their scale of building during this period of decline was therefore appropriately limited.

The Gordon Riots of 1780 had involved the Office of Works in a considerable amount of rebuilding at the King's Bench and Fleet,[3] as well as extensive surveys at Newgate, the New Gate House in Tothill Fields, the New Bridewell in St. George's Fields, and the Borough Clink, Watch House and House of Correction. The whole process of examination, repair and compensation was only completed in 1785, with Cockerell, Couse, Chambers, Craig, Taylor, James Adam and Thomas Sandby variously acting as surveyors and examiners, plus George Dance as external assessor.[4] Afterwards few repairs to the three debtors' prisons were required. But between 1790 and 1796 both the King's Bench and the Fleet underwent a series of structural alterations designed as security precautions. In 1790 the Warden of the Fleet, John

---

[1] For examples cf. 'Public Income and Expenditure, 1688–1869', *Parl. Pap.* 1868–9, xxxv, pp. 181 *et seq.*
[2] P. A. W. Collins, *Dickens and Crime* (1962), *passim.*   [3] See vol v.
[4] Works 6/108, ff. 2–3, 10–14, 18, 26, 29; Works 6/19, ff. 299, 301, 303, 305–6, 313, 324, 328, 358, 360; Works 6/20, ff. 11–14, 34–5, 318–20; T. 29/54, ff. 142, 257, 501; T. 29/55, ff. 208, 325–6; T. 29/56, ff. 536–7; Works 4/17, 29 July 1785.

Eyles, protested to the Treasury about 'divers houses and sheds' which overlooked the crumbling prison wall, a standing incentive to 'prisoners conspiring to facilitate an escape'.[1] Repairs on this occasion cost £504 17s. 5½d., more than twice the Office of Works estimate. Part of the trouble lay in the behaviour of the prisoners, who made a habit of stealing the building materials and who treated the labourers 'so roughly that one of them lay long ill, and was in great danger of losing his life'.[2] During 1792, while the wall was actually being strengthened, one celebrated prisoner, the Count de Verteillac, made his escape. Eyles was judged liable for Verteillac's debts, to the tune of £2500.[3] As a result he petitioned once more for the reconstruction of the boundary wall. And this time the cost was £7117 2s. 1½d. A solid wall was deemed more secure than additional railings, besides offering facilities for fives, 'the constant amusement of the prisoners'.[4] The Marshal of the King's Bench, William Jones, responded by demanding similar protection for his own prison: he felt himself 'in great apprehension of being ruined in his fortune owing to the insufficiency of the wall'.[5] The boundary wall was raised and the Marshal's rooms were extended, with an outside wall 'to keep off the mob in case of riots', all at a cost of £5672 3s. 3½d.[6] Scarcely had these alterations been completed when a fire in the summer of 1799 necessitated still further work, valued at £5171.[7]

Neither these works nor those of 1803–6, 1810–13 and 1814–15 made any significant alteration to the architectural or environmental character of the King's Bench and Fleet.[8] Both were still 'but the shew and name of prisons'.[9] At the Fleet, the Liberties, the racket court and the buildings of the Master's Side and Common Side (known as Bartholomew Fair), remained basically unchanged. So did the 'scenes of riot, drunkenness and disorder'. As late as 1814 the Fleet could still be described as 'the largest brothel in the Metropolis'.[10] The structural repairs and enlargements devised by Smirke and executed by Crocker in 1818 were no more than temporary expedients.[11] And Peel's scheme of 1827 to rebuild the prison in St. George's Fields, according to Smirke's designs, came to nothing.[12] It was not until 1842 that the prison was abolished. The last fragments survived until 1864.[13] The King's Bench prison

---

[1] Works 6/21, f. 168, 25 March 1790.

[2] Works 6/22, f. 34, 13 January 1792; T. 29/62, f. 29, 15 May 1790; T. 29/64, ff. 186–7, 3 February 1792; Works 5/80 (1791).

[3] *Gent's. Mag.* 1792 pt. i, p. 273. According to Loughborough, 'nothing but irresistible force (such as the riots in 1780) could be pleaded in excuse for a gaoler, who is bound to keep his prisoners in safe custody'.

[4] Works 6/22, f. 54, 27 July and f. 78, 18 December 1792; T. 29/64, ff. 472, 482; T. 29/65, ff. 114, 123, 145, 181, 217, 436, 552; T. 29/66, ff. 210, 215; Works 4/18, ff. 12, 20, 42, 166.

[5] Works 6/22, f. 180, 16 December 1794.

[6] Works 4/18, ff. 127, 132, 152, 181, 253; T. 29/69, f. 34, 28 July 1796.   [7] Works 4/18, ff. 352, 356.

[8] Works 6/23, f. 112, 3 February 1800; Works 7/19 (1802–6); Works 4/20, 23 June, 14 July 1809; Works 4/21, 26 March, 1 May, 17 September 1813, 7 January, 30 August 1814; Works 6/27, f. 101, 21 October 1813; Works 4/19, 19 June 1802, 10 June 1803, 24 February 1804, 13 and 27 June 1806; Works 6/24 f. 44, 13 June 1806; Works 4/20, 31 August 1810, 1 November 1811; Works 4/21, 9 July 1813, 2 September 1814; Works 6/25, f. 87, 7 September 1810 and f. 169, 30 August 1811; T. 29/122, f. 442, 2 April 1813.

[9] Macky, *A Journey through England* ii (1724), p. 3.

[10] 'Report from Committee on King's Bench, Fleet and Marshalsea', *Parl. Pap.* 1814–15, IV, p. 551. See also 'Report from Select Committee on Acts respecting Insolvent Debtors', *Parl. Pap.* 1819, II, pp. 321 *et seq.* For further investigations, cf. *Parl. Deb.* xxx (1815), col. 1160. For complaints about the kitchen cf. Works 6/131/1, ff. 11–12, 15 (1816).   [11] Works 6/131/1, ff. 21, 23, 26–7, 31, 47–52 (ground plans).

[12] Works 1/15, f. 136; Works 1/16, ff. 430–31; Works 1/17, f. 540; Works 6/131, ff. 32, 36.

[13] W. Thornbury, *Old and New London* ii (1873), p. 408 (view of demolition). For details of the building cf. J. Howard, *The State of the Prisons in England and Wales* (1792 ed.), pp. 217–22; C. Knight, *London* iv (1841), p. 33 (view of yard); H. P. Wheatley and P. Cunningham, *London Past and Present* ii (1891), pp. 56–8.

in St. George's Fields remained similarly unaltered. Disputes over the legal position of insolvent debtors produced riots and investigations during the 1780s and 1790s.[1] But the rows of small rooms for five hundred prisoners, the high wall, the fives courts, taverns, coffee houses and shops survived even after 1842 when the prison absorbed both its dwindling competitors, the Marshalsea and the Fleet under a new title, the Queen's Prison. During the 1820s it was known as 'the most desirable . . . place of incarceration for debtors in England'.[2] Under the direction of Marshal Jones, 'a fat, jolly man' whose periodic inspections were 'a mere farce', the establishment long maintained its eighteenth-century reputation for 'vice and debauchery'.[3] In 1823 a pamphlet was produced which set out to attract still greater numbers of insolvent debtors by describing the delights of prison life: 'each man's room is his castle . . . a happy and welcome asylum where persecution ends. . . . In the kitchen . . . the most perfect aldermanic appetite may find food for digestion, and . . . the beer . . . is considered particularly good'.[4] Not until 1862 did the King's Bench building cease to be a debtors' prison, and not until 1880 was it demolished.[5]

Meanwhile the Marshalsea had been first moved, then abolished and finally demolished. The seventeenth-century buildings off Borough High Street, Southwark, had suffered little in the Gordon Riots.[6] But by the end of the eighteenth century they were 'so much decayed as to be in danger of falling' and 'in too ruinous a state to be repaired'.[7] In 1802 the Marshal, Sir James Bland Burgess, informed both Treasury and Office of Works that 'a great part of the buildings . . . have fallen down, and . . . several persons have lately effected their escape, and . . . the Court House is in considerable danger, and unsafe to hold any more Courts therein'.[8] Without an armed guard, the prison was certainly not strong enough to hold the Admiralty prisoners, 'a desperate set of men . . . convicted of Mutiny and Sedition . . . whose escape is hourly feared by the Keepers'.[9] The Deputy Prothonotary assured Craig that 'in the event of a fit and proper place being provided . . . a considerable number [of debtors] will be induced to remain therein instead of removing themselves to the . . . King's Bench and Fleet, which is the present practice with those that can afford the expense thereof rather than remain in the present miserable and ruinous place'.[10] The search for alternative accommodation was therefore intensified. After dilatory negotiations over a period of two decades between the Treasury, the

[1] *Gent's. Mag.* 1784 pt. ii p. 635, 1785 pt. ii p. 663, 1786 pt. i p. 177, 1791 pt. i p. 578, 1791 pt. ii pp. 671, 733; *Parl. Deb.* i (1803–14) col. 319, vi (1806) col. 368, viii (1806–7) cols. 1028, 1069, ix (1807) col. 659, xii (1809) col. 138, xix (1811) cols. 109, 444, xx (1811) col. 846, xxvii (1813–14) cols. 123, 197, xxx (1815) col. 39, xxxi (1815) col. 1039, xxxiii (1816) cols. 157, 215, 1160 and N.S. xxv (1830) col. 1.
[2] T. Allen, *London, Westminster and Southwark* iv (1828), p. 478. For a less laudatory description cf. Howard *op. cit.* pp. 243–9.
[3] 'Report from Committee on King's Bench, Fleet and Marshalsea', *Parl. Pap.* 1814–15, iv, pp. 534 *et seq.*; Thornbury *op. cit.* vi, p. 61 (view of entrance). A set of twenty-eight views by J. J. Rurie, 1843, was sold at Sotheby's, 14 March 1967, lot 128. For ground plans cf. Crest 2/932; Works 38/16–17; MPE. 1090.
[4] *A Description of the King's Bench Prison* [1823], B.M. Pressmark 1128 b. 20 (map showing site location and view of interior court). The pamphlet concludes with a set of instructions on 'How to sue out a Habeas Corpus'.
[5] Works 6/131/4, ff. 45, 67, 73 (ground plan); Wheatley and Cunningham *op. cit.* ii, pp. 340–41.
[6] Works 6/19, f. 300, 14 June 1780.
[7] T. 29/60, f. 113, 31 December 1788; T. 29/64, ff. 471–2, 4 July 1792.
[8] Works 4/18, f. 223, 17 February 1797; Works 6/23, f. 19, 10 March 1797.
[9] Works 6/23, f. 72, 21 December 1798 and f. 181, 14 May 1802.
[10] Works 6/23, 21 September 1799. For a view of the old buildings cf. *Gent's. Mag.* 1803 pt. ii, p. 805, 1804 pt. i, p. 401; B.M. Maps 3905 (2); Walford, *Old and New London*, vi pp. 66–7.

Office of Works and various landowners, a site was at last chosen: the Surrey County Gaol, known as the White Lion Prison, in Southwark.[1] Removal took place in 1811, after the Office of Works had reconstructed what Howard had once called 'this sickly gaol' at a cost of £4380.[2] At the same time the Marshalsea Court was transferred from its dilapidated building, reputedly by Inigo Jones, to a new court house in Great Scotland Yard designed by Leverton and Chawner.[3]

The new Marshalsea was not altogether satisfactory. Scarcely had the prisoners arrived when a wall collapsed, killing one man and injuring another.[4] Need for expansion was soon felt, Smirke being called in to give his opinion in 1818.[5] The prisoners frequently complained of bad conditions.[6] And in 1829 an Irishman named Tighe caused something of a sensation when he exposed the whole establishment as 'the most extensive and pernicious Brothel of the metropolis'.[7] Nevertheless, with its 'oblong pile of barrack building, partitioned into squalid houses standing back to back', the Marshalsea survived as a separate institution until 1842 and as a dilapidated ruin until the 1850s. The Marshalsea Court in Scotland Yard was abolished in 1849.[8]

2. PENTONVILLE PRISON

An official inquiry into penal systems commented favourably in 1834 on that in use in Philadelphia, of separate confinement.[9] Lord John Russell, as Home Secretary, introduced legislation to facilitate its use (2 and 3 Vict. c. 56), and undertook the building of a model prison in which the experiment might be tried.[10] A ten-acre site at Pentonville was at length purchased, and designs by Major Joshua Jebb (1793–1863), surveyor general of convict prisons, were put out to tender in January 1840.[11] That of Grissell and Peto being accepted, the foundation stone was laid in April and work proceeded rapidly. Although the building came under the Home Office and

[1] For details of alternative sites, plans, land values etc. cf. Works 6/22, ff. 20–21, 30, 77, 84, 149; Works 6/23, ff. 78, 82 94, 98, 111, 114, 183, 185, 199, 261; Works 6/25, ff. 1, 2, 6; Works 4/17, 5 and 16 February, 12 and 19 June, 12 August 1789, 13 and 20 May, 3 June, 2 September, 4 and 11 November, 1791; Works 4/18, f. 6, 8 February 1793; Works 6/131/2, f. 3 20 April 1791; T. 29/61, ff. 40, 170, 210, 354, 366; T. 29/63, ff. 17, 112, 147, 488, 532; T. 29/64, f. 471; T. 27/42, f. 100; T. 27/41, f. 461; Works 1/5 f. 104, 6 September 1791; Works 6/24, ff. 267–9, 6 and 12 December 1808; T. 29/107, f. 29, 11 September 1810; T. 29/108, f. 145, 8 November 1810; Works 4/20, 12 May, 9 June 1809.
[2] Works 4/18, f. 36, 20 September 1793; T. 29/66, f. 160, 15 October 1793; Works 4/19, 4, 14 and 21 March 1800.
[3] T. 29/117, f. 560, 9 June 1812; Crest 2/932 (plans and elevations). A survey plan of 1850 is reproduced in *Survey of London* xvi, p. 208. For a view of the interior of the old Court see *Gent's Mag.* 1803, pt. ii, p. 1205.
[4] It was repaired by the Office of Works. Cf. Works 4/21, 13 and 17 May, 4 June, 2 and 16 July, 17 September, 29 October, 5 November, 24 December 1813; Works 6/26, ff. 52–4, 57, 64, 73, 76; Works 6/27, f. 106, 27 October 1813.   [5] Works 6/131/2, ff. 15 *et seq.* (1818–19).
[6] E.g. 'noxious vapours arising from the privies' (Works 6/131/2, ff. 35, 56, 68).
[7] Works 6/131/2, ff. 43–4, 50, 51. For less scandalous findings cf. 'Report from Committee on King's Bench, Fleet and Marshalsea Prisons', *Parl. Pap.* 1814–15, iv, pp. 552 *et seq.*; *Parl. Deb.* vi (1806) col. 404, xxx (1815) cols. 39–40.
[8] Wheatley and Cunningham *op. cit* ii, pp. 475–6. For plans and descriptions cf. Crest 2/932 (1843); Knight *op. cit.* v, p. 325; Allen *op. cit.* iv, pp. 492–3.
[9] *Parl. Pap.* 1834 (593) xlvi; 1835 (438) xi; *Parl. Deb.* 3rd ser. xxiv, 604 ff. See M. Grünhut, *Penal Reform* (1948), chap. iv.   [10] *Parl. Deb.*, 3rd ser. liii, 1188.
[11] Works 1/23, pp. 390, 393, 439, 464, 478, 513; 1/24, pp. 26–8, 42, 65; 2/2 pp. 369, 354, 401. For Jebb, see *D.N.B.*

was paid for by special parliamentary votes, Jebb's accounts were sent quarterly to the Works Department for checking and transmission to the Treasury.[1] The total cost was £84,164.[2]

Jebb proposed in February 1841 that Barry should be employed to design certain features of the prison in which an architectural character was desirable: houses for the governor and chaplain, the gateway and terrace walls, and porter's lodge, archway, and gates and walls in the courtyard. The cost of these parts was £8068. Barry received only 150 guineas for his drawings, the actual work falling under Jebb's supervision as in the rest of the prison.[3] The buildings were completed towards the end of 1842.

3. THE NEW GAOL, ST. JOHN'S, NEWFOUNDLAND

The Office of Works occasionally incurred advisory responsibility for works outside the United Kingdom. One instance was the New Gaol on the outskirts of St. John's, Newfoundland. This project followed naturally from the reorganisation of the colony's judicial system.[4] The gaol was one of the public works sponsored by Sir Thomas Cochrane, whose energetic Governorship spanned the period between the creation of a Supreme Court in 1825 and the establishment of a bicameral legislature in 1832–4. In November 1827 the Treasury despatched to the Office of Works a letter 'enclosing, by direction of Mr. Huskisson, a copy of one from Governor Sir Thomas Cochrane, with a memorandum of the names and number of the apartments required for the New Gaol at Newfoundland'.[5] Stephenson immediately wrote to Smirke:

> In consequence of the experience you have had in buildings of this description I have received directions to submit the same to your consideration with a requirement from the Treasury that you will, from the information furnished by these papers, make a plan and elevation for this building. The gaol is to be built with stone, and the general arrangement of the rooms described is left to your discretion together with any additional accommodation you may think requisite.[6]

Smirke had already been connected with gaols at Carlisle, Maidstone, Lincoln, Perth and Millbank, to say nothing of the King's Bench, Marshalsea and Fleet. Within less than a month a portfolio of plans was sent to the Treasury.[7] The building in question was probably the new court house and gaol erected at Harbour Grace in 1830.[8] None of Smirke's drawings appears to have survived and the prison itself has long since been demolished.

---

[1] *Parl. Deb.*, 3rd ser. liii, 1188–9; lix, 653; lxv, 91–2; Works 1/25, p. 399; 2/2, p. 403; 2/3, *passim*.
[2] E. Cresy, *Encyclopaedia of Civil Engineering* (1847), pp. 602–16, where the prison is described in detail.
[3] Works 1/25, p. 6; 1/27, p. 179; 1/28, p. 58.   [4] In accordance with 5 G. iv c. lxvii.
[5] Works 1/15, f. 498, 12 November 1827.
[6] Works 1/15, f. 504, 13 November 1827. Smirke's patron, Earl Bathurst, was Secretary of State for War and Colonies, 1812–27.
[7] Works 1/16, f. 47, 11 January 1828; Works 4/28, f. 404, 12 November 1827 and f. 456, 10 January 1828.
[8] Sir R. H. Bennycastle, *Newfoundland in 1842* i (1842), p. 156. Smirke's prison should not be confused with the central Court House and Gaol at St. John's, rebuilt in 1821 after a fire in 1817 (*Observations on the Present State of Newfoundland . . . addressed to Henry Earl Bathurst . . . by an Inhabitant of the Colony*, 1823, pp. 19, 32).

V. BRITISH EMBASSIES

Throughout the years covered by this volume accommodation for British envoys abroad was usually rented. Embassy houses were purchased only in special circumstances, and only three such buildings came under the care of the Works Department.

1. PARIS

THE Hôtel de Charost in the Rue du Faubourg St. Honoré in Paris was purchased as a residence for the British Ambassador to France by the Duke of Wellington in October, 1814. The house, built about 1720 by Mazin, was the property of Napoleon's sister, Princess Pauline Borghese.[1] Wellington described both house and stables as 'in excellent repair, and the former completely furnished, and admirably calculated for its purpose. The number of carriages attached to an Embassy [he added] will require some additional buildings for coach houses'. The British government paid, in instalments, 500,000 francs for the house, 300,000 francs for the furniture and 61,600 francs for the stables, or roughly £46,500 at the current exchange rate.[2] Annual maintenance was carried out under contract by local artisans, over £11,000 being spent on repair during the first ten years of British ownership.[3] Robert Smirke, who was sent by Treasury orders in August 1824 to inspect the building, estimated that another £4000 needed to be spent and recommended that it would be cheaper to manage work on the roofs from England. The Treasury then directed the Office of Works to arrange for the repair of the embassy and Lewis Wyatt was despatched to supervise operations. After consultations in January–February 1825 with a French architect named Bonneville and a surveyor called Beauvillain he recommended extensive repairs to the main building, the rebuilding of the dining and ball rooms, provision of a chapel, and other works and furniture to a total of some £26,800. But in April the Treasury decided to entrust more limited repairs estimated at £7000 to a French architect, as more competent to judge of the most economical mode as well as of the extent of decoration required, French houses being (a Treasury minute commented) 'in the details . . . usually less expensively finished than Houses of the same class in this country'.[4] Nevertheless, the Treasury proposed to send an English supervisor.[5] Maintenance however remained the responsibility of the Foreign Office, repairs between 1825 and 1835 amounting to some £22,000.[6]

---

[1] The building is described and illustrated by J. Vacquier, *Les Vieux Hôtels de Paris, Faubourg Saint Honoré* i (1930), pp. 11–14 and pls. 32–36. See also B. Willson, *The Paris Embassy 1814–1920* (1927).
[2] *Wellington Despatches* xii, pp. 71, 76, 88, 158, 189.   [3] Works 10/27/1, f. 2.
[4] In 1840, however, Burton represented that 'the stile of furnishing and decorating [are] much more costly [in Paris] than in London' (Burton MS. volume in Victoria and Albert Museum Library, 86 JJ2).
[5] Works 1/13, pp. 14, 79, 175–82, 228, 328, 356. Copies of Smirke's and Wyatt's reports are in the MS. volume of Decimus Burton's correspondence cited in note 4.
[6] Works 10/27/1, f. 2.

Repairs executed in 1839 under a Parisian architect J. Silveijra so greatly exceeded the estimates that the Treasury Board reviewed the cost of maintenance since 1815, and declared 'that some decided alteration is required in the manner in which this business is conducted': as an experiment they placed the buildings (with Palmerston's approval) under the direction of the Commissioners of Woods.[1] Accordingly the Commissioners took charge of the fabric under the same regulations as for palaces in England. Decimus Burton was sent out to report, and under his direction as supervising architect and that of Silveijra as resident architect or clerk of works internal repairs and redecoration were begun. Expenditure was stimulated by the appointment of a new ambassador, Lord Cowley, who told the Foreign Secretary in November 1841 that he believed the house was in such bad condition 'that it was impossible to live in it'.[2] Over £6400 were spent on repairs, decorations and furniture in 1841/3, and in 1843/4 a further £3875.[3] Burton also proposed that the extensive but dilapidated stabling should be sold and new stables built. Although legal difficulties prevented the sale, new stables were erected in 1845/6 at a cost of £3200.[4] Maintenance of the buildings and furniture averaged a little over £900 a year from 1844 to 1852.[5] Burton made an annual visit until 1850, when he was ordered to discontinue this practice.[6] The eminent French architect Hittorf,[7] called in to provide more light in the ballroom in 1851, substituted three windows for a single glazed door to the garden.[8] A new programme of repair and redecoration was begun in 1852;[9] and a general restoration, including a number of alterations, was carried out in 1858–61[10] under another French architect, F. Raveau.[11]

2. CONSTANTINOPLE

The building of a new ambassadorial residence at Constantinople in 1844–51 presented the Commissioners of Woods and Works with unusual problems: the distance, slowness of communication (the journey taking generally three weeks), and the difficulties of building in a despotic country, together with the limited

[1] *Ibid.*

[2] *Ibid.* ff. 13 *et seq.*; Works 1/24, pp. 116–7, 535, 569; 1/25, pp. 20, 51–2; 1/26, p. 188; 2/3, pp. 299–307, 338; *Diary and Correspondence of Henry Wellesley, First Lord Cowley 1790–1846*, ed. F. A. Wellesley (1936), p. 211.

[3] *Parl. Pap.* 1870 [C. 65] lxvi, A. The original accounts are in Works 5/154: the principal contractors were Guyot ('maçonnerie'), Bouilette ('menuiserie'), and Decan ('peinture'): 'maçonnerie' included plasterwork.

[4] *Ibid.*; Works 1/26, pp. 455–7; 2/4, pp. 115, 125, 146, 203; 2/5, pp. 124, 152.

[5] *Parl. Pap.* 1870 [C. 65] lxvi, A.

[6] *Parl. Pap.* 1852–3 (950) lvii, p. 49. Burton complained that he had been 'uncourteously displaced, without the usual favour of an explanation or notice of any kind from the Board' (*ibid.* p. 64, 6 October 1851).

[7] Jacques Ignace Hittorf (1792–1867); see Thieme Becker, *Allgemeines Lexikon der Bildenen Kunstler*, xvii (1924).

[8] Works 10/27/2, ff. 23–9. The cost was £221 (*Parl. Pap.* 1852–3 (950) lvii, p. 15.)

[9] See Works 10/27/4 *passim* (plan, f. 59), 10/28/1, ff. 7–80; *Parl. Pap.* 1852–3 (950) lvii, and 1857–8 (414) xxxiv (including block plan). A London architect, Benedict Albano, was employed (see p. 639).

[10] Works 10/28/3 contains the detailed accounts. It appears that the pedimental sculpture dates from this restoration: 'La sculpture d'un bas relief et des armes d'Angleterre dans les frontons sur la cour et le jardin 3,000 [francs]' is an item in an 'Etat détaillé des travaux imprévus, exécutés lors de la Restauration de l'Hôtel de l'ambassade d'Angleterre' (f. 42).

[11] D. 1872; inspector for historical monuments, Seine-Inférieure, 1850–70; see C. Bauchal, *Nouveau Dictionnaire . . . des Architectes Français* (1887), p. 716.

capabilities of the local workmen, all contributed to make the undertaking one of remarkable difficulty.

The 'palace' commenced in 1801 by Lord Elgin when ambassador to the Porte, on a site at Pera, the aristocratic suburb of Constantinople, was burned down in August 1831.[1] Designs for rebuilding made by a Signor Peverata were sent to the Treasury in January 1833, but in March 1834 Captain Harry D. Jones, R.E., was ordered to Constantinople to make plans and estimates for a new site at Therapia, halfway along the Bosphorus, as well as at Pera.[2] Though Captain Jones submitted estimates of about £22,000, exclusive of superintendence, he pointed out the extreme difficulty of setting an accurate figure:[3]

> Under this despotic Government, the Public Departments only are engaged in the erection of large Edifices of a permanent nature, and where detailed Estimates are never required; such undertakings are considered by the Persons employed, as so many favorable opportunities for reimbursing themselves for the losses they have sustained by non payment for Work performed for Individuals holding high Situations under the Government: it is therefore evident, that the actual cost of a Building, or the prices paid for the Materials, are not to be obtained. . . .

Great and open fraud was, he reported, constantly practised.

Palmerston having determined that Therapia was too far from the centre of things, Jones was sent back to obtain further information and perfect his plans for the Pera site.[4] His revised estimates of over £35,000, plus another £10,000 for completing a chapel—already under construction at the time of the fire—and building a consulate, appalled the Treasury, which refused to submit them to Parliament without further consideration.[5] Jones was recalled. Proceedings were halted by the ambassador, Viscount Ponsonby, who objected to the plans for reasons that he failed to specify though repeatedly requested to do so between July 1835 and June 1841.[6] The real difficulty was that Ponsonby preferred the climate of Therapia to that of Pera.[7] A diplomatic crisis in 1841 made the return of the ambassador to the capital essential, so Palmerston asked that the Woods and Works should send an architect there to obtain temporary accommodation for the embassy and arrange the building of a permanent residence.[8]

William James Smith,[9] assistant surveyor to Pennethorne for the Crown estates in London, was selected for this service, the first part of which he discharged successfully despite Ponsonby's refusal to co-operate.[10] The appointment of a new envoy, Sir Stratford Canning, did nothing, however, to speed the erection of a new palace. Buildings of an inferior character having been erected round the old site, Canning sought a better one and suggested that the sale of the old might realise a large profit. The new Foreign Secretary, Lord Aberdeen, made it clear that no estimate of the

[1] Works 10/1, f. 38. For the old palace see R. Walsh, *A Residence at Constantinople* (1836).
[2] Works 10/1, ff. 1–3.   [3] *Ibid.* f. 5.   [4] *Ibid.* ff. 12–14.   [5] *Ibid.* ff. 17, 20–4.   [6] *Ibid.* ff. 38–40.
[7] So did his successor, Stratford Canning: 'He disliked the climate of Pera, and Therapia was his breathing place' (S. Lane-Poole, *Life of the Rt. Hon. Stratford Canning*, 1888, ii, p. 66). The Sultan gave the British envoy an estate at Therapia in 1845.   [8] Works 10/1, ff. 38–40.
[9] Smith was engaged by the Office of Works as a professional assistant in April 1830 (Works 5/111). He knew French and Italian; and his wife may have been Spanish (Works 10/1, ff. 106–7; 10/2, ff. 178–83, 203–5).   [10] Works 10/1, ff. 30–6.

order of £40,000 would be acceptable: 'Her M[ajesty]'s Gov[ernmen]t do not see any occasion that the residence of the Embassy should be built with a view to orna-ment the Turkish Capital, or to attract the attention of passengers on the Bosphorus'.[1]

Returning to London in October 1842 Smith was ordered to prepare working drawings and estimates in communication with Seward of the Works Department.[2] He designed a rectangular structure somewhat larger than the former palace, measuring externally some 160 ft. by 120 ft. with an internal central court of about 60 ft. by 32 ft.[3] (Pl. 11B). The principal feature was a marble grand staircase, occupying the centre of one of the shorter sides. The building's general resemblance to the Reform Club, Pall Mall, is not surprising, for Barry was employed to revise the design and specification.[4] Smith's estimate, based on local prices that he had obtained, was £46,290; Seward's calculation at English prices, £57,048.[5] Finally a figure of £45,000 was adopted, an estimate of £33,000 being put before Parliament: the difference was the expected profit from the change of site. After conversations between ministers, an attic floor was added to the design, but the estimate was not altered.[6]

Aberdeen approved the plans in April 1843 and urged immediate action. The next two months, however, were taken up in settling the arrangements for Smith's return to Constantinople as superintending architect.[7] The consul-general was to act as paymaster, a device that did not always work smoothly.[8] One Luke Richardson was sent out after Smith as clerk of works, and English foremen were engaged for the masons and carpenters.[9] But in Constantinople they found that the proposed new site had been taken by the Turkish government for a cavalry hospital. Another site was purchased in November 1843, but proved to be unacceptable to the Turkish authorities.[10] Months were wasted in fruitless negotiations, until in June 1844 Lords Lincoln and Aberdeen determined that the old site must after all be employed.[11] Smith took possession on 21 August, and started work on stables and outbuildings that could initially accommodate stores and his English staff. These were substantially completed by the end of the year.[12]

Having waited so many months, the Commissioners of Woods then directed Smith not to start on the palace until he had sent comparative tables of prices, samples of materials, full plans of the foundations, particulars of the use of each room, and similar information that they well could have requested long before. But communications being slow, Smith had already begun work on the palace.[13] He had intended to rebuild two external walls on the old foundations, but finding them 'out of the upright in parts, . . . built without any footings projecting externally'

---

[1] *Ibid.* ff. 80–95.   [2] *Ibid.* f. 113; 1/26, p. 90.   [3] Works 10/2, ff. 368–9; 10/24/2, f. 278.
[4] Works 10/4, ff. 787–8, 810–20. Barry's bill 'for advice and assistance to altering and modifying Mr. Smith's Design for the Ambassador's House at Constantinople' and investigating the accounts totalling £62,000, in 1843 and 1848, was £182 10s. (Works 11/1/2, f. 159).
[5] Works 10/1, f. 138. William Tierney Clark (see *D.N.B.*), an engineer who had worked at Budapest, was consulted, and thought Smith's prices ample (*ibid.* f. 141).
[6] Works 10/3, ff. 606–9; 10/4, ff. 787–8, 810–20.
[7] Works 10/1, ff. 154, 157–9; 10/2, ff. 163, 175, 178, 203–5. While in Constantinople Smith was to be paid at the rate of £700 p.a., which he thought justified by the pains he had taken to learn Turkish (Works 10/2, ff. 178–83, 203–5).   [8] *Ibid.* ff. 208, 252–8, 345–51, 362–4.
[9] Works 1/26, pp. 223–5; 10/2, f. 224. Richardson was recommended by Robert Stephenson.
[10] Works 10/2, ff. 187–9, 220–2, 262–3.   [11] *Ibid.* ff. 279, 284.   [12] *Ibid.* ff. 309, 312, 328.
[13] *Ibid.* ff. 312–15, 323, 326, 368–9.

he had to excavate down to the solid ground, in some places a matter of twenty feet, at an additional cost of £1763.[1] Another difficulty was that the Makriqere quarry Smith had expected to use was requisitioned for the Sultan's new palace of Dolma Baktché; he found an alternative at Ayzorghia, five hours journey from Constantinople: this limestone he continued to use despite unfavourable reports from the Museum of Economic Geology. This alteration, and increases in price that he was forced to agree to, added £3500 to the cost.[2] Nor did the local masons work as well or as fast as Smith had expected: they used stone wastefully, had difficulty in carrying their work upright, and demanded higher wages. Some of the trained men were forced away to Dolma Baktché.[3] A shortage of water in the summer of 1845 caused yet more delay.[4] The joiners, too, were incompetent, unable to work columns (particularly the fluting) or projections for cornices, being unfamiliar with classical architecture.[5] Even more of the joinery than Smith had contemplated had therefore to be made in England, principally by Grissell and by Baker.[6]

By October 1846, however, the slaters were at work on the roof; but in November Smith was struck down 'with internal sufferings of no ordinary nature', and retired to Italy for four months to recuperate.[7] Back at Pera, he found the ambassador insisting on such extras as fireproof iron window shutters and Venetian blinds.[8] For the decoration of the state rooms papiermâché decorations were ordered from Bielefeld.[9] A fire that in October 1847 badly damaged the outbuildings and destroyed materials from England was a set-back, and the non-arrival of the iron shutters and window glass protracted the completion of the interior.[10] Further delays were partly the consequence of a financial crisis: in a despatch dated 2 December 1847 Smith submitted additional estimates of £31,784 for completing the palace and garden, and reinstating the buildings damaged by fire.[11] Inman, the Board's surveyor, recommended reductions of some £5800 and several months of correspondence ensued.[12] Palmerston, again at the Foreign Office, called for a strict inquiry, and in July 1848 Barry (who had himself once been at Constantinople) was asked to investigate. He pointed out that the delays over the site had involved considerable additional charges in salaries and incidentals, that alterations had been made to the original specification, and that only charges for stone and labour totalling nearly £10,000 could be regarded as exceeding Smith's estimate:[13] 'I am surprised to find the works have been executed at a cost so little beyond the amount of the original Estimate . . . which, in my opinion, could not have been effected, but for the judgement discretion and constant vigilance that must have been exercised on the part of the Architect'. Smith meanwhile protested that even if the contemporary Russian and French palaces were cheaper (which was doubtful) the work in the British was

[1] Works 10/3, ff. 603–4.   [2] Works 10/2, f. 330; 10/3, ff. 606–9.
[3] Works 10/2, ff. 374, 380, 400; 10/3, ff. 606–9.   [4] Works 10/2, f. 395.
[5] *Ibid.* f. 400; 10/3, f. 551.   [6] *Ibid.* ff. 460, 488, 570.
[7] *Ibid.* ff. 476, 483, 494.   [8] *Ibid.* ff. 497, 511.
[9] *Ibid.* ff. 525, 538, 562. The mouldings, like much of the material sent from England, suffered in transit, and Smith complained that they were not in fact papiermâché, but a plaster composition. This led to a controversy between the Board (relying on the Museum of Economic Geology's analysis) and Bielefeld as to the character of papiermâché, ended only by Bielefeld undertaking to make good whatever was required (*ibid.* ff. 698, 707, 712, 717; 10/4, ff. 727, 732, 734–6, 739, 741, 746).
[10] Works 10/3, f. 598; 10/4, ff. 839, 850.   [11] Works 10/3, ff. 601–9.   [12] *Ibid.* ff. 600 *et seq.*
[13] *Ibid.* ff. 643, 682 ff.

far superior:[1] 'However little a correct mitre or a true perpendicular or horizontal line may be appreciated elsewhere, yet I am sure that the Commissioners of Her Majesty's Woods &c would have been anything but satisfied with an officer of Theirs, had the works of the Palace here, been discreditable to England'. Convinced that there was good reason for the increased charge, the government obtained a further vote of £12,000 for 1848/9 (of which only £4000 were available for new work) and in the following session another £10,000.[2] Yet even then the completion, decoration and fitting-up of the palace were delayed by disagreements between Smith and Sir Stratford and Lady Canning,[3] as well as intervention by the economy-minded new First Commissioner, Lord Seymour.[4] Smith incurred the Board's censure by carrying out minor alterations in the domestic offices to meet the ambassador's wishes, and by ordering materials directly from London tradesmen instead of through the Office.[5] The final works were deferred over the winter of 1850–1 because the ambassador was now in residence.[6] Further complications arose over the heating apparatus, made by Messrs. Stephenson and Peill, who sent out an engineer, William Fry, to fix it. Fry claimed that the apparatus was in part defective, and also accused Smith of irregularities.[7]

The palace was practically completed in the summer and autumn of 1851 at a total cost of some £78,000 including furniture.[8] The Treasury determined that, like the Paris embassy, it should be maintained by the Works Department.[9] The rebuilding of the chapel and construction of consular buildings lie outside the period of this history, as does the restoration of the palace itself after a fire that damaged it in 1870, despite Smith's conviction of the fireproof quality of his structure.[10]

3. MADRID

The British mission in Madrid had long occupied a house in Calle de Alcalá. When the lease fell in in 1846 the government refused to buy the freehold, and Henry

---

[1] *Ibid.* ff. 657–60.   [2] *Ibid.* f. 685; 10/4, f. 751.

[3] *Ibid.* ff. 884, 947. Among other points, Smith wanted to fix an iron and glass roof over the central court; Canning vehemently opposed this, and it was deleted, though installed for a later envoy (*ibid.* ff. 756–60, 823, 833; 1/35, p. 284). But it would seem that this sort of question merely exacerbated a resentment that arose from the long-delayed occupation of the palace. Canning blamed this entirely on Smith, whom he regarded as feathering his nest by executing commissions for the Turkish government and individual ministers. Canning himself had, however, in the first instance asked Smith to provide the Turks with a plan for a hospital; Smith had obtained the Board's sanction for most of his works for the Turkish government, and had refused private commissions. Inquiry exonerated him of anything more than imprudence (Works 10/5, ff. 1022–3, 1052–6, 1065, 1075, 1182).

[4] Works 10/4, f. 966.   [5] Works 1/35, pp. 330, 338, 374.   [6] Works 1/36, p. 124.

[7] Works 1/35, p. 47; 1/36, pp. 428–30; 1/37, p. 23; 10/7, *passim.* Fry's allegations were denounced by his former employers, Messrs. Stephenson and Peill, as 'one gross tissue of vindictive falsehoods' (Works 10/7, f. 21, 25 July 1851). Fry had been drunken and insubordinate, and, when reproved by Smith, had with the Cannings' help obtained a job with the Turkish authorities before returning to England. The Cannings seem to have used Fry as a means of attacking Smith; Lord Seymour made an exhaustive inquiry and acquitted Smith, who had himself demanded an on-the-spot investigation (Works 10/5, f. 1075; 10/7, *passim*).

[8] Works 10/5, ff. 1059 (20 January 1852, when only £387 were reserved for completing various works, but extras were estimated at £1377); 1211 (13 October 1853, £79,082 5s. 3d. spent).

[9] *Ibid.* f. 1011 (6 May 1851).   [10] See Works 10/6; 10/24/2; 10/44/1.

Bulwer,[1] then British ambassador, secured the former Montezuma family residence, 9 Calle de Torija at the corner of Calle de las Rejas, for £400 p.a. from the Marqués Viudo Perija. The building was described as large and solid, with thick walls of brick and earth. Bulwer was allowed £3000 for putting it in order, and spent £3145. His architect, Domingo de la Fuerte, designed a new staircase and carriage entrance, and dignified the façades with architectural framing to the windows. A 'marble bath of great value' was also installed. The work, executed by J. Calcerada, was completed under the architect P. Garcia. When an arch over a window gave way in November 1848, the chargé d'affaires called in a Spanish government architect, José Antonio Perez, who ascribed the collapse to the cutting-away for the coach-house not having been properly girded up. Repairs were executed by the owner.[2]

On his appointment as Minister at Madrid in 1850 Lord Howden[3] received such reports of the condition of the house that he urged that an architect should be sent out. The First Commissioner of Woods chose Benedict Albano, 'an Architect of established reputation . . . who is conversant with the Spanish Language'. After careful inspection, Albano reported that Fuerte had not had a proper regard for the peculiar construction or permanent stability of the edifice, and that the subsequent repair by the owner had been wrongly planned and badly executed. He had pointed out the general dilapidation of the structure to Perija, who had undertaken to do most of the works Albano considered should fall on him. Those he refused to discharge, with others necessary on change of occupancy, Albano estimated at £1242; and repairs and alterations to the Chancery at £122.[4]

[1] 1801–72, see *D.N.B.* Ambassador at Madrid, 1843–8.
[2] Works 2/6, pp. 1–20; 2/8, pp. 264–81, 343–62.
[3] 1799–1873, see *D.N.B.* Minister at Madrid, 1850–8.   [4] Works 2/8, pp. 261–4, 338–64.

VI. ANCIENT MONUMENTS

PUBLIC interest in ancient buildings was stimulated in the early nineteenth century by the work of such topographers and historians as Lysons, Britton and Brayley, whose researches were widely disseminated in the 1830s by cheap illustrated periodicals.[1] The study of church architecture by societies at Oxford and Cambridge about 1840 helped to focus informed interest on the preservation of medieval buildings. In 1841 John Britton appeared before Joseph Hume's select committee on National Monuments,[2] and recommended the setting up of a small commission, on the lines of that instituted in France in 1837,[3] to consist of 'architects, antiquaries, amateurs, and private gentlemen', supported by public funds, to advise on the repair and preservation of national monuments. These included churches, castles, and even private houses: 'in fact', as one M.P., Ewart, summed it up, 'every thing which illustrates history, whether with regard to historical facts, society, or manners'.[4] Although the Treasury referred the committee's report to the Board of Woods and Works,[5] nothing came of Britton's suggestion.

Private endeavour then sought to supply the need: a British Archaeological Association (again inspired by French example) was founded in 1843. But Lord Lincoln, then First Commissioner of Woods and Works, who had begun to consider the problem, was contemptuous of what such societies might accomplish:[6] he wrote to Peel, 28 February 1844:

> During the last year my attention was drawn to the rapid destruction of many ancient ruins and other Architectural memorials of our History which is going on— partly for the sake of improvement of Properties, partly from ignorance of their value and other causes, but by no means more common or more generally mischievous than misjudged *reconstruction* under the name of *restoration & repair*.
>
> In France great attention has lately been paid to this subject by the Government, whilst in this Country the Societies which exist have done, & I believe can do, very little good.
>
> I requested Mr. Blore to consult Dr. Bliss of Oxford and Professor Willis of Cambridge upon this subject and submit to me their combined suggestions. In consequence Mr. Blore has addressed to me the enclosed letter and I hope you will give it your attention. It is of course capable of, and indeed requires, modification—but it will bring the matter succinctly under your notice.[7]

[1] E.g. Knight's *Penny Cyclopaedia*.

[2] *Parl. Pap.* 1841 (416) vi. The select committee was principally concerned with improving public access to national funerary monuments as a means of educating the working classes. For Britton's views see also his letter of 1837 advocating a society for the protection of ancient buildings, and that of 1840 proposing a governmental grant for preserving the 'ancient public edifices of Great Britain', printed in his *Autobiography* (1850), Appendix, pp. 140–1 and 72–81 respectively. [3] See P. Léon, *Les Monuments historiques* (Paris, 1917), pp. 52–5.

[4] *Parl. Pap.* 1841 (416) vi, q. 2168. [5] *Works* 14/131, f. 1, 21 June 1842.

[6] Not unreasonably so, given the disputes that rent the Cambridge Camden Society (for which see J. A. White, *The Cambridge Movement*, 1962) and the British Archaeological Association (see *Jnl. of the British Archaeological Association* i, 1846, pp. i–ix).

[7] Nottingham Univ., Newcastle MS. 12030. For Willis and Bliss, see *D.N.B.*

Blore's letter cannot now be found, but from the tenor of Lincoln's we may suppose it to have been on the lines of his evidence before the Hume committee of 1841:[1] that restoration was a doubtful proceeding, to be undertaken only in the last resort and with extreme care, a view Blore consistently upheld. Whether any form of historic monuments commission or inspectorate was contemplated is not clear. But the question of historic monuments had thus already been discussed by ministers when the state of Newark Castle was brought to Lincoln's notice.

This ruin was the last vestige of the Crown estate at Newark, a borough in which the influence of Lincoln's father, the Duke of Newcastle, was predominant.[2] Lincoln invited Anthony Salvin, then the leading designer of new, and restorer of old castles, to survey it.[3] In May 1844 Salvin reported that he had found part of it 'in a very dangerous state'; £700 or £800 would be useful, but he would trim his official report to whatever sum might be available.[4] In this report, forwarded by Lincoln to the Treasury in August, Salvin described how the Gate Tower was filled with earth nearly to the springing of the arches, while outside the ground had been excavated to the point of undermining the foundations. He proposed to rectify this, clear openings that had been bricked up, and cover the tops of the walls with asphalt to prevent wet penetrating. Effectual preservation could be accomplished for £650.[5] The Commissioners themselves described the ruin as one 'which in addition to its being an Object of much interest to the Inhabitants and Visitors of Newark and its Vicinity, may, from the associations connected with its early history, be considered well worthy of preservation as a National Monument of Antiquity'.[6] The Chancellor of the Exchequer sent the papers to Peel, who approved the expenditure.[7]

Meanwhile, Mr. Justice Coleridge[8] had called Lincoln's attention to the state of the Crown's castles in North Wales. At Caernarvon 'several of the spaces (curtains I think the term is) between tower & tower [are] filled up with the meanest hovels and linheys—for keeping pigs—old iron—rubbish—where these were not erected— some of the spaces are enclosed, & manure cinders &c thrown there'.[9] The mayor joined in the correspondence, and the Commissioners in November 1844 gave notice to remove the encroachments in the castle ditch.[10] Restoration might have proceeded no further had not the abutment of the arch of the Queen's Gate given way during the winter.[11] The Commissioners directed a Holyhead architect, John Provis, to secure the building: he engaged David Williams, a Caernarvon builder, to repair the arch and a considerable portion of wall on either side, 'copying the old work as closely as possible, both workmanship and Materials'.[12] But for a general report the Commissioners turned again to Salvin. He stated that the castle retained

---

[1] *Parl. Pap.* 1841 (416) vi, especially qq. 1616, 1682–3.
[2] Newark had long been a Newcastle pocket borough, and remained so after 1832, Gladstone being returned on the Duke's interest, 1833–45. When the sale of the Crown estate there was announced in 1836, the corporation and leading inhabitants persuaded the Office of Woods to reserve the castle (Crest 34/165).
[3] T. 1/4966, f. 17131/44, 20 August 1844.
[4] Nottingham Univ., Newcastle MS. 8947.   [5] Crest 34/165.   [6] T. 1/4966, f. 17131/44.
[7] *Ibid.* (unnumbered sheet). The Commissioners then let the interior of the castle for the erection of public baths (designed by Salvin), *ibid.* and Crest 34/165.
[8] See *D.N.B.*   [9] Nottingham Univ., Newcastle MS. 9011, 31 July 1844.
[10] Works 14/9, ff. 71–5; 14/10, f. 1; Crest 25/53, no. 7329. Some encroachments still remained, see Works 14/10.
[11] *Ibid.* f. 2.   [12] *Ibid.* ff. 13, 18, 20, 28–9. Provis's work cost £132 14s. 5d.

nearly all of its external features (and that were it necessary) there is sufficient detail to restore the whole of the external walls & Towers. These details are however in many instances fast disappearing, the quoin stones never having had much bond, in many places have fallen out, and parts of the walls have followed them, the same occurs to jambs of windows, doors, & loops; the tops of the Turrets are also much dilapidated & must be rebuilt, as also the parapets & battlements.[1]

Salvin's estimate for a general repair was £2478; and in 1845–7 the work was executed under his directions by Williams in a 'most satisfactory manner' at a cost of £1742.[2] Although his survey had referred to building up parts of walls that had fallen down in the various towers, he did not fill the great breaches in the Chamberlain and Queen's Towers;[3] his work was limited, as at Newark, to making the extant structure secure. 'Arvoniensis', writing to the *Archaeologia Cambrensis*, 1 December 1845, declared:

> The orders received are, to preserve the present outline—repair the whole exterior, filling up holes—mending turrets and battlements—and supplying quoins to the windows and loopholes. Those parts on the side of the ancient walls from which other rectangular walls, now fallen to pieces, had branched off, and which are marked by a vertical strip of decay, will be completely repaired, and a toothing left to indicate the spot.[4]

The third castle repaired by Salvin in 1845–8 was that at Carisbrooke. Unlike the other two, Carisbrooke was not entirely a ruin: it provided a residence for the Governor of the Isle of Wight and small sums had regularly been allowed for repairs since the Restoration;[5] a more extensive repair had been made when Thomas Orde took up residence in 1792.[6] But in 1844 Orde's descendant offered slopes adjoining the castle for sale in building lots. This provoked a great outcry locally, for it would destroy the great charm of the castle, 'the favorite resort of all Classes'. The Commissioners acted quickly and in August 1844 purchased the eight acres in question for £1250.[7] Following this, they were evidently persuaded to undertake a general repair, and Salvin's works cost about £1000.[8] It was not, however, until 1856 that the regular maintenance of the castle was entrusted to the Commissioners of Works.

Yet another building repaired at the public expense in response to local initiative at this time was Lanercost Priory, of which the ruins were also Crown property. The former nave, however, formed the parish church. When the roof of the church fell in, the vicar applied for governmental aid; Salvin made a report; and £1000 were voted in 1847/8.[9] An additional expense of £1780 was finally incurred, which brought criticism from the select committee on miscellaneous expenditure.[10]

---

[1] *Ibid.* Report, estimate and survey, 18 March 1845.   [2] *Ibid.* f. 69.

[3] See Sir L. Turner, *Thirty-one Years' Work in the Repair of Caernarvon Castle* (Caernarvon, 1902), of which there is a copy with Works 14/10.

[4] *Arch. Camb.* i (1846), p. 80 (I owe this reference to Mr. Arnold Taylor).   [5] Crest 2/1166.

[6] *Ibid.* For Orde, appointed Governor in 1791, see Sir L. B. Namier and J. Brooke (eds.) *The House of Commons, 1754–1790* (1964).

[7] Crest 2/1169 (memorial of inhabitants of Newport and district); T. 1/5000, f. 17852/44.

[8] Repairs to Newark, Carisbrooke and Caernarvon Castles, 1845–8, cost £3468 1s. 8d. (Works 2/7, pp. 205–6); of this sum, £649 related to Newark (Crest 34/165, no. 4050, 20 June 1845), and £1742 to Caernarvon (Works 14/10, f. 69).   [9] *Parl. Pap.* 1847–8, xviii, pt. i, q. 2773; pt. ii, app. p. 15.

[10] *Ibid.* pt. i. p. x; pt. ii, app. p. 34; see also *Parl. Deb.* 3rd. ser. ci, 99. Lord Morpeth would no doubt have been sympathetic, as his Dacre ancestors were buried at Lanercost.

Lord Lincoln's interest in national monuments was further shown by his commissioning Sir Richard Westmacott to report on the condition of the royal tombs in Canterbury Cathedral in July 1845.

> The statues both of Henry 4th and his Queen [reported Westmacott] are much mutilated, the Head of the Queen and Hands & Arms of both Statues requiring renewal, the Tomb itself altho much dilapidated is still in a state to leave no doubt as to a correct restoration of the Finials & Crockets and of the Canopy to the Statues.
>
> The Statue of the Black Prince is in perfect condition, but the Tomb on which it lies is in so decayed a state that unless immediately attended to I apprehend little will remain to supply examples for its renewal the material crumbling on the least pressure of the fingers, and this Tomb I strongly recommend to be restored, or reworked entirely in the same material as the present, Purbeck, which I conceive in the present instance to have been ill selected.[1]

Westmacott's estimates for restoration, including emblazonment, were £870 for Henry IV's tomb and £730 for that of the Black Prince, sums which the Treasury agreed to sanction.[2] But when the Works Department asked for further details, so as to judge of the extent to which restoration was to be carried, Westmacott replied that the work was already in hand. He was ordered to suspend it immediately, and to submit a joint report with Blore on the extent to which the work ought to be carried. Philipps, Lincoln's secretary, accompanied Blore and Westmacott to Canterbury in January 1846, and reported against a general restoration. Westmacott was instructed merely to 'put in as perfect a state as the Case admits, all that now remains of the Two Monuments in question, without replacing anything now lost', for which his estimate was only £125.[3] The work was executed by George Austin, the cathedral surveyor, and one Brusciani.[4]

Lincoln's endeavour to establish a policy respecting the preservation of national monuments may well have foundered on the Treasury's fears of the cost. In June 1845, when Thomas Wyse, at Britton's instigation, moved for a commission to consider establishing a 'Museum of National Antiquities in conjunction with a Commission for the conservation of National Monuments', it was Goulburn, the Chancellor of the Exchequer, who killed the project.[5] About a year later, the new Whig First Commissioner, Lord Morpeth, consulted Blore and the antiquarian draughtsman William Twopeny 'as to the rules by which the Commissioners of Woods and Forests should be guided in the preservation and repair of those remains of Antient art which from being the property of the Crown fall under their care'. Their report emphasized the importance of historic monuments generally, the growing public appreciation of them, and the extreme danger of 'injudicious repairs conducted with well meant but ill judged zeal'.[6] If repair was essential, careful drawings should be

---

[1] Nottingham Univ., Newcastle MS. 8858a, 15 July 1845.
[2] *Ibid.* 8861 b; Works 2/4, pp. 507 (10 September), 511 (19 September 1845).
[3] Works 1/28, pp. 364 (30 September), 449 (4 December 1845), 450; 1/29, p. 227; 1/30, pp. 87, 125, 186–7, 226.
[4] Works 1/33, p. 177. Total expenditure, including Westmacott's charge for travelling, was £157 4s.
[5] *Parl. Deb.* 3rd ser. lxxxi, 1329–34; Britton, *Autobiography*, app. p. 81. For Wyse, see p. 588 above.
[6] Works 14/131, ff. 3 *et seq.* Twopeny published *Etchings of Ancient Capitals*, and *Specimens of ancient Wood-Work* (priv. printed, 1859).

made to assist the Commissioners 'in determining as to the value and extent of the repairs to be sanctioned'; these would 'also afford evidence of the state of the building or other work of art before the repair in contemplation was executed'. Such drawings should be preserved and made accessible to the public in the British Museum. The actual state of the buildings should be described by persons selected with the greatest care: they should possess 'skilful practical knowledge . . . also a right feeling of respect for antient art, . . . supported and enlarged by a good knowledge of different styles of art which have prevailed through successive periods'. The same qualifications should be required of those under whom the repairs were executed. But this careful report was pigeon-holed, and some thirty years elapsed before the state accepted any formal responsibility for historic monuments.[1]

[1] By the Ancient Monuments Protection Act 1882, 45 and 46 Vict. cap. 73. For steps leading to this legislation see Joan Evans, *A History of the Society of Antiquaries* (1956), pp. 301, 330–3, 365–9; also M. W. Thompson, 'The First Inspector of Ancient Monuments in the Field', *Journal of the British Archaeological Assn.* 3rd ser. xxiii (1960) and references there cited, and M. W. Barley and T. B. Barry in *Antiquity* xlv (1971), pp. 215–220.

VII. CEREMONIAL OCCASIONS

UNLIKE his grandfather, George III was abstemious and unostentatious in his habits. As he reigned for sixty years, the occasions for traditional displays of monarchical pomp during this period were few. In 1805, however, after a lapse of more than thirty years, the ceremonies for the installation of Knights of the Garter were impressively revived at Windsor, only to be dropped again for 143 years.[1] George IV, while still Regent, celebrated the dynasty's centenary in 1814 with a 'Grand National Jubilee Fête' in the Parks,[2] and as King indulged his taste for splendour to the full in the ceremonies of his coronation, one of the most magnificent in English history, and the last in which the pageantry of the ritual banquet in Westminster Hall was enacted.[3] The ceremonies, postponed from 1 August 1820 to 19 July 1821 on account of the Queen's arrival, were directed by Sir Charles Long, but the arrangements in Westminster Hall and the Abbey were by long tradition the responsibility of the Office of Works.[4] Westminster Hall fell in Soane's department, but he declared that he would 'sink' under the 'frightful responsibility of the task', though he did not expect to be taken at his word.[5] Stephenson, however, entrusted the duty to Browne, the assistant Surveyor General, and Hiort, the Chief Examiner.[6] The law courts in the Hall were taken down, a wooden flooring laid, and two tiers of galleries erected on either side, supported on iron pillars with Gothic capitals cast by Moorman.[7] The traditional triumphal arch erected immediately inside the north entrance was a Gothic design by Hiort: an ogee arch flanked by thirty foot high turrets, each decorated with a niche containing the figure of a king;[8] the whole painted by T. Greenwood, Latilla (who had designed the Temple of Concord for the Jubilee Fête) and Phipps of the Office of Works. The archway was filled by a pair of massive folding doors, painted in imitation of Gothic panels, 'constructed in the manner of flood gates, . . . calculated to resist any ordinary pressure'.[9] For these works, a 1500 foot long platform, 24 feet wide, from Hall to Abbey, carpeted and with an awning, 23 temporary kitchens, of wood and brick lined with tiles, in Cotton Garden, and

---

[1] See p. 377.   [2] See p. 319.
[3] The coronation was recorded in Sir George Nayler's magnificent volume, *The Coronation of . . . George the Fourth* (1824) which realised Lord Colchester's hope that a 'suitable memorial' like Sandford's *Coronation of James II* might be published (P.R.O. 30/9/12, f. 5, 22 June 1820).
[4] Works 1/10, pp. 67-8, 115, 121, 123, 126-33, 147-9, 151-7, 161, 170, 177-9, 182, 185, 439-41, 444-5, 447-8, 455, 468, 470-4, 477, 503, 505; 4/24, pp. 192, 197, 204, 210-15, 216 (25 May 1820, ten plans, sections etc., of arrangements for the coronation of George III bought from Lt. Couse, R.A., the property of his grandfather, Kenton Couse, clerk of works at that coronation), 220, 223, 229, 239, 245; 4/25, pp. 38, 42, 48, 51-2.
[5] Soane Museum corresp. 2, xii, G. 2, f. 11 (20 July), 13 (21 July), 14 (23 July 1821).
[6] Works 4/24, p. 223. Crocker was clerk of works for the Hall and Davis for the Abbey; Phipps was to make drawings and measure the platform. All works were executed by Copeland.
[7] A drawing for the galleries by Adam Lee is in R.I.B.A. Drawings Collection J. 7/34 (5).
[8] Hiort's original design (Works 36/68/3) shows figures of knights in armour in the niches, but a 'faithful representation' of the triumphal arch in *Gent's. Mag.* 1821 (ii), p. 109 shows two crowned kings.
[9] Works 1/10, p. 435; Works 36/68, 'Book of the Coronation of George IV', containing plans, elevations and sections of Westminster Abbey and Hall as prepared for the ceremonies.

Fig. 29. Westminster Hall as arranged for the Coronation of George IV in 1821: from an engraving in the *Gentleman's Magazine* for 1821.

the fitting up of the Abbey, the Office of Works paid £52,095.[1] The increase over the £9430 of George III's coronation was due in part to the increased price of labour and materials, calculated by the Office at 276 per cent.[2]

After the extravagance of George IV, the coronation of William IV and Queen Adelaide marked a new era of retrenchment: the proceedings in the Hall were omitted, never to be revived; very little time was allowed for preparations; and the Works expenditure was reduced to £12,086.[3] Though for Queen Victoria's crowning the precedent of William IV was followed, the Board's expenditure was more than twice as great.[4] The Queen's wedding, at the Chapel Royal, St. James's Palace, was also conducted with considerable splendour.[5]

As a rule, however, royal marriages were not occasions for lavish expenditure. When the Prince of Wales was unhappily married in the Chapel Royal, St. James's, in April 1795, the total cost of alterations and fittings was in the region of £1500.[6] But the marriage of the Princess Royal to His Serene Highness the Prince of Wurtemburg two years later was rather less expensive.[7] Public processions of course required a higher level of organisation. The practice of state processions to St. Paul's Cathedral on occasions of national thanksgiving had been instituted during Queen Anne's reign and was revived under George III. When His Majesty gave thanks for his recovery in April 1789 there was a good deal of uncertainty as to procedure, and the ledgers had to be combed for precedents dating back to 1702, 1706 and 1713. In the end Chambers was responsible for the arrangements in conjunction with the Surveyor to the Dean and Chapter, Robert Mylne, and the Lord Chamberlain. In particular, the Office of Works was responsible for scaffolding inside the church and all along the route between St. James's and Temple Bar.[8] Similar arrangements were observed for the wartime thanksgiving processions in December 1797[9] and July 1814.[10]

The arrangements for funerals were rather more complicated, although here again precedents tended to be perpetuated from one occasion to the next. Royal funerals were not necessarily state occasions. The Office of Works accounts for the Duke of Cumberland's funeral at Westminster Abbey in September 1790 show expenditure totalling £672 3s. 3¾d. Samuel Wyatt held the carpentry contract,

---

[1] Works 21/14 and 21/15/1; 21/37/6; 36/1; *Parl. Pap.* 1837-8 (350) xxxvi; the total included the cost of illuminations in the Parks (Works 1/11, p. 32). There is a plan of the buildings erected in Cotton Garden by Edward Crocker in R.I.B.A. Drawings Collection J. 7/32.

[2] Works 1/10, p. 68 (4 April 1820).

[3] Works 21/15/2-45 and 21/16; *Parl. Pap.* 1837-8 (350) xxxvi. The expenses of works in the Abbey only for George IV's coronation are stated as £10,395 2s. 2d. (Works 1/18, pp. 462-4).

[4] Works 2/2, p. 293 states the cost as £31,938; but the Commissioners of Woods account (fitting up the Abbey, etc.) is given in *Parl. Pap.* 1839 (441) xxx as £30,213 2s. 10d., and £804 16s. 6d. for illuminating public buildings. The total expenses of Queen Victoria's coronation are there given as £69,421 1s. 10d., which compares with £43,159 11s. 6d. for William IV's and £243,390 6s. 2d. for George IV's (*Parl. Pap.* 1837-8 (350) xxxvi; see also Works 21/17). [5] Works 21/12/1. See p. 370 above.

[6] Works 4/18, f. 214, 16 December 1796; L.C. 1/39, 24 December 1794; Works 3/3, 24 December 1794; Works 5/85. For ceremonial details cf. *Gent's Mag.* 1795 pt. i, pp. 429-31, 475.

[7] Works 4/18, f. 242, 30 June 1797; Works 3/3, f. 78, June 1797; *Gent's Mag.* 1797 pt. i, p. 434.

[8] Works 3/3, ff. 29-30, 5-9 April 1789; Works 6/21, f. 153, 8 April and f. 162, 17 July 1789; T. 29/60, f. 346, 7 May and f. 482, 17 July 1789; *Gent's. Mag.* 1789 pt. i, pp. 367-70, 459.

[9] Works 4/18, ff. 264-6, 269-70, November–December 1797; *Gent's. Mag.* 1797 pt. ii, pp. 1057, 1059, 1065.

[10] L.C. 1/6, f. 359, 15 June, 4 August 1814, 4 September 1815; T. 29/129, f. 596, 14 June 1814; *Gent's. Mag.* 1814 pt. i, pp. 80, 87, 679.

including a 'machine to lower the corps' and Gideon Dare supplied black shields, lanterns and candlesticks.[1] But the Duke of Gloucester, Princess Amelia, the Duchess of Brunswick, Princess Charlotte and Queen Charlotte were all 'privately interred' at Windsor in 1805, 1810, 1813, 1817 and 1818, respectively. On each of these occasions all the arrangements, from crape hatbands to sable horses, were organised by the Lord Chamberlain's Office; carpentry was dealt with by the Office of Works; and tapers, candles and flambeaus were supplied by the Board of Green Cloth.[2] On quite a different scale were the state funerals of Lord Nelson and William Pitt in January and February 1806. Nelson's 'transcendant and heroic services' were rewarded by a state funeral which surpassed even that provided for the Earl of Chatham. The lying in state at Greenwich, the aquatic journey up the Thames in a royal barge, the exotic funeral car's solemn procession, the interment at St. Paul's, the transference of Wolsey's sarcophagus from Windsor, in all these arrangements the Office of Works functioned smoothly under the Lord Chamberlain's direction. The total cost of 'this mournful occasion' was £13,796 14s. 3d., of which £5260 14s. 9d. was debited to the Office of Works, Samuel Wyatt holding the carpentry contract. The Board of Green Cloth supplied 850 lbs. of candles. The Grand Funeral Car was designed 'in imitation of the hull of the Victory', hung round with allegorical devices and wreaths. The coffin, made of wood from the ship *L'Orient*, was supplied not by the Office of Works but by Messrs. Chettenden, France, Holmes and Bidwell, with decorative motifs by Ackermann. 'Within the memory of any man living', wrote one commentator, 'there has not been anything of the kind so transcendently beautiful and splendid'.[3] By comparison, Pitt's funeral was less dramatic.[4] The Office of Works spent no more than £850 5s. 9d. on the burial of 'that Illustrious and Incorruptible Patriot', although the Lord Chamberlain's Office spent a great deal more.[5] This time the interment took place in Westminster Abbey, and the arrangements followed the precedent of Chatham's funeral rather than Nelson's. Nevertheless two state funerals of exceptional importance within a matter of weeks must have placed a considerable strain upon the administration of the Office of Works.

The death of George III was the next major event of the kind. When his body lay in state in the King's Audience Chamber at Windsor Castle in February 1820, thirty thousand persons are estimated to have filed past; for his funeral St. George's Chapel was 'decorated in a style of splendour unexampled on any previous occasion'.[6] Only a few days later he was followed to the grave by his fourth son, the Duke of Kent, whose coffin, 'one of the largest which has been made for any of the Royal Family', was 7 ft. 5½ ins. in length, 'weighing altogether upwards of a ton'.[7] The

[1] Works 5/79 (1790); Works 21/4, f. 16, 19 September 1790; *Gent's. Mag.* 1790 pt. ii, pp. 856–7, 950–51.
[2] L.C. 2/38 (1); L.C. 2/36, ff. 62 *et seq.*; L.C. 2/41 (1–2); L.C. 2/36 ff. 128–32; Works 21/5/5; *Gent's. Mag.* 1805 pt. ii, pp. 869–71, 1810 pt. ii, pp. 486–8, 1817 pt. ii, pp. 449–54.
[3] For full details, accounts, press cuttings, illustrations, etc., cf. Works 4/19; L.C. 2/37; Works 6/24, ff. 20–23; L.C. 2/40; L.C. 2/38 (2); *Gent's. Mag.* 1806 pt. i, pp. 65–72. Wyatt's designs for Nelson's tomb were rejected by the Treasury in favour of Wolsey's sarcophagus from Windsor. The preparation of the vault was supervised by Mylne as surveyor to the Cathedral (Works 6/20, f. 77, 1 March 1806; Works 4/21, 3 June 1814; T. 29/91, f. 389, 13 August 1807; T. 29/93, f. 266, 2 February 1808; T. 29/122, f. 526, 6 April 1813).
[4] For comparisons between the funerals of the Duke of Albemarle (1670), the Duke of Marlborough (1722), Nelson and Pitt cf. L.C. 2/40, f. 128 *et seq.*
[5] L.C. 2/38 (2); L.C. 2/39; L.C. 2/40; *Gent's. Mag.* 1806 pt. i, pp. 264–5.
[6] *Gent's. Mag.* 1820, pt. i, pp. 172–6.   [7] *Ibid.* p. 177.

occasion was taken to transfer the coffins of the infant princes Alfred and Octavius from Westminster Abbey to rest with those of their parents. The entire proceedings cost the Office of Works £3488.[1]

When the Duke of York died in January 1827 he lay in state at St. James's Palace, where black cloth was 'so fitted up at the top as to resemble a tent, in allusion to [his] military character'. The King ordered a 'public and magnificent funeral'; but the proceedings were mismanaged, the spectacle 'by no means imposing', and the intense cold—for the interment, as was usual, took place in the late evening—was said to be the cause of much illness, some of it fatal, among the spectators.[2] The cost to the Office of Works was £1380.[3] George IV departed from the stage with much greater magnificence at an expense of £4941.[4] His lead-covered coffin enclosed in a wooden case with silver-gilt ornaments lay in state in the Great Drawing Room at Windsor, with the crowns of Great Britain and Hanover upon it, beneath banners held by gentlemen-pensioners, watched over by a hierarchy of members of the Household. On 15 July 1830 it glided along an inclined platform to the Chapel, where Greville thought the funeral was 'very well managed, and a fine sight'.[5] That of William IV was characteristically cheaper at £2990.[6] His eccentric brother, the Duke of Sussex, set a new fashion by selecting a public cemetery, Kensal Green, for his burial in 1843.[7] He was followed there by his sister Sophia five years later.[8]

---

[1] Works 1/10, pp. 29–31; 1/18, pp. 232–3; 4/24, pp. 113, 116, 119, 123, 125, 129.

[2] Greville, *Diary*, i, p. 167 (12 February 1827): '. . . the Bishop of Lincoln has died of the effects of it; Canning has been dangerously ill, . . . and the Dukes of Wellington and Montrose were both very seriously unwell for some days after'.

[3] Works 1/18, pp. 232–3; 4/28, p. 154; *Gent's. Mag.* 1827, pt. i. pp. 77–80.

[4] Works 1/18, pp. 232–3.

[5] Works 21/5/6; 4/30, pp. 241, 251, 253; *Gent's. Mag.* 1830, pt. ii, pp. 82–6; Greville, *Diary*, ii, p. 4 (18 July 1830); *Journal of Mrs. Arbuthnot*, ed. F. Bamford and Duke of Wellington ii (1950), pp. 370–1.

[6] Works 1/22, p. 340.

[7] R. Fulford, *Royal Dukes* (1933), p. 283. The Duke of Sussex doubtless made this arrangement so that he could be buried with his morganatic wife, the Duchess of Inverness. See also Works 21/5/10.

[8] D. M. Stuart, *The Daughters of George III* (1939), p. 320 (illustration opp. p. 318); Works 1/33, pp. 289, 308, 344, 409; 2/6, pp. 411–2, 446. The monument was erected at Queen Victoria's own cost. Other royal funerals, 1834–51, include Duke of Gloucester (Works 21/5/7), Princesses Augusta (21/5/9) and Sophia Matilda (21/5/11), the Duke of Cambridge (21/5/12) and Queen Adelaide (21/5/13).

VIII. THE KING'S PRIVATE ROADS

BY 1782 few of the King's private roads survived, and those that did were no longer private. Writing to the Lord Chamberlain in 1783 Chambers commented on their 'very bad condition from the great quantity of Carriages which either have a right, or are indiscriminately permitted to pass upon them'. Hampton Court Road was 'entirely open to the public'. So was Richmond Road. 'And though that from Pimlico to Fulham Bridge has barrs, and originally was confined to those alone who had Tickets, yet now, so much has been built upon the sides of the road, and so many Avenues now open to it, that it is impossible it should ever be private again'.[1] Logically enough, Chambers suggested that the three roads should become public in theory as well as in practice, thus relieving the Civil List of the cost of maintenance. James Wyatt made the same point in 1811,[2] as did Yenn in 1813.[3] But the problem remained unsolved until 1829–30.[4] In 1815 the main issue was avoided by transferring responsibility for the King's private roads from the Office of Works to the Department of Woods and Forests.[5] Not until fifteen years later was the financial burden of maintenance placed squarely upon the ratepayers of neighbouring parishes.[6]

Of the three roads, those at Hampton Court and Richmond generally proved the most expensive. But the King's Road from Pimlico to Fulham was always by far the most troublesome. The Hampton Court Road ran from Hampton Wick, across Hampton Court Green, almost as far as Hampton. For administrative purposes it was held to include the road from Teddington across Bushy Park. The Richmond Road ran from Kew Bridge to Richmond and was managed in conjunction with the road across Kew Green and the footpath parallel to the towing path from Kew Palace to Richmond. The Fulham Road, Disraeli's 'long, miscellaneous, well-watered King's Road',[7] formed a royal processional route roughly four miles long from Buckingham House to Kew, via Pimlico, Chelsea and Fulham. The road was punctuated by a series of stops and obstacles with picturesque names: the Five Fields (now Eaton Square); Great Bloody Field (now Sloane Square); the crossing of the Westbourne, known as Bloody Bridge; and six gate-lodges at Pimlico, Fighting Cocks, Church Lane, World's End, Sandy End and Fulham.[8] Administratively, this road

---

[1] Works 6/20, f. 122, 23 May 1783.   [2] Works 6/25, f. 128, 15 April 1811.
[3] Works 4/21, 19 March 1813; 'Inquiry into . . . the Office of Works', *Parl. Pap.* 1812–13, v, p. 453.
[4] *Middlesex and Hertfordshire Notes and Queries* i (1896), p. 195.
[5] Works 4/21, 20 June 1815; Works 6/27, f. 271, 20 June 1815.
[6] *British Almanac and Companion* 1831, p. 226.
[7] Benjamin Disraeli, *Lothair* i (1870), p. 264.
[8] *Victoria County History, Middlesex* ii (1911), pp. 319–20, n. 5. Compare surveys made in 1720 (B.M. Maps 3495 (134), photostat) and 1824 (MR 1519), with *Cary's Survey . . . Ten Miles Round Hampton Court* (1786). For gates and gatekeepers cf. Works 6/27, f. 275, 28 June 1815. For the environs of the King's Road, cf. T. Faulkner *Chelsea*, 2 vols. (1829), *passim*.

was surrounded by a good deal of confusion stemming from the lax enforcement of regulations regarding traffic and house-building.

Soon after taking office in 1782 Chambers discovered that gatekeepers on the Fulham Road were in the habit of selling passes for a guinea apiece: 'an abuse of considerable standing . . . a disgraceful practice, expressly contrary to His Majesty's instructions'.[1] This custom seems to have been put down, and attempts were repeatedly made to limit wheeled traffic to the carriages of gentlemen ticket-holders. But as houses, shops and public buildings encroached upon the King's Road, so the quantity of commercial traffic increased. In 1806 Henry Holland sent in a complaint about the 'great annoyance' caused by carts, pigs and horses belonging to local residents.[2] In 1807 Yenn complained of 'stage coaches from Putney and Fulham as well as Hackney coaches . . . [claiming] the privilege of coming along . . . to take up and set down passengers'.[3] In 1813 he told Wyatt that because of building-development and 'the number of avenues leading to and from the Road', 'Carriages, Carts, Drays, Stage Coaches, and every other description of horses etc. have egress and regress from one end of the road to the other'.[4] And in 1814 Craig reported the presence of 'Hackney and Stage coaches, errand and other carts'.[5] Gate lodges had been set up to guard each cross-road, at the intersection of royal and public ways; and these barricades were frequently the scene of angry scuffles between traveller and gatekeeper. In 1803 a stage coach 'was driven by the obstinacy of the coachman, through the barway at Sandy End', smashing posts, bar and gate-lodge in the process.[6] Five years later a local surgeon accused one of the gatekeepers of 'drunkenness combined with base ingratitude', for first accepting a bribe and then refusing to admit the petitioner's hackney carriage.[7] 1814 saw a lengthy dispute between two neighbouring landowners who alternately planted and uprooted a series of posts or bollards, using 'powerful destructive machinery . . . a pile driver or battering ram'.[8] And in 1815 'persons forcing their way through the Gates . . . with carts and other improper carriages' caused at least one gatekeeper, 'the widow Seymour, who keeps the White Styles bar', to retire to bed with a broken wrist.[9]

The only major change in the administration of Fulham Road between 1782 and 1815 related to the area known as the Five Fields, that is the stretch between Grosvenor Place and Sloane Square, the future Eaton Square. The presence of a section of the King's Private Road was a serious obstacle to the redevelopment of this area as a court suburb centred on Buckingham House. Earl Grosvenor therefore proposed in 1810 to circumvent this difficulty by laying out, at his own expense, a new road (Grosvenor Street West) parallel to, and ultimately replacing, the King's Private Road between the gatelodges at Pimlico and Bloody Bridge.[10] Yenn, Wyatt, Craig

    [1] Works 1/5, f. 55, 12 April 1783: letters to Lord Stormont, the Bishops of Winchester and London, Lord Hopetoun, Lord Althorp and Mr. Gibbon.   [2] Works 4/19, 31 January 1806.
    [3] Crest 2/548, 27 November 1807. Permission was given in 1806 for the Exeter and Poole mail coaches to use the King's Road because of 'the intolerable state of the road betwixt Hounslow and London' (Works 4/19, 12 January 1806; Works 6/24, f. 25, 14 December 1805; T. 29/85, f. 607, 20 December 1805).
    [4] Works 6/27, f. 58, 19 March 1813.   [5] Works 6/26, f. 139, 20 May 1814.
    [6] Works 4/19, 8 July 1803.   [7] Works 6/24, f. 185, 12 May 1808.
    [8] Works 6/27, ff. 153–4, 20 May 1814; Works 4/21, 20 May, 8 July 1814, 16 March 1815.
    [9] Works 6/26, f. 194, 16 March and f. 206, 4 April 1815.
    [10] Plan dated 13 July 1810, Liverpool Papers clxxxix (1806–12), B.M. Add. MS. 38378, f. 102.

and Nash were all asked their opinion in turn. Since the King's Road was already public in all but name few objections were raised, apart from the question of compensation for the Pimlico gatekeeper.[1] But no immediate decision as to the opening of the King's Road could be taken during George III's indisposition. So Nash suggested a sensible compromise which did much to determine the eventual character of Eaton Square as laid out by Thomas Cundy and T. and L. Cubitt during the later 1820s.[2] Grosvenor needed the old road 'for the purpose of another street out of Grosvenor Place, North of the King's Private Road, called Chester Street now begun'. Therefore the old stretch of road 'should be made exactly straight in the manner of an avenue in the middle space' between the proposed new road and Chester Street. 'And . . . a spot of ground twenty feet wide [should] be appropriated by Lord Grosvenor on each side of the King's Private Road for a row of trees to be planted, the intermediate spaces being filled up with plantation. Besides the good effect of such an avenue the plantation on each side would serve to shut out the backs of the houses of Lord Grosvenor's streets and the plantation would be a pleasing object from the back rooms of those houses'.[3] A survey of 1824 shows that the new 'parkway' had already been laid out and that the privacy of the King's Road had thus been abridged still further.[4] In this way, it was Nash's solution to the problem of the King's Private Road which supplied a basis for the axial layout of Eaton Square and struck the keynote for the future development of Belgravia.

[1] Liverpool Papers lvii (1811), B.M. Add. MS. 38246, f. 108, 15 April and f. 113, 19 April 1811.
[2] Sir John Summerson, *Georgian London* (1962 ed.), p. 195; Colvin, *Dictionary*, p. 160.
[3] Liverpool Papers lvii (1811) B.M. Add. MS. 38246 f. 256, 5 September and f. 327, 27 November 1811.
[4] MR 1519.

Appendix A

EXPENDITURE ON ROYAL PALACES AND PUBLIC BUILDINGS, 1783—1814

This table is based upon Office of Works account books, Works 5/72–103 (1783–1814), and the sums involved have been calculated to the nearest £100. Only those buildings for which the department was habitually responsible under the Civil Establishment Act 1782 are included, and no note is taken of payments deriving from extraordinary sources, such as the Privy Purse, the Duchy of Cornwall and special parliamentary grants. Contemporary distinctions between 'Ordinary' works (running repairs) and 'Extra' works (alterations and additions) have been abandoned. Simplifying the figures in this way has inevitably produced occasional distortions: bills for 'Extra' works were sometimes allowed to accumulate for several years before making their appearance in the final accounts. The figure given here for any one year therefore comprises the cost of running repairs during the twelve months ending 5 January of the following year, plus the cost of all additional work for which bills were settled during that particular year. Administrative expenses are not included. Nor are departmental salaries and allowances. These omissions, as well as minor variations in accounting and chronology, help to explain the imprecision of the totals and the discrepancies between this table and that on p. 94.

	1783	1784	1785	1786	1787	1788	1789	1790
Carlton House	—	—	—	—	—	—	—	—
Greenwich	£200	200	200	200	200	100	200	100
Hampton Court	£1800	1400	1600	1500	2200	2300	1200	2000
Kensington	£1000	1400	1000	1500	1800	700	400	900
Kew	£1900	1500	2400	1000	2000	1100	3000	1100
The King's Mews	£800	1700	1000	900	1100	900	600	1100
The King's Roads	£1400	200	400	300	300	400	300	600
Newmarket	£100	200	100	200	100	100	200	100
Buckingham House	£400	400	400	1300	600	600	1300	700
Richmond	£500	500	500	500	400	500	500	500
St. James's	£1800	2000	1800	2100	2100	1300	1700	2100
The Tower	£400	600	600	700	500	400	700	700
Westminster	£1100	300	800	1600	900	3700	3000	1800
Whitehall	£2100	1200	1900	2000	1600	1400	1900	1800
Winchester	£100	100	—	100	100	100	100	100
Windsor	£2200	2100	2200	1800	1300	1700	1400	3700
TOTAL	£15,800	13,800	14,900	15,700	16,300	15,200	16,400	17,300

	1791	*1792*	*1793*	*1794*	*1795*	*1796*	*1797*
Carlton House	—	—	—	—	—	100	1500
Greenwich	£100	100	100	100	100	700	200
Hampton Court	£1300	3700	2000	3800	3400	3700	2400
Kensington	£900	1900	1600	1300	1600	2000	2600
Kew	£1700	2800	2200	1800	2800	2500	1900
The King's Mews	£600	1700	900	1200	1500	1500	1500
The King's Roads	£500	500	700	800	800	900	700
Newmarket	£100	200	100	100	200	—	400
Buckingham House	£900	3000	1700	1000	1200	700	1800
Richmond	£700	700	700	800	600	600	500
St. James's	£2800	2300	5200	4800	2600	6100	2500
The Tower	£400	400	300	400	3800	2100	2100
Westminster	£1100	1600	5100	1500	3300	2400	2700
Whitehall	£2300	3000	4500	2500	3100	5300	2600
Winchester		200	100	—	—	—	—
Windsor	£2600	4100	2000	2600	3300	3300	3600
TOTAL	£16,000	26,200	26,800	22,600	28,300	31,900	27,000

	1798	*1799*	*1800*	*1801*	*1802*	*1803*	*1804*
Carlton House	£1100	900	1800	2200	1200	1900	2400
Greenwich	£600	200	500	600	700	800	500
Hampton Court	£3400	3400	4100	3200	3000	3000	3100
Kensington	£2300	3200	3400	3000	2100	2200	3600
Kew	£2100	2200	2400	2700	3000	2200	3100
The King's Mews	£2100	2000	2500	2100	2000	1700	2200
The King's Roads	£700	1100	1400	1300	1300	1000	1500
Newmarket	£200	100	400	200	—	900	900
Buckingham House	£1600	2600	2900	3500	6700	2600	2400
Richmond	£400	600	600	500	600	500	800
St. James's	£2300	4900	10,200	7000	3500	6500	4900
The Tower	£2400	2000	1700	1500	1300	1300	1200
Westminster	£1300	2400	1900	5100	1300	4100	2700
Whitehall	£2600	2900	2000	4900	2700	2800	7300
Winchester	—	—	—	—	—	—	—
Windsor	£3000	3600	5000	5000	5000	5900	10,600
TOTAL	£26,100	32,100	40,800	42,800	34,400	35,400	47,200

	1805	1806	1807	1808	1809	1810	1811
Carlton House	£9700	1900	1400	800	1600	2400	1300
Greenwich	£400	300	300	—	—	—	—
Hampton Court	£5100	4500	6100	4200	6200	6600	5900
Kensington	£5200	16,400	10,700	10,700	13,700	5700	4200
Kew	£2100	2300	1800	2100	3500	1500	3400
The King's Mews	£2200	1400	1000	800	2600	1200	900
The King's Roads	£1200	1500	1800	800	1800	1600	600
Newmarket	£400	—	700	1000		300	—
Buckingham House	£6200	4000	2500	1800	2300	2300	2800
Richmond	£400	600	500	500	500	600	500
St. James's	£5800	5300	5100	10,800	7100	5400	8800
The Tower	£1400	1400	1500	1300	1300	1900	1800
Westminster	£5200	3800	4400	1500	4100	2500	2200
Whitehall	£6500	5600	7100	4700	3100	4800	3700
Winchester	—	—	—	—	—	—	—
Windsor	£44,800	31,400	7500	7300	10,400	7200	6500
TOTAL	£96,200	80,400	52,400	48,300	58,200	44,000	42,600

	1812	1813	1814
Carlton House	£2800	3800	11,100
Greenwich	—	—	—
Hampton Court	£6900	6300	4500
Kensington	£4700	2100	4000
Kew	£1600	2800	1700
The King's Mews	£1400	800	900
The King's Roads	£1900	1000	2400
Newmarket	£600	600	1100
Buckingham House	£2300	1300	5600
Richmond	£500	300	300
St. James's	£5500	5600	9400
The Tower	£5100	1000	1300
Westminster	£3400	2800	1900
Whitehall	£36,400	8300	4700
Winchester	—	—	—
Windsor	£6000	4800	9600
TOTAL	£79,100	41,500	58,500

Appendix B

EXPENDITURE ON ROYAL PALACES AND PUBLIC BUILDINGS, 1815—1851

There was generally a delay of about six months, and occasionally considerably longer, before tradesmen were paid by the Office of Works or the Office of Woods and Forests. Expenditures do not, therefore, necessarily relate to the year in which they were incurred. Table II, showing costs incurred annually, reflects the actual incidence of building activity more accurately than do the tables of expenditure.

After the annexation of the Office of Works to that of Woods and Forests the works expenditures cease to be clearly ascertainable in detail as the accounts were not always drawn up under the head of buildings, particularly after 1838/9; and the sums paid to contractors are not distinguished by building or district.

These tables show sums to the nearest hundred pounds. There is an occasional minor difference between the sum of the individual figures and the total given, which is calculated directly from the complete figures.

The form '1833/4' is used solely to indicate the financial year, commencing on 1 April: this was introduced in 1832–33, when the first quarter of 1833 was added to the preceding year.

TABLE I

OFFICE OF WORKS, PAYMENTS AND CHARGES, 1815–1832,
expressed in £ hundreds

Year	Establishment	Civil List Buildings		Grant of Parliament		Woods & Forests	
		Incurred	Paid	Incurred	Paid	Incurred	Paid
1815	92	267	789	82	190	32	
1816	106	325	757	432	195	70	78
1817	104	323	440	404	525	122	138
1818	104	305	388	455	350	98	110
1819	101	360	453	428	442	98	85
1820	104	345	450	410	469	135	92
1821	105	381	431	364	327	49	89
1822	106	392	393	402	351	61	134
1823	111	413	141[1]	464	80[1]	93	32[1]
1824	116	429	747	426	601	154	196
1825	117	426	466	507	392	221	381
1826	116	463	464	327	513	203	338
1827	111	339	585	161	267	306	460
1828	107	325	434	191	209	207	329
1829	102	380	450	200	218	122	191
1830	106	409	586	160	292	74	155
1831	104	—[2]	286	506	406	110	110
1832	25		31		409		76

[1] Payments for 1823 are recorded only to 16 May, when there was a change of cashier; the remaining payments for the year are consolidated with those for 1824 (Works 5/2).

[2] This account was united with the Grant of Parliament account from 1831.

Exchequer Fee Fund		Extra works		Total		Year
Incurred	*Paid*	*Incurred*	*Paid*	*Total*		*Year*
4		5		482	*Incurred*	
	12			991	*Paid*	1815
3		24		960	*Incurred*	
	5		24	1058	*Paid*	1816
4				957	*Incurred*	
	4		5	1112	*Paid*	1817
3		85		1049	*Incurred*	
	3		113[4]	964	*Paid*	1818
4				980	*Incurred*	
	3	25[3]		1008	*Paid*	1819
3		295		1291	*Incurred*	
	4			1014	*Paid*	1820
8		281		1187	*Incurred*	
	6		356	1207	*Paid*	1821
8		114		1084	*Incurred*	
	4		430	1311	*Paid*	1822
4		385		1471	*Incurred*	
	3		108	364	*Paid*	1823
3		1910		3039	*Incurred*	
	6		1244	2795	*Paid*	1824
4		3015		4286	*Incurred*	
	3		1196	2436	*Paid*	1825
5		4948		6060	*Incurred*	
	3		3472	4790	*Paid*	1826
2		4172		5091	*Incurred*	
	4		3044	4360	*Paid*	1827
2		2640		3473	*Incurred*	
	2		2044	3019	*Paid*	1828
2		2797		3602	*Incurred*	
	2		2261	2122	*Paid*	1829
2		1175		1926	*Incurred*	
	2		1326	2361	*Paid*	1830
1		712		1434	*Incurred*	
	2		1023	1827	*Paid*	1831
	1		383	869	*Paid*	1832

[3] This arises from a re-apportioning of labour charges hitherto carried on the Civil List account.
[4] Including £2900 for Stamp Office, a building included under 'Grant of Parliament'.

TABLE II

SUMS INCURRED, BY BUILDINGS AND DISTRICTS, 1815–1831,
expressed in £ hundreds

CIVIL LIST	1815	1816	1817	1818	1819	1820
Carlton House and Stables	20*	33	35	19	26	33
Hampton Court Palace, Gardens and Home Park	23*	78	94	133	124	109
Kensington Palace and Gardens	29*	52	43	33	42	36
Royal Mews (Charing Cross) (Pimlico)	73*	14	15	13	12	12
Queen's (Buckingham) Palace	31	30	36	24	11	13
St. James's Palace (including Clarence House)	24	16	24	15	27	18
Kew Palace and Gardens		16	13	16	14	25
Windsor Castle and Queen's Lodges	24	61	63	37	97	62
GRANT OF PARLIAMENT						
Whitehall	23*	45	41	56	48	41
Westminster	9*	8	19	26	52	149
Houses of Parliament	35	39	45	49	92	70
Speaker's House	10	4	7	6	5	9
Tower of London	5*	14	30	19	9	16
Somerset House	63*	52	55	113	110	27
Mint	—	203	101	12	17	7
British Museum	—	68	45	31	20	17
King's Bench, Fleet and Marshalsea Prisons	7*	17	23	22	33	58
Horse Guards	—	—	—	52	52	42

Source: Works 5/107–111.
* From 5 April only.

1821	1822	1823	1824	1825	1826	1827	1828	1829	1830	1831
35	32	25	37	13	18	4	2	4	3	5
113	60	98	71	81	68	76	67	83	57	69
39	39	48	30	47	23	32	28	69	66	57
22	8	4	3							
				9	7	6	7	10	8	15
18	11	7	8	549	1443	856	1011	1216	334	17
95	172	71	196	119	149	91	78	74	57	43
33	42	59	74	110	99	85	82	44	43	45
27	31	33	387	868	1022	1431	890	835	512	426
43	40	91	67	187	112	24	34	100	115	40
184	72	33	9	13	4	5	12	6	7	16
40	104	205	112	112	225	159	58	41	43	67
8	6	6	33	5	14	4	4	9	4	4
16	16	9	7	18	7	4	4	7	5	5
22	123	41	48	40	38	33	34	25	18	20
21	6	6	10	33	5	4	8	2	1	1
12	18	94	307	549	375	326	159	48	139	61
16	27	17	39	29	22	12	16	12	11	12
44	46	47	58	45	66	33	31	53	33	27

TABLE III

WORKS AND PUBLIC BUILDINGS, SUMS PAID 1832/3–1850/51, expressed in £ hundreds

Year	Ordinary grant of Parliament for works and repairs	Additional works[1]	Total
1832/3	325	2251	2575
1833/4	540	990	1530
1834/5	344	1169	1513
1835/6	492	1651	2143
1836/7	719	766	1485
1837/8	513	984	1497
1838/9	571	1696	2268
1839/40	1124	1122	2246
1840/41	905	1525	2430
1841/2	1006	1579	2585
1842/3	1001	1726	2727
1843/4	1080	1470	2550
1844/5	1035	2025	3060
1845/6	1184	2614	3799
1846/7	1107	3087	4195
1847/8	1345	3365	4710
1848/9	1102	2287	3389
1849/50	974	1549	2524
1850/51	988	1562	2449

Source: L.R.R.O. 2/1–19.   [1] See Table IV for details of principal items.

TABLE IV

EXPENDITURE ON PRINCIPAL WORKS AND BUILDINGS 1832/3–1850/51, ADDITIONAL TO ORDINARY WORKS AND REPAIRS,
expressed in £ hundreds

Appropriation	1832/3	1833/4	1834/5	1835/6	1836/7	1837/8	1838/9	1839/40	1840/41
British Museum	94	14	186	262	165	261	121	241	188
Buckingham Palace	1273	430	357	497	177	103	79	15	1
Ceremonial							332		57
Claremont									33
General Post Office	13	30	13	27	23	32	34	68	150
Government Offices	54	23	33	5	12	2	2	3	1
Houses of Parliament									
(New)				8	15	180	836	651	568
(Temporary)			4	436	109	129	138	82	165
Law Courts and Offices							2	16	2
Marlborough House						88	119	46	50
National Gallery		53	228	306	165	92	27		
Prisons					2				105
Royal Pavilion, Brighton	95	8							
Trafalgar Square and Nelson Column								1	25
Westminster Hall			35	59	51	24			
Whitehall Chapel	8	9			46	67	7		
Windsor Castle[1]	713	423	314²	51					178³

Source: L.R.R.O. 2/1–19.   [1] T. 1/4398. The figures for 1832/3–1835/6 are of charges incurred.
² Includes midsummer quarter of 1835/6.   ³ Works 19/40/2.

Appropriation	1841/2	1842/3	1843/4	1844/5	1845/6	1846/7	1847/8	1848/9	1849/50	1850/51
British Museum	206	349	402	569	373	608	541	435	262	
Buckingham Palace						53	506	312	211	108
Claremont	29	6	68	31	14	21	24			
Embassies		63	92	48	178	153	125	106	67	98
General Post Office	59	37	39	87	125	248	135			
Government Offices	14	2	1	3	140	177	133	21		81
Houses of Parliament										
(New)	899	694	723	801	1453	1461	1248	1257	945	1138
(Temporary)	103	61	34	87	98	182	110	88	38	23
Kew Palm House				1	64	97	124	66	8	
Law Courts and Offices	1			11	23		177	35		
Mint		10	19	20	30	36	4			
New Economic Geology Museum							171			
Prisons	5	5	10	253						
Scotland	55	68	24		35	20	29			
Trafalgar Square and Nelson Column	32	68	48	102	69	31	39	14	19	13
Windsor Castle	171	356								

TABLE V

EXPENSES INCURRED FOR WORKS AND REPAIRS, ON PALACES AND
PUBLIC BUILDINGS, 1832/3–1838/9,
expressed in £ hundreds

Appropriation	*1832/3*	*1833/4*	*1834/5*	*1835/6*	*1836/7*	*1837/8*	*1838/9*
Hampton Court Palace, Gardens and Home Park	47	39	51	47	46	42	55
Kensington Palace and Gardens	42	31	68	77	59	58	44
Kew Palace and Gardens	29	48	25	31	67	38	26
Royal Mews		4	14	9	5	8	5
Buckingham Palace[1]					16	12	68
St. James's Palace	52	27	15	19	97	29	43
Windsor Castle[1]	22	13	25	27	41	69	35
Royal Pavilion, Brighton[1]	24	32	37	24	31	33	20
Whitehall	29	27	20	23	19	34	25
Westminster	15	5	7	12	15	9	8
Houses of Parliament[1]	50	37	38	37	34	51	56
Speaker's House	3	5	3				
Tower	9	10	3	3	4	2	6
Horse Guards	23	20	16	26	20	20	24

Source: L.R.R.O. 24/1–7.
[1] Excluding restoration and rebuilding, for which see Table IV.

TABLE VI

EXPENDITURE ON WORKS AND REPAIRS, FOR ROYAL PALACES, 1838/9–1849/50,

expressed in £ hundreds

	1838/9	1839/40	1840/41	1841/2	1842/3	1843/4	1844/5	1845/6	1846/7	1847/8	1848/9	1849/50
Hampton Court Palace, Gardens and Home Park	55	79	60	91	72	98	110	116	143	93	89	80
Kensington Palace and Gardens	47	33	26	34	38	27	21	24	21	22	7	7
Kew Palace and Gardens	27	35	33	45	40	46	58	54	110	114	57	47
Royal Mews, Pimlico	5	16	10	15	22	12	16	23	14	13	20	11
Buckingham Palace	68	98	100	15	56	24	16	48	51	19	7	8
enlargement											359	134
St. James's Palace	48	36	61	93	53	118	55	54	47	36	26	35
Windsor Castle[1]	35	19	39	43	152	188	53	115	195	114	122	168
Frogmore House					26	25	13	20	7	22	12	7
Royal Pavilion, Brighton	20	16	16	15	21	23	13	15	9	5	5	4

Source: *Parl. Pap.* 1843 (343) xxx, 1851 (374) xxxi.

[1] Excluding stables, etc. new building.

Appendix C

COMPARISON OF CONTRACT PRICES, 1824—1826

Architect: Soane

Trade	Law Courts	Board of Trade, &c.	House of Lords
Daily rate CARPENTER	4s. 9½d.–5s. 8d.	5s.*	4s. 9½d.
Contract	— 10 p.c.	— 10½ p.c.	— 10 p.c. except labour
Daily rate JOINER	5s. 0½d.–5s. 11d.	5s.–5s. 10d.*	5s. 0½d.–5s. 11d.
Contract	— 10 p.c.	— 10½ p.c.	— 10 p.c. except labour
Daily rate BRICKWORK	4s. 3½d.–4s. 9d./4s. 11d.	5s./5s. 3d.*	4s. 9d./4s. 11d.
Per rod, in mortar	£16 6s. 6d.	£14 4s.	£15
Contract	— 7½ p.c.	— 2½ p.c.	— 5 p.c. on measured, — 7½ p.c. on daywork.
Daily rate MASON	4s. 4½d.–5s. 6d.	4s. 8d.–5s. 1¼d.*	5s. 6d.
Portland stone, cu. ft.	3s. 9d.–4s. 6d.	3s. 5d.*	3s. 9d.–4s. 6d.
Contract	—10 p.c.	— 10 p.c.	— 10 p.c.
Daily rate PLASTERER	5s.–5s. 5d./5s. 9d.	5s.–5s. 9d.	5s. 5d.
Contract	— 3½ p.c.	— 3½ p.c.	— 3½ p.c.
Daily rate PLUMBER	5s. 6d.	5s. 3d.	5s. 6d.
Contract	— 10 p.c.	— 8½ p.c.	— 10 p.c.
Daily rate SMITH	4s. 7d.–5s. 3d.	5s.	4s. 7d.–5s. 6d.
Contract	— 10 p.c.	— 7½ p.c.	— 10 p.c.
FOUNDER Castings, per ton.	£15		

Notes: Daily rate: the price paid to contractors for craftsmen's labour for 'day-work'. This was generally more than the rate paid by the contractor to the craftsman. The men obtained pay increases in 1825, and the employers were allowed a higher rate in consequence: this is reflected in the range of rates, e.g. 5s. 2d.— 5s. 8d. (see p. 128 above). The difference (usually between 2d. and 4d.) between winter and summer rates is indicated by the convention '4s. 9d./4s. 11d.'

Smirke

Trade	British Museum	General Post Office	Custom House
Daily rate CARPENTER	4s. 11d./5s. 2d.*	4s. 11d.*	4s. 11d.
Contract	−13½ p.c.	−16¾ p.c.	
Daily rate JOINER	5s. 2d.*–5s. 9½d.*	4s. 11d.*	
Contract	−13½ p.c.	−16¾ p.c.	
Daily rate BRICKWORK	5s.*/5s. 2d.*	4s. 9d.*/5s.*	4s. 9d./4s. 11d.
Per rod, in mortar	£14 1s.	£13 15s.	£19 1s.
Contract	−7½ p.c.	−3½ p.c.	
Daily rate MASON	5s. 6d.*	4s. 11½d.*	5s.
Portland stone, cu. ft.	4s. 5d.–4s. 10d.	3s. 3½d.*	
Contract		−20 p.c.	
Daily rate PLASTERER	5s. 5d./5s. 9d.		
Contract			
Daily rate PLUMBER	5s. 6d.	5s. 6d.	5s. 6d.
Contract			
Daily rate SMITH	5s. 3d.		5s. 3d.
Contract			
FOUNDER			
Castings, per ton.	£12	£11–£17 10s.	

Contract rate: this is the percentage below the Office of Works schedule of prices (under constant review, see pp. 127–9) at which contractors were to be paid for all except specified items. In some agreements, most items were charged at special prices, so that comparison between contracts is very difficult. The contract percentages given here were subject to the standard deduction of two and a half per cent more.

* Special rate, not subject to deductions.

Comparison of Contract prices, 1824–1826, contd.

	Nash		Wyatville
Trade	*Royal Mews, Pimlico*[1]	*Buckingham Palace*	*Windsor Castle*
Daily rate CARPENTER Contract	5s. 2d.–5s. 11d. — 13 p.c. on deal, fir, oak; — 8½ p.c. on wainscot.	5s. 8d. — 7½ p.c.	4s. 11d.–5s. 8d. — 2½ p.c.
Daily rate JOINER Contract	5s. 4d.–5d. 11d. — 13 p.c. or — 8½ p.c.	5s. 11d. — 7½ p.c.	— 2½ p.c.
Daily rate BRICKWORK Per rod, in mortar Contract	4s. 9d./4s. 11d.	4s. 11d. £17 4s. 6d.[2] — 2½ p.c. on measured.	4s. 10d. £17 12s. special prices.
Daily rate MASON Portland stone, cu. ft. Contract	5s.–5s. 6d. [Bath stone, 3s. 9d.]	5s.–5s. 6d. [Bath stone, 3s. 11d.] — 7½ p.c. on measured.	4s. 9d. [Bath stone, 2s. 6d.] special prices.
Daily rate PLASTERER Contract	4s. 8d.–5s. 9d.	5s.–5s. 5d./5s. 9d.	4s. 8d./5s. — 2½ p.c.
Daily rate PLUMBER Contract	5s. 6d.		5s. 6d. — 5 p.c.
Daily rate SMITH Contract	5s. 3d.	5s. 3d.	5s. 3d. — 5 p.c.
FOUNDER Castings, per ton.		£17.	£22.

[1] Although the Mews was erected by contract (in gross) considerable extra works were executed at the rates given here.

[2] During the period 1825–30, the price (after deducting 2½ per cent by contract and the further standard 2½ per cent) varied between £13 8s. 6¼d. and £16 7s. 3¼d. per rod (Works 1/18, p. 516).

Sources: Works 5/125 and 126; *Parl. Pap.* 1824 (120) xvi; Soane Mus. corr. 2, xi, H.

Appendix D

PRINCIPAL OFFICE HOLDERS, 1782—1851

Dates in brackets indicate that the holder of the office was re-appointed to the same post on the re-organisation of the Office of Works in 1782, 1815, 1832 or 1851 as the case may be.

I. THE OFFICE OF WORKS 1782–1815

SURVEYOR GENERAL AND COMPTROLLER

	From			*To*	
Sir William Chambers	10 October	1782	8 March	1796	(died)
James Wyatt	16 March	1796	4 September	1813	(died)

INSPECTOR

John Jones		1782	28 August	1807	(died)

EXAMINING CLERK

Kenton Couse	10 October	1782	10 October	1790	(died)
John Woolfe sr.		1790	14 November	1793	(died)
Charles Alexander Craig	6 December	1793		1814	(retired)

RESIDENT CLERK

Richard Ripley	10 October	1782	22 January	1786	(died)
Charles Alexander Craig	1 February	1786		1793	(promoted)
Edward Crocker II (temporary)		1794			
Robert Furze Brettingham	17 June	1794		1805	(resigned)
John William Hiort	5 September	1805		1814	

FIRST ASSISTANT CLERK

George Horsley[1]	1782	1815	(retired)
John William Hiort[2]	1793	1796	
John Spence jr.[2]	1796	1805	(promoted)
— Leach[2]	1805	1807	
George Russell[2]	1807	(1815)	

SECOND ASSISTANT CLERK

Edward Crocker II	(1782)	1796	(promoted)
John William Hiort	1796	1805	(promoted)
John Spence jr.	1805	1815	

[1] From 1793 insane and on half pay.
[2] On half pay as a substitute for Horsley. Timothy Bligh acted temporarily during Russell's absence on sick leave in 1813–15.

	From		*To*

CLERK OF WORKS AT ST. JAMES'S, WHITEHALL AND WESTMINISTER

John Woolfe sr.		(1782)			1790 (transferred)
John Soane		1791			1793 (resigned)
John Woolfe jr. (temporary)					1794
John Thomas Groves	17 June	1794	24 August		1811 (died)
Charles Bacon	23 October	1811			(1815)

CLERK OF WORKS AT THE QUEEN'S HOUSE, THE MEWS, KENSINGTON AND CARLTON HOUSE

John Yenn	10 October	1782		(1815)

CLERK OF WORKS AT HAMPTON COURT AND BUSHY PARK

William Rice		(1782)	6 May		1789 (died)
Thomas Tildesley	13 May	1789	5 January		1808 (died)
Thomas Rice	12 February	1808	20 March		1810 (died)
Thomas Hardwick	19 May	1810			(1815)

CLERK OF WORKS AT THE TOWER OF LONDON, NEWMARKET, GREENWICH AND WINCHESTER

William Leach	10 October	1782			1790 (transferred)
Robert Browne sr.	26 March	1790	12 June		1796 (died)
Edward Crocker II	5 September	1796			(1815)

CLERK OF WORKS AT RICHMOND AND KEW

Thomas Fulling		(1782)		1790 (died)
Robert Browne jr.	26 March	1790		1815

CLERK OF WORKS AT WINDSOR CASTLE

Thomas Tildesley		(1782)			1789 (transferred)
Robert Browne jr.	13 May	1789			1790 (promoted)
William Leach	26 March	1790	5 April		1805 (dismissed)
William Matthew	1 July	1806			(1815)

LABOURERS IN TRUST

Whitehall and Westminster

Jason Harris		(1782)		1787 (emigrated to Ireland)
John Woolfe jr.	December 1787			1806
Adam Lee	1806			(1815)

St. James's

Thomas Bevan	1782			1799 (suspended)
—— Broadway	1800	19 July		1803 (died)
John Lawrence	1804			1813 (died)
Thomas Frederick Hunt	1813			(1815)

	From	*To*
The Queen's (Buckingham) House		
Richard Wetherill	(1782)	1803 (died)
John Andrews	1803	(1815)
Kensington		
George Marshall	(1782)	1794 (died)
William Rose	1794	1814 (died)
The Mews at Charing Cross		
Charles Alexander Craig	(1782)	1786 (promoted)
Robert Browne jr.	1786	1789 (promoted)
Thomas Clark	1789	1800
Edward Jarman	1800	1815 (retired)
The Tower of London		
Robert Browne jr.	1782	1786 (promoted)
George Meredith	1786	1793 (resigned)
William Rose	1793	1794 (promoted)
Edward Crocker II	1794	1796 (promoted)
Noah Siddons	1796	1800 (resigned)
Abraham Penbethy	1800	9 September 1814 (died)
The Speaker's House and Exchequer Offices, Westminster		
Charles Bacon	1805	1811 (promoted)
Edward Crocker II (temporary)	1811	
Hampton Court		
Mark Banks	(1782)	1800 (died)
William Pell	1800	1806 (died)
William Miles Stone	1806	1815 (dismissed)
Newmarket		
Thomas Kilvington	1782	1804 (died)
William Alexander Arnold	1806	(1815)
Carlton House		
Jeffry Wyatt	1797	1800 (resigned)
Lewis Wyatt	1800	(1815)
Richmond and Kew		
Robert Browne, sr.	(1782)	1790 (promoted)
Thomas Rice	1790	1808 (promoted)
Windsor		
John Kempshead	(1782)	22 September 1790 (died)
Robert Goodworth	1790	12 April 1812
William Child	1812	(1815)

II. THE OFFICE OF WORKS AND PUBLIC BUILDINGS 1814/15–1832

SURVEYOR GENERAL

	From		*To*	
Benjamin Charles Stephenson	November 1814	5 April	1832	

ASSISTANT SURVEYOR AND CASHIER

Robert Browne		1814		1823 (retired)
Henry Hake Seward	2 May	1823		1832

CHIEF EXAMINING CLERK

John William Hiort		1814		1832

DRAWING AND MEASURING CLERK

John Spence		1815	8 June	1825 (died)
John Phipps	June	1825		1832

FIRST ASSISTANT EXAMINING AND MEASURING CLERK

George Russell		(1815)	5 January	1822 (retired)
George Davis	5 January	1822	10 March	1823 (died)
John Phipps	March	1823	June	1825 (promoted)
William Bennett Barker	June	1825		(1832)

SECOND ASSISTANT EXAMINING AND MEASURING CLERK

George Davis	3 June	1815	4 January	1822 (promoted)
John Phipps	5 July	1822	March	1823 (promoted)
William Bennett Barker	5 July	1823	June	1825 (promoted)
Henry Joshua Robinson	5 July	1825		(1832)

FIRST COPYING CLERK

William Leckenby	28 April	1815		1832

SECOND COPYING CLERK

John Oliver French	28 April	1815	18 April	1825 (resigned)
John Mills	1 August	1825	23 September 1829 (died)	
William Madox Wyatt	10 October	1829		1832

CLERKS OF WORKS

WHITEHALL, WESTMINSTER, ST. JAMES'S PALACE AND THE KING'S MEWS

Charles Bacon		(1815)	10 June	1818 (died)
Edward Crocker II	1 July	1818	31 December 1829 (retired)	
Sydney Smirke	5 January	1830	5 April	1832

	From		To	

KENSINGTON, THE PARKS, THE QUEEN'S PALACE (to 1825), CARLTON HOUSE (to 1826) AND THE HORSE GUARDS (from 1819)

Name	From		To	
John Yenn	(1815)		10 October	1819 (retired)
Robert Charles Kidd	10 October	1819	5 January	1829 (retired)
Thomas Frederick Hunt	31 March	1829	4 January	1831 (died)
Joseph Henry Good	13 January	1831	5 April	1832

HAMPTON COURT, BUSHY PARK, RICHMOND, KEW, AND LONGFORD RIVER

Thomas Hardwick	(1815)		16 January	1829 (died)
Lewis Wyatt	26 January	1829	5 April	1832

THE TOWER OF LONDON, THE MINT, SOMERSET HOUSE, ROLLS HOUSE, KING'S BENCH, FLEET AND MARSHALSEA PRISONS, AND GREENWICH

Edward Crocker II	(1815)		30 June	1818 (transferred)
Lewis Wyatt	8 July	1818	25 January	1829 (transferred)
Sydney Smirke	16 February	1829	4 January	1830 (transferred)
Joseph Henry Good	5 January	1830	12 January	1831 (transferred)
Charles Heathcote Tatham	9 March	1831	5 April	1832

WINDSOR

William Matthew	(1815)		5 April	1832 (died 1833)

LABOURERS IN TRUST

WHITEHALL, ETC. DISTRICT

Houses of Parliament and Westminster

Adam Lee	(1815)		1832	

Whitehall and the King's Mews

Edward Crocker III	1815	29 October	1827 (resigned)
Charles Molinix	1827		1832

St. James's Palace

Thomas Frederick Hunt	(1815)	March	1829 (promoted)

(Charge then transferred to Labourer in Trust at Carlton House)

KENSINGTON, ETC. DISTRICT

Kensington

James Peacock (acting)		1815	5 July	1816
William Alexander Arnold	July	1816		?1819
James Peacock		?1819		1832

The Parks

James Peacock (acting)	July	1816	1819

The Queen's Palace (to 1825) and *Royal Mews, Pimlico* (from 1824)

John Andrews	(1815)	7 July	1818 (transferred)
John Hudson	July	1818	1832

	From		To	
Carlton House (with *St. James's Palace* from 1829)				
Lewis Wyatt		(1815) 7 July	1818 (promoted)	
John Andrews	July	1818 15 March	1820 (died)	
Joseph Morris		1820	1832	

HAMPTON COURT, ETC. DISTRICT

Hampton Court

George Slade	4 May	1815	1832

Kew and Richmond

Robert Charles Kidd		1815 21 October	1819 (promoted)
William Alexander Arnold		?1819 5 May	1829 (resigned)
John Matthew	22 May	1829	1832

EASTERN DISTRICT

Somerset House

William Bennett Barker	22 November 1815	June	1823 (promoted)
Richard Whibley	August	1823	1832

The Tower of London and *the Mint* (from 1818)

William Lush	5 April 1815 23 May	1818 (died)
Thomas Marsh	6 July 1818	1825 (absconded)
John Nixon (acting)		
John Busher	16 September 1825	1832

The Mint

Thomas Marsh	1815 25 May	1818
		(combined with the Tower)

British Museum

Lewis Joseph Phillips	29 September 1815	1825
Thomas Pulman	19 October 1825	1832

WINDSOR

William Child		(1815) 11 November	1817 (died)
William Collier	3 January	1818 25 January	1827 (died)
William Evans	30 November 1827		1832

NEWMARKET

William Alexander Arnold	(1815) 25 April	1819 (discontinued)

GENERAL POST OFFICE

John Fortune[1]	(1832)

ROYAL PAVILION, BRIGHTON

John Tyrell	1830[2]	(1832)

[1] At first employed during the rebuilding of the G.P.O. under Smirke.
[2] The Royal Pavilion was placed under the Office of Works by William IV after his accession.

III. THE OFFICE OF WOODS, FORESTS, LAND REVENUES, WORKS AND PUBLIC BUILDINGS, 1832–1851

CHIEF COMMISSIONER

	Appointed
Viscount Duncannon	22 February 1832
Sir John Cam Hobhouse	30 July 1834
Lord Granville Somerset	31 December 1834
Viscount Duncannon	7 May 1835
Earl of Lincoln	25 September 1841
Viscount Canning	10 March 1846
Viscount Morpeth (later Earl of Carlisle)	13 July 1846
Lord Seymour	15 April 1850

SECOND COMMISSIONER

	From		*To*
William Dacres Adams	22 February 1832	August	1834 (retired)
Sir B. C. Stephenson	23 August 1834	10 June	1839 (died)
Alexander Milne	18 June 1839	July	1850 (retired)
Hon. Charles Alexander Gore	28 August 1850		1851

THIRD COMMISSIONER

Sir B. C. Stephenson	22 February 1832	August	1834 (promoted)
Alexander Milne	23 August 1834	June	1839 (promoted)
Hon. Charles Alexander Gore	18 June 1839	August	1850 (promoted)
Thomas Francis Kennedy	28 August 1850		1851

DEPARTMENT OF WORKS

SURVEYOR OF WORKS AND BUILDINGS

Henry Hake Seward	1832	July	1844 (retired)
William Southcote Inman	1844		(1851)

ITINERANT SURVEYOR OF WOODS AND WORKS

Edward Jesse	1832	May	1851 (retired)
William Starie	June 1851		(1851)

ASSISTANT SURVEYOR OF WORKS AND BUILDINGS

John Phipps	1832	(1851)

SECRETARY TO THE BOARD

Alexander Milne	1832	August	1834 (promoted)

(Post abolished 1834)

SECRETARY TO THE CHIEF COMMISSIONER

Trenham Walshman Philipps	August 1834		(1851)

(Private Secretary to the Chief
Commissioner, 1827, Clerk to the Board
and Secretary to the Chief Commissioner
1834, Official Secretary to the Chief
Commissioner, 1845).

	From	*To*

MEASURING CLERK

William Bennett Barker (1832) (1851)

CLERK OF THE FURNITURE

James Robinson Sanders Cox (1832) (1851)

EXAMINING CLERK

Henry Joshua Robinson (1832) April 1843 (promoted
Accountant of Office of Woods etc.)

Joseph Bedder April 1843 (1851)
('Chief Examiner' from 1847)

CLERKS OF THE WORKS
LONDON

WHITEHALL (including Horse Guards)*
  Adam Lee 1832 28 February 1841 (retired)
  W. J. Browne 1841 May 1851 (transferred)

WESTMINSTER, SOMERSET HOUSE*
  Richard Whibley 1832 1840 (transferred)
  William J. Browne 8 August 1840 1841 (transferred)
  James Fincham April 1841 (1851)

ST. JAMES'S, PIMLICO AND CARLTON MEWS, NATIONAL GALLERY, with
KENSINGTON AND HYDE PARK 1832–3
  Joseph Morris 1832 (1851)

KENSINGTON AND HYDE PARK, with BUCKINGHAM PALACE from 1838
  John Matthew 1 January 1834 June 1837 (resigned)
  Peter Hogg August 1837 (1851)

BRITISH MUSEUM, TOWER, MINT, KING'S BENCH, MARSHALSEA AND
FLEET PRISONS, NATIONAL DEBT OFFICE, INSOLVENT DEBTORS'
COURT, GREENWICH
  Thomas Pulman 1832 (1851)

GENERAL POST OFFICE
  John Fortune (1832) (1851)

CHELSEA HOSPITAL†
  Richard Hall (1807) 1845
  William Burnett 26 January 1846 ? May 1851 (?resigned)
  W. J. Browne 26 May 1851 (1851)

* Some re-allocation of buildings between the Whitehall and Westminster Districts took place in September 1840.
† Placed under Office of Woods and Works in 1837.

<table>
<tr><td></td><td colspan="2">*From*</td><td colspan="2">*To*</td></tr>
</table>

COUNTRY

HAMPTON COURT AND BUSHY, with KEW AND RICHMOND from 1844

George Slade		1832	31 December 1833	(dismissed)
William Craib	1 January	1834	April 1845	(retired)
Henry Riley Wilson	February	1845	July 1851	(resigned)

KEW AND RICHMOND

John Matthew		1832	31 December 1833	(transferred)
George S. Robinson	1 January	1834	1844	(resigned)

[Combined with Hampton Court etc. 1844–50]

Benjamin Gregory (labourer in trust)	5 January	1851	1851	

BRIGHTON

John Tyrell		(1832)	15 January 1834	(dismissed)
Thomas Heath		1834	August 1840	(died)
R. Whibley	August	1840	25 June 1847	(dismissed)
— Fry		1847	1850	(discontinued)

WINDSOR (PARKS AND STABLES only from January 1846)

J. Busher		1832	14 January 1838	(retired)
James Whitman	14 January	1838	(1851)	

WINDSOR CASTLE

John Robson Turnbull	28 January	1846	(1851)

SCOTLAND

MASTER OF THE WORKS

Robert Reid	(1832)	March 1840	(post abolished)

CLERK OF THE WORKS

William Nixon	1 April	1840	24 March 1848	(died)
Robert Matheson	April	1848	(1851)	

THE PLATES

Plate 1

Sir William Chambers, Surveyor General and Comptroller of the Works 1782–96, from a portrait by C. F. Von Breda dated 1788 (Royal Institute of British Architects)

Plate 2

James Wyatt, Surveyor General and Comptroller of the Works, 1796–1813, from an engraving by J. Singleton after a portrait by Ozias Humphrey dated 1795 (British Museum)

Plate 3

A. John Nash, one of the architects attached to the Office of Works 1815–32, from a wax portrait by J. A. Couriguer, *circa* 1820 (National Portrait Gallery)

B. Sir John Soane, one of the architects attached to the Office of Works 1815–32, from an engraving by J. Thomson after a portrait by Sir Thomas Lawrence (Ashmolean Museum, Oxford, Hope Collection)

Plate 4

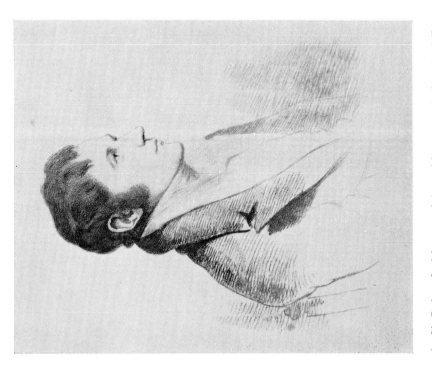

B. Sir Jeffry Wyatville, with a plan of Windsor Castle, from an engraving by H. Robinson after a portrait by Sir Thomas Lawrence dated 1829 (Ashmolean Museum, Oxford, Hope Collection)

A. Sir Robert Smirke, one of the architects attached to the Office of Works 1815–32, from an engraving by W. Daniell after a pencil drawing by George Dance published in 1808 (Ashmolean Museum, Oxford, Hope Collection)

Plate 5

B. Sir Charles Barry, architect of the new Houses of Parliament, from a portrait drawn and engraved by T. W. Harland (Ashmolean Museum, Oxford, Hope Collection)

A. Edward Blore, architect of Buckingham Palace 1831–50, from a portrait by G. Koberwein dated 1868 (National Portrait Gallery)

Plate 6

A. Buckingham Palace: Nash's east front as originally built 1825–8, from an engraving by Wallis after a drawing by A. Pugin published in 1827 (British Museum, Crace Collection XIII, 25)

B. Buckingham Palace: the east front as completed 1828–30, with the Marble Arch, from an engraving by T. Higham, *circa* 1830 (British Museum, Crace Collection XIII, 27)

Plate 7

A. Buckingham Palace: the garden front as designed by Nash, from an engraving by T. Higham dated 1831 (British Museum, Crace Collection XIII, 26)

B. Buckingham Palace: proposal by Blore for modifying the garden front, 1832 (British Museum, Additional MS. 42047, f. 13)

Plate 8

A. Buckingham Palace: the forecourt seen from the State apartments, from a drawing by T. H. Shepherd dated 1842 (Westminster City Library, Box 39, 1A)

B. Buckingham Palace: interior of the Picture Gallery before alteration in 1914, from a photograph in the Royal Library at Windsor (reproduced by gracious permission of H.M. the Queen)

Plate 9

HER MAJESTY'S STATE BALL—THE GRAND STAIRCASE AT BUCKINGHAM PALACE

Buckingham Palace: the Grand Staircase, from the *Illustrated London News* of 1855 (page 557)

Plate 10

A. Buckingham Palace: the east front as built designed by Blore in 1846, from E. W. Godwin, *Buildings and Monuments, Ancient & Modern* (1850)

B. Buckingham Palace: one of Blore's alternative designs for the east front (British Museum, Additional MS. 42047, f. 14)

Plate 11

A. Project by Nash for a palace for the Prince Regent on the site of Carlton House (Royal Collection, Buckingham Palace, reproduced by gracious permission of H.M. the Queen)

B. The British Embassy at Constantinople, from *The Builder*, 27 February 1847

Plate 12

A. Carlton House: exterior of the Gothic Conservatory designed by Thomas Hopper, from an engraving dated 1811 (Westminster City Library, Box 40, 21A)

B. Carlton House: the Gothic Dining Room designed by John Nash, from W. H. Pyne's *Royal Residencies* ii (1819)

Plate 13

Carlton House: interior of the Gothic Conservatory designed by Thomas Hopper, from W. H. Pyne's *Royal Residencies* ii (1819)

Plate 14

A. Hampton Court Palace: the Pavilions, as altered for the Duke of Gloucester in 1792–3: from an engraving in J. Hassell's *Picturesque Rides and Walks* i (1807)

B. Hampton Court Palace, the entrance front in 1826: from a pencil drawing by John Buckler (British Museum, Additional MS. 36369, f. 181)

Plate 15

A. Kew: George III's Gothic Palace from the river: from a lithograph after a drawing by W. Westall published in 1823 (Royal Botanic Gardens, Kew)

B. Kew: the main block of George III's Gothic Palace: from a contemporary engraving (Royal Botanic Gardens, Kew)

Plate 16

St. James's Palace: interior of the Chapel Royal in 1816 (Westminster City Library, Box 36, 21B)

Plate 17

A. St. James's Palace: interior of the Chapel Royal in the nineteenth century. The enlargement of the east window took place in 1840 and 1858. From a water-colour by J. Fulleylove (G.L.C. Print Collection)

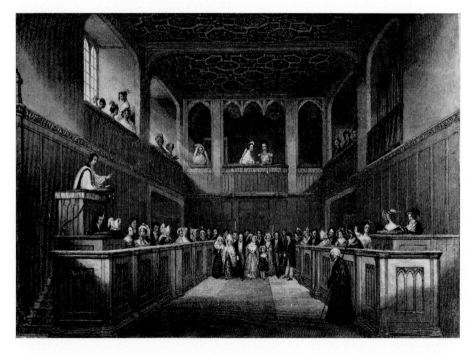

B. St. James's Palace: interior of the Chapel Royal after refitting in 1836, showing the royal closet occupied by Queen Victoria and the Prince Consort: from a drawing by T. H. Shepherd engraved in *London Interiors* (1841–4)

Plate 18

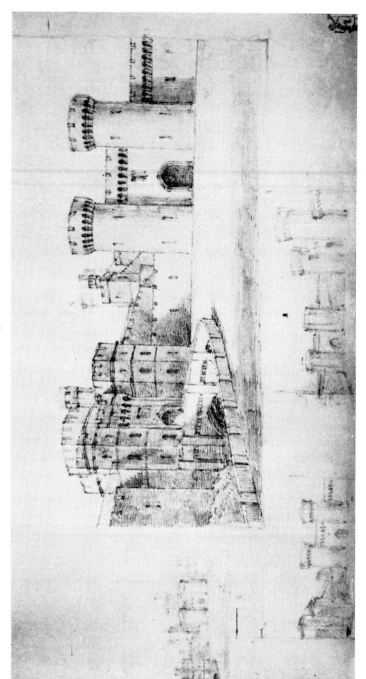

Windsor Castle: sketches by Smirke for rebuilding the Castle, 1824 (R.I.B.A. Drawings Collection J 11/29)

Plate 19

Windsor Castle: the south and east fronts as rebuilt by Wyatville: from Joseph Nash's *Views of Windsor Castle* (1848)

Plate 20

Windsor Castle: the north side of the Upper Ward before and after Wyatville's reconstruction: from a drawing by Wyatville in the Royal Library at Windsor (reproduced by gracious permission of H.M. the Queen)

Plate 21

Windsor Castle: the interior of the Upper Ward before and after Wyatville's reconstruction: from a drawing by Wyatville in the Royal Library at Windsor (reproduced by gracious permission of H.M. the Queen)

Plate 22

A. & B. Windsor Castle: views of the Round Tower before and after Wyatville's reconstruction: from W. H. Pyne's *Royal Residences* i (1819), and Joseph Nash's *Views of Windsor Castle* (1848)

Plate 23

A. Windsor Castle: the State Staircase as built by James Wyatt 1800–4: from W. H. Pyne's *Royal Residences* i (1819)

B. Windsor Castle: the State Staircase as built by Jeffry Wyatville *circa* 1830–5: from Joseph Nash's *Views of Windsor Castle* (1848)

Plate 24

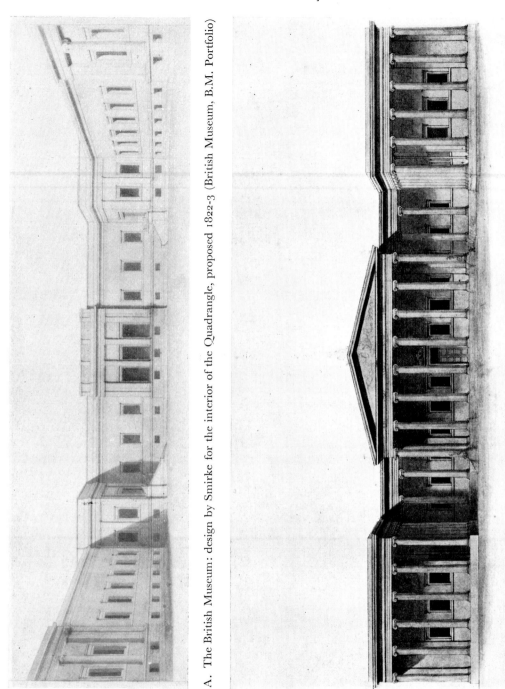

A. The British Museum: design by Smirke for the interior of the Quadrangle, proposed 1822-3 (British Museum, B.M. Portfolio)

Elevation proposed for the principal front of the Museum.

B. The British Museum: design by Smirke for the principal front, proposed 1822-3 (Dr. J. Mordaunt Crook)

Plate 25

The British Museum: the principal front as completed, with proposals for sculpture made by Smirke in 1842–4: from an engraving by F. Mackenzie

Plate 26

A. The Custom House as designed by David Laing, 1813–17: from an engraving based on a drawing by Laing (British Museum, Crace Collection VIII, 29)

B. The Custom House as reconstructed by Smirke, 1825–7: from a drawing by T. H. Shepherd engraved in *Metropolitan Improvements* (1829)

Plate 27

A. The Long Room of the Custom House as designed by David Laing, 1813–17: from Laing's *Plans of Buildings, Public and Private, executed in various parts of England* (1818)

B. The Long Room of the Custom House as reconstructed by Smirke, 1825–7: from a drawing by T. H. Shepherd engraved in *London Interiors* (1841–4)

Plate 28

A. The General Post Office designed by Smirke, 1824–9: from an engraving in *The Gentleman's Magazine* 1829, part ii, page 297

B. The Royal Mint designed by James Johnson in 1805 and completed by Smirke: from a drawing by T. H. Shepherd engraved in *London in the Nineteenth Century* (1829)

Plate 29

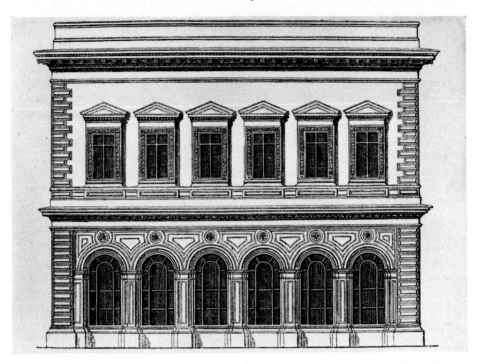

A. The Museum of Economic Geology designed by James Pennethorne and built 1847–8: the elevation to Piccadilly, from *A New Survey of London* (John Weale, 1853)

THE NEW RECORD OFFICE, CHANCERY-LANE.—Mr. PENNETHORNE, ARCHITECT.

B. The Public Record Office designed by James Pennethorne and begun in 1851: the north elevation, from *The Builder*, vol. ix (1851), p. 643

Plate 30

Trafalgar Square, as proposed by William Wilkins, the architect of the
National Gallery, *circa* 1837 (Westminster City Library, Box 14, 23A)

Plate 31

Trafalgar Square, with Nelson's Column and a layout similar to that adopted: from an engraving of 1845 (British Museum, Crace Collection XI, 124)

3A

Plate 32

The erection of Nelson's Column, showing the scaffolding, 1843 (British Museum, Crace Collection XI, 141)

Plate 33

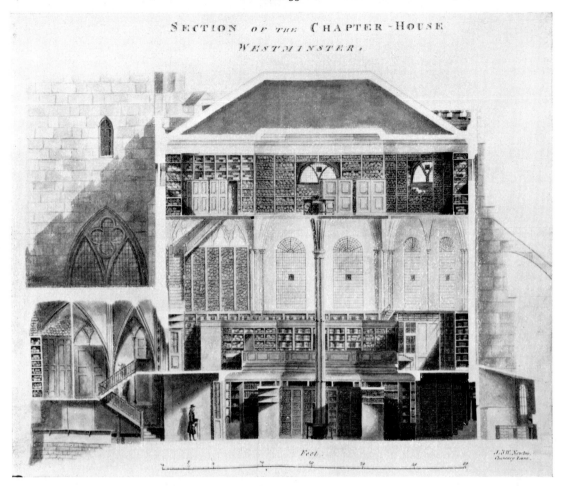

SECTION OF THE CHAPTER-HOUSE
WESTMINSTER.

Feet.

Westminster Abbey: the Chapter House in use as a Record Office, from a survey by J. & W. Newton, 1807 (Public Record Office, MPB 2/99/1)

Plate 34

A. The House of Commons before the alterations of 1800-1 (Westminster City Library, Box 56, 68B)

B. The temporary House of Commons in use from 1835 to 1851, showing the new ceiling constructed in 1836: from *London Interiors* (1841–4)

Plate 35

A. The House of Lords before the fire of 1834 (Westminster City Library, Box 56, 68A)

B. The temporary House of Lords in use from 1835 to 1847: from a drawing by T. H. Shepherd (G.L.C. Print Collection)

Plate 36

A. The east end of St. Stephen's Chapel in the eighteenth century: from a drawing by Thomas Sandby engraved by J. T. Smith for his *Antiquities of Westminster* (1837)

B. The east end of St. Stephen's Chapel as altered by James Wyatt in 1805–6: from J. T. Smith, *Antiquities of Westminster* (1837)

Plate 37

A. Old Palace Yard in 1796 (G.L.C. Print Collection)

B. Old Palace Yard in 1829: from a drawing by T. H. Shepherd engraved in *London in the Nineteenth Century* (1829)

Plate 38

A. The exterior of the Law Courts: Soane's first proposal of 1821, retaining the Tudor elevation to New Palace Yard. The eighteenth-century 'Stone Building' is on the right (Soane Museum, liii, 8, 2)

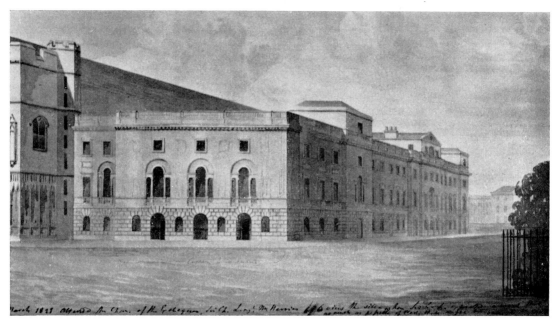

B. The exterior of the Law Courts: the design by Soane submitted in March 1823 (Soane Museum, liii, 8, 7)

Plate 39

A. The exterior of the Law Courts as built by Soane in 1823–4: from Soane's *Designs for Public and Private Buildings* (1828)

B. Drawing by Soane to show how the North elevation of the new Law Courts could be gothicised: from Soane's *Designs for Public and Private Buildings* (1828)

Plate 40

A. The north elevation of the Law Courts as altered in obedience to the Select Committee of 1824: from a drawing dated 1836 (British Museum, Crace Collection XV, 90)

B. One of Soane's drawings showing the north elevation of the Law Courts altered to meet the instructions of the Select Committee of 1824 (Soane Museum, liii, 3, 41)

Plate 41

A. New Palace Yard in 1805: from an engraving by J. Bryant in J. T. Smith's *Antiquities of Westminster* (1837)

B. New Palace Yard: a project by Soane for remodelling the north elevation of the buildings facing the Yard: from his *Designs for Public and Private Buildings* (1828)

Plate 42

A. Westminster: interior of Soane's Court of Chancery: from his *Designs for Public and Private Buildings* (1828)

B. Westminster: the Royal Entrance to the House of Lords from Old Palace Yard designed by Soane: from his *Designs for Public and Private Buildings* (1828)

Plate 43

B. Westminster: the Lord Chancellor's retiring room designed by Soane (Soane Museum, liii, 2, 59)

A. Westminster: interior of Soane's Court of King's Bench, from a drawing by J. P. Emslie dated 1883 (G.L.C. Print Collection)

Plate 44

Westminster: the Scala Regia to the House of Lords designed by Soane: from his *Designs for Public and Private Buildings* (1828)

Plate 45

NEW LIBRARY HOUSE OF COMMONS.

NEW LIBRARY HOUSE OF LORDS.

Westminster: the new libraries designed by Soane for the Houses of Lords and Commons: from his *Designs for Public and Private Buildings* (1828)

Plate 46

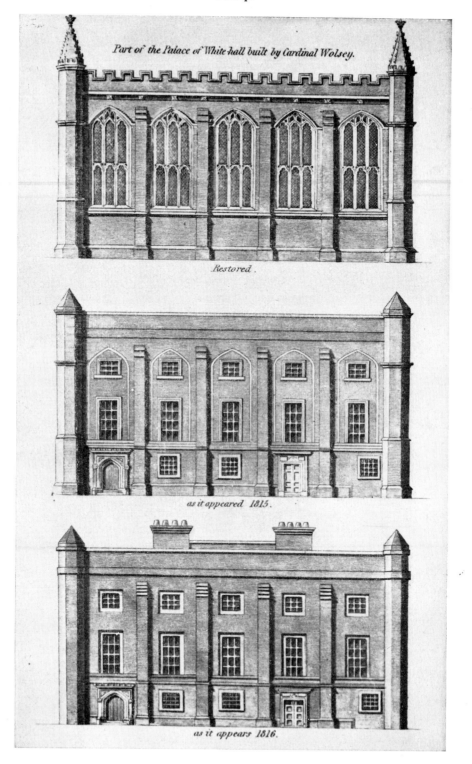

Part of the Palace of White-hall built by Cardinal Wolsey.

Restored.

as it appeared 1815.

as it appears 1816.

Whitehall: the Old Tennis Court (Home Office), showing the progressive destruction of its original features: from an engraving illustrating John Carter's complaint in the *Gentleman's Magazine* for 1816

Plate 47

A. Whitehall: one of Soane's proposals for the new Privy Council and Board of Trade Offices, with the Old Tennis Court and Dover House to the right (Soane Museum xlix, 3, 40, dated June 1824)

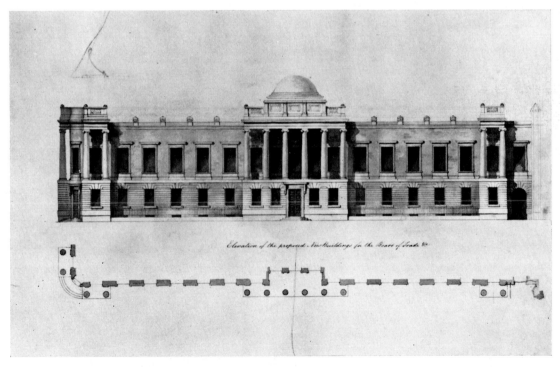

B. Whitehall: one of Soane's early designs for the new Privy Council and Board of Trade Offices (Soane Museum xlix, 3, 27, dated February 1824)

Whitehall, the Privy Council and Board of Trade Offices: an
engraving from Soane's *Designs for Public and Private Buildings*
(1828), showing alternative treatments of the Corinthian order

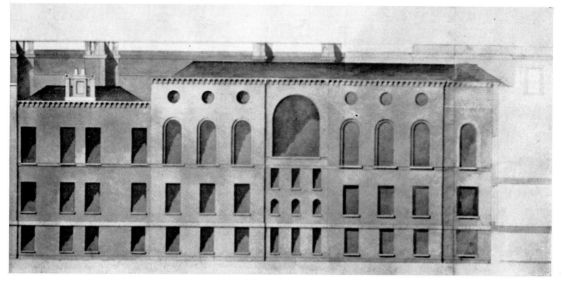

B. Whitehall: rear elevation of Soane's Privy Council and Board of Trade Offices (Soane Museum, xlix, 6, 5)

Plate 49

A. Whitehall: the Privy Council and Board of Trade Offices as built 1824–7: from an engraving by T. Higham (G.L.C. Print Collection)

B. Whitehall: the Privy Council, Board of Trade and Home Offices as remodelled by Barry 1845–6 (British Museum, Crace Collection XVI, 72)

Plate 50

Whitehall, the Privy Council Chamber designed by Soane (Soane Museum)

Plate 51

VIEW OF THE NEW STATE PAPER OFFICE TAKEN IN DUKE STR.

A. Whitehall: Soane's State Paper Office. The entrance front from Duke Street, from Soane's *Designs for Public and Private Buildings* (1828)

B. Westminster: Soane's design for new Houses of Parliament, made in 1794–6, from his *Designs for Public and Private Buildings* (1828)

Plate 52

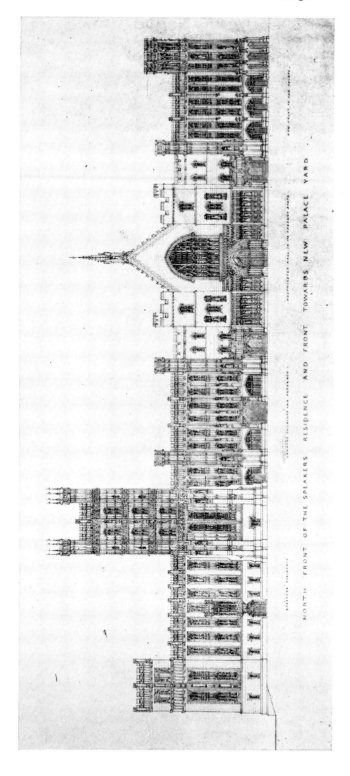

The New Houses of Parliament: Barry's first proposal for the new front to New Palace Yard. A copy of one of Barry's winning designs of 1835 (Works 29/3205), drawn on paper watermarked 1843

Plate 53

The New Houses of Parliament: Barry's revised design for the north front to New Palace Yard, as approved by the Select Committee, dated 21 April 1836 (R.I.B.A. Drawings Collection RAN 2/A/2)

Plate 54

A. The New Houses of Parliament: J. C. Buckler's Tudor Gothic design, placed second in the competition of 1835 (Works 29/47)

B. The New Houses of Parliament: David Hamilton's 'Elizabethan' design, placed third in the competition of 1835 (Works 29/56)

Plate 55

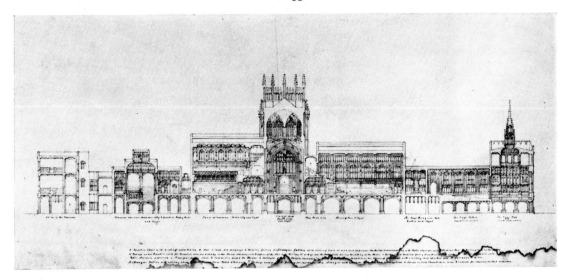

A. The New Houses of Parliament: a section through Barry's Competition design of 1835, showing the Houses of Lords and Commons, from a copy drawn on paper watermarked 1842 (Works 29/3204)

B. The New Houses of Parliament: Barry's revised design for the river front, as accepted by Parliament in 1836, from *The Athenaeum*, 21 May 1836

Plate 56

The New Houses of Parliament: the King's Tower, as envisaged in about 1837, from a drawing probably by A. W. N. Pugin (Society of Antiquaries of London)

Plate 57

The New Houses of Parliament: tracing of details of the King's stairs probably designed by A. W. N. Pugin (House of Lords Record Office)

Plate 58

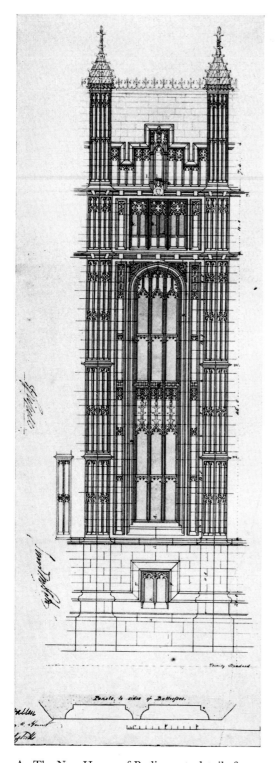

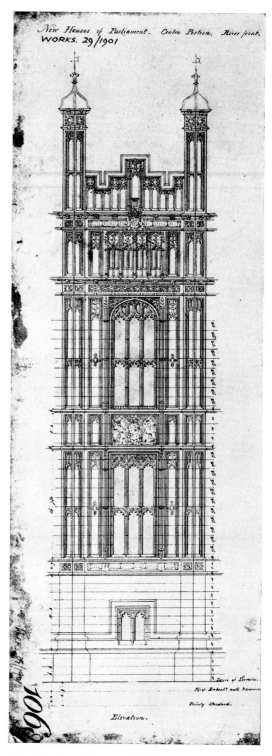

A. The New Houses of Parliament: detail of contract drawing dated 5 February 1840, showing elevation of one bay of central portion of river front (Works 29/1843)

B. The New Houses of Parliament: revised elevation for bay of central portion of river front, dated 13 January 1841 (Works 29/1901)

Plate 59

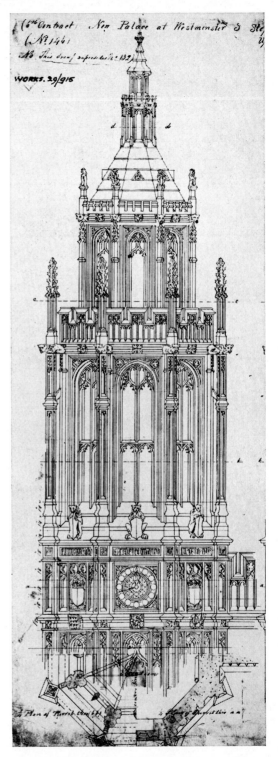

A. The New Houses of Parliament: plan and elevation of turret of St. Stephen's Porch, dated 23 December 1847 (Works 29/911)

B. The New Houses of Parliament: plan and elevation of turret of St. Stephen's Porch, dated 7 March 1848, showing revised design (Works 29/915)

Plate 60

The New Houses of Parliament: projects for the Clock Tower (R.I.B.A. Drawings Collection, RAN 2/C/1)

Plate 61

The New Houses of Parliament, sketch showing project for central tower, 1846 (Society of Antiquaries of London)

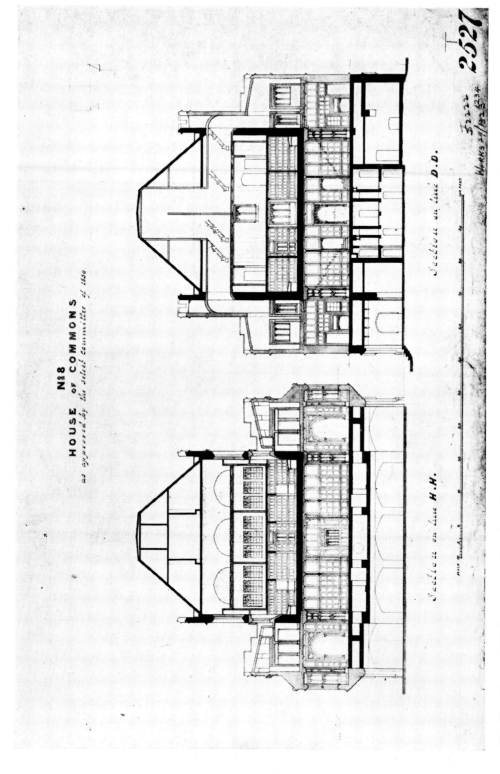

Plate 62

The New Houses of Parliament: sections through House of Commons showing alterations approved by the Select Committee of 1850, including the lowering of the ceiling (Works 29/1323)

Plate 63

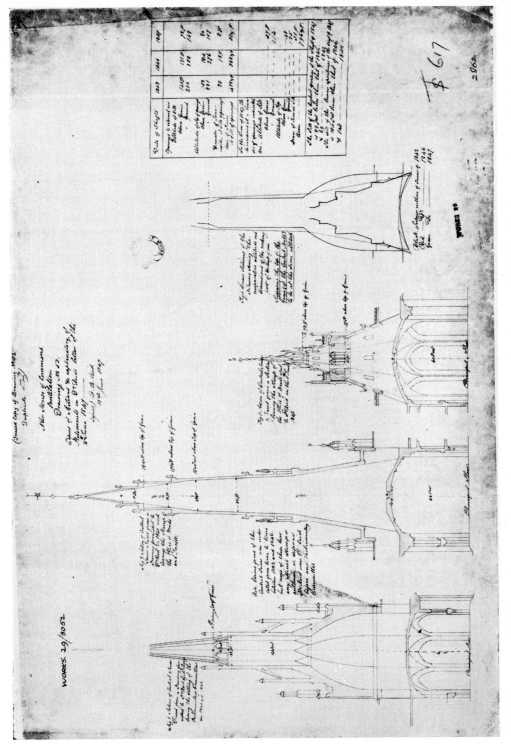

The New Houses of Parliament: tracing of drawing showing a section of Barry's successive designs for the central tower dated 1842, 1846 and 1847 (Works 29/3052)

Plate 64

The New Houses of Parliament: interior of the House of Lords, from E. W. Godwin, *Buildings and Monuments, Ancient and Modern* (1850)

Plate 65

The New Houses of Parliament: interior of the House of Commons as originally designed by Barry, from E. W. Godwin, *Buildings and Monuments, Ancient and Modern* (1850)

B. The New Houses of Parliament: building in progress in Old Palace Yard (British Museum, Crace Collection XV, 59)

Plate 66

The Tower of London in the early nineteenth century: a view from the east, from a water-colour by J. Tugman dated 1826 (the London Museum)

Index

Abbot, Charles, Speaker of the House of Commons, cr. 1st Baron Colchester,
and reconstruction of the Speaker's House, 533
   Wyatt's plan for the new House of Lords, 519
establishes Private Bill Office, 534–5
undertakes survey of national records, 488
Abbott, C. P. H., 183, 201, 218
Abbot, Charles (cr. 1st Baron Tenterden, 1827), Lord Chief Justice, 510
Abercromby, James, Speaker of the House of Commons, 534
Aberdeen, George, 4th Earl of (1784–1860),
approves new ambassadorial residence at Constantinople, 636
   Chairman, National Gallery Trustees, 462
   Foreign Secretary (1841–6), 635–6
   mentioned, 133, 213 n. 6, 384, 405, 517 n. 3, 576
Aberdeen
   King's College, 252
   Marischal College, 252–3
   post office, 254
   university, 252
Abraham, Robert, architect, 326
Academy, Royal, see Royal Academy
Accidents to workmen, 38–40
Accum, Frederick, 459
Ackermann, R., 459, 750
Adam, James, Joint Architect, 14, 24, 513, 627
Adam, Robert, architect, 27, 497
Adams, J. W., 503 n. 5
Adams, William Dacres,
   appointments held, 189 n. 3, 679
   duties at Office of Woods and Works, 191
   mentioned, 98, 189
Addington, Henry, see Sidmouth, Viscount
Adelaide, Queen (formerly Princess Adelaide of Saxe-Meiningen (q. v.) (wife of the Duke of Clarence, later William IV)
   Adelaide Cottage, 398–9

Malborough House as dower house for, 349
Ranger of Bushy Park, 339
residence at Clarence House, 370
mentioned, 321, 339 n. 11
Adelaide of Saxe-Meiningen, Princess,
marries the Duke of Clarence, 323, 339
residence, 331, 338–9
see also Adelaide, Queen
Admiralty,
offices in Whitehall, 540
Droits of, 124, 152 n. 8, 274, 405 n. 7
Adron, W. & C., marble masons, 386 n. 3
Airy, G. B., Astronomer Royal, 621
Aiton, William (1731–93) botanist and Director of Kew Gardens, 440
Aiton, William Townsend (1766–1849), botanist and Director of Kew Gardens, 440, 441, 445 n. 6
designs lodges for the grounds at Kensington Palace, 348–9
Albano, Benedict, architect, 634 n. 9, 639
Albany, Leopold, Duke of, 323
Albemarle, William Charles, 4th Earl of (1772–1849), 337
Albert, Prince Consort (husband of Queen Victoria)
and improvements to Buckingham Palace 287, 289, 290, 291, 293
   Lincoln, 211
   positioning of the statue of George IV, 493
decides on decorations at Buckingham Palace, 287
directs the construction of Osborne, 290
on Milne, 247 n. 2
   the Woods and Works, 210
presides over the (Royal) Fine Arts Commission, 226, 614
mentioned, 244, 277, 394, 396, 401
Albion Mill, Blackfriars, 357
Albon, William, 126 n. 10
Aldrick's Lodge (Thatched House Lodge, Richmond Park), 354
Alexander, D. A., architect, 328, 426

Printed in Scotland by Her Majesty's Stationery Office at HMSO Press, Edinburgh
Dd 501773 2000 4/73 (8127)